A SELECT LIBRARY

OF

NICENE AND POST-NICENE FATHERS

OF

THE CHRISTIAN CHURCH.

Second Series.

TRANSLATED INTO ENGLISH WITH PROLEGOMENA AND EXPLANATORY NOTES.

VOLUMES I,–VII,

UNDER THE EDITORIAL SUPERVISION OF

PHILIP SCHAFF, D.D., LL.D.,   AND   **HENRY WACE, D.D.,**

Professor of Church History in the   *Principal of King's College,*
Union Theological Seminary, New York.   *London.*

IN CONNECTION WITH A NUMBER OF PATRISTIC SCHOLARS OF EUROPE
AND AMERICA.

VOLUME IX.

ST. HILARY OF POITIERS.

JOHN OF DAMASCUS.

NEW YORK:

CHARLES SCRIBNER'S SONS.

OXFORD AND LONDON:

PARKER & COMPANY.

1899.

ST. HILARY OF POITIERS.

SELECT WORKS.

TRANSLATED BY

THE REV. E. W. WATSON, M.A.,
WARDEN OF THE SOCIETY OF ST. ANDREW, SALISBURY,

THE REV. L. PULLAN, M.A.,
FELLOW OF ST. JOHN'S COLLEGE, OXFORD,

AND OTHERS.

EDITED BY

THE REV. W. SANDAY, D.D., LL.D.,
LADY MARGARET PROFESSOR OF DIVINITY, AND CANON OF CHRIST CHURCH, OXFORD.

PREFACE.

THIS volume of the series of Nicene Fathers has been unfortunately delayed. When I consented in the first instance to edit the volume, it was with the distinct understanding that I could not myself undertake the translation, but that I would do my best to find translators and see the work through the press. It has been several times placed in the hands of very competent scholars; but the fact that work of this kind can only be done in the intervals of regular duties, and the almost inevitable drawback that the best men are also the busiest, has repeatedly stood in the way and caused the work to be returned to me. That it sees the light now is due mainly to the zeal, ability, and scholarship of the Rev. E. W. Watson. It was late in the day when Mr. Watson first undertook a share in the work which has since then been constantly increased. He has co-operated with me in the most loyal and efficient manner; and while I am glad to think that the whole of the Introduction and a full half of the translation are from his hand, there is hardly a page (except in the translation of the *De Synodis*, which was complete before he joined the work) which does not owe to him many and marked improvements. My own personal debt to Mr. Watson is very great indeed, and that of the subscribers to the series is, I believe, hardly less.

For the translator of Hilary has before him a very difficult task. It has not been with this as with other volumes of the series, where an excellent translation already existed and careful revision was all that was needed. A small beginning had been made for the *De Trinitate* by the late Dr. Short, Bishop of Adelaide, whose manuscript was kindly lent to one of the contributors to this volume. But with this exception no English translation of Hilary's works has been hitherto attempted. That which is now offered is the first in the field. And it must be confessed that Hilary is a formidable writer. I do not think that I know any Latin writer so formidable, unless it is Victorinus Afer, or Tertullian. And the terse, vigorous, incisive sentences of Tertullian, when once the obscurities of meaning have been mastered, run more easily into English than the involved and overloaded periods of Hilary. It is true that in a period of decline Hilary preserves more than most of his contemporaries of the tradition of Roman culture; but it is the culture of the rhetorical schools at almost the extreme point of their artificiality and mannerism. Hilary was too sincere a man and too thoroughly in earnest to be essentially mannered or artificial; but his training had taken too strong a hold upon him to allow him to express his thought with ease and simplicity. And his very merits all tended in the same direction. He has the *copia verborum*; he has the weight and force of character which naturally goes with a certain amplitude of style; he has the seriousness and depth of conviction which keeps him at a high level of dignity and gravity but is unrelieved by lighter touches.

We must take our author as we find him. But it seems to me, if I am not mistaken, that Mr. Watson has performed a real feat of translation in not only reproducing the meaning of the original but giving to it an English rendering which is so readable, flowing, and even elegant. I think it will be allowed that only a natural feeling for the rhythm and cadence of English speech, as well as for its varied harmonies of diction, could have produced the result which is now laid before the reader. And I cherish the hope, that although different degrees of success have doubtless been attained by the different contributors at least no jarring discrepancy of style will be felt throughout the volume. It will be seen that the style generally leans to the side of freedom; but I believe that it will be found to be the freedom of the scholar who is really true to his text while transfusing it into another tongue, and not the clumsy approximation which only means failure.

Few writers deserve their place in the library of Nicene and Post-Nicene Fathers more thoroughly than Hilary. He might be said to be the one Latin theologian before the age of St. Augustine and St. Leo. Tertullian had a still greater influence upon the writers who followed him. He came at a still more formative and critical time, and the *vis vivida* of his original and wayward genius has rarely been equalled. But the particular influence which Tertullian exerted in coining the terms and marking out the main lines of Latin theology came to him almost by accident. He was primarily a lawyer, and his special gift did not lie in the region of speculation. It is a strange fortune which gave to the language on which he set his stamp so great a control of the future. The influence of Hilary on the other hand is his by right. His intercourse with the East had a marked effect upon him. It quickened a natural bent for speculation unusual in the West. The reader will find in Mr. Watson's Introduction a description and estimate of Hilary's theology which is in my opinion at once accurate, candid and judicious. No attempt is made to gloss over the defects, especially in what we might call the more superficial exegesis of Hilary's argument; but behind and beneath this we feel that we are in contact with a very powerful mind. We feel that we are in contact with a mind that has seized and holds fast the central truth of the Christian system, which at that particular crisis of the Church's history was gravely imperilled. The nerve of all Hilary's thinking lies in his belief, a belief to which he clung more tenaciously than to life itself, that Christ was the Son of God not in name and metaphor only, but in fullest and deepest reality. The great Athanasius himself has not given to this belief a more impressive or more weighty expression. And when like assaults come round, as they are constantly doing, in what is in many respects the inferior arena of our own day, it is both morally bracing and intellectually helpful to go back to these protagonists of the elder time.

And yet, although Hilary is thus one of the chief builders up of a metaphysical theology in the West—although, in other words, he stands upon the direct line of the origin of the *Quicumque vult*, it is well to remember that no one could be more conscious than he was of the inadequacy of human thought and human language to deal with these high matters. The accusation of intruding with a light heart into mysteries is very far from touching him. "The heretics compel us to speak where we would far rather be silent. If anything is said, this is what must be said," is his constant burden. In this respect too Hilary affords a noble pattern not only to the Christian theologian but to the student of theology, however humble.

It has been an unfortunate necessity that use has had to be made almost throughout of an untrustworthy text. The critical edition which is being produced for the *Corpus Scrip-*

torum Ecclesiasticorum Latinorum of the Vienna Academy does not as yet extend beyond the Commentary on the Psalms (*S. Hilarii Ep. Pictaviensis Tract. super Psalmos*, recens. A. Zingerle, Vindobonae, MDCCCXCI). This is the more to be regretted as the MSS. of Hilary are rather exceptionally early and good. Most of these were used in the Benedictine edition, but not so systematically or thoroughly as a modern standard requires. It is impossible to speak decidedly about the text of Hilary until the Vienna edition is completed.

The treatise *De Synodis* was translated by the Rev. L. Pullan, and has been in print for some time. The Introduction and the translation of *De Trinitate* i.—vii. are the work of Mr. Watson. Books viii. and xii. were undertaken Mr. E. N. Bennett, Fellow of Hertford, and Books ix.—xi. by the Rev. S. C. Gayford, late Scholar of Exeter. The specimens of the Commentary on the Psalms were translated by the Rev. H. F. Stewart, Vice-Principal of the Theological College, Salisbury, who has also made himself responsible for the double Index.

A word of special thanks is due to the printers, Messrs. Parker, who have carried out their part of the work with conspicuous intelligence and with the most conscientious care.

W. SANDAY.

CHRIST CHURCH,
OXFORD,
July 12, 1898.

CONTENTS.

INTRODUCTION.

CHAPTER I.

The Life and Writings of St. Hilary of Poitiers.

St. Hilary of Poitiers is one of the greatest, yet least studied, of the Fathers of the Western Church. He has suffered thus, partly from a certain obscurity in his style of writing, partly from the difficulty of the thoughts which he attempted to convey. But there are other reasons for the comparative neglect into which he has fallen. He learnt his theology, as we shall see, from Eastern authorities, and was not content to carry on and develope the traditional teaching of the West; and the disciple of Origen, who found his natural allies in the Cappadocian school of Basil and the Gregories [1], his juniors though they were, was speaking to somewhat unsympathetic ears. Again, his Latin tongue debarred him from influence in the East, and he suffered, like all Westerns, from that deep suspicion of Sabellianism which was rooted in the Eastern Churches. Nor are these the only reasons for the neglect of Hilary. Of his two chief works, the Homilies [2] on the Psalms, important as they were in popularising the allegorical method of interpretation, were soon outdone in favour by other commentaries; while his great controversial work on the Trinity suffered from its very perfection for the purpose with which it was composed. It seems, at first sight, to be not a refutation of Arianism, or of any particular phase of Arianism, but of one particular document, the Epistle of Arius to Alexander, in which Arian doctrines are expressed; and that a document which, in the constantly shifting phases of the controversy, soon fell into an oblivion which the work of Hilary has nearly shared. It is only incidentally constructive; its plan follows, in the central portion, that of the production of Arius which he was controverting, and this negative method must have lessened its popularity for purposes of practical instruction, and in competition with such a masterpiece as the *De Trinitate* of St. Augustine. And furthermore, Hilary never does himself justice. He was a great original thinker in the field of Christology, but he has never stated his views systematically and completely. They have to be laboriously reconstructed by the collection of passages scattered throughout his works; and though he is a thinker so consistent that little or no conjecture is needed for the piecing together of his system, yet we cannot be surprised that full justice has never been done to him. He has been regarded chiefly as one of the sufferers from the violence of Constantius, as the composer of a useful conspectus of arguments against Arianism, as an unsuccessful negotiator for an understanding between the Eastern and Western Churches; but his sufferings were as nothing compared to those of Athanasius, while his influence in controversy seems to have been as small as the results of his diplomacy. It is not his practical share, in word or deed, in the conflicts of his day that is his chief title to fame, but his independence and depth as a Christian thinker. He has, indeed, exerted an important influence upon the growth of doctrine, but it has

---

[1] An actual dependence on Gregory of Nyssa has sometimes been ascribed to Hilary. But Gregory was surely too young for this. He may himself have borrowed from Hilary; but more probably both derived their common element from Eastern writers like Basil of Ancyra.

[2] This is certainly the best translation of *Tractatus*; the word is discussed on a later page.

b

been through the adoption of his views by Augustine and Ambrose; and many who have profited by his thoughts have never known who was their author.

Hilary of Poitiers, the most impersonal of writers, is so silent about himself, he is so rarely mentioned by contemporary writers—in all the voluminous works of Athanasius he is never once named,—and the ancient historians of the Church knew so little concerning him beyond what we, as well as they, can learn from his writings, that nothing more than a very scanty narrative can be constructed from these, as seen in the light of the general history of the time and combined with the few notices of him found elsewhere. But the account, though short, cannot be seriously defective. Apart from one or two episodes, it is eminently the history of a mind, and of a singularly consistent mind, whose antecedents we can, in the main, recognise, and whose changes of thought are few, and can be followed.

He was born, probably about the year 300 A.D.[3], and almost certainly, since he was afterwards its bishop, in the town, or in the district dependent upon the town, by the name of which he is usually styled. Other names, beside Hilarius, he must have had, but we do not know them. The fact that he has had to be distinguished by the name of his see, to avoid confusion with his namesake of Arles, the contemporary of St. Augustine, shews how soon and how thoroughly personal details concerning him were forgotten. The rank of his parents must have been respectable at least, and perhaps high; so much we may safely assume from the education they gave him. Birth in the Gallic provinces during the fourth century brought with it no sense of provincial inferiority. Society was thoroughly Roman, and education and literature more vigorous, so far as we can judge, than in any other part of the West. The citizen of Gaul and of Northern Italy was, in fact, more in the centre of the world's life than the inhabitant of Rome. Gaul was in the West what Roman Asia was in the East, the province of decisive importance, both for position and for wealth. And in this prosperous and highly civilised community the opportunities for the highest education were ample. We know, from Ausonius and otherwise, how complete was the provision for teaching at Bordeaux and elsewhere in Gaul. Greek was taught habitually as well as Latin. In fact, never since the days of Hadrian had educated society throughout the Empire been so nearly bilingual. It was not only that the Latin-speaking West had still to turn for its culture and its philosophy to the literature of Greece. Since the days of Diocletian the court, or at least the most important court, had resided as a rule in Asia, and Greek had tended to become, equally with Latin, the language of the courtier and the administrator. The two were of almost equal importance; if an Oriental like Ammianus Marcellinus could write, and write well, in Latin, we may be certain that, in return, Greek was familiar to educated Westerns. To Hilary it was certainly familiar from his youth; his earlier thoughts were moulded by Neoplatonism, and his later decisively influenced by the writings of Origen[4]. His literary and technical knowledge of Latin was also complete[5]. It would

---

3 The latest date which I have seen assigned for his birth is 320, by Fechtrup, in Wetzer-Welte's Encyclopædia. But this is surely inconsistent with his styling Ursacius and Valens, in his first Epistle to Constantine, 'ignorant and unprincipled youths.' This was written about the year 355, before Hilary knew much of the Arian controversy or the combatants, and was ludicrously inappropriate, for Ursacius and Valens were elderly men. He had found the words either in some of Athanasius' writings or in the records of the Council of Sardica, and borrowed them without enquiry. He could not have done so had he been only some thirty-five years of age; at fifty-five they are natural enough.

4 It is impossible to agree with Zingerle (*Comment. Wölfflin.* p. 218) that Hilary was under the necessity of using a Greek and

Latin Glossary. Such a passage as *Tract. in Ps.* cxxxviii. 43, to which he appeals, shews rather the extent than the smallness of Hilary's knowledge of Greek. What he frankly confesses, there as elsewhere, is ignorance of Hebrew. The words of Jerome (*Ep.* 34, 3 f.) about Hilary's friend, the presbyter Heliodorus, to whom he used to refer for explanations of Origen on the Psalms, are equally incapable of being employed to prove Hilary's defective Greek. Heliodorus knew Hebrew, and Hilary for want of Hebrew found Origen's notes on the Hebrew text difficult to understand, and for this reason, according to Jerome, used to consult his friend; not because he was unfamiliar with Greek.

5 His vocabulary is very poorly treated in the dictionaries; one of the many signs of the neglect into which he has fallen. There are at least twenty-four words in the *Tractatus super*

require wide special study and knowledge to fix his relation in matters of composition and rhetoric to other writers. But one assertion, that of Jerome[6], that Hilary was a deliberate imitator of the style of Quintilian, cannot be taken seriously. Jerome is the most reckless of writers; and it is at least possible to be somewhat familiar with the writings of both and yet see no resemblance, except in a certain sustained gravity, between them. Another description by Jerome of Hilary as 'mounted on Gallic buskin and adorned with flowers of Greece' is suitable enough, as to its first part, to Hilary's dignified rhetoric; the flowers of Greece, if they mean embellishments inserted for their own sake, are not perceptible. In this same passage[7] Jerome goes on to criticise Hilary's entanglement in long periods, which renders him unsuitable for unlearned readers. But those laborious, yet perfectly constructed, sentences are an essential part of his method. Without them he could not attain the effect he desires; they are as deliberate and, in their way, as successful as the eccentricities of Tacitus. But when Jerome elsewhere calls Hilary 'the Rhone of Latin eloquence[8],' he is speaking at random. It is only rarely that he breaks through his habitual sobriety of utterance; and his rare outbursts of devotion or denunciation are perhaps the more effective because the reader is unprepared to expect them. Such language as this of Jerome shews that Hilary's literary accomplishments were recognised, even though it fails to describe them well. But though he had at his command, and avowedly employed, the resources of rhetoric in order that his words might be as worthy as he could make them of the greatness of his theme[9], yet some portions of the *De Trinitate*, and most of the Homilies on the Psalms are written in a singularly equable and almost conversational style, the unobtrusive excellence of which manifests the hand of a clear thinker and a practised writer. He is no pedant[1], no laborious imitator of antiquity, distant or near; he abstains, perhaps more completely than any other Christian writer of classical education, from the allusions to the poets which were the usual ornament of prose. He is an eminently businesslike writer; his pages, where they are unadorned, express his meaning with perfect clearness; where they are decked out with antithesis or apostrophe and other devices of rhetoric, they would no doubt, if our training could put us in sympathy with him, produce the effect upon us which he designed, and we must, in justice to him, remember as we read that, in their own kind, they are excellent, and that, whether they aid us or no in entering into his argument, they never obscure his thought. Save in the few passages when corruption exists in the text, it is never safe to assert that Hilary is unintelligible. The reader or translator who cannot follow or render the argument must rather lay the blame upon his own imperfect knowledge of the language and thought of the fourth century. Where he is stating or proving truth, whether well-established or newly ascertained, he is admirably precise; and even in his more dubious speculations he never cloaks a weak argument in ambiguous language. A loftier genius might have given us in language inadequate, through no fault of his own, to the attempt some intimations of remoter truths. We must be thankful to the sober Hilary that he, with his strong sense of the limitations of our intellect, has provided a clear and accurate statement of the case against Arianism, and has widened the bounds of theological knowledge by reasonable deductions from the text of Scripture, usually convincing and always suggestive.

Psalmos which are omitted in the last edition of Georges' lexicon, and these good Latin words, not technical terms invented for purposes of argument. Among the most interesting is *quotiensque* for *quotienscumque*; an unnoticed use is the frequent *cum quando* for *quandoquidem*. Of Hilary's other writings there is as yet no trustworthy text; from them the list of new words could at least be doubled.

[6] *Ep.* 70, 5, *ad Magnum.*   [7] *Ep.* 58, 10, *ad Paulinum.*
[8] *Comm. in Gall.* ii. *pref.*
[9] Cf. *Tract. in Ps.* xiii. 1, *Trin.* i. 38.
[1] Yet he strangely reproaches his Old Latin Bible with the use of *nimis* for *ualde, Tract. in Ps.* cxxxviii. 38. This employment of relative for positive terms had been common in literature for at least a century and a half.

His training as a writer and thinker had certainly been accomplished before his conversion. His literary work done, like that of St. Cyprian, within a few years of middle life, displays, with a somewhat increasing maturity of thought, a steady uniformity of language and idiom, which can only have been acquired in his earlier days. And this assured possession of literary form was naturally accompanied by a philosophical training. Of one branch of a philosophical education, that of logic, there is almost too much evidence in his pages. He is free from the repulsive angularity which sometimes disfigures the pages of Novatian, a writer who had no great influence over him; but in the *De Trinitate* he too often refuses to trust his reader's intelligence, and insists upon being logical not only in thought but in expression. But, sound premisses being given, he may always be expected to draw the right conclusion. He is singularly free from confusion of thought, and never advances to results beyond what his premisses warrant. It is only when a false, though accepted, exegesis misleads him, in certain collateral arguments which may be surrendered without loss to his main theses, that he can be refuted; or again when, in his ventures into new fields of thought, he is unfortunate in the selection or combination of texts. But in these cases, as always, the logical processes are not in fault; his deduction is clear and honest.

Philosophy in those days was regarded as incomplete unless it included some knowledge of natural phenomena, to be used for purposes of analogy. Origen and Athanasius display a considerable interest in, and acquaintance with, physical and physiological matters, and Hilary shares the taste. The conditions of human or animal birth and life and death are often discussed [2]; he believes in universal remedies for disease [3], and knows of the employment of anæsthetics in surgery [4]. Sometimes he wanders further afield, as, for instance, in his account of the natural history of the fig-tree [5] and the worm [6], and in the curious little piece of information concerning Troglodytes and topazes, borrowed, he says, from secular writers, and still to be read in the elder Pliny [7]. Even where he seems to be borrowing, on rare occasions, from the commonplaces of Roman poetry, it is rather with the interest of the naturalist than of the rhetorician, as when he speaks in all seriousness of 'Marsian enchantments and hissing vipers lulled to sleep [8],' or recalls Lucan's asps and basilisks of the African desert as a description of his heretical opponents [9]. Perhaps his lost work, twice mentioned by Jerome [1], against the physician Dioscorus was a refutation of physical arguments against Christianity.

Hilary's speculative thought, like that of every serious adherent of the pagan creed, had certainly been inspired by Neoplatonism. We cannot take the account of his spiritual progress up to the full Catholic faith, which he gives in the beginning of the *De Trinitate*, and of which we find a less finished sketch in the Homily on Psalm lxi. § 2, as literal history. It is too symmetrical in its advance through steadily increasing light to the perfect knowledge, too well prepared as a piece of literary workmanship—it is indeed an admirable example of majestic prose, a worthy preface to that great treatise—for us to accept it, as it stands, as the record of actual experience. But we may safely see in it the evidence that Hilary had been an earnest student of the best thought of his day, and had found in Neoplatonism not only a speculative training but also the desire, which was to find its satisfaction in the Faith, for knowledge of God, and for union with Him. It was a debt which Origen, his master, shared with him; and it must have been because, as a Neoplatonist feeling after the truth, he found so much of common ground in Origen, that he was able to accept so

---

2 E.g. *Trin.* v. 11, vii. 14, ix. 4.
3 *Trin.* ii. 22.
4 *Trin.* x. 14. This is a very remarkable allusion. Celsus, vii. *præ*., confidently assumes that all surgical operations must be painful

5 *Comm. in Matt.* xxi. 8. 6 *Trin.* xi. 15.
7 *Tract. in Ps.* cxviii. *Ain.* 16; it is from Plin. N.H. 37, 32.
8 *Tract. in Ps.* lvii. 3. It suggests Virgil, Ovid, Silius, and others.
9 *Trin.* vii. 3. 1 *Ep.* 70, 5, *Vir. Ill.* 100.

fully the teaching of Alexandria. But it would be impossible to separate between the lessons which Hilary had learnt from the pagan form of this philosophy, and those which may have been new to him when he studied it in its Christian presentment. Of the influence of Christian Platonism upon him something will be said shortly. At this point we need only mention as a noteworthy indication of the fact that Hilary was not unmindful of the debt, that the only philosophy which he specifically attacks is the godless system of Epicurus, which denies creation, declares that the gods do not concern themselves with men, and deifies water or earth or atoms [2].

It was, then, as a man of mature age, of literary skill and philosophical training, that Hilary approached Christianity. He had been drawn towards the Faith by desire for a truth which he had not found in philosophy; and his conviction that this truth was Christianity was established by independent study of Scripture, not by intercourse with Christian teachers; so much we may safely conclude from the early pages of the *De Trinitate*. It must remain doubtful whether the works of Origen, who influenced his thought so profoundly, had fallen into his hands before his conversion, or whether it was as a Christian, seeking for further light upon the Faith, that he first studied them. For it is certainly improbable that he would find among the Christians of his own district many who could help him in intellectual difficulties. The educated classes were still largely pagan, and the Christian body, which was, we may say, unanimously and undoubtingly Catholic, held, without much mental activity, a traditional and inherited faith. Into this body Hilary entered by Baptism, at some unknown date. His age at the time, his employment, whether or no he was married [3], whether or no he entered the ministry of the Church of Poitiers, can never be known. It is only certain that he was strengthening his faith by thought and study.

He had come to the Faith, St. Augustine says [4], laden, like Cyprian, Lactantius and others, with the gold and silver and raiment of Egypt; and he would naturally wish to find a Christian employment for the philosophy which he brought with him. If his horizon had been limited to his neighbours in Gaul, he would have found little encouragement and less assistance. The oral teaching which prevailed in the West furnished, no doubt, safe guidance in doctrine, but could not supply reasons for the Faith. And reasons were the one great interest of Hilary. The whole practical side of Christianity as a system of life is ignored, or rather taken for granted and therefore not discussed, in his writings, which are ample enough to be a mirror of his thought. For instance, we cannot doubt that his belief concerning the Eucharist was that of the whole Church. Yet in the great treatise on the Trinity, of which no small part is given to the proof that Christ is God and Man, and that through this union must come the union of man with God, the Eucharist as a means to such union is only once introduced, and that in a short passage, and for the purpose of argument [5]. And altogether it would be as impossible to reconstruct the Christian life and thought of the day from his writings as from those of the half-pagan Arnobius. To such a mind as this the teaching which ordinary Christians needed and welcomed could bring no satisfaction, and no aid towards the interpretation of Scripture. The Western Church was, indeed, in an almost illogical position. Conviction was in advance of argument. The loyal practice of the Faith had led men on, as it were by intuition, to apprehend and firmly hold truths which the more thoughtful East was doubtfully and painfully approaching. Here, again, Hilary would be out of sympathy with his neighbours, and we cannot wonder that in such a doctrine

---

[2] *Tract. in Ps.* i. 7, lxi. 2, lxiii. 5, &c. As usual, Hilary does not name his opponents.

[3] Hilary's legendary daughte. Abra, to whom he is said to have written a letter printed in the editions of his works, is now generally abandoned by the best authorities, e.g. by Fechtrup, the writer, in Wetzer-Welte's Encyclopædia, of the best short life of Hilary.

[4] *De Doctr. Chr.* ii. 40.

[5] *Trin.* viii. 13—17.

as that of the Holy Spirit he held the conservative Eastern view. Nor were the Latin-speaking Churches well equipped with theological literature. The two [6] great theologians who had as yet written in their tongue, Tertullian and Novatian, with the former of whom Hilary was familiar, were discredited by their personal history. St. Cyprian, the one doctor whom the West already boasted, could teach disciplined enthusiasm and Christian morality, but his scattered statements concerning points of doctrine convey nothing more than a general impression of piety and soundness; and even his arrangement, in the *Testimonia*, of Scriptural evidences was a poor weapon against the logical attack of Arianism. But there is little reason to suppose that there was any general sense of the need of a more systematic theology. Africa was paralysed, and the attention of the Western provinces probably engrossed, by the Donatist strife, into which questions of doctrine did not enter. The adjustment of the relations between Church and State, the instruction and government of the countless proselytes who flocked to the Faith while toleration grew into imperial favour, must have needed all the attention that the Church's rulers could give. And these busy years had followed upon a generation of merciless persecution, during which change of practice or growth of thought had been impossible; and the confessors, naturally a conservative force, were one of the dominant powers in the Church. We cannot be surprised that the scattered notices in Hilary's writings of points of discipline, and his hortatory teaching, are in no respect different from what we find a century earlier in St. Cyprian. And men who were content to leave the superstructure as they found it were not likely to probe the foundations. Their belief grew in definiteness as the years went on, and faithful lives were rewarded, almost unconsciously, with a deeper insight into truth. But meanwhile they took the Faith as they had received it; one might say, as a matter of course. There was little heresy within the Western Church. Arianism was never prevalent enough to excite fear, even though repugnance were felt. The Churches were satisfied with faith and life as they saw it within and around them. Their religion was traditional, in no degenerate sense.

But such a religion could not satisfy ardent and logical minds, like those of St. Hilary and his two great successors, St. Ambrose and St. Augustine. To such men it was a necessity of their faith that they should know, and know in its right proportions, the truth so far as it had been revealed, and trace the appointed limits which human knowledge might not overpass. For their own assurance and for effective warfare against heresy a reasoned system of theology was necessary. Hilary, the earliest, had the greatest difficulty. To aid him in the interpretation of Scripture he had only one writer in his own tongue, Tertullian, whose teaching, in the matters which interested Hilary, though orthodox, was behind the times. His strong insistence upon the subordination of the Son to the Father, due to the same danger which still, in the fourth century, seemed in the East the most formidable, was not in harmony with the prevalent thought of the West. Thus Hilary, in his search for reasons for the Faith, was practically isolated; there was little at home which could help him to construct his system. To an intellect so self-reliant as his this may have been no great trial. Scrupulous though he was in confining his speculations within the bounds of inherited and acknowledged truth, yet in matters still undecided he exercised a singularly free judgment, now advancing beyond, now lingering behind, the usual belief of his contemporaries. In following out his thoughts, loyally yet independently, he was conscious that he was breaking what was new ground to his older fellow-Christians, almost as much as to himself, the convert

---

6 This is on the assumption, which seems probable, that Irenæus was not yet translated from the Greek. He certainly influenced Tertullian, and through him Hilary; and his doctrine of the *recapitulation* of mankind in Christ, reappearing as it does in Hilary, though not in Tertullian, suggests that our writer had made an independent study of Irenæus. Even if the present wretched translation existed, he would certainly read the Greek.

from Paganism. And that he was aware of the novelty is evident from the sparing use which he makes of that stock argument of the old controversialists, the newness of heresy. He uses it, e.g., in *Trin.* ii. 4, and uses it with effect; but it is far less prominent in him than in others.

For such independence of thought he could find precedent in Alexandrian theology, of which he was obviously a careful student and, in his free use of his own judgment upon it, a true disciple. When he was drawn into the Arian controversy and studied its literature, his thoughts to some extent were modified; but he never ceases to leave upon his reader the impression of an Oriental isolated in the West. From the Christian Platonists of Alexandria [7] come his most characteristic thoughts. They have passed on, for instance, from Philo to him the sense of the importance of the revelation contained in the divine name HE THAT IS. His peculiar doctrine of the impassibility of the incarnate Christ is derived, more probably directly than indirectly, from Clement of Alexandria. But it is to Origen that Hilary stands in the closest and most constant relations, now as a pupil, now as a critic. In fact, as we shall see, no small portion of the Homilies on the Psalms, towards the end of the work, is devoted to the controverting of opinions expressed by Origen; and by an omission which is itself a criticism he completely ignores one of that writer's most important contributions to Christian thought, the mystical interpretation of the Song of Songs. It is true that Jerome [8] knew of a commentary on that Book which was doubtfully attributed to Hilary; but if Hilary had once accepted such an exegesis he could not possibly have failed to use it on some of the numerous occasions when it must have suggested itself in the course of his writing, for it is not his habit to allow a thought to drop out of his mind; his characteristic ideas recur again and again. In some cases we can actually watch the growth of Hilary's mind as it emancipates itself from Origen's influence; as, for instance, in his psychology. He begins (*Comm. in Matt.* v. 8) by holding, with Origen and Tertullian, that the soul is corporeal; in later life he states expressly that this is not the case [9]. Yet what Hilary accepted from Origen is far more important than what he rejected. His strong sense of the dignity of man, of the freedom of the will, his philosophical belief in the inseparable connection of name and thing, the thought of the Incarnation as primarily an obscuring of the Divine glory [1], are some of the lessons which Origen has taught him. But, above all, it is to him that he owes his rudimentary doctrine concerning the Holy Spirit. Hilary says nothing inconsistent with the truth as it was soon to be universally recognised; but his caution in declining to accept, or at least to state, the general belief of Western Christendom that the Holy Spirit, since Christians are baptized in His Name as well as in that of Father and Son, is God in the same sense as They, is evidence both of his independence of the opinion around him and of his dependence on Origen. Of similar dependence on any other writer or school there is no trace. He knew Tertullian well, and there is some evidence that he knew Hippolytus and Novatian, but his thought was not moulded by theirs; and when, in the maturity of his powers, he became a fellow-combatant with Athanasius and the precursors of the great Cappadocians, his borrowing is not that of a disciple but of an equal.

There is one of St. Hilary's writings, evidently the earliest of those extant and probably the earliest of all, which may be noticed here, as it gives no sign of being written by a Bishop. It is the *Commentary on St. Matthew.* It is, in the strictest sense, a commentary, and not, like the work upon the Psalms, a series of exegetical discourses. It deals with the text of the Gospel, as it stood in Hilary's Latin version, without comment or criticism upon its peculiarities, and draws out the meaning, chiefly allegorical, not of the whole Gospel,

---

[7] Dr. Bigg's Bampton Lectures upon them are full of hints for the student of Hilary.   [8] *Vir. Ill.* 100.

[9] E.g. *Tract. in Ps.* cxxix. 4 f.   [1] E.g. *Trin.* ix. 6.

but apparently of lections that were read in public worship. A few pages at the beginning and end are unfortunately lost, but they cannot have contained anything of such importance as to alter the impression which we form of the book. In diction and grammar it is exactly similar to Hilary's later writings; the fact that it is, perhaps, somewhat more stiff in style may be due to self-consciousness of a writer venturing for the first time upon so important a subject. The exegesis is often the same as that of Origen, but a comparison of the several passages in which Jerome mentions this commentary makes it certain that it is not dependent upon him in the same way as are the Homilies on the Psalms and Hilary's lost work upon Job. Yet if he is not in this work the translator, or editor, of Origen, he is manifestly his disciple. We cannot account for the resemblance otherwise. Hilary is independently working out Origen's thoughts on Origen's lines. Origen is not named, nor any other author, except that he excuses himself from expounding the Lord's Prayer on the ground that Tertullian and Cyprian had written excellent treatises upon it[2]. This is a rare exception to his habit of not naming other writers. But, whoever the writers were from whom Hilary drew his exegesis, his theology is his own. There is no immaturity in the thought; every one of his characteristic ideas, as will be seen in the next chapter, is already to be found here. But there is one interesting landmark in the growth of the Latin theological vocabulary, very archaic in itself and an evidence that Hilary had not yet decided upon the terms that he would use. He twice[3] speaks of Christ's Divinity as 'the *theotes* which we call *deitas*.' In his later writings he consistently uses *divinitas*, except in the few instances where he is almost forced, to avoid intolerable monotony, to vary it with *deitas*; and in this commentary he would not have used either of these words, still less would he have used both, unless he were feeling his way to a fixed technical term. Another witness to the early date of the work is the absence of any clear sign that Hilary knew of the existence of Arianism. He knows, indeed, that there are heresies which impugn the Godhead of Christ[4], and in consequence states that doctrine with great precision, and frequently as well as forcibly. But it has been pointed out[5] that he discusses many texts which served, in the Arian strife, for attack or defence, without alluding to that burning question: and this would have been impossible and, indeed, a dereliction of duty, in Hilary's later life. And there is one passage[6] in which he speaks of God the Father as 'He with (or 'in') Whom the Word was *before He was born*.' The Incarnation is spoken of in words which would usually denote the eternal Generation: and if a candid reader could not be misled, yet an opportunity is given to the malevolent which Hilary or, indeed, any careful writer engaged in the Arian controversy would have avoided. The Commentary, then, is an early work, yet in no respect unworthy of its author. But though he had developed his characteristic thoughts before he began to write it, they are certainly less prominent here than in the treatises which followed. It is chiefly remarkable for its display of allegorical ingenuity. Its pages are full of fantastic interpretations of the kind which he had so great a share in introducing into Western Europe[7]. He started by it a movement which he would have been powerless to stop; that he was not altogether satisfied with the principle of allegory is shewn by the more modest use that he made of it when he composed, with fuller experience, the Homilies on the Psalms. It is, perhaps, only natural that there is little allegorism in the *De Trinitate*. Such a hot-house growth could not thrive in the keen

---

2 *Comm. in Matt.* v. 1. It may be mentioned that the chapters of the Commentary do not coincide with those of the Gospel.

3 *Comm. in Matt.* xvi. 4, *theotetam quam deitatem Latini nuncupant*, xxvi. 5, *theotetam quam deitatem nuncupamus.* The strange accusative *theotetam* makes it the more probable that we have here a specimen of the primitive Greek vocabulary of Latin Christendom of which so few examples, e.g. Baptism and Eucharist, have survived. Cyprian had probably the chief share

in destroying it; but the subject has never been examined as it deserves.

4 So especially xii. 18. There is similarly a possible allusion to Marcellus' teaching in xi. 9, which, however, may equally well be a reminiscence of some cognate earlier heresy.

5 Maffei's Introduction, § 15.

6 xxxi. 3, *penes quem erat antequam nasceretur.*

7 See Ebert, *Litteratur des Mittelalters*, i. 139.

air of controversy. As for the Commentary on St. Matthew, its chief influence has been indirect, in that St. Ambrose made large use of it in his own work upon the same Gospel. The consideration of Hilary's use of Scripture and of the place which it held in his system of theology is reserved for the next chapter, where illustrations from this Commentary are given.

About the year 350 Hilary was consecrated Bishop of Poitiers. So we may infer from his own words [8] that he had been a good while regenerate, and for some little time a bishop, on the eve of his exile in 356 A.D. Whether, like Ambrose, he was raised directly from lay life to the Episcopate cannot be known. It is at least possible that this was the case. His position as a bishop was one of great importance, and, as it must have seemed, free from special difficulties. There was a wide difference between the Church organisation of the Latin-speaking provinces of the Empire (with the exception of Central and Southern Italy and of Africa, in each of which a multitude of insignificant sees were dependent upon the autocracy of Rome and Carthage respectively) and that of the Greek-speaking provinces of the East. In the former there was a mere handful of dioceses, of huge geographical extent; in the latter every town, at least in the more civilised parts, had its bishop. The Western bishops were inevitably isolated from one another, and could exercise none of that constant surveillance over each other's orthodoxy which was, for evil as well as for good, so marked a feature of the Church life of the East. And the very greatness of their position gave them stability. The equipoise of power was too perfect, the hands in which it was vested too few, the men themselves, probably, too statesmanlike, for the Western Church to be infected with that nervous agitation which possessed the shifting multitudes of Eastern prelates, and made them suspicious and loquacious and disastrously eager for compromise. It was, in fact, the custom of the West to take the orthodoxy of its bishops for granted, and an external impulse was necessary before they could be overthrown. The two great sees with which Hilary was in immediate relation were those of Arles and Milan, and both were in Arian hands. But it needed the direct incitation of a hostile Emperor to set Saturninus against Hilary; and it was in vain that Hilary, in the floodtide of orthodox revival in the West, attacked Auxentius. The orthodox Emperor upheld the Arian, who survived Hilary by eight years and died in possession of his see. But this great and secure position of the Western bishop had its drawbacks. Hilary was conscious of its greatness [9], and strove to be worthy of it; but it was a greatness of responsibility to which neither he, nor any other man, could be equal. For in his eyes the bishop was still, as he had been in the little Churches of the past, and still might be in quiet places of the East or South, the sole priest, *sacerdos* [1], of his flock. In his exile he reminds the Emperor that he is still distributing the communion through his presbyters to the Church. This survival can have had none but evil results. It put both bishop and clergy in a false position. The latter were degraded by the denial to them of a definite status and rights of their own. Authority without influence and information in lieu of knowledge was all for which the former could hope. And this lack of any organised means of influencing a wide-spread flock—such a diocese as that of Poitiers must have been several times as large as a rural diocese of England—prevented its bishop from creating any strong public opinion within it, unless he were an evangelist with the gifts of a Martin of Tours. It was impossible for him to excite in so unwieldy a district any popular enthusiasm or devotion to himself. Unlike an Athanasius, he could be deported into exile at the Emperor's will with as little commotion as the bishop of some petty half-Greek town in Asia Minor.

---

[8] *Syn.* 91; *regeneratus pridem et in episcopatu aliquantisper manens.* The renderings 'long ago' and 'for some time' in this translation seem rather too strong.

[9] E.g. *Trin.* viii. 1. The bishop is a prince of the Church.
[1] *Sacerdos* in Hilary, as in all writers till near the end of the fourth century, means 'bishop' always.

During the first years of Hilary's episcopate there was civil turmoil in Gaul, but the Church was at peace. While the Eastern ruler Constantius favoured the Arians, partly misled by unprincipled advisers and partly guided by an unwise, though honest, desire for compromise in the interests of peace, his brother Constans, who reigned in the West, upheld the Catholic cause, to which the immense majority of his clergy and people was attached. He was slain in January, 350, by the usurper Magnentius, who, with whatever motives, took the same side. It was certainly that which would best conciliate his own subjects; but he went further, and attempted to strengthen his precarious throne against the impending attack of Constantius by negotiations with the discontented Nicene Christians of the East. He tried to win over Athanasius, who was, however, too wise to listen; and, in any case, he gained nothing by tampering with the subjects of Constantius. Constantius defeated Magnentius, pursued him, and finally slew him on the 11th August, 353, and was then undisputed master not only of the East but of the West, which he proceeded to bring into ecclesiastical conformity, as far as he could, with his former dominions.

The general history of Arianism and the tendencies of Christian thought at this time have been so fully and admirably delineated in the introduction to the translation of St. Athanasius in this series[2], that it would be superfluous and presumptuous to go over the same ground. It must suffice to say that Constantius was animated with a strong personal hatred against Athanasius, and that the prelates at his court seem to have found their chief employment in intrigues for the expulsion of bishops, whose seats might be filled by friends of their own. Athanasius was a formidable antagonist, from his strong position in Alexandria, even to an Emperor; and Constantius was attempting to weaken him by creating an impression that he was unworthy of the high esteem in which he was held. Even in the East, as yet, the Nicene doctrine was not avowedly rejected; still less could the doctrinal issue be raised in Gaul, where the truths stated in the Nicene Creed were regarded as so obvious that the Creed itself had excited little interest or attention. Hilary at this time had never heard it[3], though nearly thirty years had passed since the Council decreed it. But there were personal charges against Athanasius, of which he has himself given us a full and interesting account[4], which had done him, and were to do him, serious injury. They had been disproved publicly and completely more than once, and with great solemnity and apparent finality ten years before this, at Sardica in 343 A.D. But in a distant province, aided by the application of sufficient pressure, they might serve their turn, and if the Emperor could obtain his enemy's condemnation, and that in a region whose theological sympathies were notoriously on his side, a great step would be gained towards his expulsion from Egypt. No time was lost. In October, 353, a Council was called at Arles to consider the charges. It suited Constantius' purpose well that Saturninus of Arles, bishop of the most important see in Gaul, and the natural president, was both a courtier and an Arian. He did his work well. The assembled bishops believed, or were induced to profess that they believed, that the charges against Athanasius were not made in the interests of his theological opponents, and that the Emperor's account of them was true. The decision, condemning the accused, was almost unanimous. Even the representative of Liberius of Rome consented, to be disavowed on his return; and only one bishop, Paulinus of Treves, suffered exile for resistance. He may have been the only advocate for Athanasius, or Constantius may have thought that one example would suffice to terrify the episcopate of Gaul into submission. It is impossible to say whether Hilary was present at the Council or no. It is not probable that he was absent: and his ignorance, even later, on important points in the dispute shews that he may

---

2 By Dr. Robertson of King's College, London. This, and Professor Gwatkin's *Studies of Arianism*, are the best English accounts.

3 *Syn.* 91.
4 The *Apologia contra Arianos*, p. 100 ff. in Dr. Robertson's translation.

well have given an honest verdict against Athanasius. The new ruler's word had been given that he was guilty; nothing can yet have been known against Constantius and much must have been hoped from him. It was only natural that he should obtain the desired decision. Two years followed, during which the Emperor was too busy with warfare on the frontiers of Gaul to proceed further in the matter of Athanasius. But in the Autumn of 355 he summoned a Council at Milan, a city whose influence over Gaul was so great that it might almost be called the ecclesiastical capital of that country. Here again strong pressure was used, and the verdict given as Constantius desired. Hilary was not present at this Council; he was by this time aware of the motives of Constantius and the courtier bishops, and would certainly have shared in the opposition offered, and probably in the exile inflicted upon three of the leaders in it. These were Dionysius of Milan, who disappears from history, his place being taken by Hilary's future enemy, Auxentius, and Eusebius of Vercelli and Lucifer of Cagliari, both of whom were to make their mark in the future.

By this time Hilary had definitely taken his side, and it will be well to consider his relation to the parties in the controversy. And first as to Arianism. As we have seen, Arian prelates were now in possession of the two great sees of Arles and Milan in his own neighbourhood; and Arianisers of different shades, or at least men tolerant of Arianism, held a clear majority of the Eastern bishoprics, except in the wholly Catholic Egypt. But it is certain that, in the West at any rate, the fundamental difference of the Arian from the Catholic position was not generally recognised. Arian practice and Arian practical teaching was indistinguishable from Catholic; and unless ultimate principles were questioned, Catholic clergy might work, and the multitudes of Catholic laity might live and die, without knowing that their bishop's creed was different from their own. The Abbé Duchesne has made the very probable suggestion that the stately Ambrosian ritual of Milan was really introduced from the East by Auxentius, the Arian intruder from Cappadocia, of whom we have spoken[5]. Arian Baptism and the Arian Eucharist were exactly the same as the Catholic. They were not sceptical; they accepted all current beliefs or superstitions, and had their own confessors and workers of miracles[6]. The Bible was common ground to both parties: each professed its confidence that it had the support of Scripture. "No false system ever struck more directly at the life of Christianity than Arianism. Yet after all it held aloft the Lord's example as the Son of Man, and never wavered in its worship of Him as the Son of God[7]." And the leaders of this school were in possession of many of the great places of the Church, and asserted that they had the right to hold them; that if they had not the sole right, at least they had as good a right as the Catholics, to be bishops, and yet to teach the doctrine that Christ was a creature, not the Son. And what made things worse was that they seemed to be at one with the Catholics, and that it was possible, and indeed almost inevitable, that the multitudes who did not look below the surface should be satisfied to take them for what they seemed. Many of the Arians no doubt honestly thought that their position was a tenable one, and held their offices with a good conscience; but we cannot wonder that men like Athanasius and Hilary, aware of the sophistical nature of many of the arguments used, and knowing that some, at least, of the leaders were unscrupulous adventurers, should have regarded all Arianism and all Arians as deliberately dishonest. It seemed incredible that they could be sincerely at home in the Church, and intolerable that they should have the power of deceiving the people and persecuting true believers. It is against Arianism in the Church that Hilary's efforts are directed, not against Arianism as an external heresy. He ignores heresies outside the Church as completely as does Cyprian; they

---

[5] *Origines du culte chrétien*, p. 88.   [6] Gwatkin, *Studies of Arianism*, p. 134.   [7] Ib., p. 28.

are outside, and therefore he has nothing to do with them. But Arianism, as represented by an Auxentius or a Saturninus, is an *internum malum*[8]; and to the extirpation of this 'inward evil' the remaining years of his life were to be devoted.

His own devotion, from the time of his conversion to the Catholic Faith, which almost all around him held, was not the less sincere because it did not find its natural expression in the Nicene Creed. That document, which primarily concerned only bishops, and them only when their orthodoxy was in question, was hardly known in the West, where the bishops had as yet had little occasion for doubting one another's faith. Hilary had never heard it,—he can hardly have avoided hearing of it,—till just before his exile. In his earlier conflicts he rarely mentions it, and when he does it is in connection with the local circumstances of the East. In later life he, with Western Christendom at large, recognised its value as a rallying point for the faithful; but even then there is no attachment to the Creed for its own sake. It might almost seem that the Creed, by his defence of which Athanasius has earned such glory, owed its original celebrity to him rather than he to it. His unjust persecution and heroic endurance excited interest in the symbol of which he was the champion. If it were otherwise, there has been a strange conspiracy of silence among Western theologians. In their great works on the Trinity, Hilary most rarely, and Augustine never, allude to it; the Council of Aquileia, held in the same interests and almost at the same time as that of Constantinople in 381, absolutely ignores it[9]. The Creed, in the year 355, was little known in the West and unpopular in the East. Even Athanasius kept it somewhat in the background, from reasons of prudence, and Hilary's sympathies, as we shall see, were with the Eastern School which could accept the truth, though they disliked this expression of it.

The time had now come for Hilary, holding these views of Arianism and of the Faith, to take an active part in the conflict. We have seen that he was not at Milan; he was therefore not personally compromised, but the honour of the Church compelled him to move. He exerted himself to induce the bishops of Gaul to withdraw from communion with Saturninus, and with Ursacius and Valens, disciples of Arius during his exile on the banks of the Danube thirty years before, and now high in favour with Constantius, and his ministers, we might almost say, for the ecclesiastical affairs of the Western provinces. We do not know how many bishops were enlisted by Hilary against Saturninus. It is probable that not many would follow him in so bold a venture; even men of like mind with himself might well think it unwise. It was almost a revolutionary act; an importation of the methods of Eastern controversy into the peaceful West, for this was not the constitutional action of a synod but the private venture of Hilary and his allies. However righteous and necessary, in the interests of morality and religion, their conduct may have seemed to them, to Constantius and his advisers it must have appeared an act of defiance to the law, both of Church and State. And Hilary would certainly not win favour with the Emperor by his letter of protest, the *First Epistle to Constantius*, written about the end of the year 355. He adopts the usual tone of the time, that of exaggerated laudation and even servility towards the Emperor. Such language was, of course, in great measure conventional; we know from Cicero's letters how little superlatives, whether of flattery or abuse, need mean, and language had certainly not grown more sincere under the Empire. The letter was, in fact, a singularly bold manifesto, and one which Hilary himself must have foreseen was likely to bring upon him the

8 *Trin.* vii. 3.

9 There is much more evidence to this effect in Reuter, *Augustinische Studien*, p. 182 f. It was probably due to jealousy between West and East; cf. the way in which John of Jerusalem ignored the African decision in Pelagius' case. But the West was ignorant, as well as jealous, of the East. Even in his last years, after his sojourn in Asia Minor, Hilary believed that Jerusalem was, as had been prophesied, an uninhabited ruin; *Tr. in Ps.* cxxiv. § 2, cxxxi. §§ 18, 23, cxlvi. § 1.

punishment which had befallen the recusants at Arles and Milan. He begins (§ 1) in studiously general terms, making no mention of the provinces in which the offences were being committed, with a complaint of the tyrannical interference of civil officers in religious matters. If there is to be peace (§ 2), there must be liberty; Catholics must not be forced to become Arians. The voice of resistance was being raised; men were beginning to say that it was better to die than to see the faith defiled at the bidding of an individual. Equity required that God-fearing men should not suffer by compulsory intercourse with the teachers of execrable blasphemy, but be allowed bishops whom they could obey with a good conscience. Truth and falsehood, light and darkness could not combine. He entreated the Emperor to allow the people to choose for themselves to what teachers they would listen, with whom they would join in the Eucharist and in prayer for him. Next (§ 3) he denies that there is any purpose of treason, or any discontent. The only disturbance is that caused by Arian propagators of heresy, who are busily engaged in misleading the ignorant. He now (§ 4) prays that the excellent bishops who have been sent into exile may be restored; liberty and joy would be the result. Then (§ 5) he attacks the modern and deadly Arian pestilence. Borrowing, somewhat incautiously, the words of the Council of Sardica, now twelve years old, he gives a list of Arian chiefs which ends with "those two ignorant and unprincipled youths, Ursacius and Valens." Communion with such men as these, even communion in ignorance, is a participation in their guilt, a fatal sin. He proceeds, in § 6, to combine denunciation of the atrocities committed in Egypt with a splendid plea for liberty of conscience; it is equally vain and wicked to attempt to drive men into Arianism, and an enforced faith is, in any case, worthless. The Arians (§ 7) were themselves legally convicted long ago and Athanasius acquitted; it is a perversion of justice that the condemned should now be intriguing against one so upright and so faithful to the truth. And lastly (§ 8) he comes to the wrong just done at Milan, and tells the well-known story of the violence practised upon Eusebius of Vercelli and others in the 'Synagogue of malignants,' as he calls it. Here also he takes occasion to speak of Paulinus of Treves, exiled for his resistance at Arles two years before, where he "had withstood the monstrous crimes of those men." The conclusion of the letter is unfortunately lost, and there are one or more gaps in the body of it; these, we may judge, would only have made it more unacceptable to Constantius.

It was, indeed, from the Emperor's point of view, a most provocatory Epistle. He and his advisers were convinced that compromise was the way of peace. They had no quarrel with the orthodoxy of the West, if only that orthodoxy would concede that Arianisers were entitled to office in the Church, or would at least be silent; and they were animated by a persistent hatred of Athanasius. Moreover, the whole tendency of thought, since Constantine began to favour the Church, had run towards glorification of the Emperor as the vice-gerent of God; and the orthodox had had their full share in encouraging the idea. That a bishop, with no status to justify his interference, should renounce communion with his own superior, the Emperor's friend, at Arles; should forbid the officers of state to meddle in the Church's affairs, and demand an entirely new thing, recognition by the state as lawful members of the Church while yet they rejected the prelates whom the state recognised; should declare that peace was impossible because the conflicting doctrines were as different as light and darkness, and that the Emperor's friends were execrable heretics; should assert, while denying that he or his friends had any treasonable purpose, that men were ready to die rather than submit; should denounce two Councils, lawfully held, and demand reinstatement of those who had opposed the decision of those Councils; should, above all, take the part of Athanasius, now obviously doomed to another exile;—all this must have savoured of rebellion. And rebellion was no imaginary danger.

We have seen that Magnentius had tried to enlist Athanasius on his side against the Arian Emperor. Constantius was but a new ruler over Gaul, and had no claim, through services rendered, to its loyalty. He might reasonably construe Hilary's words into a threat that the orthodox of Gaul would, if their wishes were disregarded, support an orthodox pretender. And there was a special reason for suspicion. At this very time Constantius had just conferred the government of the West upon his cousin Julian, who was installed as Cæsar on the 6th November, 355. From the first, probably, Constantius distrusted Julian, and Julian certainly distrusted Constantius. Thus it might well seem that the materials were ready for an explosion; that a disloyal Cæsar would find ready allies in discontented Catholics.

We cannot wonder that Hilary's letter had no effect upon the policy of Constantius. It is somewhat surprising that several months elapsed before he was punished. In the spring of the year 356 Saturninus presided at a Council held at Béziers, at which Hilary was, he tells us, compelled to attend. In what the compulsion consisted we do not know. It may simply have been that he was summoned to attend; a summons which he could not with dignity refuse, knowing, as he must have done, that charges would be brought against himself. Of the proceedings of the Synod we know little. The complaints against Hilary concerned his conduct, not his faith. This latter was, of course, above suspicion, and it was not the policy of the court party to attack orthodoxy in Gaul. He seems to have been charged with exciting popular discontent; and this, as we have seen, was an accusation which his own letter had rendered plausible. He tried to raise the question of the Faith, challenging the doctrine of his opponents. But though a large majority of a council of Gallic bishops would certainly be in sympathy with him, he had no success. Their position was not threatened; Hilary, like Paulinus, was accused of no doctrinal error, and these victims of Constantius, if they had raised no questions concerning their neighbours' faith and made no objections to the Emperor's tyranny, might also have passed their days in peace. The tone of the episcopate in Gaul was, in fact, by no means heroic. If we may trust Sulpicius Severus [1], in all these Councils the opposition was prepared to accept the Emperor's word about Athanasius, and excommunicate him, if the general question of the Faith might be discussed. But the condition was evaded, and the issue never frankly raised; and, if it was cowardly, it was not unnatural that Hilary should have been condemned by the Synod, and condemned almost unanimously. Only Rodanius of Toulouse was punished with him; the sufferers would certainly have been more numerous had there been any strenuous remonstrance against the injustice. The Synod sent their decision to the Cæsar Julian, their immediate ruler. Julian took no action; he may have felt that the matter was too serious for him to decide without reference to the Emperor, but it is more likely that he had no wish to outrage the dominant Church feeling of Gaul and alienate sympathies which he might need in the future. In any case he refused to pass a sentence which he must have known would be in accordance with the Emperor's desire; and the vote of the Synod, condemning Hilary, was sent to Constantius himself. He acted upon it at once, and in the summer of the same year, 356, Hilary was exiled to the diocese, or civil district comprising several provinces, of Asia.

We now come to the most important period of Hilary's life. He was already, as we have seen, a Greek scholar and a follower of Greek theology. He was now to come into immediate contact with the great problems of the day in the field on which they were being constantly debated. And he was well prepared to take his part. He had formed his own convictions before he was acquainted with *homoousion, homoiousion* or the Nicene

---

[1] *Chron.* ii. 39.

Creed [2]. He was therefore in full sympathy with Athanasius on the main point. And his manner of treating the controversy shews that the policy of Athanasius was also, in a great measure, his. Like Athanasius, he spares Marcellus as much as possible. We know that Athanasius till the end refused to condemn him, though one of the most formidable weapons in the armoury of the Anti-Nicene party was the conjunction in which they could plausibly put their two names, as those of the most strenuous opponents of Arianism. Similarly Hilary never names Marcellus [3], as he never names Apollinaris, though he had the keenest sense of the danger involved in either heresy, and argues forcibly and often against both. Like Athanasius again, he has no mercy upon Photinus the disciple, while he spares Marcellus the master; and it is a small, though clear, sign of dependence that he occasionally applies Athanasius' nickname of *Ariomanitæ*, or 'Arian lunatics,' to his opponents. It is certain that Hilary was familiar with the writings of Athanasius, and borrowed freely from them. But so little has yet been done towards ascertaining the progress of Christian thought and the extent of each writer's contribution to it, that it is impossible to say which arguments were already current and may have been independently adopted by Hilary and by Athanasius, and for which the former is indebted to the latter [4]. Yet it is universally recognised that the debt exists; and Hilary's greatness as a theologian [5], his mastery of the subject, would embolden him to borrow and adapt the more freely that he was dealing as with an equal and a fellow-combatant in the same cause.

Athanasius and Hilary can never have met face to face. But the eyes and the agents of Athanasius were everywhere, and he must have known something of the exile and of the services of Hilary, who was, of course, well acquainted with the history of Athanasius, though, with the rest of Gaul, he may not have been whole-hearted in his defence. And now he was the more likely to be drawn towards him because this was the time of his approximation to the younger generation of the Conservative School. For it is with them that Hilary's affinities are closest and most obvious. The great Cappadocians were devoted Origenists— we know the service they rendered to their master by the publication of the *Philocalia*,— and there could be no stronger bond of union between Hilary and themselves. They were the outgrowth of that great Asiatic school to which the name of Semiarians, somewhat unkindly given by Epiphanius, has clung, and which was steadily increasing in influence over the thought of Asia, the dominant province, at this time, of the whole Empire. Gregory of Nazianzus, the eldest of the three great writers, was probably not more than twenty-five years of age when Hilary was sent into exile, and none of them can have seriously affected even his latest works. But they represented, in a more perfect form, the teaching of the best men of the Conservative School; and when we find that Hilary, who was old enough to be the father of Basil and the two Gregories, has thoughts in common with them which are not to be found in Athanasius, we may safely assign this peculiar teaching to the influence upon Hilary, predisposed by his loyalty to Origen to listen to the representatives of the Origenist tradition, of this school of theology. We see one side of this influence in Hilary's understatement of the doctrine of the Holy Ghost. The Semiarians were coming to be of one mind with the Nicenes as to the consubstantial Deity of the Son; none of them, in all probability, at this time would have admitted the

---

[2] *Syn.* 91.

[3] This sparing of Marcellus, in the case of a Western like Hilary, may have been a concession to the incapacity of the West, e.g. Julius of Rome and the Council of Sardica, to see his error. But this is not so likely as that it was a falling in with the general policy of Athanasius, as was the rare mention of the *homoousion*; cf. Gwatkin, *op. cit.* 42 n. Hilary was singularly independent of Western opinion, and his whole aim was to win the East.

[4] No such examination seems to have been made as that to which Reuter in his admirable *Augustinische Studien* has subjected some of the thoughts of St. Augustine.

[5] Harnack, *Dogmengeschichte*, ii. p. 243 n. (ed. 3). Hilary is, 'making all allowance for dependence on Athanasius, an independent thinker, who has, indeed, excelled the bishop of Alexandria as a theologian.'

consubstantial Deity of the Spirit, and the unity of their School was to be wrecked in future years upon this point. The fact that Hilary could use language so reserved upon this subject must have led them to welcome his alliance the more heartily. Neither he nor they could foresee the future of the doctrine, and both sides must have sincerely thought that they were at one. And, indeed, on Hilary's part there was a great willingness to believe in this unity, which led him, as we shall see, into an unfortunate attempt at ecclesiastical diplomacy. Another evidence of contact with this Eastern School, but at its most advanced point, is the remarkable expression, 'Only-begotten God,' which Hilary 'employs with startling freedom, evidently as the natural expression of his own inmost thought[6].' Dr. Hort, whose words these are, states that the term is used by Athanasius only twice, once in youth and once in old age; but that, on the other hand, it is familiar to two of the Cappadocians, Basil and Gregory of Nyssa. They must have learned it from some Asiatic writer known to Hilary as a contemporary, to them as successors. And when we find Hilary[7] rejecting the baptism of heretics, and so putting himself in opposition to what had been the Roman view for a century and that of Gaul since the Council of Arles in 314, and then find this opinion echoed by Gregory of Nazianzus[8], we are reminded not only of Hilary's general independence of thought, but of the circumstance that St. Cyprian found his stoutest ally in contesting this same point in the Cappadocian Firmilian. A comparison of the two sets of writings would probably lead to the discovery of more coincidences than have yet been noticed; of the fact itself, of 'the Semiarian influence so visible in the *De Synodis* of Hilary, and even in his own later work[9],' there can be no doubt.

With these affinities, with an adequate knowledge of the Greek language and a strong sympathy, as well as a great familiarity, with Greek modes of thought, Hilary found himself in the summer of the year 356 an exile in Asia Minor. It was exile in the most favourable circumstances. He was still bishop of Poitiers, recognised as such by the government, which only forbade him, for reasons of state ostensibly not connected with theology, to reside within his diocese. He held free communication with his fellow-bishops in Gaul, and was allowed to administer his own diocese, so far as administration by letter was possible, without interruption. And his diocese did not forget him. We learn from Sulpicius Severus[1] that he and the others of the little band of exiles, who had suffered at Arles, and Milan, and Béziers, were the heroes of the day in their own country. That orthodox bishops should suffer for the Faith was a new thing in the West; we cannot wonder that subsidies were raised for their support and delegations sent to assure them of the sympathy of their flocks. To a man like Hilary, of energy and ability, of recognised episcopal rank and unimpeached orthodoxy, the position offered not less but more opportunities of service than hitherto he had enjoyed. For no restriction was put upon his movements, so long as he kept within the wide bounds allotted him. He had perfect leisure for travel or for study, the money needed for the expense of his journeys, and something of the glory, still very real, with which the confessor was invested. And his movements were confined to the very region where he could learn most concerning the question of the hour, and do most for its solution. In fact, in sending Hilary into such an exile as this, Constantius had done too much, or too little; he had injured, and not advanced, his own favourite cause of unity by way of compromise. In this instance, as in those of Arius and Athanasius and many others, exile became an efficacious means for

---

6 Hort, *Two Dissertations*, p. 27.

7 *Trin.* viii. 40.

8 Cf. Gwatkin, *Studies of Arianism*, p. 130.

9 Ib., p. 159. It would not be fair to judge Hilary by the *de Synodis* alone. The would-be diplomatist, in his eagerness to bring about a reconciliation, is not quite just either to the facts or to his own feelings.

1 *Chron.* ii. 39.

the spreading and strengthening of convictions. If Hilary had no great success, as we shall see, in the Council which he attended, yet his presence, during these critical years, in a region where men were gradually advancing to the fuller truth cannot have been without influence upon their spiritual growth ; and his residence in Asia no doubt confirmed and enriched his own apprehension of the Faith.

It is certain that Hilary was busily engaged in writing his great work upon the Trinity, and that some parts of it were actually published, during his exile. But as this work in its final form would appear to belong to the next stage of Hilary's life, it will be well to postpone its consideration for the present, and proceed at once to his share in the conciliar action of the time. We have no information concerning his conduct before the year 358, but it is necessary to say something about the important events which preceded his publication of the *De Synodis* and his participation in the Council of Seleucia.

It was a time when new combinations of parties were being formed. Arianism was shewing itself openly, as it had not dared to do since Nicæa. In 357 Hilary's adversaries, Ursacius and Valens, in a Synod at Sirmium, published a creed which was Arian without concealment ; it was, indeed, as serious a blow to the Emperor's policy of compromise as anything that Athanasius or Hilary had ventured. But it was the work of friends of the Emperor, and shewed that, for the moment at any rate, the Court had been won over to the extreme party. But the forces of Conservatism were still the strongest. Within a few months, early in 358, the great Asiatic prelates, soon to be divided over the question of the Godhead of the Holy Spirit but still at one, Basil of Ancyra, Macedonius and others, met at Ancyra and repudiated Arianism while ignoring, after their manner, the Nicene definition. Then their delegates proceeded to the Court, now at Sirmium, and won Constantius back to his old position. Ursacius and Valens, who had no scruples, signed a Conservative creed, as did the weak Liberius of Rome, anxious to escape from an exile to which he had been consigned soon after the banishment of Hilary. It was a great triumph to have induced so prominent a bishop to minimise— we cannot say that he denied—his own belief and that of the Western churches. And the Asiatic leaders were determined to have the spoils of victory. Liberius, of course, was allowed to return home, for he had proved compliant, and the Conservatives had no quarrel with those who held the *homoousion*. But the most prominent of the Arian leaders, those who had the courage of their conviction, to the number, it is said, of seventy, were exiled. It is true that Constantius was quickly persuaded by other influences to restore them ; but the theological difference was embittered by the sense of personal injury, and further conflicts rendered inevitable between Conservatives and Arians.

It was with this Conservative party, victorious for the moment, that Hilary had to deal. Its leaders, and especially Basil of Ancyra, had the ear of the Emperor, and seemed to hold the future of the Church in their hands. Hilary was on friendly terms with Basil, with whom, as we have seen, he had much in common, and corresponded on his behalf with the Western Bishops. He was, indeed, by the peculiar combination in him of the Eastern and the Western, perhaps the only man who could have played the part he undertook. He was thoroughly and outspokenly orthodox, yet had no prejudice in favour of the Nicene definition. He would have been content, like the earlier generation of Eastern bishops, with a simple formulary ; the Apostles' Creed, the traditional standard of the West, satisfied the exigencies even of his own precise thought. And if a personal jealousy of Athanasius and his school on the part of the Asiatic Conservatives was one of the chief obstacles to peace, here again Hilary had certain advantages. We have seen that there was no personal communication between him and Athanasius ; he could ignore, and may even have been ignorant of, the antipathy of Asia to Alexandria. And he was no absolute follower of Athanasius' teaching. We saw that in some important respects he was an independent thinker, and that in others he is on common ground with the Cappadocians, the heirs of the best thought of such men as Basil of Ancyra. Nor could he labour under any suspicion of being involved in the heresy of Marcellus. It was an honourable tradition of Eastern Christendom to guard against the recrudescence of such heresy as his, which revived the fallacies of Paul of Samosata and of Sabellius, and seemed in Asia the most formidable of all possible errors. Marcellus had forged it as a weapon in defence of the Nicene faith; and if his doctrine were among the most formidable antagonists of Arianism, it may well have seemed that there was not much to choose between the two. And while Athanasius had never condemned Marcellus, and the West had more than once pronounced him innocent, the general feeling of the East was decisively against him, and deeply suspicious of any appearance of sympathy with him. And further, by one of those complications of personal with theological opposition which were so sadly frequent, Basil was in possession of that very see of Ancyra from which the heretic Marcellus had been expelled. Hilary, who was unconcerned in all this, saw a new hope for the Church in his Asiatic friends, and his own tendencies of thought must have been a welcome surprise to them, accustomed as they were to suspect Sabellianism in the West. The prospect, indeed, was at first sight a fair one. The Faith, it seemed, might be upheld by imperial support, now that it had advocates who were not prejudiced in the Emperor's eyes as was Athanasius; and Athanasius himself, accredited by the testimony of Asia, might recover his position. Yet Hilary was building on an unsound foundation. The Semiarian party was not united. Hilary may not have suspected, or may, in his zeal for the cause, have concealed from himself the fact, that in the doctrine of the Holy Ghost there lay the seeds of a strife which was soon to divide his allies as widely as Arius was separated from Athanasius. And these allies, as a body, were not worthy supporters of the truth. There were many sincere men among them, but these were mixed with adventurers, who used the conflict as a means of attaining office, with as few scruples as any of the other prelates who hung around the court. But the fatal obstacle to success was that the whole plan depended on the favour of Constantius. For the moment Basil and his friends possessed this, but their adversaries were men of greater dexterity and fewer scruples than they. Valens and Ursacius and their like were doing their utmost to retrieve defeat and enjoy revenge. It is significant that Athanasius, as it seems, had no share in Hilary's hopes and schemes for drawing East and West together. He had an unrivalled knowledge of the circumstances, and an open mind, willing to see good in the Semiarians; had the plan contained the elements of success it would have received his warm support.

Hilary threw himself heartily into it. He travelled, we know, extensively; so much so, that his letters from Gaul failed to reach him in the year 358. This was a serious matter. We have seen that the exiles from the West had derived great support from their flocks. Hilary's own weight as a negotiator must have depended upon the general knowledge that he did not stand alone, but represented the public opinion of a great province. For this reason, as well as for his own peace of mind, it must have been a welcome relief to him to learn, when letters came at last, that his friends had not forgotten or deserted him; and he seized the opportunity of reply to send to the bishops of all the Gallic provinces and of Britain the circular letter which we call the *De Synodis,* translated in this volume. The Introduction to it, here given, makes it unnecessary to describe its contents. It may suffice to say that it is an able and well-written attempt to explain the Eastern position to Western theologians. He shews that the Eastern creeds, which had been composed since the Nicene, were susceptible of an orthodox meaning, and felicitously brings out their merits by contrast with the unmitigated heresy of the second creed of Sirmium, which he cites at full length. It must be admitted that there is a certain amount of special pleading; that his eyes are resolutely shut to any other aspect of the documents than that which he is commending to the attention of his readers in Gaul. And he is as boldly original in his rendering of history as of doctrine. He actually describes the Council of the Dedication, which confirmed the deposition of Athanasius and propounded a compromising creed, definitely intended to displace the Nicene, as an 'assembly of the saints[2].' The West, we know, cared little for Eastern disputes and formularies. There can have been no great risk that Hilary's praise should revolt the minds of his friends, and as little hope that it would excite any enthusiasm among them. This description, and a good deal else in the *De Synodis*, was obviously meant to be read in the land where it was written. When all possible allowance is made for his sympathy with the best men among the Asiatics, and for the hopefulness with which he might naturally regard his allies, it is still impossible to think that he was quite sincere in asserting that their object in compiling ambiguous creeds was the suppression of Sabellianism and not the rejection of the *homoousion*. Yet it was natural enough that he should write as he did, for the prospect must have seemed most attractive. If this open letter could convince the Eastern bishops that they were regarded in the West not with suspicion, as teachers of the inferiority of Christ, but with admiration, as steadfast upholders of His reality, a great step was made towards union. And if Hilary could persuade his brethren in Gaul that the imperfect terms in which the East was accustomed to express its faith in Christ were compatible with sound belief, an approach could be made from that side also. And in justice to Hilary we must bear in mind that he does not fall into the error of Liberius. It was a serious fault for a Western bishop to abandon words which were, for him and for his Church, the recognised expression of the truth; it was a very different matter to argue that inadequate terms, in the mouth of those who were unhappily pledged to the use of them, might contain the saving Faith. This latter is the argument which Hilary uses. He urges the East to advance to the definiteness of the Nicene confession; he urges the West to welcome the first signs of such an advance, and meantime to recognise the truth that was half-concealed in their ambiguous documents. The attempt was a bold one, and met, as was inevitable, with severe criticism from the side of uncompromising orthodoxy, which we may for the moment leave unnoticed. What Athanasius thought of the treatise we do not know; it would be unsafe to conjecture that his own work, which bears the same title and was written in the following year, when the futility of the hope which had buoyed Hilary up had been demonstrated, was a silent criticism upon the *De Synodis* of the other. It is, at least, a success in itself, and was a step towards the ultimate victory of truth; we cannot say as much of Hilary's effort, admirable though its intention was, and though it must have contributed something to the softening of asperities. But Alexandria and Gaul were distant, and while the one excited repugnance in the Emperor's mind, the other had little influence with him. The decision seemed to lie in the hands of Basil of Ancyra and his colleagues. The men who had the ear of Constantius, and had lately induced him to banish the Arians, must in consistency use their influence for the restoration of exiles who were suffering for their opposition to Arianism; and this influence, if only the West would heartily join with them, would be strong enough to secure even the restoration of Athanasius. Such thoughts were certainly present in the mind of Hilary when he painted so bright a picture of Eastern Councils, and represented Constantius as an innocent believer, once misguided but now returned to the Faith[3]. From the Semiarian leaders, controlling the policy of Constantius, he expected peace for the Church, restoration of the exiles, the suppression of Arianism. And if to some extent he deceived himself, and was willing to believe and to persuade others that men's faith and purpose differed from what in fact it was, we must remember that it was a time of passionate earnestness, when cool judgment concerning friend or foe was almost impossible for one who was involved in that great conflict concerning the Divinity of Christ.

---

[2] *Syn.* 32.   [3] Ib. 78.

But the times were not ripe for an understanding between East and West, and the Asiatics in whom Hilary had put his trust were not, and did not deserve to be, the restorers of the Church. Their victory had been complete, but the Emperor was inconstant and their adversaries were men of talent, who had once guided his counsels and knew how to recover their position. The policy of Constantius was, as we know, one of compromise, and it might seem to him that the prevailing confusion would cease if only a sufficiently comprehensive formula could be devised and accepted. 'Specious charity and colourless indefiniteness [4]' was the policy of the new party, formed by Valens and Arians of every shade, which won the favour of Constantius within a year of the Semiarian victory. They had been mortified, had been forced to sign a confession which they disbelieved, many of them had suffered a momentary exile. Now they were to have their revenge; not only were the terms of communion to be so lax that extreme Arianism should be at home within the Church, but, as in a modern change of ministry, the Semiarians were to yield their sees to their opponents. To attain these ends a Council was necessary. The general history of the Homoean intrigues, of their division of the forces opposed to them by the assembling of a Western Council at Rimini, of an Eastern at Seleucia, and their apparent triumph, gained by shameless falsehood, in the former, would be out of place. Hilary and his Asiatic friends were concerned only with the Council which met at Seleucia in September, 359. The Emperor, who hoped for a final settlement, desired that the Council should be as large as possible, and the governors of provinces exerted themselves to collect bishops, and to forward them to Seleucia, as was usual, at the public expense. Among the rest, Hilary, who was, we must remember, a bishop with a diocese of his own, and of unimpugned orthodoxy, exiled ostensibly for a political offence, received orders to attend at the cost of the State [5]. In the Council, which numbered some 160 bishops, his Semiarian friends were in a majority of three to one; the uncompromising Nicenes of Egypt and the uncompromising Arians, taken together, did not number more than a quarter of the whole. Hilary was welcomed heartily and, as it would seem, unanimously; but he had to disclaim, on behalf of the Church in Gaul, the Sabellianism of which it was suspected, and with some reason after the Western welcome of Marcellus. He stated his faith to the satisfaction of the Council in accordance with the Nicene confession [6]. We cannot doubt that he made use of its very words, for Hilary was not the man to retreat from the position he held, and the terms of his alliance with the school of Basil of Ancyra required no such renunciation. The proceedings of the Council, in which Hilary took no public part, may be omitted. The Semiarians, strong in numbers and, as they still thought, in the Emperor's favour, swept everything before them. They adopted the ambiguous creed of the Council of the Dedication,—that Council which Hilary had lately called an 'assembly of the Saints'—for the Nicenes were a powerless minority; and they repeated their sentence of excommunication upon the Arians, who were still fewer in number. They even ventured to consecrate a successor to Eudoxius, one of the most extreme, for the great Church of Antioch. Then the Council elected a commission of ten of the leaders of the majority to present to the Emperor a report of its proceedings, and dispersed. In spite of some ominous signs of obstinacy on the part of the Arians, and of favour towards them shewn by the government officials, they seemed to have succeeded in establishing still more firmly the results attained at Ancyra two years before, and to have struck another and, as they might hope, a more effectual blow at the heretics.

But when the deputation, with whom Hilary travelled, reached Constantinople, they found that the position was entirely different from their expectation. The intriguing party, whose aim was to punish and displace the Semiarians, had contrived a double treason. They misrepresented the Western Council to the Emperor as in agreement with themselves;

4 Gwatkin, *Studies of Arianism*, p. 163. 5 Sulp. Sev. *Chron.* ii. 42.
6 Sulp. Sev. ii. 42, *iuxta ea, quæ Nicææ erant a patribus conscripta.*

and they sacrificed their more honest colleagues in Arianism. They hated those who, like Basil of Ancyra, maintained the *homoiousion*, the doctrine that the Son is of like nature with the Father ; the Emperor sincerely rejected the logical Arianism which said that He is of unlike nature. They abandoned their friends in order to induce Constantius to sacrifice his old Semiarian advisers ; and proposed with success their new Homoean formula, that the Son is 'like the Father in all things, as Scripture says.' His nature is not mentioned ; the last words were a concession to the scruples of the Emperor. We shall see presently that this rupture with the consistent Arians is a matter of some importance for the dating of Hilary's *De Trinitate ;* for the present we must follow the fortunes of himself and his allies. He had journeyed with them to Constantinople. This was, apparently, a breach of the order given him to confine himself to the diocese of Asia ; but he had already been commanded to go to Seleucia, which lay beyond those limits, and his journey to Constantinople may have been regarded as a legitimate sequel to his former journey. In any case he was not molested, and was allowed to appear, with the deputation from Seleucia, at the Court of Constantius. For the last two months of the year 359 the disputes concerning the Faith still continued. But the Emperor was firm in his determination to bring about a compromise which should embrace every one who was not an extreme and conscientious Arian, and the Homoean leaders supported him ably and unscrupulously. They falsified the sense of the Council of Rimini and denied their own Arianism, and Constantius backed them up by threats against the Seleucian deputation. Hilary, of course, had no official position, and could speak only for himself. The Western Church seemed to have decided against its own faith, and the decision of the East, represented by the ten delegates, was not yet declared, though it must have been probable that they would succumb to the pressure exercised upon them, and desert their own convictions and those of the Council whose commission they held. In these circumstances Hilary had the courage, which we cannot easily overestimate, to make a personal appeal to Constantius [7]. It is evident that as yet he is hopeful, or at least that he thinks it worth while to make an attempt. He writes with the same customary humility which we found in his former address to the Emperor. Constantius is 'most pious,' 'good and religious,' 'most gracious,' and so forth. The sincerity of the appeal is manifest ; Hilary still believes, or is trying to believe, that the Emperor, who had so lately been on the side of Basil of Ancyra and his friends, and had at their instigation humiliated and exiled their opponents, has not transferred his favour once more to the party of Valens. The address is written with great dignity of style and of matter. Hilary begins by declaring that the importance of his theme is such that it enforces attention, however insignificant the speaker may be ; yet (§ 2) his position entitles him to speak. He is a bishop, in communion with all the churches and bishops of Gaul, and to that very day distributing the Eucharist by the hands of his presbyters to his own Church. He is in exile, it is true, but he is guiltless ; falsely accused by designing men who had gained the Emperor's ear. He appeals to Julian's knowledge of his innocence ; indeed, the malice of his opponents had inflicted less of suffering upon himself than of discredit upon the administration of Julian, under which he had been condemned. The Emperor's rescript sentencing Hilary to exile was public ; it was notorious that the charges upon which the sentence was based were false. Saturninus, the active promoter, if not the instigator, of the attack, was now in Constantinople. Hilary confidently promises to demonstrate that the proceedings were a deception of Constantius, and an insult to Julian ; if he fails, he will no longer petition to be allowed to return to the exercise of his office,

7 Sulpicius Severus, *Chron.* ii. 45, says that he addressed at this time three petitions to the Emperor. This is, of course, not impossible ; but it is more likely that he had in his mind the two appeals, that before the exile and the present one, and the Invective.

but will retire to pass the rest of his days as a layman in repentance. To this end he asks to be confronted with Saturninus (§ 3), or rather takes for granted that Constantius will do as he wishes. He leaves the Emperor to determine all the conditions of the debate, in which, as he repeats, he will wring from Saturninus the confession of his falsehood. Meanwhile he promises to be silent upon the subject till the appointed time. Next, he turns to the great subject of the day. The world's danger, the guilt of silence, the judgment of God, fill him with fear; he is constrained to speak when his own salvation and that of the Emperor and of mankind is at stake, and encouraged by the consciousness of multitudes who sympathise with him. He bids the Emperor (§ 4) call back to his mind the Faith which (so he says) Constantius is longing in vain to hear from his bishops. Those whose duty is to proclaim the Faith of God are employed, instead, in composing faiths of their own, and so they revolve in an endless circle of error and of strife. The sense of human infirmity ought to have made them content to hold the Faith in the same form of words in which they had received it. At their baptism they had professed and sworn their faith, *In the Name of the Father, and of the Son, and of the Holy Ghost;* doubt or change are equally unlawful. Yet men were using the sacred words while they dishonestly assigned to them another meaning, or even were daring to depart from them. Thus to some the three sacred Names were empty terms. Hence innovations in the statement of the Faith; the search for novelties took the place of loyalty to ancient truth, and the creed of the year displaced the creed of the Gospels. Every one framed his confession according to his own desire or his own character; while creeds were multiplying, the one Faith was perishing. Since the Council of Nicæa (§ 5) there had been no end to this writing of creeds. So busily were men wrangling over words, seeking novelties, debating knotty points, forming factions and pursuing ambitions, refusing to agree and hurling anathemas at one another, that almost all had drifted away from Christ. The confusion was such that none could either teach or learn in safety. Within the last year no less than four contradictory creeds had been promulgated. There was no single point of the Faith which they or their fathers had held upon which violent hands had not been laid. And the pitiful creed which for the moment held the field was that the Son is 'like the Father'; whether this likeness were perfect or imperfect was left in obscurity. The result of constant change and ceaseless dispute was self-contradiction and mutual destruction. This search for a faith (§ 6) involved the assumption that the true Faith was not ready to the believer's hand. They would have it in writing, as though the heart were not its place. Baptism implied the Faith and was useless without its acceptance; to teach a new Christ after Baptism, or to alter the Faith then declared, was sin against the Holy Ghost. The chief cause of the continuance of the present blasphemy was the love of applause; men invented grandiloquent paraphrases in place of the Apostles' Creed, to delude the vulgar, to conceal their aberrations, to effect a compromise with other forms of error. They would do anything rather than confess that they had been wrong. When the storm arises (§ 7) the mariner returns to the harbour he had left; the spendthrift youth, with ruin in prospect, to the sober habits of his father's home. So Christians, with shipwreck of the Faith in sight and the heavenly patrimony almost lost, must return to the safety which lies in the primitive, Apostolic Baptismal Creed. They must not condemn as presumptuous or profane the Nicene confession, but eschew it as giving occasion to attacks upon the Faith and to denials of the truth on the ground of novelty. There is danger lest innovation creep in, excused as improvement of this creed; and emendation is an endless process, which leads the emenders to condemnation of each other. Hilary now (§ 8) professes his sincere admiration of Constantius' devout purpose and earnestness in seeking the truth, which he who denies is antichrist, and he who feigns is anathema. He entreats the Emperor to allow him to expound the Faith, in his own presence, before the Council which was now debating the subject at Constantinople.

His exposition shall be Scriptural; he will use the words of Christ, Whose exile and Whose bishop he is. The Emperor seeks the Faith; let him hear it not from modern volumes, but from the books of God. Even in the West it may be taught, whence shall come some that shall sit at meat in the kingdom of God. This is a matter not of philosophy, but of the teaching of the Gospel. He asks audience rather for the Emperor's sake and for God's Churches than for himself. He is sure of the faith that is in him; it is God's, and he will never change it. But (§ 9) the Emperor must bear in mind that every heretic professes that his own is the Scriptural doctrine. So say Marcellus, Photinus, and the rest. He prays (§ 10) for the Emperor's best attention; his plea will be for faith and unity and eternal life. He will speak in all reverence for Constantius' royal position, and for his faith, and what he says shall tend to peace between East and West. Finally (§ 11) he gives, as an outline of the address he proposes to deliver, the series of texts on which he will base his argument. This is what the Holy Spirit has taught him to believe. To this faith he will ever adhere, loyal to the Faith of his fathers, and the creed of his Baptism, and the Gospel as he has learnt it.

In this address, to which we cannot wonder that Constantius made no response, there is much that is remarkable. There is no doubt that Hilary's exile had been a political measure, and that the Emperor, in this as in the numerous other cases of the same kind, had acted deliberately and with full knowledge of the circumstances in the way that seemed to him most conducive to the interests of permanent peace. Hilary's assumption that Constantius had been deceived is a legitimate allusion, which no one could misunderstand, to a fact which could not be respectfully stated. That he should have spoken as he did, and indeed that he should have raised the subject at all, is a clear sign of the uncertainty of the times. A timorous appeal for mercy would have been useless; a bold statement of innocence, although, as things turned out, it failed, was an effort worth making to check the Homoean advance. Saturninus, as we saw, was one of the Court party among the bishops; and he was an enemy of Julian, who was soon to permit his deposition. Julian's knowledge of Hilary can have been but small; his exile began within a month or two of the Cæsar's arrival in Gaul, and Julian was not responsible for it. For good or for evil, he had little to say in the case. But the suspicions were already aroused which were soon to lead to Julian's revolt, and Constantius had begun to give the orders which would lessen Julian's military force, and were, as he supposed, intended to prepare his downfall. To appeal to Julian and to attack Saturninus was to remind Constantius very broadly that great interests were at stake, and that a protector might be found for the creed which he persecuted. And his double mention of the West (§§ 8, 10) as able to teach the truth, and as needing to be reconciled with the East, has a political ring. It suggests that the Western provinces are a united force, with which the Emperor must reckon. The fact that Constantius, though he did not grant the meeting in his own presence with Saturninus, which Hilary had asked for, yet did grant the substance of his prayer, allowing him to return without obstacle to his diocese, seems to shew that the Emperor felt the need for caution and concession in the West.

The theological part of the letter is even more remarkable. Its doctrine is, of course, exactly that of the *De Trinitate*. The summary of Scripture proofs for the doctrine in § 11, the allusion to unlearned fishermen who have been teachers of the Faith[8], and several other passages, are either anticipations or reminiscences of that work. But the interest of the letter lies in its bold proposal to go behind all the modern creeds, of the confusion of which a vivid picture is drawn, and revert to the baptismal formula. Here is a leading combatant on the Catholic side actually proposing to withdraw the Nicene confes-

---

[8] Cf. *Trin.* ii. 13 ff.

sion:—'Amid these shipwrecks of faith, when our inheritance of the heavenly patrimony is almost squandered, our safety lies in clinging to that first and only Gospel Faith which we confessed and apprehended at our Baptism, and in making no change in that one form which, when we welcome it and listen to it, brings the right faith [9] I do not mean that we should condemn as a godless and blasphemous writing the work of the Synod of our fathers; yet rash men make use of it as a means of gainsaying' (§ 7). The Nicene Creed [1], Hilary goes on to say, had been the starting-point of an endless chain of innovations and amendments, and thus had done harm instead of good. We have seen that Hilary was not only acting with the Semiarians, but was nearer to them in many ways than he was to Athanasius. The future of his friends was now in doubt; not only was their doctrine in danger, but, after the example they had themselves set, they must have been certain that defeat meant deposition. This was a concession which only a sense of extreme urgency could have induced Hilary to make. Yet even now he avoids the mistake of Liberius. He offers to sign no compromising creed; he only proposes that all modern creeds be consigned to the same oblivion. It was, in effect, the offer of another compromise in lieu of the Homoean; though Hilary makes it perfectly clear what is, in his eyes, the only sense in which this simple and primitive confession can honestly be made, yet assuredly those whose doctrine most widely diverged would have felt able to make it. That the proposal was sincerely meant, and that his words, uncompromising as they are in assertion of the truth, were not intended for a simple defiance of the enemy, is shewn by the list of heretics whom he advances, in § 9, in proof of his contention that all error claims to be based on Scripture. Three of them, Montanus, Manichæus and Marcion, were heretics in the eyes of an Arian as much as of a Catholic; the other three, Marcellus, Photinus and Sabellius, were those with whom the Arians were constantly taunting their adversaries. Hilary avoids, deliberately as we may be sure, the use of any name which could wound his opponents. But bold and eloquent and true as the appeal of Hilary was, it was still less likely that his petition for a hearing in Council should be granted than that he should be allowed to disprove the accusations which had led to his exile. The Homoean leaders had the victory in their hands, and they knew it, if Hilary and his friends were still in the dark. They did not want conciliation, but revenge, and this appeal was foredoomed to failure. The end of the crisis soon came. The Semiarian leaders were deposed, not on the charge of heresy, for that would have been inconsistent with the Homoean position and also with their acquiescence in the Homoean formula, but on some of those complaints concerning conduct which were always forthcoming when they were needed. Among the victims was not only Basil of Ancyra, Hilary's friend, but also Macedonius of Constantinople, who was in after days to be the chief of the party which denied the true Godhead of the Holy Ghost. He and his friends were probably unconscious at this time of the gulf which divided them from such men as Hilary, who for their part were content, in the interests of unity, with language which understated their belief, or else had not yet a clear sense of their faith upon this point. In any case it was well that the final victory of the true Faith was not won at this time, and with the aid of such allies; we may even regard it as a sign of some short-sightedness on Hilary's part that he had thrown himself so heartily into their cause. But he, at any rate, was not to suffer. The two Eastern parties, Homoean and Semiarian, which alternately ejected one another from their sees, were very evenly balanced, and though Constantius was now on the side of the former, his friendship was not to be

---

9 Reading *habet* for *habeo*, but the text is obscure.

1 It is true that the Nicene Council is not named here, but the allusion is obvious. The Conservatives had actually objected to the novelty of the Creed; and the Arians had, as Hilary goes on to say, used the pretext of novelty to destroy the Gospel. The Council of Nicæa was thirty-five years before, and is very accurately described as a 'Synod of our fathers.'

trusted. The solid orthodoxy of the West was an influence which, as Hilary had hinted, could not be ignored ; and even in the East the Nicenes were a power worth conciliating. Hence the Homoeans gave a share of the Semiarian spoils to them[2]; and it was part of the same policy, and not, as has been quaintly suggeste l, because they were afraid of his arguments, that they permitted Hilary to return to Gaul. Reasons of state as well as of ecclesiastical interest favoured his restoration.

In the late revolution, though the Faith had suffered, individual Catholics had gained. But the party to which Hilary had attached himself, and from which he had hoped so much, was crushed : and his personal advantage did not compensate, in his eyes, for the injury to truth. He has left us a memorial of his feelings in the *Invective against Constantius*, one of the bitterest documents of a controversy in which all who engaged were too earnest to spare their opponents. It is an admirable piece of rhetoric suffused with passion, not the less spontaneous because its form, according to the canons of taste of that time, is perfect. For we must remember that the education of the day was literary, its aim being to provide the recipient with a prompt and felicitous expression of his thoughts, whatever they might be. The Invective was certainly written in the first place as a relief to Hilary's own feelings ; he could not anticipate that Constantius had changed his views for the last time; that he would soon cease to be the master of Gaul, and would be dead within some eighteen months. But the existence of other attacks upon Constantius, composed about this time, makes it probable that there was some secret circulation of such documents ; and we can as little accuse the writers of cowardice, when we consider the Emperor's far-reaching power, as we can attribute to them injustice towards him.

The book begins with an animated summons to resistance :—' The time for speech is come, the time of silence past. Let us look for Christ's coming, for Antichrist is already in power. Let the shepherds cry aloud, for the hirelings are fled. Let us lay down our lives for the sheep, for the thieves have entered in and the ravening lion prowls around. With such words on our lips let us go forth to martyrdom, for the angel of Satan has transfigured himself into an angel of light.' After more Scriptural language of the same kind, Hilary goes on to say (§ 2) that, though he had been fully conscious of the extent of the danger to the Faith, he had been strictly moderate in his conduct. After the exiling of orthodox bishops at Arles and Milan, he and the bishops of Gaul had contented themselves with abstaining from communion with Saturninus, Ursacius and Valens. Other heretical bishops had been allowed a time for repentance. And even after he had been forced to attend the Synod of Béziers, refused a hearing for the charges of heresy which he wished to bring, and finally exiled, he had never, in word or writing, uttered any denunciation against his opponents, the Synagogue of Satan, who falsely claimed to be the Church of Christ. He had not faltered in his own belief, but had welcomed every suggestion that held out a hope of unity ; and in that hope he had even refrained from blaming those who associated or worshipped with the excommunicate. Setting all personal considerations on one side, he had laboured for a restoration of the Church through a general repentance. This reserve and consistency (§ 3) is evidence that what he is about to say is not due to personal irritation. He speaks in the name of Christ, and his prolonged silence makes it his duty to speak plainly. It had been happy for him had he lived in the days of Nero or Decius (§ 4). The Holy Spirit would have fired him to endure as did the martyrs of Scripture ; torments and death would have been welcome. It would have been a fair fight with an open enemy. But now (§ 5) Constantius was Antichrist, and waged his warfare by deceit and flattery. It was scourging then, pampering now ; no longer freedom in prison, but slavery at court, and gold as deadly as the sword had

---

[2] Cf. Gwatkin, *Studies of Arianism*, p. 182.

been ; martyrs no longer burnt at the stake, but a secret lighting of the fires of hell. All that seems good in Constantius, his confession of Christ, his efforts for unity, his severity to heretics, his reverence for bishops, his building of churches, is perverted to evil ends. He professes loyalty to Christ, but his constant aim is to prevent Christ from being honoured equally with the Father. Hence (§ 6) it is a clear duty to speak out, as the Baptist to Herod and the Maccabees to Antiochus. Constantius is addressed (§ 7) in the words in which Hilary would have addressed Nero or Decius or Maximian, had he been arraigned before them, as the enemy of God and His Church, a persecutor and a tyrant. But he has a peculiar infamy, worse than theirs, for it is as a pretended Christian that he opposes Christ, imprisons bishops, overawes the Church by military force, threatens and starves one council (at Rimini) into submission, and frustrates the purpose of another (Seleucia) by sowing dissension. To the pagan Emperors the Church owed a great debt (§ 8); the Martyrs with whom they had enriched her were still working daily wonders, healing the sick, casting out evil spirits, suspending the law of gravitation [3]. But Constantius' guilt has no mitigation. A nominal Christian, he has brought unmixed evil upon the Church. The victims of his perversion cannot even plead bodily suffering as an excuse for their lapse. The devil is his father, from whom he has learnt his skill in misleading. He says to Christ, *Lord, Lord,* but shall not enter the kingdom of heaven (§ 9), for he denies the Son, and therefore the fatherhood of God. The old persecutors were enemies of Christ only ; Constantius insults the Father also, by making Him lie. He is a wolf in sheep's clothing (§ 10). He loads the Church with the gold of the state and the spoil of pagan temples ; it is the kiss with which Judas betrayed his Master. The clergy receive immunities and remissions of taxation : it is to tempt them to deny Christ. He will only relate such acts of Constantius' tyranny as affect the Church (§ 11). He will not press, for he does not know the offence alleged, his conduct in branding bishops on the forehead, as convicts, and setting them to labour in the mines. But he recounts his long course of oppression and faction at Alexandria ; a warfare longer than that which he had waged against Persia [4]. Elsewhere, in the East, he had spread terror and strife, always to prevent Christ being preached. Then he had turned to the West. The excellent Paulinus had been driven from Treves, and cruelly treated, banished from all Christian society [5], and forced to consort with Montanist heretics. Again, at Milan, the soldiers had brutally forced their way through the orthodox crowds and torn bishops from the altar ; a crime like that of the Jews who slew Zacharias in the Temple. He had robbed Rome also of her bishop, whose restoration was as disgraceful to the Emperor as his banishment. At Toulouse the clergy had been shamefully maltreated, and gross irreverence committed in the Church. These are the deeds of Antichrist. Hitherto, Hilary has spoken of matters of public notoriety, though not of his own observation. Now (§ 12) he comes to the Synod of Seleucia, at which he had been present. He found there as many blasphemers as Constantius chose. Only the Egyptians, with the exception of George, the intruder into the See of Athanasius, were avowedly Homoousian.

---

[3] 'Bodies lifted up without support, women hanging by the feet without their garments falling about their face.' The other references which the Benedictine editor gives for this curious statement are evidently borrowed from this of Hilary. From the time of the first Apologists exorcism is, of course, constantly appealed to as an evidence of the truth of Christianity, but usually in somewhat perfunctory language, and without the assertion that the writer has himself seen what he records. Hilary himself does not profess to be an eye-witness.

[4] This is a telling point. Constantius had been notoriously unsuccessful in his Persian Wars.

[5] The text is corrupt, but it is not probable that Hilary means that Paulinus was first relegated to Phrygia and then to some pagan frontier district, if such there was. It is quite in Hilary's present vein to assume that because the Montanists were usually called after the province of their origin, in which they were still numerous, therefore all Phrygians were heretics and outside the pale of Christendom. If *hordeo* be read for *horreo* the passage is improved. Paulinus had either to be satisfied with rations of barley bread, the food of slaves, or else to beg from the heretics. Such treatment is very improbable, when we remember Hilary's own comfort in exile. But passions were excited, and men believed the worst of their opponents. We may compare the falsehoods in Walker's *Sufferings of the Clergy,* and in Neal's *Puritans,* which were eagerly believed in and after our own Civil War.

Yet of the one hundred and five bishops who professed the Homoeousian Creed, he found 'some piety in the words of some.' But the Anomoeans were rank blasphemers; he gives, in § 13, words from a sermon by their leader, Eudoxius of Antioch, which were quoted by the opposition, and received with the abhorrence they deserved. This party found (§ 14) that no toleration was to be expected for such doctrines, and so forged the Homoean creed, which condemned equally the *homoousion*, the *homoiousion* and the *anomoion*. Their insincerity in thus rejecting their own belief was manifest to the Council, and one of them, who canvassed Hilary's support, avowed blank Arianism in the conversation. The large Homoeousian majority (§ 15) deposed the authors of the Homoean confession, who flew for aid to Constantius, who received them with honour and allowed them to air their heresy. The tables were turned; the minority, aided by the Emperor's threats of exile, drove the majority, in the persons of their ten delegates, to conform to the new creed. The people were coerced by the prefect, the bishops threatened within the palace walls; the chief cities of the East were provided with heretical bishops. It was nothing less than making a present to the devil of the whole world for which Christ died. Constantius professed (§ 16) that his aim was to abolish unscriptural words. But what right had he to give orders to bishops or dictate the language of their sermons? A new disease needed new remedies; warfare was inevitable when fresh enemies arose. And, after all, the Homoean formula, 'like the Father,' was itself unscriptural. Scripture is adduced (§ 17) by Hilary to prove that the Son is not merely like, but equal to, the Father; and (§ 18) one in nature with Him, having (§ 19) the form and the glory of God. This 'likeness' is a trap (§ 20); chaff strewn on water, straw covering a pit, a hook hidden in the bait. The Catholic sense is the only true sense in which the word can be used, as is shewn more fully, by arguments to be found in the *De Trinitate*, in §§ 21, 22. And now he asks Constantius (§ 23) the plain question, what his creed is. He has made a hasty progress, by a steep descent, to the nethermost pit of blasphemy. He began with the Faith, which deserved the name, of Nicæa; he changed it at Antioch. But he was a clumsy builder; the structure he raised was always falling, and had to be constantly renewed; creed after creed had been framed, the safeguards and anathemas of which would have been needless had he remained steadfast to the Nicene. Hilary does not lament the creeds which Constantius had abandoned (§ 24); they might be harmless in themselves, but they represented no real belief. Yet why should he reject his own creeds? There was no such reason for his discontent with them as there had been, in his heresy, for his rejection of the Nicene. This ceaseless variety arose from want of faith; 'one Faith, one Baptism,' is the mark of truth. The result had been to stultify the bishops. They had been driven to condemn in succession the accurate *homoousion* and the harmless *homoiousion*, and even the word *ousia*, or substance. These were the pranks of a mere buffoon, amusing himself at the expense of the Church, and compelling the bishops, like dogs returning to their vomit, to accept what they had rejected. So many had been the contradictory creeds that every one was now, or had been in the past, a heretic confessed. And this result had only been attained (§ 26) by violence, as for instance in the cases of the Eastern and African bishops. The latter had committed to writing their sentence upon Ursacius and Valens; the Emperor had seized the document. It might go to the flames, as would Constantius himself, but the sentence was registered with God. Other men (§ 27) had waged war with the living, but Constantius extended his hostility to the dead; he contradicted the teaching of the saints, and his bishops rejected their predecessors, to whom they owed their orders, by denying their doctrine. The three hundred and eighteen at Nicæa were anathema to him, and his own father who had presided there. Yet though he might scorn the past, he could not control the future. The truth defined at Nicæa had been solemnly committed to writing and remained, however Constantius might contemn it. 'Give ear,' Hilary concludes, 'to the holy meaning of the words, to the unalterable determination of the Church, to the faith which thy father avowed, to the sure hope in which man must put his trust, the universal conviction of the doom of heresy; and learn therefrom that thou art the foe of God's religion, the enemy of the tombs of the saints [6], the rebellious inheritor of thy father's piety.'

Here, again, there is much of interest. Hilary's painful feeling of isolation is manifest. He had withdrawn from communion with Saturninus and the few Arians of Gaul, but has to confess that his own friends were not equally uncompromising. The Gallic bishops, with their enormous dioceses, had probably few occasions for meeting, and prudent men could easily avoid a conflict which the Arians, a feeble minority, would certainly not provoke. The bishops had been courteous, or more than courteous; and Hilary dared not protest. His whole importance as a negotiator in the East depended on the belief that he was the representative of a harmonious body of opinion. To advertise this departure from his policy of warfare would have been fatal to his influence. And if weakness, as he must have judged it, was leading his brethren at home into a recognition of Arians, Constantius and his Homoean counsellors had ingeniously contrived a still more serious break in the orthodox line of battle. There was reason in his bitter complaint of the Emperor's generosity. He was lavish with his money, and it was well worth a bishop's while to be his friend. And of this expenditure Nicenes were enjoying their share, and that without having to surrender their personal belief, for all that was required was that they should not be inquisitive as to their neighbours' heresies. But Nicene bishops, of an accommodating character, were not only holding their own; they were enjoying a share of the spoils of the routed Semiarians. It was almost a stroke of genius thus to shatter Hilary's alliance; for it was certainly not by chance that among the sees to which Nicenes, in full and formal communion with him, were preferred, was Ancyra itself, from which his chosen friend Basil had been ejected. Disgusted though Hilary must have been with such subservience, and saddened by the downfall of his friends, it is clear that the Emperor's policy had some success, even with him. His former hopes being dashed to the ground, he now turns, with an interest he had never before shewn, to the Nicene Creed as a bulwark of the Faith. And we can see the same feeling at work in his very cold recognition that there was 'some piety in the words of some' among his friends at Seleucia. It would be unjust to think of Hilary as a timeserver, but we must admit that there is something almost too businesslike in this dismission from his mind of former hopes and friendships. He looked always to a practical result in the establishment of truth, and a judgment so sound as his could not fail to see that the Asiatic negotiations were a closed chapter in his life. And his mind must have been full of the thought that he was returning to the West, which had its own interests and its own prejudices, and was impartially suspicious of all Eastern theologians; whose 'selfish coldness [7]' towards the East was, indeed, ten years later still a barrier against unity. If Hilary was to be, as he purposed, a power in the West, he must promptly resume the Western tone; and he will have succumbed to very natural infirmity if, in his disappointment, he was disposed to couple together his allies who had failed with the Emperor who had caused their failure.

The historical statements of the Invective, as has been said, cannot always be verified. The account of the Synod of Seleucia is, however, unjust to Constantius. It was the free

---

6 Hilary had previously (§ 27) asserted that 'the Apostle has taught us to communicate with the tombs of the saints.' This is an allusion to Rom. xii. 13, with the strange reading 'tombs' for 'necessities' (μνείαις for χρείαις), which has, in fact, considerable authority in the MSS. of the New Testament and in the Latin Christian writers. How far this reading may have been the cause, how far the effect, of the custom of celebrating the Eucharist at the tombs of Martyrs, it is impossible to say. The custom was by this time more than a century old, and one of its purposes was to maintain the sense of unity with the saints of the past. Constantius, by denying their doctrine, had made himself their enemy.

7 Gwatkin, *Studies of Arianism*, p. 244.

expression of the belief of Asia, and if heretics were present by command of the Emperor, an overwhelming majority, more or less orthodox, were present by the same command. But the character and policy of Constantius are delineated fairly enough. The results, disastrous both to conscience and to peace, are not too darkly drawn, and no sarcasm could be too severe for the absurd as well as degrading position to which he had reduced the Church. But the Invective is interesting not only for its contents but as an illustration of its writer's character. Strong language meant less in Latin than in English, but the passionate earnestness of these pages cannot be doubted. They are not more violent than the attacks of Athanasius upon Constantius, nor less violent than those of Lucifer; if the last author is usually regarded as pre-eminent in abuse, he deserves his reputation not because of the vigour of his denunciation, but because his pages contain nothing but railing. The change is sudden, no doubt, from respect for Constantius and hopefulness as to his conduct, but the provocation, we must remember, had been extreme. If the faith of the Fathers was intense and, in the best sense, childlike, there is something childlike also in their gusts of passion, their uncontrolled emotion in victory or defeat, the personal element which is constantly present in their controversies. Though, henceforth, ecclesiastical policy was to be but a secondary interest with Hilary, and diplomacy was to give place to a more successful attempt to influence thought, yet we can see in another sphere the same spirit of conflict; for it is evident that his labours against heresy, beside the more serious satisfaction of knowing that he was on the side of truth, are lightened by the logician's pleasure in exposing fallacy.

The deposition of the Semiarian leaders took place very early in the year 360, and Hilary's dismissal homewards, one of the same series of measures, must soon have followed. If he had formed the plan of his Invective before he left Constantinople, it is not probable that he wrote it there. It was more probably the employment of his long homeward journey. His natural route would be by the great Egnatian Way, which led through Thessalonica to Durazzo, thence by sea to Brindisi, and so to Rome and the North. It is true that the historians, or rather Rufinus, from whom the rest appear to have borrowed all their knowledge, say that Illyricum was one sphere of his labours for the restoration of the Faith. But a journey by land through Illyricum, the country of Valens and Ursacius and thoroughly indoctrinated with Arianism, would not only have been dangerous but useless. For Hilary's purpose was to confirm the faithful among the bishops and to win back to orthodoxy those who had been terrorised or deceived into error, and thus to cement a new confederacy against the Homoeans; not to make a vain assault upon what was, for the present, an impregnable position. And though the Western portion of the *Via Egnatia* did not pass through the existing political division called Illyricum, it did lie within the region called in history and literature by that name. Again, the evidence that Hilary passed through Rome is not convincing; but since it was his best road, and he would find there the most important person among those who had wavered in their allegiance to truth, we may safely accept it. He made it his business, we are told [8], to exhort the Churches through which he passed to abjure heresy and return to the true faith. But we know nothing of the places through which he passed before reaching Rome, the see of Liberius, with whom it was most desirable for him to be on friendly terms. Liberius was not so black as he has sometimes been painted, but he was not a heroic figure. His position was exactly that of many other bishops in the Western lands. They had not denied their own faith, but at one time or another, in most cases at Rimini, they had admitted that there was room in the same communion for Arian bishops and for themselves. In the case of Liberius the circumstances are involved in some obscurity, but it is clear that he had, in order to obtain remission of his exile, taken a position

---

[8] Rufinus, *Hist. Eccl.* i. 30, 31, and, dependent on him, Socrates iii. 10, and Sozomen v. 13.

which was practically that of the old Council of the Dedication [9]. Hilary, we remember, had called that Council a 'Synod of the Saints,' when speaking of it from the Eastern point of view. But he had never stooped to such a minimising of the Faith as its words, construed at the best, involved. Easterns, in their peculiar difficulties, he was hopeful enough to believe, had framed its terms in a legitimate sense; he could accept it from them, but could not use it as the expression of his own belief. So to do would have been a retrograde step; and this step Liberius had taken, to the scandal of the Church. Yet he, and all whose position in any way resembled his—all, indeed, except some few incorrigible ringleaders— were in the Church; their deflection was, in Hilary's words, an 'inward evil.' And Hilary was no Lucifer; his desire was to unite all who could be united in defence of the truth. This was the plan dictated by policy as well as by charity, and in the case of Liberius, if, as is probable, they met, it was certainly rewarded with success. Indeed, according to Rufinus, Hilary was successful at every stage of his journey. Somewhere on his course he fell in with Eusebius of Vercelli, who had been exiled at the Council of Milan, had passed his time in the region to the East of that in which Hilary had been interned, and was now profiting by the same Homoean amnesty to return to his diocese. He also had been using the opportunities of travel for the promotion of the Faith. He had come from Antioch, and therefore had probably landed at or near Naples. He was now travelling northwards, exhorting as he went. His encounter with Hilary stimulated him to still greater efforts; but Rufinus tells us [1] that he was the less successful of the two, for Hilary, 'a man by nature mild and winning, and also learned and singularly apt at persuasion, applied himself to the task with a greater diligence and skill.' They do not appear to have travelled in company; the cities to be visited were too numerous and their own time, eager as they must have been to reach their homes, too short. But their journey seems to have been a triumphal progress; the bishops were induced to renounce their compromise with error, and the people inflamed against heresy, so that, in the words of Rufinus [2], 'these two men, glorious luminaries as it were of the universe, flooded Illyricum and Italy and the Gallic provinces with their splendour, so that even from hidden nooks and corners all darkness of heresy was banished.'

In the passage just quoted Rufinus directly connects the publication of Hilary's masterpiece, usually called the *De Trinitate*, with this work of reconciliation. After speaking of his success in it, he proceeds, 'Moreover he published his books *Concerning the Faith*, composed in a lofty style, wherein he displayed the guile of the heretics and the deceptions practised upon our friends, together with the credulous and misplaced sincerity of the latter, with such skill that his ample instructions amended the errors not only of those whom he encountered, but also of those whom distance hindered him from meeting face to face.' Some of the twelve books of which the work is composed had certainly been published during his exile, and it is possible that certain portions may date from his later residence in Gaul. But a study of the work itself leads to the conclusion that Rufinus was right in the main in placing it at this stage of Hilary's life; this was certainly the earliest date at which it can have been widely influential.

The title which Hilary gave to his work as a whole was certainly *De Fide, Concerning the Faith*, the name by which, as we saw, Rufinus describes it. It is probable that its controversial purpose was indicated by the addition of *contra Arianos;* but it is certain that its present title, *De Trinitate*, was not given to it by Hilary. The word *Trinitas* is of extraordinarily rare occurrence in his writings; the only instances seem to be in *Trin.* i. 22, 36, where he is giving a very condensed summary of the contents of his work. In the actual course of his argument the word is scrupulously avoided, as it is in all his other writings. In

9 Cf. Dr. Bright, *Waymarks*, p. 217 *n*.   1 *Hist. Eccl.* i. 30, 31.
2 *Op. cit.* i. 31. The recantation of Liberius and of the Italian bishops may be read in Hilary's 12th Fragment.

this respect he resembles Athanasius, who will usually name the Three Persons rather than employ this convenient and even then familiar term. There may have been some undesirable connotation in it which he desired to avoid, though this is hardly probable; it is more likely that both Athanasius and Hilary, conscious that the use of technical terms of theology was in their times a playing with edged tools, deliberately avoided a word which was unnecessary, though it might be useful. And in Hilary's case there is the additional reason that to his mind the antithesis of truth and falsehood was One God or Two Gods[4]; that to him, more than to any other Western theologian, the developed and clearly expressed thought of Three coequal Persons was strange. Since, then, the word and the thought were rarely present in his mind, we cannot accept as the title of his work what is, after all, only a mediæval description.

The composite character of the treatise, which must still for convenience be called the *De Trinitate*, is manifest. The beginnings of several of its books, which contain far more preliminary, and often rhetorical, matter than is necessary to link them on to their predecessors, point to a separate publication of each; a course which was, indeed, necessary under the literary conditions of the time. This piecemeal publication is further proved by the elaborate summaries of the contents of previous books which are given as, e.g., at the beginning of *Trin.* x.; and by the frequent repetition of earlier arguments at a later stage, which shews that the writer could not trust to the reader's possession of the whole. Though no such attention has been devoted to the growth of this work as Noeldechen has paid to that of the treatises of Tertullian, yet some account of the process can be given. For although Hilary himself, in arranging the complete treatise, has done much to make it run smoothly and consecutively, and though the scribes who have copied it have probably made it appear still more homogeneous, yet some clues to its construction are left. The first is his description of the fifth book as the second (v. 3). This implies that the fourth is the first; and when we examine the fourth we find that, if we leave out of consideration a little preliminary matter, it is the beginning of a refutation of Arianism. It states the Arian case, explains the necessity of the term *homoousios*, gives a list of the texts on which the Arians relied, and sets out at length one of their statements of doctrine, the Epistle of Arius to Alexander, which it proceeds to demolish, in the remainder of the fourth book and in the fifth, by arguments from particular passages and from the general sense of the Old Testament. In the sixth book, for the reason already given, the Arian Creed is repeated, after a vivid account of the evils of the time, and the refutation continued by arguments from the New Testament. In § 2 of this book there is further evidence of the composite character of the treatise. Hilary says that though in the *first* book he has already set out the Arian manifesto, yet he thinks good, as he is still dealing with it, to repeat it in this *sixth*. Hilary seems to have overlooked the discrepancy, which some officious scribe has half corrected[5]. The seventh book, he says at the beginning, is the climax of the whole work. If we take the *De Trinitate* as a whole, this is a meaningless flourish; but if we look on to the eighth book, and find an elaborate introduction followed by a line of argument different from that of the four preceding books, we must be inclined to think that the seventh is the climax and termination of what has been an independent work, consisting of four books. And if we turn to the end of the seventh, and note that it alone of all the twelve has nothing that can be called a peroration, but ends in an absolutely bald and businesslike manner, we are almost forced to conclude that this is because the peroration which it once had, as the climax of the work, was unsuitable for its new position and has been wholly removed. Had Hilary written this book as one of the series of twelve, he would certainly, according to all rules of literary

---

[4] E.g. *Trin.* i. 17.
[5] Similarly in iv. 2 he alludes to the first book, meaning that which we call first, though, as we saw, in v. 3 he speaks of our fifth as his second.

propriety, have given it a formal termination. In these four books then, the fourth to the seventh, we may see the nucleus of the *De Trinitate;* not necessarily the part first written, for he says (iv. 1)[6] that some parts, at any rate, of the three first books are of earlier date, but that around which the whole has been arranged. It has a complete unity of its own, following step by step the Arian Creed, of which we shall presently speak. It is purely controversial, and quite possibly the title *Contra Arianos,* for which there is some evidence, really belongs to this smaller work, though it clung, not unnaturally, to the whole for which Hilary devised the more appropriate name *De Fide.* Concerning the date of these four books, we can only say that they must have been composed during his exile. For though he does not mention his exile, yet he is already a bishop (vi. 2), and knows about the *homoousion* (iv. 4). We have seen already that his acquaintance with the Nicene Creed began only just before his exile; he must, therefore, have written them during his enforced leisure in Asia.

In the beginning of the fourth book Hilary refers back to the proof furnished in the previous books, written some time ago, of the Scriptural character of his faith and of the unscriptural nature of all the heresies. Setting aside the first book, which does not correspond to this description, we find what he describes in the second and third. These form a short connected treatise, complete in itself. It is much more academic than that of which we have already spoken; it deals briefly with all the current heresies (ii. 4 ff.), but shews no sign that one of them, more than the others, was an urgent danger. There is none of the passion of conflict; Hilary is in the mood for rhetoric, and makes the most of his opportunities. He expatiates, for instance, on the greatness of his theme (ii. 5), harps almost to excess upon the Fisherman to whom mysteries so great were revealed (ii. 13 ff.), dilates, after the manner of a sermon, upon the condescension and the glory manifested in the Incarnation, describes miracles with much liveliness of detail (iii. 5, 20), and ends the treatise (iii. 24—26) with a nobly eloquent statement of the paradox of wisdom which is folly and folly which is wisdom, and of faith as the only means of knowing God. The little work, though it deals professedly with certain heresies, is in the main constructive. It contains far more of positive assertion of the truth, without reference to opponents, than it does of criticism of their views. In sustained calmness of tone—it recognises the existence of honest doubt (iii. 1),—and in literary workmanship, it excels any other part of the *De Trinitate,* and in the latter respect is certainly superior to the more conversational Homilies on the Psalms. But it suffers, in comparison with the books which follow, by a certain want of intensity; the reader feels that it was written, in one sense, for the sake of writing it, and written, in another sense, for purposes of general utility. It is not, as later portions of the work were, forged as a weapon for use in a conflict of life and death. Yet, standing as it does, at the beginning of the whole great treatise, it serves admirably as an introduction. It is clear, convincing and interesting, and its eloquent peroration carries the reader on to the central portion of the work, which begins with the fourth book. Except that the second book has lost its exordium, for the same reason that the seventh has lost its conclusion, the two books are complete as well as homogeneous. Of the date nothing definite can be said. There is no sign of any special interest in Arianism; and Hilary's leisure for a paper conflict with a dead foe like Ebionism suggests that he was writing before the strife had reached Gaul. The general tone of the two books is quite consistent with this; and we may regard it as more probable than not that they were composed before the exile; whether they were published at the time as a separate treatise, or laid on one side for a while, cannot be known; the former supposition is the more reasonable.

The remaining books, from the eighth to the twelfth, appear to have been written

---

6 i.e. in the passage introduced as a connecting link with the books which now precede it, when the whole work was put into its present shape.

continuously, with a view to their forming part of the present connected whole. They were, no doubt, published separately, and they, with books iv. to vii., may well be the letters (stripped, of course, in their permanent shape of their epistolary accessories) which, Hilary feared, were obtaining no recognition from his friends in Gaul. The last five have certain references back to arguments in previous books [7], while these do not refer forward, nor do the groups ii. iii. and iv.—vii. refer to one another. But books viii.—xii. have also internal references, and promise that a subject shall be fully treated in due course [8]. We may therefore assume that, when he began to write book viii., Hilary had already determined to make use of his previous minor works, and that he now proceeded to complete his task with constant reference to these. Evidences of exact date are here again lacking; he writes as a bishop and as an exile [9], and under a most pressing necessity. The preface to book viii., with its description of the dangers of the time and of Hilary's sense of the duty of a bishop, seems to represent the state of mind in which he resolved to construct the present *De Trinitate*. It is too emphatic for a mere transition from one step in a continuous discussion to another. Regarding these last five books, then, as written continuously, with one purpose and with one theological outlook, we may fix an approximate date for them by two consider- ations. They shew, in books ix. and x., that he was thoroughly conscious of the increasing peril of Apollinarianism. They shew also, by their silence, that he had determined to ignore what was one of the most obvious and certainly the most offensive of the current modes of thought. There is no refutation, except implicitly, and no mention of Anomoeanism, that extreme Arianism which pronounced the Son unlike the Father [1]. This can be explained only in one way. We have seen that Hilary thinks Arianism worth attack because it is an 'inward evil;' that he does not, except in early and leisurely work such as book ii., pay any attention to heresies which were obviously outside the Church and had an organization of their own. We have seen also that the Homoeans cast out their more honest Anomoean brethren in 359. The latter made no attempt to retrieve their position within the Church; they proceeded to establish a Church of their own, which was, so they protested, the true one. It was under Jovian (A.D. 362—363) that they consecrated their own bishop for Constantinople [2]; but the separation must have been visible for some time before that decisive step was taken. Thus, when the *De Trinitate* took its present form, Apollinarianism was risen above the Church's horizon and Anomoeanism was sunk below it. We cannot, therefore, put the completion of the work earlier than the remission of Hilary's exile; we cannot, indeed, suppose that he had leisure to make it perfect except in his home. Yet the work must have been for the most part finished before its writer reached Italy on his return; and the issue or reissue of its several portions was a natural, and certainly a powerful, measure towards the end which he had at heart.

There remains the first book, which was obviously, as Erasmus saw, the last to be composed. It is a survey of the accomplished task, beginning with that account of Hilary's spiritual birth and growth which has already been mentioned. This is a piece of writing which it is no undue praise to rank, for dignity and felicity of language, among the noblest examples of Roman eloquence. Hooker, among English authors, is the one whom it most suggests. Then there follows a brief summary of the argument of the successive books, and a prayer for the success of the work. This reads, and perhaps it was meant to read, as though it were a prayer that he might worthily execute a plan which as yet existed only in his brain; but it may also be interpreted, in the more natural sense, as a petition that his hope might not be frustrated, and that his book might appear to others what he trusted,

---

[7] E.g. ix. 31 to iii. 12, ix. 43 to vii. 17.
[8] E.g. x. 54 *in.*
[9] viii. 1, x. 4.

[1] This heresy is not even mentioned in xii. 6, where the open- ing was obvious.
[2] Dr. Gwatkin, *Studies of Arianism*, p. 226.

in his own mind, that it was, true to Scripture, sound in logic, and written with that lofty gravity which befitted the greatness of his theme.

After speaking of the construction of the work, as Hilary framed it, something must be said of certain interpolations which it has suffered. The most important are those at the end of book ix. and in x. 8, which flatly contradict his teaching[3]. They are obvious intrusions, imperfectly attested by manuscript authority, and condemned by their own character. Hilary was not the writer to stultify himself and confuse his readers by so clumsy a device as that of appending a bald denial of its truth to a long and careful exposition of his characteristic doctrine. Another passage, where the scholarship seems to indicate the work of an inferior hand, is *Trin.* x. 40, in which there is a singular misunderstanding of the Greek Testament[4]. The writer must have known Greek, for no manuscript of the Latin Bible would have suggested his mistake, and therefore he must have written in early days. It is even possible that Hilary himself was, for once, at fault in his scholarship. Yet, at the most, the interpolations are few and, where they seriously affect the sense, are easily detected[5]. Not many authors of antiquity have escaped so lightly in this respect as Hilary.

Hilary certainly intended his work to be regarded as a whole; as a treatise *Concerning the Faith*, for it had grown into something more than a refutation of Arianism. He has carefully avoided, so far as the circumstances of the time and the composite character of the treatise would allow him, any allusion to names and events of temporary interest; there is, in fact, nothing more definite than a repetition of the wish expressed in the Second Epistle to Constantius, that it were possible to recur to the Baptismal formula as the authoritative statement of the Faith[6]. It is not, like the *De Synodis*, written with a diplomatic purpose; it is, though cast inevitably in a controversial form, a statement of permanent truths. This has involved the sacrifice of much that would have been of immediate service, and deprived the book of a great part of its value as a weapon in the conflicts of the day. But we can see, by the selection he made of a document to controvert, that Hilary's choice was deliberate. It was no recent creed, no confession to which any existing body of partisans was pledged. He chose for refutation the Epistle of Arius to Alexander, written almost forty years ago and destitute, it must have seemed, of any but an historical interest. And it was no extreme statement of the Arian position. This Epistle was 'far more temperate and cautious[7]' than its alternative, Arius' letter to Eusebius. The same wide outlook as is manifest in this indifference to the interests of the moment is seen also in Hilary's silence in regard to the names of friends and foes. Marcellus, Apollinaris, Eudoxius, Acacius are a few of those whom it must have seemed that he would do well to renounce as imagined friends who brought his cause discredit, or bitter enemies to truth and its advocates. But here also he refrains; no names are mentioned except those of men whose heresies were already the commonplaces of controversy. And there is also an absolute silence concerning the feuds and alliances of the day. No notice is taken of the loyalty of living confessors or the approximation to truth of well-meaning waverers. The book contains no sign that it has any but a general object; it is, as far as possible, an impersonal refutation of error and statement of truth.

This was the deliberate purpose of Hilary, and he had certainly counted its cost in immediate popularity and success. For though, as we have seen, the work did produce, as it deserved, a considerable effect at the time of its publication, it has remained ever since, in spite of all its merits, in a certain obscurity. There can be no doubt that this is largely due to the Mezentian union with such a document as Arius' Epistle

---

3 Cf. Gore's *Dissertations*, p. 134.

4 St. Luke xxii. 32, where ἐδεήθην is translated as a passive. Christ *is entreated* for Peter. There seems to be no parallel in Latin theology.

5 E.g. the cento from the *De Trinitate* attached to the Invective against Constantius.

6 ii. 1.

7 Newman, *Arians of the Fourth Century*, ii. v. 2.

to Alexander of the decisively important section of the *De Trinitate*. The books in which that Epistle is controverted were those of vital interest for the age; and the method which Hilary's plan constrained him to adopt was such as to invite younger theologians to compete with him. Future generations could not be satisfied with his presentation of the case. And again, his plan of refuting the Arian document point by point[8], contrasting as it does with the free course of his thought in the earlier and later books, tends to repel the reader. The fourth book proves from certain texts that the Son is God; the fifth from the same texts that He is true God. Hence this part of the treatise is pervaded by a certain monotony; a cumulative impression is produced by our being led forward again and again along successive lines of argument to the same point, beyond which we make no progress till the last proof is stated. The work is admirably and convincingly done, but we are glad to hear the last of the Epistle of Arius to Alexander, and accompany Hilary in a less embarrassed enquiry.

Yet the whole work has defects of its own. It is burdened with much repetition; subjects, especially, which have been treated in books ii. and iii. are discussed again at great length in later books[9]. The frequent stress laid upon the infinity of God, the limitations of human speech and knowledge, the consequent incompleteness of the argument from analogy, the humility necessary when dealing with infinities apparently opposed[1], though it adds to the solemnity of the writer's tone and was doubtless necessary when the work was published in parts, becomes somewhat tedious in the course of a continuous reading. And something must here be said of the peculiarities of style. We saw that in places, as for instance in the beginning of the *De Trinitate*, Hilary can rise to a singularly lofty eloquence. This eloquence is not merely the unstudied utterance of an earnest faith, but the expression given to it by one whom natural talent and careful training had made a master of literary form. Yet, since his training was that of an age whose standard of taste was far from classical purity, much that must have seemed to him and to his contemporaries to be admirably effective can excite no admiration now. He prays, at the end of the first book, that his diction may be worthy of his theme, and doubtless his effort was as sincere as his prayer. Had there been less effort, there would certainly, in the judgment of a modern reader, have been more success. But he could not foresee the future, and ingenious affectations such as occur at the end of book viii. § 1, *impietati insolenti, et insolentiæ vaniloquæ, et vaniloquio seducenti*, with the jingle of rhymes which follows, are too frequent for our taste in his pages[2]. Sometimes we find purple patches which remind us of the rhetoric of Apuleius[3]; sometimes an excessive display of symmetry and antithesis, which suggests to us St. Cyprian at his worst. Yet Cyprian had the excuse that all his writings are short occasional papers written for immediate effect; neither he, nor any Latin Christian before Hilary, had ventured to construct a great treatise of theology, intended to influence future ages as well as the present. Another excessive development of rhetoric is the abuse of apostrophe, which Hilary sometimes rides almost to death, as in his addresses to the Fisherman, St. John, in the second book[4]. These blemishes, however, do not seriously affect his intelligibility. He has earned, in this as in greater matters, an unhappy reputation for obscurity, which he has, to a certain extent, deserved. His other writings, even the Commentary on St. Matthew, are free from the involved language which sometimes makes the *De Trinitate* hard to understand, and often hard to read with pleasure. When Hilary was appealing to the Emperor, or addressing his own flock, as in the Homilies on the Psalms, he has command of a style which is always clear, stately on occasion, never weak or

---

[8] v. 6.

[9] E.g. bk. iii. is largely reproduced in ix.; ii. 9 f. = xi. 46 f.

[1] E.g. i. 19, ii. 2, iii. 1, iv. 2, viii. 53, xi. 46 f.

[2] Cf. v. 1 (beginning of column 130 in Migne), x. 4.

[3] E.g. v. 3 *fin*.

[4] Cf. *Ad Const.* ii. 8, in writing which his own words in the *De Trinitate* must have come into his mind. He had probably borrowed the thought from Origen, *contra Celsum*, i. 62. Similar apostrophes are in v. 19, vi. 19 f., 33.

bald ; in these cases he resisted, or did not feel, the temptation to use the resources of his rhetoric. These, unfortunately, had for their result the production of sentences which are often marvels of grammatical contortion and elliptical ingenuity. Yet such sentences, though numerous, are of few and uniform types. In Hilary's case, as in that of Tertullian, familiarity makes the reader so accustomed to them that he instinctively expects their recurrence ; and, at their worst, they are never actual breaches of the laws of the language. A translator can hardly be an impartial judge in this matter, for constantly, in passages where the sense is perfectly clear, the ingenuity with which words and constructions are arranged makes it almost impossible to render their meaning in idiomatic terms. One can translate him out of Latin, but not into English. In this he resembles one of the many styles of St. Augustine. There are passages in the *De Trinitate*, for instance viii. 27, 28, which it would seem that Augustine had deliberately imitated ; a course natural enough in the case of one who was deeply indebted to his predecessor's thought, and must have looked with reverence upon the great pioneer of systematic theology in the Latin tongue. But this involution of style, irritating as it sometimes is, has the compensating advantage that it keeps the reader constantly on the alert. He cannot skim these pages in the comfortable delusion that he is following the course of thought without an effort.

The same attention which Hilary demands from his readers has obviously been bestowed upon the work by himself. It is the selected and compressed result not only of his general study of theology, but of his familiarity with the literature and the many phases of the great Arian controversy[5]. And he makes it clear that he is engaged in no mere conflict of wit ; his passionate loyalty to the person of Christ is the obvious motive of his writing. He has taken his side with full conviction, and he is equally convinced that his opponents have irrevocably taken theirs. There is little or no reference to the existence or even the possibility of doubt, no charitable construction for ambiguous creeds, hardly a word of pleading with those in error[6]. There is no excuse for heresy ; it is mere insanity, when it is not wilful self-destruction or deliberate blasphemy. The battle is one without quarter ; and sometimes, we must suspect, Hilary has been misled in argument by the uncompromising character of the conflict. Every reason advanced for a pernicious belief, he seems to think, must itself be bad, and be met with a direct negative. And again, in the heat of warfare he is led to press his arguments too far. Not only is the best and fullest use of Scripture made—for Hilary, like Athanasius, is marvellously imbued with its spirit as well as familiar with its letter—but texts are pressed into his service, and interpreted sometimes with brilliant ingenuity[7], which cannot bear the meaning assigned them. Yet much of this exegesis must be laid to the charge of his time, not of himself ; and in the *De Trinitate*, as contrasted with the Homilies on the Psalms ; he is wisely sparing in the use of allegorical interpretations. He remembers that he is refuting enemies, not conversing with friends. And his belief in their conscious insincerity leads to a certain hardness of tone. They will escape his conclusions if they possibly can ; he must pin them down. Hence texts are sometimes treated, and deductions drawn from them, as though they were postulates of geometry ; and, however we may admire the machine-like precision and completeness of the proof, we feel that we are reading Euclid rather than literature[8]. But this also is due to that system of exegesis, fatal to any recognition of the eloquence and poetry of Scripture, of which something will be said in the next chapter.

These, after all, are but petty flaws in so great a work. Not only as a thinker, but as a pioneer of thought, whose treasures have enriched, often unrecognised, the pages

---

5 Cf. x. 57 *in.*
6 An instance is xi. 24 *in.*

7 E.g. in his masterly treatment, from his point of view, of the Old Testament Theophanies, iv. 15 f.
8 Cf. viii. 26 f., ix. 41.

of Ambrose and Augustine and all later theologians, he deserves our reverence. Not without reason was he ranked, within a generation of his death, with Cyprian and Ambrose, as one of the three chief glories of Western Christendom [9]. Jerome and Augustine mention him frequently and with honour. This is not the place to summarise or discuss the contents of his works; but the reader cannot fail to recognise their great and varied value, the completeness of his refutation of current heresies, the convincing character of his presentation of the truth, and the originality, restrained always by scrupulous reverence as well as by intellectual caution, of his additions to the speculative development of the Faith. We recognise also the tenacity with which, encumbered as he was with the double task of simultaneously refuting Arianism and working out his own thoughts, he has adhered to the main issues. He never wanders into details, but keeps steadfastly to his course. He refrains, for instance, from all consideration of the results which Arianism might produce upon the superstructure of the Faith and upon the conduct of Christians; they are undermining the foundations, and he never forgets that it is these which he has undertaken to strengthen and defend. Our confidence in him as a guide is increased by the eminently businesslike use which he makes of his higher qualities. This is obvious in the smallest details, as, for instance, in his judicious abstinence, which will be considered in the next chapter, from the use of technical terms of theology, when their employment would have made his task easier, and might even, to superficial minds, have enhanced his reputation. We see it also in the talent which he shews in the choice of watchwords, which serve both to enliven his pages and to guide the reader through their argument. Such is the frequent antithesis of the orthodox *unitas* with the heretical *unio*, the latter a harmless word in itself and used by Tertullian indifferently with the former, but seized by the quick intelligence of Hilary to serve this special end [1]; such also, the frequent 'Not two Gods but One [2],' and the more obvious contrast between the Catholic *unum* and the Arian *unus*. Thus, in excellence of literary workmanship, in sustained cogency and steady progress of argument, in the full use made of rare gifts of intellect and heart, we must recognise that Hilary has brought his great undertaking to a successful issue; that the voyage beset with many perils, to use his favourite illustration, has safely ended in the haven of Truth and Faith.

Whether the *De Trinitate* were complete or not at the time of his return to Poitiers, after the triumphal passage through Italy, its publication in its final form must very shortly have followed. But literature was, for the present, to claim only the smaller share of his attention. Heartily as he must have rejoiced to be again in his home, he had many anxieties to face. The bishops of Gaul, as we saw from the Invective against Constantius, had been less militant against their Arian neighbours than he had wished. There had been peace in the Church; such peace as could be produced by a mutual ignoring of differences. And it may well be that the Gallican bishops, in their prejudice against the East, thought that Hilary himself had gone too far in the path of conciliation, and that his alliance with the Semiarians was a much longer step towards compromise with heresy than their own prudent neutrality. Each side must have felt that there was something to be explained. Hilary, for his part, by the publication of the *De Trinitate* had made it perfectly clear that his faith was above suspicion; and his abstinence in that work from all mention of existing parties or phases of the controversy shewed that he had withdrawn from his earlier position. He was now once more a Western bishop, concerned only with absolute truth and the interests of the Church in his own province. But he had to reckon with the sterner champions of the Nicene faith, who

---

9 Orosius, *Apol.* i.   1 E.g. iv. 42 *fin.*   2 E.g. i. 17.

had not forgotten the *De Synodis*, however much they might approve the *De Trinitate*. Some curious fragments survive of the Apology which he was driven to write by the attacks of Lucifer of Cagliari. Lucifer, one of the exiles of Milan, was an uncompromising partisan, who could recognise no distinctions among those who did not accept the Nicene Creed. All were equally bad in his eyes; no explaining away of differences or attempt at conciliation was lawful. In days to come he was to be a thorn in the side of Athanasius, and was to end his life in a schism which he formed because the Catholic Church was not sufficiently exclusive. We, who know his after history and turn with repugnance from the monotonous railing with which his writings, happily brief, are filled, may be disposed to underestimate the man. But at the time he was a formidable antagonist. He had the great advantage of being one of the little company of confessors of the Faith, whom all the West admired. He represented truly enough the feeling of the Latin Churches, now that the oppression of their leaders had awakened their hostility to Arianism. And vigorous abuse, such as the facile pen of Lucifer could pour forth, is always interesting when addressed to prominent living men, stale though it becomes when the passions of the moment are no longer felt. Lucifer's protest is lost, but we may gather from the fragments of Hilary's reply that it was milder in tone than was usual with him. Indeed, confessor writing to confessor would naturally use the language of courtesy. But it was an arraignment of the policy which Hilary had adopted, and in which he had failed, though Athanasius was soon to resume it with better success. And courteously as it may have been worded, it cannot have been pleasant for Hilary to be publicly reminded of his failure, and to have doubts cast upon his consistency; least of all when he was returning to Gaul with new hopes, but also with new difficulties. His reply, so far as we can judge of it from the fragments which remain, was of a tone which would be counted moderate in the controversies of to-day. He addresses his opponent as 'Brother Lucifer,' and patiently explains that he has been misunderstood. There is no confession that he had been in the wrong, though he fully admits that the term *homoioüsion*, innocently used by his Eastern friends, was employed by others in a heretical sense. And he points out that Lucifer himself had spoken of the 'likeness' of Son and Father, probably alluding to a passage in his existing writings[3]. The use of this *tu quoque* argument, and a certain apologetic strain which is apparent in the reply, seem to shew that Hilary felt himself at a disadvantage. He must have wished the Asiatic episode to be forgotten; he had now to make his weight felt in the West, where he had good hope that a direct and uncompromising attack upon Arianism would be successful.

For a great change was taking place in public affairs. When Hilary left Constantinople, early in the spring of the year 360, it was probably a profound secret in the capital that a rupture between Constantius and Julian was becoming inevitable. In affairs, civil and ecclesiastical, the Emperor and his favourite, the bishop Saturninus, must have seemed secure of their dominance in Gaul. But events moved rapidly. Constantius needed troops to strengthen the Eastern armies, never adequate to an emergency, for an impending war with Persia; he may also have desired to weaken the forces of Julian. He demanded men; those whom Julian detached for Eastern service refused to march, and proclaim Julian Emperor at Paris. This was in May, some months, at the least, before Hilary, delayed by his Italian labours in the cause of orthodoxy, can have reached home. Julian temporised; he kept up negotiations with Constantius, and employed his army in frontier warfare. But there could be no doubt of the issue. Conflict was inevitable, and the West could have little fear as to the result. The Western armies were the strongest in the Empire; it was with them that, in the last great trial of strength,

---

Constantine the Great had won the day, and the victory of his nephew, successful and popular both as a commander and an administrator, must have been anticipated. Julian's march against Constantius did not commence till the summer of the year 361; but long before this the rule of Constantius and the theological system for which he stood had been rejected by Gaul. The bishops had not shunned Saturninus, as Hilary had desired; most of them had been induced to give their sanction to Arianism at the Council of Rimini. While overshadowed by Constantius and his representative Saturninus, they had not dared to assert themselves. But now the moment was come, and with it the leader. Hilary's arrival in Gaul must have taken place when the conflict was visibly impending, and he can have had no hesitation as to the side he should take. Julian's rule in Gaul began but a few months before his exile, and they had probably never met face to face. But Julian had a well earned reputation as a righteous governor, and Hilary had introduced his name into his second appeal to Constantius, as a witness to his character and as suffering in fame by the injustice of Constantius. We must remember that Julian had kept his paganism carefully concealed, and that all the world, except a few intimate friends, took it for granted that he was, as the high standard of his life seemed to indicate, a sincere Christian. And now he had displaced Constantius in the supreme rule over Gaul, and Saturninus, who had by this time returned, was powerless. We cannot wonder that Hilary continued his efforts; that he went through the land, everywhere inducing the bishops to abjure their own confession made at Rimini. This the bishops, for their part, were certainly willing to do; they were no Arians at heart, and their treatment at Rimini, followed as it was by a fraudulent misrepresentation of the meaning of their words, must have aroused their just resentment. Under the rule of Julian there was no risk, there was even an advantage, in shewing their colours; it set them right both with the new Emperor and with public opinion. But it was not enough for Hilary's purpose that the 'inward evil' of a wavering faith should be amended; it was also necessary that avowed heresy should be expelled. For this the co-operation of Julian was necessary; and before it was granted Julian might naturally look for some definite pronouncement on Hilary's part. To this conjuncture, in the latter half of the year 360 or the earlier part of 361, we may best assign the publication of the Invective, already described, against Constantius. It was a renunciation of allegiance to his old master, not the less clear because the new is not mentioned. And with the name of Constantius was coupled that of Saturninus, as his abettor in tyranny and misbelief. Julian recognised the value of the Catholic alliance by giving effect to the decision of a Council held at Paris, which deposed Saturninus. Hilary had no ecclesiastical authority to gather such a Council, but his character and the eminence of his services no doubt rendered his colleagues willing to follow him; yet neither he nor they would have acted as they did without the assurance of Julian's support. Their action committed them irrevocably to Julian's cause; and it must have seemed that his expulsion of Saturninus committed him irrevocably to the orthodox side. Yet Julian, impartially disbelieving both creeds, had made the ostensible cause of Saturninus' exile, not his errors of faith, but some of those charges of misconduct which were always forthcoming when a convenient excuse was wanted for the banishment of a bishop. Saturninus was a man of the world, and very possibly his Arianism was only assumed in aid of his ambition; it is likely enough that his conduct furnished sufficient grounds for his punishment. The fall of its chief, Sulpicius Severus says, destroyed the party. The other Arian prelates, who must have been few in number, submitted to the orthodox tests, with one exception. Paternus of Périgord, a man of no fame, had the courage of his convictions. He stubbornly asserted his belief, and shared the fate of Saturninus. Thus Hilary obtained, what he had failed to get in the case of the more prominent offender, a clear precedent for the deposition of bishops guilty of Arianism.

The synodical letter, addressed to the Eastern bishops in reply to letters which some of them had sent to Hilary since his return, was incorporated by him in his History, to be mentioned hereafter [4]. The bishops of Gaul assert their orthodoxy, hold Auxentius, Valens, Ursacius and their like excommunicate, and have just excommunicated Saturninus. By his action at Paris, so Sulpicius says, Hilary earned the glory that it was by his single exertions that the provinces of Gaul were cleansed from the defilements of heresy [4a].

These events happened before Julian left the country, in the middle of the summer of 361, on his march against Constantius; or at least, if the actual proceedings were subsequent to his departure, they must have quickly followed it, for his sanction was necessary, and when that was obtained there was no motive for delay. And now, for some years, Hilary disappears from sight. He tells us nothing in his writings of the ordinary course of his life and work; even his informal and discursive Homilies cast no light upon his methods of administration, his successes or failures, and very little on the character of his flock. There was no further conflict within the Church of Gaul during Hilary's lifetime. The death of Constantius, which happened before Julian could meet him in battle, removed all political anxiety. Julian himself was too busy with the revival of paganism in the East to concern himself seriously with its promotion in the Latin-speaking provinces, from which he was absent, and for which he cared less. The orthodox cause in Gaul did not suffer by his apostasy. His short reign was followed by the still briefer rule of the Catholic Jovian. Next came Valentinian, personally orthodox, but steadily refusing to allow depositions on account of doctrine. Under him Arianism dwindled away; Catholic successors were elected to Arian prelates, and the process would have been hastened but by a few years had Hilary been permitted to expel Auxentius from Milan, as we shall presently see him attempting to do.

This was his last interference in the politics of the Church, and does not concern us as yet. His chief interest henceforth was to be in literary work; in popularising and, as he thought, improving upon the teaching of Origen. He commented upon the book of Job, as we know from Jerome and Augustine. The former says that this, and his work on the Psalms, were translations from Origen. But that is far from an accurate account of the latter work, and may be equally inaccurate concerning the former. The two fragments which St. Augustine has preserved from the Commentary on Job are so short that we cannot draw from them any conclusion as to the character of the book. If we may trust Jerome, its length was somewhat more than a quarter of that of the Homilies on the Psalms [5], in their present form. It it unfortunate, but not surprising, that the work should have fallen into oblivion. It was, no doubt, allegorical in its method, and nothing of that kind could survive in competition with Gregory the Great's inimitable *Moralia* on Job.

Hilary's other adaptation from Origen, the Homilies on the Psalms, happily remains to us. It is at least as great a work as the *De Trinitate,* and one from which we can learn even more what manner of man its writer was. For the *De Trinitate* is an appeal to all thoughtful Christians of the time, and written for future generations as well as for them; characteristic, as it is, in many ways of the author, the compass of the work and the stateliness of its rhetoric tend to conceal his personality. But the Homilies [6] on the Psalms, which would seem to have

---

[4] Fragment xi.

[4a] *Chron.* ii. 45.

[5] Jerome, *Apol. adv. Rufinum,* i. 2, says that the total length of the Commentaries on Job and the Psalms was about 40,000 lines, i.e. Virgilian hexameters. The latter, at a rough estimate, must be nearly 35,000 lines in its present state. But Jerome, as we shall see, was not acquainted with so many Homilies as have come down to us; we must deduct about 5,000 lines, and this will leave 10,000 for the Commentary on Job, making it two-sevenths of the length of the other. Jerome, however, is not careful in his statement of lengths; he calls the short *De Synodis* 'a very long book,' *Ep.* v. 2.

[6] *Tractatus* ought to be translated thus. It is the term, and the only term, used so early as this for the bishop's address to the congregation; in fact, one might almost say that *tractare, tractatus* in Christian language had no other meaning. It is an anachronism in the fourth century to render *prædicare* by 'preach;' cf. Duchesne, *Liber Pontificalis,* i. 126.

reached us in the notes of a shorthand writer, so artless and conversational is the style, shew us Hilary in another aspect.   He is imparting instruction to his own familiar congregation ; and he knows his people so well that he pours out whatever is passing through his mind.   In fact, he seems often to be thinking aloud on subjects which interest him rather than address-ing himself to the needs of his audience.   Practical exhortation has, indeed, a much smaller space than mystical exegesis and speculative Christology.   Yet abstruse questions are never made more obscure by involution of style.   The language is free and flowing, always that of an educated man who has learnt facility by practice.   And here, strange as it seems to a reader of the *De Trinitate*, he betrays a preference for poetical words [7], which shews that his renunciation of such ornament elsewhere is deliberate.   Yet, even here, he indulges in no definite reminiscences of the poets.

There remains only one trace, though it is sufficient, of the original circumstances of delivery.   The Homily on Psalm xiv. begins with the words, 'The Psalm which has been read.' The Psalms were sung as an act of worship, not read as a lesson, in the normal course of divine service ; and therefore we must assume that the Psalm to be expounded was recited, by the lector or another, as an introduction to the Homily.   We need not be surprised that such notices, which must have seemed to possess no permanent interest, have been edited away.   Many of the Homilies are too long to have been delivered on one or even two occasions, yet the ascription of praise with which Hilary, like Origen, always concludes [8] has been omitted in every case except at the end of the whole discourse.   This shews that Hilary himself, or more probably some editor, has put the work into its final shape.   But this editing of the Homilies has not extended to the excision of the numerous repetitions, which were natural enough when Hilary was delivering each as a commentary complete in itself, and do not offend us when we read the discourse on a single Psalm, though they certainly disfigure the work when regarded as a treatise on the whole Psalter.

It is probably due to the accidents of time that our present copies of the Homilies are imperfect.   We are, indeed, better off than was Jerome.   His manuscript contained Homilies on Psalms 1, 2, 51—62, 118—150, according to the Latin notation.   We have, in addition to these, Homilies which are certainly genuine on Psalms 13, 14, 63—69 ; and others on the titles of Psalms 9 and 91, which are probably spurious [9].   Some more Homilies of uncertain origin which have been fathered upon Hilary, and may be found in the editions, may be left out of account.   In the Homily on Psalm 59, § 2, he mentions one, unknown to Jerome as to ourselves, on Psalm 44 ; and this allusion, isolated though it is, suggests that the Homilies contained, or were meant to contain, a commentary on the whole Book of Psalms, composed in the order in which they stand.   There is, of course, nothing strange in the circulation in ancient times of imperfect copies ; a well-known instance is that of St. Augustine's copy of Cyprian which did not contain an epistle which has come down to us.   This series of Homilies was probably continuous as well as complete.   The incidental allusions to the events of the times contain nothing inconsistent with the supposition that he began at the beginning of the Psalter and went on to the end.   We might, indeed, construe the language of that on Psalm 52, § 13, concerning prosperous clergy, who heap up wealth for themselves and live in luxury, as an allusion to men like Saturninus, but the passage is vague, and a vivid recollection,

---

[7] E.g. *fundamen, Tr. in Ps.* cxxviii. 10, *germen,* cxxxiv. 1, *revolubilis,* ii. 23, *peccamen,* ii. 9 *fin.* and often.   The shape of sentences, though simple, is always good ; to take one test word, *sæpe,* which was almost if not quite extinct in common use, occurs fairly often near the end of a period, where it was needed for rhythm, which *frequenter* would have spoiled.   Some Psalms, e.g. xiii., xiv., are treated more rhetorically than others.

[8] Psalm li. is the only exception, due, no doubt, to careless transcription.   The Homilies on the titles of Psalms ix. and xci.

do not count ; they are probably spurious, and in any case are incomplete, as the text of the Psalms is not discussed.

[9] So Zingerle, Preface, p. xiv, to whom we owe the excellent Vienna Edition of the Homilies, the only part of Hilary's writings which has as yet appeared in a critical text.   The writer of the former of these two Homilies, in § 2, says that the title of a Psalm always corresponds to the contents.   This is quite contrary to Hilary's teaching, who frequently points out and ingeniously explains what seem to him to be discrepancies.

not a present evil, may have suggested it.   More definite, and indeed a clear note of time, is the Homily on Psalm 63, where heathenism is aggressive and is become a real danger, of which Hilary speaks in the same terms as he does of heresy.   This contrasts strongly with such language as that of the Homily on Psalm 67, § 20, where the heathen are daily flocking into the Church, or of that on Psalm 137, § 10, where paganism has collapsed, its temples are ruined and its oracles silent ; such words as the former could only have been written in the short reign of Julian.   Other indications, such as the frequent warnings against heresy and denunciations of heretics, are too general to help in fixing the date.   On the whole, it would seem a reasonable hypothesis that Hilary began his connected series of Homilies on the Psalms soon after his return to Gaul, that he had made good progress with them when Julian publicly apostatised, and that they were not completed till the better times of Valentinian.

He was conversing in pastoral intimacy with his people, and hence we cannot be surprised that he draws, perhaps unconsciously, on the results of his own previous labours. For instance, on Psalm 61, § 2, he gives what is evidently a reminiscence, yet with features of its own and not as a professed autobiography, of his mental history as described in the opening of the *De Trinitate*.   And while the direct controversy against Arianism is not avoided, there is a manifest preference for the development of Hilary's characteristic Christology, which had already occupied him in the later books of the *De Trinitate*.   We must, indeed, reconstruct his doctrine in this respect even more from the Homilies than from the *De Trinitate ;* and in the later work he not only expands what he had previously suggested, but throws out still further suggestions which he had not the length of life to present in a more perfect form.   But the Homilies contain much that is of far less permanent interest.   Wherever he can[1], he brings in the mystical interpretation of numbers, that strange vagary of the Eastern mind which had, at least from the time of Irenæus and the Epistle of Barnabas, found a congenial home in Christian thought.   This and other distortions of the sense of Scripture, which are the result in Hilary, as in Origen, of a prosaic rather than a poetical turn of mind, will find a more appropriate place for discussion at the beginning of the next chapter.   Allusions to the mode of worship of his time are very rare[2], as are details of contemporary life.   Of general encouragement to virtue and denunciation of vice there is abundance, and it repeats with striking fidelity the teaching of Cyprian.   Hilary displays the same Puritanism in regard to jewelry as does Cyprian[3], and the same abhorrence of public games and spectacles.   Of these three elements, the Christology, the mysticism, the moral teaching, the Homilies are mainly compact.   They carry on no sustained argument and contain, as has been said, a good deal of repetition.   In fact, a continuous reader will probably form a worse impression of their quality than he who is satisfied with a few pages at a time.   They are eminently adapted for selection, and the three Homilies, those on Psalms 1, 53 and 130, which have been translated for this volume, may be inadequate, yet are fairly representative, as specimens of the instruction which Hilary conveys in this work.

It has been said that the practical teaching of Hilary is that of Cyprian.   But this is not a literary debt[4]; the writer to whom almost all the exegesis is due, by borrowing of substance or of method, is Origen, except where the spirit of the fourth century has been at work.   Yet other authors have been consulted, and this not only for general information, as in the case, already cited, of the elder Pliny, but for interpretation of the Psalms.   For instance, a strange legend concerning Mount Hermon is cited on Psalm 132, § 6, from a writer whose name Hilary does not know ; and on Psalm 133, § 4, he has consulted several writers and rejects the opinion of them all.   But these authorities, whoever they may have been, were of little

---

1 E.g. in the *Instruction* or discourse preparatory to the Homilies, and in the introductory sections of that on Ps. 118 (119).

2 E.g. *Instr. in Ps.*, § 12, the fifty days of rejoicing during which Christians must not prostrate themselves in prayer, nor fast

3 Ps. 118, *Ain.*, § 16.

4 The account of exorcism given on Ps. 64, § 10, suggests Cyprian, *Ad. Don.* 5, but the subject is such a commonplace that nothing definite can be said.

importance for his purpose in comparison with Origen. Still we can only accept Jerome's assertion that the Homilies are translated from Origen in a qualified sense. Hilary was writing for the edification of his own flock, and was obliged to modify much that Origen had said if he would serve their needs, for religious thought had changed rapidly in the century which lay between the two, and a mere translation would have been as coldly received as would a reprint of some commentary of the age of George II. to-day. And Hilary's was a mind too active and independent to be the slave of a traditional interpretation. We must, therefore, expect to find a considerable divergence; and we cannot be surprised that Hilary, as he settled down to his task, grew more and more free in his treatment of Origen's exegesis.

Unhappily the remains of Origen's work upon the Psalms, though considerable, are fragmentary, and of the fragments scattered through *Catenæ* no complete or critical edition has yet been made. Still, insufficient as the material would be for a detailed study and comparison, enough survives to enable us to form a general idea of the relation between the two writers. Origen [5] composed Homilies upon the Psalter, a Commentary upon it, and a summary treatise, called the *Enchiridion*. The first of these works was Hilary's model; Origen's Homilies were diffuse extemporary expositions, ending, like Hilary's, with an ascription of praise. It is unfortunate that, of the few which survive, all treat of Psalms on which Hilary's Homilies are lost. But it is doubtful whether Hilary knew the other writings of Origen upon the Psalter. We have ourselves a very small knowledge of them, for the *Catenæ* are not in the habit of giving more than the name of the author whom they cite. Yet it may well be that some of the apparent discrepancies between the explanations given by Hilary and by Origen are due to the loss of the passage from Origen's Homily which would have agreed with Hilary, and to the survival of the different rendering given in the Commentary or the *Enchiridion*; some, no doubt, are also due to the carelessness and even dishonesty of the compilers of *Catenæ* in stating the authorship of their selections. But though it is possible that Hilary had access to all Origen's writings on the Psalms, there is no reason to suppose that he possessed a copy of his *Hexapla*. The only translation of the Old Testament which he names beside the Septuagint is that of Aquila; he is aware that there are others, but none save the Septuagint has authority or deserves respect, and his rare allusions to them are only such as we find in Origen's Homilies, and imply no such exhaustive knowledge of the variants as a possessor of the *Hexapla* would have.

A comparison of the two writers shews the closeness of their relation, and if we had Origen's complete Homilies, and not mere excerpts, the debt of Hilary would certainly be still more manifest. For the compilers of *Catenæ* have naturally selected what was best in Origen, and most suited for short extracts; his eccentricities have been in great measure omitted. Hence we may err in attributing to Hilary much that is perverse in his comments; there is an abundance of wild mysticism in the fragments of Origen, but its proportion to the whole is undoubtedly less in their present state than in their original condition. Hilary's method was that of paraphrasing, not of servile translation. There is apparently only one literal rendering of an extant passage of Origen, and that a short one [6]; but paraphrases, which often become very diffuse expansions, are constant [7]. But a just comparison between the two must embrace their differences as well as their resemblances. Hilary has exercised a silent criticism in omitting many of Origen's textual disquisitions. He gives, it is true, many various readings, but his confidence in the Septuagint often renders him indifferent in regard to

---

5 He is here cited by the volume and page of the edition by Lommatzsch. His system of interpretation is admirably described in the fourth of Dr. Bigg's Bampton Lectures, *The Christian Platonists of Alexandria*.

6 Hil. *Tr. in Ps.* 13, § 3, *his igitur ita grassantibus*, sq. = Origen (ed. Lommatzsch) xii. 38.

7 E.g. *Instr. in Ps.*, § 15 = Origen in Eusebius, *H.E.* vi. 25 (Philocalia 3), Hilary on Ps. 51, §§ 3, 7 = Origen xii. 353, 354, and very often on Ps. 118 (119), e.g. the Introduction = Or. xiii. 67 f., *Aleph*, § 12 = *ib.* 70, *Beth*, § 6 = *ib.* 71, *Caph*, §§ 4, 9 = *ib.* 82, 83, &c.

divergencies which Origen had taken seriously. The space which the latter devotes to the Greek versions Hilary employs in correcting the errors and variations of the Latin, or in explaining the meaning of Greek words. But these are matters which rather belong to the next chapter, concerning, as they do, Hilary's attitude towards Scripture. It is more significant of his tone of mind that he has omitted Origen's speculations on the resurrection of the body, preserved by Epiphanius[8], and on the origin of evil[9]. Again, Origen delights to give his readers a choice of interpretations; Hilary chooses one of those which Origen has given, and makes no mention of the other. This is his constant habit in the earlier part of the Homilies; towards the end, however, he often gives a rendering of his own, and also mentions, either as possible or as wrong, that which Origen had offered. Or else, though he only makes his own suggestion, yet it is obvious to those who have Origen at hand that he has in his mind, and is refuting for his own satisfaction, an alternative which he does not think good to lay before his audience[1]. A similar liberty with his original occurs in the Homily on Psalm 135, § 12 :—'The purposes of the present discourse and of this place forbid us to search more deeply.' This must have seemed a commonplace to his hearers; but it happens that Origen's speculations upon the passage have survived, and we can see that Hilary was rather making excuses to himself for his disregard of them than directly addressing his congregation. Apart from the numerous instances where Hilary derives a different result from the same data, there are certain cases where he accepts the current Latin text, though it differed from Origen's Greek, and draws, without any reference to Origen, his own conclusions as to the meaning[2]. These, again, seem to be confined to the latter part of the work, and may be the result of occasional neglect to consult the authorities, rather than a deliberate departure from Origen's teaching.

But the chief interest of the comparison between the writings of these two Fathers upon the Psalms lies in the insight which it affords into their respective modes of thought. Fragmentary as they are, Origen's words are a manifestly genuine and not inadequate expression of his mind; and Hilary, a recognised authority and conscious of his powers, has so moulded and transformed his original, now adapting and now rejecting, that he has made it, even on the ground which is common to both, a true and sufficient representation of his own mental attitude. The Roman contrasts broadly with the Greek. He constantly illustrates his discourse with historical incidents of Scripture, taken in their literal sense; there are few such in Origen. Origen is full, as usual, of praises of the contemplative state; in speculation upon Divine things consists for him the happiness everywhere promised to the saints. Hilary ignores abstract speculation, whether as a method of interpretation or as a hope for the future, and actually describes[3] the contemplation of God's dealings with men as merely one among other modes of preparation for eternal blessings. In the same discourse he paraphrases the words of Origen, 'He who has done all things that conduce to the knowledge of God,' by 'They who have the abiding sense of a cleansed heart[4].' Though he is the willing slave of the allegorical method, yet he revolts from time to time against its excesses in Origen; their treatment of Psalm 126, in the one case practical, in the other mystical, is a typical example[5]. Hilary's attention is fixed on concrete things; the enemies denounced in the Psalms mean for him the heretics of the day, while Origen had recognised in them the invisible agency of evil spirits[6]. The words 'Who teacheth my hands to fight' suggest to Origen intellectual weapons and victories; they remind Hilary of the 'I have

---

8 *Hæres.* 64, 12 f.

9 Origen xiii. 134. Hilary has omitted this from his Homily on Ps. 134, § 12.

1 Instances of such independence are Ps. 118, *Daleth*, § 6 (xiii. 74), 119, § 15 (*ib.* 108), 122, § 2 (*ib.* 112), 133, § 3 (*ib.* 131). The references to Origen are in brackets.

2 E.g. Ps. 118, *Heth*, § 10, 121, § 1 ; Origen xiii. 80, 111.

3 Ps. 118, *Gimel*, § 21.

4 Origen xiii. 72 ; Hilary, Ps. 118, *Gimel*, § 1.

5 Cf. also Ps. 118, *Heth*, § 7, *Koph*, § 4, with Origen xiii. 79, 98. Here again the spirit of independence manifests itself towards the end of the work.

6 Cf. Ps. 118, *Samech*, § 6 Origen xiii. 92.

overcome the world' of Christ [7].   In fact, the thought of Hilary was so charged with definite convictions concerning Christ, and so impressed with their importance, that his very earnestness and concentration betrays him into error of interpretation.   It would be an insufficient, yet not a false, contrast between him and Origen to say that the latter distorts, with an almost playful ingenuity, the single words or phrases of Scripture, while Hilary, with masterful indifference to the principles of exegesis, will force a whole chapter to render the sense which he desires.   And his obvious sincerity, his concentration of thought upon one great and always interesting doctrine, his constant appeal to what seems to be, and sometimes is, the exact sense of Scripture, and the vigour of his style, far better adapted to its purpose than that of Origen ; all these render him an even more convincing exponent than the other of the bad system of interpretation which both have adopted.   Sound theological deductions and wise moral reflections on every page make the reader willing to pardon a vicious method, for Hilary's doctrine is never based upon his exegesis of the Psalms.   No primary truth depends for him upon allegory or mysticism, and it may be that he used the method with the less caution because he looked for nothing more than that it should illustrate and confirm what was already established.   Since, then, the permanent interest of the work is that it shews us what seemed to Hilary, as a representative of his age, to be the truth, and we have in it a powerful and original presentation of that truth, we can welcome, as a quaint and not ungraceful enlivening of his argument, this ingenuity of misinterpretation.   And we may learn also a lesson for ourselves of the importance of the doctrine which he inculcates with such perseverance.   Confronting him as it did, in various aspects, at every turn and in the most unlikely places during his journey through the Psalter, his faith concerning Christ was manifestly in Hilary's eyes the vital element of religion.

The Homilies on the Psalms have never been a popular work.   Readable as they are, and free from most of the difficulties which beset the *De Trinitate*, posterity allowed them to be mutilated, and, as we saw, only a portion has come down to us.   Their chief influence, like that of the other treatise, has been that which Hilary has exercised through them upon writers of greater fame.   Ambrose has borrowed from them liberally and quite uncritically for his own exposition of certain of the Psalms ; and Ambrose, accredited by his own fame and that of his greater friend Augustine, has quite overshadowed the fame of Hilary.   The Homilies may, perhaps, have also suffered from an undeserved suspicion that anything written by the author of the *De Trinitate* would be hard to read.   They have, in any case, been little read; and yet, as the first important example in Latin literature of the allegorical method, and as furnishing the staple of a widely studied work of St. Ambrose, they have profoundly affected the course of Christian thought.   Their historical interest as well as their intrinsic value commands our respect.

In his Homily on Psalm 138, § 4, Hilary briefly mentions the Patriarchs as examples of faith, and adds, 'but these are matters of which we must discourse more suitably and fully in their proper place.'   This is a promise to which till of late no known work of our writer corresponded.   Jerome had, indeed, informed us [7a] that Hilary had composed a treatise entitled *De Mysteriis*, but no one had connected it with his words in the Homily.   It had been supposed that the lost treatise dealt with the sacraments, in spite of the facts that it is Hilary's custom to speak of types as 'mysteries,' and that the sacraments are a theme upon which he never dwells.   But in 1887 a great portion of Hilary's actual treatise on the Mysteries was recovered in the same manuscript which contained the more famous *Pilgrimage to the Holy Places* of Silvia of Aquitaine [8].   It is a short treatise of two books, unhappily mutilated at the beginning, in the middle and near the end, though the peroration has survived.   The title is

---

7 Ps. 143, § 4; Origen xiii. 149.   7a *Vir. Ill.* 100.

8 J. F Gamurrini, *S. Hilarii Tractatus de Mysteriis et Hymni, etc.*, 4to., Rome, 1887.   The *De Mysteriis* occupies pp 3—28.

lost, but there is no reason to doubt that Jerome was nearly right in calling it a *tractatus*, though he would have done better had he used the plural. It is written in the same easy style as the Homilies on the Psalms, and if it was not originally delivered as two homilies, as is probable, it must be a condensation of several discourses into a more compact form. The first book deals with the Patriarchs, the second with the Prophets, regarded as types of Christ. The whole is written from the point of view with which Hilary's other writings have made us familiar. Every deed recorded in Scripture proclaims or typifies or proves the advent of the incarnate Christ, and it is Hilary's purpose to display the whole of His work as reflected in the Old Testament, like an image in a mirror. He begins with Adam and goes on to Moses, deriving lessons from the lives of all the chief characters, often with an exercise of great ingenuity. For instance, in the history of the Fall Eve is the Church, which is sinful but shall be saved through bearing children in Baptism[9]; the burning bush is a type of the endurance of the Church, of which St. Paul speaks in 2 Cor. iv. 8[1]; the manna was found in the morning, the time of Christ's Resurrection and therefore of the reception of heavenly food in the Eucharist. They who collect too much are heretics with their excess of argument[2]. In the second book we have a fragmentary and desultory treatment of incidents in the lives of the Prophets, which Hilary ends by saying that in all the events which he has recorded we recognise 'God the Father and God the Son, and God the Son from God the Father, Jesus Christ, God and Man[3].' The peroration, in fact, reads like a summary of the argument of the *De Trinitate*. Of the genuineness of the little work there can be no doubt. Its language, its plan, its arguments are unmistakeably those of Hilary[4]. The homilies were probably delivered soon after he had finished his course on the Psalms, of which they contain some reminiscences, such as we saw are found in the later Homilies on the Psalms of earlier passages in the same. In all probability the subject matter of the *De Mysteriis* is mainly drawn from Origen. It is too short, and too much akin to Hilary's more important writings, to cast much light upon his modes of thought. He has, indeed, no occasion to speak here upon the points on which his teaching is most original and characteristic.

In this same manuscript, discovered by Gamurrini at Arezzo, are the remains of what professes to be Hilary's collection of hymns. He has always had the fame of being the earliest Latin hymn writer. This was, indeed, a task which the circumstances of his life must have suggested to him. The conflict with Arianism forced him to become the pioneer of systematic theology in the Latin tongue; it also drove him into exile in the East, where he must have acquainted himself with the controversial use made of hymnody by the Arians. Thus it was natural that he should have introduced hymns also into the West. But if the *De Trinitate* had little success, the hymns were still more unfortunate. Jerome tells us that Hilary complained of finding the Gauls unteachable in sacred song[5]; and there is no reason to suppose that he had any wide or permanent success in introducing hymns into public worship[6]. If Hilary must have the credit of originality in this respect, the honour of turning his suggestion to account belongs to Ambrose, whose fame in more respects than one is built upon foundations laid by the other. And if but a scanty remnant of the verse of Ambrose, popular as it was, survives, we cannot be surprised that not a line remains which can safely be

---

[9] Ed. Gamurrini, p. 5.   [1] Ib. p. 17.

[2] Ib. p. 21; there is the not uncommon play on the two senses of *colligere*.

[3] Ib. p. 27.

[4] It must be confessed that some authorities refuse to regard this work as the *De Mysteriis* of Hilary. Among these is Ebert, *Litteratur des Mittelalters*, p. 142, who admits that the matter might be Hilary's, but denies that the manner and style are his.

[5] *Comm. in Ep. ad Gal.* ii. *pref.*: *Hilarius in hymnorum carmine Gallos indociles vocat.* This may mean that Hilary actually used the words 'stubborn Gauls' in one of his hymns. There would be nothing extraordinary in this; the early efforts, and especially those of the Arians which Hilary imitated for a better purpose, often departed widely from the propriety of later compositions, as we shall see in one of those attributed to Hilary himself.

[6] It is true that the Fourth Council of Toledo (A.D. 633) in its 13th canon couples Hilary with Ambrose as the writer of hymns in actual use. But these canons are verbose productions, and this may be a mere literary flourish, natural enough in countrymen and contemporaries of Isidore of Seville, who knew, no doubt from Jerome's *Viri Illustres*, that Hilary was the first Latin hymn writer.

attributed to Hilary, though authorities who deserve respect have pronounced in favour of more than one of the five hymns which we must consider.

Hilary's own opinion concerning the use of hymns can best be learnt from his Homilies on Psalms 64 and 65. In the former (§ 12) the Church's delightful exercise of singing hymns at morning and evening is one of the chief tokens which she has of God's mercy towards her. In the latter (§ 1) we are told that sacred song requires the accompaniment of instrumental harmonies; that the combination to this end of different forms of service and of art produces a result acceptable to God. The lifting of the voice to God in exultation, as an act of spiritual warfare against the devil and his hosts, is given as an example of the uses of hymnody (§ 4). It is a means of putting the enemy to flight; 'Whoever he be that takes his post outside the Church, let him hear the voice of the people at their prayers, let him mark the multitudinous sound of our hymns, and in the performance of the divine Sacraments let him recognise the responses which our loyal confession makes. Every adversary must needs be affrighted, the devil routed, death conquered in the faith of the Resurrection, by such jubilant utterance of our exultant voice. The enemy will know that this gives pleasure to God and assurance to our hope, even this public and triumphant raising of our voice in song.' Original composition, both of words and music, is evidently in Hilary's mind; and we can see that he is rather recommending a useful novelty than describing an established practice. It is a remarkable coincidence that the five hymns which are called his are, in fact, a song of triumph over the devil, and a hymn in praise of the Resurrection, which are, so their editor thinks, actually alluded to in the Homily cited above; a confession of faith; and a morning hymn and one which has been taken for an evening hymn. These are exactly the subjects which correspond to Hilary's description.

But, when we come to the examination of these hymns in detail, the gravest doubts arise. The first three were discovered in the same manuscript to which we owe the *De Mysteriis*. They formed part of a small collection, which cannot have numbered more than seven or eight hymns, of which these three only have escaped, not without some mutilation. That which stands first is the confession of faith, the matter of which contains nothing that is inconsistent with Hilary's time. But beyond this, and the fact that the manuscript ascribes it to Hilary, there is nothing to suggest his authorship. It is a dreary production in a limping imitation of an Horatian metre; an involved argumentative statement of Catholic doctrine, in which it would be difficult to say whether verse or subject suffers the more from their unwonted union. The sequence of thought is helped out by the mechanical device of an alphabetical arrangement of the stanzas, but even this assistance could not make it intelligible to an ordinary congregation [7]. And the want of literary skill in the author makes it impossible to suppose that Hilary is he; classical knowledge was still on too high a level for an educated man to perpetrate such solecisms.

In the same manuscript there follow, after an unfortunate gap, the two hymns to which it has been suggested that Hilary alludes in his Homily on Psalm 65, those which celebrate the praises of the Resurrection and the triumph over Satan. The former is by a woman's hand, and the feminine forms of the language must have made it, one would think, unsuitable for congregational singing. There is no reason why the poem should not date from the fourth century; indeed, since it is written by a neophyte, that date is more probable than a later time, when adult converts to Christianity were more scarce. It has considerable merits; it is

---

7 Two of the simplest stanzas are as follows :—

Extra quam capere potest	Felix qui potuit fide
mens humana	res tantas penitus
manet Filius in Patre,	credulus assequi,
rursus quem penes sit Pater	ut incorporeo ex Deo
dignus, qui genitus est	profectus fuerit
Filius in Deum.	primogenitus Dei.

It is written in stanzas of six lines in the MS ; the metre is the second Asclepiad. Gamurrini, the discoverer, and Fechtrup (in Wetzer Welte's Encyclopædia) regard it as the work of Hilary, but the weight of opinion is against them.

fervid in tone and free in movement, and has every appearance of being the expression of genuine feeling. It is, in fact, likely enough that, if it were written in Hilary's day, he should have inserted it in a collection of sacred verse. Concerning its authorship the suggestion has been made [8] that it was written by Florentia, a heathen maiden converted by Hilary near Seleucia, who followed him to Gaul, lived, died, and was buried by him in his diocese. The story of Florentia rests on no better authority than the worthless biography of Hilary, written by Fortunatus, who, moreover, says nothing about hymns composed by her. Neither proof nor disproof is possible: unless we regard the defective Latinity as evidence in favour of a Greek origin for the authoress. The third hymn, which celebrates the triumph of Christ over Satan, may or may not be the work of the same hand as the second. It bears much more resemblance to it than to the laborious and prosaic effusion which stands first. The manuscript which contains these three hymns distinctly assigns the first, and one or more which have perished, to Hilary:—'*Incipiunt hymni eiusdem.*' Whether a fresh title stood before the later hymns, which clearly belong to another, we cannot say; the collection is too short for this to be probable. It is obvious that, if we have in this manuscript the remains of a hymn-book for actual use, it was, like ours, a compilation; brief as it was, it may have been as large as the cumbrous shape of ancient volumes would allow to be cheaply multiplied and conveniently used. Many popular treatises, as for instance some by Tertullian and Cyprian, were quite as short. Who the compiler may have been must remain unknown. We must attach some importance to the evidence of the manuscript which has restored to us the *De Mysteriis* and the Pilgrimage of Silvia; and we may reasonably suppose that this collection was made in the time, and even with the sanction, of Hilary, though we cannot accept him as the author of any of the three hymns which remain.

The spurious letter to his imaginary daughter Abra was apparently written with the ingenious purpose of fathering upon Hilary the morning hymn, *Lucis Largitor splendide.* This is a hymn of considerable beauty, in the same metre as the genuine Ambrosian hymns. But there is this essential difference, that while in the latter the rules of classical versification as regards the length of syllables are scrupulously followed, in the former these rules are ignored, and rhythm takes the place of quantity. This is a sufficient proof that the hymn is of a later date than Ambrose, and, *a fortiori*, than Hilary. There remains the so-called evening hymn, which has been supposed to be the companion to the last [9]. This, again, is alphabetical, and contains in twenty-three stanzas a confession of sin, an appeal to Christ and an assertion of orthodoxy. The rules of metre are neglected in favour of an uncouth attempt at rhythm. Latin appears to have been a dead language to the writer [1], who adorns his lines with little pieces of pagan mythology, and whose taste is indicated by his description of heretics as 'barking Sabellius and grunting Simon.' The hymn is probably the work of some bombastic monk, perhaps of the time of Charles the Great; unlike the other four, it cannot possibly date from Hilary's generation.

Omitting certain fragments of treatises of which Hilary may, or may not, have been the author [2], we now come to his attack upon Auxentius of Milan, and to the last of

---

[8] By Gamurrini in *Studî e documenti*, 1884, p. 83 f.

[9] Printed in full by Mai, *Patrum Nova Bibliotheca*, p. 490. He suspends judgment, and will not say that it is unworthy of Hilary. The Benedictine editor, Coustant, gives a few stanzas as specimens, and summarily rejects it.

[1] The four quarters of the universe are *ortus, occasus, aquilo, septentrio*; one of these last must mean the south. This would point to some German land as the home of the author; in no country of Romance tongue could such an error have been perpetrated. *Perire* is used for *perdere*, but this it not unparalleled.

[2] In Mai's *Patrum Nova Bibliotheca*, vol. i., is a short treatise on the Genealogies of Christ. The method of interpretation is the same as Hilary's, but the language is not his; and the terms used of the Virgin in §§ 11, 12, are not so early as the fourth century. In the same volume is an exposition of the beginning of St. John's Gospel in an anti-Arian sense. In spite of some difference of vocabulary, there is no strong reason why this should not be by Hilary; cf. especially, §§ 5—7. Mai also prints in the same volume a short fragment on the Paralytic (St. Matt. ix. 2), too brief for a judgment to be formed. In Pitra's *Spicilegium Solesmense*, vol. i., is a brief discussion on the first chapters of Genesis, dealing chiefly with the Fall. It appears, like the Homilies on the Psalms, to be the report of some extemporary addresses, and is more likely than any of the preceding to be the

his complete works. Dionysius of Milan had been, as we saw, a sufferer in the same cause as Hilary. But he had been still more hardly treated; he had not only been exiled, but his place had been taken by Auxentius, an Eastern Arian of the school favoured by Constantius. Dionysius died in exile, and Auxentius remained in undisputed possession of the see. He must have been a man of considerable ability; perhaps, as we have mentioned, he was the creator of the so-called Ambrosian ritual, and certainly he was the leader of the Arian party in Italy and the further West. The very fact that Constantius and his advisers chose him for so great a post as the bishopric of Milan proves that they had confidence in him. He justified their trust, holding his own without apparent difficulty at Milan and working successfully in the cause of compromise at Ariminum and elsewhere Athanasius mentions him often and bitterly as a leader of the heretics; and he must be ranked with Ursacius and Valens as one of the most unscrupulous of his party. While Constantius reigned Auxentius was, of course, safe from attack. But at the end of the year 364 Hilary thought that the opportunity was come. Since his last entry into the conflict Julian and his successor Jovian had died, and Valentinian had for some months been Emperor. He had just divided the Roman Empire with his brother Valens, himself choosing the Western half with Milan for his capital, while he gave Constantinople and the East to Valens The latter was a man of small abilities, unworthy to reign, and a convinced Arian; Valentinian, with many faults, was a strong ruler, and favoured the cause of orthodoxy. But he was, before all else, a soldier and a statesman; his orthodoxy was, perhaps, a mere acquiescence in the predominant belief among his subjects, and it had, in any case, much less influence over his conduct than had Arianism over that of Valens. It must have seemed to Hilary and to Eusebius of Vercelli that there was danger to the Church in the possession by Auxentius of so commanding a position as that of bishop of Milan, with constant access to the Emperor's ear; and especially now that the Emperor was new to his work and had no knowledge, perhaps no strong convictions, concerning the points at issue. As far as they could judge, their success or failure in displacing Auxentius would influence the fortunes of the Church for a generation at least. It would, therefore, be unjust to accuse Hilary as a mere busy-body. He interfered, it is true, outside his own province, but it was at a serious crisis; and his knowledge of the Western Church must have assured him that, if he did not act, the necessary protest would probably remain unmade.

Hilary, then, in company with his ally Eusebius, hastened to Milan in order to influence the mind of Valentinian against Auxentius, and to waken the dormant orthodoxy of the Milanese Church. For there seems to have been little local opposition to the Arian bishop: no organised congregation of Catholics in the city rejected his communion. On the other hand, there was no militant Arianism; the worship conducted by Auxentius could excite no scruples, and in his teaching he would certainly avoid the points of difference. He and his school had no desire to persecute orthodoxy because it was orthodox. From their point of view, the Faith had been settled in such a way that their own position was unassailable, and all they wished was to live and to let live. And we must remember that the Council of Rimini, disgraceful as the manner was in which its decision had been reached, was still the rule of the Faith for the Western Church. Hilary and Eusebius had induced a multitude of bishops, amid the applause of their flocks, to recant; but private expressions of opinion, however numerous, could not erase the definitions of Rimini from

<hr>

work of Hilary. It is quite in his style, but the contents are unimportant. But we must remember that the scribes were rarely content to confess that they were ignorant of the name of an author whom they transcribed; and that, being as ill-furnished with scruples as with imagination, they assigned everything that came to hand to a few familiar names. Two further works ascribed to Hilary are obviously not his. Pitra, in the volume already cited, has printed considerable remains of a Commentary on the Pauline Epistles, which really belongs to Theodore of Mopsuestia; and a Commentary on the seven Canonical Epistles, recently published in the *Spicilegium Casinense*, vol. iii., is there attributed, with much reason, to his namesake of Arles.

the records of the Church.   It was not till the year 369 that a Council at Rome expunged them.   The first object of the allies was to excite opposition to the Arian, and in this they had some success.   Auxentius, in his petition to the Emperor, which we possess, asserts that they stirred up certain of the laity, who had been in communion neither with himself nor with his predecessors, to call him a heretic.   The immediate predecessor of Auxentius was the Catholic Dionysius, and we cannot suppose that this is a fair description of Hilary's followers.   But it is probable that the malcontents were not numerous, for none but enthusiasts would venture into apparent schism on account of a heresy which was certainly not conspicuous.   How long Hilary was allowed to continue his efforts is unknown.   Valentinian reached Milan in the November of 364, and left it in the Autumn of the following year; and before his departure his decision had frustrated Hilary's purpose.   We only know that, as soon as the matter grew serious, Auxentius appealed to the Emperor.   There was no point more important in the eyes of the government than unity within the local Churches, and Auxentius, being formally in the right, must have made his appeal with much confidence.   His success was immediate.   The Emperor issued what Hilary calls a 'grievous edict[3],' the terms of which Hilary does not mention.   He only says that under the pretext, and with the desire, of unity, Valentinian threw the faithful Church of Milan into confusion.   In other words, he forbade Hilary to agitate for a separation of the people from their bishop.

But Hilary, silenced in the city, exerted himself at court.   With urgent importunity, he tells us, he pressed his charges against Auxentius, and induced the Emperor to appoint a commission to consider them.   In due time this commission met.   It consisted of two lay officials, with 'some ten' bishops as assessors[4].   Hilary and Eusebius were present, as well as the accused.   Auxentius pleaded his own cause, beginning with the unfortunate attack upon his adversaries that they had been deposed by Council, and therefore had no *locus standi* as accusers of a bishop.   This was untrue; Hilary, we know, had been banished, but his see had never been declared vacant, nor, in all probability, had that of Eusebius.   They were not intruders, like Auxentius, though even he had gained some legality for his position from the death of Dionysius in exile.   The failure of this plea was so complete that Hilary, in his account of the matter, declares that it is not worth his while to repeat his defence.   Next came the serious business of the commission.   This was not the theological enquiry after truth, but the legal question whether, in fact, the teaching of Auxentius was in conformity with recognised standards.   Hilary had asserted that his creed differed from that of the Emperor and of all other Christians, and had asserted it in very unsparing language.   He now maintained his allegation, and, in doing so, gave Auxentius a double advantage.   For he diverged into the general question of theology, while Auxentius stuck to the letter of the decisions of Rimini; and the words of Hilary had been such that he could claim to be a sufferer from calumny.   Hilary's account of the doctrinal discussion is that he forced the reluctant Auxentius by his questions to the very edge of a denial of the Faith; that Auxentius escaped from this difficulty by a complete surrender, to which Hilary pinned him down by making him sign an orthodox confession, in terms to which he had several times agreed during the course of the debate; that Hilary remitted this confession through the Quæstor, the lay president of the commission, to the Emperor.   This document, which Hilary says that he appended to his explanatory letter, is unfortunately lost.   The brief account of the matter which Auxentius gives is not inconsistent with Hilary's.   He tells us that he began by protesting that he had never known or seen Arius, and did not even know what his

---

3 *Contra Auxentium*, § 7.
4 It is clear from Hilary's account (*Contra Auxentium*, § 7) that the decision lay with the laymen. Auxentius, in his account of the matter, does not even mention the bishops.

doctrine was; he proceeded to declare that he still believed and preached the truths which he had been taught in his infancy and of which he had satisfied himself by study of Scripture; and he gives a summary of the statement of faith which he made before the commission. But he says not a word about the passage of arms between Hilary and himself, of his defeat, and of the enforced signature of a confession which contradicted his previous assertions.

Hilary's account of the proceedings must certainly be accepted. But, though his moral and dialectical victory was complete, it is obvious that he had gained no advantage for his cause. He had taunted Auxentius as an adherent of Arius. Auxentius had an immediate reply, which put his opponent in the wrong. We cannot doubt that he spoke the truth, when he said that he had never known Arius; and it certainly was the case, that in the early years of the fourth century, inadequate statements of the doctrine of the Trinity were widely prevalent and passed without dispute. It was also true that the dominant faction at the court of Constantius, of which Auxentius had been a leader, had in the most effectual way disclaimed complicity with Arianism by ejecting its honest professors from their sees and by joining with their lips in the universal condemnation of the founder of that heresy. But if this was their shame, it was also, in such circumstances as those of Auxentius, their protection. And Auxentius held one of the greatest positions in the Church, and even in the state, now that Milan was to be, so it seemed, the capital of the West. The spirit of the government at that time was one of almost Chinese reverence for official rank; and it must have seemed an outrage that the irresponsible bishop of a city, mean in comparison with Milan, should assail Auxentius in such terms as Hilary had used. Even though he had admitted, instead of repudiating, the affinity with Arius, there would have been an impropriety in the use of that familiar weapon, the labelling of a party with the name of its most discredited and unpopular member. We may be sure that Auxentius, a man of the world, would derive all possible advantage from this excessive vehemence of his adversary. In the debate itself, where Hilary would have the advantage not only of a sound cause, but of greater earnestness, we cannot be surprised that he won the victory. Auxentius was probably indifferent at heart; Hilary had devoted his life and all his talents to the cause. But such a victory could have no results, beyond lowering Auxentius in public esteem and self-respect. It does not appear from his words or from those of Hilary, that the actual creed of Rimini was imported into the dispute. It was on it that Auxentius relied; if he did not expressly contradict its terms, the debate became a mere discussion concerning abstract truth. The legal standard of doctrine was no more affected by his unwilling concession than it had been a few years before by the numerous repudiations, prompted by Hilary and Eusebius, of the vote given at Rimini. The confession which Hilary annexed in triumph to his narrative was the mere incidental expression of a private opinion, which Auxentius, in his further plea, could afford to leave unnoticed.

The commissioners no doubt made their report privately to the Emperor. We do not know its tenour, but from the sequel we may be sure that they gave it as their opinion that Auxentius was the lawful bishop of Milan. Some time passed before Valentinian spoke. Whether Hilary took any further steps to influence his decision is unknown; but we possess a memorial addressed ' to the most blessed and glorious Emperors Valentinian and Valens' by Auxentius. The two brothers were, by mutual arrangement, each sovereign within his own dominion, but they ruled as colleagues, not as rivals; and Auxentius must have taken courage from the thought that it would seem unnatural and impolitic for the elder to seize this first opportunity of proclaiming his dissent from the cherished convictions of the younger, by degrading one of the very school which his brother delighted to honour. For what had been proposed was not the silent filling of a vacant place, but the public ejection of a bishop whose station was not much less prominent than that of Athanasius himself, and his ejection on purely theological grounds. Constantius himself had rarely been so bold; his acts of oppression, as in Hilary's case, were usually cloaked by some allegation of misconduct on the victim's part. But Auxentius had more than the character of Valens and political consider-ations on which to rely. In the forefront of his defence he put the Council of Rimini. This attack by Hilary and his friends was, according to him, the attempt of a handful of men to break up the unity attained by the labours of that great assembly of six hundred bishops [5]. He declared his firm assent to all its decisions; every heresy that it had condemned he condemned. He sent with his address a copy of the Acts of the Council, and begged the Emperor to have them read to him. Its language would convince him that Hilary and Eusebius, bishops long deposed, were merely plotting universal schism. This, with his own account of the proceedings before the commission and a short statement of his belief, forms his appeal to the Emperor. It was composed with great skill, and was quite unanswerable. His actual possession of the see, the circumstances of the time, the very doctrine of the Church—for only a Council could undo what a Council had done—rendered his position unassailable. And if he was in the right, Hilary and his colleague were in the wrong. Nothing but success could have saved them from the humiliation, to which they were now subjected, of being expelled from Milan and bidden to return to their homes, while the Emperor publicly recognised Auxentius by receiving the Communion at his hands. Yet morally they had been in the right throughout. The strong legal position of Auxentius and the canons of that imposing Council of six hundred bishops behind which he screened himself had been obtained by deliberate fraud and oppression. He and his creed could not have, and did not deserve to have, any stability. Yet Valentinian was probably in the right, even in the interests of truth, in refusing to make a martyr of Auxentius. There would have been reprisals in the East, where the Catholic cause had far more to lose than had Arianism in the West; and general considerations of equity and policy must have inclined him to allow the Arian to pass the remainder of his days in peace. But we cannot wonder that Hilary failed to appreciate such reasons. He had thrown himself with all his heart into the attack, and risked in it his public credit as bishop and confessor and first of Western theologians. Hence his published account of the transaction is tinged with a pardonable shade of personal resentment. It was, indeed, necessary that he should issue a statement. The assault and the repulse were rendered conspicuous by time and place, and by the eminence of the persons engaged; and it was Hilary's duty to see that the defeat which he had incurred brought no injury upon his cause. He therefore addressed a public letter 'to the beloved brethren who abide in the Faith of the fathers and repudiate the Arian heresy, the bishops and all their flocks.' He begins by speaking of the blessings of peace, which the Christians of that day could neither enjoy nor promote, beset as they were by the forerunners of Antichrist, who boasted of the peace, in other words of the harmonious concurrence in blasphemy, which they had brought about. They bear themselves not as bishops of Christ but as priests of Antichrist. This is not random abuse (§ 2), but sober recognition of the fact, stated by St. John, that there are many Antichrists. For these men assume the cloak of piety, and pretend to preach the Gospel, with the one object of inducing others to deny Christ. It was (§ 3) the misery and folly of the day that men endeavoured to promote the cause of God by human means and the favour of the world. Hilary asks bishops, who believe in their office, whether the Apostles had secular support when by their preaching they converted the greater part of mankind. They were not adorned with palace dignities; scourged and fettered, they sang their hymns. It was in obedience to no royal edict that Paul gathered a Church for Christ;

---

5 This was a gross exaggeration. They cannot have been more than 400, and probably were less. And we must remember that the Homoean decision was only obtained by fraud, as Auxentius well knew.

he was exposed to public view in the theatre.   Nero and Vespasian and Decius were no patrons of the Church ; it was through their hatred that the truth had thriven.   The Apostles laboured with their hands and worshipped in garrets and secret places, and in defiance of senate or monarch visited, it might be said, every village and every tribe.   Yet it was these rebels who had the keys of the Kingdom of Heaven ; the more they were forbidden, the more they preached, and the power of God was made manifest.   But now (§ 4) the Faith finds favour with men.   The Church seeks for secular support, and in so doing insults Christ by the implication that His support is insufficient.   She in her turn holds out the threat of exile and prison.   It was her endurance of these that drew men to her ; now she imposes her faith by violence.   She craves for favours at the hands of her communicants ; once it was her consecration that she braved the threatenings of persecutors.   Bishops in exile spread the Faith ; now it is she that exiles bishops.   She boasts that the world loves her ; the world's hatred was the evidence that she was Christ's.   The ruin is obvious which has fallen upon the Church.   The reason is plain (§ 5).   The time of Antichrist, disguised as an angel of light, has come.   The true Christ is hidden from almost every mind and heart.   Antichrist is now obscuring the truth that he may assert falsehood hereafter.   Hence the conflicting opinions of the time, the doctrine of Arius and of his heirs, Valens, Ursacius, Auxentius and their fellows.   Their preaching of novelties concerning Christ is the work of Antichrist, who is using them to introduce his own worship.   This is proved (§ 6) by a statement of their minimising and prevaricating doctrine, which has, however, made no impression upon the guileless and well-meaning laity.   Then (§§ 7—9) comes Hilary's account of his proceedings at Milan, strongly coloured by the intensity of his feelings.   The Emperor's first refusal to interfere with Auxentius is a 'command that the Church of the Milanese, which confesses that Christ is true God, of one divinity and substance with the Father, should be thrown into confusion under the pretext, and with the desire, of unity.'   The canons of Rimini are described as those of the Thracian Nicæa ; Auxentius' protest that he had never known Arius is met by the assertion that he had been ordained to the presbyterate in an Arian Church under George of Alexandria.   Hilary refuses to discuss the Council of Rimini ; it had been universally and righteously repudiated.   His ejection from Milan, in spite of his protests that Auxentius was a liar and a renegade, is a revelation of the mystery of ungodliness.   For Auxentius (§§ 10, 11) had spoken with two contrary voices ; the one that of the confession which Hilary had driven him to sign, the other that of Rimini.   His skill in words could deceive even the elect, but he had been clearly exposed.   Finally (§ 12) Hilary regrets that he cannot state the case to each bishop and Church in person.   He begs them to make the best of his letter ; he dares not make it fully intelligible by circulating with it the Arian blasphemies which he had assailed. He bids them beware of Antichrist, and warns against love and reverence for the material structure of their churches, wherein Antichrist will one day have his seat.   Mountains and woods and dens of beasts and prisons and morasses are the places of safety ; in them some of the Prophets had lived, and some had died.   He bids them shun Auxentius as an angel of Satan, an enemy of Christ, a deceiver and a blasphemer.   'Let him assemble against me what synods he will, let him proclaim me, as he has often done already, a heretic by public advertisement, let him direct, at his will, the wrath of the mighty against me ; yet, being an Arian, he shall be nothing less than a devil in my eyes.   Never will I desire peace except with them who, following the doctrine of our fathers at Nicæa, shall make the Arians anathema and proclaim the true divinity of Christ.'

These are the concluding words of Hilary's last public utterance.   We see him again giving an unreserved adhesion, in word as well as in heart, to the Nicene confession.   It was the course dictated by policy as well as by conviction.   His cautious language in earlier days had done good service to the Church in the East, and had made it easier for those who had compromised themselves at Rimini to reconcile themselves with him and with the truth for which he stood. But by this time all whom he could wish to win had given in their adhesion; Auxentius and the few who held with him, if such there were, were irreconcileable. They took their stand upon the Council of Rimini, and their opponents found in the doctrine of Nicæa the clear and uncompromising challenge which was necessary for effective warfare. But if Hilary's doctrinal position is definite, his theory of the relations of Church and State, if indeed his indignation allowed him to think of them, is obscure. An orthodox Emperor was upholding an Arian, and Hilary, while giving Valentinian credit for personal good faith, is as eager as in the worst days of Constantius for a severance. We must, however, remember that this manifesto, though it is the expression of a settled policy in the matter of doctrine, is in other respects the unguarded outpouring of an injured feeling. And here again we find the old perplexity of the 'inward evil.' Auxentius is represented as in the Church and outside it at the same time. He is an Antichrist, a devil, all that is evil; but Hilary is threatened and it is the Church that threatens, submission to an Arian is enforced and it is the Church which enforces it [6]. And if Auxentius had adhered to the confession which Hilary had induced him to sign, all objection to his episcopate would apparently have ceased. The time had not come, if it ever can come, for the solution of such problems. Meantime Hilary did his best, so far as words could do it, to brush aside the sophistries behind which Auxentius was defending himself. The doctrine of Rimini is named that of Nicæa, in Thrace, where the discreditable and insignificant assembly met in which its terms were settled; the Church of Alexandria under the intruder George is frankly called Arian. It was an appeal to the future as well as an apology for himself. But certainly it could not move Valentinian, nor can Hilary have expected that it should. And, after all, Valentinian's action was harmless, at least. By Hilary's own confession, Auxentius had no influence for evil over his flock, and these proceedings must have warned him, if he needed the warning, that abstinence from aggressive Arianism was necessary if he would end his days in peace. The Emperor's policy remained unchanged. At the Roman Council of the year 369 the Western bishops formally annulled the proceedings of Rimini, and so deprived Auxentius of his legal position. At the same time, as the logical consequence, they condemned him to deposition, but Valentinian refused to give effect to their sentence, and Auxentius remained bishop of Milan till his death in the year 374. He had outlived Hilary and Eusebius, and also Athanasius, the promoter of the last attack upon him; he had also outlived whatever Arianism there had been in Milan. His successor, St. Ambrose, had the enthusiastic support of his people in his conflicts with Arian princes. The Church could have gained little by Hilary's success, and yet we cannot be sure that, in a broad sense, he failed. So resolute a bearing must have effectually strengthened the convictions of Valentinian and the fears of Auxentius.

There remains one work of Hilary to be considered. This was a history of the Arian controversy in such of its aspects as had fallen under his own observation. We know from Jerome's biography of Hilary that he wrote a book againt Valens and Ursacius, containing an account of the Councils of Rimini and Seleucia. They had been his adversaries throughout his career, and had held their own against him. To them, at least as much as to Constantius, the overthrow of his Asiatic friends was due, and to them he owed the favour, which must have galled him, of permission to return to his diocese. Auxentius was one of their allies, and the failure of Hilary's attack upon him made it clear that these men too, as subjects of Valentinian, were safe from merited deposition. Their worldly success was manifest; it was a natural and righteous task which Hilary undertook when he exposed their true character. It was clear that while Valens and Valentinian lived—and they were in early middle life—there would be an armed peace within the Western Church; that the overthrow of bishop by bishop in theological strife would be forbidden. The pen was the only weapon left to Hilary, and he used it to give an account of events from the time of that Council of Arles, in the year 353, which was the beginning for Gaul of the Arian conflict. He followed its course, with especial reference to Ursacius and Valens, until the year 367, or at least the end of 366; the latest incident recorded in the fragments which we possess must have happened within a few months of his death. The work was less a history than a collection of documents strung together by an explanatory narrative. It is evident that it was not undertaken as a literary effort; its aim is not the information of future generations, but the solemn indictment at the bar of public opinion of living offenders. It must have been, when complete, a singularly businesslike production, with no graces of style to render it attractive and no generalisations to illuminate its pages. Had the whole been preserved, we should have had a complete record of Hilary's life; as it is, we have thirteen valuable fragments [7], to which we owe a considerable part of our general knowledge of the time, though they tell us comparatively little of his own career. The commencement of the work has happily survived, and from it we learn the spirit in which he wrote. He begins (Fragment i. §§ 1, 2) with an exposition of St. Paul's doctrine of faith, hope, and love. He testifies, with the Apostle, that the last is the greatest. The inseparable bond, of which he is conscious, of God's love for him and his for God, has detached him from worldly interests. He, like others (§ 3), might have enjoyed ease and prosperity and imperial friendship, and have been, as they were, a bishop only in name and a burden upon the Church. But the condition imposed was that of tampering with Gospel truths, wilful blindness to oppression and the condonation of tyranny. Public opinion, ill-informed and unused to theological subtleties, would not have observed the change. But it would have been a cowardly declension from the love of Christ to which he could not stoop. He feels (§ 4) the difficulty of the task he undertakes. The devil and the heretics had done their worst, multitudes had been terrified into denial of their convictions. The story was complicated by the ingenuity in evil of the plotters, and evidence was difficult to obtain. The scene of intrigue could not be clearly delineated, crowded as it was with the busy figures of bishops and officers, putting every engine into motion against men of apostolic mind. The energy with which they propagated slander was the measure of its falsehood. They had implanted in the public mind the belief that the exiled bishops had suffered merely for refusing to condemn Athanasius; that they were inspired by obstinacy, not by principle. Out of reverence for the Emperor, whose throne is from God (§ 5), Hilary will not comment upon his usurped jurisdiction over a bishop, nor on the manner in which it was exercised; nor yet on the injustice whereby bishops were forced to pass sentence upon the accused in his absence. In this volume he will give the true causes of trouble, in comparison of which such tyranny, grievous though it be, is of small account. Once before—this, no doubt, was at Béziers—he had spoken his mind upon the matter. But that was a hasty and unprepared utterance, delivered to an audience as eager to silence him as he was to speak. He will, therefore (§ 6), give a full and consecutive narrative of events from the Council of Arles onwards, with such an account of the question there debated as will

---

[7] There are fifteen in the collection, but the second and third, which are as long as all the rest together, and are obviously extracts from the same work, are not by Hilary. He expressly says (Fragm. i. § 6) that he will commence with the Council of Arles and the exile of Paulinus. These documents narrate at great length events which began six years earlier, and with which Hilary and his province had no direct concern. This proves that the fragments are not a portion of the *Liber adversus Ursacium et Valentem*. Internal evidence proves not less clearly that they cannot be excerpts from some other work of Hilary. In Fragm. ii. § 21 we are told that, apparently in the year 349, Athanasius excommunicated Marcellus of Ancyra. It is, of course, notorious that he never did so; the mistake is one which Hilary could not possibly have made. None the less, these fragments, both in themselves and in the documents which they embody, one of our most important authorities for the transactions they narrate, and are indisputably contemporary and authentic. Nor is there any reasonable doubt as to the genuineness of the thirteen. Those of them which reveal the inconstancy of Liberius have been assailed by some Roman Catholic writers, though they are accepted by others. The same suspicion has extended to others among the fragments, because they are found in company with these revelations concerning Liberius. But the doubts have been suggested by the wish to disbelieve.

shew the true merits of Paulinus, and make it clear that nothing less than the Faith was at stake. He ends his introduction (§ 7) by warning the reader that this is a work which needs to be seriously studied. The multitude of letters and of synods which he must adduce will merely confuse and disgust him, if he do not bear in mind the dates and the persons, and the exact sense in which terms are used. Finally, he reminds him of the greatness of the subject. This is the knowledge of God, the hope of eternity; it is the duty of a Christian to acquire such knowledge as shall enable him to form and to maintain his own conclusions. The excerpts from the work have evidently been made by some one who was interested in Italy and Illyricum rather than in Gaul, and thought that the documents were more important than the narrative. Hence Hilary's character is as little illustrated as the events of his life. Nor can the date of the work be precisely fixed. It is clear that he had already taken up his final attitude of uncompromising adherence to the Nicene Symbol; that is to say, he began to write after all the waverers had been reclaimed from contact with Arianism. He must, therefore, have written the book in his latest years; and it is manifest that after he had brought the narrative down to the time of his return from exile, he continued to add to it from time to time even till the end of his life. For the last incident recorded in the Fragments, the secession from the party of Valens and Ursacius of an old and important ally, Germinius of Sirmium, must have come to his knowledge very shortly before his death. He had had little success in his warfare with error; if he and his friends had held their own, they had not succeeded either in synod or at court in overthrowing their enemies; and it is pleasant to think that this gleam of comfort came to brighten the last days of Hilary [8]. The news must have reached Gaul early in the year 367, and no subsequent event of importance can have come to his knowledge.

But though we have reached the term of Hilary's life, there remains one topic on which something must be said, his relation to St. Martin of Tours. Martin, born in Pannonia, the country of Valens and Ursacius, but converted from paganism under Catholic influences, was attracted by Hilary, already a bishop, and spent some years in his society before the outbreak of the Arian strife in Gaul. Hilary, we are told, wished to ordain him a priest, but at his urgent wish refrained, and admitted him instead to the humble rank of an exorcist. At an uncertain date, which cannot have long preceded Hilary's exile, he felt himself moved to return to his native province in order to convert his parents, who were still pagans. He succeeded in the case of his mother and of many of his countrymen. But he was soon compelled to abandon his labours, for he had, as a true disciple of Hilary, regarded it as his duty to oppose the Arianism dominant in

---

[8] This correspondence which Hilary has preserved (Fragm. xiii.—xv.) is interesting as shewing how difficult it must have been for the laity to determine who was, and who was not, a heretic, when all parties used the same Scriptural terms in commendation of themselves and condemnation of their opponents. It begins with a public letter in which Germinius makes a declaration of faith in Homoeousion terms, without any mention of the reasons which had induced him to depart from the Homoean position. This is followed by a reproachful letter, also intended for publicity, from Valens, Ursacius, and others. They had refused to attend to the rumour of his defection; but now are compelled, by his own published letter, to ask the plain question, whether or no he adheres to 'the Catholic Faith set forth and confirmed by the Holy Council at Rimini.' If he had added to the Homoean formula, which was that the Son is 'like the Father,' the words 'in substance' or 'in all things,' he had fallen into the justly condemned heresy of Basil of Ancyra. They demand an explicit statement that he never had said, and never would say, anything of the kind; and warn him that he is gravely suspected, complaints of his teaching having been made by certain of his clergy to neighbouring bishops, which they trust will be proved groundless. Germinius made no direct reply to this letter, but addressed a manifesto to a number of more sympathetic bishops, containing the Scriptural proofs of the divinity of Christ, and recalling the fact that the Homoean leaders, before their own victory, had acquiesced in the Homoeousian confession. Any teaching to the contrary is the work, not of God, but of the spirit of this world; and he entreats those whom he addresses to circulate his letter as widely as possible, lest any should fall through ignorance into the snares of the devil. Germinius was assured of safety in writing thus. Valentinian's support of Auxentius had proved that bishops might hold what opinions they would on the great question provided they were not avowed Arians. Germinius had been a leader of the Homoean party, and it is at least possible that his change of front was due to his knowledge that the Emperor, though he would not eject Homoeans, had no sympathy with them and would allow them no influence. In fact, the smaller the share of conscience, the greater the historical interest of Germinius' action as shewing the decline of Homoean influence in the West.

the province.   Opposition to the bishops on the part of a man holding so low a station in the Church was a civil as well as an ecclesiastical offence, and Martin can have expected no other treatment than that which he received, of scourging and expulsion from the province.   Hilary was by this time in exile, and Martin turned to Milan, where the heresy of the intruder Auxentius called forth his protests, which were silenced by another expulsion.   He next retired to a small island off the Italian coast, where he lived in seclusion till he heard of Hilary's return.   He hastened to Rome, so Fortunatus tells us, to meet his friend, but missed him on the way; and followed him at once to Poitiers. There Hilary gave him a site near the city, on which he founded the first monastery in that region, over which he presided for the rest of Hilary's life and for four years after his death.   In the year 371 he was consecrated bishop of Tours, and so continued till his death twenty-five years later.   It is clear that Martin was never able to exert any influence over the mind or action of Hilary, whose interests were in an intellectual sphere above his reach.   But the courage and tenacity with which Martin held and preached the Faith was certainly inspired to some considerable extent by admiration of Hilary and confidence in his teaching.   And the joy which Hilary expresses, as we have seen, in his later Homilies on the Psalms over the rapid spread of Christianity in Gaul, was no doubt occasioned by the earlier triumphs of Martin among the peasantry.   The two men were formed each to be the complement of the other.   It was the work of Hilary to prove with cogent clearness to educated Christians, that reason as well as piety dictated an acceptance of the Catholic Faith ; the mission of Martin was to those who were neither educated nor Christian, and his success in bringing the Faith home to the lives and consciences of the pagan masses marks him out as one of the greatest among the preachers of the Gospel.   Both of them actively opposed Arianism, and both suffered in the conflict.   But the confessorship of neither had any perceptible share in promoting the final victory of truth.   Their true glory is that they were fellow-labourers equally successful in widely separate parts of the same field ; and Hilary is entitled, beyond the honour due to his own achievements, to a share in that of St. Martin, whose merits he discovered and fostered.

We have now reached the end of Hilary's life.   Sulpicius Severus[9] tells us that he died in the sixth year from his return.   He had probably reached Poitiers early in the year 361 ; we have seen that the latest event recorded in the fragments of his history must have come to his knowledge early in 367.   There is no reason to doubt that this was the conclusion of the history, and no consideration suggests that Sulpicius was wrong in his date.   We may therefore assign the death of Hilary, with considerable confidence, to the year 367, and probably to its middle portion.   Of the circumstances of his death nothing is recorded.   This is one of the many signs that his contemporaries did not value him at his true worth.   To them he must have been the busy and somewhat unsuccessful man of affairs; their successors in the next generation turned away from him and his works to the more attractive writings and more commanding characters of Ambrose and Augustine.   Yet certainly no firmer purpose or more convinced faith, perhaps no keener intellect has devoted itself to the defence and elucidation of truth than that of Hilary : and it may be that Christian thinkers in the future will find an inspiration of new and fruitful thoughts in his writings.

9 *Chron.* ii. 45.

CHAPTER II.

The Theology of St. Hilary of Poitiers.

THIS Chapter offers no more than a tentative and imperfect outline of the theology of St. Hilary; it is an essay, not a monograph. Little attempt will be made to estimate the value of his opinions from the point of view of modern thought; little will be said about his relation to earlier and contemporary thought, a subject on which he is habitually silent, and nothing about the after fate of his speculations. Yet the task, thus narrowed, is not without its difficulties. Much more attention, it is true, has been paid to Hilary's theology than to the history of his life, and the student cannot presume to dispense with the assistance of the books already written [1]. But they cannot release him from the necessity of collecting evidence for himself from the pages of Hilary, and of forming his own judgment upon it, for none of them can claim completeness and they differ widely as to the views which Hilary held. There is the further difficulty that a brief statement of a theologian's opinions must be systematic. But Hilary has abstained, perhaps deliberately, from constructing a system; the scattered points of his teaching must be gathered from writings composed at various times and with various purposes. The part of his work which was, no doubt, most useful in his own day, his summary in the *De Trinitate* of the defence against Arianism, is clear and well arranged, but it bears less of the stamp of Hilary's genius than any other of his writings. His characteristic thoughts are scattered over the pages of this great controversial treatise, where the exigencies of his immediate argument often deny him full scope for their development; or else they must be sought in his Commentary on St. Matthew, where they find incidental expression in the midst of allegorical exegesis; or again, amid the mysticism and exhortation of the Homilies on the Psalms. It is in some of these last that the Christology of Hilary is most completely stated; but the Homilies were intended for a general audience, and are unsystematic in construction and almost conversational in tone. Hilary has never worked out his thoughts in consistent theological form, and many of the most original among them have failed to attract the attention which they would have received had they been presented in such a shape as that of the later books of the *De Trinitate*.

This desultory mode of composition had its advantages in life and warmth of present interest, and gives to Hilary's writings a value as historical documents which a formal and comprehensive treatise would have lacked. But it seriously increases the difficulty of the present undertaking. It was inevitable that Hilary's method, though he is a singularly consistent thinker, should sometimes lead him into self-contradiction and sometimes leave his meaning in obscurity. In such cases probabilities must be balanced, with due regard to the opinion of former theologians who have studied his writings, and a definite conclusion must be given, though space cannot be found for the considerations upon which it is based. But though the writer may be satisfied that he has, on the whole, fairly represented Hilary's belief, it is impossible that a summary of doctrine can be an adequate reflection of a great teacher's mind. Proportions are altogether changed; a doctrine once stated and then dismissed must be set down on the same scale as another to which the author recurs again

---

[1] Those which have been in constant use in the preparation of this chapter have been an excellent article by Th. Förster in the *Theologische Studien und Kritiken* for 1888, p. 645 ff., and two full and valuable papers by Dr. Baltzer on the *Theologie* and *Christologie* of Hilary in the *Programm* of the Rottweil Gymnasium for 1879 and 1889 respectively. I have unfortunately not had access to Wirthmüller's work, *Die Lehre d. hl. Hil. über die Selbstentäusserung Christi*, but the citations in Baltzer and Schwane give some clue to its contents. The Introduction to the Benedictine edition is useful, though its value is lessened by an evident desire to make Hilary conform to the accepted opinions of a later age. Dorner's great work on the *Doctrine of the Person of Christ*, in the English translation, with the *Dogmengeschichte* of Schwane (ed. 2, 1895) and that of Harnack (ed. 3, 1894) have also been constantly and profitably consulted. Indebtedness to other works is from time to time acknowledged in the notes.

and again with obvious interest. The inevitable result is an apparent coldness and stiffness and excess of method which does Hilary an injustice both as a thinker and as a writer. In the interests of orderly sequence not only must he be represented as sometimes more consistent than he really is, but the play of thought, the undeveloped suggestions, often brilliant in their originality, the striking expression given to familiar truths, must all be sacrificed, and with them great part of the pleasure and profit to be derived from his writings. For there are two conclusions which the careful student will certainly reach ; the one that every statement and argument will be in hearty and scrupulous consonance with the Creeds, the other that, within this limit, he must not be surprised at any ingenuity or audacity of logic or exegesis in explanation and illustration of recognised truths, and especially in the speculative connection of one truth with another. But the evidence that Hilary's heart, as well as his reason, was engaged in the search and defence of truth must be sought, where it will be abundantly found, in the translations given in this volume. The present chapter only purposes to set out, in a very prosaic manner, the conclusions at which his speculative genius arrived, working as it did by the methods of strict logic in the spirit of eager loyalty to the Faith.

In his effort to render a reason for his belief Hilary's constant appeal is to Scripture ; and he avails himself freely of the thoughts of earlier theologians. But he never makes himself their slave; he is not the avowed adherent of any school, and never cites the names of those whose arguments he adopts. These he adjusts to his own system of thought, and presents for acceptance, not on authority, but on their own merits. For Scripture, however, he has an unbounded reverence. Everything that he believes, save the fundamental truth of Theism, of which man has an innate consciousness, being unable to gaze upon the heavens without the conviction that God exists and has His home there [2], is directly derived from Holy Scripture. Scripture for Hilary means the Septuagint for the Old Testament, the Latin for the New. He was, as we saw, no Hebrew Scholar, and had small respect either for the versions which competed with the Septuagint or for the Latin rendering of the Old Testament, but there is little evidence [3] that he was dissatisfied with the Latin of the New ; in fact, in one instance, whether through habitual contentment with his Latin or through momentary carelessness in verifying the sense, he bases an argument on a thoroughly false interpretation [4]. Of his relation to Origen and the literary aspects of his exegetical work, something has been said in the former chapter. Here we must speak of his use of Scripture as the source of truth, and of the methods he employs to draw out its meaning.

In Hilary's eyes the two Testaments form one homogeneous revelation, of equal value throughout [5], and any part of the whole may be used in explanation of any other part. The same title of *beatissimus* is given to Daniel and to St. Paul when both are cited in *Comm. in Matt.* xxv. 3 ; indeed, he and others of his day seem to have felt that the Saints of the Old Covenant were as near to themselves as those of the New. Not many years had passed since Christians were accustomed to encourage themselves to martyrdom, in default of well-known heroes of their own faith, by the example of Daniel and his companions, or of the Seven Maccabees and their Mother. But Scripture is not only harmonious throughout, as Origen had taught ; it is also never otiose. It never repeats itself, and a significance must be sought not only in the smallest differences of language, but also in the order in which apparent synonyms occur [6] ; in fact, every detail, and every sense

---

[2] *Tr. in Ps* xxii. 2, 4.
[3] As e.g. *Trin.* vi. 45.
[4] St. John v. 44 in *Trin.* ix. 22.
[5] Thus the Book of Baruch, regarded as part of Jeremiah,

is cited with the same confidence as Isaiah and the other prophets in *Trin.* v. 39.
[6] E.g. *Tr. in Ps.* cxviii. *Aleph.* 1, cxxviii. 12, cxxxi. 8. It must be confessed that Hilary's illustrations of the principle are not always fortunate.

in which every detail may be interpreted, is a matter for profitable enquiry [7]. Hence, the text of Scripture not only bears, but demands, the most strict and literal interpretation. Hilary's explanation of the words, ' My soul is sorrowful even unto death,' in *Tract. in Ps.* cxli. 8 and *Trin.* x. 36, is a remarkable instance of his method [8]; as is the argument from the words of Isaiah, 'We *esteemed* Him stricken,' that this, so far as it signifies an actual sense of pain in Christ, is only an opinion, and a false one [9]. Similarly the language of St. Paul about the treasures of knowledge hidden in Christ is made to prove His omniscience on earth. Whatever is hidden is present in its hiding-place; therefore Christ could not be ignorant [1]. But this close adherence to the text of Scripture is combined with great boldness in its interpretation. Hilary does not venture, with Origen, to assert that some passages of Scripture have no literal sense, but he teaches that there are cases when its statements have no meaning in relation to the circumstances in which they were written [2], and uses this to enforce the doctrine, which he holds as firmly as Origen, that the spiritual meaning is the only one of serious importance [3]. All religious truth is contained in Scripture, and it is our duty to be ignorant of what lies outside it [4]. But within the limits of Scripture the utmost liberty of inference is to be admitted concerning the purpose with which the words were written and the sense to be attached to them. Sometimes, and especially in his later writings, when Hilary was growing more cautious and weaning himself from the influence of Origen, we are warned to be careful, not to read too much of definite dogmatic truth into every passage, to consider the context and occasion [5]. Elsewhere, but this especially in that somewhat immature and unguarded production, the Commentary on St. Matthew, we find a purpose and meaning, beyond the natural sense, educed by such considerations as that, while all the Gospel is true, its facts are often so stated as to be a prophecy as well as a history; or that part of an event is sometimes suppressed in the narrative in order to make the whole more perfect as a prophecy [6]. But he can derive a lesson not merely from what Scripture says but also from the discrepancies between the different texts in which it is conveyed to us. Hilary had learnt from Origen to regard the Septuagint as an independent and inspired authority for the revelation of the Old Testament. Its translators are 'those seventy elders who had a knowledge of the Law and of the Prophets which transcends the limitations and doubtfulness of the letter [7]. His confidence in their work, which is not exceeded by that of St. Augustine, encourages him to draw lessons from the differences between the Hebrew and the Septuagint titles of the Psalms. For instance, Psalm cxlii. has been furnished in the Septuagint with a title which attributes it to David when pursued by Absalom. The contents of the Psalm are appropriate neither to the circumstances nor to the date. But this does not justify us in ignoring the title. We must regard the fact that a wrong connection is given to the Psalm as a warning to ourselves not to attempt to discover its historical position, but confine ourselves to its spiritual sense. And this is not all. Another Psalm, the third, is assigned in the Hebrew to the same King in the same distress. But, though this attribution is certainly correct, here also we must follow the leading of the Septuagint, which was led to give a wrong title to one Psalm lest we should attach importance to the correct title of another. In both cases we must fix our attention not on the afflictions of David, but on the sorrows of Christ. Thus, negatively if not positively, the Septuagint must guide our judgment [8]. But Hilary often goes even further, and ventures upon a purely subjective

---

[7] Thus in *Trin.* xi. 15, in commenting on Ps. xxii. 6, he puts forward two alternative theories of the generation of worms, only one of which can be true, while both may be false. But he uses both, to illustrate two truths concerning our Lord.

[8] Cf. also *Trin.* x. 67.   [9] *Tr. in Ps.* cxxxviii. 3.

[1] *Trin.* ix. 62. There is a similar argument in § 63

[2] E.g. *Tr. in Ps.* cxxv. 1.   [3] Cf. *Tr. in Ps.* cxlii. 1.

[4] *Tr. in Ps.* cxxxii. 6.

[5] E.g. *Tr. in Ps.* lxiii. 2; *Trin.* iv. 14, ix. 59.

[6] *Comm. in Matt.* xix. 4, xxi. 13.

[7] *Tr. in Ps.* cxlii. 1; cf. *ib.* cxxxi. 24, cxxxiii. 4, cl. 1.

[8] Similar arguments are often used; cf. *Tr. in Ps.* cxlv. 1.

interpretation, which sometimes gives useful insight into the modes of thought of Gaul in the fourth century. For instance, he is thoroughly classical in taking it for granted that the Psalmist's words, 'I will lift up mine eyes unto the hills,' cannot refer to the natural feature; that he can never mean the actual mountains bristling with woods, the naked rocks and pathless precipices and frozen snows[9]. And even Gregory the Great could not surpass the prosaic grotesqueness with which Hilary declares it impious to suppose that God would feed the young ravens, foul carrion birds[1]; and that the lilies of the Sermon on the Mount must be explained away, because they wear no clothing, and because, as a matter of fact, it is quite possible for men to be more brightly attired than they[2]. Examples of such reasoning, more or less extravagant, might be multiplied from Hilary's exegetical writings; passages in which no allowance is made for Oriental imagery, for poetry or for rhetoric[3].

But though Hilary throughout his whole period of authorship uses the mystical method of interpretation, never doubting that everywhere in Scripture there is a spiritual meaning which can be elicited, and that whatever sense, consistent with truth otherwise ascertained, can be extracted from it, may be extracted, yet there is a manifest increase in sobriety in his later as compared with his earlier writings. From the riotous profusion of mysticisms in the Commentary on St. Matthew, where, for instance, every character and detail in the incident of St. John Baptist's death becomes a symbol, it is a great advance to the almost Athanasian cautiousness in exegesis of the *De Trinitate*; though even here, especially in the early books which deal with the Old Testament, there is some extravagance and a very liberal employment of the method[4]. His reasons, when he gives them, are those adduced in his other writings; the inappropriateness of the words to the time when they were written, or the plea that reverence or reason bids us penetrate behind the letter. His increasing caution is due to no distrust of the principle of mysticism.

Though Hilary was not its inventor, and was forced by the large part played by Old Testament exegesis in the Arian controversy to employ it, whether he would or not[5], yet it is certain that his hearty, though not indiscriminate[6], acceptance of the method led to its general adoption in the West. Tertullian and Cyprian had made no great use of such speculations; Irenæus probably had little influence. It was the introduction of Origen's thought to Latin Christendom by Hilary and his contemporaries which set the fashion, and none of them can have had such influence as Hilary himself. It is a strange irony of fate that so deep and original a thinker should have exerted his most permanent influence not through his own thoughts, but through this dubious legacy which he handed on from Alexandria to Europe. Yet, within certain limits, it was a sound and, for that age, even a scientific method; and Hilary might at least plead that he never allowed the system to be his master, and that it was a means which enabled him to derive from Scriptures which otherwise, to him, would be unprofitable, some measure of true and valuable instruction. It never moulds his thoughts; at the most, he regards it as a useful auxiliary. No praise can be too high for his wise and sober marshalling not so much of texts as of the collective evidence of Scripture concerning the relation of the Father and the Son in the *De Trinitate*; and if his Christology be not equally convincing, it is not the fault of his method, but of its application[7].

---

9 *Tr. in Ps.* cxx. 4.

1 Ib. cxlvi. 11.

2 *Comm. in Matt.* v. 11.

3 E.g. *Comm. in Matt.* xviii. 2; *Tr. in Ps.* cxix. 20, cxxxiv. 12, cxxxvi. 6, 7; *Trin.* iv. 38.

4 E.g. *Trin.* i. 6.

5 The unhesitating use of the Theophanies of the Old Testament as direct evidence for the divinity of Christ is noteworthy.

Similar to the usual proofs for the distinction of Persons within the Trinity, from the alternate use of plural and singular, are the arguments in *Tr. in Ps.* cxviii., *Iod*, 5, cxxvii. 4.

6 It is worth notice that he makes no use of Origen's mystical interpretation of the Canticles. Silence in such a case is itself a criticism.

7 Compare such a passage as *Trin.* x. 24 with his use of the proof-texts against Arianism.

We cannot wonder that Hilary, who owed his clear dogmatic convictions to a careful and independent study of Scripture, should have wished to lead others to the same source of knowledge. He couples it with the Eucharist as a second Table of the Lord, a public means of grace, which needs, if it is to profit the hearer, the same preparation of a pure heart and life[8]. Attention to the lessons read in church is a primary duty, but private study of Scripture is enforced with equal earnestness[9]. It must be for all, as Hilary had found it for himself, a privilege as well as a duty.

His sense of the value of Scripture is heightened by his belief in the sacredness of language. Names belong inseparably to the things which they signify; words are themselves a revelation. This is a lesson learnt from Origen; and the false antithesis between the nature and the name of God, of which, according to the Arians, Christ had the latter only, made it of special use to Hilary[1]. But if this high dignity belongs to every statement of truth, there is the less need for technical terms of theology. The rarity of their occurrence in the pages of Hilary has already been mentioned. 'Trinity'[2] is almost absent, and 'Person'[3] hardly more common; he prefers, by a turn of language which would scarcely be seemly in English, to speak of the 'embodied' Christ and of His 'Embodiment,' though Latin theology was already familiar with the 'Incarnation[4].' In fact, it would seem that he had resolved to make himself independent of technical terms and of such lines of thought as would require them. But he is never guilty of confusion caused by an inadequate vocabulary. He has the literary skill to express in ordinary words ideas which are very remote from ordinary thought, and this at no inordinate length. No one, for instance, has developed the idea of the mutual indwelling of Father and Son more fully and clearly than he; yet he has not found it necessary to employ or devise the monstrous 'circuminsession' or 'perichoresis' of later theology. And where he does use terms of current theology, or rather metaphysic, he shews that he is their master, not their slave. The most important idea of this kind which he had to express was that of the Divine substance. The word 'essence' is entirely rejected[5]; 'substance' and 'nature' are freely used as synonyms, but in such alternation that both of them still obviously belong to the sphere of literature, and not of science. They are twice used as exact alternatives, for the avoidance of monotony, in parallel clauses of *Trin.* vi. 18, 19. So also the nature of fire in vii. 29 is not an abstraction; and in ix. 36 *fin.* the Divine substance and nature are equivalents. These are only a few of many instances[6]. Here, as always, there is an abstention from abstract thoughts and terms, which indicates, on the part of a student of philosophy and of philosophical theology, a deliberate narrowing of his range of speculation. We may illustrate the purpose of Hilary by comparing his method with that of the author of a treatise on Astronomy without Mathematics. But some part of his caution is probably due to his sense of

---

8 *Tr. in Ps.* cxxvii. 10.

9 E.g. *Tr. in Ps.* xci. 10, cxviii. *Iod*, 15, cxxxiv. 1, cxxxv. 1.

1 E.g. *Trin.* vii. 13; and cf. the argument, which is also Athanasian, of vii. 31.

2 Beside the passages mentioned on p. xxx., it only occurs in the *Instructio Psalmorum*, § 13.

3 The translation of the *De Trinitate* in this volume may give a somewhat false impression in this respect. For the sake of conciseness the word *Person* has been often used in the English where it is absent, and absent designedly in the Latin. The word occurs *Trin.* iii. 23 *in.*, iv. 42, v. 10, 26, vii. 39, 40, and in a few other places.

4 *Concorporatio*, *Comm. in Matt.* vi. 1; *corporatio*, *Tr. in Ps.* i. 14, ii. 3, and often; *corporatus Deus*, *Comm. in Matt.* iv. 14, *Tr. in Ps.* li. 16; *corporalitas*, *Comm. in Matt.* iv. 14 (twice), *Instr. Ps.* vi. In the *De Trinitate* he usually prefers

a periphrasis;—*assumpta caro, assumpsit carnem. Corporatio* is used of man's dwelling in a body in *Trin.* xi. 15, and *De Mysteriis*, ed. Gamurrini, p. 5.

5 It occurs in the *De Synodis* 69, but in that work Hilary is writing as an advocate in defence of language used by others, not as the exponent of his own thoughts. It also occurs once or twice in translations from the Greek, probably by another hand than Hilary's; but from his own authorship it is completely absent.

6 *Trin.* v. 10, *Syn.* 69, 'God is One not in Person, but in nature,' *Trin.* iv. 42, 'Not by oneness of Person but by unity of substance;' vi. 35, 'the birth of a living Nature from a living Nature.' Often enough the substance or nature of God or Christ is simply a periphrasis. The two natures in the Incarnate Christ are also mentioned, though, as we shall see, Hilary here also avoids a precise nomenclature.

the inadequacy of the terms with which Latin theology was as yet equipped, and of the danger, not only to his readers' faith, but to his own reputation for orthodoxy, which might result from ingenuity in the employment or invention of technical language.

Though, as we have seen, the contemplative state is not the ultimate happiness of man, yet the knowledge of God is essential to salvation [7]; man, created in God's image, is by nature capable of, and intended for, such knowledge, and Christ came to impart it, the necessary condition on the side of humanity being purity of mind [8], and the result the elevation of man to the life of God. Hilary does not shrink from the emphatic language of the Alexandrian school, which spoke of the 'deification' of man ; God, he says, was born to be man, in order that man might be born to be God [9]. If this end is to be attained, obviously what is accepted as knowledge must be true ; hence the supreme wickedness of heresy, which destroys the future of mankind by palming upon them error for truth ; the greater their dexterity the greater, because the more deliberate, their crime. And Hilary was obviously convinced that his opponents had conceived this nefarious purpose. It is not in the language of mere conventional polemics, but in all sincerity, that he repeatedly describes them as liars who cannot possibly be ignorant of the facts which they misrepresent, inventors of sophistical arguments and falsifiers of the text of Scripture, conscious that their doom is sealed, and endeavouring to divert their minds from the thought of future misery by involving others in their own destruction [1]. He fully recognises the ability and philosophical learning displayed by them ; it only makes their case the worse, and, after all, is merely folly. But it increases the difficulties of the defenders of the Faith. For though man can and must know God, Who, for His part, has revealed Himself, our knowledge ought to consist in a simple acceptance of the precise terms of Scripture. The utmost humility is necessary ; error begins when men grow inquisitive. Our capacity for knowledge, as Hilary is never tired of insisting, is so limited that we ought to be content to believe without defining the terms of our belief. For weak as intellect is, language, the instrument which it must employ, is still less adequate to so great a task [2]. Heresy has insisted upon definition, and the true belief is compelled to follow suit [3]. Here again, in the heretical abuse of technical terms and of logical processes, we find a reason for the almost ostentatious simplicity of diction which we often find in Hilary's pages. He evidently believed that it was possible for us to apprehend revealed truth and to profit fully by it, without paraphrase or other explanation. In the case of one great doctrine, as we shall see, no necessities of controversy compelled him to develope his belief ; if he had had his way, the Faith should never have been stated in ampler terms than 'I believe in the Holy Ghost'

In a great measure he has succeeded in retaining this simplicity in regard to the doctrine of God. He had the full Greek sense of the divine unity ; there is no suggestion of the possession by the Persons of the Trinity of contrasted or complementary qualities. The revelation he would defend is that of God, One, perfect, infinite, immutable. This absolute God has manifested Himself under the name 'HE THAT IS,' to which Hilary constantly recurs. It is only through His own revelation of Himself that God can be known. But here we are faced by a difficulty ; our reason is inadequate and tends to be fallacious. The argument from analogy, which we should naturally use, cannot be a sufficient guide, since it must proceed from the finite to the infinite. Hilary has set this forth with great force and frequency, and with a picturesque variety of illustration. Again, our partial glimpses of the truth are often in apparent contradiction ; when this is the case, we need to be on our guard against the

---

7 *Tr. in Ps.* cxxxi. 6, 'The supreme achievement of Christ was to render man, instructed in the knowledge of God, worthy to be God's dwelling-place ;' cf. *ib.* § 23.

8 *Tr. in Ps.* cxviii , *Aleph.,* § 1. 9 *Trin.* x 7.

1 Cf. *Tr. in Ps.* cxix. 10 ; *Trin.* v. 1, 26, vi. 46 ff., viii 37, &c., &c.

2 *Trin.* iv. 2, xi. 44.

3 *Trin.* ii 2, *in vitium vitio coarctamur alieno.*

temptation to reject one as incompatible with the other. We must devote an equal attention to each, and believe without hesitation that both are true. The interest of the *De Trinitate* is greatly heightened by the skill and courage with which Hilary will handle some seeming paradox, and make the antithesis of opposed infinities conduce to reverence for Him of Whom they are aspects. And he never allows his reader to forget the immensity of his theme; and here again the skill is manifest with which he casts upon the reader the same awe with which he is himself impressed.

Of God as Father Hilary has little that is new to say. He is called Father in Scripture; therefore He is Father and necessarily has a Son. And conversely the fact that Scripture speaks of God the Son is proof of the fatherhood. In fact, the name 'Son' contains a revelation so necessary for the times that it has practically banished that of 'the Word,' which we should have expected Hilary, as a disciple of Origen, to employ by preference[4]. But since faith in the Father alone is insufficient for salvation[5], and is, indeed, not only insufficient but actually false, because it denies His fatherhood in ignoring the consubstantial Son, Hilary's attention is concentrated upon the relation between these two Persons. This relation is one of eternal mutual indwelling, or 'perichoresis,' as it has been called, rendered possible by Their oneness of nature and by the infinity of Both. The thought is worked out from such passages as Isaiah xlv. 14, St. John xiv. 11, with great cogency and completeness, yet always with due stress laid on the incapacity of man to comprehend its immensity. Hilary advances from this scriptural position to the profound conception of the divine self-consciousness as consisting in Their mutual recognition. Each sees Himself in His perfect image, which must be coeternal with Himself. In Hilary this is only a hint, one of the many thoughts which the urgency of the conflict with Arianism forbade him to expand. But Dorner justly sees in it 'a kind of speculative construction of the doctrine of the Trinity, out of the idea of the divine self-consciousness[6].'

The Arian controversy was chiefly waged over the question of the eternal generation of the Son. By the time that Hilary began to write, every text of Scripture which could be made applicable to the point in dispute had been used to the utmost. There was little or nothing that remained to be done in the discovery or combination of passages. Of that controversy Athanasius was the hero; the arguments which he used and those which he refuted are admirably set forth in the introduction to the translation of his writings in this series. In writing the *De Trinitate*, so far as it dealt directly with the original controversy, it was neither possible nor desirable that Hilary should leave the beaten path. His object was to provide his readers with a compendious statement of ascertained truth for their own guidance, and with an armoury of weapons which had been tried and found effective in the conflicts of the day. It would, therefore, be superfluous to give in this place a detailed account of his reasonings concerning the generation of the Son, nor would such an account be of any assistance to those who have his writings in their hands. Hilary's treatment of the Scriptural evidence is very complete, as was, indeed, necessary in a work which was intended as a handbook for practical use. The Father alone is unbegotten; the Son is truly the Son, neither created nor adopted. The Son is the Creator of the worlds, the Wisdom of God, Who alone knows the Father, Who manifested God to man in the various Theophanies of the Old Testament. His birth is without parallel, inasmuch as other births imply a previous non-existence, while that of the Son is from eternity. For the generation on the part of the Father and the birth on the part of the Son are not connected as by

---

4 *Deus Verbum* often; *Verbum* alone rarely, if ever. Dorner, with his iteration of 'Logos,' gives an altogether false impression of Hilary's vocabulary.

5 *Trin.* i. 17 and often.

6 *Doctrine of the Person of Christ*, I. ii. p. 302, English translation. The passages to which he refers are *Comm. in Matt.* xi. 12; *Tr. in Ps.* xci. 6; *Trin.* ii. 3, ix. 69. There is a good, though brief, statement of this view in Mason's *Faith of the Gospel*, p. 56.

a temporal sequence of cause and effect, but exactly coincide in a timeless eternity[7]. Hilary repudiates the possibility of illustrating this divine birth by sensible analogies; it is beyond our understanding as it is beyond time. Nor can we wonder at this, seeing that our own birth is to us an insoluble mystery. The eternal birth of the Son is the expression of the eternal nature of God. It is the nature of the One that He should be Father, of the Other that He should be Son; this nature is co-eternal with Themselves, and therefore the One is co-eternal with the Other. Hence Athanasius had drawn the conclusion that the Son is 'by nature and not by will[8]; not that the will of God is contrary to His nature, but that (if the words may be used) there was no scope for its exercise in the generation of the Son, which came to pass as a direct consequence of the Divine nature. Such language was a natural protest against an Arian abuse; but it was a departure from earlier precedent and was not accepted by that Cappadocian school, more true to Alexandrian tradition than Athanasius himself, with which Hilary was in closest sympathy. In their eyes the generation of the Son must be an act of God's will, if the freedom of Omnipotence, for which they were jealous, was to be respected; and Hilary shared their scruples. Not only in the *De Synodis* but in the *De Trinitate*[9] he assigns the birth of the Son to the omnipotence, the counsel and will of God acting in co-operation with His nature. This two-fold cause of birth is peculiar to the Son; all other beings owe their existence simply to the power and will, not to the nature of God[1]. Such being the relation between Father and Son, it is obvious that They cannot differ in nature. The word 'birth,' by which the relation is described, indicates the transmission of nature from parent to offspring; and this word is, like 'Father' and 'Son,' an essential part of the revelation. The same divine nature or substance exists eternally and in equal perfection in Both, unbegotten in the Father, begotten in the Son. In fact, the expression, 'Only-begotten God,' may be called Hilary's watchword, with such 'peculiar abundance[2]' does it occur in his writings, as in those of his Cappadocian friends. But, though the Son is the Image of the Father, Hilary in his maturer thought, when free from the influence of his Asiatic allies, is careful to avoid using the inadequate and perilous term 'likeness' to describe the relation[3]. Such being the birth, and such the unity of nature, the Son must be very God. This is proved by all the usual passages of the Old Testament, from the Creation onwards. These are used, as by the other Fathers, to prove that the Son has not the name only, but the reality, of Godhead; the reality corresponding to the nature. All things were made through Him out of nothing; therefore He is Almighty as the Father is Almighty. If man is made in the image of Both, if one Spirit belongs to Both, there can be no difference of nature between the Two. But They are not Two as possessing one nature, like human father and son, while living separate lives. God is One, with a Divinity undivided and indivisible[4]; and Hilary is never weary of denying the Arian charge that his creed involved the worship of two Gods. No analogies from created things can explain this unity. Tree and branch, fire and heat, source and stream can only illustrate Their inseparable co-existence; such comparisons, if pressed, lead inevitably to error. The true unity of Father and Son is deeper than this; deeper also than any unity, however perfect, of will with will. For it is an eternal mutual indwelling, Each perfectly corresponding with and comprehending and containing the Other, and Himself in the Other;

---

[7] *Trin.* xii. 21, 'the birth is in the generation and the generation in the birth.'

[8] *Discourses against the Arians*, iii. 58 ff.; see Robertson's notes in the Athanasius volume of this series, p. 426.

[9] E.g. *Syn.* 35, 37, 59, *Trin.* iii. 4, vi. 21, viii. 54.

[1] Cf. Baltzer, *Theologie d. hl. Hil.* p. 19 f.

[2] Hort, *Two Dissertations*, p. 21, and cf. p. xvi., above.

[3] It constantly appears, though with all due safeguards, in the *De Synodis*, where sympathy as well as policy impelled him to approximate to the language used by his friends. Similarly in *Trin.* iii. 23, he argues, from the admitted likeness, that there can be no difference. But, as we saw, this part of the *De Trinitate* is probably an early work, and does not represent Hilary's later thought. [4] *Trin.* v. 38.

and this not after the manner of earthly commingling of substances or exchange of properties. The only true comparison that can be made is with the union between Christ, in virtue of His humanity, and the believer [5] ; such is the union, in virtue of the Godhead, between Father and Son. And this unity extends inevitably to will and action. Since the Father is acting in all that the Son does, the Son is acting in all that the Father does; 'he that hath seen Me hath seen the Father.' This doctrine reconciles all our Lord's statements in the Gospel of St. John concerning His own and His Father's work.

But, notwithstanding this unity, there is a true numerical duality of Person. Sabellius, we must remember, had held for two generations the pre-eminence among heretics. To the Greek-speaking world outside Egypt the error which he and Paul of Samosata had taught, that God is one Person, was still the most dangerous of falsehoods ; the supreme victory of truth had not been won in their eyes when Arius was condemned at Nicæa, but when Paul was deposed at Antioch. The Nicene leaders had certainly counted the cost when they adopted as the test of orthodoxy the same word which Paul had used for the inculcation of error. But the *homoousion*, however great its value as a permanent safeguard of truth, was the immediate cause of alienation and suspicion. And not only did it make the East misunderstand the West, but it furnished the Arians with the most effective of instruments for widening the breach between the two forces opposed to them. They had an excuse for calling their opponents in Egypt and the West by the name of Sabellians, the very name most likely to engender distrust in Asia [6]. Hilary, who could enter with sympathy into the Eastern mind and had learnt from his own treatment at Seleucia how strong the feeling was, labours with untiring patience to dissipate the prejudice. There is no Arian plea against which he argues at greater length. The names 'Father' and 'Son,' being parts of the revelation, are convincing proofs of distinction of Person as well as of unity of nature. They prove that the nature is the same, but possessed after a different manner by Each of the Two ; by the One as ingenerate, by the Other as begotten. The word ' Image,' also a part of the revelation, is another proof of the distinction ; an object and its reflection in a mirror are obviously not one thing. Again, the distinct existence of the Son is proved by the fact that He has free volition of His own ; and by a multitude of passages of Scripture, many of them absolutely convincing, as for instance, those from the Gospel of St. John. But these two Persons, though one in nature, are not equal in dignity. The Father is greater than the Son ; greater not merely as compared to the incarnate Christ, but as compared to the Son, begotten from eternity. This is not simply by the prerogative inherent in all paternity ; it is because the Father is self-existent, Himself the Source of all being [7]. With one of his happy phrases Hilary describes it as an inferiority *generatione, non genere* [8] ; the Son is one in kind or nature with the Father, though inferior, as the Begotten, to the Unbegotten. But this inferiority is not to be so construed as to lessen our belief in His divine attributes. For instance, when He addresses the Father in prayer, this is not because He is subordinate, but because He wishes to honour the Fatherhood [9]; and, as Hilary argues at great length [1], the end, when God shall be all in all, is not to be regarded as a surrender of the Son's power, in the sense of loss. It is a mysterious final state of permanent, willing submission to the Father's will, into which He enters by the supreme expression of an obedience which has never failed. Again, our Lord's language in St. Mark xiii. 32, must not be taken as signifying ignorance on the part of the Son of His Father's purpose. For, according to St. Paul (Col. ii. 3), in Him are hid all the

---

[5] *Trin.* viii. 13 ff.

[6] Cf. *Sulp Sev.*, *Chron.* ii. 42 for the Eastern suspicion that the West held a *trionyma unio;*—one Person under three names. Sulpicius ascribes it to Arian slander, but its causes lay deeper than this.

[7] This was the doctrine of all the earlier theologians, soon to be displaced in the stress of controversy by the opinion tha the inferiority concerns the Son only as united with man. Se the citations in Westcott's *Gospel of St. John*, additional not to xiv. 28.

[8] *Tr. in Ps.* cxxxviii. 17.   [9] *Ib.* cxli. 6.

[1] *Trin.* xi. 21 ff., on 1 Cor. xv. 21 ff.

treasures of wisdom and knowledge, and therefore He must know the day and hour of judgment. He is ignorant relatively to us, in the sense that He will not betray His Father's secret [2]. Whether or no it be possible in calmer times to maintain that the knowledge and the ignorance are complementary truths which finite minds cannot reconcile, we cannot wonder that Hilary, ever on the watch against apparent concessions to Arianism, should in this instance have abandoned his usual method of balancing against each other the apparent contraries. His reasoning is, in any case, a striking proof of his intense conviction of the co-equal Godhead of the Son.

Such is Hilary's argument, very briefly stated. We may read almost all of it, where Hilary himself had certainly read it, in the *Discourses against the Arians* and elsewhere in the writings of Athanasius. How far, however, he was borrowing from the latter must remain doubtful, as must the question as to the originality of Athanasius. For the controversy was universal, and both of these great writers had the practical purpose of collecting the best arguments out of the multitude which were suggested in ephemeral literature or verbal debate. Their victory, intellectual as well as moral, over their adversaries was decisive, and the more striking because it was the Arians who had made the attack on ground chosen by themselves. The authority of Scripture as the final court of appeal was their premiss as well as that of their opponents; and they had selected the texts on which the verdict of Scripture was to be based. Out of their own mouth they were condemned, and the work done in the fourth century can never need to be repeated. It was, of course, an unfinished work. As we have seen, Hilary concerns himself with two Persons, not with three; and since he states the contrasted truths of plurality and unity without such explanation of the mystery as the speculative genius of Augustine was to supply, he leaves, in spite of all his efforts, a certain impression of excessive dualism. But these defects do not lessen the permanent value of his work. Indeed, we may even assert that they, together with some strange speculations and many instances of wild interpretation, which are, however, no part of the structure of his argument and do not affect its solidity, actually enhance its human and historical interest. The *De Trinitate* remains 'the most perfect literary achievement called forth by the Arian controversy [3].'

Hitherto we have been considering the relations within the Godhead of Father and Son, together with certain characters which belong to the Son in virtue of His eternal birth. We now come to the more original part of Hilary's teaching, which must be treated in greater detail. Till now he has spoken only of the Son; he now comes to speak of Christ, the name which the Son bears in relation to the world. We have seen that Hilary regards the Son as the Creator [4]. This was proved for him, as for Athanasius, by the passage, Proverbs viii. 22, which they read according to the Septuagint, 'The Lord hath created Me for the beginning of His ways for His Works [5].' These words, round which the controversy raged, were interpreted by the orthodox as implying that at the time, and for the purpose, of creation the Father assigned new functions to the Son as His representative. The gift of these functions, the exercise of which called into existence orders of being inferior to God, marked in Hilary's eyes a change so definite and important in the activity of the Son that it deserved to be called a second birth, not ineffable like the eternal birth, but strictly analogous to the Incarnation. This last was a creation, which brought Him within the sphere of created humanity; the creation of Wisdom for the beginning of God's ways had brought Him, though less closely, into the same relation [6], and

---

[2] *Trin.* ix. 58 ff.   [3] Bardenhewer, *Patrologie*, p. 377.
[4] This is one of Hilary's many reminiscences of Origen. Athanasius brought the Father into direct connection with the world; cf. Harnack, *Dogmengesch.* ii. 206 (ed. 3).
[5] *Trin.* xii. 35 ff. The passage is treated at much greater length in Athanasius' *Discourses against the Arians*, ii. 18 ff., where see Robertson's notes.
[6] *Trin.* xii. 45; at the Incarnation Christ is 'created in the body,' and this is connected with His creation for the beginning of the ways of God.

the Incarnation is the completion of what was begun in preparation for the creation of the world. Creation is the mode by which finite being begins, and the beginning of each stage in the connection between the infinite Son and His creatures is called, from the one point of view, a creation, from the other, a birth. We cannot fail to see here an anticipation of the opinion that 'the true Protevangelium is the revelation of Creation, or in other words that the Incarnation was independent of the Fall[7],' for the Incarnation is a step in the one continuous divine progress from the Creation to the final consummation of all things, and has not sin for its cause, but is part of the original counsel of God[8]. Together with this new office the Son receives a new name. Henceforth Hilary calls Him Christ; He is Christ in relation to the world, as He is Son in relation to the Father. From the beginning of time, then, the Son becomes Christ and stands in immediate relation to the world; it is in and through Christ that God is the Author of all things[9], and the title of Creator strictly belongs to the Son. This beginning of time, we must remember, is hidden in no remote antiquity. The world had no mysterious past; it came into existence suddenly at a date which could be fixed with much precision, some 5,600 years before Hilary's day[1], and had undergone no change since then. Before that date there had been nothing outside the Godhead; from that time forth the Son has stood in constant relation to the created world.

Christ, for so we must henceforth call Him, has not only sustained in being the universe which He created, but has also imparted to men a steadily increasing knowledge of God. For such knowledge, we remember, man was made, and his salvation depends upon its possession. All the Theophanies of the Old Testament are such revelations by Him of Himself; and it was He that spoke by the mouth of Moses and the Prophets. But however significant and valuable this Divine teaching and manifestation might be, it was not complete in itself, but was designed to prepare men's minds to expect its fulfilment in the Incarnation. Just as the Law was preliminary to the Gospel, so the appearances of Christ in human form to Abraham and to others were a foreshadowing of the true humanity which He was to assume. They were true revelations, as far as they went; but their purpose was not simply to impart so much knowledge as they explicitly conveyed, but also to lead men on to expect more, and to expect it in the very form in which it ultimately came[2]. For His self-revelation in the Incarnation was but the treading again of a familiar path. He had often appeared, and had often spoken, by His own mouth or by that of men whom He had inspired; and in all this contact with the world His one object had been to bestow upon mankind the knowledge of God. With the same object He became incarnate; the full revelation was to impart the perfect knowledge. He became man, Hilary says, in order that we might believe Him;—'to be a Witness from among us to the things of God, and by means of weak flesh to proclaim God the Father to our weak and carnal selves[3].' Here again we see the continuity of the Divine purpose, the fulfilment of the counsel which dates back to the beginning of time. If man had not sinned, he would still have needed the progressive revelation; sin has certainly modified Christ's course upon earth, but was not the determining cause of the Incarnation.

The doctrine of the Incarnation, or Embodiment as Hilary prefers to call it, is presented very fully in the *De Trinitate*, and with much originality. The Godhead of Christ is secured by His identity with the eternal Son and by the fact that at the very time of His humilia-

---

7 Westcott, essay on 'The Gospel of Creation,' in his edition of St. John's Epistles, where, however, Hilary is not mentioned.

8 Cf. *Trin.* xi. 49.

9 *Trin.* ii. 6, xii. 4, &c. He is also often named Jesus Christ in this connection, e.g. *Trin.* iv. 6.

1 According to Eusebius' computation, which Hilary would probably accept without dispute, there were 5,228 years from the Creation to our Lord's commencement of His mission in the 15th year of Tiberius, A.D. 29.

2 E.g. *Trin.* iv. 27; *Tr. in Ps.* lxviii. 19.

3 *Trin.* iii. 9; cf. St. John xvii. 3.

tion upon earth He was continuing without interruption His divine work of maintaining the existence of the worlds [4]. Indeed, by a natural protest against the degradation which the Arians would put upon Him, it is the glory of Christ upon which Hilary lays chief stress. And this is not the moral glory of submission and self-sacrifice, but the visible glory of miracles attesting the Divine presence. In the third book of the *De Trinitate* the miracles of Cana and of the feeding of the five thousand, the entrance into the closed room where the disciples were assembled, the darkness and the earthquake at the Crucifixion, are the proofs urged for His Godhead; and the wonderful circumstances surrounding the birth at Bethlehem are similarly employed in book ii. [5] Sound as the reasoning is, it is typical of a certain unwillingness on Hilary's part to dwell upon the self-surrender of Christ; he prefers to think of Him rather as the Revealer of God than as the Redeemer of men. But, apart from this preference, he constantly insists that the Incarnation has caused neither loss nor change of the Divine nature in Christ [6], and proves the point by the same words of our Lord which had been used to demonstrate the eternal Sonship. And the assumption of flesh lessens His power as little as it degrades His nature. For though it is, in one aspect, an act of submission to the will of the Father, it is, in another, an exertion of His own omnipotence. No inferior power could appropriate to itself an alien nature; only God could strip Himself of the attributes of Godhead [7].

But the incarnate Christ is as truly man as He is truly God. We have seen that He is 'created in the body'; and Hilary constantly insists that His humanity is neither fictitious nor different in kind from ours [8]. We must therefore consider what is the constitution of man. He is, so Hilary teaches, a physically composite being; the elements of which his body is composed are themselves lifeless, and man himself is never fully alive [9]. According to this physiology, the father is the author of the child's body, the maternal function being altogether subsidiary. It would seem that the mother does nothing more than protect the embryo, so giving it the opportunity of growth, and finally bring the child to birth [1]. And each human soul is separately created, like the universe, out of nothing. Only the body is engendered; the soul, wherein the likeness of man to God consists, has a nobler origin, being the immediate creation of God [2]. Hilary does not hold, or at least does not attach importance to, the tripartite division of man; for the purposes of his philosophy we consist of soul and body. We may now proceed to consider his theory of the Incarnation. This is based upon the Pauline conception of the first and second Adam. Each of these was created, and the two acts of creation exactly correspond. Christ, the Creator, made clay into the first Adam, who therefore had an earthly body. He made Himself into the second Adam, and therefore has a heavenly Body. To this end He descended from heaven and entered into the Virgin's womb. For, in accordance with Hilary's principle of interpretation [3], the word 'Spirit' must not be regarded as necessarily signifying the Holy Ghost, but one or other of the Persons of the Trinity as the context may require; and in this case it means the Son, since the question is of an act of creation, and He, and none other, is the Creator. Moreover, the correspondence between the two Adams would be as effectually broken were the Holy Ghost the Agent in the conception, as it would be were Christ's body engendered and not created. Thus

4 *Trin.* ii. 25 and often.

5 *Trin.* ii. 27. The same conclusion is constantly drawn in the *Comm. in Matt.*

6 E.g. *Trin.* ix. 4, 14, 51; *Tr. in Ps.* ii. 11, 25.

7 *Trin.* ii. 25, xii. 6, &c. 8 E.g. *Tr. in Ps.* cxxxviii. 3.

9 This, in contrast with God, Who is Life, is proved by the fact that certain bodily growths can be removed without our being conscious of the operation; *Trin.* vii. 28.

1 Cf. *Trin.* vii. 23, x. 15, 16. Similarly in the *Eumenides* 637, Æschylus makes Apollo excuse Orestes' murder of Clytæmnestra on the ground that the mother is not the parent, but only the nurse of the germ. This is contrary to Aristotle's teaching: Æschylus and Hilary evidently represent a rival current of ancient opinion.

2 *Trin.* x. 20. In *Tr. in Ps.* cxviii., *Iod*, 6, 7, this thought is developed. Man has a double origin. First, he is made after the likeness of God. This is the soul, which is immaterial and has no resemblance and owes no debt, as of effect to cause, to any other nature (i.e. substance) than God. It is not His likeness, but is after His likeness. Secondly, there is the body, composed of earthly matter.

3 *Trin.* ii. 35 f., viii. 23 f.

He is Himself not only the Author but (if the word may be used) the material of His own body [4] ; the language of St. John, that the Word *became* flesh, must be taken literally. It would be insufficient to say that the Word took, or united Himself to, the flesh [5]. But this creation of the Second Adam to be true man is not our only evidence of His humanity. We have seen that in Hilary's judgment the mother has but a secondary share in her offspring. That share, whatever it be, belongs to the Virgin ; she contributed to His growth and to His coming to birth 'everything which it is the nature of her sex to impart [6].' But though Christ is constantly said to have been born of the Virgin, He is habitually called the 'Son of Man,' not the Son of the Virgin, nor she the Mother of God. Such language would attribute to her an activity and an importance inconsistent with Hilary's theory. For no portion of her substance, he distinctly says, was taken into the substance of her Son's human body [7] ; and elsewhere he argues that St. Paul's words 'made of a woman' are deliberately chosen to describe Christ's birth as a creation free from any commingling with existing humanity [8]. But the Virgin has an essential share in the fulfilment of prophecy. For though Christ without her co-operation could have created Himself as Man, yet He would not have been, as He was fore-ordained to be, the Son of Man [9]. And since He holds that the Virgin performs every function of a mother, Hilary avoids that Valentinian heresy according to which Christ passed through the Virgin 'like water through a pipe [1],' for He was Himself the Author of a true act of creation within her, and, when she had fulfilled her office, was born as true flesh. Again, Hilary's clear sense of the eternal personal pre-existence of the Word saves him from any contact with the Monarchianism combated by Hippolytus and Tertullian, which held that the Son was the Father under another aspect. Indeed, so secure does he feel himself that he can venture to employ Monarchian theories, now rendered harmless, in explanation of the mysteries of the Incarnation. For we cannot fail to see a connection between his opinions and theirs ; and it might seem that, confident in his wider knowledge, he has borrowed not only from the arguments used by Tertullian against the Monarchian Praxeas, but also from those which Tertullian assigns to the latter. Such reasonings, we know, had been very prevalent in the West ; and Hilary's use of certain of them, in order to turn their edge by showing that they were not inconsistent with the fundamental doctrines of the Faith [2], may indicate that Monarchianism was still a real danger.

Thus the Son becomes flesh, and that by true maternity on the Virgin's part. But man is more than flesh ; he is soul as well, and it is the soul which makes him man instead of matter. The soul, as we saw, is created by a special act of God at the beginning of the separate existence of each human being ; and Christ, to be true man and not merely true flesh, created for Himself the human soul which was necessary for true humanity. He had borrowed from the Apollinarians, consciously no doubt, their interpretation of one of their favourite passages, 'The Word became flesh' ; here again we find an argument of heretics rendered harmless and adopted by orthodoxy. For the strange Apollinarian

---

[4] *Trin.* x. 16, *caro non aliunde originem sumpserat quam ex Verbo,* and *ib.* 15, 18, 25. Dorner, I. ii., p. 403, n. 1, points out that this is exactly the teaching of Gregory of Nyssa.

[5] This view that the conception by the Holy Ghost means conception by the Son is consistently held by Hilary throughout his writings. It appears in the earliest of them ; in *Comm. in Matt.* ii. 5, Christ is 'born of a woman ; . . . made flesh through the Word.' So in *Trin.* ii. 24, He is 'born of the Virgin and of the Holy Ghost, Himself ministering to Himself in this operation. . . . By His own, that is God's, overshadowing power He sowed for Himself the beginnings of His body and ordained that His flesh should commence to exist ;' and *Trin.* x. 16.

[6] *Trin.* x. 16 ; cf. *ib.* 17. In the *Instructio Psalmorum,* § 6, he speaks in more usual language ;—*adventus Domini ex virgine in hominem procreandi,* and so also in some other passages.

Dorner's view (I. ii. 403 f. and note 74, p. 533) differs from that here taken. But he is influenced (see especially p. 404) by the desire to save Hilary's consistency rather than to state his actual opinion. And Hilary was too early in the field, too anxiously employed in feeling his way past the pitfalls of heresy, to escape the danger of occasional inconsistency.

[7] *Trin.* iii. 19, *perfectum ipsa de suis non imminuta generavit.* So *ib.* ii. 25, *unigenitus Deus . . . . Virginis utero insertus accrescit.* He grew there, but nothing more. *In Virginem* exactly corresponds to *ex Virgine.*

[8] *Trin.* xii. 50 ; it would be a watering of the sense to regard *commixtio* in this passage as simply equivalent to *coitio.*

[9] *Trin.* x. 16.   [1] Irenæus, i. 1, 13.

[2] He often and emphatically repudiates the use which the Monarchians made of them, e.g. *Trin.* iv. 4.

denial to Christ of a human soul, and therefore of perfect manhood, is not only expressly contradicted[3], but repudiated on every page by the contrary assumption on which all Hilary's arguments are based. Christ, then, is 'perfect man[4], of a reasonable soul and human flesh subsisting,' for Whom the Virgin has performed the normal functions of maternity. But there is one wide and obvious difference between Hilary's mode of handling the matter and that with which we are familiar. His view concerning the mother's office forbids his laying stress upon our Lord's inheritance from her. Occasionally, and without emphasis, he mentions our Lord as the Son of David, or otherwise introduces His human ancestry[5], but he never dwells upon the subject. He neither bases upon this ancestry the truth, nor deduces from it the character, of Christ's humanity. Such is Hilary's account of the facts of the Incarnation. In his teaching there is no doubt error as well as defect, but only in the mode of explanation, not in the doctrine explained. It will help us to do him justice if we may compare the theories that have been framed concerning another great doctrine, that of the Atonement, and remember that the strangely diverse speculations of Gregory the Great and of St. Anselm profess to account for the same facts, and that, so far as definitions of the Church are concerned, we are free to accept one or other, or neither, of the rival explanations.

Christ, then, Who had been perfect God from eternity, became perfect Man by His self-wrought act of creation. Thus there was an approximation between God and man; man was raised by God, Who humbled Himself to meet Him. On the one hand the Virgin was sanctified in preparation for her sacred motherhood[6]; on the other hand there was a condescension of the Son to our low estate. The key to this is found by Hilary in the language of St. Paul. Christ emptied Himself of the form of God and took the form of a servant; this is a revelation as decisive as the same Apostle's words concerning the first and the second Adam. The form of God, wherein the Son is to the Father as the exact image reflected in a mirror, the exact impression taken from a seal, belongs to Christ's very being. He could not detach it from Himself, if He would, for it is the property of God to be eternally what He is; and, as Hilary constantly reminds us, the continuous existence of creation is evidence that there had been no break in the Son's divine activity in maintaining the universe which He had made. While He was in the cradle He upheld the worlds[7]. Yet, in some real sense, Christ emptied Himself of this form of God[8]. It was necessary that He should do so if manhood, even the sinless manhood created by Himself for His own Incarnation, was to co-exist with Godhead in His one Person[9]. This is stated as distinctly as is the correlative fact that He retained and exercised the powers and the majesty of His nature. Thus it is clear that, outside the sphere of His work for men, the form and the nature of God remained unchanged in the Son; while within that sphere the form, though not the nature, was so affected that it could truly be said to be laid aside. But when we come to Hilary's explanation of this process, we can only acquit him of inconsistency in thought by admitting the ambiguity of his language. In one group of passages he recognises the self-emptying, but minimises its importance; in another he denies that our Lord could or did empty Himself of the form of God. And again, his definitions of the word 'form' are so various as to be actually contradictory. Yet a consistent

---

3 E.g. *Trin.* x. 22 *in.* The human soul is clearly intended. Schwane, ii. 268, justly praises Hilary for greater accuracy than his contemporaries in laying stress upon each of the constituent elements of Christ's humanity, and especially upon the soul; in this respect following Tertullian and Origen.

4 In *Trin.* x. 21 f. is an argument analogous to that of the *De Synodis* concerning the Godhead. Christ is Man because He is perfectly like man, just as in the Homœusian argument He is God because He is perfectly like God.

5 E.g. *Comm. in Matt.* i.; *Tr. in Ps.* lxviii. 19.

6 *Trin.* ii. 26.   7 *Ib.* viii. 45, 47, ix. 14, &c.

8 This 'evacuation' or 'exinanition' is represented in *Tr. in Ps.* lxviii. 4 by the more precise metaphor of a vessel drained of its liquid contents.

9 Hilary has devoted his Homily on Psalm lxviii. to this subject. In § 25 he asks, 'How could He exist in the form of man while remaining in the form of God?' There are many equally emphatic statements throughout his writings.

sense, and one exceedingly characteristic of Hilary, can be derived from a comparison of his statements[1]; and in judging him we must remember that we have no systematic exposition of his views, but must gather them not only from his deliberate reasonings, but sometimes from homiletical amplifications of Scripture language, composed for edification and without the thought of theological balance, and sometimes from incidental sayings, thrown out in the course of other lines of argument. To the minimising statements belongs his description of the evacuation as a 'change of apparel[2],' and his definition of the word 'form' as meaning no more than 'face' or 'appearance[3],' as also his insistence from time to time upon the permanence of this form in Christ, not merely in His supramundane relations, but as the Son of Man[4]. On the other hand Hilary expressly declares that the 'concurrence of the two forms[5]' is impossible, they being mutually exclusive. This represents the higher form, that of God, as something more than a dress or appearance which could be changed or masked; and stronger still is the language used in the Homily on Psalm lxviii. There (§ 4) he speaks of Christ being exhausted of His heavenly nature, this being used as a synonym for the form of God, and even of His being emptied of His substance. But it is probable that the Homily has descended to us, without revision by its author, in the very words which the shorthand writer took down. This mention of 'substance' is unlike Hilary's usual language, and the antithesis between the substance which the Son had not, because He had emptied Himself of it, and the substance which He had, because He had assumed it, is somewhat infelicitously expressed. The term must certainly not be taken as the deliberate statement of Hilary's final opinion, still less as the decisive passage to which his other assertions must be accommodated; but it is at least clear evidence that Hilary, in the maturity of his thought, was not afraid to state in the strongest possible language the reality and completeness of the evacuation. The reconciliation of these apparently contradictory views concerning Christ's relation to the form of God can only be found in Hilary's idea of the Incarnation as a 'dispensation,' or series of dispensations. The word and the thought are borrowed through Tertullian[6] from the Greek 'economy'; but in Hilary's mind the notion of Divine reserve has grown till it has become, we might almost say, the dominant element of the conception. This self-emptying is a dispensation[7], whereby the incarnate Son of God appears to be, what He is not, destitute of the form of God. For this form is the glory of God, concealed by our Lord for the purposes of His human life, yet held by Hilary, to a greater extent, perhaps, than by any other theologian, to have been present with Him on earth. In words which have a wider application, and must be considered hereafter, Hilary speaks of Christ as 'emptying Himself and hiding Himself within Himself[8].' Concealment has a great part to play in Hilary's theories, and is in this instance the only explanation consistent with his doctrinal position[9].

Thus the Son made possible the union of humanity with Himself. He 'shrank from God into man[1]' by an act not only of Divine power, but of personal Divine will. He Who did this thing could not cease to be what He had been before; hence His very deed in submitting Himself to the change is evidence of His unchanged continuity of existence[2].

---

[1] Baltzer and Schwane have been followed in this matter, in opposition to Dorner.

[2] *Trin.* ix. 38, *habitus demutatio,* and similarly *ib.* 14.

[3] *Tr. in Ps.* lxviii. 25.   [4] E.g. *Trin.* viii. 45.

[5] *Trin.* ix. 14, *concursus utriusque formæ.*

[6] It is very characteristic that it lies outside Cyprian's vocabulary and range of ideas.

[7] *Trin.* ix. 38 *in.,* and especially *ib.* 39. The unity of glory departed through His obedience in the Dispensation.

[8] *Trin.* xi. 48; cf. the end of this section and xii. 6.

[9] Cf. Baltzer, *Christologie,* p. 10 f., Schwane, p. 272 f. Other explanations which have been suggested are quite inadmissible. Dorner, p. 407, takes the passage cited above about 'substance' too seriously, and wavers between the equally impossible interpretations of 'countenance' and 'personality.' Förster (l.c. p. 659) understands the word to mean 'mode of existence.' Wirthmüller, cited by Schwane, p. 273, has the courage to regard 'form of God' and 'form of a servant' as equivalent to Divinity and humanity.

[1] *Trin.* xii. 6, *decedere ex Deo in hominem.* Perhaps it should be *decidere,* as in *Tr. in Ps.* lxviii. 4.

[2] *Tr. in Ps.* lxviii. 25.

And furthermore, His assumption of the servant's form was not accomplished by a single act. His wearing of that form was one continuous act of voluntary self-repression [3], and the events of His life on earth bear frequent witness to His possession of the powers of God.

Thus in Him God is united with man; these two natures form the 'elements' or 'parts' of one Person [4]. The Godhead is superposed upon the manhood; or, as Hilary prefers to say, the manhood is assumed by Christ [5]. And these two natures are not confused [6], but simultaneously coexist in Him as the Son of Man [7]. There are not two Christs [8], nor is the one Christ a composite Being in such a sense that He is intermediate in kind between God and Man. He can speak as God and can also speak as Man; in the Homilies on the Psalms Hilary constantly distinguishes between His utterances in the one and the other nature. Yet He is one Person with two natures, of which the one dominates, though it does not extinguish, the other in every relation of His existence as the Son of Man [9]. Every act, bodily or mental, done by Him is done by both natures of the one Christ. Hence a certain indifference towards the human aspects of His life, and a tendency rather to explain away what seems humiliation than to draw out its lessons [1]. And Hilary is so impressed with the unity of Christ that the humanity, a notion for which he has no name [2], would have been in his eyes nothing more than a collective term for certain attributes of One Who is more than man, just as the body of Christ is not for him a dwelling occupied, or an instrument used, by God, but an inseparable property of Christ, Who personally is God and Man.

Hence the body of Christ has a character peculiar to itself. It is a heavenly body [3], because of its origin and because of its Owner, the Son of Man Who came down from heaven, and though on earth was in heaven still [4]. It performs the functions and experiences, the limitations of a human body, and this is evidence that it is in every sense a true, not an alien or fictitious body. Though it is free from the sins of humanity, it has our weaknesses. But here the distinction must be made, which will presently be discussed, between the two kinds of suffering, that which feels and that which only endures. Christ was not conscious of suffering from these weaknesses, which could inflict no sense of want of weariness or pain upon His body, a body not the less real because it was perfect. He took our infirmities as truly as He bore our sins. But He was no more under the dominion of the one than of the other [5]. His body was in the likeness of ours, but its reality did not consist in the likeness [6], but in the fact that He had created it a true body. Christ, by virtue of His creative power, might have made for Himself a true body, by means of which to fulfil God's purposes, that should have been free from these infirmities. It was for our sake that He did not. There would have been a true body, but it would have been difficult for us to believe it. Hence He assumed one which had for habits

---

[3] *Trin.* xi. 48, 'emptying Himself' might have been a single act; 'hiding Himself within Himself' was a sustained course of conduct.

[4] *Genus* is fairly common, though much rarer than *natura*; *pars* occurs in *Trin.* xi. 14, 15, and cf. *ib.* 40. *Elementa* is, I think, somewhat more frequent.

[5] *Trin.* xi. 40, *naturæ assumpti corporis nostri natura paternæ divinitatis invecta.* Conversely, *Trin.* ix. 54, *nova natura in Deum illata.* But such expressions are rare; *hominem ad sumpsit* is the normal phrase. In *Tr. in Ps.* lxviii. 4, he speaks as if the two natures had been forced to coalesce by a Power higher than either. But, as we have seen, in this part of the Homily Hilary's language is destitute of theological exactness.

[6] *Tr. in Ps.* liv. 2.

[7] E.g. *Trin.* ix. 11, 39, x. 16. The expression *utriusque*

naturæ persona in *Trin.* ix. 14 is susceptible of another interpretation.

[8] E.g. *Trin.* x. 22.

[9] *Trin.* x. 22, *quia totus hominis filius totus Dei filius sit.*

[1] Cf. Gore's *Dissertations*, p. 138 f. But Hilary, though he shares and even exaggerates the general tendency of his time, has also a strong sense of the danger of Apollinarianism.

[2] *Homo assumptus* is constantly used, and similarly *homo noster* for our manhood, e.g. *Trin.* ix. 7. This often leads to an awkwardness of which Hilary must have been fully conscious, though he regarded it as a less evil than the use of an abstract term.

[3] *Corpus cæleste*, x. 18.

[4] *Tr. in Ps.* ii. 11, from St. John iii. 13.

[5] *Trin.* x. 47 f.; *Tr. in Ps.* cxxxviii. 3.

[6] *Trin.* x. 25.

what are necessities to us, in order to demonstrate to us its reality [7]. It was foreordained that He should be incarnate; the mode of the Incarnation was determined by considerations of our advantage. The arguments by which this thesis is supported will be stated presently, in connection with Hilary's account of the Passion. It would be difficult to decide whether he has constructed his theory concerning the human activities of our Lord upon the basis of this preponderance of the Divine nature in His incarnate personality, or whether he has argued back from what he deems the true account of Christ's mode of life on earth, and invented the hypothesis in explanation of it. In any case he has had the courage exactly to reverse the general belief of Christendom regarding the powers normally used by Christ. We are accustomed to think that with rare exceptions, such as the Transfiguration, He lived a life limited by the ordinary conditions of humanity, to draw lessons for ourselves from His bearing in circumstances like our own, to estimate His condescension and suffering, in kind if not in degree, by our own consciousness. Hilary regards the normal state of the incarnate Christ as that of exaltation, from which He stooped on rare occasions, by a special act of will, to self-humiliation. Thus the Incarnation, though itself a declension from the pristine glory, does not account for the facts of Christ's life; they must be explained by further isolated and temporary declensions. And since the Incarnation is the one great event, knowledge and faith concerning which are essential, the events which accompany or result from it tend, in Hilary's thought, to shrink in importance. They can and must be minimised, explained away, regarded as 'dispensations,' if they seem to derogate from the Majesty of Him Who was incarnate.

When we examine the interpretation of Scripture by which Hilary reaches the desired conclusions we find it, in many instances, strange indeed. The letter of the Gospels tells us of bodily needs and of suffering; Christ, though more than man, is proved to be Man by His obvious submission to the conditions of human life. But according to Hilary all human suffering is due to the union of an imperfect soul with an imperfect body. The soul of Christ, though truly human, was perfect; His body was that of a Person Divine as well as human. Thus both elements were perfect of their kind, and therefore as free from infirmity [8] as from sin, for affliction is the lot of man not because he is man, but because he is a sinner. In contrast with the squalor of sinful humanity, glory surrounded Christ from the Annunciation onward throughout His course on earth [9]. Miracle is the attestation of His Godhead, and He Who was thus superior to the powers of nature could not be subject to the sufferings which nature inflicts. But, being omnipotent, He could subject Himself to humiliations which no power less than His own could lay upon Him, and this self-subjection is the supreme evidence of His might as well of His goodwill towards men. God, and only God, could occupy at once the cradle and the throne on high [1]. Thus in emphasizing the humiliation Hilary is extolling the majesty of Christ, and refuting the errors of Arianism. That school had made the most of Christ's sufferings, holding them a proof of His inferiority to the Father. In Hilary's eyes His power to condescend and His final victory are equally conclusive evidences of His co-equal Divinity. But if He stoops to our estate, and is at the same time God exercising His full prerogatives, here again there must be a 'dispensation.' He was truly subject to the limitations of our nature; that is a fact of revelation. But He was subject by a succession of detached acts of self-restraint, culminating in the act, voluntary like the others, of His death [2]. Of His acceptance of the ordinary infirmities of humanity we have already spoken. Hilary gives the same explanation of the Passion as he does of the thirst or

---

[7] *Trin.* x. 24. The purpose of the Old Testament Theophanies, it will be remembered, was the same. God appeared as Man, in order to make men familiar with the future reality and so more ready to believe. See *Trin.* v. 17.

[8] *Trin.* x. 14, 15.

[9] *Trin.* ii. 26 f., iii. 18 f. and often, especially in the *Comm. in Matt.*

[1] E.g. *Trin.* ix. 4, xi. 48.

[2] *Ib.* x. 11, 61.

weariness of Christ. That He could suffer, and that to the utmost, is proved by the fact that He did suffer; yet was He, or could He be, conscious of suffering? For the fulfilment of the Divine purpose, for our assurance of the reality of His work, the acts had to be done; but it was sufficient that they should be done by a dispensation, in other words, that the events should be real and yet the feelings be absent of which, had the events happened to us, we should have been conscious. To understand this we must recur to Hilary's theory of the relation of the soul to the body. The former is the organ of sense, the latter a lifeless thing. But the soul may fall below, or rise above, its normal state. Mortification of the body may set in, or drugs be administered which shall render the soul incapable of feeling the keenest pain[3]. On the other hand it is capable of a spiritual elevation which shall make it unconscious of bodily needs or sufferings, as when Moses and Elijah fasted, or the three Jewish youths walked amid the flames[4]. On this high level Christ always dwelt. Others might rise for a moment above themselves; He, not although, but because He was true and perfect Man, never fell below it. He placed Himself in circumstances where shame and wounds and death were inflicted upon Him; He had lived a life of humiliation, not only real, in that it involved a certain separation from God, but also apparent. But as in this latter respect we may no more overlook His glory than we may suppose Him ignorant, as by a dispensation He professed to be[5], so in regard to the Passion we must not imagine that He was inferior to His saints in being conscious, as they were not, of suffering[6]. So far, indeed, is He from the sense of suffering that Hilary even says that the Passion was a delight to Him[7], and this not merely in its prospective results, but in the consciousness of power which He enjoyed in passing through it. Nor could this be surprising to one who looked with Hilary's eyes upon the humanity of Christ. He enforces his view sometimes with rhetoric, as when he repudiates the notion that the Bread of Life could hunger, and He who gives the living water, thirst[8], that the hand which restored the servant's ear could itself feel pain[9], that He Who said, 'Now is the Son of Man glorified,' when Judas left the chamber, could at that moment be feeling sorrow[1], and He before Whom the soldiers fell be capable of fear[2], or shrink from the pain of a death which was itself an exertion of His own free will and power[3]. Or else he dwells upon the general character of Christ's manhood. He recognises no change in the mode of being after the Resurrection; the passing through closed doors, the sudden disappearance at Emmaus are typical of the normal properties of His body, which could heal the sick by a touch, and could walk upon the waves[4]. It is a body upon the sensibility of which the forces of nature can make no impression whatever; they can no more pain Him than the stroke of a weapon can affect air or water[5]; or, as Hilary puts it elsewhere, fear and death, which have so painful a meaning to us, were no more to Him than a shower falling upon a surface which it cannot penetrate[6]. It is not the passages of the Gospel which tell of Christ's glory, but those which speak of weakness or suffering that need to be explained; and Hilary on occasion is not afraid to explain them away. For instance, we read that when our Lord had fasted forty days and forty nights 'He was afterward an hungred.' Hilary denies that there is a connection of cause and effect. Christ's perfect body was unaffected

---

3 *Trin.* x. 14.

4 *Comm. in Matt.* iii. 2; *Trin.* x. 45. The freedom of Christian martyrs from pain is frequently noticed in early writers.

5 Cf. p. lxvi.

6 Hilary was undoubtedly influenced more than he knew by the Latin words *pati* and *dolere,* the one purely objective, the other subjective. By a line of thought which recalls that of Mozley concerning Miracles he refuses to argue from our experience to that of Christ. That He suffered, in the sense of having wounds and death inflicted upon Him, is a fact; that He was conscious of suffering is an inference, a supposition (*putatur dolere quia patitur, Tr. in Ps.* cxxxviii. 3, *fallitur ergo humanæ*

æstimationis opinio putans hunc dolere quod patitur, Trin. x. 47), and one which we are not entitled to make. In fact, the passage last cited states that He has no *natura dolendi*; so also x. 23, 35, and cf. *Tr. in Ps.* liii. 12. Or, as Hilary puts it, *Trin.* x. 24, He is subject to the *naturæ passionum* not to their *iniuriæ.*

7 *Tr. in Ps.* cxxxviii. 26.   8 *Trin.* x. 24.

9 *Ib.* 28.   1 *Ib.* 29.   2 *Ib.* 27.   3 *Ib.* 11.

4 *Ib.* 23. These instances of His power are used as a direct proof of Christ's incapacity of pain. Hilary is willing to confess that He could feel it, if it be shewn that we can follow Him in these respects.

5 *loc. cit.*   6 *Tr. in Ps.* liv. 6.

by abstinence ; but after the fast by an exertion of His will He experienced hunger [7]. So also the Agony in the Garden is ingeniously misinterpreted. He took with Him the three Apostles, and then began to be sorrowful. He was not sorrowful till He had taken them ; they, not He, were the cause. When He said, ' My soul is exceeding sorrowful, even unto death,' the last words must not be regarded as meaning that His was a mortal sorrow, but as giving a note of time. The sorrow of which He spoke was not for Himself but for His Apostles, whose flight He foresaw, and He was asserting that this sorrow would last till He died. And when He prayed that the cup might pass away from Him, this was no entreaty that He might be spared. It was His purpose to drink it. The prayer was for His disciples that the cup might pass on from Him to them ; that they might suffer for Him as martyrs full of hope, without pain or fear [8]. One passage, St. Luke xxii. 43, 44, which conflicts with his view is rejected by Hilary on textual grounds, and not without some reason [9]. He had looked for it, and found it absent, in a large number of manuscripts, both Greek and Latin. But perhaps the strangest argument which he employs is that when the Gospel tells us that Christ thirsted and hungered and wept, it does not proceed to say that He ate and drank and felt grief [9a]. Hunger and thirst, eating and drinking, were two sets of dispensations, unconnected by the relation of cause and effect ; the tears were another dispensation, not the expression of personal grief. If, as a habit, He accepts the needs and functions of our body, this does not render His own body more real, for by the act of its creation it was made truly human ; His purpose, as has been said, is to enable us to recognise its reality, which would otherwise be difficult [1]. If He wept, He had the same object ; this use of one of the evidences of bodily emotion would help us to believe [2]. And so it is throughout Christ's life on earth. He suffered but He did not feel. No one but a heretic, says Hilary, would suppose that He was pained by the nails which fixed Him to the Cross [3].

It is obvious that Hilary's theory offers a perfect defence against the two dangers of the day, Arianism and Apollinarianism. The tables are turned upon the former by emphatic insistence upon the power manifested in the humiliation and suffering of Christ. That He, being what He was, should be able to place Himself in such circumstances was the most impressive evidence of His Divinity. And if His humanity was endowed with Divine properties, much more must His Divinity rise above that inferiority to which the Arians consigned it. Apollinarianism is controverted by the demonstration of His true humanity. No language can be too strong to describe its glories ; but the true wonder is not that Christ, as God, has such attributes, but that He Who has them is very Man. The theory was well adapted for service in the controversies of the day ; for us, however we may admire the courage and ingenuity it displays, it can be no more than a curiosity of doctrinal history. Yet, whatever its defects as an explanation of the facts, the skill with which dangers on either hand are avoided, the manifest anxiety to be loyal to established doctrine, deserve recognition and respect. It has been said that Hilary ' constantly withdraws in the second clause what he has asserted in the first [4],' and in a sense it is true. For many of his statements might make him seem the advocate of an extreme doctrine of *Kenosis*, which would represent our Lord's self-emptying as

---

[7] *Comm. in Matt.* iii. 2.

[8] *Ib.* xxxi. 1—7. These were not immature speculations, abandoned by a riper judgment. The explanation of ' even unto death' is repeated, and that concerning the cup implied, in *Trin.* x. 36, 37.

[9] *Trin.* x. 41. Westcott and Hort insert it within brackets. Even if the passage be retained, Hilary has an explanation which agrees with his theory.

[9a] *Ib.* 24.

[1] *loc. cit., Tr. in Ps.* liii. 7

[2] In *Tr. in Ps.* liii. 7, there is also the moral purpose. He prays humbly. His prayer expresses no need of His own, but is meant to teach us the lesson of meekness.

[3] *Trin.* x. 45. Yet Hilary himself is not always consistent. In the purely homiletical writing of *Tr. in Ps.* lxviii. 1, he dwells upon Christ's endurance of pain. His argument obliged Him to emphasize the suffering ; it was natural, though not logical, that he should sometimes insist also upon the feeling.

[4] Harnack, *Dogmengesch.* ii. 301 *n*.

complete. But often expressed and always present in Hilary's thought, for the coherence of which it is necessary, is the correlative notion of the dispensation, whereby Christ seemed for our sake to be less than He truly was. Again, Hilary has been accused of 'sailing somewhat close to the cliffs of Docetism [5],' but all admit that he has escaped shipwreck. Various accounts of his teaching, all of which agree in acquitting him of this error, have been given; and that which has been accepted in this paper, of Christ by the very perfection of His humanity habitually living in such an ecstasy as that of Polycarp or Perpetua at their martyrdom, is a noble conception in itself and consistent with the Creeds, though it cannot satisfy us. In part, at any rate, it belonged to the lessons which Hilary had learned from Alexandria. Clement had taught, though his successor Origen rejected, the impassibility of Christ, Who had eaten and drunk only by a 'dispensation';—' He ate not for the sake of His body, which was sustained by a holy power, but that that false notion might not creep into the minds of His companions which in later days some have, in fact, conceived, that He had been manifested only in appearance. He was altogether impassible; there entered from without into Him no movement of the feelings, whether pleasure or pain [6].' Thus Hilary had what would be in his eyes high authority for his opinion. But he must have felt some doubts of its value if he compared the strange exegesis and forced logic by which it was supported with that frank acceptance of the obvious sense of Scripture in which he takes so reasonable a pride in his direct controversy with the Arians. And another criticism may be ventured. In that controversy he balances with scrupulous reverence mystery against mystery, never forgetting that he is dealing with infinities. In this case the one is made to overwhelm the other; the infinite glory excludes the infinite sorrow from his view. Here, if anywhere, Hilary needs, and may justly claim, the indulgence he has demanded. It had not been his wish to define or explain; he was content with the plain words of Scripture and the simplest of creeds. But he was compelled by the fault of others to commit a fault [7]; and speculation based on sound principles, however perilous to him who made the first attempt, had been rendered by the prevalence of heresy a necessary evil. Again, we must bear in mind that Hilary was essentially a Greek theologian, to whom the supremely interesting as well as the supremely important doctrine was that God became Man. He does not conceal or undervalue the fact of the Atonement and of the Passion as the means by which it was wrought. But, even though he had not held his peculiar theory of impassibility, he would still have thought the effort most worth making not that of realising the pains of Christ by our experience of suffering and sense of the enormity of sin, but that of apprehending the mystery of the Incarnation. For that act of condescension was greater, not only in scale but in kind, than any humiliation to which Christ, already Man, submitted Himself in His human state.

Christ, Whose properties as incarnate are thus described by Hilary, is one Person. This, of course, needs no proof, but something must be said of the use which he makes of the doctrine. It is by Christ's own work, by an act of power, even of violence [8], exercised by Him upon Himself, that the two natures are inseparably associated in Him; so inseparably that between His death and resurrection His Divinity was simultaneously present with each of the severed elements of His humanity [9]. Hence, though Hilary frequently

---

[5] The words are Förster's, *op. cit.* p. 662, and are accepted as representing their opinion by Bardenhewer, *Patrologie*, p. 382, and Baltzer, *Christologie*, p. 32.

[6] *Strom.* vi. § 71. Bigg, *Christian Platonists*, p. 71, gives other sources, by which Hilary is less likely to have been influenced, from which he may have derived this teaching. This is not the only coincidence between him and Clement.

[7] *Trin* ii. 2, *in vitium vitio coarctamur alieno.*

[8] *Tr. in Ps.* lxviii. 4. The unity is also strongly put in *Trin*. viii. 13 x. 61.

[9] *Trin*. x. 34. This was Hilary's deliberate belief. But in earlier life he had written rashly of the Holy Spirit (i.e. God the Son) surrendering His humanity to be tempted, and of the cry upon the Cross 'testifying the departure of God the Word from Him' (*Comm. in Matt.* iii. 1, xxxiii. 6). This, if it had represented Hilary's teaching in that treatise, would have proved

discriminates between Christ's utterances as God and as Man [1], he never fails to keep his reader's attention fixed upon the unity of His Person. And this unity is the more obvious because, as has been said, the Manhood in Christ is dominated by the Godhead. Though we are not allowed to forget that He is truly Man, yet as a rule Hilary prefers to speak in such words as, 'the only-begotten Son of God was crucified [2],' or to say more briefly, 'God was crucified [3].' Judas is 'the betrayer of God [4];' 'the life of mortals is renewed through the death of immortal God [5].' Such expressions are far more frequent than the balanced language, 'the Passion of Jesus Christ, our God and Lord [6],' and these again than such an exaltation of the manhood as 'the Man Jesus Christ, the Lord of Majesty [7].' But once, in an unguarded moment, an element of His humanity seems to be deified. Hilary never says that Christ's body is God, but he speaks of the spectators of the Crucifixion 'contemplating the power of the soul which by signs and deeds had proved itself God [8].'

But though distinctions may be drawn, and though for the sake of emphasis and brevity Christ may be called by the name of one only of His two natures, the essential fact is never forgotten that He is God and man, one Person in two forms, God's and the servant's. And these two natures do not stand isolated and apart, merely contained within the limits of one personality. Just as we saw that Hilary recognises a complete mutual indwelling and interpenetration of Father and Son, so he teaches that in the narrower sphere of the Incarnation there is an equally exact and comprehensive union of the Godhead and Manhood in Christ. Jesus is Christ, and Christ is Jesus [9]. Not merely is the one Christ perfect Man and perfect God, but the whole Son of Man is the whole Son of God [1]. So far is His manhood from being merged and lost in His Divinity, that the extent of the one is the measure of the other. We must not imagine that, simultaneously with the incarnate, there existed a non-incarnate Christ, respectively submitting to humiliation and ruling the worlds; nor yet must we conceive of one Christ in two unconnected states of being, as though the assumption of humanity were merely a function analogous to the guiding of the stars. On the contrary, the one Person is co-extensive with all infinity, and all action lies within His scope. Whatever He does, whether it be, or be not, in relation to humanity, and in the former case whether it be the exaltation of manhood or the self-emptying of Godhead, is done 'within the sphere of the Incarnation [2],' the sphere which embraces His whole being and His whole action. The self-emptying itself was not a self-determination, instant and complete, made before the Incarnation, but, as we saw, a process which continued throughout Christ's life on earth and was active to the end. For as He hung, deliberately self-emptied of His glory, on the Cross, He manifested His normal powers by the earthquake shock. His submission to death was the last of a consistent series of exertions of His will, which began with the Annunciation and culminated in the Crucifixion.

---

it heretical; but the whole tenour of the commentary proves that this was simply carelessness. In the Homilies on the Psalms he also writes somewhat loosely on occasion; e.g. liii. 4 *fin.*, where he mentions Christ's *former* nature, i e. the Divinity, and *ib.* 5, where he speaks of 'Him Who *after being God* (*ex Deo*) had died as man.' But only malevolence could give an evil interpretation to these passages, delivered as they were for the edification of Hilary's flock, and with no thought of theological accuracy. It is, indeed, quite possible that they were never revised, or even intended, for publication by him.

[1] E g. *Trin.* ix. 6, and often in the Homilies on the Psalms, as cxxxviii. 13.

[2] *Tr. in Ps.* liii. 12.   [3] *loc. cit.*

[4] *Tr. in Ps.* cxxxix. 15.

[5] *Trin.* x. 63. Similarly in *Tr. in Ps.* lxvii. 21, he speaks of 'the passion, the cross, the death, the burial of God.'

[6] *Tr. in Ps.* liii. 4.

[7] *Trin.* ix. 3.

[8] *Tr. in Ps.* cxli. 4. There is no evidence that the text is corrupt, though the words as they stand are rank Apollinarianism, and the more significant as dating from the maturity of Hilary's thought. But here, as often, we must remember that the Homilies are familiar addresses.

[9] *Trin.* x. 52. We must remember not only that heretical distinctions had been made, but that Christ is the name of the Son in pretemporal relation to the world (see p. lxvii.), as well as in the world.

[1] *Ib.* 22, 52.

[2] Cf. Gore, *Dissertations*, p. 211. It is in relation to the self-emptying that Hilary uses such definite language: *Trin.* xi. 48, *intra suam ipse vacuefactus potestatem . . . . Se ipsum intra se vacuefaciens continuit;* xii. 6, *se evacuavit in sese.*

Hilary estimates the cost of the Incarnation not by any episodes of Christ's life on earth, but by the fact that it brought about a real, though partial, separation or breach [3] within the Godhead. Henceforward there was in Christ the nature of the creature as well as that of the Creator; and this second nature, though it had been assumed in its most perfect form, was sundered by an infinite distance from God the Father, though indissolubly united with the Divinity of his Son. A barrier therefore was raised between them, to be overcome in due time by the elevation of manhood in and through the Son. When this elevation was complete within the Person of Christ, then the separation between Him and His Father would be at an end. He would still have true humanity, but this humanity would be raised to the level of association with the Father. In Hilary's doctrine the submission of Christ to this isolation is the central fact of Christianity, the supreme evidence of His love for men. Not only did it thus isolate Him, truly though partially, from the Father, but it introduced a strain, a 'division'[4] within His now incarnate Person. The union of natures was real, but in order that it might become perfect the two needed to be adjusted; and the humiliation involved in this adjustment is a great part of the sacrifice made by Christ. There was conflict, in a certain sense, within Himself, repression and concealment of His powers. But finally the barrier was to be removed, the loss regained, by the exaltation of the manhood into harmonious association with the Godhead of Father and of Son [5]. Then He Who had become in one Person God and Man would become for ever fully God and fully Man. The humanity would gain, the Divinity regain, its appropriate dignity [6], while each retained the reality it had had on earth.

Thus Christ's life in the world was a period of transition. He had descended; this was the time of preparation for an equal, and even loftier, ascent. We must now consider in what the preparation consisted; and here, at first sight, Hilary has involved himself in a grave difficulty. For it is manifest that his theory of Christ's life as one lived without effort, spiritual or physical, or rather as a life whose exertion consisted in a steady self-accommodation to the infirmities of men, varied by occasional and special acts of condescension to suffering, excludes the possibility of an advance, a growth in grace as well as in stature, such as Athanasius scripturally taught [7]. We might say of Hilary, as has been said of another Father, 'under his treatment the Divine history seems to be dissolved into a docetic drama [8].' In such a life it might seem that there was not merely no possibility of progress, but even an absence of identity, in the sense of continuity. The phenomena of Christ's life, therefore, are not manifestations of the disturbance and strain on which Hilary insists, for they are, when, rightly considered, proofs of His union with God and of His Divine power, not of weakness or of partial separation. It would, indeed, be vain for us to seek for sensible evidence of the process of adjustment, for it went on within the inmost being of the one Person. It did not affect the Godhead or the Manhood, both visibly revealed as aspects of the Person, but the hidden relation between the two. Our knowledge assures us that the process took place, but it is a knowledge attained by inference from what He was before and after the state of transition, not by observation of His action in that state. Both natures of the one Person were affected; 'everything'—glory as well as humiliation—'was common to the entire Person at every moment, though to each aspect in its own distinctive manner.' The entire Person entered into inequality with Himself; the actuality of each aspect, during the state of humiliation, fell short of its idea—of the idea of the Son, of the idea of the perfect man, of the idea of the God-man. It was

---

3 *Offensio, Trin.* ix. 38.
4 *Trin.* x. 22, *A se dividuus.*   5 E.g. *Trin.* ix. 38.
6 *Trin.* ix. 6. On earth Christ is *Deus* and *homo;* in glory He is *totus Deus* and *totus homo.*

7 E.g. *Discourses against the Arians,* iii. 53, p. 422 of the translation in this series.
8 Bp. Westcott on Cyril of Alexandria in St. John's Gospel (Speaker's Commentary), p. xcv.

not merely the human aspect that was at first inadequate to the Divine; for, through the medium of the voluntary 'evacuatio,' it dragged down the Divine nature also, so far as i permitted it, to its own inequality[9].' Such is the only explanation which will reconcile Hilary's various, and sometimes obscure, utterances on this great subject. It is open to the obvious and fatal objection that it cuts, instead of loosening, the knot. For it denies any connection between the dispensation of Christ's life on earth and the mystery of His assumption and exaltation of humanity; the one becomes somewhat purposeless, and the other remains unverified. But it is at least a bold and reverent speculation, not inconsistent with the Faith as a system of thought, though no place can be found for it in the Faith, regarded as a revelation of fact.

It was on behalf of mankind that this great sacrifice was made by the Son. While it separated Him from the Father, it united Him to men. We must now consider what was the spiritual constitution of the humanity which He assumed, as we have already considered the physical Man, as we saw (p. lxix.) is constituted of body and soul, an outward and an inward substance, the one earthly, the other heavenly[1]. The exact process of his creation has been revealed. First, man—that is, his soul—was made in the image of God; next, long afterwards, his body was fashioned out of dust; finally by a distinct act, man was made a living soul by the breath of God, the heavenly and earthly natures being thus coupled together[2]. The world was already complete when God created the highest, the most beautiful of His works after His own image. His other works were made by an instantaneous command; even the firmament was established by his *hand*[3]; man alone was made by the *hands* of God;—'Thy hands have made me and fashioned me.' This singular honour of being made by a process, not an act, and by the hands, not the hand or the voice, of God, was paid to man not simply as the highest of the creatures, but as the one for whose sake the rest of the universe was called into being[4]. It is, of course, the soul, made after the image of God, which has this high honour; an honour which no length of sinful ancestry can forfeit, for each soul is still separately created. Hence no human soul is akin to any other human soul; the uniformity of type is secured by each being made in the same pattern, and the dignity of humanity by the fact that this pattern is that of the Son, the Image of God. But the soul pervades the whole body with which it is associated, even as God pervades the universe[5]. The soul of each man is individual, special to himself; his brotherhood with mankind belongs to him through his body, which has therefore something of universality. Hence the relation of mankind with Christ is not through his human soul; it was 'the nature of universal flesh' which He took[6] that has made Him one with us in the Incarnation and in the Eucharist[7]. The reality of His body, as we have seen, is amply secured by Hilary; its universality is assured by the absence of any individual human paternity, which would have isolated Him from others[8]. Thus He took all humanity into His one body; He is the Church[9], for He contains her through the mystery of His body. In Him, by the same means, 'there is contained the congregation, so to speak, of the whole race of men.' Hence He spoke of Himself as the City set on a hill; the inhabitants are mankind[1]. But Christ not only

---

[9] Dorner, I. ii. 415. The liberty has been taken of putting 'Himself' for 'itself.' On the same page Dorner speaks of an 'ever increasing return of the Logos into equality with Himself.' This is a contradiction of his own explanation. God has become God-man. He could not again become simply the Logos. The key to Hilary's position is the double nature of Christ. The Godhead and the Manhood are aspects in revelation, abstractions in argument. That which connects them and gives them reality is the one Person, the object of thought and faith.

[1] *Tr. in Ps.* cxviii., *Iod*, 6, cxxix. 5.

[2] *Ib.* cxxix. 5.

[3] Isai. xlv. 12, the Old Latin, translated from the LXX.,

having the singular. This characteristic piece of exegesis is in *Tr. in Ps.* cxviii., *Iod*, 5; cf. *ib.* 7, 8.

[4] *Ib. Iod*, 1.   [5] *Tr. in Ps.* cxviii., *Koph.* 8.

[6] *Ib.* li. 16, *naturam in se universæ carnis adsumpsit, ib.* liv. 9, *universitatis nostræ caro est factus*; so also *Trin.* xi. 16*in.*, and often.

[7] This latter is the argument of *Trin.* viii. 13 f.

[8] *Trin.* ii. 24; in Him there is the *universi generis humani corpus* because He is *homo factus ex virgine.*

[9] *Tr. in Ps.* cxxv. 6.

[1] *Comm. in Matt.* iv. 12; *habitatio*, as is often the case in late Latin with abstracts, is collective. Hilary also speaks of

embraces all humanity in Himself, but the archetype after Whom, and the final cause for Whom, man was made. Every soul, when it proceeds from the hands of God, is pure, free and immortal, with a natural affinity and capacity for good [2], which can find its satisfaction only in Christ, the ideal Man. But if Christ is thus everything to man, humanity has also, in the foreordained purpose of God. something to confer upon Christ. The temporary humiliation of the Incarnation has for its result a higher glory than He possessed before [3], acquired through the harmony of the two natures.

The course of this elevation is represented by Hilary as a succession of births, in continuation of the majestic series. First there had been the eternal generation of the Son; then His creation for the ways and for the works of God, His appointment, which Hilary regards as equivalent in importance to another birth, to the office of Creator; next the Incarnation, the birth in time which makes Him what He was not before, namely Man [4]. This is followed by the birth of Baptism, of which Hilary speaks thrice [5]. He read in St. Matthew iii. 17, instead of the familiar words of the Voice from heaven, 'Thou art My Son, this day have I begotten Thee.' This was in his judgment the institution of the sacrament of Baptism; because Christ was baptized, we must follow His example. It was a new birth to Him, and therefore to us. He had been the Son; He became through Baptism the perfect Son by this fresh birth [6]. It is difficult to see what Hilary's thought was; perhaps he had not defined it to himself. But, with this reading in his copy of the Gospel, it was necessary that he should be ready with an explanation; and though there remained a higher perfection to be reached, this birth in Baptism might well be regarded as a stage in the return of Christ to His glory, an elevation of His humanity to a more perfect congruity with His Godhead. This birth is followed by another, the effect and importance of which is more obvious, that of the Resurrection, 'the birthday of His humanity to glory [7].' By the Incarnation He had lost unity with the Father; but the created nature, by the assumption of which He had disturbed the unity both within Himself and in relation to the Father, is now raised to the level on which that unity is again possible. In the Resurrection, therefore, it is restored; and this stage of Christ's achievement is regarded as a new birth [8], by which His glory becomes, as it had been before, the same as that of the Father. But now the glory is shared by His humanity; the servant's form is promoted to the glory of God [9] and the discordance comes to an end. Christ, God and Man, stands where the Word before the Incarnation stood. In this Resurrection, the only step in this Divine work which is caused by sin, His full humanity partakes. In order to satisfy all the conditions of actual human life, He died and visited the lower world [1]; and also, as man shall do, He rose again with the same body in which He had died [2]. Then comes that final state, of which something has already been said, when God shall be all in all. No further change will be possible within the Person of Christ, for his humanity, already in harmony with the Godhead, will now be transmuted. The whole Christ, Man as well as God, will become wholly God. Yet the humanity will still exist, for it is inseparable from the Divinity, and will consist, as before, of body and soul. But there will be nothing earthly or fleshly left in the body; its nature will be purely spiritual [3]. The only form in which Hilary can express this result is the seeming paradox that Christ will, by virtue of the final subjection, 'be and continue what He is not [4].' By this return of

Christ as *gerens nos*, *Trin.* x. 25, which recalls the *gestans* of Tertullian and the *portans* of Cyprian.
[2] *Tr. in Ps.* ii. 16, lvii. 3, lxii. 3, and often.
[3] *Trin.* xi. 40—42.   [4] *Tr. in Ps.* ii. 27.
[5] *Comm. in Matt.* ii. 6; *Tr. in Ps.* ii. 29; *Trin.* viii. 25. But he twice (*Trin.* vi. 23; *Tr. in Ps.* cxxxviii. 6) gives the ordinary text, without any hint that he knew of an important variant.

[6] *Tr. in Ps.* ii. 29, *ipse Deo renascebatur in filium perfectum. Trin.* viii. 25, *perfecta nativitas.*
[7] Dorner, I. ii. 417. Dorner overlooks the birth in Baptism.
[8] *Tr. in Ps.* ii. 27, liii. 14.
[9] *Ib.* cxxxviii. 19.   [1] *Ib.* liii. 14.   [2] *Ib.* lv. 12.
[3] *Trin.* xi. 40, 49.
[4] *Ib.* 40. *habens in sacramento subiectionis esse ac manere quod non est.*

the whole Christ into perfect union with God, humanity attains the purpose of its creation. He was the archetype after Whose likeness man was fashioned, and in His Person all the possibilities of mankind are attained. And this great consummation not only fulfils the destinies of humanity; it brings also an augmentation of the glory of Him Who is glorified in Christ [5].

In the fact that humanity is thus elevated in Christ consists the hope of individual men. Man in Him has, in a true sense, become God [6]; and though Hilary as a rule avoids the phrase, familiar to him in the writings of his Alexandrian teachers and freely used by Athanasius and other of his contemporaries, that men become gods because God became Man, still the thought which it conveys is constantly present to his mind. As we have seen, men are created with such elevation as their final cause; they have the innate certainty that their soul is of Divine origin and a natural longing for the knowledge and hope of things eternal [7]. But they can only rise by a process, corresponding to that by which the humanity in Christ was raised to the level of the Divinity. This process begins with the new birth in the one Baptism, and attains its completion when we fully receive the nature and the knowledge of God. We are to be members of Christ's body and partakers in Him, saved into the name and the nature of God [8]. And the means to this is knowledge of Him, received into a pure mind [9]. Such knowledge makes the soul of man a dwelling rational, pure and eternal, wherein the Divine nature, whose properties these are, may eternally abide [1]. Only that which has reason can be in union with Him Who is reason. Faith must be accurately informed as well as sincere. Christ became Man in order that we might believe Him; that He might be a witness to us from among ourselves touching the things of God [2].

We have now followed Hilary through his great theory, in which we may safely say that no other theologian entirely agrees, and which, where it is most original, diverges most widely from the usual lines of Christian thought. Yet it nowhere contradicts the accepted standards of belief; and if it errs it does so in explanation, not in the statement of the truths which it undertakes to explain. Hilary has the distinction of being the only one of his contemporaries with the speculative genius to imagine this development ending in the abolition of incongruity and in the restoration of the full majesty of the Son and of man with Him [3]. He saw that there must be such a development, and if he was wrong in tracing its course, there is a reverence and loyalty, a solidity of reasoning and steady grasp of the problems under discussion, which save him from falling into mere ingenuity or ostentation. Sometimes he may seem to be on the verge of heresy; but in each case it will be found that, whether his system be right or no, the place in it which he has found for an argument used elsewhere in the interests of error is one where the argument is powerless for evil. Sometimes—and this is the most serious reproach that can be brought against him—it must seem that his theology is abstract, moving in a region apart from the facts of human life. It must be admitted that this is the case; that though, as we shall presently see, Hilary had a clear sense of the realities of temptation and sin and of the need of redemption, and has expressed himself in these regards with the fervour and practical wisdom of an earnest and experienced pastor, still these subjects lie within the sphere of his feelings rather than of his thought. It was not his fault that he lived in the days before St. Augustine, and in the heat of an earlier controversy; and it is his conspicuous merit that in his zeal for the Divinity of Christ he traced the Incarnation back beyond the beginning of sin and found its motive in God's eternal

5 *Trin.* xi. 42, *incrementum glorificati in eo Dei.*
6 E.g. *Trin.* ix. 4, x. 7.
7 *Tr. in Ps.* lxii. 3; cf. *Comm. in Matt.* xvi. 5.
8 *Tr. in Ps.* lvi. 7, liii. 5. We must remember the importance of names in Hilary's eyes. They are not arbitrary symbols, but belong essentially to the objects which they signify. Had there been no sin, from which man needed to be saved, he would still have required raising to this name and nature.
9 *Ib.* cxviii., *Aleph*, 1, cxxxi. 6.   1 *Ib.* cxxxi. 23.
2 *Trin.* iii. 9.   3 Förster, *op. cit.*

purpose of uniting man to Himself. He does not estimate the condescension of Christ by the distance which separates the Sinless from the sinful. To his wider thought sin is not the cause of that great sequence of Divine acts of grace, but a disturbing factor which has modified its course. The measure of the love of God in Christ is the infinity He overpassed in uniting the Creator with the creature.

But before we approach the practical theology of Hilary something must be said of his teaching concerning the Third Person of the Trinity. The doctrine of the Holy Spirit is little developed in his writings. The cause was, in part, his sympathy with Eastern thought. The West, in this as in some other respects, was in advance of the contemporary Greeks; but Hilary was too independent to accept conclusions which were as yet un-reasoned[4]. But a stronger reason was that the doctrine was not directly involved in the Arian controversy. On the main question, as we have seen, he kept an open mind, and was prepared to modify from time to time the terms in which he stated the Divinity of our Lord; but in other respects he was often strangely archaic. Such is the case here; Hilary's is a logical position, but the logical process has been arrested. There is nothing in his words concerning the Holy Spirit inconsistent with the later definitions of faith[5], and it would be unfair to blame him because, in the course of a strenuous life devoted to the elucidation and defence of other doctrines, he found no time to develope this; unfair also to blame him for not recognising its full importance. In his earlier days, and while he was in alliance with the Semiarians, there was nothing to bring this doctrine prominently before his mind; in his later life it still lay outside the range of controversy, so far as he was concerned. Hilary, in fact, preferred like Athanasius to rest in the indefinite terms of the original Nicene Creed, the confession of which ended with the simple 'And in the Holy Ghost.' But there was a further and practical reason for his reserve. It was a con-stant taunt of the Arians that the Catholics worshipped a plurality of Gods. The frequency and emphasis with which Hilary denies that Christians have either two Gods or one God in solitude proves that he regarded this plausible assertion as one of the most dangerous weapons wielded by heresy. It was his object, as a skilful disputant, to bring his whole forces to bear upon them, and this in a precisely limited field of battle. To import the question of the Holy Spirit into the controversy might distract his reader's attention from the main issue, and afford the enemy an opening for that evasion which he constantly accuses them of attempting. Hence, in part, the small space allowed to so important a theme; and hence the avoidance, which we noticed, of the very word 'Trinity.' The Arians made the most of their argument about two Gods; Hilary would not allow them the opportunity of imputing to the faithful a belief in three. This might not have been a sufficient inducement, had it stood alone, but the encouragement which he received from Origen's vagueness, representative as it was of the average theology of the third century, must have predisposed him to give weight to the practical consideration. Yet Hilary has not avoided a formal statement of his belief. In *Trin.* ii. §§ 29—35, which is, as we saw, part of a summary statement of the Christian Faith, he sets it forth with Scripture proofs. But he shows clearly, by the short space he allows to it, that it is not in his eyes of co-ordinate importance with the other truths of which he treats. And the curious language in which he introduces the subject, in § 29, seems to imply that he throws it in to satisfy others rather than from his own sense of its necessary place in such a statement. The doctrine, as he here defines it, is that the Holy Spirit undoubtedly exists; the Father and the Son are the Authors of His being, and, since He is joined with Them in our confession,

---

4 Cf. Harnack, *Dogmengesch.* ii. 281. But Harnack is unjust in saying that Hilary had not made up his own mind.

5 Gwatkin, *Studies of Arianism*, p. 206 *n.* 'Hilary's belief in the deity of the Holy Spirit is hardly more doubtful than St. John's: yet he nowhere states it in so many words.'

He cannot, without mutilation of the Faith, be separated from Them. The fact that He is given to us is a further proof of His existence. Yet the title 'Spirit' is often used both for Father and for Son; in proof of this St. John iv. 24 and 2 Cor. iii. 17 are cited. Yet the Holy Spirit has a personal[6] existence and a special office in relation to us. It is through Him that we know God. Our nature is capable of knowing Him, as the eye is capable of sight; and the gift of the Spirit is to the soul what the gift of light is to the eye. Again, in xii. §§ 55, 56, the subject is introduced, as if by an after thought, and even more briefly than in the second book. As he has refused to style the Son a creature, so he refuses to give that name to the Spirit, Who has gone forth from God, and been sent by Christ. The Son is the Only-begotten, and therefore he will not say that the Spirit was begotten; yet he cannot call Him a creature, for the Spirit's knowledge of the mysteries of God, of which He is the Interpreter to men, is the proof of His oneness in nature with God. The Spirit speaks unutterable things and is ineffable in His operation. Hilary cannot define, yet he believes. It must suffice to say, with the Apostle, simply that He is the Spirit of God. The tone of § 56 seems that of silent rebuke to some excess of definition, as he would deem it, of which he had heard. To these passages must be added another in *Trin.* viii. 19 f., where the possession by Father and Son of one Spirit is used in proof of Their own unity. But in this passage there occur several instances of Hilary's characteristic vagueness. As in ii. 30, so here we are told that 'the Spirit' may mean Father or Son as well as Holy Ghost[7], and instances are given where the word has one or other of the two first significations. Thus we must set a certain number of passages where a reference in Scripture to the Holy Spirit is explained away against a number, certainly no greater, in which He is recognised; and in the latter we notice a strong tendency to understate the truth. For though we are expressly told that the Spirit is not a creature, that He is from the Father through the Son, is of one substance with Them and bears the same relation to the One that He bears to the Other[8], yet Hilary refuses with some emphasis and in a conspicuous place, at the very end of the treatise, to call Him God. But both groups of passages, those in which the Holy Ghost is recognised and those in which reason is given for non-recognition, are more than counterbalanced by a multitude in which, no doubt for the controversial reason already mentioned, the Holy Spirit is left unnamed, though it would have been most natural that allusion should be made to Him[9]. We find in Hilary 'the premisses from which the Divinity of the Holy Ghost is the necessary conclusion[1];' and there is reason to believe that he would have stated the doctrine of the Procession in the Western, not in the Eastern, form[2]; but we find a certain willingness to keep the doctrine in the background, which sufficiently indicates a failure to grasp its cardinal importance, and is, however natural in his circumstances and however interesting as evidence of his mode of thought, a blemish to the *De Trinitate*, if we seek in it a balanced exposition of the Faith[3].

We may now turn to the practical teaching of Hilary. Henceforth he will be no longer the compiler of the best Latin handbook of the Arian controversy, or the somewhat unsystematic investigator of unexplored regions of theology. We shall find him

---

6 If the word may be admitted for the sake of clearness. Hilary never calls the Spirit a Person.

7 §§ 23. 25, 30; so also ix. 69 and notably in x. 16. Similarly in *Comm in Matt.* iii. 1, the Spirit means Christ.

8 *Trin.* viii. 20, ix. 73 fin., and especially ii. 4. This last is not a reference to the Macedonian heresy, but to the logical result of Arianism.

9 *Trin.* i. 17, v. 1, 35, vii. 8, 31, viii. 31, 36, x. 6 **&c.**

1 Baltzer, *Theologie des hl. Hilarius*, p. 51.

2 *Trin.* viii. 21, xii. 55.

3 The work by Tertullian in which the doctrine of the Spirit is most fully brought out; in which, in fact, He is first expressly named God, is the *Adversus Praxean*. It was written after his secession from the Church, and Hilary, upon whom it had more influence than any other of Tertullian's writings, may have suspected that this teaching was the expression of his Montanism rather than a legitimate deduction from Scripture, and so have been misled by over caution. He may also have been influenced by such Biblical passages as Rev. xiv. 1, where the Spirit is unnamed.

often accepting the common stock of Christian ideas of his age, without criticism or attempt at improvement upon them ; often paraphrasing in even more emphatic language emphatic and apparently contradictory passages of Scripture, without any effort after harmony or balance. Yet sometimes we shall find him anticipating on one page the thoughts of later theologians, while on another he is content to repeat the views upon the same subject which had satisfied an earlier generation. His doctrine, where it is not traditional, is never more than tentative, and we must not be surprised, we must even expect, to find him inconsistent with himself.

No subject illustrates this inconsistency better than that of sin, of which Hilary gives two accounts, the one Eastern and traditional, the other an anticipation of Augustinianism. These are never compared and weighed the one against the other. In the passages where each appears, it is adduced confidently, without any reservation or hint that he is aware of another explanation of the facts of experience. The more usual account is that which is required by Hilary's doctrine of the separate creation of every human soul, which is good, because it is God's immediate work, and has a natural tendency to, and fitness for, perfection. Because God, after Whose image man is made, is free, therefore man also is free; he has absolute liberty, and is under no compulsion to good or to evil[4]. The sin which God foresees, as in the case of Esau, He does not foreordain[5]. Punishment never follows except upon sin actually committed ; the elect are they who show themselves worthy of election[6]. But the human body has defiled the soul ; in fact, Hilary sometimes speaks as though sin were not an act of will but an irresistible pressure exerted by the body on the soul. If we had no body, he says once, we should have no sin ; it is a 'body of death' and cannot be pure. This is the spiritual meaning of the ancient law against touching a corpse[7]. When the Psalmist laments that his soul cleaveth to the ground, his sorrow is that it is inseparably attached to a body of earth[8]; when Job and Jeremiah cursed the day of their birth, their anger was directed against the necessity of living surrounded by the weaknesses and vices of the flesh, not against the creation of their souls after the image of God[9]. Such language, if it stood alone, would convict its author of Manicheanism, but Hilary elsewhere asserts that the desire of the soul goes half-way to meet the invitation of sin[9a], and this latter in his normal teaching. Man has a natural proclivity to evil, an inherited weakness[1] which has, as a matter of experience, betrayed all men into actual sin, with the exception of Christ[2]. Elsewhere, however, Hilary recognises the possibility, under existing conditions, of a sinless life. For David could make the prayer, 'Take from me the way of iniquity;' of iniquity itself he was guiltless, and only needed to pray against the tendency inherent in his bodily nature[3]. But such a case is altogether exceptional; ordinary men must confide in the thought that God is indulgent, for He knows our infirmity. He is propitiated by the wish to be righteous, and in His judgment the merits of good men outweigh their sins[4]. Hence a prevalent tone of hopefulness about the future state of the baptized; even Sodom and Gomorrah, their punishment in history having satisfied the righteousness of God, shall ultimately be saved[5]. Yet God has a perfect, immutable goodness of which human goodness, though real, falls infinitely short, because He is steadfast and we are driven by varying impulses[6]. This Divine goodness is the standard and the hope set before us. It can only be attained by grace[7], and grace is freely offered. But just as the soul, being free, advances to meet sin, so it must advance to meet grace. Man must take the first step; he must wish and pray for grace, and then perseverance in

4 E.g. *Tr. in Ps.* ii. 16, li. 23.   5 *Ib.* lvii. 3.   6 *Ib.* cxviii., *Teth*, 4, lxiv. 5.   7 *Ib.* cxviii., *Gimel*, 3, 4. 8 *Ib.*, *Daleth*, 1.   9 *Ib.* cxix. 19 (12).   9a *Ib.* lxviii. 9.   1 E.g. *ib.* cxviii., *Aleph*, 8, lii. 12. *Natura infirmitatis* is a favourite phrase.

2 E.g. *ib.* lii. 9, cxviii., *Gimel*, 12, *Vau*, 6.   3 *Ib.* cxviii. *Daleth*, 8 ; cf. *He*, 16.   4 *Ib.* lii. 12.   5 *ib.* lxviii. 22, based on St. Matt. x. 15.   6 *Ib.* lii. 11, 12.   7 E.g. *ib.* cxviii., *Prolog.* 2, *Aleph*, 12, *Phe*, 3.

faith will be granted him [8], together with such a measure of the Spirit as he shall desire and deserve [9]. He will, indeed, be able to do more than he need, as David did when he spared and afterwards lamented Saul, his worst enemy, and St. Paul, who voluntarily abstained from the lawful privilege of marriage [1]. Such is Hilary's first account, 'a naive, undeveloped mode of thought concerning the origin of sin and the state of man [2].' Its inconsistencies are as obvious as their cause, the unguarded homiletical expansion of isolated passages. There is no attempt to reconcile man's freedom to be good with the fact of universal sin. The theory, so far as it is consistent, is derived from Alexandria, from Clement and Origen. It may seem not merely inadequate as theology, but philosophical rather than Christian; and its aim is, indeed, that of strengthening man's sense of moral responsibility and of heightening his courage to withstand temptation. But we must remember that Hilary everywhere assumes the union between the Christian and Christ. While this union exists there is always the power of bringing conduct into conformity with His will. Conduct, then, is, comparatively speaking, a matter of detail. Sins of action and emotion do not necessarily sever the union; a whole system of casuistry might be built upon Hilary's foundation. But false thoughts of God violate the very principle of union between Him and man. However abstract they may seem and remote from practical life, they are an insuperable barrier. For intellectual harmony, as well as moral, is necessary; and error of belief, like a key moving in a lock with whose wards it does not correspond, forbids all access to the nature and the grace of God. A good example of his relative estimate of intellectual and moral offences occurs in the Homily on Psalm i. §§ 6—8, where it is noteworthy that he does not trace back the former to moral causes [3].

Against these, the expressions of Hilary's usual opinion, must be set others in which he anticipates the language of St. Augustine in the Pelagian controversy. But certain deductions must be made, before we can rightly judge the weight of his testimony on the side of original sin. Passages where he is merely amplifying the words of Scripture must be excluded, as also those which are obviously exhibitions of unguarded rhetoric. For instance such words as these, 'Ever since the sin and unbelief of our first parent, we of later generations have had sin for the father of our body and unbelief for the mother of our soul [4],' contradicting as they do Hilary's well-known theory of the origin of the soul, cannot be regarded as giving his deliberate belief concerning sin. Again, we must be careful not to interpret strong language concerning the body (e.g. *Tr. in Ps.* cxviii., *Caph,* 5 *fin.*), as though it referred to our whole complex manhood. But after all deductions a good deal of strong Augustinianism remains. In the person of Adam God created all mankind, and all are implicated in his downfall, which was not only the beginning of evil but is a continuous power [5]. Not only as a matter of experience, is no man sinless, but no man can, by any possibility, be free from sin [6]. Because of the sin of one sentence is passed upon all [7]; the sentence of slavery which is so deep a degradation that the victim of sin forfeits even the name of man [8]. But Hilary not only states the doctrine; he approaches very nearly, on rare occasions, to the term 'original sin [9].' It follows that nothing less than a regeneration, the free gift of God, will avail [1]; and the grace by which the Christian must be maintained is also His spontaneous

---

8 *Tr. in Ps.* cxviii., *He.* 12, *Nun* 20. But in the former passage the perseverance also depends upon the Christian.

9 *Trin.* ii. 35.

1 *Tr. in Ps.* cxviii., *Nun,* 11 f.

2 Förster, *loc cit.*

3 So also the sin against the Holy Ghost is primarily intellectual, not ethical; *Comm. in Matt.* v. 15, xii. 17.

4 *Ib.* x. 23.

5 *Trin.* iv. 21; *Tr. in Ps.* lxvi. 2; *Comm. in Matt.* xviii. 6.

6 *Tr. in Ps.* cxviii., *He,* 16.

7 *Tr. in Ps.* lix. 4 *in.*

8 *Ib.* cxlii. 6, cxviii., *Ioá,* 2. In regard to the latter passage we must remember once more what importance Hilary attaches to names.

9 *Comm. in Matt.* x. 24, *originis nostræ peccata; Tr. in Ps.* cxviii., *Tau,* 6, *scit sub peccati origine et sub peccati lege se esse nitum.* Other passages must be cited from quotations in St. Augustine, but Förster, p. 676, has given reason for doubting Hilary's authorship.

1 E.g. *Comm. in Matt.* x. 24.

and unconditional gift. Faith, knowledge, Christian life, all have their origin and their maintenance from Him [2]. Such is a brief statement of Hilary's position as a forerunner of St. Augustine. The passages cited are scattered over his writings, from the earliest to the latest, and there is no sign that the more modern view was gaining ground in his mind as his judgment ripened. He had no occasion to face the question, and was content to say whatever seemed obviously to arise from the words under discussion, or to be most profitable to his audience. His Augustinianism, if it may be called so, is but one of many instances of originality, a thought thrown out but not developed. It is a symptom of revolt against the inadequate views of older theologians; but it had more influence upon the mind of his great successor than upon his own. Dealing, as he did, with the subject in hortatory writings, hardly at all, and only incidentally, in his formal treatise on the Trinity, he preferred to regard it as a matter of morals rather than of doctrine. And the dignity of man, impressed upon him by the great Alexandrians, seemed to demand for humanity the fullest liberty.

We may now turn to the Atonement, by which Christ has overcome sin. Hilary's language concerning it is, as a rule, simply Scriptural [3]. He had no occasion to discuss the doctrine, and his teaching is that which was traditional in his day, without any such anticipations of future thought as we found in his treatment of sin. Since the humanity of Christ is universal, His death was on behalf of all mankind, 'to buy the salvation of the whole human race by the offering of this holy and perfect Victim [4].' His last cry upon the Cross was the expression of His sorrow that some would not profit by His sacrifice; that He was not, as He had desired, bearing the sins of all [5]. He was able to take them upon Him because He had both natures. His manhood could do what His Godhead could not; it could atone for the sins of men. Man had been overcome by Satan; Satan, in his turn, has been overcome by Man. In the long conflict, enduring through Christ's life, of which the first pitched battle was the Temptation, the last the Crucifixion, the victory has been won by the Mediator in the flesh [6]. The devil was in the wrong throughout. He was deceived, or rather deceived himself, not recognising what it was for which Christ hungered [7]. The same delusion as to Christ's character led him afterwards to exact the penalty of sin from One Who had not deserved it [8]. Thus the human sufferings of Christ, unjustly inflicted, involve His enemy in condemnation and forfeit his right to hold mankind enslaved. Therefore we are set free [9], and the sinless Passion and death are the triumph of the flesh over spiritual wickedness and the vengeance of God upon it [1]. Man is set free, because he is justified in Christ, Who is Man. But the fact that Christ could do the works necessary to this end is proof that He is God. These works included the endurance of such suffering—in the sense, of course, which Hilary attaches to the word—as no one who was not more than man could bear. Hence he emphasises the Passion, because in so doing he magnifies the Divine nature of Him Who sustained it [2]. He sets forth the sufferings in the light of deeds, of displays of power [3], the greatest wonder being that the Son of God should have made Himself passible. Yet though it was from union with the Godhead that His humanity possessed the purity, the willingness, the power to win this victory, and though, in Hilary's words, it was immortal God Who died upon the Cross, still it was a victory won not by God but by the flesh [4]. But the Passion must not be regarded simply as an attack, ending in his own overthrow, made by Satan upon Christ. It is also a free satisfaction offered to God by Christ as Man, in order that His sufferings might release us from the punishment we had deserved, being accepted instead of ours [5]. This latter was a thought peculiarly

[2] *Tr. in Ps.* cxviii., *Vau*, 4, *Lamed*, 1; cf. *Nun*, 20.
[3] E.g. *Trin.* ix. 10; *Tr. in Ps.* cxxix. 9.
[4] *Tr. in Ps.* liii. 13 *fin.*   [5] *Comm. in Matt.* xxxiii. 6.
[6] *Ib.* iii. 2   [7] *Ib.* iii. 3.   [8] *Tr. in Ps.* lxviii. 8.

[9] *Tr. in Ps.* lxi. 2.   [1] *Trin.* ix. 7.   [2] E.g. *Trin.* x. 23, 47 *in.*
[3] E.g. *ib.* x. 11.   [4] *Comm. in Matt.* iii. 2.
[5] E.g. *Tr. in Ps.* liii. 12, 13 (translated in this volume)
lxiv. 4.

characteristic of the West, and especially of St. Cyprian's teaching; but Hilary has had his share in giving prominence to the propitiatory aspect of Christ's self-sacrifice [6]. Yet it must be confessed that the death of Christ is somewhat in the background; that Hilary is less interested in its positive value than in its negative aspect, as the cessation from earthly life and the transition to glory. Upon this, and upon the evidential importance of the Passion as a transcendent exertion of power, whereby the Son of God held Himself down and constrained Himself to suffer and die, Hilary chiefly dwells. The death has not, in his eyes, the interest of the Resurrection. The reason is that it does not belong to the course of the Incarnation as fore-ordained by God, but is only a modification of it, rendered necessary by the sinful self-will of man. Had there been no Fall, the visible, palpable flesh would still have been laid aside, though not by death upon the Cross, when Christ's work in the world was done; and there would have been some event corresponding to the Ascension, if not to the Resurrection. The body, laid aside on earth, would have been resumed in glory; and human flesh, unfallen and therefore not corrupt, yet free and therefore corruptible, would have entered into perfectly harmonious union with His Divinity, and so have been rendered safe from all possibility of evil. The purpose of raising man to the society of God was anterior to the beginnings of sin; and it is this broader conception that renders the Passion itself intelligible, while relegating it to a secondary place. But Hilary, though as a rule he mentions the subject not for its own sake but in the course of argument, has as firm a faith in the efficacy of Christ's death and of His continued intercession in His humanity for mankind [7] as he has in His triumphant Resurrection.

In regard to the manner in which man is to profit by the Atonement, Hilary shews the same inconsistency as in the case of sin. On the one hand, he lays frequent stress on knowledge concerning God and concerning the nature of sin as the first conditions of salvation; on the other, he insists, less often yet with equal emphasis, upon its being God's spontaneous gift to men, to be appropriated only by faith. We have already seen that one of Hilary's positions is that man must take the first step towards God; that if we will make the beginning He will give the increase [8]. This increase is the knowledge of God imparted to willing minds [9], which lifts them up to piety. He states strongly the superiority of knowledge to faith;—"There is a certain greater effectiveness in knowledge than in faith. Thus the writer here did not believe; he knew [1]. For faith has the reward of obedience, but it has not the assurance of ascertained truth. The Apostle has indicated the breadth of the interval between the two by putting the latter in the lower place in his list of the gifts of graces. 'To the first wisdom, to the next knowledge, to the third faith' is his message [2]; for he who believes may be ignorant even while he believes, but he who has come to know is saved by his possession of knowledge from the very possibility of unbelief [3]." This high estimation of sound knowledge was due, no doubt, to the intellectual character of the Arian conflict, in which each party retorted upon the other the charge of ignorance and folly; and it must have been confirmed by the observation that some who were conspicuous for the misinterpretation of Scripture were notorious also for moral obliquity. There was, however, that deeper reason which influenced all Hilary's thought; the conviction that if there is to be any harmony, any understanding between God and the soul of man, it must be a perfect harmony and understanding. And knowledge is pre-eminently the sphere in which this is possible, for the revelation of God is clear and precise, and unmistakeable in its import [4]. But there was another, a directly practical

---

6 Cf. Harnack, ii. 177; Schwane, ii. 271.

7 E.g. *Tr. in Ps.* liii. 4.

8 Cf. p. lxxxv. *fin.* In *Tr. in Ps.* cxviii., *Nun*, 20, Hilary says 'the reward of the consummation attained depends upon the initiative of the will;' so also *Trin.* i. 11.

9 *Tr. in Ps.* ii. 40.

1 Hilary is commenting on the words, 'I know, O Lord, that Thy judgments are right.'

2 1 Cor. xii. 8.   3 *Tr. in Ps.* cxviii., *Iod*, 12.

4 E.g. *Trin.* x. 70, xi. 1.

reason for this insistence.   Apprehension of Divine truths is the unfailing test of a Christian mind ; conduct changes and faith varies in intensity, but the facts of religion remain the same, and the believer can be judged by his attitude towards them.   Hence we cannot be surprised that Hilary maintains the insufficiency of 'simplicity of faith,' and ranks its advocates with heathen philosophers who regard purity of life as a substitute for religion. God, he says, has provided copious knowledge, with which we cannot dispense [5].   But this knowledge is to embrace not only the truth concerning God, but also concerning the realities of human life.   It is to be a knowledge of the fact that sins have been committed and an opening of the eyes to their enormity [6].   This will be followed by confession to God, by the promise to Him that we will henceforth regard sin as He regards it, and by the profession of a firm purpose to abandon it.   Here again the starting-point is human knowledge.   When the right attitude towards sin, intellectually and therefore morally, has been assumed, when there is the purpose of amendment and an earnest and successful struggle against sensual and worldly temptations, then we shall become 'worthy of the favour of God [7].'   In this light confession is habitually regarded [8] ; it is a voluntary moral act, a self-enlightenment to the realities of sin, necessarily followed by repugnance and the effort to escape, and antecedent to Divine pardon and aid.   But in contrast to this, Hilary's normal judgment, there are passages where human action is put altogether in the background.   Forgiveness is the spontaneous bounty of God, overflowing from the riches of His loving-kindness, and faith the condition of its bestowal and the means by which it is appropriated [9].   Even the Psalmist, himself perfect in all good works, prayed for mercy ; he put his whole trust in God, and so must we [1].   And faith precedes knowledge also, which is unattainable except by the believer [2].   Salvation does not come first, and then faith, but through faith is the hope of salvation ; the blind man believed before he saw [3].   Here again, as in the case of sin, we have two groups of statements without attempt at reconciliation ; but that which lays stress upon human initiative is far more numerous than the other, and must be regarded as expressing Hilary's underlying thought in his exhortations to Christian conduct, to his doctrine of which we may now turn.

We must first premise that Christ's work as our Example as well as our Saviour is fully recognised.   Many of his deeds on earth were done by way of dispensation, in order to set us a pattern of life and thought [4].   Christian life has, of course, its beginning in the free gift of Baptism, with the new life and the new faculties then bestowed, which render possible the illumination of the soul [5].   Hilary, as was natural at a time when Baptism was often deferred by professed Christians, and there were many converts from paganism, seems to contemplate that of adults as the rule ; and he feels it necessary to warn them that their Baptism will not restore them to perfect innocence.   In fact, by a strange conjecture tentatively made, he once suggests that our Baptism is that wherewith John baptized our Lord, and that the Baptism of the Holy Ghost awaits us hereafter, in cleansing fires beyond the grave or in the purification of martyrdom [6].   Hilary nowhere says in so many words that while Baptism abolishes sins previously committed, alms and other good deeds perform a similar office for later offences, but his view, which will be presently stated, concerning good works shews that he agreed in this respect with St. Cyprian ; neither, however, would hold that the good works were sufficient in ordinary cases without

---

[5] *Tr. in Ps.* cxviii., *prolog.* 4.

[6] *Ib.* cxxxv. 3 ; *confessio* is paraphrased by *professa cognitio.* Similar language is used in cxxxvii. 2 f.

[7] *Ib.* ii. 38 ; cf. lii. 12 *in.*, cxix. 11 (4).

[8] It is always confession to God directly.   There is no hint of public or ceremonial confession, or of absolution.   But Hilary's abstinence from allusion to the practical system of the Church is so complete that no argument can ever be drawn from his silence as to the existence, or the importance in his eyes, of her institutions.

[9] *Tr. in Ps.* lxvi. 2, lvi. 3.

[1] *Ib.* cxviii., *Koph*, 6.

[2] *Trin.* i. 12.   [3] *Comm. in Matt.* ix. 9.

[4] E.g. *Tr. in Ps.* liii. 7.   [5] E.g. *Trin.* i 18.

[6] *Tr. in Ps.* cxviii., *Gimel*, 5.   Hilary never mentions Confirmation.

the further purification. Martyrdoms had, of course, ceased in Hilary's day throughout the Roman empire, but it is interesting to observe that the old opinion, which had such power in the third century, still survived. The Christian, then, has need for fear, but he has a good hope, for all the baptized while in this world are still in the land of the living, and can only forfeit their citizenship by wilful and persistent unworthiness [7]. The means for maintaining the new life of effort is the Eucharist, which is equally necessary with Baptism [8]. But the Eucharist is one of the many matters of practical importance on which Hilary is almost silent, having nothing new to say, and being able to assume that his readers and hearers were well informed and of one mind with himself. His reticence is never a proof that he regarded them with indifference.

The Christian life is thus a life of hope and of high possibilities. But Hilary frankly and often recognises the serious short-comings of the average believers of his day [9]. Sometimes, in his zeal for their improvement and in the wish to encourage his flock, he even seems to condone their faults, venturing to ascribe to God what may almost be styled mere good-nature, as when he speaks of God, Himself immutable, as no stern Judge of our changefulness, but rather appeased by the wish on our part for better things than angry because we cannot perform impossibilities. But in this very passage [1] he holds up for our example the high attainment of the Saints, explaining that the Psalmist's words, 'There is none that doeth good, no not one,' refer only to those who are altogether gone out of the way and become abominable, and not to all mankind. Indeed, holding as he does that all Christians may have as much grace from God as they will take [2], and that the conduct which is therefore possible is also necessary to salvation, he could not consistently maintain the lower position. In fact, the standard of life which Hilary sets in the Homilies on the Psalms is very high. Cleanness of hand and heart is the first object at which we must aim [3], and the Law of God must be our delight. This is the lesson inculcated throughout his discourses on Psalm cxix. He recognises the complexity of life, with its various duties and difficulties, which are, however, a privilege inasmuch as there is honour to be won by victory over them [4]; and he takes a common-sense view of our powers and responsibilities [5]. But though his tone is buoyant and life in his eyes is well worth living for the Christian [6], he insists not merely upon a general purity of life, but upon renunciation of worldly pleasures. Like Cyprian, he would apparently have the wealthy believer dispose of his capital and spend his income in works of charity, without thought of economy [7]. Like Cyprian, again, he denounces the wearing of gold and jewellery [8], and the attendance at public places of amusement. Higher interests, spiritual and intellectual, must take the place of such dissipation. Sacred melody will be more attractive than the immodest dialogue of the theatre, and study of the course of the stars a more pleasing pursuit than a visit to the racecourse [9]. Yet strictly and even sternly Christian as Hilary is, he does not allow us altogether to forget that his is an age with another code than ours. Vengeance with him is a Christian motive. He takes with absolute literalness the Psalmist's imprecations [1]. Like every other emotion which he expresses, that of delight at the punishment of evil doers ought to have a place in the Christian soul. This was an inheritance from the days of persecution, which were still within the memory of living men. Cyprian often encourages the confessors to patience by the prospect of seeing the wrath of God upon their enemies; but he never gives so

---

[7] *Tr. in Ps.* li. 16, 17.

[8] E.g. *ib.* cxxxi. 23; *Trin.* viii. 13. The latter is the only passage in Hilary's writings in which the subject is discussed at length; and even here it is not introduced for its own sake.

[9] E.g. *Tr. in Ps.* i. 9 f., cxviii., *Koph*, 6. Conduct in church was not more exemplary than outside. The most innocent employment which he attributes to many of his people during the

reading of the lessons is the casting up of their business accounts, *Tr. in Ps.* cxxxv. 1.

[1] *Tr. in Ps.* lii. 9—12.

[2] *Trin.* ii. 35.

[3] *Tr. in Ps.* cxviii., *Aleph*, 1.

[4] *Ib. Phe*, 9.

[5] *Ib.* i. 12.

[6] E.g. *Trin.* i. 14, vi. 19.

[7] *Ib.* li. 21.

[8] *Ib.* cxviii., *Ain*, 16, 17.

[9] *Ib., He*, 14.

[1] E.g. *ib.* liii. 10.

strong expression to the feeling as Hilary does, when he enforces obedience to our Lord's command to turn the other cheek by the consideration that fuller satisfaction will be gained if the wrong be stored up against the Day of Judgment [2]. There is something hard and Puritan in the tone which Hilary has caught from the men of the times of persecution ; and his conflict with heretics gave him ample opportunity for indulgence in the thought of vengeance upon them. This was no mere pardonable excitement of feeling ; it was a Christian duty and privilege to rejoice in the future destruction of his opponents. But there is an even stranger difference between his standard and ours. Among the difficulties of keeping in the strait and narrow way he reckons that of truthfulness. A lie, he says, is often necessary, and deliberate falsehood sometimes useful [3]. We may mislead an assassin, and so enable his intended victim to escape ; our testimony may save a defendant who is in peril in the courts ; we may have to cheer a sick man by making light of his ailment. Such are the cases in which the Apostle says that our speech is to be 'seasoned with salt.' It is not the lie that is wrong ; the point of conscience is whether or no it will inflict injury upon another. Hilary is not alone in taking falsehood lightly [4], and allowance must be made for the age in which he lived. And his words cast light upon the history of the time. The constant accusations made against the character and conduct of theological opponents, which are so painful a feature of the controversies of the early centuries, find their justification in the principle which Hilary has stated. No harm was done, rather a benefit was conferred upon mankind, if a false teacher could be discredited in a summary and effective manner ; such was certainly a thought which presented itself to the minds of combatants, both orthodox and heterodox. Apart from these exceptions, which, however, Hilary would not have regarded as such, his standard of life, as has been said, is a high one both in faith and in practice, and his exhortation is full of strong common sense. It is, however, a standard set for educated people ; there is little attention paid to those who are safe from the dangers of intellect and wealth. The worldliness which he rebukes is that of the rich and influential ; and his arguments are addressed to the reading class, as are his numerous appeals to his audience in the Homilies on the Psalms to study Scripture for themselves. Indeed, his advice to them seems to imply that they have abundant leisure for spiritual exercises and for reflection. But he does not simply ignore the illiterate, still mostly pagans, for the work of St. Martin of Tours only began, as we saw, in Hilary's last days ; in one passage at least he speaks with the scorn of an ancient philosopher of 'the rustic mind,' which will fail to find the meaning of the Psalms [5].

Hilary is not content with setting a standard which his flock must strive to reach. He would have them attain to a higher level than is commanded, and at the same time constantly remember that they are failing to perform their duty to God. This higher life is set before his whole audience as their aim. He recognises the peculiar honour of the widow and the virgin [6], but has singularly little to say about these classes of the Christian community, or about the clergy, and no special counsel for them. The works of supererogation—the word is not his—which he preaches are within the reach of all Christians. They consist in the more perfect practice of the ordinary virtues. King

---

[2] *Tr. in Ps.* cxxxvii. 16. Cf. *Trin.* x. 55, where he refuses to believe that it was with real sorrow that our Lord wept over Jerusalem, that godless and murderous city. His tears were a 'dispensa-tion.'

[3] *Tr. in Ps.* xiv. 10, *est enim necessarium plerumque mendacium, et nonnunquam falsitas utilis est.* The latter apparently refers to his second example.

[4] Hermas, *Mand.* iii. 3, confesses to wholesale lying ; he had never heard that it was wrong. But the writer of the *Shepherd*

does not represent his mouthpiece as a model of virtue. It is more significant that Tertullian, *Pud.* 19, classes breach of trust and lying among slight sins which may happen to any one any day. This was in his strictest and most censorious period. There are grave difficulties in reconciling some of Cyprian's statements concerning his opponents with one another and with probability, but he has not ventured upon any general extenuation of the vice.

[5] *Tr. in Ps.* cxxxiv. 1.

[6] *Ib.* cxxxi. 24, cxxvii. 7, and especially cxviii., *Nun*, 14.

David 'was not content henceforth to be confined to the express commands of the Law, nor to be subject to a mere necessity of obedience.' 'The Prophet prays that these free-will offerings may be acceptable to God, because the deeds done in compliance to the Law's edict are performed under the actual compulsion of servitude [7]. As an instance he gives the character of David. His duty was to be humble; he made himself humble exceedingly, thus doing more than he was legally bound to do. He spared his enemies so far as in him lay, and bewailed their death; this was a free service to which he was bound by no compulsion. Such conduct places those who practice it on the same level with those whose lives are formally consecrated; the state of the latter being regarded, as always in early times, as admirable in itself, and not as a means towards higher things. Vigils and fasts and acts of mercy are the methods advocated by Hilary for such attainment. But they must not stand alone, nor must the Christian put his trust in them. Humility must have faith for its principle, and fasting be combined with charity [8]. And the Christian must never forget that though he may in some respects be doing more than he need, yet in others he is certainly falling short. For the conflict is unceasing; the devil, typified by the mountains in the Psalm, has been touched by God and is smoking, but is not yet burning and powerless for mischief [9]. Hence there is constant danger lest the Christian fall into unbelief or unfruitfulness, sins equally fatal [1]; he must not trust in himself, either that he can deserve forgiveness for the past or resist future temptations [2]. Nor may he dismiss his past offences from his memory. It can never cease to be good for us to confess our former sins, even though we have become righteous. St. Paul did not allow himself to forget that he had persecuted the Church of God [3]. But there is a further need than that of penitence. Like Cyprian before him and Augustine after him, Hilary insists upon the value of alms in the sight of God. The clothing of the naked, the release of the captive plead with God for the remission of our sins [4]; and the man who redeems his faults by alms is classed among those who win His favour, with the perfect in love and the blameless in faith [5].

Thus the thought of salvation by works greatly preponderates over that of salvation by grace. Hilary is fearful of weakening man's sense of moral responsibility by dwelling too much upon God's work which, however, he does not fail to recognise. Of the two great dangers, that of faith and that of life, the former seemed to him the more serious. God's requirements in that respect were easy of fulfilment; He had stated the truth and He expected it to be unhesitatingly accepted. But if belief, being an exertion of the will, was easy, misbelief must be peculiarly and fatally wicked. The confession of St. Peter, the foundation upon which the Church is built, is that Christ is God [6]; the sin against the Holy Ghost is denial of this truth [7]. These are the highest glory and the deepest shame of man. It does not seem that Hilary regarded any man, however depraved, as beyond hope so long as he did not dispute this truth; he has no code of mortal sins. But heresy concerning Christ, whatever the conduct and character of the heretic, excludes all possibility of salvation, for it necessarily cuts him off from the one Faith and the one Church which are the condition and the sphere of growth towards perfection; and the

---

[7] *Tr. in Ps.* cxviii., *Nun*, 13, 15. It is in this passage that Hilary gives his views most fully. His antithesis is between *legitima* and *voluntaria*.

[8] l.c. *Nun*, 14, *Comm. in Matt.* v. 2. In the latter passage there is a piece of practical advice which shews that public fasts were generally recognised. Hilary tells his readers that they must not take literally our Lord's command to anoint themselves when they fast. If they do, they will render themselves conspicuous and ridiculous. The passage, *Comm. in Matt.* xxvii. 5, 6, on the parables of the Virgins with their lamps and of the Talents cannot be taken, as by Förster, as evidence that Hilary rejected the later doctrine of the supererogatory righteousness of the Saints. He is speaking of the impossibility of contemporaries conveying righteousness to one another in the present life, and his words have no bearing on that doctrine.

[9] *Tr. in Ps.* cxliii. 11.   [1] *Ib.* li. 16.

[2] E.g. *ib.* lxi. 6, cxviii., *He,* 12, *Nun,* 20, *Koph,* 6.

[3] *Ib.* cxxxv. 4.   [4] *Ib.* li. 21.

[5] *Ib.* cxviii , *Lamed,* 15. Similar passages are fairly numerous; e.g. *Comm. in Matt.* iv. 26.

[6] *Trin.* vi. 36.

[7] *Comm. in Matt.* xii. 17, xxxi. 5.

severance is just, because misbelief is a wilful sin. Since, then, compliance or non-compliance with one of God's demands, that for faith in His revelation, depends upon the will, it was natural that Hilary should lay stress upon the importance of the will in regard to God's other demand, that for a Christian life. This was, in a sense, a lighter requirement, for various degrees of obedience were possible. Conduct could neither give nor deny faith, but only affect its growth, while without the frank recognition of the facts of religion no conduct could be acceptable to God. Life presents to the will a constantly changing series of choices between good and evil, while the Faith must be accepted or rejected at once and as a whole. It is clear from Hilary's insistence upon this that the difficulties, apart from heresy, with which he had to contend resembled those of Mission work in modern India. There were many who would accept Christianity as a revelation, yet had not the moral strength to live in conformity with their belief. Of such persons Hilary will not despair. They have the first essential of salvation, a clear and definite acceptance of doctrinal truth; they have also the offer of sufficient grace, and the free will and power to use it. And time and opportunity are granted, for the vicissitudes of life form a progressive education; they are, if taken aright, the school, the training-ground, for immortality [8]. This is because all Christians are in Christ, by virtue of His Incarnation. They are, as St. Paul says, complete in Him, furnished with the faith and hope they need. But this is only a preparatory completeness; hereafter they shall be complete in themselves, when the perfect harmony is attained and they are conformed to His glory [9]. Thus to the end the dignity and responsibility of mankind is maintained. But it is obvious that Hilary has failed to correlate the work of Christ with the work of the Christian. The necessity of His guidance and aid, and the manner in which these are bestowed, is sufficiently stated, and the duty of the Christian man is copiously and eloquently enforced. But the importance of Christ's work within Himself, in harmonising the two natures, has withdrawn most of Hilary's attention from His work within the believing soul; and the impression which Hilary's writings leave upon the mind concerning the Saviour and redeemed mankind is that of allied forces seeking the same end but acting independently, each in a sphere of its own.

There still remains to be considered Hilary's account of the future state. The human soul, being created after the image of God, is imperishable; resurrection is as inevitable as death [1]. And the resurrection will be in the body, for good and bad alike. The body of the good will be glorified, like that of Christ; its substance will be the same as in the present life, its glory such that it will be in all other respects a new body [2]. Indeed, the true life of man only begins when this transformation takes place [3]. No such change awaits the wicked; we shall all rise, but we shall not all be changed, as St. Paul says [4]. They remain as they are, or rather are subjected to a ceaseless process of deterioration, whereby the soul is degraded to the level of the body, while this in the case of others is raised, either instantly or by a course of purification, to the level of the soul [5]. Their last state is vividly described in language which recalls that of Virgil; crushed to powder and dried to dust they will fly for ever before the wind of God's wrath [6]. For the thoroughly good and the thoroughly bad the final state begins at the moment of death. There is no judgment for either class, but only for those whose character contains elements of both good and evil [7]. But perfect goodness is only a theoretical possibility, and Hilary is not certain of the condemnation of any except wilful unbelievers. Evil is mingled in varying proportions with good in the character of men at large; God can detect it in the very best. All therefore

[8] *Trin.* i. 14.   [9] *Ib.* ix. 8, commenting on Col. ii. 10.   [5] *Comm. in Matt.* x. 19.   [6] *Tr. in Ps.* i. 19.
[1] *Tr. in Ps.* li. 18, lxiii. 9.   [2] *Ib.* ii. 41.   [7] *Ib.* i. 19 ff., translated in this volume. For the good, see
[3] *Ib.* cxviii., *Gimel*, 3.   [4] *Ib.* lii. 17.   also *ib.* lvii. 7; for the bad, lvii. 5, *Trin.* vi 3.

need to be purified after death, if they are to escape condemnation on the Day of Judgment. Even the Mother of our Lord needs the purification of pain; this is the sword which should pierce through her soul[8]. All who are infected by sin, the heretic who has erred in ignorance among them[9], must pass through cleansing fires after death. Then comes the general Resurrection. To the good it brings the final change to perfect glory; the bad will rise only to return to their former place[1]. The multitude of men will be judged, and after the education and purification of suffering to which, by God's mercy, they have been submitted, will be accepted by Him. Hilary's writings contain no hint that any who are allowed to present themselves on the Day of Judgment will then be rejected.

We have now completed the survey of Hilary's thoughts. Many of these were strange and new to his contemporaries, and his originality, we may be sure, deprived him of some of the influence he wished to exert in the controversies of his day. Yet he shared the spirit and entered heartily into the interests and conflicts of his age, and therefore his thoughts in many ways were different from our own. To this we owe, no doubt, the preservation of his works; writings which anticipated modern opinion would have been powerless for good in that day, and would not have survived to ours. Thus from his own century to ours Hilary has been somewhat isolated and neglected, and even misunderstood. Yet he is one of the most notable figures in the history of the early Church, and must be numbered among those who have done most to make Christian thought richer and more exact. If we would appreciate him aright as one of the builders of the dogmatic structure of the Faith, we must omit from the materials of our estimate a great part of his writings, and a part which has had a wider influence than any other. His interpretation of the letter, though not of the spirit, of Scripture must be dismissed; interesting as it always is, and often suggestive, it was not his own and was a hindrance, though he did not see it, to the freedom of his thought. Yet his exegesis in detail is often admirable. For instance, it would not be easy to overpraise his insight and courage in resisting the conventional orthodoxy, sanctioned by Athanasius in his own generation and by Augustine in the next, which interpreted St. Paul's 'First-born of every creature' as signifying the Incarnation of Christ, and not His eternal generation[2]. We must omit also much that Hilary borrowed without question from current opinion; it is his glory that he concentrated his attention upon some few questions of supreme importance, and his strength, not his weakness, that he was ready to adopt in other matters the best and wisest judgments to which he had access. An intelligent, and perhaps ineffective, curiosity may keep itself abreast of the thought of the time, to quote a popular phrase; Hilary was content to survey wide regions of doctrine and discipline with the eyes of Origen and of Cyprian. This limitation of the interests of a powerful mind has enabled him to penetrate further into the mysteries of the Faith than any of his predecessors; to points, in fact, where his successors have failed to establish themselves. We cannot blame him that later theologians, starting where he left off, have in some directions advanced further still. The writings of Hilary are the quarry whence many of the best thoughts of Ambrose and of Leo are hewn. Eminent and successful as these men were, we cannot rank them with Hilary as intellectually his equals; we may even wonder how many of their conclusions they would have drawn had not Hilary supplied the premises. It is a greater honour that the unrivalled genius of Augustine is deeply indebted to him. Nor may we blame him, save lightly, for some rashness and error in his speculations. He set out, unwillingly, as we know, but not half-heartedly, upon his novel journey of exploration. He had not, as we have, centuries of criticism behind him, and could not know that some of the

---

[8] *Tr. in Ps.* cxviii., *Gimel,* 12.   [9] *Trin.* vi. 3.   [1] *Tr. in Ps.* lii. 17, lxix. 3.
[2] *Trin.* viii. 50; *Tr. in Ps.* ii. 28. Cf. Lightfoot on Col. i. 15.

avenues he followed would lead him astray. It may be that we are sober because we are, in a sense, disillusioned; that modern Christian thought which starts from the old premisses tends to excess of circumspection. And certainly Hilary would not have earned his fame as one of the most original and profound of teachers, whose view of Christology is one of the most interesting in the whole of Christian antiquity [3], had he not been inspired by a sense of freedom and of hope in his quest. Yet great as was his genius and reverent the spirit in which he worked, the errors into which he fell, though few, were serious. There are instances in which he neglects his habitual balancing of corresponding infinities; as when he shuts his eyes to half the revelation, and asserts that Christ could not be ignorant and could not feel pain. And there is that whole system of dispensations which he has built up in explanation of Christ's life on earth; a system against which our conscience and our common sense rebel, for it contradicts the plain words of Scripture and attributes to God 'a process of Divine reserve which is in fact deception [4].' We may compare Hilary's method in such cases to the architecture of Gloucester and of Sherborne, where the ingenuity of a later age has connected and adorned the massive and isolated columns of Norman date by its own light and graceful drapery of stonework. We cannot but admire the result; yet there is a certain concealment of the original design, and perhaps a perilous cutting away of the solid structure. But, in justice to Hilary, we must remember that in these speculations he is venturing away from the established standards of doctrine. When he is enunciating revealed truths, or arguing onward from them to conclusions towards which they point, he has the company of the Creeds, or at least they indicate the way he must go. But in explaining the connection between doctrine and doctrine he is left to his own guidance. It is as though a traveller, not content to acquaint himself with the highroads, should make his way over hedge and ditch from one of them to another; he will not always hit upon the best and straightest course. But at least Hilary's conclusions, though sometimes erroneous, were reached by honest and reverent reasoning, and neither ancient nor modern theology can afford to reproach him. The tendency of the former, especially after the rise of Nestorius, was to exaggerate some of his errors; and the latter has failed to develope and enforce some of his highest teaching.

This is, indeed, worthy of all admiration. On the moral side of Christianity we see him insisting upon the voluntary character of Christ's work; upon His acts of will, which are a satisfaction to God and an appeal to us [5]. On the intellectual side we find the Unity in Trinity so luminously declared that Bishop French of Lahore, one of the greatest of missionaries, had the works of Hilary constantly in his hands, and contemplated a translation of the *De Trinitate* into Arabic for the benefit of Mohammedans [6]. This was not because Hilary's explanation of our Lord's sufferings might seem to commend the Gospel to their prejudices; such a concession would have been repugnant to French's whole mode of thought. It was because in the central argument on behalf of the Godhead of Christ, where he had least scope for originality of thought, Hilary has never suffered himself to become a mere mechanical compiler. The light which he has cast upon his sub-

---

[3] Dorner, I. ii. 399.

[4] Gore, *Dissertations*, p. 151.

[5] Schwane, ii. 271, says, 'Though we reject that part of it which attributes a natural impassibility to the body of Christ, yet Hilary's exposition presents one truth more clearly than the earlier Fathers had stated it, by giving to the doctrine of the representative satisfaction of Christ its reasonable explanation as a *free* service of satisfaction. He conceives rightly of the Lord's whole life on earth, with all its troubles and infirmities, as a sacrifice of free love on the part of the God-Man; it is only his closer definition of this sacrifice that is inaccurate. . . . Hilary lays especial stress upon the freedom of the Lord's acceptance of death.' He quotes *Trin.* x. 11.

[6] He had evidently been long familiar with it (*Life*, i. 155), but the first mention of its use for missionary purposes is in 1862 (*ib.* i. 137). He began the translation into Arabic at Tunis in 1890, after his resignation of the bishopric of Lahore (ii. 333), but it seems doubtful whether he was able to make any progress with it at Muscat. His biographer says nothing of the amount actually accomplished.

ject, though clear, is never hard ; and the doctrine which, because it was attractive to himself, he has made attractive to his readers, is that of the unity of God, the very doctrine which is of supreme importance in Mohammedan eyes [7].

But, above all, it is Hilary's doctrine concerning the Incarnation as the eternal purpose of God for the union of the creature with the Creator, that must excite our interest and awaken our thoughts. He renders it, on the one hand, impossible to rate too highly the dignity of man, created to share the nature and the life of God ; impossible, on the other hand, to estimate highly enough the condescension of Christ in assuming humanity. It is by His humiliation that we are saved ; by the fact that the nature of man was taken by his Maker, not by the fact that Christ, being man, remained sinless. For sin began against God's will and after His counsel was formed ; it might deflect the march of His purpose towards fulfilment, but could no more impede its consummation than it could cause its inception. The true salvation of man is not that which rescues him, when corrupt, from sin and its consequences, but that which raises him, corruptible, because free, even though he had not become corrupt, into the safety of union with the nature of God. Human life, though pure from actual sin, would have been aimless and hopeless without the Incarnation. And the human body would have had no glory, for its glory is that Christ has taken it, worn it awhile in its imperfect state, laid it aside and finally resumed it in its perfection. All this He must have done, in accordance with God's purpose, even though the Fall had never occurred. Hence the Incarnation and the Resurrection are the facts of paramount interest ; the death of Christ, corresponding as it does to the hypothetical laying aside of the unglorified flesh, loses something of its usual prominence in Christian thought. It is represented as being primarily for Christ the moment of transition, for the Christian the act which enables him to profit by the Incarnation ; but it is the Incarnation itself whereby, in Hilary's words, we are saved into the nature and the name of God. But though we may feel that this great truth is not stated in its full impressiveness, we must allow that the thought which has taken the foremost place is no mere academic speculation. And, after all, sin and the Atonement are copiously treated in his writings, though they do not control his exposition of the Incarnation. Yet even in this there are large spaces of his argument where these considerations have a place, though only to give local colour, so to speak, and a sense of reality to the description of a purpose formed and a work done for man because he is man, not because he is fallen. But if Hilary has somewhat erred in placing the Cross in the background, he is not in error in magnifying the scope of the reconciliation [8] which includes it as in a wider horizon. Man has in Christ the nature of God ; the infinite Mind is intelligible to the finite. The Creeds are no dry statement of facts which do not touch our life ; the truths they contain are the revelation of God's self to us. Not for the pleasure of weaving theories, but in the interests of practical piety, Hilary has fused belief and conduct into the unity of that knowledge which Isaiah foresaw and St. John possessed ; the knowledge which is not a means towards life, but life itself.

---

[7] For Bishop French's view of the importance of this doctrine, see his *Life*, i. 84.

[8] Compare Bishop Lightfoot' comprehensive words on Col. i.

20. The reconciliation of mankind implies 'a restitution to a state from which they had fallen, or which was potentially theirs, or for which they were destined.'

INTRODUCTION TO THE TREATISE
DE SYNODIS.

HILARY had taken no part in the Synod held at Ancyra in the spring of A.D. 358, but he had been made acquainted with its decisions and even with the anathemas which the legates of that Synod concealed at Sirmium. He saw that these decisions marked an approach. The horror which was felt at the Sirmian *Blasphemia* by those Eusebians whose only objection to the Nicene faith was that they did not understand it, augured well for the future. At the same time the majority of the Eastern bishops were deliberately heretical. It was natural that Hilary should be anxious about the episcopate of the West.

He had been in exile about three years and had corresponded with the Western bishops. From several quarters letters had now ceased to arrive, and the fear came that the bishops did not care to write to one whose convictions were different to their own. Great was his joy when, at the end of the year 358, he received a letter which not only explained that the innocent cause of their silence was ignorance of his address, but also that they had persistently refused communion with Saturninus and condemned the *Blasphemia*.

Early in 359 he dispatched to them the *Liber de Synodis*. It is a double letter, addressed to Western bishops, but containing passages intended for Orientals, into whose hands the letter would doubtless come in time. Hilary had recognized that the orthodox of the West had kept aloof from the orthodox of the East, firstly from ignorance of events, secondly from misunderstanding of the word ὁμοούσιος, and thirdly from the feelings of distrust then prevalent. These facts determined the contents of his letter.

He begins with an expression of the delight he experienced on receiving the news that the Gallican bishops had condemned the notorious Sirmian formula. He praises the constancy of their faith.

He then mentions that he has received from certain of their number a request that he would furnish them with an account of the creeds which had been composed in the East. He modestly accedes to this request beseeching his readers not to criticise his letter until they have read the whole letter and mastered the complete argument. His aim throughout is to frustrate the heretic and assist the Catholic.

In the first or historical division of the letter he promises a transcription, with explanations, of all the creeds drawn up since the Council of Nicæa. He protests that he is not responsible for any statement contained in these creeds, and leaves his readers to judge of their orthodoxy.

The Greek confessions had already been translated into Latin, but Hilary considered it necessary to give his own independent translations, the previous versions having been half-unintelligible on account of their slavish adherence to the original.

The historical part of the book consists of fifty-four chapters (c. 10—63). It begins with the second Sirmian formula, and the opposing formula promulgated at Ancyra in A.D. 358. The Sirmian creed being given in c. 10, Hilary, before proceeding to give the twelve anathemas directed against its teaching by the bishops who assembled at Ancyra, explains the meaning of *essentia* and *substantia*. Concerning the former he says, *Essentia est res quae est, vel ex quibus est, et quae in eo quod maneat subsistit.* This *essen'ia* is therefore identical with *substantia, quia res quae est necesse est subsistat in sese.* The Ancyran anathemas are then appended, with notes and a summary.

In the second division (c. 29—33) of the historical part, Hilary considers the Dedication creed drawn up at Antioch in A.D. 341. He interprets it somewhat favourably. After stating that the creed is perhaps not sufficiently explicit in declaring the exact likeness of the Father and the Son, he excuses this inadequacy by pointing out that the Synod was not held to contradict Anomœan teaching, but teaching of a Sabellian tendency. The complete similarity of the Son's essence to that of the Father appears to him to be guarded by the phrase *Deum de Deo, totum ex toto.*

The third division (c. 34—37) contains the creed drawn up by the Synod, or Cabal Synod, which met at Philippopolis in A.D. 343. Hilary does not discuss the authority of the Synod; it was enough for his purpose that it was composed of Orientals, and that its language emphatically condemns genuine Arianism and asserts the Son is *God of God.* The anathema which the creed pronounces on those who declare the Son to have been begotten without the Father's will, is interpreted by Hilary as an assertion that the eternal Birth was not conditioned by those passions which affect human generation.

The fourth division (c. 38—61) contains the long formula drawn up at Sirmium in A.D. 351 against Photinus. The twenty-seven anathemas are then separately considered and commended. The two remaining chapters of the historical part of the work include a reflection on the many-sided character of these creeds both in their positive and negative aspects. God is *infinitus et immensus*, and therefore short statements concerning His nature may often prove misleading. The bishops have used many definitions and phrases because clearness will remove a danger. These frequent definitions would have been quite unnecessary if it had not been for the prevalence of heresy. Asia as a whole is ignorant of God, presenting a piteous contrast to the fide'ity of the Western bishops.

The theological part of the work opens in c. 64 with Hilary's exposition of his own belief. He denies that there is in God only one personality, as he denies that there is any difference of substance. The Father is greater in that He is Father, the Son is not less because He is Son. He asks his readers to remember that if his words fall short, his meaning is sound. This done, he passes to discuss the meaning of the word ὁμοούσιον. Three wrong meanings may be attributed to it. Firstly, it may be understood to deny the personal distinctions in the Trinity. Secondly, it may be thought to imply that the divine essence is capable of division. Thirdly, it may be represented as implying that the Father and the Son both equally partake of one prior substance. A short expression like ὁμοούσιος must therefore receive an exact explanation. A risk is attached to its use, but there is no risk if we understand it to mean that the Father is unbegotten and the Son derives His being from the Father, and is like Him in power, and honour, and nature. The Son is subordinate to the Father as to the Author of His being, yet it was not by a robbery that He made Himself equal with God. He is not from nothing. He is wholly God. He is not the Author of the divine life, but the Image. He is no creature, but is God. Not a second God, but one God with the Father through similarity of essence. This is the ideal meaning of ὁμοούσιος, and in this sense it is not an error to assert, but to deny, the consubstantiality.

Hilary then makes a direct appeal to the Western bishops. They might forget the contents of the word while retaining the sound, but provided that the meaning was granted what objection could be made to the word? Was the word ὁμοιούσιον free from all possible objections? Hilary (c. 72—75) shews that *really like* means *really equal.* Scripture is appealed to as proving the assertion that the Son is both like God and equal to God. This essential likeness can alone justify the statement that the Father and the Son are one.

is blasphemous to represent the similarity as a mere analogy. The similitude is a similitude of proper nature and equality. The conclusion of the argument is that the word ὁμοιούσιος, if understood, leads us to the word ὁμοούσιος which helps to guard it, and that it does not imply any separation between the Persons of the Trinity.

The saint now turns to the Eastern bishops, a small number of whom still remained faithful. He bestows upon them titles of praise, and expresses his joy at the decisions they had made, and at the Emperor's repudiation of his former mistake. With Pauline fervour Hilary exclaims that he would remain in exile all his life, if only truth might be preached.

Then, in a chapter which displays alike his knowledge of the Bible and his power of refined sarcasm, he unveils his suspicions concerning Valens and Ursacius. He doubts whether they could have been so inexperienced as to be ignorant of the meaning of the word ὁμοούσιοι when they signed the third Sirmian Creed. Furthermore he is obliged to point out a defect in the letter which the Oriental bishops wrote at the Synod of Ancyra. The word ὁμοούσιον is there rejected. The three grounds for such rejection could only be that the word was thought to imply a prior substance, or the teaching of Paul of Samosata, or that the word was not in Scripture. The first two grounds were only illusions, the third was equally fatal to the word ὁμοιούσιον. Those who intelligibly maintained ὁμοούσιον or ὁμοιούσιον, meant the same thing and condemned the same impiety (c. 82). Why should any one wish to decline the word which the Council of Nicæa had used for an end which was unquestionably good? The argument is enforced by the insertion of the Nicene Creed in full. True, the word ὁμοούσιον is quite capable of misconstruction. But the application of this test to the difficult passages in the Bible would lead to the chaos of all belief. The possible abuse of the word does not abolish its use. The authority of the eighty bishops who condemned the Samosatene abuse of it does not affect the authority of the three hundred and eighteen who ratified its Nicene meaning. Hilary adds a statement of great importance. Before he was acquainted with the term he had personally believed what it implied. The term has merely invigorated his previous faith (c. 88, cf. c. 91). In other words, Hilary tells his contemporaries and tells posterity that the word ὁμοούσιον is Scripture because it is the sense of Scripture, and is truly conservative because it alone adequately preserves the faith of the fathers. The argument is interwoven with a spirited appeal to the Eastern bishops to return to that faith as expressed at Nicæa.

The last chapter (c. 92) is addressed to the Western bishops. It modestly defends the action of Hilary in writing, and urges a corresponding energy on the part of his readers. The whole concludes with a devout prayer.

The *Liber de Synodis*, like other works in which Catholicism has endeavoured to be conciliatory, did not pass unchallenged. It satisfied neither the genuine Arian nor the violently orthodox. The notes or fragments which we call Hilary's Apology throw light upon the latter fact. Hilary has to explain that he had not meant that the Eastern bishops had stated the true faith at Ancyra, and tells his *Lord and brother Lucifer* that it was against his will that he had mentioned the word ὁμοιούσιον. We must ourselves confess that Hilary puts an interpretation on the meaning of the Eastern formulæ which would have been impossible if he had written after the Synod of Ariminum. Speaking when he did, his arguments were not only pardonable but right.

ON THE COUNCILS,

OR,

THE FAITH OF THE EASTERNS.

To the most dearly loved and blessed brethren our fellow-bishops of the province of Germania Prima and Germania Secunda, Belgica Prima and Belgica Secunda, Lugdunensis Prima and Lugdunensis Secunda, and the province of Aquitania, and the province of Novempopulana, and to the laity and clergy of Tolosa in the Provincia Narbonensis, and to the bishops of the provinces of Britain, Hilary the servant of Christ, eternal salvation in God our Lord.

I had determined, beloved brethren, to send no letter to you concerning the affairs of the Church in consequence of your prolonged silence. For when I had by writing from several cities of the Roman world frequently informed you of the faith and efforts of our religious brethren, the bishops of the East, and how the Evil One profiting by the discords of the times had with envenomed lips and tongue hissed out his deadly doctrine, I was afraid. I feared lest while so many bishops were involved in the serious danger of disastrous sin or disastrous mistake, you were holding your peace because a defiled and sinstained conscience tempted you to despair. Ignorance I could not attribute to you; you had been too often warned. I judged therefore that I also ought to observe silence towards you, carefully remembering the Lord's saying, that those who after a first and second entreaty, and in spite of the witness of the Church, neglect to hear, are to be unto us as heathen men and publicans[1].

2. But when I received the letters that your blessed faith inspired, and understood that their slow arrival and their paucity were due to the remoteness and secrecy of my place of exile, I rejoiced in the Lord that you had continued pure and undefiled by the contagion of any execrable heresy, and that you were united with me in faith and spirit, and so were partakers of that exile into which Saturninus, fearing his own conscience, had thrust me after beguiling the Emperor, and after that you had denied him communion for the whole three years ago until now. I equally rejoiced that the impious and infidel creed which was sent straightway to you from Sirmium was not only not accepted by you, but condemned as soon as reported and notified. I felt that it was now binding on me as a religious duty to write sound and faithful words to you as my fellow-bishops, who communicate with me in Christ. I, who through fear of what might have been could at one time only rejoice with my own conscience that I was free from all these errors, was now bound to express delight at the purity of our common faith. Praise God for the unshaken stability of your noble hearts, for your firm house built on the foundation of the faithful rock, for the undefiled and unswerving constancy of a will that has proved immaculate! For since the good profession at the Council of Biterræ, where I denounced the ringleaders of this heresy with some of you for my witnesses, it has remained and still continues to remain, pure, unspotted and scrupulous.

3. You awaited the noble triumph of a holy and steadfast perseverance without yielding to the threats, the powers and the assaults of Saturninus: and when all the waves of awakening blasphemy struggled against God, you who still remain with me faithful in Christ did not give way when threatened with the onset of heresy, and now by meeting that onset you have broken all its violence. Yes, brethren, you have conquered, to the abundant joy of those who share your faith: and your unimpaired constancy gained the double glory of keeping a pure conscience and giving an authoritative example. For the fame of your

[1] Matt. xiii. 15 ff.

unswerving and unshaken faith has moved certain Eastern bishops, late though it be, to some shame for the heresy fostered and supported in those regions: and when they heard of the godless confession composed at Sirmium, they contradicted its audacious authors by passing certain decrees themselves. And though they withstood them not without in their turn raising some scruples, and inflicting some wounds upon a sensitive piety, yet they withstood them so vigorously as to compel those who at Sirmium yielded to the views of Potamius and Hosius as accepting and confirming those views, to declare their ignorance and error in so doing; in fact they had to condemn in writing their own action. And they subscribed with the express purpose of condemning something else in advance [2].

4. But your invincible faith keeps the honourable distinction of conscious worth, and content with repudiating crafty, vague, or hesitating action, safely abides in Christ, preserving the profession of its liberty. You abstain from communion with those who oppose their bishops with their blasphemies and keep them in exile, and do not by assenting to any crafty subterfuge bring yourselves under a charge of unrighteous judgment. For since we all suffered deep and grievous pain at the actions of the wicked against God, within our boundaries alone is communion in Christ to be found from the time that the Church began to be harried by disturbances such as the expatriation of bishops, the deposition of priests, the intimidation of the people, the threatening of the faith, and the determination of the meaning of Christ's doctrine by human will and power. Your resolute faith does not pretend to be ignorant of these facts or profess that it can tolerate them, perceiving that by the act of hypocritical assent it would bring itself before the bar of conscience.

5. And although in all your actions, past and present, you bear witness to the uninterrupted independence and security of your faith; yet in particular you prove your warmth and fervour of spirit by the fact that some of you whose letters have succeeded in reaching me have expressed a wish that I, unfit as I am, should notify to you what the Easterns have since said in their confessions of faith. They

affectionately laid the additional burden upon me of indicating my sentiments on all their decisions. I know that my skill and learning are inadequate, for I feel it most difficult to express in words my own belief as I understand it in my heart; far less easy must it be to expound the statements of others.

6. Now I beseech you by the mercy of the Lord, that as I will in this letter according to your desire write to you of divine things and of the witness of a pure conscience to our faith, no one will think to judge me by the beginning of my letter before he has read the conclusion of my argument. For it is unfair before the complete argument has been grasped, to conceive a prejudice on account of initial statements, the reason of which is yet unknown, since it is not with imperfect statements before us that we must make a decision for the sake of investigation, but on the conclusion for the sake of knowledge. I have some fear, not about you, as God is witness of my heart, but about some who in their own esteem are very cautious and prudent but do not understand the blessed apostle's precept not to think of themselves more highly than they ought [3]: for I am afraid that they are unwilling to know all those facts, the complete account of which I will offer at the end, and at the same time they avoid drawing the true conclusion from the aforesaid facts. But whoever takes up these lines to read and examine them has only to be consistently patient with me and with himself and peruse the whole to its completion. Perchance all this assertion of my faith will result in those who conceal their heresy being unable to practise the deception they wish, and in true Catholics attaining the object which they desire.

7. Therefore I comply with your affectionate and urgent wish, and I have set down all the creeds which have been promulgated at different times and places since the holy Council of Nicæa, with my appended explanations of all the phrases and even words employed. If they be thought to contain anything faulty, no one can impute the fault to me: for I am only a reporter, as you wished me to be, and not an author. But if anything is found to be laid down in right and apostolic fashion, no one can doubt that it is no credit to the interpreter but to the originator. In any case I have sent you a faithful account of these transactions: it is for you to determine by the decision your faith inspires whether their spirit is Catholic or heretical.

8. For although it was necessary to reply to

---

[2] *Hosius*, bishop of Cordova in Spain, had been sent by Constantine to Alexandria at the outbreak of the Arian controversy. He had presided at the Council of Nicæa in 325, and had taken part in the Council of Sardica in 343, when the Nicene Creed was reaffirmed. In his extreme old age he was forced with blows to accept this extreme Arian Creed drawn up at the third Council of Sirmium in the summer of 357. This is what is stated by Socrates, and it is corroborated by Athanasius, *Hist. Arian.* c. 45, where it is added that he anathematized Arianism before dying. Hilary certainly does Hosius an injustice in declaring him to be a joint-author of the 'blasphemous' creed.

[3] Rom. xii. 3.

your letters, in which you offered me Christian communion with your faith, (and, moreover, certain of your number who were summoned to the Council which seemed pending in Bithynia did refuse with firm consistency of faith to hold communion with any but myself outside Gaul), it also seemed fit to use my episcopal office and authority, when heresy was so rife, in submitting to you by letter some godly and faithful counsel. For the word of God cannot be exiled as our bodies are, or so chained and bound that it cannot be imparted to you in any place. But when I had learnt that synods were to meet in Ancyra and Ariminum, and that one or two bishops from each province in Gaul would assemble there, I thought it especially needful that I, who am confined in the East, should explain and make known to you the grounds of those mutual suspicions which exist between us and the Eastern bishops, though some of you know those grounds ; in order that whereas you had condemned and they had anathematized this heresy that spreads from Sirmium, you might nevertheless know with what confession of faith the Eastern bishops had come to the same result that you had come to, and that I might prevent you, whom I hope to see as shining lights in future Councils, differing, through a mistake about words, even a hair's-breadth from pure Catholic belief, when your interpretation of the apostolic faith is identically the same and you are Catholics at heart.

9. Now it seems to me right and appropriate, before I begin my argument about suspicions and dissensions as to words, to give as complete an account as possible of the decisions of the Eastern bishops adverse to the heresy compiled at Sirmium. Others have published all these transactions very plainly, but much obscurity is caused by a translation from Greek into Latin, and to be absolutely literal is to be sometimes partly unintelligible.

10. You remember that in the *Blasphemia*, lately written at Sirmium, the object of the authors was to proclaim the Father to be the one and only God of all things, and deny the Son to be God : and while they determined that men should hold their peace about ὁμοούσιον and ὁμοιούσιον, they determined that God the Son should be asserted to be born not of God the Father, but of nothing, as the first creatures were, or of another essence than God, as the later creatures. And further that in saying the Father was greater in honour, dignity, splendour and majesty, they implied that the Son lacked those things which constitute the Father's superiority. Lastly, that while it is affirmed that His birth is unknow-

able, we were commanded by this Compulsory Ignorance Act not to know that He is of God : just as if it could be commanded or decreed that a man should know what in future he is to be ignorant of, or be ignorant of what he already knows. I have subjoined in full this pestilent and godless blasphemy, though against my will, to facilitate a more complete knowledge of the worth and reason of the replies made on the opposite side by those Easterns who endeavoured to counteract all the wiles of the heretics according to their understanding and comprehension.

A copy of the Blasphemia *composed at Sirmium by Osius and Potamius.*

11. Since there appeared to be some misunderstanding respecting the faith, all points have been carefully investigated and discussed at Sirmium in the presence of our most reverend brothers and fellow-bishops, Valens, Ursacius and Germinius.

It is evident that there is one God, the Father Almighty, according as it is believed throughout the whole world; and His only Son Jesus Christ our Saviour, begotten of Him before the ages. But we cannot and ought not to say that there are two Gods, for the Lord Himself said, *I will go unto My Father and your Father, unto My God and your God* [4]. So there is one God over all, as the Apostle hath taught us, *Is He the God of the Jews only ? Is He not also of the Gentiles ? Yes, of the Gentiles also: seeing it is one God, which shall justify the circumcision by faith, and the uncircumcision through faith.* And in all other things they agreed thereto, nor would they allow any difference.

But since some or many persons were disturbed by questions concerning substance, called in Greek οὐσία, that is, to make it understood more exactly, as to ὁμοούσιον, or what is called ὁμοιούσιον, there ought to be no mention made of these at all. Nor ought any exposition to be made of them for the reason and consideration that they are not contained in the divine Scriptures, and that they are above man's understanding, nor can any man declare the birth of the Son, of whom it is written, *Who shall declare His generation* [5] ? For it is plain that only the Father knows how He begat the Son, and the Son how He was begotten of the Father. There is no question that the Father is greater. No one can doubt that the Father is greater than the Son in honour, dignity, splendour, majesty, and in the very name of Father, the Son Himself testifying, *He that sent Me is greater than I* [6]. And no one

---

4 John xx. 17.   5 Is. liii. 8.   6 John xiv. 28.

is ignorant that it is Catholic doctrine that there are two Persons of Father and Son ; and that the Father is greater, and that the Son is subordinated to the Father, together with all things which the Father has subordinated to Him, and that the Father has no beginning and is invisible, immortal and impassible, but that the Son has been begotten of the Father, God of God, Light of Light, and that the generation of this Son, as is aforesaid, no one knows but His Father. And that the Son of God Himself, our Lord and God, as we read, took flesh, that is, a body, that is, man of the womb of the Virgin Mary, of the Angel announced. And as all the Scriptures teach, and especially the doctor of the Gentiles himself, He took of Mary the Virgin, man, through whom He suffered. And the whole faith is summed up and secured in this, that the Trinity must always be preserved, as we read in the Gospel, *Go ye and baptize all nations in the Name of the Father, and of the Son, and of the Holy Ghost* [7]. Complete and perfect is the number of the Trinity. Now the Paraclete, the Spirit, is through the Son : Who was sent and came according to His promise in order to instruct, teach and sanctify the apostles and all believers.

12. After these many and most impious statements had been made, the Eastern bishops on their side again met together and composed definitions of their confession. Since, however, we have frequently to mention the words essence and substance, we must determine the meaning of essence, lest in discussing facts we prove ignorant of the signification of our words. Essence is a reality which is, or the reality of those things from which it is, and which subsists inasmuch as it is permanent. Now we can speak of the essence, or nature, or genus, or substance of anything. And the strict reason why the word essence is employed is because it *is* always. But this is identical with substance, because a thing which is, necessarily subsists in itself, and whatever thus subsists possesses unquestionably a permanent genus, nature or substance. When, therefore, we say that essence signifies nature, or genus, or substance, we mean the essence of that thing which permanently exists in the nature, genus, or substance. Now, therefore, let us review the definitions of faith drawn up by the Easterns.

I. "If any one hearing that the Son is the image of the invisible God, says that the image of God is the same as the invisible God, as though refusing to confess that He is truly Son : let him be anathema."

13. Hereby is excluded the assertion of those who wish to represent the relationship of Father and Son as a matter of names, inasmuch as every image is similar in species to that of which it is an image. For no one is himself his own image, but it is necessary that the image should demonstrate him of whom it is an image. So an image is the figured and indistinguishable likeness of one thing equated with another. Therefore the Father is, and the Son is, because the Son is the image of the Father : and he who is an image, if he is to be truly an image, must have in himself his original's species, nature and essence in virtue of the fact that he is an image.

II. "And if any one hearing the Son say, *As the Father hath life in Himself, so also hath He given to the Son to have life in Himself* [8], shall say that He who has received life from the Father, and who also declares, *I live by the Father* [9], is the same as He who gave life : let him be anathema."

14. The person of the recipient and of the giver are distinguished so that the same should not be made one and sole. For since he is under anathema who has believed that, when recipient and giver are mentioned one solitary and unique person is implied, we may not suppose that the selfsame person who gave received from Himself. For He who lives and He through whom He lives are not identical, for one lives to Himself, the other declares that He lives through the Author of His life, and no one will declare that He who enjoys life and He through whom His life is caused are personally identical.

III. "And if any one hearing that the Only-begotten Son is like the invisible God, denies that the Son who is the image of the invisible God (whose image is understood to include essence) is Son in essence, as though denying His true Sonship : let him be anathema."

15. It is here insisted that the nature is indistinguishable and entirely similar. For since He is the Only-begotten Son of God and the image of the invisible God, it is necessary that He should be of an essence similar in species and nature. Or what distinction can be made between Father and Son affecting their nature with its similar genus, when the Son subsisting through the nature begotten in Him is invested with the properties of the Father, viz., glory, worth, power, invisibility, essence? And while these prerogatives of divinity are equal we neither understand the one to be less because He is Son, nor the other to be greater because

---

7 Matt. xxviii. 19.   8 John v. 26.   9 Ib. vi. 57.

He is Father: since the Son is the image of the Father in species, and not dissimilar in genus; since the similarity of a Son begotten of the substance of His Father does not admit of any diversity of substance, and the Son and image of the invisible God embraces in Himself the whole form of His Father's divinity both in kind and in amount: and this is to be truly Son, to reflect the truth of the Father's form by the perfect likeness of the nature imaged in Himself.

IV. "And if any one hearing this text, *For as the Father hath life in Himself, so also He hath given to the Son to have life in Himself*[1]; denies that the Son is like the Father even in essence, though He testifies that it is even as He has said; let him be anathema. For it is plain that since the life which is understood to exist in the Father signifies substance, and the life of the Only-begotten which was begotten of the Father is also understood to mean substance or essence, He there signifies a likeness of essence to essence."

16. With the Son's origin as thus stated is connected the perfect birth of the undivided nature. For what in each is life, that in each is signified by essence. And in the life which is begotten of life, *i.e.* in the essence which is born of essence, seeing that it is not born unlike (and that because life is of life), He keeps in Himself a nature wholly similar to His original, because there is no diversity in the likeness of the essence that is born and that begets, that is, of the life which is possessed and which has been given. For though God begat Him of Himself, in likeness to His own nature, He in whom is the unbegotten likeness did not relinquish the property of His natural substance. For He only has what He gave; and as possessing life He gave life to be possessed. And thus what is born of essence, as life of life, is essentially like itself, and the essence of Him who is begotten and of Him who begets admits no diversity or unlikeness.

V. "If any one hearing the words *formed* or *created* it and *begat me* spoken by the same lips[2], refuses to understand this *begat me* of likeness of essence, but says that *begat me* and *formed me* are the same: as if to deny that the perfect Son of God was here signified as Son under two different expressions, as Wisdom has given us to piously understand, and asserts that *formed me* and *begat me* only imply formation and not sonship: let him be anathema."

17. Those who say that the Son of God is only a creature or formation are opposed by the following argument. For this profane presumption of the impiety of heretics is based on the fact that they say they have read *The Lord formed* or *created me*, which seems to imply formation or creation; but they omit the following sentence, which is the key to the first, and from the first wrest authority for their impious statement that the Son is a creature, because Wisdom has said that she was created. But if she were created, how could she be also born? For all birth, of whatever kind, attains its own nature from the nature that begets it: but creation takes its beginning from the power of the Creator, the Creator being able to form a creature from nothing. So Wisdom, who said that she was created, does in the next sentence say that she was also begotten, using the word creation of the act of the changeless nature of her Parent, which nature, unlike the manner and wont of human parturition, without any detriment or change of self created from itself what it begat. Similarly a Creator has no need of passion or intercourse or parturition. And that which is created out of nothing begins to exist at a definite moment. And He who creates makes His object through His mere power, and creation is the work of might, not the birth of a nature from a nature that begets it. But because the Son of God was not begotten after the manner of corporeal childbearing, but was born perfect God of perfect God; therefore Wisdom says that she was created, excluding in her manner of birth every kind of corporeal process.

18. Moreover, to shew that she possesses a nature that was born and not created, Wisdom has added that she was begotten, that by declaring that she was created and also begotten, she might completely explain her birth. By speaking of creation she implies that the nature of the Father is changeless, and she also shews that the substance of her nature begotten of God the Father is genuine and real. And so her words about creation and generation have explained the perfection of her birth: the former that the Father is changeless, the latter the reality of her own nature. The two things combined become one, and that one is both in perfection: for the Son being born of God without any change in God, is so born of the Father as to be created; and the Father, who is changeless in Himself and the Son's Father by nature, so forms the Son as to beget Him. Therefore the heresy which has dared to aver that the Son of God is a creature is condemned because while the first statement shews the impassible perfection of the divinity, the second, which asserts His natural generation, crushes the

---

[1] John v. 26.　　　　　[2] Prov. viii. 22.

impious opinion that He was created out of nothing.

VI. "And if any one grant the Son only a likeness of activity, but rob Him of the likeness of essence which is the corner-stone of our faith, in spite of the fact that the Son Himself reveals His essential likeness with the Father in the words, *For as the Father hath life in Himself, so also hath He given to the Son to have life in Himself* [3], as well as His likeness in activity by teaching us that *What things soever the Father doeth, these also doeth the Son likewise* [4], such a man robs himself of the knowledge of eternal life which is in the Father and the Son, and let him be anathema."

19. The heretics when beset by authoritative passages in Scripture are wont only to grant that the Son is like the Father in might while they deprive Him of similarity of nature. This is foolish and impious, for they do not understand that similar might can only be the result of a similar nature. For a lower nature can never attain to the might of a higher and more powerful nature. What will the men who make these assertions say about the omnipotence of God the Father, if the might of a lower nature is made equal to His own? For they cannot deny that the Son's power is the same, seeing that He has said, *What things soever the Father doeth, these also doeth the Son likewise.*

No, a similarity of nature follows on a similarity of might when He says, *As the Father hath life in Himself, so also hath He given to the Son to have life in Himself.* In life is implied nature and essence; this, Christ teaches, has been given Him to have as the Father hath. Therefore similarity of life contains similarity of might: for there cannot be similarity of life where the nature is dissimilar. So it is necessary that similarity of essence follows on similarity of might: for as what the Father does, the Son does also, so the life that the Father has He has given to the Son to have likewise. Therefore we condemn the rash and impious statements of those who confess a similarity of might but have dared to preach a dissimilarity of nature, since it is the chief ground of our hope to confess that in the Father and the Son there is an identical divine substance.

VII. "And if any one professing that he believes that there is a Father and a Son, says that the Father is Father of an essence unlike Himself but of similar activity; for speaking profane and novel words against the essence of the Son and nullifying His true divine Sonship, let him be anathema."

20. By confused and involved expressions the heretics very frequently elude the truth and secure the ears of the unwary by the mere sound of common words, such as the titles Father and Son, which they do not truthfully utter to express a natural and genuine community of essence: for they are aware that God is called the Father of all creation, and remember that all the saints are named sons of God. In like manner they declare that the relationship between the Father and the Son resembles that between the Father and the universe, so that the names Father and Son are rather titular than real. For the names are titular if the Persons have a distinct nature of a different essence, since no reality can be attached to the name of father unless it be based on the nature of his offspring. So the Father cannot be called Father of an alien substance unlike His own, for a perfect birth manifests no diversity between itself and the original substance. Therefore we repudiate all the impious assertions that the Father is Father of a Son begotten of Himself and yet not of His own nature. We shall not call God Father for having a creature like Him in might and activity, but for begetting a nature of an essence not unlike or alien to Himself: for a natural birth does not admit of any dissimilarity with the Father's nature. Therefore those are anathema who assert that the Father is Father of a nature unlike Himself, so that something other than God is born of God, and who suppose that the essence of the Father degenerated in begetting the Son. For so far as in them lies they destroy the very birthless and changeless essence of the Father by daring to attribute to Him in the birth of His Only-begotten an alteration and degeneration of His natural essence.

VIII. "And if any one understanding that the Son is like in essence to Him whose Son He is admitted to be, says that the Son is the same as the Father, or part of the Father, or that it is through an emanation or any such passion as is necessary for the procreation of corporeal children that the incorporeal Son draws His life from the incorporeal Father: let him be anathema."

21. We have always to beware of the vices of particular perversions, and countenance no opportunity for delusion. For many heretics say that the Son is like the Father in divinity in order to support the theory that in virtue of this similarity the Son is the same Person as the Father: for this undivided similarity appears to countenance a belief in a single monad. For what does not differ in kind seems to retain identity of nature.

22. But birth does not countenance this

---

3 John v. 26.   4 Ib. v. 19.

vain imagination; for such identity without differentiation excludes birth. For what is born has a father who caused its birth. Nor because the divinity of Him who is being born is inseparable from that of Him who begets, are the Begetter and the Begotten the same Person; while on the other hand He who is born and He who begets cannot be unlike. He is therefore anathema who shall proclaim a similarity of nature in the Father and the Son in order to abolish the personal meaning of the word Son: for while through mutual likeness one differs in no respect from the other, yet this very likeness, which does not admit of bare union, confesses both the Father and the Son because the Son is the changeless likeness of the Father. For the Son is not part of the Father so that He who is born and He who begets can be called one Person. Nor is He an emanation so that by a continual flow of a corporeal uninterrupted stream the flow is itself kept in its source, the source being identical with the flow in virtue of the successive and unbroken continuity. But the birth is perfect, and remains alike in nature; not taking its beginning materially from a corporeal conception and bearing, but as an incorporeal Son drawing His existence from an incorporeal Father according to the likeness which belongs to an identical nature.

IX. "And if any one, because the Father is never admitted to be the Son and the Son is never admitted to be the Father, when he says that the Son is other than the Father (because the Father is one Person and the Son another, inasmuch as it is said, *There is another that beareth witness of Me, even the Father who sent Me* [5]), does in anxiety for the distinct personal qualities of the Father and the Son which in the Church must be piously understood to exist, fear that the Son and the Father may sometimes be admitted to be the same Person, and therefore denies that the Son is like in essence to the Father: let him be anathema."

23. It was said unto the apostles of the Lord, *Be ye wise as serpents, and harmless as doves* [6]. Christ therefore wished there to be in us the nature of different creatures: but in such a sort that the harmlessness of the dove might temper the serpent's wisdom, and the wisdom of the serpent might instruct the harmlessness of the dove, and that so wisdom might be made harmless and harmlessness wise. This precept has been observed in the exposition of this creed. For the former sentence of which we have spoken guarded against the teaching of a unity of person under the cloak of an essential likeness, and against the denial of the Son's birth as the result of an identity of nature, lest we should understand God to be a single monad because one Person does not differ in kind from the other. In the next sentence, by harmless and apostolic wisdom we have again taken refuge in that wisdom of the serpent to which we are bidden to be conformed no less than to the harmlessness of the dove, lest perchance through a repudiation of the unity of persons on the ground that the Father is one Person and the Son another, a preaching of the dissimilarity of their natures should again take us unawares, and lest on the ground that He who sent and He who was sent are two Persons (for the Sent and the Sender cannot be one Person) they should be considered to have divided and dissimilar natures, though He who is born and He who begets Him cannot be of a different essence. So we preserve in Father and in Son the likeness of an identical nature through an essential birth: yet the similarity of nature does not injure personality by making the Sent and the Sender to be but one. Nor do we do away with the similarity of nature by admitting distinct personal qualities, for it is impossible that the one God should be called Son and Father to Himself. So then the truth as to the birth supports the similarity of essence and the similarity of essence does not undermine the personal reality of the birth. Nor again does a profession of belief in the Begetter and the Begotten exclude a similarity of essence; for while the Begetter and the Begotten cannot be one Person, He who is born and He who begets cannot be of a different nature.

X. "And if any one admits that God became Father of the Only-begotten Son at any point in time and not that the Only-begotten Son came into existence without passion beyond all times and beyond all human calculation: for contravening the teaching of the Gospel which scorned any interval of time between the being of the Father and the Son and faithfully has instructed us that *In the beginning was the Word, and the Word was with God, and the Word was God* [7], let him be anathema."

24. It is a pious saying that the Father is not limited by times: for the true meaning of the name of Father which He bore before time began surpasses comprehension. Although religion teaches us to ascribe to Him this name of Father through which comes the

5 John v. 32.   6 Matt. x. 16.   7 John i. 1.

impassible origin of the Son, yet He is not bound in time, for the eternal and infinite God cannot be understood as having become a Father in time, and according to the teaching of the Gospel the Only-begotten God the Word is recognized even in the beginning rather to be with God than to be born.

XI. "And if any one says that the Father is older in time than His Only-begotten Son, and that the Son is younger than the Father : let him be anathema "

25. The essential likeness conformed to the Father's essence in kind is also taught to be identical in time : lest He who is the image of God, who is the Word, who is God with God in the beginning, who is like the Father, by the insertion of time between Himself and the Father should not have in Himself in perfection that which is both image, and Word, and God. For if He be proclaimed to be younger in time, He has lost the truth of the image and likeness : for that is no longer likeness which is found to be dissimilar in time. For that very fact that God is Father prevents there being any time in which He was not Father : consequently there can be no time in the Son's existence in which He was not Son. Wherefore we must neither call the Father older than the Son nor the Son younger than the Father : for the true meaning of neither name can exist without the other.

XII. "And if any one attributes the timeless substance (*i.e.* Person) of the Only-begotten Son derived from the Father to the unborn essence of God, as though calling the Father Son : let him be anathema [8]."

26. The above definition when it denied that the idea of time could be applied to the birth of the Son seemed to have given an occasion for heresy (we saw that it would be monstrous if the Father were limited by time, but that He would be so limited if the Son were subjected to time), so that by the help of this repudiation of time, the Father who is unborn might under the appellation of Son be proclaimed as both Father and Son in a single and unique Person. For in excluding time from the Son's birth it seemed to countenance the opinion that there was no birth, so that He whose birth is not in time might be considered not to have been born at all. Wherefore, lest at the suggestion of this denial of time the heresy of the unity of Persons should insinuate itself, that impiety is condemned which dares to refer the timeless birth to the unique and singular Person of the unborn essence. For it is one thing to be outside time and another to be unborn ; the first admits of birth (though outside time), the other, so far as it is, is the one sole author from eternity of its being what it is.

27. We have reviewed, beloved brethren, all the definitions of faith made by the Eastern bishops which they formulated in their assembly against the recently emerging heresy. And we, as far as we have been able, have adapted the wording of our exposition to express their meaning, following their diction rather than desiring to be thought the originators of new phrases. In these words they decree the principles of their conscience and a long maintained doctrine against a new and profane impiety. Those who compiled this heresy at Sirmium, or accepted it after its compilation, they have thereby compelled to confess their ignorance and to sign such decrees. There the Son is the perfect image of the Father : there under the qualities of an identical essence, the Person of the Son is not annihilated and confounded with the Father : there the Son is declared to be image of the Father in virtue of a real likeness, and does not differ in substance from the Father, whose image He is : there on account of the life which the Father has and the life which the Son has received, the Father can have nothing different in substance (this being implied in life) from that which the Son received to have : there the begotten Son is not a creature, but is a Person undistinguished from the Father's nature : there, just as an identical might belongs to the Father and the Son, so their essence admits of no difference : there the Father by begetting the Son in no wise degenerates from Himself in Him through any difference of nature : there, though the likeness of nature is the same in each, the proper qualities which mark this likeness are repugnant to a confusion of Persons, so that there is not one subsisting Person who is called both Father and Son : there, though it is piously affirmed that there is both a Father who sends and a Son who is sent, yet no distinction in essence is drawn between the Father and the Son, the Sent and the Sender : there the truth of God's Fatherhood is not bound by limits of time : there the Son is not later in time : there beyond all time is a perfect birth which refutes the error that the Son could not be born.

---

[8] *Substantia* is in this passage used as the equivalent of Person. The word was used by Tertullian in the sense of οὐσία, and this early Latin use of the word is the use which eventually prevailed. The meaning of the word in Hilary is influenced by its philological equivalent in Greek. At the beginning of the fourth century ὑπόστασις was used in the same sense as οὐσία. The latter word meant 'reality,' the former word 'the basis of existence.' Athanasius, however, began the practice of restricting ὑπόστασις to the divine *Persons*. Hilary consequently here uses *substantia* in this new sense of the word ὑπόστασις. The Alexandrine Council of 362 sanctioned as allowable the use of ὑπόστασις in the sense of Person, and by the end of the century the old usage practically disappeared.

28. Here, beloved brethren, is the entire creed which was published by some Easterns, few in proportion to the whole number of bishops, and which first saw light at the very time when you repelled the introduction of this heresy. The reason for its promulgation was the fact that they were bidden to say nothing of the ὁμοούσιον. But even in former times, through the urgency of these numerous causes, it was necessary at different occasions to compose other creeds, the character of which will be understood from their wording. For when you are fully aware of the results, it will be easier for us to bring to a full consummation, such as religion and unity demand, the argument in which we are interested.

An exposition of the faith of the Church made at the Council held on the occasion of the Dedication *of the church at Antioch by ninety-seven bishops there present, because of suspicions felt as to the orthodoxy of a certain bishop* 9.

29. "We believe in accordance with evangelical and apostolic tradition in one God the Father Almighty, the Creator, Maker and Disposer of all things that are, and from whom are all things.

"And in one Lord Jesus Christ, His Only-begotten Son, God through whom are all things, who was begotten of the Father, God of God, whole God of whole God, One of One, perfect God of perfect God, King of King, Lord of Lord, the Word, the Wisdom, the Life, true Light, true Way, the Resurrection, the Shepherd, the Gate, unable to change or alter, the unvarying image of the essence and might and glory of the Godhead, the first-born of all creation, who always was in the beginning with God, the Word of God, according to what is said in the Gospel, *and the Word was God,* through whom all things were made, and in whom all things subsist, who in the last days came down from above, and was born of a virgin according to the Scriptures, and was made the Lamb 1, the Mediator between God and man, the Apostle of our faith, and leader of life. For He said, *I came down*

from heaven, not to do Mine own will, but the will of Him that sent me 2. Who suffered and rose again for us on the third day, and ascended into heaven, and sitteth on the right hand of the Father, and is to come again with glory to judge the quick and the dead.

"And in the Holy Ghost, who was given to them that believe, to comfort, sanctify and perfect, even as our Lord Jesus Christ ordained His disciples, saying, *Go ye, and teach all nations, baptizing them in the name of the Father, and of the Son, and of the Holy Ghost* 3, manifestly, that is, of a Father who is truly Father, and clearly of a Son who is truly Son, and a Holy Ghost who is truly a Holy Ghost, these words not being set forth idly and without meaning, but carefully signifying the Person, and order, and glory of each of those who are named, to teach us that they are three Persons, but in agreement one.

30. "Having therefore held this faith from the beginning, and being resolved to hold it to the end in the sight of God and Christ, we say anathema to every heretical and perverted sect, and if any man teaches contrary to the wholesome and right faith of the Scriptures, saying that there is or was time, or space, or age before the Son was begotten, let him be anathema. And if any one say that the Son is a formation like one of the things that are formed, or a birth resembling other births, or a creature like the creatures, and not as the divine Scriptures have affirmed in each passage aforesaid, or teaches or proclaims as the Gospel anything else than what we have received: let him be anathema. For all those things which were written in the divine Scriptures by Prophets and by Apostles we believe and follow truly and with fear."

31. Perhaps this creed has not spoken expressly enough of the identical similarity of the Father and the Son, especially in concluding that the names Father, Son and Holy Ghost referred to *the Person and order and glory of each of those who are named to teach us that they are three Persons, but in agreement one.*

32. But in the first place we must remember that the bishops did not assemble at Antioch to oppose the heresy which has dared to declare that the substance of the Son is unlike that of the Father, but to oppose that which, in spite of the Council of Nicæa, presumed to attribute the three names to the Father. Of this we will treat in its proper place. I recollect that at the beginning of my argument I besought the patience and forbearance of my readers and hearers until the completion

---

9 The *Council at Antioch* of 341, generally known as the Dedication Council, assembled for the dedication of the great cathedral church which had been commenced there by the emperor Constantine, who did not live to see its completion. Four creeds were then drawn up, if we reckon a document which was drawn up at Antioch by a continuation of the Council in the following year. The second, and most important, of these creeds became the creed of the Semi-Nicene party. Capable of a wholly orthodox interpretation, it was insufficient of itself to repel Arianism, but not insufficient to be used as an auxiliary means of opposing it. Hilary throughout assumes that it is not to be interpreted in an Arian sense, and uses it as an introduction to Nicene theology.

1 *Lamb* is Hilary's mistake for *Man.* He doubtless read the original in a Greek manuscript which had the word ἄνθρωπον written in its abbreviated form ἄνον. This would readily be mistaken for the word ἀρνίον, lamb. The Latin word used by Hilary as a substitute for *Apostle* is *praedestinatus,* for which word it seems impossible to account.

2 John vi. 38.   3 Matt. xxviii. 19.

of my letter, lest any one should rashly rise to judge me before he was acquainted with the entire argument. I ask it again. This assembly of the saints wished to strike a blow at that impiety which by a mere counting of names evades the truth as to the Father and the Son and the Holy Ghost; which represents that there is no personal cause for each name, and by a false use of these names makes the triple nomenclature imply only one Person, so that the Father alone could be also called both Holy Ghost and Son. Consequently they declared there were three substances, meaning three subsistent Persons, and not thereby introducing any dissimilarity of essence to separate the substance of Father and Son. For the words *to teach us that they are three in substance, but in agreement one*, are free from objection, because as the Spirit is also named, and He is the Paraclete, it is more fitting that a unity of agreement should be asserted than a unity of essence based on likeness of substance.

33. Further the whole of the above statement has drawn no distinction whatever between the essence and nature of the Father and the Son. For when it is said, *God of God, whole God of whole God*, there is no room for doubting that whole God is born of whole God. For the nature of God who is of God admits of no difference, and as whole God of whole God He is in all in which the Father is. *One of One* excludes the passions of a human birth and conception, so that since He is One of One, He comes from no other source, nor is different nor alien, for He is One of One, perfect God of perfect God. Except in having a cause of its origin His birth does not differ from the birthless nature; since the perfection of both Persons is the same. *King of King.* A power that is expressed by one and the same title allows no dissimilarity of power. *Lord of Lord.* In 'Lord' also the lordship is equal: there can be no difference where domination is confessed of both without diversity. But plainest of all is the statement appended after several others, *unable to change or alter, the unvarying image of the Godhead and essence and might and glory.* For as God of God, whole God of whole God, One of One, perfect God of perfect God, King of King and Lord of Lord, since in all that glory and nature of Godhead in which the Father ever abides, the Son born of Him also subsists; He derives this also from the Father's substance that He is unable to change. For in His birth that nature from which He is born is not changed; but the Son has maintained a changeless essence since His origin is in a changeless nature. For

though He is an image, yet the image cannot alter, since in Him was born the image of the Father's essence, and there could not be in Him a change of nature caused by any unlikeness to the Father's essence from which He was begotten. Now when we are taught that He was brought into being as the first of all creation, and He is Himself said to have always been in the beginning with God as God the Word, the fact that He was brought into being shews that He was born, and the fact that He always was, shews that He is not separated from the Father by time. Therefore this Council by dividing the three substances, which it did to exclude a monad God with a threefold title, did not introduce any separation of substance between the Father and the Son. The whole exposition of faith makes no distinction between Father and Son, the Unborn and the Only-begotten, in time, or name, or essence, or dignity, or domination. But our common conscience demands that we should gain a knowledge of the other creeds of the same Eastern bishops, composed at different times and places, that by the study of many confessions we may understand the sincerity of their faith.

The Creed according to the Council of the East.

34. "We, the holy synod met in Sardica from different provinces of the East, namely, Thebaïs, Egypt, Palestine, Arabia, Phœnicia, Cœle Syria, Mesopotamia, Cilicia, Cappadocia, Pontus, Paphlagonia, Galatia, Bithynia and Hellespont, from Asia, namely, the two provinces of Phrygia, Pisidia, the islands of the Cyclades, Pamphylia, Caria, Lydia, from Europe, namely, Thrace, Hæmimontus [4], Mœsia, and the two provinces of Pannonia, have set forth this creed.

"We believe in one God, the Father Almighty, Creator and Maker of all things, from whom all fatherhood in heaven and earth is named:

"And we believe in His Only-begotten Son our Lord Jesus Christ, who before all ages was begotten of the Father, God of God, Light of Light, through whom were made all things which are in heaven and earth, visible and invisible: who is the Word and Wisdom and Might and Life and true Light: and who in the last days for our sake was incarnate, and was born of the holy Virgin, who was crucified and dead and buried, And rose from the dead on the third day, And

---

4 Mount Haemus is the mountain range which at this period formed the boundary between the provinces of Thracia and Mœsia Inferior. Hæmimontus was grouped with Mœsia Inferior under the Vicarius of Thrace.

was received into heaven, And sitteth on the right hand of the Father, And shall come to judge the quick and the dead and to give to every man according to his works : Whose kingdom remaineth without end for ever and ever. For He sitteth on the right hand of the Father not only in this age, but also in the age to come.

"We believe also in the Holy Ghost, that is, the Paraclete, whom according to His promise He sent to His apostles after His return into the heavens to teach them and to bring all things to their remembrance, through whom also the souls of them that believe sincerely in Him are sanctified.

" But those who say that the Son of God is sprung from things non-existent or from another substance and not from God, and that there was a time or age when He was not, the holy Catholic Church holds them as aliens. Likewise also those who say that there are three Gods, or that Christ is not God and that before the ages He was neither Christ nor Son of God, or that He Himself is the Father and the Son and the Holy Ghost, or that the Son is incapable of birth ; or that the Father begat the Son without purpose or will : the holy Catholic Church anathematizes."

35. In the exposition of this creed, concise but complete definitions have been employed. For in condemning those who said that the Son sprang from things non-existent, it attributed to Him a source which had no beginning but continues perpetually. And lest this source from which He drew His permanent birth should be understood to be any other substance than that of God, it also declares to be blasphemers those who said that the Son was born of some other substance and not of God. And so since He does not draw His subsistence from nothing, or spring from any other source than God, it cannot be doubted that He was born with those qualities which are God's ; since the Only-begotten essence of the Son is generated neither from things which are non-existent nor from any other substance than the birthless and eternal substance of the Father. But the creed also rejects intervals of times or ages : on the assumption that He who does not differ in nature cannot be separable by time.

36. On every side, where anxiety might be felt, approach is barred to the arguments of heretics lest it should be declared that there is any difference in the Son. For those are anathematized who say that there are three Gods : because according to God's true nature His substance does not admit a number of applications of the title, except as it is given to individual men and angels in recognition of their merit, though the substance of their nature and that of God is different. In that sense there are consequently many gods. Furthermore in the nature of God, God is one, yet in such a way that the Son also is God, because in Him there is not a different nature : and since He is God of God, both must be God, and since there is no difference of kind between them there is no distinction in their essence. A number of titular Gods is rejected ; because there is no diversity in the quality of the divine nature. Since therefore he is anathema who says there are many Gods and he is anathema who denies that the Son is God ; it is fully shewn that the fact that each has one and the same name arises from the real character of the similar substance in each : since in confessing the Unborn God the Father, and the Only-begotten God the Son, with no dissimilarity of essence between them, each is called God, yet God must be believed and be declared to be one. So by the diligent and watchful care of the bishops the creed guards the similarity of the nature begotten and the nature begetting, confirming it by the application of one name.

37. Yet to prevent the declaration of one God seeming to affirm that God is a solitary monad without offspring of His own, it immediately condemns the rash suggestion that because God is one, therefore God the Father is one and solitary, having in Himself the name of Father and of Son : since in the Father who begets and the Son who comes to birth one God must be declared to exist on account of the substance of their nature being similar in each. The faith of the saints knows nothing of the Son being incapable of birth : because the nature of the Son only draws its existence from birth. But the nature of the birth is in Him so perfect that He who was born of the substance of God is born also of His purpose and will. For from His will and purpose, not from the process of a corporeal nature, springs the absolute perfection of the essence of God born from the essence of God. It follows that we should now consider that creed which was compiled not long ago when Photinus was deposed from the episcopate.

A copy of the creed composed at Sirmium *by the Easterns to oppose Photinus.*

38. "We believe in one God the Father Almighty, the Creator and Maker, from whom every fatherhood in heaven and in earth is named.

" And in His only Son Jesus Christ our Lord, who was born of the Father before all ages, God of God, Light of Light, through whom all things were made in heaven and in earth, visible and invisible. Who is the Word and Wisdom and Might and Life and true Light: who in the last days for our sake took a body, And was born of the holy Virgin, And was crucified, And was dead and buried : who also rose from the dead on the third day, And ascended into heaven, And sitteth on the right hand of the Father, And shall come at the end of the world to judge the quick and the dead ; whose kingdom continueth without end, and remaineth for perpetual ages. For He shall be sitting at the right hand of the Father, not only in this age, but also in the age to come.

" And in the Holy Ghost, that is, the Paraclete, whom according to His promise He sent to the apostles after He ascended into heaven to teach them and to remind them of all things, through whom also are sanctified the souls of those who believe sincerely in Him.

I. " But those who say that the Son is sprung from things non-existent, or from another substance and not from God, and that there was a time or age when He was not, the holy Catholic Church regards as aliens.

II. " If any man says that the Father and the Son are two Gods : let him be anathema.

III. " And if any man says that God is one, but does not confess that Christ, God the Son of God, ministered to the Father in the creation of all things : let him be anathema.

IV. " And if any man dares to say that the Unborn God, or a part of Him, was born of Mary : let him be anathema.

V. " And if any man say that the Son born of Mary was, before born of Mary, Son only according to foreknowledge or predestination, and denies that He was born of the Father before the ages and was with God, and that all things were made through Him : let him be anathema.

VI. " If any man says that the substance of God is expanded and contracted : let him be anathema.

VII. " If any man says that the expanded substance of God makes the Son ; or names Son His supposed expanded substance : let him be anathema.

VIII. " If any man says that the Son of God is the internal or uttered Word of God : let him be anathema.

IX. " If any man says that the man alone born of Mary is the Son : let him be anathema.

X. " If any man though saying that God and Man was born of Mary, understands thereby the Unborn God : let him be anathema.

XI. " If any man hearing *The Word was made Flesh*[5] thinks that the Word was transformed into Flesh, or says that He suffered change in taking Flesh : let him be anathema.

XII. " If any man hearing that the only Son of God was crucified, says that His divinity suffered corruption, or pain, or change, or diminution, or destruction : let him be anathema.

XIII. " If any man says *Let us make man*[6] was not spoken by the Father to the Son, but by God to Himself : let him be anathema.

XIV. " If any man says that the Son did not appear to Abraham, but the Unborn God, or a part of Him : let him be anathema.

XV. " If any man says that the Son did not wrestle with Jacob as a man, but the Unborn God, or a part of Him : let him be anathema.

XVI. " If any man does not understand *The Lord rained from the Lord* to be spoken of the Father and the Son, but that the Father rained from Himself : let him be anathema. For the Lord the Son rained from the Lord the Father.

XVII. " If any man says that the Lord and the Lord, the Father and the Son are two Gods, because of the aforesaid words : let him be anathema. For we do not make the Son the equal or peer of the Father, but understand the Son to be subject. For He did not come down to Sodom without the Father's will, nor rain from Himself but *from the Lord*, to wit by the Father's authority ; nor does He sit at the Father's right hand by His own authority, but He hears the Father saying. *Sit thou on My right hand*[7].

XVIII. " If any man says that the Father and the Son and the Holy Ghost are one Person : let him be anathema.

XIX. " If any man speaking of the Holy Ghost the Paraclete says that He is the Unborn God : let him be anathema.

XX. " If any man denies that, as the Lord has taught us, the Paraclete is different from the Son ; for He said, *And the Father shall send you another Comforter, whom I shall ask*[8] : let him be anathema.

XXI. " If any man says that the Holy Spirit is a part of the Father or of the Son : let him be anathema.

XXII. " If any man says that the Father and the Son and the Holy Spirit are three Gods : let him be anathema.

XXIII. " If any man after the example of the Jews understands as said for the destruction of the Eternal Only-begotten God the words, *I am the first God, and I am the last*

---

5 John i. 14. 6 Gen. i. 26. 7 Ps. cix 1.
8 John xiv. 16.

God, and beside Me there is no God [9], which were spoken for the destruction of idols and them that are no gods: let him be anathema.

XXIV. "If any man says that the Son was made by the will of God, like any object in creation : let him be anathema.

XXV. "If any man says that the Son was born against the will of the Father : let him be anathema. For the Father was not forced against His own will, or induced by any necessity of nature to beget the Son : but as soon as He willed, before time and without passion He begat Him of Himself and shewed Him forth.

XXVI. "If any man says that the Son is incapable of birth and without beginning, saying as though there were two incapable of birth and unborn and without beginning, and makes two Gods : let him be anathema. For the Head, which is the beginning of all things, is the Son ; but the Head or beginning of Christ is God : for so to One who is without beginning and is the beginning of all things, we refer the whole world through Christ.

XXVII. "Once more we strengthen the understanding of Christianity by saying, If any man denies that Christ who is God and Son of God, personally existed before time began and aided the Father in the perfecting of all things ; but says that only from the time that He was born of Mary did He gain the name of Christ and Son and a beginning of His deity : let him be anathema."

39. The necessity of the moment urged the Council to set forth a wider and broader exposition of the creed including many intricate questions, because the heresy which Photinus was reviving was sapping our Catholic home by many secret mines. Their purpose was to oppose every form of stealthy subtle heresy by a corresponding form of pure and unsullied faith, and to have as many complete explanations of the faith as there were instances of peculiar faithlessness. Immediately after the universal and unquestioned statement of the Christian mysteries, the explanation of the faith against the heretics begins as follows.

I. "But those who say that the Son is sprung from things non-existent, or from another substance and not from God, and that there was a time or age when He was not, the holy Catholic Church regards as aliens."

40. What ambiguity is there here? What is omitted that the consciousness of a sincere faith could suggest? He does not spring from things non-existent : therefore His origin has existence. There is no other substance extant to be His origin, but that of God : therefore nothing else can be born in Him but all

that is God ; because His existence is not from nothing, and He draws subsistence from no other source. He does not differ in time : therefore the Son like the Father is eternal. And so the Unborn Father and the Only-begotten Son share all the same qualities. They are equal in years, and that very similarity between the sole-existing paternal essence and its offspring prevents distinction in any quality.

II. "If any man says that the Father and the Son are two Gods : let him be anathema.

III. "And if any man says that God is one, but does not confess that Christ who is God and eternal Son of God ministered to the Father in the creation of all things : let him be anathema."

41. The very statement of the name as our religion states it gives us a clear insight into the fact. For since it is condemned to say that the Father and the Son are two Gods, and it is also accursed to deny that the Son is God, any opinion as to the substance of the one being different from that of the other in asserting two Gods is excluded. For there is no other essence, except that of God the Father, from which God the Son of God was born before time. For since we are compelled to confess God the Father, and roundly declare that Christ the Son of God is God, and between these two truths lies the impious confession of two Gods : They must on the ground of their identity of nature and name be one in the kind of their essence if the name of their essence is necessarily one.

IV. "If any one dares to say that the Unborn God, or a part of Him, was born of Mary : let him be anathema."

42. The fact of the essence declared to be one in the Father and the Son having one name on account of their similarity of nature seemed to offer an opportunity to heretics to declare that the Unborn God, or a part of Him, was born of Mary. The danger was met by the wholesome resolution that he who declared this should be anathema. For the unity of the name which religion employs and which is based on the exact similarity of their natural essence, has not repudiated the Person of the begotten essence so as to represent, under cover of the unity of name, that the substance of God is singular and undifferentiated because we predicate one name for the essence of each, that is, predicate one God, on account of the exactly similar substance of the undivided nature in each Person.

V. "If any man say that the Son existed before Mary only according to foreknowledge or predestination, and denies that He was born of the Father before the ages and with

God, and that all things were made through Him : let him be anathema."

43. While denying that the God of us all, the Son of God, existed before He was born in bodily form, some assert that He existed according to foreknowledge and predestination, and not according to the essence of a personally subsistent nature : that is, because the Father predestined the Son to have existence some day by being born of the Virgin, He was announced to us by the Father's foreknowledge rather than born and existent before the ages in the substance of the divine nature, and that all things which He Himself spake in the prophets concerning the mysteries of His incarnation and passion were simply said concerning Him by the Father according to His foreknowledge. Consequently this perverse doctrine is condemned, so that we know that the Only-begotten Son of God was born of the Father before all worlds, and formed the worlds and all creation, and that He was not merely predestined to be born.

VI. "If any man says that the substance of God is expanded and contracted : let him be anathema."

44. To contract and expand are bodily affections : but God who is a Spirit and breathes where He listeth, does not expand or contract Himself through any change of substance. Remaining free and outside the bond of any bodily nature, He supplies out of Himself what He wills, when He wills, and where He wills. Therefore it is impious to ascribe any change of substance to such an unfettered Power.

VII. "If any man says that the expanded substance of God makes the Son, or names Son His expanded substance : let him be anathema."

45. The above opinion, although meant to teach the immutability of God, yet prepared the way for the following heresy. Some have ventured to say that the Unborn God by expansion of His substance extended Himself as far as the holy Virgin, in order that this extension produced by the increase of His nature and assuming manhood might be called Son. They denied that the Son who is perfect God born before time began was the same as He who was afterwards born as Man. Therefore the Catholic Faith condemns all denial of the immutability of the Father and of the birth of the Son.

VIII. "If any man says that the Son is the internal or uttered Word of God : let him be anathema."

46. Heretics, destroying as far as in them lies the Son of God, confess Him to be only the word, going forth as an utterance from the speaker's lips and the unembodied sound of an impersonal voice : so that God the Father has as Son a word resembling any word we utter in virtue of our inborn power of speaking. Therefore this dangerous deceit is condemned, which asserts that God the Word, who was in the beginning with God, is only the word of a voice sometimes internal and sometimes expressed.

IX. "If any man says that the man alone born of Mary is the Son: let him be anathema."

We cannot declare that the Son of God is born of Mary without declaring Him to be both Man and God. But lest the declaration that He is both God and Man should give occasion to deceit, the Council immediately adds,

X. "If any man though saying that God and Man was born of Mary, understands thereby the Unborn God : let him be anathema."

47. Thus is preserved both the name and power of the divine substance. For since he is anathema who says that the Son of God by Mary is man and not God ; and he falls under the same condemnation who says that the Unborn God became man: God made Man is not denied to be God but denied to be the Unborn God, the Father being distinguished from the Son not under the head of nature or by diversity of substance, but only by such pre-eminence as His birthless nature gives.

XI. "If any man hearing *The Word was made Flesh* thinks that the Word was transformed into Flesh, or says that He suffered change in taking Flesh : let him be anathema."

48. This preserves the dignity of the Godhead : so that in the fact that the Word was made Flesh, the Word, in becoming Flesh, has not lost through being Flesh what constituted the Word, nor has become transformed into Flesh, so as to cease to be the Word ; but the Word was made Flesh[1] in order that the Flesh might begin to be what the Word is. Else whence came to His Flesh miraculous power in working, glory on the Mount, knowledge of the thoughts of human hearts, calmness in His passion, life in His death? God knowing no change, when made Flesh lost nothing of the prerogatives of His substance.

XII. "If any man hearing that the only Son

---

[1] *The Flesh*, without ceasing to be truly flesh, is represented as becoming divine like the Word. That is, the humanity becomes so endowed with power, and knowledge, and holiness through the unction of the Holy Ghost that its natural properties are "deified." These and similar phrases are freely used by the Fathers of the fourth century, and may be compared with John i. 14, and 2 Pet. i. 4.

of God was crucified, says that His divinity suffered corruption or pain or change or diminution or destruction : let him be anathema."

49. It is clearly shewn why the Word, though He was made Flesh, was nevertheless not transformed into Flesh. Though these kinds of suffering affect the infirmity of the flesh, yet God the Word when made Flesh could not change under suffering. Suffering and change are not identical. Suffering of every kind causes all flesh to change through sensitiveness and endurance of pain. But the Word that was made Flesh, although He made Himself subject to suffering, was nevertheless unchanged by the liability to suffer. For He was able to suffer, and yet the Word was not passible. Passibility denotes a nature that is weak ; but suffering in itself is the endurance of pains inflicted, and since the Godhead is immutable and yet the Word was made Flesh, such pains found in Him a material which they could affect though the Person of the Word had no infirmity or passibility. And so when He suffered His Nature remained immutable, because like His Father, His Person is of an impassible essence, though it is born [2].

XIII. " If any man says *Let us make man*[3] was not spoken by the Father to the Son, but by God to Himself : let him be anathema.

XIV. " If any man says that the Son did not appear to Abraham [4], but the Unborn God, or a part of Him : let him be anathema.

XV. " If any man says that the Son did not wrestle with Jacob as a man [5], but the Unborn God, or a part of Him : let him be anathema.

XVI. " If any man does not understand *The Lord rained from the Lord* [6] to be spoken of the Father and the Son, but says that the Father rained from Himself : let him be anathema. For the Lord the Son rained from the Lord the Father."

50. These points had to be inserted into the creed because Photinus, against whom the synod was held, denied them. They were inserted lest any one should dare to assert that the Son of God did not exist before the Son of the Virgin, and should attach to the Unborn God with the foolish perversity of an insane heresy all the above passages which refer to the Son of God, and while applying them to

the Father, deny the Person of the Son. The clearness of these statements absolves us from the necessity of interpreting them.

XVII. " If any man says that the Lord and the Lord, the Father and the Son, are two Gods because of the aforesaid words : let him be anathema. For we do not make the Son the equal or peer of the Father, but understand the Son to be subject. For He did not come down to Sodom without the Father's will, nor rain from Himself but *from the Lord*, to wit, by the Father's authority ; nor does He sit at the Father's right hand by His own authority, but because He hears the Father saying, *Sit Thou on My right hand*[7]."

51. The foregoing and the following statements utterly remove any ground for suspecting that this definition asserts a diversity of different deities in the Lord and the Lord. No comparison is made because it was seen to be impious to say that there are two Gods : not that they refrain from making the Son equal and peer of the Father in order to deny that He is God. For, since he is anathema who denies that Christ is God, it is not on that score that it is profane to speak of two equal Gods. God is One on account of the true character of His natural essence and because from the Unborn God the Father, who is the one God, the Only-begotten God the Son is born, and draws His divine Being only from God ; and since the essence of Him who is begotten is exactly similar to the essence of Him who begat Him, there must be one name for the exactly similar nature. That the Son is not on a level with the Father and is not equal to Him is chiefly shewn in the fact that He was subjected to Him to render obedience, in that the Lord rained from the Lord and that the Father did not, as Photinus and Sabellius say, rain from Himself, as the Lord from the Lord ; in that He then sat down at the right hand of God when it was told Him to seat Himself ; in that He is sent, in that He receives, in that He submits in all things to the will of Him who sent Him. But the subordination of filial love is not a diminution of essence, nor does pious duty cause a degeneration of nature, since in spite of the fact that both the Unborn Father is God and the Only-begotten Son of God is God, God is nevertheless One, and the subjection and dignity of the Son are both taught in that by being called Son He is made subject to that name which because it implies that God is His Father is yet a name which denotes His nature. Having a name which

---

[2] *Passibility* may not be affirmed of the divine nature of Christ which is incapable of any change or limitation within itself. At the same time the Word may be said to have suffered inasmuch as the suffering affected the flesh which He assumed. This subject was afterwards carefully developed by St. John of Damascus περὶ ὀρθοδόξου πίστεως, III. 4. In c 79, Hilary criticises the Arian statement that the Son "jointly suffered," a word which meant that the divine nature of the Son shared in the sufferings which were endured by His humanity. This phrase, like the statement of Arius that the Logos was "capable of change" implied that the Son only possessed a secondary divinity.

[3] Gen. i. 26.   [4] Ib. xviii. 1.   [5] Ib. xxxii. 26.

[6] Ib. xix. 24.

[7] Ps. cx. 1.

belongs to Him whose Son He is, He is subject to the Father both in service and name; yet in such a way that the subordination of His name bears witness to the true character of His natural and exactly similar essence.

XVIII. "If any man says that the Father and the Son are one Person: let him be anathema."

52. Sheer perversity calls for no contradiction: and yet the mad frenzy of certain men has been so violent as to dare to predicate one Person with two names.

XIX. "If any man speaking of the Holy Ghost the Paraclete say that He is the Unborn God: let him be anathema."

53. The further clause makes liable to anathema the predicating Unborn God of the Paraclete. For it is most impious to say that He who was sent by the Son for our consolation is the Unborn God.

XX. "If any man deny that, as the Lord has taught us, the Paraclete is different from the Son; for He said, *And the Father shall send you another Comforter, whom I shall ask:* let him be anathema."

54. We remember that the Paraclete was sent by the Son, and at the beginning the creed explained this. But since through the virtue of His nature, which is exactly similar, the Son has frequently called His own works the works of the Father, saying, *I do the works of My Father*[8]: so when He intended to send the Paraclete, as He often promised, He said sometimes that He was to be sent from the Father, in that He was piously wont to refer all that He did to the Father. And from this the heretics often seize an opportunity of saying that the Son Himself is the Paraclete: while by the fact that He promised to pray that another Comforter should be sent from the Father, He shews the difference between Him who is sent and Him who asked.

XXI. "If any man says that the Holy Spirit is a part of the Father or of the Son: let him be anathema."

55. The insane frenzy of the heretics, and not any genuine difficulty, rendered it necessary that this should be written. For since the name of Holy Spirit has its own signification, and the Holy Spirit the Paraclete has the office and rank peculiar to His Person, and since the Father and the Son are everywhere declared to be immutable: how could the Holy Spirit be asserted to be a part either of the Father or of the Son? But since this folly is often affirmed amid other follies by godless men, it was needful that the pious should condemn it.

XXII. "If any man says that the Father and the Son and the Holy Spirit are three Gods: let him be anathema."

56. Since it is contrary to religion to say that there are two Gods, because we remember and declare that nowhere has it been affirmed that there is more than one God: how much more worthy of condemnation is it to name three Gods in the Father, Son, and Holy Ghost? Nevertheless, since heretics say this, Catholics rightly condemn it.

XXIII. "If any man, after the example of the Jews, understand as said for the destruction of the Eternal Only-begotten God, the words, *I am the first God, and I am the last God, and beside Me there is no God*[9], which were spoken for the destruction of idols and them that are no gods: let him be anathema."

57. Though we condemn a plurality of gods and declare that God is only one, we cannot deny that the Son of God is God. Nay, the true character of His nature causes the name that is denied to a plurality to be the privilege of His essence. The words, *Beside Me there is no God*, cannot rob the Son of His divinity: because beside Him who is of God there is no other God. And these words of God the Father cannot annul the divinity of Him who was born of Himself with an essence in no way different from His own nature. The Jews interpret this passage as proving the bare unity of God, because they are ignorant of the Only-begotten God. But we, while we deny that there are two Gods, abhor the idea of a diversity of natural essence in the Father and the Son. The words, *Beside Me there is no God*, take away an impious belief in false gods. In confessing that God is One, and also saying that the Son is God, our use of the same name affirms that there is no difference of substance between the two Persons.

XXIV. "If any man says that the Son was made by the will of God, like any object in creation: let him be anathema."

58. To all creatures the will of God has given substance: but a perfect birth gave to the Son a nature from a substance that is impassible and itself unborn. All created things are such as God willed them to be: but the Son who is born of God has such a personality as God has. God's nature did not produce a nature unlike itself: but the Son begotten of God's substance has derived the essence of His nature by virtue of His origin,

---

[8] John x. 37.

[9] Is. xliv. 6.

not from an act of will after the manner of creatures.

XXV. "If any man says that the Son was born against the will of the Father : let him be anathema. For the Father was not forced against His own will, or induced against His will by any necessity of nature, to beget His Son ; but as soon as He willed, before time and without passion He begat Him of Himself and shewed Him forth."

59. Since it was taught that the Son did not, like all other things, owe His existence to God's will, lest He should be thought to derive His essence only at His Father's will and not in virtue of His own nature, an opportunity seemed thereby to be given to heretics to attribute to God the Father a necessity of begetting the Son from Himself, as though He had brought forth the Son by a law of nature in spite of Himself. But such liability to be acted upon does not exist in God the Father : in the ineffable and perfect birth of the Son it was neither mere will that begat Him nor was the Father's essence changed or forced at the bidding of a natural law. Nor was any substance sought for to beget Him, nor is the nature of the Begetter changed in the Begotten, nor is the Father's unique name affected by time. Before all time the Father, out of the essence of His nature, with a desire that was subject to no passion, gave to the Son a birth that conveyed the essence of His nature.

XXVI. "If any man says that the Son is incapable of birth and without beginning, speaking as though there were two incapable of birth and unborn and without beginning, and makes two Gods : let him be anathema. For the Head, which is the beginning of all things, is the Son ; but the Head or beginning of Christ is God : for so to One who is without beginning and is the beginning of all things, we refer the whole world through Christ."

60. To declare the Son to be incapable of birth is the height of impiety. God would no longer be One : for the nature of the one Unborn God demands that we should confess that God is one. Since therefore God is one, there cannot be two incapable of birth : because God is one (although both the Father is God and the Son of God is God) for the very reason that incapability of birth is the only quality that can belong to one Person only. The Son is God for the very reason that He derives His birth from that essence which cannot be born. Therefore our holy faith rejects the idea that the Son is incapable of birth in order to predicate one God incapable of birth and consequently one God, and in order to embrace the Only-begotten nature, begotten

from the unborn essence, in the one name of the Unborn God. For the Head of all things is the Son : but the Head of the Son is God. And to one God through this stepping-stone and by this confession all things are referred, since the whole world takes its beginning from Him to whom God Himself is the beginning.

XXVII. "Once more we strengthen the understanding of Christianity by saying, If any man denies that Christ, who is God and the Son of God, existed before time began and aided the Father in the perfecting of all things ; but says that only from the time that He was born of Mary did He gain the name of Christ and Son and a beginning of His deity : let him be anathema."

61. A condemnation of that heresy on account of which the Synod was held necessarily concluded with an explanation of the whole faith that was being opposed. This heresy falsely stated that the beginning of the Son of God dated from His birth of Mary. According to evangelical and apostolic doctrine the corner-stone of our faith is that our Lord Jesus Christ, who is God and Son of God, cannot be separated from the Father in title or power or difference of substance or interval of time.

62. You perceive that the truth has been sought by many paths through the advice and opinions of different bishops, and the ground of their views has been set forth by the separate declarations inscribed in this creed. Every separate point of heretical assertion has been successfully refuted. The infinite and boundless God cannot be made comprehensible by a few words of human speech. Brevity often misleads both learner and teacher, and a concentrated discourse either causes a subject not to be understood, or spoils the meaning of an argument where a thing is hinted at, and is not proved by full demonstration. The bishops fully understood this, and therefore have used for the purpose of teaching many definitions and a profusion of words that the ordinary understanding might find no difficulty, but that their hearers might be saturated with the truth thus differently expressed, and that in treating of divine things these adequate and manifold definitions might leave no room for danger or obscurity.

63. You must not be surprised, dear brethren, that so many creeds have recently been written. The frenzy of heretics makes it necessary. The danger of the Eastern Churches is so great that it is rare to find either priest or layman that belongs to this faith, of the orthodoxy of which you may judge. Certain individuals have acted so wrongly as to support the side of evil, and the strength of the wicked

has been increased by the exile of some of the bishops, the cause of which you are acquainted with. I am not speaking about distant events or writing down incidents of which I know nothing: I have heard and seen the faults which we now have to combat. They are not laymen but bishops who are guilty. Except the bishop Eleusius[1] and his few comrades, the greater part of the ten provinces of Asia, in which I am now staying, really know not God. Would that they knew nothing about Him, for their ignorance would meet with a readier pardon than their detraction. These faithful bishops do not keep silence in their pain. They seek for the unity of that faith of which others have long since robbed them. The necessity of a united exposition of that faith was first felt when Hosius forgot his former deeds and words, and a fresh yet festering heresy broke out at Sirmium. Of Hosius I say nothing, I leave his conduct in the background lest man's judgment should forget what once he was. But everywhere there are scandals, schisms and treacheries. Hence some of those who had formerly written one creed were compelled to sign another. I make no complaint against these long-suffering Eastern bishops, it was enough that they gave at least a compulsory assent to the faith after they had once been willing to blaspheme. I think it a subject of congratulation that a single penitent should be found among such obstinate, blaspheming and heretical bishops. But, brethren, you enjoy happiness and glory in the Lord, who meanwhile retain and conscientiously confess the whole apostolic faith, and have hitherto been ignorant of written creeds. You have not needed the letter, for you abounded in the spirit. You required not the office of a hand to write what you believed in your hearts and professed unto salvation. It was unnecessary for you to read as bishops what you held when new-born converts. But necessity has introduced the custom of expounding creeds and signing expositions. Where the conscience is in danger we must use the letter. Nor is it wrong to write what it is wholesome to confess.

64. Kept always from guile by the gift of the Holy Spirit, we confess and write of our own will that there are not two Gods but one God; nor do we therefore deny that the Son

of God is also God; for He is God of God. We deny that there are two incapable of birth, because God is one through the prerogative of being incapable of birth; nor does it follow that the Unbegotten is not God, for His source is the Unborn substance. There is not one subsistent Person, but a similar substance in both Persons. There is not one name of God applied to dissimilar natures, but a wholly similar essence belonging to one name and nature. One is not superior to the other on account of the kind of His substance, but one is subject to the other because born of the other. The Father is greater because He is Father, the Son is not the less because He is Son. The difference is one of the meaning of a name and not of a nature. We confess that the Father is not affected by time, but do not deny that the Son is equally eternal. We assert that the Father is in the Son because the Son has nothing in Himself unlike the Father: we confess that the Son is in the Father because the existence of the Son is not from any other source. We recognize that their nature is mutual and similar because equal: we do not think them to be one Person because they are one: we declare that they are through the similarity of an identical nature one, in such a way that they nevertheless are not one Person.

65. I have expounded, beloved brethren, my belief in our common faith so far as our wonted human speech permitted and the Lord, whom I have ever besought, as He is my witness, has given me power. If I have said too little, nay, if I have said almost nothing, I ask you to remember that it is not belief but words that are lacking. Perhaps I shall thereby prove that my human nature, though not my will, is weak: and I pardon my human nature if it cannot speak as it would of God, for it is enough for its salvation to have believed the things of God.

66. Since your faith and mine, so far as I am conscious, is in no danger before God, and I have shewn you, as you wished, the creeds that have been set forth by the Eastern bishops (though I repeat that they were few in number, for, considering how numerous the Eastern Churches are, that faith is held by few), I have also declared my own convictions about divine things, according to the doctrine of the apostles. It remains for you to investigate without suspicion the points that mislead the unguarded temper of our simple minds, for there is now no opportunity left of hearing. And although I shall no longer fear that sentence will not be passed upon me in accordance with the whole exposition of the creed, I ask you to allow me to express

[1] *Eleusius* is criticised by Socrates II. 40, for disliking any attempt at a repudiation of the "Dedication" creed of 341, although the "Dedication" creed was little better than a repudiation of the Nicene creed. He was, in fact, a semi-Arian. But his vigorous opposition to the extreme form of Arianism and the hopefulness with which Hilary always regarded the semi-Arians, here invest him with a reputation for the "true knowledge of God." In 381 he refused to accept the Nicene creed or take part in the Council of Constantinople.

a wish that I may not have the sentence passed until the exposition is actually completed.

67. Many of us, beloved brethren, declare the substance of the Father and the Son to be one in such a spirit that I consider the statement to be quite as much wrong as right. The expression contains both a conscientious conviction and the opportunity for delusion. If we assert the one substance, understanding it to mean the likeness of natural qualities and such a likeness as includes not only the species but the genus, we assert it in a truly religious spirit, provided we believe that the one substance signifies such a similitude of qualities that the unity is not the unity of a monad but of equals. By equality I mean exact similarity so that the likeness may be called an equality, provided that the equality imply unity because it implies an equal pair, and that the unity which implies an equal pair be not wrested to mean a single Person. Therefore the one substance will be asserted piously if it does not abolish the subsistent personality or divide the one substance into two, for their substance by the true character of the Son's birth and by their natural likeness is so free from difference that it is called one.

68. But if we attribute one substance to the Father and the Son to teach that there is a solitary personal existence although denoted by two titles: then though we confess the Son with our lips we do not keep Him in our hearts, since in confessing one substance we then really say that the Father and the Son constitute one undifferentiated Person. Nay, there immediately arises an opportunity for the erroneous belief that the Father is divided, and that He cut off a portion of Himself to be His Son. That is what the heretics mean when they say the substance is one: and the terminology of our good confession so gratifies them that it aids heresy when the word ὁμοούσιος is left by itself, undefined and ambiguous. There is also a third error. When the Father and the Son are said to be of one substance this is thought to imply a prior substance, which the two equal Persons both possess. Consequently the word implies three things, one original substance and two Persons, who are as it were fellow-heirs of this one substance. For as two fellow-heirs are two, and the heritage of which they are fellow-heirs is anterior to them, so the two equal Persons might appear to be sharers in one anterior substance. The assertion of the one substance of the Father and the Son signifies either that there is one Person who has two titles, or one divided substance that has made two imperfect substances, or that there is a third prior substance which has been usurped and

assumed by two and which is called one because it was one before it was severed into two. Where then is there room for the Son's birth? Where is the Father or the Son, if these names are explained not by the birth of the divine nature but a severing or sharing of one anterior substance?

69. Therefore amid the numerous dangers which threaten the faith, brevity of words must be employed sparingly, lest what is piously meant be thought to be impiously expressed, and a word be judged guilty of occasioning heresy when it has been used in conscientious and unsuspecting innocence. A Catholic about to state that the substance of the Father and the Son is one, must not begin at that point: nor hold this word all important as though true faith did not exist where the word was not used. He will be safe in asserting the one substance if he has first said that the Father is unbegotten, that the Son is born, that He draws His personal subsistence from the Father, that He is like the Father in might, honour and nature, that He is subject to the Father as to the Author of His being, that He did not commit robbery by making Himself equal with God, in whose form He remained, that He was obedient unto death. He did not spring from nothing, but was born. He is not incapable of birth but equally eternal. He is not the Father, but the Son begotten of Him. He is not any portion of God, but is whole God. He is not Himself the source but the image; the image of God born of God to be God. He is not a creature but is God. Not another God in the kind of His substance, but the one God in virtue of the essence of His exactly similar substance. God is not one in Person but in nature, for the Born and the Begetter have nothing different or unlike. After saying all this, he does not err in declaring one substance of the Father and the Son. Nay, if he now denies the one substance he sins.

70. Therefore let no one think that our words were meant to deny the one substance. We are giving the very reason why it should not be denied. Let no one think that the word ought to be used by itself and unexplained. Otherwise the word ὁμοούσιος is not used in a religious spirit. I will not endure to hear that Christ was born of Mary unless I also hear, *In the beginning was the Word, and the Word was God*[2]. I will not hear Christ was hungry, unless I hear that after His fast of forty days He said, *Man doth not live by bread alone*[3]. I will not hear He thirsted unless I also hear, *Whosoever drinketh of the water*

2 John i. 1.   3 Matt. iv. 4.

that I shall give him shall never thirst [4]. I will not hear Christ suffered unless I hear, *The hour is come that the Son of man should be glorified* [5]. I will not hear He died unless I hear He rose again. Let us bring forward no isolated point of the divine mysteries to rouse the suspicions of our hearers and give an occasion to the blasphemers. We must first preach the birth and subordination of the Son and the likeness of His nature, and then we may preach in godly fashion that the Father and the Son are of one substance. I do not personally understand why we ought to preach before everything else, as the most valuable and important of doctrines and in itself sufficient, a truth which cannot be piously preached before other truths, although it is impious to deny it after them.

71. Beloved brethren, we must not deny that there is one substance of the Father and the Son, but we must not declare it without giving our reasons. The one substance must be derived from the true character of the begotten nature, not from any division, any confusion of Persons, any sharing of an anterior substance. It may be right to assert the one substance, it may be right to keep silence about it. You believe in the birth and you believe in the likeness. Why should the word cause mutual suspicions, when we view the fact in the same way? Let us believe and say that there is one substance, but in virtue of the true character of the nature and not to imply a blasphemous unity of Persons. Let the oneness be due to the fact that there are similar Persons and not a solitary Person.

72. But perhaps the word *similarity* may not seem fully appropriate. If so, I ask how I can express the equality of one Person with the other except by such a word? Or is to be like not the same thing as to be equal? If I say the divine nature is one I am suspected of meaning that it is undifferentiated: if I say the Persons are similar, I mean that I compare what is exactly like. I ask what position *equal* holds between *like* and *one*? I enquire whether it means similarity rather than singularity. Equality does not exist between things unlike, nor does similarity exist in one. What is the difference between those that are similar and those that are equal? Can one equal be distinguished from the other? So those who are equal are not unlike. If then those who are unlike are not equals, what can those who are like be but equals?

73. Therefore, beloved brethren, in declaring that the Son is like in all things to the Father, we declare nothing else than that He is equal. Likeness means perfect equality, and this fact we may gather from the Holy Scriptures, *And Adam lived two hundred and thirty years, and begat a son according to his own image and according to his own likeness ; and called his name Seth* [6]. I ask what was the nature of his likeness and image which Adam begat in Seth? Remove bodily infirmities, remove the first stage of conception, remove birth-pangs, and every kind of human need. I ask whether this likeness which exists in Seth differs in nature from the author of his being, or whether there was in each an essence of a different kind, so that Seth had not at his birth the natural essence of Adam? Nay, he had a likeness to Adam, even though we deny it, for his nature was not different. This likeness of nature in Seth was not due to a nature of a different kind, since Seth was begotten from only one father, so we see that a likeness of nature renders things equal because this likeness betokens an exactly similar essence. Therefore every son by virtue of his natural birth is the equal of his father, in that he has a natural likeness to him. And with regard to the nature of the Father and the Son the blessed John teaches the very likeness which Moses says existed between Seth and Adam, a likeness which is this equality of nature. He says, *Therefore the Jews sought the more to kill Him, because He not only had broken the Sabbath, but said also that God was His father, making Himself equal with God* [7]. Why do we allow minds that are dulled with the weight of sin to interfere with the doctrines and sayings of such holy men, and impiously match our rash though sluggish senses against their impregnable assertions? According to Moses, Seth is the likeness of Adam, according to John, the Son is equal to the Father, yet we seek to find a third impossible something between the Father and the Son. He is like the Father, He is the Son of the Father, He is born of Him : this fact alone justifies the assertion that they are one.

74. I am aware, dear brethren, that there are some who confess the likeness, but deny the equality. Let them speak as they will, and insert the poison of their blasphemy into ignorant ears. If they say that there is a difference between likeness and equality, I ask whence equality can be obtained? If the Son is like the Father in essence, might, glory and eternity, I ask why they decline to say He is equal? In the above creed an anathema was pronounced on any man who should say that the Father was Father of an essence unlike Himself. Therefore if He gave to Him whom

4 John iv. 13.   5 Ib. xii. 23.   6 Gen. v. 3.   7 John v. 18.

He begat without effect upon Himself a nature which was neither another nor a different nature, He cannot have given Him any other than His own. Likeness then is the sharing of what is one's own, the sharing of one's own is equality, and equality admits of no difference[8]. Those things which do not differ at all are one. So the Father and the Son are one, not by unity of Person but by equality of nature.

75. Although general conviction and divine authority sanction no difference between likeness and equality, since both Moses and John would lead us to believe the Son is like the Father and also His equal, yet let us consider whether the Lord, when the Jews were angry with Him for calling God His Father and thus making Himself equal with God, did Himself teach that He was equal with God. He says, *The Son can do nothing of Himself, but what He seeth the Father do*[9]. He shewed that the Father originates by saying *Can do nothing of Himself*, He calls attention to His own obedience by adding, *but what He seeth the Father do*. There is no difference of might, He says He can do nothing that He does not see, because it is His nature and not His sight that gives Him power. But His obedience consists in His being able only when He sees. And so by the fact that He has power when He sees, He shews that He does not gain power by seeing but claims power on the authority of seeing. The natural might does not differ in Father and Son, the Son's equality of power with the Father not being due to any increase or advance of the Son's nature but to the Father's example. In short that honour which the Son's subjection retained for the Father belongs equally to the Son on the strength of His nature. He has Himself added, *What things soever He doeth, these also doeth the Son likewise*[9a]. Surely then the likeness implies equality. Certainly it does, even though we deny it : *for these also doeth the Son likewise*. Are not things *done likewise* the same? Or do not the same things admit equality? Is there any other difference between likeness and equality, when things that are done likewise are understood to be made the same? Unless perchance any one will deny that the same things are equal, or deny that similar things are equal, for things that are done in like manner are not only declared to be equal but to be the same things.

76. Therefore, brethren, likeness of nature can be attacked by no cavil, and the Son cannot be said to lack the true qualities of the Father's nature because He is like Him. No real likeness exists where there is no equality of nature, and equality of nature cannot exist unless it imply unity, not unity of person but of kind. It is right to believe, religious to feel, and wholesome to confess, that we do not deny that the substance of the Father and the Son is one because it is similar, and that it is similar because they are one.

77. Beloved, after explaining in a faithful and godly manner the meaning of the phrases *one substance*, in Greek ὁμοούσιον, and *similar substance* or ὁμοιούσιον, and shewing very completely the faults which may arise from a deceitful brevity or dangerous simplicity of language, it only remains for me to address myself to the holy bishops of the East. We have no longer any mutual suspicions about our faith, and those which before now have been due to mere misunderstanding are being cleared away. They will pardon me if I proceed to speak somewhat freely with them on the basis of our common faith.

78. Ye who have begun to be eager for apostolic and evangelical doctrine, kindled by the fire of faith amid the thick darkness of a night of heresy, with how great a hope of recalling the true faith have you inspired us by consistently checking the bold attack of infidelity! In former days it was only in obscure corners that our Lord Jesus Christ was denied to be the Son of God according to His nature, and was asserted to have no share in the Father's essence, but like the creatures to have received His origin from things that were not. But the heresy now bursts forth backed by civil authority, and what it once muttered in secret it has of late boasted of in open triumph. Whereas in former times it has tried by secret mines to creep into the Catholic Church, it has now put forth every power of this world in the fawning manners of a false religion. For the perversity of these men has been so audacious that when they dared not preach this doctrine publicly themselves, they beguiled the Emperor to give them hearing. For they did beguile an ignorant sovereign so successfully that though he was busy with war he expounded their infidel creed, and before he was regenerate by baptism imposed a form of faith upon the churches. Opposing bishops they drove into exile. They drove me also to wish for exile, by trying to force me to commit blasphemy. May I always be an exile, if only the truth begins to be preached again! I thank God that the Emperor, through your warnings,

---

[8] *Proprietas*, or *sharing one's own*. The word *proprietas* is not here used in a technical sense. In its technical sense *proprietas* or ἰδιότης signifies the special property of each Person of the Godhead, and the word is used to secure the distinctions of the three Persons and exclude any Sabellian misunderstanding.

[9] John v. 19.   [9a] Ib.

acknowledged his ignorance, and through these your definitions of faith came to recognize an error which was not his own but that of his advisers. He freed himself from the reproach of impiety in the eyes of God and men, when he respectfully received your embassy, and after you had won from him a confession of his ignorance, shewed his knowledge of the hypocrisy of the men whose influence brought him under this reproach.

79. These are deceivers, I both fear and believe they are deceivers, beloved brethren; for they have ever deceived. This very document is marked by hypocrisy. They excuse themselves for having desired silence as to ὁμοούσιον and ὁμοιούσιον on the ground that they taught that the meaning of the words was identical. Rustic bishops, I trow, and untutored in the significance of ὁμοούσιον: as though there had never been any Council about the matter, or any dispute. But suppose they did not know what ὁμοούσιον was, or were really unaware that ὁμοιούσιον meant of a like essence. Granted that they were ignorant of this, why did they wish to be ignorant of the generation of the Son? If it cannot be expressed in words, is it therefore unknowable? But if we cannot know *how* He was born, can we refuse to know even this, that God the Son being born not of another substance but of God, has not an essence differing from the Father's? Have they not read that the Son is to be honoured even as the Father, that they prefer the Father in honour? Were they ignorant that the Father is seen in the Son, that they make the Son differ in dignity, splendour and majesty? Is this due to ignorance that the Son, like all other things, is made subject to the Father, and while thus subjected is not distinguished from them? A distinction does exist, for the subjection of the Son is filial reverence, the subjection of all other things is the weakness of things created. They knew that He suffered, but when, may I ask, did they come to know that He jointly suffered? They avoid the words ὁμοούσιον and ὁμοιούσιον, because they are not in Scripture: I enquire whence they gathered that the Son jointly suffered? Can they mean that there were two Persons who suffered? This is what the word leads us to believe. What of those words, *Jesus Christ the Son of God?* Is Jesus Christ one, and the Son of God another? If the Son of God is not one and the same inwardly and outwardly, if ignorance on such a point is permissible, then believe that they were ignorant of the meaning of ὁμοούσιον. But if on these points ignorance leads to blasphemy and yet cannot find even a false excuse, I fear that they lied

in professing ignorance of the word ὁμοιούσιον. I do not greatly complain of the pardon you extended them; it is reverent to reserve for God His own prerogatives, and mistakes of ignorance are but human. But the two bishops, Ursacius and Valens, must pardon me for not believing that at their age and with their experience they were really ignorant. It is very difficult not to think they are lying, seeing that it is only by a falsehood that they can clear themselves on another score. But God rather grant that I am mistaken than that they really knew. For I had rather be judged in the wrong than that your faith should be contaminated by communion with the guilt of heresy.

80. Now I beseech you, holy brethren, to listen to my anxieties with indulgence. The Lord is my witness that in no matter do I wish to criticise the definitions of your faith, which you brought to Sirmium. But forgive me if I do not understand certain points; I will comfort myself with the recollection that *the spirits of the prophets are subject to the prophets*[1]. Perhaps I am not presumptuous in gathering from this that I too may understand something that another does not know. Not that I have dared to hint that you are ignorant of anything according to the measure of knowledge: but for the unity of the Catholic faith suffer me to be as anxious as yourselves.

81. Your letter on the meaning of ὁμοούσιον and ὁμοιούσιον, which Valens, Ursacius and Germinius demanded should be read at Sirmium, I understand to have been on certain points no less cautious than outspoken. And with regard to ὁμοούσιον and ὁμοιούσιον your proof has left no difficulty untouched. As to the latter, which implies the similarity of essence, our opinions are the same. But in dealing with the ὁμοούσιον, or the one essence, you declared that it ought to be rejected because the use of this word led to the idea that there was a prior substance which two Persons had divided between themselves. I see the flaw in that way of taking it. Any such sense is profane, and must be rejected by the Church's common decision. The second reason that you added was that our fathers, when Paul of Samosata was pronounced a heretic, also rejected the word ὁμοούσιον, on the ground that by attributing this title to God he had taught that He was single and undifferentiated, and at once Father and Son to Himself. Wherefore the Church still regards it as most profane to exclude the different personal qualities, and, under the mask

---

[1] 1 Cor. xiv. 32.

of the aforesaid expressions, to revive the error of confounding the Persons and denying the personal distinctions in the Godhead. Thirdly you mentioned this reason for disapproving of the ὁμοούσιον, that in the Council of Nicæa our fathers were compelled to adopt the word on account of those who said the Son was a creature : although it ought not to be accepted, because it is not to be found in Scripture. Your saying this causes me some astonishment. For if the word ὁμοούσιον must be repudiated on account of its novelty, I am afraid that the word ὁμοιούσιον, which is equally absent in Scripture, is in some danger.

82. But I am not needlessly critical on this point. For I had rather use an expression that is new than commit sin by rejecting it. So, then, we will pass by this question of innovation, and see whether the real question is not reduced to something which all our fellow-Christians unanimously condemn. What man in his senses will ever declare that there is a third substance, which is common to both the Father and the Son? And who that has been reborn in Christ and confessed both the Son and the Father will follow him of Samosata in confessing that Christ is Himself to Himself both Father and Son? So in condemning the blasphemies of the heretics we hold the same opinion, and such an interpretation of ὁμοούσιον we not only reject but hate. The question of an erroneous interpretation is at an end, when we agree in condemning the error.

83. But when I at last turn to speak on the third point, I pray you to let there be no conflict of suspicions where there is peace at heart. Do not think I would advance anything hurtful to the progress of unity. For it is absurd to fear cavil about a word when the fact expressed by the word presents no difficulty. Who objects to the fact that the Council of Nicæa adopted the word ὁμοούσιον? He who does so, must necessarily like its rejection by the Arians. The Arians rejected the word, that God the Son might not be asserted to be born of the substance of God the Father, but formed out of nothing, like the creatures. This is no new thing that I speak of. The perfidy of the Arians is to be found in many of their letters and is its own witness. If the godlessness of the negation then gave a godly meaning to the assertion, I ask why we should now criticise a word which was then rightly adopted because it was wrongly denied? If it was rightly adopted, why after supporting the right should that which extinguished the wrong be called to account? Having been used as the instrument

of evil it came to be the instrument of good [2].

84. Let us see, therefore, what the Council of Nicæa intended by saying ὁμοούσιον, that is, of one substance : not certainly to hatch the heresy which arises from an erroneous interpretation of ὁμοούσιον. I do not think the Council says that the Father and the Son divided and shared a previously existing substance to make it their own. It will not be adverse to religion to insert in our argument the creed which was then composed to preserve religion.

"We believe in one God the Father Almighty, Maker of all things visible and invisible :

"And in one our Lord Jesus Christ, the Son of God, born of the Father, Only-begotten, that is, of the substance of the Father, God of God, Light of Light, Very God of very God, born not made, of one substance with the Father (which in Greek they call ὁμοούσιον) ; By whom all things were made which are in heaven and in earth, Who for our salvation came down, And was incarnate, And was made man, And suffered, And rose again the third day, And ascended into heaven, And shall come to judge the quick and the dead.

"And in the Holy Ghost.

"But those who say, There was when He was not, And before He was born He was not, And that He was made of things that existed not, or of another substance and essence, saying that God was able to change and alter, to these the Catholic Church says anathema."

Here the Holy Council of religious men introduces no prior substance divided between two Persons, but the Son born of the substance of the Father. Do we, too, deny it, or confess anything else? And after other explanations of our common faith, it says, Born not made, of one substance with the Father (which in Greek they call ὁμοούσιον). What occasion is there here for an erroneous interpretation? The Son is declared to be born of the substance of the Father, not made : lest while the word born implies His divinity, the word made should imply He is a creature. For the same reason we have *of one substance*, not to teach that there is one solitary divine Person, but that the Son is born of the substance of God and subsists from no other source, nor in any diversity caused by a difference of substance. Surely again this is our faith, that He subsists from no other source, and He is not unlike the

---

[2] *Impiare se* is used by Plautus, *Rud.* 1, 3, 8, in the sense of ἀσεβεῖν. The sentence probably refers to the misuse of the word ὁμοούσιος by Paul of Samosata.

Father. Is not the meaning here of the word ὁμοούσιον that the Son is produced of the Father's nature, the essence of the Son having no other origin, and that both, therefore, have one unvarying essence? As the Son's essence has no other origin, we may rightly believe that both are of one essence, since the Son could be born with no substance but that derived from the Father's nature which was its source.

85. But perhaps on the opposite side it will be said that it ought to meet with disapproval, because an erroneous interpretation is generally put upon it. If such is our fear, we ought to erase the words of the Apostle, *There is one Mediator between God and men, the man Christ Jesus*[3], because Photinus uses this to support his heresy, and refuse to read it because he interprets it mischievously. And the fire or the sponge should annihilate the Epistle to the Philippians, lest Marcion should read again in it, *And was found in fashion as a man*[4], and say Christ's body was only a phantasm and not a body. Away with the Gospel of John, lest Sabellius learn from it, *I and the Father are one*[5]. Nor must those who now affirm the Son to be a creature find it written, *The Father is greater than I*[6]. Nor must those who wish to declare that the Son is unlike the Father read: *But of that day and hour knoweth no man, no, not the angels which are in heaven, neither the Son, but the Father*[7]. We must dispense, too, with the books of Moses, lest the darkness be thought coeval with God who dwells in the unborn light, since in Genesis the day began to be after the night; lest the years of Methuselah extend later than the date of the deluge, and consequently more than eight souls were saved[8]; lest God hearing the cry of Sodom when the measure of its sins was full should come down as though ignorant of the cry to see if the measure of its sins was full according to the cry, and be found to be ignorant of what He knew; lest any one of those who buried Moses should have known his sepulchre when he was buried; lest these passages, as the heretics think, should prove that the contradictions of the law make it its own enemy. So as they do not understand them, we ought not to read them. And though I should not have said it myself unless forced by the argu-

ment, we must, if it seems fit, abolish all the divine and holy Gospels with their message of our salvation, lest their statements be found inconsistent; lest we should read that the Lord who was to send the Holy Spirit was Himself born of the Holy Spirit; lest He who was to threaten death by the sword to those who should take the sword, should before His passion command that a sword should be brought; lest He who was about to descend into hell should say that He would be in paradise with the thief; lest finally the Apostles should be found at fault, in that when commanded to baptize in the name of the Father, and the Son, and the Holy Ghost, they baptized in the name of Jesus only. I speak to you, brethren, to you, who are no longer nourished with milk, but with meat, and are strong[9]. Shall we, because the wise men of the world have not understood these things, and they are foolish unto them, be wise as the world is wise and believe these things foolish? Because they are hidden from the godless, shall we refuse to shine with the truth of a doctrine which we understand? We prejudice the cause of divine doctrines when we think that they ought not to exist, because some do not regard them as holy. If so, we must not glory in the cross of Christ, because it is a stumbling-block to the world; and we must not preach death in connection with the living God, lest the godless argue that God is dead.

86. Some misunderstand ὁμοούσιον; does that prevent me from understanding it? The Samosatene was wrong in using the word ὁμοούσιον; does that make the Arians right in denying it? Eighty bishops once rejected it; but three hundred and eighteen recently accepted it. And for my own part I think the number sacred, for with such a number Abraham overcame the wicked kings, and was blessed by Him who is a type of the eternal priesthood. The former disapproved of it to oppose a heretic: the latter surely approved of it to oppose a heretic. The authority of the fathers is weighty, is the sanctity of their successors trivial? If their opinions were contradictory, we ought to decide which is the better: but if both their approval and disapproval established the same fact, why do we carp at such good decisions?

87. But perhaps you will reply, 'Some of those who were then present at Nicæa have now decreed that we ought to keep silence about the word ὁμοούσιον.' Against my will I must answer: Do not the very same men rule that we must keep silence about the word ὁμοιούσιον? I beseech you that there may be

---

3 1 Tim. ii. 5.   4 Phil. ii. 7.   5 John x. 30.
6 Ib. xiv. 28.   7 Mark xiii. 32.
8 *Methuselah's* age was a favourite problem with the early Church. See Aug. *de Civ. Dei*, xv. 13. and *de pecc. orig.* ii. 23, where it is said to be one of those points on which a Christian can afford to be ignorant. According to the Septuagint, Methuselah lived for fourteen years after the deluge, so that more than 'eight souls' survived, and 1 Pet. iii. 20, appeared to be incorrect. According to the Hebrew and Vulgate there is no difficulty, as Methuselah is there represented as dying before the deluge.

9 Heb. v. 12.

found no one of them but Hosius, that old man who loves a peaceful grave too well, who shall be found to think that we ought to keep silence about both. Amid the fury of the heretics into what straits shall we fall at last, if while we do not accept both, we keep neither? For there seems to be no impiety in saying that since neither is found in Scripture, we ought to confess neither or both.

88. Holy brethren, I understand by ὁμο-ούσιον God of God, not of an essence that is unlike, not divided but born, and that the Son has a birth which is unique, of the substance of the unborn God, that He is begotten yet co-eternal and wholly like the Father. I believed this before I knew the word ὁμοούσιον, but it greatly helped my belief. Why do you condemn my faith when I express it by ὁμο-ούσιον while you cannot disapprove it when expressed by ὁμοιούσιον? For you condemn my faith, or rather your own, when you condemn its verbal equivalent. Do others misunderstand it? Let us join in condemning the misunderstanding, but not deprive our faith of its security. Do you think we must subscribe to the Samosatene Council to prevent any one from using ὁμοούσιον in the sense of Paul of Samosata? Then let us also subscribe to the Council of Nicæa, so that the Arians may not impugn the word. Have we to fear that ὁμοιούσιον does not imply the same belief as ὁμοούσιον? Let us decree that there is no difference between being of one or of a similar substance. The word ὁμοούσιον can be understood in a wrong sense. Let us prove that it can be understood in a very good sense. We hold one and the same sacred truth. I beseech you that we should agree that this truth, which is one and the same, should be regarded as sacred. Forgive me, brethren, as I have so often asked you to do. You are not Arians: why should you be thought to be Arians by denying the ὁμοούσιον?

89. But you say: 'The ambiguity of the word ὁμοούσιον troubles and offends me.' I pray you hear me again and be not offended. I am troubled by the inadequacy of the word ὁμοιούσιον. Many deceptions come from similarity. I distrust vessels plated with gold, for I may be deceived by the metal underneath: and yet that which is seen resembles gold. I distrust anything that looks like milk, lest that which is offered to me be milk but not sheep's milk: for cow's milk certainly looks like it. Sheep's milk cannot be really like sheep's milk unless drawn from a sheep. True likeness belongs to a true natural connection. But when the true natural connection exists, the ὁμοούσιον is implied. It is a likeness according to essence when one piece of metal is like another and not plated, if milk which is of the same colour as other milk is not different in taste. Nothing can be like gold but gold, or like milk that did not belong to that species. I have often been deceived by the colour of wine: and yet by tasting the liquor have recognized that it was of another kind. I have seen meat look like other meat, but afterwards the flavour has revealed the difference to me. Yes, I fear those resemblances which are not due to a unity of nature.

90. I am afraid, brethren, of the brood of heresies which are successively produced in the East: and I have already read what I tell you I fear. There was nothing whatever suspicious in the document which some of you, with the assent of certain Orientals, took on your embassy to Sirmium to be there subscribed. But some misunderstanding has arisen in reference to certain statements at the beginning which I believe you, my holy brethren, Basil, Eustathius, and Eleusius, omitted to mention lest they should give offence. If it was right to draw them up, it was wrong to bury them in silence. But if they are now unmentioned because they were wrong we must beware lest they should be repeated at some future time. Out of consideration for you I have hitherto said nothing about this: yet you know as well as I do that this creed was not identical with the creed of Ancyra. I am not talking gossip: I possess a copy of the creed, and I did not get it from laymen, it was given me by bishops.

91. I pray you, brethren, remove all suspicion and leave no occasion for it. To approve of ὁμοιούσιον, we need not disapprove of ὁμοούσιον. Let us think of the many holy prelates now at rest: what judgment will the Lord pronounce upon us if we now say anathema to them? What will be our case if we push the matter so far as to deny that they were bishops and so deny that we are ourselves bishops? We were ordained by them and are their successors. Let us renounce our episcopate, if we took its office from men under anathema. Brethren, forgive my anguish: it is an impious act that you are attempting. I cannot endure to hear the man anathematized who says ὁμοούσιον and says it in the right sense. No fault can be found with a word which does no harm to the meaning of religion. I do not know the word ὁμοιούσιον, or understand it, unless it confesses a similarity of essence. I call the God of heaven and earth to witness, that when I had heard neither word, my belief was always such that I should have interpreted ὁμοιούσιον by ὁμοούσιον. That is, I believed that nothing could be similar according to nature

unless it was of the same nature. Though long ago regenerate in baptism, and for some time a bishop, I never heard of the Nicene creed until I was going into exile, but the Gospels and Epistles suggested to me the meaning of ὁμοούσιον and ὁμοιούσιον. Our desire is sacred. Let us not condemn the fathers, let us not encourage heretics, lest while we drive one heresy away, we nurture another. After the Council of Nicæa our fathers interpreted the due meaning of ὁμοούσιον with scrupulous care; the books are extant, the facts are fresh in men's minds: if anything has to be added to the interpretation, let us consult together. Between us we can thoroughly establish the faith, so that what has been well settled need not be disturbed, and what has been misunderstood may be removed.

92. Beloved brethren, I have passed beyond the bounds of courtesy, and forgetting my modesty I have been compelled by my affection for you to write thus of many abstruse matters which until this our age were unattempted and left in silence. I have spoken what I myself believed, conscious that I owed it as my soldier's service to the Church to send to you in accordance with the teaching of the Gospel by these letters the voice of the office which I hold in Christ. It is yours to discuss, to provide and to act, that the inviolable fidelity in which you stand you may still keep with conscientious hearts, and that you may continue to hold what you hold now. Remember my exile in your holy prayers. I do not know, now that I have thus expounded the faith, whether it would be as sweet to return unto you again in the Lord Jesus Christ as it would be full of peace to die. That our God and Lord may keep you pure and undefiled unto the day of His appearing is my desire, dearest brethren.

...UCTION TO THE

DE ...RINITATE.

the *De Trinitate* was written, and the character and ...he general Introduction, it will suffice to give here ..., in the main, from the Benedictine edition.

St. Hilary's own spiritual history, the events of which ...y and symmetrically in the narrative than they had ...tells of the efforts of a pure and noble soul, impeded, ...y desires nor by indifference, to find an adequate ...o the conception of the old philosophers, and then ...ore and more of the Divine revelation in Scripture, ...he apprehension of God as revealed in the Catholic ...esult of a mere intellectual knowledge, but of belief ...ice from ignorance and fear to knowledge and peace. ...e not been charged with the sacerdotal (i.e., in the ...fice, which laid upon him the duty of caring for the ...as needed, for (§§ 15, 16) heresies were abroad, and ...that Father and Son were mere names or aspects ...e had been no true birth of the Son; and the Arian ...the name of its advocate, preferring to style it the ...openly that the Son is created and not born, and therefore is different in kind from the Father, and not, in the true sense, God. Hilary declares (§ 17) that his purpose is to refute these heresies and to demonstrate the true faith by the evidence of Scripture. He demands from his hearers a loyal belief in the Scriptures which he will cite; without such faith his arguments will not profit them (§ 18); and in § 19 he warns them of the limits of the argument from analogy, which he must employ, inadequate as it is in respect of the finite illustrations which he must use to express the infinite. Then in § 20 he speaks with a modest pride of his careful marshalling of the arguments which shall lead his readers to the right conclusion, and in §§ 21—36 he gives a summary of the contents of the work. He concludes the first Book (§§ 37, 38) with a prayer which expresses his certainty that what he holds is the truth, and entreats the Father and the Son that he may have the eloquence of language and the cogency of reasoning needed for the worthy presentation of the truth concerning Them.

BOOK II. He begins with the command to baptize all nations (St. Matt. xxviii. 19) as a summary of the faith; this by itself would suffice were not explanations rendered necessary by heretical misrepresentations of its meaning. For (§§ 3, 4) heresy is the result of Scripture misunderstood; and here we must notice that Scripture is regarded as ground common to both sides. All accept it as literally true, and combine its texts as will best serve their own purposes. Hilary, regarding all heresies as one combined opposition to the truth, makes the two objections that their arguments are mutually destructive, and that they are modern. Then in § 5 he expresses the awe with which he approaches the subject. The language which he must use is utterly inadequate, and yet he is compelled to use it. In §§ 6, 7 he begins with the notion of God as Father; in §§ 8—11 he proceeds to that of God the Son. He states the faith as it must be believed; it is not enough (§§ 12, 13) to accept the truth of Christ's miracles. The mystery, as it is revealed in St. John i. 1—4, must be the object of faith. In §§ 14—21 he expounds this passage in the face of current objections, and then triumphantly asserts that all the efforts of heresy are vain (§ 22). He advances proof-texts in § 23 against each objector, and then points out in §§ 24, 25 our indebtedness to the infinite Divine condescension thus revealed. For, in all the humiliation to which Christ stooped the Divine Majesty was still inseparably His, and was manifested both in the circumstances of His birth and in His life on earth (§§ 26—28). The book concludes (§§ 29—35) with a statement of the doctrine of the Holy Ghost, as perfect as in the undeveloped state of that doctrine was possible.

Book III. In §§ 1—4, the words, *I in the Father and the Father in Me*, are taken as typical. Man cannot comprehend, but only apprehend them. So far as they are explicable Hilary explains them. But God's self-revelation is always mysterious. The miracles of Christ are inexplicable (§§ 5—8); this is God's way, and meant to check presumption. Human wisdom is limited, and when it passes its bounds, and invades the realm of faith, it becomes folly. Next, in §§ 9—17, the passage, St. John xvii. 1 ff., is explained as proving that in the One God there are the Persons of Father and of Son, and as revealing God in the aspect of the Father. Then, in §§ 18—21, the wonderful deeds of Christ are put forth as an evidence of His wonderful birth. We must not ask how He can be coeternal with the Father, for it is in vain that we should ask how He could pass through the closed door. Either question is mere presumption. The revelation which Christ makes (§§ 22, 23) is that of God as His Father; *Unum sunt, non Unus*. And finally, in §§ 25, 26, he returns to the futility of reasoning. True wisdom is to believe where we cannot comprehend; we must trust to faith, not to proof.

Book IV. This book is in a sense the beginning of the treatise, and is sometimes cited later on as the first. Its three predecessors, he says in § 1, had been written some time before. They had contained a statement of the truth concerning the Divinity of Christ, and a summary refutation of the various heresies. He now commences his main attack upon Arianism. First (§ 2) he repeats what his difficulty is; that human language and thought cannot cope with the Infinite. Then (§ 3) he tells how the Arians explain away the eternal Sonship of Christ. As a defence against this tampering with the truth, the Church has adopted the term *Homoousion* (§§ 4—7); Hilary explains and defends its use. In § 8 he shews, by a collection of the passages of Scripture which they wrest to their own purposes, that such a definition is necessary, and in §§ 9, 10 that their use of these passages is dishonest. In § 11 he tells us exactly what the Arian teaching is, and sets it forth in one of their own formularies, the *Epistola Arii ad Alexandrum* (§§ 12, 13). In § 14 this doctrine is denounced; it does not explain, but explains away. The proclamation made through Moses, *Hear, O Israel, the Lord thy God is One*, upon which the Arians take their stand, reveals only one aspect of the truth (§ 15). It does not exhaust the truth; for God is represented as not one solitary Person in the history of creation (§§ 16—22), in the life of Abraham (§§ 23—31), and in that of Moses (§§ 32—34). And this again is the teaching of the Prophets, as is shewn by passages selected from Isaiah, Hosea, and Jeremiah (§§ 35—42).

All the evidence thus collected shews that in the Godhead there is both Father and Son, and that the Son is God.

Book V.   Hilary now points out (§ 1) the controversial strength of the Arian position. If he is silent in face of their assertion, they will claim that he agrees with them that the Son is God only in some inferior sense.   On the other hand, if he opposes them, he will seem to be contradicting the Mosaic revelation of the Divine unity.   In § 2 he recapitulates the argument of Book IV., that the witness of Scripture proves that God is not a solitary Person; that, as he says, there is *God and God*.   But the Arians had a further loophole; their creed asserted (§ 3) one true God.   They might argue that Christ is indeed God, but of a nature different from that of the Father.   In refutation of this Hilary goes once more through the history of creation (§§ 4—10), proving that the narrative reveals not only the Son's share in that work, but also His equality and oneness of nature with the Father; in other words, that He is not only God but true God.   The same truth is demonstrated from the life of Abraham (§§ 11—16).   Moreover, these self-revelations of the Son (as the Angel, on various occasions) are anticipations of the Incarnation.   He was first seen in flesh, afterwards born in flesh.   The Arians concentrate their attention on the humble conditions of Christ's human life, and so, from want of a comprehensive view, fail to discern His true Godhead. But Hilary will not anticipate the evidence of the Gospels (§§ 17, 18).   He returns to the Old Testament, and proves his point from Jacob's visions (§§ 19, 20), and by the revelations made to Moses (§§ 21—23).   After a summary and an enforcement of the preceding arguments (§§ 24, 25), he proceeds to prove from certain passages of Isaiah that the Prophet recognised the Son as true God (§§ 26—31), and that St. Paul understood him in that sense (§§ 32, 33).   Then, in §§ 34, 35, the result which has been attained is dwelt upon.   Hilary shews that it is the Arians who fail to recognise the one true God; for Christ is true God, yet not a second God.   Finally, in §§ 36—39, Moses, Isaiah, and Jeremiah are adduced as testifying that Christ is God from God, and God in God.

Book VI.   Hilary begins by lamenting the wide extension of Arianism; his love for souls leads him to combat the heresy, whose insidiousness makes it the more dangerous (§§ 1—4).   He repeats in §§ 5, 6 the same Arian creed which he had given in Book IV. The heretics here gain the appearance of orthodoxy by condemning errors inconsistent with their own; and this condemnation is designed to cast upon the Catholic faith the suspicion of complicity in such errors.   Hence he must postpone his appeal to the New Testament till he has examined them (§§ 7, 8).   Accordingly in §§ 9—12 he explains successively the doctrines of Valentinus, Manichæus, Sabellius and Hieracas, and shews that the Church rejects them all, as she does (§ 13) the doctrine which the Arians in their creed have falsely assigned to her.   Their object is to deny that the Son is coeternal with the Father and of one substance with Him (§§ 14, 15); but this denial is clean contrary to Scripture, which it is blasphemy to oppose (§§ 16, 17).   The Arians would make a creature of Christ (§ 18), to Whom, in §§ 19—21, Hilary turns with an impassioned declaration of certainty that He is very God.   He then resumes the argument, and proves that Christ is Son by birth, not by adoption, from the words both of Father and of Son as recorded in the Gospel (§§ 22—25).   This is confirmed (§§ 26, 27) by the Gospel account of His acts, which are otherwise inexplicable.   The argument is clenched by a discussion of St. John vii. 28, 29, and viii. 42 (§§ 28—31).   The true Sonship of Christ is further proved by the faith of the Apostles, whose certainty increased with their knowledge (§§ 31—35), and especially by that of St. Peter (§§ 36—38), of St. John (§§ 39—43), and of St. Paul (§§ 44, 45). To reject such a weight of testimony is to prefer Antichrist to Christ (§ 46).   And, moreover, we have the witness of those for whom He wrought miracles, of devils, of the Jews, of the Apostles in peril on the sea, of the centurion by the Cross, that Christ is truly the Son of God (§§ 47—52).

BOOK VII. The Arians are adepts at concealing their meaning; at the use of Scripture terms in unscriptural senses (§ 1). They have already been refuted by the proof that Christ is the true and coeternal Son ; and Hilary now advances to the proof of the true Divinity of Christ, which is logically inseparable from His true Sonship (§ 2). But the danger is great lest, in attacking one heresy, he should use language which would sanction others (§ 3). Yet the truth is one, while heresies are manifold. Each of them can be trusted to demolish the others, while none can establish its own case. He illustrates this by the mutually destructive arguments of Sabellius, Arius and Photinus (§§ 5—7). Christ is proved to be God by the name *God* which is given Him in Scripture : *The Word was God* (§§ 8, 9). The name is His in the strict sense, and not any derivative meaning (§§ 10, 11). Yet Father and Son are not two, but one God (§ 13). Being the Son of God, He has the nature of God, and therefore is God (§§ 14—17), and yet not one Person with the Father (§ 18). Again, His power, manifested in His works, proves His Godhead (§ 19), as does the fact that all judgment has been given Him by the Father (§ 20). Christ's own words display the truth (§ 21). The Arians are blind to the plain sense of Scripture, and are more blasphemous than the Jews ; Christ's reply to the latter meets the objections of the former (§§ 22—24). He asserts His unity with the Father (§ 25), and makes His works the proof (§ 26). The Father is in the Son and the Son is in the Father (§ 27): this is illustrated by the transmission of physical properties from parent to child and from flame to flame (§§ 28—30). In fact, the Catholic is the only rational explanation of the words of Scripture (§§ 31, 32). Again (§§ 33—38), the way to the Father is through the Son, and knowledge of the Son is knowledge of the Father. This would be impossible, were not the Son God in the same sense in which the Father is God. Thus the contrary doctrines of Sabellius and of Arius are confuted ; there is neither one Person, nor yet two Gods (§§ 39, 40). Christ calls upon us to believe the truth, and belief is not only possible but reasonable (§ 41).

BOOK VIII. Piety is necessary in a Bishop, but he needs also knowledge and dialectical skill in the face of such heresies as were rampant in Hilary's day ; for the heretics outdo the orthodox in zeal, and are masters in the art of devising pitfalls for the unwary reasoner (§§ 1—3). He maintains (§ 4) that hitherto he has established his case ; and now turns, in § 5, to the Arian interpretation of *I and the Father are One*, as meaning that They are one in will, not in nature. The fallacy of this is shewn by a comparison of the unity of Christians in Christ (§§ 7—9) ; a unity which is confessedly one of nature, yet is not more natural than that of Father and Son, of which it is a type (§ 10). And indeed the words *I and the Father are One*, are ill-adapted to express a mere harmony of will (§ 11). This gift of unity of nature could not be given, as it is, through the Incarnation and the Eucharist to Christians, unless the Givers Themselves possessed it ; i.e. unless Father and Son were One God (§§ 12—14). As a matter of fact, we have a perfect union, through the mediation of Christ, with the Father : and it is a unity of nature, a permanent abiding ; an assurance to us of the indwelling of Father in Son and Son in Father, and of the fact that Christ is not a creature, one in will with the Father, but a Son, one in nature with Him (§§ 15—18). For, again (§§ 19—21), the Mission of the Holy Ghost is jointly from the Father and the Son ; He is called sometimes the Spirit of the Father, sometimes the Spirit of the Son and this is a further proof of the unity in nature of Father and Son. Hilary now enquires (§§ 22—25) into the senses in which Scripture speaks of the Holy Spirit. Sometimes this title is given to the Father, sometimes to the Son, in both cases to save us from corporeal conceptions of God. But it is also used, in the strict sense, of the Paraclete, as on the day of Pentecost. Now the Divine Spirit dwells in Christians; but this Spirit, whether styled the Spirit of God, or the Spirit of Christ, or the Spirit of Truth, proceeding from the Father and sent by the Son, is only one Spirit. Hence the Godhead is One, and the nature of the Persons within that Godhead one also (§§ 26, 27). He next points out (§ 28) that the Arians are inconsistent in worshipping Christ, and yet styling Him a creature; for thus they fall under the curse of the Law, and forfeit the Holy Spirit. Again (§§ 29—34) the powers and graces bestowed by God are described indiscriminately as gifts of one or another Person in the Godhead. The Son, therefore, as a Giver, must be one with the Father, Who is also a Giver, and one with the Spirit. There is *One God and One Lord* (§ 35); if we deny that the Son is God, we must also deny that the Father is Lord; which is absurd. They are One God, with one Spirit, but not one Person (§ 36). St. Paul expressly says that Christ is *God over all;* an expression which must, like all the Apostle's teaching, bear the Catholic sense, and is incompatible with Arianism (§§ 37—39). The supporters of Arianism are thus alien from the faith (§ 40). After a restatement of the truth (§ 41), Hilary proceeds to deduce the Divine nature of the Son from the fact that He has been sealed by the Father (§§ 42—45). This sealing makes Him the Father's counterpart, Whose Image He thus becomes, though in the form of a servant. If He were thus the Image of God after His Incarnation, how much more before that condescension (§ 46). In § 47 he again denies that this teaching reduces the Father and the Son to one Person; and then (§§ 48—50) works out the sense in which Christ is the Image of God. It means that They are of one nature and of one power, and that the Son is the Firstborn, through Whom all things were created. But creation and also reconciliation is the joint work of Father and Son (§ 51). Christ could not have stated more explicitly than He has done His unity with the Father; the recognition of this truth is the test of the true Church (§ 52). Heresy is blind to the essential difference between the life-giving Christ and the created universe, which owes its life to Him (§ 53). In Him dwells *the whole fulness of the Godhead bodily.* The Indweller and the Indwelt are Both Persons, yet are One God; and the whole Godhead dwells in Each (§§ 54—56).

Book IX. After a summary (§ 1) of the results already obtained, Hilary returns, in § 2, to certain of the Arian proof-texts, and warns his readers that their life depends on the recognition in Christ of true God and true man, for it is this twofold nature which makes Him the Mediator (§ 3). Universal analogy and our consciousness of the capacity to rise to the life in God convince us of these two natures in Him, Who makes this rise possible (§ 4). But heresy lays hold of words spoken by Christ Incarnate, appropriate to His humility as Man, and assigns them to Him in His previous state; thus they make Him deny His true Godhead. But His utterances before the Incarnation, during His life on earth, and after His return to glory, must be carefully distinguished (§§ 5, 6). Hilary now examines the aims and achievements of Christ Incarnate, and shews that His work for men was a Divine work, accomplished by Him for us only because He was throughout both God and Man, the two natures in Him being inseparable (§§ 7—14). After reaching this conclusion from a general survey of Christ's life on earth, he examines in the light of it the Arian arguments from isolated words. They assert that Christ refused to be called *Good* or *Master.* He refused neither title, and yet declared that both belong to God only (§§ 15—18). And, indeed, He could not have associated Himself more closely than He did with the Father, while yet He kept His Person distinct (§ 19). The Father Himself bears witness to the Son; and the sin and loss of the Jews is this, that, seeing the Father's works done by Christ, they did not see in Him the Son (§§ 20, 21). The honour and glory of Christ is inseparable from that of God (§§ 22, 23). The Scribe did well to confess the Divine unity, but was still outside the Kingdom because He did not believe in Christ as God (§§ 24—27). Next, the Arian argument from the words, *This is life eternal, that they may know Thee, the only true God, and Jesus Christ Whom Thou hast sent*, is refuted by comparison with cognate passages (§§ 28—35). For, indeed, if the Father be the only true God, the Son must also be the only true God (§ 36). That Divine nature which is common to Father and Son is subject to no limitations, and the eternal generation can be illustrated by no analogy of created things (§ 37). Christ took humanity, and, since the Father's nature did not share in this, the unity was so far impaired. But humanity has been raised in Christ to God; and this could only be because His unity in the Divine nature with the Father was perfect. Otherwise the flesh which Christ took could not have entered into the Divine glory (§ 38). There is but one glory of Father and of Son; the Son sought in the Incarnation not glory for the Word but for the flesh (§§ 39, 40). The glory of Father and Son is one; in that unity the Son bestows, as well as receives, glory (§§ 41, 42), and this glory, common to Both, is evidence that the Divine nature also is common to Both (§ 42). Again, the Arians allege the words, *The Son can do nothing of Himself*, which Hilary shews, by an examination of the context, to be a support of the Catholic cause (§§ 43—46). The Son does the Father's work, not under compulsion as an inferior, but because They are One. His will is free, yet in perfect harmony with that of the Father, because of their unity of nature (§§ 47—50). The Arians also appeal to the text, *The Father is greater than I.* The Father is, in fact, greater, first as being the Unbegotten, and secondly inasmuch as the Son has condescended to the state of man, yet without forfeiting His Godhead (§ 51). But He is not greater in nature than the Son, Who is His Image; or rather, the Begetter is the greater, while the Son, as the Begotten, is not less than He, for, although begotten, He had no beginning of existence (§§ 52—57). Next, the allegation of ignorance, based on St. Mark xiii. 32, and therefore of difference in nature from God Omniscient is refuted (§§ 58—62), both by express statements of Scripture and by a consideration of the Divine character. It is only in figurative senses that God is stated in the Old Testament sometimes to come to know, sometimes to be ignorant of, particular facts (§§ 63, 64). And so it is with Christ; His ignorance is but a wise and merciful concealment of knowledge (§§ 65—67). Yet the Arians, though they admit that Christ, being superior to man, knows all the secrets of humanity, assert that He cannot penetrate the mysteries of God (§ 68). But Christ expressly declares that He can and does, for Each is in the Other and is mirrored in the Other (§ 69). The ignorance can be nothing but concealment. Only the Father knows, i.e. He has told none but the Son; the Son does not know, i.e. He wills not to reveal His knowledge (§§ 70, 71). God is unlimited; unlimited therefore in knowledge. The nature of Father and Son being one, it is impossible that the Son should be ignorant of what the Father knows. As in will, so in knowledge, They are One (§§ 72—74). And the Apostles, by repeating their question after the Resurrection, shew that they were aware that His ignorance meant reserve. And Christ did not, this time, speak of ignorance, though He withheld the knowledge which they asked (§ 75).

BOOK X. Theological differences are not the result of honest reasoning, but of reasoning distorted, as in the case of the Arians, by preconceived opinions, whose cause is sin and their result hypocrisy (§§ 1—3). Hilary has fallen on the evil times foretold by the Apostle; truth is banished and so is he, yet his sufferings do not affect his joy in the Lord (§ 4). In the preceding books he has stated the exact truth, of which he now gives a summary (§§ 5—8). But the further objection is raised that, while God is impassible, Christ in His Passion suffered fear and pain (§ 9). But He Who taught others not to fear death could not fear.

it Himself (§ 10). He died of His own free will, knowing that in three days His Body and Spirit would rise again (§§ 11, 12). Nor did He fear bodily tortures, for pain is an affection of the weak human soul, which inhabits our body, and is not felt by the body itself (§§ 13, 14). And, although the Virgin fulfilled entirely the part of a human mother, yet the Begetter was Divine. Christ, when He took the form of a servant, remained still in the form of God, and was born perfect even as the Begetter was perfect, for Mary was not the cause, but only the means, of His human life (§§ 15, 16). St. Paul draws a clear distinction between the First Man, who was earthy, and the Second Man, Who was conceived by the Holy Ghost, and in Whom what is Flesh, in one aspect, is Bread from heaven in another (§§ 17, 18). He is therefore perfect Man as well as perfect God, and did not inherit the flesh or the soul of Adam. His whole human nature is derived from the Holy Ghost, by Whom the Virgin conceived (§§ 19, 20). Again (§ 21) the Arians argue that the Word was in Jesus in the same sense in which the Spirit was in the Prophets, and reproach the Catholics with denying the true humanity of Christ. Hilary replies that just as Christ was the cause of the birth of His own human Body, so He was the Author of His own human Soul: for no soul is transmitted. Thus His human nature is complete; He has taken the form of a servant, but all the while He is in the form of God, i.e. He Who is God and also Man is one Christ, Who was born and died and rose (§ 22). In all this He endured passion but not pain, even as air or water, if pierced by a blow, is unaffected by it. The blow is real, and the Passion was real; but it was not inflicted on our limited humanity but on a human nature which could walk on water and pass through locked doors (§ 23). If it be argued that He wept, hungered, thirsted, Hilary answers that He could wipe away tears and supply needs, and therefore was not subject to them; that though He endured them, as true Man, He was not affected by them. Such sufferings are habitual with men, and He endured them to shew that He had a true Body (§ 24). For such a Body He had, although (since He was not conceived in sin) one free from the defects of our bodies; not sinful flesh, but only the likeness of sinful flesh. For He was the Word made Flesh, and continued to be true God as He had been before (§§ 25, 26). The Lord of glory suffered neither fear nor pain in His Passion, as is shewn by the powers which He exercised on the verge of death (§§ 27, 28). His utterances in the Garden and on the Cross are not evidences of pain or fear, for they may be matched by lofty expressions of calmness and hope (§§ 29—32). Thus no proof of fear or pain or weakness can be drawn from the circumstances of the Passion. Nor was the Cross a shame, for it was His road from humiliation to glory (§ 33), nor the descent to hell a degradation, for all the while He was in heaven. How different the faith of the Thief on the cross to that of the Arian! (§ 34). The argument is summed up in § 35. Next the Agony is considered. Christ does not say that He is sorrowful on account of death, but *unto death*. It is anxiety on the Apostles' account, lest their faith should fail; a fear which reached to His death, not beyond, for He knew that after His death His glory would revive their faith. This was the fear in which He was comforted by the Angel; for Himself He was fearless, being conscious of His Godhead (§§ 36—43). He was free from pain and fear, for it is the sinful body which transmits these affections to the soul. Yet even human bodies rise sometimes superior to them, e.g. Daniel and other heroes of faith: how much more Christ (§§ 44—46). In the same way we must understand His bearing our suffering and our sin (§ 47), for, as St. Paul says, His Passion was itself a triumph (§ 48). The complaint that He was forsaken by the Father is similarly explained (§ 49). The purpose of the Arian arguments is to displace the truth of Christ as very God and very man in favour of one or other heretical hypothesis, all of which the Church rejects (§§ 50—52). Our reason must recognise its limitations and be content to believe, without understanding, apparently contradictory truths (§§ 53, 54). Christ weeping over Jerusalem and at the grave of Lazarus is equally inexplicable, yet certain

(§§ 55, 56). His laying down and taking again His life is accounted for by the two natures inseparably united in one Person (§§ 57—62). After a short summary (§ 63) he returns to the union of two natures, which is the stumbling-block of worldly wisdom (§ 64), and shews it to be the only reasonable explanation of the facts (§§ 65, 66). As St. Paul says, our belief must be *according to the Scriptures;* the necessity and the rewards of faith (§§ 67—70). The seeming infirmity of Christ was assumed for our instruction and for our salvation.

BOOK XI. The Faith is one, even as God is One; but the faiths of heretics are many (§§ 1, 2). Hilary has now demonstrated the truth about Christ, so that it cannot be denied; it is attested also by miracles even in his own day (§ 3). The Arians preach another, a created Christ; and in making Christ a creature they proclaim another God, not a Father but a Creator (§ 4). The Son, as the Image, is of one nature with the Father; if He is inferior He is not the Image (§ 5). But the Arians explain the oneness away by arguments from His condescension to our estate (§ 6), and, even after His Resurrection, plead that He confesses His inequality. They argue thus from 1 Cor. xv. 24—28, a passage to which the rest of this book is devoted (§§ 7, 8). But we must recognise the mysteriousness of the truth, accepting the two sides of it, both clearly revealed though we cannot reconcile them (§ 9). They regard only one aspect; Hilary in reply proves once more that Christ is both born from God, and Himself God (§§ 10—12). But at His Incarnation He began to have as Lord the God Who had been His Father eternally (§ 13), and when He said that He was ascending to *His God,* He spoke as when He calls us His brethren (§§ 14, 15). Thus there are two senses in which God is the Father of Christ; and He Who is Father to Christ the Son is Lord to Christ the Servant (§§ 16, 17). And it was to Him as Servant that the Psalmist said, *Thy God hath anointed Thee;* the words would have no meaning if addressed to Him as Son (§§ 18, 19). It is through this lower nature that He is our Brother and God our Father, and He the Mediator (§ 20). But it is argued that His subjection at the last and the delivery of the kingdom to the Father is a proof of inequality. The passage must be taken as a whole (§§ 21, 22). There are some truths which it is difficult for man to grasp, and if we misunderstand them we must not be ashamed to confess our error (§§ 23, 24). In this passage the Arians aid their case by changing the order of the prophecy (§§ 25—27). *The end* means a final and enduring state, not the coming to an end (§ 28), and though He delivers up the kingdom He does not cease to reign (§ 29). His subjection to the Father and the subjection of all things to Him is next considered; in one sense it is figurative language, in another it proves the unity of Father and Son. The subjection of the Son means His partaking in the glory of the Father (§§ 30—36). The Transfiguration shews the glory of Christ's Body; a glory which the faithful shall share (§§ 37, 38). The righteous are His kingdom, which He, as Man, shall deliver to the Father, for *By man came also the resurrection of the dead* (§ 39). And at last God shall be all in all, humanity in Christ not being discarded, but glorified and received into the Godhead (§ 40). Christ, as well as St. Paul, has foretold this (§§ 41, 42). The Arian misrepresentation of this truth is mere folly (§ 43). Any rational explanation must assume that God's majesty cannot be augmented, even as it cannot be measured (§§ 44, 45), while our reason is limited, and so contrasted with the Divine infinity. God cannot become greater than He was in becoming *All in all.* Father and Son, after as before, must Each be as He was (§§ 46—48). All was done for us that we might be glorified, being conformed to the likeness of Him Who is the Image of the Father (§ 49).

BOOK XII. Hilary gives a final explanation of the great Arian text, *The Lord created me for a beginning of His ways;* the words must not be taken literally. Christ is not created, but Creator (§§ 1—5). If He is a creature, the Father also is a creature, for They are One in nature and in honour (§§ 6, 7). The similar passage, *I begat Thee from the womb*, is figurative; elsewhere God's Hands and Eyes are spoken of. The sense is that the Son is God from God (§§ 8—10). Nor was Christ made; He is the Son, not the handiwork, of the Father (§§ 11, 12). And His Sonship is immediate, not derivative like ours, or like that of Israel His firstborn. This latter kind of sonship has a definite beginning of existence, and an origin out of nothing (§§ 13—16). The Arian arguments fail to prove that the Sonship of Christ has either of these characters (§§ 17, 18). Truth is to be attained not by self-confident arguing but by faith (§ 19), yet it is not enough for us to avoid their reasonings; we must overthrow them (§ 20). The Son was born from eternity, being the Son of the eternal Father (§ 21). The objection that sonship involves beginning does not hold in His case (§§ 22, 23). The Son has all that the Father has; He has therefore eternity and an unconditioned existence (§ 24). He is from the Eternal, and therefore eternal Himself; from the Eternal, and therefore not from nothing. Reason cannot grasp, and therefore cannot refute, this. We must not assert that there was a time before He was born, a time when He was not (§§ 25—27). We must not argue, from the analogy of our own birth, that the truth is impossible (§ 28), nor that, because of His eternal existence, the Son was not born (§§ 29—32). Again, the Arians deny the eternal Fatherhood of God; He always existed, they say, but was not always the Father. This contradicts Scripture (§§ 33, 34). They argue that Wisdom is said to be the first of God's creatures; but creation, in this sense, is a synonym for generation, and Wisdom was antecedent to creation (§§ 35—38). Wisdom is coeternal with God (§ 39), and shared His eternal purpose of creation (§§ 40, 41). Nor may we believe that Christ was begotten simply in order to perform the creative work, as God's Minister, for Wisdom took part in the design as well as in the execution (§§ 42, 43). And again, Wisdom is spoken of as created, as an indication of Her control over created things (§ 44). The creation to be a beginning of God's ways is a separate event from the eternal generation. It means that Christ, as the Way of Life, under the Old Covenant took the semblance, under the New Covenant the substance, of the creature man, to lead us into the way. The two senses must not be confused (§§ 45—49). Yet mere inaccuracy of speech, without heretical intent, is not unpardonable (§ 50). After a final assertion (§ 51) of faith in Christ as God from God, the eternal Son, Hilary appeals to the Almighty Father, declaring his creed, his consciousness of human infirmity and of the need of faith (§§ 52, 53). The Son is the Only-begotten of God, the Second because He is the Son (§ 54). The Holy Ghost proceeds from the Father and is sent by the Son. He also is no creature, but of one nature with the God Whose mysteries He knows, and ineffable like Him Whose Spirit He is (§ 55). Finally, Hilary prays that, as he was baptized, so he may remain in the faith of Three Persons in One God.

ON THE TRINITY.

BOOK I.

1. WHEN I was seeking an employment adequate to the powers of human life and righteous in itself, whether prompted by nature or suggested by the researches of the wise, whereby I might attain to some result worthy of that Divine gift of understanding which has been given us, many things occurred to me which in general esteem were thought to render life both useful and desirable. And especially that which now, as always in the past, is regarded as most to be desired, leisure combined with wealth, came before my mind. The one without the other seemed rather a source of evil than an opportunity for good, for leisure in poverty is felt to be almost an exile from life itself, while wealth possessed amid anxiety is in itself an affliction, rendered the worse by the deeper humiliation which he must suffer who loses, after possessing, the things that most are wished and sought. And yet, though these two embrace the highest and best of the luxuries of life, they seem not far removed from the normal pleasures of the beasts which, as they roam through shady places rich in herbage, enjoy at once their safety from toil and the abundance of their food. For if this be regarded as the best and most perfect conduct of the life of man, it results that one object is common, though the range of feelings differ, to us and the whole unreasoning animal world, since all of them, in that bounteous provision and absolute leisure which nature bestows, have full scope for enjoyment without anxiety for possession.

2. I believe that the mass of mankind have spurned from themselves and censured in others this acquiescence in a thoughtless, animal life, for no other reason than that nature herself has taught them that it is unworthy of humanity to hold themselves born only to gratify their greed and their sloth, and ushered into life for no high aim of glorious deed or fair accomplishment, and that this very life was granted without the power of progress towards immortality; a life, indeed, which then we should confidently assert did not deserve to be regarded as a gift of God, since, racked by pain and laden with trouble, it wastes itself upon itself from the blank mind of infancy to the wanderings of age. I believe that men, prompted by nature herself, have raised themselves through teaching and practice to the virtues which we name patience and temperance and forbearance, under the conviction that right living means right action and right thought, and that Immortal God has not given life only to end in death; for none can believe that the Giver of good has bestowed the pleasant sense of life in order that it may be overcast by the gloomy fear of dying.

3. And yet, though I could not tax with folly and uselessness this counsel of theirs to keep the soul free from blame, and evade by foresight or elude by skill or endure with patience the troubles of life, still I could not regard these men as guides competent to lead me to the good and happy Life. Their precepts were platitudes, on the mere level of human impulse; animal instinct could not fail to comprehend them, and he who understood but disobeyed would have fallen into an insanity baser than animal unreason. Moreover, my soul was eager not merely to do the things, neglect of which brings shame and suffering, but to know the God and Father Who had given this great gift, to Whom, it felt, it owed its whole self, Whose service was its true honour, on Whom all its hopes were fixed, in Whose lovingkindness, as in a safe home and haven, it could rest amid all the troubles of this anxious life. It was inflamed with a passionate desire to apprehend Him or to know Him.

4. Some of these teachers brought forward large households of dubious deities, and under the persuasion that there is a sexual activity in divine beings narrated births and lineages from god to god. Others asserted that there were gods greater and less, of distinction propor-

tionate to their power. Some denied the existence of any gods whatever, and confined their reverence to a nature which, in their opinion, owes its being to chance-led vibrations and collisions. On the other hand, many followed the common belief in asserting the existence of a God, but proclaimed Him heedless and indifferent to the affairs of men. Again, some worshipped in the elements of earth and air the actual bodily and visible forms of created things; and, finally, some made their gods dwell within images of men or of beasts, tame or wild, of birds or of snakes, and confined the Lord of the universe and Father of infinity within these narrow prisons of metal or stone or wood. These, I was sure, could be no exponents of truth, for though they were at one in the absurdity, the foulness, the impiety of their observances, they were at variance concerning the essential articles of their senseless belief. My soul was distracted amid all these claims, yet still it pressed along that profitable road which leads inevitably to the true knowledge of God. It could not hold that neglect of a world created by Himself was worthily to be attributed to God, or that deities endowed with sex, and lines of begetters and begotten, were compatible with the pure and mighty nature of the Godhead. Nay, rather, it was sure that that which is Divine and eternal must be one without distinction of sex, for that which is self-existent cannot have left outside itself anything superior to itself. Hence omnipotence and eternity are the possession of One only, for omnipotence is incapable of degrees of strength or weakness, and eternity of priority or succession. In God we must worship absolute eternity and absolute power.

5. While my mind was dwelling on these and on many like thoughts, I chanced upon the books which, according to the tradition of the Hebrew faith, were written by Moses and the prophets, and found in them words spoken by God the Creator testifying of Himself 'I AM THAT I AM, and again, HE THAT IS *hath sent me unto you* [1].' I confess that I was amazed to find in them an indication concerning God so exact that it expressed in the terms best adapted to human understanding an unattainable insight into the mystery of the Divine nature. For no property of God which the mind can grasp is more characteristic of Him than existence, since existence, in the absolute sense, cannot be predicated of that which shall come to an end, or of that which has had a beginning, and He who now joins

continuity of being with the possession of perfect felicity could not in the past, nor can in the future, be non-existent; for whatsoever is Divine can neither be originated nor destroyed. Wherefore, since God's eternity is inseparable from Himself, it was worthy of Him to reveal this one thing, that He IS, as the assurance of His absolute eternity.

6. For such an indication of God's infinity the words 'I AM THAT I AM' were clearly adequate; but, in addition, we needed to apprehend the operation of His majesty and power. For while absolute existence is peculiar to Him Who, abiding eternally, had no beginning in a past however remote, we hear again an utterance worthy of Himself issuing from the eternal and Holy God, Who says, *Who holdeth the heaven in His palm and the earth in His hand* [2], and again, *The heaven is My throne and the earth is the footstool of My feet. What house will ye build Me or what shall be the place of My rest* [3]? The whole heaven is held in the palm of God, the whole earth grasped in His hand. Now the word of God, profitable as it is to the cursory thought of a pious mind, reveals a deeper meaning to the patient student than to the momentary hearer. For this heaven which is held in the palm of God is also His throne, and the earth which is grasped in His hand is also the footstool beneath His feet. This was not written that from throne and footstool, metaphors drawn from the posture of one sitting, we should conclude that He has extension in space, as of a body, for that which is His throne and footstool is also held in hand and palm by that infinite Omnipotence. It was written that in all born and created things God might be known within them and without, overshadowing and indwelling, surrounding all and interfused through all, since palm and hand, which hold, reveal the might of His external control, while throne and footstool, by their support of a sitter, display the subservience of outward things to One within Who, Himself outside them, encloses all in His grasp, yet dwells within the external world which is His own. In this wise does God, from within and from without, control and correspond to the universe; being infinite He is present in all things, in Him Who is infinite all are included. In devout thoughts such as these my soul, engrossed in the pursuit of truth, took its delight. For it seemed that the greatness of God so far surpassed the mental powers of His handiwork, that however far the limited mind of man might strain in the hazardous

---

[1] Exod. iii. 14.   [2] Isai. xl. 12.   [3] Ib. lxvi. 1, 2.

effort to define Him, the gap was not lessened between the finite nature which struggled and the boundless infinity that lay beyond its ken [4]. I had come by reverent reflection on my own part to understand this, but I found it confirmed by the words of the prophet, *Whither shall I go from Thy Spirit? Or whither shall I flee from Thy face? If I ascend up into heaven, Thou art there; if I go down into hell, Thou art there also; if I have taken my wings before dawn and made my dwelling in the uttermost parts of the sea (Thou art there). For thither Thy hand shall guide me and Thy right hand shall hold me* [5]. There is no space where God is not; space does not exist apart from Him. He is in heaven, in hell, beyond the seas; dwelling in all things and enveloping all. Thus He embraces, and is embraced by, the universe, confined to no part of it but pervading all.

7. Therefore, although my soul drew joy from the apprehension of this august and unfathomable Mind, because it could worship as its own Father and Creator so limitless an Infinity, yet with a still more eager desire it sought to know the true aspect of its infinite and eternal Lord, that it might be able to believe that that immeasurable Deity was apparelled in splendour befitting tbe beauty of His wisdom. Then, while the devout soul was baffled and astray through its own feebleness, it caught from the prophet's voice this scale of comparison for God, admirably expressed, *By the greatness of His works and the beauty of the things that He hath made the Creator of worlds is rightly discerned* [5a]. The Creator of great things is supreme in greatness, of beautiful things in beauty. Since the work transcends our thoughts, all thought must be transcended by the Maker. Thus heaven and air and earth and seas are fair: fair also the whole universe, as the Greeks agree, who from its beautiful ordering call it κόσμος, that is, *order*. But if our thought can estimate this beauty of the universe by a natural instinct—an instinct such as we see in certain birds and beasts whose voice, though it fall below the level of our understanding, yet has a sense clear to them though they cannot utter it, and in which, since all speech is the expression of some thought, there lies a meaning patent to themselves—must not the Lord of this universal beauty be recognised as Himself most beautiful amid all the beauty that surrounds Him? For though the splendour of His eternal glory overtax our mind's best powers, it cannot fail to see that He is beautiful. We must in truth

confess that God is most beautiful, and that with a beauty which, though it transcend our comprehension, forces itself upon our perception.

8. Thus my mind, full of these results which by its own reflection and the teaching of Scripture it had attained, rested with assurance, as on some peaceful watch-tower, upon that glorious conclusion, recognising that its true nature made it capable of one homage to its Creator, and of none other, whether greater or less; the homage namely of conviction that His is a greatness too vast for our comprehension but not for our faith. For a reasonable faith is akin to reason and accepts its aid, even though that same reason cannot cope with the vastness of eternal Omnipotence.

9. Beneath all these thoughts lay an instinctive hope, which strengthened my assertion of the faith, in some perfect blessedness hereafter to be earned by devout thoughts concerning God and upright life; the reward, as it were, that awaits the triumphant warrior. For true faith in God would pass unrewarded, if the soul be destroyed by death, and quenched in the extinction of bodily life. Even unaided reason pleaded that it was unworthy of God to usher man into an existence which has some share of His thought and wisdom, only to await the sentence of life withdrawn and of eternal death; to create him out of nothing to take his place in the world, only that when he has taken it he may perish. For, on the only rational theory of creation, its purpose was that things non-existent should come into being, not that things existing should cease to be.

10. Yet my soul was weighed down with fear both for itself and for the body. It retained a firm conviction, and a devout loyalty to the true faith concerning God, but had come to harbour a deep anxiety concerning itself and the bodily dwelling which must, it thought, share its destruction. While in this state, in addition to its knowledge of the teaching of the Law and Prophets, it learned the truths taught by the Apostle in the Gospel;—*In the beginning was the Word, and the Word was with God, and the Word was God. The same was in the beginning with God. All things were made through Him, and without Him was not anything made. That which was made in Him is life* [6], *and the life was the light of men, and the light shineth in darkness, and the darkness apprehended it not. There was a man sent from God, whose name was John. He came for witness, that he might bear witness of the light. That was the true light, which lighteneth every man that cometh*

4 Reading *mens finita* and *naturæ finitatem* for the *infinita* and *infinitatem* of the Benedictine Edition.
5 Ps. cxxxviii. (cxxxix.) 7—10.
5a Wisd. xiii. 5.

6 Cf. Hilary's explanation of this passage in Book ii. §§ 19, 20.

into this world. *He was in the world, and the world was made through Him, and the world knew Him not. He came unto His own things, and they that were His own received Him not. But to as many as received Him He gave power to become sons of God, even to them that believe on His Name; which were born, not of blood, nor of the will of man, nor of the will of the flesh, but of God. And the Word became flesh and dwelt among us, and we beheld His glory, glory as of the Only-begotten from the Father, full of grace and truth*[7]. Here the soul makes an advance beyond the attainment of its natural capacities, is taught more than it had dreamed concerning God. For it learns that its Creator is God of God; it hears that the Word is God and was with God in the beginning. It comes to understand that the Light of the world was abiding in the world and that the world knew Him not; that He came to His own possession and that they that were His own received Him not; but that they who do receive Him by virtue of their faith advance to be sons of God, being born not of the embrace of the flesh nor of the conception of the blood nor of bodily desire, but of God; finally, it learns that the Word became flesh and dwelt among us, and that His glory was seen, which, as of the Only-begotten from the Father, is perfect through grace and truth.

11. Herein my soul, trembling and distressed, found a hope wider than it had imagined. First came its introduction to the knowledge of God the Father. Then it learnt that the eternity and infinity and beauty which, by the light of natural reason, it had attributed to its Creator belonged also to God the Only-begotten. It did not disperse its faith among a plurality of deities, for it heard that He is God of God; nor did it fall into the error of attributing a difference of nature to this God of God, for it learnt that He is full of grace and truth. Nor yet did my soul perceive anything contrary to reason in God of God, since He was revealed as having been in the beginning God with God. It saw that there are very few who attain to the knowledge of this saving faith, though its reward be great, for even His own received Him not, though they who receive Him are promoted to be sons of God by a birth, not of the flesh but of faith. It learnt also that this sonship to God is not a compulsion but a possibility. for, while the Divine gift is offered to all, it is no heredity inevitably imprinted but a prize awarded to willing choice. And lest this very truth that whosoever will may become a son of God should stagger the weakness

of our faith (for most we desire, but least expect, that which from its very greatness we find it hard to hope for), God the Word became flesh, that through His Incarnation our flesh might attain to union with God the Word. And lest we should think that this incarnate Word was some other than God the Word, or that His flesh was of a body different from ours, He dwelt among us that by His dwelling He might be known as the indwelling God, and, by His dwelling among us, known as God incarnate in no other flesh than our own, and moreover, though He had condescended to take our flesh, not destitute of His own attributes; for He, the Only-begotten of the Father, full of grace and truth, is fully possessed of His own attributes and truly endowed with ours.

12. This lesson in the Divine mysteries was gladly welcomed by my soul, now drawing near through the flesh to God, called to new birth through faith, entrusted with liberty and power to win the heavenly regeneration, conscious of the love of its Father and Creator, sure that He would not annihilate a creature whom He had summoned out of nothing into life. And it could estimate how high are these truths above the mental vision of man; for the reason which deals with the common objects of thought can conceive of nothing as existent beyond what it perceives within itself or can create out of itself. My soul measured the mighty workings of God, wrought on the scale of His eternal omnipotence, not by its own powers of perception but by a boundless faith; and therefore refused to disbelieve, because it could not understand, that God was in the beginning with God, and that the Word became flesh and dwelt among us, but bore in mind the truth that with the will to believe would come the power to understand.

13. And lest the soul should stray and linger in some delusion of heathen philosophy, it receives this further lesson of perfect loyalty to the holy faith, taught by the Apostle in words inspired:—*Beware lest any man spoil you through philosophy and vain deceit, after the tradition of men, after the rudiments of the world, and not after Christ; for in Him dwelleth all the fulness of the Godhead bodily, and ye are made full in Him, Which is the Head of all principality and power; in Whom ye were also circumcised with a circumcision not made with hands, in putting off the body of the flesh, but with the circumcision of Christ; buried with Him in Baptism, wherein also ye have risen again through faith in the working of God, Who raised Him from the dead. And you, when ye were dead in sins and in the*

---

7 St. John i. 1—14.

uncircumcision of your flesh, He hath quickened with Him, having forgiven you all your sins, blotting out the bond which was against us by its ordinances, which was contrary to us ; and He hath taken it out of the way, nailing it to the Cross ; and having put off the flesh He made a show of powers openly, triumphing over them through confidence in Himself[8]. Steadfast faith rejects the vain subtleties of philosophic enquiry ; truth refuses to be vanquished by these treacherous devices of human folly, and enslaved by falsehood. It will not confine God within the limits which bound our common reason, nor judge *after the rudiments of the world* concerning Christ, *in Whom dwelleth all the fulness of the Godhead bodily*, and in such wise that the utmost efforts of the earthly mind to comprehend Him are baffled by that immeasurable Eternity and Omnipotence. My soul judged of Him as One Who, drawing us upward to partake of His own Divine nature, has loosened henceforth the bond of bodily observances ; Who, unlike the Symbolic Law, has initiated us into no rites of mutilating the flesh, but Whose purpose is that our spirit, circumcised from vice, should purify all the natural faculties of the body by abstinence from sin, that we being buried with His Death in Baptism may return to the life of eternity (since regeneration to life is death to the former life), and dying to our sins be born again to immortality, that even as He abandoned His immortality to die for us, so should we awaken from death to immortality with Him. For He took upon Him the flesh in which we have sinned that by wearing our flesh He might forgive sins ; a flesh which He shares with us by wearing it, not by sinning in it. He blotted out through death the sentence of death, that by a new creation of our race in Himself He might sweep away the penalty appointed by the former Law. He let them nail Him to the cross that He might nail to the curse of the cross and abolish all the curses to which the world is condemned. He suffered as man to the utmost that He might put powers to shame. For Scripture had foretold that He Who is God should die ; that the victory and triumph of them that trust in Him lay in the fact that He, Who is immortal and cannot be overcome by death, was to die that mortals might gain eternity. These deeds of God, wrought in a manner beyond our comprehension, cannot, I repeat, be understood by our natural faculties, for the work of the Infinite and Eternal can only be grasped by an infinite intelligence. Hence, just as

the truths that God became man, that the Immortal died, that the Eternal was buried, do not belong to the rational order but are an unique work of power, so on the other hand it is an effect not of intellect but of omnipotence that He Who is man is also God, that He Who died is immortal, that He Who was buried is eternal. We, then, are raised together by God in Christ through His death. But, since in Christ there is the fulness of the Godhead, we have herein a revelation of God the Father joining to raise us in Him Who died ; and we must confess that Christ Jesus is none other than God in all the fulness of the Deity.

14. In this calm assurance of safety did my soul gladly and hopefully take its rest, and feared so little the interruption of death, that death seemed only a name for eternal life. And the life of this present body was so far from seeming a burden or affliction that it was regarded as children regard their alphabet, sick men their draught, shipwrecked sailors their swim, young men the training for their profession, future commanders their first campaign ; that is, as an endurable submission to present necessities, bearing the promise of a blissful immortality. And further, I began to proclaim those truths in which my soul had a personal faith, as a duty of the episcopate which had been laid upon me, employing my office to promote the salvation of all men.

15. While I was thus engaged there came to light certain fallacies of rash and wicked men, hopeless for themselves and merciless towards others, who made their own feeble nature the measure of the might of God's nature. They claimed, not that they had ascended to an infinite knowledge of infinite things, but that they had reduced all knowledge, undefined before, within the scope of ordinary reason, and fixed the limits of the faith. Whereas the true work of religion is a service of obedience ; and these were men heedless of their own weakness, reckless of Divine realities, who undertook to improve upon the teaching of God.

16. Not to touch upon the vain enquiries of other heretics—concerning whom however, when the course of my argument gives occasion, I will not be silent—there are those who tamper with the faith of the Gospel by denying, under the cloak of loyalty to the One God, the birth of God the Only-begotten. They assert that there was an extension of God into man, not a descent ; that He, Who for the season that He took our flesh was Son of Man, had not been previously, nor was then, Son of God ; that there was no Divine birth in His case, but an identity of Begetter and Begotten ; and (to maintain what they consider a perfect loyalty

---

[8] Col. ii. 8—15.

to the unity of God) that there was an unbroken continuity in the Incarnation, the Father extending Himself into the Virgin, and Himself being born as His own Son. Others, on the contrary (heretics, because there is no salvation apart from Christ, Who in the beginning was God the Word with God), deny that He was born and declare that He was merely created. Birth, they hold, would confess Him to be true God, while creation proves His Godhead unreal; and though this explanation be a fraud against the faith in the unity of God, regarded as an accurate definition, yet they think it may pass muster as figurative language. They degrade, in name and in belief, His true birth to the level of a creation, to cut Him off from the Divine unity, that, as a creature called into being, He may not claim the fulness of the Godhead, which is not His by a true birth.

17. My soul has been burning to answer these insane attacks. I call to mind that the very centre of a saving faith is the belief not merely in God, but in God as a Father; not merely in Christ, but in Christ as the Son of God; in Him, not as a creature, but as God the Creator, born of God. My prime object is by the clear assertions of prophets and evangelists to refute the insanity and ignorance of men who use the unity of God (in itself a pious and profitable confession) as a cloak for their denial either that In Christ God was born, or else that He is very God. Their purpose is to isolate a solitary God at the heart of the faith by making Christ, though mighty, only a creature; because, so they allege, a birth of God widens the believer's faith into a trust in more gods than one. But we, divinely taught to confess neither two Gods nor yet a solitary God, will adduce the evidence of the Gospels and the prophets for our confession of God the Father and God the Son, united, not confounded, in our faith. We will not admit Their identity nor allow, as a compromise, that Christ is God in some imperfect sense; for God, born of God, cannot be the same as His Father, since He is His Son, nor yet can He be different in nature.

18. And you, whose warmth of faith and passion for a truth unknown to the world and its philosophers shall prompt to read me, must remember to eschew the feeble and baseless conjectures of earthly minds, and in devout willingness to learn must break down the barriers of prejudice and half-knowledge. The new faculties of the regenerate intellect are needed; each must have his understanding enlightened by the heavenly gift imparted to the soul. First he must take his stand upon the sure ground [*substantia* = ὑποστάσει] of

God, as holy Jeremiah says [9], that since he is to hear about that nature [*substantia*] he may expand his thoughts till they are worthy of the theme, not fixing some arbitrary standard for himself, but judging as of infinity. And again, though he be aware that he is partaker of the Divine nature, as the holy apostle Peter says in his second Epistle [1], yet he must not measure the Divine nature by the limitations of his own, but gauge God's assertions concerning Himself by the scale of His own glorious self-revelation. For he is the best student who does not read his thoughts into the book, but lets it reveal its own; who draws from it its sense, and does not import his own into it, nor force upon its words a meaning which he had determined was the right one before he opened its pages. Since then we are to discourse of the things of God, let us assume that God has full knowledge of Himself, and bow with humble reverence to His words. For He Whom we can only know through His own utterances is the fitting witness concerning Himself.

19. If in our discussion of the nature and birth of God we adduce certain analogies, let no one suppose that such comparisons are perfect and complete. There can be no comparison between God and earthly things, yet the weakness of our understanding forces us to seek for illustrations from a lower sphere to explain our meaning about loftier themes. The course of daily life shews how our experience in ordinary matters enables us to form conclusions on unfamiliar subjects. We must therefore regard any comparison as helpful to man rather than as descriptive of God, since it suggests, rather than exhausts, the sense we seek. Nor let such a comparison be thought too bold when it sets side by side carnal and spiritual natures, things invisible and things palpable, since it avows itself a necessary aid to the weakness of the human mind, and deprecates the condemnation due to an imperfect analogy. On this principle I proceed with my task, intending to use the terms supplied by God, yet colouring my argument with illustrations drawn from human life.

20. And first, I have so laid out the plan of the whole work as to consult the advantage of the reader by the logical order in which its books are arranged. It has been my resolve to publish no half-finished and ill-considered treatise, lest its disorderly array should resemble the confused clamour of a mob of peasants. And since no one can scale a precipice unless there be jutting ledges to aid his progress to the summit, I have here set down

---

9 xxiii. 22, according to the LXX., ἐν ὑποστάσει.
1 ii. 14.

in order the primary outlines of our ascent, leading our difficult course of argument up the easiest path ; not cutting steps in the face of the rock, but levelling it to a gentle slope, that so the traveller, almost without a sense of effort, may reach the heights.

21. Thus, after the present first book, the second expounds the mystery of the Divine birth, that those who shall be baptized in the Name of the Father and of the Son and of the Holy Ghost may know the true Names, and not be perplexed about their sense but accurately informed as to fact and meaning, and so receive full assurance that in the words which are used they have the true Names, and that those Names involve the truth.

22. After this short and simple discourse concerning the Trinity, the third book makes further progress, sure though slow. Citing the greatest instances of His power, it brings within the range of faith's understanding that saying, in itself beyond our comprehension, *I in the Father and the Father in Me*[2], which Christ utters concerning Himself. Thus truth beyond the dull wit of man is the prize of faith equipped with reason and knowledge ; for neither may we doubt God's Word concerning Himself, nor can we suppose that the devout reason is incapable of apprehending His might.

23. The fourth book starts with the doctrines of the heretics, and disowns complicity in the fallacies whereby they are traducing the faith of the Church. It publishes that infidel creed which a number of them have lately promulgated[3], and exposes the dishonesty, and therefore the wickedness, of their arguments from the Law for what they call the unity of God. It sets out the whole evidence of Law and Prophets to demonstrate the impiety of asserting the unity of God to the exclusion of the Godhead of Christ, and the treason of alleging that if Christ be God the Only-begotten, then God is not one.

24. The fifth book follows in reply the sequence of heretical assertion. They had falsely declared that they followed the Law in the sense which they assigned to the unity of God, and that they had proved from it that the true God is of one Person ; and this in order to rob the Lord Christ of His birth by their conclusion concerning the One true God, for birth is the evidence of origin. In answer I assert, step by step, what they deny ; for from the Law and the Prophets I demonstrate that there are not two gods, nor one isolated true God, neither perverting the faith in the Divine unity nor denying the birth of Christ. And since they

say that the Lord Jesus Christ, created rather than born, bears the Divine Name by gift and not by right, I have proved His true Divinity from the Prophets in such a way that, He being acknowledged very God, the assurance of His inherent Godhead shall hold us fast to the certainty that God is One.

25. The sixth book reveals the full deceitfulness of this heretical teaching. To win credit for their assertions they denounce the impious doctrine of heretics :—of Valentinus, to wit, and Sabellius and Manichæus and Hieracas, and appropriate the godly language of the Church as a cover for their blasphemy. They reprove and alter the language of these heretics, correcting it into a vague resemblance to orthodoxy, in order to suppress the holy faith while apparently denouncing heresy. But we state clearly what is the language and what the doctrine of each of these men, and acquit the Church of any complicity or fellowship with condemned heretics. Their words which deserve condemnation we condemn, and those which claim our humble acceptance we accept. Thus that Divine Sonship of Jesus Christ, which is the object of their most strenuous denial, we prove by the witness of the Father, by Christ's own assertion, by the preaching of Apostles, by the faith of believers, by the cries of devils, by the contradiction of Jews, in itself a confession, by the recognition of the heathen who had not known God ; and all this to rescue from dispute a truth of which Christ had left us no excuse for ignorance.

26. Next the seventh book, starting from the basis of a true faith now attained, delivers its verdict in the great debate. First, armed with its sound and incontrovertible proof of the impregnable faith, it takes part in the conflict raging between Sabellius and Hebion and these opponents of the true Godhead. It joins issue with Sabellius on his denial of the pre-existence of Christ, and with his assailants on their assertion that He is a creature. Sabellius overlooked the eternity of the Son, but believed that true God worked in a human body. Our present adversaries deny that He was born, assert that He was created, and fail to see in His deeds the works of very God. What both sides dispute, we believe. Sabellius denies that it was the Son who was working, and he is wrong ; but he proves his case triumphantly when he alleges that the work done was that of true God. The Church shares his victory over those who deny that in Christ was very God. But when Sabellius denies that Christ existed before the worlds, his adversaries prove to conviction that Christ's activity is from everlasting, and we are on their side in this confutation of

---

[2] St. John x. 38.
[3] The letter of Arius to Alexander ; Book iv., §§ 12, 13.

Sabellius, who recognises true God, but not God the Son, in this activity. And our two previous adversaries join forces to refute Hebion, the second demonstrating the eternal existence of Christ, while the first proves that His work is that of very God. Thus the heretics overthrow one another, while the Church, as against Sabellius, against those who call Christ a creature, against Hebion, bears witness that the Lord Jesus Christ is very God of very God, born before the worlds and born in after times as man.

27. No one can doubt that we have taken the course of true reverence and of sound doctrine when, after proving from Law and Prophets first that Christ is the Son of God, and next that He is true God, and this without breach of the mysterious unity, we proceed to support the Law and the Prophets by the evidence of the Gospels, and prove from them also that He is the Son of God and Himself very God. It is the easiest of tasks, after demonstrating His right to the Name of Son, to shew that the Name truly describes His relation to the Father; though indeed universal usage regards the granting of the name of son as convincing evidence of sonship. But, to leave no loop-hole for the trickery and deceit of these traducers of the true birth of God the Only-begotten, we have used His true Godhead as evidence of His true Sonship; to shew that He Who (as is confessed by all) bears the Name of Son of God is actually God, we have adduced His Name, His birth, His nature, His power, His assertions. We have proved that His Name is an accurate description of Himself, that the title of Son is an evidence of birth, that in His birth He retained His Divine Nature, and with His nature His power, and that that power manifested itself in conscious and deliberate self-revelation. I have set down the Gospel proofs of each several point, shewing how His self-revelation displays His power, how His power reveals His nature, how His nature is His by birthright, and from His birth comes His title to the name of Son. Thus every whisper of blasphemy is silenced, for the Lord Jesus Christ Himself by the witness of His own mouth has taught us that He is, as His Name, His birth, His nature, His power declare, in the true sense of Deity, very God of very God.

28. While its two predecessors have been devoted to the confirmation of the faith in Christ as Son of God and true God, the eighth book is taken up with the proof of the unity of God, shewing that this unity is consistent with the birth of the Son, and that the birth involves no duality in the Godhead. First

it exposes the sophistry with which these heretics have attempted to avoid, though they could not deny, the confession of the real existence of God, Father and Son; it demolishes their helpless and absurd plea that in such passages as, *And the multitude of them that believed were one soul and heart* [4], and again, *He that planteth and He that watereth are one* [5], and *Neither for these only do I pray, but for them also that shall believe on Me through their word, that they may all be one, even as Thou, Father, art in Me, and I in Thee, that they also may be in Us* [6], a unity of will and mind, not of Divinity, is expressed. From a consideration of the true sense of these texts we shew that they involve the reality of the Divine birth; and then, displaying the whole series of our Lord's self-revelations, we exhibit, in the language of Apostles and in the very words of the Holy Spirit, the whole and perfect mystery of the glory of God as Father and as Only-begotten Son. Because there is a Father we know that there is a Son; in that Son the Father is manifested to us, and hence our certainty that He is born the Only-begotten and that He is very God.

29. In matters essential to salvation it is not enough to advance the proofs which faith supplies and finds sufficient. Arguments which we have not tested may delude us into a misapprehension of the meaning of our own words, unless we take the offensive by exposing the hollowness of the enemy's proofs, and so establish our own faith upon the demonstrated absurdity of his. The ninth book, therefore, is employed in refuting the arguments by which the heretics attempt to invalidate the birth of God the Only-begotten;— heretics who ignore the mystery of the revelation hidden from the beginning of the world, and forget that the Gospel faith proclaims the union of God and man. For their denial that our Lord Jesus Christ is God, like unto God and equal with God as Son with Father, born of God and by right of His birth subsisting as very Spirit, they are accustomed to appeal to such words of our Lord as, *Why callest thou Me good? None is good save One, even God* [7]. They argue that by His reproof of the man who called Him good, and by His assertion of the goodness of God only, He excludes Himself from the goodness of that God Who alone is good and from that true Divinity which belongs only to One. With this text their blasphemous reasoning connects another, *And this is life eternal that they should*

---

4 Acts iv. 32: in this and the following passages *unum* is read.   5 1 Cor. iii. 8.   6 St. John xvii. 20, 21.
7 St. Luke xviii. 19.

know Thee the only true God, and Him Whom Thou didst send, Jesus Christ[8]. Here, they say, He confesses that the Father is the only true God, and that He Himself is neither true nor God, since this recognition of an only true God is limited to the Possessor of the attributes assigned. And they profess to be quite clear about His meaning in this passage, since He also says, *The Son can do nothing of Himself, but what He hath seen the Father doing*[9]. The fact that He can only copy is said to be evidence of the limitation of His nature. There can be no comparison between Omnipotence and One whose action is dependent upon the previous activity of Another; reason itself draws an absolute line between power and the want of power. That line is so clear that He Himself has avowed concerning God the Father, *The Father is greater than I*[1]. So frank a confession silences all demur; it is blasphemy and madness to assign the dignity and nature of God to One who disclaims them. So utterly devoid is He of the qualities of true God that He actually bears witness concerning Himself, *But of that day and hour knoweth no one, neither the angels in heaven nor the Son, but God only*[2]. A son who knows not his father's secret must, from his ignorance, be alien from the father who knows; a nature limited in knowledge cannot partake of that majesty and might which alone is exempt from the tyranny of ignorance.

30. We therefore expose the blasphemous misunderstanding at which they have arrived by distortion and perversion of the meaning of Christ's words. We account for those words by stating what manner of questions He was answering, at what times He was speaking, what partial knowledge He was deigning to impart; we make the circumstances explain the words, and do not force the former into consistency with the latter. Thus each case of variance, that for instance between *The Father is greater than I*[1], and *I and the Father are One*[3], or between *None is good save One, even God*[4], and *He that hath seen Me hath seen the Father also*[5], or a difference so wide as that between *Father, all things that are Mine are Thine, and Thine are Mine*[6], and *That they may know Thee, the only true God*[7], or between *I in the Father and the Father in Me*[8], and *But of the day and hour knoweth no one, neither the angels in heaven nor the Son, but the Father only*[9], is explained by a discrimination between gradual reve-

lation and full expression of His nature and power. Both are utterances of the same Speaker, and an exposition of the real force of each group will shew that Christ's true Godhead is no whit impaired because, to form the mystery of the Gospel faith, the birth and Name[1] of Christ were revealed gradually, and under conditions which He chose of occasion and time.

31. The purpose of the tenth book is one in harmony with the faith. For since, in the folly which passes with them for wisdom, the heretics have twisted some of the circumstances and utterances of the Passion into an insolent contradiction of the Divine nature and power of the Lord Jesus Christ, I am compelled to prove that this is a blasphemous misinterpretation, and that these things were put on record by the Lord Himself as evidences of His true and absolute majesty. In their parody of the faith they deceive themselves with words such as, *My soul is sorrowful even unto death*[2]. He, they think, must be far removed from the blissful and passionless life of God, over Whose soul brooded this crushing fear of an impending woe, Who under the pressure of suffering even humbled Himself to pray, *Father, if it be possible, let this cup pass away from Me*[3], and assuredly bore the appearance of fearing to endure the trials from which He prayed for release; Whose whole nature was so overwhelmed by agony that in those moments on the Cross He cried, *My God, My God, why hast Thou forsaken Me*[4]? forced by the bitterness of His pain to complain that He was forsaken: Who, destitute of the Father's help, gave up the ghost with the words, *Father, into Thy hands I commend My Spirit*[5]. The fear, they say, which beset Him at the moment of expiring made Him entrust His Spirit to the care of God the Father: the very hopelessness of His own condition forced Him to commit His Soul to the keeping of Another.

32. Their folly being as great as their blasphemy, they fail to mark that Christ's words, spoken under similar circumstances, are always consistent; they cleave to the letter and ignore the purpose of His words. There is the widest difference between *My soul is sorrowful even unto death*[2], and *Henceforth ye shall see the Son of Man sitting at the right hand of power*[6]; so also between *Father, if it be possible, let this cup pass away from Me*[3], and *The cup which the Father hath given Me, shall*

---

8 St. John xvii. 3.   9 Ib. v. 19.   1 Ib. xiv. 28.
2 St. Mark xiii. 32.   3 St. John x. 30.
4 St. Luke xviii. 19.   5 St. John xiv. 9.
6 Ib. xvii. 10.   7 Ib. 3.   8 Ib. xiv. 11.
9 St. Mark xiii. 32.

1 Reading *nativitas et nomen*. The clause above, which is bracketed in Migne, appears to be a gloss.
2 St. Matt. xxvi. 38.   3 Ib. 39.   4 Ib. xxvii. 46.
5 St. Luke xxiii. 46.   6 St. Matt. xxvi. 64.

I not drink it⁷? and further between *My God, My God, why hast Thou forsaken Me⁸?* and *Verily I say unto thee, To-day shalt thou be with Me in Paradise⁹*, and between *Father, into Thy hands I commend My Spirit¹*, and *Father, forgive them, for they know not what they do²;* and their narrow minds, unable to grasp the Divine meaning, plunge into blasphemy in the attempt at explanation. There is a broad distinction between anxiety and a mind at ease, between haste and the prayer for delay, between words of anguish and words of encouragement, between despair for self and confident entreaty for others; and the heretics display their impiety by ignoring the assertions of Deity and the Divine nature of Christ, which account for the one class of His words, while they concentrate their attention upon the deeds and words which refer only to His ministry on earth. I have therefore set out all the elements contained in the mystery of the Soul and Body of the Lord Jesus Christ; all have been sought out, none suppressed. Next, casting the calm light of reason upon the question, I have referred each of His sayings to the class to which its meaning attaches it, and so have shewn that He had also a confidence which never wavered, a will which never faltered, an assurance which never murmured, that, when He commended His own soul to the Father, in this was involved a prayer for the pardon of others³. Thus a complete presentment of the teaching of the Gospel interprets and confirms all (and not some only) of the words of Christ.

33. And so—for not even the glory of the Resurrection has opened the eyes of these lost men and kept them within the manifest bounds of the faith—they have forged a weapon for their blasphemy out of a pretended reverence, and even perverted the revelation of a mystery into an insult to God. From the words, *I ascend unto My Father and your Father, to My God and your God⁴*, they argue that since that Father is ours as much as His, and that God also ours and His, His own confession that He shares with us in that relation to the Father and to God excludes Him from true Divinity, and subordinates Him to God the Creator Whose creature and inferior He is, as we are, although He has received the adoption of a Son. Nay more, we must not suppose that He possesses any of the characters of the Divine nature, since the Apostle says, *But when He saith, all things are put in subjection,*

this is except Him Who did subject all things unto Him, for when all things shall have been subjected unto Him, then shall also He Himself be subjected to Him that did subject all things unto Him, that God may be all in all⁵. For, so they say, subjection is evidence of want of power in the subject and of its possession by the sovereign. The eleventh book is employed in a reverent discussion of this argument; it proves from these very words of the Apostle not only that subjection is no evidence of want of power in Christ but that it actually is a sign of His true Divinity as God the Son; that the fact that His Father and God is also our Father and God is an infinite advantage to us and no degradation to Him, since He Who has been born as Man and suffered all the afflictions of our flesh has gone up on high to our God and Father, to receive His glory as Man our Representative.

34. In this treatise we have followed the course which we know is pursued in every branch of education. First come easy lessons and a familiarity, slowly attained by practice, with the groundwork of the subject; then the student may make proof, in the business of life, of the training which he has received. Thus the soldier, when he is perfect in his exercises, can go out to battle; the advocate ventures into the conflicts of the courts when he is versed in the pleadings of the school of rhetoric; the sailor who has learned to navigate his ship in the land-locked harbour of his home may be trusted amid the storms of open seas and distant climes. Such has been our proceeding in this most serious and difficult science in which the whole faith is taught. First came simple instruction for the untaught believer in the birth, the name, the Divinity, the true Divinity of Christ; since then we have quietly and steadily advanced till our readers can demolish every plea of the heretics; and now at last we have pitted them against the adversary in the present great and glorious conflict. The mind of men is powerless with the ordinary resources of unaided reason to grasp the idea of an eternal birth, but they attain by study of things Divine to the apprehension of mysteries which lie beyond the range of common thought. They can explode that paradox concerning the Lord Jesus, which derives all its strength and semblance of cogency from a purblind pagan philosophy: the paradox which asserts, *There was a time when He was not,* and *He was not before He was born,* and *He was made out of*

---

7 St. John xviii. 11.   8 St. Matt. xxvii. 46.
9 St. Luke xxiii. 43.   1 Ib. 46.   2 Ib. 34.
3 Reading *non desiderasse.*   4 St. John xx. 17.

5 1 Cor. xv. 27, 28.

nothing, as though His birth were proof that He had previously been non-existent and at a given moment came into being, and God the Only-begotten could thus be subjected to the conception of time, as if the faith itself [by conferring the title of 'Son'] and the very nature of birth proved that there was a time when He was not. Accordingly they argue that He was born out of nothing, on the ground that birth implies the grant of being to that which previously had no being. We proclaim in answer, on the evidence of Apostles and Evangelists, that the Father is eternal and the Son eternal, and demonstrate that the Son is God of all with an absolute, not a limited, pre-existence ; that these bold assaults of their blasphemous logic —*He was born out of nothing*, and *He was not before He was born*—are powerless against Him ; that His eternity is consistent with sonship, and His sonship with eternity ; that there was in Him no unique exemption from birth but a birth from everlasting, for, while birth implies a Father, Divinity is inseparable from eternity.

35. Ignorance of prophetic diction and unskilfulness in interpreting Scripture has led them into a perversion of the point and meaning of the passage, *The Lord created Me for a beginning of His ways for His works* [6]. They labour to establish from it that Christ is created, rather than born, as God, and hence partakes the nature of created beings, though He excel them in the manner of His creation, and has no glory of Divine birth but only the powers of a transcendent creature. We in reply, without importing any new considerations or preconceived opinions, will make this very passage of Wisdom [7] display its own true meaning and object. We will show that the fact that He was created for the beginning of the ways of God and for His works, cannot be twisted into evidence concerning the Divine and eternal birth, because creation for these purposes and birth from everlasting are two entirely different things. Where birth is meant, there birth, and nothing but birth, is spoken of ; where creation is mentioned, the cause of that creation is first named. There is a Wisdom born before all things, and again there is a wisdom created for particular purposes ; the Wisdom which is from everlasting is one, the wisdom which has come into existence during the lapse of time is another.

36. Having thus concluded that we must reject the word 'creation' from our confession of faith in God the Only-begotten, we proceed to lay down the teachings of reason and of piety concerning the Holy Spirit, that the reader, whose convictions have been established by patient and earnest study of the preceding books, may be provided with a complete presentation of the faith. This end will be attained when the blasphemies of heretical teaching on this theme also have been swept away, and the mystery, pure and undefiled, of the Trinity which regenerates us has been fixed in terms of saving precision on the authority of Apostles and Evangelists. Men will no longer dare, on the strength of mere human reasoning, to rank among creatures that Divine Spirit, Whom we receive as the pledge of immortality and source of fellowship with the sinless nature of God.

37. I know, O Lord God Almighty, that I owe Thee, as the chief duty of my life, the devotion of all my words and thoughts to Thyself. The gift of speech which Thou hast bestowed can bring me no higher reward than the opportunity of service in preaching Thee and displaying Thee as Thou art, as Father and Father of God the Only-begotten, to the world in its blindness and the heretic in his rebellion. But this is the mere expression of my own desire ; I must pray also for the gift of Thy help and compassion, that the breath of Thy Spirit may fill the sails of faith and confession which I have spread, and a favouring wind be sent to forward me on my voyage of instruction. We can trust the promise of Him Who said, *Ask, and it shall be given you, seek, and ye shall find, knock, and it shall be opened unto you* [8] ; and we in our want shall pray for the things we need. We shall bring an untiring energy to the study of Thy Prophets and Apostles, and we shall knock for entrance at every gate of hidden knowledge, but it is Thine to answer the prayer, to grant the thing we seek, to open the door on which we beat. Our minds are born with dull and clouded vision, our feeble intellect is penned within the barriers of an impassable ignorance concerning things Divine ; but the study of Thy revelation elevates our soul to the comprehension of sacred truth, and submission to the faith is the path to a certainty beyond the reach of unassisted reason.

38. And therefore we look to Thy support for the first trembling steps of this undertaking, to Thy aid that it may gain strength and prosper. We look to Thee to give us the fellowship of that Spirit Who guided the Prophets and the Apostles, that we may take their words in the sense in which they spoke and assign its right shade of meaning to every

---

6 Prov. viii. 22, according to the LXX.
7 Here, as often in early writers, the Sapiential books are included under this name.

8 St. Luke xi. 9.

utterance. For we shall speak of things which they preached in a mystery; of Thee, O God Eternal, Father of the Eternal and Only-begotten God, Who alone art without birth, and of the One Lord Jesus Christ, born of Thee from everlasting. We may not sever Him from Thee, or make Him one of a plurality of Gods, on any plea of difference of nature. We may not say that He is not begotten of Thee, because Thou art One. We must not fail to confess Him as true God, seeing that He is born of Thee, true God, His Father. Grant us, therefore, precision of language, soundness of argument, grace of style, loyalty to truth. Enable us to utter the things that we believe, that so we may confess, as Prophets and Apostles have taught us, Thee, One God our Father, and One Lord Jesus Christ, and put to silence the gainsaying of heretics, proclaiming Thee as God, yet not solitary, and Him as God, in no unreal sense.

BOOK II.

1. BELIEVERS have always found their satisfaction in that Divine utterance, which our ears heard recited from the Gospel at the moment when that Power, which is its attestation, was bestowed upon us:—*Go now and teach all na'ions, baptizing them in the Name of the Father, and of the Son, and of the Holy Ghost, teaching them to observe all things whatsoever I command you; and, lo, I am with you alway, even unto the end of the world*[1]. What element in the mystery of man's salvation is not included in those words? What is forgotten, what left in darkness? All is full, as from the Divine fulness; perfect, as from the Divine perfection. The passage contains the exact words to be used, the essential acts, the sequence of processes, an insight into the Divine nature. . He bade them baptize *in the Name of the Father, and of the Son, and of the Holy Ghost*, that is with confession of the Creator and of the Only-begotten, and of the Gift. For God the Father is One, from Whom are all things; and our Lord Jesus Christ the Only-begotten, through Whom are all things, is One; and the Spirit, God's Gift to us, Who pervades all things, is also One. Thus all are ranged according to powers possessed and benefits conferred;—the One Power from Whom all, the One Offspring through Whom all, the One Gift Who gives us perfect hope. Nothing can be found lacking in that supreme Union which embraces, in Father, Son and Holy Spirit, infinity in the Eternal, His Likeness in His express Image, our enjoyment of Him in the Gift.

2. But the errors of heretics and blasphemers force us to deal with unlawful matters, to scale perilous heights, to speak unutterable words, to trespass on forbidden ground. Faith ought in silence to fulfil the commandments, worshipping the Father, reverencing with Him the Son, abounding in the Holy Ghost, but we must strain the poor resources of our language to express thoughts too great for words. The error of others compels us to err in daring to embody in human terms truths which ought to be hidden in the silent veneration of the heart.

3. For there have risen many who have given to the plain words of Holy Writ some arbitrary interpretation of their own, instead of its true and only sense, and this in defiance of the clear meaning of words. Heresy lies in the sense assigned, not in the word written; the guilt is that of the expositor, not of the text. Is not truth indestructible? When we hear the name *Father*, is not sonship involved in that Name? The Holy Ghost is mentioned by name; must He not exist? We can no more separate fatherhood from the Father or sonship from the Son than we can deny the existence in the Holy Ghost of that gift which we receive. Yet men of distorted mind plunge the whole matter in doubt and difficulty, fatuously reversing the clear meaning of words, and depriving the Father of His fatherhood because they wish to strip the Son of His sonship. They take away the fatherhood by asserting that the Son is not a Son by nature; for a son is not of the nature of his father when begetter and begotten have not the same properties, and he is no son whose being is different from that of the father, and unlike it. Yet in what sense is God a Father (as He is), if He have not begotten in His Son that same substance and nature which are His own?

4. Since, therefore, they cannot make any change in the facts recorded, they bring novel principles and theories of man's device to bear upon them. Sabellius, for instance, makes the Son an extension of the Father, and the faith in this regard a matter of words rather than of reality, for he makes one and the same Person, Son to Himself and also Father. Hebion allows no beginning to the Son of God except from Mary, and represents Him not as first God and then man, but as first man then God; declares that the Virgin did not receive into herself One previously existent, Who had been in the beginning God the Word dwelling with God, but that through the agency of the Word she bore Flesh; the 'Word' meaning in his opinion not the nature of the pre-existent Only-begotten God[2], but only the sound of an uplifted voice. Similarly certain teachers of our present day assert that the Image and Wisdom and Power of God was produced out of nothing, and in time. They do this to save God, regarded as Father of the Son, from being lowered to the Son's

---

[1] St. Matt. xxviii. 19, 20.

[2] Reading *non antea.*

level. They are fearful lest this birth of the Son from Him should deprive Him of His glory, and therefore come to God's rescue by styling His Son a creature made out of nothing, in order that God may live on in solitary perfection without a Son born of Himself and partaking His nature. What wonder that their doctrine of the Holy Ghost should be different from ours, when they presume to subject the Giver of that Holy Ghost to creation, and change, and non-existence. Thus do they destroy the consistency and completeness of the mystery of the faith. They break up the absolute unity of God by assigning differences of nature where all is clearly common to Each ; they deny the Father by robbing the Son of His true Sonship ; they deny the Holy Ghost in their blindness to the facts that we possess Him and that Christ gave Him. They betray ill-trained souls to ruin by their boast of the logical perfection of their doctrine ; they deceive their hearers by emptying terms of their meaning, though the Names remain to witness to the truth. I pass over the pitfalls of other heresies, Valentinian, Marcionite, Manichee and the rest. From time to time they catch the attention of some foolish souls and prove fatal by the very infection of their contact ; one plague as destructive as another when once the poison of their teaching has found its way into the hearer's thoughts.

5. Their treason involves us in the difficult and dangerous position of having to make a definite pronouncement, beyond the statements of Scripture, upon this grave and abstruse matter. The Lord said that the nations were to be baptized *in the Name of the Father, and of the Son, and of the Holy Ghost.* The words of the faith are clear ; the heretics do their utmost to involve the meaning in doubt. We may not on this account add to the appointed form, yet we must set a limit to their license of interpretation. Since their malice, inspired by the devil's cunning, empties the doctrine of its meaning while it retains the Names which convey the truth, we must emphasise the truth which those Names convey. We must proclaim, exactly as we shall find them in the words of Scripture, the majesty and functions of Father, Son and Holy Spirit, and so debar the heretics from robbing these Names of their connotation of Divine character, and compel them by means of these very Names to confine their use of terms to their proper meaning. I cannot conceive what manner of mind our opponents have, who pervert the truth, darken the light, divide the indivisible, rend the scatheless, dissolve the perfect unity. It may seem to them a light thing to tear

up Perfection, to make laws for Omnipotence, to limit Infinity ; as for me, the task of answering them fills me with anxiety ; my brain whirls, my intellect is stunned, my very words must be a confession, not that I am weak of utterance, but that I am dumb. Yet a wish to undertake the task forces itself upon me ; it means withstanding the proud, guiding the wanderer, warning the ignorant. But the subject is inexhaustible ; I can see no limit to my venture of speaking concerning God in terms more precise than He Himself has used. He has assigned the Names—Father, Son and Holy Ghost,—which are our information of the Divine nature. Words cannot express or feeling embrace or reason apprehend the results of enquiry carried further ; all is ineffable, unattainable, incomprehensible. Language is exhausted by the magnitude of the theme, the splendour of its effulgence blinds the gazing eye, the intellect cannot compass its boundless extent. Still, under the necessity that is laid upon us, with a prayer for pardon to Him Whose attributes these are, we will venture, enquire and speak ; and moreover—it is the only promise that in so grave a matter we dare to make—we will accept whatever conclusion He shall indicate.

6. It is the Father to Whom all existence owes its origin. In Christ and through Christ He is the source of all. In contrast to all else He is self-existent. He does not draw His being from without, but possesses it from Himself and in Himself. He is infinite, for nothing contains Him and He contains all things ; He is eternally unconditioned by space, for He is illimitable ; eternally anterior to time, for time is His creation. Let imagination range to what you may suppose is God's utmost limit, and you will find Him present there ; strain as you will there is always a further horizon towards which to strain. Infinity is His property, just as the power of making such effort is yours. Words will fail you, but His being will not be circumscribed. Or again, turn back the pages of history, and you will find Him ever present ; should numbers fail to express the antiquity to which you have penetrated, yet God's eternity is not diminished. Gird up your intellect to comprehend Him as a whole ; He eludes you. God, as a whole, has left something within your grasp, but this something is inextricably involved in His entirety. Thus you have missed the whole, since it is only a part which remains in your hands ; nay, not even a part, for you are dealing with a whole which you have failed to divide. For a part implies division, a whole is undivided, and God is everywhere and wholly present wherever He is.

Reason, therefore, cannot cope with Him, since no point of contemplation can be found outside Himself and since eternity is eternally His. This is a true statement of the mystery of that unfathomable nature which is expressed by the Name 'Father:' God invisible, ineffable, infinite. Let us confess by our silence that words cannot describe Him ; let sense admit that it is foiled in the attempt to apprehend, and reason in the effort to define. Yet He has, as we said, in ' Father' a name to indicate His nature ; He is a Father unconditioned. He does not, as men do, receive the power of paternity from an external source. He is unbegotten, everlasting, inherently eternal. To the Son only is He known, for no one knoweth the Father save the Son and him to whom the Son willeth to reveal Him, nor yet the Son save the Father [3]. Each has perfect and complete knowledge of the Other. There-fore, since *no one knoweth the Father save the Son*, let our thoughts of the Father be at one with the thoughts of the Son, the only faithful Witness, Who reveals Him to us.

7. It is easier for me to feel this concerning the Father than to say it. I am well aware that no words are adequate to describe His attributes. We must feel that He is invisible, incomprehensible, eternal. But to say that He is self-existent and self-originating and self-sustained, that He is invisible and incompre-hensible and immortal ; all this is an acknow-ledgment of His glory, a hint of our meaning, a sketch of our thoughts, but speech is power-less to tell us what God is, words cannot express the reality. You hear that He is self-existent ; human reason cannot explain such independence. We can find objects which uphold, and objects which are upheld, but that which thus exists is obviously distinct from that which is the cause of its existence. Again, if you hear that He is self-originating, no instance can be found in which the giver of the gift of life is identical with the life that is given. If you hear that He is immortal, then there is something which does not spring from Him and with which He has, by His very nature [4], no contact ; and, indeed, death is not the only thing which this word 'immortal' claims as independent of God [5]. If you hear that He is incomprehensible, that is as much as to say that He is non-existent, since contact with Him is impossible. If you say that He is invisible, a being that does not visibly exist

cannot be sure of its own existence. Thus our confession of God fails through the defects of language ; the best combination of words we can devise cannot indicate the reality and the greatness of God. The perfect knowledge of God is so to know Him that we are sure we must not be ignorant of Him, yet cannot describe Him. We must believe, must appre-hend, must worship ; and such acts of devotion must stand in lieu of definition.

8. We have now exchanged the perils of a harbourless coast for the storms of the open sea. We can neither safely advance nor safely retreat, yet the way that lies before us has greater hardships than that which lies behind. The Father is what He is, and as He is mani-fested, so we must believe. The mind shrinks in dread from treating of the Son ; at every word I tremble lest I be betrayed into treason. For He is the Offspring of the Unbegotten, One from One, true from true, living from living, perfect from perfect ; the Power of Power, the Wisdom of Wisdom, the Glory of Glory, the Likeness of the invisible God, the Image of the Unbegotten Father. Yet in what sense can we conceive that the Only-begotten is the Offspring of the Unbegotten ? Repeat-edly the Father cries from heaven, *This is My beloved Son in Whom I am well pleased* [6]. It is no rending or severance, for He that begat is without passions, and He that was born is the Image of the invisible God and bears witness, *The Father is in Me and I in the Father* [7]. It is no mere adoption, for He is the true Son of God and cries, *He that hath seen Me hath seen the Father also* [8]. Nor did He come into existence in obedience to a command as did created things, for He is the Only-begotten of the One God ; and He has life in Himself, even as He that begat Him has life, for He says, *As the Father hath life in Himself, even so gave He to the Son to have life in Himself* [9]. Nor is there a portion of the Father resident in the Son, for the Son bears witness, *All things that the Father hath are Mine* [1], and again, *And all things that are Mine are Thine, and Thine are Mine* [2], and the Apostle testifies, *For in Him dwelleth all the fulness of the Godhead bodily* [3]; and by the nature of things a portion cannot possess the whole [4]. He is the perfect Son of the perfect Father, for He Who has all has given all to Him. Yet we must not imagine that the

---

3 Cf. St. Matt. xi. 27.
4 Reading *a se*, instead of *alter*.
5 This is merely a verbal paradox, to illustrate the inadequacy of language to treat of God. God is *ex hypothesi* author of all things, and contains all things in Himself. But the negative term ' immortal ' excludes death, and its concomitants of disease, pain, &c., from God's sphere.

6 St. Matt. iii. 17 ; xvii. 5. Again in § 23 Hilary says that these words were often repeated.   7 St John x. 38.
8 Ib. xiv. 9.   9 Ib. v. 26.   1 Ib. xvi. 15.
2 Ib. xvii 10. The words which follow, "and *Whatsoever the Father hath He hath given to the Son*," printed in the editions as a Scriptural citation, are evidently a gloss which has crept into the text. The words do not occur in Scripture, but are used again by Hilary in § 10 of this Book.
3 Col. ii. 9.   4 Omitting *esse*.

Father did not give, because He still possesses, or that He has lost, because He gave to the Son.

9. The manner of this birth is therefore a secret confined to the Two. If any one lays upon his personal incapacity his failure to solve the mystery, in spite of the certainty that Father and Son stand to Each Other in those relations, he will be still more pained at the ignorance to which I confess. I, too, am in the dark, yet I ask no questions. I look for comfort to the fact that Archangels share my ignorance, that Angels have not heard the explanation, and worlds do not contain it, that no prophet has espied it and no Apostle sought for it, that the Son Himself has not revealed it. Let such pitiful complaints cease. Whoever you are that search into these mysteries, I do not bid you resume your exploration of height and breadth and depth; I ask you rather to acquiesce patiently in your ignorance of the mode of Divine generation, seeing that you know not how His creatures come into existence. Answer me this one question:—Do your senses give you any evidence that you yourself were begotten? Can you explain the process by which you became a father? I do not ask whence you drew perception, how you obtained life, whence your reason comes, what is the nature of your senses of smell, touch, sight, hearing; the fact that we have the use of all these is the evidence that they exist. What I ask is:—How do you give them to your children? How do you ingraft the senses, lighten the eyes, implant the mind? Tell me, if you can. You have, then, powers which you do not understand, you impart gifts which you cannot comprehend. You are calmly indifferent to the mysteries of your own being, profanely impatient of ignorance concerning the mysteries of God's.

10. Listen then to the Unbegotten Father, listen to the Only-begotten Son. Hear His words, *The Father is greater than I*[5], and *I and the Father are One*[6], and *He that hath seen Me hath seen the Father also*[7], and *The Father is in Me and I in the Father*[8], and *I went out from the Father*[9], and *Who is in the bosom of the Father*[1], and *Whatsoever the Father hath He hath delivered to the Son*[2], and *The Son hath life in Himself, even as the Father hath in Himself*[3]. Hear in these words the Son, the Image, the Wisdom, the Power, the Glory of God. Next mark the Holy Ghost proclaiming *Who shall declare His generation*[4]? Note[5] the

Lord's assurance, *No one knoweth the Son save the Father, neither doth any know the Father save the Son and He to whom the Son willeth to reveal Him*[6]. Penetrate into the mystery, plunge into the darkness which shrouds that birth, where you will be alone with God the Unbegotten and God the Only-begotten. Make your start, continue, persevere. I know that you will not reach the goal, but I shall rejoice at your progress. For He who devoutly treads an endless road, though he reach no conclusion, will profit by his exertions. Reason will fail for want of words, but when it comes to a stand it will be the better for the effort made.

11. The Son draws His life from that Father Who truly has life; the Only-begotten from the Unbegotten, Offspring from Parent, Living from Living. *As the Father hath life in Himself, even so gave He to the Son also to have life in Himself*[7]. The Son is perfect from Him that is perfect, for He is whole from Him that is whole. This is no division or severance, for Each is in the Other, and the fulness of the Godhead is in the Son. Incomprehensible is begotten of Incomprehensible, for none else knows Them, but Each knows the Other; Invisible is begotten of Invisible, for the Son is the Image of the invisible God, and he that has seen the Son has seen the Father also. There is a distinction, for They are Father and Son; not that Their Divinity is different in kind, for Both are One, God of God, One God Only begotten of One God Unbegotten. They are not two Gods, but One of One; not two Unbegotten, for the Son is born of the Unborn. There is no diversity, for the life of the living God is in the living Christ. So much I have resolved to say concerning the nature of their Divinity; not imagining that I have succeeded in making a summary of the faith, but recognising that the theme is inexhaustible. So faith, you object, has no service to render, since there is nothing that it can comprehend. Not so; the proper service of faith is to grasp and confess the truth that it is incompetent to comprehend its Object.

12. It remains to say something more concerning the mysterious generation of the Son; or rather this something more is everything. I quiver, I linger, my powers fail, I know not where to begin. I cannot tell the time of the Son's birth; it were impious not to be certain of the fact. Whom shall I entreat? Whom shall I call to my aid? From what books shall I borrow the terms needed to state so hard a problem? Shall I ransack the philosophy of Greece? No! I have read, *Where is*

---

5 St. John xiv. 28. 6 Ib. x. 30. 7 Ib. xiv. 9.
8 Ib. x. 38. 9 Ib. xvi. 28. 1 Ib. i. 18
2 The citation which is interpolated in § 8, where see the note, and cf. St. Matt. xi. 25.
3 St. John v. 26. 4 Isai. liii. 8. 5 Reading *observa*.

6 St. Matt. xi. 27. 7 St. John v. 26.

the wise? Where is the enquirer of this world[8]*?* In this matter, then, the world's philosophers, the wise men of paganism, are dumb: for they have rejected the wisdom of God. Shall I turn to the Scribe of the Law? He is in darkness, for the Cross of Christ is an offence to him. Shall I, perchance, bid you shut your eyes to heresy, and pass it by in silence, on the ground that sufficient reverence is shown to Him Whom we preach if we believe that lepers were cleansed, the deaf heard, the lame ran, the palsied stood, the blind (in general) received sight, the blind from his birth had eyes given to him[9], devils were routed, the sick recovered, the dead lived. The heretics confess all this, and perish.

13. Look now to see a thing not less miraculous than lame men running, blind men seeing, the flight of devils, the life from the dead. There stands by my side, to guide me through the difficulties which I have enunciated, a poor fisherman, ignorant, uneducated, fishing-lines in hand, clothes dripping, muddy feet, every inch a sailor. Consider and decide whether it were the greater feat to raise the dead or impart to an untrained mind the knowledge of mysteries so deep as he reveals by saying, *In the beginning was the Word*[1]. What means this *In the beginning was?* He ranges backward over the spaces of time, centuries are left behind, ages are cancelled. Fix in your mind what date you will for this *beginning;* you miss the mark, for even then He, of Whom we are speaking, *was.* Survey the universe, note well what is written of it, *In the beginning God made the heaven and the earth*[2]. This word *beginning* fixes the moment of creation; you can assign its date to an event which is definitely stated to have happened *in the beginning.* But this fisherman of mine, unlettered and unread, is untrammelled by time, undaunted by its immensity; he pierces beyond the beginning. For his *was* has no limit of time and no commencement; the uncreated Word *was in the beginning.*

14. But perhaps we shall find that our fisherman has been guilty of departure from the terms of the problem proposed for solution[3]. He has set the Word free from the limitations of time; that which is free lives its own life and is bound to no obedience. Let us, therefore, pay our best attention to what follows:—*And the Word was with God.* We find that it is *with God* that the Word, Which *was* before the beginning, exists unconditioned by time. The Word, Which *was,* is *with God.* He Who is absent when we seek for His origin in time[4] is present all the while with the Creator of time. For this once our fisherman has escaped; perhaps he will succumb to the difficulties which await him.

15. For you will plead that a word is the sound of a voice; that it is a naming of things, an utterance of thoughts. This Word was with God, and was in the beginning; the expression of the eternal Thinker's thoughts must be eternal. For the present I will give you a brief answer of my own on the fisherman's behalf, till we see what defence he has to make for his own simplicity. The nature, then, of a word is that it is first a potentiality, afterwards a past event; an existing thing only while it is being heard. How can we say, *In the beginning was the Word,* when a word neither exists before, nor lives after, a definite point of time? Can we even say that there is a point of time in which a word exists? Not only are the words in a speaker's mouth non-existent until they are spoken, and perished the instant they are uttered, but even in the moment of utterance there is a change from the sound which commences to that which ends a word. Such is the reply that suggests itself to me as a bystander. But your opponent the Fisherman has an answer of his own. He will begin by reproving you for your inattention. Even though your unpractised ear failed to catch the first clause, *In the beginning was the Word,* why complain of the next, *And the Word was with God?* Was it *And the Word was in God* that you heard,— the dictum of some profound philosophy? Or is it that your provincial dialect makes no distinction between *in* and *with?* The assertion is that That Which was in the beginning was *with,* not *in,* Another. But I will not argue from the beginning of the sentence; the sequel can take care of itself. Hear now the rank and the name of the Word:—*And the Word was God.* Your plea that the Word is the sound of a voice, the utterance of a thought, falls to the ground. The Word is a reality, not a sound, a Being, not a speech, God, not a nonentity.

16. But I tremble to say it; the audacity staggers me. I hear, *And the Word was God;* I, whom the prophets have taught that God is One. To save me from further fears, give me, friend Fisherman, a fuller imparting of this great mystery. Show that these assertions are consistent with the unity of God;

---

8 1 Cor. i. 20.
9 The healing of the blind man, St. John ix. 1 ff., is treated as a special case distinct from more ordinary cases of blindness.
1 St. John i. 1.   2 Gen. i. 1.
3 I.e. how to reconcile the Unity of God with the Divinity of Christ. To say that the Word is God might seem to contradict the Unity by asserting the existence of a second God.

4 Reading *a cognitione temporis.*

that there is no blasphemy in them, no explaining away, no denial of eternity. He continues, *He was in the beginning with God.* This *He was in the beginning* removes the limit of time; the word *God* shows that He is more than a voice; that He is *with God* proves that He neither encroaches nor is encroached upon, for His identity is not swallowed up in that of Another, and He is clearly stated to be present with the One Unbegotten God as God, His One and Only-begotten Son.

17. We are still waiting, Fisherman, for your full description of the Word. He was in the beginning, it may be said, but perhaps He was not before the beginning. To this also I will furnish a reply on my Fisherman's behalf. The Word could not be other than He *was*; that *was* is unconditional and unlimited. But what says the Fisherman for himself? *All things were made through Him.* Thus, since nothing exists apart from Him through Whom the universe came into being, He, the Author of all things, must have an immeasurable existence. For time is a cognisable and divisible measure of extension, not in space, but in duration. All things are from Him, without exception; time then itself is His creature.

18. But, my Fisherman, the objection will be raised that you are reckless and extravagant in your language; that *All things were made through Him* needs qualification. There is the Unbegotten, made of none; there is also the Son, begotten of the Unborn Father. This *All things* is an unguarded statement, admitting no exceptions. While we are silent, not daring to answer or trying to think of some reply, do you break in with, *And without Him was nothing made.* You have restored the Author of the Godhead to His place, while proclaiming that He has a Companion. From your saying that nothing was made *without Him*, I learn that He was not alone. He through Whom the work was done is One; He without Whom it was not done is Another: a distinction is drawn between Creator and Companion.

19. Reverence for the One Unbegotten Creator distressed me, lest in your sweeping assertion that all things were made by the Word you had included Him. You have banished my fears by your *Without Him was nothing made.* Yet this same *Without Him was nothing made* brings trouble and distraction. There was, then, something made by that Other; not made, it is true, *without Him.* If the Other did make anything, even though the Word were present at the making, then it is untrue that *through Him all things were made.* It is one thing to be the Creator's Companion, quite another to be the Creator's Self. I could find answers of my own to the previous objections; in this case, Fisherman, I can only turn at once to your words, *All things were made through Him.* And now I understand, for the Apostle has enlightened me:—*Things visible and things invisible, whether thrones or dominions or principalities or powers, all are through Him and in Him*[5].

20. Since, then, all things were made through Him, come to our help and tell us what it was that was made not without Him. *That which was made in Him is life.* That which was made *in Him* was certainly not made *without Him*; for that which was made in Him was also made *through Him.* All things were created in Him and through Him[6]. They were created in Him[7], for He was born as God the Creator. Again, nothing that was made in Him was made without Him, for the reason that God the Begotten was Life, and was born as Life, not made life after His birth; for there are not two elements in Him, one inborn and one afterwards conferred. There is no interval in His case between birth and maturity. None of the things that were created in Him was made without Him, for He is the Life which made their creation possible. Moreover God, the Son of God, became God by virtue of His birth, not after He was born. Being born the Living from the Living, the True from the True, the Perfect from the Perfect, He was born in full possession of His powers. He needed not to learn in after time what His birth was, but was conscious of His Godhead by the very fact that He was born as God of God. *I and the Father are One*[8], are the words of the Only-begotten Son of the Unbegotten. It is the voice of the One God proclaiming Himself to be Father and Son; Father speaking in the Son and Son in the Father. Hence also *He that hath seen Me hath seen the Father also*[9]; hence *All that the Father hath, He hath given to the Son*[1]; hence *As the Father hath life in Himself, so hath He given to the Son to have life in Himself*[2]; hence *No one knoweth the Father save the Son, nor the Son save the Father*[3]; hence *In Him dwelleth all the fulness of the Godhead bodily*[4].

---

5 Col. i. 16.   6 Cf. Col. i. 16.   7 I.e. potentially.
8 St. John x. 30.   9 St. John xiv. 9.   1 Ib. xvi. 15.
2 Ib. v. 26.   3 St. Matt. xi. 27.
4 Col. ii. 9. The argument of §§ 18—20 is not easy. They begin with the possible objection to *All things were made through Him*, that this would include the Father among the Son's creations. The answer is found in the following words, *Without Him was not anything made.* These show that the Son was not alone in His work; the Father is co-existent. But they raise another difficulty. What if the Father were the sole agent in creation, the Son only His inseparable Companion, yet taking no share in the work? The answer is found in the preceding words, *All things were made through Him*, amplified and explained by St. Paul when He says that it was *through Him and in Him.* *In Him*, because when the Son, the future Creator, was born, the world was potentially created; *in Him* also because He is Life, and thus the condition of all existence. Again, the truth of the words, *All things were made through Him*, is shewn by the

21. This Life is the Light of men, the Light which lightens the darkness. To comfort us for that powerlessness to describe His generation of which the prophet speaks [5], the Fisherman adds, *And the darkness comprehended Him not* [6]. The language of unaided reason was baffled and silenced; the Fisherman who lay on the bosom of the Lord was taught to express the mystery. His language is not the world's language, for He deals with things that are not of the world. Let us know what it is, if there be any teaching that you can extract from his words, more than their plain sense conveys; if you can translate into other terms the truth we have elicited, publish them abroad. If there be none—indeed, because there are none—let us accept with reverence this teaching of the fisherman, and recognise in his words the oracles of God. Let us cling in adoration to the true confession of Father and Son, Unbegotten and Only-begotten ineffably, Whose majesty defies all expression and all perception. Let us, like John, lie on the bosom of the Lord Jesus, that we too may understand and proclaim the mystery.

22. This faith, and every part of it, is impressed upon us by the evidence of the Gospels, by the teaching of the Apostles, by the futility of the treacherous attacks which heretics make on every side. The foundation stands firm and unshaken in face of winds and rains and torrents; storms cannot overthrow it, nor dripping waters hollow it, nor floods sweep it away. Its excellence is proved by the failure of countless assaults to impair it. Certain remedies are so compounded as to be of value not merely against some single disease but against all; they are of universal efficacy. So it is with the Catholic faith. It is not a medicine for some special malady, but for every ill; virulence cannot master, nor numbers defeat, nor complexity baffle it. One and unchanging it faces and conquers all its foes. Marvellous it is that one form of words should contain a remedy for every disease, a statement of truth to confront every contrivance of falsehood. Let heresy muster its forces and every sect come forth to battle. Let our answer to their challenge be that there is One Unbegotten God the Father, and One Only-begotten Son of God, perfect Offspring of perfect Parent; that the Son was begotten by no lessening of the Father or subtraction from His Substance, but that He Who possesses all things begat an all-possessing Son; a Son not emanating nor proceeding from the Father, but compact of, and inherent in, the whole Divinity of Him Who wherever He is present is present eternally; One free from time, unlimited in duration, since by Him all things were made [7], and, indeed, He could not be confined within a limit created by Himself. Such is the Catholic and Apostolic Faith which the Gospel has taught us and we avow.

23. Let Sabellius, if he dare, confound Father and Son as two names with one meaning, making of them not Unity but One Person. He shall have a prompt answer from the Gospels, not once or twice, but often repeated, *This is My beloved Son, in Whom I am well pleased* [8]. He shall hear the words, *The Father is greater than I* [9], and *I go to the Father* [1], and *Father, I thank Thee* [2], and *Glorify Me, Father* [3], and *Thou art the Son of the living God* [4]. Let Hebion try to sap the faith, who allows the Son of God no life before the Virgin's womb, and sees in Him the Word only after His life as flesh had begun. We will bid him read again, *Father, glorify Me with Thine own Self with that glory which I had with Thee before the world was* [5], and *In the beginning was the Word, and the Word was with God, and the Word was God* [6], and *All things were made through Him* [7], and *He was in the world, and the world was made through Him, and the world knew Him not* [8]. Let the preachers whose apostleship is of the newest fashion—an apostleship of Antichrist—come forward and pour their mockery and insult upon the Son of God. They must hear, *I came out from the Father* [9], and *The Son in the Father's bosom* [1], and *I and the Father are One* [2], and *I in the Father, and the Father in Me* [3]. And lastly, if they be wroth, as the Jews were, that Christ should claim God for His own Father, making Himself equal with God, they must take the answer which He gave the Jews, *Believe My works, that the Father is in Me and I in the Father* [4]. Thus our one immovable foundation, our one blissful rock of faith, is the confession from Peter's mouth, *Thou art the Son of the Living God* [5]. On it we can base an answer to every objection with which perverted ingenuity or embittered treachery may assail the truth.

24. In what remains we have the appointment of the Father's will. The Virgin, the birth, the Body, then the Cross, the death, the visit to the lower world; these things are our salvation. For the sake of

---

manner of His birth. It was instantaneous, and He was born endowed with all His powers. We may say therefore that He was the author of His own existence; *All things were made through Him*, with the necessary exception of the Father.
5 Isai. liii. 8.   6 St. John i. 4.

7 Reading *sint.*   8 St. Matt. xvii. 5.   See the note to § 8.
9 St. John xiv. 28.   1 Ib. 12.   2 Ib xi 41.
3 Ib. xvii. 5.   4 St. Matt. xvi. 17.   5 St. John xvii. 5.
6 Ib. i. 1.   7 Ib. 3.   8 Ib. 10.   9 Ib. xvi. 28.
1 Ib. i. 18.   2 Ib. x. 30.   3 Ib. xiv. 11.
4 Ib. x. 38.   5 St. Matt. xvi. 16.

mankind the Son of God was born of the Virgin and of the Holy Ghost. In this process He ministered to Himself; by His own power —the power of God—which overshadowed her He sowed the beginning of His Body, and entered on the first stage of His life in the flesh. He did it that by His Incarnation He might take to Himself from the Virgin the fleshly nature, and that through this commingling there might come into being a hallowed Body of all humanity; that so through that Body which He was pleased to assume all mankind might be hid in Him, and He in return, through His unseen existence, be reproduced in all. Thus the invisible Image of God scorned not the shame which marks the beginnings of human life. He passed through every stage; through conception, birth, wailing, cradle and each successive humiliation.

25. What worthy return can we make for so great a condescension? The One Onlybegotten God, ineffably born of God, entered the Virgin's womb and grew and took the frame of poor humanity. He Who upholds the universe, within Whom and through Whom are all things, was brought forth by common childbirth; He at Whose voice Archangels and Angels tremble, and heaven and earth and all the elements of this world are melted, was heard in childish wailing. The Invisible and Incomprehensible, Whom sight and feeling and touch cannot gauge, was wrapped in a cradle. If any man deem all this unworthy of God, the greater must he own his debt for the benefit conferred the less such condescension befits the majesty of God. He by Whom man was made had nothing to gain by becoming Man; it was our gain that God was incarnate and dwelt among us, making all flesh His home by taking upon Him the flesh of One. We were raised because He was lowered; shame to Him was glory to us. He, being God, made flesh His residence, and we in return are lifted anew from the flesh to God.

26. But lest perchance fastidious minds be exercised by cradle and wailing, birth and conception, we must render to God the glory which each of these contains, that we may approach His self-abasement with souls duly filled with His claim to reign, and not forget His majesty in His condescension. Let us note, therefore, who were attendant on His conception. An Angel speaks to Zacharias; fertility is given to the barren; the priest comes forth dumb from the place of incense; John bursts forth into speech while yet confined within his mother's womb; an Angel blesses Mary and promises that she, a virgin, shall be the mother of the Son of God. Conscious of her virginity, she is distressed at this

hard thing; the Angel explains to her the mighty working of God, saying, *The Holy Ghost shall come from above into thee, and the power of the Most High shall overshadow thee* [6]. The Holy Ghost, descending from above, hallowed the Virgin's womb, and breathing therein (for *The Spirit bloweth where it listeth* [7]), mingled Himself with the fleshly nature of man, and annexed by force and might that foreign domain. And, lest through weakness of the human structure failure should ensue, the power of the Most High overshadowed the Virgin, strengthening her feebleness in semblance of a cloud cast round her, that the shadow, which was the might of God, might fortify her bodily frame to receive the procreative power of the Spirit. Such is the glory of the conception.

27. And now let us consider the glory which accompanies the birth, the wailing and the cradle. The Angel tells Joseph that the Virgin shall bear a Son, and that that Son shall be named Emmanuel, that is, *God with us*. The Spirit foretells it through the prophet, the Angel bears witness; He that is born is God with us. The light of a new star shines forth for the Magi; a heavenly sign escorts the Lord of heaven. An Angel brings to the shepherds the news that Christ the Lord is born, the Saviour of the world. A multitude of the heavenly host flock together to sing the praise of that childbirth; the rejoicing of the Divine company proclaims the fulfilment of the mighty work. Then *glory to God in heaven, and peace on earth to men of good will* is announced. And now the Magi come and worship Him wrapped in swaddling clothes; after a life devoted to mystic rites of vain philosophy they bow the knee before a Babe laid in His cradle. Thus the Magi stoop to reverence the infirmities of Infancy; its cries are saluted by the heavenly joy of angels; the Spirit Who inspired the prophet, the heralding Angel, the light of the new star, all minister around Him. In such wise was it that the Holy Ghost's descent and the overshadowing power of the Most High brought Him to His birth. The inward reality is widely different from the outward appearance; the eye sees one thing, the soul another. A virgin bears; her child is of God. An Infant wails; angels are heard in praise. There are coarse swaddling clothes; God is being worshipped. The glory of His Majesty is not forfeited when He assumes the lowliness of flesh.

28. So was it also during His further life on earth. The whole time which He passed in

---

6 St. Luke i. 35.   7 St. John iii. 8.

human form was spent upon the works of God. I have no space for details; it must suffice to say that in all the varied acts of power and healing which He wrought, the fact is conspicuous that He was man by virtue of the flesh He had taken, God by the evidence of the works He did.

29. Concerning the Holy Spirit I ought not to be silent, and yet I have no need to speak; still, for the sake of those who are in ignorance, I cannot refrain. There is no need to speak, because we are bound to confess Him, proceeding, as He does, from Father and Son[8]. For my own part, I think it wrong to discuss the question of His existence. He does exist, inasmuch as He is given, received, retained. He is joined with Father and Son in our confession of the faith, and cannot be excluded from a true confession of Father and Son; take away a part, and the whole faith is marred. If any man demand what meaning we attach to this conclusion, he, as well as we, has read the words of the Apostle, *Because ye are sons of God, God hath sent the Spirit of His Son into our hearts, crying, Abba, Father*[9], and *Grieve not the Holy Spirit of God, in Whom ye have been sealed*[1], and again, *But we have received not the spirit of this world, but the Spirit which is of God, that we may know the things that are given unto us by God*[2], and also *But ye are not in the flesh but in the Spirit, if so be that the Spirit of God is in you. But if any man hath not the Spirit of Christ, he is not His*[3], and further, *But if the Spirit of Him that raised up Jesus from the dead dwelleth in you, He that raised up Christ from the dead shall quicken also your mortal bodies for the sake of His Spirit which dwelleth in you*[4]. Wherefore since He is, and is given, and is possessed, and is of God, let His traducers take refuge in silence. When they ask, Through Whom is He? To what end does He exist? Of what nature is He? We answer that He it is through Whom all things exist, and from Whom are all things, and that He is the Spirit of God, God's gift to the faithful. If our answer displease them, their displeasure must also fall upon the Apostles and the Prophets, who spoke of Him exactly as we have spoken. And furthermore, Father and Son must incur the same displeasure.

30. The reason, I believe, why certain people continue in ignorance or doubt is that they see this third Name, that of the Holy Spirit, often used to signify the Father or the Son. No objection need be raised to this;

whether it be Father or Son, He is Spirit, and He is holy.

31. But the words of the Gospel, *For God is Spirit*[5], need careful examination as to their sense and their purpose. For every saying has an antecedent cause and an aim which must be ascertained by study of the meaning. We must bear this in mind lest, on the strength of the words, *God is Spirit*, we deny not only the Name, but also the work and the gift of the Holy Ghost. The Lord was speaking with a woman of Samaria, for He had come to be the Redeemer for all mankind. After He had discoursed at length of the living water, and of her five husbands, and of him whom she then had who was not her husband, the woman answered, *Lord, I perceive that Thou art a prophet. Our fathers worshipped in this mountain; and ye say that in Jerusalem is the place where men ought to worship*[6]. The Lord replied, *Woman, believe Me, the hour cometh when neither in this mountain, nor in Jerusalem, shall ye worship the Father. Ye worship that which ye know not; we worship that which we know; for salvation is from the Jews. But the hour cometh, and now is, when the true worshippers shall worship the Father in the Spirit and in truth; for the Father seeketh such to worship Him. For God is Spirit, and they that worship Him must worship in the Spirit and in truth, for God is Spirit*[7]. We see that the woman, her mind full of inherited tradition, thought that God must be worshipped either on a mountain, as at Samaria, or in a temple, as at Jerusalem; for Samaria in disobedience to the Law had chosen a site upon the mountain for worship, while the Jews regarded the temple founded by Solomon as the home of their religion, and the prejudices of both confined the all-embracing and illimitable God to the crest of a hill or the vault of a building. God is invisible, incomprehensible, immeasurable; the Lord said that the time had come when God should be worshipped neither on mountain nor in temple. For Spirit cannot be cabined or confined; it is omnipresent in space and time, and under all conditions present in its fulness. Therefore, He said, they are the true worshippers who shall worship in the Spirit and in truth. And these who are to worship God the Spirit in the Spirit shall have the One for the means, the Other for the object, of their reverence: for Each of the Two stands in a different relation to the worshipper. The words, *God is Spirit*, do not alter the fact that the Holy Spirit has a Name of His own, and that He is the Gift to us. The woman who

[8] *Qui Patre et Filio auctoribus confitendus est;* A comparison with *dum et usum et auctorem eius ignorant* in § 4 makes this appear the probable translation. It might, of course, mean *confess Him on the evidence of Father and Son.*   [9] Gal. iv. 6.
[1] Eph. iv. 30.   [2] 1 Cor. ii. 12.   [3] Rom. viii. 9.   [4] Ib. 11.
[5] St. John iv. 24.   [6] Ib. 19, 20.   [7] Ib. 21—24.

confined God to hill or temple was told that God contains all things and is self-contained : that He, the Invisible and Incomprehensible, must be worshipped by invisible and incomprehensible means. The imparted gift and the object of reverence were clearly shewn when Christ taught that God, being Spirit, must be worshipped in the Spirit, and revealed what freedom and knowledge, what boundless scope for adoration, lay in this worship of God, the Spirit, in the Spirit.

32. The words of the Apostle are of like purport : *For the Lord is Spirit, and where the Spirit of the Lord is, there is liberty* [8]. To make his meaning clear he has distinguished between the Spirit, Who exists, and Him Whose Spirit He is Proprietor and Property, *He* and *His* are different in sense. Thus when he says, *The Lord is Spirit* he reveals the infinity of God ; when He adds, *Where the Spirit of the Lord is, there is liberty*, he indicates Him Who belongs to God ; for He is the Spirit of the Lord, and *Where the Spirit of the Lord is, there is liberty*. The Apostle makes the statement not from any necessity of his own argument, but in the interests of clearness. For the Holy Ghost is everywhere One, enlightening all patriarchs and prophets and the whole company of the Law, inspiring John even in his mother's womb, given in due time to the Apostles and other believers, that they might recognise the truth vouchsafed them.

33. Let us hear from our Lord's own words what is the work of the Holy Ghost within us. He says, *I have yet many things to say unto you, but ye cannot bear them now* [9]. For *it is expedient for you that I go : if I go I will send you the Advocate* [1]. And again, *I will ask the Father and He shall send you another Advocate, that He may be with you for ever, even the Spirit of truth* [2]. *He shall guide you into all truth, for He shall not speak from Himself, but whatsoever things He shall hear He shall speak, and He shall declare unto you the things that are to come. He shall glorify Me, for He shall take of Mine* [3]. These words were spoken to show how multitudes should enter the kingdom of heaven ; they contain an assurance of the goodwill of the Giver, and of the mode and terms of the Gift. They tell how, because our feeble minds cannot comprehend the Father or the Son, our faith which finds God's incarnation hard of credence shall be illumined by the gift of the Holy Ghost, the Bond of union and the Source of light.

34. The next step naturally is to listen to the Apostle's account of the powers and functions of this Gift. He says, *As many as are led by the Spirit of God, these are the children of God. For ye received not the Spirit of bondage again unto fear, but ye received the Spirit of adoption whereby we cry, Abba, Father* [4]; and again, *For no man by the Spirit of God saith anathema to Jesus, and no man can say, Jesus is Lord, but in the Holy Spirit* [5]; and he adds, *Now there are diversities of gifts, but the same Spirit, and diversities of ministrations, but the same Lord, and diversities of workings, but the same God, Who worketh all things in all. But to each one is given the enlightenment of the Spirit, to profit withal. Now to one is given through the Spirit the word of wisdom, to another the word of knowledge according to the same Spirit, to another faith in the same Spirit, to another gifts of healings in the One Spirit, to another workings of miracles, to another prophecy, to another discerning of spirits, to another kinds of tongues, to another interpretation of tongues. But all these worketh the One and same Spirit* [6]. Here we have a statement of the purpose and results of the Gift ; and I cannot conceive what doubt can remain, after so clear a definition of His Origin, His action and His powers.

35. Let us therefore make use of this great benefit, and seek for personal experience of this most needful Gift. For the Apostle says, in words I have already cited, *But we have not received the spirit of this world, but the Spirit which is of God, that we may know the things that are given unto us by God* [7]. We receive Him, then, that we may know. Faculties of the human body, if denied their exercise, will lie dormant. The eye without light, natural or artificial, cannot fulfil its office ; the ear will be ignorant of its function unless some voice or sound be heard ; the nostrils unconscious of their purpose unless some scent be breathed. Not that the faculty will be absent, because it is never called into use, but that there will be no experience of its existence. So, too, the soul of man, unless through faith it have appropriated the gift of the Spirit, will have the innate faculty of apprehending God, but be destitute of the light of knowledge. That Gift, which is in Christ, is One, yet offered, and offered fully, to all ; denied to none, and given to each according to the measure of his willingness to receive ; its stores the richer, the more earnest the desire to earn them. This gift is with us unto the end of the world, the solace of our waiting, the assurance, by the favours which He bestows, of the hope that shall be ours, the light of our minds, the sun of our souls. This Holy Spirit we must seek and must earn, and then hold fast by faith and obedience to the commands of God.

---

[8] 2 Cor. iii. 17.   [9] St. John xvi. 12.   [1] Ib. 7.
[2] Ib. xiv. 16, 17.   [3] Ib. xiv. 13, 14.

[4] Rom. viii. 14, 15.   [5] 1 Cor. xii. 3   [6] Ib. 4—11.
[7] 1 Cor. ii. 12, cited in § 29.

BOOK III.

1. THE words of the Lord, *I in the Father, and the Father in Me* [1], confuse many minds, and not unnaturally, for the powers of human reason cannot provide them with any intelligible meaning. It seems impossible that one object should be both within and without another, or that (since it is laid down that the Beings of whom we are treating, though They do not dwell apart, retain their separate existence and condition) these Beings can reciprocally contain One Another, so that One should permanently envelope, and also be permanently enveloped by, the Other, whom yet He envelopes. This is a problem which the wit of man will never solve, nor will human research ever find an analogy for this condition of Divine existence. But what man cannot understand, God can be. I do not mean to say that the fact that this is an assertion made by God renders it at once intelligible to us. We must think for ourselves, and come to know the meaning of the words, *I in the Father, and the Father in Me:* but this will depend upon our success in grasping the truth that reasoning based upon Divine verities can establish its conclusions, even though they seem to contradict the laws of the universe.

2. In order to solve as easily as possible this most difficult problem, we must first master the knowledge which the Divine Scriptures give of Father and of Son, that so we may speak with more precision, as dealing with familiar and accustomed matters. The eternity of the Father, as we concluded after full discussion in the last Book, transcends space, and time, and appearance, and all the forms of human thought. He is without and within all things, He contains all and can be contained by none, is incapable of change by increase or diminution, invisible, incomprehensible, full, perfect, eternal, not deriving anything that He has from another, but, if ought be derived from Him, still complete and self-sufficing.

3. He therefore, the Unbegotten, before time was begat a Son from Himself; not from any pre-existent matter, for all things are through the Son; not from nothing, for the Son is from the Father's self; not by way of childbirth, for in God there is neither change nor void; not as a piece of Himself cut or torn off or stretched out, for God is passionless and bodiless, and only a passible and embodied being could so be treated, and, as the Apostle says, in Christ *dwelleth all the fulness of the Godhead bodily* [2]. Incomprehensibly, ineffably, before time or worlds, He begat the Only-begotten from His own unbegotten substance, bestowing through love and power His whole Divinity upon that Birth. Thus He is the Only-begotten, perfect, eternal Son of the unbegotten, perfect, eternal Father. But those properties which He has in consequence of the Body which He took, are the fruit of His goodwill toward our salvation. For He, being invisible and bodiless and incomprehensible, as the Son of God, took upon Him such a measure of matter and of lowliness as was needed to bring Him within the range of our understanding, and perception, and contemplation. It was a condescension to our feebleness rather than a surrender of His own proper attributes.

4. He, therefore, being the perfect Father's perfect Son. the Only-begotten Offspring of the unbegotten God, who has received all from Him Who possesses all, being God from God, Spirit from Spirit, Light from Light, says boldly, *The Father in Me, and I in the Father* [3]. For as the Father is Spirit, so is the Son Spirit; as the Father is God, so is the Son God; as the Father is Light, so is the Son Light. Thus those properties which are in the Father are the source of those wherewith the Son is endowed; that is, He is wholly Son of Him Who is wholly Father; not imported from without, for before the Son nothing was; not made from nothing, for the Son is from God; not a son partially, for the fulness of the Godhead is in the Son; not a Son in some respects, but in all; a Son according to the will of Him who had the power, after a manner which He only knows. What is in the Father is in the Son also; what is in the Unbegotten is in the Only-begotten also. The One is from the Other, and they Two are a Unity; not Two made One, yet One in the Other, for that which is in Both is the same. The Father is in the Son, for the Son is from Him; the Son is in the Father, because the

---

[1] St. John xiv. 11.   [2] Col. ii. 9.   [3] St. John x. 38

Father is His sole Origin; the Only-begotten is in the Unbegotten, because He is the Only-begotten from the Unbegotten. Thus mutually Each is in the Other, for as all is perfect in the Unbegotten Father, so all is perfect in the Only-begotten Son. This is the Unity which is in Son and Father, this the power, this the love; our hope, and faith, and truth, and way, and life is not to dispute the Father's powers or to depreciate the Son, but to reverence the mystery and majesty of His birth; to set the unbegotten Father above all rivalry, and count the Only-begotten Son as His equal in eternity and might, confessing concerning God the Son that He is from God.

5. Such powers are there in God; powers which the methods of our reason cannot comprehend, but of which our faith, on the sure evidence of His action, is convinced. We shall find instances of this action in the bodily sphere as well as in the spiritual, its manifestation taking, not the form of an analogy which might illustrate the Birth, but of a deed marvellous yet comprehensible. On the wedding day in Galilee water was made wine. Have we words to tell or senses to ascertain what methods produced the change by which the tastelessness of water disappeared, and was replaced by the full flavour of wine? It was not a mixing; it was a creation, and a creation which was not a beginning, but a transformation. A weaker liquid was not obtained by admixture of a stronger element; an existing thing perished and a new thing came into being. The bridegroom was anxious, the household in confusion, the harmony of the marriage feast imperilled. Jesus is asked for help. He does not rise or busy Himself; He does the work without an effort. Water is poured into the vessels, wine drawn out in the cups. The evidence of the senses of the pourer contradicts that of the drawer. They who poured expect water to be drawn; they who draw think that wine must have been poured in. The intervening time cannot account for any gain or loss of character in the liquid. The mode of action baffles sight and sense, but the power of God is manifest in the result achieved.

6. In the case of the five loaves a miracle of the same type excites our wonder. By their increase five thousand men and countless women and children are saved from hunger; the method eludes our powers of observation. Five loaves are offered and broken; while the Apostles are dividing them a succession of new-created portions passes, they cannot tell how, through their hands. The loaf which they are dividing grows no smaller, yet their hands are continually full of the pieces. The swiftness of the process baffles sight; you follow with the eye a hand full of portions, and meantime you see that the contents of the other hand are not diminished, and all the while the heap of pieces grows. The carvers are busy at their task, the eaters are hard at work; the hungry are satisfied, and the fragments fill twelve baskets. Sight or sense cannot discover the mode of so noteworthy a miracle. What was not existent is created; what we see passes our understanding. Our only resource is faith in God's omnipotence.

7. There is no deception in these miracles of God, no subtle pretence to please or to deceive. These works of the Son of God were done from no desire for self-display; He Whom countless myriads of angels serve never deluded man. What was there of ours that He could need, through Whom all that we have was created? Did He demand praise from us who now are heavy with sleep, now sated with lust, now laden with the guilt of riot and bloodshed, now drunken from revelling;—He Whom Archangels, and Dominions, and Principalities, and Powers, without sleep or cessation or sin, praise in heaven with everlasting and unwearied voice? They praise Him because He, the Image of the Invisible God, created all their host in Himself, made the worlds, established the heavens, appointed the stars, fixed the earth, laid the foundations of the deep; because in after time He was born, He conquered death, broke the gates of hell, won for Himself a people to be His fellow-heirs, lifted flesh from corruption up to the glory of eternity. There was nothing, then, that He might gain from us, that could induce Him to assume the splendour of these mysterious and inexplicable works, as though He needed our praise. But God foresaw how human sin and folly would be misled, and knew that disbelief would dare to pass its judgment even on the things of God, and therefore He vanquished presumption by tokens of His power which must give pause to our boldest.

8. For there are many of those wise men of the world whose wisdom is folly with God, who contradict our proclamation of God from God, True from True, Perfect from Perfect, One from One, as though we taught things impossible. They pin their faith to certain conclusions which they have reached by process of logic:—*Nothing can be born of one, for every birth requires two parents*, and *If this Son be born of One, He has received a part of His Begetter: if He be a part, then Neither of the Two is perfect, for something is missing from Him from Whom the Son issued, and*

there cannot be fulness in One Who consists of a portion of Another. Thus Neither is perfect, for the Begetter has lost His fulness, and the Begotten has not acquired it. This is that wisdom of the world which was foreseen by God even in the prophet's days, and condemned through him in the words, *I will destroy the wisdom of the wise, and reject the understanding of the prudent*[4]. And the apostle says: *Where is the wise? Where is the scribe? Where is the inquirer of this world? Hath not God made foolish the wisdom of this world? For because in the wisdom of God the world through wisdom knew not God, it pleased God through the foolishness of preaching to save them that believe. For the Jews seek signs, and the Greeks seek wisdom, but we preach Christ crucified, to the Jews indeed a stumbling-block and to the Gentiles foolishness, but unto them that are called, both Jews and Greeks, Christ the power of God and the wisdom of God. Because the foolishness of God is wiser than men, and the weakness of God is stronger than men*[5].

9. The Son of God, therefore, having the charge of mankind, was first made man, that men might believe on Him; that He might be to us a witness, sprung from ourselves, of things Divine, and preach to us, weak and carnal as we are, through the weakness of the flesh concerning God the Father, so fulfilling the Father's will, even as He says, *I came not to do Mine own will, but the will of Him that sent Me*[6]. It was not that He Himself was unwilling, but that He might manifest His obedience as the result of His Father's will, for His own will is to do His Father's. This is that will to carry out the Father's will of which He testifies in the words: *Father, the hour is come; glorify Thy Son, that Thy Son may glorify Thee; even as Thou hast given Him power over all flesh, that whatsoever Thou hast given Him, He should give it eternal life. And this is life eternal, that they should know Thee the only true God, and Him Whom Thou didst send, Jesus Christ. I have glorified Thee upon earth, having accomplished the work which Thou gavest Me to do. And now, O Father, glorify Me with Thine own Self with the glory which I had with Thee before the world was. I have manifested Thy Name unto the men whom Thou hast given Me*[7]. In words short and few He has revealed the whole task to which He was appointed and assigned. Yet those words, short and few as they are, are the true faith's safeguard against every suggestion of the devil's cunning. Let us briefly consider the force of each separate phrase.

10. He says, *Father the hour is come; glorify Thy Son, that Thy Son may glorify Thee*. He says that the hour, not the day nor the time, is come. An hour is a fraction of a day. What hour must this be? The hour, of course, of which He speaks, to strengthen His disciples, at the time of His passion:—*Lo, the hour is come that the Son of Man should be glorified*[8]. This then is the hour in which He prays to be glorified by the Father, that He Himself may glorify the Father. But what does He mean? Does One who is about to give glory look to receive it? Does One who is about to confer honour make request for Himself? Is He in want of the very thing which He is about to repay? Here let the world's philosophers, the wise men of Greece, beset our path, and spread their syllogistic nets to entangle the truth. Let them ask How? and Whence? and Why? When they can find no answer, let us tell them that it is because *God has chosen the foolish things of the world to confound the wise*[9]. That is the reason why we in our foolishness understand[1] things incomprehensible to the world's philosophers. The Lord had said, *Father, the hour is come;* He had revealed the hour of His passion, for these words were spoken at the very moment; and then He added, *Glorify Thy Son*. But how was the Son to be glorified? He had been born of a virgin, from cradle and childhood He had grown to man's estate, through sleep and hunger and thirst and weariness and tears He had lived man's life: even now He was to be spitted on, scourged, crucified. And why? These things were ordained for our assurance that in Christ is pure man. But the shame of the cross is not ours; we are not sentenced to the scourge, nor defiled by spitting. The Father glorifies the Son; how? He is next nailed to the cross. Then what followed? The sun, instead of setting, fled. How so? It did not retire behind a cloud, but abandoned its appointed orbit, and all the elements of the world felt that same shock of the death of Christ. The stars in their courses, to avoid complicity in the crime, escaped by self-extinction from beholding the scene. What did the earth? It quivered beneath the burden of the Lord hanging on the tree, protesting that it was powerless to confine Him who was dying. Yet surely rock and stone will not refuse Him a resting-place. Yes, they are rent and cloven, and their strength fails. They must confess that the rock-hewn sepulchre cannot imprison the Body which awaits its burial.

11. And next? The centurion of the co-

---

4 Isaiah xxix. 14.
6 St. John vi. 38.
5 1 Cor. i. 20—25.
7 Ib. xvii. 1—6.
8 St. John xii. 23.   9 1 Cor. i. 27.   1 Reading *intelligimus*.

hort, the guardian of the cross, cries out, *Truly this was the Son of God*[2]. Creation is set free by the mediation of this Sin-offering; the very rocks lose their solidity and strength. They who had nailed Him to the cross confess that truly this is the Son of God. The outcome justifies the assertion. The Lord had said, *Glorify Thy Son*. He had asserted, by that word *Thy*, that He was God's Son not in name only, but in nature. Multitudes of us are sons of God; He is Son in another sense. For He is God's true and own Son, by origin and not by adoption, not by name only but in truth, born and not created. So, after He was glorified, that confession touched the truth; the centurion confessed Him the true Son of God, that no believer might doubt a fact which even the servant of His persecutors could not deny.

12. But perhaps some may suppose that He was destitute of that glory for which He prayed, and that His looking to be glorified by a Greater is evidence of want of power. Who, indeed, would deny that the Father is the greater; the Unbegotten greater than the Begotten, the Father than the Son, the Sender than the Sent, He that wills than He that obeys? He Himself shall be His own witness:—*The Father is greater than I*. It is a fact which we must recognise, but we must take heed lest with unskilled thinkers the majesty of the Father should obscure the glory of the Son. Such obscuration is forbidden by this same glory for which the Son prays; for the prayer, *Father glorify Thy Son*, is completed by, *That the Son may glorify Thee*. Thus there is no lack of power in the Son, Who, when He has received this glory, will make His return for it in glory. But why, if He were not in want, did He make the prayer? No one makes request except for something which he needs. Or can it be that the Father too is in want? Or has He given His glory away so recklessly that He needs to have it returned Him by the Son? No; the One has never been in want, nor the Other needed to ask, and yet Each shall give to the Other. Thus the prayer for glory to be given and to be paid back is neither a robbery of the Father nor a depreciation of the Son, but a demonstration of the power of one Godhead resident in Both. The Son prays that He may be glorified by the Father; the Father deems it no humiliation to be glorified by the Son. The exchange of glory given and received proclaims the unity of power in Father and in Son.

13. We must next ascertain what and whence this glorifying is. God, I am sure, is subject to no change; His eternity admits not of defect or amendment, of gain or of loss. It is the character of Him alone, that what He is, He is from everlasting. What He from everlasting is, it is by His nature impossible that He should ever cease to be. How then can He receive glory, a thing which He fully possesses, and of which His store does not diminish; there being no fresh glory which He can obtain, and none that He has lost and can recover? We are brought to a standstill. But the Evangelist does not fail us, though our reason has displayed its helplessness. To tell us what return of glory it was that the Son should make to the Father, he gives the words: *Even as Thou hast given Him power over all flesh, that whatsoever Thou hast given Him He may give it eternal life. And this is life eternal that they should know Thee, the only true God, and Jesus Christ Whom Thou hast sent*. The Father, then, is glorified through the Son, by His being made known to us. And the glory was this, that the Son, being made flesh, received from Him power over all flesh, and the charge of restoring eternal life to us, ephemeral beings burdened with the body. Eternal life for us was the result not of work done, but of innate power; not by a new creation, but simply by knowledge of God, was the glory of that eternity to be acquired. Nothing was added to God's glory; it had not decreased, and so could not be replenished. But He is glorified through the Son in the sight of us, ignorant, exiled, defiled, dwelling in hopeless death and lawless darkness; glorified inasmuch as the Son, by virtue of that power over all flesh which the Father gave Him, was to bestow on us eternal life. It is through this work of the Son that the Father is glorified. So when the Son received all things from the Father, the Father glorified Him; and conversely, when all things were made through the Son, He glorified the Father. The return of glory given lies herein, that all the glory which the Son has is the glory of the Father, since everything He has is the Father's gift. For the glory of Him who executes a charge redounds to the glory of Him Who gave it, the glory of the Begotten to the glory of the Begetter.

14. But in what does eternity of life consist? His own words tell us:—*That they may know Thee the only true God, and Jesus Christ Whom Thou hast sent*. Is there any doubt or difficulty here, or any inconsistency? It is life to know the true God; but the bare knowledge of Him does not give it. What, then, does He add? *And Jesus Christ Whom Thou hast sent*. In *Thee, the only true God*, the Son

pays the honour due to His Father; by the addition, *And Jesus Christ Whom Thou hast sent,* He associates Himself with the true Godhead. The believer in his confession draws no line between the Two, for his hope of life rests in Both, and indeed, the true God is inseparable from Him Whose Name follows in the creed. Therefore when we read, *That they may know Thee, the only true God, and Jesus Christ Whom Thou hast sent,* these terms of Sender and of Sent are not intended, under any semblance of distinction or discrimination, to convey a difference between the true Godhead of Father and of Son, but to be a guide to the devout confession of Them as Begetter and Begotten.

15. And so the Son glorifies the Father fully and finally in the words which follow, *I have glorified Thee on the earth, having accomplished the work which Thou hast given Me to do.* All the Father's praise is from the Son, for every praise bestowed upon the Son is praise of the Father, since all that He accomplished is what the Father had willed. The Son of God is born as man; but the power of God is in the virgin-birth. The Son of God is seen as man; but God is present in His human actions. The Son of God is nailed to the cross; but on the cross God conquers human death. Christ, the Son of God, dies; but all flesh is made alive in Christ. The Son of God is in hell; but man is carried back to heaven. In proportion to our praise of Christ for these His works, will be the praise we bring to Him from Whom Christ's Godhead is. These are the ways in which the Father glorifies the Son on earth; and in return the Son reveals by works of power to the ignorance of the heathen and to the foolishness of the world, Him from Whom He is. This exchange of glory, given and received, implies no augmentation of the Godhead, but means the praises rendered for the knowledge granted to those who had lived in ignorance of God. What, indeed, could there be which the Father, from Whom are all things, did not richly possess? In what was the Son lacking, in Whom all the fulness of the Godhead had been pleased to dwell? The Father is glorified on earth because the work which He had commanded is finished.

16. Next let us see what this glory is which the Son expects to receive from the Father; and then our exposition will be complete. The sequel is, *I have glorified Thee on the earth, having accomplished the work which Thou hast given Me to do. And now, O Father, glorify Thou Me with Thine own Self with the glory which I had with Thee before the world was. I have manifested Thy name unto men.* It is,

then, by the Son's works that the Father is glorified, in that He is recognised as God, as Father of God the Only-begotten, Who for our salvation willed that His Son should be born as man, even of a virgin; that Son Whose whole life, consummated in the Passion, was consistent with the humiliation of the virgin birth. Thus, because the Son of God, all-perfect and born from everlasting in the fulness of the Godhead, had now by incarnation become Man and was ready for His death, He prays that He may be glorified with God, even as He was glorifying His Father on the earth; for at that moment the powers of God were being glorified in the flesh before the eyes of a world that knew Him not. But what is this glory with the Father, for which He looks? It is that, of course, which He had with Him before the world was. He had the fulness of the Godhead; He has it still, for He is God's Son. But He Who was the Son of God had become the Son of man also, for *The Word was made flesh.* He had not lost His former being, but He had become what He was not before; He had not abdicated His own position, yet He had taken ours; He prays that the nature which He had assumed may be promoted to the glory which He had never renounced. Therefore, since the Son is the Word, and the Word was made flesh, and the Word was God, and was in the beginning with God, and the Word was Son before the foundation of the world; this Son, now incarnate, prayed that flesh might be to the Father what the Son had been. He prayed that flesh, born in time, might receive the splendour of the everlasting glory, that the corruption of the flesh might be swallowed up, transformed into the power of God and the purity of the Spirit. It is His prayer to God, the Son's confession of the Father, the entreaty of that flesh wherein all shall see Him on the Judgment-day, pierced and bearing the marks of the cross; of that flesh wherein His glory was foreshown upon the Mount, wherein He ascended to heaven and is set down at the right hand of God, wherein Paul saw Him and Stephen paid Him worship.

17. The name *Father* has thus been revealed to men; the question arises, What is this Father's own name? Yet surely the name of God has never been unknown. Moses heard it from the bush, Genesis announces it at the beginning of the history of creation, the Law has proclaimed and the prophets extolled it, the history of the world has made mankind familiar with it; the very heathen have worshipped it under a veil of falsehood. Men have never been left in ignorance of the name of God. And yet they were, in very truth,

in ignorance. For no man knows God unless He confess Him as Father, Father of the Only-begotten Son, and confess also the Son, a Son by no partition or extension or procession, but born of Him, as Son of Father, ineffably and incomprehensibly, and retaining the fulness of that Godhead from which and in which He was born as true and infinite and perfect God. This is what *the fulness of the Godhead* means. If any of these things be lacking, there will not be that fulness which was pleased to dwell in Him. This is the message of the Son, His revelation to men in their ignorance. The Father is glorified through the Son when men recognise that He is Father of a Son so Divine.

18. The Son, wishing to assure us of the truth of this, His Divine birth, has appointed His works to serve as an illustration, that from the ineffable power displayed in ineffable deeds we may learn the lesson of the ineffable birth. For instance, when water was made wine, and five loaves satisfied five thousand men, beside women and children, and twelve baskets were filled with the fragments, we see a fact though we cannot understand it; a deed is done, though it baffles our reason; the process cannot be followed, though the result is obvious. It is folly to intrude in the spirit of carping, when the matter into which we enquire is such that we cannot probe it to the bottom. For even as the Father is ineffable because He is Unbegotten, so is the Son ineffable because He is the Only-begotten, since the Begotten is the Image of the Unbegotten. Now it is by the use of our senses and of language that we have to form our conception of an image; and it must be by the same means that we form our idea of that which the image represents But in this case we, whose faculties can deal only with visible and tangible things, are straining after the invisible, and striving to grasp the impalpable. Yet we take no shame to ourselves, we reproach ourselves with no irreverence, when we doubt and criticise the mysteries and powers of God. How is He the Son? Whence is He? What did the Father lose by His birth? Of what portion of the Father was He born? So we ask; yet all the while there has been confronting us the evidence of works done to assure us that God's action is not limited by our power of comprehending His methods.

19. You ask what was the manner in which, as the Spirit teaches, the Son was born? I will put a question to you as to things corporal. I ask not in what manner He was born of a virgin; I ask only whether her flesh, in the course of bringing His flesh to readiness for birth, suffered any loss. As-

suredly she did not conceive Him in the common way, or suffer the shame of human intercourse, in order to bear Him: yet she bore Him, complete in His human Body, without loss of her own completeness. Surely piety requires that we should regard as possible with God a thing which we see became possible through his power in the case of a human being [3].

20. But you, whoever you are that would seek into the unsearchable, and in all seriousness form an opinion upon the mysteries and powers of God;—I turn to you for counsel, and beg you to enlighten me, an unskilled and simple believer of all that God says, as to a circumstance which I am about to mention. I listen to the Lord's words and, since I believe what is recorded, I am sure that after His Resurrection He offered Himself repeatedly in the Body to the sight of multitudes of un, believers. At any rate, He did so to Thomas who had protested that he would not believe unless he handled His wounds. His words are, *Unless I shall see in His hands the print of the nails, and put my finger into the place of the nails, and thrust my hand into His side, I will not believe* [4]. The Lord stoops to the level even of our feeble understanding; to satisfy the doubts of unbelieving minds He works a miracle of His invisible power. Do you, my critic of the ways of heaven, explain His action if you can. The disciples were in a closed room; they had met and held their assembly in secret since the Passion of the Lord. The Lord presents Himself to strengthen the faith of Thomas by meeting his challenge; He gives him His Body to feel, His wounds to handle. He, indeed, who would be recognised as having suffered wounds must needs produce the body in which those wounds were received. I ask at what point in the walls of that closed house the Lord bodily entered. The Apostle has recorded the circumstances with careful precision; *Jesus came when the doors were shut, and stood in the midst* [5]. Did He penetrate through bricks and mortar, or through stout woodwork, substances whose very nature it is to bar progress? For there He stood in bodily presence; there was no suspicion of deceit. Let the eye of your mind follow His path as He enters; let your intellectual vision accompany Him as He passes into that closed dwell-

---

[3] This is an argument against the objection that God, if Christ is His Son, must have suffered loss. If God is His Father and the sole source of His existence, Christ must have come into being by separation from the Father; i.e. the Father must have suffered diminution and lost His completeness. The answer is that a woman—and *a fortiori* the Virgin, who was the only human parent of Christ—suffers no loss of bodily completeness through becoming a mother. There is no allusion to the belief in the perpetual virginity of the Mother of our Lord.
[4] St. John xx. 25. [5] Ib. xx. 26.

ing. There is no breach in the walls, no door has been unbarred; yet lo, He stands in the midst Whose might no barrier can resist. You are a critic of things invisible; I ask you to explain a visible event. Everything remains firm as it was; no body is capable of insinuating itself through the interstices of wood and stone. The Body of the Lord does not disperse itself, to come together again after a disappearance; yet whence comes He Who is standing in the midst? Your senses and your words are powerless to account for it; the fact is certain, but it lies beyond the region of human explanation. If, as you say, our account of the Divine birth is a lie, then prove that this account of the Lord's entrance is a fiction. If we assume that an event did not happen, because we cannot discover how it was done, we make the limits of our understanding into the limits of reality. But the certainty of the evidence proves the falsehood of our contradiction. The Lord did stand in a closed house in the midst of the disciples; the Son was born of the Father. Deny not that He stood, because your puny wits cannot ascertain how He came there; renounce a disbelief in God the Only-begotten and perfect Son of God the Unbegotten and perfect Father, which is based only on the incapacity of sense and speech to comprehend the transcendent miracle of that birth.

21. Nay more, the whole constitution of nature would bear us out against the impiety of doubting the works and powers of God. And yet our disbelief tilts even against obvious truth; we strive in our fury to pluck even God from His throne. If we could, we would climb by bodily strength to heaven, would fling into confusion the ordered courses of sun and stars, would disarrange the ebb and flow of tides, check rivers at their source or make their waters flow backward, would shake the foundations of the world, in the utter irreverence of our rage against the paternal work of God. It is well that our bodily limitations confine us within more modest bounds. Assuredly, there is no concealment of the mischief we would do if we could. In one respect we are free; and so with blasphemous insolence we distort the truth and turn our weapons against the words of God.

22. The Son has said, *Father, I have manifested Thy Name unto men*. What reason is there for denunciation or fury here? Do you deny the Father? Why, it was the primary purpose of the Son to enable us to know the Father. But in fact you do deny Him when, according to you, the Son was not born of Him. Yet why should He have the name of Son if He be, as others are, an arbitrary

creation of God? I could feel awe of God as Creator of Christ as well as Founder of the universe; it were an exercise of power worthy of Him to be the Maker of Him Who made Archangels and Angels, things visible and things invisible, heaven and earth and the whole creation around us. But the work which the Lord came to do was not to enable you to recognise the omnipotence of God as Creator of all things, but to enable you to know Him as the Father of that Son Who addresses you. In heaven there are Powers beside Himself, Powers mighty and eternal; there is but one Only-begotten Son, and the difference between Him and them is not one of mere degree of might, but that they all were made through Him. Since He is the true and only Son, let us not make Him a bastard by asserting that He was made out of nothing. You hear the name *Son;* believe that He is the Son. You hear the name *Father;* fix it in your mind that He is the Father. Why surround these names with doubt and illwill and hostility? The things of God are provided with names which give a true indication of the realities; why force an arbitrary meaning upon their obvious sense? Father and Son are spoken of; doubt not that the words mean what they say. The end and aim of the revelation of the Son is that you should know the Father. Why frustrate the labours of the Prophets, the Incarnation of the Word, the Virgin's travail, the effect of miracles, the cross of Christ? It was all spent upon you, it is all offered to you, that through it all Father and Son may be manifest to you. And you replace the truth by a theory of arbitrary action, of creation or adoption. Turn your thoughts to the warfare, the conflict waged by Christ. He describes it thus:—*Father, I have manifested Thy Name unto men*. He does not say, *Thou hast created the Creator of all the heavens*, or *Thou hast made the Maker of the whole earth*. He says, *Father, I have manifested Thy Name unto men*. Accept your Saviour's gift of knowledge. Be assured that there is a Father Who begat, a Son Who was born; born in the truth of His Nature of the Father, Who is. Remember that the revelation is not of the Father manifested as God, but of God manifested as the Father.

23. You hear the words, *I and the Father are one*[6]. Why do you rend and tear the Son away from the Father? They are a unity: an absolute Existence having all things in perfect communion with that absolute Existence, from Whom He is. When you hear the Son saying, *I and the Father are one*, adjust your view o

---

facts to the Persons; accept the statement which Begetter and Begotten make concerning Themselves. Believe that They are One, even as They are also Begetter and Begotten. Why deny the common nature? Why impugn the true Divinity? You hear again, *The Father in Me, and I in the Father* [7]. That this is true of Father and of Son is demonstrated by the Son's works. Our science cannot envelope body in body, or pour one into another, as water into wine; but we confess that in Both is equivalence of power and fulness of the Godhead. For the Son has received all things from the Father; He is the Likeness of God, the Image of His substance. The words, *Image of His substance* [8], discriminate between Christ and Him from Whom He is, but only to establish Their distinct existence, not to teach a difference of nature; and the meaning of *Father in Son and Son in Father* is that there is the perfect fulness of the Godhead in Both. The Father is not impaired by the Son's existence, nor is the Son a mutilated fragment of the Father. An image implies its original; likeness is a relative term. Now nothing can be like God unless it have its source in Him; a perfect likeness can be reflected only from that which it represents; an accurate resemblance forbids the assumption of any element of difference. Disturb not this likeness; make no separation where truth shews no variance, for He Who said, *Let us make man after our image and likeness* [9], by those words *Our likeness* revealed the existence of Beings, Each like the Other. Touch not, handle not, pervert not. Hold fast the Names which teach the truth, hold fast the Son's declaration of Himself. I would not have you flatter the Son with praises of your own invention; it is well with you if you be satisfied with the written word.

24. Again, we must not repose so blind a confidence in human intellect as to imagine that we have complete knowledge of the objects of our thought, or that the ultimate problem is solved as soon as we have formed a symmetrical and consistent theory. Finite minds cannot conceive the Infinite; a being dependent for its existence upon another cannot attain to perfect knowledge either of its Creator or of itself, for its consciousness of self is coloured by its circumstances, and bounds are set which its perception cannot pass. Its activity is not self-caused, but due to the Creator, and a being dependent on a Creator [1] has perfect possession of none of its faculties, since its origin lies outside itself. Hence by an inexorable law it is folly for that being to say that it has perfect knowledge of

any matter; its powers have limits which it cannot modify, and only while it is under the delusion that its petty bounds are coterminous with infinity can it make the empty boast of possessing wisdom. For of wisdom it is incapable, its knowledge being limited to the range of its perception, and sharing the impotence of its dependent existence. And therefore this masquerade [2] of a finite nature boasting that it possesses the wisdom which springs only from infinite knowledge earns the scorn and ridicule of the Apostle, who calls its wisdom folly. He says, *For Christ sent me not to baptize, but to preach the Gospel, not in the language of wisdom, lest the cross of Christ should be made void. For the word of the cross is foolishness to them that are perishing, but unto them that are being saved it is the power of God. For it is written, I will destroy the wisdom of the wise and the understanding of the prudent I will reject. Where is the wise? Where is the scribe? Where is the enquirer of this world? Hath not God made foolish the wisdom of this world? For seeing that in the wisdom of God the world through its wisdom knew not God, God decreed through the foolishness of preaching to save them that believe. For the Jews ask for signs and the Greeks seek after wisdom, but we preach Christ crucified, unto Jews indeed a stumbling-block and to Gentiles foolishness, but unto them that are called, both Jews and Greeks, Christ the power of God and the wisdom of God. Because the weakness of God is stronger than men, and the foolishness of God is wiser than men* [3]. Thus all unbelief is foolishness, for it takes such wisdom as its own finite perception can attain, and, measuring infinity by that petty scale, concludes that what it cannot understand must be impossible. Unbelief is the result of incapacity engaged in argument. Men are sure that an event never happened, because they have made up their minds that it could not happen.

25. Hence the Apostle, familiar with the narrow assumption of human thought that what it does not know is not truth, says that he does not speak in the language of knowledge, lest his preaching should be in vain. To save himself from being regarded as a preacher of foolishness he adds that the word of the cross is foolishness to them that perish. He knew that the unbelievers held that the only true knowledge was that which formed their own wisdom, and that, since their wisdom was cognisant only of matters which lay within

---

7 St. John x. 38. 8 Heb. i. 3. 9 Gen. i. 26.
1 Omitting *in aliud.*

2 *Substitutio:* this word seems, except in technical senses of the law, to be very late and very rare. The only meaning, and that one not attested in the dictionaries, which will suit this passage, seems to be that of the jackdaw dressed in peacock's feathers.
3 1 Cor. i. 17—25.

their narrow horizon, the other wisdom, which alone is Divine and perfect, seemed foolishness to them. Thus their foolishness actually consisted in that feeble imagination which they mistook for wisdom. Hence it is that the very things which to them that perish are foolishness are the power of God to them that are saved; for these last never use their own inadequate faculties as a measure, but attribute to the Divine activities the omnipotence of heaven. God rejects the wisdom of the wise and the understanding of the prudent in this sense, that just because they recognise their own foolishness, salvation is granted to them that believe. Unbelievers pronounce the verdict of foolishness on everything that lies beyond their ken, while believers leave to the power and majesty of God the choice of the mysteries wherein salvation is bestowed. There is no foolishness in the things of God; the foolishness lies in that human wisdom which demands of God, as the condition of belief, signs and wisdom. It is the foolishness of the Jews to demand signs; they have a certain knowledge of the Name of God through long acquaintance with the Law, but the offence of the cross repels them. The foolishness of the Greeks is to demand wisdom; with Gentile folly and the philosophy of men they seek the reason why God was lifted up on the cross. And because, in consideration for the weakness of our mental powers, these things have been hidden in a mystery, this foolishness of Jews and Greeks turns to unbelief; for they denounce, as unworthy of reasonable credence, truths which their mind is inherently incapable of comprehending. But, because the world's wisdom was so foolish,—for previously through God's wisdom it knew not God, that is, the splendour of the universe, and the wonderful order which He planned for His handiwork, taught it no reverence for its Creator—God was pleased through the preaching of foolishness to save them that believe, that is, through the faith of the cross to make everlasting life the lot of mortals; that so the self-confidence of human wisdom might be put to shame, and salvation found where men had thought that foolishness dwelt. For Christ, Who is foolishness to Gentiles, and offence to Jews, is the Power of God and the Wisdom of God; because what seems weak and foolish to human apprehension in the things of God transcends in true wisdom and might the thoughts and the powers of earth.

26. And therefore the action of God must not be canvassed by human faculties; the Creator must not be judged by those who are the work of His hands. We must clothe ourselves in foolishness that we may gain wisdom; not in the foolishness of hazardous conclusions, but in the foolishness of a modest sense of our own infirmity, that so the evidence of God's power may teach us truths to which the arguments of earthly philosophy cannot attain. For when we are fully conscious of our own foolishness, and have felt the helplessness and destitution of our reason, then through the counsels of Divine Wisdom we shall be initiated into the wisdom of God; setting no bounds to boundless majesty and power, nor tying the Lord of nature down to nature's laws; sure that for us the one true faith concerning God is that of which He is at once the Author and the Witness.

BOOK IV.

1. THE earlier books of this treatise, written some time ago, contain, I think, an invincible proof that we hold and profess the faith in Father, Son, and Holy Spirit, which is taught by the Evangelists and Apostles, and that no commerce is possible between us and the heretics, inasmuch as they deny unconditionally, irrationally, and recklessly, the Divinity of our Lord Jesus Christ. Yet certain points remained which I have felt myself bound to include in this and the following books, in order to make our assurance of the faith even more certain by exposure of every one of their falsehoods and blasphemies. Accordingly, we will enquire first what are the dangers of their teaching, the risks involved by such irreverence; next, what principles they hold, and what arguments they advance against the apostolic faith to which we adhere, and by what sleight of language they impose upon the candour of their hearers; and lastly, by what method of comment they disarm the words of Scripture of their force and meaning.

2. We are well aware that neither the speech of men nor the analogy of human nature can give us a full insight into the things of God. The ineffable cannot submit to the bounds and limits of definition; that which is spiritual is distinct from every class or instance of bodily things. Yet, since our subject is that of heavenly natures, we must employ ordinary natures and ordinary speech as our means of expressing what our mind apprehends; a means no doubt unworthy of the majesty of God, but forced upon us by feebleness of our intellect, which can use only our own circumstances and our own words to convey to others our perceptions and our conclusions. This truth has been enforced already in the first book [1], but is now repeated in order that, in any analogies from human affairs which we adduce, we may not be supposed to think of God as resembling embodied natures, or to compare spiritual Beings with our passible selves, but rather be regarded as advancing the outward appearance of visible things as a clue to the inward meaning of things invisible.

3. For the heretics say that Christ is not from God, that is, that the Son is not born from the Father, and is God not by nature but by appointment; in other words, that He has received an adoption which consists in the giving of a name, being God's Son in the sense in which many are sons of God; again, that Christ's majesty is an evidence of God's widespread bounty, He being God in the sense in which there are gods many; although they admit that in His adoption and naming as God a more liberal affection than in other cases was shewn, His adoption being the first in order of time, and He greater than other adopted sons, and first in rank among the creatures because of the greater splendour which accompanied His creation. Some add, by way of confessing the omnipotence of God, that He was created into God's likeness, and that it was out of nothing that He, like other creatures, was raised up to be the Image of the eternal Creator, bidden at a word to spring from non-existence into being by the power of God, Who can frame out of nothing the likeness of Himself.

4. Moreover, they use their knowledge of the historical fact that bishops of a former time have taught that Father and Son are of one substance, to subvert the truth by the ingenious plea that this is a heretical notion. They say that this term 'of one substance,' in the Greek *homoousion*, is used to mean and express that the Father is the same as the Son; that is, that He extended Himself out of infinity into the Virgin, and took a body from her, and gave to Himself, in the body which He had taken, the name of Son. This is their first lie concerning the *homoousion*. Their next lie is that this word *homoousion* implies that Father and Son participate in something antecedent to Either and distinct from Both, and that a certain imaginary substance, or *ousia*, anterior to all matter whatsoever, has existed heretofore and been divided and wholly distributed between the Two; which proves, they say, that Each of the Two is of a nature pre-existent to Himself, and Each identical in matter with the Other. And so they profess to condemn the confession of the *homoousion* on the ground that that term does not discriminate between Father and Son, and makes the Father subsequent in time to that matter which He has in common with the Son. And they have devised this third

---

objection to the word *homoousion*, that its meaning, as they explain it, is that the Son derives His origin from a partition of the Father's substance, as though one object had been cut in two and He were the severed portion. The meaning of 'one substance,' they say, is that the part cut off from the whole continues to share the nature of that from which it has been severed ; but God, being impassible, cannot be divided, for, if He must submit to be lessened by division, He is subject to change, and will be rendered imperfect if His perfect substance leave Him, to reside in the severed portion.

5. They think also that they have a compendious refutation of Prophets, Evangelists and Apostles alike, in their assertion that the Son was born within time. They pronounce us illogical for saying that the Son has existed from everlasting ; and, since they reject the possibility of His eternity, they are forced to believe that He was born at a point in time. For if He has not always existed, there was a time when He was not ; and if there be a time when He was not, time was anterior to Him. He who has not existed everlastingly began to exist within time, while He Who is free from the limits of time is necessarily eternal. The reason they give for their rejection of the eternity of the Son is that His everlasting existence contradicts the faith in His birth ; as though by confessing that He has existed eternally, we made His birth impossible.

6. What foolish and godless fears ! What impious anxiety on God's behalf ! The meaning which they profess to detect in the word *homoousion*, and in the assertion of the eternity of the Son, is detested, rejected, denounced by the Church. She confesses one God from Whom are all things ; she confesses one Jesus Christ our Lord, through whom are all things ; One from Whom, One through Whom ; One the Source of all, One the Agent through Whom all were created. In the One from Whom are all things she recognises the Majesty which has no beginning, and in the One through Whom are all things she recognises a might coequal with His Source ; for Both are jointly supreme in the work of creation and in rule over created things. In the Spirit she recognises God as Spirit, impassible and indivisible, for she has learnt from the Lord that Spirit has neither flesh nor bones [2] ; a warning to save her from supposing that God, being Spirit, could be burdened with bodily suffering and loss. She recognises one God, unborn from everlasting ; she recognises also one Only-begotten Son of God. She confesses the Father eternal and without beginning ; she confesses also that the Son's beginning is from eternity. Not that He has no beginning, but that He is Son of the Father Who has none ; not that He is self-originated, but that He is from Him Who is unbegotten from everlasting ; born from eternity, receiving, that is, His birth from the eternity of the Father. Thus our faith is free from the guesswork of heretical perversity ; it is expressed in fixed and published terms, though as yet no reasoned defence of our confession has been put forth. Still, lest any suspicion should linger around the sense in which the Fathers have used the word *homoousion* and round our confession of the eternity of the Son, I have set down the proofs whereby we may be assured that the Son abides ever in that substance wherein He was begotten from the Father, and that the birth of His Son has not diminished ought of that Substance wherein the Father was abiding ; that holy men, inspired by the teaching of God, when they said that the Son is *homoousios* with the Father pointed to no such flaws or defects as I have mentioned [3]. My purpose has been to counteract the impression that this *ousia*, this assertion that He is *homoousios* with the Father, is a negation of the nativity of the Only-begotten Son.

7. To assure ourselves of the needfulness of these two phrases, adopted and employed as the best of safeguards against the heretical rabble of that day, I think it best to reply to the obstinate misbelief of our present heretics, and refute their vain and pestilent teaching by the witness of the evangelists and apostles. They flatter themselves that they can furnish a proof for each of their propositions ; they have, in fact, appended to each some passages or other from holy Writ ; passages so grossly misinterpreted as to ensnare none but the illiterate by the semblance of truth with which perverted ingenuity has masked their explanation.

8. For they attempt, by praising the Godhead of the Father only, to deprive the Son of His Divinity, pleading that it is written, *Hear, O Israel, the Lord thy God is One* [4], and that the Lord repeats this in His answer to the doctor of the Law who asked Him what was the greatest commandment in the Law ;— *Hear, O Israel, the Lord thy God is One* [5]. Again, they say that Paul proclaims, *For there is One God, and One Mediator between God and men* [6]. And furthermore, they insist that God alone is wise, in order to leave no wisdom for the Son, relying upon the words of the

---

2 St. Luke xxiv. 39.

3 In § 4.   4 Deut. vi. 4.   5 St. Mark xii. 29.
                 6 1 Tim. ii. 5.

Apostle, *Now to Him that is able to stablish you according to my gospel and the preaching of Jesus Christ, according to the revelation of the mystery which hath been kept in silence through age-long times, but now is manifested through the scriptures of the prophets according to the commandment of the eternal God Who is made known unto all nations unto obedience of faith; to the only wise God, through Jesus Christ, to Whom be glory for ever and ever*[7]. They argue also that He alone is true[8], for Isaiah says, *They shall bless Thee, the true God*[9], and the Lord Himself has borne witness in the Gospel, saying, *And this is life eternal that they should know Thee, the only true God, and Jesus Christ Whom Thou hast sent*[1]. Again they reason that He alone is good, to leave no goodness for the Son, because it has been said through Him, *There is none good save One, even God*[2]; and that He alone has power, because Paul has said, *Which in His own times He shall shew to us, Who is the blessed and only Potentate, the King of kings and Lord of lords*[3]. And further, they profess themselves certain that in the Father there is no change nor turning, because He has said through the prophet, *I am the Lord your God, and I am not changed*[4], and the apostle James, *With Whom there is no change*[5]; certain also that He is the righteous Judge, for it is written, *God is the righteous Judge, strong and patient*[6]; that He cares for all, because the Lord has said, speaking of the birds, *And your heavenly Father feedeth them*[7], and, *Are not two sparrows sold for a farthing? And not one of them falleth upon the ground without the will of your Father; but the very hairs of your head are numbered*[8]. They say that the Father has prescience of all things, as the blessed Susanna says, *O eternal God, that knowest secrets, and knowest all things before they be*[9]; that He is incomprehensible, as it is written, *The heaven is My throne, and the earth is the footstool of My feet. What house will ye build Me, or what is the place of My rest? For these things hath My hand made, and all these things are mine*[1]; that He contains all things, as Paul bears witness, *For in Him we live and move and have our being*[2], and the Psalmist, *Whither shall I go from Thy Spirit, and whither shall I fly from Thy face? If I climb up into heaven, Thou art there; if I go down to hell, Thou art present. If I take my wings before the light and dwell in the uttermost parts of the sea, even thither Thy hand*

shall lead me and Thy right hand shall hold me*[3]; that He is without body, for it is written, *For God is Spirit, and they that worship Him must worship in spirit and in truth*[4]; that He is immortal and invisible, as Paul says, *Who only hath immortality, and dwelleth in light unapproachable, whom no man hath seen nor can see*[5], and the Evangelist, *No one hath seen God at any time, except the Only-begotten Son, which is in the bosom of the Father*[6]; that He alone abides eternally unborn, for it is written, *I Am That I Am*, and *Thus shalt thou say to the children of Israel, I Am hath sent me unto you*[7], and through Jeremiah, *O Lord, Who art Lord*[8].

9. Who can fail to observe that these statements are full of fraud and fallacy? Cleverly as issues have been confused and texts combined, malice and folly is the character indelibly imprinted upon this laborious effort of cunning and clumsiness. For instance, among their points of faith they have included this, that they confess the Father only to be unborn; as though any one on our side could suppose that He, Who begat Him through Whom are all things, derived His being from any external source. The very fact that He bears the name of *Father* reveals Him as the cause of His Son's existence. That name of *Father* gives no hint that He who bears it is Himself descended from another, while it tells us plainly from Whom it is that the Son is begotten. Let us therefore leave to the Father His own special and incommunicable property, confessing that in Him reside the eternal powers of an omnipotence without beginning. None, I am sure, can doubt that the reason why, in their confession of God the Father, certain attributes are dwelt upon as peculiarly and inalienably His own, is that He may be left in isolated possession of them. For when they say that He alone is true, alone is righteous, alone is wise, alone is invisible, alone is good, alone is mighty, alone is immortal, they are raising up this word *alone* as a barrier to cut off the Son from His share in these attributes. He Who is alone, they say, has no partner in His properties. But if we suppose that these attributes reside in the Father only, and not in the Son also, then we must believe that God the Son has neither truth nor wisdom; that He is a bodily being compact of visible and material elements, ill-disposed and feeble and void of immortality; for we exclude Him from all these attributes of which we make the Father the solitary Possessor.

7 Rom. xvi. 25—27.
8 Omitting *solus innascibilis et,* which are out of place here.
9 Is. lxv. 16.   1 St. John xvii. 3.   2 St. Mark x. 18.
3 1 Tim. vi. 15.   4 Mal. iii. 6.   5 i. 17.
6 Ps. vii. 12.   7 St. Matt. vi. 26.   8 Ib. x. 29, 30.
9 Susanna (Daniel xiii.) 42.   1 Isai. lxvi. 1, 2.
2 Acts xvii. 28.

3 Ps. cxxxix. 6—9 (cxxxviii. 7—10).   4 St. John iv. 24.
5 1 Tim. vi. 16.   6 St. John i. 18.   7 Exod. iii. 14.
8 i. 6 (LXX).

10. We, however, who propose to discourse of that most perfect majesty and fullest Divinity which appertains to the Only-begotten Son of God, have no fear lest our readers should imagine that amplitude of phrase in speaking of the Son is a detraction from the glory of God the Father, as though every praise assigned to the Son had first been withdrawn from Him. For, on the contrary, the majesty of the Son is glory to the Father; the Source must be glorious from which He Who is worthy of such glory comes. The Son has nothing but by virtue of His birth; the Father shares all veneration received by that birthright. Thus the suggestion that we diminish the Father's honour is put to silence, for all the glory which, as we shall teach, is inherent in the Son will be reflected back, to the increased glory of Him who has begotten a Son so great.

11. Now that we have exposed their plan of belittling the Son under cover of magnifying the Father, the next step is to listen to the exact terms in which they express their own belief concerning the Son. For, since we have to answer in succession each of their allegations and to display on the evidence of Holy Scripture the impiety of their doctrines, we must append, to what they say of the Father, the decisions which they have put on record concerning the Son, that by a comparison of their confession of the Father with their confession of the Son we may follow a uniform order in our solution of the questions as they arise. They state as their verdict that the Son is not derived from any pre-existent matter, for through Him all things were created, nor yet begotten from God, for nothing can be withdrawn from God; but that He was made out of what was non-existent, that is, that He is a perfect creature of God, though different from His other creatures. They argue that He is a creature, because it is written, *The Lord hath created Me for a beginning of His ways* [9]; that He is the perfect handiwork of God, though different from His other works, they prove, as to the first point, by what Paul writes to the Hebrews, *Being made so much better than the angels, as He possesseth a more excellent name than they* [1], and again, *Wherefore, holy brethren, partakers of the heavenly calling, consider the Apostle and High Priest of our confession, Jesus Christ, who is faithful to Him that made Him* [2]. For their depreciation of the might and majesty and Godhead of the Son they rely chiefly on His own words, *The Father is greater than I* [3]. But they admit that He is not one of the common herd of creatures on the evidence of *All*

things were made through Him [4]. And so they sum up the whole of their blasphemous teaching in these words which follow :—

12. "We confess One God, alone unmade, alone eternal, alone unoriginate, alone true, alone possessing immortality, alone good, alone mighty, Creator, Ordainer and Disposer of all things, unchangeable and unalterable, righteous and good, of the Law and the Prophets and the New Testament. We believe that this God gave birth to the Only-begotten Son before all worlds, through Whom He made the world and all things; that He gave birth to Him not in semblance, but in truth, following His own Will, so that He is unchangeable and unalterable, God's perfect creature but not as one of His other creatures, His handiwork, but not as His other works; not, as Valentinus maintained, that the Son is a development of the Father; nor, as Manichæus has declared of the Son, a consubstantial part of the Father; nor, as Sabellius, who makes two out of one, Son and Father at once; nor, as Hieracas, a light from a light, or a lamp with two flames; nor as if He was previously in being and afterwards born or created afresh to be a Son, a notion often condemned by thyself, blessed Pope [5], publicly in the Church and in the assembly of the brethren. But, as we have affirmed, we believe that He was created by the will of God before times and worlds, and has His life and existence from the Father, Who gave Him to share His own glorious perfections. For, when the Father gave to Him the inheritance of all things, He did not thereby deprive Himself of attributes which are His without origination, He being the source of all things.

13. "So there are three Persons, Father, Son, and Holy Ghost. God, for His part, is the cause of all things, utterly unoriginate and separate from all; while the Son, put forth by the Father outside time, and created and established before the worlds, did not exist before He was born, but, being born outside time before the worlds, came into being as the Only Son of the Only Father. For He is neither eternal, nor co-eternal, nor co-uncreate with the Father, nor has He an existence collateral with the Father, as some say, who [6] postulate two unborn principles. But God is before all things, as being indivisible and the beginning of all. Wherefore He is before the Son also, as indeed we have learnt from thee in thy public preaching. Inasmuch then as He hath His being from God, and His glorious perfections, and His life,

---

9 Prov. viii. 22.   1 Heb. i. 4.   2 Ib. iii. 1.   4 St. John . 3.   5 Of Alexandria.
            3 St. John xiv. 28.   6 Omitting *aut aliqui.*

and is entrusted with all things, for this reason God is His source, and hath rule over Him, as being His God, since He is before Him. As to such phrases as *from Him*, and *from the womb*, and *I went out from the Father and am come*, if they be understood to denote that the Father extends a part and, as it were, a development of that one substance, then the Father will be of a compound nature and divisible and changeable and corporeal, according to them; and thus, as far as their words go, the incorporeal God will be subjected to the properties of matter[7]."

14. Such is their error, such their pestilent teaching; to support it they borrow the words of Scripture, perverting its meaning and using the ignorance of men as their opportunity of gaining credence for their lies. Yet it is certainly by these same words of God that we must come to understand the things of God. For human feebleness cannot by any strength of its own attain to the knowledge of heavenly things; the faculties which deal with bodily matters can form no notion of the unseen world. Neither our created bodily substance, nor the reason given by God for the purposes of ordinary life, is capable of ascertaining and pronouncing upon the nature and work of God. Our wits cannot rise to the level of heavenly knowledge, our powers of perception lack the strength to apprehend that limitless might. We must believe God's word concerning Himself, and humbly accept such insight as He vouchsafes to give. We must make our choice between rejecting His witness, as the heathen do, or else believing in Him as He is, and this in the only possible way, by thinking of Him in the aspect in which He presents Himself to us. Therefore let private judgment cease; let human reason refrain from passing barriers divinely set. In this spirit we eschew all blasphemous and reckless assertion concerning God, and cleave to the very letter of revelation. Each point in our enquiry shall be considered in the light of His instruction, Who is our theme; there shall be no stringing together of isolated phrases whose context is suppressed, to trick and misinform the unpractised listener. The meaning of words shall be ascertained by considering the circumstances under which they were spoken; words must be explained by circumstances, not circumstances forced into conformity with words. We, at any rate, will treat our subject completely; we will state both the circumstances under which words were spoken, and the true purport of the words. Each point shall be considered in orderly sequence.

15. Their starting-point is this; We confess, they say, One only God, because Moses says, *Hear, O Israel, the Lord thy God is One*[8]. But is this a truth which any one has ever dared to doubt? Or was any believer ever known to confess otherwise than that there is One God from Whom are all things, One Majesty which has no birth, and that He is that unoriginated Power? Yet this fact of the Unity of God offers no chance for denying the Divinity of His Son. For Moses, or rather God through Moses, laid it down as His first commandment to that people, devoted both in Egypt and in the Desert to idols and the worship of imaginary gods, that they must believe in One God. There was truth and reason in the commandment, for God, from Whom are all things, is One. But let us see whether this Moses have not confessed that He, through Whom are all things, is also God. God is not robbed, He is still God, if His Son share the Godhead. For the case is that of God from God, of One from One, of God Who is One because God is from Him. And conversely the Son is not less God because God the Father is One, for He is the Only-begotten Son of God; not eternally unborn, so as to deprive the Father of His Oneness, nor yet different from God, for He is born from Him. We must not doubt that He is God by virtue of that birth from God which proves to us who believe that God is One; yet let us see whether Moses, who announced to Israel, *The Lord thy God is One*, has also proclaimed the Godhead of the Son. To make good our confession of the Divinity of our Lord Jesus Christ we must employ the evidence of that same witness on whom the heretics rely for the confession of One Only God, which they imagine to involve the denial of the Godhead of the Son.

16. Since, therefore, the words of the Apostle, *One God the Father, from Whom are all things, and one Jesus Christ, our Lord, through Whom are all things*[9], form an accurate and complete confession concerning God, let us see what Moses has to say of the beginning of the world. His words are, *And God said, Let there be a firmament in the midst of the water, and let it divide the water from the water. And it was so, and God made the firmament, and God divided the water through the midst*[1]. Here, then, you have the God from Whom, and the God through Whom. If you deny it, you must tell us through whom it was that God's work in creation was done, or else

7 This Epistle of Arius to Alexander is translated substantially as in Newman's *Arians of the Fourth Century*, ch. II., § 5, though there are differences of some importance between Hilary's Latin version and the Greek in Athanasius *de Synodis*, § 16, from which Newman's version is made.

8 Deut. vi. 4.   9 1 Cor. viii. 6.   1 Gen. i. 6, 7.

point for your explanation to an obedience in things yet uncreated, which, when God said *Let there be a firmament*, impelled the firmament to establish itself. Such suggestions are inconsistent with the clear sense of Scripture. For all things, as the Prophet says[2], were made out of nothing; it was no transformation of existing things, but the creation into a perfect form of the non-existent. Through whom? Hear the Evangelist: *All things were made through Him.* If you ask Who this is, the same Evangelist will tell you : *In the beginning was the Word, and the Word was with God, and the Word was God. He was in the beginning with God. All things were made through Him*[3]. If you are minded to combat the view that it was the Father Who said, *Let there be a firmament*, the prophet will answer you : *He spake, and they were made ; He commanded, and they were created*[4]. The recorded words, *Let there be a firmament*, reveal to us that the Father spoke. But in the words which follow, *And it was so,* in the statement that God did this thing, we must recognise the Person of the Agent. *He spake, and they were made ;* the Scripture does not say that He willed it, and did it. *He commanded, and they were created ;* you observe that it does not say they came into existence, because it was His pleasure. In that case there would be no office for a Mediator between God and the world which was awaiting its creation. God, from Whom are all things, gives the order for creation which God, through Whom are all things, executes. Under one and the same Name we confess Him Who gave and Him Who fulfilled the command. If you dare to deny that *God made* is spoken of the Son, how do you explain *All things were made through Him?* Or the Apostle's words, *One Jesus Christ, our Lord, through Whom are all things?* Or, *He spake, and they were made?* If these inspired words succeed in convincing your stubborn mind, you will cease to regard that text, *Hear, O Israel, the Lord thy God is One,* as a refusal of Divinity to the Son of God, since at the very foundation of the world He Who spoke it proclaimed that His Son also is God. But let us see what increase of profit we may draw from this distinction of God Who commands and God Who executes. For though it is repugnant even to our natural reason to suppose that in the words, *He commanded, and they were made,* one single and isolated Person is intended, yet, for the avoidance of all doubts, we must expound the events which followed upon the creation of the world.

17. When the world was complete and its inhabitant was to be created, the words spoken concerning him were, *Let Us make man after Our image and likeness*[5]. I ask you, Do you suppose that God spoke those words to Himself? Is it not obvious that He was addressing not Himself, but Another? If you reply that He was alone, then out of His own mouth He confutes you, for He says, *Let Us make man after Our image and likeness.* God has spoken to us through the Lawgiver in the way which is intelligible to us ; that is, He makes us acquainted with His action by means of language, the faculty with which He has been pleased to endow us. There is, indeed, an indication of the Son of God[6], through Whom all things were made, in the words, *And God said, Let there be a firmament,* and in, *And God made the firmament,* which follows : but lest we should think these words of God were wasted and meaningless, supposing that He issued to Himself the command of creation, and Himself obeyed it,— for what notion could be further from the thought of a solitary God than that of giving a verbal order to Himself, when nothing was necessary except an exertion of His will?— He determined to give us a more perfect assurance that these words refer to Another beside Himself. When He said, *Let Us make man after Our image and likeness,* His indication of a Partner demolishes the theory of His isolation. For an isolated being cannot be partner to himself; and again, the words, *Let Us make,* are inconsistent with solitude, while *Our* cannot be used except to a companion. Both words, *Us* and *Our,* are inconsistent with the notion of a solitary God speaking to Himself, and equally inconsistent with that of the address being made to a stranger who has nothing in common with the Speaker. If you interpret the passage to mean that He is isolated, I ask you whether you suppose that He was speaking with Himself? If you do not understand that He was speaking with Himself, how can you assume that He was isolated? If He were isolated, we should find Him described as isolated ; if He had a companion, then as not isolated. *I* and *Mine* would describe the former state ; the latter is indicated by *Us* and *Our.*

18. Thus, when we read, *Let Us make man after Our image and likeness,* these two words *Us* and *Our* reveal that there is neither one isolated God, nor yet one God in two dissimilar Persons ; and our confession must be framed in harmony with the second as well as with the first truth. For the words *our image*—not *our images*—prove that there is

---

2 2 Macc. vii. 28.   3 St. John i. 1—3.
4 Ps clxviii. 5.   5 Gen. i. 26.   6 Reading *Filii.*

one nature possessed by Both But an argument from words is an insufficient proof, unless its result be confirmed by the evidence of facts ; and accordingly it is written, *And God made man ; after the image of God made He him* [7]. If the words He spoke, I ask, were the soliloquy of an isolated God, what meaning shall we assign to this last statement? For in it I see a triple allusion, to the Maker, to the being made, and to the image. The being made is man ; God made him, and made him in the image of God. If Genesis were speaking of an isolated God, it would certainly have been *And made him after His own image*. But since the book was foreshowing the Mystery of the Gospel, it spoke not of two Gods, but of God and God, for it speaks of man made through God in the image of God. Thus we find that God wrought man after an image and likeness common to Himself and to God , that the mention of an Agent forbids us to assume that He was isolated ; and that the work, done after an image and likeness which was that of Both, proves that there is no difference in kind between the Godhead of the One and of the Other.

19. It may seem waste of time to bring forward further arguments, for truths concerning God gain no strength by repetition ; a single statement suffices to establish them. Yet it is well for us to know all that has been revealed upon the subject, for though we are not responsible for the words of Scripture, yet we shall have to render an account for the sense we have assigned to them. One of the many commandments which God gave to Noah is, *Whoso sheddeth man's blood, for his blood shall his life be shed, for after the image of God made I man* [8]. Here again is the distinction between likeness, creature, and Creator. God bears witness that He made man after the image of God. When He was about to make man, because He was speaking of Himself, yet not to Himself, God said, *After our image;* and again, after man was made, *God made man after the image of God*. It would have been no inaccuracy of language, had He said, addressing Himself, *I have made man after My image*, for He had shewn that the Persons are one in nature by, *Let us make man after Our image* [9]. But for the more perfect removal of all doubt as to whether God be, or be not, a solitary Being, when He made man He made him, we are told, *After the image of God*.

20. If you still wish to assert that God the Father in solitude said these words to Himself, I can go with you as far as to admit the possibility that He might in solitude have spoken to Himself as if He were conversing with a companion, and that it is credible that He wished the words *I have made man after the image of God* to be equivalent to *I have made man after My own image*. But your own confession of faith will refute you. For you have confessed that all things are from the Father, but all through the Son ; and the words, *Let Us make man*, shew that the Source from Whom are all things is He Who spoke thus, while *God made him after the image of God* clearly points to Him through Whom the work was done.

21. And furthermore, to make all self-deception unlawful, that Wisdom, which you have yourself confessed to be Christ, shall confront you with the words, *When He was establishing the fountains under the heaven, when He was making strong the foundations of the earth. I was with Him, setting them in order. It was I, over Whom He rejoiced. Moreover, I was daily rejoicing in His sight, all the while that He was rejoicing in the world that He had made, and in the sons of men* [1]. Every difficulty is removed ; error itself must recognise the truth. There is with God Wisdom, begotten before the worlds ; and not only present with Him, but setting in order, for She was *with Him, setting them in order*. Mark this work of setting in order, or arranging. The Father, by His commands, is the Cause ; the Son, by His execution of the things commanded, sets in order. The distinction between the Persons is marked by the work assigned to Each. When it says *Let us make*, creation is identified with the word of command ; but when it is written, *I was with Him, setting them in order*, God reveals that He did not do the work in isolation. For He was rejoicing before Him, Who, He tells us, rejoiced in return ; *Moreover, I was daily rejoicing in His sight, all the while that He was rejoicing in the world that He had made, and in the sons of men*. Wisdom has taught us the reason of Her joy. She rejoiced because of the joy of the Father, Who rejoices over the completion of the world and over the sons of men. For it is written, *And God saw that they were good*. She rejoices that God is well pleased with His work, which has been made through Her, at His command. She avows that Her joy results from the Father's gladness over the finished world and over the sons of men ; over the sons of men, because in the one man Adam the whole human race had begun its course. Thus in the creation of the world there is no mere soliloquy of an isolated Father ; His Wisdom is His partner

7 Gen. i. 27.   8 Ib. ix. 6.   9 i.e. by the word *Our*.   1 Prov. viii. 28—31.

in the work, and rejoices with Him when their conjoint labour ends.

22. I am aware that the full explanation of these words involves the discussion of many and weighty problems. I do not shirk them, but postpone them for the present, reserving their consideration for later stages of the enquiry. For the present I devote myself to that article of the blasphemers' faith, or rather faithlessness, which asserts that Moses proclaims the solitude of God. We do not forget that the assertion is true in the sense that there is One God, from Whom are all things; but neither do we forget that this truth is no excuse for denying the Godhead of the Son, since Moses throughout the course of his writings clearly indicates the existence of God and God. We must examine how the history of God's choice, and of the giving of the Law, proclaims God co-ordinate with God.

23. After God had often spoken with Abraham, Sarah was moved to wrath against Hagar, being jealous that she, the mistress, was barren, while her handmaid had conceived a son. Then, when Hagar had departed from her sight, the Spirit speaks thus concerning her, *And the angel of the Lord said unto Hagar, Return to thy mistress, and submit thyself under her hands. And the angel of the Lord said unto her, I will multiply thy seed exceedingly, and it shall not be numbered for multitude*, and again, *And she called the Name of the Lord that spake with her, Thou art God, Who hast seen me* [2]. It is the Angel of God Who speaks [3], and speaks of things far beyond the powers which a messenger, for that is the meaning of the word, could have. He says, *I will multiply thy seed exceedingly, and it shall not be numbered for multitude*. The power of multiplying nations lies outside the ministry of an angel. Yet what says the Scripture of Him Who is called the Angel of God, yet speaks words which belong to God alone? *And she called the Name of the Lord that spake with her, Thou art God, Who hast seen me.* First He is the Angel of God; then He is the Lord, for *She called the Name of the Lord;* then, thirdly, He is God, for *Thou art God, Who hast seen me.* He Who is called the Angel of God is also Lord and God. The Son of God is also, according to the prophet, the *Angel of great counsel* [4]. To discriminate clearly between the Persons, He is called the Angel of God; He Who is God from God is also the Angel of

God, but, that He may have the honour which is His due, He is entitled also Lord and God.

24. In this passage the one Deity is first the Angel of God, and then, successively, Lord and God. But to Abraham He is God only. For when the distinction of Persons had first been made, as a safeguard against the delusion that God is a solitary Being, then His true and unqualified name could safely be uttered. And so it is written, *And God said to Abraham, Behold Sarah thy wife shall bear thee a son, and thou shalt call his name Isaac; and I will establish My covenant with him for an everlasting covenant, and with his seed after him. And as for Ishmael, behold, I have heard thee and have blessed him, and will multiply him exceedingly; twelve nations shall he beget, and I will make him a great nation* [5]. Is it possible to doubt that He Who was previously called the Angel of God is here, in the sequel, spoken of as God? In both instances He is speaking of Ishmael; in both it is the same Person Who shall multiply him. To save us from supposing that this was a different Speaker from Him who had addressed Hagar, the Divine words expressly attest the identity, saying, *And I have blessed him, and will multiply him.* The blessing is repeated from a former occasion, for Hagar had already been addressed; the multiplication is promised for a future day, for this is God's first word to Abraham concerning Ishmael. Now it is God Who speaks to Abraham; to Hagar the Angel of God had spoken. Thus God and the Angel of God are One; He Who is the Angel of God is also God the Son of God. He is called the Angel because He is the *Angel of great counsel;* but afterwards He is spoken of as God, lest we should suppose that He Who is God is only an angel. Let us now repeat the facts in order. The Angel of the Lord spoke to Hagar; He spoke also to Abraham as God. One Speaker addressed both. The blessing was given to Ishmael, and the promise that he should grow into a great people.

25. In another instance the Scripture reveals through Abraham that it was God Who spoke. He receives the further promise of a son, Isaac. Afterwards there appear to him three men. Abraham, though he sees three, worships One, and acknowledges Him as Lord. Three were standing before him, Scripture says, but he knew well Which it was that he must worship and confess. There was nothing in outward appearance to distinguish them, but by the eye of faith, the vision of the soul, he knew his Lord. Then the Scripture goes on, *And He said unto him, I will*

---

[2] Gen. xvi. 9, 10, 13.
[3] The parenthesis which follows: 'Now *angel of God* has two senses, that of Him Who is, and that of Him Whose He is,' interrupts the sense and seems quite out of place. The same distinction in the case of the word Spirit, in Book II. § 32 may be compared.
[4] Isaiah ix. 6 (LXX).

[5] Gen. xvii. 19, 20.

certainly return unto thee at this time hereafter, and Sarah thy wife shall have a son[5]; and afterwards the Lord said to Him, *I will not conceal from Abraham My servant the things that I will do*[7]; and again, *Moreover the Lord said, The cry of Sodom and Gomorrah is filled up, and their sins are exceeding great*[8]. Then after long discourse, which for the sake of brevity shall be omitted, Abraham, distressed at the destruction which awaited the innocent as well as the guilty, said, *In no wise wilt Thou, Who judgest the earth, execute this judgment. And the Lord said, If I find in Sodom fifty righteous within the city, then I will spare all the place for their sakes*[9]. Afterwards, when the warning to Lot, Abraham's brother, was ended, the Scripture says, *And the Lord rained upon Sodom and upon Gomorrah brimstone and fire from the Lord out of heaven*[1]; and, after a while, *And the Lord visited Sarah as He had said, and did unto Sarah as He had spoken, and Sarah conceived and bare Abraham a son in his old age, at the set time of which God had spoken to him*[2]. And afterwards, when the handmaid with her son had been driven from Abraham's house, and was dreading lest her child should die in the wilderness for want of water, the same Scripture says, *And the Lord God heard the voice of the lad, where he was, and the Angel of God called to Hagar out of heaven, and said unto her, What is it, Hagar? Fear not, for God hath heard the voice of the lad from the place where he is. Arise, and take the lad, and hold his hand, for I will make him a great nation*[3].

26. What blind faithlessness it is, what dulness of an unbelieving heart, what headstrong impiety, to abide in ignorance of all this, or else to know and yet neglect it! Assuredly it is written for the very purpose that error or oblivion may not hinder the recognition of the truth. If, as we shall prove, it is impossible to escape knowledge of the facts, then it must be nothing less than blasphemy to deny them. This record begins with the speech of the Angel to Hagar, His promise to multiply Ishmael into a great nation and to give him a countless offspring. She listens, and by her confession reveals that He is Lord and God. The story begins with His appearance as the Angel of God; at its termination He stands confessed as God Himself. Thus He Who, while He executes the ministry of declaring the *great counsel* is God's Angel, is Himself in name and nature God. The name corresponds to the nature; the nature is not falsified to make it conform to the name.

Again, God speaks to Abraham of this same matter; he is told that Ishmael has already received a blessing, and shall be increased into a nation; *I have blessed him*, God says. This is no change from the Person indicated before; He shews that it was He Who had already given the blessing. The Scripture has obviously been consistent throughout in its progress from mystery to clear revelation; it began with the Angel of God, and proceeds to reveal that it was God Himself Who had spoken in this same matter.

27. The course of the Divine narrative is accompanied by a progressive development of doctrine. In the passage which we have discussed God speaks to Abraham, and promises that Sarah shall bear a son. Afterwards three men stand by him; he worships One and acknowledges Him as Lord. After this worship and acknowledgment by Abraham, the One promises that He will return hereafter at the same season, and that then Sarah shall have her son. This One again is seen by Abraham in the guise of a man, and salutes him with the same promise. The change is one of name only; Abraham's acknowledgment in each case is the same. It was a Man whom he saw, yet Abraham worshipped Him as Lord; he beheld, no doubt, in a mystery the coming Incarnation. Faith so strong has not missed its recognition; the Lord says in the Gospel, *Your father Abraham rejoiced to see My day; and he saw it, and was glad*[4]. To continue the history; the Man Whom he saw promised that He would return at the same season. Mark the fulfilment of the promise, remembering meanwhile that it was a Man Who made it. What says the Scripture? *And the Lord visited Sarah.* So this Man is the Lord, fulfilling His own promise. What follows next? *And God did unto Sarah as He had said.* The narrative calls His words those of a Man, relates that Sarah was visited by the Lord, proclaims that the result was the work of God. You are sure that it was a Man who spoke, for Abraham not only heard, but saw Him. Can you be less certain that He was God, when the same Scripture, which had called Him Man, confesses Him God? For its words are, *And Sarah conceived, and bare Abraham a son in his old age, and at the set time of which God had spoken to him.* But it was the Man who had promised that He would come. Believe that He was nothing more than man; unless, in fact, He Who came was God and Lord. Connect the incidents. It was, confessedly, the Man who promised that He would come that Sarah might con-

6 Gen. xviii. 10.   7 Ib. 17.   8 Ib. 20.   9 Ib. 25, 26.
1 Ib. xix. 24.   2 Ib. xxi. 1, 2.   3 Ib. 17, 18.

4 St. John viii. 56.

ceive and bear a son. And now accept instruction, and confess the faith; it was the Lord God Who came that she might conceive and bear. The Man made the promise in the power of God; by the same power God fulfilled the promise. Thus God reveals Himself both in word and deed. Next, two of the three men whom Abraham saw depart; He Who remains behind is Lord and God. And not only Lord and God, but also Judge, for Abraham stood before the Lord and said, *In no wise shalt Thou do this thing, to slay the righteous with the wicked, for then the righteous shall be as the wicked. In no wise wilt Thou, Who judgest the whole earth, execute this judgment*[5]. Thus by all his words Abraham instructs us in that faith, for which he was justified; he recognises the Lord from among the three, he worships Him only, and confesses that He is Lord and Judge.

28. Lest you fall into the error of supposing that this acknowledgment of the One was a payment of honour to all the three whom Abraham saw in company, mark the words of Lot when he saw the two who had departed; *And when Lot saw them, he rose up to meet them, and he bowed himself with his face toward the ground; and he said, Behold, my lords, turn in to your servant's house*[6]. Here the plural *lords* shews that this was nothing more than a vision of angels; in the other case the faithful patriarch pays the honour due to One only. Thus the sacred narrative makes it clear that two of the three were mere angels; it had previously proclaimed the One as Lord and God by the words, *And the Lord said unto Abraham, Wherefore did Sarah laugh, saying, Shall I then bear a child? But I am grown old. Is anything from God impossible? At this season I will return to thee hereafter, and Sarah shall have a son*[7]. The Scripture is accurate and consistent; we detect no such confusion as the plural used of the One God and Lord, no Divine honours paid to the two angels. Lot, no doubt, calls them *lords*, while the Scripture calls them angels. The one is human reverence, the other literal truth.

29. And now there falls on Sodom and Gomorrah the vengeance of a righteous judgment. What can we learn from it for the purposes of our enquiry? *The Lord rained brimstone and fire from the Lord.* It is *The Lord from the Lord;* Scripture makes no distinction, by difference of name, between Their natures, but discriminates between Themselves. For we read in the Gospel, *The Father judgeth no man, but hath given all judgment to the*

Son[8]. Thus what the Lord gave, the Lord had received from the Lord.

30. You have now had evidence of God the Judge as Lord and Lord; learn next that there is the same joint ownership of name in the case of God and God. Jacob, when he fled through fear of his brother, saw in his dream a ladder resting upon the earth and reaching to heaven, and the angels of God ascending and descending upon it, and the Lord resting above it, Who gave him all the blessings which He had bestowed upon Abraham and Isaac. At a later time God spoke to him thus: *And God said unto Jacob, Arise, go up to the place Bethel, and dwell there, and make there an altar unto God, that appeared unto thee when thou fleddest from the face of thy brother*[9]. God demands honour for God, and makes it clear that that demand is on behalf of Another than Himself. *He who appeared to thee when thou fleddest* are His words: He guards carefully against any confusion of the Persons. It is God Who speaks, and God of Whom He speaks. Their majesty is asserted by the combination of Both under Their true Name of God, while the words plainly declare Their several existence.

31. Here again there occur to me considerations which must be taken into account in a complete treatment of the subject. But the order of defence must adapt itself to the order of attack, and I reserve these outstanding questions for discussion in the next book. For the present, in regard to God Who demanded honour for God, it will suffice for me to point out that He Who was the Angel of God, when He spoke with Hagar, was God and Lord when He spoke of the same matter with Abraham; that the Man Who spoke with Abraham was also God and Lord, while the two angels, who were seen with the Lord and whom He sent to Lot, are described by the prophet as angels, and nothing more. Nor was it to Abraham only that God appeared in human guise; He appeared as Man to Jacob also. And not only did He appear, but, so we are told, He wrestled; and not only did He wrestle, but He was vanquished by His adversary. Neither the time at my disposal, nor the subject, will allow me to discuss the typical meaning of this wrestling. It was certainly God Who wrestled, for Jacob prevailed against God, and Israel saw God.

32. And now let us enquire whether elsewhere than in the case of Hagar the Angel of God has been discovered to be God Himself. He has been so discovered, and found to be not only God, but the God of Abraham

---

5 Gen. xviii. 25.   6 Ib. xix. 1, 2.   7 Ib. xviii. 13, 14.   8 St. John v. 22.   9 Gen. xxxv. 1.

and of Isaac and of Jacob. For the Angel of the Lord appeared to Moses from the bush; and Whose voice, think you, are we to suppose was heard? The voice of Him Who was seen, or of Another? There is no room for deception; the words of Scripture are clear: *And the Angel of the Lord appeared unto him in a flame of fire from a bush*, and again, *The Lord called unto him from the bush, Moses, Moses, and he answered, What is it? And the Lord said, Draw not nigh hither, put off thy shoes from off thy feet, for the place whereon thou standest is holy ground. And He said unto him, I am the God of Abraham, and the God of Isaac, and the God of Jacob*[1]. He who appeared in the bush speaks from the bush; the place of the vision and of the voice is one; He Who speaks is none other than He Who was seen. He Who is the Angel of God when the eye beholds Him, is the Lord when the ear hears Him, and the Lord Whose voice is heard is recognised as the God of Abraham, and of Isaac, and of Jacob. When He is styled the Angel of God, the fact is revealed that He is no self-contained and solitary Being: for He is the Angel of God. When He is designated Lord and God, He receives the full title which is due to His nature and His name. You have, then, in the Angel Who appeared from the bush, Him Who is Lord and God.

33. Continue your study of the witness borne by Moses; mark how diligently he seizes every opportunity of proclaiming the Lord and God. You take note of the passage, *Hear, O Israel, the Lord thy God is One*[2]. Note also the words of that Divine song of his; *See, See, that I am the Lord, and there is no God beside Me*[3]. While God has been the Speaker throughout the poem, he ends with, *Rejoice, ye heavens, together with Him, and let all the sons of God praise Him. Rejoice, O ye nations, with His people, and let all the Angels of God do Him honour*[4]. God is to be glorified by the Angels of God, and He says, *For I am the Lord, and there is no God beside Me*. For He is God the Only-begotten, and the title 'Only-begotten' excludes all partnership in that character, just as the title 'Unoriginate' denies that there is, in that regard, any who shares the character of the Unoriginate Father. The Son is One from One. There is none unoriginate except God the Unoriginate, and so likewise there is none only-begotten except God the Only-begotten. They stand Each single and alone, being respectively the One Unoriginate and

the One Only-begotten. And so They Two are One God, for between the One, and the One Who is His offspring, there lies no gulf of difference of nature in the eternal Godhead. Therefore He must be worshipped by the sons of God and glorified by the angels of God. Honour and reverence is demanded for God from the sons and from the angels of God. Notice Who it is that shall receive this honour, and by whom it is to be paid. It is God, and they are the sons and angels of God. And lest you should imagine that honour is not demanded for God Who shares our nature[5], but that Moses is thinking here of reverence due to God the Father,—though, indeed, it is in the Son that the Father must be honoured—examine the words of the blessing bestowed by God upon Joseph, at the end of the same book. They are, *And let the things that are well-pleasing to Him that appeared in the bush come upon the head and crown of Joseph*[6]. Thus God is to be worshipped by the sons of God; but God Who is Himself the Son of God. And God is to be reverenced by the angels of God; but God Who is Himself the Angel of God. For God appeared from the bush as the Angel of God, and the prayer for Joseph is that he may receive such blessings as He shall please. He is none the less God because He is the Angel of God; and none the less the Angel of God because He is God. A clear indication is given of the Divine Persons; the line is definitely drawn between the Unbegotten and the Begotten. A revelation of the mysteries of heaven is granted, and we are taught not to dream of God as dwelling in solitude, when angels and sons of God shall worship Him Who is God's Angel and His Son.

34. Let this be taken as our answer from the books of Moses, or rather as the answer of Moses himself. The heretics imagine that they can use his assertion of the Unity of God in disproof of the Divinity of God the Son; a blasphemy in defiance of the clear warning of their own witness, for whenever he confesses that God is One he never fails to teach the Son's Divinity. Our next step must be to adduce the manifold utterance of the prophets concerning the same Son.

35. You know the words, *Hear, O Israel, the Lord thy God is One;* would that you knew them aright! As you interpret them, I seek in vain for their sense. It is said in the Psalms, *God, Thy God, hath anointed Thee*[7]. Impress upon the reader's mind the distinction between

[1] Exod. iii. 2, 4—6.　[2] Deut. vi. 4.　[3] Ib. xxxii. 39.　[4] Ib. 43 (LXX.)　[5] *Dei naturalis*: cf. Book ix. § 39.　[6] Deut xxxiii. 16.　[7] Ps. xlv. 7 (xliv. 8).

VOL. IX.　　G

the Anointer and the Anointed; discriminate between the *Thee* and the *Thy*: make it clear to Whom and of Whom the words are spoken. For this definite confession is the conclusion of the preceding passage, which runs thus; *Thy throne, O God, is for ever and ever; the sceptre of Thy kingdom is a right sceptre. Thou hast loved righteousness and hated iniquity.* And then he continues, *Therefore God, Thy God, hath anointed Thee.* Thus the God of the eternal kingdom, in reward for His love of righteousness and hatred of iniquity, is anointed by His God. Surely some broad difference is drawn, some gap too wide for our mental span, between these names? No; the distinction of Persons is indicated by *Thee* and *Thy*, but nothing suggests a difference of nature. *Thy* points to the Author, *Thee* to Him Who is the Author's offspring. For He is God from God, as these same words of the prophet declare, *God, Thy God, hath anointed Thee.* And His own words bear witness that there is no God anterior to God the Un-originate; *Be ye My witnesses, and I am witness, saith the Lord God, and My Servant Whom I have chosen, that ye may know and believe and understand that I am, and before Me there is no other God, nor shall be after Me*[8]. Thus the majesty of Him that has no beginning is declared, and the glory of Him that is from the Unoriginate is safeguarded; for *God, Thy God, hath anointed Thee.* That word *Thy* declares His birth, yet does not contradict His nature[9]; *Thy God* means that the Son was born from Him to share the Godhead. But the fact that the Father is God is no obstacle to the Son's being God also, for *God, Thy God, hath anointed Thee.* Mention is made both of Father and of Son; the one title of *God* conveys the assurance that in character and majesty They are One.

36. But lest these words, *For I am, and before Me there is no other God, nor shall be after Me*, be made a handle for blasphemous presumption, as proving that the Son is not God, since after the God, Whom no God precedes, there follows no other God, the purpose of the passage must be considered. God is His own best interpreter, but His chosen Servant joins with Him to assure us that there is no God before Him, nor shall be after Him. His own witness concerning Himself is, indeed, sufficient, but He has added the witness of the Servant Whom He has chosen. Thus we have the united testimony of the Two, that there is no God before Him; we accept the truth, because all things

are from Him. We have Their witness also that there shall be no God after Him; but They do not deny that God has been born from Him in the past. Already there was the Servant speaking thus, and bearing witness to the Father; the Servant born in that tribe from which God's elect was to spring. He sets forth also the same truth in the Gospels: *Behold, My Servant Whom I have chosen, My Beloved in Whom My soul is well pleased*[1]. This is the sense, then, in which God says, *There is no other God before Me, nor shall be after Me.* He reveals the infinity of His eternal and unchanging majesty by this as-sertion that there is no God before or after Himself. But He gives His Servant a share both in the bearing of witness and in the possession of the Name of God.

37. The fact is obvious from His own words. For He says to Hosea the prophet, *I will no more have mercy upon the house of Israel, but will altogether be their enemy. But I will have mercy upon the children of Judah, and will save them in the Lord their God*[2]. Here God the Father gives the name of God, without any ambiguity, to the Son, in Whom also He chose us before countless ages. *Their God,* He says, for while the Father, being Unori-ginate, is independent of all, He has given us for an inheritance to His Son. In like manner we read, *Ask of Me, and I will give Thee the Gentiles for Thine inheritance*[3]. None can be God to Him from Whom are all things[4], for He is eternal and has no beginning; but the Son has God, from Whom He was born, for His Father. Yet to us the Father is God and the Son is God; the Father reveals to us that the Son is our God, and the Son teaches that the Father is God over us. The point for us to remember is that in this passage the Father gives to the Son the name of God, the title of His own unoriginate majesty. But I have commented sufficiently on these words of Hosea.

38. Again, how clear is the declaration made by God the Father through Isaiah concerning our Lord! He says, *For thus saith the Lord, the holy God of Israel, Who made the things to come, Ask me concerning your sons and your daughters, and concerning the works of My hands command ye Me. I have made the earth and man upon it, I have commanded all the stars, I have raised up a King with righteous-ness, and all His ways are straight. He shall build My city, and shall turn back the captivity of My people, not for price nor reward, saith the Lord of Sabaoth. Egypt shall labour*

---

8 Is. xliii. 10.
9 His human nature also; cf. next §, and Book xi. § 18.

1 St. Matt. xii. 18.   2 Hos. i. 6, 7.   3 Ps. ii. 8.
4 i.e. We cannot say *Thy God* of the Father.

and the merchandise of the Ethiopians and Sabeans. Men of stature shall come over unto Thee and shall be Thy servants, and shall follow after Thee, bound in chains, and shall worship Thee and make supplication unto Thee, for God is in Thee and there is no God beside Thee. For Thou art God, and we knew it not, O God of Israel, the Saviour. All that resist Him shall be ashamed and confounded, and shall walk in confusion[5]. Is any opening left for gainsaying, or excuse for ignorance? If blasphemy continue, is it not in brazen defiance that it survives? God from Whom are all things, Who made all by His command, asserts that He is the Author of the universe, for, unless He had spoken, nothing had been created. He asserts that He has raised up a righteous King, who builds for Himself, that is, for God, a city, and turns back the captivity of His people, for no gift nor reward, for freely are we all saved. Next, He tells how after the labours of Egypt, and after the traffic of Ethiopians and Sabeans, men of stature shall come over to Him. How shall we understand these labours in Egypt, this traffic of Ethiopians and Sabeans? Let us call to mind how the Magi of the East worshipped and paid tribute to the Lord; let us estimate the weariness of that long pilgrimage to Bethlehem of Judah. In the toilsome journey of the Magian princes we see the labours of Egypt to which the prophet alludes. For when the Magi executed, in their spurious, material way, the duty ordained for them by the power of God, the whole heathen world was offering in their person the deepest reverence of which its worship was capable. And these same Magi presented gifts of gold and frankincense and myrrh from [6] the merchandise of the Ethiopians and Sabeans; a thing foretold by another prophet, who has said, *The Ethiopians shall fall down before His face, and His enemies shall lick the dust. The Kings of Tharsis shall offer presents, the Kings of the Arabians and Sabeans shall bring gifts, and there shall be given to Him of the gold of Arabia*[7]. The Magi and their offerings stand for the labour of Egypt and for the merchandise of Ethiopians and Sabeans; the adoring Magi represent the heathen world, and offer the choicest gifts of the Gentiles to the Lord Whom they adore.

39. As for the men of stature who shall come over to Him and follow Him in chains, there is no doubt who they are. Turn to the Gospels; Peter, when he is to follow his Lord, is girded up. Read the Apostles:

Paul, the servant of Christ, boasts of his bonds. Let us see whether this 'prisoner of Jesus Christ' conforms in his teaching to the prophecies uttered by God concerning God His Son. God had said, *They shall make supplication, for God is in Thee*. Now mark and digest these words of the Apostle:—*God was in Christ, reconciling the world to Himself*[8]. And then the prophecy continues, *And there is no God beside Thee*. The Apostle promptly matches this with *For there is one Jesus Christ, our Lord, through Whom are all things*[9]. Obviously there can be none other but He, for He is One. The third prophetic statement is, *Thou art God, and we knew it not*. But Paul, once the persecutor of the Church, says, *Whose are the fathers, from Whom is Christ, Who is God over all*[1]. Such is to be the message of these men in chains; men of stature, indeed, they will be, and shall sit on twelve thrones to judge the tribes of Israel, and shall follow their Lord, witnesses to Him in teaching and in martyrdom.

40. Thus God is in God, and it is God in Whom God dwells. But how is *There is no God beside Thee* true, if God be within Him? Heretic! In support of your confession of a solitary Father you employ the words, *There is no God beside Me;* what sense can you assign to the solemn declaration of God the Father, *There is no God beside Thee*, if your explanation of *There is no God beside Me* be a denial of the Godhead of the Son? To whom, in that case, can God have said, *There is no God beside Thee?* You cannot suggest that this solitary Being said it to Himself. It was to the King Whom He summoned that the Lord said, by the mouth of the men of stature who worshipped and made supplication, *For God is in Thee*. The facts are inconsistent with solitude. *In Thee* implies that there was One present within range, if I may say so, of the Speaker's voice. The complete sentence, *God is in Thee*, reveals not only God present, but also God abiding in Him Who is present. The words distinguish the Indweller from Him in Whom He dwells, but it is a distinction of Person only, not of character. God is in Him, and He, in Whom God is, is God. The residence of God cannot be within a nature strange and alien to His own. He abides in One Who is His own, born from Himself. God is in God, because God is from God. *For Thou art God, and we knew it not, O God of Israel, the Saviour*.

41. My next book is devoted to the refutation of your denial that God is in God; for the

---

[5] Is. xlv. 11—16.   [6] Reading *ex* for *et*.
[7] Ps. lxxi. (lxxii.) 9, 10.

[8] 2 Cor. v. 19.   [9] 1 Cor. viii. 6.   [1] Rom. ix. 5.

prophet continues, *All that resist Him shall be ashamed and confounded and shall walk in confusion.* This is God's sentence, passed upon your unbelief. You set yourself in opposition to Christ, and it is on His account that the Father's voice is raised in solemn reproof; for He, Whose Godhead you deny, is God. And you deny it under cloak of reverence for God, because He says, *There is no other God beside Me.* Submit to shame and confusion; the Unoriginate God has no need of the dignity you offer; He has never asked for this majesty of isolation which you attribute to Him. He repudiates your officious interpretation which would twist His words, *There is no other God beside Me,* into a denial of the Godhead of the Son Whom He begat from Himself. To frustrate your purpose of demolishing the Divinity of the Son by assigning the Godhead in some special sense to Himself, He rounds off the glories of the Only-begotten by the attribution of absolute Divinity:—*And there is no God beside Thee.* Why make distinctions between exact equivalents? Why separate what is perfectly matched? It is the peculiar characteristic of the Son of God that there is no God beside Him; the peculiar characteristic of God the Father that there is no God apart from Him. Use His words concerning Himself; confess Him in His own terms, and entreat Him as King; *For God is in Thee, and there is no God beside Thee. For Thou art God, and we knew it not, O God of Israel, the Saviour.* A confession couched in words so reverent is free from the taint of presumption: its terms can excite no repugnance. Above all, we must remember that to refuse it means shame and ignominy. Brood in thought over these words of God; employ them in your confession of Him, and so escape the threatened shame. For if you deny the Divinity of the Son of God, you will not be augmenting the glory of God by adoring Him in lonely majesty; you will be slighting the Father by refusing to reverence the Son. In faith and veneration confess of the Unoriginate God that there is no God beside Him; claim for God the Only-begotten that apart from Him there is no God.

42. As you have listened already to Moses and Isaiah, so listen now to Jeremiah inculcating the same truth as they:—*This is our God, and there shall be none other likened unto Him, Who hath found out all the way of knowledge, and hath given it unto Jacob His servant and to Israel His beloved. Afterward did He shew Himself upon earth and dwelt among men [2].* For previously he had said, *And He is Man, and Who shall know Him [3]?* Thus you have God seen on earth and dwelling among men. Now I ask you what sense you would assign to *No one hath seen God at any time, save the Only-begotten Son, which is in the bosom of the Father [4],* when Jeremiah proclaims God seen on earth and dwelling among men? The Father confessedly cannot be seen except by the Son; Who then is This who was seen and dwelt among men? He must be our God, for He is God visible in human form, Whom men can handle. And take to heart the prophet's words, *There shall be none other likened to Him.* If you ask how this can be, listen to the remainder of the sentence, lest you be tempted to deny to the Father His share of the confession, *Hear, O Israel, the Lord thy God is One.* The whole passage is, *There shall be none likened unto Him, Who hath found out all the way of knowledge, and hath given it unto Jacob His servant and to Israel His beloved. Afterward did He shew Himself upon earth and dwelt among men.* For there is one Mediator between God and Men, Who is both God and Man; Mediator both in giving of the Law and in taking of our body. Therefore none other can be likened unto Him, for He is One, born from God into God, and He it was through Whom all things were created in heaven and earth, through Whom times and worlds were made. Everything, in fine, that exists owes its existence to His action. He it is that instructs Abraham, that speaks with Moses, that testifies to Israel, that abides in the prophets, that was born through the Virgin from the Holy Ghost, that nails to the cross of His passion the powers that are our foes, that slays death in hell, that strengthens the assurance of our hope by His Resurrection, that destroys the corruption of human flesh by the glory of His Body. Therefore none shall be likened unto Him. For these are the peculiar powers of God the Only-begotten; He alone was born from God, the blissful Possessor of such great prerogatives. No second god can be likened unto Him, for He is God from God, not born from any alien being. There is nothing new or strange or modern created in Him. When Israel hears that its God is one, and that no second god is likened, that men may deem him God, to God Who is God's Son, the revelation means that God the Father and God the Son are One altogether, not by confusion of Person but by unity of substance. For the prophet forbids us, because God the Son is God, to liken Him to some second deity.

BOOK V.

1. OUR reply, in the previous books, to the mad and blasphemous doctrines of the heretics has led us with open eyes into the difficulty that our readers incur an equal danger whether we refute our opponents, or whether we forbear. For while unbelief with boisterous irreverence was thrusting upon us the unity of God, a unity which devout and reasonable faith cannot deny, the scrupulous soul was caught in the dilemma that, whether it asserted or denied the proposition, the danger of blasphemy was equally incurred. To human logic it may seem ridiculous and irrational to say that it can be impious to assert, and impious to deny, the same doctrine, since what it is godly to maintain it must be godless to dispute; if it serve a good purpose to demolish a statement, it may seem folly to dream that good can come from supporting it. But human logic is fallacy in the presence of the counsels of God, and folly when it would cope with the wisdom of heaven; its thoughts are fettered by its limitations, its philosophy confined by the feebleness of natural reason. It must be foolish in its own eyes before it can be wise unto God; that is, it must learn the poverty of its own faculties and seek after Divine wisdom. It must become wise, not by the standard of human philosophy, but of that which mounts to God, before it can enter into His wisdom, and its eyes be opened to the folly of the world. The heretics have ingeniously contrived that this folly, which passes for wisdom, shall be their engine. They employ the confession of One God, for which they appeal to the witness of the Law and the Gospels in the words, *Hear, O Israel, the Lord thy God is One*[1]. They are well aware of the risks involved, whether their assertion be met by contradiction or passed over in silence; and, whichever happens, they see an opening to promote their heresy. If sacred truth, pressed with a blasphemous intent, be met by silence, that silence is construed as consent; as a confession that, because God is One, therefore His Son is not God, and God abides in eternal solitude. If, on the other hand, the heresy involved in their bold argument be met by contradiction, this opposition is branded as a departure from the true Gospel faith, which states in precise terms the unity of God, or else they cast in the opponent's teeth that he has fallen into the contrary heresy, which allows but one Person of Father and of Son[2]. Such is the deadly artifice, wearing the aspect of an attractive innocence, which the world's wisdom, which is folly with God, has forged to beguile us in this first article of their faith, which we can neither confess nor deny without risk of blasphemy. We walk between dangers on either hand; the unity of God may force us into a denial of the Godhead of His Son, or, if we confess that the Father is God and the Son is God, we may be driven into the heresy of interpreting the unity of Father and of Son in the Sabellian sense. Thus their device of insisting upon the *One God* would either shut out the Second Person from the Godhead, or destroy the Unity by admitting Him as a second God, or else make the unity merely nominal. For unity, they would plead, excludes a Second; the existence of a Second is destructive of unity; and Two cannot be One.

2. But we who have attained this wisdom of God, which is folly to the world, and purpose, by means of the sound and saving profession of true faith in the Lord, to unmask the snake-like treachery of their teaching; we have so laid out the plan of our undertaking as to gain a vantage ground for the display of the truth without entangling ourselves in the dangers of heretical assertion. We carefully avoid either extreme; not denying that God is One, yet setting forth distinctly, on the evidence of the Lawgiver who proclaims the unity of God, the truth that there is God and God. We teach that it is by no confusion of the Two that God is One; we do not rend Him in pieces by preaching a plurality of Gods, nor yet do we profess a distinction only in name. But we present Him as God and God, postponing at present for fuller discussion hereafter the question of the Divine unity. For the Gospels tell us that Moses taught the truth when he proclaimed that God is One; and Moses by his proclamation of One God confirms the lesson of the Gospels, which tell of God and God.

---

[1] Deut. vi. 4; St. Mark xii. 29.

[2] Reading *recideretve*.

Thus we do not contradict our authorities, but base our teaching upon them, proving that the revelation to Israel of the unity of God gives no sanction to the refusal of Divinity to the Son of God; since he who is our authority for asserting that there is One God is our authority also for confessing the Godhead of His Son.

3. And so the arrangement of our treatise follows closely the order of the objections raised. Since the next article of their blasphemous and dishonest confession is, *We confess One true God*[3], the whole of this second[4] book is devoted to the question whether the Son of God be true God. For it is clear that the heretics have ingeniously contrived this arrangement of first naming *One God* and then *One true God*, in order to detach the Son from the name and nature of God; since the thought must suggest itself that, truth being inherent in the One God, it must be strictly confined to Him. And therefore, since it is clear beyond a doubt that Moses, when he proclaimed the unity of God, meant therein to assert the Divinity of the Son, let us return to the leading passages in which his teaching is conveyed, and enquire whether or no he wishes us to believe that the Son, Who, as he has taught us, is God, is also true God. It is clear that the truth, or genuineness, of a thing is a question of its nature and its powers. For instance, true wheat is that which grows to a head with the beard bristling round it, which is purged from the chaff and ground to flour, compounded into a loaf and taken for food, and renders the nature and the uses of bread. Thus natural powers are the evidence of truth; and let us see, by this test, whether He, Whom Moses calls God, be true God. We will defer for the present our discourse concerning this One God, Who is also true God, lest, if I fail at once to take up their challenge and uphold the One True God in the two Persons of Father and of Son, eager and anxious souls be oppressed by dangerous doubts.

4. And now, since we accept as common ground the fact that God recognises His Son as God, I ask you: how does the creation of the world disprove our assertion that the Son is true God? There is no doubt that all things are through the Son, for, in the Apostle's words, *All things are through Him, and in Him*[5]. If all things are through Him, and all were made out of nothing, and none otherwise than through Him, in what element of true Godhead is He defective, Who possesses both the nature and the power of God? He had at His disposal the powers of the Divine nature, to bring into being the non-existent and to create at His pleasure. For *God saw that they were good*[6].

5. When the Law says, *And God said, Let there be a firmament*, and then adds, *And God made the firmament*, it introduces no other distinction than that of Person. It indicates no difference of power or nature, and makes no change of name. Under the one title of *God* it reveals, first, the thought of Him Who spoke, and then the action of Him Who created. The language of the narrator says nothing to deprive Him of Divine nature and power; nay rather, how precisely does it inculcate His true Godhead. The power to give effect to the word of creation belongs only to that Nature with Whom to speak is the same as to fulfil. How then is He not true God, Who creates, if He is true God, Who commands? If the word spoken was truly Divine, the deed done was truly Divine also. God spake, and God created; if it was true God Who spake, He Who created was true God also; unless indeed, while the presence of true Godhead was displayed in the speech of the One, its absence was manifested in the action of the Other. Thus in the Son of God we behold the true Divine nature. He is God, He is Creator, He is Son of God, He is omnipotent. It is not merely that He can do whatever He will, for will is always the concomitant of power; but He can do also whatever is commanded Him. Absolute power is this, that its possessor can execute as Agent whatever His words as Speaker can express. When unlimited power of expression is combined with unlimited power of execution, then this creative power, commensurate with the commanding word, possesses the true nature of God. Thus the Son of God is not false God, nor God by adoption, nor God by gift of the name, but true God. Nothing would be gained by the statement of the arguments by which His true Godhead is opposed. His possession of the name and of the nature of God is conclusive proof. He, by Whom all things were made, is God. So much the creation of the world tells me about Him. He is God, equal with God in name; true God, equal with true God in power. The might of God is revealed to us in the creative word; the might of God is manifested also in the creative act. And now again I ask by what authority you deny, in your confession of Father and Son, the true Divine nature of

---

3 From the beginning of the Arian Creed, Book iv. § 12.
4 The first three books are regarded as preliminary. The direct refutation began with Book iv.
5 Col. i. 16.

6 i.e. His freedom of action is proved by His satisfaction with the result.

Him Whose name reveals His power, Whose power proves His right to the Name.

6. My reader must bear in mind that I am silent about the current objections through no forgetfulness, and no distrust of my cause. For that constantly cited text, *The Father is greater than I*, and its cognate passages are perfectly familiar to me, and I have my interpretation of them ready, which makes them witness to the true Divine nature of the Son. But it serves my purpose best to adhere in reply to the order of attack, that our pious effort may follow close upon the progress of their impious scheme, and when we see them diverge into godless heresy we may at once obliterate the track of error. To this end we postpone to the end of our work the testimony of the Evangelists and Apostles, and join battle with the blasphemers for the present on the ground of the Law and the Prophets, silencing their crooked argument, based on misinterpretation and deceit, by the very texts with which they strive to delude us. The sound method of demonstrating a truth is to expose the fallacy of the objections raised against it; and the disgrace of the deceiver is complete if his own lie be converted into an evidence for the truth. And, indeed, the universal experience of mankind has learned that falsehood and truth are incompatible, and cannot be reconciled or made coherent; that by their very nature they are among those opposites which are eternally repugnant, and can never combine or agree.

7. This being the case, I ask how a distinction can be made in the words, *Let Us make man after Our own image and likeness*, between a true God and a false. The words express a meaning, the meaning is the outcome of thought; the thought is set in motion by truth. Let us follow the words back to their meaning, and learn from the meaning the thought, and from the thought attain to the underlying truth. Thy enquiry is, whether He to Whom the words *Let Us make man after Our own image and likeness* were spoken, was not thought of as true by Him Who spoke; for they undoubtedly express the feeling and thought of the Speaker. In saying *Let Us make*, He clearly indicates One in no discord with Himself, no alien or powerless Being, but One endowed with power to do the thing of which He speaks. His own words assure us that this is the sense in which we must understand that they were spoken.

8. To assure us still more fully of the true Godhead manifested in the nature and work of the Son, He, Who expressed His meaning in the words I have cited, shews that His thought was suggested by the true Divinity of Him to Whom He said, *After Our own image and likeness*. How is He falsely called God, to Whom the true God says, *After Our own image and likeness?* *Our* is inconsistent with isolation, and with difference either in purpose or in nature. Man is created, taking the words in their strict sense, in Their common image. Now there can be nothing common to the true and to the false. God, the Speaker, is speaking to God; man is being created in the image of Father and of Son. The Two are One in name and One in nature. It is only one image after which man is made. The time has not yet come for me to discuss this matter; hereafter I will explain what is this image of God the Father and of God the Son into which man was created. For the present we will stick to the question, was, or was not, He true God, to Whom the true God said, *Let Us make man after Our own image and likeness?* Separate, if you can, the true from the false elements in this image common to Both; in your heretical madness divide the indivisible. For They Two are One, of Whose one image and likeness man is the one copy.

9. But now let us continue our reading of this Scripture, to shew how the consistency of truth is unaffected by these dishonest objections. The next words are, *And God made man; after the image of God made He him.* The image is in common; God made man after the image of God. I would ask him who denies that God's Son is true God, in what shape he supposes that God made man? He must bear constantly in mind that all things are through the Son; heretical ingenuity must not, for its own purposes, twist this passage into action on the part of the Father. If, therefore, man is created through God the Son after the image of God the Father, he is created also after the image of the Son; for all admit that the words *After Our image and likeness* were spoken to the Son. Thus His true Godhead is as explicitly asserted by the Divine words as manifested in the Divine action; so that it is God Who moulds man into the image of God, Who reveals Himself as God, and, moreover, as true God. For His joint possession of the Divine image proves Him true God, while His creative action displays Him as God the Son.

10. What wild insanity of abandoned souls! What blind audacity of reckless blasphemy! You hear of God and God; you hear of *Our image*. Why suggest that One is, and One is not, true God? Why distinguish between God by nature and God in name? Why, under pretext of defending the faith, do you destroy the faith? Why struggle to

pervert the revelation of One God, One true God, into a denial that God is One and true? Not yet will I stifle your insane efforts with the clear words of Evangelists and Prophets, in which Father and Son appear not as one Person, but as One in nature, and Each as true God. For the present the Law, unaided, annihilates you. Does the Law ever speak of One true God, and One not true? Does it ever speak of Either, except by the name of God, which is the true expression of Their nature? It speaks of God and God; it speaks also of God as One. Nay, it does more than so describe Them. It manifests Them as true God and true God, by the sure evidence of Their joint image. It begins by speaking of Them first by their strict name of God; then it attributes true Godhead to Both in common. For when man, Their creature, is created after the image of Both, sound reason forces the conclusion that Each of Them is true God.

11. But let us travel once more in our journey of instruction over the lessons taught in the holy Law of God. The Angel of God speaks to Hagar; and this same Angel is God. But perhaps His being the Angel of God means that He is not true God. For this title seems to indicate a lower nature; where the name points to a difference in kind, it is thought that true equality must be absent. The last book has already exposed the hollowness of this objection; the title of Angel informs us of His office, not of His nature. I have prophetic evidence for this explanation; *Who maketh His angels spirits, and His ministers a flaming fire*[7]. That flaming fire is His ministers; that spirit which comes, His angels. These figures shew the nature and the power of His messengers, or angels, and of His ministers. This spirit is an angel, that flaming fire a minister, of God. Their nature adapts them for the function of messenger or minister. Thus the Law, or rather God through the Law, wishing to indicate God the Son as a Person, yet as bearing the same name with the Father, calls Him the Angel, that is, the Messenger, of God. The title *Messenger* proves that He has an office of His own; that His nature is truly Divine is proved when He is called God. But this sequence, first Angel, then God, is in the order of revelation, not in Himself. For we confess Them Father and Son in the strictest sense, in such equality that the Only-begotten Son, by virtue of His birth, possesses true Divinity from the Unbegotten Father. This revelation of Them as Sender and as Sent is but another

expression for Father and Son; not contradicting the true Divine nature of the Son, nor cancelling His possession of the Godhead as His birthright. For none can doubt that the Son by His birth partakes congenitally of the nature of His Author, in such wise that from the One there comes into being an indivisible Unity, because One is from One.

12. Faith burns with passionate ardour; the burden of silence is intolerable, and my thoughts imperiously demand an utterance. Already, in the preceding book I have departed from the intended method of my demonstration. I was denouncing that blasphemous sense in which the heretics speak of One God, and expounding the passages in which Moses speaks of God and God. I hastened on with a precipitate, though devout, zeal to the true sense in which we hold the unity of God. And now again, wrapped up in the pursuit of another enquiry, I have suffered myself to wander from the course, and, while I was engaged upon the true Divinity of the Son, the ardour of my soul has hurried me on before the time to make the confession of true God as Father and as Son. But our own faith must wait its proper place in the treatise. This preliminary statement of it has been made as a safeguard for the reader; it shall be so developed and explained hereafter as to frustrate the schemes of the gainsayer.

13. To resume the argument; this title of office indicates no difference of nature, for He, Who is the Angel of God, is God. The test of His true Godhead shall be, whether or no His words and acts were those of God. He increases Ishmael into a great people, and promises that many nations shall bear his name. Is this, I ask, within an angel's power? If not, and this is the power of God, why do you refuse true Divinity to Him Who, on your own confession, has the true power of God? Thus He possesses the true and perfect powers of the Divine nature. True God, in all the types in which He reveals Himself for the world's salvation, is not, nor ever can be, other than true God.

14. Now first, I ask, what is the meaning of these terms, 'true God' and 'not true God'? If any one says to me 'This is fire, but not true fire; water, but not true water,' I can attach no intelligible meaning to his words. What difference in kind can there be between one true specimen, and another true specimen, of the same class? If a thing be fire, it must be true fire; while its nature remains the same it cannot lose this character of true fire. Deprive water of its watery nature, and by so doing you destroy it as true water; let it

---

7 Psalm civ. (ciii.) 4.

remain water, and it will inevitably still be true water. The only way in which an object can lose its nature is by losing its existence; if it continue to exist it must be truly itself. If the Son of God is God, then He is true God; if He is not true God, then in no possible sense is He God at all. If He has not the nature, then He has no right to the name; if, on the contrary, the name which indicates the nature is His by inherent right, then it cannot be that He is destitute of that nature in its truest sense.

15. But perhaps it will be argued that, when the Angel of God is called God, He receives the name as a favour, through adoption, and has in consequence a nominal, not a true, Godhead. If He gave us an inadequate revelation of His Divine nature at the time when He was styled the Angel of God, judge whether He has not fully manifested His true Godhead under the name of a nature lower than the angelic. For a Man spoke to Abraham, and Abraham worshipped Him as God. Pestilent heretic! Abraham confessed Him, you deny Him, to be God. What hope is there for you, in your blasphemy, of the blessings promised to Abraham? He is Father of the Gentiles, but not for you; you cannot go forth from your regeneration to join the household of his seed, through the blessings given to his faith. You are no son, raised up to Abraham from the stones; you are a generation of vipers, an adversary of his belief. You are not the Israel of God, the heir of Abraham, justified by faith; for you have disbelieved God, while Abraham was justified and appointed to be the Father of the Gentiles through that faith wherein he worshipped the God Whose word he trusted. God it was Whom that blessed and faithful Patriarch worshipped then; and mark how truly He was God, to Whom, in His own words, all things are possible. Is there any, but God alone, to Whom nothing is impossible? And He, to Whom all things are possible, does He fall short of true Divinity?

16. I ask further, Who is this God Who overthrew Sodom and Gomorrah? For *the Lord rained from the Lord*[8]; was it not the true Lord from the true Lord? Have you any alternative to this Lord, and Lord? Or any other meaning for the terms, except that in Lord, and Lord, their Persons are distinguished? Bear in mind that Him Whom you have confessed as *Alone true*, you have also confessed as *Alone the righteous Judge*[9]. Now mark that the Lord who rains from the Lord, and slays not the just with the unjust, and judges the whole earth, is both Lord and also righteous Judge, and also rains from the Lord. In the face of all this, I ask you Which it is that you describe as alone the righteous Judge. The Lord rains from the Lord; you will not deny that He Who rains from the Lord is the righteous Judge, for Abraham, the Father of the Gentiles—but not of the unbelieving Gentiles—speaks thus : *In no wise shalt Thou do this thing, to slay the righteous with the wicked, for then shall the righteous be as the wicked. In no wise shalt Thou, Who judgest the earth, execute this judgment*[1]. This God, then, the righteous Judge, is clearly also the true God. Blasphemer! Your own falsehood confutes you. Not yet do I bring forward the witness of the Gospels concerning God the Judge; the Law has told me that He is the Judge. You must deprive the Son of His judgeship before you can deprive Him of His true Divinity. You have solemnly confessed that He Who is the only righteous Judge is also the only true God; your own statements bind you to the admission that He Who is the righteous Judge is also true God. This Judge is the Lord, to Whom all things are possible, the Promiser of eternal blessings, Judge of righteous and of wicked. He is the God of Abraham, worshipped by him. Fool and blasphemer that you are, your shameless readiness of tongue must invent some new fallacy, if you are to prove that He is not true God.

17. His merciful and mysterious self-revelations are in no wise inconsistent with His true heavenly nature; and His faithful saints never fail to penetrate the guise He has assumed in order that faith may see Him. The types of the Law foreshew the mysteries of the Gospel; they enable the Patriarch to see and to believe what hereafter the Apostle is to gaze on and publish. For, since the Law is the shadow of things to come, the shadow that was seen was a true outline of the reality which cast it. God was seen and believed and worshipped as Man, Who was indeed to be born as Man in the fulness of time. He takes upon Him, to meet the Patriarch's eye, a semblance which foreshadows the future truth. In that old day God was only seen, not born, as Man; in due time He was born, as well as seen. Familiarity with the human appearance, which He took that men might behold Him, was to prepare them for the time when He should, in very truth, be born as Man. Then it was that the shadow took substance, the semblance reality, the vision

---

8 Gen. xix. 24.
9 Book iv. § 12. The latter expression is cited inaccurately.

1 Gen. xviii. 25.

life. But God remained unchanged, whether He were seen in the appearance, or born in the reality, of manhood. The resemblance was perfect between Himself, after His birth, and Himself, as He had been seen in vision. As He was born, so He had appeared ; as He had appeared, so was He born. But, since the time has not yet come for us to compare the Gospel account with that of the prophet Moses, let us pursue our chosen course through the pages of the Law. Hereafter we shall prove from the Gospels that it was the true Son of God Who was born as Man; for the present, we are shewing from the Law that it was true God, the Son of God, Who appeared to the Patriarchs in human form. For when One appeared to Abraham as Man, He was worshipped as God and proclaimed as Judge ; and when the Lord rained from the Lord, beyond a doubt the Law tells us that the Lord rained from the Lord in order to reveal to us the Father and the Son. Nor can we for a moment suppose that when the Patriarch, with full knowledge, worshipped the Son as God, he was blind to the fact that it was true God Whom he worshipped.

18. But godless unbelief finds it very hard to apprehend the true faith. Their capacity for devotion has never been expanded by belief, and is too narrow to receive a full presentment of the truth. Hence the unbelieving soul cannot grasp the great work done by God in being born as Man to accomplish the salvation of mankind; in the work of its salvation it fails to see the power of God. They think of the travail of His birth, the feebleness of infancy, the growth of childhood, the attainment of maturity, of bodily suffering and of the Cross with which it ended, and of the death upon the Cross ; and all this conceals His true Godhead from their eyes. Yet He had called into being all these capacities for Himself, as additions to His nature ; capacities which in His true Divine nature He had not possessed. Thus He acquired them without loss of His true Divinity, and ceased not to be God when He became Man; when He, Who is God eternally, became Man at a point in time. They cannot see an exercise of the true God's power in His becoming what He was not before, yet never ceasing to be His former Self. And yet there would have been no acceptance of our feeble nature, had not He by the strength of His own omnipotent nature, while remaining what He was, come to be what previously He was not. What blindness of heresy, what foolish wisdom of the world, which cannot see that the reproach of Christ

is the power of God, the folly of faith the wisdom of God! So Christ in your eyes is not God because He, Who was from eternity, was born, because the Unchangeable grew with years, the Impassible suffered, the Living died, the Dead lives ; because all His history contradicts the common course of nature ! Is not all this simply to say that He, being God, was omnipotent? Not yet, ye holy and venerable Gospels, do I turn your pages, to prove from them that Christ Jesus, amid these changes and sufferings, is God. For the Law is the forerunner of the Gospels, and the Law must teach us that, when God clothed Himself in infirmity, He lost not His Godhead. The types of the Law are our convincing assurance of the mysteries of the Gospel faith.

19. Be with me now in thy faithful spirit, holy and blessed Patriarch Jacob, to combat the poisonous hissings of the serpent of unbelief. Prevail once more in thy wrestling with the Man, and, being the stronger, once more entreat His blessing. Why pray for what thou mightest demand from thy weaker Opponent? Thy strong arm has vanquished Him Whose blessing thou prayest. Thy bodily victory is in broad contrast to thy soul's humility, thy deeds to thy thoughts. It is a Man whom thou holdest powerless in thy strong grasp ; but in thine eye this Man is true God, and God not in name only, but in nature. It is not the blessing of a God by adoption that thou dost claim, but the true God's blessing. With Man thou strivest ; but face to face thou seest God. What thou seest with the bodily eye is different far from what thou beholdest with the vision of faith. Thou hast felt Him to be weak Man ; but thy soul has been saved because it saw God in Him. When thou wast wrestling thou wast Jacob ; thou art Israel now, through faith in the blessing which thou didst claim. According to the flesh, the Man is thy inferior, for a type of His passion in the flesh ; but thou canst recognise God in that weak flesh, for a sign of His blessing in the Spirit. The witness of the eye does not disturb thy faith ; His feebleness does not mislead thee into neglect of His blessing. Though He is Man, His humanity is no bar to His being God, His Godhead no bar to His being true God ; for, being God, He must indeed be true[2].

20. The Law in its progress still follows the sequence of the Gospel mystery, of which it is the shadow ; its types are a faithful anticipation of the truths taught by the Apostles. In the vision of his dream the blessed Jacob saw God ; this was the revelation of a mystery, not

---

[2] Omitting *et benedicendo et transferendo et nuncupando.*

a bodily manifestation. For there was shown to him the descent of angels by the ladder, and their ascent to heaven, and God resting above the ladder; and the vision, as it was interpreted, foretold that his dream should some day become a revealed truth. The Patriarch's words, *The house of God and the gate of heaven,* shew us the scene of his vision; and then, after a long account of what he did, the narrative proceeds thus: *And God said unto Jacob, Arise, and go up to the place Bethel, and dwell there: and make there a Sacrifice unto God, that appeared unto thee when thou fleddest from the face of Esau*[3]. If the faith of the Gospel has access through God the Son to God the Father, and if it is only through God that God can be apprehended, then shew us in what sense This is not true God, Who demands reverence for God, Who rests above the heavenly ladder. What difference of nature separates the Two, when Both bear the one name which indicates the one nature? It is God Who was seen; it is also God Who speaks about God Who was seen. God cannot be apprehended except through God; even as also God accepts no worship from us except through God. We could not understand that the One must be reverenced, unless the Other had taught us reverence for Him; we could not have known that the One is God, unless we had known the Godhead of the Other. The revelation of mysteries holds its appointed course; it is by God that we are initiated into the worship of God. And when one name, which tells of one nature, combines the Father with the Son, how can the Son so fall beneath Himself as to be other than true God?

21. Human judgment must not pass its sentence upon God. Our nature is not such that it can lift itself by its own forces to the contemplation of heavenly things. We must learn from God what we are to think of God; we have no source of knowledge but Himself. You may be as carefully trained as you will in secular philosophy; you may have lived a life of righteousness. All this will contribute to your mental satisfaction, but it will not help you to know God. Moses was adopted as the son of the queen, and instructed in all the wisdom of the Egyptians; he had, moreover, out of loyalty to his race avenged the wrong of the Hebrew by slaying the Egyptian[4], and yet he knew not the God Who had blessed his fathers. For when he left Egypt through fear of the discovery of his deed, and was living as a shepherd in the land of Midian, he saw a fire in the bush, and the bush unconsumed.

Then it was that he heard the voice of God, and asked His name, and learned His nature. Of all this he could have known nothing except through God Himself. And we, in like manner, must confine ourselves, in whatever we say of God, to the terms in which He has spoken to our understanding concerning Himself.

22. It is the Angel of God Who appeared in the fire from the bush; and it is God Who spoke from the bush amid the fire. He is manifested as Angel; that is His office, not His nature. The name which expresses His nature is given you as God; for the Angel of God is God. But perhaps He is not true God. Is the God of Abraham, then, the God of Isaac, the God of Jacob, not true God? For the Angel Who speaks from the bush is their God eternally. And, lest you insinuate that the name is His only by adoption, it is the absolute God Who speaks to Moses. These are His words:—*And the Lord said unto Moses, I Am that I Am; and He said, Thus shalt thou say unto the children of Israel, He that is hath sent me unto you*[5]. God's discourse began as the speech of the Angel, in order to reveal the mystery of human salvation in the Son. Next He appears as the God of Abraham, and the God of Isaac, and the God of Jacob, that we may know the name which is His by nature. Finally it is the God *that is* Who sends Moses to Israel, that we may have full assurance that in the absolute sense He is God.

23. What further fictions can the futile folly of insane blasphemy devise? Do you still persist in your nightly sowing of tares, predestined to be burnt, among the pure wheat, when the knowledge of all the Patriarchs contradicts you? Nay more: if you believed Moses, you would believe also in God, the Son of God; unless perchance you deny that it was of Him that Moses spoke. If you propose to deny that, you must listen to the words of God:—*For had ye believed Moses, ye would have believed Me also, for he wrote of Me*[6]. Moses, indeed, will refute you with the whole volume of the Law, ordained through angels, which he received by the hand of the Mediator. Enquire whether He, Who gave the Law, were not true God; for the Mediator was the Giver. And was it not to meet God that Moses led out the people to the Mount? Was it not God Who came down into the Mount? Or was it, perhaps, only by a fiction or an adoption, and not by right of nature, that He, Who did all this, bore the name of God? Mark the blare of the trumpets, the flashing of the torches,

3 Gen. xxxv. 1.
4 This act is used as the evidence of Moses' righteousness.
5 Exod. iii. 14. 6 St. John v. 46.

the clouds of smoke, as from a furnace, rolling over the mountain, the terror of conscious impotence on the part of man in the presence of God, the confession of the people, when they prayed Moses to be their spokesman, that at the voice of God they would die. Is He, in your judgment, not true God, when simple dread lest He should speak filled Israel with the fear of death? He Whose voice could not be borne by human weakness? In your eyes is He not God, because He addressed you through the weak faculties of a man, that you might hear, and live 7? Moses entered the Mount; in forty days and nights he gained the knowledge of the mysteries of heaven, and set it all in order according to the vision of the truth which was revealed to him there. From intercourse with God, Who spoke with him, he received the reflected splendour of that glory on which none may gaze? his corruptible countenance was transfigured into the likeness of the unapproachable light of Him, with Whom he was dwelling. Of this God he bears witness, of this God he speaks; he summons the angels of God to come and worship Him amid the gladness of the Gentiles, and prays that the blessings which please Him may descend upon the head of Joseph. In face of such evidence as this, dare any man say that He has nothing but the name of God, and deny His true Divinity?

24. This long discussion has, I believe, brought out the truth that no sound argument has ever been adduced in favour of a distinction between One Who is, and One Who is not, true God, in those passages where the Law speaks of God and God, of Lord and Lord. I have proved that these terms are inconsistent with difference between Them in name or in nature, and that we can use the name as a test of the nature, and the nature as a clue to the name. Thus I have shewn that the character, the power, the attributes, the name of God are inherent in Him Whom the Law has called God. I have shewn also that the Law, gradually unfolding the Gospel mystery, reveals the Son as a Person by manifesting God as obedient, in the creation of the world, to the words of God, and in the formation of man making what is the joint image of God, and of God; and again, that in the judgment of the men of Sodom the Lord is Judge from the Lord; that, in the giving of blessings and ordaining of the mysteries of the Law, the Angel of God is God. Thus, in support of the saving confession of God as ever manifested in the Persons of Father and of Son, we have shewn how the Law teaches

the true Godhead by the use of the strict name of God; for, while the Law states clearly that They are Two, it casts no shadow of doubt upon the true Godhead of either.

25. And now the time has come for us to put a stop to that cunning artifice of heresy, by which they pervert the devout and godly teachings of the Law into a support for their own godless delusion. They preface their denial of the Son of God with the words, *Hear, O Israel, the Lord thy God is One;* and then, because their blasphemy would be refuted by the identity of name, since the Law speaks of God and God, they invoke the authority of the prophetic words, *They shall bless Thee, the true God,* to prove that the name is not used in the true sense. They argue that these words teach that God is One, and that God, the Son of God, has His name only and not His nature; and that therefore we must conclude that the true God is one Person only. But perhaps you imagine, fool, that we shall contradict these texts of yours, and so deny that there is one true God. Assuredly we do not contradict them by a confession conceived in your sense. Our faith receives them, our reason accepts them, our words declare them. We recognise One God, and Him true God. The name of God has no dangers for our confession, which proclaims that in the nature of the Son there is the One true God. Learn the meaning of your own words, recognise the One true God, and then you will be able to make a faithful confession of God, One and true. It is the words of our faith which you are turning into the instrument of your blasphemy, preserving the sound and perverting the sense. Masquerading in a foolish garb of imaginary wisdom, under cover of loyalty to truth you are the truth's destroyer. You confess that God is One and true, on purpose to deny the truth which you confess. Your language claims a reputation for piety on the strength of its impiety, for truth on the strength of its falsehood. Your preaching of One true God leads up to a denial of Him. For you deny that the Son is true God, though you admit that He is God, but God in name only, not in nature. If His birth be in name, not in nature, then you are justified in denying His true right to the name; but if He be truly born as God, how then can He fail to be true God by virtue of His birth? Deny the fact, and you may deny the consequence; if you admit the fact, how can He be other than Himself? No being can alter its own essential nature. About His birth I shall speak presently; meantime I will refute your blasphemous falsehoods concerning His true Divine nature by the utterances of prophets. But I shall

---

7 Reading *viveres.*

take care that in our assertion of the One true God I give no cover to the Sabellian heresy that the Father is one Person with the Son, and none to that slander against the Son's true Godhead, which you evolve out of the unity of the One true God.

26. Blasphemy is incompatible with wisdom; where the fear of God, which is the beginning of wisdom, is absent, no glimmer of intelligence survives. An instance of this is seen in the heretics' citation of the prophet's words, *And they shall bless Thee, the true God*, as evidence against the Godhead of the Son. First, we see here the folly, which clogs unbelief in the misunderstanding or (if it were understood) in the suppression of the earlier part of the prophecy: and again we see it in their fraudulent interpolation of that one little word, not to be found in the book itself. This proceeding is as stupid as it is dishonest, since no one would trust them so far as to accept their reading without referring for corroboration to the prophetic text. For that text does not stand thus: *They shall bless Thee, the true God*, but thus: *They shall bless the true God*[8]. There is no slight difference between *Thee, the true God* and *The true God*. If *Thee* be retained, the pronoun of the second person implies that Another is being addressed; if *Thee* be omitted, *True God*, the object of the sentence, is the Speaker.

27. To ensure that our explanation of the passage shall be complete and certain, I cite the words in full:—*Therefore thus saith the Lord, Behold, they that serve Me shall eat, but ye shall be hungry, behold, they that serve Me shall drink, but ye shall be thirsty, behold, they that serve Me shall rejoice with gladness, but ye shall cry for sorrow of your heart, and shall howl for vexation of spirit. For ye shall leave your name for a rejoicing unto My chosen, but the Lord shall slay you. But My servants shall be called by a new name, which shall be blessed upon earth; and they shall bless the true God, and they that swear upon the earth shall swear by the true God*[9]. There is always a good reason for any departure from the accustomed modes of expression, but novelty is also made an opportunity for misinterpretation. The question here is, Why, when so many earlier prophecies have been uttered concerning God, and the name *God*, alone and without epithet, has sufficed hitherto to indicate the Divine majesty and nature, the Spirit of prophecy should now foretell through Isaiah that the *true* God was to be blessed, and that men should swear upon earth by the *true* God. First, we must bear in mind that this discourse

was spoken concerning times to come. Now, I ask, was not He, in the mind of the Jews, true God, Whom men used then to bless, and by whom they swore? The Jews, unaware of the typical meaning of their mysteries, and therefore ignorant of God the Son, worshipped God simply as God, and not as Father[1]; for, if they had worshipped Him as Father, they would have worshipped the Son also. It was *God*, therefore, Whom they blessed and by Whom they swore. But the prophet testifies that it is *true* God Who shall be blessed hereafter; calling Him *true God*, because the mysteriousness of His Incarnation was to blind the eyes of some to His true Godhead. When falsehood was to be published abroad, it was necessary that the truth should be clearly stated. And now let us review this passage, clause by clause.

28. *Therefore thus saith the Lord, Behold, they that serve Me shall eat, but ye shall be hungry; behold, they that serve Me shall drink, but ye shall be thirsty*. Note that one clause contains two different tenses, in order to teach truth concerning two different times; *They that serve Me shall eat*. Present piety is rewarded with a future prize, and similarly present godlessness shall suffer the penalty of future thirst and hunger. Then He adds, *Behold, they that serve Me shall rejoice with gladness, but ye shall cry for sorrow of your heart, and shall howl for vexation of spirit*. Here again, as before, there is a revelation for the future and for the present. They who serve now shall rejoice with gladness, while they who do not serve shall abide in crying and howling through sorrow of heart and vexation of spirit. He proceeds, *For ye shall leave your name for a rejoicing unto My chosen, but the Lord shall slay you*. These words, dealing with a future time, are addressed to the carnal Israel, which is taunted with the prospect of having to surrender its name to the chosen of God. What is this name? Israel, of course; for to Israel the prophecy was addressed. And now I ask, What is Israel to-day? The Apostle gives the answer:—They who are in the spirit, not in the letter, they who walk in the Law of Christ, are the Israel of God[2].

29. Furthermore, we must form a conclusion why it is that the words cited above, *Therefore thus saith the Lord*, are followed by *But the Lord shall slay you*, and as to the meaning of the next sentence, *But my servants shall be called by a new name, which shall be blessed upon earth*. There can be no doubt that both *Therefore thus saith the*

---

8 Isai. lxv. 16.   9 Ib. 13—16.   1 Cf. Book iii. § 17.   2 Cf. Rom. ii. 29.

Lord, and afterwards *But the Lord shall slay you*, prove that it was the Lord Who both spoke, and also purposed to slay, Who meant to reward His servants with that new name, Who was well known to have spoken through the prophets and was to be the judge of the righteous and of the wicked. And thus the remainder of this revelation of the mystery of the Gospel removes all doubt concerning the Lord as Speaker and as Slayer. It continues:—*But My servants shall be called by a new name, which shall be blessed upon earth.* Here everything is in the future. What then is this new name of a religion; a name which shall be blessed upon earth? If ever in past ages there were a blessing upon the name *Christian*, it is not a new name. But if this hallowed name of our devotion towards God be new, then this new title of *Christian*, awarded to our faith, is that heavenly blessing which is our reward upon earth.

30. And now come words in perfect harmony with the inward assurance of our faith. He says, *And they shall bless the true God, and they that swear upon earth shall swear by the true God.* And indeed they who in God's service have received the new name shall bless God; and moreover the God by Whom they shall swear is the true God. What doubt is there as to Who this true God is, by Whom men shall swear and Whom they shall bless, through Whom a new and blessed name shall be given to them that serve Him? I have on my side, in opposition to the blasphemous misrepresentations of heresy, the clear and definite evidence of the Church's faith; the witness of the new name which Thou, O Christ, hast given, of the blessed title which Thou hast bestowed in reward of loyal service. It swears that Thou art true God. Every mouth, O Christ, of them that believe tells that Thou art God. The faith of all believers swears that Thou art God, confesses, proclaims, is inwardly assured, that Thou art true God.

31. And thus this passage of prophecy, taken with its whole context, clearly describes as God both Him Whom we serve for the new name's sake, and Him through Whom the new name is blessed upon earth. It tells us Who it is that is blessed as true God, and Who is sworn by as true God. And this is the confession of faith made, in the fulness of time, by the Church in loyal devotion to Christ her Lord. We can see how exactly the words of prophecy conform to the truth, by their refraining from the insertion of that pronoun of the second person. Had the words been *Thee, the true God*, then they might have been interpreted as spoken to

another. *The true God* can refer to none but the Speaker. The passage, taken by itself, shews to Whom it refers; the preceding words, taken in connexion with it, declare Who the Speaker is Who makes this confession of God. They are these:—*I have appeared openly to them that asked not for Me, and I have been found of them that sought Me not. I said, Here am I, unto a nation that called not on My name. I have spread out My hands all the day to an unbelieving and gainsaying people* [3]. Could a dishonest attempt to suppress the truth be more completely exposed, or the Speaker be more distinctly revealed as true God, than here? Who, I demand, was it that appeared to them that asked not for Him, and was found of them that sought Him not? What nation is it that formerly called not on His name? Who is it that spread out His hands all the day to an unbelieving and gainsaying people? Compare with these words that holy and Divine Song of Deuteronomy [4], in which God, in His wrath against them that are no Gods, moves the unbelievers to jealousy against those that are no people and a foolish nation. Conclude for yourself, Who it is that makes Himself manifest to them that knew Him not; Who, though one people is His own, becomes the possession of strangers; Who it is that spreads out His hands before an unbelieving and gainsaying people, nailing to the cross the writing of the former sentence against us [5]. For the same Spirit in the prophet, whom we are considering, proceeds thus in the course of this one prophecy, which is connected in argument as well as continous in utterance:—*But My servants shall be called by a new name, which shall be blessed upon earth, and they shall bless the true God, and they that swear upon the earth shall swear by the true God.*

32. If heresy, in its folly and wickedness, shall attempt to entice the simple-minded and uninstructed away from the true belief that these words were spoken in reference to God the Son, by feigning that they are an utterance of God the Father concerning Himself, it shall hear sentence passed upon the lie by the Apostle and Teacher of the Gentiles. He interprets all these prophecies as allusions to the passion of the Lord and to the times of Gospel faith, when he is reproving the unbelief of Israel, which will not recognise that the Lord is come in the flesh. His words are:—*For whosoever shall have called upon the name of the Lord shall be saved. How shall they call on Him in Whom they have not believed? But how shall they believe*

3 Isai. lxv. 1, 2.   4 Deut. xxxii. 21.   5 Cf. Col. ii. 14

in Him of Whom they have not heard? And how shall they hear without a preacher? And how shall they preach, except they have been sent? As it is written, How beautiful are the feet of them that proclaim peace, of them that proclaim good things. But all do not obey the Gospel. For Esaias saith, Lord, who hath believed our report? So then faith cometh by hearing, and hearing through the word. But I say, Have they not heard? Yes verily, their sound went into all the earth, and their words unto the ends of the world. But I say, Did not Israel know? First Moses saith, I will provoke you to jealousy against them that are no people, and against a foolish nation I will anger you. Moreover Esaias is bold, and saith, I appeared unto them that seek Me not, I was found by them that asked not after Me. But to Israel what saith He? All day long I have stretched forth My hands to a people that hearken not[6]. Who art thou that hast mounted up through the successive heavens, knowing not whether thou wert in the body or out of the body, and canst explain more faithfully than he the words of the prophet? Who art thou that hast heard, and mayst not tell, the ineffable mysteries of the secret things of heaven, and hast proclaimed with greater assurance the knowledge granted thee by God for revelation? Who art thou that hast been foreordained to a full share of the Lord's suffering on the Cross, and first has been caught up to Paradise and drawn nobler teaching from the Scriptures of God than this chosen vessel? If there be such a man, has he been ignorant that these are the deeds and words of the true God, proclaimed to us by His own true and chosen Apostle that we may recognise in Him their Author?

33. But it may be argued that the Apostle was not inspired by the Spirit of prophecy when he borrowed these prophetic words; that he was only interpreting at random the words of another man, and though, no doubt, everything the Apostle says of himself comes to him by revelation from Christ, yet his knowledge of the words of Isaiah is only derived from the book. I answer that in the beginning of that utterance in which it is said that the servants of the true God shall bless Him and swear by Him, we read this adoration by the prophet:—From everlasting we have not heard, nor have our eyes seen God, except Thee, and Thy works which Thou wilt do for them that await Thy mercy[7]. Isaiah says that he has seen no God but Him. For he did actually see the glory of God, the mystery of Whose taking flesh from the Virgin

he foretold. And if you, in your heresy, do not know that it was God the Only-begotten Whom the prophet saw in that glory, listen to the Evangelist:—These things said Esaias, when he saw His glory, and spake of Him[8]. The Apostle, the Evangelist, the Prophet combine to silence your objections. Isaiah did see God; even though it is written, No one hath seen God at any time, save the Only-begotten Son Who is in the bosom of the Father; He hath declared Him[9], it was God Whom the prophet saw. He gazed upon the Divine glory, and men were filled with envy at such honour vouchsafed to his prophetic greatness. For this was the reason why the Jews passed sentence of death upon him.

34. Thus the Only-begotten Son, Who is in the bosom of the Father, has told us of God, Whom no man has seen. Either disprove the fact that the Son has thus informed us, or else believe Him Who has been seen, Who appeared to them who knew Him not, and became the God of the Gentiles who called not upon Him and spread out His hands before a gainsaying people. And believe this also concerning Him, that they who serve Him are called by a new name, and that on earth men bless Him and swear by Him as true God. Prophecy tells, the Gospel confirms, the Apostle explains, the Church confesses, that He Who was seen is true God; but none venture to say that God the Father was seen. And yet the madness of heresy has run to such lengths that, while they profess to recognise this truth, they really deny it. They deny it by means of the newfangled and godless device of evading the truth, while making a studied pretence of adhesion to it. For when they confess one God, alone true and alone righteous, alone wise, alone unchangeable, alone immortal, alone mighty, they attach to Him a Son different in substance, not born from God to be God, but adopted through creation to be a Son, having the name of God not by nature, but as a title received by adoption; and thus they inevitably deprive the Son of all those attributes which they accumulate upon the Father in His lonely majesty.

35. The distorted mind of heresy is incapable of knowing and confessing the One true God; the sound faith and reason necessary for such confession is incompatible with unbelief. We must confess Father and Son before we can apprehend God as One and true. When we have known the mysteries of man's salvation, accomplished in us through the power of regeneration unto life in the

---

6 Rom. x. 13—21.   7 Isai. lxiv. 4.   8 St. John xii. 41.   9 Ib. i. 18.

Father and the Son, then we may hope to penetrate the mysteries of the Law and the Prophets. Godless ignorance of the teaching of Evangelists and Apostles cannot frame the thought of One true God. Out of the teaching of Evangelists and Apostles we shall present the sound doctrine concerning Him, in accurate agreement with the faith of true believers. We shall present Him in such wise that the Only-begotten, Who is of the substance of the Father, shall be known as indivisible and inseparable in nature, not in Person. We shall set forth God as One, because God is from the nature of God. But we shall also establish this doctrine of the perfect unity of God upon the words of the Prophets, and make them the foundations of the Gospel structure, proving that there is One God, with one Divine nature, by the fact that God the Only-begotten is never classed apart as a second God. For throughout this book of our treatise we have followed the same course as in its predecessor; the same methods which proved there that the Son is God, have proved here that He is true God. I trust that our explanation of each passage has been so convincing that we have now manifested Him as true God as effectually as we formerly demonstrated His Godhead. The remainder of the book shall be devoted to the proof that He, Who is now recognised as true God, must not be regarded as a second God. Our disproof of the notion of a second God will further establish the unity; and this truth shall be displayed as not inconsistent with the personal existence of the Son, while yet it maintains the unity of nature in God and God.

36. The true method of our enquiry demands that we should begin with him, through whom God first manifested Himself to the world, that is, with Moses, by whose mouth God the Only-begotten thus declared Himself; *See, see that I am God, and there is no God beside Me* [1]. That godless heresy must not assign these words to God, the unbegotten Father, is clear by the sense of the passage and by the evidence of the Apostle who, as we have already stated [2], has taught us to understand this whole discourse as spoken by God the Only-begotten. The Apostle also points out the words, *Rejoice, O ye nations, with His people* [3] as those of the Son, and in corroboration further cites this :—*And there shall be a root of Jesse, and One that shall arise to rule the nations; in Him shall the nations trust* [4]. Thus Moses by the words, *Rejoice,*

O ye nations, with His people indicates Him Who said, *There is no God beside Me;* and the Apostle refers the same words to our Lord Jesus Christ, God the Only-begotten, in Whose rising as a king from the root of Jesse, according to the flesh, the hope of the Gentiles rests. And therefore we must now consider the meaning of these words, that we, who know that they were spoken by Him, may ascertain in what sense He spoke them.

37. That true and absolute and perfect doctrine, which forms our faith, is the confession of God from God and God in God, by no bodily process but by Divine power, by no transfusion from nature into nature but through the secret and mighty working of the One nature; God from God, not by division or extension or emanation, but by the operation of a nature which brings into existence, by means of birth, a nature One with itself. The facts shall receive a fuller treatment in the next book, which is to be devoted to an exposition of the teaching of the Evangelists and Apostles; for the present we must maintain our assertion and belief by means of the Law and the Prophets. The nature with which God is born is necessarily the same as that of His Source. He cannot come into existence as other than God, since His origin is from none other than God. His nature is the same, not in the sense that the Begetter also was begotten—for then the Unbegotten, having been begotten, would not be Himself— but that the substance of the Begotten consists in all those elements which are summed up in the substance of the Begetter, Who is His only Origin. Thus it is due to no external cause that His origin is from the One, and that His existence partakes the Unity; their is no novel element in Him, because His life is from the Living : no element absent, because the Living begot Him to partake His own life. Hence, in the generation of the Son, the incorporeal and unchangeable God begets, in accordance with His own nature, God incorporeal and unchangeable; and this perfect birth of incorporeal and unchangeable God from incorporeal and unchangeable God involves, as we see in the light of the revelation of God from God, no diminution of the Begetter's substance. And so God the Only-begotten bears witness through the holy Moses; *See, see that I am God, and there is no God beside Me.* For there is no second Divine nature, and so there can be no God beside Him, since He is God, yet by the powers of His nature God is also in Him. And because He is God and God is in Him, there is no God beside Him; for God, than Whom there is no other Source of Deity, is

---

1 Deut. xxxii. 39.   2 Book iv. § 33.
        3 Deut. xxxii. 43 (Rom xv. 10).
        4 Isai. xi. 10 (Rom. xv. 12).

in Him, and consequently there is within Him not only His own existence, but the Author of that existence.

38. This saving faith which we profess is sustained by the spirit of prophecy, speaking with one voice through many mouths, and never, through long and changing ages, bearing an uncertain witness to the truths of revelation. For instance, the words which, as we are told through Moses, were spoken by God the Only-begotten, are confirmed for our better instruction by the prophetic spirit, speaking this time through those men of stature,—*For God is in Thee, and there is no God beside Thee. For Thou art God, and we knew it not, O God of Israel, the Saviour.* Let heresy fling itself with its utmost effort of despair and rage against this declaration of a name and nature inseparably joined, and rend in twain, if its furious struggles can, a union perfect in title and in fact. God is in God and beside Him there is no God. Let heresy, if it can, divide the God within from the God within Whom He is, and classify, Each after His kind, the members of that mystic union. For when He says *God is in Thee,* He teaches that the true nature of God the Father is present in God the Son; for we must understand that it is the God *Who is* [5] that is in Him. And when He adds, *And there is no God beside Thee,* He shews that outside Him there is no God, since God's dwelling is within Himself. And the third assertion, *Thou art God and we knew it not,* sets forth for our instruction what must be the confession of the devout and believing soul. When it has learnt the mysteries of the Divine birth, and the name *Emmanuel* which the angel announced to Joseph, it must cry, *Thou art God, and we knew it not, O God of Israel, the Saviour.* It must recognise the subsistence of the Divine nature in Him, in-asmuch as God is in God, and the non-existence of any other God except the true. For, He being God and God being in Him, the delusion of another God, of what kind soever, must be surrendered. Such is the message of the prophet Isaiah; he bears witness to the indivisible and inseparable Godhead of Father and of Son.

39. Jeremiah also, a prophet equally inspired, has taught that God the Only-begotten is of a nature one with that of God the Father. His words are:—*This is our God, and there shall be none other likened unto Him, Who hath found out all the way of knowledge, and hath given it unto Jacob His servant, and to Israel His beloved. Afterward He was seen upon earth, and dwelt among men* [6]. Why try to transform the Son of God into a second God? Learn to recognise and to confess the One True God. No second God is likened to Christ, and so can claim to be God. He is God from God by nature and by birth, for the Source of His Godhead is God. And, again, He is not a second God, for no other is likened unto Him; the truth that is in Him is nothing else than the truth of God. Why link together, in pretended devotion to the unity of God, true and false, base and genuine, unlike and unlike? The Father is God and the Son is God. God is in God; beside Him there is no God, and none other is likened unto Him so as to be God. If in these Two you shall recognise the Unity, instead of the solitude, of God, you will share the Church's faith, which confesses the Father in the Son. But if, in ignorance of the heavenly mystery, you insist that God is One in order to enforce the doctrine of His isolation, then you are a stranger to the knowledge of God, for you deny that God is in God.

[5] Exod. iii. 14.

[6] Baruch iii. 35—37.

BOOK VI.

1. It is with a full knowledge of the dangers and passions of the time that I have ventured to attack this wild and godless heresy, which asserts that the Son of God is a creature. Multitudes of Churches, in almost every province of the Roman Empire, have already caught the plague of this deadly doctrine; error, persistently inculcated and falsely claiming to be the truth, has become ingrained in minds which vainly imagine that they are loyal to the faith. I know how hardly the will is moved to a thorough recantation, when zeal for a mistaken cause is encouraged by the sense of numbers and confirmed by the sanction of general approval. A multitude under delusion can only be approached with difficulty and danger. When the crowd has gone astray, even though it know that it is in the wrong, it is ashamed to return. It claims consideration for its numbers, and has the assurance to command that its folly shall be accounted wisdom. It assumes that its size is evidence of the correctness of its opinions; and thus a falsehood which has found general credence is boldly asserted to have established its truth.

2. For my own part, it was not only the claim which my vocation has upon me, the duty of diligently preaching the Gospel which, as a bishop, I owe to the Church, that has led me on. My eagerness to write has increased with the increasing numbers endangered and enthralled by this heretical theory. There was a rich prospect of joy in the thought of multitudes who might be saved, if they could know the mysteries of the right faith in God, and abandon the blasphemous principles of human folly, desert the heretics and surrender themselves to God; if they would forsake the bait with which the fowler snares his prey, and soar aloft in freedom and safety, following Christ as Leader, prophets as instructors, apostles as guides, and accepting the perfect faith and sure salvation in the confession of Father and of Son. So would they, in obedience to the words of the Lord, *He that honoureth not the Son honoureth not the Father which hath sent Him* [1], be setting themselves to honour the Father, through honour paid to the Son.

3. For of late the infection of a mortal evil has gone abroad among mankind, whose ravages have dealt destruction and death on every hand. The sudden desolation of cities smitten, with their people in them, by earthquake to the ground, the terrible slaughter of recurring wars, the widespread mortality of an irresistible pestilence, have never wrought such fatal mischief as the progress of this heresy throughout the world. For God, unto Whom all the dead live, destroys those only who are self-destroyed. From Him Who is to be the Judge of all, Whose Majesty will temper with mercy the punishment allotted to the mistakes of ignorance, they who deny Him can expect not even judgment, but only denial.

4. For this mad heresy does deny; it denies the mystery of the true faith by means of statements borrowed from our confession, which it employs for its own godless ends. The confession of their misbelief, which I have already cited in an earlier book, begins thus:—" We confess one God, alone unmade, alone eternal, alone unoriginate, alone true, alone possessing immortality, alone good, alone mighty." Thus they parade the opening words of our own confession, which runs, "One God, alone unmade and alone unoriginate," that this semblance of truth may serve as introduction to their blasphemous additions. For, after a multitude of words in which an equally insincere devotion to the Son is expressed, their confession continues, "God's perfect creature, but not as one of His other creatures, His Handiwork, but not as His other works." And again, after an interval in which true statements are occasionally interspersed in order to veil their impious purpose of alleging, as by sophistry they try to prove, that He came into existence out of nothing, they add, "He created and established before the worlds, did not exist before He was born." And lastly, as though every point of their false doctrine, that He is to be regarded neither as Son nor as God, were guarded impregnably against assault, they continue:—"As to such phrases as *from Him*, and *from the womb*, an *I went out from the Father and am come*, if the be understood to denote that the Father e

---

[1] St. John v. 23.

tends a part and, as it were, a development of that one substance, then the Father will be of a compound nature and divisible and changeable and corporeal, according to them; and thus, as far as their words go, the incorporeal God will be subjected to the properties of matter." But, as we are now about to cover the whole ground once more, employing this time the language of the Gospels as our weapon against this most godless heresy, it has seemed best to repeat here, in the sixth book, the whole heretical document, though we have already given a full copy of it in the fourth[2], in order that our opponents may read it again, and compare it, point by point, with our reply, and so be forced, however reluctant and argumentative, by the clear teaching of the Evangelists and Apostles, to recognise the truth. The heretical confession is as follows:—

5. "We confess one God, alone unmade, alone eternal, alone unoriginate, alone possessing immortality, alone good, alone mighty, Creator, Ordainer and Disposer of all things, unchangeable and unalterable, righteous and good, of the Law and the Prophets and the New Testament. We believe that this God gave birth to the Only-begotten Son before all worlds, through Whom He made the world and all things, that He gave birth to Him not in semblance, but in truth, following His own will, so that He is unchangeable and unalterable, God's perfect Creature, but not as one of His other creatures, His Handiwork, but not as His other works; not, as Valentinus maintained, that the Son is a development of the Father, nor, as Manichæus has declared of the Son, a consubstantial part of the Father, nor, as Sabellius, who makes two out of One, Son and Father at once, nor, as Hieracas, a light from a light, or a lamp with two flames, nor, as if He was previously in being and afterwards born, or created afresh, to be a Son, a notion often condemned by thyself, blessed Pope, publicly in the Church, and in the assembly of the brethren. But, as we have affirmed, we believe that He was created by the will of God before times and worlds, and has His life and existence from the Father, Who gave Him to share His own glorious perfections. For, when the Father gave to Him the inheritance of all things, He did not thereby deprive Himself of attributes which are His without origination, He being the source of all things.

6. "So there are three Persons, Father, Son and Holy Ghost. God, for His part, is the Cause of all things, utterly unoriginate

and separate from all; while the Son, put forth by the Father outside time, and created and established before the worlds, did not exist before He was born, but, being born outside time before the worlds, came into being as the Only Son of the Only Father. For He is neither eternal, nor co-eternal, nor co-uncreate with the Father, nor has He an existence collateral with the Father, as some say who postulate two unborn principles. But God is before all things, as being indivisible and the beginning of all. Wherefore He is before the Son also, as indeed we have learnt from thee in thy public preaching. Inasmuch then as He has His being from God, and His glorious perfections, and His life, and is entrusted with all things, for this reason God is His Source. For He rules over Him, as being His God, since He is before Him. As to such phrases as *from Him*, and *from the womb*, and *I went out from the Father and am come*, if they be understood to denote that the Father extends a part and, as it were, a development of that one Substance, then the Father will be of a compound nature and divisible and changeable and corporeal, according to them; and thus, as far as their words go, the incorporeal God will be subjected to the properties of matter[3]."

7. Who can fail to see here the slimy windings of the serpent's track: the coiled adder, with forces concentrated for the spring, concealing the deadly weapon of its poisonous fangs within its folds? Presently we shall stretch it out and examine it, and expose the venom of this hidden head. For their plan is first to impress with certain sound statements, and then to infuse the poison of their heresy. They speak us fair, in order to work us secret harm. Yet, amid all their specious professions, I nowhere hear God's Son entitled God; I never hear sonship attributed to the Son. They say much about His having the name of Son, but nothing about His having the nature. That is kept out of sight, that He may seem to have no right even to the name. They make a show of unmasking other heresies to conceal the fact that they are heretics themselves. They strenuously assert that there is One only, One true God, to the end that they may strip the Son of God of His true and personal Divinity.

8. And therefore, although in the two last books I have proved from the teaching of the Law and Prophets that God and God, true God and true God, true God the Father

---

[2] Reading *quarto* instead of *primo*; but cf. v. § 3.

[3] The *Epistola Arii ad Alexandrum*, repeated from Book iv §§ 12. 13, where see the notes. The only difference in the text is that this copy omits *alone true*, at the beginning.

and true God the Son, must be confessed as One true God, by unity of nature and not by confusion of Persons, yet, for the complete presentation of the faith, I must also adduce the teaching of the Evangelists and Apostles. I must show from them that true God, the Son of God, is not of a different, an alien nature from that of the Father, but possesses the same Divinity while having a distinct existence through a true birth. And, indeed, I cannot think that any soul exists so witless as to fancy that, although we know God's self-revelations, yet we cannot understand them; that, if they can be understood, would not wish to understand, or would dream that human reason can devise improvements upon them. But before I begin to discuss the facts contained in these saving mysteries, I must first humble the pride with which these heretics rebuke the names of other heresies. I shall hold up to the light this ingenious cloak for their own impiety. I shall shew that this very means of concealing the deadliness of their teaching serves rather to reveal and betray it, and is a widely effectual warning of the true character of this honeyed poison.

9. For instance, these heretics would have it that the Son of God is not from God; that God was not born from God out of, and in, the nature of God. To this end, when they have solemnly borne witness to "One God, alone true," they refrain from adding "The Father." And then, in order to escape from confessing one true Godhead of Father and of Son by a denial of the true birth, they proceed, "Not, as Valentinus maintained, that the Son is a development of the Father." Thus they think to cast discredit upon the birth of God from God by calling it a "development," as though it were a form of the Valentinian heresy. For Valentinus was the author of foul and foolish imaginations; beside the chief God, he invented a whole household of deities and countless powers called æons, and taught that our Lord Jesus Christ was a development mysteriously brought about by a secret action of will. The faith of the Church, the faith of the Evangelists and Apostles, knows nothing of this imaginary development, sprung from the brain of a reckless and senseless dreamer. It knows nothing of the "Depth" and "Silence" and the thrice ten æons of Valentinus. It knows none but One God the Father, from Whom are all things, and One Jesus Christ, our Lord, through Whom are all things, Who is God born from God. But it occurred to them that He, in being born as God from God, neither withdrew anything from the Divinity of His Author nor was Himself born

other than God; that He became God not by a new beginning of Deity but by birth from the existing God; and that every birth appears, as far as human faculties can judge, to be a development, so that even that birth might be regarded as a development. And these considerations have induced them to make an attack upon the Valentinian heresy of development as a means of destroying faith in the true birth of the Son. For the experience of common life leads worldly wisdom to suppose that there is no great difference between a birth and a development. The mind of man, dull and slow to grasp the things of God, needs to be constantly reminded of the principle, which I have stated more than once[4], that analogies drawn from human experience are not of perfect application to the mysteries of Divine power; that their only value is that this comparison with material objects imparts to the spirit such a notion of heavenly things that we may rise, as by a ladder of nature, to an apprehension of the majesty of God. But the birth of God must not be judged by such development as takes place in human births. When One is born from One, God born from God, the circumstances of human birth enable us to apprehend the fact; but a birth which presupposes intercourse and conception and time and travail can give us no clue to the Divine method. When we are told that God was born from God, we must accept it as true that He was born, and be content with that. We shall, however, in the proper place discourse of the truth of the Divine birth, as the Gospels and the Apostles set it forth. Our present duty has been to expose this device of heretical ingenuity, this attack upon the true birth of Christ, concealed under the form of an attack upon a so-called development.

10. And then, in continuation of this same fraudulent assault upon the faith, their confession proceeds thus:—"Nor, as Manichæus has declared of the Son, a consubstantial part of the Father." They have already denied that He is a development, in order to escape from the admission of His birth; now they introduce, labelled with the name of Manichæus, the doctrine that the Son is a portion of the one Divine substance, and deny it, in order to subvert the belief in God from God. For Manichæus, the furious adversary of the Law and Prophets, the strenuous champion of the devil's cause and blind worshipper of the sun, taught that That which was in the Virgin's womb was a portion of the one Divine

4 E.g. i. § 10, iv. § 2; reading *non semel.*

substance, and that by the Son we must understand a certain piece of God's substance, which was cut off, and made its appearance in the flesh. And so they make the most of this heresy that in the birth of the Son there was a division of the one substance, and use it as a means of evading the doctrine of the birth of the Only-begotten, and the very name of the unity of substance. Because it is sheer blasphemy to speak of a birth resulting from division of the one substance, they deny any birth; all forms of birth are joined in the condemnation which they pass upon the Manichæan notion of birth by severance. And again, they abolish the unity of substance, both name and thing, because the heretics hold that the unity is divisible; and deny that the Son is God from God, by refusing to believe that He is truly possessed of the Divine nature. Why does this mad heresy profess a fictitious reverence, a senseless anxiety? The faith of the Church does, as these insane propounders of error remind us, condemn Manichæus, for she knows nothing of the Son as a portion. She knows Him as whole God from whole God, as One from One, not severed but born. She is assured that the birth of God involves neither impoverishment of the Begetter nor inferiority of the Begotten. If this be the Church's own imagining, reproach her with the follies of a wisdom falsely claimed; but if she have learned it from her Lord, confess that the Begotten knows the manner of His begetting. She has learnt from God the Only-begotten these truths, that Father and Son are One, and that in the Son the fulness of the Godhead dwells. And therefore she loathes this attribution to the Son of a portion of the one substance; and, because she knows that He was truly born of God, she worships the Son as rightful Possessor of true Divinity. But, for the present, let us defer our full answer to these several allegations, and hasten through the rest of their denunciations.

11. What follows is this:—" Nor, as Sabellius, who makes two out of One, Son and Father at once." Sabellius holds this in wilful blindness to the revelation of the Evangelists and Apostles. But what we see here is not one heretic honestly denouncing another. It is the wish to leave no point of union between Father and Son that prompts them to reproach Sabellius with his division of an indivisible Person; a division which does not result in the birth of a second Person, but cuts the One Person into two parts, one of which enters the Virgin's womb[5]. But we

confess a birth; we reject this confusion of two Persons in One, while yet we cleave to the Divine unity. That is, we hold that *God from God* means unity of nature; for that Being, Who, by a true birth from God, became God, can draw His substance from no other source than the Divine. And since He continues to draw His being, as He drew it at first, from God, He must remain true God for ever; and hence They Two are One, for He, Who is God from God, has no other than the Divine nature, and no other than the Divine origin. But the reason why this blasphemous Sabellian confusion of two Persons into One is here condemned is that they wish to rob the Church of her true faith in Two Persons in One God. But now I must examine the remaining instances of this perverted ingenuity, to save myself from the reputation of a censorious judge of sincere enquirers, moved rather by dislike than genuine fear. I shall shew, by the terms with which they wind up their confession, what is the deadly conclusion which they have skilfully contrived shall be its inevitable issue.

12. Their next clause is:—" Nor, as Hieracas, a light from a light, or a lamp with two flames, nor as if He was previously in being, and afterwards born, or created afresh, to be a Son." Hieracas ignores the birth of the Only-begotten, and, in complete unconsciousness of the meaning of the Gospel revelations, talks of two flames from one lamp. This symmetrical pair of flames, fed by the supply of oil contained in one bowl, is His illustration of the substance of Father and Son. It is as though that substance were something separate from Either Person, like the oil in the lamp, which is distinct from the two flames, though they depend upon it for their existence; or like the wick, of one material throughout and burning at both ends, which is distinct from the flames, yet provides them and connects them together. All this is a mere delusion of human folly, which has trusted to itself, and not to God, for knowledge. But the true faith asserts that God is born from God, as light from light, which pours itself forth without self-diminution, giving what it has yet having what it gave. It asserts that by His birth He was what He is, for as He is so was He born; that His birth was the gift of the existing Life, a gift which did not lessen the store from which it was taken; and that They Two are One, for He, from Whom He is born, is as Himself, and He that was born has neither another source nor another nature, for He is Light from Light. It is in order to draw men's faith away from this, the true doctrine, that

---

5 Reading *virginem*.

this lantern or lamp of Hieracas is cast in the teeth of those who confess Light from Light. Because the phrase has been used in an heretical sense, and condemned both now and in earlier days, they want to persuade us that there is no true sense in which it can be employed. Let heresy forthwith abandon these groundless fears, and refrain from claiming to be the protector of the Church's faith on the score of a reputation for zeal earned so dishonestly. For we allow nothing bodily, nothing lifeless, to have a place among the attributes of God; whatever is God is perfect God. In Him is nothing but power, life, light, blessedness, Spirit. That nature contains no dull, material elements; being immutable, it has no incongruities within it. God, because He is God, is unchangeable; and the unchangeable God begat God. Their bond of union is not, like that of two flames, two wicks of one lamp, something outside Themselves. The birth of the Only-begotten Son from God is not a prolongation in space, but a begetting; not an extension [6], but Light from Light. For the unity of light with light is a unity of nature, not unbroken continuation.

13. And again, what a wonderful example of heretical ingenuity is this :—" Nor as if He were previously in being, and afterwards born, or created afresh, to be a Son." God, since He was born from God, was assuredly not born from nothing, nor from things non-existent. His birth was that of the eternally living nature. Yet, though He is God, He is not identical with the pre-existing God; God was born from God Who existed before Him; in, and by, His birth He partook of the nature of His Source. If we are speaking words of our own, all this is mere irreverence; but if, as we shall prove, God Himself has taught us how to speak, then the necessity is laid upon us of confessing the Divine birth in the sense revealed by God. And it is this unity of nature in Father and in Son, this ineffable mystery of the living birth, which the madness of heresy is struggling to banish from belief, when it says, " Nor as if He were previously in being, and afterwards born, or created afresh, to be a Son." Now who is senseless enough to suppose that the Father ceased to be Himself; that the same Person Who had previously existed was afterwards born, or created afresh, to be the Son? That God disappeared, and that His disappearance was followed by an emergence in birth, when, in fact, that birth is evidence of the continuous existence of its Author? Or who is so insane

as to suppose that a Son can come into existence otherwise than through birth? Who so void of reason as to say that the birth of God resulted in anything else than in God being born? The abiding God was not born, but God was born from the abiding God; the nature bestowed in that birth was the very nature of the Begetter. And God by His birth, which was from God into God, received, because His was a true birth, not things new-created but things which were and are the permanent possession of God. Thus it is not the pre-existent God that was born; yet God was born, and began to exist, out of and with the properties of God. And thus we see how heresy, throughout this long prelude, has been treacherously leading up to this most blasphemous doctrine. Its object being to deny God the Only-begotten, it starts with what purports to be a defence of truth, to go on to the assertion that Christ is born not from God but out of nothing, and that His birth is due to the Divine counsel of creation from the non-existent.

14. And then again, after an interval designed to prepare us for what is coming, their heresy delivers this assault ;—" While the Son, put forth outside time, and created and established before the worlds, did not exist before He was born." This " He did not exist before He was born " is a form of words by which the heresy flatters itself that it gains two ends; support for its blasphemy, and a screen for itself if its doctrine be arraigned. A support for its blasphemy, because, if He did not exist before He was born, He cannot be of one nature with His eternal Origin. He must have His beginning out of nothing, if He have no powers but such as are coeval with His birth. And a screen for its heresy, for if this statement be condemned, it furnishes a ready answer. He that did exist, it will be said, could not be born; being in existence already, He could not possibly come into being by passing through the process of birth, for the very meaning of birth is the entry into existence of the being that is born. Fool and blasphemer! Who dreams of birth in the case of Him Who is the unborn and eternal? How can we think of God, *Who is* [7], being born, when being born implies the process of birth? It is the birth of God the Only-begotten from God His Father that you are striving to disprove, and it was your purpose to escape the confession of that truth by means of this " He did not exist before He was born;" the confession that God, from Whom the Son of God was born, did

---

exist eternally, and that it is from His abiding nature that God the Son draws His existence through birth. If, then, the Son is born from God, you must confess that His is a birth of that abiding nature; not a birth of the pre-existing God, but a birth of God from God the pre-existent.

15. But the fiery zeal of this heresy is such that it cannot restrain itself from passionate outbreak. In its effort to prove, in conformity with its assertion that He did not exist before He was born, that the Son was born from the non-existent, that is, that He was not born from God the Father to be God the Son by a true and perfect birth, it winds up its confession by rising in rage and hatred to the highest pitch of possible blasphemy :— "As to such phrases as *from Him*, and *from the womb*, and *I went out from the Father and am come*, if they be understood to denote that the Father extends a part, and, as it were, a development of that one substance, then the Father will be of a compound nature and divisible and changeable and corporeal, according to them; and thus, as far as their words go, the incorporeal God will be subjected to the properties of matter." The defence of the true faith against the falsehoods of heresy would indeed be a task of toil and difficulty, if it were needful for us to follow the processes of thought as far as they have plunged into the depths of godlessness. Happily for our purpose it is shallowness of thought that has engendered their eagerness to blaspheme. And hence, while it is easy to refute the folly, it is difficult to amend the fool, for he will neither think out right conclusions for himself, nor accept them when offered by another. Yet I trust that they who in pious ignorance, not in wilful folly bred of self-conceit, are enchained by error, will welcome correction. For our demonstration of the truth will afford convincing proof that heresy is nothing else than folly.

16. You said in your unreason, and you are still repeating to-day, ignorant that your wisdom is a defiance of God, "As to such phrases as *from Him*, and *from the womb*, and *I went out from the Father and am come*," I ask you, Are these phrases, or are they not, words of God? They certainly are His; and, since they are spoken by God about Himself, we are bound to accept them exactly as they were spoken. Concerning the phrases themselves, and the precise force of each, we shall speak in the proper place. For the present I will only put this question to the intelligence of every reader; When we see *From Himself*, are we to take it as equivalent to "From some one else," or to "From nothing," or are

we to accept it as the truth? It is not "From some one else," for it is *From Himself;* that is, His Godhead has no other source than God. It is not "From nothing," for it is *From Himself;* a declaration of the nature from which His birth is. It is not "Himself," but *From Himself;* a statement that They are related as Father and Son. And next, when the revelation *From the womb* is made, I ask whether we can possibly believe that He is born from nothing, when the truth of His birth is clearly indicated in terms borrowed from bodily functions. It is not because He has bodily members, that God records the generation of the Son in the words, *I bore Thee from the womb before the morning star* [8]. He uses language which assists our understanding to assure us that His Only-begotten Son was ineffably born of His own true Godhead. His purpose is to educate the faculties of men up to the knowledge of the faith, by clothing Divine verities in words descriptive of human circumstances. Thus, when He says, *From the womb*, He is teaching us that His Only-begotten was, in the Divine sense, born, and did not come into existence by means of creation out of nothing. And lastly, when the Son said, *I went forth from the Father and am come*, did He leave it doubtful whether His Divinity were, or were not, derived from the Father? He went out from the Father; that is, He had a birth, and the Father, and no other, gave Him that birth. He bears witness that He, from Whom He declares that He came forth, is the Author of His being. The proof and interpretation of all this shall be given hereafter.

17. But meanwhile let us see what ground these men have for the confidence with which they forbid us to accept as true the utterances of God concerning Himself; utterances, the authenticity of which they do not deny. What more grievous insult could be flung by human folly and insolence at God's self-revelation, than a condemnation of it, shewn in correction? For not even doubt and criticism will satisfy them. What more grievous than this profane handling and disputing of the nature and power of God? Than the presumption of saying that, if the Son is from God, then God is changeable and corporeal, since He has extended or developed a part of Himself to be His Son? Whence this anxiety to prove the immutability of God? We confess the birth, we proclaim the Only-begotten, for so God has taught us. You, in order to banish the birth and the Only-begotten from the faith of the Church, confront us with an unchangeable

<hr>

[8] Psalm cix. (cx.) 3.

God, incapable, by His nature, of extension or development. I could bring forward instances of birth, even in natures belonging to this world, which would refute this wretched delusion that every birth must be an extension. And I could save you from the error that a being can come into existence only at the cost of loss to that which begets it, for there are many examples of life transmitted, without bodily intercourse, from one living creature to another. But it would be impious to deal in evidences, when God has spoken; and the utmost excess of madness to deny His authority to give us a faith, when our worship is a confession that He alone can give us life. For if life comes through Him alone, must not He be the Author of the faith which is the condition of that life? And if we hold Him an untrustworthy witness concerning Himself, how can we be sure of the life which is His gift?

18. For you attribute, most godless of heretics, the birth of the Son to an act of creative will; you say that He is not born from God, but that He was created and came into existence by the choice of the Creator. And the unity of the Godhead, as you interpret it, will not allow Him to be God, for, since God remains One, the Son cannot retain His original nature in that state into which He has been born. He has been endowed, through creation, you say, with a substance different from the Divine, although, being in a sense the Only-begotten, He is superior to God's other creatures and works. You say that He was raised up, that He in His turn might perform the task committed to Him of raising up the created world; but that His birth did not confer upon Him the Divine nature. He was born, according to you, in the sense that He came into existence out of nothing. You call Him a Son, not because He was born from God, but because He was created by God. For you call to mind that God has deemed even holy men worthy of this title, and you consider that it is assigned to the Son in exactly the same sense in which the words, *I have said, Ye are Gods, and all of you sons of the Most High* [9], were spoken; that is, that He bears the name through the Giver's condescension, and not by right of nature. Thus, in your eyes, He is Son by adoption, God by gift of the title, Only-begotten by favour, Firstborn in date, in every sense a creature, in no sense God. For you hold that His generation was not a birth from God, in the natural sense, but the beginning of the life of a created substance.

19. And now, Almighty God, I first must pray Thee to forgive my excess of indignation, and permit me to address Thee; and next to grant me, dust and ashes as I am, yet bound in loyal devotion to Thyself, freedom of utterance in this debate. There was a time when I, poor wretch, was not; before my life and consciousness and personality began to exist. It is to Thy mercy that I owe my life; and I doubt not that Thou, in Thy goodness, didst give me my birth for my good, for Thou, Who hast no need of me, wouldst never have made the beginning of my life the beginning of evil. And then, when Thou hadst breathed into me the breath of life and endowed me with the power of thought, Thou didst instruct me in the knowledge of Thyself, by means of the sacred volumes given us through Thy servants Moses and the prophets. From them I learnt Thy revelation, that we must not worship Thee as a lonely God. For their pages taught me of God, not different from Thee in nature but One with Thee in mysterious unity of substance. I learnt that Thou art God in God, by no mingling or confusion but by Thy very nature, since the Divinity which is Thyself dwells in Him Who is from Thee. But the true doctrine of the perfect birth revealed that Thou, the Indwelt, and Thou, the Indweller, are not One Person, yet that Thou dost dwell in Him Who is from Thee. And the voices of Evangelists and Apostles repeat the lesson, and the very words which fell from the holy mouth of Thy Only-begotten are recorded, telling how Thy Son, God the Only-begotten from Thee the Unbegotten God, was born of the Virgin as man to fulfil the mystery of my salvation; how Thou dwellest in Him, by virtue of His true generation from Thyself, and He in Thee, because of the nature given in His abiding birth from Thee.

20. What is this hopeless quagmire of error into which Thou hast plunged me? For I have learnt all this and have come to believe it; this faith is so ingrained into my mind that I have neither the power nor the wish to change it. Why this deception of an unhappy man, this ruin of a poor wretch in body and soul, by deluding him with falsehoods concerning Thyself? After the Red Sea had been divided, the splendour on the face of Moses, descending from the Mount, deceived me. He had gazed, in Thy presence, upon all the mysteries of heaven, and I believed his words, dictated by Thee, concerning Thyself. And David, the man that was found after Thine own heart, has betrayed me to destruction, and Solomon, who was thought worthy of the gift of Divine Wisdom, and Isaiah, who saw the Lord of Sabaoth and prophesied, and Jeremiah consecrated in the womb, before he was fashioned,

---

9 Psalm lxxxi. (lxxxii.) 6.

to be the prophet of nations to be rooted out and planted in, and Ezekiel, the witness of the mystery of the Resurrection, and Daniel, the man beloved, who had knowledge of times, and all the hallowed band of the Prophets; and Matthew also, chosen to proclaim the whole mystery [1] of the Gospel, first a publican, then an Apostle, and John, the Lord's familiar friend, and therefore worthy to reveal the deepest secrets of heaven, and blessed Simon, who after his confession of the mystery was set to be the foundation-stone of the Church, and received the keys of the kingdom of heaven, and all his companions who spoke by the Holy Ghost, and Paul, the chosen vessel, changed from persecutor into Apostle, who, as a living man, abode under the deep sea [2] and ascended into the third heaven, who was in Paradise before his martyrdom, whose martyrdom was the perfect offering of a flawless faith; all have deceived me.

21. These are the men who have taught me the doctrines which I hold, and so deeply am I impregnated with their teaching that no antidote can release me from their influence. Forgive me, O God Almighty, my powerlessness to change, my willingness to die in this belief. These propagators of blasphemy, for so they seem to me, are a product of these last times, too modern to avail me. It is too late for them to correct the faith which I received from Thee. Before I had ever heard their names, I had put my trust in Thee, had received regeneration from Thee and become Thine, as still I am. I know that Thou art omnipotent; I look not that Thou shouldst reveal to me the mystery of that ineffable birth which is secret between Thyself and Thy Only-begotten. Nothing is impossible with Thee, and I doubt not that in begetting Thy Son Thou didst exert Thy full omnipotence. To doubt it would be to deny that Thou art omnipotent. For my own birth teaches me that Thou art good, and therefore I am sure that in the birth of Thine Only-begotten Thou didst grudge Him no good gift. I believe that all that is Thine is His, and all that is His is Thine. The creation of the world is sufficient evidence to me that Thou art wise; and I am sure that Thy Wisdom, Who is like Thee, must have been begotten from Thyself. And Thou art One God, in very truth, in my eyes; I will never believe that in Him, Who is God from Thee, there is ought that is not Thine. Judge me in Him, if it be sin in me that, through Thy Son, I have trusted too well in Law and Prophets and Apostles.

22. But this wild talk must cease; the rhetoric of exposing heretical folly must give place to the drudgery of framing arguments. So, I trust, those among them who are capable of being saved will set their faces towards the true faith taught by the Evangelists and Apostles, and recognise Him Who is the true Son of God, not by adoption but by nature. For the plan of our reply must be that of first proving that He is the Son of God, and therefore fully endowed with that Divine nature in the possession of which His Sonship consists. For the chief aim of the heresy, which we are considering, is to deny that our Lord Jesus Christ is true God and truly the Son of God. Many evidences assure us that our Lord Jesus Christ is, and is revealed to be, God the Only-begotten, truly the Son of God. His Father bears witness to it, He Himself asserts it, the Apostles proclaim it, the faithful believe it, devils confess it, Jews deny it, the heathen at His passion recognised it. The name of God is given Him in the right of absolute ownership, not because He has been admitted to joint use with others of the title. Every work and word of Christ transcends the power of those who bear the title of sons; the foremost lesson that we learn from all that is most prominent in His life is that He is the Son of God, and that He does not hold the name of Son as a title shared with a widespread company of friends.

23. I will not weaken the evidence for this truth by intermixing words of my own. Let us hear the Father, when the baptism of Jesus Christ was accomplished, speaking, as often, concerning His Only-begotten, in order to save us from being misled by His visible body into a failure to recognise Him as the Son. His words are:— *This is My beloved Son, in Whom I am well pleased* [3]. Is the truth presented here with dim outlines? Is the proclamation made in uncertain tones? The promise of the Virgin birth brought by the angel from the Holy Ghost, the guiding star of the Magi, the reverence paid Him in His cradle, the majesty, attested by the Baptist, of Him Who condescended to be baptized; all these are deemed an insufficient witness to His glory. The Father Himself speaks from heaven, and His words are, *This is My Son.* What means this evidence, not of titles, but of pronouns? Titles may be appended to names at will; pronouns are a sure indication of the persons to whom they refer. And here we have, in *This* and *My*, the clearest of indications. Mark the true meaning and the purpose of the words. You have read,

---

[1] Reading *et ad omne.* [2] Cf. 2 Cor. xi. 25. [3] St. Matt. iii. 17.

I have begotten sons, and have raised them up[4]; but you did not read there *My sons*, for He had begotten Himself those sons by division among the Gentiles, and from the people of His inheritance. And lest we should suppose that the name *Son* was given as an additional title to God the Only-begotten, to signify His share by adoption in some joint heritage, His true nature is expressed by the pronoun which gives the indubitable sense of ownership. I will allow you to interpret the word *Son*, if you will, as signifying that Christ is one of a number, if you can furnish an instance where it is said of another of that number, *This is My Son*. If, on the other hand, *This is My Son* be His peculiar designation, why accuse the Father, when He asserts His ownership, of making an unfounded claim? When He says *This is My Son*, may we not paraphrase His meaning thus:—" He has given to others the title of sons, but He Himself is My own Son; I have given the name to multitudes by adoption, but this Son is My very own. Seek not for another, lest you lose your faith that This is He. By gesture and by voice, by *This*, and *My*, and *Son*, I declare Him to you." And now what reasonable excuse remains for lack of faith? This, and nothing less than this, it was that the Father's voice proclaimed. He willed that we should not be left in ignorance of the nature of Him Who came to be baptized, that He might fulfil all righteousness; that by the voice of God we might recognise as the Son of God Him Who was visible as Man, to accomplish the mystery of our salvation.

24. And again, because the life of believers was involved in the confession of this faith,—for there is no other way to eternal life than the assurance that Jesus Christ, God the Only-begotten, is the Son of God—the Apostles heard once more the voice from heaven repeating the same message, in order to strengthen this life-giving belief, in negation of which is death. When the Lord, apparelled in splendour, was standing upon the Mountain, with Moses and Elias at His side, and the three Pillars of the churches who had been chosen as witnesses to the truth of the vision and the voice, the Father spoke thus from heaven:— *This is My beloved Son in Whom I am well pleased; hear Him*[5]. The glory which they saw was not sufficient attestation of His majesty; the voice proclaims, *This is My Son*. The Apostles cannot face the glory of God; mortal eyes grow dim in its presence. The trust of Peter and James and John fails them,

and they are prostrate in fear. But this solemn declaration, spoken from the Father's knowledge, comes to their relief; He is revealed as His Father's own true Son. And over and above the witness of *This* and *My* to His true Sonship, the words are uttered, *Hear Him*. It is the witness of the Father from heaven, in confirmation of the witness borne by the Son on earth; for we are bidden to *hear Him*. Though this recognition by the Father of the Son removes all doubt, yet we are bidden also to accept the Son's self-revelation. When the Father's voice commands us to shew our obedience by hearing Him, we are ordered to repose an absolute confidence in the words of the Son. Since, therefore, the Father has manifested His will in this message to us to hear the Son, let us hear what it is that the Son has told us concerning Himself.

25. I can conceive of no man so destitute of ordinary reason as to recognise in each of the Gospels confessions by the Son of the humiliation to which He has submitted in taking a body upon Him,—as for instance His words, often repeated, *Father, glorify Me*[6], and *Ye shall see the Son of Man*[7], and *The Father is greater than I*[8], and, more strongly, *Now is My soul troubled exceedingly*[9], and even this, *My God, My God, why hast Thou forsaken me*[9a]? and many more, of which I shall speak in due time,—and yet, in the face of these constant expressions of His humility, to charge Him with presumption because He calls God His Father, as when He says, *Every plant, which my heavenly Father hath not planted, shall be rooted up*[1], or, *Ye have made my Father's house an house of merchandise*[2]. I can conceive of no one foolish enough to regard His assertion, consistently made, that God is His Father, not as the simple truth sincerely stated from certain knowledge, but as a bold and baseless claim. We cannot denounce this constantly professed humility as an insolent demand for the rights of another, a laying of hands on what is not His own, an appropriation of powers which only God can wield. Nor, when He calls Himself the Son, as in, *For God sent not His Son into this world to condemn the world, but that the world through Him might be saved*[3], and in, *Dost thou believe on the Son of God*[4]? can we accuse Him of what would be an equal presumption with that of calling God His Father. But what else is it than such an accusation, if we allow to Jesus Christ the name of Son by adoption only? Do we not

4 Isai. i. 2.   5 St. Matt. xvii. 5.

6 St. John xvii. 5 ; cf. xiii. 32, xvi. 14, xvii. 1.
7 St. Matt. xxvi. 64.   8 St. John xiv. 28.   9 Ib. xii 27.
9a St. Matt. xxvii. 46.   1 Ib. xv. 13.   2 St. John ii. 16.
3 Ib. iii. 17.   4 Ib. ix. 35.

charge Him, when He calls God His Father, with daring to make a baseless claim? The Father's voice from heaven says *Hear Him.* I hear Him saying, *Father, I thank Thee* [5], and *Say ye that I blasphemed, because I said, I am the Son of God* [6]? If I may not believe these names, and assume that they mean what they assert, how am I to trust and to understand? No hint is given of an alternative meaning. The Father bears witness from heaven, *This is My Son;* the Son on His part speaks of *My Father's house,* and *My Father.* The confession of that name gives salvation, when faith is demanded in the question, *Dost thou believe on the Son of God?* The pronoun *My* indicates that the noun which follows belongs to the speaker. What right, I demand, have you heretics to suppose it otherwise? You contradict the Father's word, the Son's assertion; you empty language of its meaning, and distort the words of God into a sense they cannot bear. On you alone rests the guilt of this shameless blasphemy, that God has lied concerning Himself.

26. And thus, although nothing but a sincere belief that these names are truly significant,—that, when we read, *This is My Son* and *My Father,* the words really indicate Persons of Whom, and to Whom, they were spoken—can make them intelligible, yet, lest it be supposed that *Son* and *Father* are titles, the one merely of adoption, the other merely of dignity, let us see what are the attributes attached, by the Son Himself, to His name of Son. He says, *All things are delivered Me of My Father, and no one knoweth the Son but the Father, neither knoweth any the Father save the Son, and he to Whom the Son will reveal Him* [7]. Are the words of which we are speaking, *This is My Son* and *My Father,* consistent, or are they not, with *No one knoweth the Son but the Father, neither knoweth any the Father save the Son?* For it is only by witness mutually borne that the Son can be known through the Father, and the Father through the Son. We hear the voice from heaven; we hear also the words of the Son. We have as little excuse for not knowing the Son, as we have for not knowing the Father. All things are delivered unto Him; from this *All* there is no exception. If They possess an equal might; if They share an equal mutual knowledge, hidden from us; if these names of Father and Son express the relation between Them, then, I demand, are They not in truth what They are in name, wielders of the same omnipotence, shrouded in the same

impenetrable mystery? God does not speak in order to deceive. The Fatherhood of the Father, the Sonship of the Son, are literal truths. And now learn how facts bear out the verities which these names reveal.

27. The Son speaks thus:—*For the works which the Father hath given Me to finish, the same works which I do, bear witness of Me that the Father hath sent Me; and the Father Himself which hath sent Me hath borne witness of Me* [8]. God the Only-begotten proves His Sonship by an appeal not only to the name, but to the power; the works which He does are evidence that He has been sent by the Father. What, I ask, is the fact which these works prove? That He was sent. That He was sent, is used as a proof of His sonlike obedience and of His Father's authority: for the works which He does could not possibly be done by any other than Him Who is sent by the Father. Yet the evidence of His works fails to convince the unbelieving that the Father sent Him. For He proceeds, *And the Father Himself which hath sent Me hath borne witness of Me; and ye have neither heard His voice nor seen His shape* [9]. What was this witness of the Father concerning Him? Turn over the pages of the Gospels and review their contents. Read us other of the attestations given by the Father beside those which we have heard already; *This is My beloved Son, in Whom I am well pleased,* and *Thou art My Son.* John, who heard these words, needed them not, for He knew the truth already. It was for our instruction that the Father spoke. But this is not all. John in the wilderness was honoured with this revelation; the Apostles were not to be denied the same assurance. It came to them in the very same words, but with an addition which John did not receive. He had been a prophet from the womb, and needed not the commandment, *Hear Him.* Yes; I will hear Him, and will hear none but Him and His Apostle, who heard for my instruction. Even though the books contained no further witness, borne by the Father to the Son, than that He is the Son, I have, for confirmation of the truth, the evidence of His Father's works which He does. What is this modern slander that His name is a gift by adoption, His Godhead a lie, His titles a pretence? We have the Father's witness to His Sonship; by works, equal to the Father's, the Son bears witness to His own equality with the Father. Why such blindness to His obvious possession of the true Sonship which He both claims and displays. It is not through condescending

kindness on the part of God the Father that Christ bears the name of Son ; not by holiness that He has earned the title, as many have won it by enduring hardness in confession of the faith. Such sonship is not of right ; it is by a favour, worthy of Himself, that God bestows the title. But that which is indicated by *This*, and *My*, and *Hear Him*, is different in kind from the other. It is the true and real and genuine Sonship.

28. And indeed the Son never makes for Himself a lower claim than is contained in this designation, given Him by His Father. The Father's words, *This is My Son*, reveal His nature ; those which follow, *Hear Him*, are a summons to us to listen to the mystery and the faith which He came down from heaven to bring ; to learn that, if we would be saved, our confession must be a copy of His teaching. And in like manner the Son Himself teaches us, in words of His own, that He was truly born and truly came ;— *Ye neither know Me, nor know ye whence I am, for I am not come of Myself, but He that sent Me is true, Whom ye know not, but I know Him. for I am from Him, and He hath sent Me* [9a]. No man knows the Father ; the Son often assures us of this. The reason why He says that none knows Him but Himself, is that He is from the Father. Is it, I ask, as the result of an act of creation, or of a genuine birth, that He is from Him? If it be an act of creation, then all created things are from God. How then is it that none of them know the Father, when the Son says that the reason why He has this knowledge is that He is from Him? If He be created, not born, we shall observe in Him a resemblance to other beings who are from God. Since all, on this supposition, are from God, why is He not as ignorant of the Father as are the others? But if this knowledge of the Father be peculiar to Him, Who is from the Father, must not this circumstance also, that He is from the Father, be peculiar to Him? That is, must He not be the true Son born from the nature of God? For the reason why He alone knows God is that He alone is from God. You observe, then, a knowledge, which is peculiar to Himself, resulting from a birth which also is peculiar to Himself. You recognise that it is not by an act of creative power, but through a true birth, that He is from the Father ; and that this is why He alone knows the Father, Who is unknown to all other beings which are from Him.

29. But He immediately adds, *For I am from Him, and He hath sent Me*, to debar

heresy from the violent assumption that His being from God dates from the time of His Advent. The Gospel revelation of the mystery proceeds in a logical sequence ; first He is born, then He is sent. Similarly, in the previous declaration, we were told of ignorance [1], first as to Who He is, and then as to whence He is. For the words, *I am from Him, and He hath sent Me*, contain two separate statements, as also do the words, *Ye neither know Me, nor know ye whence I am.* Every man is born in the flesh ; yet does not universal consciousness make every man spring from God? How then can Christ assert that either He, or the source of His being, is unknown? He can only do so by assigning His immediate parentage to the ultimate Author of existence ; and, when He has done this, He can demonstrate their ignorance of God by their ignorance of the fact that He is the Son of God. Let the victims of this wretched delusion reflect upon the words, *Ye neither know Me, nor know ye whence I am.* All things, they argue, are from nothing ; they allow of no exception. They even dare to misrepresent God the Only-begotten as sprung from nothing. How can we explain this ignorance of Christ, and of the origin of Christ, on the part of the blasphemers? The very fact that, as the Scripture says, they know not whence He is, is an indication of that unknowable origin from which He springs. If we can say of a thing that it came into existence out of nothing, then we are not ignorant of its origin ; we know that it was made out of nothing, and this is a piece of definite knowledge. Now He Who came is not the Author of His own being ; but He Who sent Him is true, Whom the blasphemers know not. He it was Who sent Him ; and they know not that He was the Sender. Thus the Sent is from the Sender ; from Him Whom they know not as His Author. The reason why they know not Who Christ is, is that they know not from Whom He is. None can confess the Son who denies that He was born ; none can understand that He was born who has formed the opinion that He is from nothing. And indeed He is so far from being made out of nothing, that the heretics cannot tell whence He is.

30. They are blankly ignorant who separate the Divine name from the Divine nature ; ignorant, and content to be ignorant. But let them listen to the reproof which the Son inflicts upon unbelievers for their want of this knowledge, when the Jews said that God was their Father :—*If God were your Father, ye*

9a St. John vii. 28, 29　　　　　　　1 Reading *nesciretur*; cf. St. John vii. 28 in § 28.

would surely love Me; for I went forth from God, and am come; neither am I come of Myself, but He sent Me². The Son of God has here no word of blame for the devout confidence of those who combine the confession that He is true God, the Son of God, with their own claim to be God's sons. What He is blaming is the insolence of the Jews in daring to claim God as their Father, when meanwhile they did not love Him, the Son :— *If God were your Father, ye would surely love Me; for I went forth from God*. All, who have God for their Father through faith, have Him for Father through that same faith whereby we confess that Jesus Christ is the Son of God. But to confess that He is the Son in a sense which covers the whole company of saints; to say, in effect, that He is one of the sons of God ;—what faith is there in that? Are not all the rest, feeble created beings though they be, in that sense sons? In what does the eminence of a faith, which has confessed that Jesus Christ is the Son of God, consist, if He, as one of a multitude of sons, have the name only, and not the nature, of the Son? This unbelief has no love for Christ ; it is a mockery of the faith for these perverters of the truth to claim God as their Father. If He were their Father, they would love Christ because He had gone forth from God. And now I must enquire the meaning of this going forth from God. His going forth is obviously different from His coming, for the two are mentioned side by side in this passage, *I went forth from God and am come*. In order to elucidate the separate meanings of *I went forth from God and I am come*, He immediately subjoins, *Neither am I come of Myself, but He sent Me*. He tells us that He is not the source of His own existence in the words, *Neither am I come of Myself*. In them He tells us that He has proceeded forth a second time from God³, and has been sent by Him. But when He tells us that they who call God their Father must love Himself because He has gone forth from God, He makes His birth the reason for their love. *Went forth* carries back our thoughts to the incorporeal birth, for it is by love of Christ, Who was born from Him, that we must gain the right of devoutly claiming God for our Father. For when the Son says, *He that hateth Me hateth My Father also*⁴, this *My* is the assertion of a relation to the Father which is shared by none. On the other hand, He condemns the man who claims God as his Father, and loves not the

Son, as using a wrongful liberty with the Father's name ; since he who hates Him, the Son, must hate the Father also, and none can be devoted to the Father save those who love the Son. For the one and only reason which He gives for loving the Son is His origin from the Father. The Son, therefore, is from the Father, not by His Advent, but by His birth⁵ ; and love for the Father is only possible to those who believe that the Son is from Him.

31. To this the Lord's words bear witness ;—*I will not say unto you that I will pray the Father for you, for the Father Himself loveth you, because ye have loved Me, and believe that I went forth from God, and am come from the Father into this world*⁶. A complete faith concerning the Son, which accepts and loves the truth that He went forth from God, has access to the Father without need of His intervention. The confession that the Son was born and sent from God wins for it direct audience and love from Him. Thus the narrative of His birth and coming must be taken in the strictest and most literal sense. *I went forth from God*, He says, conveying that His nature is exactly that which was given Him by His birth ; for what being but God could go forth from God, that is, could enter upon existence by birth from Him? Then He continues, *And am come from the Father into this world*. To assure us that this going forth from God means birth from the Father, He tells us that He came from the Father into this world. The latter statement refers to His incarnation, the former to His nature. And again, His putting on record first the fact of His going forth from God, and then His coming from the Father, forbids us to identify the going with the coming. Coming from the Father, and going forth from God, are not synonymous ; they might be paraphrased as 'Birth' and 'Presence,' and are as different in meaning as these. It is one thing to have gone forth from God, and entered by birth upon a substantial existence ; another to have come from the Father into this world to accomplish the mysteries of our salvation.

32. In the order of our defence, as I have arranged it in my mind, this has seemed the most convenient place for proving that, thirdly⁷, the Apostles believed our Lord Jesus Christ to be the Son of God, not merely in name but in nature, not by adoption but by birth.

---

² St. John viii. 42.   3 i.e. in the Incarnation.
4 St. John xv. 23.

5 *Nativitas* here, as normally in Hilary, means the eternal generation.
6 St. John xvi. 26—28.
7 Firstly, the Father's witness is given in §§ 23—27 ; secondly, the Son's, §§ 28—31 ; thirdly, that of the Apostles, §§ 32—46.

It is true that there remain unmentioned many and most weighty words of God the Only-begotten concerning Himself, in which the truth of His Divine birth is set so clearly forth as to silence any whisper of objection. Yet since it would be unwise to burden the reader's mind with an accumulation of evidence, and ample proof has been already given of the genuineness of His birth, I will hold back the remainder of His utterances till later stages of our enquiry. For we have so arranged the course of our argument that now, after hearing the Father's witness and the Son's self-revelation, we are to be instructed by the Apostles' faith in the true and, as we must confess, the truly born Son of God. We must see whether they could find in the words of the Lord, *I went forth from God*, any other meaning than this, that there was in Him a birth of the Divine nature.

33. After many dark sayings, spoken in parables by Him Whom they already knew as the Christ foretold by Moses and the Prophets, Whom Nathanael had confessed as the Son of God and King of Israel, Who had Himself reproached Philip, in his question about the Father, for not perceiving, by the works which He did, that the Father was in Him and He in the Father; after He had already often taught them that He was sent from the Father; still, it was not till they had heard Him assert that He had gone forth from God that they confessed, in the words which immediately follow in the Gospel;— *His disciples say unto Him, Now speakest Thou plainly, and speakest no proverb. Now therefore we are sure that Thou knowest all things, and needest not that any man should ask Thee ; by this we believe that Thou wentest forth from God* [8]. What was there so marvellous in this form of words, *Went forth from God*, which He had used? Had ye seen, O holy and blessed men, who for the reward of your faith have received the keys of the kingdom of heaven and power to bind and to loose in heaven and earth, works so great, so truly Divine, wrought by our Lord Jesus Christ, the Son of God ; and do ye yet profess that it was not until He had first told you that He had gone forth from God that ye attained the knowledge of the truth? And yet ye had seen water at the marriage turned into the marriage wine ; one nature becoming another nature, whether it were by change, or by development, or by creation. And your hands had broken up the five loaves into a meal for that great multitude, and when all were satisfied ye had found that twelve baskets were needed to contain the fragments of the loaves ; a small quantity of matter, in the process of relieving hunger, had multiplied into a great quantity of matter of the same nature. And ye had seen withered hands recover their suppleness, the tongues of dumb men loosened into speech, the feet of the lame made swift to run, the eyes of the blind endowed with vision, and life restored to the dead. Lazarus, who stank already, had risen to his feet at a word. He was summoned from the tomb and instantly came forth, without a pause between the word and its fulfilment. He was standing before you, a living man, while yet the air was carrying the odour of death to your nostrils. I speak not of other exertions of His mighty, His Divine powers. And is it, in spite of all this, only after ye heard Him say, *I went forth from God*, that ye understood Who He is that had been sent from heaven? Is this the first time that the truth had been told you without a proverb? The first time that the powers of His nature made it manifest to you that He went forth from God? And this in spite of His silent scrutiny of the purposes of your will, of His needing not to ask you concerning anything as though He were ignorant, of His universal knowledge? For all these things, done in the power and in the nature of God, are evidence that He must have gone forth from God.

34. By this the holy Apostles did not understand that He had gone forth, in the sense of having been sent, from God. For they had often heard Him confess, in His earlier discourses, that He was sent ; but what they hear now is the express statement that He had gone forth from God. This opens their eyes to perceive from His works His Divine nature. The fact that He had gone forth from God makes clear to them His true Divinity, and so they say, *Now therefore we are sure that Thou knowest all things, and needest not that any man should ask Thee ; by this we believe that Thou wentest forth from God*. The reason why they believe that He went forth from God is that He both can, and does, perform the works of God. Their perfect assurance of His Divine nature is the result of their knowledge, not that He is come from God, but that He did go forth from God. Accordingly we find that it is this truth, now heard for the first time, which clenches their faith. The Lord had made two statements ; *I went forth from God*, and *I am come from the Father into this world*. One of these, *I am come from the Father into this world*, they had often heard, and it awakens no surprise. But their reply makes it manifest that they now believe and understand the other, that is, *I went forth*

---

8 St. John xvi. 29, 30.

from God. Their answer, *By this we believe that Thou wentest forth from God,* is a response to it, and to it only; they do not add, 'And art come from the Father into this world.' The one statement is welcomed with a declaration of faith; the other is passed over in silence. The confession was wrung from them by the sudden presentation of a new truth, which convinced their reason and constrained them to avow their certainty. They knew already that He, like God, could do all things; but His birth, which accounted for that omnipotence, had not been revealed. They knew that He had been sent from God, but they knew not that He had gone forth from God. Now at last, taught by this utterance to understand the ineffable and perfect birth of the Son, they confess that He had spoken to them without a proverb.

35. For God is not born from God by the ordinary process of a human childbirth; this is no case of one being issuing from another by the exertion of natural forces. That birth is pure and perfect and stainless; indeed, we must call it rather a proceeding forth than a birth. For it is One from One; no partition, or withdrawing, or lessening, or efflux, or extension, or suffering of change, but the birth of living nature from living nature. It is God going forth from God, not a creature picked out to bear the name of God. His existence did not take its beginning out of nothing, but went forth from the Eternal; and this going forth is rightly entitled a birth, though it would be false to call it a beginning. For the proceeding forth of God from God is a thing entirely different from the coming into existence of a new substance. And though our apprehension of this truth, which is ineffable, cannot be defined in words, yet the teaching of the Son, as He reveals to us that He went forth from God, imparts to it the certainty of an assured faith.

36. A belief that the Son of God is Son in name only, and not in nature, is not the faith of the Gospels and of the Apostles. If this be a mere title, to which adoption is His only claim; if He be not the Son in virtue of having proceeded forth from God, whence, I ask, was it that the blessed Simon Bar-Jona confessed to Him, *Thou art the Christ, the Son of the living God*[9]? Because He shared with all mankind the power of being born as one of the sons of God through the sacrament of regeneration? If Christ be the Son of God only in this titular way, what was the revelation made to Peter, not by flesh and blood, but by the Father in heaven?

What praise could he deserve for making a declaration which was universally applicable? What credit was due to Him for stating a fact of general knowledge? If He be Son by adoption, wherein lay the blessedness of Peter's confession, which offered a tribute to the Son to which, in that case, He had no more title than any member of the company of saints? The Apostle's faith penetrates into a region closed to human reasoning. He had, no doubt, often heard, *He that receiveth you receiveth Me, and He that receiveth Me receiveth Him that sent Me*[1]. Hence he knew well that Christ had been sent; he had heard Him, Whom he knew to have been sent, making the declaration, *All things are delivered unto Me of the Father, and no one knoweth the Son but the Father, neither knoweth any one the Father save the Son*[2]. What then is this truth, which the Father now reveals to Peter, which receives the praise of a blessed confession? It cannot have been that the names of 'Father' and 'Son' were novel to him; he had heard them often. Yet he speaks words which the tongue of man had never framed before:—*Thou art the Christ, the Son of the living God.* For though Christ, while dwelling in the body, had avowed Himself to be the Son of God, yet now for the first time the Apostle's faith had recognised in Him the presence of the Divine nature. Peter is praised not merely for his tribute of adoration, but for his recognition of the mysterious truth; for confessing not Christ only, but Christ the Son of God. It would clearly have sufficed for a payment of reverence, had he said, *Thou art the Christ,* and nothing more. But it would have been a hollow confession, had Peter only hailed Him as Christ, without confessing Him the Son of God. And so his words *Thou art*[3] declare that what is asserted of Him is strictly and exactly true to His nature. Next, the Father's utterance, *This is My Son,* had revealed to Peter that he must confess *Thou art the Son of God,* for in the words *This is,* God the Revealer points Him out, and the response, *Thou art,* is the believer's welcome to the truth. And this is the rock of confession whereon the Church is built. But the perceptive faculties of flesh and blood cannot attain to the recognition and confession of this truth. It is a mystery, Divinely revealed, that Christ must be not only named, but believed, the Son of God. Was it only the Divine name; was it not rather the Divine nature that was revealed to Peter? If it were the name, he had

[1] St. Matt. x. 40.   [2] Ib. xi. 27.
[3] St. Hilary takes them as an allusion to the *I am (qui est)* of Exodus iii. 14.

heard it often from the Lord, proclaiming Himself the Son of God. What honour, then, did he deserve for announcing the name? No; it was not the name; it was the nature, for the name had been repeatedly proclaimed.

37. This faith it is which is the foundation of the Church; through this faith the gates of hell cannot prevail against her. This is the faith which has the keys of the kingdom of heaven. Whatsoever this faith shall have loosed or bound on earth shall be loosed or bound in heaven. This faith is the Father's gift by revelation; even the knowledge that we must not imagine a false Christ, a creature made out of nothing, but must confess Him the Son of God, truly possessed of the Divine nature. What blasphemous madness and pitiful folly is it, that will not heed the venerable age and faith of that blessed martyr, Peter himself, for whom the Father was prayed that his faith might not fail in temptation; who twice repeated the declaration of love for God that was demanded of him, and was grieved that he was tested by a third renewal of the question, as though it were a doubtful and wavering devotion, and then, because this third trial had cleansed him of his infirmities, had the reward of hearing the Lord's commission, *Feed My sheep*, a third time repeated; who, when all the Apostles were silent, alone recognised by the Father's revelation the Son of God, and won the pre-eminence of a glory beyond the reach of human frailty by his confession of his blissful faith! What are the conclusions forced upon us by the study of his words? He confessed that Christ is the Son of God; you, lying bishop of the new apostolate, thrust upon us your modern notion that Christ is a creature, made out of nothing. What violence is this, that so distorts the glorious words? The very reason why he is blessed is that he confessed the Son of God. This is the Father's revelation, this the foundation of the Church, this the assurance of her permanence. Hence has she the keys of the kingdom of heaven, hence judgment in heaven and judgment on earth. Through revelation Peter learnt the mystery hidden from the beginning of the world, proclaimed the faith, published the Divine nature, confessed the Son of God. He who would deny all this truth and confess Christ a creature, must first deny the apostleship of Peter, his faith, his blessedness, his episcopate, his martyrdom. And when he has done all this, he must learn that he has severed himself from Christ; for it was by confessing Him that Peter won these glories.

38. Do you think, wretched heretic of to-day, that Peter would have been the more blessed now, if he had said, 'Thou art Christ, God's perfect creature, His handiwork, though excelling all His other works. Thy beginning was from nothing, and through the goodness of God, Who alone is good, the name of Son has been given Thee by adoption, although in fact Thou wast not born from God?' What answer, think you, would have been given to such words as these, when this same Peter's reply to the announcement of the Passion, *Be it far from Thee, Lord; this shall not be*, was rebuked with, *Get thee behind Me, Satan, thou art an offence unto Me*[4]? Yet[5] Peter could plead his human ignorance in extenuation of his guilt, for as yet the Father had not revealed all the mystery of the Passion; still, mere defect of faith was visited with this stern condemnation. Now, why was it that the Father did not reveal to Peter your true confession, this faith in an adopted creature? I fancy that God must have grudged him the knowledge of the truth; that He wanted to postpone it to a later age, and keep it as a novelty for your modern preachers. Yes; you may have a change of faith, if the keys of heaven are changed. You may have a change of faith, if there is a change in that Church against which the gates of hell shall not prevail. You may have a change of faith, if there shall be a fresh apostolate, binding and loosing in heaven what it has bound and loosed on earth. You may have a change of faith, if another Christ the Son of God, beside the true Christ, shall be preached. But if that faith which confesses Christ as the Son of God, and that faith only, received in Peter's person every accumulated blessing, then perforce the faith which proclaims Him a creature, made out of nothing, holds not the keys of the Church and is a stranger to the apostolic faith and power. It is neither the Church's[6] faith, nor is it Christ's.

39. Let us therefore cite every example of a statement of the faith made by an Apostle. All of them, when they confess the Son of God, confess Him not as a nominal and adoptive Son, but as Son by possession of the Divine nature. They never degrade Him to the level of a creature, but assign Him the splendour of a true birth from God. Let John speak to us, while he is waiting, just as he is, for the coming of the Lord; John, who was left behind and appointed to a destiny hidden in the counsel of God, for he is not told that he shall not die, but only that he shall tarry. Let him speak to us in his own familiar voice:—*No one hath seen God at*

---

4 St. Matt. xvi. 22, 23.   5 Omitting *nec.*
6 Reading *ecclesiæ.*

any time, except the Only-begotten Son, Which is in the bosom of the Father [7]. It seemed to him that the name of Son did not set forth with sufficient distinctness His true Divinity, unless he gave an external support to the peculiar majesty of Christ by indicating the difference between Him and all others. Hence he not only calls Him the Son, but adds the further designation of the *Only-begotten*, and so cuts away the last prop from under this imaginary adoption. For the fact that He is Only-begotten is proof positive of His right to the name of Son.

40. I defer the consideration of the words, *which is in the bosom of the Father*, to a more appropriate place. My present enquiry is into the sense of *Only-begotten*, and the claim upon us which that sense may make. And first let us see whether the word mean, as you assert, a perfect creature of God ; *Only-begotten* being equivalent to perfect, and *Son* a synonym for creature. But John described the Only-begotten Son as God, not as a perfect creature. His words, *Which is in the bosom of the Father*, shew that he anticipated these blasphemous designations ; and, indeed, he had heard his Lord say, *For God so loved the world that He gave His Only-begotten Son, that whosoever believeth in Him should not perish but have everlasting life* [8]. God, Who loved the world, gave His Only-begotten Son as a manifest token of His love. If the evidence of His love be this, that He bestowed a creature upon creatures, gave a worldly being on the world's behalf, granted one raised up from nothing for the redemption of objects equally raised up from nothing, this cheap and petty sacrifice is a poor assurance of His favour towards us. Gifts of price are the evidence of affection : the greatness of the surrender of the greatness of the love. God, Who loved the world, gave not an adopted Son, but His own, His Only-begotten. Here is personal interest, true Sonship, sincerity ; not creation, or adoption, or pretence. Herein is the proof of His love and affection, that He gave His own, His Only-begotten Son.

41. I appeal not now to any of the titles which are given to the Son ; there is no loss in delay when it is the result of an embarrassing abundance of choice. My present argument is that a successful result implies a sufficient cause ; some clear and cogent motive must underlie every effectual performance. And so the Evangelist has been obliged to reveal his motive in writing. Let us see what is the purpose which he confesses ;—*But these things are written that ye may believe that Jesus is the Christ, the Son of God* [9]. The one reason which he alleges for writing his Gospel is that all may believe that Jesus is the Christ, the Son of God. If it be sufficient for salvation to believe that He is the Christ, why does he add *The Son of God?* But if the true faith be nothing less than the belief that Christ is not merely Christ, but Christ the Son of God, then assuredly the name of Son is not attached to Christ as a customary appendage due to adoption, seeing that it is essential to salvation. If then salvation consists in the confession of the name, must not the name express the truth? If the name express the truth, by what authority can He be called a creature? It is not the confession of a creature, but the confession of the Son, which shall give us salvation.

42. To believe, therefore, that Jesus Christ is the Son of God is true salvation, is the acceptable service of an unfeigned faith. For we have no love within us towards God the Father except through faith in the Son. Let us hear Him speaking to us in the words of the Epistle ;—*Every one that loveth the Father loveth Him that is born from Him* [1]. What, I ask, is the meaning of being born from Him? Can it mean, perchance, being created by Him? Does the Evangelist lie in saying that He was born from God, while the heretic more correctly teaches that He was created? Let us all listen to the true character of this teacher of heresy. It is written, *He is antichrist, that denieth the Father and the Son* [2]. What will you do now, champion of the creature, conjurer up of a novel Christ out of nothing? Hear the title which awaits you, if you persist in your assertion. Or do you think that perhaps you may still describe the Father and the Son as Creator and Creature, and yet by an ingenious ambiguity of language escape being recognised as antichrist? If your confession embraces a Father in the true sense, and a Son in the true sense, then I am a slanderer, assailing you with a title of infamy which you have not deserved. But if in your confession all Christ's attributes are spurious and nominal, and not His own, then learn from the Apostle the right description of such a faith as yours ; and hear what is the true faith which believes in the Son. The words which follow are these ;—*He that denieth the Son, the same hath not the Father : he that confesseth the Son hath both the Son and the Father* [3]. He that denies the Son is destitute of the Father ; he that confesses and has the Son has the Father also. What room is there here for adoptive names? Does not every word tell of the Divine nature? Learn how completely that nature is present.

---

7 St. John i. 18.   8 Ib. iii. 16.   9 St. John xx. 31.   1 1 John v 1.   2 Ib. ii. 22.
3 Ib. 23.

43. John speaks thus;—*For we know that the Son of God is come, and was incarnate for us, and suffered, and rose again from the dead and took us for Himself, and gave us a good understanding that we may know Him that is true, and may be in His true Son Jesus Christ. He is true and is life eternal and our resurrection*[4]. Wisdom doomed to an evil end, void of the Spirit of God, destined to possess the spirit and the name of Antichrist, blind to the truth that the Son of God came to fulfil the mystery of our salvation, and unworthy in that blindness to perceive the light of that sovereign knowledge! For this wisdom asserts that Jesus Christ is no true Son of God, but a creature of His, Who bears the Divine name by adoption. In what dark oracle of hidden knowledge was the secret learnt? To whose research do we owe this, the great discovery of the day? Were you he that lay upon the bosom of the Lord? You he to whom in the familiar intercourse of love He revealed the mystery? Was it you that alone followed Him to the foot of the Cross? And while He was charging you to receive Mary as your Mother, did He teach you this secret, as the token of His peculiar love for yourself? Or did you run to the Sepulchre, and reach it sooner even than Peter, and so gain this knowledge there? Or was it amid the throngs of angels, and sealed books whose clasps none can open, and manifold influences of the signs of heaven, and unknown songs of the eternal choirs, that the Lamb, your Guide, revealed to you this godly doctrine, that the Father is no Father, the Son no Son, nor nature nature, nor truth truth? For you transform all these into lies. The Apostle, by that most excellent knowledge that was granted him, speaks of the Son of God as true. You assert His creation, proclaim His adoption, deny His birth. While the true Son of God is eternal life and resurrection to us, for him, in whose eyes He is not true, there is neither eternal life nor resurrection. And this is the lesson taught by John, the disciple beloved of the Lord.

44. And the persecutor, who was converted to be an Apostle and a chosen vessel, delivers the very same message. What discourse is there of his which does not presuppose the confession of the Son? What Epistle of his that does not begin with a confession of that mysterious truth? When he says, *We were reconciled to God by the death of His Son*[5], and, *God sent His Son to be the likeness of the flesh of sin*[6], and again, *God is faithful, by Whom ye were called unto the fellowship of His Son*[7], is any loophole left for heretical misrepresentation? *His Son, Son of God;* so we read, but nothing is said of His adoption, or of God's creature. The name expresses the nature; He is God's Son, and therefore the Sonship is true. The Apostle's confession asserts the genuineness of the relation. I see not how the Divine nature of the Son could have been more completely stated. That Chosen Vessel has proclaimed in no weak or wavering voice that Christ is the Son of Him Who, as we believe, is the Father. The Teacher of the Gentiles, the Apostle of Christ, has left us no uncertainty, no opening for error in his presentation of the doctrine. He is quite clear upon the subject of children by adoption; of those who by faith attain so to be and so to be named. In his own words, *For as many as are led by the Spirit of God, they are the sons of God. For ye have not received the spirit of bondage again unto fear, but ye have received the Spirit of adoption, whereby we cry, Abba, Father*[8]. This is the name granted to us, who believe, through the sacrament of regeneration; our confession of the faith wins us this adoption. For our work done in obedience to the Spirit of God gives us the title of sons of God. *Abba, Father,* is the cry which we raise, not the expression of our essential nature. For that essential nature of ours is untouched by that tribute of the voice. It is one thing for God to be addressed as Father; another thing for Him to be the Father of His Son.

45. But now let us learn what is this faith concerning the Son of God, which the Apostle holds. For though there is no single discourse, among the many which he delivered concerning the Church's doctrine, in which he mentions the Father without also making confession of the Son, yet, in order to display the truth of the relation which that name conveys with the utmost definiteness of which human language is capable, he speaks thus :— *What then? If God be for us, who can be against us? Who spared not His own Son, but delivered Him up for us*[9]. Can *Son*, by any remaining possibility, be a title received through adoption, when He is expressly called God's own Son? For the Apostle, wishing to make manifest the love of God towards us, uses a kind of comparison, to enable us to estimate how great that love is, when He says that it was His own Son Whom God did not

---

4 1 John v. 20. The long interpolation, which resembles a creed, is only found twice elsewhere (Codex Toletanus and the so-called Speculum of Augustine), and, though evidently from the Greek, never in that language.
5 Rom. v. 10.

6 1 John viii. 3.   7 1 Cor. i. 9.   8 Rom. viii. 14, 15.
                        9 Ib. 31, 32.

spare. He suggests the thought that this was no sacrifice of an adopted Son, on behalf of those whom He purposed to adopt, of a creature for creatures, but of His Son for strangers, His own Son for those to whom He had willed to give a share in the name of sons. Seek out the full import of the term, that you may understand the extent of the love. Consider the meaning of *own;* mark the genuineness of the Sonship which it implies. For the Apostle now describes Him as God's own Son; previously he had often spoken of Him as God's Son, or Son of God. And though many manuscripts, through a want of apprehension on the part of the translators, read in this passage *His Son,* instead of *His own Son,* yet the original Greek, the tongue in which the Apostle wrote, is more exactly rendered by *His own* than by *His* [1]. And though the casual reader may discern no great difference between *His own* and *His,* yet the Apostle, who in all his other statements had spoken of *His Son,* which is, in the Greek, τὸν ἑαυτοῦ υἱόν, in this passage uses the words ὅς γε τοῦ ἰδίου υἱοῦ οὐκ ἐφείσατο, that is, *Who spared not His own Son,* expressly and emphatically indicating His true Divine nature. Previously he had declared that through the Spirit of adoption there are many sons; now his object is to point to God's own Son, God the Only-begotten.

46. This is no universal and inevitable error; they who deny the Son cannot lay the fault upon their ignorance, for ignorance of the truth which they deny is impossible. They describe the Son of God as a creature who came into being out of nothing. If the Father has never asserted this, nor the Son confirmed it, nor the Apostles proclaimed it, then the daring which prompts their allegation is bred not of ignorance, but of hatred for Christ. When the Father says of His Son, *This is* [2], and the Son of Himself, *It is He that talketh with Thee* [3], and when Peter confesses *Thou art* [4], and John assures us, *This is the true God* [5], and Paul is never weary of proclaiming Him as God's own Son, I can conceive of no other motive for this denial than hatred. The plea of want of familiarity with the subject cannot be urged in extenuation of their guilt. It is the suggestion of that Evil One, uttered now through these prophets and forerunners of his coming; he will utter it himself hereafter when he comes as Antichrist. He is using this novel engine of assault to shake us in our saving confession of the faith. His first object is to pluck from our hearts the confident assurance of the Divine nature of the Son; next, he would fill our minds with the notion of Christ's adoption, and leave no room for the memory of His other claims. For they who hold that Christ is but a creature, must regard Christ as Antichrist, since a creature cannot be God's own Son, and therefore He must lie in calling Himself the Son of God. Hence also they who deny that Christ is the Son of God must have Antichrist for their Christ.

47. What is the hope of which this futile passion of yours is in pursuit? What is the assurance of your salvation which emboldens you with blasphemous licence of tongue to maintain that Christ is a creature, and not a Son? It was your duty to know this mystery from the Gospels, and to hold the knowledge fast. For though the Lord can do all things, yet He resolved that every one who prays for His effectual help must earn it by a true confession of Himself. Not, indeed, that the suppliant's confession could augment the power of Him, Who is the Power of God; but the earning was to be the reward of faith. So, when He asked Martha, who was entreating Him for Lazarus, whether she believed that they who had believed in Him should not die eternally, her answer expressed the trust of her soul;— *Yea, Lord, I believe that Thou art the Christ, the Son of God, Who art come into this world* [6]. This confession is eternal life; this faith has immortality. Martha, praying for her brother's life, was asked whether she believed this. She did so believe. What life does the denier expect, from whom does he hope to receive it, when this belief, and this only, is eternal life? For great is the mystery of this faith, and perfect the blessedness which is the fruit of this confession.

48. The Lord had given sight to a man blind from his birth; the Lord of nature had removed a defect of nature. Because this blind man had been born for the glory of God, that God's work might be made manifest in the work of Christ, the Lord did not delay till the man had given evidence of his faith by a confession of it. But though he knew not at the time Who it was that had bestowed the great gift of eyesight, yet afterwards he earned a knowledge of the faith. For it was not the dispelling of his blindness that won him eternal life. And so, when the man was already healed and had suffered

---

[1] Yet *His own (proprius)* is on the whole characteristic of the Old Latin MSS. still in existence. This passage is important as indicating the independence of scribes. Hilary seems to take it for granted that each will modify at his discretion the text from which he is copying.
[2] St. Matt. iii. 17, again an allusion to Exod. iii. 14.
[3] St. John ix. 37. [4] St. Matt. xvi. 16; cf. Exod. iii. 14.
[5] 1 John v. 20.

[6] St. John xi. 27.

ejection from the synagogue, the Lord put to him the question, *Dost thou believe on the Son of God[7]?* This was to save him from the thought of loss, in exclusion from the synagogue, by the certainty that confession of the true faith had restored him to immortality. When the man, his soul still unenlightened, made answer, *Who is He, Lord, that I may believe on Him[8]?* The Lord's reply was, *Thou hast both seen Him, and it is He that talketh with thee.* For He was minded to remove the ignorance of the man whose sight he had restored, and whom He was now enriching with the knowledge of so glorious a faith. Does the Lord demand from this man, as from others, who prayed Him to heal them, a confession of faith as the price of their recovery? Emphatically not. For the blind man could already see when he was thus addressed. The Lord asked the question in order to receive the answer, *Lord, I believe[9].* The faith which spoke in that answer was to receive not sight, but life[1]. And now let us examine carefully the force of the words. The Lord asks of the man, *Dost thou believe on the Son of God?* Surely, if a simple confession of Christ, leaving His nature in obscurity, were a complete expression of the faith, the terms of the question would have been, 'Dost thou believe in Christ?' But in days to come almost every heretic was to make a parade of that name, confessing Christ and yet denying that He is the Son: and therefore He demands, as the condition of faith, that we should believe in what is peculiar to Himself, that is, in His Divine Sonship. What is the profit of faith in the Son of God, if it be faith in a creature, when He requires of us faith in Christ, not the creature, but the Son, of God.

49. Did devils fail to understand the full meaning of this name of Son? For we are valuing the heretics at their true worth if we refute them no longer by the teaching of Apostles, but out of the mouth of devils. They cry, and cry often, *What have I to do with Thee, Jesus, Thou Son of God most High[2]?* Truth wrung this confession from them against their will; their reluctant obedience is a witness to the force of the Divine nature within Him. When they fly from the bodies they have long possessed, it is His might that conquers them; their confession of His nature is an act of reverence. These transactions display Christ as the Son of God both in power and in name. Can you hear, amid all these cries of devils confessing Him, Christ once styled a creature, or God's condescension in adopting Him once named?

50. If you will not learn Who Christ is from those that know Him, learn it at least from those that know Him not. So shall the confession, which their ignorance is forced to make, rebuke your blasphemy. The Jews did not recognise Christ, come in the body, though they knew that the true Christ must be the Son of God. And so, when they were employing false witnesses, without one word of truth in their testimony, against Him, their priest asked Him, *Art Thou the Christ, the Son of the Blessed[3]?* They knew not that in Him the mystery was fulfilled; they knew that the Divine nature was the condition of its fulfilment. They did not ask whether Christ be the Son of God; they asked whether He were Christ, the Son of God. They were wrong as to the Person, not as to the Sonship, of Christ. They did not doubt that Christ is the Son of God; and thus, while they asked whether He were the Christ, they asked without denying that the Christ is the Son of God. What, then, of your faith, which leads you to deny what even they, in their blindness, confessed? The perfect knowledge is this, to be assured that Christ, the Son of God, Who existed before the worlds, was also born of the Virgin. Even they, who know nothing of His birth from Mary, know that He is the Son of God. Mark the fellowship with Jewish wickedness in which your denial of the Divine Sonship has involved you! For they have put on record the reason of their condemnation:—*And by our Law He ought to die, because He made Himself the Son of God[4].* Is not this the same charge which you are blasphemously bringing against Him, that, while you pronounce Him a creature, He calls Himself the Son? He confesses Himself the Son, and they declare Him guilty of death; you too deny that He is the Son of God. What sentence do you pass upon Him? You have the same repugnance to His claim as had the Jews. You agree with their verdict; I want to know whether you will quarrel about the sentence. Your offence, in denying that He is the Son of God, is exactly the same as theirs, though their guilt is less, for they sinned in ignorance. They knew not that Christ was born of Mary, yet they never doubted that Christ must be the Son of God. You are perfectly aware of the fact that Christ was born of Mary, yet you refuse Him the name of Son of God. If they come to the faith, there awaits them an unimperilled salvation, because of their past

---

7 St. John ix. 35.   8 Ib. ix. 36.   9 Ib. 38.
1 Reading *vitam.*   2 St. Luke viii 28.

3 St. Mark xiv. 61.   4 St. John xix. 7.

ignorance. Every gate of safety is shut to you, because you persist in denying a truth which is obvious to you. For you are not ignorant that He is the Son of God; you know it so well that you allow Him the name as a title of adoption, and feign that He is a creature adorned, like others, with the right to call Himself a Son. You rob Him, as far as you can, of the Divine nature; if you could, you would rob Him of the Divine name as well. But, because you cannot, you divorce the name from the nature; He is called a Son, but He shall not be the true Son of God.

51. The confession of the Apostles, for whom by a word of command the raging wind and troubled sea were restored to calm, was an opportunity for you. You might have confessed, as they did, that He is God's true Son; you might have borrowed their very words, *Of a truth, this is the Son of God*[5]. But an evil spirit of madness is driving you on to shipwreck of your life; your reason is distracted and overwhelmed, like the ocean tormented by the fury of the storm.

52. If this witness of the voyagers seem inconclusive to you because they were Apostles, —though to me it comes with the greater weight for the same reason, though it surprises me the less,—accept at any rate a corroboration given by the Gentiles. Hear how the soldier of the Roman cohort, one of the stern guard around the Cross, was humbled to the faith. The centurion sees the mighty workings of Christ's power; and this is the witness borne by him :—*Truly this was the Son of God*[6]. The truth was forced upon him, after Christ had given up the ghost, by the torn veil of the Temple, and the earth that shook, and the rocks that were rent, and the sepulchres that were opened, and the dead that rose. And it was the confession of an unbeliever. The deeds that were done convinced him that Christ's nature was omnipotent; he names Him the Son of God, being assured of His true Divinity. So cogent was the proof, so strong the man's conviction, that the force of truth conquered his will, and even he who had nailed Christ to the Cross was driven to confess that He is the Lord of eternal glory, truly the Son of God.

---

5 St. Matt. xiv. 33.

6 St. Matt. xxvii. 54.

BOOK VII.

1. THIS is the seventh book of our treatise against the wild extravagance of modern heresy. In order of place it must follow its predecessors ; in order of importance, as an exposition of the mysteries of the right faith, it precedes and excels them all. I am well aware how hard and steep is the path of evangelical instruction up which we are mounting. The fears inspired by consciousness of my own incapacity are plucking me back, but the warmth of faith urges me on ; the assaults of heresy heat my blood, and the dangers of the ignorant excite my compassion. I fear to speak, and yet I cannot be silent. A double dread subdues my spirit ; it may be that speech, it may be that silence, will render me guilty of a desertion of the truth. For this cunning heresy has hedged itself round with marvellous devices of perverted ingenuity. First there is the semblance of devotion ; then the language carefully chosen to lull the suspicions of a candid listener ; and again, the accommodation of their views to secular philosophy ; and finally, their withdrawing of attention from manifest truth by a pretended explanation of Divine methods. Their loud profession of the unity of God is a fraudulent imitation of the faith ; their assertion that Christ is the Son of God a play upon words for the delusion of their hearers ; their saying that He did not exist before He was born a bid for the support of the world's philosophers ; their confession of God as incorporeal and immutable leads, by a display of fallacious logic, up to a denial of the birth of God from God. They turn our arguments against ourselves ; the Church's faith is made the engine of its own destruction. They have contrived to involve us in the perplexing position of an equal danger, whether we reason with them or whether we refrain. For they use the fact that we allow certain of their assumptions to pass unchallenged as an argument on behalf of those which we do contradict.

2. We call to mind that in the preceding books the reader has been urged to study the whole of that blasphemous manifesto[1], and mark how it is animated throughout by the one aim of propagating the belief that our Lord Jesus Christ is neither God, nor Son of God. Its authors argue that He is permitted to use the names of God and of Son by virtue of a certain adoption, though neither Godhead nor Sonship be His by nature. They use the fact, true in itself, that God is immutable and incorporeal, as an argument against the birth of the Son from Him. They value the truth, that God the Father is One, only as a weapon against our faith in the Godhead of Christ ; pleading that an incorporeal nature cannot be rationally conceived as generating another, and that our faith in One God is inconsistent with the confession of God from God. But our earlier books have already refuted and foiled this argument of theirs by an appeal to the Law and the Prophets. Our defence has followed, step by step, the course of their attack. We have set forth God from God, and at the same time confessed One true God ; shewing that this presentation of the faith neither falls short of the truth by ascribing singleness of Person to the One true God, nor adds to the faith by asserting the existence of a second Deity. For we confess neither an isolated God, nor yet two Gods. Thus, neither denying that God is One nor maintaining that He is alone, we hold the straight road of truth. Each Divine Person is in the Unity, yet no Person is the One God. Next, our purpose being to demonstrate the irrefragable truth of this mystery by the evidence of the Evangelists and Apostles, our first duty has been to make our readers acquainted with the nature, truly subsisting and truly born, of the Son of God ; to demonstrate that He has no origin external to God, and was not created out of nothing, but is the Son, born from God. This is a truth which the evidence adduced in the last book has placed beyond all doubt. The assertion that He bears the name of Son by virtue of adoption has been put to silence, and He stands fo:th as a true Son by a true birth. Our present task is to prove from the Gospels that, because He is true Son, He is true God also. For unless He be true Son He cannot be true God, nor true God unless He be true Son.

3. Nothing is more harassing to human nature than the sense of impending danger. If calamities unknown or unanticipated befall

1 The *Epistola Arii ad Alexandrum*; see Books iv. 12, vi. 5.

us, we may need pity, yet we have been free from care; no load of anxiety has oppressed us. But he whose mind is full of possibilities of trouble suffers already a torment in his fear. I, who now am venturing out to sea, am a mariner not unused to shipwreck, a traveller who knows by experience how brigands lurk in the forests, an explorer of African deserts aware of the danger from scorpions and asps and basilisks[2]. I enjoy no instant of relief from the knowledge and fear of present danger. Every heretic is on the watch, noting every word as it drops from my mouth. The whole progress of my argument is infested with ambuscades and pitfalls and snares. It is not of the road, of its hardness or steepness, that I complain; I am following in the footsteps of the Apostles, not choosing my own path. My trouble is the constant peril, the constant dread, of wandering into some ambush, of stumbling into some pit, of being entangled in some net. My purpose is to proclaim the unity of God, in the sense of the Law and Prophets and Apostles. Sabellius is at hand, eager with cruel kindness to welcome me, on the strength of this unity, and swallow me up in his own destruction. If I withstand him, and deny that, in the Sabellian sense, God is One, a fresh heresy is ready to receive me, pointing out that I teach the existence of two Gods. Again, if I undertake to tell how the Son of God was born from Mary, Photinus, the Ebion of our day, will be prompt to twist this assertion of the truth into a confirmation of his lie. I need mention no other heresies, save one; all the world knows that they are alien from the Church. It is one that has been often denounced, often rejected, yet it preys upon our vitals still. Galatia[3] has reared a large brood of godless assertors of the unity of God. Alexandria[4] has sown broadcast, over almost the whole world, her denial, which is an affirmation, of the doctrine of two Gods. Pannonia[5] upholds her pestilent doctrine that the only birth of Jesus Christ was from the Virgin. And the Church, distracted by these rival faiths, is in danger of being led by means of truth into a rejection of truth. Doctrines are being forced upon her for godless ends, which, according to the use that is made of them, will either support or overthrow the faith. For instance, we cannot, as true believers, assert that God is One, if we mean by it that He is alone; for faith in a lonely God denies the Godhead of the Son. If, on the other hand, we assert, as we truly can, that the Son is God, we are in danger, so they fondly imagine, of deserting the truth that God is One. We are in peril on either hand; we may deny the unity or we may maintain the isolation. But it is a danger which has no terrors for the *foolish things of the world*[6]. Our adversaries are blind to the fact that His assertion that He is not alone is consistent with unity; that though He is One He is not solitary.

4. But I trust that the Church, by the light of her doctrine, will so enlighten the world's vain wisdom, that, even though it accept not the mystery of the faith, it will recognise that in our conflict with heretics we, and not they, are the true representatives of that mystery. For great is the force of truth; not only is it its own sufficient witness, but the more it is assailed the more evident it becomes; the daily shocks which it receives only increase its inherent stability. It is the peculiar property of the Church that when she is buffeted she is triumphant, when she is assaulted with argument she proves herself in the right, when she is deserted by her supporters she holds the field. It is her wish that all men should remain at her side and in her bosom; if it lay with her, none would become unworthy to abide under the shelter of that august mother, none would be cast out or suffered to depart from her calm retreat. But when heretics desert her or she expels them, the loss she endures, in that she cannot save them, is compensated by an increased assurance that she alone can offer bliss. This is a truth which the passionate zeal of rival heresies brings into the clearest prominence. The Church, ordained by the Lord and established by His Apostles, is one for all; but the frantic folly of discordant sects has severed them from her. And it is obvious that these dissensions concerning the faith result from a distorted mind, which twists the words of Scripture into conformity with its opinion, instead of adjusting that opinion to the words of Scripture. And thus, amid the clash of mutually destructive errors, the Church stands revealed not only by her own teaching, but by that of her rivals. They are ranged, all of them, against her; and the very fact that she stands single and alone is her sufficient answer to their godless delusions. The hosts of heresy assemble themselves against her; each of them can defeat all the others, but not one can win a victory for itself. The only victory is the triumph which the Church celebrates over them all. Each heresy wields against its adversary some weapon

---

[2] Cf. Lucan. IX. 696 ff.   [3] Marcellus of Ancyra.
[4] Arius.   [5] Photinus of Sirmium.

[6] 1 Cor. i. 27.

already shattered, in another instance, by the Church's condemnation. There is no point of union between them, and the outcome of their internecine struggles is the confirmation of the faith.

5. Sabellius sweeps away the birth of the Son, and then preaches the unity of God; but he does not doubt that the mighty Nature, which acted in the human Christ, was God. He shuts his eyes to the revealed mystery of the Sonship; the works done seem to him so marvellous that he cannot believe that He who performed them could undergo a true generation. When he hears the words, *He that hath seen Me hath seen the Father also* [7], he jumps to the blasphemous conclusion of an inseparable and indistinguishable identity of nature in Father and Son, because he fails to see that the revelation of the birth is the mode in which Their unity of nature is manifested to us. For the fact that the Father is seen in the Son is a proof of the Son's Divinity, not a disproof of His birth. Thus our knowledge of Each of Them is conditioned by our knowledge of the Other, for there is no difference of nature between them; and, since in this respect they are One, a reverent study of the character of Either will give us a true insight into the nature of Both For, indeed, it is certain that He, Who was in the form of God, must in His self-revelation present Himself to us in the exact aspect of the form of God [8]. Again, this perverse and insane delusion derives a further encouragement from the words, *I and the Father are One* [9]. From the fact of unity in the same nature they have impiously deduced a confusion of Persons; their interpretation, that the words signify a single Power, contradicts the tenour of the passage. For *I and the Father are One* does not indicate a solitary God. The use of the conjunction *and* shews clearly that more than one Person is signified; and *are* requires a plurality of subject. Moreover, the *One* is not incompatible with a birth. Its sense is, that the Two Persons have the one nature in common. The *One* is inconsistent with difference; the *are* with identity.

6. Set our modern heresy in array against the delusion, equally wild, of Sabellius; let them make the best of their case. The new heretics will advance the passage. *The Father is greater than I* [1]. Neglecting the mystery of the Divine birth, and the mystery of God's emptying Himself and taking flesh, they will argue the inferiority of His nature from His assertion that the Father is the greater. They will plead against Sabellius that Christ is a Son, in so far as One can be a Son who is inferior to the Father and needs to ask for restoration to His glory, and fears to die and indeed did die. In reply Sabellius will adduce His deeds in evidence of His Divine nature; and while our novel heresy, to escape the admission of Christ's true Sonship, will heartily agree with him that God is One, Sabellius will emphatically assert the same article of the faith, in the sense that no Son exists. The one side lays stress upon the action of the Son; the other urges that in that action God is manifest. The one will demonstrate the unity, the other disprove the identity. Sabellius will defend his position thus:—"The works that were done could have been done by no other nature than the Divine. Sins were remitted, the sick were healed, the lame ran, the blind saw, the dead lived. God alone has power for this. The words *I and the Father are One* could only have been spoken from self-knowledge; no nature, outside the Father's, could have uttered them. Why then suggest a second substance, and urge me to believe in a second God? These works are peculiar to God; the One God wrought them." His adversaries, animated by a hatred, equally venomous, for the faith, will argue that the Son is unlike in nature to God the Father:—"You are ignorant of the mystery of your salvation. You must believe in a Son through Whom the worlds were made, through Whom man was fashioned, Who gave the Law through Angels, Who was born of Mary, Who was sent by the Father, was crucified, dead and buried, Who rose again from the dead and is at the right hand of God, Who is the Judge of quick and dead. Unto Him we must rise again, we must confess Him, we must earn our place in His kingdom." Each of the two enemies of the Church is fighting the Church's battle. Sabellius displays Christ as God by the witness of the Divine nature manifested in His works; Sabellius' antagonists confess Christ, on the evidence of the revealed faith, to be the Son of God.

7. Again, how glorious a victory for our faith is that in which Ebion—in other words, Photinus—both wins the day and loses it! He castigates Sabellius for denying that the Son of God is Man, and in his turn has to submit to the reproaches of Arian fanatics for failing to see that this Man is the Son of God. Against Sabellius he calls the Gospels to his aid, with their evidence concerning the Son of Mary; Arius deprives him of this ally by proving that the Gospels make Christ some-

---

7 St. John xiv. 9.   8 Cf. Phil. ii. 6.   9 St. John x 30.
1 Ib. xiv. 28.

thing more than the Son of Mary. Sabellius denies that there is a Son of God; against him Photinus elevates man to the place of Son. Photinus will hear nothing of a Son born before the worlds; against him, Arius denies that the only birth of the Son of God was His human birth. Let them defeat one another to their hearts' content, for every victory which each of them wins is balanced by a defeat. Our present adversaries are routed in the matter of the Divine nature of the Son; Sabellius in the matter of the Son's revealed existence; Photinus is convicted of ignorance, or else of falsehood, in his denial of the Son's birth before the worlds. Meanwhile the Church, whose faith is based upon the teaching of Evangelists and Apostles, holds fast, against Sabellius, her assertion that the Son exists; against Arius, that He is God by nature; against Photinus, that He created the universe. And she is the more convinced of her faith, in that they cannot combine to contradict it. For Sabellius points to the works of Christ in proof of the Divinity of Him Who wrought them, though he knows not that the Son was their Author. The Arians grant Him the name of Son, though they confess not that the true nature of God dwelt in Him. Photinus maintains His manhood, though in maintaining it he forgets that Christ was born as God before the worlds. Thus, in their several assertions and denials, there are points in which each heresy is in the right in defence or attack; and the result of their conflicts is that the truth of our confession is brought into clearer light.

8. I felt that I must spare a little space to point this out. It has been from no love for amplification, but that it might serve as a warning. First, I wished to expose the vague and confused character of this crowd of heresies, whose mutual feuds turn, as we have seen, to our advantage. Secondly, in my warfare against the blasphemous doctrines of modern heresy; that is, in my task of proclaiming that both God the Father and God the Son are God,—in other words, that Father and Son are One in name, One in nature, One in the kind of Divinity which they possess,—I wished to shield myself from any charge which might be brought against me, either as an advocate of two Gods or of one lonely and isolated Deity. For in God the Father and God the Son, as I have set them forth, no confusion of Persons can be detected; nor in my exposition of Their common nature can any difference between the Godhead of the One and of the Other be discerned. In the preceding book I have sufficiently refuted, by the witness of the

Gospels, those who deny the subsistence of God the Son by a true birth from God; my present duty is to shew that He, Who in the truth of His nature is Son of God, is also in the truth of His nature God. But this proof must not degenerate into the fatal profession of a solitary God, or of a second God. It shall manifest God as One yet not alone; but in its care to avoid the error of making Him lonely it shall not fall into the error of denying His unity.

9. Thus we have all these different assurances of the Divinity of our Lord Jesus Christ:—His name, His birth, His nature, His power, His own assertion. As to the name, I conceive that no doubt is possible. It is written, *In the beginning was the Word, and the Word was with God, and the Word was God*[2]. What reason can there be for suspecting that He is not what His name indicates? And does not this name clearly describe His nature? If a statement be contradicted, it must be for some reason. What reason, I demand, is there in this instance for denying that He is God? The name is given Him, plainly and distinctly, and unqualified by any incongruous addition which might raise a doubt. The Word, we read, which was made flesh, was none other than God. Here is no loophole for any such conjecture as that He has received this name as a favour or taken it upon Himself, so possessing a titular Godhead which is not His by nature.

10. Consider the other recorded instances in which this name was given by favour or assumed. To Moses it was said, *I have made thee a god to Pharaoh*[3]. Does not this addition, *to Pharaoh*, account for the title? Did God impart to Moses the Divine nature? Did He not rather make Moses a god in the sight of Pharaoh, who was to be smitten with terror when Moses' serpent swallowed the magic serpents and returned into a rod, when he drove back the venomous flies which he had called forth, when he stayed the hail by the same power wherewith he had summoned it, and made the locusts depart by the same might which had brought them; when in the wonders that he wrought the magicians saw the finger of God? That was the sense in which Moses was appointed to be god to Pharaoh; he was feared and entreated, he chastised and healed. It is one thing to be appointed a god; it is another thing to be God. He was made a god to Pharaoh; he had not that nature and that name wherein God consists. I call to mind another instance

---

[2] St. John i. 1.   [3] Exod. vii. 1.

of the name being given as a title; that where it is written, *I have said, Ye are gods* [4]. But this is obviously the granting of a favour. *I have said* proves that it is no definition, but only a description by One Who chooses to speak thus. A definition gives us knowledge of the object defined; a description depends on the arbitrary will of the speaker. When a speaker is manifestly conferring a title, that title has its origin only in the speaker's words, not in the thing itself. The title is not the name which expresses its nature and kind.

11. But in this case the *Word* in very truth is God; the essence of the Godhead exists in the Word, and that essence is expressed in the Word's name. For the name *Word* is inherent in the Son of God as a consequence of His mysterious birth, as are also the names *Wisdom* and *Power*. These, together with the substance which is His by a true birth, were called into existence to be the Son of God [5]; yet, since they are the elements of God's nature, they are still immanent in Him in undiminished extent, although they were born from Him to be His Son. For, as we have said so often, the mystery which we preach is that of a Son Who owes His existence not to division but to birth. He is not a segment cut off, and so incomplete, but an Offspring born, and therefore perfect; for birth involves no diminution of the Begetter, and has the possibility of perfection for the Begotten. And therefore the titles of those substantive properties [6] are applied to God the Only-begotten, for when He came into existence by birth it was they which constituted His perfection; and this although they did not thereby desert the Father, in Whom, by the immutability of His nature, they are eternally present. For instance, the Word is God the Only-begotten, and yet the Unbegotten Father is never without His Word. Not that the nature of the Son is that of a sound which is uttered. He is God from God, subsisting through a true birth; God's own Son, born from the Father, indistinguishable from Him in nature, and therefore inseparable. This is the lesson which His title of the Word is meant to teach us. And in the same way Christ is the Wisdom and the Power of God; not that He is, as He is often regarded [7], the inward activity of the Father's might or thought, but that His nature, possessing through birth a true substantial existence, is indicated by these names of inward forces. For an object, which has by birth an existence of its own, cannot be regarded as a property; a property is necessarily inherent in some being and can have no independent existence. But it was to save us from concluding that the Son is alien from the Divine nature of His Father that He, the Only-begotten from the eternal God His Father, born as God into a substantial existence of His own, has had Himself revealed to us under these names of properties, of which the Father, out of Whom He came into existence, has suffered no diminution. Thus He, being God, is nothing else than God. For when I hear the words, *And the Word was God*, they do not merely tell me that the Son was called God; they reveal to my understanding that He is God. In those previous instances, where Moses was called god and others were styled gods, there was the mere addition of a name by way of title. Here a solid essential truth is stated; *The Word was God*. That *was* indicates no accidental title, but an eternal reality, a permanent element of His existence, an inherent character of His nature.

12. And now let us see whether the confession of Thomas the Apostle, when he cried, *My Lord and My God*, corresponds with this assertion of the Evangelist. We see that he speaks of Him, Whom he confesses to be God, as *My God*. Now Thomas was undoubtedly familiar with those words of the Lord, *Hear, O Israel, the Lord thy God is One*. How then could the faith of an Apostle become so oblivious of that primary command as to confess Christ as God, when life is conditional upon the confession of the Divine unity? It was because, in the light of the Resurrection, the whole mystery of the faith had become visible to the Apostle. He had often heard such words as, *I and the Father are One*, and, *All things that the Father hath are Mine*, and, *I in the Father and the Father in Me* [3]; and now he can confess that the name of God expresses the nature of Christ, without peril to the faith. Without breach of loyalty to the One God, the Father, his devotion could now regard the Son of God as God, since he believed that everything contained in the nature of the Son was truly of the same nature with the Father. No longer need he fear that such a confession as his was the proclamation of a second God, a treason against the unity of the Divine nature; for it was not a second God Whom that perfect birth of the Godhead had brought into being. Thus it was with full knowledge of the mystery of the Gospel that Thomas confessed his Lord and his God. It was not a title of honour;

---

4 Psalm lxxxi. (lxxxii.) 6.
5 I.e. These are the elements of which His Person is composed by the eternal generation.
6 Word, Wisdom, Power.   7 By the Sabellians.

8 St. John x. 30, xvi. 15, xiv. 11.

it was a confession of nature. He believed that Christ was God in substance and in power. And the Lord, in turn, shews that this act of worship was the expression not of mere reverence, but of faith, when He says, *Because thou hast seen, thou hast believed; blessed are they which have not seen, and have believed.* For Thomas had seen before he believed. But, you ask, What was it that Thomas believed? That, beyond a doubt, which is expressed in his words, *My Lord and my God.* No nature but that of God could have risen by its own might from death to life; and it is this fact, that Christ is God, which was confessed by Thomas with the confidence of an assured faith. Shall we, then, dream that His name of God is not a substantial reality, when that name has been proclaimed by a faith based upon certain evidence? Surely a Son devoted to His Father, One Who did not His own will but the will of Him that sent Him, Who sought not His own glory but the glory of Him from Whom He came, would have rejected the adoration involved in such a name as destructive of that unity of God which had been the burden of His teaching. Yet, in fact, He confirms this assertion of the mysterious truth, made by the believing Apostle; He accepts as His own the name which belongs to the nature of the Father. And He teaches that they are blessed who, though they have not seen Him rise from the dead, yet have believed, on the assurance of the Resurrection, that He is God.

13. Thus the name which expresses His nature proves the truth of our confession of the faith. For the name, which indicates any single substance, points out also any other substance of the same kind; and, in this instance, there are not two substances but one substance, of the one kind. For the Son of God is God; this is the truth expressed in His name. The one name does not embrace two Gods; for the one name *God* is the name of one indivisible nature. For since the Father is God and the Son is God, and that name which is peculiar to the Divine nature is inherent in Each, therefore the Two are One. For the Son, though He subsists through a birth from the Divine nature, yet preserves the unity in His name; and this birth of the Son does not compel loyal believers to acknowledge two Gods, since our confession declares that Father and Son are One, both in nature and in name. Thus the Son of God has the Divine name as the result of His birth. Now the second step in our demonstration was to be that of shewing that it is by virtue of His birth that He is God. I have still

to bring forward the evidence of the Apostles that the Divine name is used of Him in an exact sense; but for the present I purpose to continue our enquiry into the language of the Gospels.

14. And first I ask what new element, destructive of His Godhead, can have been imported by birth into the nature of the Son? Universal reason rejects the supposition that a being can become different in nature, by the process of birth, from the being to which its birth is due; although we recognise the possibility that from parents, different in kind, an offspring sharing the nature of both, yet diverse from either, may be propagated. The fact is familiar in the case of beasts, both tame and wild. But even in this case there is no real novelty; the new qualities already exist, concealed in the two different parental natures, and are only developed by the connexion. The birth of their joint offspring is not the cause of that offspring's difference from its parents. The difference is a gift from them of various diversities, which are received and combined in one frame. When this is the case as to the transmission and reception even of bodily differences, is it not a form of madness to assert that the birth of God the Only-begotten was the birth from God of a nature inferior to Himself? For the giving of birth is a function of the true nature of the transmitter of life; and without the presence and action of that true nature there can be no birth. The object of all this heat and passion is to prove that there was no birth, but a creation, of the Son of God; that the Divine nature is not His origin and that He does not possess that nature in His personal subsistence, but draws, from what was non-existent, a nature different in kind from the Divine. They are angry because He says, *That which is born of the flesh is flesh, and that which is born of the Spirit is Spirit* [9]. For, since God is a Spirit, it is clear that in One born from Him there can be nothing alien or different from that Spirit from which He was born. Thus the birth of God constitutes Him perfect God. And hence also it is clear that we must not say that He began to exist, but only that He was born. For there is a sense in which beginning is different from birth. A thing which begins to exist either comes into existence out of nothing, or developes out of one state into another, ceasing to be what it was before; so, for instance, gold is formed out of earth, solids melt into liquids, cold changes to warmth, white to red, water

---

9 St. John iii. 6.

breeds moving creatures, lifeless objects turn into living. In contrast to all this, the Son of God did not begin, out of nothing, to be God, but was born as God; nor had He an existence of another kind before the Divine. Thus He Who was born to be God had neither a beginning of His Godhead, nor yet a development up to it. His birth retained for Him that nature out of which He came into being; the Son of God, in His distinct existence, is what God is, and is nothing else.

15. Again, any one who is in doubt concerning this matter may gain from the Jews an accurate knowledge of Christ's nature; or rather learn that He was truly born from the Gospel, where it is written, *Therefore the Jews sought the more to kill Him because He not only broke the Sabbath, but said also that God was His own Father, making Himself equal with God*[1]. This passage is unlike most others in not giving us the words spoken by the Jews, but the Apostle's explanation of their motive in wishing to kill the Lord. We see that no plea of misapprehension can excuse the wickedness of these blasphemers; for we have the Apostle's evidence that the true nature of Christ was fully revealed to them. They could speak of His birth :—*He said that God was His Father, making Himself equal with God*. Was not His clearly a birth of nature from nature, when He published the equality of His nature by speaking of God, by name, as His own Father? Now it is manifest that equality consists in the absence of difference between those who are equal. Is it not also manifest that the result of birth must be a nature in which there is an absence of difference between Son and Father? And this is the only possible origin of true equality; birth can only bring into existence a nature equal to its origin. But again, we can no more hold that there is equality where there is confusion, than we can where there is difference. Thus equality, as of the image[2], is incompatible with isolation and with diversity; for equality cannot dwell with difference, nor yet in solitude.

16. And now, although we have found the sense of Scripture, as we understand it, in harmony with the conclusions of ordinary reason, the two agreeing that equality is incompatible either with diversity or with isolation, yet we must seek a fresh support for our contention from actual words of our Lord. For only so can we check that licence of arbitrary interpretation whereby these bold traducers of the faith would even venture to cavil at the Lord's solemn self-revelation. His answer to the Jews was this :—*The Son can do nothing of Himself but what He seeth the Father do; for what things soever He doeth, these also doeth the Son likewise. For the Father loveth the Son, and sheweth Him all things that Himself doeth; and He will shew Him greater works than these, that ye may marvel. For as the Father raiseth up the dead and quickeneth them, even so the Son quickeneth whom He will. For the Father judgeth no man, but hath given all judgment to the Son, that all may honour the Son even as they honour the Father. He that honoureth not the Son honoureth not the Father which hath sent Him*[3]. The course of our argument, as I had shaped it in my mind, required that each several point of the debate should be handled singly; that, since we had been taught that our Lord Jesus Christ, the Son of God, is God in name, in birth, in nature, in power, in self-revelation, our demonstration of the faith should establish each successive point in that order. But His birth is a barrier to such a treatment of the question; for a consideration of it includes a consideration of His name and nature and power and self-revelation. For His birth involves all these, and they are His by the fact that He is born. And thus our argument concerning His birth has taken such a course that it is impossible for us to keep these other matters back for separate discussion in their turn.

17. The chief reason why the Jews wished to kill the Lord was that, in calling God His Father, He had made Himself equal with God; and therefore He put His answer, in which He reproved their evil passion, into the form of an exposition of the whole mystery of our faith. For just before this, when He had healed the paralytic and they had passed their judgment upon Him that He was worthy of death for breaking the Sabbath, He had said, *My Father worketh hitherto, and I work*[4]. Their jealousy had been inflamed to the utmost by the raising of Himself to the level of God which was involved in this use of the name of Father. And now He wishes to assert His birth and to reveal the powers of His nature, and so He says, *I say unto you, the Son can do nothing of Himself, but what He seeth the Father do*. These opening words of His reply are aimed at that wicked zeal of the Jews, which hurried them on even to the desire of slaying Him. It is in reference to the charge of breaking the Sabbath that He says, *My Father worketh hitherto, and I work*. He wished them to

---

[1] St. John v. 18. [2] Heb. i. 3. [3] St. John v. 19—22. [4] Ib. v. 17.

understand that His practice was justified by Divine authority; and He taught them by the same words that His work must be regarded as the work of the Father, Who was working in Him all that He wrought. And again, it was to subdue the jealousy awakened by His speaking of God as His Father that He uttered those words, *Verily, verily, I say unto you, the Son can do nothing of Himself, but what He seeth the Father do.* Lest this making of Himself equal to God, as having the name and nature of God's Son, should withdraw men's faith from the truth that He had been born, He says that the Son can do nothing but what He sees the Father do. Next, in confirmation of the saving harmony of truths in our confession of Father and of Son, He displays this nature which is His by birth; a nature which derives its power of action not from successive gifts of strength to do particular deeds, but from knowledge. He shews that this knowledge is not imparted by the Father's performance of any bodily work, as a pattern, that the Son may imitate what the Father has previously done; but that, by the action of the Divine nature, He had come to share the subsistence of the Divine nature, or, in other words, had been born as Son from the Father. He told them that, because the power and the nature of God dwelt consciously within Him, it was impossible for Him to do anything which He had not seen the Father doing; that, since it is in the might of the Father that God the Only-begotten performs His works, His liberty of action coincides in its range with His knowledge of the powers of the nature of God the Father; a nature inseparable from Himself, and lawfully owned by Him in virtue of His birth. For God sees not after a bodily fashion, but possesses, by His nature, the vision of Omnipotence.

18. The next words are, *For what things soever He*—the Father—*doeth, these also doeth the Son likewise.* This *likewise* is added to indicate His birth; *whatsoever* and *same* to indicate the true Divinity of His nature. *Whatsoever* and *same* make it impossible that there should be any actions of His that are different from, or outside, the actions of the Father. Thus He, Whose nature has power to do all the same things as the Father, is included in the same nature with the Father. But when, in contrast with this, we read that all these same things are done by the Son *likewise*, the fact that the works are like those of Another is fatal to the supposition that He Who does them works in isolation. Thus the same things that the Father does are all done likewise by the Son. Here we have clear proof of His true birth,

and at the same time a convincing attestation of the Mystery of our faith, which, with its foundation in the Unity of the nature of God, confesses that there resides in Father and Son an indivisible Divinity. For the Son does the same things as the Father, and does them likewise; while acting in like manner He does the same things. Two truths are combined in one proposition; that His works are done likewise proves His birth; that they are the same works proves His nature.

19. Thus the progressive revelation contained in our Lord's reply is at one with the progressive statement of truth in the Church's confession of faith. Neither of them divides the nature, and both declare the birth. For the next words of Christ are, *For the Father loveth the Son, and sheweth Him all things that Himself doeth; and He will shew Him greater works than these, that ye may marvel. For as the Father raiseth up the dead, and quickeneth them, even so the Son quickeneth whom He will.* Can there be any other purpose in this revelation of the manner in which God works, except that of inculcating the true birth; the faith in a subsisting Son born from the subsisting God, His Father? The only other explanation is that God the Only-begotten was so ignorant that He needed the instruction conveyed in this shewing; but the reckless blasphemy of the suggestion makes this alternative impossible. For He, knowing, as He does, everything that He is taught, has no need of the teaching. And accordingly, after the words, *The Father loveth the Son, and sheweth Him all things that Himself doeth,* we are next informed that all this shewing is for our instruction in the faith; that the Father and the Son may have their equal share in our confession, and we be saved, by this statement that the Father shews all that He does to the Son, from the delusion that the Son's knowledge is imperfect. With this object He goes on to say, *And He will shew Him greater works than these, that ye may marvel. For as the Father raiseth up the dead and quickeneth them, even so the Son quickeneth whom He will.* We see that the Son has full knowledge of the future works which the Father will shew Him hereafter. He knows that He will be shewn how, after His Father's example, He is to give life to the dead. For He says that the Father will shew to the Son things at which they shall marvel; and at once proceeds to tell them what these things are;— *For as the Father raiseth up the dead and quickeneth them, even so the Son quickeneth whom He will.* The power is equal because the nature is one and the same. The shewing of the works is an aid, not to ignorance in

Him, but to faith in us. It conveys to the Son no knowledge of things unknown, but it imparts to us the confidence to proclaim His birth, by assuring us that the Father has shewn to Him all the works that He Himself can do. The terms used in this Divine discourse have been chosen with the utmost deliberation, lest any vagueness of language should suggest a difference of nature between the Two. Christ says that the Father's works were shewn Him, instead of saying that, to enable Him to perform them, a mighty nature was given Him. Hereby He wishes to reveal to us that this shewing was a substantive part of the process of His birth, since, simultaneously with that birth, there was imparted to Him by the Father's love a knowledge of the works which the Father willed that He should do. And again, to save us from being led, by this declaration of the shewing, to suppose that the Son's nature is ignorant and therefore different from the Father's, He makes it clear that He already knows the things that are to be shewn Him. So far, indeed, is He from needing the authority of precedent to enable Him to act, that He is to give life to whom He will. To will implies a free nature, subsisting with power to choose in the blissful exercise of omnipotence.

20. And next, lest it should seem that to give life to whom He will is not within the power of One Who has been truly born, but is only the prerogative of ingenerate Omnipotence, He hastens to add, *For the Father judgeth no man, but hath given all judgment to the Son.* The statement that all judgment is given teaches both His birth and His Sonship; for only a nature which is altogether one with the Father's could possess all things; and a Son can possess nothing, except by gift. But all judgment has been given Him, for He quickens whom He will. Now we cannot suppose that judgment is taken away from the Father, although He does not exercise it; for the Son's whole power of judgment proceeds from the Father's, being a gift from Him. And there is no concealment of the reason why judgment has been given to the Son, for the words which follow are, *But He hath given all judgment to the Son, that all men may honour the Son even as they honour the Father. He that honoureth not the Son honoureth not the Father Which hath sent Him.* What possible excuse remains for doubt, or for the irreverence of denial? The reason for the gift of judgment is that the Son may receive an honour equal to that which is paid to the Father; and thus he who dishonours the Son is guilty of dishonouring the Father also. How, after this proof, can we imagine that the nature given Him by birth is different from the Father's, when He is the Father's equal in work, in power, in honour, in the punishment awarded to gainsayers? Thus this whole Divine reply is nothing else than an unfolding of the mystery of His birth. And the only distinction that it is right or possible to make between Father and Son is that the Latter was born; yet born in such a sense as to be One with His Father.

21. Thus the Father works hitherto and the Son works. In Father and Son you have the names which express Their nature in relation to Each other. Note also that it is the Divine nature, that through which God works, that is working here. And remember, lest you fall into the error of imagining that the operation of two unlike natures is here described, how it was said concerning the blind man, *But that the works of God may be made manifest in him, I must work the works of Him that sent Me* [5]. You see that in his case the work wrought by the Son is the Father's work; and the Son's work is God's work. The remainder of the discourse which we are considering also deals with works; but my defence is at present only concerned with assigning the whole work to Both, and pointing out that They are at one in Their method of working, since the Son is employed upon that work which the Father does hitherto. The sanction contained in this fact that, by virtue of His Divine birth, the Father is working with Him in all that He does, will save us from supposing that the Lord of the Sabbath was doing wrong in working on the Sabbath. His Sonship is not affected, for there is no confusion of His Divinity with the Father's, and no negation of it; His Godhead is not affected, for His Divine nature is untouched. Their unity is not affected, for no difference is revealed to sever Them; and Their unity is not presented in such a light as to contradict Their distinct existence. First recognise the Sonship of the Son; *The Son can do nothing of Himself, but what He seeth the Father do.* Here His birth is manifest; because of i. He can do nothing of Himself till He sees it being done. He cannot be unbegotten, because He can do nothing of Himself; He has no power of initiation, and therefore He must have been born. But the fact that He can see the Father's works proves that He has the comprehension which belongs to the conscious Possessor of Divinity. Next, mark that He does possess this true Divine nature;— *For what things soever He doeth, these also doeth*

---

the Son likewise. And now that we have seen Him endowed with the powers of that nature, note how this results in unity, how one nature dwells in the Two ;—*That all men may honour the Son, even as they honour the Father.* And then, lest reflection on this unity entangle you in the delusion of a solitary and self-contained God, take to heart the mystery of the faith manifested in these words, *He that honoureth not the Son honoureth not the Father Which hath sent Him.* The rage and cunning of heresy may do their worst; our position is impregnable. He is the Son, because He can do nothing of Himself; He is God, because, whatever the Father does, He does the same; They Two are One, because He is equal in honour to the Father and does the very same works; He is not the Father, because He is sent. So great is the wealth of mysterious truth contained in this one doctrine of the birth! It embraces His name, His nature, His power, His self-revelation ; for everything conveyed to Him in His birth must be contained in that nature from which His birth is derived. Into His nature no element of any substance different in kind from that of His Author is introduced, for a nature which springs from one nature only must be entirely one with that nature which is its parent. An unity is that which, containing no discordant elements, is one in kind with itself ; an unity constituted through birth cannot be solitary ; for solitude can have but a single occupant, while an unity constituted through birth implies the conjunction of Two.

22. And furthermore, let His own Divine words bear witness to Himself. He says, *They that are of My sheep hear My voice, and I know them, and they follow Me ; and I give unto them eternal life, and they shall never perish, neither shall any man pluck them out of My hand. That which My Father hath given Me is greater than all, and no man shall be able to pluck them out of My Father's hand. I and the Father are one*[6]. What lethargy can blunt so utterly the edge of our understanding as to render so precise a statement for one moment obscure to us? What proud sophistry can play such pranks with human docility as to persuade those, who have learnt from these words the knowledge of what God is, that they must not recognise God in Him, Whose Godhead was here revealed to them? Heresy ought either to bring forward other Gospels in support of its doctrine ; or else, if our existing Gospels are the only documents which teach of God, why do they not believe the lessons taught? If they are the only

source of knowledge, why not draw faith, as well as knowledge, from them? Yet now we find that their faith is held in defiance of their knowledge ; and hence it is a faith rooted not in knowledge, but in sin ; a faith of bold irreverence, instead of reverent humility, towards the truth confessedly known. God the Only-begotten, as we have seen, fully assured of His own nature, reveals with the utmost precision of language the mystery of His birth. He reveals it, ineffable though it is, in such wise that we can believe and confess it ; that we can understand that He was born and believe that He has the nature of God and is One with the Father, and One with Him in such a sense that God is not alone nor Son another name for Father, but that in very truth He is the Son. For, firstly, He assures us of the powers of His Divine nature, saying of His sheep, *and no man shall pluck them out of My hand.* It is the utterance of conscious power, this confession of free and irresistible energy, that will allow no man to pluck His sheep from His hand. But more than this ; not only has He the nature of God, but He would have us know that that nature is His by birth from God, and hence He adds, *That which the Father has given Me is greater than all.* He makes no secret of His birth from the Father, for what He received from the Father He says is greater than all. And He Who received it, received it at His birth, not after His birth, and yet it came to Him from Another, for He received it [7]. But He, Who received this gift from Another, forbids us to suppose that He Himself is different in kind from That Other, and does not eternally subsist with the same nature as that of Him Who gave the gift, by saying, *No man shall be able to pluck them out of My Father's hand.* None can pluck them out of His hand, for He has received from His Father that which is greater than all things. What, then, means this contradictory assertion that none can pluck them from His Father's hand? It is the Son's hand which received them from the Father, the Father's hand which gave them to the Son : in what sense is it said that what cannot be plucked from the Son's hand cannot be plucked from the Father's hand? Hear, if you wish to know :—*I and the Father are one.* The Son's hand is the Father's hand. For the Divine nature does not deteriorate or cease to be the same in passing through birth : nor yet is this sameness a bar to our faith in the birth, for in that birth no alien element was admitted into His nature. And here He

---

6 St. John x. 27—30.

7 I.e. He is not Unbegotten.

speaks of the Son's hand, which is the hand of the Father, that by a bodily similitude you may learn the power of the one Divine nature which is in Both; for the nature and the power of the Father is in the Son. And lastly, that in this mysterious truth of the birth you may discern the true and indistinguishable unity of the nature of God, the words were spoken, *I and the Father are One.* They were spoken that in this unity we might see neither difference nor solitude; for They are Two, and yet no second nature came into being through that true birth and generation.

23. There still remains, if I read them aright, the same desire in these maddened souls, though their opportunity for fulfilling it is lost. Their bitter hearts still cherish a longing for mischief which they can no longer hope to satisfy. The Lord is on His throne in heaven, and the furious hatred of heresy cannot drag Him, as the Jews did, to the Cross. But the spirit of unbelief is the same, though now it takes the form of rejecting His Godhead. They bid defiance to His words, though they cannot deny that He spoke them. They vent their hatred in blasphemy; instead of stones they shower abuse. If they could they would bring Him down from His throne to a second crucifixion. When the Jews were moved to wrath by the novelty of Christ's teaching we read, *The Jews therefore took up stones to stone Him. He answered them, Many good works have I shewed you from the Father; for which of those works do ye stone Me? The Jews answered Him, For a good work we stone Thee not, but for blasphemy; and because Thou, being a man, makest Thyself God*[8]. I bid you, heretic, to recognise herein your own deeds, your own words. Be sure that you are their partner, for you have made their unbelief your pattern. It was at the words, *I and the Father are One,* that the Jews took up stones. Their godless irritation at the revelation of that saving mystery hurried them on even to an attempt to slay. There is no one whom you can stone; but is your guilt in denying Him less than theirs? The will is the same, though it is frustrated by His throne in heaven. Nay, it is you that are more impious than the Jew. He lifted his stone against the Body, you lift yours against the Spirit; he as he thought, against man, you against God; he against a sojourner on earth, you against Him that sits upon the throne of majesty; he against One Whom he knew not, you against Him Whom you confess; he against

the mortal Christ, you against the Judge of the universe. The Jew says, *Being Man;* you say, 'Being a creature.' You and he join in the cry, *Makest Thyself God,* with the same insolence of blasphemy. You deny that He is God begotten of God; you deny that He is the Son by a true birth; you deny that His words, *I and the Father are One,* contain the assertion of one and the same nature in Both. You foist upon us in His stead a modern, a strange, an alien god; you make Him God of another kind from the Father, or else not God at all, as not subsisting by a birth from God.

24. The mystery contained in those words, *I and the Father are One,* moves you to wrath. The Jew answered, *Thou, being a man makest Thyself God;* your blasphemy is a match for his:—'Thou, being a creature, makest Thyself God.' You say, in effect, 'Thou art not a Son by birth, Thou art not God in truth; Thou art a creature, excelling all other creatures. But Thou wast not born to be God, for I refuse to believe that the incorporeal God gave birth to Thy nature. Thou and the Father are not One. Nay more. Thou art not the Son, Thou art not like God, Thou art not God.' The Lord had His answer for the Jews; an answer that meets the case of your blasphemy even better than it met theirs:—*Is it not written in the Law, I said, Ye are gods? If, therefore, He called them gods, unto whom the word of God came, and the Scripture cannot be broken, say ye of Me, Whom the Father hath sanctified and sent into this world, that I have blasphemed, because I said I am the Son of God? If I do not the works of the Father, believe Me not; but if I do, and ye will not believe Me, believe the works, that ye may know and be sure that the Father is in Me, and I in Him*[9]. The matter of this reply was dictated by that of the blasphemous attack upon Him. The accusation was that He, being a man, made Himself God. Their proof of this allegation was His own statement, *I and the Father are One.* He therefore sets Himself to prove that the Divine nature, which is His by birth, gives Him the right to assert that He and the Father are One. He begins by exposing the absurdity, as well as the insolence, of such a charge as that of making Himself God, though He was a man. The Law had conferred the title upon holy men; the word of God, from which there is no appeal, had given its sanction to the public use of the name. What blasphemy, then, could there be in the assumption of the title of Son of

---

[8] St. John x. 31—33.

[9] St. John x. 34—38.

God by Him Whom the Father had sanctified and sent into the world? The unalterable record of the Word of God has confirmed the title to those to whom the Law assigned it. There is an end, therefore, of the charge that He, being a man, makes Himself God, when the Law gives the name of *gods* to those who are confessedly men. And further, if other men may use this name without blasphemy, there can obviously be no blasphemy in its use by the Man Whom the Father has sanctified,—and note here that throughout this argument He calls Himself Man, for the Son of God is also Son of Man— since He excels the rest, who yet are guilty of no irreverence in styling themselves gods. He excels them, in that He has been hallowed to be the Son, as the blessed Paul says, who teaches us of this sanctification :—*Which He had promised afore by His prophets in the Holy Scriptures, concerning His Son, Which was made of the seed of David according to the flesh, and was appointed to be the Son of God with power, according to the spirit of sanctification* [1]. Thus the accusation of blasphemy on His part, in making Himself God, falls to the ground. For the Word of God has conferred this name upon many men; and He, Who was sanctified and sent by the Father, did no more than proclaim Himself the Son of God.

25. There remains, I conceive, no possibility of doubt but that the words, *I and the Father are One*, were spoken with regard to the nature which is His by birth. The Jews had rebuked Him because by these words He, being a man, made Himself God. The course of His answer proves that, in this *I and the Father are One*, He did profess Himself the Son of God, first in name, then in nature, and lastly by birth. For *I* and *Father* are the names of substantive Beings; *One* is a declaration of Their nature, namely, that it is essentially the same in Both; *are* forbids us to confound Them together; *are one*, while forbidding confusion, teaches that the unity of the Two is the result of a birth. Now all this truth is drawn out from that name, the Son of God, which He being sanctified by the Father, bestows upon Himself; a name, His right to which is confirmed by His assertion, *I and the Father are One*. For birth cannot confer any nature upon the offspring other than that of the parent from whom that offspring is born.

26. Once more, God the Only-begotten has summed up for us, in words of His own, the whole revealed mystery of the faith. When He had given His answer to the charge that He, being a man, made Himself God, He determined to shew that His words, *I and the Father are One*, are a clear and necessary conclusion; and therefore He thus pursued His argument;— *Ye say that I have blasphemed, because I said, I am the Son of God. If I do not the works of the Father, believe Me not; but if I do, and ye will not believe Me, believe the works, that ye may know and be sure that the Father is in Me, and I in the Father.* After this, heresy that still persists in its course perpetrates a wilful outrage in conscious despair; the assertion of unbelief is deliberate shamelessness. They who make it take pride in folly and are dead to the faith, for it is not ignorance, but madness, to contradict this saying. The Lord had said, *I and the Father are One;* and the mystery of His birth, which He revealed, was the unity in nature of Father and Son. Again, when He was accused for claiming the Divine nature, He justified His claim by advancing a reason; —*If I do not the works of the Father, believe Me not.* We are not to believe His assertion that He is the Son of God, unless He does His Father's works. Hence we see that His birth has given Him no new or alien nature, for His doing of the Father's works is to be the reason why we must believe that He is the Son. What room is there here for adoption, or for leave to use the name, or for denial that He was born from the nature of God, when the proof that He is God's Son is that He does the works which belong to the Father's nature? No creature is equal or like to God, no nature external to His is comparable in might to Him; it is only the Son, born from Himself, Whom we can without blasphemy liken and equal to Him. Nothing outside Himself can be compared to God without insult to His august majesty. If any being, not born from God's self, can be discovered that is like Him and equal to Him in power, then God, in admitting a partner to share His throne, forfeits His pre-eminence. No longer is God One, for a second, indistinguishable from Himself, has arisen. On the other hand, there is no insult in making His own true Son His equal. For then that which is like Him is His own; that which is compared with Him is born from Himself; the Power that can do His own works is not external to Him. Nay more, it is an actual heightening of His glory, that He has begotten Omnipotence, and yet not severed that Omnipotent nature from Himself. The Son performs the Father's works, and on that ground demands that we should believe that He is God's Son. This is no

---

[1] Rom. i. 2—4.

claim of mere arrogance ; for He bases it upon His works, and bids us examine them. And He bears witness that these works are not His own, but His Father's. He would not have our thoughts distracted by the splendour of the deeds from the evidence for His birth. And because the Jews could not penetrate the mystery of the Body which He had taken, the Humanity born of Mary, and recognise the Son of God, He appeals to His deeds for confirmation of His right to the name ;—*But if I do them, and ye will not believe Me, believe the works.* First, He would not have them believe that He is the Son of God, except on the evidence of God's works which He does. Next, if He does the works, yet seems unworthy, in His bodily humility, to bear the Divine name, He demands that they shall believe the works. Why should the mystery of His human birth hinder our recognition of His birth as God, when He that is Divinely born fulfils every Divine task by the agency of that Manhood which He has assumed? If we believe not the Man, for the works' sake, when He tells us that He is the Son of God, let us believe the works when they, which are beyond a doubt the works of God, are manifestly wrought by the Son of God. For the Son of God possesses, in virtue of His birth, everything that is God's ; and therefore the Son's work is the Father's work because His birth has not excluded Him from that nature which is His source and wherein He abides, and because He has in Himself that nature to which He owes it that He exists eternally.

27. And so the Son, Who does the Father's works and demands of us that, if we believe not Him, at least we believe His works, is bound to tell us what the point is as to which we are to believe the works. And He does tell us in the words which follow :—*But if I do, and ye will not believe Me, believe the works, that ye may know and be sure that the Father is in Me, and I in Him.* It is the same truth as is contained in *I am the Son of God*, and *I and the Father are One.* This is the nature which is His by birth ; this the mystery of the saving faith, that we must not divide the unity, nor separate the nature from the birth, but must confess that the living God was in truth born from the living God. God, Who is Life, is not a Being built up of various and lifeless portions ; He is Power, and not compact of feeble elements, Light, intermingled with no shades of darkness, Spirit, that can harmonise with no incongruities. All that is within Him is One ; what is Spirit is Light and Power and Life, and what is Life is Light and Power and Spirit. He Who says,

I am, and I change not[2], can suffer neither change in detail nor transformation in kind. For these attributes, which I have named, are not attached to different portions of Him, but meet and unite, entirely and perfectly, in the whole being of the living God. He is the living God, the eternal Power of the living Divine nature ; and that which is born from Him, according to the mysterious truth which He reveals, could not be other than living. For when He said, *As the living Father hath sent Me, and I live through the Father*[3], He taught that it is through the living Father that He has life in Himself. And, moreover, when He said, *For as the Father hath life in Himself, so hath He given to the Son also to have life in Himself*[4], He bore witness that life, to the fullest extent, is His gift from the living God. Now if the living Son was born from the living Father, that birth took place without a new nature coming into existence. Nothing new comes into existence when the Living is begotten by the Living ; for life was not sought out from the non-existent to receive birth ; and Life, which receives its birth from Life, must needs, because of that unity of nature and because of the mysterious event of that perfect and ineffable birth, live always in Him that lives and have the life of the Living in Himself.

28. I call to mind that, at the beginning of our treatise[5], I gave the warning that human analogies correspond imperfectly to their Divine counterparts, yet that our understanding receives a real, if incomplete, enlightenment by comparing the latter with visible types. And now I appeal to human experience in the matter of birth, whether the source of their children's being remain not within the parents. For though the lifeless and ignoble matter, which sets in motion the beginnings of life, pass from one parent into the other, yet these retain their respective natural forces. They have brought into existence a nature one with their own, and therefore the begetter is bound up with the existence of the begotten ; and the begotten, receiving birth through a force transmitted, yet not lost, by the begetter, abides in that begetter. This may suffice as a statement of what happens in a human birth. It is inadequate as a parallel to the perfect birth of God the Only-begotten; for humanity is born in weakness and from the union of two unlike natures, and maintained in life by a combination of lifeless substances. Again, humanity does not enter at once into the exercise of its appointed life

2 Mal. iii. 6.   3 St. John vi. 57.   4 Ib. v. 26.
5 Book i. § 19, iv. § 9, vi. § 9.

and never fully lives that life, being always encumbered with a multitude of members which decay and are insensibly discarded. In God, on the other hand, the Divine life is lived in the fullest sense, for God is Life; and from Life nothing that is not truly living can be born. And His birth is not by way of emanation but results from an act of power. Thus, since God's life is perfect in its intensity, and since that which is born from Him is perfect in power, God has the power of giving birth but not of suffering change. His nature is capable of increase [6], not of diminution, for He continues in, and shares the life of, that Son to Whom He gave in birth a nature like to, and inseparable from, His own. And that Son, the Living born from the Living, is not separated by the event of His birth from the nature that begat Him.

29. Another analogy which casts some light upon the meaning of the faith is that of fire, as containing fire in itself and as abiding in fire. Fire contains the brightness of light, the heat which is its essential nature, the property of destroying by combustion the flickering inconstancy of flame. Yet all the while it is fire, and in all these manifestations there is but one nature. Its weakness is that it is dependent for its existence upon inflammable matter, and that it perishes with the matter on which it has lived. A comparison with fire gives us, in some measure, an insight into the incomparable nature of God; it helps us to believe in the properties of God that we find them, to a certain extent, present in an earthly element. I ask, then, whether in fire derived from fire there is any division or separation. When one flame is kindled from another, is the original nature cut off from the derived, so as not to abide in it? Does it not rather follow on, and dwell in the second flame by a kind of increase, as it were by birth? For no portion has been cut off from the nature of the first flame, and yet there is light from light. Does not the first flame live on in the second, which owes its existence, though not by division, to the first? Does not the second still dwell in the first, from which it was not cut off; from which it went forth, retaining its unity with the substance to which its nature belongs? Are not the two one, when it is physically impossible to derive light from light by division, and logically impossible to distinguish between them in nature.

30. These illustrations, I repeat, must only be used as aids to apprehension of the faith, not as standards of comparison for the Divine majesty. Our method is that of using bodily instances as a clue to the invisible. Reverence and reason justify us in using such help, which we find used in God's witness to Himself, while yet we do not aspire to find a parallel to the nature of God. But the minds of simple believers have been distressed by the mad heretical objection that it is wrong to accept a doctrine concerning God which needs, in order to become intelligible, the help of bodily analogies. And therefore, in accordance with that word of our Lord which we have already cited, *That which is born of the flesh is flesh, but that which is born of the Spirit is Spirit* [7], we have thought it expedient, since God is Spirit, to give to these comparisons a certain place in our argument. By so doing we shall avert from God the charge that He has deceived us in using these analogies; shewing, as we have done, that such illustrations from the nature of His creatures enable us to grasp the meaning of God's self-revelation to us.

31. We see how the living Son of the living Father, He Who is God from God, reveals the unity of the Divine nature, indissolubly One and the same, and the mystery of His birth in these words, *I and the Father are One.* Because the seeming arrogance of them engendered a prejudice against Him, He made it more clear that He had spoken in the conscious possession of Divinity by saying, *Ye say that I have blasphemed because I said, I am the Son of God;* thus shewing that the oneness of His nature with that of God was due to birth from God. And then, to clench their faith in His birth by a positive assertion, and to guard them, at the same time, from imagining that the birth involves a difference of nature, He crowns His argument with the words, *Believe the works, that the Father is in Me, and I in the Father.* Does His birth, as here revealed, display His Divinity as not His by nature, as not His own by right? Each is in the Other; the birth of the Son is from the Father only; no alien or unlike nature has been raised to Godhead and subsists as God. God from God, eternally abiding, owes His Godhead to none other than God. Import, if you see your opportunity, two gods into the Church's faith; separate Son from Father as far as you can, consistently with the birth which you admit; yet still the Father is in the Son, and the Son is in the Father, and this by no interchange of emanations but by the perfect birth of the living nature. Thus you cannot add together God the Father and God the Son, and count Them as two Gods,

---

[6] Cf. the next section.

[7] St. John iii. 6.

for They Two are One God. You cannot confuse Them together, for They Two are not One Person. And so the Apostolic faith rejects two gods; for it knows nothing of two Fathers or two Sons. In confessing the Father it confesses the Son; it believes in the Son in believing in the Father. For the name of Father involves that of Son, since without having a son none can be a father. Evidence of the existence of a son is proof that there has been a father, for a son cannot exist except from a father. When we confess that God is One we deny that He is single; for the Son is the complement of the Father, and to the Father the Son's existence is due. But birth works no change in the Divine nature; both in Father and in Son that nature is true to its kind. And the right expression for us of this unity of nature is the confession that They, being Two by birth and generation, are One God, not one Person.

32. We will leave it to him to preach two Gods, who can preach One God without confessing the unity: he shall proclaim that God is solitary, who can deny that there are two Persons, Each dwelling in the Other by the power of Their nature and the mystery of birth given and received. And that man may assign a different nature to Each of the Two, who is ignorant that the unity of Father and of Son is a revealed truth. Let the heretics blot out this record of the Son's self-revelation, *I in the Father and the Father in Me;* then, and not till then, shall they assert that there are two Gods, or one God in loneliness. There is no hint of more natures than one in what we are told of Their possession of the one Divine nature. The truth that God is from God does not multiply God by two: the birth destroys the supposition of a lonely God. And again, because They are interdependent They form an unity; and that They are interdependent is proved by Their being One from One. For the One, in begetting the One, conferred upon Him nothing that was not His own; and the One, in being begotten, received from the One only what belongs to one. Thus the apostolic faith, in proclaiming the Father, will proclaim Him as One God, and in confessing the Son will confess Him as One God; since one and the same Divine nature exists in Both, and because, the Father being God and the Son being God, and the one name of God expressing the nature of Both, the term 'One God' signifies the Two. God from God, or God in God, does not mean that there are two Gods, for God abides, One from One, eternally with the one Divine nature and the one Divine name; nor does God dwindle down to a single

Person, for One and One can never be in solitude.

33. The Lord has not left in doubt or obscurity the teaching conveyed in this great mystery; He has not abandoned us to lose our way in dim uncertainty. Listen to Him as He reveals the full knowledge of this faith to His Apostles;—*I am the Way and the Truth and the Life; no man cometh unto the Father but through Me. If ye know Me, ye know My Father also; and from henceforth ye shall know Him, and have seen Him. Philip saith unto Him, Lord, shew us the Father, and it sufficeth us. Jesus saith unto him, Have I been so long time with you, and ye have not known Me, Philip? He that hath seen Me hath seen the Father also. How sayest thou, Shew us the Father? Dost thou not believe Me, that I am in the Father, and the Father is in Me? The words that I speak unto you I speak not of Myself, but the Father that dwelleth in Me, He doeth His works. Believe Me, that I am in the Father, and the Father in Me; or else believe for the very works' sake*[8]. He Who is the Way leads us not into by-paths or trackless wastes: He Who is the Truth mocks us not with lies; He Who is the Life betrays us not into delusions which are death. He Himself has chosen these winning names to indicate the methods which He has appointed for our salvation. As the Way, He will guide us to the Truth; the Truth will establish us in the Life. And therefore it is all-important for us to know what is the mysterious mode, which He reveals, of attaining this life. *No man cometh to the Father but through Me.* The way to the Father is through the Son. And now we must enquire whether this is to be by a course of obedience to His teaching, or by faith in His Godhead. For it is conceivable that our way to the Father may be through adherence to the Son's teaching, rather than through believing that the Godhead of the Father dwells in the Son. And therefore let us, in the next place, seek out the true meaning of the instruction given us here. For it is not by cleaving to a preconceived opinion, but by studying the force of the words, that we shall enter into possession of this faith.

34. The words which follow those last cited are, *If ye know Me, ye know My Father also.* It is the Man, Jesus Christ, Whom they behold. How can a knowledge of Him be a knowledge of the Father? For the Apostles see Him wearing the aspect of that human nature which belongs to Him: but God is not encumbered with body and flesh, and

---

[8] St. John xiv. 6—11.

is incognisable by those who dwell in our weak and fleshly body. The answer is given by the Lord, Who asserts that under the flesh, which, in a mystery, He had taken, His Father's nature dwells within Him. He sets the facts in their due order thus;—*If ye know Me, ye know My Father also; and from henceforth ye shall know Him, and have seen Him.* He makes a distinction between the time of sight, and the time of knowledge. He says that from henceforth they shall know Him, Whom they had already seen; and so shall possess, from the time of this revelation onward, the knowledge of that nature, on which, in Him, they long had gazed.

35. But the novel sound of these words disturbed the Apostle Philip. A Man is before their eyes; this Man avows Himself the Son of God, and declares that when they have known Him they will know the Father. He tells them that they have seen the Father, and that, because they have seen Him, they shall know Him hereafter. This truth is too broad for the grasp of weak humanity; their faith fails in the presence of these paradoxes. Christ says that the Father has been seen already and shall now be known; and this, although sight, is knowledge. He says that if the Son has been known, the Father has been known also; and this though the Son has imparted knowledge of Himself through the bodily senses of sight and sound, while the Father's nature, different altogether from that [9] of the visible Man, which they know, could not be learnt from their knowledge of the nature of Him Whom they have seen. He has also often borne witness that no man has seen the Father. And so Philip broke forth, with the loyalty and confidence of an Apostle, with the request, *Lord, shew us the Father, and it sufficeth us.* He was not tampering with the faith; it was but a mistake made in ignorance. For the Lord had said that the Father had been seen already and henceforth should be known; but the Apostle had not understood that He had been seen. Accordingly he did not deny that the Father had been seen, but asked to see Him. He did not ask that the Father should be unveiled to his bodily gaze, but that he might have such an indication as should enlighten him concerning the Father Who had been seen. For he had seen the Son under the aspect of Man, but cannot understand how he could thereby have seen the Father. His adding, *And it sufficeth us,* to the prayer, *Lord, shew us the Father,* reveals clearly that it was a mental, not a bodily vision of the Father which he

desired. He did not refuse faith to the Lord's words, but asked for such enlightenment to his mind as should enable him to believe; for the fact that the Lord had spoken was conclusive evidence to the Apostle that faith was his duty. The consideration which moved him to ask that the Father might be shewn, was that the Son had said that He had been seen, and should be known because He had been seen. There was no presumption in this prayer that He, Who had already been seen, should now be made manifest.

36. And therefore the Lord answered Philip thus;—*Have I been so long time with you, and ye have not known Me, Philip?* He rebukes the Apostle for defective knowledge of Himself; for previously He had said that when He was known the Father was known also. But what is the meaning of this complaint that for so long they had not known Him? It means this; that if they had known Him, they must have recognised in Him the Godhead which belongs to His Father's nature. For His works were the peculiar works of God. He walked upon the waves, commanded the winds, manifestly, though none could tell how, changed the water into wine and multiplied the loaves, put devils to flight, healed diseases, restored injured limbs and repaired the defects of nature, forgave sins and raised the dead to life. And all this He did while wearing flesh; and He accompanied the works with the assertion that He was the Son of God. Hence it is that He justly complains that they did not recognise in His mysterious human birth and life the action of the nature of God, performing these deeds through the Manhood which He had assumed.

37. And therefore the Lord reproached them that they had not known Him, though He had so long been doing these works, and answered their prayer that He would shew them the Father by saying, *He that hath seen Me hath seen the Father also.* He was not speaking of a bodily manifestation, of perception by the eye of flesh, but by that eye of which He had once spoken;—*Say not ye, There are yet four months, and then cometh harvest? Behold, I say unto you, Lift up your eyes and look on the fields; for they are white to harvest* [1]. The season of the year, the fields white to harvest are allusions equally incompatible with an earthly and visible prospect. He was bidding them lift the eyes of their understanding to contemplate the bliss of the final harvest. And so it is with His present words, *He that hath seen Me hath seen the Father also.* It was not the carnal body,

---

9 Reading *ab ea.*

1 St. John iv. 35.

which He had received by birth from the Virgin, that could manifest to them the image and likeness of God. The human aspect which He wore could be no aid towards the mental vision of the incorporeal God. But God was recognised in Christ, by such as recognised Christ as the Son on the evidence of the powers of His Divine nature; and a recognition of God the Son produces a recognition of God the Father. For the Son is in such a sense the Image, as to be One in kind with the Father, and yet to indicate that the Father is His Origin. Other images, made of metals or colours or other materials by various arts, reproduce the appearance of the objects which they represent. Yet can lifeless copies be put on a level with their living originals? Painted or carved or molten effigies with the nature which they imitate? The Son is not the Image of the Father after such a fashion as this; He is the living Image of the Living. The Son that is born of the Father has a nature in no wise different from His; and, because His nature is not different, He possesses the power of that nature which is the same as His own. The fact that He is the Image proves that God the Father is the Author of the birth of the Only-begotten, Who is Himself revealed as the Likeness and Image of the invisible God. And hence the likeness, which is joined in union with the Divine nature, is indelibly His, because the powers of that nature are inalienably His own.

38. Such is the meaning of this passage, *Have I been so long time with you, and ye have not known Me, Philip? He that hath seen Me hath seen the Father also. How sayest thou, Shew us the Father? Dost thou not believe Me, that I am in the Father, and the Father is in Me?* It is only the Word of God, of Whom we men are enabled, in our discourse concerning Divine things, to reason. All else that belongs to the Godhead is dark and difficult, dangerous and obscure. If any man propose to express what is known in other words than those supplied by God, he must inevitably either display his own ignorance, or else leave his readers' minds in utter perplexity. The Lord, when He was asked to shew the Father, said, *He that hath seen Me hath seen the Father also.* He that would alter this is an antichrist, he that would deny it is a Jew, he that is ignorant a Pagan. If we find ourselves in difficulty, let us lay the fault to our own reason; if God's declaration seem involved in obscurity, let us assume that our want of faith is the cause. These words state with precision that God is not solitary, and yet that there are no differences within the

Divine nature. For the Father is seen in the Son, and this could be the case neither if He were a lonely Being, nor yet if He were unlike the Son. It is through the Son that the Father is seen: and this mystery which the Son reveals is that They are One God, but not one Person. What other meaning can you attach to this saying of the Lord's, *He that hath seen Me hath seen the Father also?* This is no case of identity; the use of the conjunction *also* shews that the Father is named in addition to the Son. These words, *The Father also*, are incompatible with the notion of an isolated and single Person. No conclusion is possible but that the Father was made visible through the Son, because They are One and are alike in nature. And, lest our faith in this regard should be left in any doubt, the Lord proceeded, *How sayest thou, Shew us the Father?* The Father had been seen in the Son; how then could men be ignorant of the Father? What need could there be for Him to be shewn?

39. Again, the unity of Begetter and Begotten, manifested in sameness of nature and true oneness of kind, proves that the Father was seen in His true nature. And this is shewn by the Lord's next words, *Believe ye not that I am in the Father, and the Father in Me?* In no other words than these, which the Son has used, can the fact be stated that Father and Son, being alike in nature, are inseparable. The Son, Who is the Way and the Truth and the Life, is not deceiving us by some theatrical transformation of names and aspects, when He, while wearing Manhood, styles Himself the Son of God. He is not falsely concealing the fact that He is God the Father[2]; He is not a single Person[3] Who hides His features under a mask, that we may imagine that Two are present. He is not a solitary Being, now posing as His own Son, and again calling Himself the Father; tricking out one unchanging nature with varying names. Far removed from this is the plain honesty of the words. The Father is the Father, and the Son is the Son. But these names, and the realities which they represent, contain no innovation upon the Divine nature, nothing inconsistent, nothing alien. For the Divine nature, being true to itself, persists in being itself; that which is from God is God. The Divine birth imports neither diminution nor difference into the Godhead, for the Son is born into, and subsists with, a nature that is within the Divine nature and is like to it, and the Father sought out no alien element

---

[2] Sabellianism.
[3] *Personalis* occurs here for the first time; *persona* is found in iii. 23, v. 26.

to be mingled in the nature of His Only-begotten Son, but endowed Him with all things that are His own, and this without loss to the Giver. And thus the Son is not destitute of the Divine nature, for, being God, He is from God and from none other; and He is not different from God, but is indeed nothing else than God, for that which is begotten from God is the Son, and the Son only, and the Divine nature, in receiving birth as a Son, has not forfeited its Divinity. Thus the Father is in the Son, the Son is in the Father, God is in God. And this is not by the combination of two harmonious, though different, kinds of being, nor by the incorporating power of an ampler substance exercised upon a lesser; for the properties of matter make it impossible that things which enclose others should also be enclosed by them. It is by the birth of living nature from living nature. The substance remains the same, birth causes no deterioration in the Divine nature; God is not born from God to be ought else than God. Herein is no innovation, no estrangement, no division. It is sin to believe that Father and Son are two Gods, sacrilege to assert that Father and Son are one solitary God, blasphemy to deny the unity, consisting in sameness of kind, of God from God.

40. Lest they, whose faith conforms to the Gospel, should regard this mystery as something vague and obscure, the Lord has expounded it in this order;—*Dost thou not believe Me, that I am in the Father, and the Father is in Me? The words that I speak unto you I speak not of Myself, but the Father that dwelleth in Me, He doeth His works.* In what other words than these could, or can, the possession of the Divine nature by Father and Son be declared, consistently with prominence for the Son's birth? When He says, *The words that I speak unto you I speak not of Myself*, He neither suppresses His personality, nor denies His Sonship, nor conceals the presence in Himself of His Father's Divine nature. While speaking of Himself—and that He does so speak is proved by the pronoun *I*—He speaks as abiding in the Divine substance; while speaking not of Himself, He bears witness to the birth which took place in Him of God from God His Father. And He is inseparable and indistinguishable in unity of nature from the Father; for He speaks, though He speaks not of Himself. He Who speaks, though He speak not of Himself, necessarily exists, inasmuch as He speaks; and, inasmuch as He speaks not of Himself, He makes it manifest that His words are not His own. For He has added, *But the Father that dwelleth in Me, He doeth His*

works. That the Father dwells in the Son proves that the Father is not isolated and alone; that the Father works through the Son proves that the Son is not an alien or a stranger. There cannot be one Person only, for He speaks not of Himself; and, conversely, They cannot be separate and divided when the One speaks through the voice of the Other. These words are the revelation of the mystery of Their unity. And again, They Two are not different One from the Other, seeing that by Their inherent nature Each is in the Other; and They are One, seeing that He, Who speaks, speaks not of Himself, and He, Who speaks not of Himself, yet does speak. And then, having taught that the Father both spoke and wrought in Him, the Son establishes this perfect unity as the rule of our faith;—*But the Father that dwelleth in Me, He doeth His works. Believe Me, that I am in the Father, and the Father in Me; or else believe for the very works' sake.* The Father works in the Son; but the Son also works the works of His Father.

41. And so, lest we should believe and say that the Father works in the Son through His own omnipotent energy, and not through the Son's possession, as His birthright, of the Divine nature, Christ says, *Believe Me, that I am in the Father, and the Father in Me.* What means this, *Believe Me?* Clearly it refers back to the previous, *Shew us the Father.* Their faith—that faith which had demanded that the Father should be shewn—is confirmed by this command to believe. He was not satisfied with saying, *He that hath seen Me hath seen the Father also.* He goes further, and expands our knowledge, so that we can contemplate the Father in the Son, remembering meanwhile that the Son is in the Father. Thus He would save us from the error of imagining a reciprocal emanation of the One into the Other, by teaching Their unity in the One nature through birth given and received. The Lord would have us take Him at His word, lest our hold upon the faith be shaken by His condescension in assuming Humanity. If His flesh, His body, His passion seem to make His Godhead doubtful, let us at least believe, on the evidence of the works, that God is in God and God is from God, and that They are One. For by the power of Their nature Each is in the Other. The Father loses nothing that is His because it is in the Son, and the Son receives His whole Sonship from the Father. Bodily natures are not created after such a fashion that they mutually contain each other, or possess the perfect unity of one abiding nature. In their case it would be impossible that an Only-

begotten Son could exist eternally, inseparable from the true Divine nature of His Father. Yet this is the peculiar property of God the Only-begotten, this the faith revealed in the mystery of His true birth, this the work of the Spirit's power, that to be, and to be in God, is for Christ the same thing; and that this being in God is not the presence of one thing within another, as a body inside another body, but that the life and subsistence of Christ is such that He is within the subsisting God, and within Him, yet having a subsistence of His own. For Each subsists in such wise as not to exist apart from the Other, since They are Two through birth given and received, and therefore only one Divine nature exists. This is the meaning of the words, *I and the Father are One*, and *He that hath seen Me hath seen the Father also*, and *I in the Father and the Father in Me*. They tell us that the Son Who is born is not different or inferior to the Father; that His possession, by right of birth, of the Divine nature as Son of God, and therefore nothing else than God, is the supreme truth conveyed in the mysterious revelation of the One Godhead in Father and Son. And therefore the doctrine of the generation of the Only-begotten is guiltless of ditheism, for the Son of God, in being born into the Godhead, manifested in Himself the nature of God His Begetter.

BOOK VIII.

1. THE Blessed Apostle Paul in laying down the form for appointing a bishop and creating by his instructions an entirely new type of member of the Church, has taught us in the following words the sum total of all the virtues perfected in him:—*Holding fast the word according to the doctrine of faith that he may be able to exhort to sound doctrine and to convict gainsayers. For there are many unruly men, vain talkers and deceivers* [1]. For in this way he points out that the essentials of orderliness and morals are only profitable for good service in the priesthood if at the same time the qualities needful for knowing how to teach and preserve the faith are not lacking, for a man is not straightway made a good and useful priest [2] by a merely innocent life or by a mere knowledge of preaching. For an innocent minister is profitable to himself alone unless he be instructed also ; while he that is instructed has nothing to support his teaching unless he be innocent. For the words of the Apostle do not merely fit a man for his life in this world by precepts of honesty and uprightness, nor on the other hand do they educate in expertness of teaching a mere Scribe of the Synagogue for the expounding of the Law : but the Apostle is training a leader of the Church, perfected by the perfect accomplishment of the greatest virtues, so that his life may be adorned by his teaching, and his teaching by his life. Accordingly he has provided Titus, the person to whom his words were addressed, with an injunction as to the perfect practice of religion to this effect :—*In all things shewing thyself an ensample of good works, teaching with gravity sound words that cannot be condemned, that the adversary may be ashamed, having nothing disgraceful or evil to say of us* [3]. This teacher of the Gentiles and elect doctor of the Church, from his consciousness of Christ who spoke and dwelt within him, knew well that the infection of tainted speech would spread abroad, and that the corruption of pestilent doctrine would furiously rage against the sound form of faithful words, and infusing the poison of its own evil tenets into the inmost soul, would creep on with deep-seated mischief. For it is of these that he says, *Whose word spreadeth like a cancer* [4], tainting the health of the mind, invaded by it with a secret and stealthy contagion. For this reason, he wished that there should be in the bishop the teaching of sound words, a good conscience in the faith and expertness in exhortation to withstand wicked and false and wild gainsayings. For there are many who pretend to the faith, but are not subject to the faith, and rather set up a faith for themselves than receive that which is given, being puffed up with the thoughts of human vanity, knowing the things they wish to know and unwilling to know the things that are true ; since it is a mark of true wisdom sometimes to know what we do not like. However, this will-wisdom is followed by foolish preaching, for what is foolishly learnt must needs be foolishly preached. Yet how great an evil to those who hear is foolish preaching, when they are misled into foolish opinions by conceit of wisdom ! And for this cause the Apostle described them thus : *There are many unruly, vain talkers and deceivers* [5]. Hence we must utter our voice against arrogant wickedness and boastful arrogance and seductive boastfulness,—yes, we must speak against such things through the soundness of our doctrine, the truth of our faith, the sincerity of our preaching, so that we may have the purity of truth and the truth of sound doctrine.

2. The reason why I have just mentioned this utterance of the Apostle is this ; men of crooked minds and false professions, void of hope and venomous of speech, lay upon me the necessity of inveighing against them, because under the guise of religion they instil deadly doctrines, infectious thoughts and corrupt desires into the simple minds of their hearers. And this they do with an utter disregard of the true sense of the apostolic teaching, so that the Father is not a Father, nor the Son, Son, nor the Faith, the Faith. In resisting their wild falsehoods, we have extended the course of our reply so far, that after proving from the Law that God and God were distinct and that very God was in very God, we then shewed from the teaching of evangelists and

---

[1] Tit. i. 9, 10.   [2] i.e. bishop.
[3] Tit. ii. 7, 8.   [4] 2 Tim. ii. 17.   [5] Tit. i. 9.

apostles the perfect and true birth of the Only-begotten God; and lastly, we pointed out in the due course of our argument that the Son of God is very God, and of a nature identical with the Father's, so that the faith of the Church should neither confess that God is single nor that there are two Gods. For neither would the birth of God allow God to be solitary, nor would a perfect birth allow different natures to be ascribed to two Gods. Now in refuting their vain speaking we have a twofold object, first that we may teach what is holy and perfect and sound, and, that our discourse should not by straying through any by-paths and crooked ways, and struggling out of devious and winding tunnels, seem rather to search for the truth than declare it. Our second object is that we should reveal to the conviction of all men the folly and absurdity of those crafty arguments of their vain and deceitful opinions which are adapted to a plausible show of seductive truth. For it is not enough for us to have pointed out what things are good, unless they are understood to be absolutely good by our refutation of their opposites.

3. But as it is the nature and endeavour of the good and wise to prepare themselves wholly for securing either the reality or the opportunity of some precious hope lest their preparedness should in some respects fall short of that which they look for,—so in like manner those who are filled with the madness of heretical frenzy make it their chiefest anxiety to labour with all the ingenuity of their impiety against the truth of pious faith, in order that against those who are religious they may establish their own irreligion; that they may surpass the hope of our life in the hopelessness of their own, and that they may spend more thought over false than we spend over true teaching. For against the pious assertions of our faith they have carefully devised such objections of their impious misbelief, as first to ask whether we believe in one God, next, whether Christ also be God, lastly, whether the Father is greater than the Son, in order that when they hear us confess that God is one they may use our reply to shew that Christ cannot be God. For they do not enquire concerning the Son whether He be God; all they wish for in asking questions about Christ is to prove that He is not a Son, that by entrapping men of simple faith they may through the belief in one God divert them from the belief in Christ as God, on the ground that God is no longer one if Christ also must be acknowledged as God. Again with what subtlety of worldly wisdom do they contend when they say, If God is one, whosoever that other shall be shewn to be, he will not be God. For if there be another God He can no longer be one, since nature does not permit that where there is another there should be one only, or that where there is only one there should be another. Afterwards, when by the crafty cunning of this insidious argument they have misled those who are ready to believe and listen, they then apply this proposition (as if they could now establish it by an easier method), that Christ is God rather in name than in nature, because this generic name in Him can destroy in none that only true belief in one God: and they contend that through this the Father is greater than the Son, because, the natures being different, as there is but one God, the Father is greater from the essential character of His nature; and that the Other is only called Son while He is really a creature subsisting by the will of the Father, because He is less than the Father; and also that He is not God, because God being one does not admit of another God, since he who is less must necessarily be of a nature alien from that of the person who is greater. Again, how foolish they are in their attempts to lay down a law for God when they maintain that no birth can take place from one single being, because throughout the universe birth arises from the union of two; moreover, that the unchangeable God cannot accord from Himself birth to one who is born, because that which is changeless is incapable of addition, nor can the nature of a solitary and single being contain within itself the property of generation.

4. We, on the contrary, having by spiritual teaching arrived at the faith of the evangelists and apostles, and following after the hope of eternal blessedness by our confession of the Father and the Son, and having proved out of the Law the mystery of God and God, without overstepping the limits of our faith in one God, or failing to proclaim that Christ is God, have adopted this method of reply from the Gospels, that we declare the true nativity of Only-begotten God from God the Father, because that through this He was both very God and not alien from the nature of the One very God, and thus neither could His Godhead be denied nor Himself be described as another God, because while the birth made Him God, the nature within him of one God of God did not separate Him off as another God. And although our human reason led us to this conclusion, that the names of distinct natures could not meet together in the same nature, and not be one, where the essence of each did not differ in kind; nevertheless, it seemed good that we should prove this from the ex-

press sayings of our Lord, Who after frequently making known that the God of our faith and hope was One, in order to affirm the mystery of the One God, while declaring and proving His own Godhead, said, *I and the Father are one;* and, *If ye had known Me, ye would have known My Father also;* and, *He that hath seen Me hath seen the Father also;* and, *Believe Me, that the Father is in Me, and I in the Father: or else believe for the very works' sake* [6]. He has signified His own birth in the name *Father,* and declares that in the knowledge of Himself the Father is known. He avows the unity of nature, when those who see Him see the Father. He bears witness that He is indivisible from the Father, when He dwells in the Father Who dwells in Him. He possesses the confidence of self-knowledge when He demands credit for His words from the operations of His power. And thus in this most blessed faith of the perfect birth, every error, as well that of two Gods as of a single God, is abolished, since They Who are one in essence are not one person, and He Who is not one person with HIM WHO IS, is yet so free from difference from Him that They Two are One God.

5. Now seeing that heretics cannot deny these things because they are so clearly stated and understood, they nevertheless pervert them by the most foolish and wicked lies so as afterwards to deny them. For the words of Christ, *I and the Father are one* [7], they endeavour to refer to a mere concord of unanimity, so that there may be in them a unity of will not of nature, that is, that they may be one not by essence of being, but by identity of will. And they apply to the support of their case the passage in the Acts of the Apostles, *Now of the multitude of them that believed the heart and soul were one* [8], in order to prove that a diversity of souls and hearts may be united into one heart and soul through a mere conformity of will. Or else they cite those words to the Corinthians, *Now he that planteth and he that watereth are one* [9], to shew that, since They are one in Their work for our salvation, and in the revelation of one mystery, Their unity is an unity of wills. Or again, they quote the prayer of our Lord for the salvation of the nations who should believe in Him: *Neither for these only do I pray, but for them also that shall believe on Me through their Word; that they all may be one; even as Thou, Father, art in Me, and I in Thee, that they also may be in Us* [1], to shew that since men cannot, so to speak, be fused back

into God or themselves coalesce into one undistinguished mass, this oneness must arise from unity of will, while all perform actions pleasing to God, and unite one with another in the harmonious accord of their thoughts, and that thus it is not nature which makes them one, but will.

6. He clearly knows not wisdom who knows not God. And since Christ is Wisdom he must needs be beyond the pale of wisdom who knows not Christ or hates Him [2]. As, for instance, they do who will have it that the Lord of Glory, and King of the Universe, and Only-begotten God is a creature of God and not His Son, and in addition to such foolish lies shew a still more foolish cleverness in the defence of their falsehood. For even putting aside for a little that essential character of unity which exists in God the Father and God the Son, they can be refuted out of the very passages which they adduce.

7. For as to those whose soul and heart were one, I ask whether they were one through faith in God? Yes, assuredly, through faith, for through this the soul and heart of all were one. Again I ask, is the faith one or is there a second faith? One undoubtedly, and that on the authority of the Apostle himself, who proclaims one faith even as one Lord, and one baptism, and one hope, and one God [3]. If then it is through faith, that is, through the nature of one faith, that all are one, how is it that thou dost not understand a natural unity in the case of those who through the nature of one faith are one? For all were born again to innocence, to immortality, to the knowledge of God, to the faith of hope. And if these things cannot differ within themselves because there is both one hope and one God, as also there is one Lord and one baptism of regeneration; if these things are one rather by agreement than by nature, ascribe a unity of will to those also who have been born again into them. If, however, they have been begotten again into the nature of one life and eternity, then, inasmuch as their soul and heart are one, the unity of will fails to account for their case who are one by regeneration into the same nature.

8. These are not our own conjectures which we offer, nor do we falsely put together any of these things in order to deceive the ears of our hearers by perverting the meaning of words; but holding fast the form of sound teaching we know and preach the things which are true. For the Apostle shews that this unity of the faithful arises from the nature of the sacraments when he writes to the Ga-

---

6 St. John x. 30; xiv. 7, 9, 10, 11.   7 Ib. x. 30.
8 Acts iv. 32.   9 1 Cor. iii. 8.   1 St. John xvii. 20, 21.

2 Reading *odit.*   3 Eph. iv. 4, 5.

latians. *For as many of you as were baptized into Christ did put on Christ. There is neither Jew nor Greek, there is neither bond nor free, there is neither male nor female; for ye are all one in Christ Jesus* [4]. That these are one amid so great diversities of race, condition, sex,—is it from an agreement of will or from the unity of the sacrament, since these have one baptism and have all put on one Christ? What, therefore, will a concord of minds avail here when they are one in that they have put on one Christ through the nature of one baptism?

9. Or, again, since he who plants and he who waters are one, are they not one because, being themselves born again in one baptism they form a ministry of one regenerating baptism? Do not they do the same thing? Are they not one in One? So they who are one through the same thing are one also by nature, not only by will, inasmuch as they themselves have been made the same thing and are ministers of the same thing and the same power.

10. Now the contradiction of fools always serves to prove their folly, because with regard to the faults which they contrive by the devices of an unwise or crooked understanding against the truth, while the latter remains unshaken and immovable the things which are opposed to it must needs be regarded as false and foolish. For heretics in their attempt to deceive others by the words, *I and the Father are one* [5], that there might not be acknowledged in them the unity and like essence of deity, but only a oneness arising from mutual love and an agreement of wills—these heretics, I say, have brought forward an instance of that unity, as we have shewn above, even from the words of our Lord, *That they all may be one, as Thou Father art in Me, and I in Thee, that they also may be in Us* [6]. Every man is outside the promises of the Gospel who is outside the faith in them, and by the guilt of an evil understanding has lost all simple hope. For to know not what thou believest demands not so much excuse as a reward, for the greatest service of faith is to hope for that which thou knowest not. But it is the madness of most consummate wickedness either not to believe things which are understood or to have corrupted the sense in which one believes.

11. But although the wickedness of man can pervert his intellectual powers, nevertheless the words retain their meaning. Our Lord prays to His Father that those who shall believe in Him may be one, and as He is in the Father and the Father in Him, so all may be one in Them. Why

dost thou bring in here an identity of mind, why a unity of soul and heart through agreement of will? For there would have been no lack of suitable words for our Lord, if it were will that made them one, to have prayed in this fashion,—Father, as We are one in will, so may they also be one in will, that we may all be one through agreement. Or could it be that He Who is the Word was unacquainted with the meaning of words? and that He Who is Truth knew not how to speak the truth? and He Who is Wisdom went astray in foolish talk? and He Who is Power was compassed about with such weakness that He could not speak what He wished to be understood? He has clearly spoken the true and sincere mysteries of the faith of the Gospel. And He has not only spoken that we may comprehend, He has also taught that we may believe, saying, *That they all may be one, as Thou Father art in Me, and I in Thee, that they also may be in Us.* For those first of all is the prayer of whom it is said, *That they all may be one.* Then the promotion of unity is set forth by a pattern of unity, when He says, *as Thou, Father, art in Me, and I in Thee, that they also may be in Us,* so that as the Father is in the Son and the Son in the Father, so through the pattern of this unity all might be one in the Father and the Son.

12. But because it is proper to the Father alone and the Son that They should be one by nature because God is from God, and the Only-begotten from the Unbegotten can subsist in no other nature than that of His origin; so that He Who was begotten should exist in the substance of His birth, and the birth should possess no other and different truth of deity than that from which it issued; for our Lord has left us in no doubt as to our belief by asserting throughout the whole of the discourse which follows the nature of this complete unity. For the next words are these, *That the world may believe that Thou didst send Me* [7]. Thus the world is to believe that the Son has been sent by the Father because all who shall believe in Him will be one in the Father and the Son. And how they will be so we are soon told,—*And the glory which Thou hast given Me I have given unto them* [8]. Now I ask whether glory is identical with will, since will is an emotion of the mind while glory is an ornament or embellishment of nature. So then it is the glory received from the Father that the Son hath given to all who shall believe in Him, and certainly not will. Had this been given, faith would carry with

---

4 Gal. iii. 27, 28.   5 St. John x. 30.   6 Ib. xvii. 21.

7 St. John xvii. 21.   8 Ib. 22.

it no reward, for a necessity of will attached to us would also impose faith upon us. However He has shewn what is effected by the bestowal of the glory received, *That they may be one, even as We are one*[9]. It is then with this object that the received glory was bestowed, that all might be one. So now all are one in glory, because the glory given is none other than that which was received: nor has it been given for any other cause than that all should be one. And since all are one through the glory given to the Son and by the Son bestowed upon believers, I ask how can the Son be of a different glory from the Father's, since the glory of the Son brings all that believe into the unity of the Father's glory. Now it may be that the utterance of human hope in this case may be somewhat immoderate, yet it will not be contrary to faith; for though to hope for this were presumptuous, yet not to have believed it is sinful, for we have one and the same Author both of our hope and of our faith. We will treat of this matter more clearly and at greater length in its own place, as is fitting. Yet in the meantime it is easily seen from our present argument that this hope of ours is neither vain nor presumptuous. So then through the glory received and given all are one. I hold the faith and recognise the cause of the unity, but I do not yet understand how it is that the glory given makes all one.

13. Now our Lord has not left the minds of His faithful followers in doubt, but has explained the manner in which His nature operates, saying, *That they may be one, as We are one: I in them and Thou in Me, that they may be perfected in one*[1]. Now I ask those who bring forward a unity of will between Father and Son, whether Christ is in us to-day through verity of nature or through agreement of will. For if in truth the Word has been made flesh and we in very truth receive the Word made flesh as food from the Lord, are we not bound to believe that He abides in us naturally, Who, born as a man, has assumed the nature of our flesh now inseparable from Himself, and has conjoined the nature of His own flesh to the nature of the eternal Godhead in the sacrament by which His flesh is communicated to us? For so are we all one, because the Father is in Christ and Christ in us. Whosoever then shall deny that the Father is in Christ naturally must first deny that either he is himself in Christ naturally, or Christ in him, because the Father in Christ and Christ in us make us one in Them. Hence, if indeed Christ has taken to Himself the flesh of our body, and that Man Who was born from Mary was indeed Christ, and we indeed receive in a mystery the flesh of His body—(and for this cause we shall be one, because the Father is in Him and He in us),—how can a unity of will be maintained, seeing that the special property of nature received through the sacrament is the sacrament of a perfect unity[2]?

14. The words in which we speak of the things of God must be used in no mere human and worldly sense, nor must the perverseness of an alien and impious interpretation be extorted from the soundness of heavenly words by any violent and headstrong preaching. Let us read what is written, let us understand what we read, and then fulfil the demands of a perfect faith. For as to what we say concerning the reality of Christ's nature within us, unless we have been taught by Him, our words are foolish and impious. For He says Himself, *My flesh is meat indeed, and My blood is drink indeed. He that eateth My flesh and drinketh My blood abideth in Me, and I in him*[3]. As to the verity of the flesh and blood there is no room left for doubt. For now both from the declaration of the Lord Himself and our own faith, it is verily flesh and verily blood. And these when eaten and drunk, bring it to pass that both we are in Christ and Christ in us. Is not this true? Yet they who affirm that Christ Jesus is not truly God are welcome to find it false. He therefore Himself is in us through the flesh and we in Him, whilst together with Him our own selves are in God.

15. Now how it is that we are in Him through the sacrament of the flesh and blood bestowed upon us, He Himself testifies, saying, *And the world will no longer see Me, but ye shall see Me; because I live ye shall live also; because I am in My Father, and ye in Me, and I in you*[4]. If He wished to indicate a mere unity of will, why did He set forth a kind of gradation and sequence in the completion of the unity, unless it were that, since He was in the Father through the nature of Deity, and we on the contrary in Him through His birth in the body, He would have us believe that He is in us through the mystery of the sacraments? and thus there might be taught a perfect unity through a Mediator, whilst, we abiding in Him, He abode in the Father, and as abiding in the Father abode

---

[9] St. John xvii. 22.   [1] Ib. 22, 23.

[2] If in the Sacrament we hold real communion with the Father and the Son, the union of Father and Son on which it is based must be also real, and not a mere concord of will.
[3] St. John vi. 55, 56.   [4] Ib. xiv. 19, 20.

also in us; and so we might arrive at unity with the Father, since in Him Who dwells naturally in the Father by birth, we also dwell naturally, while He Himself abides naturally in us also.

16. Again, how natural this unity is in us He has Himself testified on this wise,—*He who eateth My flesh and drinketh My blood abideth in Me, and I in him*[5]. For no man shall dwell in Him, save him in whom He dwells Himself, for the only flesh which He has taken to Himself is the flesh of those who have taken His. Now He had already taught before the sacrament of this perfect unity, saying, *As the living Father sent Me, and I live through the Father, so he that eateth My flesh shall himself also live through Me*[6]. So then He lives through the Father, and as He lives through the Father in like manner we live through His flesh. For all comparison is chosen to shape our understanding, so that we may grasp the subject of which we treat by help of the analogy set before us. This is the cause of our life that we have Christ dwelling within our carnal selves through the flesh, and we shall live through Him in the same manner as He lives through the Father. If, then, we live naturally through Him according to the flesh, that is, have partaken of the nature of His flesh, must He not naturally have the Father within Himself according to the Spirit since He Himself lives through the Father? And He lives through the Father because His birth has not implanted in Him an alien and different nature, inasmuch as His very being is from Him yet is not divided from Him by any barrier of an unlikeness of nature, for within Himself He has the Father through the birth in the power of the nature.

17. I have dwelt upon these facts because the heretics falsely maintain that the union between Father and Son is one of will only, and make use of the example of our own union with God, as though we were united to the Son and through the Son to the Father by mere obedience and a devout will, and none of the natural verity of communion were vouchsafed us through the sacrament of the Body and Blood; although the glory of the Son bestowed upon us through the Son abiding in us after the flesh, while we are united in Him corporeally and inseparably, bids us preach the mystery of the true and natural unity.

18. So we have made our reply to the folly of our violent opponents, merely to prove the emptiness of their falsehoods and so prevent them from misleading the unwary by the error of their vain and foolish statements. But the faith of the Gospel did not of necessity require our answer. The Lord prayed on our behalf for our union with God, but God keeps His own unity and abides in it. It is not through any mysterious appointment of God that they are one, but through a birth of nature, for God loses nothing in begetting Him from Himself. They are one, for the things which are not plucked out of His hand are not plucked out of the hand of the Father[7], for, when He is known, the Father is known, for, when He is seen, the Father is seen, for what He speaks the Father speaks as abiding in Him, for in His works the Father works, for He is in the Father and the Father in Him[8]. This proceeds from no creation but from birth; it is not brought about by will but by power; it is no agreement of mind that speaks, it is nature; because to be created and to be born are not one and the same, any more than to will and to be able; neither is it the same thing to agree and to abide.

19. Thus we do not deny a unanimity between the Father and the Son,—for heretics are accustomed to utter this falsehood, that since we do not accept concord by itself as the bond of unity we declare Them to be at variance. But let them listen how it is that we do not deny such a unanimity. The Father and the Son are one in nature, honour, power, and the same nature cannot will things that are contrary. Moreover, let them listen to the testimony of the Son as touching the unity of nature between Himself and the Father, for He says, *When that advocate is come, Whom I shall send to you from the Father, the Spirit of truth Who proceedeth from the Father, He shall testify of Me*[9]. The Advocate shall come and the Son shall send Him from the Father, and He is the Spirit of truth Who proceedeth from the Father. Let the whole following of heretics arouse the keenest powers of their wit; let them now seek for what lies they can tell to the unlearned, and declare what that is which the Son sends from the Father. He Who sends manifests His power in that which He sends. But as to that which He sends from the Father, how shall we regard it, as received or sent forth or begotten? For His words that He will *send from the Father* must imply one or other of these modes of sending. And He will send from the Father that Spirit of truth which proceedeth from the Father; He therefore

---

5 St. John vi. 56.   6 Ib. 57.

7 St. John x. 28, 29.   8 Ib. xiv. 7, 9, 10, 12.
9 Ib. xv. 26.

cannot be the Recipient, since He is revealed as the Sender. It only remains to make sure of our conviction on the point, whether we are to believe an egress of a co-existent Being, or a procession of a Being begotten.

20. For the present I forbear to expose their licence of speculation, some of them holding that the Paraclete Spirit comes from the Father or from the Son. For our Lord has not left this in uncertainty, for after these same words He spoke thus,— *I have yet many things to say unto you, but ye cannot bear them now. When He, the Spirit of truth, is come, He shall guide you into all truth: for He shall not speak from Himself: but what things soever He shall hear, these shall He speak; and He shall declare unto you the things that are to come. He shall glorify Me: for He shall receive of Mine and shall declare it unto you. All things whatsoever the Father hath are Mine: therefore said I, He shall receive of Mine and shall declare it unto you*[1]. Accordingly He receives from the Son, Who is both sent by Him, and proceeds from the Father. Now I ask whether to receive from the Son is the same thing as to proceed from the Father. But if one believes that there is a difference between receiving from the Son and proceeding from the Father, surely to receive from the Son and to receive from the Father will be regarded as one and the same thing. For our Lord Himself says, *Because He shall receive of Mine and shall declare it unto you. All things whatsoever the Father hath are Mine: therefore said I, He shall receive of Mine and shall declare it unto you.* That which He will receive,—whether it will be power, or excellence, or teaching,—the Son has said must be received from Him, and again He indicates that this same thing must be received from the Father. For when He says that all things whatsoever the Father hath are His, and that for this cause He declared that it must be received from His own, He teaches also that what is received from the Father is yet received from Himself, because all things that the Father hath are His. Such a unity admits no difference, nor does it make any difference from whom that is received, which given by the Father is described as given by the Son. Is a mere unity of will brought forward here also? All things which the Father hath are the Son's, and all things which the Son hath are the Father's. For He Himself saith, *And all Mine are Thine, and Thine are Mine*[2]. It is not yet the place to shew why He spoke thus, *For He shall receive of Mine:* for this

points to some subsequent time, when it is revealed that He shall receive. Now at any rate He says that He will receive of Himself, because all things that the Father had were His. Dissever if thou canst the unity of the nature, and introduce some necessary unlikeness through which the Son may not exist in unity of nature. For the Spirit of truth proceedeth from the Father and is sent from the Father by the Son. All things that the Father hath are the Son's; and for this cause whatever He Who is to be sent shall receive, He shall receive from the Son, because all things that the Father hath are the Son's. The nature in all respects maintains its law, and because Both are One that same Godhead is signified as existing in Both through generation and nativity; since the Son affirms that that which the Spirit of truth shall receive from the Father is to be given by Himself. So the frowardness of heretics must not be allowed an unchecked licence of impious beliefs, in refusing to acknowledge that this saying of the Lord,—that because all things which the Father hath are His, therefore the Spirit of truth shall receive of Him,—is to be referred to unity of nature.

21. Let us listen to that chosen vessel and teacher of the Gentiles, when he had already commended the faith of the people of Rome because of their understanding of the truth. For wishing to teach the unity of nature in the case of the Father and the Son, he speaks thus, *But ye are not in the flesh but in the Spirit, if indeed the Spirit of God is in you. But if any have not the Spirit of Christ, he is none of His. But if Christ is in you, the body indeed is dead through sin, but the Spirit is life through righteousness. But if the Spirit of Him Who raised up Christ from the dead dwelleth in you; He Who raised up Christ from the dead shall also quicken your mortal bodies, because of His Spirit Who dwelleth in you*[3]. We are all spiritual if the Spirit of God dwells in us. But this Spirit of God is also the Spirit of Christ, and though the Spirit of Christ is in us, yet His Spirit is also in us Who raised Christ from the dead, and He Who raised Christ from the dead shall quicken our mortal bodies also on account of His Spirit that dwelleth in us. We are quickened therefore on account of the Spirit of Christ that dwelleth in us, through Him Who raised Christ from the dead. And since the Spirit of Him Who raised Christ from the dead dwells in us, and yet the Spirit of Christ is in us, nevertheless the Spirit Which is in us cannot but be the Spirit of God. Separate,

---

[1] St. John xvi. 12—15. [2] Ib. xvii. 10. [3] Rom. viii. 9—11.

then, O heretic, the Spirit of Christ from the Spirit of God, and the Spirit of Christ raised from the dead from the Spirit of God Which raises Christ from the dead; when the Spirit of Christ that dwelleth in us is the Spirit of God, and when the Spirit of Christ Who was raised from the dead is yet the Spirit of God Who raises Christ from the dead.

22. And now I ask whether thou thinkest that in the Spirit of God is signified a nature or a property belonging to a nature. For a nature is not identical with a thing belonging to it, just as neither is a man identical with what belongs to a man, nor fire with what belongs to fire itself, and in like manner God is not the same as that which belongs to God.

23. For I am aware that the Son of God is revealed under the title *Spirit of God* in order that we may understand the presence of the Father in Him, and that the term *Spirit of God* may be employed to indicate Either, and that this is shewn not only on the authority of prophets but of evangelists also, when it is said, *The Spirit of the Lord is upon Me; therefore He hath anointed Me*[4]. And again, *Behold My Servant Whom I have chosen, My beloved in Whom My soul is well pleased, I will put My Spirit upon Him*[5]. And when the Lord Himself bears witness of Himself, *But if I in the Spirit of God cast out devils, then has the kingdom of God come upon you*[6]. For the passages seem without any doubt to denote either Father or Son, while they yet manifest the excellence of nature.

24. For I think that the expression 'Spirit of God' was used with respect to Each, lest we should believe that the Son was present in the Father or the Father in the Son in a merely corporeal manner, that is, lest God might be thought to abide in one position and exist nowhere else apart from Himself. For a man or any other thing like him, when he is in one place, cannot be in another, because what is in one place is confined to the place where it is: his nature cannot allow him to be everywhere when he exists in some one position. But God is a living Force, of infinite power, present everywhere and nowhere absent, and manifests His whole self through His own, and signifies that His own are nought else than Himself, so that where they are He may be understood to be Himself. Yet we must not think that, after a corporeal fashion, when He is in one place He ceases to be everywhere, for through His own things He is still present in all places, while the things

which are His are none other than His own self. Now these things have been said to make us understand what is meant by 'nature.'

25. Now I think that it ought to be clearly understood that God the Father is denoted by the Spirit of God, because our Lord Jesus Christ declared that the Spirit of the Lord was upon Him since He anoints Him and sends Him to preach the Gospel. For in Him is made manifest the excellence of the Father's nature, disclosing that the Son partakes of His nature even when born in the flesh through the mystery of this spiritual unction, since after the birth ratified in His baptism this intimation of His inherent Sonship was heard as a voice bore witness from Heaven :—*Thou art My Son; this day have I begotten Thee*[7]. For not even He Himself can be understood as resting upon Himself or coming to Himself from Heaven, or as bestowing on Himself the title of Son : but all this demonstration was for our faith, in order that under the mystery of a complete and true birth we should recognise that the unity of the nature dwells in the Son Who had begun to be also man. We have thus found that in the Spirit of God the Father is designated; but we understand that the Son is indicated in the same way, when He says: *But if I in the Spirit of God cast out devils, then has the kingdom of God come upon you.* That is, He shews clearly that He, by the power of His nature, casts out devils, which cannot be cast out save by the Spirit of God. The phrase 'Spirit of God' denotes also the Paraclete Spirit, and that not only on the testimony of prophets but also of apostles, when it is said :—*This is that which was spoken through the Prophet, It shall come to pass on the last day, saith the Lord, I will pour out of My Spirit upon all flesh, and their sons and their daughters shall prophesy*[8]. And we learn that all this prophecy was fulfilled in the case of the Apostles, when, after the sending of the Holy Spirit, they all spake with the tongues of the Gentiles.

26. Now we have of necessity set these things forth with this object, that in whatever direction the deception of heretics betakes itself, it might yet be kept in check by the boundaries and limits of the gospel truth. For Christ dwells in us, and where Christ dwells God dwells. And when the Spirit of Christ dwells in us, this indwelling means not that any other Spirit dwells in us than the Spirit of God. But if it is understood that Christ dwells in us through the Holy

---

4 St. Luke iv. 18.   5 St. Matt. xii. 18.   6 Ib. 28.   7 Ps. ii. 8, cf. St. Matt. iii. 17, &c.   8 Acts ii. 16, 17.

Spirit, we must yet recognise this Spirit of God as also the Spirit of Christ. And since the nature dwells in us as the nature of one substantive Being, we must regard the nature of the Son as identical with that of the Father, since the Holy Spirit Who is both the Spirit of Christ and the Spirit of God is proved to be a Being of one nature. I ask now, therefore, how can They fail to be one by nature? The Spirit of Truth proceeds from the Father, He is sent by the Son and receives from the Son. But all things that the Father hath are the Son's, and for this cause He Who receives from Him is the Spirit of God, but at the same time the Spirit of Christ. The Spirit is a Being of the nature of the Son, but the same Being is of the nature of the Father. He is the Spirit of Him Who raised Christ from the dead; but this is no other than the Spirit of Christ Who was so raised. The nature of Christ and of God must differ in some respect so as not to be the same, if it can be shewn that the Spirit which is of God is not the Spirit of Christ also.

27. But you, heretic, as you wildly rave and are driven about by the Spirit of your deadly doctrine the Apostle seizes and constrains, establishing Christ for us as the foundation of our faith, being well aware also of that saying of our Lord, *If a man love Me, he will also keep My word; and My Father will love him, and We will come unto him, and make Our abode with him* [9]. For by this He testified that while the Spirit of Christ abides in us the Spirit of God abides in us, and that the Spirit of Him that was raised from the dead differs not from the Spirit of Him that raised Him from the dead. For they come and dwell in us: and I ask whether they will come as aliens associated together and make Their abode, or in unity of nature? Nay, the teacher of the Gentiles contends that it is not two Spirits—the Spirits of God and of Christ—that are present in those who believe, but the Spirit of Christ which is also the Spirit of God. This is no joint indwelling, it is one indwelling: yet an indwelling under the mysterious semblance of a joint indwelling, for it is not the case that two Spirits indwell, nor is one that indwells different from the other. For there is in us the Spirit of God and there is also in us the Spirit of Christ, and when the Spirit of Christ is in us there is also in us the Spirit of God. And so since what is of God is also of Christ, and what is of Christ is also of God, Christ cannot be anything different from what God is. Christ, therefore, is God, one Spirit with God.

28. Now the Apostle asserts that those words in the Gospel, *I and the Father are one* [9a], imply unity of nature and not a solitary single Being, as he writes to the Corinthians, *Wherefore I give you to understand, that no man in the Spirit of God calleth Jesus anathema* [1]. Perceivest thou now, O heretic, in what spirit thou callest Christ a creature? For since they are under a curse who have served the creature more than the Creator—in affirming Christ to be a creature, learn what thou art, since thou knowest full well that the worship of the creature is accursed. And observe what follows, *And no one can call Jesus Lord, but in the Holy Spirit* [2]. Dost thou perceive what is lacking to thee, when thou deniest Christ what is His own? If thou holdest that Christ is Lord through His Divine nature, thou hast the Holy Spirit. But if He be Lord merely by a name of adoption thou lackest the Holy Spirit, and art animated by a spirit of error: because no one can call Jesus Lord, but in the Holy Spirit. But when thou sayest that He is a creature rather than God, although thou stylest Him Lord, still thou dost not say that He is the Lord. For to thee He is Lord as one of a common class and by a familiar name, rather than by nature. Yet learn from Paul His nature.

29. For the Apostle goes on to say, *Now there are diversities of gifts, but there is the same Spirit; and there are diversities of ministrations but one and the same Lord; and there are diversities of workings but the same God, Who worketh all things in all. But to each one is given the manifestation of the Spirit for that which profiteth* [3]. In this passage before us we perceive a fourfold statement: in the diversity of gifts it is the same Spirit, in the diversity of ministrations it is the very same Lord, in the diversity of workings it is the same God, and in the bestowal of that which is profitable there is a manifestation of the Spirit. And in order that the bestowal of what is profitable might be recognised in the manifestation of the Spirit, he continues: *To one indeed is given through the Spirit the word of wisdom; and to another the word of knowledge according to the same Spirit; to another faith in the same Spirit; to another the gift of healing in the same Spirit; to another the working of miracles; to another prophecy; to another discerning of spirits; to another kinds of tongues; to another the interpretation of tongues* [4].

30. And indeed that which we called the fourth statement, that is the manifestation of the Spirit in the bestowal of what is profitable,

---

[9] St. John xiv. 23.

[9a] St. John x. 30.   [1] 1 Cor. xii. 3.   [2] Ibid.
[3] Ib. 4—7.   [4] Ib. 8—10.

VOL. IX.   L

has a clear meaning. For the Apostle has enumerated the profitable gifts through which this manifestation of the Spirit took place. Now in these diverse activities that Gift is set forth in no uncertain light of which our Lord had spoken to the apostles when He taught them *not to depart from Jerusalem; but wait, said He, for the promise of the Father which ye heard from My lips: for John indeed baptized with water, but ye shall be baptized with the Holy Ghost, which ye shall also receive not many days hence*[5]. And again: *But ye shall receive power when the Holy Ghost cometh upon you; and ye shall be My witnesses in Jerusalem, and in all Judæa, and in Samaria, and unto the uttermost part of the earth*[6]. He bids them wait for the promise of the Father of which they had heard from His lips. We may be sure that here[7] we have a reference to the Father's same promise. Hence it is by these miraculous workings that the manifestation of the Spirit takes place. For the gift of the Spirit is manifest, where wisdom makes utterance and the words of life are heard, and where there is the knowledge that comes of God-given insight, lest after the fashion of beasts through ignorance of God we should fail to know the Author of our life; or by faith in God, lest by not believing the Gospel of God, we should be outside His Gospel; or by the gift of healings, that by the cure of diseases we should bear witness to His grace Who bestoweth these things; or by the working of miracles, that what we do may be understood to be the power of God, or by prophesy, that through our understanding of doctrine we might be known to be taught of God; or by discerning of spirits, that we should not be unable to tell whether any one speaks with a holy or a perverted spirit; or by kinds of tongues, that the speaking in tongues may be bestowed as a sign of the gift of the Holy Spirit; or by the interpretation of tongues, that the faith of those that hear may not be imperilled through ignorance, since the interpreter of a tongue explains the tongue to those who are ignorant of it. Thus in all these things distributed to each one to profit withal there is the manifestation of the Spirit, the gift of the Spirit being apparent through these marvellous advantages bestowed upon each.

31. Now the blessed Apostle Paul in revealing the secret of these heavenly mysteries, most difficult to human comprehension, has preserved a clear enunciation and a carefully worded caution in order to shew that these diverse gifts are given through the Spirit and in the Spirit (for to be given through the Spirit and in the Spirit is not the same thing), because the granting of a gift which is exercised in the Spirit is yet bestowed through the Spirit. But he sums up these diversities of gifts thus: *Now all these things worketh one and the same Spirit, dividing to each one as He will*[8]. Now, therefore, I ask what Spirit works these things, dividing to each one according as He wills: is it He by Whom or He in Whom there is this distribution of gifts[9]? But if any one shall dare to say that it is the same Person which is indicated, the Apostle will refute so faulty an opinion, for he says above, *And there are diversities of workings, but the same God Who worketh all things in all*. So there is one Who distributes and another in Whom the distribution is vouchsafed. Yet know that it is always God Who worketh all these things, but in such a way that Christ works, and the Son in His working performs the Father's work. And if in the Holy Spirit thou confessest Jesus to be Lord, understand the force of that threefold indication in the Apostle's letter; forasmuch as in the diversities of gifts, it is the same Spirit, and in the diversities of ministrations it is the same Lord, and in the diversities of workings it is the same God; and again, one Spirit that worketh all things distributing to each according as He will. And grasp the idea if thou canst that the Lord in the distribution of ministrations, and God in the distribution of workings, are this one and the same Spirit Who both works and distributes as He will; because in the distribution of gifts there is one Spirit, and the same Spirit works and distributes.

32. But if this one Spirit of one Divinity, one in both God and Lord through the mystery of the birth, does not please thee, then point out to me what Spirit both works and distributes these diverse gifts to us, and in what Spirit He does this. But, thou must shew me nothing but what accords with our faith, because the Apostle shews us Who is to be understood, saying, *For as the body is one, and hath many members, and all the members of the body, being many, are one body, so also is Christ*[9a]. He affirms that diversities of gifts come from one Lord Jesus Christ Who is the body of all Because after he had made known the Lord in ministration, and made known also God in workings, he yet shews that one Spirit both works and distributes all these things, distri

5 Acts i. 4, 5.   6 Ib. 8.   7 i.e. in 1 Cor. xii. 8 f.

8 1 Cor. xii 11.
9 Hilary's interpretation of this passage is not strictly Trinitarian. His view is that there are two Divine Persons at work, the Father and the Son, and that Both are embraced under the common name of 'Spirit.' Compare ii. 30, and the exegesis St. John iv. 24, which follows.
9a 1 Cor. xii. 12.

buting these varieties of His gracious gifts for the perfecting of one body.

33. Unless perchance we think that the Apostle did not keep to the principle of unity in that he said, *And there are diversities of ministrations, and the same Lord, and there are diversities of workings, but the same God*[1]. So that because he referred ministrations to the Lord and workings to God, he does not appear to have understood one and the same Being in ministrations and operations. Learn how these members which minister are also members which work, when he says, *Ye are the body of Christ, and of Him members indeed. For God hath set some in the Church, first apostles,* in whom is the word of wisdom; *secondly prophets,* in whom is the gift of knowledge; *thirdly teachers,* in whom is the doctrine of faith; *next mighty works,* among which are the *healing of diseases, the power to help, governments* by the prophets, and gifts of either speaking or interpreting *divers kinds of tongues.* Clearly these are the Church's agents of ministry and work of whom the body of Christ consists; and God has ordained them. But perhaps thou maintainest that they have not been ordained by Christ, because it was God Who ordained them. But thou shalt hear what the Apostle says himself: *Now to each one of us was the grace given according to the measure of the gift of Christ.* And again, *He that descended is the same also that ascended far above all the heavens that He might fill all things. And he gave some to be apostles; and some, prophets; and some, evangelists; and some, pastors and teachers; for the perfecting of the saints, for the work of ministering*[2]. Are not then the gifts of ministration Christ's, while they are also the gifts of God?

34. But if impiety has assumed to itself that because he says, *The same Lord and the same God*[3], they are not in unity of nature, I will support this interpretation with what you deem still stronger arguments. For the same Apostle says, *But for us there is one God, the Father, of Whom are all things, and we in Him, and one Lord Jesus Christ, through Whom are all things, and we through Him*[4]. And again, *One Lord, one faith, one baptism, one God and Father of all, Who is both through all, and in us all*[5]. By these words *one God* and *one Lord* it would seem that to God only is attributed, as to one God, the property of being God; since the property of oneness does not admit of partnership with another. Verily how rare and hard to attain are such spiritual gifts! How truly is the manifestation

of the Spirit seen in the bestowal of such useful gifts! And with reason has this order in the distribution of graces been appointed, that the foremost should be the word of wisdom; for true it is, *And no one can call Jesus Lord but in the Holy Spirit*[6], because but through this word of wisdom Christ could not be understood to be Lord; that then there should follow next the word of understanding, that we might speak with understanding what we know, and might know the word of wisdom; and that the third gift should consist of faith, seeing that those leading and higher graces would be unprofitable gifts did we not believe that He is God. So that in the true sense of this greatest and most noble utterance of the Apostle no heretics possess either the word of wisdom or the word of knowledge or the faith of religion, inasmuch as wilful wickedness, being incapable of understanding, is void of knowledge of the word and of genuineness of faith. For no one utters what he does not know; nor can he believe that which he cannot utter; and thus when the Apostle preached one God, a proselyte as He was from the Law, and called to the gospel of Christ, he has attained to the confession of a perfect faith. And lest the simplicity of a seemingly unguarded statement might afford heretics any opportunity for denying through the preaching of one God the birth of the Son, the Apostle has set forth one God while indicating His peculiar attribute in these words, *One God the Father, of Whom are all things, and we in Him*[7], in order that He Who is God might also be acknowledged as Father. Afterwards, inasmuch as this bare belief in one God the Father would not suffice for salvation, he added, *And one, our Lord Jesus Christ, through Whom are all things, and we through Him,* shewing that the purity of saving faith consists in the preaching of one God and one Lord, so that we might believe in one God the Father and one Lord Jesus Christ. For he knew full well how our Lord had said, *For this is the will of My Father, that every one that seeth the Son and believeth on Him should have eternal life*[8]. But in fixing the order of the Church's faith, and basing our faith upon the Father and the Son, he has uttered the mystery of that indivisible and indissoluble unity and faith in the words *one God and one Lord.*

35. First of all, then, O heretic that hast no part in the Spirit which spake by the Apostle, learn thy folly. If thou wrongly employest the confession of one God to deny the Godhead of

---

[1] 1 Cor. xii. 5, 6. [2] Eph. iv. 7. 10—12.
[3] 1 Cor. xii. 5, 6. [4] Ib. viii. 6. [5] Eph. iv. 5, 6. [6] 1 Cor. xii. 3. [7] Ib. viii. 6. [8] St. John vi. 40.

Christ, on the ground that where one God exists He must be regarded as solitary, and that to be One is characteristic and peculiar to Him Who is One,—what sense wilt thou assign to the statement that Jesus Christ is one Lord? For if, as thou assertest, the fact that the Father alone is God has not left to Christ the possibility of Godhead, it must needs be also according to thee that the fact of Christ being one Lord does not leave God the possibility of being Lord, seeing that thou wilt have it that to be One must be the essential property of Him Who is One. Hence if thou deniest that the one Lord Christ is also God, thou must needs deny that the one God the Father is also Lord. And what will the greatness of God amount to if He be not Lord, and the power of the Lord if He be not God: since it (viz., the greatness or power) causes that to be God which is Lord, and makes that Lord which is God?

36. Now the Apostle, maintaining the true sense of the Lord's saying, *I and the Father are one* [9], whilst He asserts that Both are One, signifies that Both are One not after the manner of the soleness of a single being, but in the unity of the Spirit; for one God the Father and one Christ the Lord, since Each is both Lord and God, do not yet admit in our creed either two Gods or two Lords. So then Each is one, and though one, neither is sole. We shall not be able to express the mystery of the faith except in the words of the Apostle. For there is one God and one Lord, and the fact that there is one God and one Lord proves that there is at once Lordship in God, and Godhead in the Lord. Thou canst not maintain a union of person, so making God single; nor yet canst thou divide the Spirit, so preventing the Two from being One [1]. Nor in the one God and one Lord wilt thou be able to separate the power, so that He Who is Lord should not also be God, and He Who is God should not also be Lord. For the Apostle in the enunciation of the Names has taken care not to preach either two Gods or two Lords. And for this reason he has employed such a method of teaching as in the one Lord Christ to set forth also one God, and in the one God the Father to set forth also one Lord. And, not to misguide us into the blasphemy that God is solitary, which would destroy the birth of the Only-begotten God, he has confessed both Father and Christ.

37. Unless perchance the frenzy of utter desperation will venture to rush to such lengths that, inasmuch as the Apostle has called Christ Lord, no one ought to acknowledge Him as aught else save Lord, and that because He has the property of Lord He has not the true Godhead. But Paul knows full well that Christ is God, for he says, *Whose are the fathers, and of whom is Christ, Who is God over all* [2]. It is no creature here who is reckoned as God; nay, it is the God of things created Who is God over all.

38. Now that He Who is God over all is also Spirit inseparable from the Father, learn also from that very utterance of the Apostle, of which we are now speaking. For when he confessed one God the Father from Whom are all things, and one Lord Jesus Christ through Whom are all things; what difference, I ask, did he intend by saying that all things are from God and that all things are through Christ? Can He possibly be regarded as of a nature and spirit separable from Himself, He from Whom and through Whom are all things? For all things have come into being through the Son out of nothing, and the Apostle has referred them to God the Father, *From Whom are all things*, but also to the Son, *through Whom are all things*. And I find here no difference, since by Each is exercised the same power. For if with regard to the subsistence of the universe it was an exact sufficient statement that things created are from God, what need was there to state that the things which are from God are through Christ, unless it be one and the same thing to be through Christ and from God? But as it has been ascribed to Each of Them that They are Lord and God in such wise that each title belongs to Both, so too *from Whom* and *through Whom* is here referred to Both; and this to shew the unity of Both, not to make known God's singleness. The language of the Apostle affords no opening for wicked error, nor is his faith too exalted for careful statement. For he has guarded himself by those specially appropriate words from being understood to mean two Gods or a solitary God: for while he rejects oneness of person he yet does not divide the unity of Godhead. For this *from Whom are all things* and *through Whom are all things*, although it did not posit a solitary Deity in the sole possession of majesty, must yet set forth One not different in efficiency, since *from Whom are all things* and *through Whom are all things* must signify an Author of the same nature engaged in the same work. He affirms, moreover, that Each is properly of the same nature. For after announcing the depth of the riches and wisdom and

9 St. John x. 30.   1 See § 31, *supr.*, and note.   2 Rom. ix. 5.

knowledge of God, and after asserting the mystery of His inscrutable judgments and avowing our ignorance of His ways past finding out, he has yet made use of the exercise of human faith, and rendered this homage to the depth of the unsearchable and inscrutable mysteries of heaven, *For of Him and through Him and in Him are all things: to Him be glory for ever. Amen*[3]. He employs to indicate the one nature, that which cannot but be the work of one nature.

39. For whereas he has specially ascribed to God that all things are from Him, and he has assigned as a peculiar property to Christ, that all things are through Him, and it is now the glory of God that from Him and through Him and in Him are all things; and whereas the Spirit of God is the same as the Spirit of Christ, or whereas in the ministration of the Lord and in the working of God, one Spirit both works and divides, They cannot but be one Whose properties are those of one; since in the same Lord the Son, and in the same God the Father, one and the same Spirit distributing in the same Holy Spirit accomplishes all things. How worthy is this saint of the knowledge of exalted and heavenly mysteries, adopted and chosen to share in the secret things of God, preserving a due silence over things which may not be uttered, true apostle of Christ! How by the announcement of his clear teaching has he restrained the imaginations of human wilfulness, confessing, as he does, one God the Father and one Lord Jesus Christ, so that meanwhile no one can either preach two Gods or one solitary God; although He Who is not one person cannot multiply into two Gods, nor on the other hand can They Who are not two Gods be understood to be one single person; while meantime the revelation of God as Father demonstrates the true nativity of Christ.

40. Thrust out now your quivering and hissing tongues, ye vipers of heresy, whether it be thou Sabellius or thou Photinus, or ye who now preach that the Only-begotten God is a creature. Whosoever denies the Son shall hear of one God the Father, because inasmuch as a father becomes a father only by having a son, this name *Father* necessarily connotes the existence of the Son. And again, let him who takes away from the Son the unity of an identical nature, acknowledge one Lord Jesus Christ. For unless through unity of the Spirit He is one Lord, room will not be left for God the Father to be Lord. Again, let him who holds the Son to have become Son in time and by His

Incarnation, learn that through Him are all things and we through Him, and that His timeless Infinity was creating all things before time was. And meanwhile let him read again that there is one hope of our calling, and one baptism, and one faith; if, after that, he oppose himself to the preaching of the Apostle, he, being accursed because he framed strange doctrines of his own device, is neither called nor baptized nor believing; because in one God the Father and in one Lord Jesus Christ there lies the one faith of one hope and baptism. And no alien doctrine can boast that it has a place among the truths which belong to one God and Lord and hope and baptism and faith.

41. So then the one faith is, to confess the Father in the Son and the Son in the Father through the unity of an indivisible nature, not confused but inseparable, not intermingled but identical, not conjoined but coexisting, not incomplete but perfect. For there is birth not separation, there is a Son not an adoption; and He is God, not a creature. Neither is He a God of a different kind, but the Father and Son are one: for the nature was not altered by birth so as to be alien from the property of its original. So the Apostle holds the faith of the Son abiding in the Father and the Father in the Son when he proclaims that for him there is one God the Father and one Lord Christ, since in Christ the Lord there was also God, and in God the Father there was also Lord, and They Two are that unity which is God, and They Two are also that unity which is the Lord, for reason indicates that there must be something imperfect in God unless He be Lord, and in the Lord unless He were God. And so since Both are one, and Both are implied under either name, and neither exists apart from the unity, the Apostle has not gone beyond the preaching of the Gospel in his teaching, nor does Christ when He speaks in Paul differ from the words which He spake while abiding in the world in bodily form.

42. For the Lord had said in the gospels, *Work not for the meat which perisheth, but for the meat which abideth unto life eternal, which the Son of Man shall give unto you: for Him the Father, even God, hath sealed. They said therefore unto Him, What must we do that we may work the works of God? And He said unto them, This is the work of God, that ye believe on Him Whom He hath sent*[4]. In setting forth the mystery of His Incarnation and His Godhead our Lord has also uttered the teaching of our faith and hope that we

---

3 Rom. xi. 36.

4 St. John vi. 27—29.

should work for food, not that which perisheth but that which abideth for ever; that we should remember that this food of eternity is given us by the Son of Man; that we should know the Son of Man as sealed by God the Father; that we should know that this is the work of God, even faith in Him Whom He has sent. And Who is it Whom the Father has sent? Even He Whom the Father has sealed. And Who is He Whom the Father has sealed? In truth, the Son of Man, even He who gives the food of eternal life. And further who are they to whom He gives it? They who shall work for the food that does not perish. Thus, then, the work for this food is at the same time the work of God, namely, to believe on Him Whom He has sent. But these words are uttered by the Son of Man. And how shall the Son of Man give the food of life eternal? Why, he knows not the mystery of his own salvation, who knows not that the Son of Man, bestowing food unto life eternal, has been sealed by God the Father. At this point I now ask in what sense are we to understand that the Son of Man has been sealed by God the Father?

43. Now we ought to recognise first of all that God has spoken not for Himself but for us, and that He has so far tempered the language of His utterance as to enable the weakness of our nature to grasp and understand it. For after being rebuked by the Jews for having made Himself the equal of God by professing to be the Son of God, He had answered that He Himself did all things that the Father did, and that He had received all judgment from the Father; moreover that He must be honoured even as the Father. And in all these things having before declared Himself Son, He had made Himself equal to the Father in honour, power and nature. Afterwards He had said that as the Father had life in Himself, so He had given the Son to have life in Himself, wherein He signified that by virtue of the mystery of the birth He possessed the unity of the same nature. For when He says that He has what the Father has, He means that He has the Father's self. For that God is not after human fashion of a composite being, so that in Him there is a difference of kind between Possessor and Possessed; but all that He is is life, a nature, that is, complete, absolute and infinite, not composed of dissimilar elements but with one life permeating the whole. And since this life was in such wise given as it was possessed, although the fact that it was given manifestly reveals the birth of the Recipient, it yet does not involve a difference of kind since the life given was such as was possessed.

44. Therefore after this manifold and precise revelation of the presence of the Father's nature in Himself, He goes on to say, *For Him hath the Father sealed, even God*[5]. It is the nature of a seal to exhibit the whole form of the figure graven upon it, and that an impression taken from it reproduces it in every respect; and since it receives the whole of that which is impressed, it displays also in itself wholly whatever has been impressed upon it. Yet this comparison is not adequate to exemplify the Divine birth, because in seals there is a matter, difference of nature, and an act of impression, whereby the likeness of stronger natures is impressed upon things of a more yielding nature. But the Only-begotten God, Who was also through the Mystery of our salvation the Son of Man, desiring to point out to us the likeness of His Father's proper nature in Himself, said that He was sealed by God; because the Son of Man was about to give the food of eternal life, and that we thereby might perceive in Him the power of giving food unto eternity, in that He possessed within Himself all the fulness of His Father's form, even of the God Who sealed Him: so that what God had sealed should display in itself none other than the form of the God Who sealed it. These things indeed the Lord spake to the Jews, who could not receive His saying because of unbelief.

45. But in us the preacher of the Gospel by the Spirit of Christ Who spake through him, instils the knowledge of this His proper nature when he says, *Who, being in the form of God, thought it not a thing to grasp at that He was equal with God, but emptied Himself, taking the form of a servant*[6]. For He, Whom God had sealed, could be nought else than the form of God, and that which has been sealed in the form of God must needs present at the same time imaged forth within itself all that God possesses. And for this cause the Apostle taught that He Whom God sealed is God abiding in the form of God. For when about to speak of the Mystery of the body assumed and born in Him, he says, *He thought it not a thing to grasp at that He was equal with God, but emptied Himself, taking the form of a servant*[7]. As regards His being in the form of God, by virtue of God's seal upon Him, he still remained God. But inasmuch as He was to take the form of a

5 St. John vi. 27.
6 Phil. ii. 6, 7. The sense in which Hilary understands *non rapinam arbitratus est*, is to be seen in his explanation, *non sibi rapiens esse se æqualem Deo* (see just below).
7 Ibid.

servant and become obedient unto death, not grasping at His equality with God, He emptied Himself through obedience to take the form of a slave. And He emptied Himself of the form of God, that is, of that wherein He was equal with God—not that He regarded His equality with God as any encroachment,—although He was in the form of God and equal with God and sealed by God as God.

46. At this point I ask whether He Who abides as God in the form of God is a God of another kind, as we perceive in the case of seals in respect of the likenesses which stamp and those which are stamped, since a steel die impressed upon lead or a gem upon wax shapes the figure cut in it or imprints that which stands in relief upon it. But if there be any one so foolish and senseless as to think that that, pertaining to Himself, which God fashions to be God, is aught but God, and that He Who is in the form of God is in any respect anything else save God after the mystery of His Incarnation and of His humility, made perfect through obedience even unto the death of the cross, he shall hear, by the confession of things in heaven and things on earth and things under the earth and of every tongue, that Jesus is in the glory of God the Father. If then, when His form had become that of a slave He abides in such glory, how, I ask, did He abide when in the form of God? Must not Christ the Spirit have been in the nature of God—for this is what is meant by 'in the glory of God'—when Christ as Jesus, that is, born as man, exists in the glory of God the Father?

47. In all things the blessed Apostle preserves the unchangeable teaching of the Gospel faith. The Lord Jesus Christ is proclaimed as God in such wise that neither does the Apostle's faith, by calling Him a God of a different order, fall away to the confession of two Gods, nor by making God the Son inseparable from the Father does it leave an opening for the unholy doctrine of a single and solitary God. For when he says, *in the form of God* and *in the glory of the Father,* the Apostle neither teaches that They differ one from another, nor allows us to think of Him as not existing. For He Who is in the form of God neither ends by becoming another God nor Himself loses His Godhead: for He cannot be severed from the form of God since He exists in it, nor is He, Who is in the form of God, not God. Just as He Who is in the glory of God cannot be aught else than God, and, since He is God in the glory of God, cannot be proclaimed as another god and one different from the true God, seeing that by reason of the fact that He is in the glory of

God He possesses naturally from Him in Whose glory He is, the property of divinity.

48. But there is no danger that the one faith will cease to be such through diversity in its preaching. The Evangelist had taught that our Lord said, *He that hath seen Me, hath seen the Father also* [8]. But has Paul, the teacher of the Gentiles, forgotten or kept back the meaning of the Lord's words, when he says, *Who is the image of the invisible God* [9]? I ask whether He is the visible likeness of the invisible God, and whether the infinite God can also be presented to view under the likeness of a finite form? For a likeness must needs repeat the form of that of which it is the likeness. Let those, however, who will have a nature of a different sort in the Son determine what sort of likeness of the invisible God they wish the Son to be. Is it a bodily likeness exposed to the gaze, and moving from place to place with human gait and motion? Nay, but let them remember that according to the Gospels and the Prophets both Christ is a Spirit and God is a Spirit. If they confine this Christ the Spirit within the bounds of shape and body, such a corporeal Christ will not be the likeness of the invisible God, nor will a finite limitation represent that which is infinite.

49. But, as it is, neither did the Lord leave us in doubt: *He who hath seen Me, hath seen the Father also;* nor was the Apostle silent as to His nature, *Who is the image of the invisible God.* For the Lord had said, *If I do not the works of My Father, believe Me not* [1], teaching them to see the Father in Himself in that He did the works of the Father; that through perceiving the power of His nature they might understand the nature of that power which they perceived. Wherefore the Apostle proclaiming that this is the image of God, says, *Who is the image of the invisible God, the first-born of all creation; for in Him were all things made in the heavens and upon the earth, things visible and things invisible, whether thrones or dominions or principalities or powers; all things have been created through Him and in Him, and He is before all, and for Him all things consist. And He is the head of the body, the Church, Who is the beginning, the first-born from the dead, that in all things He might have the pre-eminence. For it was the good pleasure of the Father that in Him should all the fulness dwell, and through Him all things should be reconciled to Him* [2]. So through the power of these works He is the image of God. For assuredly the Creator of things invisible is not

---

[8] St. John xiv. 9.   [9] Col. i. 15.   [1] St. John x. 37.
[2] Col. i. 15—20.

compelled by any necessity inherent in His nature to be the visible image of the invisible God. And lest He should be regarded as the likeness of the form and not of the nature, He is styled the likeness of the invisible God in order that we may understand by His exercise of the powers (not the invisible attributes) of the Divine nature, that that nature is in Him.

50. He is accordingly the first-born of every creature because in Him all things were created. And lest any one should dare to refer to any other than Him the creation of all things in Himself, he says, *All things have been created through Him and in Him, and He is before all, and for Him all things consist.* All things then consist for Him Who is before all things, and in Whom are all things. Now this indeed describes the origin of created things. But concerning the dispensation by which He assumed our body, he adds, *And He is the head of the body, the Church: Who is the beginning, the first-born from the dead: that in all things He might have the pre-eminence. For it was the good pleasure of the Father that in Him should all the fulness dwell, and that through Him all things should be reconciled to Him.* The Apostle has assigned to the spiritual mysteries their material effects. For He Who is the image of the invisible God is Himself the head of His body, the Church, and He Who is the first-born of every creature is at the same time the beginning, the first born from the dead: that in all things He might have the pre-eminence, being for us the Body, while He is also the image of God, since He, Who is the first-born of created things, is at the same time the first-born for eternity; so that as to Him things spiritual, being created in the First-born, owe it that they abide, even so all things human also owe it to Him that in the First-born from the dead they are born again into eternity. For He is Himself the beginning, Who as Son is therefore the image, and because the image, is of God. Further He is the first-born of every created thing, possessing in Himself the origin of the universe: and again He is the head of His body, the Church, and the first-born from the dead, so that in all things He has the pre-eminence. And because all things consist for Him, in Him the fulness of the Godhead is pleased to dwell, for in Him all things are reconciled through Him to Him, through Whom all things were created in Himself.

51. Do you now perceive what it is to be the image of God? It means that all things are created in Him through Him. Whereas all things are created in Him, understand that He, Whose image He is, also creates all things in Him. And since all things which are create[d] in Him are also created through Him, recognise that in Him Who is the image there is present the nature of Him, Whose image He is. For through Himself He creates the things which are created in Him, just as through Himself all things are reconciled in Him. Inasmuch as they are reconciled in Him, recognise in Him the nature of the Father's unity, reconciling all things to Himself in Him. Inasmuch as all things are reconciled through Him, perceive Him reconciling to the Father in Himself all things which He reconciled through Himself. For the same Apostle says, *But all things are from God, Who reconciled us to Himself through Christ, and gave unto us the ministry of reconciliation: to wit, that God was in Christ reconciling the world unto Himself*[3]. Compare with this the whole mystery of the faith of the Gospel. For He Who is seen when Jesus is seen, Who works in His works, and speaks in His words, also reconciles in His reconciliation. And for this cause, in Him and through Him there is reconciliation, because the Father abiding in Him through a like nature restored the world to Himself by reconciliation through and in Him.

52. Thus God out of regard for human weakness has not set forth the faith in bare and uncertain statements. For although the authority of our Lord's mere words of itself compelled their acceptance, He nevertheless has informed our reason by a revelation which explains their meaning, that we might learn to know His words, *I and the Father are one*[4], by means of that which was itself the cause of the unity in question. For in saying that the Father speaks in His words, and works through His working, and judges through His judgment, and is seen in His manifestation, and reconciles through His reconciliation, and abides in Him, while He in turn abides in the Father,—what more fitting words, I ask, could He have employed in His teaching to suit the faculties of our reason, that we might believe in Their unity, than those by which, through the truth of the birth and the unity of the nature, it is declared that whatever the Son did and said, the Father said and did in the Son? This says nothing of a nature foreign to Himself, or added by creation to God, or born into Godhead by a partition of God, but it betokens the divinity of One Who by a perfect birth is begotten perfect God, Who has so confident an assurance of His nature that He says, *I in the Father and the Father in Me*[5], and again, *All things whatsoever the Father hath are Mine*[6]. For nought

3 2 Cor. v. 18, 19.   4 St. John x. 30.
5 Ib. xiv. 11.   6 Ib. xvi. 15.

of the Godhead is lacking in Him, in Whose working and speaking and manifestation God works and speaks and is beheld. They are not two Gods, Who in their working and words and manifestation put on a semblance of unity. Neither is He a solitary God, Who in the works and words and sight of God, Himself worked and spoke and was seen as God. The Church understands this. The Synagogue does not believe, philosophy does not know, that being One of One, Whole of Whole, God and Son, He has neither by His birth deprived the Father of His completeness, nor failed to possess the same completeness in Himself by right of His birth. And whosoever is caught in this folly of unbelief is a disciple either of the Jews or of the heathen.

53. Now that you may understand the saying of the Lord, when He said, *All things whatsoever the Father hath are Mine*[7], learn the teaching and faith of the Apostle who said, *Take heed lest any lead you astray through philosophy and vain deceit, after the tradition of men, after the elements of the world and not after Christ; for in Him dwelleth the fulness of Godhead bodily*[8]. That man is of the world and savours of the teaching of men and is the victim of philosophy, who does not know Christ to be the true God, who does not recognise in Him the fulness of Godhead. The mind of man knows only that which it understands, and the world's powers of belief are limited, since it judges according to the laws of the material elements that that alone is possible which it can see or do. For the elements of the world have come into being out of nothing, but Christ's continuity of existence did not begin in the non-existent, nor did He ever begin to exist, but He took from the beginning a beginning which is eternal. The elements of the world are either without life, or have issued out of this stage into life, but Christ is life, born to be living God from the living God. The elements of the world have been established by God, but they are not God: Christ as God of God is Himself wholly all that God is. The elements of the world, since they are within it, cannot possibly rise out of their condition and cease to be within it, but Christ, while having God within Himself through the Mystery, is Himself in God. The elements of the universe, generating from themselves creatures with a life like their own, do indeed through the exercise of their bodily functions bestow upon them from their own bodies the beginnings of life, but they are not themselves present as living beings in their offspring, whereas in Christ all the fulness of the Godhead is present in bodily shape.

54. Now I ask, whose Godhead is it whereof the fulness dwells in Him? If it be not that of the Father, what other God do you, misleading preacher of one God, thrust upon me as Him Whose Godhead dwells fully in Christ? But if it be that of the Father, inform me how this fulness dwells in Him in bodily fashion. If you hold that the Father abides in the Son in bodily fashion, the Father, while dwelling in the Son, will not exist in Himself. If on the other hand, and this is more true, the Godhead abiding in Him in bodily shape displays within Him the verity of the nature of God from God, inasmuch as God is in Him, abiding neither through condescension nor through will but by birth, true and wholly in bodily fulness according as He is; and inasmuch as, in the whole compass of His being, He was born by His divine birth to be God, and within the Godhead there is no difference or dissimilarity, except that in Christ He dwells in bodily form, and yet whatever dwells in Him bodily is according to the fulness of Godhead; why follow after the doctrines of men? Why cleave to the teaching of empty falsehoods? Why talk of 'agreement' or 'harmony of will' or 'a creature?' The fulness of Godhead dwells in Christ bodily.

55. The Apostle has herein held fast to the canon of his faith, by teaching that the fulness of the Godhead dwelt in Christ bodily; and this, in order that the teaching of the faith might not degenerate into an unholy profession of a oneness of Persons or sinful frenzy break forth into the belief of two different natures. For the fulness of Godhead which dwells in Christ in bodily fashion is neither solitary nor separable; for the fulness in bodily form does not admit any partition from the other bodily fulness, and the indwelling Godhead cannot be regarded as also the dwelling-place of the Godhead. And Christ is so constituted that the fulness of Godhead dwells in Him in bodily fashion, and that this fulness must be held one in nature with Christ. Lay hands on every chance that offers for your quibbles, sharpen the points of your blasphemous wit. Name, at least, the imaginary being whose fulness of Godhead it is which dwells in Christ in bodily fashion. For He is Christ, and there is dwelling in Him in bodily fashion the fulness of Godhead.

56. And if you would know what it is to 'dwell in bodily fashion,' understand what it is to speak in one that speaks, to be seen in one who is seen, to work in one who works, to be God in God, whole of whole, one of one; and thus learn what is meant by the

---

7 St. John xvi. 15.   8 Col. ii. 8, 9.

fulness of God in bodily shape. Remember, too, that the Apostle does not keep silence on the question, whose Godhead it is, which dwells fully in Christ in bodily fashion, for he says, *For the invisible things of Him since the creation of the world are clearly seen, being perceived through the things that are made, even His everlasting power and divinity*[9]. So it is His Godhead that dwells in Christ in bodily fashion, not partially but wholly, not parcelwise but in fulness; and so dwelling that the Two are one, and so one, that the One Who is God does not differ from the Other Who is God: Both so equally divine, as a perfect birth engendered perfect God. And the birth exists thus in its perfection, because the fulness of the Godhead dwells bodily in God born of God.

---

[9] Rom. i. 20.

BOOK IX.

1. In the last book we treated of the indistinguishable nature of God the Father and God the Son, and demonstrated that the words, *I and the Father are One*[1], go to prove not a solitary God, but a unity of the Godhead unbroken by the birth of the Son: for God can be born only of God, and He that is born God of God must be all that God is. We reviewed, although not exhaustively, yet enough to make our meaning clear, the sayings of our Lord and the Apostles, which teach the inseparable nature and power of the Father and the Son; and we came to the passage in the teaching of the Apostle, where he says, *Take heed lest there shall be any one that leadeth you astray through philosophy and vain deceit, after the tradition of men, after the rudiments of the world, and not after Christ; for in Him dwelleth all the fulness of the Godhead bodily*[2]. We pointed out that here the words, *in Him dwelleth all the fulness of the Godhead bodily*, prove Him true and perfect God of His Father's nature, neither severing Him from, nor identifying Him with, the Father. On the one hand we are taught that, since the incorporeal God dwelt in Him bodily, the Son as God begotten of God is in natural unity with the Father: and on the other hand, if God dwelt in Christ, this proves the birth of the personal Christ in Whom He dwelt[3]. We have thus, it seems to me, more than answered the irreverence of those who refer to a unity or agreement of will such words of the Lord as, *He that hath seen Me hath seen the Father*[4], or, *The Father is in Me and I in the Father*[5], or, *I and the Father are One*[6], or, *All things whatsoever the Father hath are Mine*[7]. Not daring to deny the words themselves, these false teachers, in the mask of religion, corrupt the sense of the words. For instance, it is true that where the unity of nature is proclaimed, the agreement of will cannot be denied; but in order to set aside that unity which follows from the birth, they profess merely a relationship of mutual harmony. But the blessed Apostle, after many indubitable statements of the real truth, cuts short their rash and profane assertions, by saying, *in Christ dwelleth all the fulness of the Godhead bodily*, for by the bodily indwelling of the incorporeal God in Christ is taught the strict unity of Their nature. It is, therefore, not a matter of words, but a real truth that the Son was not alone, but the Father abode in Him: and not only abode, but also worked and spoke: not only worked and spoke, but also manifested Himself in Him. Through the Mystery of the birth the Son's power is the power of the Father, His authority the Father's authority, His nature the Father's nature. By His birth the Son possesses the nature of the Father: as the Father's image, He reproduces from the Father all that is in the Father, because He is the reality as well as the image of the Father, for a perfect birth produces a perfect image, and the *fulness of the Godhead dwelling bodily in Him* indicates the truth of His nature.

2. All this is indeed as it is: He, Who is by nature God of God, must possess the nature of His origin, which God possesses, and the indistinguishable unity of a living nature cannot be divided by the birth of a living nature. Yet nevertheless the heretics, under cover of the saving confession of the Gospel faith, are stealing on to the subversion of the truth: for by forcing their own interpretations on words uttered with other meanings and intentions, they are robbing the Son of His natural unity. Thus to deny the Son of God, they quote the authority of His own words, *Why callest thou Me good? None is good, save one, God*[8]. These words, they say, proclaim the Oneness of God: anything else, therefore, which shares the name of God, cannot possess the nature of God, for God is One. And from His words, *This is life eternal, that they should know Thee the only true God*[9], they attempt to establish the theory that Christ is called God by a mere title, not as being very God. Further, to exclude Him from the

---

[1] St. John x. 30. [2] Col. ii. 8, 9.
[3] *Subsistentis Christi = subsistentia distincti Christi* (see footnote in the Benedictine Edition). God the Father dwelt in Christ. But the Dweller must be personally distinct from Christ, in Whom He dwelt: and as the only distinction between the Father and Christ is that of Begetter and Begotten, therefore the words 'God dwelt in Christ' prove the generation of Christ.
[4] St. John xiv. 9. [5] Ib. x. 38. [6] Ib. 30. [7] Ib. xvi. 15.

[8] St. Mark x. 18 (cf. St. Matt. xix. 17, St. Luke xviii. 19). The Greek is οὐδεὶς ἀγαθὸς, εἰ μὴ εἷς ὁ θεός, 'save one, even God' (R.V.). The application of this text by the Arians depends upon the omission of the article ὁ.
[9] St. John xvii. 3.

proper nature of the true God, they quote, *The Son can do nothing of Himself except that which He hath seen the Father do*[1]. They use also the text, *The Father is greater than I*[2] Finally, when they repeat the words, *Of that day and that hour knoweth no one, neither the angels in heaven, nor the Son, but the Father only*[3], as though they were the absolute renunciation of His claim to divinity, they boast that they have overthrown the faith of the Church. The birth, they say, cannot raise to equality the nature which the limitation of ignorance degrades. The Father's omniscience and the Son's ignorance reveal unlikeness in the Divinity, for God must be ignorant of nothing, and the ignorant cannot be compared with the omniscient. All these passages they neither understand rationally, nor distinguish as to their occasions, nor apprehend in the light of the Gospel mysteries, nor realize in the strict meaning of the words; and so they impugn the divine nature of Christ with crude and insensate rashness, quoting single detached utterances to catch the ears of the unwary, and keeping back either the sequel which explains or the incidents which prompted them, though the meaning of words must be sought in the context before or after them.

3. We will offer later an explanation of these texts in the words of the Gospels and Epistles themselves. But first we hold it right to remind the members of our common faith, that the knowledge of the Eternal is presented in the same confession which gives eternal life[4]. He does not, he cannot know his own life, who is ignorant that Christ Jesus was very God, as He was very man. It is equally perilous, whether we deny that Christ Jesus was God the Spirit, or that He was flesh of our body : *Every one therefore who shall confess Me before men, him will I also confess before My Father which is in Heaven. But whosoever shall deny Me before men, him will I also deny before My Father which is in heaven*[5]. So said the Word made flesh; so taught the man Jesus Christ, the Lord of majesty, constituted Mediator in His own person for the salvation of the Church, and being in that very mystery of Mediatorship between men and God, Himself one Person, both man and God. For He, being of two natures united for that Mediatorship, is the full reality of each nature; while abiding in each, He is wanting in neither; He does not cease to be God because He becomes man, nor fail to be man

because He remains for ever God. This is the true faith for human blessedness, to preach at once the Godhead and the manhood, to confess the Word and the flesh, neither forgetting the God, because He is man, nor ignoring the flesh, because He is the Word.

4. It is contrary to our experience of nature, that He should be born man and still remain God; but it accords with the tenor of our expectation, that being born man, He still remained God, for when the higher nature is born into the lower, it is credible that the lower should also be born into the higher. And, indeed, according to the laws and habits of nature, the working of our expectation even anticipates the divine mystery. For in every thing that is born, nature has the capacity for increase, but has no power of decrease. Look at the trees, the crops, the cattle. Regard man himself, the possessor of reason. He always expands by growth, he does not contract by decrease; nor does he ever lose the self into which he has grown. He wastes indeed with age, or is cut off by death; he undergoes change by lapse of time, or reaches the end allotted to the constitution of life, yet it is not in his power to cease to be what he is; I mean that he cannot make a new self by decrease from his old self, that is, become a child again from an old man. So the necessity of perpetual increase, which is imposed on our nature by natural law, leads us on good grounds to expect its promotion into a higher nature, since its increase is according to, and its decrease contrary to, nature. It was God alone Who could become something other than before, and yet not cease to be what He had ever been ; Who could shrink within the limits of womb, cradle, and infancy, yet not depart from the power of God. This is a mystery, not for Himself, but for us. The assumption of our nature was no advancement for God, but His willingness to lower Himself is our promotion, for He did not resign His divinity but conferred divinity on man.

5. The Only-begotten God, therefore, when He was born man of the Virgin, and in the fulness of time was about in His own person to raise humanity to divinity, always maintained this form of the Gospel teaching. He taught, namely, to believe Him the Son of God, and exhorted to preach Him the Son of Man; man saying and doing all that belongs to God; God saying and doing all that belongs to man. Yet never did He speak without signifying by the twofold aspect of these very utterances both His manhood and His divinity. Though He proclaimed one God the Father, He declared Himself to be in the

---

[1] St. John v. 19.   [2] Ib. xiv. 28.
[3] St. Mark xiii. 32 ; cf. St. Matt. xxiv. 36.
[4] Alluding to St. John xvii. 3, quoted in c. 2.
[5] St. Matt. x. 32, 33.

nature of the one God, by the truth of His generation. Yet in His office as Son and His condition as man, He subjected Himself to God the Father, since everything that is born must refer itself back to its author, and all flesh must confess itself weak before God. Here, accordingly, the heretics find opportunity to deceive the simple and ignorant. These words, uttered in His human character, they falsely refer to the weakness of His divine nature; and because He was one and the same Person in all His utterances, they claim that He spake always of His entire self.

6. We do not deny that all the sayings which are preserved of His, refer to His nature. But, if Jesus Christ be man and God, neither God for the first time, when He became man, nor then ceasing to be God, nor after He became Man in God less than perfect man and perfect God, then the mystery of His words must be one and the same with that of His nature. When according to the time indicated, we disconnect His divinity from humanity, then let us also disconnect His language as God from the language of man; when we confess Him God and man at the same time, let us distinguish at the same time His words as God and His words as man; when after His manhood and Godhead, we recognise again the time when His whole manhood is wholly God, let us refer to that time all that is revealed concerning it[6]. It is one thing, that He was God before He was man, another, that He was man and God, and another, that after being man and God, He was perfect man and perfect God. Do not then confuse the times and natures in the mystery of the dispensation, for according to the attributes of His different natures, He must speak of Himself in relation to the mystery of His humanity, in one way before His birth, in another while He was yet to die, and in another as eternal.

7. For our sake, therefore, Jesus Christ, retaining all these attributes, and being born man in our body, spoke after the fashion of our nature without concealing that divinity belonged to His own nature. In His birth, His passion, and His death, He passed through all the circumstances of our nature, but He bore them all by the power of His own. He was Himself the cause of His birth, He willed to suffer what He could not suffer, He died though He lives for ever. Yet God did all

this, not merely through man, for He was born of Himself, He suffered of His own free will, and died of Himself. He did it also as man, for He was really born, suffered and died. These were the mysteries of the secret counsels of heaven, determined before the world was made. The Only-begotten God was to become man of His own will, and man was to abide eternally in God. God was to suffer of His own will, that the malice of the devil, working in the weakness of human infirmity, might not confirm the law of sin in us, since God had assumed our weakness. God was to die of His own will, that no power, after that the immortal God had constrained Himself within the law of death, might raise up its head against Him, or put forth the natural strength which He had created in it. Thus God was born to take us into Himself, suffered to justify us, and died to avenge us; for our manhood abides for ever in Him, the weakness of our infirmity is united with His strength, and the spiritual powers of iniquity and wickedness are subdued in the triumph of our flesh, since God died through the flesh.

8. The Apostle, who knew this mystery, and had received the knowledge of the faith through the Lord Himself, was not unmindful, that neither the world, nor mankind, nor philosophy could contain Him, for he writes, *Take heed, lest there shall be any one that leadeth you astray through philosophy and vain deceit, after the tradition of men, after the rudiments of the world, and not after Jesus Christ, for in Him dwelleth all the fulness of the Godhead bodily, and in Him ye are made full, Who is the head of all principalities and powers*[7]. After the announcement that in Christ dwelleth all the fulness of the Godhead bodily, follows immediately the mystery of our assumption, in the words, *in Him ye are made full*. As the fulness of the Godhead is in Him, so we are made full in Him. The Apostle says not merely *ye are made full*, but, *in Him ye are made full;* for all who are, or shall be, regenerated through the hope of faith to life eternal, abide even now in the body of Christ; and afterwards they shall be made full no longer in Him, but in themselves, at the time of which the Apostle says, *Who shall fashion anew the body of our humiliation, that it may be conformed to the body of His glory*[8]. Now, therefore, we are made full in Him, that is, by the assumption of His flesh, for in Him dwelleth the fulness of the Godhead bodily. Nor has this our hope a light authority in Him. Our fulness in Him constitutes His

---

[6] The three periods referred to in these three sentences are (1) before the Incarnation: we can assign only to His Godhead the words Christ uses in reference to this period, because He was not yet man. (2) The Incarnation: we must distinguish whether He is speaking of Himself as man or as God. (3) After the Resurrection, when His manhood remains, but is perfected in the Godhead.

[7] Col. ii. 8—10.

[8] Phil. iii. 21.

headship and principality over all power, as it is written, *That in His name every knee should bow, of things in heaven, and things on earth, and things below, and every tongue confess that Jesus is Lord in the glory of God the Father* [1]. Jesus shall be confessed in the glory of God the Father, born in man, yet now no longer abiding in the infirmity of our body, but in the glory of God. Every tongue shall confess this. But though all things in heaven and earth shall bow the knee to Him, yet herein He is head of all principalities and powers, that to Him the whole universe shall bow the knee in submission, in Whom we are made full, Who through the fulness of the Godhead dwelling in Him bodily, shall be confessed in the glory of God the Father.

9. But after the announcement of the mystery of Christ's nature, and our assumption, that is, the fulness of Godhead abiding in Christ, and ourselves made full in Him by His birth as man, the Apostle continues the dispensation of human salvation in the words, *In whom ye were also circumcised with a circumcison not made with hands, in the stripping off of the body of the flesh, but with the circumcision of Christ, having been buried with Him in baptism, wherein ye were also raised with Him through faith in the working of God, who raised Him from the dead* [2]. We are circumcised not with a fleshly circumcision but with the circumcision of Christ, that is, we are born again into a new man; for, being buried with Him in His baptism, we must die to the old man, because the regeneration of baptism has the force of resurrection. The circumcision of Christ does not mean the putting off of foreskins, but to die entirely with Him, and by that death to live henceforth entirely to Him. For we rise again in Him through faith in God, Who raised Him from the dead; wherefore we must believe in God, by Whose Working Christ was raised from the dead, for our faith rises again in and with Christ.

10. Then is completed the entire mystery of the assumed manhood, *And you being dead through your trespasses and the uncircumcision of your flesh, you I say, did He quicken together with Him, having forgiven you all your trespasses, blotting out the bond written in ordinances, that was against us, which was contrary to us; and He hath taken it out of the way, nailing it to the cross, and having put off from Himself His flesh, He hath made a shew of powers, triumphing over them in Himself* [3].

The worldly man cannot receive the faith of the Apostle, nor can any language but that of the Apostle explain his meaning. God raised Christ from the dead; Christ in Whom the fulness of the Godhead dwelt bodily. But He quickened us also together with Him, forgiving us our sins, blotting out the bond of the law of sin, which through the ordinances made aforetime was against us, taking it out of the way, and fixing it to His cross, stripping Himself of His flesh by the law of death, holding up the powers to shew, and triumphing over them in Himself. Concerning the powers and how He triumphed over them in Himself, and held them up to shew, and the bond which he blotted out, and the life which He gave us, we have already spoken [4]. But who can understand or express this mystery? The working of God raises Christ from the dead; the same working of God quickens us together with Christ, forgives our sins, blots out the bond, and fixes it to the cross; He puts off from Himself His flesh, holds up the powers to shew, and triumphs over them in Himself. We have the working of God raising Christ from the dead, and we have Christ working in Himself the very things which God works in Him, for it was Christ who died, stripping from Himself His flesh. Hold fast then to Christ the man, raised from the dead by God, and hold fast to Christ the God, working out our salvation when He was yet to die. God works in Christ, but it is Christ Who strips from Himself His flesh and dies. It was Christ who died, and Christ Who worked with the power of God before His death, yet it was the working of God which raised the dead Christ, and it was none other who raised Christ from the dead but Christ Himself, Who worked before His death, and put off His flesh to die.

11. Do you understand already the Mysteries of the Apostle's Faith? Do you think to know Christ already? Tell me, then, Who is it Who strips from Himself His flesh, and what is that flesh stripped off? I see two thoughts expressed by the Apostle, the flesh stripped off, and Him Who strips it off: and then I hear of Christ raised from the dead by the working of God. If it is Christ Who is raised from the dead, and God Who raises Him; Who, pray, strips from Himself the flesh? Who raises Christ from the dead, and quickens us with Him? If the dead Christ be not the same as the flesh stripped off, tell me the name of the flesh stripped off, and expound me the nature of Him Who strips it off. I find that Christ the God, Who was raised from the dead, is the

---

[1] Phil. ii. 10, 11. The Greek is εἰς δόξαν, κ.τ.λ. 'to the glory of God the Father' (R.V.). There is also another reading in Hilary's text in this place, 'in gloriam' instead of 'in gloria;' but the latter is demanded by the context. See c. 42.
[2] Col. ii. 11, 12.   [3] Ib. 13—15.

[4] See I. 13.

same as He Who stripped from Himself His flesh, and that flesh, the same as Christ Who was raised from the dead; then I see Him holding principalities and powers up to shew, and triumphing in Himself. Do you understand this triumphing in Himself? Do you perceive that the flesh stripped off, and He Who strips it off, are not different from one another? He triumphs in Himself, that is in that flesh which He stripped from Himself. Do you see that thus are proclaimed His humanity and His divinity, that death is attributed to the man, and the quickening of the flesh to the God, though He Who dies and He Who raises the dead to life are not two, but one Person? The flesh stripped off is the dead Christ: He Who raises Christ from the dead is the same Christ Who stripped from Himself the flesh. See His divine nature in the power to raise again, and recognise in His death the dispensation of His manhood. And though either function is performed by its proper nature, yet remember that He Who died, and raised to life, was one, Christ Jesus.

12. I remember that the Apostle often refers to God the Father as raising Christ from the dead; but he is not inconsistent with himself or at variance with the Gospel faith, for the Lord Himself says:— *Therefore doth the Father love Me, because I lay down My life, that I may take it again. No one shall take it from Me, but I lay it down of Myself. I have power to lay it down, and I have power to take it again. This command have I received from the Father* [5]: and again, when asked to shew a sign concerning Himself, that they might believe in Him, He says of the Temple of His body, *Destroy this Temple, and in three days I will raise it up* [6]. By the power to take His soul again and to raise the Temple up, He declares Himself God, and the Resurrection His own work: yet He refers all to the authority of His Father's command. This is not contrary to the meaning of the Apostle, when He proclaims Christ, the *power of God and the wisdom of God* [7], thus referring all the magnificence of His work to the glory of the Father: for whatever Christ does, the power and the wisdom of God does: and whatever the power and the wisdom of God does, without doubt God Himself does, Whose power and wisdom Christ is. So Christ was raised from the dead by the working of God; for He Himself worked the works of God the Father with a nature indistinguishable from God's. And our faith in the Resurrection rests on the God Who raised Christ from the dead.

13. It is this preaching of the double aspect of Christ's Person which the blessed Apostle emphasises. He points out in Christ His human infirmity, and His divine power and nature. Thus to the Corinthians he writes, *For though He was crucified through weakness, yet He liveth through the power of God* [8], attributing His death to human infirmity, but His life to divine power: and again to the Romans, *For the death, that He died unto sin, He died once: but the life, that He liveth, He liveth unto God. Even so reckon ye yourselves also to be dead unto sin, but alive unto God in Christ Jesus* [9], ascribing His death to sin, that is, to our body, but His life to God, Whose nature it is to live. We ought, therefore, he says, to die to our body, that we may live to God in Christ Jesus, Who after the assumption of our body of sin, lives now wholly unto God, uniting the nature He shared with us with the participation of divine immortality.

14. I have been compelled to dwell briefly on this, lest we should forget our Lord Jesus Christ is being treated of as a Person of two natures, since He, Who was abiding in the form of God, took the form of a servant, in which He was obedient even unto death. The obedience of death has nothing to do with the form of God, just as the form of God is not inherent in the form of a servant. Yet through the Mystery of the Gospel Dispensation the same Person is in the form of a servant and in the form of God, though it is not the same thing to take the form of a servant and to be abiding in the form of God; nor could He Who was abiding in the form of God, take the form of a servant without emptying Himself, since the combination of the two forms would be incongruous. Yet it was not another and a different Person Who emptied Himself and Who took the form of a servant. To take anything cannot be predicated of some one who is not, for he only can take who exists. The emptying of the form does not then imply the abolition of the nature: He emptied Himself, but did not lose His self: He took a new form, but remained what He was. Again, whether emptying or taking, He was the same Person: there is, therefore, a mystery, in that He emptied Himself, and took the form of a servant, but He does not come to an end, so as to cease to exist in emptying Himself, and to be non-existent when He took. The emptying availed to bring about the taking of the servant's form, but not to prevent Christ, Who was in the form of God, from continuing to be Christ, for it was in very deed Christ Who took the form of a servant. When He emptied Himself to become Christ the man, while continuing to be Christ the Spirit, the

5 St. John x. 17, 18.   6 Ib. ii 19.   7 1 Cor. i. 24.   8 2 Cor. xiii. 4.   9 Rom. vi. 10, 11.

changing of His bodily fashion, and the assumption of another nature in His body, did not put an end to the nature of His eternal divinity, for He was one and the same Christ when He changed His fashion, and when He assumed our nature.

15. We have now expounded the Dispensation of the Mysteries, through which the heretics deceive certain of the unlearned into ascribing to infirmity in the divinity, what Christ said and did through His assumed human nature, and attributing to the form of God what is appropriate only to the form of the servant. Let us pass on, then, to answer their statements in detail. We can always safely distinguish the two kinds of utterances, since the only true faith lies in the confession of Jesus Christ as Word and flesh, that is, God and Man. The heretics consider it necessary to deny that our Lord Jesus Christ by virtue of His nature was divine, because He said, *Why callest thou Me good? None is good save one, God*[1]. Now a satisfactory answer must stand in direct relation to the matter of enquiry, for only in that case will it furnish a reply to the question put. At the outset, then, I would ask these misinterpreters, "Do you think that the Lord resented being called good?" Would He rather have been called bad, as seems to be signified by the words, *Why callest thou Me good?* I do not think any one is so unreasonable as to ascribe to Him a confession of wickedness, when it was He Who said, *Come unto Me, all ye that labour, and are heavy laden, and I will refresh you. Take My yoke upon you, and learn of Me: for I am meek and lowly of heart, and ye shall find rest unto your souls. For My yoke is easy and My burden is light*[2]. He says He is meek and lowly: can we believe that He was angry because He was called good? The two propositions are inconsistent. He Who witnesses to His own goodness would not repudiate the name of Good. Plainly, then, He was not angry because He was called good: and if we cannot believe that He resented being called good, we must ask what was said of Him which He did resent.

16. Let us see, then, how the questioner styled Him, beside calling Him good. He said, *Good Master, what good thing shall I do*[3]? adding to the title of "good" that of master. If Christ then did not chide because He was called good, it must have been because He was called "good Master." Further the manner of His reproof shews that it was the

disbelief of the questioner, rather than the name of master, or of good, which He resented. A youth, who prides himself upon the observance of the law, but did not know the end of the law[4], which is Christ, who thought himself justified by works, without perceiving that Christ came to *the lost sheep of the house of Israel*[5], and to those who believe that the law cannot save through the faith of justification[6], questioned the Lord of the law, the Only-begotten God, as though He were a teacher of the common precepts and the writings of the law. But the Lord, abhorring this declaration of irreverent unbelief, which addresses Him as a teacher of the law, answered, *Why callest thou Me good?* and to shew how we may know, and call Him good, He added, *None is good, save one, God*, not repudiating the name of good, if it be given to Him as God.

17. Then, as a proof that He resents the name "good master," on the ground of the unbelief, which addresses Him as a man, He replies to the vain-glorious youth, and his boast that he had fulfilled the law, *One thing thou lackest; go, sell whatsoever thou hast, and give to the poor, and thou shalt have treasure in heaven; and come, follow Me.* There is no shrinking from the title of "good" in the promise of heavenly treasures, no reluctance to be regarded as "master" in the offer to lead the way to perfect blessedness. But there is reproof of the unbelief which draws an earthly opinion of Him from the teaching, that goodness belongs to God alone. To signify that He is both good and God, He exercises the functions of goodness, opening the heavenly treasures, and offering Himself as guide to them. All the homage offered to Him as man He repudiates, but he does not disown that which He paid to God; for at the moment when He confesses that the one God is good, His words and actions are those of the power and the goodness and the nature of the one God.

18. That He did not shrink from the title of good, or decline the office of master, but resented the unbelief which perceived no more in Him than body and flesh, may be proved from the difference of His language, when the apostles confessed Him their Master, *Ye call Me Master, and Lord, and ye say well, for so I am*[7]; and on another occasion, *Be ye not called masters, for Christ is your Master*[8]. From the faithful, to whom He is master, He accepts the title with words of praise, but here

---

[1] St. Mark x. 18; cf. St. Matt. xix. 17; St. Luke xviii. 19, and note on c. 2 of this book.
[2] S. Matt. xi. 28, 30.   [3] Ib. xix. 16.

[4] Rom. x. 4.   [5] St. Matt. xv. 24; cf. x. 6.
[6] Cf. Rom. viii. 3, "What the law could not do;" and Gal. iii. 11 ff., "No man is justified by the law in the sight of God .... the law is not of faith."
[7] St. John xiii. 13.   [8] St. Matt. xxiii. 10.

He rejects the name " good master," when He is not acknowledged to be the Lord and the Christ, and pronounces the one God alone good, but without distinguishing Himself from God, for He calls Himself Lord, and Christ, and guide to the heavenly treasures.

19. The Lord always maintained this definition of the faith of the Church, which consists in teaching that there is one God the Father, but without separating Himself from the mystery of the one God, for He declared Himself, by the nature which is His by birth, neither a second God, nor the sole God. Since the nature of the One God is in Him, He cannot be God of a different kind from Him ; His birth requires that, being Son, it should be with a perfect Sonship 9. So He can neither be separated from God nor merged in God. Hence He speaks in words deliberately chosen, so that whatever He claims for the Father, He signifies in modest language to be appropriate to Himself also. Take as an instance the command, *Believe in God, and believe also in Me* 1. He is identified with God in honour; how, pray, can He be separated from His nature? He says, *Believe in Me also,* just as He said *Believe in God.* Do not the words *in Me* signify His nature? Separate the two natures, but you must separate also the two beliefs. If it be life, that we should believe in God without Christ, strip Christ of the name and qualities of God. But if perfect life is given to those who believe in God, only when they believe in Christ also, let the careful reader ponder the meaning of the saying, *Believe in God, and believe in Me also,* for these words, uniting faith in Him with faith in God, unite His nature to God's. He enjoins first of all the duty of belief in God, but adds to it the command that we should believe in Himself also ; which implies that He is God, since they who believe in God must also believe in Him. Yet He excludes the suggestion of a unity contrary to religion 2, for the exhortation *Believe in God, believe in Me also,* forbids us to think of Him as alone in solitude.

20. In many, nay almost all His discourses, He offers the explanation of this mystery, never separating Himself from the divine unity, when He confesses God the Father, and never characterising God as single and solitary, when He places Himself in unity with Him. But nowhere does He more plainly teach the mystery of His unity and His birth than when

He says, *But the witness which I have is greater than that of John, for the works which the Father hath given Me to accomplish, the very works that I do, bear witness of Me, that the Father hath sent Me, and the Father which sent Me, He hath borne witness of Me. Ye have neither heard His voice at any time nor seen His form. And ye have not His word abiding in you, for Whom He sent, Him ye believe not* 3. How can the Father be truly said to have borne witness of the Son, when neither He Himself was seen, nor His voice heard? Yet I remember that a voice was heard from Heaven, which said, *This is My beloved Son, in Whom I have been well pleased ; hear ye Him* 4. How can it be said that they did not hear the voice of God, when the voice which they heard itself asserted that it was the Father's voice? But perhaps the dwellers in Jerusalem had not heard what John had heard in the solitude of the desert. We must ask, then, " How did the Father bear witness in Jerusalem?" It is no longer the witness given to John, who heard the voice from heaven, but a witness greater than that of John. What that witness is He goes on to say, *The works which the Father hath given me to accomplish, the very works which I do, bear witness of Me, that the Father hath sent Me.* We must admit the authority of the testimony, for no one, except the Son sent of the Father, could do such works. His works are therefore His testimony. But what follows? *And the Father, which sent Me, He hath borne witness of Me. Ye have neither heard His voice at any time, nor seen His form, and ye have not His word abiding in you.* Are they blameless, in that they did not know the testimony of the Father, Who was never heard or seen amongst them, and Whose word was not abiding in them? No, for they cannot plead that His testimony was hidden from them ; as Christ says, the testimony of His works is the testimony of the Father concerning Him. His works testify of Him that He was sent of the Father ; but the testimony of these works is the Father's testimony ; since, therefore, the working of the Son is the Father's testimony, it follows of necessity that the same nature was operative in Christ, by which the Father testifies of Him. So Christ, Who works the works, and the Father Who testifies through them, are revealed as possessing one inseparable nature through the birth, for the operation of Christ

9 i.e. including personal distinction from the Father, cf. c. 1, and note.
1 St. John xiv. 1.
2 i.e. such as Sabellius had taught by extending the unity of nature into a unity of person. There is a unity of nature in the Godhead, but a union of Persons.

3 St. John v. 36—38.
4 St. Matt. xvii. 5, the occasion of the Transfiguration. But the context shews that Hilary is referring to the voice heard at the baptism, where all the three Evangelists (St. Matt. iii. 17, St. Mark i. 11. St. Luke iii. 22), according to the commonly received text agree in omitting the words, " Hear ye Him."

is signified to be itself the testimony of God concerning Him.

21. They are not, therefore, acquitted of blame for not recognising the testimony; for the works of Christ are the Father's testimony concerning Him. Nor can they plead ignorance of the testimony on the ground that they had not heard the voice of the Testifier, nor seen His form, nor had His word abiding in them. For immediately after the words, *Ye have neither heard His voice at any time, nor seen His form, and ye have not His word abiding in you*, He points out why the voice was not heard, nor the form seen, and the word did not abide in them, though the Father had testified concerning Him: *For Whom He sent, Him ye believe not;* that is, if they had believed Him, they would have heard the voice of God, and seen the form of God, and His word would have been in them, since through the unity of Their nature the Father is heard and manifested and possessed in the Son. Is He not also the expression of the Father, since He was sent from Him? Does He distinguish Himself by any difference of nature from the Father, when He says that the Father, testifying of Him, was neither heard, nor seen, nor understood, because they did not believe in Him, Whom the Father sent? The Only-begotten God does not, therefore, separate Himself from God when He confesses God the Father; but, proclaiming by the word "Father" His relationship to God, He includes Himself in the honour due to God.

22. For, in this very same discourse in which He pronounces that His works testify of Him that He was sent of the Father, and asserts that the Father testifies of Him, that He was sent from Him, He says, *The honour of Him, Who alone is God, ye seek not*[5]. This is not, however, a bare statement, without any previous preparation for the belief in His unity with the Father. Hear what precedes it, *Ye will not come to Me that ye may have life. I receive not glory from men. But I know you, that ye have not the love of God in yourselves. I am come in My Father's name, and ye receive Me not: if another shall come in His name*[6], *him ye will receive. How can ye believe, which receive glory from men, and the glory of Him, Who alone is God, ye seek not*[7]? He disdains the glory of men, for glory should rather be sought of God. It is the mark of unbelievers to receive glory of one another: for what glory can man give to man? He says He knows that the love of God is not in them, and pronounces, as the cause, that they do not receive Him coming in His Father's name. "Coming in His Father's name:" what does that mean but "coming in the name of God?" Is it not because they rejected Him Who came in the name of God, that the love of God is not in them? Is it not implied that He has the nature of God, when He says, *Ye will not come to Me that ye may have life.* Hear what He said of Himself in the same discourse, *Verily, verily, I say unto you, the hour cometh, and now is, when the dead shall hear the voice of the Son of God; and they that hear shall live*[8]. He comes in the name of the Father: that is, He is not Himself the Father, yet is in the same divine nature as the Father: for as Son and God it is natural for Him to come in the name of the Father. Then, another coming in the same name they will receive: but he is one from whom men will expect glory, and to whom they will give glory in return, though he will feign to have come in the name of the Father. By this, doubtless, is signified the Antichrist, glorying in his false use of the Father's name. Him they will glorify, and will be glorified of him: but the glory of Him, Who alone is God, they will not seek.

23. They have not the love of God in them, He says, because they rejected Him coming in the name of the Father, but accepted another, who came in the same name, and received glory of one another, but neglected the glory of Him, Who is the only true God. Is it possible to think that He separates Himself from the glory of the only God, when He gives as the reason why they seek not the glory of the only God, that they receive Antichrist, and Himself they will not receive? To reject Him is to neglect the glory of the only God; is not, then, His glory the glory of the only God, if to receive Him stedfastly was to seek the glory of the only God? This very discourse is our witness: for at its beginning we read, *That all may honour the Son, even as they honour the Father. He that honoureth not the Son, honoureth not the Father which sent Him*[9]. It is only things of the same nature that are equal in honour; equality of honour denotes that there is no separation between the honoured. But with the revelation of the birth is combined, the demand for equality of honour. Since the Son is to be honoured as

---

5 St. John v. 44. The usual text of the Greek is τὴν δόξαν τὴν παρὰ τοῦ μόνου θεοῦ, "the glory that cometh from the only God" (R.V.).

6 At the close of this chapter, Hilary speaks as if these words were, "if another shall come in His (i e. the Father's) name," though the Latin "si alius venerit in nomine suo," is ambiguous and the Greek, "ἐὰν ἄλλος ἔλθῃ ἐν τῷ ὀνόματι τῷ ἰδίῳ," quite excludes this translation

7 St. John v. 40—44.

8 St. John v. 25.   9 Ib. v. 23.

the Father[1], and since they seek not the honour of Him, Who is the only God, He is not excluded from the honour of the only God, for His honour is one and the same as that of God : just as *He that honoureth not the Son, honoureth not the Father also,* so he who seeks not the honour of the only God, seeks not the honour of Christ also. Accordingly the honour of Christ is inseparable from the honour of God. By His words, when the news of Lazarus' sickness was brought to Him, He illustrates the complete identification of Father and Son in honour : *This sickness is not unto death, but for the glory of God, that the Son of Man may be glorified through him*[2] Lazarus dies for the glory of God, that the Son of God may be glorified through him. Is there any doubt that the glory of the Son of God is the glory of God, when the death of Lazarus, which is glorious to God, glorifies the Son of God? Thus Christ is declared to be one in nature with God the Father through His birth, since the sickness of Lazarus is for the glory of God, and at the same time the Mystery of the faith is not violated, for the Son of God is to be glorified through Lazarus. The Son of God is to be regarded as God, yet He is none the less to be confessed also Son of God : for by glorifying God through Lazarus, the Son of God is glorified.

24. By the mystery of the divine nature we are forbidden to separate the birth of the living Son from His living Father The Son of God suffers no such change of kind, that the truth of His Father's nature does not abide in Him. For even where, by the confession of One God only, He seems to disclaim for Himself the nature of God by the term "only," nevertheless, without destroying the belief in one God, He places Himself in the unity of the Father's nature. Thus, when the Scribe asked Him, which is the chief commandment of the law, He answered, *Hear, O Israel, the Lord our God is one Lord : thou shalt love the Lord thy God with all thy heart, and with all thy soul, and with all thy spirit, and with all thy strength. This is the first commandment. And the second is like unto it, Thou shalt love thy neighbour as thyself. There is none other commandment greater than these*[3]. They think that He severs Himself from the nature and worship of the One God when He pronounces as the chief commandment, *Hear, O Israel, the Lord our God is one Lord,* and does not even make Himself the object of worship in the second

commandment, since the law bids us to love our neighbour, as it bids us to believe in one God. Nor must we pass over the answer of the Scribe, *Of a truth thou hast well said, that God is one, and there is none other but He : and to love Him with all the heart, and all the strength and all the soul, and to love his neighbour as himself, this is greater than all whole burnt offerings and sacrifices*[4]. The answer of the Scribe seems to accord with the words of the Lord, for He too proclaims the innermost and inmost love of one God, and professes the love of one's neighbour as real as the love of self, and places love of God and love of one's neighbour above all the burnt offerings of sacrifices. But let us see what follows.

25. *And when Jesus saw that he answered discreetly, He said unto him, Thou art not far from the kingdom of God*[5]. What is the meaning of such moderate praise? Believe in one God, and love Him with all thy soul, and with all thy strength, and with all thy heart, and love thy neighbour as thyself; if this be the faith which makes man perfect for the Kingdom of God, why is not the Scribe already within, instead of *not far from the Kingdom of Heaven?* It is in another strain that He grants the Kingdom of Heaven to those who clothe the naked, feed the hungry, give drink to the thirsty, and visit the sick and the prisoner, *Come, ye blessed of My Father, inherit the kingdom prepared for you from the foundation of the world*[6]; or rewards the poor in spirit, *Blessed are the poor in spirit : for theirs is the Kingdom of Heaven*[7]. Their gain is perfect, their possession complete, their inheritance of the kingdom prepared for them is secured. But was this young man's confession short of theirs? His ideal of duty raises love of neighbour to the level of love of self; what more did he want to attain to the perfection of good conduct? To be occasionally charitable, and ready to help, is not perfect love ; but perfect love has fulfilled the *whole* duty of charity, when a man leaves no debt to his neighbour unpaid, but gives him as much as he gives himself. But the Scribe was debarred from perfection, because he did not know the mystery which had been accomplished. He received, indeed, the praise of the Lord for his profession of faith, he heard the reply that he was not far from the kingdom, but he was not put in actual possession of the blessed hope. His course, though ignorant, was favourable ; he put the love of God before all things, and charity towards his neighbour on a level with love of self. And

[1] Following the punctuation of the older Editions, and placing the full stop after, instead of before, the sentence "cum Filius ita honorandus ut Pater sit."
[2] St. John xi. 4, "through him"=through Lazarus. The Greek is δι' αὐτῆς, "thereby " (R.V.).
[3] St. Mark xii. 29—31; cf. Matt. xxii. 36—40.

[4] St. Mark xii. 52, 33.   [5] Ib. 34.
[6] St. Matt. xxv. 34.   [7] Ib. v. 3 ; cf. Luke vi 20.

when he ranked the love of God even higher than charity towards his neighbour, he broke through the law of burnt offerings and sacrifices; and that was not far from the mystery of the Gospel.

26. We may perceive also, from the words of our Lord Himself, why He said, *Thou art not far from the Kingdom of Heaven*, rather than, *Thou shalt be in the Kingdom of Heaven*. Then follows: *And no man after that durst ask Him any question. And Jesus answered and said, as He taught in the Temple, How say the Scribes that the Christ is the Son of David? David himself saith in the Holy Spirit, The Lord said unto my Lord, Sit Thou on My right hand, till I make Thine enemies the footstool of Thy feet* (Ps. cx. 1). *David himself calleth Him Lord, and whence is He his Son*[8]? The Scribe is not far from the Kingdom of God when he confesses one God, Who is to be loved above all things. But his own statement of the law is a reproach to him that the mystery of the law has escaped him, that he does not know Christ the Lord, the Son of God, by the nature of His birth to be included in the confession of the one God. The confession of one God according to the law seemed to leave no room for the Son of God in the mystery of the one Lord; so He asks the Scribe, how he can call Christ the Son of David, when David calls Him his Lord, since it is against the order of nature that the son of so great a Patriarch should be also his Lord. He would bid the Scribe, who regards Him only in respect of His flesh, and His birth from Mary, the daughter of David, to remember that, in respect of His Spirit, He is David's Lord rather than his son; that the words, *Hear, O Israel, the Lord our God is one Lord*, do not sever Christ from the mystery of the One Lord, since so great a Patriarch and Prophet calls Him his Lord, as the Son begotten of the Lord before the morning star. He does not pass over the law, or forget that none other is to be confessed Lord, but without violating the faith of the law, He teaches that He is Lord, in that He had His being by the mystery of a natural birth from the substance of the incorporeal God. He is one, born of one, and the nature of the one Lord has made Him by nature Lord.

27. What room is any longer left for doubt? The Lord Himself proclaiming that the chief commandment of the law is to confess and love the one Lord, proves Himself to be Lord not by words of His own, but by the Prophet's testimony, always signifying, however, that He

's Lord, because He is the Son of God. By virtue of His birth He abides in the mystery of the one God, for the birth transmitting with it, as it did, the nature of God is not the issuing forth of another God with a different nature; and, because the generation is real, neither is the Father degraded from being Lord, nor is the Son born less than Lord. The Father retains His authority, the Son obtains His nature. God the Father is one Lord, but the Only-begotten God the Lord is not separated from the One, since He derives His nature as Lord from the one Lord. Thus by the law Christ teaches that there is one Lord; by the witness of the prophets He proves Himself Lord also.

28. May the faith of the Gospel ever profit thus by the rash contentions of the ungodly to defend itself with the weapons of their attack, and conquering with the arms prepared for its destruction, prove that the words of the one Spirit are the doctrine of the one faith! For Christ is none other than He is preached, namely the true God, and abiding in the glory of the one true God. Just as He proclaims Himself Lord out of the law, even when He seems to deny the fact, so in the Gospels He proves Himself the true God, even when He appears to confess the opposite. To escape the acknowledgment that He is the true God, the heretics plead that He said, *And this is life eternal, that they should know Thee, the only true God, and Him Whom Thou didst send, even Jesus Christ*[9]. When He says, *Thee, the only true God*, they think He excludes Himself from the reality of God by the restriction of solitariness; for the only true God cannot be understood except as a solitary God. It is true the Apostolic faith does not suffer us to believe in two true Gods, for nothing which is foreign to the nature of the one God can be put on equality with the truth of that nature; and there is more than one God in the reality of the one God, if there exists outside the nature of the only true God a true God of another kind, not possessing by virtue of His birth the same nature with Him.

29. But by these very words He proclaims Himself plainly to be true God in the nature of the only true God. To understand this, let our answer proceed from statements which He made previously, though the connection is unbroken right down to these words. We can then establish the faith step by step, and let the confidence of our freedom rest at last on the summit of our argument, the true Godhead of Christ. There comes first the mystery

---

8 St. Mark xii. 34—37.   9 St. John xvii. 3.

of His words, *He that hath seen Me, hath seen the Father; and, Do ye not believe Me that I am in the Father and the Father in Me? The words that I say unto you, I speak not from Myself; but the Father abiding in Me, Himself doeth His works. Believe Me that I am in the Father and the Father in Me: or else believe Me for the very works' sake* [1]. At the close of this discourse, teeming with deep mysteries, follows the reply of the disciples, *Now know we that Thou knowest all things, and needest not that any man should ask thee: by this we believe that Thou camest forth from God* [2]. They perceived in Him the nature of God by the divine powers which He exercised; for to know all things, and to read the thoughts of the heart belongs to the Son, not to the mere messenger of God. They confessed, therefore, that He was come from God, because the power of the divine nature was in Him.

30. The Lord praised their understanding, and answered not that He was sent from, but that He was come out from, God, signifying by the words "come out from" the great fact of His birth from the incorporeal God. He had already proclaimed the birth in the same language, when He said, *Ye love Me, and believe that I came out from the Father, and came from the Father into this world* [3]. He had come from the Father into this world, because He had come out from God. To shew that He signifies His birth by the coming out, He adds that He has come from the Father; and since He had come out from God, because He had come from the Father, that "coming out," followed, as it is, by the confession of the Father's name, is simply and solely the birth. To the Apostles, then, as understanding this mystery of His coming out, He continues, *Ye believe now, Behold the hour cometh, yea is come, that ye shall be scattered, every man to his own, and shall leave Me alone: yet I am not alone, because the Father is with Me* [4]. He would shew that the "coming out" is not a separation from God the Father, but a birth, which by His being born continues in Him the nature of God the Father, and therefore He adds that He is not alone, but the Father is with Him; in power, that is, and unity of nature, for the Father was abiding in Him, speaking in His words, and working in His works. Lastly to shew the reason of this whole discourse, He adds, *These things I have spoken to you, that in Me ye may have peace. In this world ye shall have tribulation: but be of good cheer, for I have overcome the world* [5]. He has spoken these things unto them, that in Him they may abide in peace, not torn asunder by the passion of dissension over debates about the faith. He was left alone, but was not alone, for He had come out from God, and there abode still in Him the God, from Whom He had come out. Therefore he bade them, when they were harassed in the world, to wait for His promises, for since He had come out from God, and God was still in Him, He had conquered the world.

31. Then, finally, to express in words the whole Mystery, He raised His eyes to heaven, and said, *Father, the hour is come: glorify Thy Son, that Thy Son may glorify Thee. Even as Thou gavest Him authority over all flesh, that, whatsoever Thou hast given Him, to them He should give eternal life* [6]. Do you call Him weak because He asks to be glorified? So be it, if He does not ask to be glorified in order that He may Himself glorify Him by Whom He is glorified. Of the receiving and giving of glory we have spoken in another book [7], and it would be superfluous to go over the question again. But of this at least we are certain, that He prays for glory in order that the Father may be glorified by granting it. But perhaps He is weak in that He *receives* power over all flesh. And indeed the receiving of power might be a sign of weakness if He were not able to give to those whom He receives life eternal. Yet the very fact of receiving is used to prove inferiority of nature. It might, if Christ were not true God by birth as truly as is the Unbegotten. But if the receiving of power signifies neither more nor less than the Birth, by which He received all that He has, that gift does not degrade the Begotten, because it makes Him perfectly and entirely what God is. God Unbegotten brought God Only-begotten to a perfect birth of divine blessedness: it is, then, the mystery of the Father to be the Author of the Birth, but it is no degradation to the Son to be made the perfect image of His Author by a real birth. The giving of power over all flesh, and this, in order that to all flesh might be given eternal life, postulates the Fatherhood of the Giver and the Divinity of the Receiver: for by giving is signified that the One is the Father, and in receiving the power to give eternal life, the Other remains God the Son. All power is therefore natural and congenital to the Son of God; and though it is given, that does not separate Him from His Author, for that which is given is the property of His Author,

---

[1] St. John xiv. 9—11. [2] Ib. xvi. 30.
[3] Ib. 27, 28. [4] Ib. 31, 32.
[5] St. John xvi. 33. [6] Ib. xvii. 1, 2. [7] See iii. 12.

power to bestow eternal life, to change the corruptible into the incorruptible. The Father gave all, the Son received all; as is plain from His words, *All things, whatsoever the Father hath, are Mine* [8]. He is not speaking here of species of created things, and processes of material change [1], but He unfolds to us the glory of the blessed and perfect Divinity, and teaches us that God is here manifested as the sum of His attributes, His power, His eternity, His providence, His authority; not that we should think that He possesses these as something extraneous to Himself, but that by these His qualities He Himself has been expressed in terms partly comprehensible by our sense. The Only-begotten, therefore, taught that He had all that the Father has, and that the Holy Spirit should receive of Him: as He says, *All things, whatsoever the Father hath, are Mine; therefore I said, He shall take of Mine* [2]. All that the Father hath are His, delivered and received: but these gifts do not degrade His divinity, since they give Him the same attributes as the Father.

32. These are the steps by which He advances the knowledge of Himself. He teaches that He is come out from the Father, proclaims that the Father is with Him, and testifies that He has conquered the world. He is to be glorified of the Father, and will glorify Him: He will use the power He has received, to give to all flesh eternal life. Then hear the crowning point, which concludes the whole series, *And this is life eternal, that they should know Thee, the only true God, and Him Whom Thou didst send, even Jesus Christ* [3]. Learn, heretic, to confess, if you cannot believe, the faith which gives eternal life. Separate, if you can, Christ from God, the Son from the Father, God over all from the true God, the One from the Only: if, as you say, eternal life is to believe in one only true God without Jesus Christ. But if there is no eternal life in a confession of the only true God, which separates Christ from Him, how, pray, can Christ be separated from the true God for our faith, when He is not separable for our salvation?

33. I know that laboured solutions of difficult questions do not find favour with the reader, but it will perhaps be to the advantage of the faith if I permit myself to postpone for a time the exposition of the full truth, and

wrestle against the heretics with these words of the Gospel. You hear the statement of the Lord, *This is life eternal, that they should know Thee, the only true God, and Him Whom Thou didst send, even Jesus Christ.* What is it, pray, which suggests to you that Christ is not the true God? No further indication is given to shew you what you should think of Christ. There is nothing but *Jesus Christ:* not *Son of Man,* as He generally called Himself: not *Son of God,* as He often declared Himself: not *the living bread which cometh down from Heaven* [4], as He repeated to the scandal of many. He says, *Thee, the only true God, and Him Whom Thou didst send, even Jesus Christ,* omitting all His usual names and titles, natural and assumed. Hence, if the confession of the only true God, and of Jesus Christ, gives us eternal life, without doubt the name Jesus Christ has here the full sense of that of God.

34. But perhaps by saying, *Thee the only,* Christ severs Himself from communion and unity with God. Yes, but after the words, *Thee the only true God,* does He not immediately continue, *and Him Whom Thou didst send, even Jesus Christ?* I appeal to the sense of the reader: what must we believe Christ to be, when we are commanded to believe in Him also, as well as the Father the only true God? Or, perhaps, if the Father is the only true God, there is no room for Christ to be God. It might be so, if, because there is one God the Father, Christ were not the one Lord [5]. The fact that God the Father is one, leaves Christ none the less the one Lord: and similarly the Father's one true Godhead makes Christ none the less true God: for we can only obtain eternal life if we believe in Christ, as well as in the only true God

35. Come, heretic, what will your fatuous doctrine instruct us to believe of Christ; Christ, Who dispenses eternal life, Who is glorified of, and glorifies, the Father, Who overcame the world, Who, deserted, is not alone, but has the Father with Him, Who came out from God, and came from the Father? He is born with such divine powers; what of the nature and reality of God will you allow Him? It is in vain that we believe in the only true God the Father, unless we believe also in Him, Whom He sent, even Jesus Christ. Why do you hesitate? Tell us, what is Christ to be confessed? You deny what has been written: what is left, but to believe what has not been written? O unhappy wilfulness! O falsehood striving against the truth! Christ is united in belief and con-

---

[8] St. John xvi. 15.
[1] i.e. He does not mean by *whatsoever the Father hath* the created world: nor is the giving and receiving to be understood in a material sense, cf. c. 72.
[2] St. John xvi. 15. The 'He' is the Holy Ghost; see the context.
[3] Ib. xvii. 3.

[4] St. John vi. 51.　　[5] 1 Cor. viii. 6: see above, c. 32.

fession with the only true God the Father: what faith is it, pray, to deny Him to be true God, and to call Him a creature, when it is no faith to believe in the only true God without Christ? But you are narrow, heretic, and unable to receive the Holy Spirit. The sense of the heavenly words escapes you; stung with the asp's poison of error, you forget that Christ is to be confessed true God in the faith of the only true God, if we would obtain eternal life.

36. But the faith of the Church, while confessing the only true God the Father, confesses Christ also. It does not confess Christ true God without the Father the only true God; nor the Father the only true God without Christ. It confesses Christ true God, because it confesses the Father the only true God. Thus the fact that God the Father is the only true God constitutes Christ also true God. The Only-begotten God suffered no change of nature by His natural birth: and He Who, according to the nature of His divine origin was born God from the living God, is, by the truth of that nature, inalienable from the only true God. Thus there follows from the true divine nature its necessary result, that the outcome of true divinity must be a true birth, and that the one God could not produce from Himself a God of a second kind. The mystery of God consists neither in simplicity, nor in multiplicity: for neither is there another God, Who springs from God with qualities of His own nature, nor does God remain as a single Person, for the true birth of the Son teaches us to confess Him as Father. The begotten God did not, therefore, lose the qualities of His nature: He possesses the natural power of Him, Whose nature He retains in Himself by a natural birth. The divinity in Him is not changed, or degenerate, for if His birth had brought with it any defect, it would more justly cast upon the Nature, through which He came into being, the reflection of having failed to implant in its offspring the properties of itself. The change would not degrade the Son, Who had passed into a new substance by birth, but the Father, Who had been unable to maintain the constancy of His nature in the birth of the Son, and had brought forth something external and foreign to Himself.

37. But, as we have often said, the inadequacy of human ideas has no corresponding inadequacy in the unity of God the Father and God the Son: as though there were extension, or series, or flux, like a spring pouring forth its stream from the source, or a tree supporting its branch on the stem, or fire giving out its heat into space. In these cases we have expansion without any separation: the parts are bound together and do not exist of themselves, but the heat is in the fire, the branch in the tree, the stream in the spring. So the thing itself alone has an independent existence; the one does not pass into the other, for the tree and the branch are one and the same, as also the fire and the heat, the spring and the stream. But the Only-begotten God is God, subsisting by virtue of a perfect and ineffable birth, true Scion of the Unbegotten God, incorporeal offspring of an incorporeal nature, living and true God of living and true God, God of a nature inseparable from God. The fact of birth does not make Him God with a different nature, nor did the generation, which produced His substance, change its nature in kind.

38. But in the dispensation of the flesh which He assumed, and through the obedience whereby He emptied Himself of the form of God, Christ, born man, took to Himself a new nature, not by loss of virtue or nature but by change of fashion. He emptied Himself of the form of God and took the form of a servant, when He was born. But the Father's nature, with which He was in natural unity, was not affected by this assumption of flesh; while Christ, though abiding in the virtue of His nature, yet in respect of the humanity assumed in this temporal change, lost together with the form of God the unity with the divine nature also. But the Incarnation is summed up in this, that the whole Son, that is, His manhood as well as His divinity, was permitted by the Father's gracious favour to continue in the unity of the Father's nature, and retained not only the powers of the divine nature, but also that nature's self. For the object to be gained was that man might become God. But the assumed manhood could not in any wise abide in the unity of God, unless, through unity with God, it attained to unity with the nature of God. Then, since God the Word was in the nature of God, the Word made flesh would in its turn also be in the nature of God. Thus, if the flesh were united to the glory of the Word, the man Jesus Christ could abide in the glory of God the Father, and the Word made flesh could be restored to the unity of the Father's nature, even as regards His manhood, since the assumed flesh had obtained the glory of the Word. Therefore the Father must reinstate the Word in His unity, that the offspring of His nature might again return to be glorified in Himself: for the unity had been infringed by the new dispensation, and could only be restored perfect as before if the Father glorified with Himself the flesh assumed by the Son.

39. For this reason, having already so well prepared their minds for the understanding of this belief, the Lord follows up the words, *And this is eternal life, that they should know Thee, the only true God, and Him Whom Thou didst send, even Jesus Christ*, with a reference to the obedience displayed in His incarnation, *I have glorified Thee on the earth, I have accomplished the work which Thou gavest Me to do*[6]. And then, that we might know the reward of His obedience, and the secret purpose of the whole divine plan, He continued, *And now, O Father, glorify Thou Me with Thine own self, with the glory which I had with Thee before the world was*[7]. Does any one deny that Christ remained in the nature of God, or believe Him separable and distinct from the only true God? Let him tell us what is the meaning of this prayer, *And now, O Father, glorify Thou Me with Thine own self*. For what purpose should the Father glorify Him with His own self? What is the signification of these words? What follows from their signification? The Father neither stood in need of glory, nor had He emptied Himself of the form of His glory. How should He glorify the Son with His own self, and with that glory which He had with Him before the world was made? And what is the sense of *which He had with Him?* Christ does not say, " The glory which I had before the world was made, when I was with Thee," but, *The glory which I had with Thee*. When *I was with Thee* would signify, " when I dwelt by Thy side :" but *which I had with Thee* teaches the Mystery of His nature. Further, *Glorify Me with Thyself* is not the same as " Glorify Me." He does not ask merely that He may be glorified, that He may have some special glory of His own, but prays that He may be glorified of the Father with Himself. The Father was to glorify Him with Himself, that He might abide in unity with Him as before, since the unity with the Father's glory had left Him through the obedience of the Incarnation. And this means that the glorifying should reinstate Him in that nature, with which He was united by the Mystery of His divine birth; that He might be glorified of the Father with Himself; that He should resume all that He had had with the Father before ; that the assumption of the servant's form should not estrange from Him the nature of the form of God, but that God should glorify in Himself the form of the servant, that it might become for ever the form of God, since He, Who had before abode in the form of God, was now in the form of a servant.

And since the form of a servant was to be glorified in the form of God, it was to be glorified in Him in Whose form the fashion of the servant's form was to be honoured.

40. But these words of the Lord are not new, or attested now for the first time in the teaching of the Gospels, for He testified to this very mystery of God the Father glorifying the Son with Himself by the noble joy at the fulfilment of His hope, with which He rejoiced at the very moment when Judas went forth to betray Him. Filled with joy that His purpose was now to be fully accomplished. He said, *Now is the Son of Man glorified and God is glorified in Him. If God is glorified in Him, He hath glorified Him in Himself, and straightway hath He glorified Him*[8]. How can we whose souls are burdened with bodies of clay, whose minds are polluted and stained with foul consciousness of sin, be so puffed up as to judge of His divine claim? How can we set up ourselves to criticise His heavenly nature, rebelling against God with our unhallowed and blasphemous disputations? The Lord enunciated the faith of the Gospel in the simplest words that could be found, and fitted His discourses to our understanding, so far as the weakness of our nature allowed Him, without saying anything unworthy of the majesty of His own nature. The signification of His opening words cannot, I think, be doubted, *Now is the Son of Man glorified;* that is, all the glory which He obtains is not for the Word but for His flesh : not for the birth of His Godhead, but for the dispensation of His manhood born into the world. What then, may I ask, is the meaning of what follows, *And God is glorified in Him?* I hear that God is glorified in Him ; but what that can be according to your interpretation, heretic, I do not know. God is glorified in Him, in the Son of Man, that is : tell me, then, is the Son of Man the same as the Son of God? And since the Son of Man is not one and the Son of God another, but He Who is Son of God is Himself also Son of Man, Who, pray, is the God Who is glorified in this Son of Man, Who is also Son of God?

41. So God is glorified in the Son of Man, Who is also Son of God. Let us see, then, what is this third clause which is added, *If God is glorified in Him, God hath also glorified Him in Himself.* What, pray, is this secret mystery? God, in the glorified Son of Man, glorifies a glorified God in Himself! The glory of God is in the Son of Man, and the glory of God is in the glory of the Son

---

6 St. John xvii. 3, 4.　　　7 Ib. 5.　　　8 St. John xiii. 31, 32.

of Man. God glorifies in Himself, but man is not glorified through himself. Again the God Who is glorified in the man, though He receives the glory, yet is Himself none other than God. But since in the glorifying of the Son of Man, the God, Who glorifies, glorifies God in Himself, I recognise that the glory of Christ's nature is taken into the glory of that nature which glorifies His nature. God does not glorify Himself, but He glorifies in Himself God glorified in man. And this "glorifies in Himself," though it is not a glorifying of Himself, yet means that He took the nature, which He glorified, into the glory of His own nature. Since the God, Who glorifies the God glorified in man, glorifies Him in Himself, He proves that the God Whom He glorifies is in Himself, for He glorifies Him in Himself. Come, heretic, whoever you be, produce the inextricable objections of your tortuous doctrine ; though they bind themselves in their own tangles, yet, marshal them as you will, we shall not be in danger of sticking in their snares. The Son of Man is glorified ; God is glorified in Him ; God glorifies in Himself Him, Who is glorified in the man. It is not the same that the Son of Man is glorified, as that God is glorified in the Son of Man, or that God glorifies in Himself Him, Who is glorified in the man. Express in the terms of your unholy belief, what you mean by God being glorified in the Son of Man. It must certainly be either Christ Who is glorified in the flesh, or the Father Who is glorified in Christ. If it is Christ Christ is manifestly God, Who is glorified in the flesh. If it is the Father, we are face to face with the mystery of the unity, since the Father is glorified in the Son. Thus, if you allow it to be Christ, despite yourself you confess Him God ; if you understand it of God the Father, you cannot deny the nature of God the Father in Christ. Let this be enough concerning the glorified Son of Man and God glorified in Him. But when we consider that God glorifies in Himself God, Who is glorified in the Son of Man, by what loophole, pray, can your profane doctrine escape from the confession that Christ is very God according to the verity of His nature? God glorifies in Himself Christ, Who was born a man; is Christ then outside Him, when He glorifies Him in Himself? He restores to Christ in Himself the glory which He had with Himself, and now that the servant's form, which He assumed, is in turn assumed into the form of God, God Who is glorified in man is glorified in Himself; He was in God's self before the dispensation, by which He emptied Himself, and now He is united with God's self

both in the form of the servant, and in the nature belonging to His birth. For His birth did not make Him God of a new and foreign nature, but by generation He was made natural Son of a natural Father. After His human birth, when He is glorified in His manhood, He shines again with the glory of His own nature ; the Father glorifies Him in Himself, when He is assumed into the glory of His Father's nature, of which He had emptied Himself in the dispensation.

42. The words of the Apostle's faith are a barrier against your reckless and frenzied profanity, which forbids you to turn the freedom of speculation into licence, and wander into error. *Every tongue, he says, shall confess that Jesus is Lord in the glory of God the Father* [9]. The Father has glorified Him in Himself, therefore He must be confessed in the glory of the Father. And if He is to be confessed in the Father's glory, and the Father has glorified Him in Himself, is He not plainly all that His Father is, since the Father has glorified Him in Himself and He is to be confessed in the Father's glory? He is now not merely in the glory of God, but in the glory of God the Father. The Father glorifies Him, not with a glory from without, but in Himself. By taking Him back into that glory, which belongs to Himself, and which He had with Him before, the Father glorifies Him with Himself and in Himself. Therefore this confession is inseparable from Christ even in the humiliation of His manhood, as He says, *And this is eternal life, that they should know Thee, the only true God, and Him, Whom Thou didst send, even Jesus Christ* [1]; for firstly there is no life eternal in the confession of God the Father without Jesus Christ, and secondly Christ is glorified in the Father. Eternal life is precisely this, to know the only true God and Him, Whom He sent, even Jesus Christ ; deny that Christ is true God, if you can have life by believing in God without Him. As for the truth that God the Father is the only true God ; let this be untrue of the God Christ, unless Christ's glory is wholly in the only true God the Father. For if the Father glorifies Him in Himself, and the Father is the only true God, Christ is not outside the only true God, since the Father, Who is the only true God, glorifies in Himself Christ, Who is raised into the glory of God. And in that He is glorified by the only true God in Himself, He is not estranged from the only

---

9 Phil. ii. 11. The Greek is εἰς δόξαν θεοῦ πατρός, *to the glory of God the Father* (R.V.): see note on c. 8.
1 St. John xvii. 3.

true God, for He is glorified by the true God in Himself, the only God.

43. But perhaps the godless unbeliever meets the pious believer with the assertion that we cannot understand of the true God a confession of powerlessness, such as, *Verily, verily, I say unto you, The Son can do nothing of Himself, but what He hath seen the Father doing*[2]. If the twofold anger[3] of the Jews had not demanded a twofold answer, it would indeed have been a confession of weakness, that the Son could do nothing of Himself, except what He had seen the Father doing. But Christ was answering in the same sentence the double charge of the Jews, who accused Him of violating the Sabbath, and of making Himself equal with God by calling God His Father. Do you think, then, that by fixing attention upon the form of His reply you can withdraw it for the substance? We have already treated of this passage in another book[4]; yet as the exposition of the faith gains rather than loses by repetition, let us ponder once more on the words, since the occasion demands it of us.

44. Hear how the necessity for the reply arose:—*And for this cause did the Jews persecute Jesus, and sought to kill Him, because He did these things on the Sabbath*[5]. Their anger was so kindled against Him, that they desired to kill Him, because He did His works on the Sabbath. But let us see also, what the Lord answered, *My Father worketh even until now, and I work*[6]. Tell us, heretic, what is that work of the Father; since through the Son, and in the Son, are all things, visible and invisible? You, who are wise beyond the Gospels, have doubtless obtained from some other secret source of learning the knowledge of the Father's work, to reveal Him to us. But the Father works in the Son, as the Son Himself says, *The words that I say unto you, I speak not from Myself, but the Father who abideth in Me, He doeth His works*[7]. Do you grasp the meaning of the words, *My Father worketh even until now?* He speaks that we may recognise in Him the power of the Father's nature employing the nature, which has that power, to work on the Sabbath. The Father works in Him while He works; without doubt, then, He works along with the working of the Father, and therefore He says, *My Father worketh even until now*, that this present work of His words and actions may be regarded as the working of the Father's

nature in Himself. This *worketh even until now* identifies the time with the moment of speaking, and therefore we must regard Him as referring to that very work of the Father's which He was then doing, for it implies the working of the Father at the very time of His words. And lest the Faith, being restricted to a knowledge of the Father only, should fail of the hope of eternal life, He adds at once, *And I work;* that is, what the Father worketh even until now, the Son also worketh. Thus He expounds the whole of the faith; for the work which is *now*, belongs to the present time; and if the Father works, and the Son works, no union exists between them, which merges them into a single Person[8]. But the wrath of the bystanders is now redoubled. Hear what follows, *For this cause, therefore, the Jews sought the more to kill Him, because He not only broke the Sabbath, but because He called God His own Father, making Himself equal with God*[1]. Allow me here to repeat that, by the judgment of the Evangelist and by common consent of mankind, the Son is in equality with the Father's nature; and that equality cannot exist except by identity of nature. The begotten cannot derive what it is save from its source and the thing generated cannot be foreign to that which generates it, since from that alone has it come to be what it is. Let us see, then, what the Lord replied to this double outburst of wrath, *Verily, verily, I say unto you, the Son can do nothing of Himself, but what He hath seen the Father doing: for what things soever He doeth, these the Son also doeth in like manner*[2].

45. Unless we regard these words as an integral part of His statement, we do them violence by forcing upon them an arbitrary and unbelieving interpretation. But if His answer refers to the grounds of their anger, our faith expresses rightly what He meant to teach, and the perversity of the ungodly is left without support for its profane delusion. Let us see then whether this reply is suitable to an accusation of working on the Sabbath. *The Son can do nothing of Himself, but what He hath seen the Father doing.* He has said just above, *My Father worketh even until now, and I work.* If by virtue of the authority of the Father's nature within Him, all that He works, He works with the Father in Him, and the Father works even until now on the Sabbath, then the Son, Who pleads the authority of the Father's working, is acquitted of blame.

---

[2] St. John v. 19.
[3] Ib. 18. The Jews sought the more to kill Him, because He not only broke the Sabbath, but also called God His own Father, making Himself equal with God.
[4] Book vii. 15 ff.   [5] St. John v. 16.   [6] Ib. 17.
[7] Ib. xiv. 10.

[8] That both Father and Son work implies that They are two distinct Persons and forbids us to suppose a union of Father and Son, which merges them into one Person.
[1] St. John v. 18.   [2] Ib. 19.

For the words, *can do nothing*, refer not to strength but to authority; He can do nothing of Himself, except what He has seen. Now, to have seen does not confer the power to do, and therefore He is not weak, if He can do nothing without having seen, but His authority is shewn to depend on seeing. Again the words, *unless He hath seen*, signify the consciousness derived from seeing, as when He says to the Apostles, *Behold I say unto you, Lift up your eyes, and look on the fields, that they are white already unto harvest*[3]. With the consciousness that the Father's nature is abiding in Him, and working in Him when He works, to forestall the idea that the Lord of the Sabbath has violated the Sabbath, He pronounces that, *The Son can do nothing of Himself, but what He hath seen the Father doing*. And thus He demonstrates that His every action springs from His consciousness of the nature working within Him; when He works on the Sabbath, the Father *worketh even until now* on the Sabbath. In what follows, however, He refers to the second cause of their indignation, *For what things soever He doeth, the Son doeth in like manner*. Is it false that, *what things soever the Father doeth, the Son doeth in like manner?* Does the Son of God admit a distinction between the Father's power and working and His own? Does He shrink from claiming the equality of homage befitting an equal in power and nature? If He does, disdain His weakness, and degrade Him from equality of nature with the Father. But He Himself says only a little later, *That all may honour the Son, even as they honour the Father. He that honoureth not the Son, honoureth not the Father which sent Him*[4]. Discover, if you can, the inferiority, when Both are equal in honour; make out the weakness, when Both work with the same power.

46. Why do you misrepresent the occasion of the reply in order to detract from His divinity? To the working on the Sabbath He answers that He can do nothing of Himself, but what He hath seen the Father doing: to demonstrate His equality, He professes to do what things soever the Father doeth. Enforce your charge of weakness, by His answer concerning the Sabbath, if you can disprove that *what things soever the Father doeth, the Son doeth in like manner*. But if *what things soever* includes all things without exception; in what is He found weak, when there is nothing that the Father doeth, which He cannot also do? Where is His claim to equality refuted by any episode of weakness, when one and the same honour is demanded for Him and for the Father? If Both have the same power in operation, and both claim the same reverence in worship, I cannot understand what dishonour of inferiority can exist, since Father and Son possess the same power of operation, and equality of honour.

47. Although we have treated this passage as the facts themselves explain it, yet to prove that the Lord's words, *The Son can do nothing of Himself, but what He hath seen the Father doing*, so far from supporting this unholy degradation of His nature, testify to His conscious possession of the nature of the Father, by Whose authority He worked on the Sabbath, let us shew them that we can produce another saying of the Lord, which bears upon the question, *I do nothing of Myself, but as the Father taught Me, I speak these things. And He that sent Me is with Me: He hath not left Me alone, for I do always the things that are pleasing to Him*[5]. Do you feel what is implied in the words, *The Son can do nothing, but what He hath seen the Father doing?* Or what a mystery is contained in the saying, *I can do nothing of myself*, and *He hath not left me alone, for I do always the things that are pleasing to Him?* He does nothing of Himself, because the Father abides in Him; can you reconcile with this the fact that the Father does not leave Him, because He does the things which are pleasing to Him? Your interpretation, heretic, sets up a contradiction between these two statements, that He does nothing of Himself, unless taught of the Father abiding in Him, and that the Father abides in Him, because He does always the things which are pleasing to Him. For if the Father's abiding in Him means that He does nothing of Himself, how could He have deserved that the Father should abide in Him, by doing always the things which are pleasing to the Father. It is no merit, not to do of oneself what one does. Conversely, how are the Son's deeds pleasing to the Father, if the Father Himself, abiding in the Son, be their Author? Impiety, thou art in a sore strait; the well-armed piety of the faith hath hemmed thee in. The Son is either an Agent, or He is not. If He is not an Agent, how does He please by his acts? If He is an Agent, in what sense are deeds, done *not of Himself*, His own? On the one hand, He must have done the things which are pleasing; on the other, it is no merit to have done, yet not of oneself, what one does.

48. But, my opponent, the unity of Their nature is such, that the several action of

Each implies the conjoint action of Both, and Their joint activity a several activity of Each. Conceive the Son acting, and the Father acting through Him. He acts not of Himself, for we have to explain how the Father abides in Him. He acts in His own Person, for in accordance with His birth as the Son, He does Himself what is pleasing. His acting *not of Himself* would prove Him weak, were it not the case that He so acts that what He does is pleasing to the Father. But He would not be in the unity of the divine nature, if the deeds which He does, and wherein He pleases, were not His own, and He were merely prompted to action by the Father abiding in Him. The Father then in abiding in Him, teaches Him, and the Son in acting, acts not of Himself; while, on the other hand, the Son, though not acting of Himself, acts Himself, for what He does is pleasing. Thus is the unity of Their nature retained in Their action, for the One, though He acts Himself, does not act of Himself, while the Other, Who has abstained from action, is yet active.

49. Connect with this that saying, which you lay hold of to support the imputation of infirmity, *All that the Father giveth Me shall come unto Me, and him that cometh to Me I will in no wise cast out ; for I am come down from heaven not to do Mine own will, but the will of the Father that sent Me* [6]. But, perhaps you say, the Son has no freedom of will : the weakness of His nature subjects Him to necessity, and He is denied free-will, and subjected to necessity that He may not reject those who are given to Him and come from the Father. Nor was the Lord content to demonstrate the mystery of the Unity by His action in not rejecting those who are given to Him, nor seeking to do His own will instead of the will of Him that sent Him, but when the Jews, after the repetition of the words, *Him that sent Me,* began to murmur, He confirms our interpretation by saying, *Every one who heareth from the Father and learneth, cometh unto Me. Not that any man hath seen the Father, save He which is from God, He hath seen the Father. Verily, verily, I say unto you, he that believeth in Me hath eternal life* [7]. Now, tell me first, where has the Father been heard, and where has He taught His hearers? No one hath seen the Father, save Him Who is from God : has any one ever heard Him Whom no one has ever seen? He that has heard from the Father, comes to the Son : and he that has heard the teaching of the Son, has heard the teaching of the

Father's nature, for its properties are revealed in the Son. When, therefore, we hear the Son teaching, we must understand that we are hearing the teaching of the Father. No one hath seen the Father, yet he who comes to the Son, hears and learns from the Father to come : it is manifest, therefore, that the Father teaches through the words of the Son, and, though seen of none, speaks to us in the manifestation of the Son, because the Son, by virtue of His perfect birth, possesses all the properties of His Father's nature. The Only-begotten God desiring, therefore, to testify of the Father's authority, yet inculcating His own unity with the Father's nature, does not cast out those who are given to Him of the Father, or work His own will instead of the will of Him that sent Him : not that He does not will what He does, or is not Himself heard when He teaches ; but in order that He may reveal Him Who sent Him, and Himself the Sent, under the aspect of one indistinguishable nature, He shews all that He wills, and says, and does, to be the will and works of the Father.

50. But He proves abundantly that His will is free by the words, *As the Father raiseth the dead and quickeneth them, even so the Son also quickeneth whom He will* [8]. When the equality of Father and Son in power and honour is indicated, then the freedom of the Son's will is made manifest : when Their unity is demonstrated, His conformity to the Father's will is signified, for what the Father wills, the Son does. But to do is something more than to obey a will : the latter would imply external necessity, while to do another's will requires unity with him, being an act of volition. In doing the will of the Father the Son teaches that through the identity of Their nature His will is the same in nature with the Father's, since all that He does is the Father's will. The Son plainly wills all that the Father wills, for wills of the same nature cannot dissent from one another. It is the will of the Father which is revealed in the words, *For this is the will of My Father, that every one that beholdeth the Son and believeth in Him, should have eternal life, and that I should raise Him up at the last day* [9]. Hear now, whether the will of the Son is discordant with the Father's, when He says, *Father, those whom Thou hast given Me, I will that where I am they also may be with Me* [1]. Here is no doubt that the Son wills : for while the Father wills that those who believe in the Son should have eternal life, the Son wills that the believer should be

---

6 St. John vi. 37, 38.   7 Ib. 45—47.   8 St. John v. 21.   9 Ib. vi. 40.   1 Ib. xvii. 24.

where He is. For is it not eternal life to dwell together with Christ? And does He not grant to the believer in Him all perfection of blessing when He says, *No one hath known the Son save the Father, neither hath any known the Father save the Son, and he to whomsoever the Son willeth to reveal Him*[2]? Has He not freedom of will, when He wills to impart to us the knowledge of the Father's mystery? Is not His will so free that He can bestow on whom He will the knowledge of Himself and His Father? Thus Father and Son are manifestly joint Possessors of a nature common to Both through birth and common through unity: for the Son is free of will, but what He does willingly is an act of the Father's will.

51. He who has not grasped the manifest truths of the faith, obviously cannot have an understanding of its mysteries; because he has not the doctrine of the Gospel he is an alien to the hope of the Gospel. We must confess the Father to be in the Son and the Son in the Father, by unity of nature, by might of power, as equal in honour as Begetter and Begotten. But perhaps you say, the witness of our Lord Himself is contrary to this declaration, for He says, *The Father is greater than I*[3]. Is this, heretic, the weapon of your profanity? Are these the arms of your frenzy? Has it escaped you, that the Church does not admit two Unbegotten, or confess two Fathers? Have you forgotten the Incarnation of the Mediator, with the birth, the cradle, the childhood, the passion, the cross and the death belonging to it? When you were born again, did you not confess the Son of God, born of Mary? If the Son of God, of Whom these things are true, says, *The Father is greater than I*, can you be ignorant that the Incarnation for your salvation was an emptying of the form of God, and that the Father, unaffected by this assumption of human conditions, abode in the blessed eternity of His own incorrupt nature without taking our flesh? We confess that the Only-begotten God, while He abode in the form of God, abode in the nature of God, but we do not at once reabsorb into the substance of the divine unity His unity bearing the form of a servant. Nor do we teach that the Father is in the Son, as if He entered into Him bodily; but that the nature which was begotten by the Father of the same kind as His own, possessed by nature the nature which begot it[4]: and that this nature, abiding in the

form of the nature which begot it, took the form of human nature and weakness. Christ possessed all that was proper to His nature: but the form of God had departed from Him, for by emptying Himself of it, He had taken the form of a servant. The divine nature had not ceased to be, but still abiding in Him, it had taken upon itself the humility of earthly birth, and was exercising its proper power in the fashion of the humility it assumed. So God, born of God, being found as man in the form of a servant, but acting as God in His miracles, was at once God as His deeds proved, and yet man, for He was found in the fashion of man

52. Therefore, in the discourse we have expounded above, He had borne witness to the unity of His nature with the Father's: *He that hath seen Me, hath seen the Father also*[5]: *The Father is in Me, and I in the Father*[6]. These two passages perfectly agree, since Both Persons are of equal nature; to behold the Son is the same as to behold the Father; that the One abides in the One shows that They are inseparable And lest they should misunderstand Him, as though when they beheld His body, they beheld the Father in Him, He had added, *Believe Me, that I am in the Father and the Father in Me: or else believe Me for the very works' sake*[7]. His power belonged to His nature, and His working was the exercise of that power; in the exercise of that power, then, they might recognise in Him the unity with the Father's nature. In proportion as any one recognised Him to be God in the power of His nature, he would come to know God the Father, present in that mighty nature. The Son, Who is equal with the Father, shewed by His works that the Father could be seen in Him: in order that we, perceiving in the Son a nature like the Father's in its power, might know that in Father and Son there is no distinction of nature.

53. So the Only-begotten God, just before He finished His work in the flesh, and completed the mystery of taking the servant's form, in order to establish our faith, thus speaks, *Ye heard how I said unto you, I go away, and I come unto you. If ye loved Me, ye would rejoice, because I go unto the Father; for the Father is greater than I*[8]. He has already in an earlier part of this very discourse unfolded in all its aspects the teaching of His divine nature: can we, then, on the strength

---

[2] St. Matt. xi. 27.   [3] St. John xiv. 28.
[4] The unity of the Father and the Son does not mean that the Son's body was derived from the Father, as in human conception the father is *in* the son: but the Son Who derived His incorporeal nature from the Father at the generation, afterwards

assumed a human body for the Incarnation. Thus Hilary clears himself of any Patripassian or Marcellian construction which might be put on his words.
[5] St. John xiv. 9.   [6] Ib. x. 38: cf. xiv. 10, 11.
[7] Ib. xiv. 11.   [8] Ib. 28.

of this confession deprive the Son of that equality, which His true birth has perfected in Him? Or is it an indignity to the Only-begotten God, that the Unbegotten God is His Father, seeing that His Only-begotten birth from the Unbegotten gives Him the Only-begotten nature? He is not the source of His own being, nor did He, being Himself non-existent, bring to pass His own birth out of nothing; but, existing as a living nature and from a living nature, He possesses the power of that nature, and declares the authority of that nature, by bearing witness to His honour, and in His honour to the grace belonging to the birth He received. He pays to the Father the tribute of obedience to the will of Him Who sent Him, but the obedience of humility does not dissolve the unity of His nature: He becomes obedient unto death, but, after death, He is above every name [9].

54. But if His equality is doubted because the Name is given Him after He put off the form of God, we dishonour Him by ignoring the mystery of the humility which He assumed. The birth of His humanity brought to Him a new nature, and His form was changed in His humility, by the assumption of a servant's form, but now the giving of the Name restores to Him equality of form. Ask yourself what it is, which is given. If the gift be something pertaining to God, the grant to the receiving nature does not impair the divinity of the giving nature. Again, the words, *And gave Him the Name*, involve a mystery in the giving, but the giving of the Name does not make it another name. To Jesus is given, that to Him, *Every knee shall bow of things in heaven, and things on earth, and things under the earth, and every tongue confess that Jesus is Lord in the glory of God the Father* [1]. The honour is given Him that He should be confessed in the glory of God the Father. Do you hear Him say, *The Father is greater than I?* Know Him also, of Whom it is said in reward of His obedience, *And gave unto Him the Name which is above every name* [2]; hear Him Who said, *I and the Father are one; He that hath seen Me, hath seen the Father also; I am in the Father, and the Father in Me.* Consider the honour of the confession which is granted Him, that Jesus is Lord in the glory of God the Father. When, then, is the Father greater than the Son? Surely, when He gives Him the Name above every name. And on the other hand, when is it that the Son and the Father are one? Surely, when every tongue confesses that Jesus is

Lord in the glory of God the Father. If, then, the Father is greater through His authority to give, is the Son less through the confession of receiving? The Giver is greater: but the Receiver is not less, for to Him it is given to be one with the Giver. If it is not given to Jesus to be confessed in the glory of God the Father, He is less than the Father. But if it is given Him to be in that glory, in which the Father is, we see in the prerogative of giving, that the Giver is greater, and in the confession of the gift, that the Two are One. The Father is, therefore, greater than the Son: for manifestly He is greater, Who makes another to be all that He Himself is, Who imparts to the Son by the mystery of the birth the image of His own unbegotten nature, Who begets Him from Himself into His own form, and restores Him again from the form of a servant to the form of God, Whose work it is that Christ, born God according to the Spirit in the glory of the Father, but now Jesus Christ dead in the flesh, should be once more God in the glory of the Father. When, therefore, Christ says that He is going to the Father, He reveals the reason why they should rejoice if they loved Him, because the Father is greater than He.

55. After the explanation that love is the source of this joy, because love rejoices that Jesus is to be confessed in the glory of God the Father, He next expresses His claim to receive back that glory, in the words, *For the prince of this world cometh, and he hath nothing in Me* [3]. The prince of this world hath nothing in Him: for being found in fashion as a man, He dwelt in the likeness of the flesh of sin, yet apart from the sin of the flesh, and in the flesh condemned sin by sin [4]. Then, giving obedience to the Father's command as His only motive, He adds, *But that the world may know that I love the Father, even as the Father gave Me commandment, so I do. Arise, let us go hence* [5]. In His zeal to do the Father's commandment, He rises and hastens to complete the mystery of His bodily passion. But the next moment He unfolds the mystery of His assumption of flesh. Through this assumption we are in Him, as the branches in the vinestock [6]; and unless He had become the

---

9 Phil. ii. 8, 9.   1 Ib. 10, 11.   2 Ib. 9.

3 St. John xiv. 30.
4 Rom. viii. 3. Here Hilary's *de peccato peccatum . . . condemnans* must mean 'by means of sin.' In Latin of this date *de* is often instrumental.
5 St. John xiv. 31. The words 'but that the world . . . . even so I do,' are generally connected with the previous sentence, and the last sentence, 'Arise, let us go hence,' is regarded as the breaking off of the discourse. But the words, 'But that the world,' &c., do not stand in very clear connection with the previous sentence, and the view here suggested has much to be said for it.
6 St. John xv. 1, 2.

Vine, we could have borne no good fruit. He exhorts us to abide in Himself, through faith in His assumed body, that, since the Word has been made flesh, we may be in the nature of His flesh, as the branches are in the Vine. He separates the form of the Father's majesty from the humiliation of the assumed flesh by calling Himself the Vine, the source of unity for all the branches, and the Father the careful Husbandman, Who prunes away its useless and barren branches to be burnt in the fire. In the words, *He that hath seen Me, hath seen the Father also,* and *The words that I say unto you, I speak not of Myself, but the Father abiding in Me, He doth His works,* and *Believe Me, that I am in the Father, and the Father in Me,* He reveals the truth of His birth and the mystery of His Incarnation. He then continues the thread of His discourse, until He comes to the saying, *The Father is greater than I;* and after this, to complete the meaning of these words, He hastens to add the illustration of the husbandman, the vine, and the branches, which directs our notice to His submission to bodily humiliation. He says that, because the Father is greater than Himself, He is going to the Father, and that love should rejoice, that He is going to the Father, that is, to receive back His glory from the Father: with Him, and in Him, to be glorified not with a brand-new honour, but with the old, not with some strange honour but with that which He had with Him before. If then Christ shall not enter into Him with glory, to abide in the glory of God, you may disparage His nature: but if the glory which He receives is the proof of His Godhead, recognise that it as Giver of this proof that the Father is the greater.

56. Why do you distort the Incarnation into a blasphemy? Why pervert the mystery of salvation into a weapon of destruction? The Father, Who glorifies the Son, is greater: The Son, Who is glorified in the Father, is not less. How can He be less, when He is in the glory of God the Father? And how can the Father not be greater? The Father therefore is greater, because He is Father: but the Son, because He is Son, is not less. By the birth of the Son the Father is constituted greater: the nature that is His by birth, does not suffer the Son to be less. The Father is greater, for the Son prays Him to render glory to manhood He has assumed. The Son is not less, for He receives back His glory with the Father. Thus are consummated at once the mystery of the Birth, and the dispensation of the Incarnation. The Father, as Father, and as glorifying Him Who now is Son of Man, is greater: Father and Son are one, in that the Son, born of the Father, after assuming an earthly body is taken back to the glory of the Father.

57. The birth, therefore, does not constitute His nature inferior, for He is in the form of God, as being born of God. And though by their very signification, 'Unbegotten' and 'Begotten' seem to be opposed, yet the Begotten cannot be excluded from the nature of the Unbegotten, for there is none other from whom He could derive His substance. He does not indeed share in the supreme majesty of being unbegotten; but He has received from the Unbegotten God the nature of divinity. Thus faith confesses the eternity of the Only-begotten God, though it can give no meaning to begetting or beginning in His case. His nature forbids us to say that He ever began to be, for His birth lies beyond the beginnings of time. But while we confess Him existent before all ages, we do not hesitate to pronounce Him born in timeless eternity, for we believe His birth, though we know it never had a beginning.

58 Seeking to disparage His nature, the heretics lay hold of such sayings as, *The Father is greater than I,* or, *But of that day and hour knoweth no one, not even the angels in heaven, neither the Son, but the Father only[7].* It is turned to a reproach against the Only-begotten God that He did not know the day and the hour: that, though God, born of God, He is not in the perfection of divine nature, since He is subjected to the limitation of ignorance; that is, an external force stronger than Himself, triumphing, as it were, over His weakness, makes Him captive to this infirmity. And, indeed, it is with an apparent right to claim that this confession is inevitable, that the heretics, in their frenzy, would drive us to such a blasphemous interpretation. The words are those of the Lord Himself, and what, it may be asked, could be more unholy than to corrupt His express assertion by our attempt to explain it away.

59. But, before we investigate the meaning and occasion of these words, let us first appeal to the judgment of common sense. Is it credible, that He, Who stands to all things as the Author of their present and future, should not know all things? If all things are through and in Christ, and in such a way through Christ that they are also in Him, must not that, which is both in Him and through Him, be also in His knowledge, when that knowledge, by virtue of a nature which cannot be

---

7 St. Matt. xxiv. 36 ; St. Mark xiii. 32.

nescient, habitually apprehends what is neither in, nor through Him[8]? But that which derives from Him alone its origin, and has in Him alone the efficient cause of its present state and future development, can that be beyond the ken of His nature, through which is effected, and in which is contained, all that it is and shall be? Jesus Christ knows the thoughts of the mind, as it is now, stirred by present motives, and as it will be to-morrow, aroused by the impulse of future desires. Hear the witness of the Evangelist, *For Jesus knew from the beginning who they were that believed not, and who it was that should betray Him*[9]. By its virtue His nature could perceive the unborn future, and foresee the awakening of passions yet dormant in the mind: do you believe that it did not know what is through itself, and within itself? He is Lord of all that belongs to others, is He not Lord of His own? Remember what is written of Him, *All things have been created through Him, and in Him: and He is before all things*[9a]: or again, *For it was the good pleasure of the Father, that in Him should all the fulness dwell, and through Him to reconcile all things unto Himself*[1], all fulness is in Him, all things were made through Him, and are reconciled in Him, and for that day of reconciliation we wait expectant; did He not, then, know it, when its time was in His hands, and fixed by His mystery, for it is the day of His coming, of which the Apostle wrote, *When Christ, Who is your life, shall be manifested, then shall ye also with Him be manifested in glory*[2]. No one is ignorant of that which is through himself and within himself: shall Christ come, and does He not know the day of His coming? It is His day, for the same Apostle says, *The day of the Lord shall come as a thief in the night*[3]: can we believe, then, that He did not know it? Human natures, so far as in them lies, foresee what they determine to do: knowledge of the end desired accompanies the desire to act: does not He Who is born God, know what is in, and through, Himself? The times are through Him, the day is in His hand, for the future is constituted through Him, and the Dispensation of His coming is in His power: is His understanding so dull, that the sense of His torpid nature does not tell Him what He has Himself determined? Is He like the brute and the beast, which, animated by no reason or foresight, not even conscious of acting but driven to and fro by the impulse of irrational desire, proceed to their end with fortuitous and uncertain course?

60. But, again, how can we believe that the Lord of glory, because He was able not to know the day of His own coming, was of a discordant and imperfect nature, subject to the necessity of coming, but ignorant of the day of His coming? This would make God weaker than the power of ignorance, which took from Him the prerogative of knowledge. Then, too, how we redouble occasions of blasphemy, if we impute not only infirmity to Christ, but also defect to God the Father, saying that He defrauded of foreknowledge of this day the Only-begotten God, the Son of His love, and in malice denied Him certainty concerning the future consummation: suffered Him to know the day and hour of His passion, but withheld from Him the day of His power, and the hour of His glory among His Saints: took from Him the knowledge of His blessedness, while He granted Him prescience of His death? The trembling conscience of man dare not presume to think thus of God, or ascribe to Him such taint of human fickleness, that the Father should deny anything to the Son, or the Son, Who was born as God, should possess an imperfect knowledge.

61. But God can never be anything but love, or anything but the Father: and He, Who loves, does not envy; He Who is Father, is wholly and entirely Father. This name admits of no compromise: no one can be partly father, and partly not. A father is father in respect of his whole personality; all that he is is present in the child, for paternity by piecemeal is impossible: not that paternity extends to self-generation, but that a father is altogether father in all his qualities, to the offsprings born of him. According to the constitution of human bodies, which are made of dissimilar elements, and composed of various parts, the father must be father of the whole, since a perfect birth hands on to the child all the different elements and parts, which are in the father. The father is, therefore, father of all that is his; the birth proceeds from the whole of himself, and constitutes the whole of the child. God, however, has no body, but simple essence: no parts, but an all-embracing whole: nothing quickened, but everything living. God is therefore all life, and all one, not compounded of parts, but perfect in His simplicity, and, as the Father, must be Father to His begotten in all that He Himself is, for the perfect birth of the Son makes Him perfect Father in all that He has. So, if He is proper Father to the Son the Son must possess all the

---

8 Christ was conscious, e.g., of the sinfulness of men.
9 St. John vi. 64. 9a Col. i. 16. 1 Ib. 19.
2 Ib. iii. 4. 3 1 Thess. v. 2.

properties of the Father. Yet how can this be, if the Son has not the quality of prescience, if there is anything from His Author, which is wanting in His birth? To say that there is one of God's properties which He has not, is almost equivalent to saying that He has none of them. And what is proper to God, if not the knowledge of the future, a vision, which embraces the invisible and unborn world, and has within its scope that which is not yet, but is to be?

62. Moreover Paul, the teacher of the Gentiles, forestalls the impious falsehood, that the Only-begotten God was partially nescient. Listen to his words, *Being instructed in love, unto all riches of the fulness of understanding, unto knowledge of the mystery of God, even Christ, in Whom are all the treasures of wisdom and knowledge hidden* [4]. God, even Christ, is the mystery, and all the treasures of wisdom and knowledge are hidden in Him. But a portion is one thing, the whole another: a part is not the same as *all*, nor can *all* be called a part. If the Son does not know the day, all the treasures of knowledge are not in Him; but He has all the treasures of knowledge in Him, therefore He is not ignorant of the day. But we must remember that those treasures of knowledge were *hidden* in Him, though not, because hidden, therefore wanting. As in God, they are in Him: as in the mystery, they are hidden. But Christ, the mystery of God, in Whom are all the treasures of knowledge hidden, is not Himself hidden from our eyes and minds. Since then He is Himself the mystery, let us see whether He is ignorant when He does not know. If elsewhere His profession of ignorance does not imply that He does not know, here also it will be wrong to call Him ignorant, if He does not know. In Him are hidden all the treasures of knowledge, and so His ignorance is an economy rather than ignorance. Thus we can assign a reason for His ignorance, without the assumption that He did not know.

63. Whenever God says that He does not know, He professes ignorance indeed, but is not under the defect of ignorance. It is not because of the infirmity of ignorance that He does not know, but because it is not yet the time to speak, or the divine Plan to act. Thus He says to Abraham, *The cry of Sodom and Gomorrah is full, and their sin is very grievous. Therefore I will go down now, and see if they have done altogether according to the cry of it: and if not, I will know* [5]. Here we perceive God not knowing that which notwithstanding He knows. He knows that their

sins are very grievous, but He comes down again to see whether they have done altogether, and to know if they have not. We observe, then, that He is not ignorant, although He does not know, but that, when the time comes for action, He knows. This knowledge is not, therefore, a change from ignorance, but the coming of the fulness of time. He waits still to know, but we cannot suppose that He does not know: therefore His not knowing what He knows, and His knowing what He does not know, is nothing else than a divine economy in word and deed.

64. We cannot, then, doubt that the knowledge of God depends on the occasion and not on any change on His part: by the occasion being meant the occasion, not of obtaining but of declaring knowledge, as we learn from His words to Abraham, *Lay not thine hand upon the lad, neither do thou anything unto him, for now I know that thou fearest thy God, and hast not withheld thy beloved son, for My sake* [6]. God knows now, but that *now I know* is a profession of previous ignorance: yet it is not true, that until now God did not know the faith of Abraham, for it is written, *Abraham believed in God, and it was counted to him for righteousness* [7], and therefore this *now I know* marks the time when Abraham received this testimony, not when God began to know. Abraham had proved, by the sacrifice of his son, the love he bore to God, and God knew it at the time He spoke: but as we cannot suppose that He did not know before, we must for this reason suppose that He took knowledge of it then because He spoke.

By way of example, we have chosen for our consideration this passage out of many in the Old Testament, which treat of the knowledge of God, in order to shew that when God does not know, the cause lies, not in His ignorance, but in the occasion.

65. We find our Lord in the Gospels knowing, yet not knowing, many things. Thus He does not know the workers of iniquity, who glory in their mighty works and in His name, for He says to them, *Then will I swear, I never knew you; depart from Me, all ye that work iniquity* [8]. He declares with an oath even, that He does not know them, but nevertheless He knows them to be workers of iniquity. He does not know them, not because He does not know, but because by the iniquity of their deeds they are unworthy of His knowledge, and He even confirms His denial with the sanctity of an oath. By the virtue of His nature He could not be

[4] Col. ii. 2, 3.   [5] Gen. xviii. 20, 21.   [6] Gen. xxii. 12.   [7] Ib. xv. 6.   [8] St. Matt. vii. 23.

VOL. IX.   N

ignorant, by the mystery of His will He refused to know. Again the Unbegotten God does not know the foolish virgins; He is ignorant of those who were too careless to have their oil ready, when He entered the chamber of His glorious coming. They come and implore, and so far from not knowing them, He cries, *Verily, I say unto you, I know you not*[9]. Their coming and their prayer compel Him to recognise them, but His profession of ignorance refers to His will, not to His nature: they are unworthy to be known of Him to Whom nothing is unknown. Hence, in order that we should not impute His ignorance to infirmity, He says immediately to the Apostles, *Watch therefore, for ye know not the day nor the hour*[1]. When He bids them watch, for they know not the day or the hour, He points out that He knew not the virgins, because through sleep and neglect they had no oil, and therefore were unworthy to enter into His chamber.

66. The Lord Jesus Christ, then, Who *searcheth the heart and the reins*[2], has no weakness in His nature, that He should not know, for, as we perceive, even the fact of His ignorance proceeds from the omniscience of His nature. Yet if any there be, who impute to Him ignorance, let them tremble, lest He Who knows their thoughts should say to them, *Wherefore think ye evil in your hearts*[3]? The All-knowing, though not ignorant of thoughts and deeds, sometimes enquires as if He were, as for instance when He asks the woman who it was that touched the hem of His garment, or the Apostles, why they quarrelled among themselves, or the mourners, where the sepulchre of Lazarus was: but His ignorance was not ignorance, except in words. It is against reason that He should know from afar the death and burial of Lazarus, but not the place of his sepulchre: that He should read the thoughts of the mind, and not recognise the faith of the woman: that He should not need to ask concerning anything[4], yet be ignorant of the dissension of the Apostles. But He, Who knows all things, sometimes by a practice of economy professes ignorance, even though He is not ignorant. Thus, in the case of Abraham, God concealed His knowledge for a time: in that of the foolish virgins and the workers of iniquity, He refused to recognise the unworthy: in the mystery of the Son of Man, His asking, as if ignorant, expressed His humanity. He accommodated Himself to the reality of His birth in the flesh in everything to which the weakness of our nature is subject, not in such wise that He became weak in His divine nature, but that God, born man, assumed the weaknesses of humanity, yet without thereby reducing His unchangeable nature to a weak nature, for the unchangeable nature was that wherein He mysteriously assumed flesh. He, Who was God is man, but, being man, has not ceased to remain God. Conducting Himself then as one born man, and proving Himself such, though remaining God the Word, He often uses the language of man (though God, speaking as God, makes frequent use of human terms), and does not know that which it is not yet time to declare, or which is not deserving of His recognition.

67. We can now understand why He said that He knew not the day. If we believe Him to have been really ignorant, we contradict the Apostle, who says, *In Whom are all the treasures of wisdom and knowledge hidden*[5]. There is knowledge which is hidden in Him, and because it has to be hidden, it must sometimes for this purpose be professed as ignorance, for once declared, it will no longer be secret. In order, therefore, that the knowledge may remain hidden, He declares that He does not know. But if He does not know, in order that the knowledge may remain hidden, this ignorance is not due to His nature, which is omniscient, for He is ignorant solely in order that it may be hidden. Nor is it hard to see why the knowledge of the day is hidden. He exhorts us to watch continually with unrelaxing faith, and withholds from us the security of certain knowledge, that our minds may be kept on the stretch by the uncertainty of suspense, and while they hasten towards and continually look for the day of His coming, may always watch in hope; and that, though we know the time must come, its very uncertainty may make us careful and vigilant. Thus the Lord says, *Therefore be ye also ready, for ye know not what hour the Son of Man shall come*[6]; and again, *Blessed is that servant whom His lord, when He cometh, shall find so doing*[7]. The ignorance is, therefore, a means not to delude, but to encourage in perseverance. It is no loss to be denied a knowledge which it is an advantage not to have, for the security of knowledge might breed negligence of the faith, which now is concealed, while the uncertainty of expectation keeps us continually prepared, even as the master of the house, with the fear of loss before his eyes, watches and guards against the dreaded com-

---

9 St. Matt. xxv. **12.**   1 Ib. xxv. **13.**
2 Rev. ii. 23.   3 St. Matt. ix. 4.
4 St. John xvi. 30. The Greek is ἵνα τίς σε ἐρωτᾷ, 'that any one should ask thee' (R.V.).

5 Col. ii. 3.   6 St. Matt. xxiv. 44.   7 Ib. 46.

ing of the thief, who chooses the time of sleep for his work.

68. Manifestly, therefore, the ignorance of God is not ignorance but a mystery: in the economy of His actions and words and manifestations, He does not know and at the same time He knows, or knows and at the same time does not know. But we must ask, whether it may not be through the Son's infirmity that He knows not what the Father knows. He could perhaps read the thoughts of the human heart, because His stronger nature can unite itself with a weaker in all its movements, and by the force of its power, as it were, pass through and through the feeble nature. But a weaker nature is powerless to penetrate a stronger: light things may be penetrated by heavy, rare by dense, liquid by solid, but the heavy are impenetrable to the light, the dense to the rare, and the solid to the liquid: the strong are not exposed to the weak, but the weak are penetrated by the strong. Therefore, the heretics say, the Son knew not the thoughts of the Father, because, being Himself weak, He could not approach the more powerful and enter into Him, or pass through Him.

69. Should any one presume, not merely to speak thus of the Only-begotten God in the rashness of his tongue, but even to think so in the wickedness of his heart, let him hear what the Apostle thought of the Holy Ghost, from the words he wrote to the Corinthians, *But unto us God revealed them through the Spirit: for the Spirit searcheth all things, yea the deep things of God. For who among men knoweth the things of a man, which are in him, save the spirit of the man which is in him? Even so the things which are in God, none knoweth, save the Spirit of God* [8]. But let us cast aside these empty illustrations of material things, and measure God born of God, Spirit of Spirit, by His own powers and not by earthly conditions. Let us measure Him not by our own senses, but by His divine claims. Let us believe Him Who said, *He that hath seen Me hath seen the Father also* [9]. Let us not forget that He said, *Believe, if only by My works, that the Father is in Me, and I in the Father* [1], and again, *I and the Father are one* [2]. If the names which correspond to realities, when intelligibly used, impart to us any true information, then He Who is seen in Another by the eye of understanding is not different in nature from that Other; not different in kind, since He abides in the Father, and the Father in Him; not separate, since Both are One. Perceive their unity in the indivisibility of their nature, and apprehend the mystery of that indivisible nature by regarding the One as the mirror of the Other. But remember that He is the mirror, not as the image reflected by the splendour of a nature outside Himself, but as being a living nature, indistinguishable from the Father's living nature, derived wholly from the whole of His Father's, having the Father's in Him because He is the Only-begotten, and abiding in the Father, because He is God.

70. The heretics cannot deny that the Lord used these words to signify the mystery of His birth, but they attempt to escape from them by referring them to a harmony of will. They make the unity of God the Father and God the Son not one of divinity, but merely of will: as if the divine teaching were poor in expression and the Lord could not have said, *I and the Father are one in will;* or as if those words could have the same meaning as *I and the Father are one;* or as if He meant, *He that hath seen My will, hath seen the will of My Father also,* but, being unskilled in statement, tried to express that idea in the words, *He that hath seen Me hath seen the Father also:* or as if the divine vocabulary did not contain the terms, *The will of My Father is in Me, and My will is in the Father,* but this thought could be expressed by *I in the Father and the Father in Me.* All this is nauseous and irreverent nonsense; common sense condemns the judgment of such silly fancies, as that the Lord could not say what He wanted, or did not say what He said. True, we find Him speaking in parables and allegories, but it is a different thing to strengthen one's words with illustrations, or satisfy the dignity of the subject with the help of suggestive proverbs, or adapt one's language to the needs of the moment. But this passage concerning the unity, of which we are speaking, does not allow us to look for the meaning outside the plain sound of the words. If Father and Son are one, in the sense that They are one in will, and if separable natures cannot be one in will, because their diversity of kind and nature must draw them into diversities of will and judgment, how can They be one in will, not being one in knowledge? There can be no unity of will between ignorance and knowledge. Omniscience and nescience are opposites, and opposites cannot be of the same will.

71. But perhaps it may be held to confirm the Son in His confession of ignorance that He says the Father alone knows. But unless He had plainly said that the Father alone knows, it would have been a matter of the greatest danger for our under-

---

[8] 1 Cor. ii. 10, 11.   [9] St. John xiv. 9.
[1] St. John x. 38; cf. xiv. 11.   [2] Ib. x. 30.

standing, since we might have thought that He Himself did not know. For, since His ignorance is due to the economy of hidden knowledge, and not to a nature capable of ignorance, now that He says the Father alone knows, we cannot believe that He does not know; for, as we said above, God's knowledge is not the discovery of what He did not know, but its declaration. The fact that the Father alone knows, is no proof that the Son is ignorant: He says that He does not know, that others may not know: that the Father alone knows, to shew that He Himself also knows. If we say that God came to know the love of Abraham [3], when He ceased to conceal His knowledge, it follows that only because He did not conceal it from the Son, can the Father be said to know the day, for God does not learn by sudden perception, but declares His knowledge with the occasion. If, then, the Son according to the mystery does not know the day, that He may not reveal it: on the other hand, only by the fact that He has revealed it can the Father be proved to know the day.

72. Far be it from us to imagine vicissitudes of bodily change in the Father and Son, as though the Father sometimes spoke to the Son, and sometimes was silent. We remember, indeed, that a voice was sometimes uttered from heaven for us, that the power of the Father's words might confirm for us the mystery of the Son, as the Lord says, *This voice hath not come from Heaven for My sake but for your sakes* [4]. But the divine nature can dispense with the various combinations necessary for human functions, the motion of the tongue, the adjustment of the mouth, the forcing of the breath, and the vibration of the air. God is a simple Being: we must understand Him by devotion, and confess Him by reverence. He is to be worshipped, not pursued by our senses, for a conditioned and weak nature cannot grasp with the guesses of its imagination the mystery of an infinite and omnipotent nature. In God is no variability, no parts, as of a composite divinity, that in Him will should follow inaction, speech silence, or work rest, or that He should not will, without passing from some other mental state to volition, or speak, without breaking the silence with His voice, or act, without going forth to labour. He is not subject to the laws of nature, for nature has received its law from Him: He never suffers weakness or change when He acts, for His power is boundless, as the Lord said, *Father, all things are possible unto Thee* [5]. He can do more than

human sense can conceive. The Lord does not deprive even Himself of the quality of omnipotence, for He says, *What things soever the Father doeth, these the Son also doeth in like manner* [6]. Nothing is difficult, when there is no weakness; for only a power which is weak to effect, knows the need of effort. The cause of difficulty is the weakness of the motive force; a force of limitless power rises above the conditions of impotence.

73. We have established this point to exclude the idea that after silence God spoke to the Son, or after ignorance the Son began to know. To reach our intelligence terms must be used applicable to our own nature: thus we do not understand communication except by word of mouth, or comprehend the opposite of nescience except as knowledge. Thus the Son does not know the day for the reason that He does not reveal it: the Father, He says, alone knows it for the reason that He reveals it to the Son alone. But, as we have said, Christ is conscious of no such natural impediments as an ignorance which must be removed before He can come to know, or a knowledge which is not His before the Father begins to speak. He declares the unity of His nature, as the only-begotten, with the Father, by the unmistakeable words, *All things whatsoever the Father hath, are Mine* [7]. There is no mention here of coming into possession: it is one thing, to be the Possessor of things external to Him; another, to be self-contained and self-existent. The former is to possess heaven and earth and the universe, the latter to be able to describe Himself by His own properties, which are His, not as something external and subject, but as something of which He Himself subsists. When He says, therefore, that all things which the Father has, are His, He alludes to the divine nature, and not to a joint ownership of gifts bestowed. For referring to His words that the Holy Spirit should take of His [8], He says, *All things whatsoever the Father hath are Mine, therefore said I, He shall take of Mine*: that is, the Holy Spirit takes of His, but takes also of the Father's: and if He receives of the Father's, He receives also of His. The Holy Spirit is the Spirit of God, and does not receive of a creature, but teaches us that He receives all these gifts, because they are all God's. All things that belong to the Father are the Spirit's; but we must not think that whatever He received of the Son, He did not receive of the Father also; for all that the Father hath belongs equally to the Son.

---

3 Gen. xxii. 12 : see c. 64.   4 St. John xii. 30.
        5 St. Mark xiv. 36.

6 St. John v. 19.   7 Ib. xvi. 15.
8 Ib. 14. "He shall glorify Me, for He shall take of Mine, and shall declare it unto you."

74. So the nature of Christ needed no change, or question, or answer, that it should advance from ignorance to knowledge, or ask of One Who had continued in silence, and wait to receive His answer: but, abiding perfectly in mysterious unity with Him, it received of God its whole being as it derived from Him its origin. And, further, it received all that belonged to the whole being of God, namely, His knowledge and His will. What the Father knows, the Son does not learn by question and answer; what the Father wills, the Son does not will by command. Since all that the Father has, is His, it is the property of His nature to will and know, exactly as the Father wills and knows. But to prove His birth He often expounds the doctrine of His Person, as when He says, *I came not to do Mine own will, but the will of Him that sent Me* [9]. He does the Father's will, not His own, and by *the will of Him that sent Me*, He means His Father. But that He Himself wills the same, is unmistakeably declared in the words, *Father, those whom Thou hast given Me, I will, that, where I am, they also may be with Me* [1]. The Father wills that we should be with Christ, in Whom, according to the Apostle, He chose us before the foundation of the world [2], and the Son wills the same, namely that we should be with Him. His will is, therefore, the same in nature as the Father's will, though to make plain the fact of the birth it is distinguished from the Father's.

75. The Son is ignorant, then, of nothing which the Father knows, nor does it follow, because the Father alone knows, that the Son does not know. Father and Son abide in unity of nature, and the ignorance of the Son belongs to the divine Plan of silence, seeing that in Him are hidden all the treasures of wisdom and knowledge. This the Lord Himself testified, when He answered the question of the Apostles concerning the times, *It is not yours to know times or moments, which the Father hath set within His own authority* [3]. The knowledge is denied them, and not only that, but the anxiety to learn is forbidden, because it is not theirs to know these times. Yet now that He is risen, they ask again, though their question on the former occasion had been met with the reply, that not even the Son knew. They cannot possibly have understood literally that the Son did not know, for they ask Him again as though He did know. They perceived in the mystery of His ignorance a divine Plan of silence, and now, after His resurrection, they renew the question, thinking that the time has come to speak. And the Son no longer denies that He knows, but tells them that it is not theirs to know, because the Father has set it within His own authority. If, then, the Apostles attributed it to the divine Plan, and not to weakness, that the Son did not know the day, shall we say that the Son knew not the day for the simple reason that He was not God? Remember, God the Father set the day within His authority, that it might not come to the knowledge of man, and the Son, when asked before, replied that He did not know, but now, no longer denying His knowledge, replies that it is theirs not to know, for the Father has set the times not in His own *knowledge*, but in His own *authority*. The day and the moment are included in the word 'times': can it be, then, that He, Who was to restore Israel to its kingdom, did not Himself know the day and the moment of that restoration? He instructs us to see an evidence of His birth in this exclusive prerogative of the Father, yet He does not deny that He knows: and while He proclaims that the possession of this knowledge is withheld from ourselves, He asserts that it belongs to the mystery of the Father's authority.

[4] We must not therefore think, because He said He did not know the day and the moment, that the Son did not know. As man He wept, and slept, and sorrowed, but God is incapable of tears, or fear, or sleep. According to the weakness of His flesh He shed tears, slept, hungered, thirsted, was weary, and feared, yet without impairing the reality of His Only-begotten nature; equally so must we refer to His human nature, the words that He knew not the day or the hour.

---

9 St. John vi. 38. Hilary means that by the mention of two wills, our Lord teaches the personal distinction of the Father and the Son: cf. cc. 49, 50.

1 St. John xvii. 24.   2 Eph. i. 4.   3 Acts i. 7.

4 This last paragraph is omitted from many MSS., though contained in several of high authority. It offers a different explanation from that which Hilary has adopted in the rest of the book (see especially c. 59), where he maintains that Christ avoided revealing what He really knew, by saying that He did not know. The line adopted here is the same as that in the passage found by Erasmus and inserted by him in Book x. c. 8. This is one of several interpolations made in later, though still early, times to correct or supplement Hilary's teaching; cf. x. 8, with the note.

BOOK X.

1. It is manifest that there is nothing which men have ever said which is not liable to opposition. Where the will dissents the mind also dissents: under the bias of opposing judgment it joins battle, and denies the assertions to which it objects. Though every word we say be incontrovertible if gauged by the standard of truth, yet so long as men think or feel differently, the truth is always exposed to the cavils of opponents, because they attack, under the delusion of error or prejudice, the truth they misunderstand or dislike. For decisions once formed cling with excessive obstinacy: and the passion of controversy cannot be driven from the course it has taken, when the will is not subject to the reason. Enquiry after truth gives way to the search for proofs of what we wish to believe; desire is paramount over truth. Then the theories we concoct build themselves on names rather than things: the logic of truth gives place to the logic of prejudice: a logic which the will adjusts to defend its fancies, not one which stimulates the will through the understanding of truth by the reason. From these defects of partisan spirit arise all controversies between opposing theories. Then follows an obstinate battle between truth asserting itself, and prejudice defending itself: truth maintains its ground and prejudice resists. But if desire had not forestalled reason: if the understanding of the truth had moved us to desire what was true: instead of trying to set up our desires as doctrines, we should let our doctrines dictate our desires; there would be no contradiction of the truth, for every one would begin by desiring what was true, not by defending the truth of that which he desired.

2. Not unmindful of this sin of wilfulness, the Apostle, writing to Timothy, after many injunctions to bear witness to the faith and to preach the word, adds, *For the time will come when they will not endure sound doctrine, but having itching ears will heap up teachers to themselves after their own lusts, and will turn away their ears from the truth, and turn aside unto fables* [1]. For when their unhallowed zeal shall drive them beyond the endurance of sound doctrine, they will heap up teachers for their lusts, that is, construct schemes of doctrine to suit their own desires, not wishing to be taught, but getting together teachers who will tell them what they wish: that the crowd of teachers whom they have ferreted out and gathered together, may satisfy them with the doctrines of their own tumultuous desires. And if these madmen in their godless folly do not know with what spirit they reject the sound, and yearn after the corrupt doctrine, let them hear the words of the same Apostle to the same Timothy, *But the Spirit saith expressly that in the last days some shall fall away from the faith, giving heed to seducing spirits, and doctrines of devils through the hypocrisy of lying talk* [2]. What advancement of doctrine is it to discover what one fancies, and not what one ought to learn? Or what piety in doctrine is it not to desire what one ought to learn, but to heap up doctrine after our desires? But this is what the promptings of seducing spirits supply. They confirm the falsehoods of pretended godliness, for a canting hypocrisy always succeeds to defection from the faith: so that at least in word the reverence is retained, which the conscience has lost. Even that pretended piety they make impious by all manner of lies, violating by schemes of false doctrine the sacredness of the faith: for they pile up doctrines to suit their desires, and not according to the faith of the Gospel. They delight, with an uncontrollable pleasure, to have their itching ears tickled by the novelty of their favourite preaching; they estrange themselves utterly from the hearing of the truth, and surrender themselves entirely to fables: so that their incapacity for either speaking or understanding the truth invests their discourse with what is, to them, a semblance of truth.

3. We have clearly fallen on the evil times prophesied by the Apostle; for nowadays teachers are sought after who preach not God but a creature [3]. And men are more zealous for what they themselves desire, than for what the sound faith teaches. So far have their itching ears stirred them to listen to what they desire, that for the moment that preaching

[1] 2 Tim. iv. 3, 4.

[2] 1 Tim. iv. 1, 2.
[3] i.e. the Arians, who maintained that Jesus was created (*creatura*) and not God.

alone rules among their crowd of doctors which estranges the Only-begotten God from the power and nature of God the Father, and makes Him in our faith either a God of the second order, or not a God at all; in either case a damning profession of impiety, whether one profess two Gods by making different grades of divinity; or else deny divinity altogether to Him Who drew His nature by birth from God. Such doctrines please those whose ears are estranged from the hearing of the truth and turned to fables, while the hearing of this our sound faith is not endured, and is driven bodily into exile with its preachers.

4. But though many may heap up teachers according to their desires, and banish sound doctrine, yet from the company of the Saints the preaching of truth can never be exiled. From our exile we shall speak by these our writings, and the Word of God which cannot be bound will run unhindered, warning us of this time which the Apostle prophesied. For when men shew themselves impatient of the true message, and heap up teachers according to their own human desires, we can no longer doubt about the times, but know that while the preachers of sound doctrine are banished [4], truth is banished too. We do not complain of the times: we rejoice rather, that iniquity has revealed itself in this our exile, when, unable to endure the truth, it banishes the preachers of sound doctrine, that it may heap up for itself teachers after its own desires. We glory in our exile, and rejoice in the Lord, that in our person the Apostle's prophecy should be fulfilled.

5. In the earlier books, then, while maintaining the profession of a faith, I trust, sincere, and a truth uncorrupted, we arranged the method of our answer throughout, so that (though such are our limitations, that human language can never be safe from exception) no one could contradict us without an open profession of godlessness. For so completely have we demonstrated the true meaning of those texts which they cunningly filch from the Gospels and appropriate for their own teaching, that if any one denies it, he cannot escape on the plea of ignorance, but is condemned out of his own mouth of godlessness. Further, we have, according to the gift of the Holy Ghost, so cautiously proceeded throughout in our proof of the faith, that no charge could possibly be trumped up against us. For it is their way to fill the ears of the unwary with declarations that we deny the birth of Christ [5],

when we preach the unity of the Godhead; and they say that by the text, *I and the Father are one* [6], we confess that God is solitary: thus, according to them, we say that the Unbegotten God descended into the Virgin, and was born man, and that He refers [7] the opening word 'I' to the dispensation of His flesh, but adds to it the proof of His divinity, *And the Father*, as being the Father of Himself as man; and further, that, consisting of two Persons, human and divine, He said of Himself, *We are one* [8].

6. But we have always maintained the birth existing out of time: we have taught that God the Son is God of the same nature with God the Father, not co-equal with the Unbegotten, for He was not Himself Unbegotten, but, as the Only-begotten, not unequal because begotten; that the Two are One, not by the giving of a double name to one Person, but by a true begetting and being begotten; that neither are there two Gods, different in kind, in our faith, nor is God solitary because He is one, in the sense in which we confess the mystery of the Only-begotten God: but that the Son is both indicated in the name of, and exists in, the Father, Whose name and Whose nature are in Him, while the Father by His name implies, and abides in, the Son, since a son cannot be spoken of, or exist, except as born of a father. Further, we say that He is the living copy of the living nature, the impression of the divine seal upon the divine nature, so undistinguished from God in power and kind, that neither His works nor His words nor His form are other than the Father's: but that, since the image by nature possesses the nature of its author, the Author also has worked and spoken and appeared through His natural image.

7. But by the side of this timeless and ineffable generation of the Only-begotten, which transcends the perception of human understanding, we taught as well the mystery of God born to be man from the womb of the Virgin, shewing how according to the plan of the Incarnation, when He emptied Himself of the form of God and took the form of a servant, the weakness of the assumed humanity did not weaken the divine nature, but that Divine power was imparted to humanity without the virtue of divinity being lost in the human form. For when God was born to be man the purpose was not that the Godhead should be lost, but that, the Godhead remaining, man should be born to

---

4 Reading 'exsulantibus' with the Benedictine Edition (Paris, 1693); Migne (Paris, 1844), 'exultantibus.'
5 i.e. The generation of the second Person from the first Person of the Trinity.

6 St. John x. 30.   7 Supply, 'referat.'
8 The Arians accused the Catholics of a Sabellian denial of the Trinity and a Patripassian view of the Incarnation, i.e. that the unborn God became man.

be God. Thus Emmanuel is His name, which is *God with us* [9], that God might not be lowered to the level of man, but man raised to that of God. Nor, when He asks that He may be glorified [1], is it in any way a glorifying of His divine nature, but of the lower nature He assumed: for He asks for that glory which He had with God before the world was made.

8. As we are answering all, even their most insensate statements, we come now to the discussion of the unknown hour [2]. Now, even if, as they say, the Son had not known it, this could give no ground for an attack upon His Godhead as the Only-begotten. It was not in the nature of things that His birth should avail to put His beginning back, until it was equivalent to the existence which is unbegotten, and had no beginning; and the Father reserves as His prerogative, to demonstrate His authority as the Unbegotten, the fixing of this still undetermined day. Nor may we conclude that in His Person there is any defect in that nature which contained by right of birth all the fulness of that nature which a perfect birth could impart. Nor again could the ignorance of day and hour be imputed in the Only-begotten God to a lower degree of Divinity. It is to demonstrate against the Sabellian heretics that the Father's authority is without birth or beginning, that this prerogative of unbegotten authority is not granted to the Son [3]. But if, as we have maintained, when He said that He knew not the day, He kept silence not from ignorance, but in accordance with the Divine Plan, all occasion for irreverent declarations must be removed, and the blasphemous teachings of heresy thwarted, that the truth of the Gospel may be illustrated by the very words which seem to obscure it.

9. Thus the greater number of them will not allow Him to have the impassible nature of God because He feared His Passion and shewed Himself weak by submitting to suffering [4]. They assert that He Who feared and felt pain could not enjoy that confidence of power which is above fear, or that incorruption of spirit which is not conscious of suffering: but, being of a nature lower than God the Father, He trembled with fear at human suffering, and groaned before the violence of bodily pain. These impious assertions are based on the words, *My soul is sorrowful even unto death* [5], and *Father if it be possible let this cup pass away from He* [6], and also, *My God, My God, why hast Thou forsaken He* [7]? to which they also add, *Father, into Thy hands I commend My Spirit* [8]. All these words of our holy faith they appropriate to the use of their unholy blasphemy: that He feared, Who was sorrowful, and even prayed that the cup might be taken away from Him; that He felt pain, because He complained that God had deserted Him in His suffering; that He was infirm, because He commended His Spirit to the Father. His doubts and anxieties preclude us, they say, from assigning to Him that likeness to God which would belong to a nature equal to God as being born His Only-begotten. He proclaims His own weakness and inferiority by the prayer to remove the cup, by the complaint of desertion and the commending of His Spirit.

10. Now first of all, before we shew from these very texts, that He was subject to no infirmity of fear or sorrow on His own account, let us ask, "What can we find for Him to fear, that the dread of an unendurable pain should have seized Him?" The objects of His fear, which they allege, are, I suppose, suffering and death. Now I ask those who are of this opinion, "Can we reasonably suppose that He feared death, Who drove away the terrors of death from His Apostles, exhorting them to the glory of martyrdom with the words, *He that doth not take his cross and follow after Me is not worthy of Me*; and, *He that findeth his life shall lose it, and he that hath lost his life for My sake shall find it* [1]? If to die for Him is life, what pain can we think He had to suffer in the mystery of death, Who rewards with life those

9 St. Matt. i. 23.   1 St. John xvii. 5.

2 "Of that day and that hour knoweth no one, not even the Angels of Heaven, neither the Son, but the Father only." St. Matt. xxiv. 36; cf. St. Mark xiii. 32.

3 Hilary is granting for the moment that the Son really was ignorant of the day and hour; this, he says, could be no argument for the inequality of the Son: it would serve, however, to disprove the Sabellian identification of the Son and the Father by shewing that this knowledge was the possession of the Father only. Erasmus inserted here a passage which he found in a MS:—"and this shews us that the saying of the Word referred to the mystery of human perfection: that He, Who bore our infirmities, should take upon Himself also the infirmity of human ignorance, and that He should say He knew not the day, just as He knew not where they had laid Lazarus, or who it was when the woman touched the hem of His garment: being infirm in knowledge as He was infirm in weeping, in the endurance of weariness, hunger, and thirst, He did not disdain even the error of ignorance: especially when we consider how, when He rose from the dead, and was about to ascend up to, and above, the heavens, the Apostles approached Him as no longer ignorant, but knowing, and determining this His day, and put exactly the same question to Him of which He was silent during the dispensation of His humanity: that it might be made plain by their repeated question, that they understood His statement, 'I know not,' of an ignorance which He took upon Himself, not essential to His nature." The passage is utterly inconsistent with Hilary's teaching both here and in ix. 58 f., and is an obvious and clumsy interpolation.

4 Throughout the whole of this discussion of Christ's sufferings. Hilary distinguishes the feeling of pain (*dolere, dolor*) from the physical cause of pain, i.e. the cutting and piercing of the body (*pati, passio*). Christ's body suffered (*pati*) but He could not feel pain (*dolere*): see c. 23.

5 St. Matt. xxvi. 38.   6 Ib. 39.   7 Ib. xxvii. 46.

8 St. Luke xxiii. 46.   1 St. Matt. x. 38, 39.

who die for Him? Could death make Him fear what could be done to the body, when He exhorted the disciples, *Fear not those which kill the body* [2] ?

11. Further, what terror had the pain of death for Him, to Whom death was an act of His own free will? In the human race, death is brought on either by an attack upon the body of an external enemy, such as fever, wound, accident or fall: or our bodily nature is overcome by age, and yields to death. But the Only-begotten God, Who had the power of laying down His life, and of taking it up again [3], after the draught of vinegar, having borne witness that His work of human suffering was finished, in order to accomplish in Himself the mystery of death, bowed His head and gave up His Spirit [4]. If it has been granted to our mortal nature of its own will to breathe its last breath, and seek rest in death; if the buffeted soul may depart, without the breaking up of the body, and the spirit burst forth and flee away, without being as it were violated in its own home by the breaking and piercing and crushing of limbs; then fear of death might seize the Lord of life; if, that is, when He gave up the ghost and died, His death were not an exercise of His own free will. But if He died of His own will, and through His own will gave back His Spirit, death had no terror, because it was in His own power.

12. But perchance with the fearfulness of human ignorance, He feared the very power of death, which He possessed; so, though He died of His own accord, He feared because He was to die. If any think so, let them ask "To which was death terrible, to His Spirit or to His body?" If to His body, are they ignorant that the Holy One should not see corruption [5], that within three days He was to revive the temple of His body [6]? But if death was terrible to His Spirit, should Christ fear the abyss of hell, while Lazarus was rejoicing in Abraham's bosom? It is foolish and absurd, that He should fear death, Who could lay down His soul, and take it up again, Who, to fulfil the mystery of human life, was about to die of His own free will. He cannot fear death Whose power and purpose in dying is to die but for a moment: fear is incompatible with willingness to die, and the power to live again, for both of these rob death of his terrors.

13. But was it perhaps the physical pain of hanging on the cross, or the rough cords with which He was bound, or the cruel wounds, where the nails were driven in, that dismayed Him? Let us see of what body the Man Jesus was, that pain should dwell in His crucified, bound, and pierced body.

14. The nature of our bodies is such, that when endued with life and feeling by conjunction with a sentient soul, they become something more than inert, insensate matter. They feel when touched, suffer when pricked, shiver with cold, feel pleasure in warmth, waste with hunger, and grow fat with food. By a certain transfusion of the soul, which supports and penetrates them, they feel pleasure or pain according to the surrounding circumstances. When the body is pricked or pierced, it is the soul which pervades it that is conscious, and suffers pain. For instance a flesh-wound is felt even to the bone, while the fingers feel nothing when we cut the nails which protrude from the flesh. And if through some disease a limb becomes withered, it loses the feeling of living flesh: it can be cut or burnt, it feels no pain whatever, because the soul is no longer mingled with it. Also when through some grave necessity part of the body must be cut away, the soul can be lulled to sleep by drugs, which overcome the pain, and produce in the mind a death-like forgetfulness of its power of sense. Then limbs can be cut off without pain: the flesh is dead to all feeling, and does not heed the deep thrust of the knife, because the soul within it is asleep. It is, therefore, because the body lives by admixture with a weak soul, that it is subject to the weakness of pain.

15. If the Man Jesus Christ began His bodily life with the same beginning as our body and soul, if He were not, as God, the immediate Author of His own body and soul alike, when He was fashioned in the likeness and form of man, and born as man, then we may suppose that He felt the pain of our body; since by His beginning, a conception like ours, He had a body animated with a soul like our own. But if through His own act He took to Himself flesh from the Virgin, and likewise by His own act joined a soul to the body thus conceived, then the nature of His suffering must have corresponded with the nature of His body and soul. For when He emptied Himself of the form of God and received the form of a servant when the Son of God was born also Son of Man, without losing His own self and power, God the Word formed the perfect living Man. For how was the Son of God born Son of Man, how did He receive the form of a servant, still remaining in the form of God, unless (God the Word being

2 St. Matt. x. 28. 3 St. John x. 18. 4 Ib. xix. 30.
5 Ps. xv. 10.
6 St. John ii. 19; St. Matt. xxvi. 16, xxvii. 40; St. Mark xiv. 58.

able of Himself to take flesh from the Virgin and to give that flesh a soul, for the redemption of our soul and body), the Man Christ Jesus was born perfect, and made in the form of a servant by the assumption of the body, which the Virgin conceived? For the Virgin conceived, what she conceived, from the Holy Ghost alone [7], and though for His birth in the flesh she supplied from herself that element, which women always contribute to the seed planted in them, still Jesus Christ was not formed by an ordinary human conception. In His birth, the cause of which was transmitted solely by the Holy Ghost, His mother performed the same part as in all human conceptions: but by virtue of His origin He never ceased to be God.

16. This deep and beautiful mystery of His assumption of manhood the Lord Himself reveals in the words, *No man hath ascended into heaven, but He that descended from heaven, even the Son of Man which is in heaven* [8]. 'Descended from heaven' refers to His origin from the Spirit: for though Mary contributed to His growth in the womb and birth all that is natural to her sex, His body did not owe to her its origin. The 'Son of Man' refers to the birth of the flesh conceived in the Virgin; 'Who is in heaven' implies the power of His eternal nature: an infinite nature, which could not restrict itself to the limits of the body, of which it was itself the source and base. By the virtue of the Spirit and the power of God the Word, though He abode in the form of a servant, He was ever present as Lord of all, within and beyond the circle of heaven and earth. So He descended from heaven and is the Son of Man, yet is in heaven: for the Word made flesh did not cease to be the Word. As the Word, He is in heaven, as flesh He is the Son of Man. As Word made flesh, He is at once from heaven, and Son of Man, and in heaven, for the power of the Word, abiding eternally without body, was present still in the heaven He had left: to Him and to none other the flesh owed its origin. So the Word made flesh, though He was flesh, yet never ceased to be the Word.

17. The blessed Apostle also perfectly describes this mystery of the ineffable birth of Christ's body in the words, *The first man was from the soil of the ground, the second man from heaven* [1]. Calling Him 'Man' he expresses His birth from the Virgin, who in the exercise of her office as mother, performed the duties of her sex in the conception and birth of man. And when he says, *The second man from heaven* he testifies His origin from the Holy Ghost, Who came upon the Virgin [2]. As He is then man, and from heaven, this Man was born of the Virgin, and conceived of the Holy Ghost. So speaks the Apostle.

18. Again the Lord Himself revealing this mystery of His birth, speaks thus: *I am the living bread Who have descended from Heaven: if any one shall eat of My bread he shall live for ever* [3]: calling Himself the Bread since He is the origin of His own body. Further, that it may not be thought the Word left His own virtue and nature for the flesh, He says again that it is *His* bread; since He is the bread which descends from heaven, His body cannot be regarded as sprung from human conception, because it is shewn to be from heaven. And His language concerning *His bread* is an assertion that the Word took a body, for He adds, *Unless ye eat the flesh of the Son of Man and drink His blood, ye have not life in you* [4]. Hence, inasmuch as the Being Who is Son of Man descended also as bread from heaven, by the 'Bread descending from heaven' and by the 'Flesh and Blood of the Son of Man' must be understood His assumption of the flesh, conceived by the Holy Ghost, and born of the Virgin.

19. Being, then, Man with this body, Jesus Christ is both the Son of God and Son of Man, Who emptied Himself of the form of God, and received the form of a servant. There is not one Son of Man and another Son of God; nor one in the form of God, and another born perfect man in the form of a servant: so that, as by the nature determined for us by God, the Author of our being, man is born with body and soul, so likewise Jesus Christ, by His own power, is God and Man with flesh and soul, possessing in Himself whole and perfect manhood, and whole and perfect Godhead.

20. Yet many, with the art by which they seek to prove their heresy, are wont to delude the ears of the unlearned with the error, that as the body and soul of Adam both sinned, so the Lord must have taken the soul and body of Adam from the Virgin, and that it was not the whole Man that she conceived from the Holy Ghost [5]. If they had understood the

---

7 Omitting 'suo:' or retaining it 'His (i.e. the Word's) Holy Spirit.'
8 St. John iii. 13.
1 1 Cor. xv. 47. One copy reads *de terra terrenus*, of the earth, earth

2 Luke i. 35. "The Holy Ghost shall come upon thee, and the power of the Most High shall overshadow thee."
3 St. John vi. 51.   4 Ib. vi. 54.
5 Apollinaris argued that if Christ were perfect God and perfect man, there would be two Christs, the Son of God by nature and the Son of God by adoption. Hence He taught that Christ was partly God and partly man; that He received from the Virgin His body and the lower, irrational soul which is the

mystery of the Incarnation, these men would have understood at the same time the mystery that the Son of Man is also Son of God. As if in receiving so much from the Virgin, He received from her His soul also; whereas though flesh is always born of flesh, every soul is the direct work of God.

21. With a view to deprive of substantive divinity the Only-begotten God, Who was God the Word with God in the beginning, they make Him merely the utterance of the voice of God. The Son is related to God His Father, they say, as the words to the speaker. They are trying to creep into the position, that it was not God the eternal Word, abiding in the form of God, Who was born as Christ the Man, Whose life therefore springs from a human origin, not from the mystery of a spiritual conception; that He was not God the Word, making Himself man by birth from the Virgin, but the Word of God dwelling in Jesus as the spirit of prophecy dwelt in the prophets. They accuse us of saying that Christ was born man with body and soul different from ours. But we preach the Word made flesh, Christ emptying Himself of the form of God and taking the form of a servant, perfect according to the fashion of human form, born a man after the likeness of ourselves: that, being true Son of God, He is indeed true Son of Man, neither the less Man because born of God, nor the less God because Man born of God.

22. But as He by His own act assumed a body from the Virgin, so He assumed from Himself a soul; though even in ordinary human birth the soul is never derived from the parents. If, then, the Virgin received from God alone the flesh which she conceived, far more certain is it that the soul of that body can have come from God alone. If, too, the same Christ be the Son of Man, Who is also the Son of God (for the whole Son of Man is the whole Son of God), how ridiculous is it to preach besides the Son of God, the Word made flesh, another, I know not whom, inspired, like a prophet, by God the Word; whereas our Lord Jesus Christ is both Son of Man and Son of God. Yet because His soul was sorrowful unto death, and because He had the power to lay down His soul and the power to take it up again, they want to derive it from some alien source, and not from the Holy Ghost, the Author of His body's conception: for God the Word became man without departing from the mys-

tery of His own nature. He was born also not to be at one time two separate beings, but that it might be made plain, that He Who was God before He was Man, now that He has taken humanity, is God and Man. How could Jesus Christ, the Son of God, have been born of Mary, except by the Word becoming flesh: that is by the Son of God, though in the form of God, taking the form of a slave? When He Who was in the form of God took the form of a slave, two contraries were brought together[6]. Thus it was just as true, that He received the form of a slave, as that He remained in the form of God. The use of the one word 'form' to describe both natures compels us to recognise that He truly possessed both. He is in the *form* of a servant, Who is also in the *form* of God[7]. And though He is the latter by His eternal nature, and the former in accordance with the divine Plan of Grace, the word has its true significance equally in both cases, because He *is* both: as truly in the form of God as in the form of Man. Just as to take the form of a servant is none other than to be born a man, so to be in the form of God is none other than to be God: and we confess Him as one and the same Person, not by loss of the Godhead, but by assumption of the manhood: in the form of God through His divine nature, in the form of man from His conception by the Holy Ghost, being found in fashion as a man. That is why after His birth as Jesus Christ, His suffering, death, and burial, He also rose again. We cannot separate Him from Himself in all these diverse mysteries, so that He should be no longer Christ; for Christ, Who took the form of a servant, was none other than He Who was in the form of God: He Who died was the same as He Who was born: He Who rose again as He Who died; He Who is in heaven as He Who rose again; lastly, He Who is in heaven as He Who before descended from heaven.

23. So the Man Jesus Christ, Only-begotten God, as flesh and as Word at the same time Son of Man and Son of God, without ceasing to be Himself, that is, God, took true humanity after the likeness of our humanity. But when, in this humanity, He was struck with blows, or smitten with wounds, or bound with ropes, or lifted on high, He felt the force of suffering, but without its pain. Thus a dart passing through water, or piercing a flame, or wounding the air, inflicts all that it is its nature to do: it

---

condition of bodily life; while His rational Spirit was Divine. On this theory the 'whole man,' as Hilary says, was not born of the Virgin. Hilary denies the threefold division. The soul in every case, Christ's included, is, he says, the immediate work of God.

6 i.e. the infinite nature of God, and the finite nature of man.
7 *Form* since the time of Aristotle meant the qualities which constituted the distinctive essence of a thing.

passes through, it pierces, it wounds; but all this is without effect on the thing it strikes; since it is against the order of nature to make a hole in water, or pierce flame, or wound the air, though it is the nature of a dart to make holes, to pierce and to wound. So our Lord Jesus Christ suffered blows, hanging, crucifixion and death: but the suffering which attacked the body of the Lord, without ceasing to be suffering, had not the natural effect of suffering. It exercised its function of punishment with all its violence; but the body of Christ by its virtue suffered the violence of the punishment, without its consciousness. True, the body of the Lord would have been capable of feeling pain like our natures, if our bodies possessed the power of treading on the waters, and walking over the waves without weighing them down by our tread or forcing them apart by the pressure of our steps, if we could pass through solid substances, and the barred doors were no obstacle to us. But, as only the body of our Lord could be borne up by the power of His soul in the waters, could walk upon the waves, and pass through walls, how can we judge of the flesh conceived of the Holy Ghost on the analogy of a human body? That flesh, that is, that Bread, is from Heaven; that humanity is from God. He had a body to suffer, and He suffered: but He had not a nature [8] which could feel pain. For His body possessed a unique nature of its own; it was transformed into heavenly glory on the Mount, it put fevers to flight by its touch, it gave new eyesight by its spittle.

24. It may perhaps be said, 'We find Him giving way to weeping, to hunger and thirst: must we not suppose Him liable to all the other affections of human nature?' But if we do not understand the mystery of His tears, hunger, and thirst, let us remember that He Who wept also raised the dead to life: that He did not weep for the death of Lazarus, but rejoiced [1]; that He Who thirsted, gave from Himself rivers of living water [2]. He could not be parched with thirst, if He was able to give the thirsty drink. Again, He Who hungered could condemn the tree which offered no fruit for His hunger [3]: but how could His nature be overcome by hunger if He could strike the green tree barren by His word? And if, beside the mystery of weeping, hunger and thirst, the flesh He assumed, that is His entire manhood, was exposed to our weaknesses: even then it was not left to suffer from their indignities. His weeping was not for Himself; His thirst needed no water to quench it; His hunger no food to stay it. It is never said that the Lord ate or drank or wept when He was hungry, or thirsty, or sorrowful. He conformed to the habits of the body to prove the reality of His own body, to satisfy the custom of human bodies by doing as our nature does. When He ate and drank, it was a concession, not to His own necessities, but to our habits.

25. For Christ had indeed a body, but unique, as befitted His origin. He did not come into existence through the passions incident to human conception: He came into the form of our body by an act of His own power. He bore our collective humanity in the form of a servant, but He was free from the sins and imperfections of the human body: that we might be in Him, because He was born of the Virgin, and yet our faults might not be in Him, because He is the source of His own humanity, born as man but not born under the defects of human conception. It is this mystery of His birth which the Apostle upholds and demonstrates, when he says, *He humbled Himself, taking the form of a servant, being made in the likeness of a man and being formed in fashion as a man* [4]: that is, in that He took the form of a servant, He was born in the form of a man: in that He was made in the likeness of a man, and formed in fashion as a man, the appearance and reality of His body testified His humanity, yet, though He was formed in fashion as a man, He knew not what sin was. For His conception was in the likeness of our nature, not in the possession of our faults. For lest the words, *He took the form of a servant*, might be understood of a natural birth, the Apostle adds, *made in the likeness of a man, and formed in fashion as a man*. The truth of His birth is thus prevented from suggesting the defects incident to our weak natures, since the *form of a servant* implies the reality of His birth, and *found in fashion as a man*, the likeness of our nature. He was of Himself born man through the Virgin, and found in the likeness of our degenerate body of sin: as the Apostle testifies in his letter to the Romans, *For what the law could not do, in that it was weak through the flesh, God sending His Son in the likeness of flesh of sin, condemned sin of sin* [5]. He was not *found in the fashion of a man*: but *found in fashion* as a man: nor was His flesh the flesh of sin, but the likeness of the flesh of

---

[8] Erasmus mentions an insertion in one MS. here, which explains what Hilary implies throughout the chapter; 'weak as ours from sin,' i.e. weakness is the proper penalty for sin: pain is only a secondary and adventitious effect of the weakness of human nature brought on by sin. Christ then atoned completely for sin, by suffering, without feeling pain.

[1] St. John xi. 15, 'Lazarus is dead. And I am glad for your sakes, that I was not there, to the intent that ye may believe.'

[2] St. John vii. 38.   [3] St. Matt. xxi. 19 and St. Mark xi. 3.

[4] Phil. ii. 7.   [5] Rom. viii. 3.

sin. Thus the fashion of flesh implies the truth of His birth, and the likeness of the flesh of sin removes Him from the imperfections of human weakness. So the Man Jesus Christ as man was truly born, as Christ had no sin in His nature: for, on His human side, He was born, and could not but be a man; on His divine side, He could never cease to be Christ. Since then Jesus Christ was man, He submitted as man to a human birth: yet as Christ He was free from the infirmity of our degenerate race.

26. The Apostles' belief prepares us for the understanding of this mystery; when it testifies that Jesus Christ was found in fashion as a man and was sent in the likeness of the flesh of sin. For being fashioned as a man, He is in the form of a servant, but not in the imperfections of a servant's nature; and being in the likeness of the flesh of sin, the Word is indeed flesh, but is in the likeness of the flesh of sin and not the flesh of sin itself. In like manner Jesus Christ being man is indeed human, but even thus cannot be aught else but Christ, born as man by the birth of His body, but not human in defects, as He was not human in origin. The Word made flesh could not but be the flesh that He was made; yet He remained always the Word, though He was made flesh. As the Word made flesh could not vacate the nature of His Source, so by virtue of the origin of His nature He could not but remain the Word: but at the same time we must believe that the Word is that flesh which He was made; always, however, with the reserve, that when He dwelt among us, the flesh was not the Word, but was the flesh of the Word dwelling in the flesh.

Though we have proved this, still we will see whether in the whole range of suffering, which He endured, we can anywhere detect in our Lord the weakness of bodily pain. We will put off for a time the discussion of the passages on the strength of which heresy has attributed fear to our Lord; now let us turn to the facts themselves: for His words cannot signify fear if His actions display confidence.

27. Do you suppose, heretic, that the Lord of glory feared to suffer? Why, when Peter made this error through ignorance, did He not call him 'Satan' and a 'stumbling-block [6]?' Thus was Peter, who deprecated the mystery of the Passion, established in the faith by so sharp a rebuke from the lips of the gentle Christ, Whom not flesh and blood, but the Father in Heaven had revealed to him [7].

What phantom hope are you chasing when you deny that Christ is God, and attribute to Him fear of suffering? He afraid, Who went forth to meet the armed bands of His captors? Weakness in His body, at Whose approach the pursuers reeled and broke their ranks and fell prone, unable to endure His Majesty as He offered Himself to their chains? What weakness could enthral His body, Whose nature had such power?

28. But perhaps He feared the pain of wounds. Say then, What terror had the thrust of the nail for Him Who merely by His touch restored the ear that was cut off? You who assert the weakness of the Lord, explain this work of power at the moment when His flesh was weak and suffering. Peter drew his sword and smote: the High Priest's servant stood there, lopped of his ear. How was the flesh of the ear restored from the bare wound by the touch of Christ? Amidst the flowing blood, and the wound left by the cleaving sword, when the body was so maimed, whence sprang forth an ear which was not there? Whence came that which did not exist before? Whence was restored that which was wanting? Did the hand, which created an ear, feel the pain of the nails? He prevented another from feeling the pain of a wound: did He feel it Himself? His touch could restore the flesh that was cut off; was He sorrowful because He feared the piercing of His own flesh? And if the body of Christ had this virtue, dare we allege infirmity in that nature, whose natural force could counteract all the natural infirmities of man?

29. But, perhaps, in their misguided and impious perversity, they infer His weakness from the fact that His soul was sorrowful unto death [8]. It is not yet the time to blame you, heretic, for misunderstanding the passage. For the present I will only ask you, Why do you forget that when Judas went forth to betray Him, He said, *Now is the Son of Man glorified [9]?* If suffering was to glorify Him, how could the fear of it have made Him sorrowful? How, unless He was so void of reason, that He feared to suffer when suffering was to glorify Him?

30. But perhaps He may be thought to have feared to the extent that He prayed that the cup might be removed from Him: *Abba, Father, all things are possible unto Thee: remove this cup from Me [1].* To take the narrowest ground of argument, might you not have refuted for yourself this dull impiety by your own reading of the words, *Put up thy sword into its sheath: the cup which My Father hath given Me, shall I not drink it [2]?* Could fear

---

6 St. Matt. xvi. 22, 23.   7 Ib. xvi. 16.   8 St. Matt. xxvi. 38.   9 St. John xiii. 31.
1 St. Mark xiv. 36.   2 St. John xviii. 11.

induce Him to pray for the removal from Him of that which, in His zeal for the Divine Plan, He was hastening to fulfil? To say He shrank from the suffering He desired is not consistent. You allow that He suffered willingly: would it not be more reverent to confess that you had misunderstood this passage, than to rush with blasphemous and headlong folly to the assertion that He prayed to escape suffering, though you allow that He suffered willingly?

31. Yet, I suppose, you will arm yourself also for your godless contention with these words of the Lord, *My God, My God, why hast Thou forsaken Me* [3]? Perhaps you think that after the disgrace of the cross, the favour of His Father's help departed from Him, and hence His cry that He was left alone in His weakness. But if you regard the contempt, the weakness, the cross of Christ as a disgrace, you should remember His words, *Verily I say unto you, From henceforth ye shall see the Son of Man sitting at the right hand of power, and coming with the clouds of Heaven* [4].

32. Where, pray, can you see fear in His Passion? Where weakness? Or pain? Or dishonour? Do the godless say He feared? But He proclaimed with His own lips His willingness to suffer. Do they maintain that He was weak? He revealed His power, when His pursuers were stricken with panic and dared not face Him. Do they contend that He felt the pain of the wounds in His flesh? But He shewed, when He restored the wounded flesh of the ear, that, though He was flesh, He did not feel the pain of fleshly wounds. The hand which touched the wounded ear belonged to His body: yet that hand created an ear out of a wound: how then can that be the hand of a body which was subject to weakness?

33. But, they say, the cross was a dishonour to Him; yet it is because of the cross that we can now see the Son of Man sitting on the right hand of power, that He Who was born man of the womb of the Virgin has returned in His Majesty with the clouds of heaven. Your irreverence blinds you to the natural relations of cause and event: not only does the spirit of godlessness and error, with which you are filled, hide from your understanding the mystery of faith, but the obtuseness of heresy drags you below the level of ordinary human intelligence. For it stands to reason that whatever we fear, we avoid: that a weak nature is a prey to terror by its very feebleness: that whatever feels pain

possesses a nature always liable to pain: that whatever dishonours is always a degradation. On what reasonable principle, then, do you hold that our Lord Jesus Christ feared that towards which He pressed: or awed the brave, yet trembled Himself with weakness: or stopped the pain of wounds, yet felt the pain of His own: or was dishonoured by the degradation of the cross, yet through the cross sat down by God on high, and returned to His Kingdom?

34. But perhaps you think your impiety has still an opportunity left to see in the words, *Father, into Thy hands I commend My Spirit* [5], a proof that He feared the descent into the lower world, and even the necessity of death. But when you read these words and could not understand them, would it not have been better to say nothing, or to pray devoutly to be shewn their meaning, than to go astray with such barefaced assertions, too mad with your own folly to perceive the truth? Could you believe that He feared the depths of the abyss, the scorching flames, or the pit of avenging punishment, when you listen to His words to the thief on the cross, *Verily, I say unto thee, To-day shalt thou be with Me in Paradise* [6]? Such a nature with such power could not be shut up within the confines of the nether world, nor even subjected to fear of it. When He descended to Hades, He was never absent from Paradise (just as He was always in Heaven when He was preaching on earth as the Son of Man), but promised His martyr [7] a home there, and held out to him the transports of perfect happiness. Bodily fear cannot touch Him Who reaches indeed down as far as Hades, but by the power of His nature is present in all things everywhere. As little can the abyss [8] of Hell and the terrors of death lay hold upon the nature which rules the world, boundless in the freedom of its spiritual power, confident of the raptures of Paradise; for the Lord Who was to descend to Hades, was also to dwell in Paradise. Separate, if you can, from His indivisible nature a part which could fear punishment: send the one part of Christ to Hades to suffer pain, the other, you must leave in Paradise to reign: for the thief says, *Remember me when Thou comest in Thy Kingdom.* It was the groan he heard, I suppose, when the nails pierced the hands of our Lord, which provoked in him this blessed confession of faith: he learnt the Kingdom of Christ from His weakened and stricken body! He begs

---

3 St. Mark xv. 34; St. Matt. xxvii. 46.
4 St. Matt. xxvi. 64; ct. xvi. 27.

5 St. Luke xxiii. 46.   6 Ib. 43.
7 i.e. the thief on the cross.
8 In Biblical and Patristic Latin *chaos* had acquired the sense of χάσμα; cf. Rönsch, *Itala u. Vulgata*, p. 250.

that Christ will remember him when He comes in His Kingdom : *you* say that Christ feared as He hung dying upon the cross. The Lord promises him, *To-day shalt thou be with Me in Paradise; you* would subject Christ to Hades and fear of punishment. Your faith has the opposite expectation. The thief confessed Christ in His Kingdom as He hung on the cross, and was rewarded with Paradise from the cross : you who impute to Christ the pain of punishment and the fear of death, will fail of Paradise and His Kingdom.

35. We have now seen the power that lay in the acts and words of Christ. We have incontestably proved that His body did not share the infirmity of a natural body, because its power could expel the infirmities of the body : that when He suffered, suffering laid hold of His body, but did not inflict upon it the nature of pain : and this because, though the form of our body was in the Lord, yet He by virtue of His origin was not in the body of our weakness and imperfection. He was conceived of the Holy Ghost and born of the Virgin, who performed the office of her sex, but did not receive the seed of His conception from man [9]. She brought forth a body, but one conceived of the Holy Ghost; a body possessing inherent reality, but with no infirmity in its nature. That body was truly and indeed body, because it was born of the Virgin : but it was above the weakness of our body, because it had its beginning in a spiritual conception.

36. But even now that we have proved what was the faith of the Apostle, the heretics think to meet it by the text, *My soul is sorrowful even unto death* [1]. These words, they say, prove the consciousness of natural infirmity which made Christ begin to be sorrowful. Now, first, I appeal to common intelligence : what do we mean by *sorrowful unto death?* It cannot signify the same as 'to be sorrowful because of death :' for where there is sorrow because of death, it is the death that is the cause of the sadness. But a sadness even to death [2] implies that death is the finish, not the cause, of the sadness. If then He was sorrowful even *to* death, not *because of* death, we must enquire, whence came His sadness? He was sorrowful, not for a certain time, or for a period which human ignorance could not determine, but even unto death. So far from His sadness being caused by His death, it was removed by it.

37. That we may understand what was the cause of His sadness, let us see what precedes and follows this confession of sadness : for in the Passover supper our Lord completely signified the whole mystery of His Passion and our faith. After He had said that they should all be offended in Him [3], but promised that He would go before them into Galilee [4], Peter protested that though all the rest should be offended, he would remain faithful and not be offended [5]. But the Lord knowing by His Divine Nature what should come to pass, answered that Peter would deny Him thrice : that we might know from Peter how the others were offended, since even he lapsed into so great peril to his faith by the triple denial. After that, He took Peter, James and John, chosen, the first two to be His martyrs, John to be strengthened for the proclamation of the Gospel, and declared that He was sorrowful unto death. Then He went before, and prayed, saying, *My Father, if it is possible, let this cup pass from Me; yet, not as I will, but as Thou wilt* [6]. He prays that the cup may pass from Him, when it was certainly already before Him : for even then was being fulfilled that pouring forth of His blood of the New Testament for the sins of many. He does not pray that it may not be with Him ; but that it may pass away from Him. Then He prays that His will may not be done, and wills that what He wishes to be effected, may not be granted Him. For He says, *Yet not as I will, but as Thou wilt* : signifying by His spontaneous prayer for the cup's removal His fellowship with human anxiety, yet associating Himself with the decree of the Will which He shares inseparably with the Father. To shew, moreover, that He does not pray for Himself, and that He seeks only a conditional fulfilment of what He desires and prays for, He prefaces the whole of this request with the words, *My Father, if it is possible.* Is there anything for the Father the possibility of which is uncertain? But if nothing is impossible to the Father, we can see on what depends this condition, *if it is possible* [7] : for this prayer is immediately followed by the words, *And He came to His disciples and findeth them sleeping, and saith to Peter, Could ye not watch one hour with Me? Watch and pray that ye enter not into temptation : for the spirit indeed is willing,*

---

9 Reading 'susceptis elementis.'
1 St. Matt. xxvi. 38 ; St. Mark xiv. 34.
2 *Usque ad mortem :* up to, as far as death. The Latin gives more colour to this interpretation of Hilary than the English translation 'even unto death.'

3 St. Matt. xxvi. 31 ; St. Mark xiv. 27 ; cf. St. John xvi. 32.
4 St. Matt. xxvi. 32 ; St. Mark xiv. 28 ; cf. xvi. 7.
5 St. Matt. xxvi. 33.
6 St. Matt. xxvi. 39 ; St. Mark xiv. 36 ; St. Luke xxii. 42.
7 i.e. the possibility that the disciples may not endure the temptation of the cup : that it might abide with them instead of passing away. See the explanation in the next chapter.

but the flesh is weak [8]. Is the cause of this sadness and this prayer any longer doubtful? He bids them watch and pray with Him for this purpose, that they may not enter into temptation ; *for the spirit indeed is willing, but the flesh is weak.* They were under the promise made in the constancy of faithful souls, not to be offended, yet, through weakness of the flesh, they were to be offended It is not, therefore, for Himself that He is sorrowful, and prays : it is for those whom He exhorts to watchfulness and prayer, lest the cup of suffering should be their lot : lest that cup which He prays may pass away from Him, should abide with them.

38. And the reason He prayed that the cup might be removed from Him, if that were possible, was that, though with God nothing is impossible, as Christ Himself says, *Father, all things are possible to Thee* [9], yet for man it is impossible to withstand the fear of suffering, and only by trial can faith be proved. Wherefore, as Man He prays for men that the cup may pass away, but as God from God, His will is in unison with the Father's effectual will. He teaches what He meant by *If it is possible*, in His words to Peter, *Lo, Satan hath sought you that He might sift you as wheat : but I have prayed for thee that thy faith may not fail* [1]. The cup of the Lord's Passion was to be a trial for them all, and He prays the Father for Peter that his faith may not fail : that when he denied through weakness, at least he might not fail of penitential sorrow, for repentance would mean that faith survived.

39. The Lord was sorrowful then unto death because in presence of the death, the earthquake, the darkened day, the rent veil, the opened graves, and the resurrection of the dead, the faith of the disciples would need to be established which had been so shaken by the terror of the night arrest, the scourging, the striking, the spitting upon, the crown of thorns, the bearing of the cross, and all the insults of the Passion, but most of all by the condemnation to the accursed cross. Knowing that all this would be at an end after His Passion, He was sad unto death. He knew, too, that the cup could not pass away unless He drank it, for He said, *My Father, this cup cannot pass from Me unless I drink it : Thy will be done* [2] : that is, with the completion of His Passion, the fear of the cup would pass away which could not pass away

unless He drank it : the end of that fear would follow only when His Passion was completed and terror destroyed [3], because after His death, the stumbling-block of the disciples' weakness would be removed by the glory of His power.

40. Although by His words, *Thy will be done*, He surrendered the Apostles to the decision of His Father's will, in regard to the offence of the cup, that is, of His Passion, still He repeated His prayer a second and a third time. After that He said, *Sleep on now, and take your rest* [4]. It is not without the consciousness of some secret reason that He Who had reproached them for their sleep, now bade them sleep on, and take their rest. Luke is thought to have given us the meaning of this command. After He had told us how Satan had sought to sift the Apostles as it were wheat, and how the Lord had been entreated that the faith of Peter might not fail [5], he adds that the Lord prayed earnestly, and then that an angel stood by Him comforting Him, and as the angel stood by Him, He prayed the more earnestly, so that the sweat poured from His body in drops of blood [6]. The Angel was sent, then, to watch over the Apostles, and when the Lord was comforted by him, so that He no longer sorrowed for them, He said, without fear of sadness, *Sleep on now, and take your rest.* Matthew and Mark are silent about the angel, and the request of the devil : but after the sorrowfulness of His soul, the reproach of the sleepers, and the prayer that the cup may be taken away, there must be some good reason for the command to the sleepers which follows ; unless we assume that He Who was about to leave them, and Himself had received comfort from the Angel sent to Him, meant to abandon them to their sleep, soon to be arrested and kept in durance.

41. We must not indeed pass over the fact that in many manuscripts, both Latin and Greek, nothing is said of the angel's coming or the Bloody Sweat. But while we suspend judgment, whether this is an omission, where it is wanting, or an interpolation, where it is found (for the discordance of the copies leaves the question uncertain), let not the heretics encourage themselves that herein lies a confirmation of His weakness, that He needed the help and comfort of an angel. Let them remember the Creator of the angels needs not the support of His creatures. Moreover His comforting must be explained

---

8 St. Matt. xxvi. 40, 41 ; St. Mark xiv. 37, 38 ; cf. St. Luke xxii. 45, 46.
9 St. Mark xiv. 36.   1 St. Luke xxii. 31, 32.
2 St. Matt. xxvi. 42. The Greek is :—' My Father, if this cup cannot pass away except I drink of it, Thy will be done.'

3 Reading ' non nisi finito.'   4 St. Matt. xxvi. 45.
5 This is a mistranslation of St. Luke xxii. 32, ἐδεήθην being taken as passive.
6 St. Luke xxii. 43, 44. The Greek is ὡσεί, ' as it were drops of blood.'

in the same way as His sorrow. He was sorrowful for us, that is, on our account; He must also have been comforted for us, that is, on our account. If He sorrowed concerning us, He was comforted concerning us. The object of His comfort is the same as that of His sadness. Nor let any one dare to impute the Sweat to a weakness, for it is contrary to nature to sweat blood[7]. It was no infirmity, for His power reversed the law of nature. The bloody sweat does not for one moment support the heresy of weakness, while it establishes against the heresy which invents an apparent body[8], the reality of His body. Since, then, His fear was concerning us, and His prayer on our behalf, we are forced to the conclusion that all this happened on our account, for whom He feared, and for whom He prayed.

42. Again the Gospels fill up what is lacking in one another: we learn some things from one, some from another, and so on, because all are the proclamation of the same spirit. Thus John, who especially brings out the working of spiritual causes in the Gospel, preserves this prayer of the Lord for the Apostles, which all the others passed over: how He prayed, namely, *Holy Father, keep them in Thy Name . . . . while I was with them I kept them in Thy Name: those whom Thou gavest Me I have kept*[9]. That prayer was not for Himself but for His Apostles; nor was He sorrowful for Himself, since He bids them pray that they be not tempted; nor is the angel sent to Him, for He could summon down from Heaven, if He would, twelve thousand angels[1]; nor did He fear because of death when He was troubled unto death. Again, He does not pray that the cup may pass over Himself, but that it may pass *away from* Himself, though before it could pass away He must have drunk it. But, further, 'to pass away' does not mean merely to leave the place,' but 'not to exist any more at all:' which is shewn in the language of the Gospels and Epistles: for example, *Heaven and earth shall pass away, but My word shall not perish*[2]: also the Apostle says, *Behold the old things are passed away; they are become new*[3]. And again, *The fashion of this world*

shall pass away[4]. The cup, therefore, of which He prays to the Father, cannot pass away unless it be drunk; and when He prays, He prays for those whom He preserved, so long as He was with them, whom He now hands over to the Father to preserve. Now that He is about to accomplish the mystery of death He begs the Father to guard them. The presence of the angel who was sent to Him (if this explanation be true) is not of doubtful significance. Jesus shewed His certainty that the prayer was answered when, at its close, He bade the disciples sleep on. The effect of this prayer and the security which prompted the command, 'sleep on,' is noticed by the Evangelist in the course of the Passion, when he says of the Apostles just before they escaped from the hands of the pursuers, *That the word might be fulfilled which He had spoken, Of those whom Thou hast given Me I lost not one of them*[5]. He fulfils Himself the petition of His prayer, and they are all safe; but He asks that those whom He has preserved the Father will now preserve in His own Name. And they are preserved: the faith of Peter does not fail: it cowered, but repentance followed immediately.

43. Combine the Lord's prayer in John, the request of the devil in Luke, the sorrowfulness unto death, and the protest against sleep, followed by the command, *Sleep on,* in Matthew and Mark, and all difficulty disappears. The prayer in John, in which He commends the Apostles to His Father, explains the cause of His sorrowfulness, and the prayer that the cup may pass away. It is not from Himself that the Lord prays the suffering may be taken away. He beseeches the Father to preserve the disciples during His coming passion. In the same way, the prayer against Satan[6] in St. Luke explains the confidence with which He permitted the sleep He had just forbidden.

44. There was, then, no place for human anxiety and trepidation in that nature, which was more than human. It was superior to the ills of earthly flesh; a body not sprung from earthly elements, although His origin as Son of Man was due to the mystery of the conception by the Holy Ghost. The power of the Most High imparted its power to the body which the Virgin bare from the conception of the Holy Ghost. The animated body derives its conscious existence from association with a soul, which is diffused throughout it, and quickens it to perceive pains inflicted from without. Thus the soul, warned by the happy

---

[7] The Greek is ἐγένετο δὲ ὁ ἱδρὼς αὐτοῦ ὡσεὶ θρόμβοι αἵματος. His sweat became as it were great drops of blood '(R.V.): see supra.

[8] i.e. all sects with Docetic tenets, who would not allow Christ have had a real human body, but only to have appeared in bodily shape, like a ghost.

[9] St. John xvii. 11, 12. Hilary omits after 'keeping them in Thy Name,' the words 'which Thou hast given Me, that they may be one even as We are One.'

[1] St. Matt. xxvi. 53.

[2] St. Mark xiii. 31. In the Greek the same word παρέρχεσθαι is used in both cases, but Hilary uses *transire* in the first, *praeterire* in the second instance. [3] 2 Cor. v. 17.

[4] 1 Cor. vii. 31.   [5] St. John xviii. 9.
[6] i.e. St. Luke xxvi. 31, 32, as quoted above, c. 38.

glow of its own heavenly faith and hope, soars above its own origin in the beginnings of an earthly body, and raises [6a] that body to union with itself in thought and spirit, so that it ceases to feel the suffering of that which, all the while, it suffers. Why need we then say more about the nature of the Lord's body, that of the Son of Man Who came down from heaven? Even earthly bodies can sometimes be made indifferent to the natural necessities of pain and fear.

45. Did the Jewish children fear the flames blazing up with the fuel cast upon them in the fiery furnace at Babylon? Did the terror of that terrible fire prevail over their nature, conceived though it was like ours [7]? Did they feel pain, when the flames surrounded them? Perhaps, however, you may say they felt no pain, because they were not burnt: the flames were deprived of their burning nature. To be sure it is natural to the body to fear burning, and to be burnt by fire. But through the spirit of faith their earthly bodies (that is, bodies which had their origin according to the principles of natural birth) could neither be burnt nor made afraid. What, therefore, in the case of men was a violation of the order of nature, produced by faith in God, cannot be judged in God's case natural, but as an activity of the Spirit commencing with His earthly origin. The children were bound in the midst of the fire; they had no fear as they mounted the blazing pile: they felt not the flame as they prayed: though in the midst of the furnace, they could not be burnt. Both the fire and their bodies lost their proper natures; the one did not burn, the others were not burnt. Yet in all other respects, both fire and bodies retained their natures: for the bystanders were consumed, and the ministers of punishment were themselves punished. Impious heretic, you will have it that Christ suffered pain from the piercing of the nails, that He felt the bitterness of the wound, when they were driven through His hands: why, pray, did not the children fear the flames? Why did they suffer no pain? What was the nature in their bodies, which overcame that of fire? In the zeal of their faith and the glory of a blessed martyrdom they forgot to fear the terrible; should Christ be sorrowful from fear of the cross, Christ, Who even if He had been conceived with our sinful origin, would have been still God upon the cross, Who was to judge the world and reign for ever and ever? Could He forget such a reward, and tremble with the anxiety of dishonourable fear?

46. Daniel, whose meat was the scanty portion of a prophet [8], did not fear the lions' den. The Apostles rejoiced in suffering and death for the Name of Christ. To Paul his sacrifice was the crown of righteousness [9]. The Martyrs sang hymns as they offered their necks to the executioner, and climbed with psalms the blazing logs piled for them. The consciousness of faith takes away the weakness of nature, transforms the bodily senses that they feel no pain, and so the body is strengthened by the fixed purpose of the soul, and feels nothing except the impulse of its enthusiasm. The suffering which the mind despises in its desire of glory, the body does not feel, so long as the soul invigorates it. It is, then, a natural effect in man, that the zeal of the soul glowing for glory should make him unconscious of suffering, heedless of wounds, and regardless of death. But Jesus Christ the Lord of glory, the hem of Whose garment can heal, Whose spittle and word can create; for the man with the withered hand at His command stretched it forth whole, he who was born blind felt no more the defect of his birth, and the smitten ear was made sound as the other; dare we think of His pierced body in that pain and weakness, from which the spirit of faith in Him rescued the glorious and blessed Martyrs?

47. The Only-begotten God, then, suffered in His person the attacks of all the infirmities to which we are subject; but He suffered them in the power of His own nature, just as He was born in the power of His own nature, for at His birth He did not lose His omnipotent nature by being born. Though born under human conditions, He was not so conceived: His birth was surrounded by human circumstances, but His origin went beyond them. He suffered then in His body after the manner of our infirm body, yet bore the sufferings of our body in the power of His own body. To this article of our faith the prophet bears witness when he says, *He beareth our sins and grieveth for us: and we esteemed Him stricken, smitten, and afflicted: He was wounded for our transgressions and made weak for our sins* [1]. It is then a mistaken opinion of human judgment, which thinks He felt pain because He suffered. He bore our sins, that is, He assumed our body of sin, but was Himself sinless. He was sent in the likeness of the flesh of sin, bearing sin indeed in His flesh but *our* sin. So too He felt pain for us, but not with our senses; He was found in fashion as a man, with a body which could

6a. Reading *efficit*.   7 Dan. iii. 23.

8 Dan. i. 8—16.   9 2 Tim. iv. 6, 8.
1 Isai. liii. 4, 5. Hilary translates from the Septuagint. The Hebrew and the Vulgate differ, cf. the English Version, "Surely He hath borne our griefs" (instead of "our sins").

feel pain, but His nature could not feel pain; for, though His fashion was that of a man, His origin was not human, but He was born by conception of the Holy Ghost.

For the reasons mentioned, He was esteemed 'stricken, smitten and afflicted.' He took the form of a servant: and 'man born of a Virgin' conveys to us the idea of One Whose nature felt pain when He suffered. But though He was wounded it was 'for our transgressions.' The wound was not the wound of His own transgressions: the suffering not a suffering for Himself. He was not born man for His own sake, nor did He transgress in His own action. The Apostle explains the principle of the Divine Plan when he says, *We beseech you through Christ to be reconciled to God. Him, Who knew no sin, He made to be sin on our behalf*[2]. To condemn sin through sin in the flesh, He Who knew no sin was Himself made sin; that is, by means of the flesh to condemn sin in the flesh, He became flesh on our behalf but knew not flesh[3]: and therefore was wounded because of our transgressions.

48. Again, the Apostle knows nothing in Christ about fear of pain. When He wishes to speak of the dispensation of the Passion, He includes it in the mystery of Christ's Divinity. *Forgiving us all our trespasses, blotting out the bond written in ordinances, that was against us, which was contrary to us: taking it away, and nailing it to the cross; stripping off from Himself His flesh, He made a shew of principalities and powers openly triumphing over them in Himself*[4]. Was that the power, think you, to yield to the wound of the nail, to wince under the piercing blow, to convert itself into a nature that can feel pain? Yet the Apostle, who speaks as the mouthpiece of Christ[5], relating the work of our salvation through the Lord, describes the death of Christ as 'stripping off from Himself His flesh, boldly putting to shame the powers and triumphing over them in Himself.' If His passion was a necessity of nature and not the free gift of your salvation: if the cross was merely the suffering of wounds, and not the fixing upon Himself of the decree of death made out against you: if His dying was a violence done by death, and not the stripping off of the flesh by the power of God: lastly, if His death itself was anything but a dishonouring of powers, an act of boldness, a triumph: then ascribe to Him infirmity, because He was therein subject to necessity and nature, to force, to

fear and disgrace. But if it is the exact opposite in the mystery of the Passion, as it was preached to us, who, pray, can be so senseless as to repudiate the faith taught by the Apostles, to reverse all feelings of religion, to distort into the dishonourable charge of natural weakness, what was an act of free-will, a mystery, a display of power and boldness, a triumph? And what a triumph it was, when He offered Himself to those who sought to crucify Him, and they could not endure His presence: when He stood under sentence of death, Who shortly was to sit on the right hand of power: when He prayed for His persecutors while the nails were driven through Him: when He completed the mystery as He drained the draught of vinegar; when He was numbered among the transgressors and meanwhile granted Paradise: that when He was lifted on the tree, the earth quaked: when He hung on the cross, sun and day were put to flight: that He left His own body, yet called life back to the bodies of others[6]: was buried a corpse and rose again God: as man suffered all weaknesses for our sakes, as God triumphed in them all.

49. There is still, the heretics say, another serious and far reaching confession of weakness, all the more so because it is in the mouth of the Lord Himself, *My God, My God, why hast Thou forsaken Me*[7]? They construe this into the expression of a bitter complaint, that He was deserted and given over to weakness. But what a violent interpretation of an irreligious mind! how repugnant to the whole tenor of our Lord's words! He hastened to the death, which was to glorify Him, and after which He was to sit on the right hand of power; with all those blessed expectations could He fear death, and therefore complain that His God had betrayed Him to its necessity, when it was the entrance to eternal blessedness?

50. Further their heretical ingenuity presses on in the path prepared by their own godlessness, even to the entire absorption of God the Word into the human soul, and consequent denial that Jesus Christ, the Son of Man, was the same as the Son of God. So either God the Word ceased to be Himself while He performed the function of a soul in giving life to a body[8], or the man who was born was not the Christ at all, but the Word dwelt in him, as the Spirit dwelt in the prophets[9].

---

[6] Allusion to St. Matt. xxvii. 52, "many bodies of the saints that had fallen asleep were raised."
[7] St. Matt. xxvii. 46.
[8] Apollinaris' heresy that in Christ the place of the ordinary human soul was supplied by the Logos, the second Person in the Trinity.
[9] This doctrine was held by Marcellus of Ancyra (Sozomen, *H.E* II. 33), and Photinus: cp. also what Sozomen (VII. 7) says of Hebion.

---

[2] 2 Cor. v. 20, 21. The Greek is ὑπὲρ χριστοῦ, 'on behalf of Christ.'
[3] i.e. flesh in the bad sense, "the flesh of sin."
[4] Col. ii. 13—15.   [5] 2 Cor. xii. 3.

These absurd and perverse errors have grown in boldness and godlessness till they assert that Jesus Christ was not Christ until He was born of Mary. He Who was born was not a pre-existent Being, but began at that moment to exist [9a].

Hence follows also the error that God the Word, as it were some part of the Divine power extending itself in unbroken continuation, dwelt within that man who received from Mary the beginning of his being, and endowed him with the power of Divine working : though that man lived and moved by the nature of his own soul [1].

51. Through this subtle and mischievous doctrine they are drawn into the error that God the Word became soul to the body, His nature by self-humiliation working the change upon itself, and thus the Word ceased to be God ; or else, that the Man Jesus, in the poverty and remoteness from God of His nature, was animated only by the life and motion of His own human soul, wherein the Word of God, that is, as it were, the might of His uttered voice, resided. Thus the way is opened for all manner of irreverent theorising : the sum of which is, either that God the Word was merged in the soul and ceased to be God : or that Christ had no existence before His birth from Mary, since Jesus Christ, a mere man of ordinary body and soul, began to exist only at His human birth and was raised to the level of the Power, which worked within Him, by the extraneous force of the Divine Word extending itself into Him. Then when God the Word, after this extension, was withdrawn, He cried, *My God, My God, why hast Thou forsaken Me?* or at least when the divine nature of the Word once more gave place within Him to a human soul, He Who had hitherto relied on His Father's help, now separated from it, and abandoned to death, bemoaned His solitude and chid His deserter. Thus in every way arises a deadly danger of error in belief, whether it be thought that the cry of complaint denotes a weakness of nature in God the Word, or that God the Word was not pre-existent because the birth of Jesus Christ from Mary was the beginning of His being.

52. Amid these irreverent and ill-grounded theories the faith of the Church, inspired by the teaching of the Apostles, has recognised a birth of Christ, but no beginning. It knows of the dispensation, but of no division [2] : it re-fuses to make a separation in Jesus Christ [3], whereby Jesus is one and Christ another ; nor does it distinguish the Son of Man from the Son of God, lest perhaps the Son of God be not regarded as Son of Man also. It does not absorb the Son of God in the Son of Man ; nor does it by a tripartite belief [3a] tear asunder Christ, Whose coat woven from the top throughout was not parted, dividing Jesus Christ into the Word, a body and a soul ; nor, on the other hand, does it absorb the Word in body and soul. To it He is perfectly God the Word, and perfectly Christ the Man. To this alone we hold fast in the mystery of our confession, namely, the faith that Christ is none other than Jesus, and the doctrine that Jesus is none other than Christ.

53. I am not ignorant how much the grandeur of the divine mystery baffles our weak understanding, so that language can scarcely express it, or reason define it, or thought even embrace it. The Apostle, knowing that the most difficult task for an earthly nature is to apprehend, unaided, God's mode of action (for then our judgment were keener to discern than God is mighty to effect), writes to his true son according to the faith, who had received the Holy Scripture from his childhood, *As I exhorted thee to tarry at Ephesus, when I was going into Macedonia, that thou mightest charge certain men not to teach a different doctrine, neither to give heed to fables and endless genealogies, the which minister questionings, rather than the edification of God which is in faith* [4]. He bids him forbear to handle wordy genealogies and fables, which minister endless questionings. The edification of God, he says, is in faith : he limits human reverence to the faithful worship of the Almighty, and does not suffer our weakness to strain itself in the attempt to see what only dazzles the eye. If we look at the brightness of the sun, the sight is strained and weakened : and sometimes when we scrutinise with too curious gaze the source of the shining light, the eyes lose their natural power, and the sense of sight is even destroyed. Thus it happens that through trying to see too much we see nothing at all. What must we then expect in the case of God, the Sun of Righteousness? Will not foolishness be their reward, who would be over wise? Will not dull and brainless stupor usurp the place of the burning light of intelligence? A lower nature cannot understand the principle of a higher : nor can Heaven's mode of thought be revealed to human conception, for whatever is within the range of a limited con-

---

9a See note 9.
[1] The preaching of Sabellius, cf. I. 16, *protensio sit potius quam descensio,* 'an extension rather than a descent.'
[2] i.e. it realises the plan by which the second Person of the Trinity chose to take a human form, but refuses to separate the Divine from the human in Jesus.

3 Reading *partitur* for MSS. *patitur.*
3a Apollinarianism.   4 1 Tim. i. 3, 4.

sciousness, is itself limited. The divine power exceeds therefore the capacity of the human mind. If the limited strains itself to reach so far, it becomes even feebler than before. It loses what certainty it had: instead of seeing heavenly things it is only blinded by them. No mind can fully comprehend the divine: it punishes the obstinacy of the curious by depriving them of their power. Would we look at the sun we must remove as much of his brilliancy as we need, in order to see him: if not, by expecting too much, we fall short of the possible. In the same way we can only hope to understand the purposes of Heaven, so far as is permitted. We must expect only what He grants to our apprehension: if we attempt to go beyond the limit of His indulgence, it is withdrawn altogether. There is that in God which we *can* perceive: it is visible to all if we are content with the possible. Just as with the sun we can see something, if we are content to see what can be seen, but if we strain beyond the possible we lose all: so is it with the nature of God. There is that which we *can* understand if we are content with understanding what we can: but aim beyond your powers and you will lose even the power of attaining what was within your reach.

54. The mystery of that other timeless birth I will not yet touch upon: its treatment demands an ampler space than this. For the present I will speak of the Incarnation only. Tell me, I pray, ye who pry into the secrets of Heaven, the mystery of Christ born of a Virgin and His nature; whence will you explain that He was conceived and born of a Virgin? What was the physical cause of His origin according to your disputations? How was He formed within His mother's womb? Whence His body and His humanity? And lastly, what does it mean that the *Son of Man descended from heaven Who remained in heaven* [5]? It is not possible by the laws of bodies for the same object to remain and to descend: the one is the change of downward motion; the other the stillness of being at rest. The Infant wails but is in Heaven: the Boy grows but remains ever the immeasurable God. By what perception of human understanding can we comprehend that He ascended where He was before, and He descended Who remained in heaven? The Lord says, *What if ye should behold the Son of Man ascending thither where He was before* [6]? The Son of Man ascends where He was before: can sense apprehend this? The Son

of Man descends from heaven, Who is in heaven: can reason cope with this? The Word was made flesh: can words express this? The Word becomes flesh, that is, God becomes Man: the Man is in heaven: the God is from heaven. He ascends Who descended: but He descends and yet does not descend. He is as He ever was, yet He was not ever what He is. We pass in review the causes, but we cannot explain the manner: we perceive the manner, and we cannot understand the causes. Yet if we understand Christ Jesus even thus, we shall know Him: if we seek to understand Him further we shall not know Him at all.

55. Again, how great a mystery of word and act it is that Christ wept, that His eyes filled with tears from the anguish of His mind [7]. Whence came this defect in His soul that sorrow should wring tears from His body? What bitter fate, what unendurable pain, could move to a flood of tears the Son of Man Who descended from heaven? Again, what was it in Him which wept? God the Word? or His human soul? For though weeping is a bodily function, the body is but a servant; tears are, as it were, the sweat of the agonised soul. Again, what was the cause of His weeping? Did He owe to Jerusalem the debt of His tears, Jerusalem, the godless parricide, whom no suffering could requite for the slaughter of Apostles and Prophets, and the murder of her Lord Himself? He might weep for the disasters and death which befall mankind: but could He grieve for the fall of that doomed and desperate race? What, I ask, was this mystery of weeping? His soul wept for sorrow; was not it the soul which sent forth the Prophets? Which would so often have gathered the chickens together under the shadow of His wings [8]? But God the Word cannot grieve, nor can the Spirit weep: nor could His soul possibly do anything before the body existed. Yet we cannot doubt that Jesus Christ truly wept [9].

56. No less real were the tears He shed for Lazarus [1]. The first question here is, What was there to weep for in the case of Lazarus? Not his death, for that was not unto death, but for the glory of God: for the Lord says, *That sickness is not unto death, but for the glory of God, that the Son of God may be honoured through him* [2]. The death which

5 St. John iii. 13.   6 Ib. vi. 62.

7 St. Luke xix. 41.
8 St. Matt. xxiii. 37; St. Luke xiii. 34.
9 The human soul in Jesus alone could feel grief and weep: yet it was the divine Spirit which sent forth the prophets: for the human soul began to exist only in conjunction with His human body.
1 St. John xi. 35.
2 Ib. 4.   The Greek is δι' αὐτῆς, through it.

was the cause of God's being glorified could not bring sorrow and tears. Nor was there any occasion for tears in His absence from Lazarus at the time of his death. He says plainly, *Lazarus is dead, and I rejoice for your sakes that I was not there, to the intent that ye may believe* [3]. His absence then, which aided the Apostles' belief, was not the cause of His sorrow : for with the knowledge of Divine omniscience, He declared the death of the sick man from afar. We can find, then, no necessity for tears, yet He wept. And again I ask, To whom must we ascribe the weeping? To God, or the soul, or the body? The body, of itself, has no tears except those it sheds at the command of the sorrowing soul. Far less can God have wept, for He was to be glorified in Lazarus. Nor is it reason to say His soul recalled Lazarus from the tomb : can a soul linked to a body, by the power of its command, call another soul back to the dead body from which it has departed? Can He grieve Who is about to be glorified? Can He weep Who is about to restore the dead to life? Tears are not for Him Who is about to give life, or grief for Him Who is about to receive glory. Yet He Who wept and grieved was also the Giver of life.

57. If there are many points which we treat scantily it is not because we have nothing to say, or do not know what has already been said ; our purpose is, by abstaining from too laborious a process of argument, to render the results as attractive as possible to the reader. We know the deeds and words of our Lord, yet we know them not : we are not ignorant of them, yet they cannot be understood. The facts are real, but the power behind them is a mystery. We will prove this from His own words, *For this reason doth the Father love Me, because I lay down My life that I may take it up again. No one taketh it from Me, but I lay it down of Myself. I have power to lay it down and I have power to take it up again. This commandment received I from the Father* [4]. He lays down His life of Himself, but I ask *who* lays it down? We confess, without hesitation, that Christ is God the Word : but on the other hand, we know that the Son of Man was composed of a soul and a body : compare the angel's words to Joseph, *Arise, and take the child and His mother, and go into the land of Israel; for they are dead who sought the soul of the child* [5]. Whose soul is it? His body's, or God's? If His body's, what power has the body to lay down the soul, when it is only by the working of the

soul that it is quickened into life? Again, how could the body, which apart from the soul is inert and dead, receive a command from the Father? But if, on the other hand, any man suppose that God the Word laid aside His soul, that He might take it up again, he must prove that God the Word died, that is, remained without life and feeling like a dead body, and took up His soul again to be quickened once more into life by it.

58. But, further, no one who is endued with reason can impute to God a soul ; though it is written in many places that the soul of God hates sabbaths and new moons : and also that it delights in certain things [6]. But this is merely a conventional expression to be understood in the same way as when God is spoken of as possessing body, with hands, and eyes, and fingers, and arms, and heart. As the Lord said, *A Spirit hath not flesh and bones* [7]: He then Who *is,* and *changeth not* [8], cannot have the limbs and parts of a tangible body. He is a simple and blessed nature, a single, complete, all-embracing Whole. God is therefore not quickened into life, like bodies, by the action of an indwelling soul, but is Himself His own life.

59. How does He then lay down His soul, or take it up again? What is the meaning of this command He received? God could not lay it down, that is, die, or take it up again, that is, come to life. But neither did the body receive the command to take it up again ; it could not do so of itself, for He said of the Temple of His body, *Destroy this temple and after three days I will raise it up* [9]. Thus it is God Who raises up the temple of His body. And Who lays down His soul to take it again? The body does not take it up again of itself : it is raised up by God. That which is raised up again must have been dead, and that which is living does not lay down its soul. God then was neither dead nor buried : and yet He said, *In that she has poured this ointment upon My body she did it for My burial* [1]. In that it was poured upon His body it was done for His burial : but the *His* is not the same as *Him.* It is quite another use of the pronoun when we say, 'it was done for the burial of *Him,*' and when we say, '*His* body was anointed :' nor is the sense the same in '*His* body was buried,' and '*He* was buried.'

60. To grasp this divine mystery we must see the God in Him without ignoring the Man ; and the Man without ignoring the God. We must not divide Jesus Christ, for the Word was made flesh : yet we must not call Him

---

3 St. John 14, 15.   4 Ib. x. 17, 18.   5 St. Matt. ii. 20.

6 E.g. Isai. i. 14.   7 St. Luke xxiv. 39.   8 Mal. iii 6.
9 St. John ii. 19.   1 St. Matt. xxvi. 12.

buried, though we know He raised Himself again: must not doubt His resurrection, though we dare not deny He was buried [2]. Jesus Christ was buried, for He died: He died, and even cried out at the moment of death, *My God, My God, why hast Thou forsaken Me?* Yet He, Who uttered these words, said also: *Verily I say unto thee, This day shalt thou be with Me in Paradise* [3], and He Who promised Paradise to the thief cried aloud, *Father, into Thy hands I commend My Spirit; and having said this He gave up the Ghost* [4].

61. Ye who trisect Christ into the Word, the soul and the body, or degrade the whole Christ, even God the Word, into a single member of our race, unfold to us this mystery of great godliness which was manifested in the flesh [4a]. What Spirit did Christ give up? Who commended His Spirit into the hands of His Father? Who was to be in Paradise that same day? Who complained that He was deserted of God? The cry of the deserted betokens the weakness of the dying: the promise of Paradise the sovereign power of the living God. To commend His Spirit denoted confidence: to give up His Spirit implied His departure by death. Who then, I demand, was it Who died? Surely He Who gave up His Spirit? but Who gave up His Spirit? Certainly He Who commended it to His Father. And if He Who commended His Spirit is the same as He Who gave it up and died, was it the body which commended its soul, or God Who commended the body's soul? I say 'soul,' because there is no doubt it is frequently synonymous with 'spirit,' as might be gathered merely from the language here: Jesus gave up His 'Spirit' when He was on the point of death. If, therefore, you hold the conviction that the body commended the soul, that the perishable commended the living, the corruptible the eternal, that which was to be raised again, that which abides unchanged, then, since He Who commended His Spirit to the Father was also to be in Paradise with the thief that same day, I would fain know if, while the sepulchre received Him, He was abiding in heaven, or if He was abiding in heaven, when He cried out that God had deserted Him.

62. It is one and the same Lord Jesus Christ, the Word made flesh, Who expresses Himself in all these utterances, Who is man when He says He is abandoned to death: yet while man still rules in Paradise as God, and though reigning in Paradise, as Son of God

commends His Spirit to His Father, as Son of Man gives up to death the Spirit He commended to the Father. Why do we then view as a disgrace that which is a mystery? We see Him complaining that He is left to die, because He is Man: we see Him, as He dies, declaring that He reigned in Paradise, because He is God. Why should we harp, to support our irreverence, on what He said to make us understand His death, and keep back what He proclaimed to demonstrate His immortality? The words and the voice are equally His, when He complains of desertion, and when He declares His rule: by what method of heretical logic do we split up our belief and deny that He Who died was at the same time He Who rules? Did He not testify both equally of Himself, when He commended His Spirit, and when He gave it up? But if He is the same, Who commended His Spirit, and gave it up, if He dies when ruling and rules when dead: then the mystery of the Son of God and Son of Man means that He is One, Who dying reigns, and reigning dies.

63. Stand aside then, all godless unbelievers, for whom the divine mystery is too great, who do not know that Christ wept not for Himself but for us, to prove the reality of His assumed manhood by yielding to the emotion common to humanity: who do not perceive that Christ died not for Himself, but for our life, to renew human life by the death of the deathless God: who cannot reconcile the complaint of the deserted with the confidence of the Ruler: who would teach us that because He reigns as God and complains that He is dying, we have here a dead man and the reigning God. For He Who dies is none other than He Who reigns, He Who commends His spirit than He Who gives it up: He Who was buried, rose again: ascending or descending He is altogether one.

64. Listen to the teaching of the Apostle and see in it a faith instructed not by the understanding of the flesh but by the gift of the Spirit. *The Greeks seek after wisdom,* he says, *and the Jews ask for a sign; but we preach Christ crucified, to the Jews a stumbling block, and unto Gentiles foolishness; but unto them that are called, both Jews and Greeks, Christ Jesus, the power of God, and the wisdom of God* [5]. Is Christ divided here so that Jesus the crucified is one, and Christ, the power and wisdom of God, another? This is to the Jews a stumbling-block and unto the Gentiles foolishness; but to us Christ Jesus is the power of God, and the wisdom of God: wisdom, how-

---

[2] Hilary is playing on the mystery of the two natures in one Person. We cannot say the God-nature was buried: nor that the human nature brought itself back to life: yet Jesus Christ died, was buried, and rose again.
[3] St. Luke xxiii. 43. [4] Ib. 46. [4a] 1 Tim. iii. 16.

[5] 1 Cor. i. 23, 24.

ever, not known of the world, nor understood by a secular philosophy. Hear the same blessed Apostle when he declares that it has not been understood, *We speak the wisdom of God, which hath been hidden in a mystery, which God foreordained before the world for our glory: which none of the rulers of this world has known: for had they known it, they would not have crucified the Lord of Glory* [6]. Does not the Apostle know that this wisdom of God is hidden in a mystery, and cannot be known of the rulers of this world? Does he divide Christ into a Lord of Glory and a crucified Jesus? Nay, rather, he contradicts this most foolish and impious idea with the words, *For I determined to know nothing among you, save Jesus Christ, and Him crucified* [7].

65. The Apostle knew nothing else, and he determined to know nothing else: we men of feebler wit, and feebler faith, split up, divide and double Jesus Christ, constituting ourselves judges of the unknown, and blaspheming the hidden mystery. For us Christ crucified is one, Christ the wisdom of God another: Christ Who was buried different from Christ Who descended from Heaven: the Son of Man not at the same time also Son of God. We teach that which we do not understand: we seek to refute that which we cannot grasp. We men improve upon the revelation of God: we are not content to say with the Apostle, *Who shall lay anything to the charge of God's elect? It is God that justifieth, who is he that condemneth? It is Christ Jesus, that died, yea, rather, that was raised from the dead, Who is at the right hand of God, Who also maketh intercession for us* [8]. Is He Who intercedes for us other than He Who is at the right hand of God? Is not He Who is at the right hand of God the very same Who rose again? Is He Who rose again other than He Who died? He Who died than He Who condemns us? Lastly, is not He Who condemns us also God Who justifies us? Distinguish, if you can, Christ our accuser from God our defender, Christ Who died from Christ Who condemns, Christ sitting at the right hand of God and praying for us from Christ Who died. Whether, therefore, dead or buried, descended into Hades or ascended in.o Heaven, all is one and the same Chri.t: as the Apostle says, *Now this ' He ascended' what is it, but that He also descended to the lower parts of the earth? He that descended is the same also that ascended far above all heavens, that He may fill all things* [9]. How far then shall we push our babbling ignorance and blasphemy, professing

to explain what is hidden in the mystery of God? *He that descended is the same also that ascended.* Can we longer doubt that the Man Christ Jesus rose from the dead, ascended above the heavens and is at the right hand of God? We cannot say His body descended into Hades, which lay in the grave. If then He Who descended is one with Him, Who ascended; if His body did not go down into Hades, yet really arose from the dead, and ascended into heaven, what remains, except to believe in the secret mystery, which is hidden from the world and the rulers of this age, and to confess that, ascending or descending, He is but One, one Jesus Christ for us, Son of God and Son of Man, God the Word and Man in the flesh, Who suffered, died, was buried, rose again, was received into heaven, and sitteth at the right hand of God: Who possesses in His one single self, according to the Divine Plan and nature, in the form of God and in the form of a servant, the Human and Divine without separation or division.

66. So the Apostle moulding our ignorant and haphazard ideas into conformity with truth says of this mystery of the faith, *For He was crucified through weakness but He liveth through the power of God* [1]. Preaching the Son of Man and Son of God, Man through the Divine Plan, God through His eternal nature, he says, that He Who was crucified through weakness is He Who lives through the power of God. His weakness arises from *the form of a servant*, His nature remains because of the *form of God*. He took the form of a servant, though He was in form of God: therefore there can be no doubt as to the mystery according to which He both suffered and lived. There existed in Him both weakness to suffer, and power of God to give life: and hence He Who suffered and lived cannot be more than One, or other than Himself.

67. The Only-begotten God suffered indeed all that men can suffer: but let us express ourselves in the words and faith of the Apostle. He says, *For I delivered unto you first of all how that Christ died for our sins, according to the Scriptures, and that He was buried, and that He rose again the third day according to the Scriptures* [2]. This is no unsupported statement of his own, which might lead to error, but a warning to us to confess that Christ died and rose after a real manner, not a nominal, since the fact is certified by the full weight of Scripture authority; and that we must understand His death in that exact sense in which Scripture declares it. In his

---

[6] 1 Cor. ii. 7, 8.   [7] Ib 2.   [8] Rom. viii. 33, 34.
[9] Eph. iv. 9, 10.

[1] 2 Cor. xiii. 4.   [2] 1 Cor. xv. 3, 4.

regard for the perplexities and scruples of the weak and sensitive believer, he adds these solemn concluding words, *according to the Scriptures*, to his proclamation of the death and the resurrection. He would not have us grow weaker, driven about by every wind of vain doctrine, or vexed by empty subtleties and false doubts: he would summon faith to return, before it were shipwrecked, to the haven of piety, believing and confessing the death and resurrection of Jesus Christ, Son of Man and Son of God, *according to the Scriptures*, this being the safeguard of reverence against the attack of the adversary, so to understand the death and resurrection of Jesus Christ, as it was written of Him. There is no danger in faith : the reverent confession of the hidden mystery of God is always safe. Christ was born of the Virgin, but conceived of the Holy Ghost *according to the Scriptures*. Christ wept, but *according to the Scriptures* : that which made Him weep was also a cause of joy. Christ hungered ; but *according to the Scriptures*, He used His power as God against the tree which bore no fruit, when He had no food. Christ suffered : but *according to the Scriptures*, He was about to sit at the right hand of Power. He complained that He was abandoned to die : but *according to the Scriptures*, at the same moment He received in His kingdom in Paradise the thief who confessed Him. He died : but *according to the Scriptures*, He rose again and sits at the right hand of God. In the belief of this mystery there is life : this confession resists all attack.

68. The Apostle is careful to leave no room for doubt : we cannot say, "Christ was born, suffered, was dead and buried, and rose again : but how, by what power, by what division of parts of Himself? Who wept? Who rejoiced? Who complained? Who descended? and Who ascended?" He rests the merits of faith entirely on the confession of unquestioning reverence. *The righteousness*, he says, *which is of faith saith thus, Say not in thy heart, Who hath ascended into heaven, that is, to bring Christ down : or Who hath descended into the abyss : that is, to bring Christ up from the dead? But what saith the Scripture? Thy word is nigh, in thy mouth, and in thy heart ; that is, the word of faith which we preach : because if thou shalt confess with thy mouth Jesus as Lord, and shalt believe in thy heart, that God hath raised Him up from the dead, thou shalt be saved* [3]. Faith perfects the righteous man : as it is written, *Abraham believed God and it was reckoned unto him for*

righteousness [4]. Did Abraham impugn the word of God, when he was promised the inheritance of the Gentiles, and an abiding posterity as many as the sand or the stars for multitude? To the reverent faith, which trusts implicitly on the omnipotence of God, the limits of human weakness are no barrier. Despising all that is feeble and earthly in itself, it believes the divine promise, even though it exceeds the possibilities of human nature. It knows that the laws which govern man are no hindrance to the power of God, Who is as bountiful in the performance as He is gracious in the promise. Nothing is more righteous than Faith. For as in human conduct it is equity and self-restraint that receive our approval, so in the case of God, what is more righteous for man than to ascribe omnipotence to Him, Whose Power He perceives to be without limits?

69. The Apostle then looking in us for the righteousness which is of Faith, cuts at the root of incredulous doubt and godless unbelief. He forbids us to admit into our hearts the cares of anxious thought, and points to the authority of the Prophet's words, *Say not in thy heart, Who hath ascended into heaven* [5]? Then He completes the thought of the Prophet's words with the addition, *That is to bring Christ down*. The perception of the human mind cannot attain to the knowledge of the divine : but neither can a reverent faith doubt the works of God. Christ needed no human help, that any one should ascend into heaven to bring Him down from His blessed Home to His earthly body. It was no external force which drove Him down to the earth. We must believe that He came, even as He did come : it is true religion to confess Jesus Christ not brought down, but descending. The mystery both of the time and the method of His coming, belongs to Him alone. We may not think because He came but recently, that therefore He must have been brought down, nor that His coming in time depended upon another, who brought Him down.

Nor does the Apostle give room for unbelief in the other direction. He quotes at once the words of the Prophet, *Or Who hath descended into the abyss* [6], and adds immediately the explanation, *That is to bring Christ back from the dead*. He is free to return into heaven, Who was free to descend to the earth. All hesitation and doubt is then removed. Faith reveals what omnipotence plans : his-

---

3 Rom. x. 6—9.

4 Gen. xv. 16 ; Rom. iv. 3.
5 Deut. xxx. 12. The context is the assurance of Moses, that "the law is not hidden from thee, neither is it far off," but "the word is very nigh unto thee, in thy mouth, and in thy heart."
6 Deut. xxx. 13. E.V. Who shall go over the sea for us?

tory relates the effect, God Almighty was the cause.

70. But there is demanded from us an unwavering certainty. The Apostle expounding the whole secret of the Scripture passes on, *Thy word is nigh, in thy mouth and in thy heart*[7]. The words of our confession must not be tardy or deliberately vague : there must be no interval between heart and lips, lest what ought to be the confession of true reverence become a subterfuge of infidelity. The word must be near us, and within us ; no delay between the heart and the lips ; a faith of conviction as well as of words. Heart and lips must be in harmony, and reveal in thought and utterance a religion which does not waver. Here too, as before, the Apostle adds the explanation of the Prophet's words, *That is the word of Faith, which we preach ; because if thou shalt confess with thy mouth Jesus as Lord, and shalt believe in thy heart that God hath raised Him up from the dead, thou shalt be saved.* Piety consists in rejecting doubt, righteousness in believing, salvation in confessing. Trifle not with ambiguities, be not stirred up to vain babblings, do not debate in any way the powers of God, or impose limits upon His might, cease searching again and again for the causes of unsearchable mysteries : confess rather that Jesus is the Lord, and believe that God raised Him from the dead ; herein is salvation. What folly is it to depreciate the nature and character of Christ, when this alone is salvation, to know that He is the Lord. Again, what an error of human vanity to quarrel about His resurrection, when it is enough for eternal life to believe that God raised Him up. In simplicity then is faith, in faith righteousness, and in confession true godliness. For God does not call us to the blessed life through arduous investigations. He does not tempt us with the varied arts of rhetoric. The way to eternity is plain and easy ; believe that Jesus was raised from the dead by God and confess that He is the Lord. Let no one therefore wrest into an occasion for impiety, what was said because of our ignorance. It had to be proved to us, that Jesus Christ died, that we might live in Him.

71. If then He said, *My God, My God, why hast Thou forsaken Me*[8], and *Father, into Thy hands I commend My Spirit*[9], that we might be sure that He did die, was not this, in His care for our faith, rather a scattering of our doubts, than a confession of His weakness ? When He was about to restore Lazarus, He prayed to the Father : but what need had He of prayer, Who said, *Father, I thank Thee, that Thou hast heard Me ; and I know that Thou hearest Me always, but because of the multitude I said it, that they may believe that Thou didst send Me*[1] ? He prayed then for us, that we may know Him to be the Son ; the words of prayer availed Him nothing, but He said them for the advancement of our faith. He was not in want of help, but we of teaching. Again He prayed to be glorified ; and immediately was heard from heaven the voice of God the Father glorifying Him : but when they wondered at the voice, He said, *This voice hath not come for My sake, but for your sakes*[2]. The Father is besought for us, He speaks for us : may all this lead us to believe and confess ! The answer of the Glorifier is granted not to the prayer for glory, but to the ignorance of the bystanders : must we not then regard the complaint of suffering, when He found His greatest joy in suffering, as intended for the building up of our faith ? Christ prayed for His persecutors, because they knew not what they did. He promised Paradise from the cross, because He is God the King. He rejoiced upon the cross, that all was finished when He drank the vinegar, because He had fulfilled all prophecy before He died. He was born for us, suffered for us, died for us, rose again for us. This alone is necessary for our salvation, to confess the Son of God risen from the dead : why then should we die in this state of godless unbelief ? If Christ, ever secure of His divinity, made clear to us His death, Himself indifferent to death, yet dying to assure that it was true humanity that He had assumed : why should we use this very confession of the Son of God that for us He became Son of Man and died as the chief weapon to deny His divinity ?

---

[7] Deut. xxx. 14.

[8] St. Mark xv. 34.   [9] St. Luke xxiii. 46.
[1] St. John xi. 41, 42.   [2] Ib. xii. 30.

BOOK XI.

1. THE Apostle in his letter to the Ephesians, reviewing in its manifold aspects the full and perfect mystery of the Gospel, mingles with other instructions in the knowledge of God the following: *As ye also were called in one hope of your calling; One Lord, one faith, one baptism, one God and Father of all, and through all, and in us all*[1]. He does not leave us in the vague and misleading paths of an indefinite teaching, or abandon us to the shifting fancies of imagination, but limits the unimpeded license of intellect and desire by the appointment of restraining barriers. He gives us no opportunity to be wise beyond what he preached, but defines in exact and precise language the faith fixed for all time, that there may be no excuse for instability of belief. He declares one faith, as he preaches one Lord, and pronounces one baptism, as he declares one faith of one Lord, that as there is one faith of one Lord, so there may be one baptism of one faith in one Lord. And since the whole mystery of the baptism and the faith is not only in one Lord, but also in one God, he completes the consummation of our hope by the confession of one God. The one baptism and the one faith are of one God, as they are of one Lord. Lord and God are each one, not by union of person but by distinction of properties: for, on the one hand, it is the property of Each to be one, whether of the Father in His Fatherhood, or of the Son in His Sonship, and on the other hand, that property of individuality, which Each possesses, constitutes for Each the mystery of His union with the Other. Thus the one Lord Christ cannot take away from God the Father His Lordship, or the one God the Father deny to the one Lord Christ His Godhead. If, because God is one, Christ is not also by nature divine, then we cannot allow that the one God is Lord, because there is one Lord Christ: that is, on the supposition that by their 'oneness' is signified not the mystery, but an exclusive unity. So there is one baptism and one faith of one Lord, as of one God.

2. But how can it be any longer one faith, if it does not steadfastly and sincerely confess one Lord and one God the Father: and how can the faith which is not one faith confess one Lord and one God the Father? Further, how can the faith be one, when its preachers are so at variance? One comes teaching that the Lord Jesus Christ, being in the weakness of our nature, groaned with anguish when the nails pierced His hands, that He lost the virtue of His own power and nature, and shrank shuddering from the death which threatened Him. Another even denies the cardinal doctrine of the Generation and pronounces Him a creature. Another will call Him, but not think Him, God on the ground that religion allows us to speak of more Gods than One, but He, Whom we recognise as God, must be conscious of sharing the divine nature[2]. Again, how can Christ the Lord be one, when some say that as God He feels no pain, others make Him weak and fearful: to some He is God in name, to others God in nature: to some the Son by Generation, to others the Son by appellation? And if this is so, how can God the Father be one in the faith, when to some He is Father by His authority, to others Father by generation, in the sense that God is Father of the universe?

And yet, who will deny that whatever is not the one faith, is not faith at all? For in the one faith there is one Lord Christ, and God the Father is one. But the one Lord Jesus Christ is not one in the truth of the confession, as well as in name, unless He is Son, unless He is God[3], unless He is unchangeable, unless His Sonship and His Godhead have been eternally present in Him. He who preaches Christ other than He is, that is, other than Son and God, preaches another Christ. Nor is he in the one faith of the one baptism, for in the teaching of the Apostle the one faith is the faith of that one baptism, in which the one Lord is Christ, the Son of God Who is also God.

3. Yet it cannot be denied that Christ was Christ. It cannot be that He was incognisable to mankind. The books of the prophets have set their seal upon Him: the ful-

---

[1] Eph. iv. 4—6.

[2] The text is very corrupt here, but the meaning seems to be that, while we have the authority of the Bible to speak of God, if we do not attach its full meaning to the word (e.g. Psalm lxxxii. 6, "I have said, 'Ye are Gods,'"), yet if we use the name in its proper significance it is blasphemous to call Christ God. The reading of the earlier editions and some MSS., 'duos dici irreligiosum est, et Deum non intelligi,' is probably a gloss to soften the difficulty.

[3] Reading 'unus est, si filius sit, si Deus sit.'

ness of the times, which waxes daily, witnesses of Him : by the working of wonders the tombs of Apostles and Martyrs proclaim Him : the power of His name reveals Him : the unclean spirits confess Him, and the devils howling in their torment call aloud His name. In all we see the dispensation of His power. But our faith must preach Him as He is, namely, one Lord not in name but in confession, in one faith of one baptism : for on our faith in one Lord Christ depends our confession of one God the Father.

4. But these teachers of a new Christ, who deny to Him all that is His, preach another Lord Christ as well as another God the Father. The One is not the Begetter but the Creator, the Other not begotten, but created. Christ is therefore not very God, because He is not God by birth, and faith cannot recognise a Father in God, because there is no generation to constitute Him Father. They glorify God the Father indeed, as is His right and due, when they predicate of Him a nature unapproachable, invisible, inviolable, ineffable, and infinite, endued with omniscience and omnipotence, instinct with love, moving in all and permeating all, immanent and transcendent, sentient in all sentient existence. But when they proceed to ascribe to Him the unique glory of being alone good, alone omnipotent, alone immortal, who does not feel that this pious praise aims to exclude the Lord Jesus Christ from the blessedness, which by the reservation ' alone ' is restricted to the glory of God? Does it not leave Christ in sinfulness and weakness and death, while the Father reigns in solitary perfection? Does it not deny in Christ a natural origin from God the Father, in the fear lest He should be thought to inherit by a birth, which bestows upon the Begotten the same virtue of nature as the Begetter, a blessedness natural to God the Father alone?

5. Unlearned in the teaching of the Gospels and Apostles, they extol the glory of God the Father, not, however, with the sincerity of a devout believer, but with the cunning of impiety, to wrest from it an argument for their wicked heresy. Nothing, they say, can be compared with His nature : therefore the Only-begotten God is excluded from the comparison, because He possesses a lower and weaker nature. And this they say of God, the living image of the living God, the perfect form of His blessed nature, the only-begotten offspring of His unbegotten substance ; Who is not truly the image of God unless He possesses the perfect glory of the Father's blessedness, and reproduces in its exactitude the likeness of His whole nature. But if the Only-

begotten God is the image of the Unbegotten God, the verity of that perfect and supreme nature resides in Him and makes Him the image of the very God. Is the Father omnipotent? The weak Son is not the image of omnipotence. Is He good? The Son, Whose divinity is of a lower stamp, does not reflect in His sinful nature the image of goodness. Is He incorporeal? The Son, Whose very spirit is confined to the limits of a body, is not in the form of the Incorporeal. Is He ineffable? The Son, Whom language can define, Whose nature the tongue can describe, is not the image of the Ineffable. Is He the true God? The Son possesses only a fictitious divinity, and the false cannot be the image of the True. The Apostle, however, does not ascribe to Christ a portion of the image, or a part of the form, but pronounces Him unreservedly the image of the invisible God and the form of God[4]. And how could He declare more expressly the divine nature of the Son of God, than by saying that Christ is the image of the invisible God even in respect of His invisibility : for if the substance of Christ were discernible how could He be the image of an invisible nature?

6. But, as we pointed out in the former books, they seize the Dispensation of the assumed manhood as a pretext to dishonour His divinity, and distort the Mystery of our salvation into an occasion of blasphemy. Had they held fast the faith of the Apostle, they would neither have forgotten that He, Who was in the form of God, took the form of a servant, nor made use of the servant's form to dishonour the form of God (for the form of God includes the fulness of divinity), but they would have noted, reasonably and reverently, the distinction of occasions[5] and mysteries, without dishonouring the divinity, or being misled by the Incarnation of Christ. But now, when we have, I am convinced, proved everything to the utmost, and pointed out the power of the divine nature underlying the birth of the assumed body, there is no longer room for doubt. He Who was at once man and the Only-begotten God performed all things by the power of God, and in the power of God accomplished all things through a true human nature. As begotten of God He possessed the nature of divine omnipotence, as born of the Virgin He had a perfect and entire humanity. Though He had a real body, He subsisted in the nature of God, and though He subsisted in the nature of God, He abode in a real body.

---

[4] Cf. Col. i. 15, and Phil. ii. 6.
[5] i.e. the occasions when Christ was speaking of His humanity and those when He was referring to His divine nature.

7. In our reply we have followed Him to the moment of His glorious death, and taking one by one the statements of their unhallowed doctrine, we have refuted them from the teaching of the Gospels and the Apostle. But even after His glorious resurrection there are certain things which they have made bold to construe as proofs of the weakness of a lower nature, and to these we must now reply. Let us adopt once more our usual method of drawing out from the words themselves their true signification, that so we may discover the truth precisely where they think to overthrow it. For the Lord spoke in simple words for our instruction in the faith, and His words cannot need support or comment from foreign and irrelevant sayings.

8. Among their other sins the heretics often employ as an argument the words of the Lord, *I ascend unto My Father and your Father, and My God and your God* [6]. His Father is also their Father, His God their God ; therefore He is not in the nature of God, for He pronounces God the Father of others as of Himself, and His unique Sonship ceases when He shares with others the nature and the origin which make Him Son and God. But let them add further the words of the Apostle, *But when He saith All things are put in subjection, He is excepted Who did subject all things unto Him. And when all things have been subjected unto Him, then shall He Himself be subjected unto Him, that did subject all things unto Himself, that God may be all in all* [7], whereby, since they regard that subjection as a proof of weakness, they may dispossess Him of the virtue of His Father's nature, because His natural infirmity subjected Him to the dominion of a stronger nature. And after that, let them adopt their very strongest position and their impregnable defence, before which the truth of the Divine birth is to be demolished ; namely, that if He is subjected, He is not God; if His God and Father is ours also, He shares all in common with creatures, and therefore is Himself also a creature : created of God and not begotten, since the creature has its substance out of nothing, but the begotten possesses the nature of its author.

9. Falsehood is always infamous, for the liar throwing off the bridle of shame dares to gainsay the truth, or else at times he hides behind some veil of pretext, that he may appear to defend with modesty what is shameless in intention. But in this case, when they sacrilegiously use the Scriptures to degrade the dignity of our Lord, there is no room for the blush or the false excuse ; for there are occasions when even pardon accorded to ignorance is refused, and wilful misconstruction is exposed in its naked profanity. Let us postpone for a moment the exposition of this passage in the Gospel, and ask them first whether they have forgotten the preaching of the Apostle, who said, *Without controversy great is the mystery of godliness, which was manifested in the flesh, justified in the Spirit, seen of angels, preached among the nations, believed on in the world, received up in glory* [8]. Who is so dull that he cannot comprehend that the mystery of godliness is simply the Dispensation of the flesh assumed by the Lord ? At the outset then, he who does not agree in this confession is not in the faith of God. For the Apostle leaves no doubt that all must confess that the hidden secret of our salvation is not the dishonour of God, but the mystery of great godliness, and a mystery no longer kept from our eyes, but manifested in the flesh ; no longer weak through the nature of flesh, but justified in the Spirit. And so by the justification of the Spirit is removed from our faith the idea of fleshly weakness ; through the manifestation of the flesh is revealed that which was secret, and in the unknown cause of that which was secret is contained the only confession, the confession of the mystery of great godliness. This is the whole system of the faith set forth by the Apostle in its proper order. From godliness proceeds the mystery, from the mystery the manifestation in the flesh, from the manifestation in the flesh the justification in the Spirit : for the mystery of godliness which was manifested in the flesh, to be truly a mystery, was manifested in the flesh through the justification of the Spirit. Again, we must not forget what manner of justification in the Spirit is this manifestation in the flesh : for the mystery which was manifested in the flesh, justified in the Spirit, seen of angels, preached among the nations, and believed on in this world, this same mystery was received up in glory. Thus is it in every way a mystery of great godliness, when it is manifested in the flesh, when it is justified in the Spirit, when it is seen of angels, when it is preached among the nations, when it is believed on in the world, and when it is received up in glory. The preaching follows the seeing, and the believing the preaching, and the consummation of all is the receiving up in glory : for the assumption into glory is the mystery of great godliness, and by faith in the Dispensation we are prepared to be received up, and to be conformed to the glory of the Lord. The assumption of flesh is there-

---

[6] St. John xx. 17.   [7] 1 Cor. xv. 27, 28.   [8] 1 Tim. iii. 16.

fore also the mystery of great godliness, for through the assumption of flesh the mystery was manifested in the flesh. But we must believe that the manifestation in the flesh also is this same mystery of great godliness, for His manifestation in the flesh is His justification in the Spirit, and His assumption into glory. And now what room does our faith leave for any to think that the secret of the Dispensation of godliness is the enfeebling of the divinity, when through the assumption of glory is to be confessed the mystery of great godliness? What was 'infirmity' is now the 'mystery:' what was 'necessity' becomes 'godliness[9].' And now let us turn to the meaning of the Evangelist's words, that the secret of our salvation and our glory may not be converted into an occasion of blasphemy.

10. You credit with the weight of irresistible authority, heretic, that saying of the Lord, *I ascend to My Father and your Father, and My God and your God*[1]. The same Father, you say, is His Father and ours, the same God His God and ours. He partakes, therefore, of our weakness, for in the possession of the same Father we are not inferior as sons, and in the service of the same God we are equal as servants. Since, then, we are of created origin and a servant's nature, but have a common Father and God with Him, He is in common with our nature a creature and a servant. So runs this infatuated and unhallowed teaching. It produces also the words of the Prophet, *Thy God hath anointed Thee, O God*, to prove that Christ does not partake of that glorious nature which belongs to God, since the God Who anoints Him is preferred before Him as His God[2].

11. We do not know Christ the God unless we know God the Begotten. But to be born God is to belong to the nature of God, for the name Begotten signifies indeed the manner of His origin, but does not make Him different in kind from the Begetter. And if so, the Begotten owes indeed to His Author the source of His being, but is not dispossessed of the nature of that Author, for the birth of God can arise but from one origin, and have but one nature. If its origin is not from God, it is not a birth; if it is anything but a birth, Christ is not God. But He *is* God of God, and therefore God the Father stands to God the Son as God of His birth and Father of His nature, for the birth of God is from God, and in the specific nature of God.

12. See in all that He said, how carefully the Lord tempers the pious acknowledgment of His debt, so that neither the confession of the birth could be held to reflect upon His divinity, nor His reverent obedience to infringe upon His sovereign nature. He does not withhold the homage due from Him as the Begotten, Who owed to His Author His very existence, but He manifests by His confident bearing the consciousness of participation in that nature, which belongs to Him by virtue of the origin whereby He was born as God. Take, for instance, the words, *He that hath seen Me, hath seen the Father also*[3], and, *The words that I say, I speak not from Myself*[4]. He does not speak from Himself: therefore He receives from His Author that which He says. But if any have seen Him, they have seen the Father also: they are conscious, by this evidence, given to shew that God is in Him, that a nature, one in kind with that of God, was born from God to subsist as God. Take again the words, *That which the Father hath given unto Me, is greater than all*[5], and, *I and the Father are one*[6]. To say that the Father gave, is a confession that He received His origin: but the unity of Himself with the Father is a property of His nature derived from that origin. Take another instance, *He hath given all judgment unto the Son, that all may honour the Son even as they honour the Father*[7]. He acknowledges that the judgment is given to Him, and therefore He does not put His birth in the background: but He claims equal honour with the Father, and therefore He does not resign His nature. Yet another example, *I am in the Father, and the Father is in Me*[8], and, *The Father is greater than I*[9]. The One is in the Other: recognise, then, the divinity of God, the Begotten of God: the Father is greater than He: perceive, then, His acknowledgment of the Father's authority. In the same way He says, *The Son can do nothing of Himself but what He hath seen the Father doing: for what things soever He doeth, these the Son also doeth in like manner*[1]. He doeth nothing of Himself: that is, in accordance with His birth the Father prompts His actions: yet what things soever the Father doeth, these the Son also doeth in like manner; that is, He subsists as nothing less than God, and by the Father's omnipotent nature residing in Him, can do all that God the Father does. All is uttered in agreement with His unity of Spirit with the Father, and the properties of that nature,

---

9 i.e. the Incarnation is the Mystery of godliness, not the infirmity of necessity.
1 St. John xx. 17.
2 Ps. xlv. 7. The general reading is, "Therefore God, thy God, &c." (R.V.).

3 St. John xiv. 9.   4 Ib. 10.   5 Ib. x. 29.
6 Ib. 30.   7 Ib. v. 22, 23.   8 Ib. xiv. 11 ; cf. x. 38.
9 Ib. xiv. 28.   1 Ib. v. 19.

which He possesses by virtue of His birth. That birth, which brought Him into being, constituted Him divine, and His being reveals the consciousness of that divine nature. God the Son confesses God His Father, because He was born of Him; but also, because He was born, He inherits the whole nature of God.

13. So the Dispensation of the great and godly mystery makes Him, Who was already Father of the divine Son, also His Lord in the created form which He assumed, for He, Who was in the form of God, was found also in the form of a servant. Yet He was not a servant, for according to the Spirit He was God the Son of God. Every one will agree also that there is no servant where there is no lord. God is indeed Father in the Generation of the Only-begotten God, but only in the case that the Other is a servant can we call Him Lord as well as Father. The Son was not at the first a servant by nature, but afterwards began to be by nature something which He was not before. Thus the Father is Lord on the same grounds as the Son is servant. By the Dispensation of His nature the Son had a Lord, when He made Himself a servant by the assumption of manhood.

14. Being, then, in the form of a servant, Jesus Christ, Who before was in the form of God, said as a man, *I ascend to My Father and your Father, and My God and your God.* He was speaking as a servant to servants: how can we then dissociate the words from Christ the servant, and transfer them to that nature, which had nothing of the servant in it? For He Who abode in the form of God took upon Him the form of a servant, this form being the indispensable condition of His fellowship as a servant with servants. It is in this sense that God is His Father and the Father of men, His God and the God of servants. Jesus Christ was speaking as a man in the form of a servant to men and servants; what difficulty is there then in the idea, that in His human aspect the Father is His Father as ours, in His servant's nature God is His God as all men's?

15. These, then, are the words with which He prefaces the message, *Go unto My brethren, and say to them, I ascend unto My Father and your Father, and My God and your God.* I ask, Are they to be understood as His brethren with reference to the form of God or to the form of a servant? And has our flesh kinship with Him in regard to the fulness of the Godhead dwelling in Him, that we should be reckoned His brothers in respect of His divinity? No, for the Spirit of prophecy recognises clearly in what respect we

are the brethren of the Only-begotten God. It is as *a worm and no man* [2] that He says, *I will declare Thy name unto My brethren* [3]. As a worm, which is born without the ordinary process of conception, or else comes up into the world, already living, from the depths of the earth, He speaks here in manifestation of the fact that He had assumed flesh and also brought it up, living, from Hades. Throughout the Psalm He is foretelling by the Spirit of prophecy the mysteries of His Passion: it is therefore in respect of the Dispensation, in which He suffered, that He has brethren. The Apostle also recognises the mystery of this brotherhood, for he calls Him not only the firstborn from the dead [4], but also the firstborn among many brethren [5]. Christ is the Firstborn among many brethren in the same sense in which He is Firstborn from the dead: and as the mystery of death concerns His body, so the mystery of brotherhood also refers to His flesh. Thus God has brethren according to His flesh, for the Word became flesh and dwelt amongst us [6]: but the Only-begotten Son, unique as the Only-begotten, has no brethren.

16. By assuming flesh, however, He acquired our nature in our totality, and became all that we are, but did not lose that which He was before. Both before by His heavenly origin, and now by His earthly constitution, God is His Father. By His earthly constitution God is His Father, since all things are from God the Father, and God is Father to all things, since from Him and in Him are all things. But to the Only-begotten God, God is Father, not only because the Word became flesh; His Fatherhood extends also to Him Who was, as God the Word, with God in the beginning. Thus, when the Word became flesh, God was His Father both by the birth of God the Word, and by the constitution of His flesh: for God is the Father of all flesh, though not in the same way that He is Father to God the Word. But God the Word, though He did not cease to be God, really did become flesh: and while He thus dwelt He was still truly the Word, just as when the Word became flesh He was still truly God as well as man. For to 'dwell' can only be said of one who abides in something: and to 'become flesh' of one who is born. He dwelt among us; that is, He assumed our flesh. The Word became flesh and dwelt among us; that is, He was God in the reality of our body. If Christ Jesus, the man according to the flesh, robbed God the Word of the divine nature, or was

---

[2] Ps. xxii. 6.   [3] Ib. 22.
[4] Col. i. 18.   [5] Rom. viii. 29.   [6] St. John i. 14.

not according to the mystery of godliness also God the Word, then it reduces His nature to our level that God is His Father, and our Father, His God and our God. But if God the Word, when He became the man Christ Jesus, did not cease to be God the Word, then God is at the same time His Father and ours, His God and ours, only in respect of that nature, by which the Word is our brother, and the message to His brethren, *I ascend unto My Father and your Father, and My God and your God*, is not that of the Only-begotten God the Word, but of the Word made flesh.

17. The Apostle here speaks in carefully guarded words, which by their definiteness can give no occasion to the ungodly. We have seen that the Evangelist makes the Lord use the word ' Brethren ' in the preface to the message, thus signifying that the whole message, being addressed to His brethren, refers to His fellowship in that nature which makes Him their brother. Thus he makes manifest that the mystery of godliness, which is here proclaimed, is no degradation of His divinity. The community with Him, by which God is our Father and His, our God and His, exists in regard to the Dispensation of the flesh : we are counted His brethren, because He was born into the body. No one disputes that God the Father is also the God of our Lord Jesus Christ, but this reverent confession offers no occasion for irreverence. God is His God, but not as possessing a different order of divinity from His. He was begotten God of the Father, and born a servant by the Dispensation : and so God is His Father because He is God of God, and God is His God, because He is flesh of the Virgin. All this the Apostle confirms in one short and decisive sentence, *Making mention of you in my prayers that the God of our Lord Jesus Christ, the Father of glory, may give unto you a spirit of wisdom and revelation* [7]. When he speaks of Him as Jesus Christ, he mentions His God : when his theme is the glory of Christ, he calls God His Father. To Christ, as having glory, God is Father : to Christ, as being Jesus, God is God. For the angel, when speaking of Christ the Lord, Who should be born of Mary, calls Him by the name ' Jesus [8] : ' but to the prophets Christ the Lord is ' Spirit [9].' The Apostle's words in this passage seem to many, on account of the Latin, somewhat obscure, for Latin has no articles, which the beautiful and logical usage of Greek employs. The Greek runs, ὁ Θεὸς τοῦ Κυρίου ἡμῶν Ἰησοῦ Χριστοῦ, ὁ πατὴρ τῆς δόξης, which we might translate into

Latin, if the usage of the article were permitted, ' Ille Deus illius Domini nostri Jesu Christi, ille pater illius claritatis ' (The God of the Lord [of us] Jesus Christ, the Father of the glory). In this form ' *The* God of *the* Jesus Christ,' and ' *the* Father of *the* glory,' the sentence expresses, so far as we can comprehend them, certain truths of His nature. Where the glory of Christ is concerned, God is His Father ; where Christ is Jesus, there the Father is His God. In the Dispensation by which He is a servant, He has as God Him Whom, in the glory by which He is God, He has as Father.

18. Time and the lapse of ages make no difference to a Spirit [1]. Christ is one and the same Christ, whether in the body, or abiding by the Spirit in the prophets. Speaking through the mouth of the holy Patriarch David, He says, *Thy God, O God, hath anointed Thee with the oil of gladness above Thy fellows* [2], which refers to no less a mystery than the Dispensation of His assumption of flesh. He, Who now sends the message to His brethren that their Father is His Father, and their God His God, announced Himself then as anointed by His God above His fellows. No one is fellow to the Only-begotten Christ, God the Word : but we know that we are His fellows by the assumption which made Him flesh. That anointing did not exalt the blessed and incorruptible Begotten Who abides in the nature of God, but it established the mystery of His body, and sanctified the manhood which He assumed. To this the Apostle Peter witnesses, *Of a truth in this city were they gathered together against Thy holy Son Jesus, Whom Thou didst anoint* [3] : and on another occasion, *Ye know that the saying was published through all Judæa, beginning from Galilee, after the baptism which John preached : even Jesus of Nazareth, how that God anointed Him with the Holy Ghost and with power* [4]. Jesus was anointed, therefore, that the mystery of the regeneration of flesh might be accomplished. Nor are we left in doubt how He was thus anointed with the Spirit of God and with power, when we listen to the Father's voice, as it spoke when He came up out of the Jordan, *Thou art My Son, this day have I begotten Thee* [5]. Thus is testified the sanctification of His flesh, and in this testimony we must recognise His anointing with the power of the Spirit.

---

7 Eph. i. 16, 17.   8 St. Matt. i. 21 ; St. Luke i. 31.   9 i.e. divine.

1 By ' Spirit' Hilary means God considered as a spiritual (as opposed to a material) Being : cf. in the previous chapter, " to the prophets Christ the Lord is ' Spirit.'"   2 Ps. xlv. 7.   3 Acts iv. 27.   4 Ib. x. 37, 38.   5 Ps. ii. 7. The last words occur neither in St. Matt. (iii. 17), nor St. Mark (i. 11), nor St. Luke (iii. 22) : but there is evidence of the existence of such a reading. See Tischendorf, *Nov. Test. Græc.*, on St. Matt. iii. 17, and St. Luke iii. 22.

19. But the Word was God, and with God in the beginning, and therefore the anointing could neither be related nor explained, if it referred to that nature, of which we are told nothing, except that it was in the beginning And in fact He Who was God had no need to anoint Himself with the Spirit and power of God, when He was Himself the Spirit and power of God. So He, being God, was anointed by His God *above His fellows*. And, although there were many Christs (i.e. anointed persons) according to the Law before the Dispensation of the flesh, yet Christ, Who was anointed above His fellows, came *after* them, for He was preferred above His anointed fellows. Accordingly, the words of the prophecy bring out the fact that the anointing took place in time, and comparatively late in time. *Thou hast loved righteousness and hated iniquity: therefore Thy God, O God, hath anointed Thee with the oil of gladness above Thy fellows.* Now, a fact which follows later upon other facts, cannot be dated before them. That a reward be deserved postulates as a prior condition the existence of one who can deserve it, for merit earned implies that there has been one capable of acquiring it. If, therefore, we attribute the birth of the Only-begotten God to this anointing, which is His reward for loving righteousness and hating iniquity, we shall be regarding Him not as born, but as promoted by unction, to be the Only-begotten God. But then we imply that He advanced with gradual progress and promotion to perfect divinity, and that He was not born God, but afterwards for His merit anointed God. Thus we shall make Christ as God Himself conditioned, whereas He is the final cause of all conditions; and what becomes then of the Apostle's words, *All things are through Him and in Him, and He is before all, and in Him all things consist* [6]? The Lord Jesus Christ was not deified because of anything, or by means of anything, but was born God: God by origin, not promoted to divinity for any cause after His birth, but as the Son; and one in kind with God because begotten of Him. His anointing then, though it is the result of a cause, did not enhance that in Him, which could not be made more perfect. It concerned that part of Him which was to be made perfect through the perfection of the Mystery: that is, our manhood was sanctified in Christ by unction. If then the prophet here also teaches us the dispensation of the servant, for which Christ is anointed by His God above His fellows, and that because

He loved righteousness and hated iniquity, then surely the words of the prophet must refer to that nature in Christ, by which He has fellows through His assumption of flesh. Can we doubt this when we note how carefully the Spirit of prophecy chooses His words? God is anointed by His God; that is, in His own nature He is God, but in the dispensation of the anointing God is His God. God is anointed: but tell me, is that Word anointed, Who was God in the beginning? Manifestly not, for the anointing comes after His divine birth. It was then not the begotten Word, God with God in the beginning, Who was anointed, but that nature in God which came to Him through the dispensation later than His divinity [7]: and when His God anointed Him, He anointed in Him the whole nature of the servant, which He assumed in the mystery of His flesh.

20. Let no one then defile with his godless interpretations the mystery of great godliness which was manifested in the flesh, or reckon himself equal to the Only-begotten in respect of His divine substance. Let Him be our brother and our fellow, inasmuch as the Word made flesh dwelt among us, inasmuch as the man Jesus Christ is Mediator between God and man. Let Him, after the manner of servants, have a common Father and a common God with us, and as anointed above His fellows, let Him be of the same nature as His anointed fellows, though His be an unction of special privilege. In the mystery of the Mediatorship let Him be at once very man and very God, Himself God of God, but having a common Father and God with us in that community by which He is our brother.

21. But perhaps that subjection, that delivering of the kingdom, and lastly that end betoken the dissolution of His nature, or the loss of His power, or the enfeebling of His divinity. Many argue thus: Christ is included in the common subjection of all to God, and by the condition of subjection loses His divinity: He surrenders His Kingdom, therefore He is no longer King: the end which overtakes Him entails as its consequence the loss of His power.

22. It will not be out of place here if we review the full meaning of the Apostle's teaching upon this subject. Let us take, then, each single sentence and expound it, that we may grasp the entire Mystery by comprehending it in its fulness. The words of the Apostle are, *For since by man came death, by man came*

---

6 Col. i. 16, 17.

7 Reading 'quam' instead of quâ.

also the resurrection of the dead. For as in Adam all die, so also in Christ are all made alive. But each in his own order: Christ the firstfruits, then they that are Christ's at His coming. Then cometh the end, when He shall have delivered the Kingdom to God, even the Father, when He shall have emptied all authority and all power. For He must reign until He put all enemies under His feet. The last enemy that shall be conquered is death. But when He saith, All things are put in subjection, He is excepted Who did subject all things unto Him. But when all things have been subjected to Him, then shall He also Himself be subjected to Him, that did subject all things unto Him, that God may be all in all [8].

23. The Apostle who was chosen not of men nor through man, but through Jesus Christ, to be the teacher of the Gentiles [9], expounds in language as express as he can command the secrets of the heavenly Dispensations. He who had been caught up into the third heaven and had heard unspeakable words [1], reveals to the perception of human understanding as much as human nature can receive. But he does not forget that there are things which cannot be understood in the moment of hearing. The infirmity of man needs time to review before the true and perfect tribunal of the mind, that which is poured indiscriminately into the ears. Comprehension follows the spoken words more slowly than hearing, for it is the ear which hears, but the reason which understands, though it is God Who reveals the inner meaning to those who seek it. We learn this from the words written among many other exhortations to Timothy, the disciple instructed from a babe in the Holy Scriptures by the glorious faith of his grandmother and mother [2]: *Understand what I say, for the Lord shall give thee understanding in all things* [3]. The exhortation to understand is prompted by the difficulty of understanding. But God's gift of understanding is the reward of faith, for through faith the infirmity of sense is recompensed with the gift of revelation. Timothy, that 'man of God' as the Apostle witnesses of him [4], Paul's true child in the faith [5], is exhorted to understand because the Lord will give him understanding in all things: let us, therefore, knowing that the Lord will grant us understanding in all things, remember that the Apostle exhorts us also to understand.

24. And if, by an error incident to human nature, we be clinging to some preconception of our own, let us not reject the advance in knowledge through the gift of revelation. If we have hitherto used only our own judgment, let that not make us ashamed to change its decisions for the better. Guiding this advance wisely and carefully, the same blessed Apostle writes to the Philippians, *Let us therefore as many as be perfect, be thus minded: and if in anything ye are otherwise minded, this also shall God reveal unto you. Only, wherein we have hastened, in that same let us walk* [6]. Reason cannot anticipate with preconceptions the revelation of God. For the Apostle has here shewn us wherein consists the wisdom of those who have the perfect wisdom, and for those who are otherwise minded, he awaits the revelation of God, that they may obtain the perfect wisdom. If any, then, have otherwise conceived this profound dispensation of the hidden knowledge, and if that which we offer them is in any respect more right or better approved, let them not be ashamed to receive the perfect wisdom, as the Apostle advises, through the revelation of God, and if they hate to abide in untruth let them not love ignorance more. If to them, who had another wisdom, God has revealed this also, the Apostle exhorts them to hasten on the road in which they have started, to cast aside the notions of their former ignorance, and obtain the revelation of perfect understanding by the path into which they have eagerly entered. Let us, therefore, keep on in the path along which we have hastened: or, if the error of our wandering steps has delayed our eager haste, let us, notwithstanding, start again through the revelation of God towards the goal of our desire, and not turn our feet from the path. We have hastened towards Christ Jesus the Lord of Glory, the King of the eternal ages, in Whom are restored all things in Heaven and in earth, by Whom all things consist, in Whom and with Whom we shall abide for ever. So long as we walk in this path we have the perfect wisdom: and if we have another wisdom, God will reveal to us what is the perfect wisdom. Let us, then, examine in the light of the Apostle's faith the mystery of the words before us: and let our treatment be, as it always has been, a refutation from the actual truth of the Apostle's confession of every interpretation, which they would profanely foist upon his words.

25. Three assertions are here disputed, which, in the order in which the Apostle makes them, are first the end, then the delivering, and lastly the subjection. The object is to prove that Christ ceases to exist at the

8 1 Cor. xv. 21—28.   9 Cf. Gal. i. 1.
1 Cf. 2 Cor. xii. 2, 4.   2 Cf. 2 Tim. i. 5 ; iii. 15.
3 2 Tim. ii. 7.   4 1 Tim. v.. 11.   5 Ib. i. 2.

6 Phil. iii. 15, 16.

end, that He loses His kingdom, when He delivers it up, that He strips Himself of the divine nature, when He is subjected to God.

26. At the outset take note that this is not the order of the Apostle's teaching, for in that order the surrender of the Kingdom is first, then the subjection, and lastly the end. But every cause is itself the result of its particular cause, so that, in every chain of causation, each cause, itself producing a result, has inevitably its underlying antecedent. Thus the end will come, but when He has delivered the Kingdom to God. He will deliver the Kingdom, but when He has abolished all authority and power. He will abolish all authority and power, because He must reign. He will reign until He has put all enemies under His feet. He will put all enemies under His feet, because God has subjected everything under His feet. God has so subjected them as to make death the last enemy to be conquered by Him. Then, when all things are subjected unto God. except Him Who subjected all things unto Him, He too will be subjected unto Him, Who subjects all to Himself. But the cause of the subjection is none other than that God may be all in all; and therefore the end is that God is all in all.

27. Before going any further we must now enquire whether the end is a dissolution, or the delivering a forfeiture, or the subjection an enfeebling of Christ. And if we find that these are contraries, which cannot be connected as causes and effects, we shall be able to understand the words in the true sense in which they were spoken.

28. *Christ is the end of the law*[7]; but, tell me, is He come to destroy it or to fulfil it? And if Christ, the end of the law, does not destroy it, but fulfils it (as He says, *I am come not to destroy the law but to fulfil it*[8]), is not the end of the law, so far from being its dissolution, the very opposite, namely its final perfection? All things are advancing towards an end, but that end is a condition of rest in the perfection, which is the goal of their advance, and not their abolition. Further, all things exist for the sake of the end, but the end itself is not the means to anything beyond: it is an ultimate, all-embracing whole, which rests in itself. And because it is self-contained, and works for no other time or object than itself, the goal is always that to which our hopes are directed. Therefore the Lord exhorts us to wait with patient and reverent faith until the end comes: *Blessed is He that endureth to the end*[9]. It is not a blessed dissolution, which awaits us,

nor is non-existence the fruit, and annihilation the appointed reward of faith : but the end is the final attainment of the promised blessedness, and they are blessed who endure until the goal of perfect happiness is reached, when the expectation of faithful hope has no object beyond. Their end is to abide with unbroken rest in that condition, towards which they are pressing. Similarly, as a deterrent, the Apostle warns us of the end of the wicked, *Whose end is perdition, ... but our expectation is in heaven*[1]. Suppose then we interpret the end as a dissolution, we are forced to acknowledge that, since there is an end for the blessed and for the wicked, the issue levels the godly with the ungodly, for the appointed end of both is a common annihilation. What of our expectation in heaven, if for us as well as for the wicked the end is a cessation of being? But even if there remains for the saints an expectation, whereas for the wicked there waits the end they have deserved, we cannot conceive that end as a final dissolution. What punishment would it be for the wicked to be beyond the feeling of avenging torments, because the capability of suffering has been removed by dissolution? The end is, therefore, a culminating and irrevocable condition which awaits us, reserved for the blessed and prepared for the wicked.

29. We can therefore no longer doubt that by the end is meant an ultimate and final condition and not a dissolution. We shall have something more to say upon this subject, when we come to the explanation of this passage, but for the present this is enough to make our meaning clear. Let us, therefore, turn now to the delivering of the Kingdom, and see whether it means a surrender of rule, whether the Son by delivering ceases to possess that which He delivers to the Father. If this is what the wicked contend in their unreasoning infatuation, they must allow that the Father, by delivering, lost all, when He delivered all to the Son, if delivery implies the surrender of that which is delivered. For the Lord said, *All things have been delivered unto Me of My Father*[2], and again, *All authority hath been given unto Me in heaven and earth*[3]. If, therefore, to deliver is to yield possession, the Father no longer possessed that which He delivered. But if the Father did not cease to possess that which He delivered, neither does the Son surrender that which He delivers. Therefore, if He did not lose by the delivering that which He delivered, we must recognise that only the Dispensation explains how the

---

7 Rom. x. 4. 8 St. Matt. v. 17.
9 St. Matt. x. 22 ; cf. St. Mark xiii 13.

1 Phil. iii. 19, 20. The Greek paraphrased 'expectation,' is πολίτευμα, 'citizenship' (R.V.), or 'commonwealth' (marg.).
2 St. Luke x. 22. 3 St. Matt. xxviii. 18.

Father still possesses what He delivered, and the Son does not forfeit what He gave.

30. As to the subjection, there are other facts which come to the help of our faith, and prevent us from putting an indignity on Christ upon this score, but above all this passage contains its own defence. First, however, I appeal to common reason : is the subjection still to be understood as the subordination of servitude to lordship, weakness to power, meanness to honour, qualities the opposite of one another ? Is the Son in this manner subjected to the Father by the distinction of a different nature ? If, indeed, we would think so, we shall find in the Apostle's words a preventive for such errors of the imagination. When all things are subjected to Him, says He, then must He be subjected to Him, Who subjects all things to Himself; and by this 'then' he means to denote the temporal Dispensation. For if we put any other construction on the subjection, Christ, though then to be subjected, is not subjected now, and thus we make Him an insolent and impious rebel, whom the necessity of time, breaking as it were and subduing His profane and overweening pride, will reduce to a tardy obedience. But what does He Himself say ? *I am not come to do Mine own will, but the will of Him that sent Me*[4]: and again, *Therefore hath the Father loved Me because I do all things that are pleasing unto Him*[5]*:* and, *Father, Thy will be done*[6]. Or hear the Apostle, *He humbled Himself, becoming obedient even unto death*[7]. Although He humbled Himself, His nature knew no humiliation : though He was obedient, it was a voluntary obedience, for He became obedient by humbling Himself. The Only-begotten God humbled Himself, and obeyed His Father even to the death of the Cross : but as what, as man or as God, is He to be subjected to the Father, when all things have been subjected to Him ? Of a truth this subjection is no sign of a fresh obedience, but the Dispensation of the Mystery, for the allegiance is eternal, the subjection an event within time. The subjection is then in its signification simply a demonstration of the Mystery.

31. What that is must be understood in view of this same hope of our faith. We cannot be ignorant that the Lord Jesus Christ rose again from the dead, and sits at the right hand of God, for we have also the witness of the Apostle, *According to the working of the strength of His might, which He wrought in Christ, when He raised Him from the dead, and made Him to sit at His right hand in the heavenly places above all rule and authority and power and dominion, and every name that is named not only in this world but also in that which is to come, and put all things in subjection under His feet*[8]. The language of the Apostle, as befits the power of God, speaks of the future as already past : for that which is to be wrought by the completion of time already exists in Christ, in Whom is all fulness, and 'future' refers only to the temporal order of the Dispensation, not to a new development. Thus, God has put all things under His feet, though they are still to be subjected. By their subjection, conceived as already past, is expressed the immutable power of Christ : by their subjection, as future, is signified their consummation at the end of the ages as the result of the fulness of time.

32. The meaning of the abolishing of every power which is against Him is not obscure. The prince of the air, the power of spiritual wickedness, shall be delivered to eternal destruction, as Christ says, *Depart from Me, ye cursed, into the eternal fire which My Father hath prepared for the devil and his angels*[9]. The abolishing is not the same as the subjecting. To abolish the power of the enemy is to sweep away for ever his prerogative of power, so that by the abolition of his power is brought to an end the rule of his kingdom. Of this the Lord testifies when He says, *My kingdom is not of this world*[1] : as He had once before testified that the ruler of that kingdom is the prince of the world, whose power shall be destroyed by the abolition of the rule of His kingdom[2]. A subjection, on the other hand, which implies obedience and allegiance, is a proof of submission and mutability.

33. So when their authority is abolished, His enemies shall be subjected : and so subjected, that He shall subject them to Himself. Moreover He shall so subject them to Himself, that God shall subject them to Him. Was the Apostle ignorant, think you, of the force of these words in the Gospel, *No one cometh to Me, except the Father draw Him to Me*[3] which stand side by side with those other words, *No one cometh unto the Father but by Me*[4]: just as in this Epistle Christ subjects His enemies to Himself, yet God subjects them to Him, and He witnesses throughout this, his work of subjection, that God is working in Him? Except through Him there is no approach to the Father, but there is also no approach to Him, unless the Father draw

---

4 St. John vi. 38.   5 Cf. ib. viii. 29.
6 Cf. St. Matt. xxvi. 39, 42; St. Mark xiv. 36; St. Luke xxii. 42.   7 Phil. ii. 8.

8 Eph. i. 19 b—22 a.   9 St. Matt. xxv. 41.
1 St. John xviii. 36.
2 Ib. xvi. 11. "The prince of this world hath been judged."
3 Ib. vi. 44   4 Ib. xiv. 6.

us. Understanding Him to be the Son of God, we recognise in Him the true nature of the Father. Hence, when we learn to know the Son, God the Father calls us: when we believe the Son, God the Father receives us; for our recognition and knowledge of the Father is in the Son, Who shews us in Himself God the Father, Who draws us, if we be devout, by His fatherly love into a mutual bond with His Son. So then the Father draws us, when, as the first condition, He is acknowledged Father: but no one comes to the Father except through the Son, because we cannot know the Father, unless faith in the Son is active in us, since we cannot approach the Father in worship, unless we first adore the Son, while if we know the Son, the Father draws us to eternal life and receives us. But each result is the work of the Son, for by the preaching of the Father, Whom the Son preaches, the Father brings us to the Son, and the Son leads us to the Father. The statement of this Mystery was necessary for the more perfect understanding of the present passage, to shew that through the Son the Father draws us and receives us; that we might understand the two aspects, the Son subjecting all to Himself, and the Father subjecting all to Him. Through the birth the nature of God is abiding in the Son, and does that which He Himself does. What He does God does, but what God does in Him, He Himself does: in the sense that where He acts Himself we must believe the Son of God acts; and where God acts, we must perceive the properties of the Father's nature existing in Him as the Son.

34. When authorities and powers are abolished, His enemies shall be subjected under His feet. The same Apostle tells who are these enemies, *As touching the Gospel they are enemies for your sakes, but as touching the election they are beloved for the fathers' sake* [5]. We remember that they are enemies of the cross of Christ; let us remember also that, because they are beloved for the fathers' sake, they are reserved for the subjection, as the Apostle says, *I would not, brethren, have you ignorant of this mystery, lest ye be wise in your own conceits, that a hardening in part hath befallen Israel, until the fulness of the Gentiles be come in, and so all Israel shall be saved, even as it is written, There shall come out of Sion a Deliverer, and shall turn away ungodliness from Jacob: and this is the covenant from Me to them, when I have taken away their sins* [6]. So His enemies shall be subjected under His feet.

35. But we must not forget what follows the subjection, namely, *Last of all is death conquered by Him* [7]. This victory over death is nothing else than the resurrection from the dead: for when the corruption of death is stayed, the quickened and now heavenly nature is made eternal, as it is written, *For this corruptible must put on incorruption, and this mortal must put on immortality. But when this mortal shall have put on immortality, then shall come to pass the saying that is written, Death is swallowed up in strife. O death, where is thy sting? O death, where is thy strife* [8]? In the subjection of His enemies death is conquered; and, death conquered, life immortal follows. The Apostle tells us also of the special reward attained by this subjection which is made perfect by the subjection of belief: *Who shall fashion anew the body of our humiliation, that it may be conformed to the body of His glory, according to the works of His power, whereby He is able to subject all things to Himself* [9]. There is then another subjection, which consists in a transition from one nature to another, for our nature ceases, so far as its present character is concerned, and is subjected to Him, into Whose form it passes. But by 'ceasing' is implied not an end of being, but a promotion into something higher. Thus our nature by being merged into the image of the other nature which it receives, becomes subjected through the imposition of a new form.

36. Hence the Apostle, to make his explanation of this Mystery complete, after saying that death is the last enemy to be conquered, adds: *But when He saith, All things are put in subjection except Him, Who did subject all things to Him, then must He be subjected to Him, that did subject all things to Him, that God may be all in all* [1]. The first step of the Mystery is that all things are subjected to Him: then He is subjected to Him, Who subjects all things to Himself. As we are subjected to the glory of the rule of His body, so He also, reigning in the glory of His body, is by the same Mystery in turn subjected to Him, Who subjects all things to Himself. And we are subjected to the glory of His body, that we may share that splendour with which He reigns in the body, since we shall be conformed to His body.

37. Nor are the Gospels silent concerning the glory of His present reigning body. It is written that the Lord said, *Verily, I say unto you, there be some of them that stand here, which*

---

5 Rom. xi. 28. 6 Ib. 25—27.

7 Cf. 1 Cor. xv. 26.
8 Ib. 53—55. The reading 'strife' instead of 'victory' arose from the confusion of νεῖκος (= strife) and νῖκος (= victory) in the original Greek.
9 Phil. iii. 21. 1 1 Cor. xv. 27, 28.

shall not taste of death till they see the Son of Man coming in His Kingdom. And it came to pass, after six days Jesus taketh with Him Peter and James and John His brother, and bringeth them up into a high mountain apart. And Jesus was transfigured before them, and His face did shine as the sun, and His garments became as snow [2]. Thus was shewn to the Apostles the glory of the body of Christ coming into His Kingdom: for in the fashion of His glorious Transfiguration, the Lord stood revealed in the splendour of His reigning body.

38. He promised also to the Apostles the participation in this His glory. *So shall it be in the end of the world. The Son of Man shall send forth His angels, and they shall gather together out of His Kingdom all things that cause stumbling, and them that do iniquity, and He shall send them into the furnace of fire: there shall be the weeping and gnashing of teeth. Then shall the righteous shine forth as the sun in the Kingdom of their Father. He that hath ears to hear, let him hear* [3]. Were their natural and bodily ears closed to the hearing of the words, that the Lord should need to admonish them to hear? Yet the Lord, hinting at the knowledge of the Mystery, commands them to listen to the doctrine of the faith. In the end of the world all things that cause stumbling shall be removed from His Kingdom. We see the Lord then reigning in the splendour of His body, until the things that cause stumbling are removed. And we see ourselves, in consequence, conformed to the glory of His body in the Kingdom of the Father, shining as with the splendour of the sun, the splendour in which He shewed the fashion of His Kingdom to the Apostles, when He was transfigured on the mountain.

39. He shall deliver the Kingdom to God the Father, not in the sense that He resigns His power by the delivering, but that we, being conformed to the glory of His body, shall form the Kingdom of God. It is not said, *He shall deliver up His Kingdom*, but, *He shall deliver up the Kingdom* [4], that is, deliver up to God us who have been made the Kingdom by the glorifying of His body. He shall deliver us into the Kingdom, as it is said in the Gospel, *Come, ye blessed of My Father, inherit the Kingdom prepared for you from the foundation of the world* [5]. The just shall shine like the sun in the Kingdom of their Father, and the Son shall deliver to the Father, as His Kingdom, those whom He has called into His Kingdom, to whom also He has promised the blessedness of this Mystery, *Blessed are the*

pure in heart, for they shall see God [6]. While He reigns, He shall remove all things that cause stumbling, and then the just shall shine as the sun in the Kingdom of the Father. Afterwards He shall deliver the Kingdom to the Father, and those whom He has handed to the Father, as the Kingdom, shall see God. He Himself witnesses to the Apostles what manner of Kingdom this is: *The Kingdom of God is within you* [7]. Thus it is as King that He shall deliver up the Kingdom, and if any ask Who it is that delivers up the Kingdom, let him hear, *Christ is risen from the dead, the firstfruits of them that sleep; since by man came death, by man came also the resurrection of the dead* [8]. All that is said on the point before us concerns the Mystery of the body, since Christ is the firstfruits of the dead. Let us gather also from the words of the Apostle by what Mystery Christ rose from the dead: *Remember that Christ hath risen from the dead, of the seed of David* [9]. Here he teaches that the death and resurrection are due only to the Dispensation by which Christ was flesh.

40. In His body, the same body though now made glorious, He reigns until the authorities are abolished, death conquered, and His enemies subdued. This distinction is carefully preserved by the Apostle: the authorities and powers are *abolished*, the enemies are *subjected* [1]. Then, when they are subjected, He, that is the Lord, shall be subjected to Him that subjecteth all things to Himself, that God may be all in all [2], the nature of the Father's divinity imposing itself upon the nature of our body which was assumed. It is thus that God shall be all in all: according to the Dispensation He becomes by His Godhead and His manhood the Mediator between men and God, and so by the Dispensation He acquires the nature of flesh, and by the subjection shall obtain the nature of God in all things, so as to be God not in part, but wholly and entirely. The end of the subjection is then simply that God may be all in all, that no trace of the nature of His earthly body may remain in Him. Although before this time the two were combined within Him, He must now become God only; not, however, by casting off the body, but by translating it through subjection; not by losing it through dissolution, but by transfiguring it in glory: adding humanity to His divinity, not divesting Himself of divinity by His humanity. And He is subjected, not that He may cease to be, but that God may be all in all, having, in the mystery of the subjection, to continue to be

---

2 St. Matt. xvi. 28—xvii. 2.   3 Ib. xiii. 40—43.
4 1 Cor. xv. 24.   5 St. Matt. xxv. 34.
6 St. Matt. v. 8.   7 St. Luke xvii. 21.   8 1 Cor. xv. 20, 21.
9 2 Tim. ii. 8.   1 1 Cor. xv. 24, 25.   2 Ib. 28.

that which He no longer is [3], not having by dissolution to be robbed of Himself, that is, to be deprived of His being.

41. We have a sufficient and sacred guarantee for this belief in the authority of the Apostle. Through the Dispensation, and within time, the Lord Jesus Christ, the firstfruits of them that sleep, is to be subjected, that God may be all in all, and this subjection is not the debasement of His divinity, but the promotion of His assumed nature, for He Who is God and Man is now altogether God. But some may think that, when we say He was both glorified in the body whilst reigning in the body, and is hereafter to be subjected that God may be all in all, our belief finds no support for itself in the Gospels nor yet in the Epistles. We will, therefore, produce testimony of our faith, not only from the words of the Apostle, but also from our Lord's mouth. We will shew that Christ said first with His own lips what He afterwards said by the mouth of Paul.

42. Does He not reveal to His Apostles the Dispensation of this glory by the express signification of the words, *Now is the Son of Man glorified, and God is glorified in Him. If God hath been glorified in Him, God hath glorified Him in Himself, and straightway hath He glorified Him* [4]. In the words, *Now is the Son of Man honoured, and God is honoured in Him*, we have first the glory of the Son of Man, then the glory of God in the Son of Man. So there is first signified the glory of the body, which it borrows from its association with the divine nature : and then follows the promotion to a fuller glory derived from an addition to the glory of the body. *If God hath been honoured in Him, God hath honoured Him in Himself, and straightway hath God honoured Him.* God has glorified Him in Himself, because He has already been glorified in Him. *God was glorified in Him :* this refers to the glory of the body, for by this glory is expressed in a human body the glory of God, in the glory of the Son of Man is seen the divine glory. *God was glorified in Him, and therefore hath God glorified Him in Himself :* that is, by His promotion to the Godhead, whose glory was increased in Him, God has glorified Him in Himself. Already before this He was reigning in the glory which springs from the divine glory : from henceforth, however, He is Himself to pass into the divine glory. *God hath glorified Him in Himself :*

that is, in that nature by which God is what He is. *That God may be all in all :* that His whole being, leaving behind the Dispensation by which He is man, may be eternally transformed into divinity. Nor is the time of this hidden from us : *And God hath glorified Him in Himself, and straightway hath He glorified Him.* At the moment when Judas arose to betray Him, He signified as present the glory which He would obtain after His Passion through the Resurrection, but assigned to the future the glory with which God would glorify Him with Himself. The glory of God is seen in Him in the power of the Resurrection, but He Himself, out of the Dispensation of subjection, will be taken eternally into the glory of God, that is, into God, the all in all.

43. But what absurd folly is it of the heretics to regard as unattainable for God that goal to which man hopes to attain, to imply that He is powerless to effect in Himself that which He is mighty to effect in us. It is not the language of reason or common sense to say that God is bound by some necessity of His nature to consult our happiness, but cannot bestow the like blessings upon Himself. God does not, indeed, need any further blessedness, for His nature and power stand fast in their eternal perfection. But although in the Dispensation, that mystery of great godliness, He Who is God became man, He is not powerless to make Himself again entirely God, for without doubt He will transform us also into that which as yet we are not. The final sequel of man's life and death is the resurrection : the assured reward of our warfare is immortality and incorruption, not the ceaseless persistence of everlasting punishment, but the unbroken enjoyment and happiness of eternal glory. These bodies of earthly origin shall be exalted to the fashion of a higher nature, and conformed to the glory of the Lord's body. But what then of God found in the form of a servant ? Though already, while still in the form of a servant, glorified in the body, shall He not be also conformed to God? Shall He bestow upon us the form of His glorified body, and yet be able to do for His own body nothing more than He does for Himself in common with us ? For the most part the heretics interpret the words, *Then shall He be subjected to Him that did subject all things to Himself, that God may be all in all*, as if they meant that the Son is to be subjected to God the Father, in order that by the subjection of the Son, God the Father may be all in all. But is there still lacking in God some perfection which He is to obtain by the subjection of the Son ? Can they believe that God does not already possess that final accession

---

[3] The humanity is eternal, although He is no longer man.

[4] St. John xiii. 31, 32. There is another reading in the text of Hilary, *glorificabit*, "shall glorify Him in Himself," and though it is not well supported by MS. authority, and in ix. 40 all the MSS. agree in the perfect *honorificavit*, the future is favoured by the last two sentences of this chapter. The variation between *honoured* and *glorified* shews the confusion of texts which preceded the Vulgate and caused it to be welcomed.

of blessed divinity, because it is said that by the coming of the fulness of time He shall be made all in all?

44. To me, who hold that God cannot be known except by devotion, even to answer such objections seems no less unholy than to support them. What presumption to suppose that words can adequately describe His nature, when thought is often too deep for words, and His nature transcends even the conceptions of thought! What blasphemy even to discuss whether anything is lacking in God, whether He is Himself full, or it remains for Him to be fuller than His fulness! If God, Who is Himself the source of His own eternal divinity, were capable of progress, that He should be greater to-day than yesterday, He could never reach the time when nothing would be wanting to Him, for the nature to which advance is still possible must always in its progress leave some ground ahead still untrodden: if it be subject to the law of progress, though always progressing it must always be susceptible of further progress. But to Him, Who abides in perfect fulness, Who for ever is, there is no fulness left by which He can be made more full, for perfect fulness cannot receive an accession of further fulness. And this is the attitude of thought in which reverence contemplates God, namely, that nothing is wanting to Him, that He is full.

45. But the Apostle does not neglect to say with what manner of confession we should bear witness of God. *O the depth of the riches both of the wisdom and of the knowledge of God! How unsearchable are His judgments, and His ways past tracing out! For who hath known the mind of the Lord? Or who hath been His counsellor? Or who hath first given to Him, and it shall be recompensed unto him?* For *of Him, and through Him, and in Him are all things. To Him be the glory for ever and ever* [5]. No earthly mind can define God, no understanding can penetrate with its perception to sound the depth of His wisdom. His judgments defy the searching scrutiny of His creatures: the trackless paths of His knowledge baffle the zeal of all pursuers. His ways are plunged in the depths of incomprehensibility: nothing can be fathomed or traced to the end in the things of God. No one has ever been taught to know His mind, no one besides Himself ever permitted to share His counsel. But all this applies to us men only, and not to Him, through Whom are all things, the *Angel of mighty Counsel* [6], Who said, *No one knoweth the Son save the Father: neither doth any one know the Father save the Son, and him*

to whom the Son hath willed to reveal Him [7]. It is to curb our own feeble intellect, when it strains itself to fathom the depth of the divine nature with its descriptions and definitions, that we must re-echo the language of the Apostle's exclamation, lest we should attempt by rash conjecture to snatch from God more than He has been pleased to reveal to us.

46. It is a recognised axiom of natural philosophy, that nothing falls within the scope of the senses unless it is subjected to their observation, as for instance an object placed before the eyes, or an event posterior to the birth of human sense and intelligence. The former we can see and handle, and therefore the mind is qualified to pass a verdict upon it, since it can be examined by the senses of touch and sight. The latter, which is an event in time, produced or constituted since the origin of man, falls within the limits in which the discerning sense may claim to pass judgment, since it is not prior in time to our perception and reason. For our sight cannot perceive the invisible, since it only distinguishes the seen; our reason cannot project itself into the time when it was not, because it can only judge of that, to which it is prior in time. And even within these limits, the infirmity which is bound up with its nature robs it of absolutely certain knowledge of the sequence of cause and effect. How much less then can it go back behind the time when it had its origin, and comprehend with its perception things which existed before it in the realms of eternity?

47. The Apostle then recognised that nothing can fall within our knowledge, except it be posterior in time to the faculty of sense. Accordingly when he had asserted the depth of the wisdom of God, the infinity of His inscrutable judgments, the secret of His unsearchable ways, the mystery of His unfathomable mind, the incomprehensibility of His uncommunicated counsel, he continued, *For who hath first given to Him, and it shall be recompensed unto him again? For of Him, and through Him, and in Him are all things.* The eternal God is neither subject to limitation, nor did human reason and intelligence exercise their functions before He had His being. His whole being is therefore a depth, which we can neither examine nor penetrate. We say His *whole* being, not to define it as limited, but to understand it in its unlimited boundlessness: because of no one has He received His being, no antecedent giver can claim service from Him in return for a gift bestowed: *for*

5 Rom. xi. 33—36.
6 Isai. ix. 6 in the LXX. and Old Latin.
7 St. Matt. xi. 27.

of Him and through Him and in Him are all things. He does not lack things that are of Him and through Him and in Him. The Source and Maker of all, Who contains all, Who is beyond all, does not need that which is within Him, the Creator His creatures, the Possessor His possessions. Nothing is prior to Him, nothing derived from any other than Him, nothing beyond Him. What element of fulness is still lacking in God, which time will supply to make Him all in all? Whence can He receive it, if outside Him is nothing, and while nothing is outside Him, He is eternally Himself? And if He is eternally Himself, and there is nothing outside Him, with what increase shall He be made full, by what addition shall He be made other than He is? Did He not say, *I am and I change not* [8]? What possibility is there of change in Him? What scope for progress? What is prior to eternity? What more divine than God? The subjection of the Son will not therefore make God to be all in all, nor will any cause perfect Him, from Whom and through Whom and in Whom are all causes. He remains God as He ever was, and He needs nothing further, for what He is, He is eternally of Himself and for Himself.

48. But neither is it necessary for the Only-begotten God that He should change. He is God, and that is the name of full and perfect divinity. For, as we said before, the meaning of the repeated glorifying, and the cause of the subjection is that God may be all in all: but it is a Mystery, not a necessity, that God is to be all in all. Christ abode in the form of God when He assumed the form of a servant, not being subjected to change, but emptying Himself; hiding within Himself, and remaining master of Himself though He was emptied. He constrained Himself even to the form and fashion of a man, lest the weakness of the assumed humility should not be able to endure the immeasurable power of His nature. His unbounded might contracted itself, until it could fulfil the duty of obedience even to the endurance of the body to which it was yoked. But since He was self-contained even when He emptied Himself, His authority suffered no diminution, for in the humiliation of the emptying He exercised within Himself the power of that authority which was emptied.

49. It is therefore for the promotion of us, the assumed humanity, that God shall be all in all. He Who was found in the form of a servant, though He was in the form of God, is now again to be confessed in the glory of God the Father: that is, without doubt He dwells in the form of God, in Whose glory He is to be confessed. All is therefore a dispensation only, and not a change of His nature; for He abides still in Him, in Whom He ever was. But there intervenes a new nature, which began in Him with His human birth, and so all that He obtains is on behalf of that nature which before was not God, since after the Mystery of the Dispensation God is all in all. It is, therefore, we who are the gainers, we who are promoted, for we shall be conformed to the glory of the body of God. Further the Only-begotten God, despite His human birth, is nothing less than God, Who is all in all. That subjection of the body, by which all that is fleshly in Him, is swallowed up into the spiritual nature, will make Him to be God and all in all, since He is Man also as well as God; and His humanity which advances towards this goal is ours also. We shall be promoted to a glory conformable to that of Him Who became Man for us, being renewed unto the knowledge of God, and created again in the image of the Creator, as the Apostle says, *Having put off the old man with his doings, and put on the new man, which is being renewed unto the knowledge of God, after the image of Him that created him* [9]. Thus is man made the perfect image of God. For, being conformed to the glory of the body of God, he is exalted to the image of the Creator, after the pattern assigned to the first man. Leaving sin and the old man behind, he is made a new man unto the knowledge of God, and arrives at the perfection of his constitution, since through the knowledge of his God he becomes the perfect image of God. Through godliness he is promoted to immortality, through immortality he shall live for ever as the image of his Creator.

---

[8] Mal. iii. 6.

[9] Col. iii. 9, 10.

BOOK XII.

1. At length, with the Holy Ghost speeding our way, we are approaching the safe, calm harbour of a firm faith. We are in the position of men, long tossed about by sea and wind, to whom it very often happens, that while great heaped-up waves delay them for a time around the coasts near the ports, at last that very surge of the vast and dreadful billows drives them on into a trusty, well-known anchorage. And this, I hope, will befall us, as we struggle in this twelfth book against the storm of heresy; so that while we venture our trusty bark therein upon the wave of this grievous impiety, this very wave may bring us to the haven of rest for which we long. For while all are driven about by the uncertain wind of doctrine, there is panic here and danger there, and then again there often is even shipwreck, because it is maintained on prophetic authority that God Only-begotten is a creature—so that to Him there belongs not birth but creation, because it has been said in the character of Wisdom, *The Lord created Me as the beginning of His ways*[1]. This is the greatest billow in the storm they raise, this is the big wave of the whirling tempest: yet when we have faced it, and it has broken without damage to our ship, it will speed us forward even to the all-safe harbour of the shore for which we long.

2. Yet we do not rest, like sailors, on uncertain or on idle hopes: whom, as they shape their course to their wish, and not by assured knowledge, at times the shifting, fickle winds forsake or drive from their course. But we have by our side the unfailing Spirit of faith, abiding with us by the gift of the Only-begotten God, and leading us to smooth waters in an unwavering course. For we recognise the Lord Christ as no creature, for indeed He is none such; nor as something that has been made, since He is Himself the Lord of all things that are made; but we know Him to be God, God the true generation of God the Father. All we indeed, as His goodness has thought fit, have been named and adopted as sons of God: but He is to God the Father the one, true Son, and the true and perfect birth, which abides only in the knowledge of the Father and the Son. But this only,

and this alone, is our religion, to confess Him as the Son not adopted but born, not chosen but begotten. For we do not speak of Him either as made, or as not born; since we neither compare the Creator to His creatures, nor falsely speak of birth without begetting. He does not exist of Himself, Who exists through birth; nor is He not born, Who is the Son; nor can He, Who is the Son, come to exist otherwise than by being born, because He is the Son.

3. Moreover no one doubts that the assertions of impiety always contradict and resist the assertions of religious faith; and that that cannot be piously held now which is already condemned as impiously conceived; as, for instance, the discrepancy and variance which these new correctors of the apostolic faith maintain between the Spirit of the Evangelists and that of Prophets; or their assertion that the Prophets prophesied one thing and the Evangelists preached another, since Solomon calls upon us to adore a creature, while Paul convicts those who serve a creature. And certainly these two texts do not seem to agree together, according to the blasphemous theory, whereby the Apostle, who was trained by the law, and separated by divine appointment, and spoke through Christ speaking in him, either was ignorant of the prophecy, or was not ignorant but contradicted it; and thus did not know Christ to be a creature when he named Him the Creator; and forbade the worship of a creature, warning us that the Creator alone is to be served, and saying, *Who changed the truth of God into a lie, and served the creature, passing by the Creator Who is blessed for ever and ever*[2].

4. Does Christ, Who is God, speaking in Paul, fail to refute this impiety of falsehood? Does He fail to condemn this lying perversion of truth? For through the Lord Christ all things were created; and therefore it is His proper name that He should be the Creator. Does not both the reality and the title of His creative power belong to Him? Melchisedec is our witness, thus declaring God to be Creator of heaven and earth: *Blessed be Abraham of God most high, Who created heaven and earth*[3]. The prophet

---

[1] Prov. viii. 22. [2] Rom i. 23 [3] Gen. xiv. 19.

Hosea also is witness, saying, *I am the Lord thy God, that establish the heavens and create the earth, Whose hands have created all the host of heaven*[4]. Peter too is witness, writing thus, *Committing your souls as to a faithful Creator*[5]. Why do we apply the name of the work to the Maker of that work? Why do we give the same name to God and to our fellowmen? He is our Creator, He is the Creator of all the heavenly host.

5. Since by the faith of the Apostles and Evangelists these statements are referred in their meaning to the Son, through Whom all things were made, how shall He be made equal to the very works of His hands, and be in the same category of nature as all other things? In the first place our human intelligence repudiates this statement that the Creator is a creature; since creation comes to exist by means of the Creator. But if He is a creature, He is both subject to corruption and exposed to the suspense of waiting, and is subjected to bondage. For the same blessed Apostle Paul says: *For the long expectation of the creature waiteth for the revelation of the sons of God. For the creature was subject to vanity, not of its own will, but on account of Him Who has made it subject in hope. Because also the creature itself shall be freed from the slavery of corruption into the liberty of the glory of the children of God*[6]. If, therefore, Christ is a creature, it must needs be that He is in uncertainty, hoping always with a tedious expectation, and that His long expectation, rather than ours, is waiting, and that while He waits He is subjected to vanity, and is subjected through a subjection due to necessity, not of His own will. But since He is subjected not of His own will, He must needs be also a bondservant; moreover since He is a bondservant He must needs also be dwelling in a corruptible nature. For the Apostle teaches that all these things belong to the creature, and that, when it shall be freed from these through a long expectation, it will shine with a glory proper to man. But what a thoughtless and impious assertion about God is this, to imagine Him exposed, through the insults which the creature bears, to such mockeries as that He should hope and serve, and be under compulsion and receive recognition, and be freed hereafter into a condition which is ours, not His; while really it is of His gift that we make our little progress.

6. But our impiety, by the licence of this forbidden language, waxes apace with yet deeper faithlessness; asserting that since the Son is a creature it is bound to maintain that the Father also does not differ from a creature. For Christ, remaining in the form of God, took the form of a servant; and if He is a creature Who is in the form of God, God can never be separate from the creature, because there is a creature in the form of God. But to be in the form of God can only be understood to mean, remaining in the nature of God; whence also God is a creature, because there is a creature with His nature. But He Who was in the form of God, did not grasp at being equal with God, because from equality with God, that is, from the form of God, He descended into the form of a servant. But He could not descend from God into man, except by emptying Himself, as God, of the form of God. But when He emptied Himself, He was not effaced, so as not to be; since then He would have become other in kind than He had been. For neither did He, Who emptied Himself within Himself, cease to be Himself; since the power of His might remains even in the power of emptying Himself; and the transition into the form of a servant does not mean the loss of the nature of God, since to have put off the form of God is nothing less than a mighty act of divine power.

7. But to be in this way in the form of God is nothing else than to be equal with God: so that equality of honour is owed to the Lord Jesus Christ, Who is in the form of God, as He Himself says, *That all men may honour the Son, even as they honour the Father. He that honoureth not the Son honoureth not the Father Who sent Him*[7]. There is never a difference between things which does not also imply a different degree of honour. The same objects deserve the same reverence; for otherwise the highest honour will be unworthily bestowed on those which are inferior, or with insult to the superior the inferior will be made equal to them in honour. But if the Son, regarded as a creation rather than a birth, be treated with a reverence equal to that paid the Father, then we grant no special meed of honour to the Father, since we charge ourselves with only such reverence towards Him as is shewn to a creature. But since He is equal to God the Father, inasmuch as He is born as God from Him, He is also equal to Him in honour, for He is a Son and not a creature.

8. This again is a notable utterance of the Father concerning Him: *From the womb, before the morning star I begat Thee*[8]. Here, as we have often said already, nothing derogatory

4 Hos. xiii. 4 (LXX.). 5 1 Pet. iv. 19. 6 Rom. viii. 19—21. 7 St. John v. 23. 8 Ps. cix. 3 (LXX.).

to God is implied in the concession to our weakness of understanding; as though, because He said that He begat Him *from the womb,* He were therefore composed of inner and outer parts, which unite to form His members, and owed His being to the same causes within time to which earthly bodies owe theirs; when in fact He Whose existence is due to no natural necessities, free and perfect, and eternal Lord of all nature, in explanation of the true character of the birth of His O ly-begotten, points to power of His own unchangeable nature. For though Spirit be born of Spirit (consistently, be it remembered, with the true character of Spirit, through which itself is also Spirit), nevertheless its only cause for being born lies within those perfect and unchangeable causes. And though it is from a perfect and unchangeable cause that it is born, it must needs be born from that cause, in accordance with the true character of that cause. Now the necessary process of human birth is conditioned by the causes which operate upon the womb. But as God is not made up of parts, but is unchangeable as being Spirit, for God is Spirit, He is subject to no natural necessity working within Him. But since He was telling us of the birth of Spirit from Spirit, He instructed our understanding by an example from causes which work among us : not to give an example of the manner of birth, but to declare the fact of generation; not that the example might prove Him subject to necessity, but that it might enlighten our mind. If, therefore, God Only-begotten is a created being, what meaning is there in a revelation which uses the common facts of human birth to indicate that He was divinely generated?

9. For often by means of these members of our bodies, God illustrates for us the method of His own operations, enlightening our intelligence by using terms commonly understood : as when He says, *Whose hands created all the host of heaven* [9] *;* or again, *The eyes of the Lord are upon the righteous* [1] *;* or again, *I have found David, the son of Jesse, a man after My own heart* [2]*.* Now by the heart is denoted the desire, to which David was well-pleasing through the uprightness of his character; and knowledge of the whole universe, whereby nothing is beyond God's ken, is expressed under the term 'eyes;' and His creative activity, whereby nothing exists which is not of God, is understood by the name of 'hands.' Therefore as God wills and foresees and does everything, and even in the use

of terms denoting bodily action must be understood to have no need of the assistance of a body ; surely, now, in the statement that He begat from the womb, the idea is brought forward not of a human origin produced by a bodily act, but of a birth which must be understood as spiritual, since in the other cases where members are spoken of, this is done to represent to us other active powers in God.

10. Therefore since heart is put for desire, and eyes for sight, and hands for work achieved,—and yet, without in any way being made up of parts, God desires and foresees and acts, these same operations being expressed by the words heart, and eyes, and hand,—is not the meaning of the phrase that *He begat from the womb* an assertion of the reality of the birth? Not that He begat the Son from His womb, just as neither does He act by means of a hand, nor see by means of eyes, nor desire by means of a heart. But since by the employment of these terms it is made clear that He really acts and sees and wills everything, so from the word 'womb' it is clear that He really begat from Himself Him Whom He begat; not that he made use of a womb, but that He purposed to express reality. Just in the same way He does not will or see or act through bodily faculties, but uses the names of these members in order that through the services performed by corporeal forces we may understand the power of forces which are not corporeal.

11. Now the constitution of human society does not allow, nor indeed do the words of our Lord's teaching permit, that the disciple should be above his master, or the slave rule over his lord; because, in these contrasted positions, subordination to knowledge is the fitting state of ignorance, and unconditional submission the appointed lot of servitude. And since it is the common judgment of all that this is so, whose rashness now shall induce us to say or think that God is a creature, or that the Son has been made? For nowhere do we find that our Master and Lord spake thus of Himself to His servants and disciples, or that He taught that His birth was a creation or a making. Moreover, the Father never bore witness to Him as being aught else but a Son, nor did the Son profess that God was aught else than His own true Father, assuredly affirming that He was born, not made nor created, as He says, *Every one that loveth the Father, loveth also the Son Who is born of Him* [3].

[9] Hos. xiii. 4, according to LXX.   [1] Ps. xxxiv. 15.
   [2] Acts xiii. 22 ; cf. Ps. lxxxix. 20.

[3] 1 St. John v. 1.

12. On the other hand His works in creation are acts of making and not a birth through generation. For the heaven is not a son, neither is the earth a son, nor is the world a birth; for of these it is said, *All things were made through Him*[4]; and by the prophet, *The heavens are the works of Thy hands*[5]; and by the same prophet, *Neglect not the works of Thy hands*[6]. Is the picture a son of the painter, or the sword a son of the smith, or the house a son of the architect? These are the works of their making: but He alone is the Son of the Father Who is born of the Father.

13. And we indeed are sons of God, but sons because the Son has made us such. For we were once sons of wrath, but have been made sons of God through the Spirit of adoption, and have earned that title by favour, not by right of birth. And since everything that is made, before it was made, was not, so we, although we were not sons, have been made what we are. For formerly we were not sons: but after we have earned the name we are such. Moreover, we have not been born, but made; not begotten, but purchased. For God purchased a people for Himself, and by this act begat them. But we never learn that God begat sons in the strict sense of the term. For He does not say, "I have begotten and brought up *My* sons," but only, *I have begotten and brought up sons*[7].

14. Yet perchance inasmuch as He says, *My firstborn Son Israel*[8], some one will interpret the fact that He said, *My firstborn*, so as to deprive the Son of the characteristic property of birth; as though, because God also applied to Israel the epithet *Mine*, the adoption of those who have been made sons was misrepresented as though it were an actual birth, and therefore the phrase used of Him, *This is My beloved Son*[9], is not solely applicable to the birth of God, since the epithet *My* is (so it is asserted) shared with those who clearly were not born sons. But that they were not really born, although they are said to have been born, is shewn even from that passage where it is said, *A people which shall be born, whom the Lord hath made*[1].

15. Therefore the people of Israel is born, in such wise that it is made; nor do we take the assertion that it is born as contradictory to the fact that it is made. For it is a son by adoption, not by generation; nor is this its true character, but its title. For although the words, *My firstborn* are written of

it; there is yet a great and wide difference between *My beloved Son*, and *My firstborn son*. For where there is birth, there we see, *My beloved Son*; but where there is a choice from among the nations, and adoption through an act of will, there is *My firstborn son*. Here the people is God's, in regard to its character as firstborn; in the former case the fact that He is God's, relates to His character as a Son. Again, in a case of birth the father's ownership comes first, and then his love; in a case of adoption the primary fact is that the son is made a firstborn, and then comes the ownership. Thus to Israel, adopted for a son out of all the peoples of the earth, properly belonged the character of a firstborn; but to Him alone, Who is born God, properly belongs the character of a Son. Accordingly there is no true and complete birth where sonship is imputed rather than real: since it is not doubtful that that people, which is born into a state of sonship, is also made. But since it would not have been what it is now become, and inasmuch as its birth is but a name for its being made, it has no true birth, since it was something else before it was born. And for this reason it was not before it was born, that is, before it was made, because that which is a son from among the nations was a nation before it was a son, and accordingly it is not truly a son, because it was not always a son. But God Only-begotten was neither at any time not a Son, nor was He anything before He was a Son, nor is He Himself anything except a Son. And so He Who is always a Son, has rendered it impossible for us to think of Him that there was a time when He was not.

16. For indeed human births involve a previous non-existence, because, as a first reason, all are born from those, all of whom formerly were not. For although each one who is born has his origin from one who has been, nevertheless that very parent, from whom he is born, was not before he was born. Again, as a second reason, he who is born, is born after that he was not, for time existed before he was born. For if he is born to-day, in the time which was yesterday, he was not; and he has come into a state of being from a state of not being; and our reason enforces that that which is born to-day did not exist yesterday. And so it remains that his birth, by virtue of which he is, took place after a state of non-existence; since necessarily to-day implies the previous existence of yesterday, so that it is true of it that there was a time when it was not. And these facts hold good of the origin of everything relating to man: all receive a beginning, previously to which they

4 St. John i. 3.   5 Ps. cii. 25.   6 Ib. cxxxviii. 8.
7 Is. i. 2 (LXX.).   8 Ex. iv. 22.   9 St. Matt. xvii. 5.
       1 Ps. xxi. 32 (LXX.).

had not been : firstly, as we have explained, in respect of time, and then in respect of cause. And in respect of time indeed there is no doubt that things which now begin to be, formerly were not ; and this is true also in respect of cause, since it is certain that their existence is not derived from a cause within themselves. For think over all the causes of beginnings, and direct your understanding to their antecedents : you will find that nothing began by self-causation, since nothing is born by the free act of the parent, but all things are created what they are through the power of God. Whence also it is a natural property of each class of things by virtue of actual heredity, that it once was not and then began to be, beginning after time began, and existing within time. And while all existing things have an origin later than that of time, their causes also, in their turn, were once non-existent, being born from things which once were not. Even Adam, the first parent of the human race, was formed from the earth, which was made out of nothing, and after time, that is to say, after the heaven and earth, and the day and the sun, moon and stars, and he had no first beginning in being born, and began to be when he once had not been.

17. But for God Only-begotten, Who is preceded by no antecedent time, the possibility is excluded that at some time He was not, since that "some time" thus becomes prior to Him ; and again, the assertion that He was not involves the notion of time : whence time will not begin to be after Him, but He Himself will begin to be after time, and, inasmuch as He was not before He was born, the very period when He was not will take precedence of Him. Further, He Who is born from Him Who really *is*, cannot be understood to have been born from that which was not : since He Who really *is*, is the cause of His existing, and His birth cannot have its origin in that which is not. And therefore since in His case it is not true either in regard of time that He ever was not, or in regard of the Father, that is, the Author of His being, that He has come into existence out of nothing, He has left no possibility with regard to Himself either of His having been born out of nothing, or of His not having existed before He was born.

18. Now I am not ignorant that most of those, whose mind being dulled by impiety does not accept the mystery of God, or who through the strong influence of a hostile spirit are ready to manifest, under the cover of reverence, a mad passion for disparaging God, are wont to make strange assertions in the ears of simple-minded men. They assert that since we say that the Son always has been, and that He never has been anything which He has not always been, we are therefore declaring that He is without birth, inasmuch as He always has been ; since, according to the workings of human reason, that which always has existed cannot possibly have been born : since (so they urge) the cause of a thing being born, is that something, which was not, may come into existence, while the coming into existence of something which was not, means nothing else, according to the judgment of common sense, than its being born. They may add those arguments, subtle enough and pleasant to hear ;—"If He was born, He began to be ; at the time when He began to be, He was not : and when He was not, it cannot be that He was." By such proofs let them maintain that it is the language of reasonable piety to say, " He was not before He was born : because in order that He might come to be, One Who was not, not One Who was, was born. Nor did He Who was, require a birth, although He Who was not was born, to the end that He might come to be."

19. Now, first of all, men professing a devout knowledge of divine things, in matters where the truth preached by Evangelists and Apostles shewed the way, ought to have laid aside the intricate questions of a crafty philosophy, and rather to have followed after the faith which rests in God : because the sophistry of a syllogistical question easily disarms a weak understanding of the protection of its faith, since treacherous assertion lures on the guileless defender, who tries to support his case by enquiry into facts, till at last it robs him, by means of his own enquiry, of his certainty ; so that the answerer no longer retains in his consciousness a truth which by his admission he has surrendered. For what answer accommodates itself so well to the questioner's purpose, as the admission on our part, when we are asked, "Does anything exist before it is born?" that that which is born, did not previously exist? For it is contrary both to nature and to necessary reason that a thing which already exists should be born : since a thing must needs be born in order that it may come to be, and not because it already existed. But when we have made this concession, because it is rightly made, we lose the certainty of our faith, and being ensnared we fall in with their impious and unchristian designs.

20. But the blessed Apostle Paul, taking precaution against this, as we have often shewn, warned us to be on our guard, saying: *Take heed lest any man spoil you through philosophy and vain deceit, according to the tradition of men, according to the elements of the world, and*

not according to Christ, in Whom dwelleth all the fulness of the Godhead bodily [2]. Therefore we must be on our guard against philosophy, and methods which rest upon traditions of men we must not so much avoid as refute. Any concession that we make must imply not that we are out-argued but that we are confused, for it is right that we, who declare that Christ is the power of God and the wisdom of God, should not flee from the doctrines of men, but rather overthrow them; and we must restrain and instruct the simple-minded lest they be spoiled by these teachers. For since God can do all things, and in His wisdom can do all things wisely, for neither is His purpose unarmed with power nor His power unguided by purpose, it behoves those who proclaim Christ to the world, to face the irreverent and faulty doctrines of the world with the knowledge imparted by that wise Omnipotence, according to the saying of the blessed Apostle: *For our weapons are not carnal but powerful for God, for the casting down of strongholds, casting down reasonings and every high thing which is exalted against the knowledge of God* [3]. The Apostle did not leave us a faith which was bare and devoid of reason; for although a bare faith may be most mighty to salvation, nevertheless, unless it is trained by teaching, while it will have indeed a secure retreat to withdraw to in the midst of foes, it will yet be unable to maintain a safe and strong position for resistance. Its position will be like that which a camp affords to a weak force after a flight; not like the undismayed courage of men who have a camp to hold. Therefore we must beat down the insolent arguments which are raised against God, and destroy the fastnesses of fallacious reasoning, and crush cunning intellects which lift themselves up to impiety, with weapons not carnal but spiritual, not with earthly learning but with heavenly wisdom; so that in proportion as divine things differ from human, so may the philosophy of heaven surpass the rivalry of earth.

21. Accordingly let misbelief abandon its efforts; let it not think, because it does not understand, that we deny a truth which, in fact, we alone rightly understand and believe. For while we declare in so many words that He was born, nevertheless we do not assert that He was ever not born [3a]. For it is not the same thing to be not born and to be born: since the latter term expresses origin derived from some other, the former origin derived from none. And it is one thing to exist always, as the Eter-

nal, without any source of being, and another to be co-eternal with a Father, having Him for the Source of being. For where a father is the source of being, there also is birth; and further, where the Source of being is eternal, the birth also is eternal: for since birth comes from the source of being, birth which comes from an eternal Source of being must be eternal. Now everything which always exists, is also eternal. But nevertheless, not everything which is eternal is also not born; since that which is born from eternity has eternally the character of having been born; but that which is not born is ingenerate as well as eternal. But if that which has been born from the Eternal is not born eternal, it will follow that the Father also is not an eternal Source of being. Therefore if any measure of eternity is wanting to Him Who has been born of the eternal Father, clearly the very same measure is wanting to the Author of His being; since what belongs in an infinite degree to Him Who begets, belongs in an infinite degree to Him also Who is born. For neither reason nor intelligence allows of any interval between the birth of God the Son and the generation by God the Father; since the generation consists in the birth, and the birth in the generation. Thus each of these events coincides exactly with the other; neither took place unless both took place. Therefore that which owes its existence to both these events cannot be eternal unless they both are eternal; since neither of the two correlatives, apart from the other, has any reality, because it is impossible for one to exist without the other.

22. But some one, who cannot receive this divine mystery, will say, "Everything which has been born, once was not; since it was born in order that it might come into existence."

23. But does any one doubt that all human beings that have been born, at one time were not? It is, however, one thing to be born of some one who once was not, and another to be born of One Who always is. For every state of infancy, since previously it had no existence, began from some point of time. And this again, growing up into childhood, still later urges on youth to fatherhood. Yet the man was not always a father, for he advanced to youth through boyhood, and to boyhood through original infancy. Therefore he who was not always a father, also did not always beget: but where the Father is eternal, the Son also is eternal. And so if you hold, whether by argument or by instinct, that God, in the mystery of our knowledge of Whom one property is that He is Father, was not always the Father of

---

the begotten Son, you hold also, as a matter of understanding and of knowledge, that the Son, Who was begotten, did not always exist. But if the property of fatherhood be co-eternal with the Father, then necessarily also the property of sonship must be co-eternal with the Son. And how will it square with our language or our understanding to maintain that He was not before He was born, Whose property it is that He always was what He has been born.

24. And so God Only-begotten, containing in Himself the form and image of the invisible God, in all things which are properties of God the Father is equal to Him by virtue of the fulness of true Godhead in Himself. For, as we have shewn in the former books, in respect of power and veneration He is as mighty and as worthy of honour as the Father: so also, inasmuch as the Father is always Father, He too, inasmuch as He is the Son, possesses the like property of being always the Son. For according to the words spoken to Moses, *He Who is, hath sent Me unto you*[4], we obtain the unambiguous conception that absolute being belongs to God; since that which *is*, cannot be thought of or spoken of as not being. For being and not being are contraries, nor can these mutually exclusive descriptions be simultaneously true of one and the same object: for while the one is present, the other must be absent. Therefore, where anything *is*, neither conception nor language will admit of its not being. When our thoughts are turned backwards, and are continually carried back further and further to understand the nature of Him Who is, this sole fact about Him, that He is, remains ever prior to our thoughts; since that quality, which is infinitely present in God, always withdraws itself from the backward gaze of our thoughts, though they reach back to an infinite distance. The result is that the backward straining of our thoughts can never grasp anything prior to God's property of absolute existence; since nothing presents itself, to enable us to understand the nature of God, even though we go on seeking to eternity, save always the fact that God always is. That then which has both been declared about God by Moses, that of which our human intelligence can give no further explanation; that very quality the Gospels testify to be a property of God Only-begotten; since in the beginning was the Word, and since the Word was with God, and since He was the true Light, and since God Only-begotten is in the bosom of the

Father[5], and since Jesus Christ is God over all[6].

25. Therefore He *was*, and He *is*, since He is from Him Who always is what He is. But to be from Him, that is to say, to be from the Father, is birth. Moreover, to be always from Him, Who always is, is eternity; but this eternity is derived not from Himself, but from the Eternal. And from the Eternal nothing can spring but what is eternal: for if the Offspring is not eternal, then neither is the Father, Who is the source of generation, eternal. Now since it is the special characteristic of His being that His Father always exists, and that He is always His Son, and since eternity is expressed in the name HE THAT IS, therefore, since He possesses absolute being, He possesses also eternal being. Moreover, no one doubts that generation implies birth, and that birth points to one existing from that time forth, and not to one who does not continue. Furthermore, there can be no doubt that no one who already was in existence could be born. For no cause of birth can accrue to Him, Who of Himself continues eternal. But God Only-begotten, Who is the Wisdom of God, and the Power and the Word of God, since He was born, bears witness to the Father as the source of His being. Since He was born of One, Who eternally exists, He was not born of nothing. Since He was born before times eternal, His birth must necessarily be prior to all thought. There is no room for the verbal quibble, " He was not, before He was born." For if He is within the range of our thought, in the sense that He was not before He was born, then both our thought and time are prior to His birth; since everything which once was not, is within the compass of thought and time, by the very meaning of the assertion that it once was not, which separates off, within time, a period when it did not exist. But He is from the Eternal, and yet has always been; He is not ingenerate, yet never was non-existent; since to have always been transcends time, and to have been born is birth.

26. And so we confess that God Only-begotten was born, but born before times eternal: since we must make our confession within such limits as the express preaching of Apostles and Prophets assigns to us; though at the same time human thought cannot grasp any intelligible idea of birth out of time, since it is inconsistent with the nature of earthly beings that any of them should be born before all times. But when we make this assertion,

---

4 Ex. iii. 14 (in LXX.).   5 St. John i. 1, 9, 18.   6 Rom. ix. 5.

how can we reconcile with it, as part of the same doctrine, the contradictory statement that before His birth He was not, when according to the Apostle He is God Only-begotten before times eternal? If, therefore, the belief that He was born before times eternal is not only the reasonable conclusion of human intelligence, but the confession of thoughtful faith, then, since birth implies some author of being, and what surpasses all time is eternal, and whatever is born before times eternal transcends earthly perception, we are certainly exalting by impious self-will a notion of human reason, if we maintain in a carnal sense that before He was born He was not, since He is born eternal, beyond human perception or carnal intelligence. And again, whatever transcends time is eternal.

27. For we can embrace all time in imagination or knowledge, since we know that what is now to-day, did not exist yesterday, because what was yesterday is not now; and on the other hand what is now, is only now and was not also yesterday. And by imagination we can so span the past that we have no doubt that before some city was founded, there existed a time in which that city had not been founded. Since, therefore, all time is the sphere of knowledge or imagination, we judge of it by the perceptions of human reason; hence we are considered to have reasonably asserted about anything, "It was not, before it was born," since antecedent time is prior to the origin of every single thing. But on the other hand, since in things of God, that is to say, in regard to the birth of God, there is nothing that is not before time eternal: it is illogical to use of Him the phrase "before He was born," or to suppose that He Who possesses before times eternal the eternal promise, is merely (in the language of the blessed Apostle[7]) in hope of eternal life, which God Who cannot lie has promised before times eternal, or to say that once He was not. For reason rejects the notion that He began to exist after anything, Who, so we must confess, existed before times eternal.

28. We may grant that for anything to be born before times eternal is not the way of human nature, nor a matter which we can understand; and yet in this we believe God's declarations about Himself. How then does the infidelity of our own day assert, according to the conceptions of human intelligence, that that had no existence before it was born, which the Apostolic faith tells us was, in some manner inconceivable to the human[8] understanding, always born, or in other words

existed before times eternal? For what is born before time is always born; since that which exists before time eternal, always exists. But what has always been born, cannot at any time have had no existence; since non-existence at a given time is directly contrary to eternity of existence. Moreover, existing always excludes the idea of not having existed always. And the idea of not having existed always being excluded by the postulate that He has always been born, we cannot conceive the supposition that He did not exist before He was born. For it is obvious that He Who was born before times eternal, has always been born, although we can form no positive conception of anything having been born before all time. For if we must confess (as is clearly necessary) that He has been born before every creature, whether invisible or corporeal, and before all ages and times eternal, and before all perception, Who always exists through the very fact that He has been so born;—then by no manner of thought can it be conceived that before He was born, He did not exist; since He Who has been born before times eternal, is prior to all thought, and we can never think that once He did not exist, when we have to confess that He always exists.

29. But our opponent cunningly anticipates us with this carping objection. "If," he urges, "it is inconceivable that He did not exist before He was born, it must be conceivable that One Who already existed was born."

30. I will ask this objector in reply, whether he remembers my calling Him anything else than born, and whether I did not say that existence before times eternal and birth have the same meaning in the case of Him that was. For the birth of One already existing is not really birth, but a self-wrought change through birth, and the eternal existence of One Who is born means that in His birth He is prior to any conception of time, and that there is no room for the mind to suppose that at any time He was unborn. And so an eternal birth before times eternal is not the same as existence before being born. But to have been born always before times eternal excludes the possibility of having had no existence before birth.

31. Again, this same fact excludes the possibility of saying that He existed before He was born; because He Who transcends perception transcends it in every respect. For if the notion of being born, though always existing, transcends thought, it is equally impossible that the notion that He did not exist before He was born should be a subject of thought. And so, since we must confess

that to have been always born means for us nothing beyond the fact of birth, the question whether He did or did not exist before He was born cannot be determined under our conditions of thought; since this one fact that He was born before times eternal ever eludes the grasp of our thought. So He was born and yet has always existed; He Who does not allow anything else to be understood or said about Him than that He was born. For since He is prior to time itself, within which thought exists (since time eternal is previous to thought), He debars thought from determining concerning Him, whether He was or was not before He was born; since existence before birth is incompatible with the idea of birth, and previous non-existence involves the idea of time. Therefore, while the infinity of times eternal is fatal to any explanation involving the idea of time—that is to say, to the notion that He did not exist; His birth equally forbids any that is inconsistent with it,—that is to say, the notion that He existed before He was born. For if the question of His existence or His non-existence can be determined under our conditions of thought, then the birth itself must be after time; for He Who does not always exist must, of necessity, have begun to be after some given point of time.

32. Therefore the conclusion reached by faith and argument and thought is that the Lord Jesus both was born and always existed: since if the mind survey the past in search of knowledge concerning the Son, this one fact, and nothing else, will be constantly present to the enquirer's perception, that He was born and always existed. As therefore it is a property of God the Father to exist without birth, so also it must belong to the Son to exist always through birth. But birth can declare nothing except that there is a Father, and the title Father nothing else except that there is a birth. For neither those names, nor the nature of the case, will allow of any intermediate position. For either He was not always a Father, unless there was always also a Son; or if He was always a Father, there was always also a Son; since whatever period of time is denied to the Son, to make His sonship non-eternal, just so much the Father lacks of having been always a Father: so that although He was always God, nevertheless He cannot have been also a Father for the same infinity during which He is God.

33. Now the declarations of impiety even go so far as not only [9] to ascribe to the Son birth in time, but also generation in time [9a] to the Father; because the process of generation and the birth take place within one period.

34. But, heretic, do you consider it pious and devout to confess that God indeed always existed, yet was not always Father? For if it is pious for you to think so, you must then condemn Paul of impiety, when he says that the Son existed before times eternal [1]: you must also accuse Wisdom itself, when it bears witness concerning itself that it was founded before the ages: for it was present with the Father when He was preparing the heaven. But in order that you may assign to God a beginning of His being a Father, first determine the starting-point at which the times must have begun. For if they had a beginning, the Apostle is a liar for declaring them to be eternal. For you all are accustomed to reckon the times from the creation of the sun and the moon, since it is written of them, *And let them be for signs and for times and for years* [2]. But He Who is before the heaven, which in your view is even before time, is also before the ages. Nor is He merely before the ages, but also before the generations of generations which precede the ages. Why do you limit things divine and infinite by what is perishable and earthly and narrow? With regard to Christ, Paul knows of nothing except an eternity of times. Wisdom does not say that it is after anything, but before everything. In your judgment the times were established by the sun and the moon; but David shews that Christ remains before the sun, saying, *His name is before the sun* [3]. And lest you should think that the things of God began with the formation of this universe, he says again, *And for generations of generations before the moon* [4]. These great men counted worthy of prophetic inspiration look down upon time: every opening is barred whereby human perception might penetrate behind the birth, which transcends times eternal. Yet let the faith of a devout imagination accept this as limit of its speculations, remembering that the Lord Jesus Christ, God Only-begotten, is born in a manner to be acknowledged as a perfect birth, and in the reverence paid to His divinity, not forgetting that He is eternal.

35. But we are accused of lying, and together with us the doctrine preached by the Apostle is attacked, because while it confesses the birth, it asserts the eternity of that birth: the result being that, while the birth bears witness to an Author of being, the assertion of eternity in the mystery of the divine birth transgresses the limits of human thought. For

---

9 Reading *non solum*.　　9a Reading *generationis*.

1 Tit. i. 2.　　2 Gen. i. 14.　　3 Ps. lxxi. 17 (in LXX.).
4 Ib. 5 (LXX.).

there *is* brought forward against us the declaration of Wisdom concerning itself, when it taught that it was created in these words : *The Lord created Me for the beginning of His ways* [5].

36. And, O wretched heretic! you turn the weapons granted to the Church against the Synagogue, against belief in the Church's preaching, and distort against the common salvation of all the sure meaning of a saving doctrine. For you maintain by these words that Christ is a creature, instead of silencing the Jew, who denies that Christ was God before eternal ages, and that His power is active in all the working and teaching of God, by these words of the living Wisdom! For Wisdom has in this passage asserted that it had been created for the beginning of the ways of God and for His works from the commencement of the ages, lest perchance it might be supposed that it did not subsist before Mary; yet has not employed this word 'create.l' in order to signify that its birth was a creation, since it was created for the beginning of God's ways and for His works. Nay rather lest any one should suppose that this beginning of the ways, which is indeed the starting-point for the human knowledge of things divine, was meant to subordinate an infinite birth to conditions of time, Wisdom declared itself established before the ages. For, since it is one thing to be created for the beginning of the ways and for the works of God, and another to be established before the ages, the establishing was intended to be understood as prior to the creation; and the very fact of its being established for God's works before the ages was intended to point to the mystery of the creation; since the establishing is before the ages, but the creation for the beginning of the ways and for the works of God is after the commencement of the ages.

37. But now, lest the terms 'creation' and 'establishing' should be an obstacle to belief in the divine birth, these words follow, *Before He made the earth, before He made firm the mountains, before all the hills He begat Me* [6]. Thus He is begotten before the earth, Who is established before the ages; and not only before the earth, but also before the mountains and hills. And indeed in these expressions, since Wisdom speaks of itself, more is meant than is said. For all objects which are used to convey the idea of infinity must be of such a kind as to be subsequent in point of time to no single thing and to no class of things. But things existing in time cannot

possibly be fitted to indicate eternity; because, from the very fact that they are posterior to other things, they are incapable of suggesting the thought of infinity as a beginning, themselves having their own beginning in time. For what wonder is it, that God should have begotten the Lord Christ before the earth, when the origin of the angels is found to be prior to the creation of the earth? Or why should He, Who was said to be begotten before the earth, be also declared to be born before the mountains, and not only before the mountains but also before the hills; the hills being mentioned, as an afterthought, after the mountains, and reason requiring that there should be a world before mountains could exist? For such reasons it cannot be supposed that these words were used merely in order that He might be understood to exist prior to hills and mountains and earth, Who surpasses by the eternity of His own infinity things which are themselves prior to earth and mountains and hills.

38. But this divine discourse has not left our understandings unenlightened, since it explains the reason of the phrase in what follows :—*God made the regions, both the uninhabitable parts and the heights which are inhabited under the heaven. When He was preparing the heaven, I was with Him; and when He was setting apart His own seat. When above the winds He made the clouds huge in the upper air, and when He placed securely the springs under the heaven, and when He made firm the foundations of the earth, I was by Him, joining all things together* [7]. What period in time is here? Or how far are the conceptions of human intelligence allowed to reach beyond the infinite birth of God Only-begotten? By means of things whose creation we can conceive in our mind, it is not possible to understand the generation of Him, Who is prior to all these things; and hence we cannot maintain that He came, indeed, first in time, yet was not infinite, inasmuch as the only privilege bestowed upon Him was a birth prior to things temporal. For in that case, since they, by their constitution, are subject to the conditions of time, He, though prior to them all, would be equally subject to conditions of time, because their creation within time would define the time of His birth, namely that He was born before then; for that which is antecedent to temporal things stands in the same relation to time as they.

39. But the voice of God, our instruction in true wisdom, speaks what is perfect, and expresses the absolute truth, when it teaches

---

5 Prov. viii. 22 (LXX.).   6 Ib. 24, 25 (LXX.).   7 Prov. viii. 26—30 (LXX.).

that itself is prior not merely to things of time, but even to things infinite. For when the heaven was being prepared, it was present with God. Is the preparation of the heaven an act of God within time; so that an impulse of thought suddenly surprised His mind, as though it had been previously dull and inert, and after the fashion of men He sought for materials and instruments for fashioning the heaven? Nay, the prophet's conception of the working of God is far different, when He says, *By the word of the Lord were the heavens established, and all their power by the breath of His mouth* [8]. Yet the heavens needed the command of God, that they might be established; for their arrangement and excellence in this firm unshaken constitution, which they display, did not arise from the blending and commingling of some kind of matter, but from the breath of the mouth of God. What then does it mean, that Wisdom begotten of God was present with Him, when He was preparing the heaven? For neither does the creation of heaven consist in a preparation of material, nor does it consist with the nature of God to linger over preliminary thoughts concerning His work. For everything, which there is in created things, was always with God: for although these things in respect of their creation have a beginning, nevertheless they have no beginning in respect of the knowledge and power of God. And here the prophet is our witness, saying, *O God, Who hast made all things which shall be* [9]. For although things future, in so far as they are to be created, are still to be made, yet to God, with Whom there is nothing new or sudden in creation, they have already been made; since there is a dispensation of times for their creation, and in the prescient working of the divine power they have already been made. Here, therefore, Wisdom, in teaching that it was born before the ages, teaches that it is not merely prior to things which have been created, but is even co-eternal with what is eternal, to wit, with the preparation of the heaven, and the setting apart of the abode of God. For this abode was not set apart at the time when it was actually made, for setting apart and fashioning an abode are different things. Nor again was the heaven formed at the time when it was (ideally) prepared, for Wisdom was with God both when He prepared and when He set apart the heaven. And afterwards it was fashioning the heaven by the side of God Who formed it: it proves its eternity by its presence with

Him as He prepares; it reveals its functions, when it fashions by the side of God Who forms. Therefore, in the passage before us it said that it was begotten even before the earth and mountains and hills, because it meant to teach that it was present at the preparation of the heaven; in order that it might shew that, even when the heaven was being prepared, this work was already finished in the counsel of God, for to Him there is nothing new.

40. For the preparation for creation is perpetual and eternal: nor was the frame of this universe actually made by isolated acts of thought, in the sense that first the heaven was thought of, and afterwards there came into God's mind a thought and plan concerning the earth; that He thought of each part singly, so that first the earth was spread out as a plain, and then through better counsels was made to rise up in mountains, and yet again was diversified with hills, and in the fourth place was also made habitable even in the heights; that so the heaven was prepared and the abode of God set apart, and huge clouds in the upper air held the exhalations caught up by the winds; then afterwards sure springs began to run under the heaven, and, last of all, the earth was made firm with strong foundations. For Wisdom declares that it is prior to all these things. But since all things under the heaven were made through God, and Christ was present at the fashioning of the heaven, and preceded even the eternity of the heaven which was prepared, this fact does not allow us to think in respect to God of disconnected thoughts on details, since the whole preparation of these things is co-eternal with God. For although, as Moses teaches, each act of creation had its proper order;—the making the firmament solid, the laying bare of the dry land, the gathering together of the sea, the ordering of the stars, the generation by the waters and the earth when they brought forth living creatures out of themselves; yet the creation of the heaven and earth and other elements is not separated by the slightest interval in God's working, since their preparation had been completed in like infinity of eternity in the counsel of God.

41. Thus, though Christ was present in God with these infinite and eternal decrees, He has granted to us nothing more than a knowledge of the fact of His birth; in order that, just as an apprehension of the birth is the means which leads to faith in God, so also the knowledge of the eternity of His birth might avail to sustain piety; since neither reason nor experience allow us to speak of any but an eternal Son as proceeding from a Father Who is eternal.

8 Ps. xxxii 6 (LXX.).
9 Is. xlv. 11 (LXX. but altered from the 3rd person to the 2nd).

42. But perhaps the word 'creation,' and its employment of Him, disturbs us. Certainly the word 'creation' would disturb us, if birth before the ages and creation for the beginning of the ways of God and for His works were not affirmed of Him. For birth cannot be understood to denote creation, since the birth precedes causation, but the creation takes place through causation. For before the preparation of the heaven and before the commencement of the ages was He established, Who was created for the beginning of the ways of God and for His works. Is it possible that to be created for the beginning of the ways of God and for His works, means the same as to be born before all things? No : one of these ideas relates to time employed in action, but the other bears a sense which has no relation to time.

43. Or perhaps you wish the assertion that He was created for the works to be understood in the sense that He was created on account of the works; in other words that Christ was created for the sake of performing the works. In that case He exists as a servant and a builder of the universe, and was not born the Lord of Glory; He was created for the service of forming the ages, and was not always the beloved Son and the King of the ages. But, although the general understanding of Christians contradicts this impious thought of yours, recognising that it is one thing to be created for the beginning of the ways of God and for His works, and another to be born before the ages, yet this very same passage thwarts your purpose of falsely asserting that the Lord Christ was created, on account of the formation of the universe, since it shews that God the Father is the Maker and Former of the universe, and shews it convincingly, since Christ Himself was present fashioning by the side of Him Who was forming all things. But, while all Scripture was designed to speak of the Lord Jesus Christ as the Creator of the universe, Wisdom, to destroy all occasion for impiety, has here declared that though God the Father was the Constructor of the universe, yet itself was not absent from Him while constructing it, since it was present with Him even when He was preparing it beforehand, and that when the Father formed the universe, Wisdom also was fashioning it by the side of Him Who formed it, and was present with Him even when He prepared it. Whence Wisdom would have us understand that it was not created on account of God's works [1], by the very fact that it had been present at

the eternal preparation of works yet to be, and proves Scripture not to be false, by the fact that it fashioned the universe by the side of God when He formed it.

44. Learn at last, heretic, from the revelation of Catholic teaching, what is the meaning of the saying that Christ was created for the beginning of the ways of God and for His works ; and be taught by the words of Wisdom itself the folly of your impious dulness. For thus it begins : *If I shall declare unto you the things which are done every day, I will remember to recount those things which are from of old* [2]. For Wisdom had said before, *You, O men, I entreat, and I utter my voice to the sons of men. O ye simple, understand subtilty, moreover, ye unlearned, apply your heart* [3] ; and again, *Through Me kings reign, and mighty men decree justice. Through Me princes are magnified, and through Me despots possess the earth* [4] ; and again, *I walk in the ways of equity, and move in the midst of the paths of justice; that I may divide substance to those that love Me, and fill their treasuries with good things* [5]. Wisdom is not silent about its daily work. And firstly entreating all men, it advises the simple to understand subtilty, and the unlearned to apply their heart, in order that a zealous and diligent reader may ponder the different and separate meanings of the words. And so it teaches that by its methods and ordinances all success, all attainment of knowledge or fame or wealth, is achieved : it shews that within itself are contained the reigns of kings and the prudence of the mighty, and the famous works of princes, and the justice of despots who possess the earth ; that it moreover does not mingle with wicked deeds and has no part in acts of injustice ; and that all this is done by Wisdom in order that, by taking part in every work of equity and justice, it may supply to those that love it, a wealth of eternal goods and incorruptible treasures. Therefore Wisdom, after declaring that it will relate the things which are done every day, promises that it will also be mindful to recount the things which are from of old. And now what blindness is it, to think that things were performed before the beginning of the ages, which are expressly declared to date merely from the beginning of the ages ! For every work among those which date from the beginning of the ages is itself posterior to that beginning : but on the contrary, things which are before the beginning of the ages, precede the ordering of the ages, which are later than they. And so Wisdom, after declaring that

---

[1] Reading *per id ipsum ea neque propter opera.*

[2] Prov. viii. 21 (LXX.).   [3] Ib. 4, 5.   [4] Ib. 15, 16.
[5] Ib. 20, 21.

it is mindful to speak of the things which date from the beginning of the ages, says, *The Lord created Me for the beginning of His ways for His works,* by these words denoting things performed from the date of the beginning of the ages. Thus Wisdom's teaching concerns not a generation declared to precede the ages, but a dispensation which began with the ages themselves.

45. We must also enquire what is the meaning of the saying that God, born before the ages, was again created for the beginning of the ways of God and for His works. This surely is said because where there is a birth before the commencement of the ages, there is the eternity of an endless generation: but where the same birth is represented as a creation from the commencement of the ages, for the ways of God and for His works, it is applied as the creative cause to the works and to the ways. And first, since Christ is Wisdom, we must see whether He is Himself the beginning of the way of the works of God. Of this, I think, there is no doubt; for He says, *I am the way,* and, *No man cometh to the Father except through Me* [6]. A way is the guide of those who go, the course marked out for those who hasten, the safeguard of the ignorant, a teacher, so to speak, of things unknown and longed for. Therefore He is created for the beginning of the ways, for the works of God; because He is the Way and leads men to the Father. But we must seek for the purpose of this creation, which is from the commencement of the ages. For it is also the mystery of the last dispensation, wherein Christ was again created in bodily form, and declared that He was the way of the works of God. Again, He was created for the ways of God from the commencement of the ages, when, subjecting Himself to the visible form of a creature, He took the form of a created being.

46. And so let us see for what ways of God, and for what works of God, Wisdom was created from the commencement of the ages, though born of God before all ages. Adam heard the voice of One walking in Paradise. Do you think that His approach could have been heard, had He not assumed the guise of a created being? Is not the fact, that He was heard as He walked, proof that He was present in a created form? I do not ask in what guise He spoke to Cain and Abel and Noah, and in what guise He was near to Enoch also, blessing him. An Angel speaks to Hagar, and certainly He is also God. Has He the same form, when He appears like an Angel, as He has in that nature, by virtue of which He is God? Certainly the form of an Angel is revealed, where afterwards mention is made of the nature of God. But why should I speak of an Angel? He comes as a man to Abraham. Under the guise of a man, in the shape of that created being, is not Christ present in that nature, which He possesses as being also God? A man speaks, and is present in the body, and is nourished by food; and yet God is adored. Surely He Who was an Angel is now also man, in order to save us from the assumption that any of these diverse aspects of one state, that of the creature, is His natural form as God. Again, He comes to Jacob in human shape, and even grasps him for wrestling; and He takes hold with His hands, and struggles with His limbs, and bends His flanks, and adopts every movement and gesture of ours. But again He is revealed, this time to Moses, and as a fire; in order that you might learn to believe that this created nature was to provide Him with an outward guise, not to embody the reality of His nature. He possessed, at that moment, the power of burning, but He did not assume the destructive property which is inherent in the nature of fire, for the fire evidently burned and yet the bush was not injured.

47. Glance over the whole course of time, and realise in what guise He appeared to Joshua the son of Nun, a prophet bearing His name, or to Isaiah, who relates that he saw Him, as the Gospel also bears witness [7], or to Ezekiel, who was admitted even to knowledge of the Resurrection, or to Daniel, who confesses the Son of Man in the eternal kingdom of the ages, or to all the rest to whom He presented Himself in the form of various created beings, *for the ways of God and for the works of God,* that is to say, to teach us to know God, and to profit our eternal state. Why does this method, expressly designed for human salvation, bring about at the present time such an impious attack upon His eternal birth? The creation, of which you speak, dates from the commencement of the ages; but His birth is without end, and before the ages. Maintain by all means that we are doing violence to words, if a Prophet, or the Lord, or an Apostle, or any oracle whatever has described by the name of creation the birth of His eternal divinity. In all these manifestations God, Who is a consuming fire, is present, as created, in such a manner that He could lay aside the created form by the same power by which He assumed it, being

---

[6] St. John xiv. 6.

[7] St. John xii. 41.

able to destroy again that which had come into existence merely that it might be looked upon.

48. But that blessed and true birth of the flesh conceived within the Virgin the Apostle has named both a creating and a making, for then there was born both the nature and form of our created being. And without doubt in his view this name belongs to Christ's true birth as a man, since he says, *But when the fulness of the time came, God sent His Son, made of a woman, made under the law, in order that He might redeem those who are under the law, that we might obtain the adoption of sons* [8]. And so He is God's own Son, Who is made in human form and of human origin; nor is He only made but also created, as it is said: *Even as the truth is in Jesus, that ye put away, according to your former manner of life, that old man, which becomes corrupt according to the lusts of deceit. However, be ye renewed in the spirit of your mind, and put ye on that new man, which is created according to God* [9]. So the new man is to be put on Who has been created according to God. For He Who was Son of God was born also Son of Man. This was not the birth of the divinity, but the creating of the flesh; the new Man taking the title of the race, and being created according to God Who was born before the ages. And how the new man was created according to God, he explains in what follows, adding, *in righteousness, and in holiness, and in truth* [1]. For there was no guile in Him; and He has been made unto us righteousness and sanctification, and is Himself the Truth. This, then, is the Christ, created a new man according to God, Whom we put on.

49. If, then, Wisdom, in saying that it was mindful of the things which have been performed since the beginning of the ages, said that it was created for the works of God and for the ways of God; and yet, while saying that it was created, taught that it was established before the ages, lest we should suppose that the mystery of that created form, so variously and frequently assumed, involved some change in its nature;—for although the firmness with which it was established would not allow of any disturbance that could overthrow it, yet, lest the establishment might seem to mean something less than birth, Wisdom declared itself to be begotten before all things:—if this is so, why is the term 'creation' now applied to the birth of that which was both begotten before all things, and also established before the ages? Because that which

was established before the ages was created anew from the commencement of the ages for the beginning of the ways of God and for His works. In this sense must we understand the difference between creation from the commencement of the ages and that birth which precedes the ages and all things. Impiety at least has not this excuse, that it can plead error as the cause of its profanity.

50. For although the weakness of the understanding might hinder the perceptions of a man devoutly disposed, so that, even after this explanation, he might fail to grasp the meaning of "creation," nevertheless, even the letter of the Apostle's saying, when he applies [2] the term "making" to a true birth, should have sufficed for a sincere, if not intelligent, belief, that the term "creation" was designed to conduce to a belief in generation. For when the Apostle was minded to assert the birth of One from one Parent, that is to say, the birth of the Lord from a virgin without a conception due to human passions, he clearly had a definite purpose in calling Him "made of a woman," Whom he knew and had frequently asserted to have been born. He desired that the 'birth' should point to the reality of the generation, and the 'making' should testify to the birth of One from one Parent; because the term 'making' excludes the idea of a conception by means of human intercourse, it being expressly stated that He was *made* of a virgin, though it is equally certain that He was born and not made. But see, heretic, how impious you are. No sentence of prophet, or evangelist, or apostle has said that Jesus Christ was created from God, rather than born from Him: yet you deny the birth, and assert the creation, but not according to the Apostle's meaning, when he said that He was made, lest there should be any doubt that He was born as One from one Parent. You make your assertion in a most impious sense, implying that God did not derive His being by way of birth conveying nature; although a creature would rather have come into being out of nothing. This is the primary infection in your unhappy mind, not that you term birth a creating, but that you adapt your faith to the idea of creation instead of birth. And yet while it would mark a poor intellect, still it would not mark a man entirely undevout, if you had called Christ created, in order that men might recognise His impassible birth from God, as being that of One from One.

51. But none of these phrases does a firm

---

[8] Gal. iv. 4, 5. [9] Eph. iv. 21—24. [1] Ib. 24.

* *Deputantis*, conj. edd. Benedict.

apostolic faith permit. For it knows in what dispensation of time Christ was created, and in what eternity of times He was born. Moreover, He was born God of God, and the divinity of His true birth and perfect generation is not doubtful. For in relation to God we acknowledge only two modes of being, birth and eternity: birth, moreover, not after anything, but before all things, so that birth only bears witness to a Source of being, and does not predicate any incongruity between the offspring and the Source of being. Still, by common admission, this birth, because it is from God, implies a secondary position in respect to the Source of being, and yet cannot be separated from that Source, since any attempt of thought to pass beyond acceptance of the fact of birth, must also necessarily penetrate the mystery of the generation. And so this is the only pious language to use about God: to know Him as Father, and with Him to know also Him, Who is the Son born of Him. Nor assuredly are we taught anything concerning God, except that He is the Father of God the Only-begotten and the Creator. So let not human weakness overreach itself; and let it make this only confession, in which alone lies its salvation—that, before the mystery of the Incarnation, it is ever assured, concerning the Lord Jesus Christ, of this one fact that He had been born.

52. For my part, so long as I shall have the power by means of this Spirit Whom Thou hast granted me, Holy Father, Almighty God, I will confess Thee to be not only eternally God, but also eternally Father. Nor will I ever break out into such folly and impiety, as to make myself the judge of Thy omnipotence and Thy mysteries, nor shall this weak understanding arrogantly seek for more than that devout belief in Thy infinitude and faith in Thy eternity, which have been taught me. I will not assert that Thou wast ever without Thy Wisdom, and Thy Power, and Thy Word, without God Only-begotten, my Lord Jesus Christ. The weak and imperfect language, to which our nature is limited, does not dominate my thoughts concerning Thee, so that my poverty of utterance should choke faith into silence. For although we have a word and wisdom and power of our own, the product of our free inward activity, yet Thine is the absolute generation of perfect God, Who is Thy Word and Wisdom and Power; so that He can never be separated from Thee, Who in these names of Thy eternal properties is shewn to be born of Thee. Yet His birth is only so far shewn as to make manifest the fact that Thou art the Source of His being; yet sufficiently to confirm our belief in His infinity, inasmuch as it is related that He was born before times eternal.

53. For in human affairs Thou hast set before us many things of such a sort, that though we do not know their cause, yet the effect is not unknown; and reverence inculcates faith, where ignorance is inherent in our nature. Thus when I raised to Thy heaven these feeble eyes of mine, my certainty regarding it was limited to the fact that it is Thine. For seeing therein these orbits where the stars are fixed, and their annual revolutions, and the Pleiades and the Great Bear and the Morning Star, each having their varied duties in the service which is appointed them, I recognise Thy presence, O God, in these things whereof I cannot gain any clear understanding. And when I view the marvellous swellings of Thy sea, I know that I have failed to comprehend not merely the origin of the waters but even the movements of this changeful expanse; yet I grasp at faith in some reasonable cause, although it is one that I cannot see, and fail not to recognise Thee in these things also, which I do not know. Furthermore, when in thought I turn to the earth, which by the power of hidden agencies causes to decay all the seeds which it receives, quickens them when decayed, multiplies them when quickened, and makes them strong when multiplied; in all these changes I find nothing which my mind can understand, yet my ignorance helps towards recognising Thee, for though I know nothing of the nature that waits on me, I recognise Thee by actual experience of the advantages I possess. Moreover, though I do not know myself, yet I perceive so much that I marvel at Thee the more because I am ignorant of myself. For without understanding it, I perceive a certain motion or order or life in my mind when it exercises its powers; and this very perception I owe to Thee, for though Thou deniest the power of understanding my natural first beginning, yet Thou givest that of perceiving nature with its charms. And since in what concerns myself I recognise Thee, ignorant as I am, so recognising Thee I will not in what concerns Thee cherish a feebler faith in Thy omnipotence, because I do not understand. My thoughts shall not attempt to grasp and master the origin of Thy Only-begotten Son, nor shall my faculties strain to reach beyond the truth that He is my Creator and my God.

54. His birth is before times eternal. If anything exist which precedes eternity, it will be something which, when eternity is comprehended, still eludes comprehension. And this something is Thine, and is Thy Only-begotten;

no portion, nor extension, nor any empty name devised to suit some theory of Thy mode of action. He is the Son, a Son born of Thee, God the Father, Himself true God, begotten by Thee in the unity of Thy nature, and meet to be acknowledged after Thee, and yet with Thee, since Thou art the eternal Author of His eternal origin. For since He is from Thee, He is second to Thee; yet since He is Thine, Thou art not to be separated from Him. For we must never assert that Thou didst once exist without Thy Son, lest we should be reproaching Thee either with imperfection, as then unable to generate, or with superfluousness after the generation. And so the exact meaning for us of the eternal generation is that we know Thee to be the eternal Father of Thy Only-begotten Son, Who was born of Thee before times eternal.

55. But, for my part, I cannot be content by the service of my faith and voice, to deny that my Lord and my God, Thy Only-begotten, Jesus Christ, is a creature; I must also deny that this name of ' creature' belongs to Thy Holy Spirit, seeing that He proceeds from Thee and is sent through Him, so great is my reverence for everything that is Thine. Nor, because I know that Thou alone art unborn and that the Only-begotten is born of Thee, will I refuse to say that the Holy Spirit was begotten, or assert that He was ever created. I fear the blasphemies which would be insinuated against Thee by such use of this title 'creature,' which I share with the other beings brought into being by Thee. Thy Holy Spirit, as the Apostle says, searches and knows Thy deep things, and as Intercessor for me speaks to Thee words I could not utter; and shall I express or rather dishonour, by the title 'creature,' the power of His nature, which subsists eternally, derived from Thee through Thine Only-begotten? Nothing, except what belongs to Thee, penetrates into Thee; nor can the agency of a power foreign and strange to Thee measure the depth of Thy boundless majesty. To Thee belongs whatever enters into Thee; nor is anything strange to Thee, which dwells in Thee through its searching power.

56. But I cannot describe Him, Whose pleas for me I cannot describe. As in the revelation that Thy Only-begotten was born of Thee before times eternal, when we cease to struggle with ambiguities of language and difficulties of thought, the one certainty of His birth remains; so I hold fast in my consciousness the truth that Thy Holy Spirit is from Thee and through Him, although I cannot by my intellect comprehend it. For in Thy spiritual things I am dull, as Thy Only-begotten says, *Marvel not that I said unto thee, ye must be born anew. The Spirit breathes where it will, and thou hearest the voice of it; but dost not know whence it comes or whither it goes. So is every one who is born of water and of the Holy Spirit* [3]. Though I hold a belief in my regeneration, I hold it in ignorance; I possess the reality, though I comprehend it not. For my own consciousness had no part in causing this new birth, which is manifest in its effects. Moreover the Spirit has no limits; He speaks when He will, and what He will, and where He will. Since, then, the cause of His coming and going is unknown, though the watcher is conscious of the fact, shall I count the nature of the Spirit among created things, and limit Him by fixing the time of His origin? Thy servant John says, indeed, that all things were made through the Son [4], Who as God the Word was in the beginning, O God, with Thee. Again, Paul recounts all things as created in Him, in heaven and on earth, visible and invisible [5]. And, while he declared that everything was created in Christ and through Christ, he thought, with respect to the Holy Spirit, that the description was sufficient, when he called Him Thy Spirit. With these men, peculiarly Thine elect, I will think in these matters; just as, after their example, I will say nothing beyond my comprehension about Thy Only-begotten, but simply declare that He was born, so also after their example I will not trespass beyond that which human intellect can know about Thy Holy Spirit, but simply declare that He is Thy Spirit. May my lot be no useless strife of words, but the unwavering confession of an unhesitating faith!

57. Keep, I pray Thee, this my pious faith undefiled, and even till my spirit departs, grant that this may be the utterance of my convictions: so that I may ever hold fast that which I professed in the creed of my regeneration, when I was baptized in the Father, and the Son, and the Holy Spirit. Let me, in short, adore Thee our Father, and Thy Son together with Thee; let me win the favour of Thy Holy Spirit, Who is from Thee, through Thy Only-begotten. For I have a convincing Witness to my faith, Who says, *Father, all Mine are Thine, and Thine are Mine* [6], even my Lord Jesus Christ, abiding in Thee, and from Thee, and with Thee, for ever God: Who is blessed for ever and ever. Amen.

---

3 St. John iii. 7, 8.   4 Ib. i. 1, 3.   5 Col. i. 16.
6 St. John xvii. 10.

INTRODUCTION TO THE
HOMILIES ON PSALMS I., LIII., CXXX.

SOME account of St. Hilary's *Homilies on the Psalms* has already been given in the Introduction to this volume, pp. xl.—xlv. A few words remain to be said concerning his principle of exposition. This may be gathered from his own statement in the fifth section of the *Instructio Psalmorum*, the discourse preliminary to the Homilies :—'There is no doubt that the language of the Psalms must be interpreted by the light of the teaching of the Gospel. Thus, whoever he be by whose mouth the Spirit of prophecy has spoken, the whole purpose of his words is our instruction concerning the glory and power of the coming, the Incarnation, the Passion, the kingdom of our Lord Jesus Christ, and of our resurrection. Moreover, all the prophecies are shut and sealed to worldly sense and pagan wisdom, as Isaiah says, *And all these words shall be unto you as the sayings of this book which is sealed*[1]. . . . The whole is a texture woven of allegorical and typical meanings, whereby are spread before our view all the mysteries of the Only-begotten Son of God, Who was to be born in the body, to suffer, to die, to rise again, to reign for ever with those who share His glory because they believed on Him, to be the Judge of the rest of mankind.' It is true that Hilary from time to time discriminates, and sometimes very shrewdly, between passages which must, and others which must not, be thus interpreted, but for the most part the commentary is theological and therefore mystical. The Psalter is not used for the establishment of doctrine. No position for which Hilary had not another and an independent defence is maintained on the strength of an allegorical explanation, and no deductions are drawn from such allegories. They are simply used for the cumulative confirmation of truth otherwise revealed. The result is a commentary much more illustrative of Hilary's own thought than of that of the writers of the Psalms ; and great as are the merits of the Homilies, they are counter-balanced by obvious and serious defects. There is, of course, little interest taken in the circumstances in which the Psalms were written. They are, in Hilary's eyes, essentially prophecies, and he is content as a rule to describe the writer simply as 'the Prophet.' And as with the history, so with the spirit of the Psalter. There is little evidence that he recognised in it the noblest and most perfect expression of human devotion towards God, and still less that he appreciated the elevation of its poetry. For the latter failure there is ample excuse. The Septuagint and Old Latin versions of the Psalms have for us venerable antiquity and sacred associations, but they can hardly be said to appeal to the imagination. Now while Hilary of course regarded the Greek translation as authoritative on account both of our Lord's use of it and of general consent, he treats it not as literature but rather in the spirit of a lawyer interpreting and applying the terms of an ancient charter. Nor is it likely that the Latin version would move Hilary as it sometimes moves us who read it to-day and find a certain dignity and power in its unpolished sentences. Its roughness could only shock, and its obscurity perplex, one who, as we have said already (Intr. iii.), could think and express himself clearly in what was to him a living and a cultivated language. But with all his disadvantages he has produced a great and profoundly Christian work, of permanent value and interest and of abiding influence upon thought, theological and moral. For in these Homilies, and not least in those which are here translated, the Roman genius for moral reflection is manifest, and the pattern set which St. Ambrose was to follow with success in such work as his *De officiis ministrorum.*

---

[1] Is. xxix. 11.

HOMILIES ON THE PSALMS.

PSALM I.

THE primary condition of knowledge for reading the Psalms is the ability to see as whose mouthpiece we are to regard the Psalmist as speaking, and who it is that he addresses. For they are not all of the same uniform character, but of different authorship and different types. For we constantly find that the Person of God the Father is being set before us, as in that passage of the eighty-eighth Psalm : *I have exalted one chosen out of My people, I have found David My servant, with My holy oil have I anointed him. He shall call Me, Thou art my Father and the upholder of my salvation. And I will make him My first-born, higher than the kings of the earth*[1]*;* while in what we might call the majority of Psalms the Person of the Son is introduced, as in the seventeenth : *A people whom I have not known hath served Me*[2]*;* and in the twenty-first: *they parted My garments among them and cast lots upon My vesture*[3]. But the contents of the first Psalm forbid us to understand it either of the Person of the Father or of the Son : *But his will hath been in the law of the Lord, and in His Law will he meditate day and night.* Now in the Psalm in which we said the Person of the Father is intended, the terms used are exactly appropriate, for instance : *He shall call Me, Thou art my Father, my God and the upholder of my salvation ;* and in that one in which we hear the Son speaking, He proclaims Himself to be the author of the words by the very expressions He employs, saying, *A people whom I have not known hath served Me.* That is to say, when the Father on the one hand says : *He shall call Me ;* and the Son on the other hand says : *a people hath served Me,* they shew that it is They Themselves Who are speaking concerning Themselves. Here, however, where we have *But his will hath been in the Law of the Lord ;* obviously it is not the Person of the Lord speaking concerning Himself, but the person of another, extolling the happiness of that man whose will is in the Law of the Lord.

Here, then, we are to recognise the person of the Prophet by whose lips the Holy Spirit speaks, raising us by the instrumentality of his lips to the knowledge of a spiritual mystery.

2. And as he says this we must enquire concerning what man we are to understand him to be speaking. He says: *Happy is the man who hath not walked in the counsel of the ungodly nor stood in the way of sinners, and hath not sat in the seat of pestilence. But his will hath been in the Law of the Lord, and in His Law will he meditate day and night. And he shall be like a tree planted by the rills of water, that will yield its fruit in its own season. His leaf also shall not wither, and all things, whatsoever he shall do, shall prosper.* I have discovered, either from personal conversation or from their letters and writings, that the opinion of many men about this Psalm is, that we ought to understand it to be a description of our Lord Jesus Christ, and that it is His happiness which is extolled in the verses following. But this interpretation is wrong both in method and reasoning, though doubtless it is inspired by a pious tendency of thought, since the whole of the Psalter is to be referred to Him : the time and place in His life to which this passage refers must be ascertained by the sound method of knowledge guided by reason.

3. Now the words which stand at the beginning of the Psalm are quite unsuited to the Person and Dignity of the Son, while the whole contents are in themselves a condemnation of the careless haste that would use them to extol Him. For when it is said, *and his will hath been in the Law of the Lord,* how (seeing that the Law was given by the Son of God) can a happiness which depends on his will being in the Law of the Lord be attributed to Him Who is Himself Lord of the Law? That the Law is His He Himself declares in the seventy-seventh Psalm, where He says: *Hear My Law, O My people : incline your ears unto the words of My mouth. I will open My mouth in a parable*[4]. And the

---

[1] Ps. lxxxviii. (lxxxix.), 20 ff.   [2] Ib. xvii. (xviii.), 45.
[3] Ib. xxi. (xxii.), 19.

[4] Ps. lxxvii. (lxxviii.), 1.

Evangelist Matthew further asserts that these words were spoken by the Son, when he says: *For this cause spake He in parables that the saying might be fulfilled: I will open My mouth in parables* [5]. The Lord then gave fulfilment in act to His own prophecy, speaking in the parables in which He had promised that He would speak. But how can the sentence, *and he shall be like a tree planted by the rills of water*,—wherein growth in happiness is set forth in a figure—be possibly applied to His Person, and a tree be said to be more happy than the Son of God, and the cause of His happiness, which would be the case if an analogy were established between Him and it in respect of growth towards happiness? Again, since according to Wisdom [5a] and the Apostle, He is both before the ages and before times eternal, and is the First-born of every creature; and since in Him and through Him all things were created, how can He be happy by becoming like objects created by Himself? For neither does the power of the Creator need for its exaltation comparison with any creature, nor does the immemorial age of the First-born allow of a comparison involving unsuitable conditions of time, as would be the case if He were compared to a tree. For that which shall be at some point of future time cannot be looked upon as having either previously existed or as now existing anywhere. But whatsoever already is does not need any extension of time to begin existence, because it already possesses continuous existence from the date of its beginning up till the present.

4. And so, since these words are understood to be inapplicable to the divinity of the Only-begotten Son of God, our Lord Jesus Christ, we must suppose him, who is here extolled as happy by the Prophet, to be the man who strives to conform himself to that body which the Lord assumed and in which He was born as man, by zeal for justice and perfect fulfilment of all righteousness. That this is the necessary interpretation will be shewn as the exposition of the Psalm proceeds.

5. The Holy Spirit made choice of this magnificent and noble introduction to the Psalter, in order to stir up weak man to a pure zeal for piety by the hope of happiness, to teach him the mystery of the Incarnate God, to promise him participation in heavenly glory, to declare the penalty of the Judgment, to proclaim the two-fold resurrection, to shew forth the counsel of God as seen in His award. It is indeed after a faultless and mature design that He has laid the foundation of this great prophecy [6]; His will being that the hope connected with the happy man might allure weak humanity to zeal for the Faith; that the analogy of the happiness of the tree might be the pledge of a happy hope, that the declaration of His wrath against the ungodly might set the bounds of fear to the excesses of ungodliness, that difference in rank in the assemblies of the saints might mark difference in merit, that the standard appointed for judging the ways of the righteous might shew forth the majesty of God.

But let us now deal with the subject matter and the words which express it.

6. *Happy is the man who hath not walked in the counsel of the ungodly nor stood in the way of sinners, and hath not sat in the seat of pestilence. But his will hath been in the Law of the Lord, and in His Law will he meditate day and night.*

The Prophet recites five kinds of caution as continually present in the mind of the happy man: the first, not to walk in the counsel of the ungodly, the second, not to stand in the way of sinners, the third, not to sit in the seat of pestilence, next, to set his will in the Law of the Lord, and lastly, to meditate therein by day and by night. There must, therefore, be a distinction between the ungodly and the sinner, between the sinner and the pestilent; chiefly because here the ungodly has a counsel, the sinner a way, the pestilent a seat, and again, because the question is of walking, not standing, in the counsel of the ungodly; of standing, not walking, in the way of the sinner. Now, if we would understand the reason of these facts, we must note the precise difference between the sinner and the undutiful [7], that so it may become clear why to the sinner is assigned a way, and to the undutiful a counsel; next, why the question is of standing in the way, and of walking in the counsel, whereas men are accustomed to connect standing with a counsel, and walking with a way.

Not every man that is a sinner is also undutiful: but the undutiful man cannot fail to be a sinner. Let us take an instance from general experience. Sons, though they be drunken and profligate and spendthrift, can yet love their fathers; and with all these vices, and, therefore, not free from guilt, may yet be free from undutifulness. But the undutiful, though they may be models of continence and frugality, are, by the mere fact of despising the parent, worse transgressors than if they were guilty of every sin that lies outside the category of undutifulness.

---

5 St. Matt. xiii. 35.   5a Prov. viii. 22.   6 i.e. the Psalter.

7 *Impius*, which is elsewhere in the Homily translated *ungodly*, is here rendered *undutiful*, in order to preserve to some extent the sense of *undutiful towards parents* in which Hilary, with true Roman appreciation of the *patria potestas*, uses it in this passage.

7. There is no doubt then that, as this instance proves, the undutiful (or ungodly) must be distinguished from the sinner. And, indeed, general opinion agrees to call those men ungodly who scorn to search for the knowledge of God, who in their irreverent mind take for granted that there is no Creator of the world, who assert that it arrived at the order and beauty which we see by chance movements, who, in order to deprive their Creator of all power to pass judgment on a life lived rightly or in sin, will have it that man comes into being and passes out of it again by the simple operation of a law of nature.

Thus, all the counsel of these men is wavering, unsteady, and vague, and wanders about in the same familiar paths and over the same familiar ground, never finding a resting-place, for it fails to reach any definite decision. They have never in their system risen to the doctrine of a Creator of the world, for instead of answering our questions as to the cause, beginning, and duration of the world, whether the world is for man, or man for the world, the reason of death, its extent and nature, they press in ceaseless motion round the circle of this godless argument and find no rest in these imaginings.

8. There are, besides, other counsels of the ungodly, i.e., of those who have fallen into heresy, unrestrained by the laws of either the New Testament or the Old. Their reasoning ever takes the course of a vicious circle; without grasp or foothold to stay them they tread their interminable round of endless indecision. Their ungodliness consists in measuring God, not by His own revelation, but by a standard of their choosing; they forget that it is as godless to make a God as to deny Him; if you ask them what effect these opinions have on their faith and hope, they are perplexed and confused, they wander from the point and wilfully avoid the real issue of the debate. Happy is the man then who hath not walked in this kind of counsel of the ungodly, nay, who has not even entertained the wish to walk therein, for it is a sin even to think for a moment of things that are ungodly.

9. The next condition is, that the man who has not walked in the counsel of the ungodly shall not stand in the way of sinners. For there are many whose confession concerning God, while it acquits them of ungodliness, yet does not set them free from sin; those, for example, who abide in the Church but do not observe her laws; such are the greedy, the drunken, the brawlers, the wanton, the proud, hypocrites, liars, plunderers. No doubt we are urged towards these sins by the promptings of our natural instincts; but it is good for us to withdraw from the path into which we are being hurried and not to stand therein, seeing that we are offered so easy a way of escape. It is for this reason that the man who has not stood in the way of sinners is happy, for while nature carries him into that way, religious belief draws him back.

10. Now the third condition for gaining happiness is not to sit in the seat of pestilence. The Pharisees sat as teachers in Moses' seat, and Pilate sat in the seat of judgment: of what seat then are we to consider the occupation pestilential? Not surely of that of Moses, for it is the occupants of the seat and not the occupation of it that the Lord condemns when He says: *The Scribes and Pharisees sit on Moses' seat; whatsoever they bid you do, that do; but do not ye after their work* [8]. The occupation of that seat is not pestilential, to which obedience is enjoined by the Lord's own word. That then must be really pestilential, the infection of which Pilate sought to avoid by washing his hands. For many, even God-fearing men, are led astray by the canvassing for worldly honours; and desire to administer the law of the courts, though they are bound by those of the Church.

But although they bring to the discharge of their duties a religious intention, as is shewn by their merciful and upright demeanour, still they cannot escape a certain contagious infection arising from the business in which their life is spent. For the conduct of civil cases does not suffer them to be true to the holy principles of the Church's law, even though they wish it. And without abandoning their pious purpose they are compelled, against their will, by the necessary conditions of the seat they have won, to use, at one time invective, at another, insult, at another, punishment; and their very position makes them authors as well as victims of the necessity which constrains them, their system being as it were impregnated with the infection. Hence this title, *the seat of pestilence*, by which the Prophet describes their seat, because by its infection it poisons the very will of the religiously minded.

11. But the fact that he has not walked in the counsel of the ungodly, nor stood in the way of sinners, nor sat in the seat of pestilence, does not constitute the perfection of the man's happiness. For the belief that one God is the Creator of the world, the avoidance of sin by the pursuit of unassuming goodness, the preference of the tranquil leisure of private life to the grandeur of public position—all this may be found even in a pagan. But here

---

[8] St. Matt. xxiii. 2.

the Prophet, in portraying in the likeness of God the man that is perfect—one who may serve as a noble example of eternal happiness—points to the exercise by him of no commonplace virtues, and to the words, *But his will hath been in the Law of the Lord*, for the attainment of perfect happiness. To refrain from what has gone before is useless unless his mind be set on what follows, *But his will hath been in the Law of the Lord*. The Prophet does not look for fear. The majority of men are kept within the bounds of Law by fear; the few are brought under the Law by will: for it is the mark of fear not to dare to omit what it is afraid of, but of perfect piety to be ready to obey commands. This is why that man is happy whose will, not whose fear, is in the Law of God.

12. But then sometimes the will needs supplementing; and the mere desire for perfect happiness does not win it, unless performance wait upon intention. The Psalm, you remember, goes on: *And in His Law will he meditate day and night.* The man achieves the perfection of happiness by unbroken and unwearied meditation in the Law. Now it may be objected that this is impossible owing to the conditions of human infirmity, which require time for repose, for sleep, for food: so that our bodily circumstances preclude us from the hope of attaining happiness, inasmuch as we are distracted by the interruption of our bodily needs from our meditation by day and night. Parallel to this passage are the words of the Apostle, *Pray without ceasing* [9]. As though we were bound to set at naught our bodily requirements and to continue praying without any interruption! Meditation in the Law, therefore, does not lie in reading its words, but in pious performance of its injunctions; not in a mere perusal of the books and writings, but in a practical meditation and exercise in their respective contents, and in a fulfilment of the Law by the works we do by night and day, as the Apostle says: *Whether ye eat or drink, or whatsoever ye do, do all to the glory of God* [1]. The way to secure uninterrupted prayer is for every devout man to make his life one long prayer by works acceptable to God and always done to His glory: thus a life lived according to the Law by night and day will in itself become a nightly and daily meditation in the Law.

13. But now that the man has found perfect happiness by keeping aloof from the counsel of the ungodly and the way of sinners and the seat of pestilence, and by gladly meditating in the Law of God by day and by night, we are next to be shewn the rich fruit that this happiness he has won will yield him. Now the anticipation of happiness contains the germ of future happiness. For the next verse runs: *And he shall be like a tree planted beside the rills of water, which shall yield its fruit in its own season, whose leaf also shall not fall off.* This may perhaps be deemed an absurd and inappropriate comparison, in which are extolled a planted tree, rills of water, the yielding of fruit, its own time, and the leaf that falls not. All this may appear trivial enough to the judgment of the world. But let us examine the teaching of the Prophet and see the beauty that lies in the objects and words used to illustrate happiness.

14. In the book of Genesis [2], where the lawgiver depicts the paradise planted by God, we are shewn that every tree is fair to look upon and good for food; it is also stated that there stands in the midst of the garden a tree of Life and a tree of the knowledge of good and evil; next that the garden is watered by a stream that afterwards divides into four heads. The Prophet Solomon teaches us what this tree of Life is in his exhortation concerning Wisdom: *She is a tree of life to all them that lay hold upon her, and lean upon her* [3]. This tree then is living; and not only living, but, furthermore, guided by reason; guided by reason, that is, in so far as to yield fruit, and that not casually nor unseasonably, but in its own season. And this tree is planted beside the rills of water in the domain of the Kingdom of God, that is, of course, in Paradise, and in the place where the stream as it issues forth is divided into four heads. For he does not say, *Behind the rills of water*, but, *Beside the rills of water*, at the place where first the heads receive each their flow of waters. This tree is planted in that place whither the Lord, Who is Wisdom, leads the thief who confessed Him to be the Lord, saying: *Verily I say unto thee, to day shalt thou be with Me in Paradise* [4]. And now that we have shewn upon prophetic warrant that Wisdom, which is Christ, is called the tree of Life in accordance with the mystery of the coming Incarnation and Passion, we must go on to find support for the strict truth of this interpretation from the Gospels. The Lord with His own lips compared Himself to a tree when the Jews said that He cast out devils in Beelzebub: *Either make the tree good*, said He, *and its fruit good; or else make the tree corrupt, and its fruit corrupt; for the tree is known by its fruit* [5]; because although to cast out devils is an excellent fruit, they said He was Beelzebub,

9 1 Thess. v. 17.   1 1 Cor. x. 31.   2 Gen. ii. 9.   3 Prov. iii. 18.   4 St. Luke xxiii. 43.   5 St. Matt. xii. 33.

whose fruits are abominable. Nor yet did He hesitate to teach that the power that makes the tree happy resided in His Person, when on the way to the Cross He said: *For if they do these things in the green tree, what shall be done in the dry* [6]? Declaring by this image of the green tree that there was nothing in Him that was subject to the dryness of death.

15. That happy man, then, will become like unto this tree when he shall be transplanted, as the thief was, into the garden and set to grow beside the rills of water : and his planting will be that happy new planting which cannot be uprooted, to which the Lord refers in the Gospels when He curses the other kind of planting and says: *Every planting that My Father hath not planted shall be rooted up* [7]. This tree, therefore, will yield its fruits. Now in all other passages where God's Word teaches some lesson from the fruits of trees, it mentions them as making fruit rather than as yielding fruit, as when it says: *A good tree cannot make evil fruits* [8], and when in Isaiah the complaint about the vine is: *I looked that it should make grapes, and it made thorns* [9]. But this tree will yield its fruits, being supplied with free-will and understanding for the purpose. For it will yield its fruits in its own season. And, pray, in what season? In the season, of course, of which the Apostle speaks: *That He might make known unto you also the mystery of His Will, according to His good pleasure which He hath purposed in Himself, in the dispensation of the fulness of time* [1]. This, then, is the dispensation of time, by which is regulated the right moment of receiving, in the case of the recipients, and of giving, in that of the giver; for the giver has choice of the season. But delay in point of time depends upon the fulness of times. For the dispensation of yielding fruit waits upon the fulness of time. Now what, you ask, is this fruit that is to be dispensed? That assuredly of which this same Apostle is speaking when he says: *And He will change our vile body, that it may be fashioned like His glorious body* [2]. Thus He will give us those fruits of His which He has already brought to perfection in that man whom He has chosen to Himself, who is portrayed under the image of a tree, whose mortality He has utterly done away and has raised him to share in His own immortality.

This man then will be happy like that tree, when at length he stands surrounded by the glory of God, being made like unto the Lord.

16. *But the leaf of this tree shall not fall off.* There is no ground for wonder that its leaves do not fall off, seeing that its fruits will not drop to the ground, either because they are forced off by ripeness, or shaken off by external violence, but it will yield them, distributing them by an act of reasoned service. Now the spiritual significance of the leaves is made clear by a comparison based upon material objects. We see that leaves are made to sprout round the fruits about which they cluster, for the express purpose of protecting them, and of forming a kind of fence to the young and tender shoots. What the leaves signify, then, is the teaching of God's words in which the promised fruits are clothed. For it is these words that kindly shade our hopes, that shield and protect them from the rough winds of this world. These leaves, then, that is the words of God, shall not fall: for the Lord Himself has said : *Heaven and earth shall pass away, but My words shall not pass away* [3], for of the words that have been spoken by God not one shall fail or fall.

17. Now that the leaves of the tree we speak of are not valueless but are a source of health to the nations is testified by St. John in the Apocalypse, where he says: *And He shewed me a river of water of life, bright as crystal, proceeding out of the throne of God and of the Lamb; in the midst of the street of it and on either side of the river the tree of life, bearing twelve manner of fruits, yielding its fruit every month: and the leaves of the tree are for the healing of the nations* [4].

Bodily manifestations so reveal the mysteries of heaven that, although matter by itself cannot convey the full spiritual meaning, yet to regard them only in their material aspect is to mutilate them. We should have expected to hear that there were trees, not one tree, standing on either side of the river shewn to the saint. But because the tree of Life in the sacrament of Baptism is in every case one, supplying to those that come to it on every side the fruits of the apostolic message, so there stands on either side of the river one tree of Life. There is one Lamb seen amid the throne of God, and one river, and one tree of Life : three figures wherein are comprised the mysteries of the Incarnation, Baptism and Passion, whose leaves, that is to say, the words of the Gospel, bring healing to the nations through the teaching of a message that cannot fall to the ground.

18. *And all things whatsoever he doeth shall prosper.* Never again shall His gift and His statutes be set at naught, as they were in the case of Adam, who by his sin in breaking the

---

6 St. Luke xxiii. 31.   7 St. Matt. xv. 13.   8 Ib. vii. 18.
9 Is. v. 2.   1 Eph. i. 9.   2 Phil. iii. 21.

3 St. Matt. xxiv. 35.   4 Apoc. xxii. 1.

Law lost the happiness of an assured immortality; but now, thanks to the redemption wrought by the tree of Life, that is, by the Passion of the Lord, all that happens to us is eternal and eternally conscious of happiness, in virtue of our future likeness to that tree of Life. For all their doings shall prosper, being wrought no longer amid shift and change nor in human weakness, for corruption will be swallowed up in incorruption, weakness in endless life, the form of earthly flesh in the form of God. This tree, then, planted and yielding its fruit in its own season, shall that happy man resemble, himself being planted in the Garden, that what God has planted may abide, never to be rooted up, in the Garden where all things done by God shall be guided to a prosperous issue, apart from the decay that belongs to human weakness and to time, and has to be uprooted.

19. The next point after the prophet had set forth the man's perfect happiness was for him to declare what punishment remained for the ungodly. Thus there ensues: *The ungodly are not so, but are like the dust which the wind driveth away from the face of the earth.* The ungodly have no possible hope of having the image of the happy tree applied to them; the only lot that awaits them is one of wandering and winnowing, crushing, dispersion and unrest; shaken out of the solid framework of their bodily condition, they must be swept away to punishment in dust, a plaything of the wind. They shall not be dissolved into nothing, for punishment must find in them some stuff to work on, but ground into particles, imponderable, unsubstantial, dry, they shall be tossed to and fro, and make sport for the punishment that gives them never rest. Their punishment is recorded by the same Prophet in another place where he says: *I will beat them small as the dust before the wind, like the mire of the streets I will destroy them* [5].

Thus as there is an appointed type for happiness, so is there one for punishment. For as it is no hard task for the wind to scatter the dust, and as men who walk through the mud of the streets are hardly aware that they have been treading on it, so it is easy for the punishment of hell to destroy and disperse the ungodly, the logical result of whose sins is to melt them into mud and crush them into dust, reft of all solid substance, for dust and mud they are, and being merely mud and dust are good for nothing else than punishment.

20. And the Prophet, seeing that the change of their solid substance into dust will deprive them of all share in the boon of fruit to be bestowed upon the happy man in season by the tree, has accordingly added: *Therefore the ungodly shall not rise again in the Judgment.* The fact that they shall not rise again does not convey sentence of annihilation upon these men, for indeed they will exist as dust; it is the resurrection to Judgment that is denied them. Non-existence will not enable them to miss the pain of punishment; for while that which will be non-existent would escape punishment, they, on the other hand, will exist to be punished, for they will be dust. Now to become dust, whether by being dried to dust or ground to dust, involves not loss of the state of existence, but a change of state. But the fact that they will not rise again to Judgment makes it clear that they have lost, not the power to rise, but the privilege of rising to Judgment. Now what we are to understand by the privilege of rising again and being judged is declared by the Lord in the Gospels where He says: *He that believeth on Me is not judged: he that believeth not hath been judged already. And this is the judgment, that the light is come into the world, and men loved the darkness rather than the light* [6].

21. The terms of this utterance of the Lord are disturbing to inattentive hearers and careless, hasty readers. For by saying, *He that believeth on Me shall not be judged*, He exempts believers, and by adding: *But he that believeth not hath been judged already*, He excludes unbelievers, from judgment. If, then, He has thus exempted believers and debarred unbelievers, allowing the chance of judgment neither to one class nor the other, how can He be considered consistent when he adds thirdly: *And this is the judgment, that the light is come into the world, and men loved the darkness rather than the light?* For there can apparently be no place left for judgment, since neither believers nor unbelievers are to be judged. Such no doubt will be the conclusion drawn by inattentive hearers and hasty readers. The utterance, however, has an appropriate meaning and a rational interpretation of its own.

22. He that believes, says Christ, is not judged. And is there any need to judge a believer? Judgment arises out of ambiguity, and where ambiguity ceases, there is no call for trial and judgment. Hence not even unbelievers need be judged, because there is no doubt about their being unbelievers; but after exempting believers and unbelievers alike from judgment, the Lord added a case for judgment and human agents upon whom it must be

---

exercised. For some there are who stand midway between the godly and the ungodly, having affinities to both, but strictly belonging to neither class, because they have come to be what they are by a combination of the two. They may not be assigned to the ranks of belief, because there is in them a certain infusion of unbelief; they may not be ranged with unbelief, because they are not without a certain portion of belief. For many are kept within the pale of the church by the fear of God; yet they are tempted all the while to worldly faults by the allurements of the world. They pray, because they are afraid; they sin, because it is their will. The fair hope of future life makes them call themselves Christians; the allurements of present pleasure make them act like heathen. They do not abide in ungodliness, because they hold the name of God in honour; they are not godly because they follow after things contrary to godliness. And they cannot help loving those things best which can never enable them to be what they call themselves, because their desire to do such works is stronger than their desire to be true to their name. And this is why the Lord, after saying that believers would not be judged and that unbelievers had been judged already, added that *This is the judgment, that the light is come into the world, and men loved the darkness rather than the light.*

These, then, are they whom the judgment awaits which unbelievers have already had passed upon them and believers do not need: because they have loved darkness more than light; not that they did not love the light too, but because their love of darkness is the more active. For when two loves are matched in rivalry, one always wins the preference; and their judgment arises from the fact that, though they loved Christ, they yet loved darkness more. These then will be judged; they are neither exempted from judgment like the godly, nor have they already been judged like the ungodly; but judgment awaits them for the love which they have deliberately preferred.

23. It is precisely the scheme and system thus laid down in the Gospel that the Prophet has followed, when he says: *Therefore the ungodly shall not rise again in the Judgment, nor sinners in the counsel of the righteous.* He leaves no judgment for the ungodly, because they have been judged already; on the other hand, he has refused to sinners, who as we shewed in our former discourse [7] are to be distinguished from the ungodly, the counsel of

the righteous, because they are to be judged. For ungodliness causes the former to be judged beforehand, but sin keeps the latter to be judged hereafter. Thus ungodliness having already been judged is not admitted to the judgment of sinners, while again sinners, who are yet to be judged, are deemed unworthy of enjoying the counsel of the righteous, who will not be judged.

24. The source of this distinction lies in the following words: *For the Lord knoweth the way of the righteous, but the way of the ungodly shall perish.* Sinners do not come near the counsel of the righteous for this reason, that the Lord knows the way of the righteous. Now He knows, not by an advance from ignorance to knowledge, but because He condescends to know. For there is no play of human emotions in God that He should know or not know anything. The blessed Apostle Paul declared how we were known of God when he said: *If any man among you is a prophet or spiritual, let him take knowledge of the things which I write unto you, that they are of the Lord: but if any man does not know, he is not known* [8].

Thus he shews that those are known of God who know the things of God: they are to come to be known when they know, that is, when they attain to the honour of being known through the merit of their known godliness, in order that the knowledge may be seen to be a growth on the part of him who is known, and not a growth on the part of one who knows not.

Now God shews clearly in the cases of Adam and Abraham that He does not know sinners, but does know believers. For it was said to Adam when he had sinned: *Adam, where art thou* [9]? Not because God knew not that the man whom He still had in the garden was there still, but to shew, by his being asked where he was, that he was unworthy of God's knowledge by the fact of having sinned. But Abraham, after being for a long time unknown—the word of God came to him when he was seventy years of age—was, upon his proving himself faithful to the Lord, admitted to intimacy with God by the following act of high condescension: *Now I know that thou fearest the Lord thy God, and for My sake thou hast not spared thy dearly loved son* [1].

God certainly was not ignorant of the faith of Abraham, which He had already reckoned to him for righteousness when he believed about the birth of Isaac: but now because he had given a signal instance of his fear in offering his son, he is at last known, approved, rendered worthy of being not unknown. It is

---

[7] This proves that the Homily in its original form consisted of two parts.

[8] 1 Cor. xiv. 37.   [9] Gen. iii. 9.   [1] Ib. xxii. 12.

in this way then that God both knows and knows not—Adam the sinner is not known, and Abraham the faithful is known, is worthy, that is, of being known by God Who surely knows all things. The way of the righteous, therefore, who are not to be judged is known by God : and this is why sinners, who are to be judged, are set far from their counsel ; while the ungodly shall not rise again to judgment, because their way has perished, and they have already been judged by Him Who said : *The Father judgeth no man*, but hath given all judgment unto the Son, our Lord Jesus Christ, Who is blessed for ever and ever. Amen.

PSALM LIII. (LIV.).

For the end among the hymns, of the meaning of David when the Ziphims came and said to Saul: behold. is not David hid with us ?

Save me, O God, by Thy name, and judge me by Thy power. Hear my prayer, O God ; give ear unto the words of my mouth, and so on.

1. The doctrines of the Gospel were well known to holy and blessed David in his capacity of Prophet, and although it was under the Law that he lived his bodily life, he yet fulfilled, as far as in him lay, the requirements of the Apostolic behest and justified the witness borne to him by God in the words : *I have found a man after My own heart, David, the son of Jesse*[2]. He did not avenge himself upon his foes by war, he did not oppose force of arms to those that laid wait for him, but after the pattern of the Lord, Whose name and Whose meekness alike he foreshadowed, when he was betrayed he entreated, when he was in danger he sang psalms, when he incurred hatred he rejoiced ; and for this cause he was found a man after God's own heart. For although twelve legions of angels might have come to the help of the Lord in His hour of passion, yet that He might perfectly fulfil His service of humble obedience, He surrendered Himself to suffering and weakness, only praying with the words : *Father into Thy hands I commend My spirit*[3]. After the same pattern, David, whose actual sufferings prophetically foretold the future sufferings of the Lord, opposed not his enemies either by word or act ; in obedience to the command of the Gospel, he would not render evil for evil, in imitation of his Master's meekness, in his affliction, in his betrayal, in his flight, he called upon the Lord and was content to use His weapons only in his contest with the ungodly.

2. Now to this Psalm is prefixed a title arising out of an historical event ; but before the event is described we are instructed as to the scope, time and application of the incidents underlying it. First we have : *For the end of the meaning of that David.* Then there follows : *When the Ziphims came and said to Saul: behold, is not David hid with us ?* Thus David's betrayal by the Ziphims awaits for its interpretation the end. This shews that what was actually being done to David contained a type of something yet to come ; an innocent man is harassed by railing, a prophet is mocked by reviling words, one approved by God is demanded for execution, a king is betrayed to his foe. So the Lord was betrayed to Herod and Pilate by those very men in whose hands He ought to have been safe. The Psalm then awaits the end for its interpretation, and finds its meaning in the true David, in Whom is the end of the Law, that David who holds the keys and opens with them the gate of knowledge, in fulfilling the things foretold of Him by David.

3. The meaning of the proper name, according to the exact sense of the Hebrew, affords us no small assistance in interpreting the passage. *Ziphims* mean what we call sprinklings of the face ; these were called in Hebrew *Ziphims*. Now, by the Law, sprinkling was a cleansing from sins ; it purified the people through faith by the sprinkling of blood, of which this same blessed David thus speaks : *Thou shalt sprinkle me with hyssop and I shall be cleansed*[4] ; the Law, through faith, providing as a temporary substitute, in the blood of whole burnt-offerings, a type of the sprinkling with the blood of the Lord, which was to be. But this people, like the people of the Ziphims, being sprinkled on their face and not in their faith, and receiving the cleansing drops on their lips and not in their hearts, turned faithless and traitors towards their David, as God had foretold by the Prophet : *This people honoureth Me with their lips, but their heart is far from Me*[5]. They were ready to betray David because, the faith of their heart being dead, they had performed all the mystical ceremonies of the Law with deceitful face.

4. *Save me, O God, by Thy Name, and judge me by Thy power. Hear my prayer, O God ; give ear unto the words of my mouth.*

---

[2] Acts xiii. 22 (cp. 1 Sam. xiii. 14).　　[3] St. Luke xxiii. 46.　　[4] Ps. l. (li.) 9.　　[5] Is. xxix. 13.

The suffering of the Prophet David is, according to the account we have given of the title, a type of the Passion of our God and Lord Jesus Christ. This is why his prayer also corresponds in sense with the prayer of Him, Who being the Word was made flesh : in such wise that He Who suffered all things after the manner of man, in everything He said, spoke after the manner of man ; and He who bore the infirmities and took on Him the sins of men approached God in prayer with the humility proper to men. This interpretation, even though we be unwilling and slow to receive it, is required by the meaning and force of the words, so that there can be no doubt that everything in the Psalm is uttered by David as His mouthpiece. For he says : *Save me, O God, by Thy name.* Thus prays in bodily humiliation, using the words of His own Prophet, the Only-begotten Son of God, Who at the same time was claiming again the glory which He had possessed before the ages. He asks to be saved by the Name of God whereby He was called and wherein He was begotten, in order that the Name of God which rightly belonged to His former nature and kind might avail to save Him in that body wherein He had been born.

5. And because the whole of this passage is the utterance of One in the form of a servant—of a servant obedient unto the death of the Cross—which He took upon Him and for which He supplicates the saving help of the Name that belongs to God, and being sure of salvation by that Name, He immediately adds : *and judge Me by Thy power.* For now, as the reward for His humility in emptying Himself and assuming the form of a servant, in the same humility in which He had assumed it, He was asking to resume the form which He shared with God, having saved to bear the Name of God that humanity in which as God He had obediently condescended to be born. And in order to teach us that the dignity of this Name whereby He prayed to be saved is something more than an empty title, He prays to be judged by the power of God. For a right award is the essential result of judgment, as the Scripture says : *Becoming obedient unto death* [6], *yea, the death of the Cross. Wherefore also God highly exalted Him and gave unto Him the name which is above every name.* Thus, first of all the name which is above every name is given unto Him ; then next, this is a judgment of decisive force, because by the power of God, He, Who after being God had died as man, rose again from death as man to be God, as the Apostle says : *He was crucified*

from weakness, yet He liveth by the power of God [7], and again : *For I am not ashamed of the Gospel : for it is the power of God unto salvation to every one that believeth* [8]. For by the power of the Judgment human weakness is rescued to bear God's name and nature ; and thus as the reward for His obedience He is exalted by the power of this judgment unto the saving protection of God's name ; whence He possesses both the Name and the Power of God. Again, if the Prophet had begun this utterance in the way men generally speak, he would have asked to be judged by mercy or kindness, not by power. But judgment by power was a necessity in the case of One Who being the Son of God was born of a virgin to be Son of Man, and Who now being Son of Man was to have the Name and power of the Son of God restored to Him by the power of judgment.

6. Next there follows : *Hear my prayer, O God, give ear unto the words of my mouth.* The obvious thing for the Prophet to say was, *O God, hear me.* But because he is speaking as the mouthpiece of Him, Who alone knew how to pray, we are given a constantly reiterated demand that prayer shall be heard. The words of St. Paul teach us that no man knows how he ought to pray : *For we know not how to pray as we ought* [9]. Man in his weakness, therefore, has no right to demand that his prayer shall be heard : for even the teacher of the Gentiles does not know the true object and scope of prayer, and that, after the Lord had given a model. What we are shewn here is the perfect confidence of Him, Who alone sees the Father, Who alone knows the Father, Who alone can pray the whole night through—the Gospel tells us that the Lord continued all night in prayer—Who in the mirror of words has shewn us the true image of the deepest of all mysteries in the simple words we use in prayer. And so, in making the demand that His prayer should be heard, he added, in order to teach us that this was the prerogative of His perfect confidence : *Give ear unto the words of My mouth.* Now can any man suppose that it is a human confidence which can thus desire that the words of his mouth should be heard? Those words, for instance, in which we express the motions and instincts of the mind, either when anger inflames us, or hatred moves us to slander, or pain to complaint, when flattery makes us fawn, when hope of gain or shame of the truth begets the lie, or resentment over injury, the insult? Was there ever any man at all points so pure and patient in his life as not to be liable to these failings of human insta-

6 Phil. ii. 8 ff.   7 2 Cor. xiii. 4.   8 Rom. i. 16.   9 Ib. viii. 26.

bility? He alone could confidently desire this Who did no sin, in Whose mouth was no deceit, Who gave His back to the smiters, Who turned not His cheek from the blow, Who did not resent scorn and spitting, Who never crossed the will of Him, to Whose Will ordering it all He gave in all points glad obedience.

7. He has next added the reason why He prays for His words to be heard : *For strangers are risen up against Me and violent men have sought after My soul; they have not set God before their eyes.* The Only-begotten Son of God, the Word of God and God the Word— although assuredly He could Himself do all things that the Father could, as He says: *What things soever the Father doeth, the Son also doeth in like manner*[1], while the name describing the divine nature which was His inseparably involved the inseparable possession of divine power,— yet in order that He might present to us a perfect example of human humility, both prayed for and underwent all things that are the lot of man. Sharing in our common weakness He prayed the Father to save Him, so that He might teach us that He was born man under all the conditions of man's infirmity. This is why He was hungry and thirsty, slept and was weary, shunned the assemblies of the ungodly, was sad and wept, suffered and died. And it was in order to make it clear that He was subject to all these conditions, not by His nature, but by assumption, that when He had undergone them all He rose again. Thus all His complaints in the Psalms spring from a mental state belonging to our nature. Nor must it cause surprise if we take the words of the Psalms in this sense, seeing that the Lord Himself testified, if we believe the Gospel, that the Psalms spiritually foretold His Passion.

8. Now they were *strangers that rose up against Him.* For these are no sons of Abraham, nor sons of God, but a brood of vipers, servants of sin, a Canaanitish seed, their father an Amorite and their mother a daughter of Heth, inheriting diabolical desires from the devil their parent. Further it is *the violent* that seek after His soul; such as was Herod when he asked the chief priests where Christ should be born, such as was the whole synagogue when it bore false witness against Him. But in deeming this soul to be of human nature and weakness *they set not God before their eyes;* for God had stooped from that estate wherein He abode as God, even to the beginnings of human birth; that is, He became Son of Man Who before was the Son

of God. For the Son of God is none other than He Who is Son of Man, and Son of Man not in partial measure but born so, the Form of God divesting Itself of that which It was and becoming that which It was not, that so It might be born into a soul and body of Its own. Hence He is both Son of God and Son of Man, hence both God and Man : in other words the Son of God was born with the attributes derived from human birth, the Nature of God condescending to assume the nature of one born as man who is wholly moulded of soul and flesh. Wherefore strangers, when they rise up against Him, and the mighty, when they seek after that soul of His, which in the Gospels is often sad and cast down, set not God before their eyes, because God it was, and the Son of God existing from out the ages, that was born with the attributes of human nature, was born as man, that is, with our body and our soul, by a virgin birth ; the mighty and glorious works He wrought never opened their eyes to the fact that the Son of Man Whose soul they were seeking had come to be man with a beginning of life after an eternal existence as Son of God.

9. The introduction of a pause[2] marks a change of person. He no longer speaks but is addressed. For now the prophetic utterance assumes a general character. Thus immediately after the prayer addressed to God, he has added, in order that the confidence of the speaker might be understood to have obtained what He was asking even in the very moment of asking: *Behold, God is My helper and the Lord is the upholder of My soul. He has requited evil unto Mine enemies.* To each separate petition he has assigned its proper result, thus teaching us both that God does not neglect to hear, and that to look for a pledge of His pitifulness in hearing our several petitions is not a thing unreasonable. For to the words, *For strangers are risen up against Me,* the corresponding statement is : *God is My helper;* while with regard to *and the violent have sought after My soul,* the exact result of the hearing of His prayer is expressed in the words : *and the Lord is the upholder of My soul;* lastly the statement, *they have not set God before their eyes,* is appropriately balanced by, *He hath requited evil unto Mine enemies.* Thus God both gives help against those that rise up, and upholds the soul of His Holy One when it is sought by the violent, and when He is not set before the eyes, nor considered by the ungodly, He requites upon His enemies the very evils which they had wrought; so that while without think-

---

[1] St. John v. 19.

[2] *Diapsalmus,* see Suicer, s.v. and Dict. of Bible, *Selah.*

ing upon God they seek the soul of the righteous and rise up against Him, He is saved and upheld, and they find that He Whom, absorbed in their wicked works, they did not consider, avenges their malice by turning it against themselves.

10. Let pure religion, therefore, have this confidence, and doubt not that amid the persecutions at the hand of man and the dangers to the soul, it still has God for its helper, knowing that, if at length it comes to a violent and unjust death, the soul on leaving the tabernacle of the body finds rest with God its upholder; let it have, moreover, perfect assurance of requital in the thought that all evil deeds return upon the heads of those that work them. God cannot be charged with injustice, and perfect goodness is unstained by the impulses and motions of an evil will. He does not awaken mischief out of malice, but requites it in vengeance; He does not inflict it because He wishes us ill, but He aims it against our sins. For these evils are universally appointed as instruments of retribution without destruction of life, such being the sternly just ord'nance of that righteous judgment. But these evils are warded off from the righteous by the law of righteousness, and are turned back upon the unrighteous by the righteousness of that judgment. Each proceeding is equally just; for the righteous, because they are righteous, the warning exhibition of evil without actual infliction; for the wicked, because they so deserve, the punitive infliction of evil; the righteous will not suffer it, though it is displayed to them; the wicked will never cease to suffer it, because it is displayed to them.

11. After this there is a return to the Person of God, to Whom the petition was at the first addressed : *Destroy them by Thy truth*. Truth confounds falsehood, and lying is destroyed by truth. We have shewn that the whole of the foregoing prayer is the utterance of that human nature in which the Son of God was born ; so here it is the voice of human nature calling upon God the Father to destroy His enemies in His truth. What this truth is, stands beyond doubt ; it is of course He Who said : *I am the Life, the Way, the Truth* [3]. And the enemies were destroyed by the truth when, for all their attempts to win Christ's condemnation by false witness, they heard that He was risen from the dead and had to admit that He had resumed His glory in all the reality of Godhead. Ere long they found, in ruin and destruction by famine and war, their reward for crucifying God ; for they condemned the Lord of Life to death, and paid no heed to God's truth displayed in Him through His glorious works. And thus the Truth of God destroyed them when He rose again to resume the majesty of His Father's Glory, and gave proof of the truth of that perfect Divinity which He possessed.

12. Now in view of our repeated, nay our unbroken assertion both that it was the Only-begotten Son of God Who was uplifted on the cross, and that He was condemned to death Who is eternal by virtue of the origin which is His by the nature which He derives from the eternal Father, it must be clearly understood that He was subjected to suffering of no natural necessity, but to accomplish the mystery of man's salvation ; that He submitted to suffering of His own Will, and not under compulsion. And although this suffering did not belong to His nature as eternal Son, the immutability of God being proof against the assault of any derogatory disturbance, yet it was freely undertaken, and was intended to fulfil a penal function without, however, inflicting the pain of penalty upon the sufferer: not that the suffering in question was not of a kind to cause pain, but because the divine Nature feels no pain. God suffered, then, by voluntarily submitting to suffering ; but although He underwent the sufferings in all the fulness of their force, which necessarily causes pain to the sufferers, yet He never so abandoned the powers of His Nature as to feel pain.

13. For next there follows : *I will sacrifice unto Thee freely*. The sacrifices of the Law, which consisted of whole burnt-offerings and oblations of goats and of bulls, did not involve an expression of free will, because the sentence of a curse was pronounced on all who broke the Law. Whoever failed to sacrifice laid himself open to the curse. And it was always necessary to go through the whole sacrificial action because the addition of a curse to the commandment forbad any trifling with the obligation of offering. It was from this curse that our Lord Jesus Christ redeemed us, when, as the Apostle says: *Christ redeemed us from the curse of the law, being made curse for us, for it is written : cursed is every one that hangeth on a tree* [4]. Thus He offered Himself to the death of the accursed that He might break the curse of the Law, offering Himself voluntarily a victim to God the Father, in order that by means of a voluntary victim the curse which attended the discontinuance of the regular victim might be removed. Now of this sacrifice mention is made in another passage of the

Psalms: *Sacrifice and offering thou wouldest not, but a body hast thou prepared for me* [4a]*;* that is, by offering to God the Father, Who refused the legal sacrifices, the acceptable offering of the body which He received. Of which offering the holy Apostle thus speaks: *For this He did once for all when He offered Himself up* [5], securing complete salvation for the human race by the offering of this holy, perfect victim.

14. Then He gives thanks to God the Father for the accomplishment of all these acts: *I will give thanks unto Thy name, O Lord, for it is good, for Thou hast delivered Me out of all affliction.* He has assigned to each clause its strict fulfilment. Thus at the beginning He had said: *Save Me, O God, by Thy name;* after the prayers had been heard it was right that there should follow a corresponding ascription of thanks, in order that confession might be made to His name by Whose name He had prayed to be saved, and that inasmuch as He had asked for help against the strangers that rose up against Him, He might set on record that He had received it in the burst of joy expressed in the words: *Thou hast delivered Me out of all affliction.* Then in respect of the fact that the violent in seeking after His soul did not set God before their eyes, He has declared His eternal possession of unchangeable divinity in the words: *And Mine eye hath looked down upon Mine enemies.* For the Only-begotten Son of God was not cut off by death. It is true that in order to take the whole of our nature upon Him He submitted to death, that is to the apparent severance of soul and body, and made His way even to the realms below, the debt which man must manifestly pay: but He rose again and abides for ever and looks down with an eye that death cannot dim upon His enemies, being exalted unto the glory of God and born once more Son of God after becoming Son of Man, as He had been Son of God when He first became Son of Man, by the glory of His resurrection. He looks down upon His enemies to whom He once said: *Destroy this temple, and in three days I will build it up* [6]. And so, now that this temple of His body has been built again, He surveys from His throne on high those who sought after His soul, and, set far beyond the power of human death, He looks down from heaven upon those who wrought His death, He who suffered death, yet could not die, the God-Man, our Lord Jesus Christ, Who is blessed for ever and ever. Amen.

[4a] Ps. xxxix. (xl.) 7.   [5] Heb. vii. 27.   [6] St. John ii. 19.

PSALM CXXX. (CXXXI.).

O Lord, my heart is not exalted, neither have mine eyes been lifted up.

1. This Psalm, a short one, which demands an analytical rather than a homiletical treatment, teaches us the lesson of humility and meekness. Now, as we have in a great number of other places spoken about humility, there is no need to repeat the same things here. Of course we are bound to bear in mind in how great need our faith stands of humility when we hear the Prophet thus speaking of it as equivalent to the performance of the highest works: *O Lord, my heart is not exalted.* For a troubled heart is the noblest sacrifice in the eyes of God. The heart, therefore, must not be lifted up by prosperity, but humbly kept within the bounds of meekness through the fear of God.

2. *Neither have mine eyes been lifted up.* The strict sense of the Greek here conveys a different meaning; οὐδὲ ἐμετεωρίσθησαν οἱ ὀφθαλμοί μου, that is, have not been lifted up from one object to look on another. Yet the eyes must be lifted up in obedience to the Prophet's words: *Lift up your eyes and see who hath displayed all these things* [7]. And the Lord says in the gospel: *Lift up your eyes, and look on the fields, that are white unto harvest* [8]. The eyes, then, are to be lifted up: not, however, to transfer their gaze elsewhere, but to remain fixed once for all upon that to which they have been raised.

3. Then follows: *Neither have I walked amid great things, nor amid wonderful things that are above me.* It is most dangerous to walk amid mean things, and not to linger amid wonderful things. God's utterances are great; He Himself is wonderful in the highest: how then can the psalmist pride himself as on a good work for not walking amid great and wonderful things? It is the addition of the words, *which are above me,* that shews that the walking is not amid those things which men commonly regard as great and wonderful.

[7] Is. xl. 26.   [8] St. John iv. 35.

For David, prophet and king as he was, once was humble and despised and unworthy to sit at his father's table; but he found favour with God, he was anointed to be king, he was inspired to prophesy. His kingdom did not make him haughty, he was not moved by hatreds: he loved those that persecuted him, he paid honour to his dead enemies, he spared his incestuous and murderous children. In his capacity of sovereign he was despised, in that of father he was wounded, in that of prophet he was afflicted; yet he did not call for vengeance as a prophet might, nor exact punishment as a father, nor requite insults as a sovereign. And so he did not walk amid things great and wonderful which were above him.

4. Let us see what comes next: *If I was not humble-minded but have lifted up my soul.* What inconsistency on the Prophet's part! He does not lift up his heart: he does lift up his soul. He does not walk amid things great and wonderful that are above him; yet his thoughts are not mean. He is exalted in mind: and cast down in heart. He is humble in his own affairs: but he is not humble in his thought. For his thought reaches to heaven, his soul is lifted up on high. But his heart, *out of which proceed,* according to the Gospel, *evil thoughts, murders, adulteries, fornications, thefts, false witness, railings*[9], is humble, pressed down beneath the gentle yoke of meekness. We must strike a middle course, then, between humility and exaltation, so that we may be humble in heart but lifted up in soul and thought.

---

9 St. Matt. xv. 19.

5. Then he goes on: *Like a weaned child upon his mother's breast, so wilt thou reward my soul.* We are told that when Isaac was weaned Abraham made a feast because now that he was weaned he was on the verge of boyhood and was passing beyond milk food. The Apostle feeds all that are imperfect in the faith and still babes in the things of God with the milk of knowledge. Thus to cease to need milk marks the greatest possible advance. Abraham proclaimed by a joyful feast that his son had come to stronger meat, and the Apostle refuses bread to the carnal-minded and those that are babes in Christ. And so the Prophet prays that God, because he has not lifted up his heart, nor walked amid things great and wonderful that are above him, because he has not been humble-minded but did lift up his soul, may reward his soul, lying like a weaned child upon his mother: that is to say that he may be deemed worthy of the reward of the perfect, heavenly and living bread, on the ground that by reason of his works already recorded he has now passed beyond the stage of milk.

6. But he does not demand this living bread from heaven for himself alone, he encourages all mankind to hope for it by saying: *Let Israel hope in the Lord from henceforth and for evermore.* He sets no temporal limit to our hope, he bids our faithful expectation stretch out into infinity. We are to hope for ever and ever, winning the hope of future life through the hope of our present life which we have in Christ Jesus our Lord, Who is blessed for ever and ever. Amen.

INDEX.

I. INDEX OF SUBJECTS.

Intr. = Introduction.   T. = De Trin.   S. = De Syn.   Ps. = Hom. in Psalmos.

II. INDEX OF TEXTS.

JOHN OF DAMASCUS.

EXPOSITION OF THE ORTHODOX FAITH.

TRANSLATED BY

THE REV. S. D. F. SALMOND, D.D., F.E.I.S.,

PRINCIPAL OF THE FREE CHURCH COLLEGE, ABERDEEN.

NOTE.

———

IN the difficult task of translating the *De Fide Orthodoxa*—a task made the more difficult at times by the condition of the text,—I am indebted for much to my son, James L. Salmond, M.A., M.B., formerly of Balliol College, Oxford. There still remain passages of doubtful interpretation. It was intended to furnish a larger body of Notes and also an account of John and his writings. It has been found advisable, however, to complete the volume without these.

S. D. F. SALMOND.

ABERDEEN,
   1 *Sept.* 1898.

CONTENTS OF DOGMATIC CHAPTERS.

BOOK I.

BOOK II.

CONTENTS OF DOGMATIC CHAPTERS.

PROLOGUE.

FROM THE LATIN OF THE EDITION OF MICHAEL LEQUIEN, AS GIVEN IN MIGNE'S PATROLOGY.

AFTER the rules of Christian dialectic and the review of the errors of ancient heresies comes at last the book "Concerning the Orthodox Faith." In this book John of Damascus retains the same order as was adopted by Theodoret in his "Epitome of Divine Dogmas," but takes a different method. For the former, by the sheer weight of his own genius, framed various kinds of arguments against heretics, adducing the testimony of the sacred page, and thus he composed a concise treatise of Theology. Our author, however, did not confine himself to Scripture, but gathered together also the opinions of the holy Fathers, and produced a work marked with equal perspicuity and brevity, and forming an unexhausted storehouse of tradition in which nothing is to be found that has not been either sanctioned by the œcumenical synods or accepted by the approved leaders of the Church.

He followed, indeed, chiefly Gregory of Nazianzus, who, from the great accuracy of his erudition in divine matters, earned the title "The Theologian," and who has left scarcely any chapter of Christian learning untouched in his surviving works, and is free from any taint or suspicion of the slightest error. John had read his books with such assiduity that he seemed to hold them all in the embrace of his faithful memory. Wherefore throughout this work you may hear not so much John of Damascus as Gregory the Theologian expounding the mysteries of the orthodox faith. John further made use of Basil the Great, of Gregory of Nyssa, and especially of Nemesius, bishop of Emesa in Syria, the most beloved of all; likewise of Cyril of Alexandria, Leo the Great, Leontius of Byzantium, the martyr Maximus: also of Athanasius, Chrysostom, Epiphanius, and, not to mention others, that writer who took the name of Dionysius the Areopagite. Out of all these he culled on every hand the flower of their opinions, and concocted most sweet honey of soundest doctrine. For his aim was, not to strike out views of his own or anything novel, but rather to collect into one single theological work the opinions of the ancients which were scattered through various volumes. And, indeed, in order that the reader may more readily perceive the method of this most careful teacher, we shall carefully note in the margin the names of the authors and of the books from which he copied each separate opinion.

To John of Damascus, therefore, belongs the merit of being the first to compose a volume packed with the sentences of catholic teachers. Accordingly his authority among theologians was always weighty, not only in the East but even in the West and with the Latins: all the more so after the translation into Latin of his book "Concerning the Orthodox Faith," by Burgundio, a citizen of Pisa, during the Pontificate of Eugenius the Third. Further it was this translation that was used by that master of sentences, St. Thomas, and other later theologians, down till the time when at the beginning of the 16th century Jacobus Faber Stapulensis attempted to produce a more perfect translation than was the old one with its uncouth and barbarous diction. But as this one, too, had many faults, Jacobus Billius, in the course of the same century, completed a version of greater elegance but yet lacking in carefulness and brevity. For, as Combefis remarked, "in translating the Damascene Billius shewed the rawness of a recruit." Combefis himself, however, considered the translation of Billy of no little worth; for when he was toiling at a new edition of the works of John of Damascus, he did not think it necessary to make a new translation once more, but was quite content to emend the earlier one. For he was rightly aware that all the most learned interpreters of lengthy tomes slip into many errors, and that it is much easier to improve on the errors of others than to detect one's own. Thus our translation will represent that of Billius purged of its blemishes and restored to a more concise style. But in order that our edition should go forth in a more accurate shape than the rest, besides using the older translations and the various copies to the number of twenty or more codices, collated by my own hand, I have moreover revised the Greek phraseology and diction in those places of the Greek Fathers which the Damascene has massed together. Nay, further, omitting both the shorter commentaries of

Faber on each chapter and also the longer ones of Judocus Clictoveus of Neoportua, neither of whom contributes much, if anything, to the intelligent understanding of the Greek Fathers, I have attempted by fuller annotations to place before the eyes of all a specimen of eastern theology, drawn alike from those teachers whom the Damascene copied and from Greeks of later date whom I had the privilege of consulting.

The customary division among the Latins of the work "Concerning the Orthodox Faith" into four books is found in no Greek codex, nor in the Greek edition of Verona. And, further, that division is not met with in the old manuscripts of the original Latin translation, except as a chance note written in ink by a second and later hand on the margins of some of them. Hence Marcus Hopperus appears to be mistaken in ascribing in the dedicatory epistle of the Graeco-Latin edition of Basil the division into four books to the Latin translator: that is, unless I am mistaken, to Faber, whose edition he published. Traces of this, however, exist in the books of St. Thomas Aquinas. I therefore hold that this mode of division was devised and introduced by the Latins in imitation of the four books of "Sentences" of Peter Lombard. Codex Regius *n.* 3445, and that is a very late one, alone seems to divide the "De Fide Orthodoxa" into two parts, the first, or περὶ τῆς θεολογίας, dealing indeed with the one triune God, the Creator and Provider, and the second, or περὶ τῆς οἰκονομίας, with God Incarnate, the Redeemer and Rewarder. But an objection to this division is the clear connection between chapter 43, in which the Incarnation, or "Oeconomia Divina," is discussed, and the words which immediately precede it in the end of chapter 42, which is entitled "On Praedestination," making either chapter part of one continuous discussion. This fault cannot be taken to the other division into four parts. But in order not to startle the reader accustomed to the former division with too much novelty, I have, following Hopperus, assigned indeed to the Greek chapters the same numbers as were marked in the Greek codices, but I have not hesitated to divide the Latin translation into four books.

I have come across no edition of the old Latin translation; but the version of Jacobus Faber was issued in Paris by Judocus Clictoveus from the press of Henry Stephen in the year 1512, along with commentaries. Next, in the year 1535, Henry Pet, the printer of Basle, published the existing works of St. John of Damascus, and amongst them the four books "Concerning the Orthodox Faith, as translated by Jacobus Faber of Stapula," but without any commentary. After some years the same Henry in a second edition added the shorter commentaries of Clictoveus, and again in the edition published in the year 1537. In the preface to these editions there occurs among others the following sentence, "Now for the first time are added annotations explaining all the difficulties and the hard and lofty passages." For of a truth I know no older edition in which those explanations, such as they are, are given. Further, the author of these is asserted by Henricus Gravius, of the order of Preachers, in his own Latin edition of the works of holy John of Damascus, which he brought out at Cologne from the press of Peter Quentel, in the year 1546, to have been Jacobus Faber, and of a surety indeed in certain places, and in especial where the most holy mystery of the Eucharist is under discussion, the annotations are somewhat frigid in character and do not express with sufficient fulness the catholic faith. And this cannot be said without pain, for the sake of a man whom otherwise I should look up to as worthy of veneration, as almost one of my own house, had he not proved himself a traitor to his ancestral religion or at least somewhat too partial to innovators. As to the edition of our Gravius, learned as he was in both Latin and Greek, he revised the translation, Jacobus Faber's translation, and compared it with the Greek text and illustrated it with very short scholia, "for the sake of heretics," as he said in the dedicatory letter to Oswald, especially where they themselves try in vain to shake the doctrine of the Church as stated by the Damascene.

The book "Concerning the Orthodox Faith" Donatus Veronensis caused to be printed at Verona first in Greek only, and presented it to Clement the Seventh in the year 1531. Not till the year 1548 did he produce a version containing both the Greek and Latin, and again in the year 1575. Next, in the year 1577, Jacobus Billy published at Paris his own translation without the Greek text: and it was printed again in that same city in the years 1603 and 1617.

Here it will not be superfluous to call to mind that the great part of the first book, as they say, of the work "Concerning the Orthodox Faith" exists as the sixth volume of the works of Cyril of Alexandria, inscribed in that teacher's name, a result to be doubtless attributed to the carelessness of some copyist who found these writings of the Damascene along with others of Cyril.

AN EXACT EXPOSITION OF THE ORTHODOX FAITH.

BOOK I.

CHAPTER I.

That the Deity is incomprehensible, and that we ought not to pry into and meddle with the things which have not been delivered to us by the holy Prophets, and Apostles, and Evangelists.

No one hath seen God at any time; the Only-begotten Son, which is in the bosom of the Father, He hath declared Him [1]. The Deity, therefore, is ineffable and incomprehensible. *For no one knoweth the Father, save the Son, nor the Son, save the Father* [2]. And the Holy Spirit, too, so knows the things of God as the spirit of the man knows the things that are in him [3]. Moreover, after the first and blessed nature no one, not of men only, but even of supramundane powers, and the Cherubim, I say, and Seraphim themselves, has ever known God, save he to whom He revealed Himself.

God, however, did not leave us in absolute ignorance. For the knowledge of God's existence has been implanted by Him in all by nature. This creation, too, and its maintenance, and its government, proclaim the majesty of the Divine nature [4]. Moreover, by the Law and the Prophets [5] in former times, and afterwards by His Only-begotten Son, our Lord and God and Saviour Jesus Christ, He disclosed to us the knowledge of Himself as that was possible for us. All things, therefore, that have been delivered to us by Law and Prophets and Apostles and Evangelists we receive, and know, and honour [6], seeking for nothing beyond these. For God, being good, is the cause of all good, subject neither to envy nor to any passion [7]. For envy is far removed from the Divine nature, which is both passionless and only good. As knowing all things, therefore, and providing for what

is profitable for each, He revealed that which it was to our profit to know; but what we were unable [8] to bear He kept secret. With these things let us be satisfied, and let us abide by them, not removing everlasting boundaries, nor overpassing the divine tradition [9].

CHAPTER II.

Concerning things utterable and things unutterable, and things knowable and things unknowable.

It is necessary, therefore, that one who wishes to speak or to hear of God should understand clearly that alike in the doctrine of Deity and in that of the Incarnation [1], neither are all things unutterable nor all utterable; neither all unknowable nor all knowable [2]. But the knowable belongs to one order, and the utterable to another; just as it is one thing to speak and another thing to know. Many of the things relating to God, therefore, that are dimly understood cannot be put into fitting terms, but on things above us we cannot do else than express ourselves according to our limited capacity; as, for instance, when we speak of God we use the terms *sleep*, and *wrath*, and *regardlessness*, *hands*, too, and *feet*, and such like expressions.

We, therefore, both know and confess that God is without beginning, without end, eternal and everlasting, uncreate, unchangeable, invariable, simple, uncompound, incorporeal, invisible, impalpable, uncircumscribed, infinite, incognisable, indefinable, incomprehensible, good, just, maker of all things created, almighty, all-ruling, all-surveying, of all overseer, sovereign, judge; and that God is One, that

[1] St. John i. 18 (R.V.).   [2] St. Matt. xi. 27.
[3] 1 Cor. ii. 11.   [4] Wisd. xiii. 5.
[5] *Greg. Naz., Orat.* 34.   [6] *Dionys., De div. nom.,* c. 1.
[7] *Greg. Naz., Orat.* 34.

[8] Reading ὑπὲρ δὲ οὐκ ἐδυνάμεθα for ὑπὲρ δὲ οὖν ἐδυνάμεθα. *Cod. Reg.* 3379 gives καὶ ὁ οὐ δυνάμεθα.
[9] Prov. xxii. 28.
[1] τά τε τῆς θεολογίας, τά τε τῆς οἰκονομίας.
[2] *Dionys., De div. nom.* c. 1; *Greg. Naz., Orat.* 34 and 37.

:s to say, one essence[3]; and that He is known[4], and has His being in three subsistences, in Father, I say, and Son and Holy Spirit; and that the Father and the Son and the Holy Spirit are one in all respects, except in that of not being begotten, that of being begotten, and that of procession; and that the Only-begotten Son and Word of God and God, in His bowels of mercy, for our salvation, by the good pleasure of God and the co-operation of the Holy Spirit, being conceived without seed, was born uncorruptedly of the Holy Virgin and Mother of God, Mary, by the Holy Spirit, and became of her perfect Man; and that the Same is at once perfect God and perfect Man, of two natures, Godhead and Manhood, and in two natures possessing intelligence, will and energy, and freedom, and, in a word, perfect according to the measure and proportion proper to each, at once to the divinity, I say, and to the humanity, yet to one composite person[5]; and that He suffered hunger and thirst and weariness, and was crucified, and for three days submitted to the experience of death and burial, and ascended to heaven, from which also He came to us, and shall come again. And the Holy Scripture is witness to this and the whole choir of the Saints.

But neither do we know, nor can we tell, what the essence[6] of God is, or how it is in all, or how the Only-begotten Son and God, having emptied Himself, became Man of virgin blood, made by another law contrary to nature, or how He walked with dry feet upon the waters[7]. It is not within our capacity, therefore, to say anything about God or even to think of Him, beyond the things which have been divinely revealed to us, whether by word or by manifestation, by the divine oracles at once of the Old Testament and of the New[8].

CHAPTER III.

Proof that there is a God.

That there is a God, then, is no matter of doubt to those who receive the Holy Scriptures, the Old Testament, I mean, and the New; nor indeed to most of the Greeks. For, as we said[9], the knowledge of the existence of God is implanted in us by nature. But since the wickedness of the Evil One has prevailed so mightily against man's nature as even to drive some into denying the existence of God, that most foolish and woefulest pit of destruction (whose folly David, revealer of the Divine meaning, exposed when

he said[9], *The fool said in his heart, There is no God*), so the disciples of the Lord and His Apostles, made wise by the Holy Spirit and working wonders in His power and grace, took them captive in the net of miracles and drew them up out of the depths of ignorance[1] to the light of the knowledge of God. In like manner also their successors in grace and worth, both pastors and teachers, having received the enlightening grace of the Spirit, were wont, alike by the power of miracles and the word of grace, to enlighten those walking in darkness and to bring back the wanderers into the way. But as for us who[2] are not recipients either of the gift of miracles or the gift of teaching (for indeed we have rendered ourselves unworthy of these by our passion for pleasure), come, let us in connection with this theme discuss a few of those things which have been delivered to us on this subject by the expounders of grace, calling on the Father, the Son, and the Holy Spirit.

All things, that exist, are either created or uncreated. If, then, things are created, it follows that they are also wholly mutable. For things, whose existence originated in change, must also be subject to change, whether it be that they perish or that they become other than they are by act of will[3]. But if things are un-created they must in all consistency be also wholly immutable. For things which are opposed in the nature of their existence must also be opposed in the mode of their existence, that is to say, must have opposite properties: who, then, will refuse to grant that all existing things, not only such as come within the province of the senses, but even the very angels, are subject to change and transformation and movement of various kinds? For the things appertaining to the rational world, I mean angels and spirits and demons, are subject to changes of will, whether it is a progression or a retrogression in goodness, whether a struggle or a surrender; while the others suffer changes of generation and destruction, of increase and decrease, of quality and of movement in space. Things then that are mutable are also wholly created. But things that are created must be the work of some maker, and the maker cannot have been created. For if he had been created, he also must surely have been created by some one, and so on till we arrive at something uncreated. The Creator, then, being uncreated, is also wholly immutable. And what could this be other than Deity?

---

3 οὐσία, substance, being.
4 ὑποστάσεσι, hypostases, persons.
5 μιᾷ δὲ συνθέτῳ ὑποστάσει.   6 οὐσία, *substance, being.*
7 *Dionys., De div. nom.,* c. 2.   8 Ibid. c. 1.
9 *Supr.* c 1; cf. *Greg. Naz., Orat.* 34.

9 Ps. xiv. 1 (E.V.).
1 The readings vary between ἀγνωσίας and ἀγνοίας.
2 *Greg. Naz., Orat.* 34.
3 Reading προαίρεσιν; a variant is τροπήν.

And even the very continuity of the creation, and its preservation and government, teach us that there does exist a Deity, who supports and maintains and preserves and ever provides for this universe. For how [4] could opposite natures, such as fire and water, air and earth, have combined with each other so as to form one complete world, and continue to abide in indissoluble union, were there not some omnipotent power which bound them together and always is preserving them from dissolution?

What is it that gave order to things of heaven and things of earth, and all those things that move in the air and in the water, or rather to what was in existence before these, viz., to heaven and earth and air and the elements of fire and water? What [5] was it that mingled and distributed these? What was it that set these in motion and keeps them in their unceasing and unhindered course [6]? Was it not the Artificer of these things, and He Who hath implanted in everything the law whereby the universe is carried on and directed? Who then is the Artificer of these things? Is it not He Who created them and brought them into existence. For we shall not attribute such a power to the spontaneous [7]. For, supposing their coming into existence was due to the spontaneous; what of the power that put all in order [8]? And let us grant this, if you please. What of that which has preserved and kept them in harmony with the original laws of their existence [9]? Clearly it is something quite distinct from the spontaneous [1]. And what could this be other than Deity [2]?

CHAPTER IV.

Concerning the nature of Deity : that it is incomprehensible.

It is plain, then, that there is a God. But what He is in His essence and nature is absolutely incomprehensible and unknowable. For it is evident that He is incorporeal [3]. For how could that possess body which is infinite, and boundless, and formless, and intangible and invisible, in short, simple and not compound? How could that be immutable [4] which is circumscribed and subject to passion? And how could that be passionless which is composed of elements and is resolved again into them? For combination [5] is the beginning of conflict, and conflict of separation, and separation of dissolution, and dissolution is altogether foreign to God [6].

Again, how will it also be maintained [7] that God permeates and fills the universe? as the Scriptures say, *Do not I fill heaven and earth, saith the Lord* [8]? For it is an impossibility [9] that one body should permeate other bodies without dividing and being divided, and without being enveloped and contrasted, in the same way as all fluids mix and commingle.

But if some say that the body is immaterial, in the same way as the fifth body [1] of which the Greek philosophers speak (which body is an impossibility), it will be wholly subject to motion like the heaven. For that is what they mean by the fifth body. Who then is it that moves it? For everything that is moved is moved by another thing. And who again is it that moves that? and so on to infinity till we at length arrive at something motionless. For the first mover is motionless, and that is the Deity. And must not that which is moved be circumscribed in space? The Deity, then, alone is motionless, moving the universe by immobility [2]. So then it must be assumed that the Deity is incorporeal.

But even this gives no true idea of His essence, to say that He is unbegotten, and without beginning, changeless and imperishable, and possessed of such other qualities as we are wont to ascribe to God and His environment [3]. For these do not indicate what He is, but what He is not [4]. But when we would explain what

---

[4] Athan., Cont. Gent.   [5] Various reading, Who.

[6] Greg. Naz., Orat. 34.

[7] The Greek is τῷ αὐτομάτῳ, to the automatic; perhaps = to the accidental, or, to chance.

[8] Or, Whose was the disposing of them in order?

[9] Or, Whose are the preserving of them, and the keeping of them in accordance with the principles under which they were first placed?

[1] παρὰ τὸ αὐτόματον; or, quite other than the spontaneous, or, than chance.

[2] Athan., De Incarn. Verbi, near the beginning. Greg. Naz., Orat. 34.

[3] Various reading, It is evident that the divine (τὸ Θεῖον) is incorporeal.

[4] Text, ἄτρεπτον. Most MSS. read σεπτόν. So, too, Greg. Naz., Orat. 34, from which these words are taken. An old interpretation is 'venerabile est.' But in the opinion of Combefis, Gregory's text is corrupt, and ἄτρεπτον should be read, which reading is also supported by various authorities, including three Cod. Reg.: cf. also De Trinit. in Cyril.

[5] σύνθεσις.

[6] Greg. Naz., Orat. 32, 34.

[7] Text, σωθήσεται: various reading, συνθήσεται.

[8] Jer. xxiii. 24.   [9] Greg. Naz. ut supr.

[1] The reference is to the Pythagorean and Aristotelian ideas of the heavens as being like the body of Deity, something uncorrupt, different from the four elements, and therefore called a fifth body or element (στοιχεῖον). In his Meteor. i. 3, De Cœlo i. 3, &c., Aristotle speaks of the Ether as extending from the heaven of the fixed stars down to the moon, as of a nature specially adapted for circular motion, as the first element in rank; but as the fifth, "if we enumerate beginning with the elements directly known by the senses . . . . the subsequently so-called πέμπτον στοιχεῖον, quinta essentia." The other elements, he taught, had the upward motion, or the downward: the earth having the attribute of heaviness, and its natural place in the world being the lowest; fire being the light element, and "its place the sphere next adjoining the sphere of the ether" See Ueberweg's History of Philosophy, Vol. I. p. 167, Morris's translation. and the chapter on the De Cœlo in Grote's Aristotle, Vol II. pp. 389, &c.

[2] Greg. Naz. ut supr.

[3] Or, such as are said to exist in the case of God, or in relation to God. The Greek is, ὅσα περὶ Θεοῦ, ἢ περὶ Θεὸν εἶναι λέγεται.

[4] Greg. Naz. ut supr.

the essence of anything is, we must not speak only negatively. In the case of God, however, it is impossible to explain what He is in His essence, and it befits us the rather to hold discourse about His absolute separation from all things [5]. For He does not belong to the class of existing things : not that He has no existence [6], but that He is above all existing things, nay even above existence itself. For if all forms of knowledge have to do with what exists, assuredly that which is above knowledge must certainly be also above essence [7] : and, conversely, that which is above essence [7] will also be above knowledge.

God then is infinite and incomprehensible : and all that is comprehensible about Him is His infinity and incomprehensibility. But all that we can affirm concerning God does not shew forth God's nature, but only the qualities of His nature [8]. For when you speak of Him as good, and just, and wise, and so forth, you do not tell God's nature but only the qualities of His nature [9]. Further there are some affirmations which we make concerning God which have the force of absolute negation : for example, when we use the term darkness, in reference to God, we do not mean darkness itself, but that He is not light but above light : and when we speak of Him as light, we mean that He is not darkness.

CHAPTER V.

Proof that God is one and not many.

We have, then, adequately demonstrated that there is a God, and that His essence is incomprehensible. But that God is one [1] and not many is no matter of doubt to those who believe in the Holy Scriptures. For the Lord says in the beginning of the Law : *I am the Lord thy God, which have brought thee out of the land of Egypt. Thou shalt have no other Gods before Me* [2]. And again He says, *Hear, O Israel, the Lord our God is one Lord* [3]. And in Isaiah the prophet we read, *For I am the first God and I am the last, and beside Me there is no God. Before Me there was not any God, nor after Me will there be any God, and beside Me there is no God* [4]. And the Lord, too, in the holy gospels

speaketh these words to His Father, *And this is life eternal, that they may know Thee the only true God* [5]. But with those that do not believe in the Holy Scriptures we will reason thus.

The Deity is perfect [6], and without blemish in goodness, and wisdom, and power, without beginning, without end, everlasting, uncircumscribed [7], and in short, perfect in all things. Should we say, then, that there are many Gods, we must recognise difference among the many. For if there is no difference among them, they are one rather than many. But if there is difference among them, what becomes of the perfectness ? For that which comes short of perfection, whether it be in goodness, or power, or wisdom, or time, or place, could not be God. But it is this very identity in all respects that shews that the Deity is one and not many [8].

Again, if there are many Gods, how can one maintain that God is uncircumscribed ? For where the one would be, the other could not be [9].

Further, how could the world be governed by many and saved from dissolution and destruction, while strife is seen to rage between the rulers ? For difference introduces strife [1]. And if any one should say that each rules over a part, what of that which established this order and gave to each his particular realm ? For this would the rather be God. Therefore, God is one, perfect, uncircumscribed, maker of the universe, and its preserver and governor, exceeding and preceding all perfection.

Moreover, it is a natural necessity that duality should originate in unity [2].

CHAPTER VI.

Concerning the Word and the Son of God : a reasoned proof.

So then this one and only God is not Wordless [3]. And possessing the Word, He will have it not as without a subsistence, nor as having had a beginning, nor as destined to cease to be. For there never was a time when God was not Word : but He ever possesses His own Word, begotten of Himself, not, as our word is, without a subsistence and dissolving into air, but having a subsistence in Him and

5 *Greg. Naz., Orat.* 32, 34. The Greek is, οἰκειότερον δὲ μᾶλλον ἐκ τῆς ἀπάντων ἀφαιρέσεως ποιεῖσθαι τὸν λόγον. It may be given thus :—*It is more in accordance with the nature of the case rather to discourse of Him in the way of abstracting from Him all that belongs to us.*
6 *Dionys., De Myst. Theolog.*
7 Or, *above being ;* ὑπὲρ οὐσίαν·
8 Or, *but only the things which relate to His nature.* The Greek is, ὅσα δὲ λέγομεν ἐπὶ Θεοῦ καταφαντικῶς, οὐ τὴν φύσιν, ἀλλὰ τὰ περὶ τὴν φύσιν δηλοῖ.
9 Or, *the things that relate to His nature.*   2 Exod. xx. 2, 3.
1 Various reading, *but that He is one.*
3 Deut. vi. 4.   4 Isai. xliii. 10.

5 St. John xvii. 3.
6 See *Thomas Aquin. I. quæst.* 11, *Art.* 4 ; also cf. Book iv., c. 21 beneath. The question of the unity of the Deity is similarly dealt with by those of the Fathers who wrote against the Marcionites and the Manichæans, and by Athenagoras.
7 Or, *infinite ;* ἀπερίγραπτον.
8 *Infr. lib.* iv. c. 21.   9 *Greg. Nyss., Prol. Catech.*
1 *Greg. Naz., Orat.* 35.
2 Cf. *Dionys., De div. nom.,* c. 5, 13.
3 ἄλογον ; *without Word,* or, without Reason.

life and perfection, not proceeding out of Himself but ever existing within Himself[4]. For where could it be, if it were to go outside Him? For inasmuch as our nature is perishable and easily dissolved, our word is also without subsistence. But since God is everlasting and perfect, He will have His Word subsistent in Him, and everlasting and living, and possessed of all the attributes of the Begetter. For just as our word, proceeding as it does out of the mind, is neither wholly identical with the mind nor utterly diverse from it (for so far as it proceeds out of the mind it is different from it, while so far as it reveals the mind, it is no longer absolutely diverse from the mind, but being one in nature with the mind, it is yet to the subject diverse from it), so in the same manner also the Word of God[5] in its independent subsistence is differentiated[6] from Him from Whom it derives its subsistence[7]: but inasmuch as it displays in itself the same attributes as are seen in God, it is of the same nature as God. For just as absolute perfection is contemplated in the Father, so also is it contemplated in the Word that is begotten of Him.

CHAPTER VII.

Concerning the Holy Spirit, a reasoned proof.

Moreover the Word must also possess Spirit[8]. For in fact even our word is not destitute of spirit; but in our case the spirit is something different from our essence[9]. For there is an attraction and movement of the air which is drawn in and poured forth that the body may be sustained. And it is this which in the moment of utterance becomes the articulate word, revealing in itself the force of the word[1]. [2]But in the case of the divine nature, which is simple and uncompound, we must confess in all piety that there exists a Spirit of God, for the Word is not more imperfect than our own word. Now we cannot, in piety, consider the Spirit to be something foreign that gains admission into God from without, as is the case with compound natures like us. Nay, just as, when we heard[3] of the Word of God, we considered it to be not without subsistence, nor the product of learning, nor the mere utterance of voice, nor as passing into the air and perishing, but as being essentially subsisting, endowed with free volition, and energy, and omnipotence: so also, when we have learnt about the Spirit of God, we contemplate it as the companion of the Word and the revealer of His energy, and not as mere breath without subsistence. For to conceive of the Spirit that dwells in God as after the likeness of our own spirit, would be to drag down the greatness of the divine nature to the lowest depths of degradation. But we must contemplate it as an essential power, existing in its own proper and peculiar subsistence, proceeding from the Father and resting in the Word[4], and shewing forth the Word, neither capable of disjunction from God in Whom it exists, and the Word Whose companion it is, nor poured forth to vanish into nothingness[5], but being in subsistence in the likeness of the Word, endowed with life, free volition, independent movement, energy, ever willing that which is good, and having power to keep pace with the will in all its decrees[6], having no beginning and no end. For never was the Father at any time lacking in the Word, nor the Word in the Spirit.

Thus because of the unity in nature, the error of the Greeks in holding that God is many, is utterly destroyed: and again by our acceptance of the Word and the Spirit, the dogma of the Jews is overthrown: and there remains of each party[7] only what is profitable[8]. On the one hand of the Jewish idea we have the unity of God's nature, and on the other, of the Greek, we have the distinction in subsistences and that only[9].

---

4 *Greg. Nyss.*, *Catech.*, c. 1.
5 In R. 2427 is added, 'Who is the Son.'
6 διήρηται, i.e. distinguished from the Father. Objection is taken to the use of such a verb as suggestive of division. It is often employed, however, by Greg. Naz. (e.g. *Orat.* 34) to express the distinction of persons. In many passages of Gregory and other Fathers the noun διαίρεσις is used to express the distinction of one thing from another: and in this sense it is opposed both to the Sabellian confusion and the Arian division.
7 Reading ὑπόστασιν. Various reading, ὕπαρξιν, *existence*.
8 The Greek theologians, founding on the primary sense of the Greek term Πνεῦμα, and on certain passages of Scripture in which the word seemed to retain that sense more or less (especially Psalm xxxiii. 6 in the Vulgate rendering, verbo Dei cœli formati sunt: et spiritu oris ejus omnis virtus eorum), spoke of the Holy Ghost as proceeding from the Father like the breath of His mouth in the utterance or emission of His Word. See ch. 15 of this Book, where we have the sentence, οὐδεμία γὰρ ὁρμὴ ἄνευ πνεύματος. Compare also such passages as these—*Greg. Naz.*, *Orat.* i. 3; *Cyril. Alex.*, *Thes.*, assert. 34, *De Trin.* dial. 2, p 425, and 7, pp.634, 640; *Basil, Contra Eunom.*, B.V., and *De Spiritu Sancto*, ch. 18; *Greg. Scholar.*, *Contra Latin.*, *de process. Spiritus Sancti*, i. 4, where we have the statement οὕτω καὶ τὸ ἅγιον Πνεῦμα ὥσπερ ὁρμὴ καὶ κίνησις, ἐνδοτέρα τῆς ὑπερφυοῦς ἐκείνης οὐσίας, *so the Holy Spirit is like an impulse and movement within that supernatural essence.*
9 Or, *substance*; οὐσία.
1 Text, φανεροῦσα: various reading, φέρουσα (cf. *Cyril, De Trinitate*).
2 *Greg. Nyss.*, *Catech.*, c. 2.

3 Text, ἀκούσαντες: variant, ἀκούοντες (so in *Cyril*).
4 So Cyril speaks frequently of the Holy Spirit as *proceeding from the Father* and *being* (εἶναι) and *abiding* (μένειν) *in the Son*; as also of the Spirit as *being of the Son and having His nature in Him* (ἐξ αὐτοῦ καὶ ἐμπεφυκὼς αὐτῷ). The idea seems to have been that as the Son is in the bosom of the Father so the Spirit is in the bosom of the Son. The Spirit was compared again to the *e ergy*, the *natural, living energy of the Son* (ἐνέργεια φυσικὴ καὶ ζῶσα, τὸ ἐνεργὲς τοῦ υἱοῦ), Cyril, Dial 7 ad Hermiam. Such terms as προβολεὺς ἐκφαντορικοῦ πνεύματος, the *Producer*, or, *Emitter of the revealing Spirit*, and the ἔκφανσις or ἔλλαμψις, the *revealing*, the *forth-shewing*, were also used to express the procession of the one eternal Person from the Other as like the emission or forth-shewing of light from light.
5 *Greg. Naz.*, *Orat.* 37, 44.
6 Text, πρὸς πᾶσαν πρόθεσιν: variant, θέλησιν in almost all the codices.   7 αἵρεσις.   8 *Greg. Orat.* 38, and elsewhere.
9 *Greg. Nyss.*, *Catech.*, c. 3.

But should the Jew refuse to accept the Word and the Spirit, let the divine Scripture confute him and curb his tongue. For concerning the Word, the divine David says, *For ever, O Lord, Thy Word is settled in heaven*[1]. And again, *He sent His Word and healed them*[2]. But the word that is uttered is not sent, nor is it for ever settled[3]. And concerning the Spirit, the same David says, *Thou sendest forth Thy Spirit, they are created*[4]. And again, *By the word of the Lord were the heavens made: and all the host of them by the breath of His mouth*[5]. Job, too, says, *The Spirit of God hath made me, and the breath of the Almighty hath given me life*[6]. Now the Spirit which is sent and makes and stablishes and conserves, is not mere breath that dissolves, any more than the mouth of God is a bodily member. For the conception of both must be such as harmonizes with the Divine nature[7].

CHAPTER VIII.

Concerning the Holy Trinity.

We believe, then, in One God, one beginning[8], having no beginning, uncreate, unbegotten, imperishable and immortal, everlasting, infinite, uncircumscribed, boundless, of infinite power, simple, uncompound, incorporeal, without flux, passionless, unchangeable, unalterable, unseen, the fountain of goodness and justice, the light of the mind, inaccessible; a power known by no measure, measurable only by His own will alone (for all things that He wills He can[9]), creator of all created things, seen or unseen, of all the maintainer and preserver, for all the provider, master and lord and king over all, with an endless and immortal kingdom: having no contrary, filling all, by nothing encompassed, but rather Himself the encompasser and maintainer and original possessor of the universe, occupying[1] all essences intact[2] and extending beyond all things, and being separate from all essence as being super-essential[3] and above all things and absolute God, absolute goodness, and absolute fulness[4]: determining all sovereignties and ranks, being placed above all sovereignty and rank, above essence and life and word and thought: being Himself very light and goodness and life and essence, inasmuch as He does not derive His being from another, that is to say, of those things that exist: but being Himself the fountain of being to all that is, of life to the living, of reason to those that have reason; to all the cause of all good: perceiving all things even before they have become: one essence, one divinity, one power, one will, one energy, one beginning, one authority, one dominion, one sovereignty, made known in three perfect subsistences and adored with one adoration, believed in and ministered to by all rational creation[5], united without confusion and divided without separation (which indeed transcends thought). (We believe) in Father and Son and Holy Spirit whereinto also we have been baptized[6]. For so our Lord commanded the Apostles to baptize, saying, *Baptizing them in the name of the Father, Son, and Holy Spirit*[7].

(We believe) in one Father, the beginning[8], and cause of all: begotten of no one: without cause or generation, alone subsisting: creator of all: but Father of one only by nature, His Only-begotten Son and our Lord and God and Saviour Jesus Christ, and Producer[9] of the most Holy Spirit. And in one Son of God, the Only-begotten, our Lord, Jesus Christ: begotten of the Father, before all the ages: Light of Light, true God of true God: begotten, not made, consubstantial with the Father, through Whom all things are made: and when we say He was before all the ages we shew that His birth is without time or beginning: for the Son of God was not brought into being out of nothing[1], He that is the effulgence of the glory, the impress of the Father's subsistence[2], the living wisdom and power[3], the Word possessing interior subsistence[4], the essential and perfect and living image[5] of the unseen God. But always He was with the Father and in Him[6], everlastingly and without beginning begotten of Him. For there never was

---

[1] Ps. cxix. 89.　　　　[2] Ib. cvii. 30.
[3] Text, διαμένει: variant, μένει　　[4] Ps. civ. 30.
[5] Ib. xxxiii 6.　　　　[6] Job xxxiii. 4.
[7] Basil, De Spir. Sancto, ad Amphil. c. 18.
[8] Or, principle, ἀρχήν.　　[9] Cf. Ps. cxxxv. 6.
[1] Or, penetrating, ἐπιβατεύουσαν.　　[2] ἀχράντως.
[3] ὑπερούσιον.
[4] ὑπέρθεον, ὑπεράγαθον, ὑπερπλήρη.

[5] Greg. Naz., Orat. 13, n. 32.
[6] An argument much used against the Arians, the Macedonians, and the Sabellians. See e.g. Athan , ad Serap. Epist. 1 and 2; Basil, Contra Eunom., bk. iii., and De Spiritu Sancto, ch. 10, 12; Greg. Naz., Orat. 34.
[7] St. Matt. xviii. 19.　　[8] Or, principle, ἀρχήν.
[9] προβολέα. The term προβολή, rendered prolatio by Tertullian and Hilary, was rejected as unsuitable to the idea of the Divine procession, e.g. by Athanasius, who in his Expos. Fidei denies that the Word is ἀπόῤῥοια, efflux, or τμῆσις, segmen, or προβολή, emissio or prolatio; and by Jerome, Adv. Ruf., Apol. 2, his reason being that the word had been used by Gnostics in speaking of the emanations of Æons, Greg. Naz., however, Orat. 13. 35, speaks of the Father as γεννήτωρ and προβολεύς, and of the Spirit as πρόβλημα.
[1] Greg. Naz., Orat. 36.　　　　[2] Ibid,
[3] 1 Cor. i. 24.
[4] The Word enhypostatic, ὁ Λόγος ἐνυπόστατος.
[5] Heb. i. 3.
[6] The Arians admitted that the Son is in the Father, in the sense in which all created things are in God. Basil (De Spiritu Sancto, ch. 25, Orat. in princip. evang. Joan.) takes the preposition σύν, in, to express the idea of the σύναφεια, or conjunction of the two. The Scholiast on the present passages calls attention to the two prepositions with and in as denoting the Son's eternal existence and His union with the Father, as the shining is with the light, and comes from it without separation. Basil, De Spir. Sancto, ch. 26, holds it better to say that the Spirit is one with (συνεῖναι) the Father and the Son than that He is in (ἐνεῖναι) the Father and the Son.

a time when the Father was and the Son was not, but always the Father and always the Son, Who was begotten of Him, existed together. For He could not have received the name Father apart from the Son: for if He were without the Son[7], He could not be the Father: and if He thereafter had the Son, thereafter He became the Father, not having been the Father prior to this, and He was changed from that which was not the Father and became the Father. This is the worst form of blasphemy[8]. For we may not speak of God as destitute of natural generative power: and generative power means, the power of producing from one's self, that is to say, from one's own proper essence, that which is like in nature to one's self[9].

In treating, then, of the generation of the Son, it is an act of impiety[1] to say that time comes into play and that the existence of the Son is of later origin than the Father. For we hold that it is from Him, that is, from the Father's nature, that the Son is generated. And unless we grant that the Son co-existed from the beginning with the Father, by Whom He was begotten, we introduce change into the Father's subsistence, because, not being the Father, He subsequently became the Father[2]. For the creation, even though it originated later, is nevertheless not derived from the essence of God, but is brought into existence out of nothing by His will and power, and change does not touch God's nature. For generation means that the begetter produces out of his essence offspring similar in essence. But creation and making mean that the creator and maker produces from that which is external, and not out of his own essence, a creation of an absolutely dissimilar nature[3].

Wherefore in God, Who alone is passionless and unalterable, and immutable, and ever so continueth, both begetting and creating are passionless[4]. For being by nature passionless and not liable to flux, since He is simple and uncompound, He is not subject to passion or flux either in begetting or in creating, nor has He need of any co-operation. But generation in Him is without beginning and everlasting, being the work of nature and producing out of His own essence, that the Begetter may not undergo change, and that He may not be God first and God last, nor receive any accession: while creation in the case of God[5], being the work of will, is not co-eternal

with God. For it is not natural that that which is brought into existence out of nothing should be co-eternal with what is without beginning and everlasting. There is this difference in fact between man's making and God's. Man can bring nothing into existence out of nothing[6], but all that he makes requires pre-existing matter for its basis[7], and he does not create it by will only, but thinks out first what it is to be and pictures it in his mind, and only then fashions it with his hands, undergoing labour and trouble[8], and often missing the mark and failing to produce to his satisfaction that after which he strives. But God, through the exercise of will alone, has brought all things into existence out of nothing. Now there is the same difference between God and man in begetting and generating. For in God, Who is without time and beginning, passionless, not liable to flux, incorporeal, alone and without end[1], generation is without time and beginning, passionless and not liable to flux, nor dependent on the union of two[2]: nor has His own incomprehensible generation beginning or end. And it is without beginning because He is immutable: without flux because He is passionless and incorporeal: independent of the union of two again because He is incorporeal but also because He is the one and only God, and stands in need of no co-operation: and without end or cessation because He is without beginning, or time, or end, and ever continues the same. For that which has no beginning has no end: but that which through grace is endless is assuredly not without beginning, as, witness, the angels[3].

Accordingly the everlasting God generates His own Word which is perfect, without beginning and without end, that God, Whose nature and existence are above time, may not engender in time. But with man clearly it is otherwise, for generation is with him a matter of sex, and destruction and flux and increase and body clothe him round about[4], and he possesses a nature which is male or female. For the male requires the assistance of the female. But may He Who surpasses all, and transcends all thought and comprehension, be gracious to us.

The holy catholic and apostolic Church,

---

[7] Greg. Naz., Orat. 35.
[8] Cyril, Thesaurus, assert. 4 and 5.   [9] Ibid., assert. 6.
[1] Ibid., assert. 4.   [2] Greg. Naz., Orat. 29.
[3] Text, ἀνόμοιον παντελῶς, variant, ἀνόμοιον παντελῶς κατ' οὐσίαν, cf. also Cyrill.
[4] Greg. Naz., Orat. 29 and 35.
[5] On this distinction between *generation* and *creation*, com-

pare *Athan., Contra Arianos, Or.* 2, 3; *Basil, Contra Eunom.*, bk. iv.; *Cyril, Thes., assert.* 3. &c.
[6] Greg. Naz., Orat. 29.   [7] Cyril, Thes., assert. 7 and 18.
[8] Greg. Naz., Orat. 29.
[1] Cyril, Thes., assert. 5, 6, and 16; Greg., Orat. 35.
[2] ἀρρεύστως γεννᾷ καὶ ἐκτὸς συνδυασμοῦ. This argument is repeatedly made in refutation both of Gnostic ideas of emanation and Arian misrepresentations of the orthodox doctrine. Cf. *Athan., De Synodis; Epiph., Hæres.* 69; *Hilary, De Trin.* iii. iv.; *Greg. Naz., Orat.* 35.
[3] Infra, Book ii. c. 3.
[4] Greg. Naz., Orat. 45.

then, teaches the existence at once of a Father and of His Only-begotten Son, born of Him without time and flux and passion, in a manner incomprehensible and perceived by the God of the universe alone: just as we recognise the existence at once of fire and the light which proceeds from it: for there is not first fire and thereafter light, but they exist together. And just as light is ever the product of fire, and ever is in it and at no time is separate from it, so in like manner also the Son is begotten of the Father and is never in any way [5] separate from Him, but ever is in Him [6]. But whereas the light which is produced from fire without separation, and abideth ever in it, has no proper subsistence of its own distinct from that of fire (for it is a natural quality of fire), the Only-begotten Son of God, begotten of the Father without separation and difference and ever abiding in Him, has a proper subsistence of its own distinct from that of the Father.

The terms, 'Word' and 'effulgence,' then, are used because He is begotten of the Father without the union of two, or passion, or time, or flux, or separation [7]: and the terms 'Son' and 'impress of the Father's subsistence,' because He is perfect and has subsistence [8] and is in all respects similar to the Father, save that the Father is not begotten [9]: and the term 'Only-begotten' [1] because He alone was begotten alone of the Father alone. For no other generation is like to the generation of the Son of God, since no other is Son of God. For though the Holy Spirit proceedeth from the Father, yet this is not generative in character but processional. This is a different mode of existence, alike incomprehensible and unknown, just as is the generation of the Son. Wherefore all the qualities the Father has are the Son's, save that the Father is unbegotten [2], and this exception involves no difference in essence nor dignity [3], but only a different mode of coming into existence [4]. We have an analogy in Adam, who was not begotten (for God Himself moulded him), and Seth, who was begotten (for he is Adam's son), and Eve, who proceeded out of Adam's rib (for she was not begotten). These do not differ from each other in nature, for they are human beings: but they differ in the mode of coming into existence [5].

For one must recognise that the word ἀγένητον with only one 'ν' signifies "uncreate" or "not having been made," while ἀγέννητον written with double 'ν' means "unbegotten." According to the first significance essence differs from essence: for one essence is uncreate, or ἀγένητον with one 'ν,' and another is create or γενητή. But in the second significance there is no difference between essence and essence. For the first subsistence of all kinds of living creatures is ἀγέννητος but not ἀγένητος. For they were created by the Creator, being brought into being by His Word, but they were not begotten, for there was no pre-existing form like themselves from which they might have been born.

So then in the first sense of the word the three absolutely divine subsistences of the Holy Godhead agree [6]: for they exist as one in essence and uncreate [7]. But with the second signification it is quite otherwise. For the Father alone is ingenerate [8], no other subsistence having given Him being. And the Son alone is generate, for He was begotten of the Father's essence without beginning and without time. And only the Holy Spirit proceedeth from the Father's essence, not having been generated but simply proceeding [9]. For this is the doctrine of Holy Scripture. But the nature of the generation and the procession is quite beyond comprehension.

And this also it behoves [1] us to know, that the names Fatherhood, Sonship and Procession, were not applied to the Holy Godhead by us: on the contrary, they were communicated to us by the Godhead, as the divine apostle says, *Wherefore I bow the knee to the Father, from Whom is every family in heaven and on earth* [2]. But if we say [3] that the Father is the origin of the Son and greater than the

---

5 Text, μηδ' ὅλως. Variant in many codices is μηδαμῶς, as in the previous sentence.

6 *Greg. Naz., Orat.* bk. i., *Cont. Eun.*, p. 66; *Cyril, Thes., assert.* 5.   7 *Greg. Naz., Orat.* 36.

8 ἐνυπόστατον; enhypostatic. See Suicer, *Thesaurus, sub voce.*

9 *Greg. Naz., Orat.* 23, 37 and 39.   1 Cf. *ibid.* 23, 36.

2 *Athan., Contra Arian., Orat.* 2; *Basil, Contra Eunom.* iv.; *Greg. Naz., Orat.* 35.   3 ἀξιώματι.

4 *Basil*, bk. ii. and iv.   5 *Greg. Naz., Orat.* 36 and 37.

6 *Man. Dialog. contr. Arian.*

7 *Cyril, Thes., assert.* 1, p. 12.   8 *Greg. Naz., Orat.* 35.

9 St. John xv. 26.

1 Cf. *Basil, Contra Eunom.*, v.; *Athan., Contra Arian*, ii.; *Cyril, Thes., assert.* 32; *Epiphan., Hæres.* 73, &c.

2 Ephes. iii. 14 and 15: *Cyril, Thes., assert.* 32: *Dionys., De divin. nom.*, c. 1.

3 In the first Book of his *Contra Arianos* Athanasius refers to Christ's word in St. John xiv. 28. He remarks that He does not say "the Father is better (κρείσσων) than I," lest it should be inferred that the Son is not equal to the Father in Divine nature, but of another nature; but "the Father is *greater* (μείζων) than I," that is to say, not in dignity or age, but as being begotten of the Father. And further, that by the word "greater" He indicates the peculiar property of the substance (τῆς οὐσίας τὴν ἰδιότητα). This declaration of our Lord's was understood in the same way by Basil, Gregory Nazianzenus, Cyril and others of the Greek Fathers, and by Hilary among the Latin Fathers. In the ixth and xth Books of his *De Trinitate* Hilary refers to this, and says that the Father is called '*greater*' *propter auctoritatem*, meaning by *auctoritas* not *power*, but what the Greeks understand by αἰτιότης, causation, principle or authorship of being. So also Soebadius says that the Father is rightly called '*greater*,' because He alone is without an author of His being. But Latin theologians usually spoke of the Father as '*greater*,' not because He is *Father*, but because the Son was made Man. To this effect also Athanasius expresses himself in his *De hum. carne suscepta*, while Gregory Nazianzenus speaks otherwise in his *Orat.* 36.

Son, we do not suggest any precedence in time or superiority in nature of the Father over the Son[4] (for through His agency He made the ages[5]), or superiority in any other respect save causation. And we mean by this, that the Son is begotten of the Father and not the Father of the Son, and that the Father naturally is the cause of the Son : just as we say in the same way not that fire proceedeth from light, but rather light from fire. So then, whenever we hear it said that the Father is the origin of the Son and greater than the Son, let us understand it to mean in respect of causation. And just as we do not say that fire is of one essence and light of another, so we cannot say that the Father is of one essence and the Son of another : but both are of one and the same essence[6]. And just as we say that fire has brightness[7] through the light proceeding from it, and do not consider the light of the fire as an instrument ministering to the fire, but rather as its natural force : so we say that the Father creates all that He creates through His Only-begotten Son, not as though the Son were a mere instrument serving[8] the Father's ends, but as His natural and subsistential force[9]. And just as we say both that the fire shines and again that the light of the fire shines, *So all things whatsoever the Father doeth, these also doeth the Son likewise*[9a]. But whereas light possesses no proper subsistence of its own, distinct from that of the fire, the Son is a perfect subsistence[1], inseparable from the Father's subsistence, as we have shewn above. For it is quite impossible to find in creation an image that will illustrate in itself exactly in all details the nature of the Holy Trinity. For how could that which is create and compound, subject to flux and change, circumscribed, formed and corruptible, clearly shew forth the super-essential divine essence, unaffected as it is in any of these ways ? Now it is evident that all creation is liable to most of these affections, and all from its very nature is subject to corruption.

Likewise we believe also in one Holy Spirit, the Lord and Giver of Life : Who proceedeth from the Father and resteth in the Son : the object of equal adoration and glorification with the Father and Son, since He is co-essential and co-eternal[2] : the Spirit of God, direct, authoritative[3], the fountain of wisdom,

and life, and holiness : God existing and addressed along with Father and Son : uncreate, full, creative, all-ruling, all-effecting, all-powerful, of infinite power, Lord of all creation and not under any lord[4] : deifying, not deified[5] : filling, not filled : shared in, not sharing in : sanctifying, not sanctified : the intercessor, receiving the supplications of all : in all things like to the Father and Son : proceeding from the Father and communicated through the Son, and participated in by all creation, through Himself creating, and investing with essence and sanctifying, and maintaining the universe : having subsistence, existing in its own proper and peculiar subsistence, inseparable and indivisible from Father and Son, and possessing all the qualities that the Father and Son possess, save that of not being begotten or born. For the Father is without cause and unborn : for He is derived from nothing, but derives from Himself His being, nor does He derive a single quality from another[6]. Rather He is Himself the beginning and cause of the existence of all things in a definite and natural manner. But the Son is derived from the Father after the manner of generation, and the Holy Spirit likewise is derived from the Father, yet not after the manner of generation, but after that of procession. And we have learned that there is a difference[7] between generation and procession, but the nature of that difference we in no wise understand. Further, the generation of the Son from the Father and the procession of the Holy Spirit are simultaneous.

All then that the Son and the Spirit have is from the Father, even their very being[8] : and unless the Father is, neither the Son nor the Spirit is. And unless the Father possesses a certain attribute, neither the Son nor the Spirit possesses it : and through the Father[9], that is, because of the Father's existence[1], the Son and the Spirit exist[2], and through the Father, that is, because of the Father having the qualities, the Son and the Spirit have all their qualities, those of being unbegotten, and of birth and of procession being excepted[3]. For in these *hypo-*

---

4 St. John xiv. 28.   5 τοὺς αἰῶνας: Heb i. 3.
6 *Greg. Naz., Orat.* 37 ; *Athan., Contr. Arian.,* bk. i.
7 φαίνειν, *shines.*
8 See *Cyril, Ad Herm.,* dial. 2 ; *Irenæus.* iv. 14, v. 6, and *John of Damascus,* himself in his *Dial. Contr. Manich.*
9 *Greg. Naz., Orat.* 13, 31 and 37.
9a St. John v. 19.
1 τέλεια ὑπόστασις ; *a perfect hypostasis.*
2 *Greg. Naz., Orat.* 37.   3 ἡγεμονικόν.

4 *Greg. Naz., Orat.* 49.   5 θεοῦν οὐ θεούμενον.
6 Text οὐ γὰρ ἔκ τινος· ἐξ ἑαυτοῦ γὰρ τὸ εἶναι ἔχει, οὐδέ τι τῶν ὅσαπερ ἔχει ἐξ ἑτέρου ἔχει· Another reading is, οὐ γὰρ ἔκ τινος τὸ εἶναι ἔχει, οὐδέ τι τῶν ὅσα ἔχει, i.e. *for He does not derive His being nor any one of His qualities from any one.*
7 See *Greg. Naz., Orat.* 29, 35 ; *Thomas Aquin.,* I. *Quæst.* 35, art 1.
8 *Greg. Naz., Orat.* 25.
9 See *Athan., Contra Arian., Orat.* 3 ; *Greg. Naz., Orat.* 35. So Augustine (*Contr. Max.* iii. 14, *De Trin.* xv.). Epiphanius (*Anchor.*), and Gregory of Nyssa (*Epist. ad Ablab.*) teach that the Spirit *proceeds,* and is not *begotten,* because He is both of the Father and the Son, while the Son is only of the Father.
1 Reading, διὰ τὸ εἶναι τὸν Πατέρα: a variant is, διὰ τὸ εἶναι αὐτὸν Πατέρα, as also in *Cyrilli, De Trinitate.*
2 *Greg. Naz., Orat.* 23.   3 *Ibid., Orat.,* 25.

static or *personal* properties alone do the three holy subsistences [3a] differ from each other, being indivisibly divided not by essence but by the distinguishing mark of their proper and peculiar subsistence.

Further we say that each of [4] the three has a perfect subsistence, that we may understand not one compound perfect nature made up of three imperfect elements, but one simple essence, surpassing and preceding perfection, existing in three perfect subsistences [5]. For all that is composed of imperfect elements must necessarily be compound. But from perfect subsistences no compound can arise. Wherefore we do not speak of the form as from subsistences, but as in subsistences [6]. But we speak of those things as imperfect which do not preserve the form of that which is completed out of them. For stone and wood and iron are each perfect in its own nature, but with reference to the building that is completed out of them each is imperfect : for none of them is in itself a house.

The subsistences then we say are perfect, that we may not conceive of the divine nature as compound. For compoundness is the beginning of separation. And again we speak of the three subsistences as being in each other [7], that we may not introduce a crowd and multitude of Gods [8]. Owing to the three subsistences, there is no compoundness or confusion : while, owing to their having the same essence and dwelling in one another, and being the same in will, and energy, and power, and authority, and movement, so to speak, we recognise the indivisibility and the unity of God. For verily there is one God, and His word and Spirit.

Marg. MS. Concerning the distinction of the three subsistences : and concerning the thing itself and our reason and thought in relation to it.

One ought, moreover, to recognise that it is one thing to look at a matter as it is, and another thing to look at it in the light of reason and thought. In the case of all created things, the distinction of the subsistences is observed in actual fact. For in actual fact Peter is seen to be separate from Paul. But the community and connection and unity are apprehended by reason and thought. For it is by the mind that we perceive that Peter and Paul are of the same

nature and have one common nature [9]. For both are living creatures, rational and mortal : and both are flesh, endowed with the spirit of reason and understanding [1]. It is, then, by reason that this community of nature is observed. For here indeed the subsistences do not exist one within the other. But each privately and individually, that is to say, in itself, stands quite separate, having very many points that divide it from the other. For they are both separated in space and differ in time, and are divided in thought, and power, and shape, or form, and habit, and temperament and dignity, and pursuits, and all differentiating properties, but above all, in the fact that they do not dwell in one another but are separated. Hence it comes that we can speak of two, three, or many men.

And this may be perceived throughout the whole of creation, but in the case of the holy and superessential and incomprehensible Trinity, far removed from everything, it is quite the reverse. For there the community and unity are observed in fact, through the co-eternity of the subsistences, and through their having the same essence and energy and will and concord of mind [2], and then being identical in authority and power and goodness—I do not say similar but identical—and then movement by one impulse [3]. For there is one essence, one goodness, one power, one will, one energy, one authority, one and the same, I repeat, not three resembling each other. But the three subsistences have one and the same movement. For each one of them is related as closely to the other as to itself : that is to say that the Father, the Son, and the Holy Spirit are one in all respects, save those of not being begotten, of birth and of procession. But it is by thought that the difference is perceived [4]. For we recognise one God : but only in the attributes of Fatherhood, Sonship, and Procession, both in respect of cause and effect and perfection of subsistence, that is, manner of existence, do we perceive difference [5]. For with reference to the uncircumscribed Deity we cannot speak of separation in space, as we can in our own case. For the subsistences dwell in one another, in no wise confused but cleaving together, according to the word of the Lord,

---

3a υπόστασεις ; *hypostases.*
4 See *Athan., Contra Arian., Orat.* 5.
5 *Greg. Naz., Orat.* 13 and 29 : *At'ian., Orat. Contr. Arian.*
6 The Greek is όθεν ουδέ λέγομεν τὸ εἶδος ἐξ ὑποστάσεων, ἀλλ' ἐν ὑποστάσεων. See *Basil., Orat. Contr. Sabell., Ar. et Eunom.*
7 See *Greg. Naz., Orat.* 1 and 37.
8 *Greg. Naz., Orat.* 29, 34 and 40.

9 *Greg. Naz., Orat.* 37.   1 *Ibid.* 32.
2 τὴν τῆς γνώμης σύμπνοιαν ; *co-operation of judgment,* or, *disposition.*
3 *Greg. Naz., Orat.* 40. The Greek is singular and difficult : τὸ ἓν ἐξαλμα τῆς κινήσεως ; *the one forthleaping of the motion,* or *movement.* Origen speaks of ἡ ἀπ' αὐτοῦ κίνησις (I. 436 A.). In Athanasius (I. 253 C.) κίνησις has the metaphorical sense of *indignation.*
4 *Greg. Naz., Orat.* 37 ; *Greg. Nyss., Epist. ad Ablab. et Orat.* 32.
5 *Basil., Epist.* 43.

I am in the Father, and the Father in Me[6]: nor can one admit difference in will or judgment or energy or power or anything else whatsoever which may produce actual and absolute separation in our case. Wherefore we do not speak of three Gods, the Father, the Son, and the Holy Spirit, but rather of one God, the holy Trinity, the Son and Spirit being referred to one cause[7], and not compounded or coalesced according to the synæresis of Sabellius. For, as we said, they are made one not so as to commingle, but so as to cleave to each other, and they have their being in each other[8] without any coalescence or commingling. Nor do the Son and the Spirit stand apart, nor are they sundered in essence according to the diæresis of Arius[9]. For the Deity is undivided amongst things divided, to put it concisely: and it is just like three suns cleaving to each other without separation and giving out light mingled and conjoined into one. When, then, we turn our eyes to the Divinity, and the first cause and the sovereignty and the oneness and sameness, so to speak, of the movement and will of the Divinity, and the identity in essence and power and energy and lordship, what is seen by us is unity[1]. But when we look to those things in which the Divinity is, or, to put it more accurately, which are the Divinity, and those things which are in it through the first cause without time or distinction in glory or separation, that is to say, the subsistences of the Son and the Spirit, it seems to us a

Trinity that we adore[2]. The Father is one Father, and without beginning, that is, without cause: for He is not derived from anything. The Son is one Son, but not without beginning, that is, not without cause: for He is derived from the Father. But if you eliminate the idea of a beginning from time, He is also without beginning: for the creator of times cannot be subject to time. The Holy Spirit is one Spirit, going forth from the Father, not in the manner of Sonship but of procession; so that neither has the Father lost His property of being unbegotten because He hath begotten, nor has the Son lost His property of being begotten because He was begotten of that which was unbegotten (for how could that be so?), nor does the Spirit change either into the Father or into the Son because He hath proceeded and is God. For a property is quite constant. For how could a property persist if it were variable, moveable, and could change into something else? For if the Father is the Son, He is not strictly the Father: for there is strictly one Father. And if the Son is the Father, He is not strictly the Son: for there is strictly one Son and one Holy Spirit.

Further, it should be understood that we do not speak of the Father as derived from any one, but we speak of Him as the Father of the Son. And we do not speak of the Son as Cause[3] or Father, but we speak of Him both as from the Father, and as the Son of the Father. And we speak likewise of the Holy Spirit as from the Father, and call Him the Spirit of the Father. And we do not speak of the Spirit as from the Son[4]: [5] but yet we call Him the Spirit of the Son. *For if any one hath not the Spirit of Christ, he is none of His*[6], saith the divine apostle. And we confess that He is manifested and imparted to us through the Son. *For He breathed upon His Disciples*, says he, *and said, Receive ye the Holy Spirit*[7]. It is just the same as in the case of the sun from which come both the ray and the radiance (for the sun itself is the source of both the ray and the radiance), and it is through the ray that the radiance is imparted to us, and it is the radiance itself by which we are lightened and in which we participate. Further we do not speak of the Son of the Spirit, or of the Son as derived from the Spirit[8].

---

6 St. John xiv. 11.
7 εἰς ἓν αἴτιον. So elsewhere it is put, ὥσπερ μία ἀρχή, κατὰ τοῦτο εἰς Θεός. The three Persons or Subsistences are yet One God, because of the one Principle of Being whence Son and Spirit derive. So the Father is said to be the ἕνωσις ἐξ οὗ καὶ πρὸς ὃν ἀνάγεται τὰ ἑξῆς.
8 The Greek runs thus:—καὶ τὴν ἐν ἀλλήλαις περιχώρησιν ἔχουσι δίχα πάσης συναλοιφῆς καὶ συμφύρσεως. The term περιχώρησις, *circumincessio, immanentia*, was meant to express the peculiarity of the relations of the Three Divine Persons or Subsistences—their Indwelling in each other, the fact that, while they are distinct they yet are in one another, the Coinherence which implies their equal and identical Godhead. "In the Trinity," says Bishop Bull (*Defence of the Nicene Creed*, bk. iv. ch. iv., secs. 13, 14), "the circumincession is most proper and perfect, forasmuch as the Persons mutually contain Each Other, and all the three have an immeasureable whereabouts (*immensum ubi*, as the Schoolmen express it), so that wherever one Person is there the other two exist; in other words They are all everywhere. . . . This outcome of the circumincession of the Persons in the Trinity is so far from introducing Sabellianism, that it is of great use, as Petavius has also observed, for (establishing) the diversity of the Persons, and for confuting that heresy. For, in order to that mutual existence (in each other) which is discerned in the Father, the Son, and the Holy Ghost, it is absolutely necessary that there should be some distinction between these who are thus joined together—that is, that those that exist mutually in each other should be different in reality, and not in mode of conception only; for that which is simply one is not said to exist in itself, or to interpenetrate itself. . . . Lastly, this is to be especially considered—that this circumincession of the Divine Persons is indeed a very great mystery, which we ought rather religiously to adore than curiously to pry into. No similitude can be devised which shall be in every respect apt to illustrate it; no language avails worthily to set it forth, seeing that it is an union which far transcends all other unions."
9 *Greg., Orat.* 29; *Dionys., De div. nom., c.* 2.
1 *Greg. Naz., Orat.* 37.

2 *Greg. Naz., Orat.* 19 and 29.
3 Text, αἴτιον: variant, ἀναίτιον, *causeless*.
4 *Maxim. Epist. ad Marin.*
5 ἐκ τοῦ Υἱοῦ δὲ τὸ Πνεῦμα οὐ λέγομεν. See also ch. xii., καὶ Υἱοῦ Πνεῦμα οὐχ ὡς ἐξ αὐτοῦ, and at the close of the *Epist. ad Jordan.*, Πνεῦμα Υἱοῦ μὴ ἐξ Υἱοῦ.
6 Rom. viii. 9.   7 St. John xx. 29.
8 *Greg. Naz., Orat.* 37.

CHAPTER IX.

Concerning what is affirmed about God.

The Deity is simple and uncompound. But that which is composed of many and different elements is compound. If, then, we should speak of the qualities of being uncreate and without beginning and incorporeal and immortal and everlasting and good and creative and so forth as essential differences in the case of God, that which is composed of so many qualities will not be simple but must be compound. But this is impious in the extreme. Each then of the affirmations about God should be thought of as signifying not what He is in essence, but either something that it is impossible to make plain, or some relation to some of those things which are contrasts or some of those things that follow the nature, or an energy [9].

It appears then [9a] that the most proper of all the names given to God is " He that is," as He Himself said in answer to Moses on the mountain, *Say to the sons of Israel, He that is hath sent Me* [1]. For He keeps all being in His own embrace [2], like a sea of essence infinite and unseen. Or as the holy Dionysius says, " He that is good [3]." For one cannot say of God that He has being in the first place and goodness in the second.

The second name of God is ὁ Θεός, derived from θέειν [4], to run, because He courses through all things, or from αἴθειν, to burn: *For God is a fire consuming all evil* [5]: or from θεᾶσθαι, because He is all-seeing [6]: for nothing can escape Him, and over all He keepeth watch. For He saw all things before they were, holding them timelessly in His thoughts; and each one conformably to His voluntary and timeless thought [7], which constitutes predetermination and image and pattern, comes into existence at the predetermined time [8].

The first name then conveys the notion of His existence and of the nature of His existence: while the second contains the idea of energy. Further, the terms ' without

beginning,' ' incorruptible,' ' unbegotten,' as also ' uncreate,' ' incorporeal,' ' unseen,' and so forth, explain what He is not : that is to say, they tell us that His being had no beginning, that He is not corruptible, nor created, nor corporeal, nor visible [9]. Again, goodness and justice and piety and such like names belong to the nature [1], but do not explain His actual essence. Finally, Lord and King and names of that class indicate a relationship with their contrasts : for the name Lord has reference to those over whom the lord rules, and the name King to those under kingly authority, and the name Creator to the creatures, and the name Shepherd to the sheep he tends.

CHAPTER X.

Concerning divine union and separation.

Therefore all these names must be understood as common to deity as a whole, and as containing the notions of sameness and simplicity and indivisibility and union : while the names Father, Son and Spirit, and causeless and caused, and unbegotten and begotten, and procession contain the idea of separation : for these terms do not explain His essence, but the mutual relationship [2] and manner of existence [3].

When, then, we have perceived these things and are conducted from these to the divine essence, we do not apprehend the essence itself but only the attributes of the essence : just as we have not apprehended the essence of the soul even when we have learnt that it is incorporeal and without magnitude and form : nor again, the essence of the body when we know that it is white or black, but only the attributes of the essence. Further, the true doctrine [4] teacheth that the Deity is simple and has one simple energy, good and energising in all things, just as the sun's ray, which warms all things and energises in each in harmony with its natural aptitude and receptive power, having obtained this form of energy from God, its Maker.

But quite distinct is all that pertains to the divine and benignant incarnation of the divine Word. For in that neither the Father nor the Spirit have any part at all, unless so far as regards approval and the working of inexplicable miracles which the God-Word,

---

9 The Greek runs :—ἡ σχέσιν τινὰ πρὸς τὶ τῶν ἀντιδιαστελλομένων, ἢ τι τῶν παρεπομένων τῇ φύσει, ἢ ἐνέργειαν.

9a Rendered in the Septuagint Version, Ἐγώ εἰμι ὁ ὤν. Some of the Fathers made much of the fact that it is not the neuter form τὸ ὄν.

1 Exod. iii. 14.   2 *Greg. Naz., Orat.* 36.

3 *Dionys., De div. nom.* c. 2, 3 and 4. This sentence and the next are absent in some MSS., and are rather more obscurely stated than is usual with John of Damascus.

4 In his *Cratylus* Plato gives this etymology, and Eusebius quotes it in his *Prep. Evangel.* i. Clement of Alexandria refers to it more than once in his *Strom.*, bk. iv., and in his *Protrept.*, where he says—*Sidera θέους ἐκ τοῦ θέειν, deos a currendo nominarunt.*

5 Deut. iv. 24.   6 2 Mach. x. 5.

7 κατὰ τὴν θελητικὴν αὐτοῦ ἄχρονον ἔννοιαν. See *Thomas Aquin.*, I., II. *Quæst.* 17, *Art.* 1, where he says, *est actus rationis, præsupposito tamen actu voluntatis.*

8 This sentence is absent in some MSS., being added at the end of the chapter with the mark σχόλ.

9 *Dionys., De div. nom.*, c. 5.

1 παρέπονται τῇ φύσει ; *follow the nature,* are *consequents of the nature,* or *accompany it.*

2 *Greg. Naz., Orat.* 45 ; cf. also *Epist. ad Evagr.*, and *Greg. Nyss., Epist. ad Ablab.; Dionys., De div. nom.,* c. 2 ; *Basil, Epist.* 43 ad *Greg. fratr.*

3 *Dionys., De div. nom.,* c. 2 ; *Greg. Naz., Orat.* 37 and 45 ; *Nyss. Epist. ad. Ablab.*

4 ὁ δὲ ἀληθὴς λόγος.

having become man [5] like us, worked, as unchangeable God and son of God [6].

CHAPTER XI.

Concerning what is affirmed about God as though He had body.

Since we find many terms used symbolically in the Scriptures concerning God which are more applicable to that which has body, we should recognise that it is quite impossible for us men clothed about with this dense covering of flesh to understand or speak of the divine and lofty and immaterial energies of the Godhead, except by the use of images and types and symbols derived from our own life [7]. So then all the statements concerning God, that imply body, are symbols, but have a higher meaning: for the Deity is simple and formless. Hence by God's eyes and eyelids and sight we are to understand His power of overseeing all things and His knowledge, that nothing can escape: for in the case of us this sense makes our knowledge more complete and more full of certainty. By God's ears and hearing is meant His readiness to be propitiated and to receive our petitions: for it is this sense that renders us also kind to suppliants, inclining our ear to them more graciously. God's mouth and speech are His means of indicating His will; for it is by the mouth and speech that we make clear the thoughts that are in the heart: God's food and drink are our concurrence to His will, for we, too, satisfy the necessities of our natural appetite through the sense of taste. And God's sense of smell is His appreciation of our thoughts of and good will towards Him, for it is through this sense that we appreciate sweet fragrance. And God's countenance is the demonstration and manifestation of Himself through His works, for our manifestation is through the countenance. And God's hands mean the effectual nature of His energy, for it is with our own hands that we accomplish our most useful and valuable work. And His right hand is His aid in prosperity, for it is the right hand that we also use when making anything of beautiful shape or of great value, or where much strength is required. His handling is His power of accurate discrimination and exaction, even in the minutest and most secret details, for those whom we have handled cannot conceal from us aught within themselves. His feet and walk are His advent and presence, either for the purpose of bringing succour to the needy, or vengeance against enemies, or to perform any other action, for it is by using our feet that we come to arrive at any place. His oath is the unchangeableness of His counsel, for it is by oath that we confirm our compacts with one another. His anger and fury are His hatred of and aversion to all wickedness, for we, too, hate that which is contrary to our mind and become enraged thereat [8]. His forgetfulness and sleep and slumbering are His delay in taking vengeance on His enemies and the postponement of the accustomed help to His own. And to put it shortly, all the statements made about God that imply body have some hidden meaning and teach us what is above us by means of something familiar to ourselves, with the exception of any statement concerning the bodily sojourn of the God-Word. For He for our safety took upon Himself the whole nature of man [9], the thinking spirit, the body, and all the properties of human nature, even the natural and blameless passions.

CHAPTER XII.

Concerning the Same.

The following, then, are the mysteries which we have learned from the holy oracles, as the divine Dionysius the Areopagite said [1]: that God is the cause and beginning of all: the essence of all that have essence: the life of the living: the reason of all rational beings: the intellect of all intelligent beings: the recalling and restoring of those who fall away from Him: the renovation and transformation of those that corrupt that which is natural: the holy foundation of those who are tossed in unholiness: the steadfastness of those who have stood firm: the way of those whose course is directed to Him and the hand stretched forth to guide them upwards. And I shall add He is also the Father of all His creatures (for God, Who brought us into being out of nothing, is in a stricter sense our Father than are our parents who have derived both being and begetting from Him [2]): the shepherd of those who follow and are tended by Him: the radiance of those who are enlightened: the initiation of the initiated: the deification of the deified: the peace of those at discord: the simplicity of those who love simplicity: the unity of those who worship unity: of all beginning the beginning, super-essential be-

---

[5] Text, ἄνθρωπος, which is absent in some codices and in Dionys., De div. nom., from which these words are taken.
[6] Greg. Naz., Orat. 24: Dionys., De div. nom., c. 2.
[7] Dionys., De div. nom., c. 1; De Cœl. Hier., c. 15.

[8] Greg. Naz., Orat. 37.
[9] Text, πάντα τὸν ἄνθρωπον: variant, ἅπαντα.
[1] Dionys., De div. nom., c. 1.
[2] Athan., Orat. 2, Cont. Arian.; Cyril, Thes., assert. 13.

cause above all beginning[3]: and the good revelation of what is hidden, that is, of the knowledge of Him so far as that is lawful for and attainable by each.

Further and more accurately concerning the divine names[4].

The Deity being incomprehensible is also assuredly nameless. Therefore since we know not His essence, let us not seek for a name for His essence. For names are explanations of actual things[5]. But God, Who is good and brought us out of nothing into being that we might share in His goodness, and Who gave us the faculty of knowledge, not only did not impart to us His essence, but did not even grant us the knowledge of His essence. For it is impossible for nature to understand fully the super-natural[6]. Moreover, if knowledge is of things that are[7], how can there be knowledge of the super-essential? Through His unspeakable goodness, then, it pleased Him to be called by names that we could understand, that we might not be altogether cut off from the knowlege of Him but should have some notion of Him, however vague. Inasmuch, then, as He is incomprehensible, He is also unnameable. But inasmuch as He is the cause of all and contains in Himself the reasons and causes of all that is, He receives names drawn from all that is, even from opposites: for example, He is called light and darkness, water and fire: in order that we may know that these are not of His essence but that He is super-essential and unnameable: but inasmuch as He is the cause of all, He receives names from all His effects.

Wherefore, of the divine names, some have a negative signification, and indicate that He is super-essential[8]: such are "non-essential[9]," "timeless," "without beginning," "invisible": not that God is inferior to anything or lacking in anything (for all things are His and have become from Him and through Him and endure in Him[9a]), but that He is preeminently separated from all that is. For He is not one of the things that are, but over all things. Some again have an affirmative signification, as indicating that He is the cause of all things. For as the cause of all that is and of all essence, He is called both Ens and Essence. And as the cause of all reason and wisdom, of the rational and the wise, He is called both reason and rational, and wisdom and wise. Similarly He is spoken of as Intellect and Intellectual, Life and Living, Power and Powerful, and so on with all the rest. Or rather those names are most appropriate to Him which are derived from what is most precious and most akin to Himself. That which is immaterial is more precious and more akin to Himself than that which is material, and the pure than the impure, and the holy than the unholy: for they have greater part in Him. So then, sun and light will be more apt names for Him than darkness, and day than night, and life than death, and fire and spirit and water, as having life, than earth, and above all, goodness than wickedness: which is just to say, being more than not being. For goodness is existence and the cause of existence, but wickedness is the negation of goodness, that is, of existence. These, then, are the affirmations and the negations, but the sweetest names are a combination of both: for example, the super-essential essence, the Godhead that is more than God, the beginning that is above beginning and such like. Further there are some affirmations about God which have in a pre-eminent degree the force of denial: for example, darkness: for this does not imply that God is darkness but that He is not light, but above light.

God then is called Mind and Reason and Spirit and Wisdom and Power, as the cause of these, and as immaterial, and maker of all, and omnipotent[9b]. And these names are common to the whole Godhead, whether affirmative or negative. And they are also used of each of the subsistences of the Holy Trinity in the very same and identical way and with their full significance[1]. For when I think of one of the subsistences, I recognise it to be perfect God and perfect essence: but when I combine and reckon the three together, I know one perfect God. For the Godhead is not compound but in three perfect subsistences, one perfect indivisible and uncompound God. And when I think of the relation of the three subsistences to each other, I perceive that the Father is super-essential Sun, source of goodness, fathomless sea of essence, reason, wisdom, power, light, divinity: the generating and productive source

---

3 Text reads, ὡς ὑπάρχιος: surely a misprint for ὡς ὑπεράρχιος.

4 This chapter is not found in the oldest copies, but only in a few of the latest date. In *Cod. Reg.* 3109 it comes in after bk. iv. c. 9, and in *Cod. Reg.* 3451, after bk. ii. c. 2.

5 *Greg. Naz.*, *Orat.* 36.

6 *Dionys.*, *De div. nom.*, c. 1.

7 Text, εἰ δὲ καὶ τῶν ὄντων αἱ γνωσεις, τὸ ὑπερούσιον πῶς γνωθήσεται; a variant, εἰ δὲ αἱ φύσεις ἄγνωστοι, αὐτὸ ὑπερούσιον πῶς γνωθήσεται. *If the natures are unknown how can the super-essential itself be known?*

8 Or, super-substantial, ὑπερούσιος.

9 ἀνούσιος, non-substantial, without substance.

9a Coloss. i. 17.

9b *Dionys.*, *De div. nom.*, c. 5.

1 Text, ἀπαραλείπτως: variant, ἀπαραλλάκτως, *unchangeably*, an adverb used by the Greeks in connection with the equality of the divine persons.

of good hidden in it. He Himself then is mind, the depth of reason, begetter of the Word, and through the Word the Producer[2] of the revealing Spirit. And to put it shortly, the Father has no reason[3], wisdom, power, will[4], save the Son Who is the only power of the Father, the immediate[5] cause of the creation of the universe: as perfect subsistence begotten of perfect subsistence in a manner known to Himself, Who is and is named the Son. And the Holy Spirit is the power of the Father revealing the hidden mysteries of His Divinity, proceeding from the Father through the Son in a manner known to Himself, but different from that of generation. Wherefore the Holy Spirit is the perfecter of the creation of the universe. All the terms, then, that are appropriate to the Father, as cause, source, begetter, are to be ascribed to the Father alone: while those that are appropriate to the caused, begotten Son, Word, immediate power, will, wisdom, are to be ascribed to the Son: and those that are appropriate to the caused, processional, manifesting, perfecting power, are to be ascribed to the Holy Spirit. The Father is the source and cause of the Son and the Holy Spirit: Father of the Son alone and producer of the Holy Spirit. The Son is Son, Word, Wisdom, Power, Image, Effulgence, Impress of the Father and derived from the Father. But the Holy Spirit is not the Son of the Father but the Spirit of the Father as proceeding from the Father. For there is no impulse without Spirit. And we speak also of the Spirit of the Son, not as though proceeding from Him, but as proceeding through Him from the Father. For the Father alone is cause.

CHAPTER XIII.

Concerning the place of God: and that the Deity alone is uncircumscribed.

Bodily place is the limit of that which contains, by which that which is contained is contained[6]: for example, the air contains but the body is contained[7]. But it is not the whole of the containing air which is the place of the contained body, but the limit of the containing air, where it comes into contact with the contained body: and the reason is clearly because that which contains is not within that which it contains.

But there is also mental place where mind is active, and mental and incorporeal nature exists: where mind dwells and energises and is contained not in a bodily but in a mental fashion. For it is without form, and so cannot be contained as a body is. God, then, being immaterial[8] and uncircumscribed, has not place. For He is His own place, filling all things and being above all things, and Himself maintaining all things[9]. Yet we speak of God having place and the place of God where His energy becomes manifest. For He penetrates everything without mixing with it, and imparts to all His energy in proportion to the fitness and receptive power of each: and by this I mean, a purity both natural and voluntary. For the immaterial is purer than the material, and that which is virtuous than that which is linked with vice. Wherefore by the place of God is meant that which has a greater share in His energy and grace. For this reason the Heaven is His throne. For in it are the angels who do His will and are always glorifying Him[1]. For this is His rest and the earth is His footstool[2]. For in it He dwelt in the flesh among men[3]. And His sacred flesh has been named the foot of God. The Church, too, is spoken of as the place of God: for we have set this apart for the glorifying of God as a sort of consecrated place wherein we also hold converse with Him. Likewise also the places in which His energy becomes manifest to us, whether through the flesh or apart from flesh, are spoken of as the places of God.

But it must be understood that the Deity is indivisible, being everywhere wholly in His entirety and not divided up part by part like that which has body, but wholly in everything and wholly above everything.

Marg. MS. Concerning the place of angel and spirit, and concerning the uncircumscribed.

The angel, although not contained in place with figured form as is body, yet is spoken of as being in place because he has a mental presence and energises in accordance with his nature, and is not elsewhere but has his mental limitations there where he energises. For it is impossible to energise at the same time in different places. For to God alone belongs the power of energising everywhere

---

2 προβολεύς, Lat. productor, *Emitter.*
3 Or, *Word*; λόγος.
4 θέλησις, cf. *Cyril, Th., assert.* 7 ; *Athan., Contr. Arian.* 4 ; *Greg. Nyss., Contr. Eunom.,* p. 345.
5 ἡ μονὴ δύναμις τοῦ Πατρός, ἡ προκαταρτικὴ τῆς τῶν πάντων ποιήσεως. The ἡ προκαταρτικὴ is understood by some to mean the *primordial* or *immediate Cause,* by others to be better rendered as the *primordial Power* or *Energy.* Basil in his *De Spiritu Sancto* speaks of the *Father* as the *primordial Cause* (προκαταρτικὴ αἰτία) in the creation of the world.
6 *Arist., Physic,* bk. iv. 4.
7 Text, οἷον ὁ ἀὴρ περιέχει, τὸ δὲ σῶμα περιέχεται· οὐχ ὅλος δὲ ὁ περιέχων ἀήρ, &c. Variant, οἷον ὁ ἀὴρ περιέχει τόδε σῶμα, οὐχ ὅλος, &c.

8 ἄϋλος ὤν. *Greg. Naz., Orat.* 34, *Greg. Nyss., De anim. et resurr.,* &c., speak of God as *nowhere* and as *everywhere.*
9 *Greg. Naz., Orat.* 34.   1 *Isai.* vi. 1, *seq.*
2 *Isai.* lxvi. 1.   3 *Baruch* iii. 38.

at the same time. The angel energises in different places by the quickness of his nature and the promptness and speed by which he can change his place: but the Deity, Who is everywhere and above all, energises at the same time in diverse ways with one simple energy.

Further the soul is bound up with the body, whole with whole and not part with part : and it is not contained by the body but contains it as fire does iron, and being in it energises with its own proper energies.

That which is comprehended in place or time or apprehension is circumscribed : while that which is contained by none of these is uncircumscribed. Wherefore the Deity alone is uncircumscribed, being without beginning and without end, and containing all things, and in no wise apprehended [4]. For He alone is incomprehensible and unbounded, within no one's knowledge and contemplated by Himself alone. But the angel is circumscribed alike in time (for His being had commencement) and in place (but mental space, as we said above) and in apprehension. For they know somehow the nature of each other and have their bounds perfectly defined by the Creator. Bodies in short are circumscribed both in beginning and end, and bodily place and apprehension.

Marg. MS. From various sources concerning God and the Father, and the Son, and the Holy Spirit. And concerning the Word and the Spirit.

The Deity, then, is quite unchangeable and invariable. For all things which are not in our hands He hath predetermined by His foreknowledge, each in its own proper and peculiar time and place. And accordingly *the Father judgeth no one, but hath given all judgment to the Son* [5]. For clearly the Father and the Son and also the Holy Spirit judged as God. But the Son Himself will descend in the body as man, and will sit on the throne of Glory (for descending and sitting require circumscribed body), and will judge all the world in justice.

All things are far apart from God, not in place but in nature. In our case, thoughtfulness, and wisdom, and counsel come to pass and go away as states of being. Not so in the case of God : for with Him there is no happening or ceasing to be : for He is invariable and unchangeable : and it would not be right to speak of contingency in connection with Him. For goodness is concomitant with essence. He who longs alway after God, he

seeth Him : for God is in all things. Existing things are dependent on that which is, and nothing can be unless it is in that which is. God then is mingled with everything, maintaining their nature : and in His holy flesh the God-Word is made one in subsistence and is mixed with our nature, yet without confusion.

No one seeth the Father, save the Son and the Spirit [6].

The Son is the counsel and wisdom and power of the Father. For one may not speak of quality in connection with God, from fear of implying that He was a compound of essence and quality.

The Son is from the Father, and derives from Him all His properties : *hence He cannot do ought of Himself* [7]. For He has not energy peculiar to Himself and distinct from the Father [8].

That God Who is invisible by nature is made visible by His energies, we perceive from the organisation and government of the world [9].

The Son is the Father's image, and the Spirit the Son's, through which Christ dwelling in man makes him after his own image [1].

The Holy Spirit is God, being between the unbegotten and the begotten, and united to the Father through the Son [2]. We speak of the Spirit of God, the Spirit of Christ, the mind of Christ, the Spirit of the Lord, the very Lord [3], the Spirit of adoption, of truth, of liberty, of wisdom (for He is the creator of all these) : filling all things with essence, maintaining all things, filling the universe with essence, while yet the universe is not the measure of His power.

God is everlasting and unchangeable essence, creator of all that is, adored with pious consideration.

God is also Father, being ever unbegotten, for He was born of no one, but hath begotten His co-eternal Son : God is likewise Son, being always with the Father, born of the Father timelessly, everlastingly, without flux or passion, or separation from Him. God is also Holy Spirit, being sanctifying power, subsistential, proceeding from the Father without separation, and resting in the Son, identical in essence with Father and Son.

Word is that which is ever essentially present with the Father. Again, word is also the natural movement of the mind, according to which it is moved and thinks and considers,

---

[4] *Greg. Naz., Orat. 44.*   [5] St. John v. 22.

[6] St. John vi. 46.   [7] Ibid. v. 30.   [8] *Greg., Orat.* 36.
[9] Wisd. xii. 5.   [1] *Basil, Cont. Eun.*, bk. v.
■ μέσον τοῦ ἀγεννήτου καὶ τοῦ γεννητοῦ, καὶ δι' Υἱοῦ τῷ Πατρὶ συναπτόμενον.
[3] αὐτοκύριος.

being as it were its own light and radiance. Again, word is the thought that is spoken only within the heart. And again, word is the utterance[4] that is the messenger of thought. God therefore is Word[5] essential and enhypostatic: and the other three kinds of word are faculties of the soul, and are not contemplated as having a proper subsistence of their own. The first of these is the natural offspring of the mind, ever welling[6] up naturally out of it: the second is the thought: and the third is the utterance.

The Spirit has various meanings. There is the Holy Spirit: but the powers of the Holy Spirit are also spoken of as spirits: the good messenger is also spirit: the demon also is spirit: the soul too is spirit: and sometimes mind also is spoken of as spirit. Finally the wind is spirit and the air is spirit.

CHAPTER XIV.

The properties of the divine nature.

Uncreate, without beginning, immortal, infinite, eternal, immaterial[7], good, creative, just, enlightening, immutable, passionless, uncircumscribed, immeasurable, unlimited, undefined, unseen, unthinkable, wanting in nothing, being His own rule and authority, all-ruling, life-giving, omnipotent, of infinite power, containing and maintaining the universe and making provision for all: all these and such like attributes the Deity possesses by nature, not having received them from elsewhere, but Himself imparting all good to His own creations according to the capacity of each.

The subsistences dwell and are established firmly in one another. For they are inseparable and cannot part from one another, but keep to their separate courses within one another, without coalescing or mingling, but cleaving to each other. For the Son is in the Father and the Spirit: and the Spirit in the Father and the Son: and the Father in the Son and the Spirit, but there is no coalescence or commingling or confusion[8]. And there is one and the same motion: for there is one impulse and one motion of the three subsistences, which is not to be observed in any created nature.

Further the divine effulgence and energy, being one and simple and indivisible, assuming many varied forms in its goodness among what is divisible and allotting to each the component parts of its own nature, still remains simple and is multiplied without division among the divided, and gathers and converts the divided into its own simplicity[9]. For all things long after it and have their existence in it. It gives also to all things being according to their several natures[1], and it is itself the being of existing things, the life of living things, the reason of rational beings, the thought of thinking beings. But it is itself above mind and reason and life and essence.

Further the divine nature has the property of penetrating all things without mixing with them and of being itself impenetrable by anything else. Moreover, there is the property of knowing all things with a simple knowledge and of seeing all things, simply with His divine, all-surveying, immaterial eye, both the things of the present, and the things of the past, and the things of the future, before they come into being[2]. It is also sinless, and can cast sin out, and bring salvation: and all that it wills, it can accomplish, but does not will all it could accomplish. For it could destroy the universe but it does not will so to do[3].

---

4 προφορικός is absent in MSS. but added by a second hand in one codex.

5 οὐσιώδης τέ ἐστι καὶ ἐνυπόστατος. Against the Sabellian doctrine, the views of Paul of Samosata, &c.

6 πηγαζόμενον.

7 Text, τὸ ἄϋλον: in one codex there is added as emendation or explanation, τὸ ἁπλοῦν, τὸ ἀσύνθετον.

8 *Greg. Naz., Orat.* 1, 13 and 40.

9 *Dionys., De div. nom.,* c. 5.

1 Text, καθὼς ἔχει φύσεως: in the margin of the manuscript is ὡς ἔχουσι.

2 Dan. ii. 22.   3 *Greg., Orat.* 40.

BOOK II.

CHAPTER I.

Concerning aeon or age.

HE created the ages Who Himself was before the ages, Whom the divine David thus addresses, *From age to age Thou art* [1]. The divine apostle also says, *Through Whom He created the ages* [2].

It must then be understood that the word age has various meanings, for it denotes many things. The life of each man is called an age. Again, a period of a thousand years is called an age [3]. Again, the whole course of the present life is called an age: also the future life, the immortal life after the resurrection [4], is spoken of as an age. Again, the word age is used to denote, not time nor yet a part of time as measured by the movement and course of the sun, that is to say, composed of days and nights, but the sort of temporal motion and interval that is co-extensive with eternity [5]. For age is to things eternal just what time is to things temporal.

Seven ages [6] of this world are spoken of, that is, from the creation of the heaven and earth till the general consummation and resurrection of men. For there is a partial consummation, viz., the death of each man: but there is also a general and complete consummation, when the general resurrection of men will come to pass. And the eighth age is the age to come.

Before the world was formed, when there was as yet no sun dividing day from night, there was not an age such as could be measured [7], but there was the sort of temporal motion and interval that is co-extensive with eternity. And in this sense there is but one age, and God is spoken of as αἰώνιος [8] and προαιώνιος, for the age or aeon itself is His creation. For God, Who alone is without beginning, is Himself the Creator of all things, whether age or any other existing thing. And when I say God, it is evident that I mean the Father and His Only-begotten Son, our Lord, Jesus Christ, and His all-holy Spirit, our one God.

But we speak also of ages of ages, inasmuch as the seven ages of the present world include many ages in the sense of lives of men, and the one age embraces all the ages, and the present and the future are spoken of as age of age. Further, everlasting (i.e. αἰώνιος) life and everlasting punishment prove that the age or aeon to come is unending [9]. For time will not be counted by days and nights even after the resurrection, but there will rather be one day with no evening, wherein the Sun of Justice will shine brightly on the just, but for the sinful there will be night profound and limitless. In what way then will the period of one thousand years be counted which, according to Origen [1], is required for the complete restoration? Of all the ages, therefore, the sole creator is God Who hath also created the universe and Who was before the ages.

CHAPTER II.

Concerning the creation.

Since, then, God, Who is good and more than good, did not find satisfaction in self-contemplation, but in His exceeding goodness wished certain things to come into existence which would enjoy His benefits and share in His goodness, He brought all things out of nothing into being and created them, both what is invisible and what is visible. Yea, even man, who is a compound of the visible and the invisible. And it is by thought that He creates, and thought is the basis of the work, the Word filling it and the Spirit perfecting it [2].

CHAPTER III.

Concerning angels.

HE is Himself the Maker and Creator of the angels: for He brought them out of nothing into being and created them after His own image, an incorporeal race, a sort of spirit or immaterial fire: in the words of the divine David, *He maketh His angels spirits, and His ministers a flame of fire* [3]: and He has described their lightness and the ardour, and

---

[1] Ps. xc. 2. [2] Hebr. i. 2.
[3] *Arist., De Cœlo*, bk. 1, text 100.
[4] St. Matt. xii. 32 ; St. Luke vii. 34.
[5] *Greg. Naz.. Orat.* 35, 38. 42.
[6] *Basil, De Struct.*, hom. 2 ; *Greg. Naz., Orat.* 44.
[7] *Greg. Naz., Orat.* 44.
[8] αἰώνιος, 'eternal,' but also 'secular,' 'aeonian,' 'age-long.'

[9] Variant, καὶ ἀπέραντον δηλοῖ. In Regg. αἰῶνος is absent.
[1] See his *Contr. Cels*, iv. Cf. *Justin Martyr. Apol.* 1; *Basil. Hex.*, hom. 3; *Greg. Nyss.. Orat. Catech.* 26, &c.
[2] *Greg. Naz., Orat.* 38, 42 ; *Dionys., De Eccl. Hier.*, ch. 4.
[3] Ps. civ. 4.

heat, and keenness and sharpness with which they hunger for God and serve Him, and how they are borne to the regions above and are quite delivered from all material thought [4].

An angel, then, is an intelligent essence, in perpetual motion, with free-will, incorporeal, ministering to God, having obtained by grace an immortal nature: and the Creator alone knows the form and limitation of its essence. But all that we can understand is, that it is incorporeal and immaterial. For all that is compared with God Who alone is incomparable, we find to be dense and material. For in reality only the Deity is immaterial and incorporeal.

The angel's nature then is rational, and intelligent, and endowed with free-will, changeable in will, or fickle. For all that is created is changeable, and only that which is uncreated is unchangeable. Also all that is rational is endowed with free-will. As it is, then, rational and intelligent, it is endowed with free-will: and as it is created, it is changeable, having power either to abide or progress in goodness, or to turn towards evil.

It is not susceptible of repentance because it is incorporeal. For it is owing to the weakness of his body that man comes to have repentance.

It is immortal, not by nature [5] but by grace [6]. For all that has had beginning comes also to its natural end. But God alone is eternal, or rather, He is above the Eternal: for He, the Creator of times, is not under the dominion of time, but above time.

They are secondary intelligent lights derived from that first light which is without beginning, for they have the power of illumination; they have no need of tongue or hearing, but without uttering words [7] they communicate to each other their own thoughts and counsels [8].

Through the Word, therefore, all the angels were created, and through the sanctification by the Holy Spirit were they brought to perfection, sharing each in proportion to his worth and rank in brightness and grace [9].

They are circumscribed: for when they are in the Heaven they are not on the earth: and when they are sent by God down to the earth they do not remain in the Heaven. They are not hemmed in by walls and doors, and bars and seals, for they are quite unlimited. Unlimited, I repeat, for it is not as they really are that they reveal themselves to the worthy men [1] to whom God wishes them to appear, but in a changed form which the beholders are capable of seeing. For that alone is naturally and strictly unlimited which is uncreated. For every created thing is limited by God Who created it.

Further, apart from their essence they receive the sanctification from the Spirit: through the divine grace they prophesy [2]: they have no need of marriage for they are immortal.

Seeing that they are minds they are in mental places [3], and are not circumscribed after the fashion of a body. For they have not a bodily form by nature, nor are they extended in three dimensions. But to whatever post they may be assigned, there they are present after the manner of a mind and energise, and cannot be present and energise in various places at the same time.

Whether they are equals in essence or differ from one another we know not. God, their Creator, Who knoweth all things, alone knoweth. But they differ [4] from each other in brightness and position, whether it is that their position is dependent on their brightness, or their brightness on their position: and they impart brightness to one another, because they excel one another in rank and nature [5]. And clearly the higher share their brightness and knowledge with the lower.

They are mighty and prompt to fulfil the will of the Deity, and their nature is endowed with such celerity that wherever the Divine glance bids them there they are straightway found. They are the guardians of the divisions of the earth: they are set over nations and regions, allotted to them by their Creator: they govern all our affairs and bring us succour. And the reason surely is because they are set over us by the divine will and command and are ever in the vicinity of God [6].

With difficulty they are moved to evil, yet they are not absolutely immoveable: but now they are altogether immoveable, not by nature but by grace and by their nearness to the Only Good [7].

They behold God according to their capacity, and this is their food [8].

They are above us for they are incorporeal, and are free of all bodily passion, yet are not passionless: for the Deity alone is passionless.

---

[4] *Greg. Naz.*, *Orat.* 38.   [5] *Nemes.*, ch. **1**.
[6] Text, χάριτι. R. 2930, κατὰ χάριν.
[7] ἄνευ λόγου προφορικοῦ : *without word of utterance.*
[8] *Greg. Naz.*, *Orat.* 38.   *Ibid.* 34.

[1] Text, ἀξίοις. R. 2930, ἀγίοις.
[2] *Theodoret, Epist. de div. decr.*, ch. **8**.
[3] ἐν νοητοῖς καὶ τόποις. Cf. bk. i. 17.
[4] See *Greg. Naz.*, *Orat.* 34. And cf. *Cyril, Thesaur.* 31, p. 266; *Epiph., Hæres.* 64.
[5] *Dionys., De Cæl. Hier.*, ch. 3; *Greg. Naz., Orat.* 34.
[6] *Dionys., De Cæl. Hier.*, ch. 9; *Greg. Naz.*, *Orat.* 34.
[7] *Greg. Naz.*, *Orat.* 38.
[8] Text, τροφήν. Variant, τρυφήν, cf. *Dionys., De Cæl. Hier.*, ch. 7.

They take different forms at the bidding of their Master, God, and thus reveal themselves to men and unveil the divine mysteries to them.

They have Heaven for their dwelling-place, and have one duty, to sing God's praise and carry out His divine will.

Moreover, as that most holy, and sacred, and gifted theologian, Dionysius the Areopagite [9], says, All theology, that is to say, the holy Scripture, has nine different names for the heavenly essences [1]. These essences that divine master in sacred things divides into three groups, each containing three. And the first group, he says, consists of those who are in God's presence and are said to be directly and immediately one with Him, viz., the Seraphim with their six wings, the many-eyed Cherubim and those that sit in the holiest thrones. The second group is that of the Dominions, and the Powers, and the Authorities; and the third, and last, is that of the Rulers and Archangels and Angels.

Some, indeed [2], like Gregory the Theologian, say that these were before the creation of other things. He thinks that the angelic and heavenly powers were first and that thought was their function [3]. Others, again, hold that they were created after the first heaven was made. But all are agreed that it was before the formation of man. For myself, I am in harmony with the theologian. For it was fitting that the mental essence should be the first created, and then that which can be perceived, and finally man himself, in whose being both parts are united.

But those who say that the angels are creators of any kind of essence whatever are the mouth of their father, the devil. For since they are created things they are not creators. But He Who creates and provides for and maintains all things is God, Who alone is uncreate and is praised and glorified in the Father, the Son, and the Holy Spirit.

CHAPTER IV.

Concerning the devil and demons.

He who from among these angelic powers was set over [4] the earthly realm, and into whose hands God committed the guardianship of the earth, was not made wicked in nature but was good, and made for good ends, and re-ceived from his Creator no trace whatever of evil in himself. But he did not sustain the brightness and the honour which the Creator had bestowed [5] on him, and of his free choice was changed from what was in harmony to what was at variance with his nature, and became roused against God Who created him, and determined to rise in rebellion against Him [6]: and he was the first to depart from good and become evil [7]. For evil is nothing else than absence of goodness, just as darkness also is absence of light. For goodness is the light of the mind, and, similarly, evil is the darkness of the mind. Light, therefore, being the work of the Creator and being made good (for *God saw all that He made, and behold they were exceeding good* [8]) produced darkness at His free-will. But along with him an innumerable host of angels subject to him were torn away and followed him and shared in his fall. Wherefore, being of the same nature [9] as the angels, they became wicked, turning away at their own free choice from good to evil [1].

Hence they have no power or strength against any one except what God in His dispensation hath conceded to them, as for instance, against Job [2] and those swine that are mentioned in the Gospels [3]. But when God has made the concession they do prevail, and are changed and transformed into any form whatever in which they wish to appear.

Of the future both the angels of God and the demons are alike ignorant: yet they make predictions. God reveals the future to the angels and commands them to prophesy, and so what they say comes to pass. But the demons also make predictions, sometimes because they see what is happening at a distance, and sometimes merely making guesses: hence much that they say is false and they should not be believed, even although they do often, in the way we have said, tell what is true. Besides they know the Scriptures.

All wickedness, then, and all impure passions are the work of their mind. But while the liberty to attack man has been granted to them, they have not the strength to overmaster any one: for we have it in our power to receive or not to receive the attack [4]. Wherefore there has been prepared for the

9 *Dionys., De Cæl. Hier.*, ch. 6.
1 But cf. *August., Enchir.*, ch. 8; *Greg. Naz., Orat.* 34; *Greg. Nyss., Contra Eunom., Orat.* 1; *Chrysost., De incomprehens., hom.* 3, &c.
2 See *Epiph., Hæres.* 6, n. 4 and 5; *Basil, Hex.* 1; *Chrysost.*, 2 *Hom. in Gen.; Theodor., Quæst.* 3 *in Gen.*
3 *Greg. Naz., Orat.* 2.
4 πρωτοστάτης. Cf. *Chrysost., Epist. ad Ephes., hom.* 4, &c.

5 Text, ἐδωρήσατο. R. 1986, ἐχαρίσατο.
6 See *Iren.*, bk. iv. c. 48, &c.
7 *Greg. Nyss., Orat. Catech.*, cp. 6.   8 Gen. i. 31.
9 See *Greg. Naz., Orat.* 19, 38; *Chrysost., In S. Babyl. Or.* 2; *Basil, In Jesaiam.*, ch. 1, &c.
1 *Quæst. ad Antioch.* 10.   2 Job i. 12.
3 St. Mark v. 13.
4 *Vide* Iambl., *De Myst.*, ch. 11, sect. 4.

devil and his demons, and those who follow him, fire unquenchable and everlasting punishment [5].

Note, further, that what in the case of man is death is a fall in the case of angels. For after the fall there is no possibility of repentance for them, just as after death there is for men no repentance [6].

CHAPTER V.
Concerning the visible creation.

Our God Himself, Whom we glorify as Three in One, *created the heaven and the earth and all that they contain* [7], and brought all things out of nothing into being : some He made out of no pre-existing basis of matter, such as heaven, earth, air, fire, water : and the rest out of these elements that He had created, such as living creatures, plants, seeds. For these are made up of earth, and water, and air, and fire, at the bidding of the Creator.

CHAPTER VI.
Concerning the Heaven.

The heaven is the circumference of things created, both visible and invisible. For within its boundary are included and marked off both the mental faculties of the angels and all the world of sense. But the Deity alone is uncircumscribed, filling all things, and surrounding all things, and bounding all things, for He is above all things, and has created all things.

Since [8], therefore, the Scripture speaks of heaven, and heaven of heaven [9], and heavens of heavens [1], and the blessed Paul says that he was snatched away to the third heaven [2], we say that in the cosmogony of the universe we accept the creation of a heaven which the foreign philosophers, appropriating the views of Moses, call a starless sphere. But further, God called the firmament also heaven [3], which He commanded to be in the midst of the waters, setting it to divide the waters that are above the firmament from the waters that are below the firmament. And its nature, according to the divine Basilius [4], who is versed in the mysteries of divine Scripture, is delicate as smoke. Others, however, hold that it is watery in nature, since it is set in the midst of the waters : others say it is composed of the four elements : and lastly, others speak of it as a filth body, distinct from the four elements [5].

Further, some have thought that the heaven encircles the universe and has the form of a sphere, and that everywhere it is the highest point, and that the centre of the space enclosed by it is the lowest part : and, further, that those bodies that are light and airy are allotted by the Creator the upper region : while those that are heavy and tend to descend occupy the lower region, which is the middle. The element, then, that is lightest and most inclined to soar upwards is fire, and hence they hold that its position is immediately after the heaven, and they call it ether, and after it comes the lower air. But earth and water, which are heavier and have more of a downward tendency, are suspended in the centre. Therefore, taking them in the reverse order, we have in the lowest situation earth and water : but water is lighter than earth, and hence is more easily set in motion : above these on all hands, like a covering, is the circle of air, and all round the air is the circle of ether, and outside all is the circle of the heaven.

Further, they say that the heaven moves in a circle and so compresses all that is within it, that they remain firm and not liable to fall asunder.

They say also that there are seven zones of the heaven [6], one higher than the other. And its nature, they say, is of extreme fineness, like that of smoke, and each zone contains one of the planets. For there are said to be seven planets : Sol, Luna, Jupiter, Mercury, Mars, Venus and Saturn. But sometimes Venus is called Lucifer and sometimes Vesper. These are called planets because their movements are the reverse of those of the heaven. For while the heaven and all other stars move from east to west, these alone move from west to east. And this can easily be seen in the case of the moon, which moves each evening a little backwards.

All, therefore, who hold that the heaven is in the form of a sphere, say that it is equally removed and distant from the earth at all points, whether above, or sideways, or below. And by ' below ' and ' sideways ' I mean all that comes within the range of our senses. For it follows from what has been said, that the heaven occupies the whole of the upper region and the earth the whole of the lower. They say, besides, that the heaven encircles the earth in the manner of a sphere, and bears along with it in its most rapid revolutions sun, moon and stars, and that when the sun is over the earth it becomes day there, and when it is under the earth it is

5 St. Matt. xxv. 41.
6 Nemes., De Nat. Hom., ch. 1.   7 Ps. cxlvi. 6.
8 Cf. Chrysost., In Genes., hom. 4 ; Basil, Hex. hom. 3, &c.
9 Ps. cxv. 16.   1 Ib. cxlviii. 4.   2 2 Cor. xii. 2.
3 Gen. i. 8.   4 Basil, Hom. 1 in Hexaëmeron.
5 The Peripatetics. See Nemes., ch. 5.

6 Basil, Hom. 3, in Hexaëmeron.

night. And, again, when the sun goes under the earth it is night here, but day yonder.

Others have pictured the heaven as a hemisphere. This idea is suggested by these words of David, the singer of God, *Who stretchest out the heavens like a curtain*[7], by which word he clearly means a tent: and by these from the blessed Isaiah, *Who hath established the heavens like a vault*[8]*:* and also because when the sun, moon, and stars set, they make a circuit round the earth from west to north, and so reach once more the east[9]. Still, whether it is this way or that, all things have been made and established by the divine command, and have the divine will and counsel for a foundation that cannot be moved. *For He Himself spoke and they were made: He Himself commanded and they were created. He hath also established them for ever and ever: He hath made a decree which will not pass*[1].

The heaven of heaven, then, is the first heaven which is above the firmament[2]. So here we have two heavens, for God called the firmament also Heaven[3]. And it is customary in the divine Scripture to speak of the air also as heaven, because we see it above us. *Bless Him*, it says, *all ye birds of the heaven*, meaning of the air. For it is the air and not the heaven that is the region in which birds fly. So here we have three heavens, as the divine Apostle said[4]. But if you should wish to look upon the seven zones as seven heavens there is no injury done to the word of truth. For it is usual in the Hebrew tongue to speak of heaven in the plural, that is, as heavens, and when a Hebrew wishes to say heaven of heaven, he usually says heavens of heavens, and this clearly means heaven of heaven[5], which is above the firmament, and the waters which are above the heavens, whether it is the air and the firmament, or the seven zones of the firmament, or the firmament itself which are spoken of in the plural as heavens according to the Hebrew custom.

All things, then, which are brought into existence are subject to corruption according to the law of their nature[6], and so even the heavens themselves are corruptible. But by the grace of God they are maintained and preserved[7]. Only the Deity, however, is by nature without beginning and without end[8]. Wherefore it has been said, *They will perish, but Thou dost endure*[1]*:* nevertheless, the heavens will not be utterly destroyed. For

they will wax old and be wound round as a covering, and will be changed, and there will be a new heaven and a new earth[2].

For the great part the heaven is greater than the earth, but we need not investigate the essence of the heaven, for it is quite beyond our knowledge.

It must not be supposed that the heavens or the luminaries are endowed with life[3]. For they are inanimate and insensible[4]. So that when the divine Scripture saith, *Let the heavens rejoice and the earth be glad*[5], it is the angels in heaven and the men on earth that are invited to rejoice. For the Scripture is familiar with the figure of personification, and is wont to speak of inanimate things as though they were animate: for example[6], *The sea saw it and fled: Jordan was driven back*[7]. And again, *What ailed thee, O thou sea, that thou fleddest? thou, O Jordan, that thou was driven back*[8]*?* Mountains, too, and hills are asked the reason of their leaping in the same way as we are wont to say, *the city was gathered together*, when we do not mean the buildings, but the inhabitants of the city: again, *the heavens declare the glory of God*[9], does not mean that they send forth a voice that can be heard by bodily ears, but that from their own greatness they bring before our minds the power of the Creator: and when we contemplate their beauty we praise the Maker as the Master-Craftsman[1].

CHAPTER VII.

Concerning light, fire, the luminaries, sun, moon and stars.

Fire is one of the four elements, light and with a greater tendency to ascend than the others. It has the power of burning and also of giving light, and it was made by the Creator on the first day. For the divine Scripture says, *And God said, Let there be light, and there was light*[2]. Fire is not a different thing from what light is, as some maintain. Others again hold that this fire of the universe is above the air[3] and call it ether. In the beginning, then, that is to say on the first day, God created light, the ornament and glory of the whole visible creation. For take away light and all things remain in undistinguishable darkness, incapable of displaying their native beauty. *And God called the light day, but the darkness*

---

7 Ps. civ. 2.　　　　　　　8 Is. xl. 22.
9 Chrysost., *Hom.* 14 and 17, *ad Hebr.*
1 Ps. cxlviii. 5, 6.　　　　2 *Greg. Nyss. de opif. Hom.*
3 Gen. i. 8.　　　4 2 Cor. xii. 2.　　　5 Ps. cxlviii. 4.
6 Plato, *Tim.*　　7 *Basil Hom.* 1 and 3, *in Hexaëmeron.*
8 Just., *quæst.* 93.　　　1 Ps. cii. 26.

2 Apoc. xxi. 1.　　　　　3 Cf. *August., Retract.*. ii. 2.
4 *Basil, Hom.* 13, *in Hexaëmeron.*　　5 Ps. xcvi. 11.
6 Text, ὡς τό. N. καὶ τὸ ἀνάπαλιν.　　7 Ps. cxiv. 3.
8 Ibid. 5.　　　　　　　9 Ibid. xix. 1.
1 *Basil, Hom.* 1 and 3, *in Hexaëmeron.*　　2 Gen. i. 3.
3 Text, ὑπερ. Variant, ὑπο, but this does not agree with the view of the author or the ancients.

He called night [4]. Further, darkness is not any essence, but an accident : for it is simply absence of light. The air, indeed, has not light in its essence [5]. It was, then, this very absence of light from the air that God called darkness : and it is not the essence of air that is darkness, but the absence of light which clearly is rather an accident than an essence. And, indeed, it was not night, but day, that was first named, so that day is first and after that comes night. Night, therefore, follows day. And from the beginning of day till the next day is one complete period of day and night. For the Scripture says, *And the evening and the morning were one day* [6].

When, therefore, in the first three days the light was poured forth and reduced at the divine command, both day and night came to pass [7]. But on the fourth day God created the great luminary, that is, the sun, to have rule and authority [8] over the day : for it is by it that day is made : for it is day when the sun is above the earth, and the duration of a day is the course of the sun over the earth from its rising till its setting. And He also created the lesser luminaries, that is, the moon and the stars, to have rule and authority [1] over the night, and to give light by night. For it is night when the sun is under the earth, and the duration of night is the course of the sun under the earth from its rising till its setting. The moon, then, and the stars were set to lighten the night : not that they are in the daytime under the earth, for even by day stars are in the heaven over the earth : but the sun conceals both the stars and the moon by the greater brilliance of its light and prevents them from being seen.

On these luminaries the Creator bestowed the first-created light : not because He was in need of other light, but that that light might not remain idle. For a luminary is not merely light, but a vessel for containing light [2].

There are, we are told, seven planets amongst these luminaries, and these move in a direction opposite to that of the heaven : hence the name planets. For, while they say that the heaven moves from east to west, the planets move from west to east ; but the heaven bears the seven planets along with it by its swifter motion. Now these are the names of the seven planets : Luna, Mercury, Venus, Sol, Mars, Jupiter, Saturn, and in

each zone of heaven is, we are told, one of these seven planets :

In the first and highest	Saturn	♄
In the second	Jupiter	♃
In the third	Mars	♂
In the fourth	Sol	☉
In the fifth	Venus	♀
In the sixth	Mercury	☿
In the seventh and lowest	Luna	☾

The course which the Creator [3] appointed for them to run is unceasing and remaineth fixed as He established them. For the divine David says, *The moon and the stars which Thou establishedst* [4], and by the word ' establishedst,' he referred to the fixity and unchangeableness of the order and series granted to them by God. For He appointed them for seasons, and signs, and days and years. It is through the Sun that the four seasons are brought about. And the first of these is spring : for in it God created all things [5], and even down to the present time its presence is evidenced by the bursting of the flowers into bud, and this is the equinoctial period, since day and night each consist of twelve hours. It is caused by the sun rising in the middle, and is mild and increases the blood, and is warm and moist, and holds a position midway between winter and summer, being warmer and drier than winter, but colder and moister than summer. This season lasts from March 21st till June 24th. Next, when the rising of the sun moves towards more northerly parts, the season of summer succeeds, which has a place midway between spring and autumn, combining the warmth of spring with the dryness of autumn : for it is dry and warm, and increases the yellow bile. In it falls the longest day, which has fifteen hours, and the shortest night of all, having only nine hours. This season lasts from June 24th till September 25th. Then when the sun again returns to the middle, autumn takes the place of summer. It has a medium amount of cold and heat, dryness and moisture, and holds a place midway between summer and winter, combining the dryness of summer with the cold of winter. For it is cold and dry, and increases the black bile. This season, again, is equinoctial, both day and night consisting of twelve hours, and it lasts from September 25th till December 25th. And when the rising of the sun sinks to its smallest and lowest point, i.e. the south, winter is reached, with its cold and moisture. It occupies a place midway between autumn and spring, combining the cold of autumn

---

4 Gen. i. 5.   5 *Basil, Hom. 2, in Hexaëmeron.*
6 Gen. i. 5.   7 *Basil, Hom. 2, in Hexaëmeron.*
8 Text, ἐξουσίαν : variant. ἐξουσίας.
1 Variant here also, ἐξουσίας.
2 *Basil, Hom. 6, in Hexaëmeron.*

3 Text, ὁ Δημιουργός.   Variant, ὁ δημιουργήσας.
4 Ps. viii. 3.   5 *Basil, Hom. 6, in Hexaëmeron.*

and the moisture of spring. In it falls the shortest day, which has only nine hours, and the longest night, which has fifteen : and it lasts from December 25th till March 21st. For the Creator made this wise provision that we should not pass from the extreme of cold, or heat, or dryness, or moisture, to the opposite extreme, and thus incur grievous maladies. For reason itself teaches us the danger of sudden changes.

So, then, it is the sun that makes the seasons, and through them the year : it likewise makes the days and nights, the days when it rises and is above the earth, and the nights when it sets below the earth : and it bestows on the other luminaries, both moon and stars, their power of giving forth light.

Further, they say that there are in the heaven twelve signs made by the stars, and that these move in an opposite direction to the sun and moon, and the other five planets, and that the seven planets pass across these twelve signs. Further, the sun makes a complete month in each sign and traverses the twelve signs in the same number of months. These, then, are the names of the twelve signs and their respective months :—

The Ram, which receives the sun on the 21st of March.
The Bull, 　　　on the 23rd of April.
The Twins, 　　on the 24th of May.
The Crab, 　　　on the 24th of June.
The Virgin, 　　on the 25th of July.
The Scales, 　　on the 25th of September.
The Scorpion, 　on the 25th of October.
The Archer, 　　on the 25th of November.
Capricorn, 　　on the 25th of December.
Aquarius, 　　　on the 25th of January.
The Fish, 　　　on the 24th of February.

But the moon traverses the twelve signs each month, since it occupies a lower position and travels through the signs at a quicker rate. For if you draw one circle within another, the inner one will be found to be the lesser : and so it is that owing to the moon occupying a lower position its course is shorter and is sooner completed.

Now the Greeks declare that all our affairs are controlled by the rising and setting and collision[6] of these stars, viz., the sun and moon : for it is with these matters that astrology has to do. But we hold that we get from them signs of rain and drought, cold and heat, moisture and dryness, and of the various winds, and so forth[7], but no sign whatever as to our actions. For we have

been created with free wills by our Creator and are masters over our own actions. Indeed, if all our actions depend on the courses of the stars, all we do is done of necessity[8] : and necessity precludes either virtue or vice. But if we possess neither virtue nor vice, we do not deserve praise or punishment, and God, too, will turn out to be unjust, since He gives good things to some and afflicts others. Nay, He will no longer continue to guide or provide for His own creatures, if all things are carried and swept along in the grip of necessity. And the faculty of reason will be superfluous to us : for if we are not masters of any of our actions, deliberation is quite superfluous. Reason, indeed, is granted to us solely that we might take counsel, and hence all reason implies freedom of will.

And, therefore, we hold that the stars are not the causes of the things that occur, nor of the origin of things that come to pass, nor of the destruction of those things that perish. They are rather signs of showers and changes of air. But, perhaps, some one may say that though they are not the causes of wars, yet they are signs of them. And, in truth, the quality of the air which is produced[1] by sun, and moon, and stars, produces in various ways different temperaments, and habits, and dispositions[2]. But the habits are amongst the things that we have in our own hands, for it is reason that rules, and directs, and changes them.

It often happens, also, that comets arise. These are signs of the death of kings[3], and they are not any of the stars that were made in the beginning, but are formed at the same time by divine command and again dissolved[4]. And so not even that star which the Magi saw at the birth of the Friend and Saviour of man, our Lord, Who became flesh for our sake, is of the number of those that were made in the beginning. And this is evidently the case because sometimes its course was from east to west, and sometimes from north to south ; at one moment it was hidden, and at the next it was revealed : which is quite out of harmony with the order and nature of the stars.

It must be understood, then, that the moon derives its light from the sun ; not that God was unable to grant it light of its own, but in order that rhythm and order may be impressed upon nature, one part ruling, the other being ruled, and that we might thus be taught to live in community and to share

---

6 Text, συγκρούσεως. Variants, συγκράσεως and συγκρίσεως.
7 Basil, Hom. 6, in Hexaëmeron.

8 Nemes., de Nat. Hom., ch. 34.
1 Text, ποιουμένη. Variant, ποιούμενον.
2 Basil, Hom. 6, in Hexaëmeron.
3 Text, θάνατον δηλοῦντα βασίλεων. Variant, θανάτων βασιλέων : also θάνατον, ἢ ἀνάδειξιν σημαίνουσι βασιλέων.
4 Basil, Christi Nativit.

our possessions with one another, and to be under subjection, first to our Maker and Creator, our God and Master, and then also to the rulers set in authority over us by Him: and not to question why this man is ruler and not I myself, but to welcome all that comes from God in a gracious and reasonable spirit.

The sun and the moon, moreover, suffer eclipse, and this demonstrates the folly of those who worship the creature in place of the Creator [5], and teaches us how changeable and alterable all things are. For all things are changeable save God, and whatever is changeable is liable to corruption in accordance with the laws of its own nature.

Now the cause of the eclipse of the sun is that the body of the moon is interposed like a partition-wall and casts a shadow, and prevents the light from being shed down on us [6]: and the extent of the eclipse is proportional to the size of the moon's body that is found to conceal the sun. But do not marvel that the moon's body is the smaller. For many declare that the sun is many times larger even than the earth, and the holy Fathers say that it is equal to the earth: yet often a small cloud, or even a small hill or a wall quite conceals it.

The eclipse of the moon, on the other hand, is due to the shadow the earth casts on it when it is a fifteen days' moon and the sun and moon happen to be at the opposite poles of the highest circle, the sun being under the earth and the moon above the earth. For the earth casts a shadow and the sun's light is prevented from illuminating the moon, and therefore it is then eclipsed.

It should be understood that the moon was made full by the Creator, that is, a fifteen days' moon: for it was fitting that it should be made complete [7]. But on the fourth day, as we said, the sun was created. Therefore the moon was eleven days in advance of the sun, because from the fourth to the fifteenth day there are eleven days. Hence it happens that in each year the twelve months of the moon contain eleven days fewer than the twelve months of the sun. For the twelve months of the sun contain three hundred and sixty-five and a quarter days, and so because the quarter becomes a whole, in four years an extra day is completed, which is called bissextile. And that year has three hundred and sixty-six days. The years of the moon, on the other hand, have three hundred and fifty-

four days. For the moon wanes from the time of its origin, or renewal, till it is fourteen and three-quarter days' old, and proceeds to wane till the twenty-ninth and a half day, when it is completely void of light. And then when it is once more connected with the sun it is reproduced and renewed, a memorial of our resurrection. Thus in each year the moon gives away eleven days to the sun, and so in three years the intercalary month of the Hebrews arises, and that year comes to consist of thirteen months, owing to the addition of these eleven days [8].

It is evident that both sun and moon and stars are compound and liable to corruption according to the laws of their various natures. But of their nature we are ignorant. Some, indeed, say that fire when deprived of matter is invisible, and thus, that when it is quenched it vanishes altogether. Others, again, say that when it is quenched it is transformed into air [9].

The circle of the zodiac has an oblique motion and is divided into twelve sections called zodia, or signs: each sign has three divisions of ten each, i.e. thirty divisions, and each division has sixty very minute subdivisions. The heaven, therefore, has three hundred and sixty-five degrees: the hemisphere above the earth and that below the earth each having one hundred and eighty degrees.

The abodes of the planets.

The Ram and the Scorpion are the abode of Mars: the Bull and the Scales, of Venus [1]: the Twins and the Virgin, of Mercury: the Crab, of the Moon: the Lion, of the Sun: the Archer and the Fish, of Jupiter: Capricorn and Aquarius, of Saturn.

Their altitudes.

The Ram has the altitude of the Sun: the Bull, of the Moon: the Crab, of Jupiter: the Virgin, of Mars: the Scales, of Saturn: Capricorn, of Mercury: the Fish, of Venus.

The phases of the moon.

It is in conjunction whenever it is in the same degree as the sun: it is born when it is fifteen degrees distant from the sun: it rises when it is crescent-shaped, and this occurs twice [2], at which times it is sixty degrees distant from the sun: it is half-full twice, when it is ninety degrees from the sun: twice it is gibbous, when it is one hundred

---

[5] Rom. i. 25.
[6] Text, διαναδοθῆναι: variants, διαδοθῆναι and δοθῆναι.
[7] Sever. Gabal., De opif. mundi, III.

[8] Ibid. De opif. mundi, III.
[9] Nemes., ch. 5.   [1] Vide Porph., de antro Nymph.
[2] Text, δίς. R. 4 has δεύτερον.

and twenty degrees from the sun : it is twice a full moon, giving full light, when it is a hundred and fifty degrees from the sun : it is a complete moon when it is a hundred and eighty degrees distant from the sun. We say twice, because these phases occur both when the moon waxes and when it wanes. In two and a half days the moon traverses each sign.

CHAPTER VIII.

Concerning air and winds.

Air is the most subtle element, and is moist and warm : heavier, indeed, than fire : but lighter than earth and water : it is the cause of respiration and voice : it is colourless, that is, it has no colour by nature : it is clear and transparent, for it is capable of receiving light : it ministers to three of our senses, for it is by its aid that we see, hear and smell : it has the power likewise of receiving heat and cold, dryness and moisture, and its movements in space are up, down, within, without, to the right and to the left, and the cyclical movement.

It does not derive its light from itself, but is illuminated by sun, and moon, and stars, and fire. And this is just what the Scripture means when it says, *And darkness was upon the deep* 3 ; for its object is to shew that the air has not derived its light from itself, but that it is quite a different essence from light.

And wind is a movement of air : or wind is a rush of air which changes its name as it changes the place whence it rushes 4.

Its place is in the air. For place is the circumference of a body. But what is it that surrounds bodies but air ? There are, moreover, different places in which the movement of air originates, and from these the winds get their names. There are in all twelve winds. It is said that air is just fire after it has been extinguished, or the vapour of heated water. At all events, in its own special nature the air is warm, but it becomes cold owing to the proximity of water and earth, so that the lower parts of it are cold, and the higher warm 5.

These then are the winds 6 : Caecias, or Meses, arises in the region where the sun rises in summer. Subsolanus, where the sun rises at the equinoxes. Eurus, where it rises in winter. Africus, where it sets in winter. Favonius, where it sets at the equinoxes, and Corus, or Olympias, or Iapyx, where it sets in summer. Then come Auster and Aquilo,

whose blasts oppose one another. Between Aquilo and Caecias comes Boreas : and between Eurus and Auster, Phoenix or Euronotus ; between Auster and Africus, Libonotus or Leuconotus : and lastly, between Aquilo and Corus, Thrascias, or Cercius, as it is called by the inhabitants of that region.

[These 7, then, are the races which dwell at the ends of the world : beside Subsolanus are the Bactriani : beside Eurus, the Indians : beside Phoenix, the Red Sea and Ethiopia : beside Libonotus, the Garamantes, who are beyond Systis : beside Africus, the Ethiopians and the Western Mauri : beside Favonius, the columns of Hercules and the beginnings of Libya and Europe : beside Corus, Iberia, which is now called Spain : beside Thrascia, the Gauls and the neighbouring nations : beside Aquilo, the Scythians who are beyond Thrace : beside Boreas, Pontus, Maeotis and the Sarmatae : beside Caecias, the Caspian Sea and the Sacai.]

CHAPTER IX.

Concerning the waters.

Water also is one of the four elements, the most beautiful of God's creations. It is both wet and cold, heavy, and with a tendency to descend, and flows with great readiness. It is this the Holy Scripture has in view when it says, *And darkness was upon the face of the deep. And the Spirit of God moved upon the face of the waters* 8. For the deep is nothing else than a huge quantity of water whose limit man cannot comprehend. In the beginning, indeed, the water lay all over the surface of the earth. And first God created the firmament to divide the water above the firmament from the water below the firmament. For in the midst of the sea of waters the firmament was established at the Master's decree. And out of it God bade the firmament arise, and it arose. Now for what reason was it that God placed water above the firmament ? It was because of the intense burning heat of the sun and ether 1. For immediately under the firmament is spread out the ether 2, and the sun and moon and stars are in the firmament, and so if water had not been put above it the firmament would have been consumed by the heat 3.

Next, God bade the waters be gathered together into one mass 4. But when the Scrip-

---

3 Gen. i. 2.   4 *Sever. Gabal., Hom. 1 in Hexaëm.*
5 *Nemes., De Nat. Hom.* i., ch. 5.
6 These are absent in edit. Veron.

7 This paragraph is absent in almost all the copies.
8 Gen. i. 2.   1 See *Basil, Hexaëm., Hom.* 3.
2 Text, ὑφήπλωται. Variant, ἐφήπλωται.
3 *Basil, Hom.* 2 *in Hexaëm.*; *Sever. Gabal., Orat. de opific. mundi.*
4 Gen. i. 9.

ture speaks of one mass it evidently does not mean that they were gathered together into one place : for immediately it goes on to say, *And the gatherings of the waters He called seas*[5] *:* but the words signify that the waters were separated off in a body from the earth into distinct groups. Thus the waters were gathered together into their special collections and the dry land was brought to view. And hence arose the two seas that surround Egypt, for it lies between two seas. These collections contain[6] various seas and mountains, and islands, and promontories, and harbours, and surround various bays and beaches, and coastlands. For the word beach is used when the nature of the tract is sandy, while coastland signifies that it is rocky and deep close into shore, getting deep all on a sudden. In like manner arose also the sea that lies where the sun rises, the name of which is the Indian Sea : also the northern sea called the Caspian. The lakes also were formed in the same manner.

The ocean, then, is like a river encircling the whole earth, and I think it is concerning it that the divine Scripture says, *A river went out of Paradise*[7]. The water of the ocean is sweet and potable[8]. It is it that furnishes the seas with water which, because it stays a long time in the seas and stands unmoved, becomes bitter : for the sun and the waterspouts draw up always the finer parts. Thus it is that clouds are formed and showers take place, because the filtration makes the water sweet.

This is parted into four first divisions, that is to say, into four rivers. The name of the first is Pheison, which is the Indian Ganges ; the name of the second is Geon, which is the Nile flowing from Ethiopia down to Egypt : the name of the third is Tigris, and the name of the fourth is Euphrates. There are also very many other mighty rivers of which some empty themselves into the sea and others are used up in the earth. Thus the whole earth is bored through and mined, and has, so to speak, certain veins through which it sends up in springs the water it has received from the sea. The water of the spring thus depends for its character on the quality of the earth. For the sea water is filtered and strained through the earth and thus becomes sweet. But if the place from which the spring arises is bitter or briny, so

also is the water that is sent up[9]. Moreover, it often happens that water which has been closely pent up bursts through with violence, and thus it becomes warm. And this is why they send forth waters that are naturally warm.

By the divine decree hollow places are made in the earth, and so into these the waters are gathered. And this is how mountains are formed. God, then, bade the first water produce living breath, since it was to be by water and the Holy Spirit that moved upon the waters in the beginning[1], that man was to be renewed. For this is what the divine Basilius said : Therefore it produced living creatures, small and big ; whales and dragons, fish that swim in the waters, and feathered fowl. The birds form a link between water and earth and air : for they have their origin in the water, they live on the earth and they fly in the air. Water, then, is the most beautiful element and rich in usefulness, and purifies from all filth, and not only from the filth of the body but from that of the soul, if it should have received the grace of the Spirit[2].

Concerning the seas[3].

The Ægean Sea is received by the Hellespont, which ends at Abydos and Sestus : next, the Propontis, which ends at Chalcedon and Byzantium : here are the straits where the Pontus arises. Next, the lake of Maeotis. Again, from the beginning of Europe and Libya it is the Iberian Sea, which extends from the pillars of Hercules to the Pyrenees mountain. Then the Ligurian Sea as far as the borders of Etruria. Next, the Sardinian Sea, which is above Sardinia and inclines downwards to Libya. Then the Etrurian Sea, which begins at the extreme limits of Liguria and ends at Sicily. Then the Libyan Sea. Then the Cretan, and Sicilian, and Ionian, and Adriatic Seas, the last of which is poured out of the Sicilian Sea, which is called the Corinthian Gulf, or the Alcyonian Sea. The Saronic Sea is surrounded by the Sunian and Scyllæan Seas. Next is the Myrtoan Sea and the Icarian Sea, in which are also the Cyclades. Then the Carpathian, and Pamphylian, and Egyptian Seas : and, thereafter, above the Icarian Sea, the Ægean Sea pours itself out. There is also the coast of Europe from the mouth of the Tanais River to the Pillars of Hercules, 609,709 stadia : and that of Libya from the Tigris, as far as the mouth of the Canobus, 209,252

---

[5] Gen. i. 10.
[6] Text, συνήχθησαν. R. 2927 has διέστησαν: Edit. Veron. Reg. 3362 has ὅθεν συνέστησαν: Colb. 1 has ὅθεν συνέστη.
[7] Gen. ii. 10.
[8] For ποταμὸς δὲ ὁ γλυκὺ ὕδωρ ἔχων ἐστί, reading πότιμον καὶ γλυκὺ ὕδωρ ἔχων.

[9] Basil, Hom. 4 in Hexaëm.   [1] Gen. i. 2.
[2] Sever. Gabal., Orat. 4, De opific. mundi : Basil, Hom. 8.
[3] This chapter is wanting in certain copies, Reg. 7, Colb. 1, R. 2930. In Cod. Hil. it is given after the chapter On Creation.

stadia : and lastly, that of Asia from the Canobus to the Tanais, which, including the Gulf, is 4,111 stadia. And so the full extent of the seaboard of the world that we inhabit with the gulfs is 1,309,072 stadia [4].

CHAPTER X.

Concerning earth and its products.

The earth is one of the four elements, dry, cold, heavy, motionless, brought into being by God, out of nothing on the first day. *For in the beginning*, he said, *God created the heaven and the earth* [5] *:* but the seat and foundation of the earth no man has been able to declare. Some, indeed, hold that its seat is the waters : thus the divine David says, *To Him Who established the earth on the waters* [6]. Others place it in the air. Again some other says, *He Who hangeth the earth on nothing* [7]. And, again, David, the singer of God, says, as though the representative of God, *I bear up the pillars of it* [8], meaning by "pillars" the force that sustains it. Further, the expression, *He hath founded it upon the seas* [9], shews clearly that the earth is on all hands surrounded with water. But whether we grant that it is established on itself, or on air or on water, or on nothing, we must not turn aside from reverent thought, but must admit that all things are sustained and preserved by the power of the Creator.

In the beginning, then, as the Holy Scripture says [1], it was hidden beneath the waters, and was unwrought, that is to say, not beautified. But at God's bidding, places to hold the waters appeared, and then the mountains came into existence, and at the divine command the earth received its own proper adornment, and was dressed in all manner of herbs and plants, and on these, by the divine decree, was bestowed the power of growth and nourishment, and of producing seed to generate their like. Moreover, at the bidding of the Creator it produced also all manner of kinds of living creatures, creeping things, and wild beasts, and cattle. All, indeed, are for the seasonable use of man : but of them some are for food, such as stags, sheep, deer, and such like : others for service such as camels, oxen, horses, asses, and such like : and others for enjoyment, such as apes, and among birds, jays and parrots, and such like. Again, amongst plants and herbs some are fruit bearing, others edible, others fragrant and flowery, given to us for our enjoyment,

for example, the rose and such like, and others for the healing of disease. For there is not a single animal or plant in which the Creator has not implanted some form of energy capable of being used to satisfy man's needs. For He Who knew all things before they were, saw that in the future man would go forward in the strength of his own will, and would be subject to corruption, and, therefore, He created all things for his seasonable use, alike those in the firmament, and those on the earth, and those in the waters.

Indeed, before the transgression all things were under his power. For God set him as ruler over all things on the earth and in the waters. Even the serpent [2] was accustomed to man, and approached him more readily than it did other living creatures, and held intercourse with him with delightful motions [3]. And hence it was through it that the devil, the prince of evil, made his most wicked suggestion to our first parents [4]. Moreover, the earth of its own accord used to yield fruits, for the benefit of the animals that were obedient to man, and there was neither rain nor tempest on the earth. But after the transgression, when he was compared with the unintelligent cattle and became like to them [5], after he had contrived that in him irrational desire should have rule over reasoning mind and had become disobedient to the Master's command, the subject creation rose up against him whom the Creator had appointed to be ruler : and it was appointed for him that he should till with sweat the earth from which he had been taken.

But even now wild beasts are not without their uses, for, by the terror they cause, they bring man to the knowledge of his Creator and lead him to call upon His name. And, further, at the transgression the thorn sprung out of the earth in accordance with the Lord's express declaration and was conjoined with the pleasures of the rose, that it might lead us to remember the transgression on account of which the earth was condemned to bring forth for us thorns and prickles [6].

That this is the case is made worthy of belief from the fact that their endurance is secured by the word of the Lord, saying, *Be fruitful and multiply, and replenish the earth* [7].

Further, some hold that the earth is in the form of a sphere, others that it is in that of a cone. At all events it is much smaller

---

[4] *Vide* Strab. bk. **ii.**   [5] Gen. i. 1.
[6] Ps. cxxxvi. 6.   [7] Job xxvi. 7.
[8] Ps. lxxv. 3.   [9] Ibid. xxiv. 2.   [1] Gen. i. 2.

[2] In this John does not follow Basil in his *De Paradiso.*
[3] *Basil. Hom. de Parad.*
[4] Gen. iii. 1.   [5] Ps. xlix. 12.   [6] *Basil, Hom. de Parad.*
[7] Gen. i. 22.

than the heaven, and suspended almost like a point in its midst. And it will pass away and be changed. But blessed is the man who inherits the earth promised to the meek [8].

For the earth that is to be the possession of the holy is immortal. Who, then, can fitly marvel at the boundless and incomprehensible wisdom of the Creator? Or who can render sufficient thanks to the Giver of so many blessings [9]?

[There are also provinces, or prefectures, of the earth which we recognise: Europe embraces thirty-four, and the huge continent of Asia has forty-eight of these provinces, and twelve canons as they are called [1].]

CHAPTER XI.

Concerning Paradise.

Now when God was about to fashion man out of the visible and invisible creation in His own image and likeness to reign as king and ruler over all the earth and all that it contains, He first made for him, so to speak, a kingdom in which he should live a life of happiness and prosperity [2]. And this is the divine paradise [3], planted in Eden by the hands of God, a very storehouse of joy and gladness of heart (for "Eden" [4] means luxuriousness [5]). Its site is higher in the East than all the earth: it is temperate and the air that surrounds it is the rarest and purest: evergreen plants are its pride, sweet fragrances abound, it is flooded with light, and in sensuous freshness and beauty it transcends imagination: in truth the place is divine, a meet home for him who was created in God's image: no creature lacking reason made its dwelling there but man alone, the work of God's own hands.

In its midst [6] God planted the tree of life and the tree of knowledge [7]. The tree of knowledge was for trial, and proof, and exercise of man's obedience and disobedience: and hence it was named the tree of the knowledge of good and evil, or else it was because to those who partook of it was given power to know their own nature. Now this is a good thing for those who are mature, but an evil thing for the immature and those whose appetites are too strong [8], being like solid food to tender babes still in need of milk [9]. For our Creator, God, did not intend us to be burdened with care and troubled about many things, nor to take thought about, or make provision for, our own life. But this at length was Adam's fate: for he tasted and knew that he was naked and made a girdle round about him: for he took fig-leaves and girded himself about. But before they took of the fruit, *They were both naked, Adam and Eve, and were not ashamed* [1]. For God meant that we should be thus free from passion, and this is indeed the mark of a mind absolutely void of passion. Yea, He meant us further to be free from care and to have but one work to perform, to sing as do the angels, without ceasing or intermission, the praises of the Creator, and to delight in contemplation of Him and to cast all our care on Him. This is what the Prophet David proclaimed to us when He said, *Cast thy burden on the Lord, and He will sustain thee* [2]. And, again, in the Gospels, Christ taught His disciples saying, *Take no thought for your life what ye shall eat, nor for your body what ye shall put on* [3] And further, *Seek ye first the Kingdom of God and His righteousness and all these things shall be added unto you* [4]. And to Martha He said, *Martha, Martha, thou art careful and troubled about many things: but one thing is needful: and Mary hath chosen that good part, which shall not be taken away from her* [5], meaning, clearly, sitting at His feet and listening to His words.

The tree of life, on the other hand, was a tree having the energy that is the cause of life, or to be eaten only by those who deserve to live and are not subject to death. Some, indeed, have pictured Paradise as a realm of sense [6], and others as a realm of mind. But it seems to me, that, just as man is a creature, in whom we find both sense and mind blended together, in like manner also man's most holy temple combines the properties of sense and mind, and has this twofold expression: for, as we said, the life in the body is spent in the most divine and lovely region, while the life in the soul is passed in a place far more sublime and of more surpassing beauty, where God makes His home, and where He wraps man about as with a glorious garment, and robes him in His grace, and delights and sustains him like an angel with the sweetest of all fruits, the contemplation of Himself. Verily it has been fitly named the tree of life. For since the

8 St. Matt. v. 5.
9 *Method , Cont. Orig. apud Epiph. Hæres.* 64.
1 Only *Cod. Reg.* 3451 has this paragraph.
2 *Greg. Nyss., De opif. Hom.,* ch. 2.
3 See the treatise of *Anastas. II. Antiochen.,* on the *Hexaëmeron,* bk. vii.
4 Ἐδεμ, *Edem,* in the text. Basil, *Hom de Parad.*
5 See 2 Kings xix. 12; Isai. xxxvii. 12; Ezek. xxvii. 23.
6 See Chrysost., *In Gen. Hom.* 16, Theodor., *Quæst.* 27, &c.
7 Gen. ii. 9.
8 Text, τὴν ἔφεσιν λιχνοτέροις. Variant τὴν αἴσθησιν, &c.

9 *Greg. Naz., Orat.* 38 and 42: *Method., ap Epiph. Hæres.* 64.
1 Gen. ii. 25.   2 Ps. lv. 22.
3 St. Matt. vi. 25.   4 Ibid. 33.   5 St. Luke x. 41, 42.
6 *Nemes., de Nat. Hom.,* ch. 1.

life is not cut short by death, the sweetness of the divine participation is imparted to those who share it. And this is, in truth, what God meant by every tree, saying, *Of every tree in Paradise thou mayest freely eat*[7]. For the 'every' is just Himself in Whom and through Whom the universe is maintained. But the tree of the knowledge of good and evil was for the distinguishing between the many divisions of contemplation, and this is just the knowledge of one's own nature, which, indeed, is a good thing for those who are mature and advanced in divine contemplation (being of itself a proclamation of the magnificence of God), and have no fear of falling[8], because they have through time come to have the habit of such contemplation, but it is an evil thing to those still young and with stronger appetites, who by reason of their insecure hold on the better part, and because as yet they are not firmly established in the seat of the one and only good, are apt to be torn and dragged away from this to the care of their own body.

Thus, to my thinking, the divine Paradise is twofold, and the God-inspired Fathers handed down a true message, whether they taught this doctrine or that. Indeed, it is possible to understand by every tree the knowledge of the divine power derived from created things. In the words of the divine Apostle, *For the invisible things of Him from the creation of the world are clearly seen, being understood by the things that are made*[9]. But of all these thoughts and speculations the sublimest is that dealing with ourselves, that is, with our own composition. As the divine David says, *The knowledge of Thee from me*[1], that is from my constitution, was made a wonder[2]. But for the reasons we have already mentioned, such knowledge was dangerous for Adam who had been so lately created[3].

The tree of life too may be understood as that more divine thought that has its origin in the world of sense, and the ascent through that to the originating and constructive cause of all. And this was the name He gave to every tree, implying fulness and indivisibility, and conveying only participation in what is good. But by the tree of the knowledge of good and evil, we are to understand that sensible and pleasurable food which, sweet though it seems, in reality brings him who partakes of it into communion

with evil. For God says, *Of every tree in Paradise thou mayest freely eat*[4]. It is, methinks, as if God said, *Through all My creations thou art to ascend to Me thy creator, and of all the fruits thou mayest pluck one, that is, Myself who am the true life: let every thing bear for thee the fruit of life, and let participation in Me be the support of your own being. For in this way thou wilt be immortal. But of the tree of the knowledge of good and evil, thou shalt not eat of it: for in the day that thou eatest thereof thou shalt surely die*[5]. For sensible food is by nature for the replenishing of that which gradually wastes away and it passes into the draught and perisheth: and he cannot remain incorruptible who partakes of sensible food.

CHAPTER XII.
Concerning Man.

IN this way, then, God brought into existence mental essence[6], by which I mean, angels and all the heavenly orders. For these clearly have a mental and incorporeal nature: "incorporeal" I mean in comparison with the denseness of matter. For the Deity alone in reality is immaterial and incorporeal. But further He created in the same way sensible essence[7], that is heaven and earth and the intermediate region; and so He created both the kind of being that is of His own nature (for the nature that has to do with reason is related to God, and apprehensible by mind alone), and the kind which, inasmuch as it clearly falls under the province of the senses, is separated from Him by the greatest interval. And it was also fit that there should be a mixture of both kinds of being, as a token of still greater wisdom and of the opulence of the Divine expenditure as regards natures, as Gregorius, the expounder of God's being and ways, puts it, and to be a sort of connecting link between the visible and invisible natures[8]. And by the word "fit" I mean, simply that it was an evidence of the Creator's will, for that will is the law and ordinance most meet, and no one will say to his Maker, "Why hast Thou so fashioned me?" For the potter is able at his will to make vessels of various patterns out of his clay[9], as a proof of his own wisdom.

Now this being the case, He creates with His own hands man of a visible nature and an invisible, after His own image and likeness: on the one hand man's body He formed of earth, and on the other his reasoning and

7 Gen. ii. 16.   8 *Greg. Naz., Orat.* 38 and 42.
9 Rom. i. 20.   1 Ps. cxxxix. 6.
2 εθαυμαστώθη ή γνῶσίς σου ἐξ ἐμοῦ, τουτέστιν, ἐκ τῆς ἐμῆς κατασκευῆς. Basil, Gregory Naz., Anastasius II.. Antiochenus and others render it so, following the LXX. version, and not the Hebrew text.
3 *Maxim., in Script.* p. 10.

4 Gen. ii. 16.   5 Ibid. 17.
6 τὴν νοητὴν οὐσίαν *rational being*
7 τὴν αισθητήν; *material being, being perceptible by sense.*
8 *Greg. Naz., Orat.* 38 and 42.   9 Rom. ix. 21.

thinking soul[1] He bestowed upon him by His own inbreathing, and this is what we mean by "after His image." For the phrase "after His image" clearly refers[2] to the side of his nature which consists of mind and free will, whereas "after His likeness" means likeness in virtue so far as that is possible.

Further, body and soul were formed at one and the same time[3], not first the one and then the other, as Origen so senselessly supposes.

God then made man without evil, upright, virtuous, free from pain and care, glorified with every virtue, adorned with all that is good, like a sort of second microcosm within the great world[4], another angel capable of worship, compound, surveying the visible creation and initiated into the mysteries of the realm of thought, king over the things of earth, but subject to a higher king, of the earth and of the heaven, temporal and eternal, belonging to the realm of sight and to the realm of thought, midway between greatness and lowliness, spirit and flesh: for he is spirit by grace, but flesh by overweening pride: spirit that he may abide and glorify his Benefactor, and flesh that he may suffer, and suffering may be admonished and disciplined when he prides himself in his greatness[5]: here, that is, in the present life, his life is ordered as an animal's, but elsewhere, that is, in the age to come, he is changed and—to complete the mystery—becomes deified by merely inclining himself towards God; becoming deified, in the way of participating in the divine glory and not in that of a change into the divine being[6].

But God made him by nature sinless, and endowed him with free will. By sinless, I mean not that sin could find no place in him (for that is the case with Deity alone), but that sin is the result of the free volition he enjoys rather than an integral part of his nature[7]; that is to say, he has the power to continue and go forward in the path of goodness, by co-operating with the divine grace, and likewise to turn from good and take to wickedness, for God has conceded this by conferring freedom of will upon him. For there is no virtue in what is the result of mere force[8].

The soul, accordingly[9], is a living essence, simple, incorporeal, invisible in its proper nature to bodily eyes, immortal, reasoning and intelligent, formless, making use of an organised body, and being the source of its powers of life, and growth, and sensation, and generation[1], mind being but its purest part and not in any wise alien to it; (for as the eye to the body, so is the mind to the soul); further it enjoys freedom and volition and energy, and is mutable, that is, it is given to change, because it is created. All these qualities according to nature it has received of the grace of the Creator, of which grace it has received both its being and this particular kind of nature.

Marg. The different applications of "incorporeal." We understand two kinds of what is incorporeal and invisible and formless: the one is such in essence, the other by free gift: and likewise the one is such in nature, and the other only in comparison with the denseness of matter. God then is incorporeal by nature, but the angels and demons and souls are said to be so by free gift, and in comparison with the denseness of matter.

Further, body is that which has three dimensions, that is to say, it has length and breadth and depth, or thickness. And every body is composed of the four elements; the bodies of living creatures, moreover, are composed of the four humours.

Now there are, it should be known, four elements: earth which is dry and cold: water which is cold and wet: air which is wet and warm: fire which is warm and dry. In like manner there are also four humours, analogous to the four elements: black bile, which bears an analogy to earth, for it is dry and cold: phlegm, analogous to water, for it is cold and wet: blood, analogous to air[2], for it is wet and warm: yellow bile, the analogue to fire, for it is warm and dry. Now, fruits are composed of the elements, and the humours are composed of the fruits, and the bodies of living creatures consist of the humours and dissolve back into them. For every thing that is compound dissolves back into its elements.

Marg. That man has community alike with inanimate things and animate creatures, whe-

[1] Ψυχὴν λογικήν.
[2] Cf. *Chrysostom, Hom. in Gen.* 9; *Anastasius, Hom. in Hex.* 7; *Clem. Alex., Strom.* II.; *Basil, Hom. de hom. Struct.* 1; *Greg. Nyss., De opif. hom.,* ch. 16; *Iren., Hær.* v. 8, &c.
[3] Cf. *Greg. Naz., Orat.* 31; *Jerome, Epist.* 82; *August., De Genesi,* x. 28, &c.
[4] ἐν μικρῷ μέγαν, is read in *Nazianz. Hom.* 38 and 42: so also in Nicetas, who says that 'the world is small in comparison with man, for whose sake all was made.' But Combefis emended it.
[5] The text read, τῷ μεγέθει φιλοτιμούμενος· τὸ δὲ ἵνα πάσχων ὑπομιμνήσκηται, καὶ παιδεύηται ζῷον. On the basis of various manuscripts and the works of Gregory of Nazianzum, it is corrected so—ἵνα πάσχῃ, καὶ πάσχων, ὑπομιμνήσκηται, καὶ παιδεύηται τῷ μεγέθει φιλοτιμούμενον.
[6] *Greg. Naz., Orat.* 38 and 42.
[7] Reading, οὐχ ὡς ἐν τῇ φύσει, for ἀλλ' οὐκ ἐν τῇ φύσει.

[8] *Athan. lib. de inob. contr. Apoll.*
[9] The Fathers objected to Aristotle's definition of the soul as the ἐντελέχεια πρώτη σώματος φυσικοῦ ὀργανικοῦ taking it to imply that the soul had no independent existence but was dissolved with the body. Cicero explains it otherwise, *Tusc. Quæst.,* bk. 1.
[1] *Maxim., opus de Anima.*
[2] Supplying the words, τῷ ὕδατι, ψυχρὸν γὰρ καὶ ὑγρόν· αἷμα, ἀναλογοῦν.

ther they are devoid of or possess the faculty of reason.

Man, it is to be noted, has community with things inanimate, and participates in the life of unreasoning creatures, and shares in the mental processes of those endowed with reason. For the bond of union between man and inanimate things is the body and its composition out of the four elements : and the bond between man and plants consists, in addition to these things, of their powers of nourishment and growth and seeding, that is, generation : and finally, over and above these links man is connected with unreasoning animals by appetite, that is anger and desire, and sense and impulsive movement.

There are then five senses, sight, hearing, smell, taste, touch. Further, impulsive movement consists in change from place to place, and in the movements of the body as a whole, and in the emission of voice and the drawing of breath. For we have it in our power to perform or refrain from performing these actions.

Lastly, man's reason unites him to incorporeal and intelligent natures, for he applies his reason and mind and judgment to everything, and pursues after virtues, and eagerly follows after piety, which is the crown of the virtues. And so man is a microcosm.

Moreover, it should be known that division and flux and change [3] are peculiar to the body alone. By change, I mean change in quality, that is in heat and cold and so forth : by flux, I mean change in the way of depletion [4], for dry things and wet things and spirit [5] suffer depletion, and require repletion : so that hunger and thirst are natural affections. Again, division is the separation of the humours, one from another, and the partition into form and matter [6].

But piety and thought are the peculiar properties of the soul. And the virtues are common to soul and body, although they are referred to the soul as if the soul were making use of the body.

The reasoning part, it should be understood, naturally bears rule over that which is void of reason. For the faculties of the soul are divided into that which has reason, and that which is without reason. Again, of that which is without reason there are two divisions : that which does not listen to reason, that is to say, is disobedient to reason, and that which listens and obeys reason. That which does not listen or obey reason is the vital or pulsating faculty,

and the spermatic or generative faculty, and the vegetative or nutritive faculty : to this belong also the faculties of growth and bodily formation. For these are not under the dominion of reason but under that of nature. That which listens to and obeys reason, on the other hand is divided into anger and desire. And the unreasoning part of the soul is called in common the pathetic and the appetitive [7]. Further, it is to be understood, that impulsive movement [8] likewise belongs to the part that is obedient to reason.

The part [9] which does not pay heed to reason includes the nutritive and generative and pulsating faculties : and the name " vegetative [9a] " is applied to the faculties of increase and nutriment and generation, and the name " vital " to the faculty of pulsation.

Of the faculty of nutrition, then, there are four forces : an attractive force which attracts nourishment : a retentive force by which nourishment is retained and not suffered to be immediately excreted : an alterative force by which the food is resolved into the humours : and an excretive force, by which the excess of food is excreted into the draught and cast forth.

The forces again [1], inherent in a living creature are, it should be noted, partly psychical, partly vegetative, partly vital. The psychical forces are concerned with free volition, that is to say, impulsive movement and sensation. Impulsive movement includes change of place and movement of the body as a whole, and phonation and respiration. For it is in our power to perform or refrain from performing these acts. The vegetative and vital forces, however, are quite outside the province of will. The vegetative, moreover, include the faculties of nourishment and growth, and generation, and the vital power is the faculty of pulsation. For these go on energising whether we will it or not.

Lastly, we must observe that of actual things, some are good, and some are bad. A good thing in anticipation constitutes desire : while a good thing in realisation constitutes pleasure. Similarly an evil thing in anticipation begets fear, and in realisation it begets pain. And when we speak of good in this connection we are to be understood to mean both real and apparent good : and, similarly, we mean real and apparent evil.

3 τομή, καὶ ῥεῦσις, καὶ μεταβολή.
4 Nemes., ae Nat. Hom., ch. 1.   5 Or, breath, πνεῦμα.
6 Nemes., de Nat. Hom., ch. 1.
7 παθητικὸν καὶ ὀρεκτικόν.
8 ἡ καθ' ὁρμὴν κίνησις.
9 The following three paragraphs, as found in manuscripts and the old translation, are placed at the end of ch. 32, " Concerning Anger," but do not suit the context there.
9a Supplying the word φυτικόν trom Nemesius.
1 Nemes., ch. 23.

CHAPTER XIII.

Concerning Pleasures.

There are pleasures of the soul and pleasures of the body. The pleasures of the soul are those which are the exclusive possession of the soul, such as the pleasures of learning and contemplation. The pleasures of the body, however, are those which are enjoyed by soul and body in fellowship, and hence are called bodily pleasures : and such are the pleasures of food and intercourse and the like. But one could not find any class of pleasures[2] belonging solely to the body[3].

Again, some pleasures are true, others false. And the exclusively intellectual pleasures consist in knowledge and contemplation, while the pleasures of the body depend upon sensation. Further, of bodily pleasures[4], some are both natural and necessary, in the absence of which life is impossible, for example the pleasures of food which replenishes waste, and the pleasures of necessary clothing. Others are natural but not necessary, as the pleasures of natural and lawful intercourse. For though the function that these perform is to secure the permanence of the race as a whole, it is still possible to live a virgin life apart from them. Others, however, are neither natural nor necessary, such as drunkenness, lust, and surfeiting to excess. For these contribute neither to the maintenance of our own lives nor to the succession of the race, but on the contrary, are rather even a hindrance. He therefore that would live a life acceptable to God must follow after those pleasures which are both natural and necessary : and must give a secondary place to those which are natural but not necessary, and enjoy them only in fitting season, and manner, and measure ; while the others must be altogether renounced.

Those then are to be considered moral[5] pleasures which are not bound up with pain, and bring no cause for repentance, and result in no other harm and keep[6] within the bounds of moderation, and do not draw us far away from serious occupations, nor make slaves of us.

CHAPTER XIV.

Concerning Pain.

There are four varieties of pain, viz., anguish[7], grief[8], envy, pity. Anguish is pain without utterance : grief is pain that is heavy to bear like a burden : envy is pain over the good fortune of others : pity is pain over the evil fortune of others.

CHAPTER XV.

Concerning Fear.

Fear is divided into six varieties : viz., shrinking[9], shame, disgrace, consternation, panic, anxiety[9a]. Shrinking[9b] is fear of some act about to take place. Shame is fear arising from the anticipation of blame : and this is the highest form of the affection. Disgrace is fear springing from some base act already done, and even for this form there is some hope of salvation. Consternation is fear originating in some huge product of the imagination. Panic is fear caused by some unusual product of the imagination. Anxiety is fear of failure, that is, of misfortune : for when we fear that our efforts will not meet with success, we suffer anxiety.

CHAPTER XVI.

Concerning Anger.

Anger is the ebullition[1] of the heart's blood[2] produced by bilious exhalation or turbidity. Hence it is that the words χολή and χόλος[3] are both used in the sense of anger. Anger is sometimes lust for vengeance. For when we are wronged or think that we are wronged, we are distressed, and there arises this mixture of desire and anger.

There are three forms of anger : rage, which the Greeks also call χολή or χόλος, μῆνις and κότος. When anger arises and begins to be roused, it is called rage or χολή or χόλος. Wrath again implies that the bile endures, that is to say, that the memory of the wrong abides : and indeed the Greek word for it, μῆνις, is derived from μένειν, and means what abides and is transferred to memory. Rancour, on the other hand, implies watching for a suitable moment for revenge, and the Greek word for it is κότος from κεῖσθαι.

Anger further is the satellite of reason, the vindicator of desire. For when we long after anything and are opposed in our desire by some one, we are angered at that person, as though we had been wronged : and reason evidently deems that there are just grounds for displeasure in what has happened, in the

---

2 Reading, οὐκ ἂν εὕροι τις ἰδίας ἡδονάς.
3 Nemes., ch. 18 : Chrys., Hom. in Joan., 74.
4 See Chrysostom, Hom. in Joannem, 74 ; Cicero, De fin. bon. et mal., 1.
5 καλάς, honourable, good.
6 Text, χωροῦσας. Variant, παραχωροῦσας.
7 ἄχος. 8 ἄχθος.

9 ὄκνος, dread. 9a ἀγωνία.
9b Nemesius and certain manuscripts give these species of fear in a different order, viz., dread, consternation, panic, anxiety, shame, disgrace.
1 ζέσις, boiling.
2 τοῦ περὶ καρδίαν αἵματος, the blood about the heart.
3 Nemes., ch. 21.

case of those who, like us, have in the natural course of things to guard their own position.

CHAPTER XVII.

Concerning Imagination.

Imagination [4] is a faculty of the unreasoning part of the soul. It is through the organs of sense that it is brought into action, and it is spoken of as sensation. And further, what is imagined [5] and perceived is that which comes within the scope of the faculty of imagination and sensation. For example, the sense of sight is the visual faculty itself, but the object of sight is that which comes within the scope of the sense of sight, such as a stone or any other such object. Further, an imagination is an affection of the unreasoning part of the soul which is occasioned by some object acting upon the sensation. But an appearance [6] is an empty affection of the unreasoning part of the soul, not occasioned by any object acting upon the sensation. Moreover the organ of imagination is the anterior ventricle of the brain.

CHAPTER XVIII.

Concerning Sensation.

Sensation is that faculty of the soul whereby material objects can be apprehended or discriminated. And the sensoria are the organs or members through which sensations are conveyed. And the objects of sense are the things that come within the province of sensation. And lastly, the subject of sense is the living animal which possesses the faculty of sensation. Now there are five senses, and likewise five organs of sense.

The first sense is sight: and the sensoria or organs of sight are the nerves of the brain and the eyes. Now sight is primarily perception of colour, but along with the colour it discriminates the body that has colour, and its size and form, and locality, and the intervening space and the number [7]: also whether it is in motion or at rest, rough or smooth, even or uneven, sharp or blunt, and finally whether its composition is watery or earthy, that is, wet or dry.

The second sense is hearing, whereby voices and sounds are perceived. And it distinguishes these as sharp or deep, or smooth or loud. Its organs are the soft nerves of the brain, and the structure of the ears. Further, man and the ape are the only animals that do not move their ears.

The third sense is smell, which is caused by the nostrils transmitting the vapours to the brain: and it is bounded by the extreme limits of the anterior ventricle of the brain. It is the faculty by which vapours are perceived and apprehended. Now, the most generic distinction between vapours is whether they have a good or an evil odour, or form an intermediate class with neither a good nor an evil odour. A good odour is produced by the thorough digestion in the body of the humours. When they are only moderately digested the intermediate class is formed, and when the digestion is very imperfect or utterly wanting, an evil odour results.

The fourth sense is taste: it is the faculty whereby the humours are apprehended or perceived, and its organs of sense are the tongue, and more especially the lips, and the palate (which the Greeks call οὐρανίσκος), and in these are nerves that come from the brain and are spread out, and convey to the dominant part of the soul the perception or sensation they have encountered [8]. The so-called gustatory qualities of the humours are these:— sweetness, pungency, bitterness, astringency, acerbity, sourness, saltness, fattiness, stickiness; for taste is capable of discriminating all these. But water has none of these qualities, and is therefore devoid of taste. Moreover, astringency is only a more intense and exaggerated form of acerbity.

The fifth sense is touch, which is common to all living things [9]. Its organs are nerves which come from the brain and ramify all through the body. Hence the body as a whole, including even the other organs of sense, possesses the sense of touch. Within its scope come heat and cold, softness and hardness, viscosity and brittleness [1], heaviness and lightness: for it is by touch alone that these qualities are discriminated. On the other hand, roughness and smoothness, dryness and wetness, thickness and thinness, up and down, place and size, whenever that is such as to be embraced in a single application of the sense of touch, are all common to touch and sight, as well as denseness and rareness, that is porosity, and rotundity if it is small, and some other shapes. In like manner also by the aid of memory and thought perception of the nearness of a body is possible, and similarly perception of number up to two or three, and such small and easily reckoned figures. But it is by sight rather than touch that these things are perceived.

The Creator, it is to be noted, fashioned

---

4 φανταστικόν.   5 Or, *presented.*
6 See *Aristotle, De anima*, III. c. 7.   7 *Nemes.,* ch. 71.

8 *Nemes.,* ch. 9.   9 Ibid., ch. 8.
1 ξηρόν is added in some MSS. but wrongly: for it is what is perceived by touch alone that is here spoken of, whereas, below, we are told that dryness is recognised also by sight; so also in Nemesius.

all the other organs of sense in pairs, so that if one were destroyed, the other might fill its place. For there are two eyes, two ears, two orifices of the nose, and two tongues, which in some animals, such as snakes, are separate, but in others, like man, are united. But touch is spread over the whole body with the exception of bones, nerves, nails, horns, hairs, ligaments, and other such structures.

Further, it is to be observed that sight is possible only in straight lines, whereas smell and hearing are not limited to straight lines only, but act in all directions. Touch, again, and taste act neither in straight lines, nor in every direction, but only when each comes near to the sensible objects that are proper to it.

CHAPTER XIX.
Concerning Thought.

The faculty of thought deals with judgments and assents, and impulse to action and disinclinations, and escapes from action: and more especially with thoughts connected with what is thinkable, and the virtues and the different branches of learning, and the theories of the arts and matters of counsel and choice [2]. Further, it is this faculty which prophesies the future to us in dreams, and this is what the Pythagoreans, adopting the Hebrew view, hold to be the one true form of prophecy. The organ of thought then is the mid-ventricle of the brain, and the vital spirit it contains [3].

CHAPTER XX.
Concerning Memory.

The faculty of memory is the cause [4] and storehouse of remembrance and recollection. For memory is a fantasy [5] that is left behind of some sensation and thought [6] manifesting itself in action; or the preservation [7] of a sensation and thought [8]. For the soul comprehends objects of sense through the organs of sense, that is to say, it perceives, and thence arises a notion: and similarly it comprehends the objects of thought through the mind, and thence arises a thought. It is then the preservation of the types of these notions and thoughts that is spoken of as memory.

Further, it is worthy of remark that the apprehension of matters of thought depends on learning, or natural process of thought, and not on sensation. For though objects of sense are retained in the memory by themselves, only such objects of thought are remembered as we have learned, and we have no memory of their essence.

Recollection is the name given to the recovery of some memory lost by forgetfulness. For forgetfulness is just loss of memory. The faculty of imagination [9] then, having apprehended material objects through the senses, transmits this to the faculty of thought or reason (for they are both the same), and this after it has received and passed judgment on it, passes it on to the faculty of memory. Now the organ of memory is the posterior ventricle of the brain, which the Greeks call the παρεγκεφαλίς, and the vital spirit it contains.

CHAPTER XXI.
Concerning Conception and Articulation.

Again the reasoning part of the soul is divided into conception and articulation. Conception is an activity of the soul originating in the reason without resulting in utterance. Accordingly, often, even when we are silent we run through a whole speech in our minds, and hold discussions in our dreams. And it is this faculty chiefly which constitutes us all reasoning beings. For those who are dumb by birth or have lost their voice through some disease or injury, are just as much reasoning beings. But articulation by voice or in the different dialects requires energy: that is to say, the word is articulated by the tongue and mouth, and this is why it is named articulation. It is, indeed, the messenger of thought, and it is because of it that we are called speaking beings.

CHAPTER XXII.
Concerning Passion and Energy.

Passion is a word with various meanings. It is used in regard to the body, and refers to diseases and wounds, and again, it is used in reference to the soul, and means desire and anger. But to speak broadly and generally, passion is an animal affection which is succeeded by pleasure and pain. For pain succeeds passion, but is not the same thing as passion. For passion is an affection of things without sense, but not so pain. Pain then is not passion, but the sensation of passion: and it must be considerable, that is to say,

2 Nemes., ch. 11.
3 Greg. Nyss., De opif. Hom., ch. 13.
4 Text, αἴτιον. R. 2930, ἀγγεῖον.
5 φαντασία.
6 καὶ νοήσεως is wanting in some MSS, nor is it found in Nemesius, who borrowed his description from Origen.
7 Text, σωτηρία. Variant, σωρεία, a heaping up, "coacervatio." Faber has "confirmatio," which is nearer σωτηρία, conservatio, which is found in Nemesius, &c.
8 Nemes., ch. 13.

9 τὸ φαντστικόν, the faculty of fantasy.

it must be great enough to come within the scope of sense.

Again, the definition of passions of the soul is this: Passion is a sensible activity of the appetitive faculty, depending on the presentation to the mind of something good or bad. Or in other words, passion is an irrational activity of the soul, resulting from the notion of something good or bad. For the notion of something good results in desire, and the notion of something bad results in anger. But passion considered as a class, that is, passion in general, is defined as a movement in one thing caused by another. Energy, on the other hand, is a drastic movement, and by "drastic" is meant that which is moved of itself. Thus, anger is the energy manifested by the part of the soul where anger resides, whereas passion involves the two divisions of the soul, and in addition the whole body when it is forcibly impelled to action by anger. For there has been caused movement in one thing caused by another, and this is called passion.

But in another sense energy is spoken of as passion. For energy is a movement in harmony with nature, whereas passion is a movement at variance with nature. According, then, to this view, energy may be spoken of as passion when it does not act in accord with nature, whether its movement is due to itself or to some other thing. Thus, in connection with the heart, its natural pulsation is energy, whereas its palpitation, which is an excessive and unnatural movement, is passion and not energy.

But it is not every activity of the passionate part of the soul that is called passion, but only the more violent ones, and such as are capable of causing sensation: for the minor and unperceived movements are certainly not passions. For to constitute passion there is necessary a considerable degree of force, and thus it is on this account that we add to the definition of passion that it is a sensible activity. For the lesser activities escape the notice of the senses, and do not cause passion.

Observe also that our soul possesses twofold faculties, those of knowledge, and those of life. The faculties of knowledge are mind, thought, notion, presentation, sensation: and the vital or appetitive faculties are will and choice. Now, to make what has been said clearer, let us consider these things more closely, and first let us take the faculties of knowledge.

Presentation and sensation then have already been sufficiently discussed above. It is sensation that causes a passion, which is called presentation, to arise in the soul, and from presentation comes notion. Thereafter thought,

weighing the truth or falseness of the notion, determines what is true: and this explains the Greek word for thought, διάνοια, which is derived from διανοεῖν, meaning to think and discriminate. That, however, which is judged[1] and determined to be true, is spoken of as mind.

Or to put it otherwise: The primary activity of the mind, observe, is intelligence, but intelligence applied to any object is called a thought, and when this persists and makes on the mind an impression of the object of thought, it is named reflection, and when reflection dwells on the same object and puts itself to the test, and closely examines the relation of the thought to the soul, it gets the name prudence. Further, prudence, when it extends its area forms the power of reasoning, and is called conception, and this is defined as the fullest activity of the soul, arising in that part where reason resides, and being devoid of outward expression: and from it proceeds the uttered word spoken by the tongue. And now that we have discussed the faculties of knowledge, let us turn to the vital or appetitive faculties.

It should be understood that there is implanted in the soul by nature a faculty of desiring that which is in harmony with its nature, and of maintaining in close union all that belongs essentially to its nature: and this power is called will or θέλησις. For the essence both of existence and of living yearns after activity both as regards mind and sense, and in this it merely longs to realise its own natural and perfect being. And so this definition also is given of this natural will: will is an appetite, both rational and vital, depending only on what is natural. So that will[2] is nothing else than the natural and vital and rational appetite of all things that go to constitute nature, that is, just the simple faculty. For the appetite of creatures without reason, since it is irrational, is not called will.

Again βούλησις or wish is a sort of natural will, that is to say, a natural and rational appetite for some definite thing. For there is seated in the soul of man a faculty of rational desire. When, then, this rational desire directs itself naturally to some definite object it is called wish. For wish is rational desire and longing for some definite thing.

Wish, however, is used both in connection with what is within our power, and in connection with what is outside our power, that is, both with regard to the possible and the impossible. For we wish often to indulge lust or to be temperate, or to sleep and the

---

[1] Cf. 1 Cor. i. 10.   [2] *Max. ad Marin. et ad Incert.* p. 98.

like, and these are within our power to accomplish, and possible. But we wish also to be kings, and this is not within our power, or we wish perchance never to die, and this is an impossibility.

The wish [3], then, has reference to the end alone, and not to the means by which the end is attained. The end is the object of our wish, for instance, to be a king or to enjoy good health: but the means by which the end is attained, that is to say, the manner in which we ought to enjoy good health, or reach the rank of king, are the objects of deliberation [4]. Then after wish follow inquiry and speculation (ζήτησις and σκέψις), and after these, if the object is anything within our power, comes counsel or deliberation (βουλή or βούλευσις): counsel is an appetite for investigating lines of action lying within our own power. For one deliberates, whether one ought to prosecute any matter or not, and next, one decides which is the better, and this is called judgment (κρίσις). Thereafter, one becomes disposed to and forms a liking for that in favour of which deliberation gave judgment, and this is called inclination (γνώμη). For should one form a judgment and not be disposed to or form a liking for the object of that judgment, it is not called inclination. Then, again, after one has become so disposed, choice or selection (προαίρεσις and ἐπιλογή) comes into play. For choice consists in the choosing and selecting of one of two possibilities in preference to the other. Then one is impelled to action, and this is called impulse (ὁρμή): and thereafter it is brought into employment, and this is called use (χρῆσις). The last stage after we have enjoyed the use is cessation from desire.

In the case, however, of creatures without reason, as soon as appetite is roused for anything, straightway arises impulse to action. For the appetite of creatures without reason is irrational, and they are ruled by their natural appetite. Hence, neither the names of will or wish are applicable to the appetite of creatures without reason. For will is rational, free and natural desire, and in the case of man, endowed with reason as he is, the natural appetite is ruled rather than rules. For his actions are free, and depend upon reason, since the faculties of knowledge and life are bound up together in man. He is free in desire, free in wish, free in examination and investigation, free in deliberation, free in judgment, free in inclination, free in choice,

free in impulse, and free in action where that is in accordance with nature.

But in the case of God [5], it is to be remembered, we speak of wish, but it is not correct to speak of choice. For God does not deliberate, since that is a mark of ignorance, and no one deliberates about what he knows. But if counsel is a mark of ignorance, surely choice [6] must also be so. God, then, since He has absolute knowledge of everything, does not deliberate [7].

Nor in the case of the soul of the Lord do we speak of counsel or choice, seeing that He had no part in ignorance. For, although He was of a nature that is not cognisant of the future, yet because of His oneness in subsistence with God the Word, He had knowledge of all things, and that not by grace, but, as we have said, because He was one in subsistence [8]. For He Himself was both God and Man, and hence He did not possess the will that acts by opinion [9] or disposition. While He did possess the natural and simple will which is to be observed equally in all the personalities of men, His holy soul had not opinion [1] (or, disposition) that is to say, no inclination opposed to His divine will, nor aught else contrary to His divine will. For opinion (or, disposition) differs as persons differ, except in the case of the holy and simple and uncompound and indivisible Godhead [2]. There, indeed, since the subsistences are in nowise divided or separated, neither is the object of will divided. And there, since there is but one nature, there is also but one natural will. And again, since the subsistences are unseparated, the three subsistences have also one object of will, and one activity. In the case of men, however, seeing that their nature is one, their natural will is also one, but since their subsistences [3] are separated and divided from each other, alike in place and time, and disposition to things, and in many other respects, for this reason their acts of will and their opinions are different. But in the case of our Lord Jesus Christ, since He possesses different natures, His natural wills, that is, His volitional faculties belonging to Him as God and as Man are also different. But since the subsistence is one, and He Who exercises

---

3 τὸ βουλητόν.
4 *Max. Dial. cum Pyrrh. et Epist. 1 ad Marin.*

5 Thomas Aquinas (1--2, *Quæst.* 4, *a.* 1 and 2) lays down the position, in accordance with John of Damascus, that there is no "counsel" in God *quatenus est appetitus inquisitivus*, but that there is *quantum ad certitudinem judicii*. Basil (*Hexaëm. Hom.* 1), arguing against the ancient philosophers who taught that the world was made ἀπροαιρέτως, affirms "counsel" in God in the latter sense.
6 *Max., Epist. 1 ad Marin.*
7 Text, ὁ δὲ Θεὸς πάντα εἰδὼς ἁπλῶς, οὐ βουλεύεται. Various reading is, ὁ δὲ Θεὸς πάντα αἰδῶς ἁπλῶς βούλεται.
8 *Max., Dial. cum Pyrrh.*
9 διὸ οὐδὲ γνωμικὸν εἶχε θέλημα.   1 γνωμήν.
2 *v. infr.,* lib. iii. ch. 14.   3 Or, *personalities.*

the will is one, the object of the will [4], that is, the gnomic will [5], is also one, His human will evidently following His divine will, and willing that which the divine will willed it to will.

Further note, that will (θέλησις) and wish (βούλησις) are two different things: also the object of will (τὸ θελητόν) and the capacity for will (θελητικόν), and the subject that exercises will (ὁ θέλων), are all different. For will is just the simple faculty of willing, whereas wish is will directed to some definite object. Again, the object of will is the matter underlying the will, that is to say, the thing that we will: for instance, when appetite is roused for food. The appetite pure and simple, however, is a rational will. The capacity for will, moreover, means that which possesses the volitional faculty, for example, man. Further, the subject that exercises will is the actual person who makes use of will.

The word τὸ θέλημα, it is well to note, sometimes denotes the will, that is, the volitional faculty, and in this sense we speak of natural will: and sometimes it denotes the object of will, and we speak of will (θέλημα γνωμικόν) depending on inclination [6].

CHAPTER XXIII.
Concerning Energy.

All the faculties [7] we have already discussed, both those of knowledge and those of life, both the natural and the artificial, are, it is to be noted, called energies. For energy [8] is the natural force and activity of each essence: or again, natural energy is the activity innate in every essence: and so, clearly, things that have the same essence have also the same energy, and things that have different natures have also different energies. For no essence can be devoid of natural energy.

Natural energy again is the force in each essence by which its nature is made manifest. And again: natural energy is the primal, eternally-moving force of the intelligent soul: that is, the eternally-moving word of the soul, which ever springs naturally from it. And yet again: natural energy [9] is the force and activity of each essence which only that which is not lacks.

But actions [9a] are also called energies: for

instance, speaking, eating, drinking, and such like. The natural affections [9b] also are often called energies, for instance, hunger, thirst, and so forth [1]. And yet again, the result of the force is also often called energy.

Things are spoken of in a twofold way as being potential and actual. For we say that the child at the breast is a potential scholar, for he is so equipped that, if taught, he will become a scholar. Further, we speak of a potential and an actual scholar, meaning that the latter is versed in letters, while the former has the power of interpreting letters, but does not put it into actual use: again, when we speak of an actual scholar, we mean that he puts his power into actual use, that is to say, that he really interprets writings.

It is, therefore, to be observed that in the second sense potentiality and actuality go together; for the scholar is in the one case potential, and in the other actual.

The primal and only true energy of nature is the voluntary or rational and independent life which constitutes our humanity. I know not how those who rob the Lord of this can say that He became man [2].

Energy is drastic activity of nature: and by drastic is meant that which is moved of itself.

CHAPTER XXIV.
Concerning what is Voluntary and what is Involuntary.

The voluntary [3] implies a certain definite action, and so-called involuntariness also implies a certain definite action. Further, many attribute true involuntariness not only to suffering, but even to action. We must then understand action to be rational energy. Actions are followed by praise or blame, and some of them are accompanied with pleasure and others with pain; some are to be desired by the actor, others are to be shunned: further, of those that are desirable, some are always so, others only at some particular time. And so it is also with those that are to be shunned. Again, some actions enlist pity and are pardonable, others are hateful and deserve punishment. Voluntariness, then, is assuredly followed by praise or blame, and renders the action pleasurable and desirable to the actor, either for all time or for the moment of its performance. Involuntariness, on the other hand, brings merited pity or pardon in its train, and renders the act painful and unde-

---

4 Text, θελητόν, as given by Faber. Variant, θελητικόν.
5 τὸ γνωμικὸν θέλημα, the will of individual opinion, or, the dispositional will.
6 Or, acting by opinion, or disposition.
7 Anast. Sin. in Ὁδηγ., from Greg. Nyss., p. 44; Clem. Alex. ap. Max., p. 151
8 The Greek ἐνέργεια being a term with a large connotation is explained as meaning in different cases operation (operatio), action (actio), and act (actus). Nemesius defines actio as operatio rationalis, actus as perfectio potentiæ.
9 Cf. Anast. Sin. in Ὁδηγός, p. 43; John of Dam., Dialect. c. 30; Greg. Nyss., in Maximus, II., p. 155.
9a πράξεις. So πρᾶξις is defined as ἐνέργεια λογική in the following chapter.

9b τὰ πάθη. Cf. Instit. Elem., c. 9; Greg. Nyss., Cont. Eunom., v. p. 170.
1 Max., Dial. cum Pyrrh.
2 Greg. Nyss. ap. Max., p. 155.
3 Cf. Greg. Nyss., in Maxim.; Nemes., ch. 29.

sirable to the doer, and makes him leave it in a state of incompleteness even though force is brought to bear upon him.

Further, what is involuntary depends in part on force and in part on ignorance. It depends on force when the creative beginning or cause is from without, that is to say, when one is forced by another without being at all persuaded, or when one does not contribute to the act on one's own impulse, or does not co-operate at all, or do on one's own account that which is exacted by force [4]. Thus we may give this definition: "An involuntary act is one in which the beginning is from without, and where one does not contribute at all on one's own impulse to that to which one is forced." And by beginning we mean the creative cause. An involuntary act depends, on the other hand, on ignorance, when one is not the cause of the ignorance one's self, but events just so happen. For, if one commits murder while drunk, it is an act of ignorance, but yet not involuntary [5]: for one was one's self responsible for the cause of the ignorance, that is to say, the drunkenness. But if while shooting at the customary range one slew one's father who happened to be passing by, this would be termed an ignorant and involuntary act.

As, then, that which is involuntary is in two parts, one depending on force, the other on ignorance, that which is voluntary is the opposite of both. For that which is voluntary is the result neither of force nor of ignorance [6]. A voluntary act, then, is one of which the beginning or cause originates in an actor, who knows each individual circumstance through which and in which the action takes place. By "individual" is meant what the rhetoricians call circumstantial elements: for instance, the actor, the sufferer, the action (perchance a murder), the instrument, the place, the time, the manner, the reason of the action.

Notice that there are certain things that occupy a place intermediate between what is voluntary and what is involuntary. Although they are unpleasant and painful we welcome them as the escape from a still greater trouble; for instance, to escape shipwreck we cast the cargo overboard [7].

Notice also that children and irrational creatures perform voluntary actions, but these do not involve the exercise of choice: further, all our actions that are done in anger and without previous deliberation are voluntary actions, but do not in the least involve free choice [8]. Also, if a friend suddenly appears on the scene, or if one unexpectedly lights on a treasure, so far as we are concerned it is quite voluntary, but there is no question of choice in the matter. For all these things are voluntary, because we desire pleasure from them, but they do not by any means imply choice, because they are not the result of deliberation. And deliberation must assuredly precede choice, as we have said above.

CHAPTER XXV.

Concerning what is in our own power, that is, concerning Free-will [9].

The first enquiry involved in the consideration of free-will, that is, of what is in our own power, is whether anything is in our power [1]: for there are many who deny this. The second is, what are the things that are in our power, and over what things do we have authority? The third is, what is the reason for which God Who created us endued us with free-will? So then we shall take up the first question, and firstly we shall prove that of those things which even our opponents grant, some are within our power. And let us proceed thus.

Of all the things that happen, the cause is said to be either God, or necessity, or fate, or nature, or chance, or accident. But God's function has to do with essence and providence: necessity deals with the movement of things that ever keep to the same course: fate with the necessary accomplishment of the things it brings to pass (for fate itself implies necessity): nature with birth, growth, destruction, plants and animals; chance with what is rare and unexpected. For chance is defined as the meeting and concurrence of two causes, originating in choice but bringing to pass something other than what is natural: for example, if a man finds a treasure while digging a ditch [2]: for the man who hid the treasure did not do so that the other might find it, nor did the finder dig with the purpose of finding the treasure: but the former hid it that he might take it away when he wished, and the other's aim was to dig the ditch: whereas something happened quite different from what both had in view. Accident again deals with casual occurrences that take place among lifeless or irrational things, apart from nature and art. This then is their doctrine. Under which, then, of these categories are we to bring what happens through the agency of

---

4 *Nemes.*, ch. 30.   5 Ibid., ch. 31.   6 Ibid., ch. 32.
7 Ibid., ch. 30.

8 *Nemes.*, ch. 33.   9 τοῦ αὐτεξουσίου. See also III. 34.
1 *Nemes.*, ch. 39.
2 Text, ταφρον. Variant, τάφον.

man, if indeed man is not the cause and beginning of action [3]? for it would not be right to ascribe to God actions that are sometimes base and unjust : nor may we ascribe these to necessity, for they are not such as ever continue the same : nor to fate, for fate implies not possibility only but necessity : nor to nature, for nature's province is animals and plants : nor to chance, for the actions of men are not rare and unexpected : nor to accident, for that is used in reference to the casual occurrences that take place in the world of lifeless and irrational things. We are left then with this fact, that the man who acts and makes is himself the author of his own works, and is a creature endowed with free-will.

Further, if man is the author of no action, the faculty of deliberation is quite superfluous: for to what purpose could deliberation be put if man is the master of none of his actions? for all deliberation is for the sake of action. But to prove that the fairest and most precious of man's endowments is quite superfluous would be the height of absurdity. If then man deliberates, he deliberates with a view to action. For all deliberation is with a view to and on account of action.

CHAPTER XXVI.
Concerning Events [4].

Of events [5], some are in our hands, others are not. Those then are in our hands which we are free to do or not to do at our will, that is all actions that are done voluntarily (for those actions are not called voluntary the doing of which is not in our hands), and in a word, all that are followed by blame or praise and depend on motive and law. Strictly all mental [6] and deliberative acts are in our hands. Now deliberation is concerned with equal possibilities : and an ' equal possibility' is an action that is itself within our power and its opposite, and our mind makes choice of the alternatives, and this is the origin of action. The actions, therefore, that are in our hands are these equal possibilities : e.g. to be moved or not to be moved, to hasten or not to hasten, to long for unnecessaries or not to do so, to tell lies or not to tell lies, to give or not to give, to rejoice or not to rejoice as fits the occasion, and all such actions as imply virtue or vice in their performance, for we are free to do or not to do these at our pleasure. Amongst equal possibilities also

are included the arts, for we have it in our power to cultivate these or not as we please.

Note, however, that while the choice of what is to be done is ever in our power, the action itself often is prevented by some dispensation of the divine Providence [7].

CHAPTER XXVII.
Concerning the reason of our endowment with Free-will.

We hold, therefore, that free-will [8] comes on the scene at the same moment as reason, and that change and alteration are congenital to all that is produced. For all that is produced is also subject to change [9]. For those things must be subject to change whose production has its origin in change. And change consists in being brought into being out of nothing, and in transforming a substratum of matter into something different. Inanimate things, then, and things without reason undergo the afore-mentioned bodily changes, while the changes of things endowed with reason depend on choice. For reason consists of a speculative and a practical part. The speculative part is the contemplation of the nature of things, and the practical consists in deliberation and defines the true reason for what is to be done. The speculative side is called mind or wisdom, and the practical side is called reason or prudence. Every one, then, who deliberates does so in the belief that the choice of what is to be done lies in his hands, that he may choose what seems best as the result of his deliberation, and having chosen may act upon it. And if this is so, free-will must necessarily be very closely related to reason. For either man is an irrational being, or, if he is rational, he is master of his acts and endowed with free-will. Hence also creatures without reason do not enjoy free-will : for nature leads them rather than they nature, and so they do not oppose the natural appetite, but as soon as their appetite longs after anything they rush headlong after it. But man, being rational, leads nature rather than nature him, and so when he desires aught he has the power to curb his appetite or to indulge it as he pleases. Hence also creatures devoid of reason are the subjects neither of praise nor blame, while man is the subject of both praise and blame [1].

Note also that the angels, being rational, are endowed with free-will, and, inasmuch as they are created, are liable to change. This

---

3 Text, πράξεως. MSS. πράξεων, as in Nemesius.
4 περὶ τῶν γινομένων.   5 Nemes., ch. 40.
6 τὰ ψυχικὰ πάντα.

7 Nemes., ch. 37.
8 This is supplied by Combefis from Nemesius.
9 Nemes., ch. 41.
1 This sentence is omitted in Basil and some MSS.

in fact is made plain by the devil who, although made good by the Creator, became of his own free-will the inventor of evil, and by the powers who revolted with him [2], that is the demons, and by the other troops of angels who abode in goodness.

CHAPTER XXVIII.

Concerning what is not in our hands.

Of things that are not in our hands some have their beginning or cause in those that are in our power, that is to say, the recompenses of our actions both in the present and in the age to come, but all the rest are dependent on the divine will. For the origin of all things is from God, but their destruction has been introduced by our wickedness for our punishment or benefit. For God did not create death, neither does He take delight in the destruction of living things [3]. But death is the work rather of man, that is, its origin is in Adam's transgression, in like manner as all other punishments. But all other things must be referred to God. For our birth is to be referred to His creative power; and our continuance to His conservative power; and our government and safety to His providential power; and the eternal enjoyment of good things by those who preserve the laws of nature in which we are formed is to be ascribed to His goodness. But since some deny the existence of Providence, let us further devote a few words to the discussion of Providence.

CHAPTER XXIX.

Concerning Providence.

Providence, then, is the care that God takes over existing things. And again : Providence is the will of God through which all existing things receive their fitting issue [4]. But if Providence is God's will, according to true reasoning all things that come into being through Providence must necessarily be both most fair and most excellent, and such that they cannot be surpassed. For the same person must of necessity be creator of and provider for what exists: for it is not meet nor fitting that the creator of what exists and the provider should be separate persons. For in that case they would both assuredly be deficient, the one in creating, the other in providing [5]. God therefore is both Creator and Provider, and His creative and preserving and providing power is simply His good-will. For *whatsoever the Lord pleased that did He*

in heaven and in earth [6], and *no one resisted His will* [7]. He willed that all things should be and they were. He wills the universe to be framed and it is framed, and all that He wills comes to pass.

That He provides, and that He provides excellently [8], one can most readily perceive thus. God alone is good and wise by nature. Since then He is good, He provides : for he who does not provide is not good. For even men and creatures without reason provide for their own offspring according to their nature, and he who does not provide is blamed. Again, since He is wise, He takes the best care over what exists.

When, therefore, we give heed to these things we ought to be filled with wonder at all the works of Providence, and praise them all [9], and accept them all without enquiry, even though they are in the eyes of many unjust, because the Providence of God is beyond our ken and comprehension, while our reasonings and actions and the future are revealed to His eyes alone. And by "all" I mean those that are not in our hands : for those that are in our power are outside the sphere of Providence and within that of our Free-will.

Now the works of Providence are partly according to the good-will [2] (of God) and partly according to permission [3]. Works of good-will include all those that are undeniably good, while works of permission are . . . . . . [4]. For Providence often permits the just man to encounter misfortune in order that he may reveal to others the virtue that lies concealed within him [5], as was the case with Job [6]. At other times it allows something strange to be done in order that something great and marvellous might be accomplished through the seemingly-strange act, as when the salvation of men was brought about through the Cross. In another way it allows the pious man to suffer sore trials in order that he may not depart from a right conscience nor lapse into pride on account of the power and grace granted to him, as was the case with Paul [7].

One man is forsaken for a season with a view to another's restoration, in order that others when they see his state may be taught a lesson [8], as in the case of Lazarus and the rich man [9]. For it belongs to our nature to be

6 Ps. cxxxv. 6.   7 Rom. ix. 19.   8 *Nemes.*, ch. 44.
9 The words πάντα ἐπαινεῖν are wanting in *Cod. R.* 2 and in *Nemes.*, ch. 44.
2 κατ᾿ εὐδοκίαν.   3 κατὰ συγχώρησιν.
4 There is a hiatus here in Edit. Veron. and in *Cod. R.* 2927. Various readings are found in other MSS., some with no sense and others evidently supplied by librarians. It is best supplied from *Nemesius*, ch. 44, τῆς δὲ συγχωρήσεως πολλὰ εἴδη, " but there are many forms of concession."
5 *Nemes* , ch. 44.   6 Job i. 11.   7 2 Cor. xii. 7.
8 *Nemes.*, ch. 44.   9 St. Luke xvi. 19.

---

2 Nemesius speaks of this at greater length.
3 Wisd. i. 13.   4 *Nemes.*, ch. 43.   5 Ibid.; ch. 42.

cast down when we see persons in distress. Another is deserted by Providence in order that another may be glorified, and not for his own sin or that of his parents, just as the man who was blind from his birth ministered to the glory of the Son of Man [1]. Again another is permitted to suffer in order to stir up emulation in the breasts of others, so that others by magnifying the glory of the sufferer may resolutely welcome suffering in the hope of future glory and the desire for future blessings, as in the case of the martyrs. Another is allowed to fall at times into some act of baseness in order that another worse fault may be thus corrected, as for instance when God allows a man who takes pride in his virtue and righteousness to fall away into fornication in order that he may be brought through this fall into the perception of his own weakness and be humbled and approach and make confession to the Lord.

Moreover, it is to be observed [2] that the choice of what is to be done is in our own hands [3] : but the final issue depends, in the one case when our actions are good, on the co-operation of God, Who in His justice brings help according to His foreknowledge to such as choose the good with a right conscience, and, in the other case when our actions are to evil, on the desertion by God, Who again in His justice stands aloof in accordance with His foreknowledge [4].

Now there are two forms of desertion : for there is desertion in the matters of guidance and training, and there is complete and hopeless desertion. The former has in view the restoration and safety and glory of the sufferer, or the rousing of feelings of emulation and imitation in others, or the glory of God : but the latter is when man, after God has done all that was possible to save him, remains of his own set purpose blind and uncured, or rather incurable, and then he is handed over to utter destruction, as was Judas [5]. May God be gracious to us, and deliver us from such desertion.

Observe further that the ways of God's providence are many, and they cannot be explained in words nor conceived by the mind.

And remember that all the assaults of dark and evil fortune contribute to the salvation of those who receive them with thankfulness, and are assuredly ambassadors of help.

Also one must bear in mind [6] that God's original wish was that all should be saved and come to His Kingdom [7]. For it was not for punishment that He formed us but to share in His goodness, inasmuch as He is a good God. But inasmuch as He is a just God, His will is that sinners should suffer punishment.

The first then is called God's antecedent will and pleasure, and springs from Himself, while the second is called God's consequent will and permission, and has its origin in us. And the latter is two-fold ; one part dealing with matters of guidance and training, and having in view our salvation, and the other being hopeless and leading to our utter punishment, as we said above. And this is the case with actions that are not left in our hands [8].

But of actions that are in our hands the good ones depend on His antecedent goodwill and pleasure, while the wicked ones depend neither on His antecedent nor on His consequent will, but are a concession to free-will. For that which is the result of compulsion has neither reason nor virtue in it. God [9] makes provision for all creation and makes all creation the instrument of His help and training, yea often even the demons themselves, as for example in the cases of Job and the swine [1].

CHAPTER XXX.

Concerning Prescience and Predestination.

We ought to understand [2] that while God knows all things beforehand, yet He does not predetermine all things [3]. For He knows beforehand those things that are in our power, but He does not predetermine them. For it is not His will that there should be wickedness nor does He choose to compel virtue. So that predetermination is the work of the divine command based on fore-knowledge [4]. But on the other hand God predetermines those things which are not within our power in accordance with His prescience. For already God in His prescience has pre-judged all things in accordance with His goodness and justice.

Bear in mind, too [5], that virtue is a gift from God implanted in our nature, and that He Himself is the source and cause of all good,

1 St. John ix. 1.   2 Nemes., ch. 37.
3 Cf. Nemes., c. 27; also Cicero's statement on Providence in the Academ. Quest.
4 See the reference in Migne.   5 St. Matt. xxvi. 24.
6 See Chrysostom, Hom. 1, in Epist. ad Ephes., and Hom. 18, in Epist. ad Hebræos.

7 1 Tim. ii. 4.
8 These words are wanting in two MSS.
9 This last sentence is absent in one Codex.
1 St. Matt. viii. 30 seqq.
2 Chrys., Hom. 12 in Epist. ad Ephes.
3 Cf. Maximus, Vita, n. 8; Just. Martyr, Apol. 1 ; Tatian, Or. ad Græcos ; Origen, Ep. ad Rom. 1 ; Jerome, on Ezek. c. xxiv., &c.
4 Act. S. Max.
5 Cf. Clem. Alex., Strom., bk. vi. ; Jerome, on Ep. ad Gal., ch. 1 ; Greg. Naz , Carmen de virt. hum.

and without His co-operation [6] and help we cannot will or do any good thing. But we have it in our power either to abide in virtue and follow God, Who calls us into ways of virtue, or to stray from paths of virtue, which is to dwell in wickedness, and to follow the devil who summons but cannot compel us. For wickedness is nothing else than the withdrawal of goodness, just as darkness is nothing else than the withdrawal of light. While then we abide in the natural state we abide in virtue, but when we deviate from the natural state, that is from virtue, we come into an unnatural state and dwell in wickedness [7].

Repentance is the returning from the unnatural into the natural state, from the devil to God, through discipline and effort.

Man then the Creator made male, giving him to share in His own divine grace, and bringing him thus into communion with Himself: and thus it was that he gave in the manner of a prophet the names to living things, with authority as though they were given to be his slaves. For having been endowed with reason and mind, and free-will after the image of God, he was fitly entrusted with dominion over earthly things by the common Creator and Master of all.

But since God in His prescience [8] knew that man would transgress and become liable to destruction, He made from him a female to be a help to him like himself; a help, indeed, for the conservation of the race after the transgression from age to age by generation. For the earliest formation is called 'making' and not 'generation.' For 'making' is the original formation at God's hands, while 'generation' is the succession from each other made necessary by the sentence of death imposed on us on account of the transgression.

This man He [9] placed in Paradise, a home that was alike spiritual and sensible. For he lived in the body on the earth in the realm of sense, while he dwelt in the spirit among the angels, cultivating divine thoughts, and being supported by them: living in naked simplicity a life free from artificiality, and being led up through His creations to the one and only Creator, in Whose contemplation he found joy and gladness [1].

When therefore He had furnished his nature with free-will, He imposed a law on him, not to taste of the tree of knowledge. Concerning this tree, we have said as much as is necessary in the chapter about Paradise, at least as much as it was in our power to say. And with this command He gave the promise that, if he should preserve the dignity of the soul by giving the victory to reason, and acknowledging his Creator and observing His command, he should share eternal blessedness and live to all eternity, proving mightier than death: but if forsooth he should subject the soul to the body, and prefer the delights of the body, comparing himself in ignorance of his true dignity to the senseless beasts [2], and shaking off his Creator's yoke, and neglecting His divine injunction, he will be liable to death and corruption, and will be compelled to labour throughout a miserable life. For it was no profit to man to obtain incorruption while still untried and unproved, lest he should fall into pride and under the judgment of the devil. For through his incorruption the devil, when he had fallen as the result of his own free choice, was firmly established in wickedness, so that there was no room for repentance and no hope of change: just as, moreover, the angels also, when they had made free choice of virtue became through grace immoveably rooted in goodness.

It was necessary, therefore, that man should first be put to the test (for man untried and unproved [3] would be worth nothing [4]), and being made perfect by the trial through the observance of the command should thus receive incorruption as the prize of his virtue. For being intermediate between God and matter he was destined, if he kept the command, to be delivered from his natural relation to existing things and to be made one with God's estate, and to be immoveably established in goodness, but, if he transgressed and inclined the rather to what was material, and tore his mind from the Author of his being, I mean God, his fate was to be corruption, and he was to become subject to passion instead of passionless, and mortal instead of immortal, and dependent on connection and unsettled generation. And in his desire for life he would cling to pleasures as though they were necessary to maintain it, and would fearlessly abhor those who sought to deprive him of these, and transfer his desire from God to matter, and his anger from the real enemy of his salvation to his own brethren. The

[6] Cf. *Clem. Alex., Quis dives salvetur; Greg. Naz., Orat.* 31; *Chrysost., Hom.* 45 *in Joann., Hom. in Ep. ad Hebr.* xii. 2, *Hom.* 15 *in Ep. ad Rom.; Cyril, De ador. in Spir. et ver.,* p. 25; *Petavius, Dogm.,* vol. i., bk. ix. c. 4, &c.

[7] Cf. *infra,* bk. iii. ch. 14.

[8] ὁ προγνώστης Θεός. See *Athanas., in Psalm* 1; *Chrysost. in Hom.* 18 *in Gen.; Greg. Nyss., De opif. hom.; Athanas., Minor, Quest.* 50 *ad Antioch.; Thomas Aquinas* I., *Quæst.* 98, *Art.* 2.

[9] *Greg. Nyss., De opif.,* ch. 20.

[1] Text, εὐφραινόμενος. Variant, σεμνυνόμενος.

[2] Ps. xlix. 12.

[3] ἀδόκιμος; in *Cod. R.* 2 ἀδοκίμαστον.

[4] This parenthesis is absent in almost all codices and in the translations of Faber, &c.

envy of the [5] devil then was the reason of man's fall. For that same demon, so full of envy and with such a hatred of good, would not suffer us to enjoy the pleasures of heaven, when he himself was kept below on account of his arrogance, and hence the false one tempts miserable man with the hope of Godhead, and leading him up to as great a height of arrogance as himself, he hurls him down into a pit of destruction just as deep.

---

[5] Cf. *Greg. Naz., Orat.* 38 and 42; *Cyril Alex., Cont. Anthrop.*, I. 8; *Anast. II. Antioch., Hexaëm.* vi.; *Chrysost., Hom.* 10 *in Ep. ad Rom., Hom.* 5 *in Ep. ad Epes., &c.*

BOOK III.

CHAPTER I.

Concerning the Divine Œconomy and God's care over us, and concerning our salvation.

MAN, then, was thus snared by the assault of the arch-fiend, and broke his Creator's command, and was stripped of grace and put off his confidence with God, and covered himself with the asperities of a toilsome life (for this is the meaning of the fig-leaves[1]); and was clothed about with death, that is, mortality and the grossness of flesh (for this is what the garment of skins signifies); and was banished from Paradise by God's just judgment, and condemned to death, and made subject to corruption. Yet, notwithstanding all this, in His pity, God, Who gave him his being, and Who in His graciousness bestowed on him a life of happiness, did not disregard man[2]. But He first trained him in many ways and called him back, by groans and trembling, by the deluge of water, and the utter destruction of almost the whole race[3], by confusion and diversity of tongues[4], by the rule[5] of angels[6], by the burning of cities[7], by figurative manifestations of God, by wars and victories and defeats, by signs and wonders, by manifold faculties, by the law and the prophets: for by all these means God earnestly strove to emancipate man from the wide-spread and enslaving bonds of sin, which had made life such a mass of iniquity, and to effect man's return to a life of happiness. For it was sin that brought death like a wild and savage beast into the world[8] to the ruin of the human life. But it behoved the Redeemer to be without sin, and not made liable through sin to death, and further, that His nature should be strengthened and renewed, and trained by labour and taught the way of virtue which leads away from corruption to the life eternal: and, in the end, is revealed the mighty ocean of love to man that is about Him[9]. For the very Creator and Lord Himself undertakes a struggle[1] in behalf of the work of His own hands, and learns by toil to become Master. And since the enemy snares man by the hope of Godhead, he himself is snared in turn by the screen of flesh, and so are shown at once the goodness and wisdom, the justice and might of God. God's goodness is revealed in that He did not disregard[2] the frailty of His own handiwork, but was moved with compassion for him in his fall, and stretched forth His hand to him: and His justice in that when man was overcome He did not make another victorious over the tyrant, nor did He snatch man by might from death, but in His goodness and justice He made him, who had become through his sins the slave of death, himself once more conqueror and rescued like by like, most difficult though it seemed: and His wisdom is seen in His devising the most fitting solution of the difficulty[3]. For by the good pleasure of our God and Father, the Only-begotten Son and Word of God and God, Who is in the bosom of the God and Father[4], of like essence with the Father and the Holy Spirit, Who was before the ages, Who is without beginning and was in the beginning, Who is in the presence of the God and Father, and is God and made in the form of God[5], bent the heavens and descended to earth: that is to say, He humbled without humiliation His lofty station which yet could not be humbled, and condescends to His servants[6], with a condescension ineffable and incomprehensible: (for that is what the descent signifies). And God being perfect becomes perfect man, and brings to perfection the newest of all new things[7], the only new thing under the Sun, through which the boundless might of God is manifested. For what greater thing is there, than that God should become Man? And the Word became flesh without being changed, of the Holy Spirit, and Mary the holy and ever-virgin one, the mother of God. And He acts as mediator between God and man, He the only lover of man conceived in the Virgin's chaste womb without will[8] or desire, or any connection with man or pleasurable generation, but through the

---

[1] Gen. iii. 7; cf. *Greg. Naz., Orat.* 38 and 42; *Greg. Nyss., Orat. Catech.* c. 8.
[2] Text, παρεῖδεν. Variant, περιεῖδεν.   [3] Gen. vi. 13.
[4] Ibid. xi. 7.   [5] ἐπιστασία, *care*, or *dominion*.
[6] Gen. xviii. 1 *seqq.*   [7] Ibid xix. 1 *seqq.*
[8] Wisd. ii. 24.   [9] *Greg. Naz., Orat.* 12 and 3°.
[1] Text, πάλην. Variant, πλάσιν, cf. "plasmationem" (Faber).

[2] Text, παρεῖδε. Variant, περιεῖδεν.
[3] *Greg. Nyss., Orat. Cathec.*, ch 20 *et seqq.*
[4] St. John i. 18.   [5] Phil. ii. 6.
[6] "Condescends to His servants" is absent in some **MSS.**
[7] Eccles. i. 10.   [8] *Greg. Nyss., Cat.* ch. 16.

Holy Spirit and the first offspring of Adam. And He becomes obedient to the Father Who is like unto us, and finds a remedy for our disobedience in what He had assumed from us, and became a pattern of obedience to us without which it is not possible to obtain salvation [8].

CHAPTER II.

Concerning the manner in which the Word[9] was conceived, and concerning His divine incarnation.

The angel of the Lord was sent to the holy Virgin, who was descended from David's line [1]. *For it is evident that our Lord sprang out of Judah, of which tribe no one turned his attention to the altar* [2], as the divine apostle said: but about this we will speak more accurately later. And bearing glad tidings to her, he said, *Hail thou highly favoured one, the Lord is with thee* [3]. And she was troubled at his word, and the angel said to her, *Fear not, Mary, for thou hast found favour with God, and shalt bring forth a Son and shalt call His name Jesus* [4]; for He shall save His people from their sins [5]. Hence it comes that Jesus has the interpretation Saviour. And when she asked in her perplexity, *How can this be, seeing I know not a man* [6]*?* the angel again answered her, *The Holy Spirit shall come upon thee, and the power of the Highest shall overshadow thee. Therefore also that holy thing which shall be born of thee* [7] *shall be called the Son of God* [8]. And she said to him, *Behold the handmaid of the Lord: be it unto me according to Thy word* [9].

So then, after the assent of the holy Virgin, the Holy Spirit descended on her, according to the word of the Lord which the angel spake, purifying her [1], and granting her power to receive the divinity of the Word, and likewise power to bring forth [2]. And then was she overshadowed [3] by the enhypostatic Wisdom and Power of the most high God, the Son of God Who is of like essence with the Father as of Divine seed, and from her holy and most pure blood He formed flesh animated with the spirit of reason and thought, the first-fruits of our compound nature [4]: not by procreation but by creation through the Holy Spirit: not developing the fashion of the body by gradual additions but perfecting it at once, He Himself, the very Word of God, standing to the flesh in the relation of subsistence. For the divine Word was not made one with flesh that had an independent pre-existence [5], but taking up His abode in the womb of the holy Virgin, He unreservedly in His own subsistence took upon Himself through the pure blood of the eternal Virgin a body of flesh animated with the spirit of reason and thought, thus assuming to Himself the first-fruits of man's compound nature, Himself, the Word, having become a subsistence in the flesh. So that [6] He is at once flesh, and at the same time flesh of God the Word, and likewise flesh animated, possessing both reason and thought [7]. Wherefore we speak not of man as having become God, but of God as having become Man [8]. For being by nature perfect God, He naturally became likewise perfect Man: and did not change His nature nor make the dispensation [9] an empty show, but became, without confusion or change or division, one in subsistence with the flesh, which was conceived of the holy Virgin, and animated with reason and thought, and had found existence in Him, while He did not change the nature of His divinity into the essence of flesh, nor the essence of flesh into the nature of His divinity, and did not make one compound nature out of His divine nature and the human nature He had assumed [1].

CHAPTER III.

Concerning Christ's two natures, in opposition to those who hold that He has only one [2].

For the two natures were united with each other without change or alteration, neither the divine nature departing from its native simplicity, nor yet the human being either changed into the nature of God or reduced to non-existence, nor one compound nature being produced out of the two. For the compound nature [3] cannot be of the same essence as either of the natures out of which it is compounded, as made one thing out of others: for example, the body is composed of the four elements, but is not of the same essence as fire or air, or water or earth, nor does it keep these names. If, therefore, after the union, Christ's nature was, as the heretics

---

[8] *Athan., De salut. adv. Christi.*
[9] Text, τοῦ Λόγου. Variant, τοῦ Θεοῦ Λόγου: so *Dei Verbi* (Faber).
　[1] St. Luke i. 27.　　[2] Hebr. vii. 14.　　[3] St. Luke i. 28.
[4] Ibid. 30, 31.　　[5] St. Matt. i 21.　　[6] St. Luke i. 34.
[7] "Of thee" is wanting in some MSS.　　[8] St. Luke i. 35.
[9] Ibid. 38.　　　　　[1] Ibid. 27, 28.
　[2] *Greg. Naz.*, Orat. 38 and 42.
[3] Cf. *Athan., Ep. ad Serap., De Spiritu Sancto; Greg. Nyss., Contr. Apoll.* 6, 25; *Rufinus, Exp. Symb.; Tertullian, De Carne Christi* and *Contr. Prax.; Hilary, De Trin.* II. 26.
[4] *Basil, Christi Nativ.*

[5] *Cyril, Apolog.* 5 and 8 *anathem.*
[6] Cf. *Greg. Naz.*, 1 *Ep. ad Cledon; Cyril,* 1 *Ep. ad Nestor.; Theodor., Ep. ad Joan. Antioch.*, &c.
[7] *Cyril., Epist. ad Monach.*　　[8] *Procl., Epist.* 2 *ad Arm.*
[9] τὴν οἰκονομίαν, *the œconomy, the Incarnation.*
　[1] *Cod. R.* 2428 adds here some statements taken from the *Dissertation against the Nestorians.*
　[2] κατὰ Μονοφυσιτῶν: these words are absent in MSS.
　[3] Cf. *Eulogius* and also *Polemon* in the *Collect. Contr. Severianos.*

hold, a compound unity, He had changed from a simple into a compound nature [4], and is not of the same essence as the Father Whose nature is simple, nor as the mother, who is not a compound of divinity and humanity. Nor will He then be in divinity and humanity: nor will He be called either God or Man, but simply Christ: and the word Christ will be the name not of the subsistence, but of what in their view is the one nature.

We, however, do not give it as our view that Christ's nature is compound, nor yet that He is one thing made of other things and differing from them as man is made of soul and body, or as the body is made of the four elements, but hold [5] that, though He is constituted of these different parts He is yet the same [6]. For we confess that He alike in His divinity and in His humanity both is and is said to be perfect God, the same Being, and that He consists of two natures, and exists in two natures [7]. Further, by the word "Christ" we understand the name of the subsistence, not in the sense of one kind, but as signifying the existence of two natures. For in His own person He anointed Himself; as God anointing His body with His own divinity, and as Man being anointed. For He is Himself both God and Man. And the anointing is the divinity of His humanity. For if Christ, being of one compound nature, is of like essence to the Father, then the Father also must be compound and of like essence with the flesh, which is absurd and extremely blasphemous [8].

How, indeed, could one and the same nature come to embrace opposing and essential differences? For how is it possible that the same nature should be at once created and uncreated, mortal and immortal, circumscribed and uncircumscribed?

But if those who declare that Christ has only one nature should say also that that nature is a simple one, they must admit either that He is God pure and simple, and thus reduce the incarnation to a mere pretence, or that He is only man, according to Nestorius. And how then about His being "perfect in divinity and perfect in humanity"? And when can Christ be said to be of two natures, if they hold that He is of one composite nature after the union? For it is surely clear to every one that before the union Christ's nature was one.

But this is what leads the heretics [9] astray, viz., that they look upon nature and subsistence as the same thing [1]. For when we speak of the nature of men as one [2], observe that in saying this we are not looking to the question of soul and body. For when we compare together the soul and the body it cannot be said that they are of one nature. But since there are very many subsistences of men, and yet all have the same kind of nature [3]: for all are composed of soul and body, and all have part in the nature of the soul, and possess the essence of the body, and the common form: we speak of the one nature of these very many and different subsistences; while each subsistence, to wit, has two natures, and fulfils itself in two natures, namely, soul and body.

But [4] a common form cannot be admitted in the case of our Lord Jesus Christ. For neither was there ever, nor is there, nor will there ever be another Christ constituted of deity and humanity, and existing in deity and humanity at once perfect God and perfect man. And thus in the case of our Lord Jesus Christ we cannot speak of one nature made up of divinity and humanity, as we do in the case of the individual made up of soul and body [5]. For in the latter case we have to do with an individual, but Christ is not an individual. For there is no predicable form of Christlihood, so to speak, that He possesses. And therefore we hold that there has been a union of two perfect natures, one divine and one human; not with disorder or confusion, or intermixture [6], or commingling, as is said by the God-accursed Dioscorus and by Eutyches [7] and Severus, and all that impious company: and not in a personal or relative manner, or as a matter of dignity or agreement in will, or equality in honour, or identity in name, or good pleasure, as Nestorius, hated of God, said, and Diodorus and Theodorus of Mopsuestia, and their diabolical tribe: but by synthesis, that is, in subsistence, without change or confusion or alteration or difference or separation, and we confess that in two perfect natures there is but one subsistence of the Son of God incarnate [8]; holding that there is one and the same subsistence belong-

---

[4] *Max Epist. ad Joan. cubic.* p. 279.
[5] *Ibid.* p. 286.
[6] ἐξ ἑτέρων τὰ αὐτά. *Cod. R.* 3 reads ταῦτα. See also *Cyril, Ep.* 2 *ad Success.*
[7] Cf. *Niceph. Call., Hist.* xviii. 46.
[8] *Eulog. apud Max.,* t. ii. p. 145.

[9] Cf. *Sever., Ep.* 2 *ad Joannem.*
[1] *Anast. Sinaita, in* Ὁδηγῷ, ch. 9; *Leontius, contr. Nest. et Eutych.*
[2] *Greg. Naz., Ep. ad Cled.,* 1.
[3] τὸν αὐτὸν ἐπιδέχονται λόγον τῆς φύσεως; perhaps—*all admit the same account of the nature,—all can be dealt with in the same way in respect of nature.*
[4] *Leontius, Contr. Sev. et Eutych. Max. loc. cit.,* p. 277.
[5] Reading ὥσπερ ἐπὶ ἀτόμου, &c. These words are omitted in *Cod. S. Hil. Reg.* 10, Colb. 3, and N.
[6] ἢ σύγκρασιν, ἢ ἀνάκρασιν. The MSS. omit the latter.
[7] The word Εὐτυχῆς. however, is omitted by the best copies.
[8] *Procl., Epist.* 2 *ad Arm.*

ing to His divinity and His humanity, and granting that the two natures are preserved in Him after the union, but we do not hold that each is separate and by itself, but that they are united to each other in one compound subsistence. For we look upon the union as essential, that is, as true and not imaginary. We say that it is essential[9], moreover, not in the sense of two natures resulting in one compound nature, but in the sense of a true union of them in one compound subsistence of the Son of God, and we hold that their essential difference is preserved. For the created remaineth created, and the uncreated, uncreated : the mortal remaineth mortal; the immortal, immortal : the circumscribed, circumscribed : the uncircumscribed, uncircumscribed : the visible, visible : the invisible, invisible. "The one part is all glorious with wonders : while the other is the victim of insults[1]."

Moreover, the Word appropriates to Himself the attributes of humanity : for all that pertains to His holy flesh is His : and He imparts to the flesh His own attributes by way of communication[2] in virtue of the interpenetration of the parts[3] one with another, and the oneness according to subsistence, and inasmuch as He Who lived and acted both as God and as man, taking to Himself either form and holding intercourse with the other form, was one and the same[4]. Hence it is that the Lord of Glory is said to have been crucified[5], although His divine nature never endured the Cross, and that the Son of Man is allowed to have been in heaven before the Passion, as the Lord Himself said[6]. For the Lord of Glory is one and the same with Him Who is in nature and in truth the Son of Man, that is, Who became man, and both His wonders and His sufferings are known to us, although His wonders were worked in His divine capacity, and His sufferings endured as man. For we know that, just as is His one subsistence, so is the essential difference of the nature preserved. For how could difference be preserved if the very things that differ from one another are not preserved ? For difference is the difference between things that differ. In so far as Christ's natures differ from one another, that is, in the matter of essence, we hold that Christ unites in Himself two extremes : in respect of His divinity

He is connected with the Father and the Spirit, while in respect of His humanity He is connected with His mother and all mankind. And in so far as His natures are united, we hold that He differs from the Father and the Spirit on the one hand, and from the mother and the rest of mankind on the other. For the natures are united in His subsistence, having one compound subsistence, in which He differs from the Father and the Spirit, and also from the mother and us.

CHAPTER IV.

Concerning the manner of the Mutual Communication[8].

Now we have often said already that essence is one thing and subsistence another, and that essence signifies the common and general form[9] of subsistences of the same kind, such as God, man, while subsistence marks the individual, that is to say, Father, Son, Holy Spirit, or Peter, Paul. Observe, then, that the names, divinity and humanity, denote essences or natures : while the names, God and man, are applied both in connection with natures, as when we say that God is incomprehensible essence, and that God is one, and with reference to subsistences, that which is more specific having the name of the more general applied to it, as when the Scripture says, *Therefore God, thy God, hath anointed thee*[1], or again, *There was a certain man in the land of Uz*[2], for it was only to Job that reference was made.

Therefore, in the case of our Lord Jesus Christ, seeing that we recognise that He has two natures but only one subsistence compounded of both, when we contemplate His natures we speak of His divinity and His humanity, but when we contemplate the subsistence compounded of the natures we sometimes use terms that have reference to His double nature, as "Christ," and "at once God and man," and "God Incarnate;" and sometimes those that imply only one of His natures, as "God" alone, or "Son of God," and "man" alone, or "Son of Man;" sometimes using names that imply His loftiness and sometimes those that imply His lowliness. For He Who is alike God and man is one, being the former from the Father ever without[3] cause, but having become the latter afterwards for His love towards man[4].

---

9 *Greg. Naz., Hom.* 5. See also John's *Dialect.*, 65.
1 *Leo papa, Epist.* 10, ch. 4.
2 κατὰ τὸν ἀντιδόσεως τρόπον, *in the way of a communication of properties.*
3 διὰ τὴν εἰς ἄλληλα τῶν μερῶν περιχώρησιν. See *Leont., De Sect.*, 7, *Contr. Nest. et Eutych.*, I.
4 *Leo papa, Epist.* 10, ch. 4.   5 1 Cor. ii. 8.
6 St. John iii. 13.

8 Cf. *Athan., De Salut. adv. Christi* ; *Greg. Naz., Orat.* 38; *Greg. Nyss., Contr. Apoll.* ; *Leont., Contr. Nestor. et Eutych.*, bk. 1; *Thomas Aquinas, III., quæst.* 16, art. 4, 5.
9 εἶδος, *form, class, species.*
1 Ps. xlv. 7.   2 Job i. 1.
3 ἀεὶ ἀναιτίως ἐκ Πατρός.   4 *Greg. Naz., Orat.* 35.

When, then, we speak of His divinity we do not ascribe to it the properties of humanity. For we do not say that His divinity is subject to passion or created. Nor, again, do we predicate of His flesh or of His humanity the properties of divinity : for we do not say that His flesh or His humanity is uncreated. But when we speak of His subsistence, whether we give it a name implying both natures, or one that refers to only one of them, we still attribute to it the properties of both natures. For Christ, which name implies both natures, is spoken of as at once God and man, created and uncreated, subject to suffering and incapable of suffering : and when He is named Son of God and God, in reference to only one of His natures, He still keeps the properties of the co-existing nature, that is, the flesh, being spoken of as God who suffers, and as the Lord of Glory crucified [5], not in respect of His being God but in respect of His being at the same time man. Likewise also when He is called Man and Son of Man, He still keeps the properties and glories of the divine nature, a child before the ages, and man who knew no beginning ; it is not, however, as child or man but as God that He is before the ages, and became a child in the end. And this is the manner of the mutual communication, either nature giving in exchange to the other its own properties through the identity of the subsistence and the interpenetration of the parts with one another. Accordingly we can say of Christ : *This our God was seen upon the earth and lived amongst men* [6], and *This man is uncreated and impassible and uncircumscribed.*

CHAPTER V.

Concerning the number of the Natures.

In the case, therefore, of the Godhead [7] we confess that there is but one nature, but hold that there are three subsistences actually existing, and hold that all things that are of nature and essence are simple, and recognise the difference of the subsistences only in the three properties of independence of cause and Fatherhood, of dependence on cause and Sonship, of dependence on cause and procession [8]. And we know further that these are indivisible and inseparable from each other and united into one, and interpenetrating one another without confusion. Yea, I repeat, united

without confusion, for they are three although united, and they are distinct, although inseparable. For although each has an independent existence, that is to say, is a perfect subsistence and has an individuality of its own, that is, has a special mode of existence, yet they are one in essence and in the natural properties, and in being inseparable and indivisible from the Father's subsistence, and they both are and are said to be one God. In the very same way, then, in the case of the divine and ineffable dispensation [9], exceeding all thought and comprehension, I mean the Incarnation of the One God the Word of the Holy Trinity, and our Lord Jesus Christ, we confess that there are two natures, one divine and one human, joined together with one another and united in subsistence [1], so that one compound subsistence is formed out of the two natures : but we hold that the two natures are still preserved, even after the union, in the one compound subsistence, that is, in the one Christ, and that these exist in reality and have their natural properties ; for they are united without confusion, and are distinguished and enumerated without being separable. And just as the three subsistences of the Holy Trinity are united without confusion, and are distinguished and enumerated without being separable [2], the enumeration not entailing division or separation or alienation or cleavage among them (for we recognise one God the Father, the Son and the Holy Spirit), so in the same way the natures of Christ also, although they are united, yet are united without confusion ; and although they interpenetrate one another, yet they do not permit of change or transmutation of one into the other [3]. For each keeps its own natural individuality strictly unchanged. And thus it is that they can be enumerated without the enumeration introducing division. For Christ, indeed, is one, perfect both in divinity and in humanity. For it is not the nature of number to cause separation or unity, but its nature is to indicate the quantity of what is enumerated, whether these are united or separated : for we have unity, for instance, when fifty stones compose a wall, but we have separation when the fifty stones lie on the ground ; and again, we have unity when we speak of coal having two natures, namely, fire and wood, but we have separation in that the nature of fire is one thing, and the nature of wood another thing ;

---

5 1 Cor. ii. 8.
6 Baruch iii. 38 : these words are absent in many MSS.
7 *Leont., Resp. ad argum. Sever.*
8 For καὶ τῇ αἰτιατῇ καὶ υἱκῇ, καὶ τῇ αἰτιατῇ καὶ ἐκπορευτῇ we get καὶ τῇ αἰτιατικῇ, καὶ υἱκῇ, καὶ πορευτῇ in *Cod. Colb. D,* Cod. Reg. 3, and so Faber also.

9 οἰκονομίας, *incarnation.*
1 *Leont., Resp. ad argum. Sever.*
2 See *Leont., Act. 7. De Sect.,* with reference to one of the arguments of the Nestorians ; also *Greg. Naz., Orat.* 36 ; *Max., Ep.* 1 *ad Joan. Cubic.*
3 *Infr.* ch. vii. : Basil, *Epist.* 4; and Bk. *De Spir. Sanct* ch. 17

for these things are united and separated not by number, but in another way. So, then, just as even though the three subsistences of the Godhead are united with each other, we cannot speak of them as one subsistence because we should confuse and do away with the difference between the subsistences, so also we cannot speak of the two natures of Christ as one nature, united though they are in subsistence, because we should then confuse and do away with and reduce to nothing the difference between the two natures.

CHAPTER VI.

That in one of its subsistences the divine nature is united in its entirety to the human nature, in its entirety and not only part to part.

What is common and general is predicated of the included particulars. Essence, then, is common as being a form [4], while subsistence is particular. It is particular not as though it had part of the nature and had not the rest, but particular in a numerical sense, as being individual. For it is in number and not in nature that the difference between subsistences is said to lie. Essence, therefore, is predicated of subsistence, because in each subsistence of the same form the essence is perfect. Wherefore subsistences do not differ from each other in essence but in the accidents which indeed are the characteristic properties, but characteristic of subsistence and not of nature. For indeed they define subsistence as essence along with accidents. So that the subsistence contains both the general and the particular, and has an independent existence [5], while essence has not an independent existence but is contemplated in the subsistences. Accordingly when one of the subsistences suffers, the whole essence, being capable of suffering [6], is held to have suffered in one of its subsistences as much as the subsistence suffered, but it does not necessarily follow, however, that all the subsistences of the same class should suffer along with the suffering subsistence.

Thus, therefore, we confess that the nature of the Godhead is wholly and perfectly in each of its subsistences, wholly in the Father, wholly in the Son, and wholly in the Holy Spirit. Wherefore also the Father is perfect God, the Son is perfect God, and the Holy Spirit is perfect God. In like manner, too, in the Incarnation of the Trinity of the One God the Word of the Holy Trinity, we hold

that in one of its subsistences the nature of the Godhead is wholly and perfectly united with the whole nature of humanity, and not part united to part [7]. The divine Apostle in truth says that *in Him dwelleth all the fulness of the Godhead bodily* [8], that is to say in His flesh. And His divinely-inspired disciple, Dionysius, who had so deep a knowledge of things divine, said that the Godhead as a whole had fellowship with us in one of its own subsistences [9]. But we shall not be driven to hold that all the subsistences of the Holy Godhead, to wit the three, are made one in subsistence with all the subsistences of humanity. For in no other respect did the Father and the Holy Spirit take part in the incarnation of God the Word than according to good will and pleasure. But we hold that to the whole of human nature the whole essence of the Godhead was united. For God the Word omitted none of the things which He implanted in our nature when He formed us in the beginning, but took them all upon Himself, body and soul both intelligent and rational, and all their properties. For the creature that is devoid of one of these is not man. But He in His fulness took upon Himself me in my fulness, and was united whole to whole that He might in His grace bestow salvation on the whole man. For what has not been taken cannot be healed [1].

The Word of God [2], then, was united to flesh through the medium of mind which is intermediate between the purity of God and the grossness of flesh [3]. For the mind holds sway over soul and body, but while the mind is the purest part of the soul God is that of the mind. And when it is allowed [4] by that which is more excellent, the mind of Christ gives proof of its own authority [5], but it is under the dominion of and obedient to that which is more excellent, and does those things which the divine will purposes.

Further the mind has become the seat of the divinity united with it in subsistence, just as is evidently the case with the body too, not as an inmate [6], which is the impious error into which the heretics fall when they say that one bushel cannot contain two bushels, for they are judging what is immaterial by material standards. How indeed could Christ be called perfect God and perfect man, and be said to be of like essence with the Father and

4 εἶδος, *form, class, species.*
5 These words are found only in *Cod. Reg.* 2927.
6 The words οὐσία παθητή and πέπονθε are omitted in some editions.

7 Against Arius, Apollinaris and the Severians.
8 Col. ii. 9.   9 *Dion., De div. nom.,* ch. 2.
1 *Athan., De salut. adv. Christ: Greg. Naz., Epist.* 1 *ad Cled. et Orat.* 1 : *Cyril, in* John viii.
2 Cf. *Greg. Naz., Orat.* 1, &c.
3 *Greg., Orat.* 1, 38—51.
4 περιχωρεῖται ὑπὸ τοῦ κρείττονος.
5 *Infr.,* ch. xviii.
6 οὐ σύνοικος. It is proposed to read αὐτοῦ σύνοικος, or ὡς σύνοικος.

with us, if only part of the divine nature is joined in Him to part of the human nature [7]?

We hold, moreover, that our nature has been raised from the dead and has ascended to the heavens and taken its seat at the right hand of the Father: not that all the persons of men have risen from the dead and taken their seat at the right hand of the Father, but that this has happened to the whole of our nature in the subsistence of Christ [8]. Verily the divine Apostle says, *God hath raised us up together and made us sit together in Christ* [9].

And this further we hold, that the union took place through common essences. For every essence is common to the subsistences contained in it, and there cannot be found a partial and particular nature, that is to say, essence: for otherwise we would have to hold that the same subsistences are at once the same and different in essence, and that the Holy Trinity in respect of the divinity is at once the same and different in essence. So then the same nature is to be observed in each of the subsistences, and when we said that the nature of the word became flesh, as did the blessed Athanasius and Cyrillus, we mean that the divinity was joined to the flesh. Hence we cannot say "The nature of the Word suffered;" for the divinity in it did not suffer, but we say that the human nature, not by any means, however, meaning [1] all the subsistences of men, suffered in Christ, and we confess further that Christ suffered in His human nature. So that when we speak of the nature of the Word we mean the Word Himself. And the Word has both the general element of essence and the particular element of subsistence.

CHAPTER VII.

Concerning the one compound subsistence of God the Word.

We hold then that the divine subsistence of God the Word existed before all else and is without time and eternal, simple and uncompound, uncreated, incorporeal, invisible, intangible, uncircumscribed, possessing all the Father possesses, since He is of the same essence with Him, differing from the Father's subsistence in the manner of His generation and the relation of the Father's subsistence, being perfect also and at no time separated from the Father's subsistence: and in these last days, without leaving the Father's bosom, took up His abode in an uncircumscribed manner in the womb of the holy Virgin, without the instrumentality of seed, and in an incomprehensible manner known only to Himself, and causing the flesh derived from the holy Virgin to subsist in the very subsistence that was before all the ages.

So then He was both in all things and above all things and also dwelt in the womb of the holy Mother of God, but in it by the energy of the incarnation. He therefore became flesh and He took upon Himself thereby the first-fruits of our compound nature [2], viz., the flesh animated with the intelligent and rational soul, so that the very subsistence of God the Word was changed into the subsistence of the flesh, and the subsistence of the Word, which was formerly simple, became compound [3], yea compounded of two perfect natures, divinity and humanity, and bearing the characteristic and distinctive property of the divine Sonship of God the Word in virtue of which it is distinguished from the Father and the Spirit, and also the characteristic and distinctive properties of the flesh, in virtue of which it differs from the Mother and the rest of mankind, bearing further the properties of the divine nature in virtue of which it is united to the Father and the Spirit, and the marks of the human nature in virtue of which it is united to the Mother and to us. And further it differs from the Father and the Spirit and the Mother and us in being at once God and man. For this we know to be the most special property of the subsistence of Christ.

Wherefore we confess Him, even after the incarnation, the one Son of God, and likewise Son of Man, one Christ, one Lord, the only-begotten Son and Word of God, one Lord Jesus. We reverence His two generations, one from the Father before time and beyond cause and reason and time and nature, and one in the end for our sake, and like to us and above us; for our sake because it was for our salvation, like to us in that He was man born of woman [4] at full time [5], and above us because it was not by seed, but by the Holy Spirit and the Holy Virgin Mary [6], transcending the laws of parturition. We proclaim Him not as God only, devoid of our humanity, nor yet as man only, stripping Him of His divinity, nor as two distinct persons, but as one and the same, at once God and man, perfect God and perfect man, wholly God and wholly man, the same being wholly God, even though He was also

7 *Greg., Epist. 1 ad Cled.*
8 *Athan., De salut. adv. Christ.*   9 Ephes. ii. 6.
1 Text, ὑπεμφαίνοντες. Variant, ἐμφαίνομεν.

2 ἀπαρχὴν τοῦ ἡμετέρου φυράματος.
3 σύνθετον γενέσθαι τὴν πρότερον ἀπλῆν οὖσαν τοῦ Λόγου ὑπόστασιν, σύνθετον δὲ ἐκ δύο τελείων φύσεων.
4 Text, καὶ χρόνῳ κινήσεως. Various readings, καὶ τρόπῳ κινήσεως: καὶ χρόνῳ καὶ κινήσει: καὶ νόμῳ κινήσεως.
5 Cf. *Ruf., Expos. Symb.*; Epiph., in the epilogue to his *De Hær.*; *Joan. Scyth., Epist. Dionys.* 4.
6 Μαρίας is absent in most MSS.

flesh and wholly man, even though He was also most high God. And by "perfect God" and "perfect man" we mean to emphasize the fulness and unfailingness of the natures : while by "wholly God" and "wholly man" we mean to lay stress on the singularity and individuality of the subsistence.

And we confess also that there is one incarnate nature of God the Word, expressing by the word "incarnate 7 " the essence of the flesh, according to the blessed Cyril 8. And so the Word was made flesh and yet did not abandon His own proper immateriality : He became wholly flesh and yet remained wholly uncircumscribed. So far as He is body He is diminished and contracted into narrow limits, but inasmuch as He is God He is uncircumscribed, His flesh not being coextensive with His uncircumscribed divinity.

He is then wholly perfect God, but yet is not simply 9 God : for He is not only God but also man. And He is also wholly 1 perfect man but not simply 2 man, for He is not only man but also God. For "simply 2" here has reference to His nature, and "wholly 1" to His subsistence, just as "another thing" would refer to nature, while "another 3" would refer to subsistence 4.

But observe 5 that although we hold that the natures of the Lord permeate one another, yet we know that the permeation springs from the divine nature. For it is that that penetrates and permeates all things, as it wills, while nothing penetrates it : and it is it, too, that imparts to the flesh its own peculiar glories, while abiding itself impassible and without participation in the affections of the flesh. For if the sun imparts to us his energies and yet does not participate in ours, how much the rather must this be true of the Creator and Lord of the Sun 6.

CHAPTER VIII.

In reply to those who ask whether 7 the natures of the Lord are brought under a continuous or a discontinuous quantity 8.

If any one asks concerning the natures of the Lord if they are brought under a con-

tinuous or discontinuous quantity 9, we will say that the natures of the Lord are neither one body nor one superficies 1, nor one line, nor time, nor place, so as to be reduced to a continuous quantity. For these are the things that are reckoned continuously.

Further note that number deals with things that differ, and it is quite impossible to enumerate things that differ from one another in no respect : and just so far as they differ are they enumerated : for instance, Peter and Paul are not counted separately in so far as they are one. For since they are one in respect of their essence they cannot be spoken of as two natures, but as they differ in respect of subsistence they are spoken of as two subsistences. So that number deals with differences, and just as the differing objects differ from one another so far they are enumerated.

The natures of the Lord, then, are united without confusion so far as regards subsistence, and they are divided without separation according to the method and manner of difference. And it is not according to the manner in which they are united that they are enumerated, for it is not in respect of subsistence that we hold that there are two natures of Christ : but according to the manner in which they are divided without separation they are enumerated, for it is in respect of the method and manner of difference that there are two natures of Christ. For being united in subsistence and permeating one another, they are united without confusion, each preserving throughout its own peculiar and natural difference. Hence, since they are enumerated according to the manner of difference, and that alone, they must be brought under a discontinuous quantity.

Christ, therefore 2, is one, perfect God and perfect man : and Him we worship along with the Father and the Spirit, with one obeisance, adoring even His immaculate flesh and not holding that the flesh is not meet for worship : for in fact it is worshipped in the one subsistence of the Word, which indeed became subsistence for it. But in this we do not do homage to that which is created. For we worship Him, not as mere flesh, but as flesh united with divinity, and because His two natures are brought under the one person and one subsistence of God the Word. I fear to touch coal because of the fire bound up with the wood. I worship the twofold nature of Christ because of the divinity that is in Him bound up with flesh. For I do not

7 *Expositio fidei a Patribus Nicænis contra Paul. Samos. III. p. conc. Ephes.*
8 *Commonit. ad Eulog. et Epist. 2 ad Success.* ; cf. *supr.* ch. vi. *et infr.* ch. xi.
9 ὅλος μὲν οὖν ἐστι Θεὸς τέλειος, οὐχ ὅλον δὲ Θεός.
1 ὅλος.   2 ὅλον.
3 *Greg. Naz., Orat.* 51.
4 The following is added in R. 2927: ἐν πᾶσι μὲν ἦν, καὶ ὑπὲρ τὰ πάντα, καὶ ἐν τῇ γάστρι τῆς Θεομήτορος, ἀλλ' ἐν ταύτῃ τε, ἐνεργείᾳ τῆς σαρκώσεως. This is assuredly an interpolation.
5 *v. supr.* ch. iii.   6 *Leontius de sectis, Act.* 3.
7 Directed against the Severians. See *Leont., De Sect., Act.* 7 ; *Greg. Naz., Orat.* 37.
8 ὑπὸ τὸ συνεχὲς πόσον ἀνάγονται αἱ τοῦ Κυρίου φύσεις, ἢ ὑπὸ τὸ διωρισμένον.

9 Text, ἀνάγονται. Variants, ἀναφέροιτο and διαφέροιτο.
1 μία ἐπιφάνεια.
2 *Cyril, De Anath.* 8 *cont. Theod.*

introduce a fourth person [3] into the Trinity. God-forbid! but I confess one person of God the Word and of His flesh, and the Trinity remains Trinity, even after the incarnation of the Word.

In reply [4] to those who ask whether the two natures are brought under a continuous or a discontinuous quantity.

The natures of the Lord are neither one body nor one superficies, nor one line, nor place, nor time, so as to be brought under a continuous quantity : for these are the things that are reckoned continuously. But the natures of the Lord are united without confusion in respect of subsistence, and are divided without separation according to the method and manner of difference. And according to the manner in which they are united they are not enumerated. For we do not say that the natures of Christ are two subsistences or two in respect of subsistence. But according to the manner in which they are divided without division, are they enumerated. For there are two natures according to the method and manner of difference. For being united in subsistence and permeating one another they are united without confusion, neither having been changed into the other, but each preserving its own natural difference even after the union. For that which is created remained created, and that which is uncreated, uncreated. By the manner of difference, then, and in that alone, they are enumerated, and thus are brought under discontinuous quantity. For things which differ from each other in no respect cannot be enumerated, but just so far as they differ are they enumerated ; for instance, Peter and Paul are not enumerated in those respects in which they are one : for being one in respect of their essence they are not two natures nor are they so spoken of. But inasmuch as they differ in subsistence they are spoken of as two subsistences. So that difference is the cause of number.

CHAPTER IX.

In reply to the question whether there is any Nature that has no Subsistence.

For although [5] there is no nature without subsistence, nor essence apart from person

(since in truth it is in persons and subsistences that essence and nature are to be contemplated), yet it does not necessarily follow that the natures that are united to one another in subsistence should have each its own proper subsistence. For after they have come together into one subsistence, it is possible that neither should they be without subsistence, nor should each have its own peculiar subsistence, but that both should have one and the same subsistence [6]. For since one and the same subsistence of the Word has become the subsistence of the natures, neither of them is permitted to be without subsistence, nor are they allowed to have subsistences that differ from each other, or to have sometimes the subsistence of this nature and sometimes of that, but always without division or separation they both have the same subsistence—a subsistence which is not broken up into parts or divided, so that one part should belong to this, and one to that, but which belongs wholly to this and wholly to that in its absolute entirety. For the flesh of God the Word did not subsist as an independent subsistence, nor did there arise another subsistence besides that of God the Word, but as it existed in that it became rather a subsistence which subsisted in another, than one which was an independent subsistence. Wherefore, neither does it lack subsistence altogether, nor yet is there thus introduced into the Trinity another subsistence.

CHAPTER X.
Concerning the Trisagium (" the Thrice Holy").

This being so [7], we declare that the addition which the vain-minded Peter the Fuller made to the Trisagium or " Thrice Holy " Hymn is blasphemous [8]; for it introduces a fourth person into the Trinity, giving a separate place to the Son of God, Who is the truly subsisting power of the Father, and a separate place to Him Who was crucified as though He were different from the " Mighty One," or as though the Holy Trinity was considered passible, and the Father and the Holy Spirit suffered on the Cross along with the Son. Have done with this blasphemous [9] and nonsensical interpolation! For we hold the words " Holy God " to refer to the Father, without limiting the title of divinity to Him alone, but acknowledging also as God the Son and the Holy Spirit : and the words

---

3 The Apollinarians attacked the orthodox as ἀνθρωπολάτραι, *man-worshippers*, and as making the Trinity a Quaternity by their doctrine of two perfect natures in Christ. See *Greg. Naz., Ep.* 1 *ad Cled.* ; *Athanas., Ep ad Epictet.* ; *Anastas. Antioch., De Operationibus* ; *Cyril, Contr. Nestor.* 1.
4 See Migne on the position of this section.
5 Another allegation of the Severian party is in view here. See *Leont., De Sect., Act.* 7, *Contr. Nestor. et Eutych.* I. ; *John of Dam., Dialect.* 29.

6 *Leont., De sect., Act* 7.
7 *Dam., Epist. ad Jord. Archim.*
8 Text, βλάσφημον. Variant, βλασφημίαν.

"Holy and Mighty" we ascribe to the Son, without stripping the Father and the Holy Spirit of might: and the words "Holy and Immortal" we attribute to the Holy Spirit, without depriving the Father and the Son of immortality. For, indeed, we apply all the divine names simply and unconditionally to each of the subsistences in imitation of the divine Apostle's words . *But to us there is but one God, the Father, of Whom are all things, and we in Him: and one Lord Jesus Christ by Whom are all things, and we by Him* [1] [2]. And, nevertheless, we follow Gregory the Theologian [3] when he says, "But to us there is but one God, the Father, of Whom are all things, and one Lord Jesus Christ, through Whom are all things, and one Holy Spirit, in Whom are all things :" for the words " of Whom" and "through Whom" and "in Whom" do not divide the natures (for neither the prepositions nor the order of the names could ever be changed), but they characterise the properties of one unconfused nature. And this becomes clear from the fact that they are once more gathered into one, if only one reads with care these words of the same Apostle, *Of Him and through Him and in Him are all things: to Him be the glory for ever and ever. Amen* [4].

For that the "Trisagium" refers not to the Son alone [5], but to the Holy Trinity, the divine and saintly Athanasius and Basil and Gregory, and all the band of the divinely-inspired Fathers bear witness: because, as a matter of fact, by the threefold holiness the Holy Seraphim suggest to us the three subsistences of the superessential Godhead. But by the one Lordship they denote the one essence and dominion of the supremely-divine Trinity. Gregory the Theologian of a truth says [6], "Thus, then, the Holy of Holies, which is completely veiled by the Seraphim, and is glorified with three consecrations, meet together in one lordship and one divinity." This was the most beautiful and sublime philosophy of still another of our predecessors.

Ecclesiastical historians [7], then, say that once when the people of Constantinople were offering prayers to God to avert a threatened calamity [8], during Proclus' tenure of the office

of Archbishop, it happened that a boy was snatched up from among the people, and was taught by angelic teachers the "Thrice Holy" Hymn, "Thou Holy God, Holy and Mighty One, Holy and Immortal One, have mercy upon us:" and when once more he was restored to earth, he told what he had learned, and all the people sang the Hymn, and so the threatened calamity was averted. And in the fourth holy and great Œcumenical Council, I mean the one at Chalcedon, we are told that it was in this form that the Hymn was sung; for the minutes of this holy assembly so record it [9]. It is, therefore, a matter for laughter and ridicule that this "Thrice Holy" Hymn, taught us by the angels, and confirmed by the averting of calamity [1], ratified and established by so great an assembly of the holy Fathers, and sung first by the Seraphim as a declaration of the three subsistences of the Godhead, should be mangled and forsooth emended to suit the view of the stupid Fuller as though he were higher than the Seraphim. But oh ! the arrogance ! not to say folly ! But we say it thus, though demons should rend us in pieces, "Do Thou, Holy God, Holy and Mighty One, Holy and Immortal One, have mercy upon us."

CHAPTER XI.

Concerning the Nature as viewed in Species and in Individual, and concerning the difference between Union and Incarnation: and how this is to be understood, "The one Nature of God the Word Incarnate."

Nature [2] is regarded either abstractly as a matter of pure thought [3] (for it has no independent existence): or commonly in all subsistences of the same species as their bond of union, and is then spoken of as nature viewed in species: or universally as the same, but with the addition of accidents, in one subsistence, and is spoken of as nature viewed in the individual, this being identical with nature viewed in species [4]. God the Word Incarnate, therefore, did not assume the nature that is regarded as an abstraction in pure thought (for this is not incarnation, but only an imposture and a figment of incarnation), nor the nature viewed in species (for He did not

---

[1] 1 Cor. viii. 5.
[2] These words which refer to the Holy Spirit are absent in R. 2930 and in 1 Cor. viii., but are present in other Codices and in *Basil, De Spirit. Sancto*, and in *Greg. Naziauz., Orat.* 39, and further in the Damascene himself in *Parallel.* and elsewhere, and could not be omitted here.
[3] *Orat.* 39.   [4] Rom. xi. 36.
[5] *Vid. Epist. ad Jordan.*
[6] *Orat.* 42. at the beginning.
[7] *Epist. ad Petrum Fullonem ; Theoph., Ad Arn.* 5930.
[8] See *Niceph. Call., Hist.* xviii. 51.

[9] *Conc. Chal., Act.* 1, at the end.
[1] In *Cod. S. Hil.* is written above the line ἢ θεηλάτου ὀργῆς παύσει, which explains the author's meaning.
[2] *Niceph. Call., Hist.* xviii. 51, speaks of this Hymn and also the φῶς ἱλαρόν as coming from the Apostles themselves. The writer of the Life of Basil supposed to be Amphilochius of Iconium, declares that the *Trisagium* was recited by Basil at Nicæa.
[3] ἡ ψιλῇ θεωρίᾳ κατανοεῖται.
[4] This division is absent in some copies and is not restored in the old translation, but is not superfluous.

assume all the subsistences) : but the nature viewed in the individual, which is identical with that viewed in species. For He took on Himself the elements of our compound nature, and these not as having an independent existence or as being originally an individual, and in this way assumed by Him, but as existing in His own subsistence. For the subsistence of God the Word in itself became the subsistence of the flesh, and accordingly " the Word became flesh [5] " clearly without any change, and likewise the flesh became Word without alteration, and God became man. For the Word is God, and man is God, through having one and the same subsistence. And so it is possible to speak of the same thing as being the nature of the Word and the nature in the individual. For it signifies strictly and exclusively neither the individual, that is, the subsistence, nor the common nature of the subsistences, but the common nature as viewed and presented in one of the subsistences.

Union, then, is one thing, and incarnation is something quite different. For union signifies only the conjunction, but not at all that with which union is effected. But incarnation (which is just the same as if one said " the putting on of man's nature ") signifies that the conjunction is with flesh, that is to say, with man, just as the heating of iron [6] implies its union with fire. Indeed, the blessed Cyril himself, when he is interpreting the phrase, " one nature of God the Word Incarnate," says in the second epistle to Sucensus, ' For if we simply said ' the one nature of the Word ' and then were silent, and did not add the word ' incarnate,' but, so to speak, quite excluded the dispensation [7], there would be some plausibility in the question they feign to ask, ' If one nature is the whole, what becomes of the perfection in humanity, or how has the essence [8] like us come to exist ? ' But inasmuch as the perfection in humanity and the disclosure of the essence like us are conveyed in the word ' incarnate,' they must cease from relying on a mere straw " Here, then, he placed the nature of the Word over nature itself. For if He had received nature instead of subsistence, it would not have been absurd to have omitted the " incarnate." For when we say simply one subsistence of God the Word, we do not err [9]. In like manner, also, Leontius the Byzantine [1] considered this phrase to refer to nature, and not to subsistence. But in the Defence which he wrote

in reply to the attacks that Theodoret made on the second anathema, the blessed Cyril [2] says this : " The nature of the Word, that is, the subsistence, which is the Word itself." So that " the nature of the Word " means neither the subsistence alone, nor " the common nature of the subsistence," but " the common nature viewed as a whole in the subsistence of the Word."

It has been said, then, that the nature of the Word became flesh, that is, was united to flesh : but that the nature of the Word suffered in the flesh we have never heard up till now, though we have been taught that Christ suffered in the flesh. So that " the nature of the Word " does not mean " the subsistence." It remains, therefore, to say that to become flesh is to be united with the flesh, while the Word having become flesh means that the very subsistence of the Word became without change the subsistence of the flesh. It has also been said that God became man, and man God. For the Word which is God became without alteration man. But that the Godhead became man, or became flesh, or put on the nature of man, this we have never heard. This, indeed, we have learned, that the Godhead was united to humanity in one of its subsistences, and it has been stated that God took on a different form or essence [3], to wit our own. For the name God is applicable to each of the subsistences, but we cannot use the term Godhead in reference to subsistence. For we are never told that the Godhead is the Father alone, or the Son alone, or the Holy Spirit alone. For " Godhead " implies " nature," while " Father " implies subsistence. just as " Humanity " implies nature, and " Peter " subsistence. But " God " indicates the common element of the nature, and is applicable derivatively to each of the subsistences, just as " man " is. For He Who has divine nature is God, and he who has human nature is man.

Besides all this, notice [4] that the Father and the Holy Spirit take no part at all in the incarnation of the Word except in connection with the miracles, and in respect of good will and purpose.

CHAPTER XII.

That the holy Virgin is the Mother of God : an argument directed against the Nestorians.

Moreover we proclaim the holy Virgin to be

---

5 St. John i. 14.
6 τοῦ σιδήρου is absent in some codices and also in the old translation.
7 τὴν οἰκονομίαν, *the incarnation.*
8 ἡ καθ' ἡμᾶς οὐσία.
9 *Supr.* ch. 6 and 7.   1 *Leont., De sect. Act.* 8.

2 *Cyril, Defens. II., Anath. cont. Theod.*
3 ὁ Θεὸς μορφοῦται, ἤτοι οὐσιοῦται τὸ ἀλλότριον. Gregory of Nazianzum in his *Carmen* used the term οὐσιοῦσθαι of the Word after the assumption of our nature. See also *Dionys., De div. nom.,* ch. 2 ; *Ep. ad Carmen,* 4 ; &c.
4 *Dion., De div. nom.,* ch. 8.

in strict truth [5] the Mother of God [6]. For inasmuch as He who was born of her was true God, she who bare the true God incarnate is the true mother of God. For we hold that God was born of her, not implying that the divinity of the Word received from her the beginning of its being, but meaning that God the Word Himself, Who was begotten of the Father timelessly before the ages, and was with the Father and the Spirit without beginning and through eternity, took up His abode in these last days for the sake of our salvation in the Virgin's womb, and was without change made flesh and born of her. For the holy Virgin did not bare mere man but true God: and not mere God but God incarnate, Who did not bring down His body from Heaven, nor simply passed through the Virgin as channel, but received from her flesh of like essence to our own and subsisting in Himself [7]. For if the body had come down from heaven and had not partaken of our nature, what would have been the use of His becoming man? For the purpose of God the Word becoming man [8] was that the very same nature, which had sinned and fallen and become corrupted, should triumph over the deceiving tyrant and so be freed from corruption, just as the divine apostle puts it, *For since by man came death, by man came also the resurrection of the dead* [9]. If the first is true the second must also be true.

Although [1], however, he says, *The first Adam is of the earth earthy; the second Adam is the Lord from Heaven* [2], he does not say that His body is from heaven, but emphasises the fact that He is not mere man. For, mark, he called Him both Adam and Lord, thus indicating His double nature. For Adam is, being interpreted, earth-born: and it is clear that man's nature is earth-born since he is formed from earth, but the title Lord signifies His divine essence.

And again the Apostle says: *God sent forth His only-begotten Son, made of a woman* [3]. He did not say "made by a woman." Wherefore the divine apostle meant that the only-begotten Son of God and God is the same as He who was made man of the Virgin, and that He who was born of the Virgin is the same as the Son of God and God.

But He was born after the bodily fashion inasmuch as He became man, and did not take up His abode in a man formed beforehand, as in a prophet, but became Himself

in essence and truth man, that is He caused flesh animated with the intelligent and reasonable to subsist in His own subsistence, and Himself became subsistence for it. For this is the meaning of "made of a woman." For how could the very Word of God itself have been made under the law, if He did not become man of like essence with ourselves?

Hence it is with justice and truth that we call the holy Mary the Mother of God. For this name embraces the whole mystery of the dispensation. For if she who bore Him is the Mother of God, assuredly He Who was born of her is God and likewise also man. For how could God, Who was before the ages, have been born of a woman unless He had become man? For the son of man must clearly be man himself. But if He Who was born of a woman is Himself God, manifestly He Who was born of the Father in accordance with the laws of an essence that is divine and knows no beginning, and He Who was in the last days born of the Virgin in accordance with the laws of an essence that has beginning and is subject to time, that is, an essence which is human, must be one and the same. The name in truth signifies the one subsistence and the two natures and the two generations of our Lord Jesus Christ.

But we never say that the holy Virgin is the Mother of Christ [4] because it was in order to do away with the title Mother of God, and to bring dishonour on the Mother of God, who alone is in truth worthy of honour above all creation, that the impure and abominable Judaizing Nestorius [5], that vessel of dishonour, invented this name for an insult [6]. For David the king, and Aaron, the high priest, are also called *Christ* [7], for it is customary to make kings and priests by anointing: and besides every God-inspired man may be called *Christ*, but yet he is not by nature God: yea, the accursed Nestorius insulted Him Who was born of the Virgin by calling Him God-bearer [8]. May it be far from us to speak of or think of Him as God-bearer only [9], Who is in truth God incarnate. For the Word Himself became flesh, having been in truth conceived of the Virgin, but coming forth as God with the assumed nature which, as soon as He was brought forth into being, was deified by Him, so that these three things took place simultaneously, the assumption of our nature, the coming into being, and the

---

5 See especially *Greg. Naz., Ep.* 1 *ad Cled.; Theod., Hær. fab.,* v. 18.
  6 *Greg. Naz., Epist. I. ad Cledon.*   7 *Ibid.*
  8 *Infr.* ch. 18.   9 1 Cor. xv. 21.   1 *Greg. Naz., ibid.*
  2 1 Cor. xv. 47.   3 Gal. iv. 4.

4 χριστοτόκος, as opposed to θεοτόκος.
5 *Cyril, ad Monachos, Epist.* 1.
6 ὡς ἐπηρεαζομένην is absent in Vegelinus.
7 i.e. *Anointed One.*
8 θεοφόρος, *Deigerus.* See *Greg. Naz., Ep.* 2, *ad Cled. Basil, De Spir. Sanc.,* ch. 5, &c.
9 *Cyril, cont. Nest.,* bk. 1.

deification of the assumed nature by the Word. And thus it is that the holy Virgin is thought of and spoken of as the Mother of God, not only because of the nature of the Word, but also because of the deification of man's nature, the miracles of conception and of existence being wrought together, to wit, the conception the Word, and the existence of the flesh in the Word Himself. For the very Mother of God in some marvellous manner was the means of fashioning the Framer of all things and of bestowing manhood on the God and Creator of all, Who deified the nature that He assumed, while the union preserved those things that were united just as they were united, that is to say, not only the divine nature of Christ but also His human nature, not only that which is above us but that which is of us. For He was not first made like us and only later became higher than us, but ever [1] from His first coming into being He existed with the double nature, because He existed in the Word Himself from the beginning of the conception. Wherefore He is human in His own nature, but also, in some marvellous manner, of God and divine. Moreover He has the properties of the living flesh : for by reason of the dispensation [2] the Word received these which are, according to the order of natural motion, truly natural [3].

CHAPTER XIII.

Concerning the properties of the two Natures.

Confessing, then, the same Jesus Christ, our Lord, to be perfect God and perfect man, we hold that the same has all the attributes of the Father save that of being ingenerate, and all the attributes of the first Adam, save only his sin, these attributes being body and the intelligent and rational soul ; and further that He has, corresponding to the two natures, the two sets of natural qualities belonging to the two natures : two natural volitions, one divine and one human, two natural energies, one divine and one human, two natural free-wills, one divine and one human, and two kinds of wisdom and knowledge, one divine and one human. For being of like essence with God and the Father, He wills and energises freely as God, and being also of like essence with us He likewise wills and energises freely as man. For His are the miracles and His also are the passive states.

CHAPTER XIV.

Concerning the volitions and free-wills of our Lord Jesus Christ.

Since, then, Christ has two natures, we hold that He has also two natural wills and two natural energies. But since His two natures have one subsistence, we hold that it is one and the same person who wills and energises naturally in both natures, of which, and in which, and also which is Christ our Lord : and moreover that He wills and energises without separation but as a united whole. For He wills and energises in either form in close communion with the other [4]. For things that have the same essence have also the same will and energy, while things that are different in essence are different in will and energy [5] ; and *vice versa*, things that have the same will and energy have the same essence, while things that are different in will and energy are different in essence.

Wherefore [6] in the case of the Father and Son and Holy Spirit we recognise, from their sameness in will and energy, their sameness in nature. But in the case of the divine dispensation [7] we recognise from their difference in will and energy the difference of the two natures, and as we perceive the difference of the two natures we confess that the wills and energies also are different. For just as the number of the natures of one and the same Christ, when considered and spoken of with piety, do not cause a division of the one Christ but merely bring out the fact that the difference between the natures is maintained even in the union, so it is with the number of wills and energies that belong essentially to His natures. (For He was endowed with the powers of willing and energising in both natures, for the sake of our salvation) It does not introduce division : God forbid ! but merely brings out the fact that the differences between them are safe-guarded and preserved even in the union. For we hold that wills and energies are faculties belonging to nature, not to subsistence ; I mean those faculties of will and energy by which He Who wills and energises does so. For if we allow that they belong to subsistence, we will be forced to say that the three subsistences of the Holy Trinity have different wills and different energies.

For it is to be noted [8] that willing and the manner of willing are not the same thing. For to will is a faculty of nature, just as

---

[1] ἀεί is absent in Vegelinus.
[2] οἰκονομίας λόγῳ, *by reason of the incarnation.*
   Reading γινόμενα, for which Cod. R. 2930 gives ὑπῆρχον.

[4] *Leo, Epist.* 10, *ad Flavian.*
[5] *Max., Disp. cum Pyrrho.*
[6] *Supr.,* bk. ii. ch. 22.
[7] οἰκονομίας. *incarnation.*
[8] *Max., Dial. cum Pyrrho ; Anast.* in Ὁδηγός, ch. 6, p. 40.

seeing is, for all men possess it; but the manner of willing does not depend on nature but on our judgment, just as does also the manner of seeing, whether well or ill. For all men do not will in the same way, nor do they all see in the same way. And this also we will grant in connection with energies. For the manner of willing, or seeing, or energising, is the mode of using the faculties of will and sight and energy, belonging only to him who uses them, and marking him off from others by the generally accepted difference.

Simple willing then is spoken of as volition or the faculty of will [9], being a rational propension [1] and natural will; but in a particular way willing, or that which underlies volition, is the object of will [2], and will dependent on judgment [3]. Further that which has innate in it the faculty of volition is spoken of as capable of willing [4]: as for instance the divine is capable of willing, and the human in like manner. But he who exercises volition, that is to say the subsistence, for instance Peter, is spoken of as willing.

Since, then [5], Christ is one and His subsistence is one, He also Who wills both as God and as man is one and the same. And since He has two natures endowed with volition, inasmuch as they are rational (for whatever is rational is endowed with volition and free-will), we shall postulate two volitions or natural wills in Him. For He in His own person is capable of volition in accordance with both His natures. For He assumed that faculty of volition which belongs naturally to us. And since Christ, Who in His own person wills according to either nature, is one, we shall postulate the same object of will in His case, not as though He wills only those things which He willed naturally as God (for it is no part of Godhead to will to eat or drink and so forth), but as willing also those things which human nature requires for its support [6], and this without involving any opposition in judgment, but simply as the result of the individuality of the natures. For then it was that He thus willed naturally, when His divine volition so willed and permitted the flesh to suffer and do that which was proper to it.

But that volition is implanted in man by nature [7] is manifest from this. Excluding the divine life, there are three forms of life: the vegetative, the sentient, and the intellectual.

The properties of the vegetative life are the functions of nourishment, and growth, and production: that of the sentient life is impulse: and that of the rational and intellectual life is freedom of will. If, then, nourishment belongs by nature to the vegetative life and impulse to the sentient, freedom of will by nature belongs to the rational and intellectual life. But freedom of will is nothing else than volition. The Word, therefore, having become flesh, endowed with life and mind and free-will, became also endowed with volition.

Further, that which is natural is not the result of training: for no one learns how to think, or live, or hunger, or thirst, or sleep. Nor do we learn how to will: so that willing is natural.

And again: if in the case of creatures devoid of reason nature rules, while nature is ruled in man who is moved of his own free-will and volition, it follows, then, that man is by nature endowed with volition.

And again: if man has been made after the image of the blessed and super-essential Godhead, and if the divine nature is by nature endowed with free-will and volition, it follows that man, as its image, is free by nature and volitive [8]. For the fathers defined freedom as volition [9].

And further: if to will is a part of the nature of every man and not present in some and absent in others, and if that which is seen to be common to all is a characteristic feature of the nature that belongs to the individuals of the class, surely, then, man is by nature endowed with volition [10].

And once more: if the nature receives neither more nor less, but all are equally endowed with volition and not some more than others, then by nature man is endowed with volition [10]. So that since man is by nature endowed with volition, the Lord also must be by nature endowed with volition, not only because He is God, but also because He became man. For just as He assumed our nature, so also He has assumed naturally our will. And in this way the Fathers said that He formed our will in Himself [11].

If the will is not natural, it must be either hypostatic or unnatural. But if it is hypostatic, the Son must thus, forsooth, have a different will from what the Father has: for that which is hypostatic is characteristic of subsistence only. And if it is unnatural, will must be a defection from nature: for

9 τὸ μὲν ἁπλῶς θέλειν, θέλησις, ἤτοι ἡ θελητικὴ δύναμις.
1 ὄρεξις.
2 θέλητον, willed, the thing willed.
3 θέλημα γνωμικόν. dispositional volition, will of judgment.
4 θελητικόν, volitive. Volitivum, volitive, is the Scholastic translation θελητικόν.
5 Max., Dial. cum Pyrrh.   6 Max., ibid.
7 Max., ibid.

8 θελητικός, endowed with volition.
9 θέλησις, will.   10 θελητικός.
11 καὶ κατὰ τοῦτο οἱ Πατέρες τὸ ἡμέτερον ἐν ἑαυτῷ τυπῶσαι αὐτὸν ἔφησαν θέλημα: and according to this the Fathers said that He typified, moulded, had the form of our will in Himself.

what is unnatural is destructive of what is natural.

The God and Father of all things wills either as Father or as God. Now if as Father, His will will be different from that of the Son, for the Son is not the Father. But if as God, the Son is God and likewise the Holy Spirit is God, and so volition is part of His nature, that is, it is natural.

Besides [12], if according to the view of the Fathers, those who have one and the same will have also one and the same essence, and if the divinity and humanity of Christ have one and the same will, then assuredly these have also one and the same essence.

And again : if according to the view of the Fathers the distinction between the natures is not seen in the single will, we must either, when we speak of the one will, cease to speak of the different natures in Christ or, when we speak of the different natures of Christ, cease to speak of the one will.

And further [1], the divine Gospel says, *The Lord came into the borders of Tyre and Sidon and entered into a house, and would have no man know it ; but He could not be hid* [2]. If, then, His divine will is omnipotent, but yet, though He would, He could not be hid, surely it was as man that He would and could not, and so as man He must be endowed with volition.

And once again [3], the Gospel tells us that, *He, having come into the place, said ' I thirst' : and they gave Him some vinegar mixed with gall, and when He had tasted it He would not drink* [4]. If, then, on the one hand it was as God that He suffered thirst and when He had tasted would not drink, surely He must be subject to passion [5] also as God, for thirst and taste are passions [6]. But if it was not as God but altogether as man that He was athirst, likewise as man He must be endowed with volition [7].

Moreover, the blessed Paul the Apostle says, *He became obedient unto death, even the death of the cross* [8]. But obedience is subjection of the real will, not of the unreal will. For that which is irrational is not said to be obedient or disobedient [9]. But the Lord having become obedient to the Father, became so not as God but as man. For as God

He is not said to be obedient or disobedient. For these things are of the things that are under one's hand [1], as the inspired Gregorius said [2]. Wherefore, then, Christ is endowed with volition as man.

While, however, we assert that will is natural, we hold not that it is dominated by necessity, but that it is free. For if it is rational, it must be absolutely free. For it is not only the divine and uncreated nature that is free from the bonds of necessity, but also the intellectual and created nature. And this is manifest : for God, being by nature good and being by nature the Creator and by nature God, is not all this of necessity. For who is there to introduce this necessity ?

It is to be observed further [3], that freedom of will is used in several senses, one in connection with God, another in connection with angels, and a third in connection with men. For used in reference to God it is to be understood in a superessential manner, and in reference to angels it is to be taken in the sense that the election is concomitant with the state [4], and admits of the interposition of no interval of time at all : for while the angel possesses free-will by nature, he uses it without let or hindrance, having neither antipathy on the part of the body to overcome nor any assailant. Again, used in reference to men, it is to be taken in the sense that the state is considered to be anterior in time to the election. For man is free and has free-will by nature, but he has also the assault of the devil to impede him and the motion of the body : and thus through the assault and the weight of the body, election comes to be later than the state.

If, then, Adam [5] obeyed of his own will and ate of his own will, surely in us the will is the first part to suffer. And if the will is the first to suffer, and the Word Incarnate did not assume this with the rest of our nature, it follows that we have not been freed from sin.

Moreover, if the faculty of free-will which is in nature is His work and yet He did not assume it, He either condemned His own workmanship as not good, or grudged us the comfort it brought, and so deprived us of the full benefit, and shewed that He was Himself subject to passion since He was not willing or not able to work out our perfect salvation.

Moreover, one cannot speak of one com-

---

[12] *Greg. Nyss., Cont. Apollin* and others, *Act.* 10, *sext. syn.*
[1] *Max., Agatho pap. Epist. Syn. in VI Syn., Act.* 4.
[2] St Mark vii. 24.   [3] *Max., ibid.*
[4] St. Matt. xxvii. 33 and 34 ; St. John xix. 28 and 29.
[5] ἐμπαθής, *passible, sensible, possessed of sensibility.*
[6] πάθος, *sensibility.*
[7] In N. is added : καὶ εἰ ἐν τῇ ἡμέρᾳ τοῦ πάθους λέγει· Πάτερ, εἰ δυνατόν, παρελθέτω τὸ ποτήριον τοῦτο ἀπ' ἐμοῦ. Πλὴν οὐχ ὡς ἐγὼ θέλω, ἀλλ' ὡς σύ. Ἰδοὺ δύο θελήσεις, θεϊκὴ ἅμα καὶ ἀνθρωπίνη.
[8] Phil. ii. 8.   [9] *Max., ut supr.*

[1] τῶν ὑπὸ χεῖρα γὰρ ταῦτα.
[2] *Orat.* 36, some distance from the beginning.
[3] *Max., Disp. cum Pyrrh.*
[4] ὡς συντρεχούσης τῇ ἕξει τῆς προχειρίσεως, **the choice,** or **decision,** *being synchronous with the moral disposition.*
[5] *Max., Disp. cum Pyrrh.*

pound thing made of two wills in the same way as a subsistence is a composition of two natures. Firstly because the compositions are of things in subsistence (*hypostasis*), not of things viewed in a different category, not in one proper to them [6]: and secondly, because if we speak of composition of wills and energies, we will be obliged to speak of composition of the other natural properties, such as the uncreated and the created, the invisible and the visible, and so on. And what will be the name of the will that is compounded out of two wills? For the compound cannot be called by the name of the elements that make it up. For otherwise we should call that which is compounded of natures nature and not subsistence. And further, if we say that there is one compound will in Christ, we separate Him in will from the Father, for the Father's will is not compound. It remains, therefore, to say that the subsistence of Christ alone is compound and common, as in the case of the natures so also in that of the natural properties.

And we cannot [7], if we wish to be accurate, speak of Christ as having judgment (γνώμη) and preference [8]. For judgment is a disposition with reference to the decision arrived at after investigation and deliberation concerning something unknown, that is to say, after counsel and decision. And after judgment comes preference [9], which chooses out and selects the one rather than the other. But the Lord being not mere man but also God, and knowing all things, had no need of inquiry and investigation, and counsel, and decision, and by nature made whatever is good His own and whatever is bad foreign to Him [1]. For thus says Isaiah the prophet, *Before the child shall know to prefer the evil, he shall choose the good ; because before the child knows good or evil, he refuses wickedness by choosing the good* [2]. For the word " before " proves that it is not with investigation and deliberation, as is the way with us, but as God and as subsisting in a divine manner in the flesh, that is to say, being united in subsistence to the flesh, and because of His very existence and all-embracing knowledge, that He is possessed of good in His own nature. For the virtues are natural qualities [3], and are implanted in all by nature and in equal measure, even if we do not all in equal measure employ our natural energies. By the transgression we were driven

from the natural to the unnatural [4]. But the Lord led us back from the unnatural into the natural [5]. For this is what is the meaning of *in our image, after our likeness* [6]. And the discipline and trouble of this life were not designed as a means for our attaining virtue which was foreign to our nature, but to enable us to cast aside the evil that was foreign and contrary to our nature : just as on laboriously removing from steel the rust which is not natural to it but acquired through neglect, we reveal the natural brightness of the steel.

Observe further that the word judgment (γνώμη) is used in many ways and in many senses. Sometimes it signifies exhortation : as when the divine apostle says, *Now concerning virgins I have no commandment of the Lord ; yet I give my judgment* [7] : sometimes it means counsel, as when the prophet David says, *They have taken crafty counsel against Thy people* [8] : sometimes it means a decree, as when we read in Daniel, *Concerning whom* (or, *what*) *went this shameless decree forth* [9] *?* At other times it is used in the sense of belief, or opinion, or purpose, and, to put it shortly, the word judgment has twenty-eight [1] different meanings.

CHAPTER XV.

Concerning the energies in our Lord Jesus Christ.

We hold, further, that there are two energies [2] in our Lord Jesus Christ. For He possesses on the one hand, as God and being of like essence with the Father, the divine energy, and, likewise, since He became man and of like essence to us, the energy proper to human nature [3].

But observe that energy and capacity for energy, and the product of energy, and the agent of energy, are all different. Energy is the efficient (δραστική) and essential activity of nature : the capacity for energy is the nature from which proceeds energy : the product of energy is that which is effected by energy : and the agent of energy is the person or subsistence which uses the energy. Further, sometimes energy is used in the sense of the product of energy, and the product of energy in that of energy, just as the terms creation and creature are sometimes transposed. For we say " all creation," meaning creatures.

---

6 πρῶτον μὲν, ὅτι αἱ συνθέσεις τῶν ἐν ὑποστάσει ὄντων, καὶ οὐ τῶν ἑτέρῳ λόγῳ, καὶ οὐκ ἰδίῳ θεωρουμένων εἰσί.
7 *Max., Dial. cum Pyrrh.*　　8 *Max., Epist. ad Marin.*
9 προαίρεσις.
1 Basil, on Ps. xliv., or rather on Isaiah vii.
2 Is. vii. 16, sec. LXX.
3 Φυσικαὶ μὲν γάρ εἰσιν αἱ ἀρεταί ; cf. Cicero, *De leg.* 1.

4 *Supr.*, bk. ii., ch. 30.　　5 *Max., Dial. cum Pyrrh.*
6 Gen. i. 26.　　7 1 Cor. vii. 25.　　8 Ps. lxxxiii. 3.
9 Dan. ii. 15. περὶ τίνος ἐξῆλθεν ἡ γνώμη ἡ ἀναιδὴς αὕτη. In our A.V., *Why is the decree so hasty from the king?*
1 Text, κατὰ εἴκοσι ὀκτώ : Variants, κατὰ κοινοῦ, κατὰ πολύ, secundum multa (old trans.), and secundum plurima (Faber). Maximus gave 28 meanings of γνώμη.
2 Cf. *Anast., De operationibus,* I. ; *Joan. Scyth, Con. Sever.* VIII.. &c.
3 *Supr.* bk. ii. : *Max., Dial. cum Pyrrh.*

Note also that energy is an activity and is energised rather than energises; as Gregory the Theologian says in his thesis concerning the Holy Spirit[4]: "If energy exists, it must manifestly be energised and will not energise: and as soon as it has been energised, it will cease."

Life itself, it should be observed, is energy, yea, the primal energy of the living creature: and so is the whole economy of the living creature, its functions of nutrition and growth, that is, the vegetative side of its nature, and the movement stirred by impulse, that is, the sentient side, and its activity of intellect and free-will. Energy, moreover, is the perfect realisation of power. If, then, we contemplate all these in Christ, surely we must also hold that He possesses human energy.

The first thought[5] that arises in us is called energy: and it is simple energy not involving any relationship, the mind sending forth the thoughts peculiar to it in an independent and invisible way, for if it did not do so it could not justly be called mind. Again, the revelation and unfolding of thought by means of articulate speech is said to be energy. But this is no longer simple energy that involves no relationship, but it is considered in relation as being composed of thought and speech. Further, the very relation which he who does anything bears to that which is brought about is energy: and the very thing that is effected is called energy[6]. The first belongs to the soul alone, the second to the soul making use of the body, the third to the body animated by mind, and the last is the effect[7]. For the mind sees beforehand what is to be and then performs it thus by means of the body. And so the hegemony belongs to the soul, for it uses the body as an instrument, leading and restraining it. But the energy of the body is quite different, for the body is led and moved by the soul. And with regard to the effect, the touching and handling and, so to speak, the embrace of what is effected, belong to the body, while the figuration and formation belong to the soul. And so in connection with our Lord Jesus Christ, the power of miracles is the energy of His divinity, while the work of His hands and the willing and the saying, *I will, be thou clean*[8], are the energy of His humanity. And as to the effect, the breaking of the loaves[9], and the fact that the leper heard the "I will," belong to His humanity, while the multiplication of the loaves and the purification of the leper belong to His divinity. For through both, that is through the energy of the body and the energy of the soul, He displayed one and the same, cognate and equal divine energy. For just as we saw that His natures were united and permeate one another, and yet do not deny that they are different but even enumerate them, although we know they are inseparable, so also in connection with the wills and the energies we know their union, and we recognise their difference and enumerate them without introducing separation. For just as the flesh was deified without undergoing change in its own nature, in the same way also will and energy are deified without transgressing their own proper limits. For whether He is the one or the other, He is one and the same, and whether He wills and energises in one way or the other, that is as God or as man, He is one and the same.

We must, then, maintain that Christ has two energies in virtue of His double nature. For things that have diverse natures, have also different energies, and things that have diverse energies, have also different natures. And so conversely, things that have the same nature have also the same energy, and things that have one and the same energy have also one and the same essence[1], which is the view of the Fathers, who declare the divine meaning[2]. One of these alternatives, then, must be true: either, if we hold that Christ has one energy, we must also hold that He has but one essence, or, if we are solicitous about truth, and confess that He has according to the doctrine of the Gospels and the Fathers two essences, we must also confess that He has two energies corresponding to and accompanying them. For as He is of like essence with God and the Father in divinity, He will be His equal also in energy. And as He likewise is of like essence with us in humanity He will be our equal also in energy. For the blessed Gregory, bishop of Nyssa, says[3], "Things that have one and the same energy, have also absolutely the same power." For all energy is the effect of power. But it cannot be that uncreated and created nature have one and the same nature or power or energy. But if we should hold that Christ has but one energy, we should attribute to the divinity of the Word the passions of the intelligent spirit, viz. fear and grief and anguish.

If they should say[4], indeed, that the holy

4 *Orat.* 37, near the beginning.
5 *Anast. Antioch., De operationibus.*
6 καὶ αὐτὸ τὸ ἀποτελούμενον; cf. *Max., ad Marin.* II.
7 *Max.* tom. ii., *Dogmat. ad Marin.*, p. 124.
8 St. Matt. viii. 3.   9 St. John vi. 11.

1 See *Act.* 10 *sextae synodi.*
2 Text, θεηγόρους. Variant, θεοφόρους.
3 *Orat. de natura et hyp.* Also in *Basil.* 43.
4 *Max., Dial. cum Pyrrh.*

Fathers said in their disputation concerning the Holy Trinity, " Things that have one and the same essence have also one and the same energy, and things which have different essences have also different energies," and that it is not right to transfer to the dispensation what has reference to matters of theology, we shall answer that if it has been said by the Fathers solely with reference to theology. and if the Son has not even after the incarnation the same energy as the Father [5], assuredly He cannot have the same essence. But to whom shall we attribute this, *My Father worketh hitherto and I work* [6] : and this, *What things soever He seeth the Father doing, these also doeth the Son likewise* [7]: and this, *If ye believe not Me, believe My works* [8] : and this, *The work which I do bear witness concerning Me* [9] : and this, *As the Father raised up the dead and quickeneth them, even so the Son quickeneth whom He will* [1]. For all these shew not only that He is of like essence to the Father even after the incarnation, but that He has also the same energy.

And again : if the providence that embraces all creation is not only of the Father and the Holy Spirit, but also of the Son even after the incarnation, assuredly since that is energy, He must have even after the incarnation the same energy as the Father.

But if we have learnt from the miracles that Christ has the same essence as the Father, and since the miracles happen to be the energy of God, assuredly He must have even after the incarnation the same energy as the Father.

But, if there is one energy belonging to both His divinity and His humanity, it will be compound, and will be either a different energy from that of the Father, or the Father, too, will have a compound energy. But if the Father has a compound energy, manifestly He must also have a compound nature.

But if they should say that together with energy is also introduced personality [2], we shall reply that if personality is introduced along with energy, then the true converse must hold good that energy is also introduced along with personality ; and there will be also three energies of the Holy Trinity just as there are three persons or subsistences, or there will be one person and one subsistence just as there is only one energy. Indeed, the holy Fathers have maintained with one voice that things that have the same essence have also the same energy.

But further, if personality is introduced along with energy, those who divine that neither one nor two energies of Christ are to be spoken of, do not maintain that either one or two persons of Christ are to be spoken of.

Take the case of the flaming sword ; just as in it the natures of the fire and the steel are preserved distinct [3], so also are their two energies and their effects. For the energy of the steel is its cutting power, and that of the fire is its burning power, and the cut is the effect of the energy of the steel, and the burn is the effect of the energy of the fire : and these are kept quite distinct in the burnt cut, and in the cut burn, although neither does the burning take place apart from the cut after the union of the two, nor the cut apart from the burning : and we do not maintain on account of the two-fold natural energy that there are two flaming swords, nor do we confuse the essential difference of the energies on account of the unity of the flaming sword. In like manner also, in the case of Christ, His divinity possesses an energy that is divine and omnipotent while His humanity has an energy such as is our own. And the effect of His human energy was His taking the child by the hand and drawing her to Himself, while that of His divine energy was the restoring of her to life [4]. For the one is quite distinct from the other, although they are inseparable from one another in theandric energy. But if, because Christ has one subsistence, He must also have one energy, then, because He has one subsistence, He must also have one essence.

And again : if we should hold that Christ has but one energy, this must be either divine or human, or neither. But if we hold that it is divine [5], we must maintain that He is God alone, stripped of our humanity. And if we hold that it is human, we shall be guilty of the impiety of saying that He is mere man. And if we hold that it is neither divine nor human, we must also hold that He is neither God nor man, of like essence neither to the Father nor to us. For it is as a result of the union that the identity in hypostasis arises, but yet the difference between the natures is not done away with. But since the difference between the natures is preserved, manifestly also the energies of the natures will be preserved. For no nature exists that is lacking in energy.

If Christ our Master [6] has one energy, it must be either created or uncreated ; for

5 *Max , Dial. cum Pyrrh.*   6 St. John v. **17.**   7 *Ibid.* **19.**
8 *Ibid.* x. 38.   9 *Ibid.* v. 36.   1 *Ibid.* 21.   2 *Max., ibid.*

3 *Maxim., lib. De duab. vol. et Dial. cum Pyrrh.*
4 St Luke viii. 54 ; *Max., Dial. cum Pyrrh.*
5 *Max., ibid.*   6 *Max., ibid.*

between these there is no energy, just as there is no nature. If, then, it is created, it will point to created nature alone, but if it is uncreated, it will betoken uncreated essence alone. For that which is natural must completely correspond with its nature : for there cannot exist a nature that is defective. But the energy [7] that harmonises with nature does not belong to that which is external : and this is manifest because, apart from the energy that harmonises with nature, no nature can either exist or be known. For through that in which each thing manifests its energy, the absence of change confirms its own proper nature.

If Christ has one energy, it must be one and the same energy that performs both divine and human actions. But there is no existing thing which abiding in its natural state can act in opposite ways : for fire does not freeze and boil, nor does water dry up and make wet. How then could He Who is by nature God, and Who became by nature man, have both performed miracles, and endured passions with one and the same energy?

If, then, Christ assumed the human mind, that is to say, the intelligent and reasonable soul, undoubtedly He has always thought, and will think for ever. But thought is the energy of the mind : and so Christ, as man, is endowed with energy, and will be so for ever.

Indeed, the most wise and great and holy John Chrysostom says in his interpretation of the Acts, in the second discourse [8], "One would not err if he should call even His passion action : for in that He suffered all things, He accomplished that great and marvellous work, the overthrow of death, and all His other works."

If all energy is defined as essential movement of some nature, as those who are versed in these matters say, where does one perceive any nature that has no movement, and is completely devoid of energy, or where does one find energy that is not movement of natural power? But, as the blessed Cyril says [9], no one in his senses could admit that there was but one natural energy of God and His creation [1]. It is not His human nature that raises up Lazarus from the dead, nor is it His divine power that sheds tears : for the shedding of tears is peculiar to human nature while the life is peculiar to the enhypostatic

life. But yet they are common the one to the other, because of the identity in subsistence. For Christ is one, and one also is His person or subsistence, but yet He has two natures, one belonging to His humanity, and another belonging to His divinity. And the glory, indeed, which proceeded naturally from His divinity became common to both through the identity in subsistence, and again on account of His flesh that which was lowly became common to both. For He Who is the one or the other, that is God or man, is one and the same, and both what is divine and what is human belong to Himself. For while His divinity performed the miracles, they were not done apart from the flesh, and while His flesh performed its lowly offices, they were not done apart from the divinity. For His divinity was joined to the suffering flesh, yet remaining without passion, and endured the saving passions, and the holy mind was joined to the energising divinity of the Word, perceiving and knowing what was being accomplished.

And thus His divinity communicates its own glories to the body while it remains itself without part in the sufferings of the flesh. For His flesh did not suffer through His divinity in the same way that His divinity energised through the flesh. For the flesh acted as the instrument of His divinity. Although, therefore, from the first conception there was no division at all between the two forms [2], but the actions of either form through all the time became those of one person, nevertheless we do not in any way confuse those things that took place without separation, but recognise from the quality of its works what sort of form anything has.

Christ, then, energises according to both His natures [3], and either nature energises in Him in communion with the other, the Word performing through the authority and power of its divinity all the actions proper to the Word, i.e. all acts of supremacy and sovereignty, and the body performing all the actions proper to the body, in obedience to the will of the Word that is united to it, and of whom it has become a distinct part. For He was not moved of Himself to the natural passions [4], nor again did He in that way recoil from the things of pain, and pray for release from them, or suffer what befel from without, but He was moved in conformity with His nature, the Word willing and allowing Him œconomically [5] to suffer that, and to do the

---

[7] Text, ἡ δὲ κατὰ φύσιν ἐνέργεια. Variant, εἰ δέ.
[8] Hom. 1.
[9] Thes., xxxii , ch. 2 ; Act. 10, sextae Synodi.
[1] The Monotheletes made much of the case of the raising of the daughter of Jairus. See Cyril, In Joan., p. 351 ; Max., Dial. cum Pyrrh., Epist. ad Nicand., Epist. ad Mon. Sicil.; Scholiast in Collect. cont. Severum, ch. 20.

[2] οἰκονομῶς, in incarnate form.   [3] Leo, Epist. cit.
[4] οὐ γὰρ ἀφ᾽ ἑαυτοῦ πρὸς τὰ φυσικὰ πάθη τὴν ὁρμὴν ἐποιεῖτο, οὐδ᾽ αὐτὴν ἐκ τῶν λυπη ῶν ἀφορμὴν καὶ παραίτησιν.
[5] The term is μορφή, as in Phil. ii. 6, 7.

things proper to Him, that the truth might be confirmed by the works of nature.

Moreover, just as [6] He received in His birth of a virgin superessential essence, so also He revealed His human energy in a superhuman way, walking with earthly feet on unstable water, not by turning the water into earth, but by causing it in the superabundant power of His divinity not to flow away nor yield beneath the weight of material feet. For not in a merely human way did He do human things: for He was not only man, but also God, and so even His sufferings brought life and salvation: nor yet did He energise as God, strictly after the manner of God, for He was not only God, but also man, and so it was by touch and word and such like that He worked miracles.

But if any one [7] should say, "We do not say that Christ has but one nature, in order to do away with His human energy, but we do so because [8] human energy, in opposition to divine energy, is called passion (πάθος)," we shall answer that, according to this reasoning, those also who hold that He has but one nature do not maintain this with a view to doing away with His human nature, but because human nature in opposition to divine nature is spoken of as passible (παθητική). But God forbid that we should call the human activity passion, when we are distinguishing it from divine energy. For, to speak generally, of nothing is the existence recognised or defined by comparison or collation. If it were so, indeed, existing things would turn out to be mutually the one the cause of the other. For if the human activity is passion because the divine activity is energy, assuredly also the human nature must be wicked because the divine nature is good, and, by conversion and opposition, if the divine activity is called energy because the human activity is called passion, then also the divine nature must be good because the human nature is bad. And so all created things must be bad, and he must have spoken falsely who said, And God saw every thing that He had made, and, behold, it was very good [9].

We, therefore, maintain [1] that the holy Fathers gave various names to the human activity according to the underlying notion. For they called it power, and energy, and difference, and activity, and property, and quality, and passion, not in distinction from the divine activity, but power, because it is a conservative

and invariable force; and energy, because it is a distinguishing mark, and reveals the absolute similarity between all things of the same class; and difference, because it distinguishes; and activity, because it makes manifest; and property, because it is constituent and belongs to that alone, and not to any other; and quality, because it gives form; and passion, because it is moved. For all things that are of God and after God suffer in respect of being moved, forasmuch as they have not in themselves motion or power. Therefore, as has been said, it is not in order to distinguish the one from the other that it has been named, but it is in accordance with the plan implanted in it in a creative manner by the Cause that framed the universe. Wherefore, also, when they spoke of it along with the divine nature they called it energy. For he who said, "For either form energises close communion with the other [2]," did something quite different from him who said, And when He had fasted forty days, He was afterwards an hungered [3]: (for He allowed His nature to energise when it so willed, in the way proper to itself [4],) or from those who hold there is a different energy in Him or that He has a twofold energy, or now one energy and now another [5]. For these statements with the change in terms [5a] signify the two energies. Indeed, often the number is indicated both by change of terms and by speaking of them as divine and human [6]. For the difference is difference in differing things, but how do things that do not exist differ?

CHAPTER XVI.

In reply to those who say [7], "If man has two natures and two energies, Christ must be held to have three natures and as many energies."

Each individual man, since he is composed of two natures, soul and body, and since these natures are unchangeable in him, could appropriately be spoken of as two natures: for he preserves even after their union the natural properties of either. For the body is not immortal, but corruptible; neither is the soul mortal, but immortal: and the body is not invisible nor the soul visible to bodily eyes: but the soul is rational and intellectual, and incorporeal, while the body is dense and visible, and irrational. But things that are opposed to one another in essence have not

---

6 *Dion.*, ch. 2, *De div. nom. et Epist.* 4.
7 *Max.*, *Dial cum Pyrrh.*
8 See the reply of Maximus in the *Dialogue cum Pyrrh.*
9 Gen. i. 31.
1 *Max.*, *Opusc. Polem.*, pp. 31, 32.

2 *Leo, Epist.* 10.   3 St. Matt. iv. 2.
4 *Nyss., adv. Apoll.*   5 Chrysost., *Hom. in S. Thom.*
5a δι' ἀντωνυμίας.   6 *Cyril, in Joan.*, bk. viii.
7 This is directed to another argument of the Severians. Cf. *Leont., De Sect.*, 7, *Contr. Nest. et Eutych.*, I.

one nature, and, therefore, soul and body cannot have one essence.

And again: if man is a rational and mortal animal, and every definition is explanatory of the underlying natures, and the rational is not the same as the mortal according to the plan of nature, man then certainly cannot have one nature, according to the rule of his own definition.

But if man should at any time be said to have one nature, the word "nature" is here used instead of "species," as when we say that man does not differ from man in any difference of nature. But since all men are fashioned in the same way, and are composed of soul and body, and each has two distinct natures, they are all brought under one definition. And this is not unreasonable, for the holy Athanasius spake of all created things as having one nature forasmuch as they were all produced, expressing himself thus in his Oration against those who blasphemed the Holy Spirit: "That the Holy Spirit is above all creation, and different from the nature of things produced and peculiar to divinity, we may again perceive. For whatever is seen to be common to many things, and not more in one and less in another, is called essence [8]. Since, then, every man is composed of soul and body, accordingly we speak of man as having one nature. But we cannot speak of our Lord's subsistence as one nature: for each nature preserves, even after the union, its natural properties, nor can we find a class of Christs. For no other Christ was born both of divinity and of humanity to be at once God and man."

And again: man's unity in species is not the same thing as the unity of soul and body in essence. For man's unity in species makes clear the absolute similarity between all men, while the unity of soul and body in essence is an insult to their very existence, and reduces them to nothingness: for either the one must change into the essence of the other, or from different things something different must be produced, and so both would be changed, or if they keep to their own proper limits there must be two natures. For, as regards the nature of essence the corporeal is not the same as the incorporeal. Therefore, although holding that man has one nature, not because the essential quality of his soul and that of his body are the same, but because the individuals included under the species are exactly the same, it is not necessary for us to maintain that Christ also

has one nature, for in this case there is no species embracing many subsistences.

Moreover, every compound [9] is said to be composed of what immediately composes it. For we do not say that a house is composed of earth and water, but of bricks and timber. Otherwise, it would be necessary to speak of man as composed of at least five things, viz., the four elements and soul. And so also, in the case of our Lord Jesus Christ we do not look at the parts of the parts, but at those divisions of which He is immediately composed, viz., divinity and humanity.

And further, if by saying that man has two natures we are obliged to hold that Christ has three, you, too, by saying that man is composed of two natures must hold that Christ is composed of three natures: and it is just the same with the energies. For energy must correspond with nature: and Gregory the Theologian bears witness that man is said to have and has two natures, saying, "God and man are two natures, since, indeed, soul and body also are two natures [1]." And in his discourse "Concerning Baptism" he says, "Since we consist of two parts, soul and body, the visible and the invisible nature, the purification is likewise twofold, that is, by water and Spirit [2]."

CHAPTER XVII.
Concerning the deification of the nature of our Lord's flesh and of His will.

It is worthy of note [3] that the flesh of the Lord is not said to have been deified and made equal to God and God in respect of any change or alteration, or transformation, or confusion of nature: as Gregory the Theologian [4] says, "Whereof the one deified, and the other was deified, and, to speak boldly, made equal to God: and that which anointed became man, and that which was anointed became God [5]." For these words do not mean any change in nature, but rather the œconomical union (I mean the union in subsistence by virtue of which it was united inseparably with God the Word), and the permeation of the natures through one another, just as we saw that burning permeated the steel. For, just as we confess that God became man without change or alteration, so we consider that the flesh became God without change. For because the Word became flesh, He did not overstep the limits of His own divinity nor abandon

[8] *Epist. 2 ad Serap.*, towards the end; *Collect.*, as above, c. 19.

[9] *Anast., Collect.*, ch. 19. [1] *Epist.* 1, *ad Cledon.*
[2] *Orat.* 4. not far from the beginning.
[3] Cf. *Greg. Naz., Orat.* 38, 39, 42, 51; *Niceph., C. P. adv. Ep. Euseb.*, c. 50; *Euthym., Panopl.*, II. 7.
[4] *Greg., Orat.* 42.
[5] *Id., Orat.* 39; *Max. bk. De duabus voluntatibus.*

the divine glories that belong to Him: nor, on the other hand, was the flesh, when deified, changed in its own nature or in its natural properties. For even after the union, both the natures abode unconfused and their properties unimpaired. But the flesh of the Lord received the riches of the divine energies through the purest union with the Word, that is to say, the union in subsistence, without entailing the loss of any of its natural attributes. For it is not in virtue of any energy of its own but through the Word united to it, that it manifests divine energy: for the flaming steel burns, not because it has been endowed in a physical way with burning energy, but because it has obtained this energy by its union with fire [6].

Wherefore the same flesh was mortal by reason of its own nature and life-giving through its union with the Word in subsistence. And we hold that it is just the same with the deification of the will [7]; for its natural activity was not changed but united with His divine and omnipotent will, and became the will of God, made man [8]. And so it was that, though He wished, He could not of Himself escape [9], because it pleased God the Word that the weakness of the human will, which was in truth in Him, should be made manifest. But He was able to cause at His will the cleansing of the leper [1], because of the union with the divine will.

Observe further, that the deification of the nature and the will points most expressly and most directly both to two natures and two wills. For just as the burning does not change into fire the nature of the thing that is burnt, but makes distinct both what is burnt, and what burned it, and is indicative not of one but of two natures, so also the deification does not bring about one compound nature but two, and their union in subsistence. Gregory the Theologian, indeed, says, "Whereof the one deified, the other was deified [2]," and by the words "whereof," "the one," "the other," he assuredly indicates two natures.

CHAPTER XVIII.

Further concerning volitions and free-wills: minds, too, and knowledges and wisdoms.

When we say that Christ is perfect God [3] and perfect man, we assuredly attribute to Him all the properties natural to both the Father and mother. For He became man

in order that that which was overcome might overcome. For He Who was omnipotent did not in His omnipotent authority and might lack the power to rescue man out of the hands of the tyrant. But the tyrant would have had a ground of complaint if, after He had overcome man, God should have used force against him. Wherefore God in His pity and love for man wished to reveal fallen man himself as conqueror, and became man to restore like with like.

But that man is a rational and intelligent animal, no one will deny. How, then, could He have become man if He took on Himself flesh without soul, or soul without mind? For that is not man. Again, what benefit would His becoming man have been to us if He Who suffered first was not saved, nor renewed and strengthened by the union with divinity? For that which is not assumed is not remedied. He, therefore, assumed the whole man, even the fairest part of him, which had become diseased, in order that He might bestow salvation on the whole. And, indeed, there could never exist a mind that had not wisdom and was destitute of knowledge. For if it has not energy or motion, it is utterly reduced to nothingness.

Therefore, God the Word [4], wishing to restore that which was in His own image, became man. But what is that which was in His own image, unless mind? So He gave up the better and assumed the worse. For mind [5] is in the border-land between God and flesh, for it dwells indeed in fellowship with the flesh, and is, moreover, the image of God. Mind, then, mingles with mind, and mind holds a place midway between the pureness of God and the denseness of flesh. For if the Lord assumed a soul without mind, He assumed the soul of an irrational animal.

But if the Evangelist said that *the Word was made flesh* [6], note that in the Holy Scripture sometimes a man is spoken of as a soul, as, for example, *with seventy-five souls came Jacob into Egypt* [7]: and sometimes a man is spoken of as flesh, as, for example, *All flesh shall see the salvation of God* [8]. And accordingly the Lord did not become flesh without soul or mind, but man. He says, indeed, Himself, *Why seek ye to kill Me, a Man that hath told you the truth [9]?* He, therefore, assumed flesh animated with the spirit of reason and mind, a spirit that holds sway

6 *Max , Epist. ad Nicandr.*   7 *Greg. Naz., Orat.* 36.
8 *Ibid.* 35, p. 595.   9 St. Mark vii. 24.
1 St. Matt. viii. 3.   2 *Greg. Naz., Orat.* 42.
3 Against the Apollinarians and the Monotheletes. Cf. *Max.*, *ut supra*, II p. 151.

4 *Greg. Naz., Carm. sen. adv. Apollin., Epist. ad Cled.*, and elsewhere.
5 See also ch. 6 above, and Gregory's lines against the Apollinarians.
6 St. John i. 14.
7 Gen. xlvi. 27, ap. LXX.; Acts vii. 14.
8 Is. xl. 5; St. Luke iii. 6.   9 St. John viii. 40.

over the flesh but is itself under the dominion of the divinity of the Word.

So, then, He had by nature, both as God and as man, the power of will. But His human will was obedient and subordinate to His divine will, not being guided by its own inclination, but willing those things which the divine will willed. For it was with the permission of the divine will that He suffered by nature what was proper to Him[1]. For when He prayed that He might escape the death, it was with His divine will naturally willing and permitting it that He did so pray and agonize and fear, and again when His divine will willed that His human will should choose the death, the passion became voluntary to Him[2]. For it was not as God only, but also as man, that He voluntarily surrendered Himself to the death. And thus He bestowed on us also courage in the face of death. So, indeed, He said before His saving passion, *Father, if it be possible, let this cup pass from Me[3],*" manifestly as though He were to drink the cup as man and not as God. It was as man, then, that He wished the cup to pass from Him : but these are the words of natural timidity. *Nevertheless*, He said, *not My will,* that is to say, not in so far as I am of a different essence from Thee, *but Thy will be done[4]*, that is to say, My will and Thy will, in so far as I am of the same essence as Thou. Now these are the words of a brave heart. For the Spirit of the Lord, since He truly became man in His good pleasure, on first testing its natural weakness was sensible of the natural fellow-suffering involved in its separation from the body, but being strengthened by the divine will it again grew bold in the face of death. For since He was Himself wholly God although also man, and wholly man although also God, He Himself as man subjected in Himself and by Himself His human nature to God and the Father, and became obedient to the Father, thus making Himself the most excellent type and example for us.

Of His own free-will, moreover, He exercised His divine and human will. For freewill is assuredly implanted in every rational nature. For to what end would it possess reason, if it could not reason at its own freewill? For the Creator hath implanted even in the unreasoning brutes natural appetite to compel them to sustain their own nature. For devoid of reason, as they are, they cannot guide their natural appetite but are guided by it. And so, as soon as the appetite for anything has sprung up, straightway arises also the impulse for action. And thus they do not win praise or happiness for pursuing virtue, nor punishment for doing evil. But the rational nature, although it does possess a natural appetite, can guide and train it by reason wherever the laws of nature are observed. For the advantage of reason consists in this, the free-will, by which we mean natural activity in a rational subject. Wherefore in pursuing virtue it wins praise and happiness, and in pursuing vice it wins punishment.

So that the soul[5] of the Lord being moved of its own free-will willed, but willed of its free-will those things which His divine will willed it to will. For the flesh was not moved at a sign from the Word, as Moses and all the holy men were moved at a sign from heaven. But He Himself, Who was one and yet both God and man, willed according to both His divine and His human will. Wherefore it was not in inclination but rather in natural power that the two wills of the Lord differed from one another. For His divine will was without beginning and all-effecting, as having power that kept pace with it, and free from passion ; while His human will had a beginning in time, and itself endured the natural and innocent passions, and was not naturally omnipotent. But yet it was omnipotent because it truly and naturally had its origin in the God-Word.

CHAPTER XIX.
Concerning the theandric energy.

When the blessed Dionysius[6] says that Christ exhibited to us some sort of novel theandric energy[7], he does not do away with the natural energies by saying that one energy resulted from the union of the divine with the human energy : for in the same way we could speak of one new nature resulting from the union of the divine with the human nature. For, according to the holy Fathers, things that have one energy have also one essence. But he wished to indicate the novel and ineffable manner in which the natural energies of Christ manifest themselves, a manner befitting the ineffable manner in which the natures of Christ mutually permeate one another, and further how strange and wonderful and, in the nature of things, unknown was His life as man[8], and lastly the manner of

---

[1] *Sophron., Epist. Synod.*
[2] See *Cyril, In Joann.,* ch. **x.**
[3] St. Matt. xxvi. 39 ; St. Luke xxii. **22.**   [4] Ibid.

[5] *Max., Dial. cum Pyrrh. ; Greg. Naz., Ep. 1, ad Cledon.*
[6] *Dionys., Epist. 4, ad Caium.*
[7] See *Severus, Ep. 3, ad Joann. Hegum. ; Anastas. Sinai. Hodegus,* p. 240.   [8] *Max., Dial. cum Pyrrh.*

the mutual interchange arising from the ineffable union. For we hold that the energies are not divided and that the natures do not energise separately, but that each conjointly in complete community with the other energises with its own proper energy [9]. For the human part did not energise merely in a human manner, for He was not mere man; nor did the divine part energise only after the manner of God, for He was not simply God, but He was at once God and man. For just as in the case of natures we recognise both their union and their natural difference, so is it also with the natural wills and energies.

Note, therefore, that in the case of our Lord Jesus Christ, we speak sometimes of His two natures and sometimes of His one person: and the one or the other is referred to one conception. For the two natures are one Christ, and the one Christ is two natures. Wherefore it is all the same whether we say "Christ energises according to either of His natures," or "either nature energises in Christ in communion with the other." The divine nature, then, has communion with the flesh in its energising, because it is by the good pleasure of the divine will that the flesh is permitted to suffer and do the things proper to itself, and because the energy of the flesh is altogether saving, and this is an attribute not of human but of divine energy. On the other hand the flesh has communion with the divinity of the Word in its energising, because the divine energies are performed, so to speak, through the organ of the body, and because He Who energises at once as God and man is one and the same.

Further observe [1] that His holy mind also performs its natural energies, thinking and knowing that it is God's mind and that it is worshipped by all creation, and remembering the times He spent on earth and all He suffered, but it has communion with the divinity of the Word in its energising and orders and governs the universe, thinking and knowing and ordering not as the mere mind of man, but as united in subsistence with God and acting as the mind of God.

This, then, the theandric energy makes plain that when God became man, that is when He became incarnate, both His human energy was divine, that is deified, and not without part in His divine energy, and His divine energy was not without part in His human energy, but either was observed in conjunction with the other. Now this manner of speaking is called a periphrasis, viz., when one embraces two things in one statement [2]. For just as in the case of the flaming sword we speak of the cut burn as one, and the burnt cut as one, but still hold that the cut and the burn have different energies and different natures, the burn having the nature of fire and the cut the nature of steel, in the same way also when we speak of one theandric energy of Christ, we understand two distinct energies of His two natures, a divine energy belonging to His divinity, and a human energy belonging to His humanity.

CHAPTER XX.

Concerning the natural and innocent passions [2a].

We confess [3], then, that He assumed all the natural and innocent passions of man. For He assumed the whole man and all man's attributes save sin. For that is not natural, nor is it implanted in us by the Creator, but arises voluntarily in our mode of life as the result of a further implantation by the devil, though it cannot prevail over us by force. For the natural and innocent passions are those which are not in our power, but which have entered into the life of man owing to the condemnation by reason of the transgression; such as hunger, thirst, weariness, labour, the tears, the corruption, the shrinking from death, the fear, the agony with the bloody sweat, the succour at the hands of angels because of the weakness of the nature, and other such like passions which belong by nature to every man.

All, then, He assumed that He might sanctify all. He was tried and overcame in order that He might prepare victory for us and give to nature power to overcome its antagonist, in order that nature which was overcome of old might overcome its former conqueror by the very weapons wherewith it had itself been overcome.

The wicked one [4], then, made his assault from without, not by thoughts prompted inwardly, just as it was with Adam. For it was not by inward thoughts, but by the serpent that Adam was assailed. But the Lord repulsed the assault and dispelled it like vapour, in order that the passions which assailed him and were overcome might be easily subdued by us, and that the new Adam should save the old.

[9] Leo, *Epist. 1 ad Flav.*
[1] Perhaps from *Joann. Scythop.*, bk. viii.; cf. *Niceph., C. P. Antirrh.*, III. 59.

[2] *Max., Dogm. ad Marin.*, p. 43.
[2a] Or, *sensibilities*.
[3] Cf. *Greg. Nyss., Contr. Apoll.*; *Leont., De Sect., Act.* 10; *Anastas.. Hodegus*, 13, &c.
[4] Cf. *Athanas., De Salut. Adventu Christi.*

Of a truth our natural passions were in harmony with nature and above nature in Christ. For they were stirred in Him after a natural manner when He permitted the flesh to suffer what was proper to it : but they were above nature because that which was natural did not in the Lord assume command over the will. For no compulsion is contemplated in Him but all is voluntary. For it was with His will that He hungered and thirsted and feared and died.

CHAPTER XXI.

Concerning ignorance and servitude.

He assumed, it is to be noted [5], the ignorant and servile nature [6]. For it is man's nature to be the servant of God, his Creator, and he does not possess knowledge of the future. If, then, as Gregory the Theologian holds, you are to separate the realm of sight from the realm of thought, the flesh is to be spoken of as both servile and ignorant, but on account of the identity of subsistence and the inseparable union the soul of the Lord was enriched with the knowledge of the future as also with the other miraculous powers. For just as the flesh of men is not in its own nature life-giving, while the flesh of our Lord which was united in subsistence with God the Word Himself, although it was not exempt from the mortality of its nature, yet became life-giving through its union in subsistence with the Word, and we may not say that it was not and is not for ever life-giving : in like manner His human nature does not in essence possess the knowledge of the future, but the soul of the Lord through its union with God the Word Himself and its identity in subsistence was enriched, as I said, with the knowledge of the future as well as with the other miraculous powers.

Observe further [7] that we may not speak of Him as servant. For the words servitude and mastership are not marks of nature but indicate relationship, to something, such as that of fatherhood and sonship. For these do not signify essence but relation.

It is just as we said, then, in connection with ignorance, that if you separate with subtle thoughts, that is, with fine imaginings, the created from the uncreated, the flesh is a servant, unless it has been united with God the Word [8]. But how can it be a servant when

t is once united in subsistence? For since Christ is one, He cannot be His own servant and Lord. For these are not simple predications but relative. Whose servant, then, could He be? His Father's? The Son, then, would not have all the Father's attributes, if He is the Father's servant and yet in no respect His own. Besides, how could the apostle say concerning us who were adopted by Him, *So that you are no longer a servant but a son* [9], if indeed He is Himself a servant? The word servant, then, is used merely as a title, though not in the strict meaning : but for our sakes He assumed the form of a servant and is called a servant among us. For although He is without passion, yet for our sake He was the servant of passion and became the minister of our salvation. Those, then, who say that He is a servant divide the one Christ into two, just as Nestorius did. But we declare Him to be Master and Lord of all creation, the one Christ, at once God and man, and all-knowing. *For in Him are all the treasures of wisdom and knowledge, the hidden treasures* [1].

CHAPTER XXII.

Concerning His growth.

He is, moreover, said to grow in wisdom and age and grace [2], increasing in age indeed and through the increase in age manifesting the wisdom that is in Him [3]; yea, further, making men's progress in wisdom and grace, and the fulfilment of the Father's goodwill, that is to say, men's knowledge of God and men's salvation, His own increase, and everywhere taking as His own that which is ours. But those who hold that He progressed in wisdom and grace in the sense of receiving some addition to these attributes, do not say that the union took place at the first origin of the flesh, nor yet do they give precedence to the union in subsistence, but giving heed [4] to the foolish Nestorius they imagine some strange relative union and mere indwelling, *understanding neither what they say nor whereof they affirm* [5]. For if in truth the flesh was united with God the Word from its first origin, or rather if it existed in Him and was identical in subsistence with Him, how was it that it was not endowed completely with all wisdom and grace? not that it might itself participate in the grace, nor share by grace in what belonged to the Word, but rather by reason of the union in subsistence, since both what is human and

5 *Greg. Naz., Orat.* 36.
6 *Photius, Cod.* 230; *Eulog.,* bk. x., *Ep.* 35; *Sophron., Ep. ad Serg.; Leont., De Sect., Act.* 10.
7 Cf. *Sophron., Ep. ad. Serg.,* who refers to the *Duliani* Δουλιανοί); the opinions of Felix and Elipandas, condemned at the Synod of Frankfort; and *Thomas Aquinas, III., Quaest.* 20, *Art.* 1.
8 *Greg. Naz., Orat.* 24.

9 Gal. iv. 7.   1 Col. ii. 3.   2 St. Luke ii. 52.
3 *Athanas., Contr. Arian.,* bk. iv. ; *Greg. Naz., Ep.* I. *ad Cled.,* and *Orat.* 20; *Cyril, Contr. Nest.,* bk. iii. ; *Greg. Nyss.. Contr. Apoll.,* ll. 28, &c.
4 Text has πειθομαι : surely it should be πειθόμενοι.
5 1 Tim. i. 1.

what is divine belong to the one Christ, and that He Who was Himself at once God and man should pour forth like a fountain over the universe His grace and wisdom and plenitude of every blessing.

CHAPTER XXIII.
Concerning His Fear.

The word fear has a double meaning. For fear is natural when the soul is unwilling to be separated from the body, on account of the natural sympathy and close relationship implanted in it in the beginning by the Creator, which makes it fear and struggle against death and pray for an escape from it. It may be defined thus: natural fear is the force whereby we cling to being with shrinking[6]. For if all things were brought by the Creator out of nothing into being, they all have by nature a longing after being and not after non-being. Moreover the inclination towards those things that support existence is a natural property of them. Hence God the Word when He became man had this longing, manifesting, on the one hand, in those things that support existence, the inclination of His nature in desiring food and drink and sleep, and having in a natural manner made proof of these things, while on the other hand displaying in those things that bring corruption His natural disinclination in voluntarily shrinking in the hour of His passion before the face of death. For although what happened did so according to the laws of nature, yet it was not, as in our case, a matter of necessity. For He willingly and spontaneously accepted that which was natural. So that fear itself and terror and agony belong to the natural and innocent passions and are not under the dominion of sin.

Again, there is a fear which arises from treachery of reasoning and want of faith, and ignorance of the hour of death, as when we are at night affected by fear at some chance noise. This is unnatural fear, and may be thus defined : unnatural fear is an unexpected shrinking. This our Lord did not assume. Hence He never felt fear except in the hour of His passion, although He often experienced a feeling of shrinking in accordance with the dispensation. For He was not ignorant of the appointed time.

But the holy Athanasius in his discourse against Apollinarius says that He did actually feel fear. " Wherefore the Lord said: *Now is My soul troubled*[7]. The 'now' indeed means just ' when He willed,' but yet points to what actually was. For He did not speak of what

was not, as though it were present, as if the things that were said only apparently happened. For all things happened naturally and actually." And again, after some other matters, he says, " In nowise does His divinity admit passion apart from a suffering body, nor yet does it manifest trouble and pain apart from a pained and troubled soul, nor does it suffer anguish and offer up prayer apart from a mind that suffered anguish and offered up prayer. For, although these occurrences were not due to any overthrow of nature, yet they took place to shew forth His real being[8]." The words " these occurrences were not due to any overthrow of His nature," prove that it was not involuntarily that He endured these things.

CHAPTER XXIV.
Concerning our Lord's Praying.

Prayer is an uprising of the mind to God or a petitioning of God for what is fitting. How then did it happen that our Lord offered up prayer in the case of Lazarus, and at the hour of His passion? For His holy mind was in no need either of any uprising towards God, since it had been once and for all united in subsistence with the God Word, or of any petitioning of God. For Christ is one. But it was because He appropriated to Himself our personality and took our impress on Himself, and became an ensample for us, and taught us to ask of God and strain towards Him, and guided us through His own holy mind in the way that leads up to God. For just as He[9] endured the passion, achieving for our sakes a triumph over it, so also He offered up prayer, guiding us, as I said, in the way that leads up to God, and " fulfilling all righteousness[1] " on our behalf, as He said to John, and reconciling His Father to us, and honouring Him as the beginning and cause, and proving that He is no enemy of God. For when He said in connection with Lazarus, *Father, I thank Thee that Thou hast heard Me. And I know that Thou hearest Me always, but because of the people which stand by I said it, that they may believe that Thou hast sent Me*[2], is it not most manifest to all that He said this in honour of His Father as the cause even of Himself, and to shew that He was no enemy of God[3]?

Again, when he said, *Father, if it be possible, let this cup pass from Me: yet, not as I will*

6 *Max., Dial. cum Pyrrh.*   7 St. John xii. 27.

---

8 *S. Athanas., De salutari adventu Christi, contra Apollina-rem* towards the end.
9 St. Matt., *Greg. Naz , Orat.* 36.   1 St. Matt. iii. 15.
2 St. John xi 42.
3 *Greg. Naz., Orat.* 42 ; *Chyrs., Hom. 63 in Joan.*

but as Thou wilt [4], is it not clear to all [5] that He said this as a lesson to us to ask help in our trials only from God, and to prefer God's will to our own, and as a proof that He did actually appropriate to Himself the attributes of our nature, and that He did in truth possess two wills, natural, indeed, and corresponding with His natures but yet in no wise opposed to one another? "Father" implies that He is of the same essence, but "if it be possible" does not mean that He was in ignorance (for what is impossible to God?), but serves to teach us to prefer God's will to our own. For that alone is impossible which is against God's will and permission [6]. "But not as I will but as Thou wilt," for inasmuch as He is God, He is identical with the Father, while inasmuch as He is man, He manifests the natural will of mankind. For it is this that naturally seeks escape from death.

Further, these words, *My God, My God, why hast Thou forsaken Me* [7]? He said as making our personality His own [8]. For neither would God be regarded with us as His Father, unless one were to discriminate with subtle imaginings of the mind between that which is seen and that which is thought, nor was He ever forsaken by His divinity: nay, it was we who were forsaken and disregarded. So that it was as appropriating our personality that He offered these prayers [9].

CHAPTER XXV.
Concerning the Appropriation.

It is to be observed [1] that there are two appropriations [2] : one that is natural and essential, and one that is personal and relative. The natural and essential one is that by which our Lord in His love for man took on Himself our nature and all our natural attributes, becoming in nature and truth man, and making trial of that which is natural: but the personal and relative appropriation is when any one assumes the person of another relatively, for instance, out of pity or love, and in his place utters words concerning him that have no connection with himself. And it was in this way that our Lord appropriated both our curse and our desertion, and such other things as are not natural: not that He Himself was or became such, but that He took upon Himself our personality and ranked Himself as

one of us. Such is the meaning in which this phrase is to be taken : *Being made a curse for our sakes* [3].

CHAPTER XXVI.
Concerning the Passion of our Lord's body, and the Impassibility of His divinity.

The Word of God then itself endured all in the flesh, while His divine nature which alone was passionless remained void of passion. For since the one Christ, Who is a compound of divinity and humanity, and exists in divinity and humanity, truly suffered, that part which is capable of passion suffered as it was natural it should, but that part which was void of passion did not share in the suffering. For the soul, indeed, since it is capable of passion shares in the pain and suffering of a bodily cut, though it is not cut itself but only the body : but the divine part which is void of passion does not share in the suffering of the body.

Observe, further [4], that we say that God suffered in the flesh, but never that His divinity suffered in the flesh, or that God suffered through the flesh. For if, when the sun is shining upon a tree, the axe should cleave the tree, and, nevertheless, the sun remains uncleft and void of passion, much more will the passionless divinity of the Word, united in subsistence to the flesh, remain void of passion when the body undergoes passion [5]. And should any one pour water over flaming steel, it is that which naturally suffers by the water, I mean, the fire, that is quenched, but the steel remains untouched (for it is not the nature of steel to be destroyed by water) : much more, then, when the flesh suffered did His only passionless divinity escape all passion although abiding inseparable from it. For one must not take the examples too absolutely and strictly: indeed, in the examples, one must consider both what is like and what is unlike, otherwise it would not be an example. For, if they were like in all respects they would be identities, and not examples, and all the more so in dealing with divine matters. For one cannot find an example that is like in all respects whether we are dealing with theology or the dispensation.

CHAPTER XXVII.
Concerning the fact that the divinity of the Word remained inseparable from the soul

---

4 St. Matt. xxvi. 39.   5 *Chyrs. in Cat. in St. Matt. xxvi.*
6 *Greg., Orat.* 36.   7 St. Matt. xxvii. 46.
8 *Greg. Naz., Orat.* 36 ; *Cyril, De recta fide ; Athanas., Contr. Arian.,* bk. iv.
9 *Greg. Nyss., Orat.* 38.
1 *Max. ad Marin. in solut.* 1 *dubit. Theod.*
2 *Greg. Naz., Orat.* 36 ; *Athanas., De Salut. adv. Christi.*

3 Gal. iii. 15.   4 *Photius, Cod.* 46.
5 *Athan., De salut. adv. Christi.*

and the body, even at our Lord's death, and that His subsistence continued one.

Since our Lord Jesus Christ was without sin (*for He committed no sin, He Who took away the sin of the world, nor was there any deceit found in His mouth* [6]) He was not subject to death, since death came into the world through sin [7]. He dies, therefore, because He took on Himself death on our behalf, and He makes Himself an offering to the Father for our sakes. For we had sinned against Him, and it was meet that He should receive the ransom for us, and that we should thus be delivered from the condemnation. God forbid that the blood of the Lord should have been offered to the tyrant [8]. Wherefore death approaches, and swallowing up the body as a bait is transfixed on the hook of divinity, and after tasting of a sinless and life-giving body, perishes, and brings up again all whom of old he swallowed up. For just as darkness disappears on the introduction of light, so is death repulsed before the assault of life, and brings life to all, but death to the destroyer.

Wherefore, although [9] He died as man and His Holy Spirit was severed from His immaculate body, yet His divinity remained inseparable from both, I mean, from His soul and His body, and so even thus His one hypostasis was not divided into two hypostases. For body and soul received simultaneously in the beginning their being in the subsistence [9a] of the Word, and although they were severed from one another by death, yet they continued, each of them, having the one subsistence of the Word. So that the one subsistence of the Word is alike the subsistence of the Word, and of soul and body. For at no time had either soul or body a separate subsistence of their own, different from that of the Word, and the subsistence of the Word is for ever one, and at no time two. So that the subsistence of Christ is always one. For, although the soul was separated from the body topically, yet hypostatically they were united through the Word.

CHAPTER XXVIII.

Concerning Corruption and Destruction.

The word corruption [1] has two meanings [2]. For it signifies all the human sufferings, such as hunger, thirst, weariness, the piercing with nails, death, that is, the separation of soul and body, and so forth. In this sense we say that our Lord's body was subject to corruption. For He voluntarily accepted all these things. But corruption means also the complete resolution of the body into its constituent elements, and its utter disappearance, which is spoken of by many preferably as destruction. The body of our Lord did not experience this form of corruption, as the prophet David says, *For Thou wilt not leave my soul in hell, neither wilt Thou suffer Thine holy one to see corruption* [3].

Wherefore to say, with that foolish Julianus and Gaïanus, that our Lord's body was incorruptible, in the first sense of the word, before His resurrection is impious. For if it were incorruptible it was not really, but only apparently, of the same essence as ours, and what the Gospel tells us happened, viz. the hunger, the thirst, the nails, the wound in His side, the death, did not actually occur. But if they only apparently happened, then the mystery of the dispensation is an imposture and a sham, and He became man only in appearance, and not in actual fact, and we are saved only in appearance, and not in actual fact. But God forbid, and may those who so say have no part in the salvation [4]. But we have obtained and shall obtain the true salvation. But in the second meaning of the word "corruption," we confess that our Lord's body is incorruptible, that is, indestructible, for such is the tradition of the inspired Fathers. Indeed, after the resurrection of our Saviour from the dead, we say that our Lord's body is incorruptible even in the first sense of the word. For our Lord by His own body bestowed the gifts both of resurrection and of subsequent incorruption even on our own body, He Himself having become to us the firstfruits both of resurrection and incorruption, and of passionlessness [5]. For as the divine Apostle says, *This corruptible must put on incorruption* [6].

CHAPTER XXIX.

Concerning the Descent to Hades.

The soul [7] when it was deified descended into Hades, in order that, just as the Sun of Righteousness [8] rose for those upon the earth, so likewise He might bring light to those who sit under the earth in darkness

6 Is. liii. 9 ; St. John i. 29.   7 Rom. v. 12.
8 *Greg., Orat.* 42.
9 Cf. *Epiph., Hæres.* 69 ; *Greg. Nyss., Contr. Eunom.,* II. p. 55.
9ª ὑπόστασις, *hypostasis.*
1 *Leont. De sect., Act.* 10, and *Dial. cont. Aphthartodoc.*
2 *Anast Sinait., Hodegus,* p. 295.

3 Ps. xvi. 10.   4 *Anast. Sinait., Hodegus,* p. 293.
5 1 Cor. xv. 20.   6 Ibid. 53.
7 Cf. *Ruf., Expos. Symbol. Apost.; Cassian, Contr. Nestor.* bk. vi.; *Cyril, Catech.* 14.
8 Mal. iv. 2.

and shadow of death[9] : in order that just as He brought the message of peace to those upon the earth, and of release to the prisoners, and of sight to the blind [1], and became to those who believed the Author of everlasting salvation and to those who did not believe a reproach of their unbelief[2], so He might become the same to those in Hades[3] : *That every knee should bow to Him, of things in heaven, and things in earth and things under the earth*[4]. And thus after He had freed those who had been bound for ages, straightway He rose again from the dead, shewing us the way of resurrection.

---

[9] Is. ix. 2.   [1] Is. lxi. 1 ; St. Luke iv. 19.   [2] 1 Pet. iii. 19.   [3] *Iren.*, iv. 45 ; *Greg. Naz., Orat.* 42.   [4] Phil. ii. 10.

BOOK IV.

CHAPTER I.

Concerning what followed the Resurrection.

After Christ was risen from the dead He laid aside all His passions, I mean His corruption or hunger or thirst or sleep or weariness or such like. For, although He did taste food after the resurrection [1], yet He did not do so because it was a law of His nature (for He felt no hunger), but in the way of œconomy, in order that He might convince us of the reality of the resurrection, and that it was one and the same flesh which suffered and rose again [2]. But He laid aside none of the divisions of His nature, neither body nor spirit, but possesses both the body and the soul intelligent and reasonable, volitional and energetic, and in this wise He sits at the right hand of the Father, using His will both as God and as man in behalf of our salvation, energising in His divine capacity to provide for and maintain and govern all things, and remembering in His human capacity the time He spent on earth, while all the time He both sees and knows that He is adored by all rational creation. For His Holy Spirit knows that He is one in substance with God the Word, and shares as Spirit of God and not simply as Spirit the worship accorded to Him. Moreover, His ascent from earth to heaven, and again, His descent from heaven to earth, are manifestations of the energies of His circumscribed body. *For He shall so come again to you,* saith he, *in like manner as ye have seen Him go into Heaven* [3].

CHAPTER II.

Concerning the sitting at the right hand of the Father.

We hold, moreover, that Christ sits in the body at the right hand of God the Father, but we do not hold that the right hand of the Father is actual place. For how could He that is uncircumscribed have a right hand limited by place? Right hands and left hands belong to what is circumscribed. But we

understand the right hand of the Father to be the glory and honour of the Godhead in which the Son of God, who existed as God before the ages, and is of like essence to the Father, amd in the end became flesh, has a seat in the body, His flesh sharing in the glory. For He along with His flesh is adored with one adoration by all creation [4].

CHAPTER III.

In reply to those who say [5], " If Christ has two natures, either ye do service to the creature in worshipping created nature, or ye say that there is one nature to be worshipped, and another not to be worshipped."

Along with the Father and the Holy Spirit we worship the Son of God, Who was incorporeal before He took on humanity, and now in His own person is incarnate and has become man though still being also God. His flesh, then, in its own nature [6], if one were to make subtle mental distinctions between what is seen and what is thought, is not deserving of worship since it is created. But as it is united with God the Word, it is worshipped on account of Him and in Him. For just as the king deserves homage alike when unrobed and when robed, and just as the purple robe, considered simply as a purple robe, is trampled upon and tossed about, but after becoming the royal dress receives all honour and glory, and whoever dishonours it is generally condemned to death: and again, just as wood in itself [7] is not of such a nature that it cannot be touched, but becomes so when fire is applied to it, and it becomes charcoal, and yet this is not because of its own nature, but because of the fire united to it, and the nature of the wood is not such as cannot be touched, but rather the charcoal or burning wood: so also the flesh, in its own nature, is not to be worshipped, but is worshipped in the incarnate God Word, not because of itself, but because of its union in subsistence with God the Word. And we do not say that

---

[1] St. Luke xxiv. 43.
[2] *Theodor., Dial. 2; Greg. Naz., Orat.* 49, *Ep.* 1 *ad Cled.*
[3] Acts i. 11.

[4] *Athan. Jun.,* p. 45, *ad Ant.; Basil, De Spiritu Sancto,* ch. 6.
[5] Against the Apollinarians, &c. Cf. *Greg. Naz., Ep. ad Cled.,* 11.
[6] *Athan.,* bk. i., *Cont. Apoll. Epist. ad Adelph. Epiphan. Ancor.,* § 51.
[7] A simile much used by the Fathers : cf. *supr.,* bk. iii., ch. 8.

we worship mere flesh, but God's flesh, that is, God incarnate.

CHAPTER IV.

Why it was the Son of God, and not the Father or the Spirit, that became man : and what having become man He achieved.

The Father is Father[8] and not Son[9]: the Son is Son and not Father: the Holy Spirit is Spirit and not Father or Son. For the individuality[9a] is unchangeable. How, indeed, could individuality continue to exist at all if it were ever changing and altering? Wherefore the Son of God became Son of Man in order that His individuality might endure. For since He was the Son of God, He became Son of Man, being made flesh of the holy Virgin and not losing the individuality of Sonship[1].

Further, the Son of God became man, in order that He might again bestow on man that favour for the sake of which He created him. For He created him after His own image, endowed with intellect and free-will, and after His own likeness, that is to say, perfect in all virtue so far as it is possible for man's nature to attain perfection. For the following properties are, so to speak, marks of the divine nature : viz. absence of care and distraction and guile, goodness, wisdom, justice, freedom from all vice. So then, after He had placed man in communion with Himself (for having made him for incorruption[2], He led him up through communion with Himself to incorruption), and when moreover, through the transgression of the command we had confused and obliterated the marks of the divine image, and had become evil, we were stripped of our communion with God (for what communion hath light with darkness[3]?): and having been shut out from life we became subject to the corruption of death : yea, since He gave us to share in the better part, and we did not keep it secure, He shares in the inferior part, I mean our own nature, in order that through Himself and in Himself He might renew that which was made after His image and likeness, and might teach us, too, the conduct of a virtuous life, making through Himself the way thither easy for us, and might by the communication of life deliver us from corruption, becoming

Himself the firstfruits of our resurrection, and might renovate the useless and worn vessel calling us to the knowledge of God that He might redeem us from the tyranny of the devil, and might strengthen and teach us how to overthrow the tyrant through patience and humility[4].

The worship of demons then has ceased : creation has been sanctified by the divine blood : altars and temples of idols have been overthrown, the knowledge of God has been implanted in men's minds, the co-essential Trinity, the uncreate divinity, one true God, Creator and Lord of all receives men's service : virtues are cultivated, the hope of resurrection has been granted through the resurrection of Christ, the demons shudder at those men who of old were under their subjection. And the marvel, indeed, is that all this has been successfully brought about through His cross and passion and death. Throughout all the earth the Gospel of the knowledge of God has been preached ; no wars or weapons or armies being used to rout the enemy, but only a few, naked, poor, illiterate, persecuted and tormented men, who with their lives in their hands, preached Him Who was crucified in the flesh and died, and who became victors over the wise and powerful. For the omnipotent power of the Cross accompanied them. Death itself, which once was man's chiefest terror, has been overthrown, and now that which was once the object of hate and loathing is preferred to life. These are the achievements of Christ's presence : these are the tokens of His power. For it was not one people that He saved, as when through Moses He divided the sea and delivered Israel out of Egypt and the bondage of Pharaoh[5] ; nay, rather He rescued all mankind from the corruption of death and the bitter tyranny of sin : not leading them by force to virtue, not overwhelming them with earth or burning them with fire, or ordering the sinners to be stoned, but persuading men by gentleness and long-suffering to choose virtue and vie with one another, and find pleasure in the struggle to attain it. For, formerly, it was sinners who were persecuted, and yet they clung all the closer to sin, and sin was looked upon by them as their God : but now for the sake of piety and virtue men choose persecutions and crucifixions and death.

Hail! O Christ, the Word and Wisdom and Power of God, and God omnipotent! What can we helpless ones give Thee in return for

---

8 *Greg. Naz., Orat.* 37; *Fulg., De fid. ad Petrum; Thomas Aquinas, III., quæst.* 3, Art. 6.
9 *Greg. Naz., Orat.* 39.
9a ἡ ἰδιότης, Latin, *proprietas*, the propriety, that which is distinctive of each.
1 Text, καὶ οὐκ ἐκστὰς τῆς ὑἱκῆς ἰδιότητος. R. 1 has, καὶ οὐκ ἐξέστη τῆς οἰκείας ἰδιότητος, and the old trans. is "et non secessit a propria proprietate.'
2 Wisd. ii. 23.   3 2 Cor. vi. 14.

4 *Athan., De Incarn.; Cyril, In Joan.,* bk. i.
5 Ex. xiv. 16.

all these good gifts? For all are Thine, and Thou askest naught from us save our salvation, Thou Who Thyself art the Giver of this, and yet art grateful to those who receive it, through Thy unspeakable goodness. Thanks be to Thee Who gave us life, and granted us the grace of a happy life, and restored us to that, when we had gone astray, through Thy unspeakable condescension.

CHAPTER V.

In reply to those who ask if Christ's subsistence is create or uncreate.

The subsistence [6] of God the Word before the Incarnation was simple and uncompound, and incorporeal and uncreate: but after it became flesh, it became also the subsistence of the flesh, and became compounded of divinity which it always possessed, and of flesh which it had assumed: and it bears the properties of the two natures, being made known in two natures: so that the one same subsistence is both uncreate in divinity and create in humanity, visible and invisible. For otherwise we are compelled either to divide the one Christ and speak of two subsistences, or to deny the distinction between the natures and thus introduce change and confusion.

CHAPTER VI.

Concerning the question, when Christ was called.

The mind was not united with God the Word, as some falsely assert [7], before the Incarnation by the Virgin and from that time called Christ. That is the absurd nonsense of Origen [8], who lays down the doctrine of the priority of the existence of souls. But we hold that the Son and Word of God became Christ after He had dwelt in the womb of His holy ever-virgin Mother, and became flesh without change, and that the flesh was anointed with divinity. For this is the anointing of humanity, as Gregory the Theologian says [9]. And here are the words of the most holy Cyril of Alexandria which he wrote to the Emperor Theodosius [1]: "For I indeed hold that one ought to give the name Jesus Christ neither to the Word that is of God if He is without humanity, nor yet to the temple born of woman if it is not united with the Word. For the Word that is of God is understood to be Christ when united with humanity in

ineffable manner in the union of the œconomy [2]." And again, he writes to the Empresses thus [3]: "Some hold that the name 'Christ' is rightly given to the Word that is begotten of God the Father, to Him alone, and regarded separately by Himself. But we have not been taught so to think and speak. For when the Word became flesh, then it was, we say, that He was called Christ Jesus. For since He was anointed with the oil of gladness, that is the Spirit, by Him Who is God and Father, He is for this reason [4] called Christ. But that the anointing was an act that concerned Him as man could be doubted by no one who is accustomed to think rightly." Moreover, the celebrated Athanasius says this in his discourse "Concerning the Saving Manifestation:" "The God Who was before the sojourn in the flesh was not man, but God in God, being invisible and without passion, but when He became man, He received in addition the name of Christ because of the flesh, since, indeed, passion and death follow in the train of this name."

And although the holy Scripture [4] says, *Therefore God, thy God, hath anointed thee with the oil of gladness [5]*, it is to be observed that the holy Scripture often uses the past tense instead of the future, as for example here: *Thereafter He was seen upon the earth and dwelt among men [6]*. For as yet God was not seen nor did He dwell among men when this was said. And here again: *By the rivers of Babylon, there we sat down; yea we wept [7]*. For as yet these things had not come to pass.

CHAPTER VII.

In answer to those who enquire whether the holy Mother of God bore two natures, and whether two natures hung upon the Cross.

ἀγένητον and γενητόν, written with one 'ν' [8] and meaning uncreated and created, refer to nature: but ἀγέννητον and γεννητόν, that is to say, unbegotten and begotten, as the double 'ν' indicates, refer not to nature but to subsistence. The divine nature then is ἀγένητος, that is to say, uncreate, but all things that come after the divine nature are γένητα, that is, created. In the divine and uncreated nature, therefore, the property of being ἀγέννητον or unbegotten is contemplated in the Father (for He was not begotten), that of being γέννητον or begotten in the Son (for He has been eternally begotten of the Father),

---

6 ὑπόστασις, hypostasis.
7 See *Sophr.*, *Ep. ad Serg.*; *Origen*, Περὶ ἀρχῶν, II. 6; *Ruf., Expos. Symb.*, &c.
8 *Origen*, Περὶ ἀρχῶν, bk. ii., ch. 6.
9 *Orat.* 36, near the end.   1 *Edit. Paris*, p. 25.

2 καθ' ἕνωσιν οἰκονομικήν, *in the union of the Incarnation.*
3 *Edit. Paris*, p. 54.   4 Ps. xlv. 7.
5 Some copies omit the last five words.   6 Bar. iii. 38.
7 Ps. cxxxvii. 1.   8 *Supr.*, bk. i. ch. 9.

and that of procession in the Holy Spirit. Moreover of each species of living creatures, the first members were ἀγέννητα but not ἀγένητα: for they were brought into being by their Maker, but were not the offspring of creatures like themselves. For γένεσις is creation, while γέννησις or begetting is in the case of God the origin of a co-essential Son arising from the Father alone, and in the case of bodies, the origin of a co-essential subsistence arising from the contact of male and female. And thus we perceive that begetting refers not to nature but to subsistence 9. For if it did refer to nature, τὸ γέννητον and τὸ ἀγέννητον, i.e. the properties of being begotten and unbegotten, could not be contemplated in one and the same nature. Accordingly the holy Mother of God bore a subsistence revealed in two natures; being begotten on the one hand, by reason of its divinity, of the Father timelessly, and, at last, on the other hand, being incarnated of her in time and born in the flesh.

But if our interrogators should hint that He Who is begotten of the holy Mother of God is two natures, we reply, " Yea ! He is two natures : for He is in His own person God and man. And the same is to be said concerning the crucifixion and resurrection and ascension. For these refer not to nature but to subsistence. Christ then, since He is in two natures, suffered and was crucified in the nature that was subject to passion. For it was in the flesh and not in His divinity that He hung upon the Cross. Otherwise, let them answer us, when we ask if two natures died. No, we shall say. And so two natures were not crucified but Christ was begotten, that is to say, the divine Word having become man was begotten in the flesh, was crucified in the flesh, suffered in the flesh, while His divinity continued to be impassible."

CHAPTER VIII.

How the Only-begotten Son of God is called first-born.

He who is first begotten is called first-born [1], whether he is only-begotten or the first of a number of brothers. If then the Son of God was called first-born, but was not called Only-begotten, we could imagine that He was the first-born of creatures, as being a creature [2]. But since He is called both first-born and Only-begotten, both senses must be preserved in His case. We say that He is first-born of all creation [3] since both He Himself is of God and creation is of God, but as He Himself is born alone and timelessly of the essence of God the Father, He may with reason be called Only-begotten Son, first-born and not first-created. For the creation was not brought into being out of the essence of the Father, but by His will out of nothing [4]. And He is called First-born among many brethren [5], for although being Only-begotten, He was also born of a mother. Since, indeed, He participated just as we ourselves do in blood and flesh and became man, while we too through Him became sons of God, being adopted through the baptism, He Who is by nature Son of God became first-born amongst us who were made by adoption and grace sons of God, and stand to Him in the relation of brothers. Wherefore He said, *I ascend unto My Father and your Father* [6]. He did not say "our Father," but " My Father," clearly in the sense of Father by nature, and "your Father," in the sense of Father by grace. And "My God and your God [7]." He did not say "our God," but " My God : " and if you distinguish with subtle thought that which is seen from that which is thought, also "your God," as Maker and Lord.

CHAPTER IX.

Concerning Faith and Baptism.

We confess one baptism for the remission of sins and for life eternal. For baptism declares the Lord's death. We are indeed " buried with the Lord through baptism [8]," as saith the divine Apostle. So then, as our Lord died once for all, we also must be baptized once for all, and baptized according to the Word of the Lord, *In the Name of the Father, and of the Son, and of the Holy Spirit* [9], being taught the confession in Father, Son, and Holy Spirit. Those [1], then, who, after having been baptized into Father, Son, and Holy Spirit, and having been taught that there is one divine nature in three subsistences, are rebaptized, these, as the divine Apostle says, crucify the Christ afresh. *For it is impossible*, he saith, *for those who were once enlightened, &c., to renew them again unto repentance : seeing they crucify to themselves the Christ afresh, and put Him to an open shame* [2]. But those who were not bap-

---

9 *Euthym.*, p. 2, *tit.* 8.
1 See the Scholiast on Gregory Nyssenus in *Cod. Reg.* 3451.
2 *Vid. apud Greg. Nyss.*, bk. iii., *contr. Eunom.*

3 Col. i 15.   4 *Athan., Expos. Fidei.*   5 Rom. viii. 29.
6 St. John xx. 17.   7 Ibid.   8 Col. ii. 12.
9 St. Matt. xxviii. 19.
1 See *Clem. Alex., Strom.*, bk. i. ; *Basil, Ep. ad Amphiloch.* 2 ; *Irenæus*, i. 8 ; *Theodor., Hær. fab.* c. 12 ; *Euseb., Hist. Eccles.* vii. 9 ; *Trullan Canon* 95 ; *Tertull., De Bapt.*, c 1, &c.
2 Heb. vi. 4.

tized into the Holy Trinity, these must be baptized again. For although the divine Apostle says : *Into Christ and into His death were we baptized* [3], he does not mean that the invocation of baptism must be in these words, but that baptism is an image of the death of Christ. For by the three immersions [4], baptism signifies the three days of our Lord's entombment [5]. The baptism then into Christ means that believers are baptized into Him. We could not believe in Christ if we were not taught confession in Father, Son, and Holy Spirit [6]. For Christ is the Son of the Living God [7], Whom the Father anointed with the Holy Spirit [8] : in the words of the divine David, *Therefore God, thy God, hath anointed thee with the oil of gladness above thy fellows* [9]. And Isaiah also speaking in the person of the Lord says, *The Spirit of the Lord is upon me because He hath anointed me* [1]. Christ, however, taught His own disciples the invocation and said, *Baptizing them in the Name of the Father, and of the Son, and of the Holy Spirit* [2]. For since Christ made us for incorruption [3][4], and we transgressed His saving command. He condemned us to the corruption of death in order that that which is evil should not be immortal, and when in His compassion He stooped to His servants and became like us, He redeemed us from corruption through His own passion. He caused the fountain of remission to well forth for us out of His holy and immaculate side [5], water for our regeneration, and the washing away of sin and corruption; and blood to drink as the hostage of life eternal. And He laid on us the command to be born again of water and of the Spirit [6], through prayer and invocation, the Holy Spirit drawing nigh unto the water [7]. For since man's nature is twofold, consisting of soul and body, He bestowed on us a twofold purification, of water and of the Spirit : the Spirit renewing that part in us which is after His image and likeness, and the water by the grace of the Spirit cleansing the body from sin and delivering it from corruption, the water indeed expressing the image of death, but the Spirit affording the earnest of life.

For from the beginning *the Spirit of God moved upon the face of the waters* [8], and anew

the Scripture witnesseth that water has the power of purification [9]. In the time of Noah God washed away the sin of the world by water [1]. By water every impure person is purified [2], according to the law, even the very garments being washed with water. Elias shewed forth the grace of the Spirit mingled with the water when he burned the holocaust by pouring on water [3]. And almost everything is purified by water according to the law : for the things of sight are symbols of the things of thought. The regeneration, however, takes place in the spirit : for faith has the power of making us sons (of God [4]), creatures as we are, by the Spirit, and of leading us into our original blessedness.

The remission of sins, therefore, is granted alike to all through baptism : but the grace of the Spirit is proportional to the faith and previous purification. Now, indeed, we receive the firstfruits of the Holy Spirit through baptism, and the second birth is for us the beginning and seal and security and illumination [5] of another life.

It behoves us, then, with all our strength to steadfastly keep ourselves pure from filthy works, that we may not, like the dog returning to his vomit [6], make ourselves again the slaves of sin. For faith apart from works is dead, and so likewise are works apart from faith [7]. For the true faith is attested by works.

Now we are baptized [8] into the Holy Trinity because those things which are baptized have need of the Holy Trinity for their maintenance and continuance, and the three subsistences cannot be otherwise than present, the one with the other. For the Holy Trinity is indivisible.

The first baptism [9] was that of the flood for the eradication of sin. The second [1] was through the sea and the cloud : for the cloud is the symbol of the Spirit and the sea of the water [2]. The third baptism was that of the Law : for every impure person washed himself with water, and even washed his garments, and so entered into the camp [3]. The fourth [4] was that of John [5], being preliminary and leading those who were baptized to repentance, that they might believe in Christ : *I,*

---

3 Rom vi. 3.
4 See *Basil., De Spir. Sanct.*, c. 28, and *Ep.* 39; *Jerome, Contr. Lucif.; Theodor., Hær.* III. 4; *Socrates, Hist.* c. 23; *Sozomen, Hist.* VI. 26.
5 *Auct., Quaest. ad Antioch.*
6 *Basil., De Bapt.*, bk. i. ch. 12.   7 St. Matt. xvi. 16.
8 Acts x. 38.   9 Ps. xlv. 7.   1 Is. lxi. 1.
2 St. Matt. xxviii 19.
3 Text, ἐπ᾿ ἀφθαρσίαν. Variant, ἐπ᾿ ἀφθαρσίᾳ; old interpretation, 'in incorruption.'   4 *Method., De Resurr.*
5 St. John xix. 34.   6 Ibid. iii. 5.   7 *Greg., Orat.* 48.
8 Gen. i. 2.

9 Lev. xv. 10.   1 Gen. vi. 17.
2 Text, καθαίρεται. Variant in many Codices is ἐκάθαιρετο. On one margin is, ἡ ἐκεκάθαρτο.
3 III. Reg. xviii. 32.
4 πίστις γὰρ υἱοθετεῖν οἶδε.
5 Text, φωτισμός, illumination. In R. 2626 is added, καὶ ἁγιασμός, which Faber translates,"et illuminatio et sanctificatio." In R. 2024, ἁγιασμός is read instead of φωτισμός.
6 2 Pet. ii 22.   7 James ii. 26.
8 *Greg. Naz , Orat.* 40; *Athan. ad Serap. De Spir. Sancto.*
9 *Greg. Theol., Orat.* 39.   1 Gen. vii. 17.
2 1 Cor. x. 1.   3 Lev. xiv. 8.
4 *Greg., Orat.* 40; *Basil. Hom. de Bapt.; Chrys. in Matt. Hom.* 10, and others.
5 Cf. *Basil, De Bapt.*, I. 2.

indeed, he said, *baptize you with water; but He that cometh after me, He will baptize you in the Holy Spirit and in fire* [6]. Thus John's purification with water was preliminary to receiving the Spirit. The fifth was the baptism of our Lord, whereby He Himself was baptized. Now He is baptized not as Himself requiring purification but as making my purification His own, that He may break the heads of the dragons on the water [7], that He may wash away sin and bury all the old Adam in water, that He may sanctify the Baptist, that He may fulfil the Law, that He may reveal the mystery of the Trinity, that He may become the type and ensample to us of baptism. But we, too, are baptized in the perfect baptism of our Lord, the baptism by water and the Spirit. Moreover [8], Christ is said to baptize with fire: because in the form of flaming tongues He poured forth on His holy disciples the grace of the Spirit: as the Lord Himself says, *John truly baptized with water: but ye shall be baptized with the Holy Spirit and with fire, not many days hence* [9]: or else it is because of the baptism of future fire wherewith we are to be chastised [1]. The sixth is that by repentance and tears, which baptism is truly grievous. The seventh is baptism by blood and martyrdom [2], which baptism Christ Himself underwent in our behalf [3], He Who was too august and blessed to be defiled with any later stains [4]. The eighth [5] is the last, which is not saving, but which destroys evil [6]: for evil and sin no longer have sway: yet it punishes without end [7].

Further, the Holy Spirit [8] descended in bodily form as a dove, indicating the firstfruits of our baptism and honouring the body: since even this, that is the body, was God by the deification; and besides the dove was wont formerly to announce the cessation of the flood. But to the holy Apostles He came down in the form of fire [9]: for He is God, and *God is a consuming fire* [1].

Olive oil [2] is employed in baptism as significant of our anointing [3], and as making us anointed, and as announcing to us through the Holy Spirit God's pity: for it was the fruit of the olive that the dove brought to those who were saved from the flood [4].

John was baptized, putting his hand upon the divine head of his Master, and with his own blood.

It does not behove [5] us to delay baptism when the faith of those coming forward is testified to by works. For he that cometh forward deceitfully to baptism will receive condemnation rather than benefit.

CHAPTER X.
Concerning Faith.

Moreover, faith is twofold. For *faith cometh by hearing* [6]. For by hearing the divine Scriptures we believe in the teaching of the Holy Spirit. The same is perfected by all the things enjoined by Christ, believing in work, cultivating piety, and doing the commands of Him Who restored us. For he that believeth not according to the tradition of the Catholic Church, or who hath intercourse with the devil through strange works, is an unbeliever.

But again, *faith is the substance of things hoped for, the evidence of things not seen* [7], or undoubting and unambiguous hope alike of what God hath promised us and of the good issue of our prayers. The first, therefore, belongs to our will, while the second is of the gifts of the Spirit.

Further, observe that by baptism we cut [8] off all the covering which we have worn since birth, that is to say, sin, and become spiritual Israelites and God's people.

CHAPTER XI.
Concerning the Cross and here further concerning Faith.

The word ' Cross' *is foolishness to those that perish, but to us who are saved it is the power of God* [9]. For *he that is spiritual judgeth all things, but the natural man receiveth not the things of the Spirit* [1]. For it is foolishness to those who do not receive in faith and who do not consider God's goodness and omnipotence, but search out divine things with human and natural reasonings. For all the things that are of God are above nature and reason and conception. For should any one consider how and for what purpose God brought all things out of nothing into being, and aim at arriving at that by natural reasonings, he fails to comprehend it. For knowledge of this kind belongs to spirits and demons. But if any one, under the guidance of faith, should consider the divine goodness

---

6 St. Matt. iii. 11.   7 Ps. lxxiv. 13.
8 *Greg. Naz., Orat.* 40.   9 Acts i. 5.
1 *Greg. Naz., Orat.* 40.   2 Id. ibid.   3 St. Luke xii. 50.
4 Text, ὡς λίαν . . . ὅσον. Variants, ὅσων and ὁ καί.
5 *Greg Naz., Orat.* 40.   6 See *Basil, De Spir. Sanct.,* c. 13.
7 οὐ σωτήριον, ἀλλὰ τῆς μὲν κακίας ἀναιρετικόν· οὐκ ἔτι γὰρ κακία καὶ ἁμαρτία πολιτεύεται· κόλαζον δὲ ἀτελεύτητα.
8 *Greg. Naz., Orat.* 39.
9 *Greg. Naz., Orat.* 44: Acts ii. 3.   1 Deut. iv. 24.
2 Cf., *Allab., De Cousens,* bk. iii., c. 16; *Cyril of Jerus., Catech. Myst.* 2.
3 Reading, χρίσιν. Variant, χάριν.   4 Gen. viii. 11.

5 *Greg. Naz., Orat.* 40.   6 Rom. x. 17.
7 Heb. xi. 1.   8 περιτεμνόμεθα, *circumcise.*
9 1 Cor. i. 23.   1 Ibid ii. 14, 15.

and omnipotence and truth and wisdom and justice, he will find all things smooth and even, and the way straight. *But without faith it is impossible to be saved*[2]. For it is by faith that all things, both human and spiritual, are sustained. For without faith neither does the farmer[3] cut his furrow, nor does the merchant commit his life to the raging waves of the sea on a small piece of wood, nor are marriages contracted nor any other step in life taken. By faith we consider that all things were brought out of nothing into being by God's power. And we direct all things, both divine and human, by faith. Further, faith is assent free from all meddlesome inquisitiveness[4].

Every action, therefore, and performance of miracles by Christ are most great and divine and marvellous: but the most marvellous of all is His precious Cross. For no other thing has subdued death, expiated the sin of the first parent[5], despoiled Hades, bestowed the resurrection, granted the power to us of contemning the present and even death itself, prepared the return to our former blessedness, opened the gates of Paradise[6], given our nature a seat at the right hand of God, and made us the children and heirs of God[7], save the Cross of our Lord Jesus Christ. For by the Cross[8] all things have been made right. *So many of us*, the apostle says, *as were baptized into Christ, were baptized into His death*[9], and *as many of you as have been baptized into Christ, have put on Christ*[1]. Further, *Christ is the power of God and the wisdom of God*[2]. Lo! the death of Christ, that is, the Cross, clothed us with the enhypostatic wisdom and power of God. And the power of God is the Word of the Cross, either because God's might, that is, the victory over death, has been revealed to us by it, or because, just as the four extremities of the Cross are held fast and bound together by the bolt in the middle, so also by God's power the height and the depth, the length and the breadth, that is, every creature visible and invisible, is maintained[3].

This was given to us as a sign on our forehead, just as the circumcision was given to Israel: for by it we believers are separated and distinguished from unbelievers. This is the shield and weapon against, and trophy over, the devil. *This is the seal that the destroyer may not touch you*[4], as saith the

Scripture. This is the resurrection of those lying in death, the support of the standing, the staff of the weak, the rod of the flock, the safe conduct of the earnest, the perfection of those that press forwards, the salvation of soul and body, the aversion of all things evil, the patron of all things good, the taking away of sin, the plant of resurrection, the tree of eternal life.

So, then, this same truly precious and august tree[5], on which Christ hath offered Himself as a sacrifice for our sakes, is to be worshipped as sanctified by contact with His holy body and blood; likewise the nails, the spear, the clothes, His sacred tabernacles which are the manger, the cave, Golgotha, which bringeth salvation[6], the tomb which giveth life, Sion, the chief stronghold of the churches and the like, are to be worshipped. In the words of David, the father of God[7], *We shall go into His tabernacles, we shall worship at the place where His feet stood*[8]. And that it is the Cross that is meant is made clear by what follows, *Arise, O Lord, into Thy Rest*[9]. For the resurrection comes after the Cross. For if of those things which we love, house and couch and garment, are to be longed after, how much the rather should we long after that which belonged to God, our Saviour[1], by means of which we are in truth saved.

Moreover we worship even the image of the precious and life-giving Cross, although made of another tree, not honouring the tree (God forbid) but the image as a symbol of Christ. For He said to His disciples, admonishing them, *Then shall appear the sign of the Son of Man in Heaven*[2], meaning the Cross. And so also the angel of the resurrection said to the woman, *Ye seek Jesus of Nazareth which was crucified*[3]. And the Apostle said, *We preach Christ crucified*[4]. For there are many Christs and many Jesuses, but one crucified. He does not say speared but crucified. It behoves us, then, to worship the sign of Christ[5]. For wherever the sign may be, there also will He be. But it does not behove us to worship the material of which the image of the Cross is composed, even though it be gold or precious stones, after it is destroyed, if that should happen. Everything, therefore, that is dedicated to God we worship, conferring the adoration on Him.

The tree of life which was planted by God in Paradise pre-figured this precious Cross.

[2] Heb. xi. 6. [3] Basil. in Ps. cxv. [4] Basil, cit. loc.
[5] Text, προπάτορος ἁμαρτία. Variant, προπατ. Ἀδὰμ ἁμαρτ.
[6] Text, ἠνοίχθησαν. Variant, ἠνοίγησαν.
[7] Cyril, Hier. catech. i. 14.
[8] Text, διὰ σταυροῦ. Variant, δί αὐτοῦ.
[9] Rom. vi. 3. [1] Gal. iii. 27. [2] Cor. i. 24.
[3] Basil. in Is. xi. [4] Exod. xii 23.

[5] Cf. Cyril. Contr. Jul., bk. vi.
[6] Text, ὁ Γοργοθᾶς, ὁ σωτήριος. Variant, ὁ σταυρός
[7] ὁ θεοπάτωρ Δαβίδ. Cf. Dionysiaster, Ep. 8.
[8] Ps cxxxii. 7. [9] Ibid. 8.
[1] Text, Σωτῆρος. Variant, σταυρός.
[2] St. Matt. xxiv. 30. [3] St. Mark xvi. 6. [4] 1 Cor. i. 22.
[5] Text, Χριστοῦ. Variant, σταυροῦ.

For since death was by a tree, it was fitting that life and resurrection should be bestowed by a tree [6]. Jacob, when He worshipped the top of Joseph's staff, was the first to image the Cross, and when he blessed his sons with crossed hands [7] he made most clearly the sign of the cross. Likewise [8] also did Moses' rod, when it smote the sea in the figure of the cross and saved Israel, while it overwhelmed Pharaoh in the depths; likewise also the hands stretched out crosswise and routing Amalek; and the bitter water made sweet by a tree, and the rock rent and pouring forth streams of water [9], and the rod that meant for Aaron the dignity of the high priesthood [1]: and the serpent lifted in triumph on a tree as though it were dead [2], the tree bringing salvation to those who in faith saw their enemy dead, just as Christ was nailed to the tree in the flesh of sin which yet knew no sin [3]. The mighty Moses cried [4], *You will see your life hanging on the tree before your eyes*, and Isaiah likewise, *I have spread out my hands all the day unto a faithless and rebellious people* [5]. But may we who worship this [6] obtain a part in Christ the crucified. Amen.

CHAPTER XII.

Concerning Worship towards the East.

It is not without reason or by chance that we worship towards the East. But seeing that we are composed of a visible and an invisible nature, that is to say, of a nature partly of spirit and partly of sense, we render also a twofold worship to the Creator; just as we sing both with our spirit and our bodily lips, and are baptized with both water and Spirit, and are united with the Lord in a twofold manner, being sharers in the mysteries and in the grace of the Spirit.

Since, therefore, God [7] is spiritual light [8], and Christ is called in the Scriptures Sun of Righteousness [1] and Dayspring [2], the East is the direction that must be assigned to His worship. For everything good must be assigned to Him from Whom every good thing arises. Indeed the divine David also says, *Sing unto God, ye kingdoms of the earth: O sing praises unto the Lord: to Him that rideth upon the Heavens of heavens towards the East* [3]. More-

over the Scripture also says, *And God planted a garden eastward in Eden; and there He put the man whom He had formed* [4]: and when he had transgressed His command He expelled him and made him to dwell over against the delights of Paradise [5], which clearly is the West. So, then, we worship God seeking and striving after our old fatherland. Moreover the tent of Moses [6] had its veil and mercy seat [7] towards the East. Also the tribe of Judah as the most precious pitched their camp on the East [8]. Also in the celebrated temple of Solomon the Gate of the Lord was placed eastward. Moreover Christ, when He hung on the Cross, had His face turned towards the West, and so we worship, striving after Him. And when He was received again into Heaven He was borne towards the East, and thus His apostles worship Him, and thus He will come again in the way in which they beheld Him going towards Heaven [9]; as the Lord Himself said, *As the lightning cometh out of the East and shineth* [1] *even unto the West, so also shall the coming of the Son of Man be* [2].

So, then, in expectation of His coming we worship towards the East. But this tradition of the apostles is unwritten. For much that has been handed down to us by tradition is unwritten [3].

CHAPTER XIII.

Concerning the holy and immaculate Mysteries of the Lord.

God [4] Who is good and altogether good and more than good, Who is goodness throughout, by reason of the exceeding riches of His goodness did not suffer Himself, that is His nature, only to be good, with no other to participate therein, but because of this He made first the spiritual and heavenly powers: next the visible and sensible universe: next man with his spiritual and sentient nature. All things, therefore, which he made, share in His goodness in respect of their existence. For He Himself is existence to all, since all things that are, are in Him [5], not only because it was He that brought them out of nothing into being, but because His energy preserves and maintains all that He made: and in especial the living creatures. For both in that they exist and in that they

6 Gen. ii. and iii.   7 Heb. xi. 21.
8 Auct., *Quest. ad Antioch.*, 9, 63.
9 Num. xx.   1 Exod. iv.   2 Ibid.
3 Text, οὐκ εἰδυίᾳ. Variant, εἰδώς.
4 *Iren.*, bk. v., c 18.   5 Isai. lxv. 2.
6 Text, τοῦτο. Variants, τοῦτον and τούτῳ.
7 *Basil, De Spir. Sanct.*, c. 27; *Alcuin, De Trin.* ii. 5: *Wal. Strabo, De reb. eccles*, c. 4; *Hon. August., Gemma Animæ.* c. 950.
8 1 St. John i. 5.   1 Mal. iv. 2.
2 Zach. iii. 8, vi. 12; St. Luke i. 78.   3 Ps. lxviii. 32, 33.

4 Gen. ii. 8.
5 Text, ὃν παραβάντα ἐξώρισεν, ἀπέναντί τε τοῦ Παραδείσου τῆς τρυφῆς κατῴκισεν. Variants, ὃν παραβάντα, τῆς τρυφῆς ἐξώρισεν, and ὃν παραβάντα, τοῦ παραδείσου τῆς τρυφῆς ἐξώρισεν, ἀπέναντί τε τοῦ παραδείσου κατῴκισεν.
6 Levit. xvi. 14.   7 Ibid. 2.   8 Num. ii. 3.
9 Acts i. 11.
1 Text, φαίνεται. Variant, φθάνει. The old translation gives occupat.   2 St Matt. xxiv. 27.
3 *Basil, De Spiritu Sancto*, ch. 27.
4 *Greg. Naz., Orat* 42: *Dion. De div. nom.*, ch. 3.
5 Rom. xi. 36.

enjoy life they share in His goodness. But in truth those of them that have reason have a still greater share in that, both because of what has been already said and also because of the very reason which they possess. For they are somehow more clearly akin to Him, even though He is incomparably higher than they.

Man, however, being endowed with reason and free will, received the power of continuous union with God through his own choice, if indeed he should abide in goodness, that is in obedience to his Maker. Since, however, he transgressed the command of his Creator and became liable to death and corruption, the Creator and Maker of our race, because of His bowels of compassion, took on our likeness, becoming man in all things but without sin, and was united to our nature [6]. For since He bestowed on us His own image and His own spirit and we did not keep them safe, He took Himself a share in our poor and weak nature, in order that He might cleanse us and make us incorruptible, and establish us once more as partakers of His divinity.

For it was fitting that not only the first-fruits of our nature should partake in the higher good but every man who wished it, and that a second birth should take place and that the nourishment should be new and suitable to the birth, and thus the measure of perfection be attained. Through His birth, that is, His incarnation, and baptism and passion and resurrection, He delivered our nature from the sin of our first parent and death and corruption, and became the first-fruits of the resurrection, and made Himself the way and image and pattern, in order that we, too, following in His footsteps, may become by adoption what He is Himself by nature [7], sons and heirs of God and joint heirs with Him [8]. He gave us therefore, as I said, a second birth in order that, just as we who are born of Adam are in his image and are the heirs of the curse and corruption, so also being born of Him we may be in His likeness and heirs [9] of His incorruption and blessing and glory.

Now seeing that this Adam is spiritual, it was meet that both the birth and likewise the food should be spiritual too, but since we are of a double and compound nature, it is meet that both the birth should be double and likewise the food compound. We were therefore given a birth by water and Spirit: I mean, by the holy baptism [1]: and the food is the very

bread of life, our Lord Jesus Christ, Who came down from heaven [2]. For when He was about to take on Himself a voluntary death for our sakes, on the night on which He gave Himself up, He laid a new covenant on His holy disciples and apostles, and through them on all who believe on Him. In the upper chamber, then, of holy and illustrious Sion, after He had eaten the ancient Passover with His disciples and had fulfilled the ancient covenant, He washed His disciples' feet [3] in token of the holy baptism. Then having broken bread He gave it to them saying, *Take, eat, this is My body broken for you for the remission of sins* [4]. Likewise also He took the cup of wine and water and gave it to them saying, *Drink ye all of it: for this is My blood, the blood of the New Testament which is shed for you for the remission of sins. This do ye in remembrance of Me. For as often as ye eat this bread and drink this cup, ye do shew the death of the Son of man and confess His resurrection until He come* [5].

If then the Word of God is quick and energising [6], and the Lord did all that He willed [7]; if He said, Let there be light and there was light, let there be a firmament and there was a firmament [8]; if the heavens were established by the Word of the Lord and all the host of them by the breath of His mouth [9]; if the heaven and the earth, water and fire and air and the whole glory of these, and, in sooth, this most noble creature, man, were perfected by the Word of the Lord; if God the Word of His own will became man and the pure and undefiled blood of the holy and ever-virginal One made His flesh without the aid of seed [1], can He not then make the bread His body and the wine and water His blood? He said in the beginning, *Let the earth bring forth grass* [2], and even until this present day, when the rain comes it brings forth its proper fruits, urged on and strengthened by the divine command. God said, *This is My body*, and *This is My blood*, and *this do ye in remembrance of Me*. And so it is at His omnipotent command until He come: for it was in this sense that He said *until He come*: and the overshadowing power of the Holy Spirit becomes through the invocation the rain to this new tillage [3]. For just as God made all that He made by the energy of the Holy Spirit, so also now the energy of the

---

6 Heb. ii. 17.   7 Rom. vii. 17.
8 Variant, φύσει καὶ κληρονόμοι τῆς αὐτοῦ γενώμεθα χάριτος, καὶ αὐτοῦ υἱοὶ, καὶ συγκληρονόμοι.
9 Text, κληρονομήσωμεν. Variant, κληρονομήσαντες.
1 *Chrys. in Matt., Hom.* 83; St. John iii. 3.

2 St. John vi. 48.   3 Ibid. xiii.
4 St. Matt. xxvi. 26; *Liturg. S. Jacobi.*
5 St. Matt. xxvi. 27, 28; St. Mark xiv. 22—24; St. Luke xxii. 19, 20; 1 Cor. xi. 24—26.
6 Heb. iv. 12.   7 Ps. cxxxv. 6.   8 Gen. i. 3 and 6.
9 Ps. xxxiii. 6.
1 Text, καὶ τὰ τῆς . . . καθαρὰ καὶ ἀμώμητα αἵματα ἑαυτῷ. Variant, καὶ ἐκ τῶν τῆς . . . καθαρῶν καὶ ἀμωμήτων αἱμάτων ἑαυτῷ.
2 Gen. i. 11.
3 *Iren.*, bk. iv., ch. 35; *Fulg., Ad Monim.*, bk. ii., ch. 6; *Chrys., De prod. Judæ; Greg. Nyss., Catech.*, &c.

Spirit performs those things that are supernatural and which it is not possible to comprehend unless by faith alone. *How shall this be*, said the holy Virgin, *seeing I know not a man?* And the archangel Gabriel answered her: *The Holy Spirit shall come upon thee, and the power of the Highest shall overshadow thee*[4]. And now you ask, how the bread became Christ's body and the wine and water Christ's blood. And I say unto thee, "The Holy Spirit is present and does those things which surpass reason and thought."

Further, bread and wine[5] are employed: for God knoweth man's infirmity: for in general man turns away discontentedly from what is not well-worn by custom: and so with His usual indulgence He performs His supernatural works through familiar objects: and just as, in the case of baptism, since it is man's custom to wash himself with water and anoint himself with oil, He connected the grace of the Spirit with the oil and the water and made it the water of regeneration, in like manner since it is man's custom to eat and to drink water and wine[6], He connected His divinity with these and made them His body and blood in order that we may rise to what is supernatural through what is familiar and natural.

The body which is born of the holy Virgin is in truth body united with divinity, not that the body which was received up into the heavens descends, but that the bread itself and the wine are changed into God's body and blood[7]. But if you enquire how this happens, it is enough for you to learn that it was through the Holy Spirit, just as the Lord took on Himself flesh that subsisted in Him and was born of the holy Mother of God through the Spirit. And we know nothing further save that the Word of God is true and energises and is omnipotent, but the manner of this cannot be searched out[8]. But one can put it well thus, that just as in nature the bread by the eating and the wine and the water by the drinking are changed into the body and blood of the eater and drinker, and do not[9] become a different body from the former one, so the bread of the table[1] and the wine and water are supernaturally changed by the invocation and presence of the Holy Spirit into the body and blood of Christ, and are not two but one[2] and the same.

Wherefore to those who partake worthily with faith, it is for the remission of sins and for life everlasting and for the safe-guarding of soul and body; but to those who partake unworthily without faith, it is for chastisement and punishment, just as also the death of the Lord became to those who believe life and incorruption for the enjoyment of eternal blessedness, while to those who do not believe and to the murderers of the Lord it is for everlasting chastisement and punishment.

The bread and the wine are not merely figures of the body and blood of Christ (God forbid!) but the deified body of the Lord itself: for the Lord has said, "This is My body," not, this is a figure of My body: and "My blood," not, a figure of My blood. And on a previous occasion He had said to the Jews, *Except ye eat the flesh of the Son of Man and drink His blood, ye have no life in you. For My flesh is meat indeed and My blood is drink indeed.* And again, *He that eateth Me, shall live*[3][4].

Wherefore with all fear and a pure conscience and certain faith let us draw near and it will assuredly be to us as we believe, doubting nothing. Let us pay homage to it in all purity both of soul and body: for it is twofold. Let us draw near to it with an ardent desire, and with our hands held in the form of the cross[5] let us receive the body of the Crucified One: and let us apply our eyes and lips and brows and partake of the divine coal, in order that the fire of the longing, that is in us, with the additional heat derived from the coal may utterly consume our sins and illumine our hearts, and that we may be inflamed and deified by the participation in the divine fire. Isaiah saw the coal[6]. But coal is not plain wood but wood united with fire: in like manner also the bread of the communion[7] is not plain bread but bread united with divinity. But a body[8] which is united with divinity is not one nature, but has one nature belonging to the body and another belonging to the divinity that is united to it, so that the compound is not one nature but two.

With bread and wine Melchisedek, the priest of the most high God, received Abraham on his return from the slaughter of the Gentiles[9]. That table pre-imaged this mystical table, just as that priest was a type and image of Christ, the true high-priest[1]. *For thou art a priest for ever after the order of Melchisedek*[2]. Of this

---

4 St. Luke i. 34, 35.   5 *Nyss., Orat., Catech.*, ch. 37.
6 *Clem., Constit.*, bk. viii.; *Justin Martyr, Apol.* i.; *Iren.*, v. 2.
7 *Greg. Nyss., Orat. Catech.*, c. 37.
8 *Simile Nyss. loc. cit.*   9 οὐ is absent in some MSS.
1 The Greek is ὁ τῆς προθέσεως οἶνος, *the bread of the prothesis*. It is rendered *panis propositionis* in the old translations. These phrases designate the *Shewbread* in the LXX. and the Vulgate. The πρόθεσις is explained as a smaller table placed on the right side of the altar, on which the priests make ready the bread and the cup for consecration. See the note in Migne.
2 See *Niceph., C.P., Antirr.* ii. 3.

3 St. John vi. 51—55.
4 ζωὴν αἰώνιον is added in many MSS.
5 *Cyril Hierosol., Cat. Mystag.* 5; *Chrys. Hom.* 3 *in Epist ad Ephes.; Trull. can.* 101.
6 Is. vi. 6.   7 See *Cyril Alex.* on Isaiah vi.
8 *Vide Basil, ibid.*   9 Gen. xiv. 18.
1 Lev. xiv.   2 Ps. cx. 4.

bread the show-bread was an image [3]. This surely is that pure and bloodless sacrifice which the Lord through the prophet said is offered to Him from the rising to the setting of the sun [4].

The body and blood of Christ are making for the support of our soul and body, without being consumed or suffering corruption, not making for the draught (God forbid!) but for our being and preservation, a protection against all kinds of injury, a purging from all uncleanness: should one receive base gold, they purify it by the critical burning lest in the future we be condemned with this world. They purify from diseases and all kinds of calamities; according to the words of the divine Apostle [5], *For if we would judge ourselves, we should not be judged. But when we are judged, we are chastened of the Lord, that we should not be condemned with the world.* This too is what he says, *So that he that partaketh of the body and blood of Christ unworthily, eateth and drinketh damnation to himself* [6]. Being purified by this, we are united to the body of Christ and to His Spirit and become the body of Christ.

This bread is the first-fruits [7] of the future bread which is ἐπιούσιος, i.e. necessary for existence. For the word ἐπιούσιον signifies either the future, that is Him Who is for a future age, or else Him of Whom we partake for the preservation of our essence. Whether then it is in this sense or that, it is fitting to speak so of the Lord's body. For the Lord's flesh is life-giving spirit because it was conceived of the life-giving Spirit. For what is born of the Spirit is spirit. But I do not say this to take away the nature of the body, but I wish to make clear its life-giving and divine power [8].

But if some persons called the bread and the wine antitypes [9] of the body and blood of the Lord, as did the divinely inspired Basil, they said so not after the consecration but before the consecration, so calling the offering itself.

Participation is spoken of; for through it we partake of the divinity of Jesus. Communion, too, is spoken of, and it is an actual communion, because through it we have communion with Christ and share in His flesh and His divinity: yea, we have communion and are united with one another through it. For since we partake of one bread, we all become one body of Christ and one blood, and members one of another, being of one body with Christ.

With all our strength, therefore, let us beware lest we receive communion from or grant it to heretics; *Give not that which is holy unto the dogs, saith the Lord, neither cast ye your pearls before swine* [1], lest we become partakers in their dishonour and condemnation. For if union is in truth with Christ and with one another, we are assuredly voluntarily united also with all those who partake with us. For this union is effected voluntarily and not against our inclination. *For we are all one body because we partake of the one bread,* as the divine Apostle says [2].

Further, antitypes of future things are spoken of, not as though they were not in reality Christ's body and blood, but that now through them we partake of Christ's divinity, while then we shall partake mentally [3] through the vision alone.

CHAPTER XIV.

Concerning our Lord's genealogy and concerning the holy Mother of God [4].

Concerning the holy and much-lauded ever-virgin one, Mary, the Mother of God, we have said something in the preceding chapters, bringing forward what was most opportune, viz., that strictly and truly she is and is called the Mother of God. Now let us fill up the blanks. For she being pre-ordained by the eternal prescient counsel of God and imaged forth and proclaimed in diverse images and discourses of the prophets through the Holy Spirit, sprang at the pre-determined time from the root of David, according to the promises that were made to him. *For the Lord hath sworn, He saith in truth to David, He will not turn from it: of the fruit of Thy body will I set upon Thy throne* [5]. And again, *Once have I sworn by My holiness, that I will not lie unto David. His seed shall endure for ever, and His throne as the sun before Me. It shall be established for ever as the moon, and as a faithful witness in heaven* [6]. And Isaiah says: *And there shall come out a rod out of the stem of Jesse and a branch shall grow out of his roots* [7].

But that Joseph is descended from the tribe of David is expressly demonstrated by Matthew and Luke, the most holy evangelists. But Matthew derives Joseph from David through Solomon, while Luke does so through Nathan; while over the holy Virgin's origin both pass in silence.

One ought to remember that it was not the custom of the Hebrews nor of the divine Scripture to give genealogies of women; and

---

3 Text, εἰκόνιζον. Variant, εἰκονίζουσι.
4 Mal. i. 11.   5 1 Cor. xi. 31, 32.
6 Ibid. 29.   7 Cyril, loc. cit.
8 St. John vi. 63.   9 Anastas., Hodegus, ch. 23.

1 St. Matt. vii. 6.   2 1 Cor. x. 17.
3 Text, νοητῶς διὰ μόνης τῆς Θέας: νοητῶς is wanting in some, Reg. 2928 having διὰ μόνης τῆς Θείας ἐνώσεως.
4 In *Reg.* 2428 is added καὶ Ἰωσὴφ τοῦ μνήστορος.
5 Ps. cxxxii. 11.   6 Ibid. lxxxix 35, 36, 37.   7 Is. xi. 1.

the law was to prevent one tribe seeking wives from another [8]. And so since Joseph was descended from the tribe of David and was a just man (for this the divine Gospel testifies), he would not have espoused the holy Virgin contrary to the law; he would not have taken her unless she had been of the same tribe [8a]. It was sufficient, therefore, to demonstrate the descent of Joseph.

One ought also to observe [9] this, that the law was that when a man died without seed, this man's brother should take to wife the wife of the dead man and raise up seed to his brother [1]. The offspring, therefore, belonged by nature to the second, that is, to him that begat it, but by law to the dead.

Born then of the line of Nathan, the son of David, Levi begat Melchi [2] and Panther: Panther begat Barpanther, so called. This Barpanther begat Joachim: Joachim begat the holy Mother of God [3][4]. And of the line of Solomon, the son of David, Mathan had a wife [5] of whom he begat Jacob. Now on the death of Mathan, Melchi, of the tribe of Nathan, the son of Levi and brother of Panther, married the wife of Mathan, Jacob's mother, of whom he begat Heli. Therefore Jacob and Heli became brothers on the mother's side, Jacob being of the tribe of Solomon and Heli of the tribe of Nathan. Then Heli of the tribe of Nathan died childless, and Jacob his brother, of the tribe of Solomon, took his wife and raised up seed to his brother and begat Joseph. Joseph, therefore, is by nature the son of Jacob, of the line of Solomon, but by law he is the son of Heli of the line of Nathan.

Joachim then [6] took to wife that revered and praiseworthy woman, Anna. But just as the earlier Anna [7], who was barren, bore Samuel by prayer and by promise, so also this Anna by supplication and promise from God bare the Mother of God in order that she might not even in this be behind the matrons of fame [8]. Accordingly it was grace (for this is the interpretation of Anna) that bore the lady: (for she became truly the Lady of all created things in becoming the Mother of the Creator). Further, Joachim [9] was born in the house of the *Probatica* [1], and was brought up to the temple. Then planted in

the House of God and increased by the Spirit, like a fruitful olive tree, she became the home of every virtue, turning her mind away from every secular and carnal desire, and thus keeping her soul as well as her body virginal, as was meet for her who was to receive God into her bosom: for as He is holy, He finds rest among the holy [2]. Thus, therefore, she strove after holiness, and was declared a holy and wonderful temple fit for the most high God.

Moreover, since the enemy of our salvation was keeping a watchful eye on virgins, according to the prophecy of Isaiah, who said, *Behold a virgin shall conceive and bare a Son and shall call His name Emmanuel, which is, being interpreted, ' God with us* [3],' in order that *he who taketh the wise in their own craftiness* [4] may deceive him who always glorieth in his wisdom, the maiden is given in marriage to Joseph by the priests, a new book to him who is versed in letters [5]: but the marriage was both the protection of the virgin and the delusion of him who was keeping a watchful eye on virgins. But when the fulness of time was come, the messenger of the Lord was sent to her, with the good news of our Lord's conception. And thus she conceived the Son of God, the hypostatic power of the Father, *not of the will of the flesh nor of the will of man* [6], that is to say, by connection and seed, but by the good pleasure of the Father and co-operation of the Holy Spirit. She ministered to the Creator in that He was created, to the Fashioner in that He was fashioned, and to the Son of God and God in that He was made flesh and became man from her pure and immaculate flesh and blood, satisfying the debt of the first mother. For just as the latter was formed from Adam without connection, so also did the former bring forth the new Adam, who was brought forth in accordance with the laws of parturition and above the nature of generation.

For He who was of the Father, yet without mother, was born of woman without a father's co-operation. And so far as He was born of woman, His birth was in accordance with the laws of parturition, while so far as He had no father, His birth was above the nature of generation: and in that it was at the usual time (for He was born on the completion of the ninth month when the tenth was just beginning), His birth was in accordance with the laws of parturition, while in that it was painless it was above the laws of generation. For, as pleasure did not precede

---

[8] Num. xxxvi. 6 *seqq.*   [8a] σκήπτρου.
[9] Cf. *Julius Afric., Ep. ad Aristidem*, cited in *Eusebius, Hist. Eccles.* i 7.
[1] Deut. xxv. 5.   [2] See the note in Migne.
[3] Text, τὴν ἁγίαν Θεοτόκον. Variant, τὴν ἁγίαν Ἄνναν.
[4] St. Luke iii. 24 *seqq.*
[5] R. 2926 adds "Etnan," the name being taken from Julius Africanus.
[6] *Epiph., Hæres.* 79.   [7] 1 Sam. i. 2.
[8] *Greg. Nyss., Orat. in nativ. Dom.: Eustath. in Hexaëm.*
[9] *Epiph., Hæres.* 79.
[1] τῆς προβατικῆς, *the Sheep-gate.*

[2] Ps. xviii. 25, 26.
[3] Is. vii. 14; St. Matt. i. 23.   [4] 1 Cor. iii. 19; Job v. 13.
[5] Is. xxix. 11.   [6] St. John i. 13.

it, pain did not follow it, according to the prophet who says, *Before she travailed, she brought forth*, and again, *before her pain came she was delivered of a man-child*[7]. The Son of God incarnate, therefore, was born of her, not a divinely-inspired [8] man but God incarnate ; not a prophet anointed with energy but by the presence of the anointing One in His completeness, so that the Anointer became man and the Anointed God, not by a change of nature but by union in subsistence. For the Anointer and the Anointed were one and the same, anointing in the capacity of God Himself as man. Must there not therefore be a Mother of God who bore God incarnate? Assuredly she who played the part of the Creator's servant and mother is in all strictness and truth in reality God's Mother and Lady and Queen over all created things. But just as He who was conceived kept her who conceived still virgin, in like manner also He who was born preserved her virginity intact, only passing through her and keeping her closed [9]. The conception, indeed, was through the sense of hearing, but the birth through the usual path by which children come, although some tell tales of His birth through the side of the Mother of God. For it was not impossible for Him to have come by this gate, without injuring her seal in any way.

The ever-virgin One thus remains even after the birth still virgin, having never at any time up till death consorted with a man. For although it is written, *And knew her not till she had brought forth her first-born Son*[1], yet note that he who is first-begotten is first-born, even if he is only-begotten. For the word "first-born" means that he was born first, but does not at all suggest the birth of others. And the word "till" signifies the limit of the appointed time but does not exclude the time thereafter. For the Lord says, *And lo, I am with you always, even unto the end of the world*[2], not meaning thereby that He will be separated from us after the completion of the age. The divine apostle, indeed, says, *And so shall we ever be with the Lord*[3], meaning after the general resurrection.

For could it be possible that she, who had borne God and from experience of the subsequent events had come to know the miracle, should receive the embrace of a man. God forbid! It is not the part of a chaste mind to think such thoughts, far less to commit such acts

But this blessed woman, who was deemed worthy of gifts that are supernatural, suffered those pains, which she escaped at the birth, in the hour of the passion, enduring from motherly sympathy the rending of the bowels, and when she beheld Him, Whom she knew to be God by the manner of His generation, killed as a malefactor, her thoughts pierced her as a sword, and this is the meaning of this verse : *Yea, a sword shall pierce through thy own soul also*[4] [5]. But the joy of the resurrection transforms the pain, proclaiming Him, Who died in the flesh, to be God.

CHAPTER XV.

Concerning the honour due to the Saints and their remains.

To the saints honour must be paid as friends of Christ, as sons and heirs of God : in the words of John the theologian and evangelist, *As many as received Him, to them gave He power to become sons of God*[6]. *So that they are no longer servants, but sons : and if sons, also heirs, heirs of God and joint heirs with Christ*[7] : and the Lord in the holy Gospels says to His apostles, *Ye are My friends*[8]. *Henceforth I call you not servants, for the servant knoweth not what his lord doeth*[9]. And further, if the Creator and Lord of all things is called also King of Kings and Lord of Lords[1] and God of Gods, surely also the saints are gods and lords and kings. For of these God is and is called God and Lord and King. *For I am the God of Abraham*, He said to Moses, *the God of Isaac and the God of Jacob*[2]. And God made Moses a god to Pharaoh[3]. Now I mean gods and kings and lords not in nature, but as rulers and masters of their passions, and as preserving a truthful likeness to the divine image according to which they were made (for the image of a king is also called king), and as being united to God of their own free-will and receiving Him as an indweller and becoming by grace through participation with Him what He is Himself by nature. Surely, then, the worshippers and friends and sons of God are to be held in honour? For the honour shewn to the most thoughtful of fellow-servants is a proof of good feeling towards the common Master[4].

These are made treasuries and pure habitations of God : *For I will dwell in them*,

---

7 Is. lxvi. 7.   8 θεοφόρος.   9 Ezek. xliv. 2.
1 St. Matt. i. 25.   2 Ibid xxviii. 20.   3 1 Thess. iv. 17.

4 St. Luke ii. 35.
5 In R. 2926 is added, ὅπερ αὐτῇ προείρηκεν ὁ Θεοδόχος Συμεὼν, τὸν Κύριον ἐναγκαλισάμενος.
6 St. John i. 12.   7 Gal. iv. 7 : Rom. viii. 17.
8 St. John xv. 14.   9 Ibid. 15.   1 Apoc. xix. 16.
2 Ex. iii. 6.   3 Ibid. vii. 1.
4 *Basil, Orat. in 40 Martyr.*

said God, *and walk in them, and I will be their God*[5]. The divine Scripture likewise saith that the souls of the just are in God's hand[6] and death cannot lay hold of them. For death is rather the sleep of the saints than their death. *For they travailed in this life and shall to the end*[7], and *Precious in the sight of the Lord is the death of His saints*[8]. What, then, is more precious than to be in the hand of God? For God is Life and Light, and those who are in God's hand are in life and light.

Further, that God dwelt even in their bodies in spiritual wise[8a], the Apostle tells us, saying, *Know ye not that your bodies are the temples of the Holy Spirit dwelling in you?*[9], and *The Lord is that Spirit*[1], and *If any one destroy the temple of God, him will God destroy*[2]. Surely, then, we must ascribe honour to the living temples of God, the living tabernacles of God. These while they lived stood with confidence before God.

The Master Christ made the remains of the saints to be fountains of salvation to us, pouring forth manifold blessings and abounding in oil of sweet fragrance : and let no one disbelieve this[3]. For if water burst in the desert from the steep and solid rock at God's will[4] and from the jaw-bone of an ass to quench Samson's thirst[5], is it incredible that fragrant oil should burst forth from the martyrs' remains? By no means, at least to those who know the power of God and the honour which He accords His saints.

In the law every one who toucheth a dead body was considered impure[6], but these are not dead. For from the time when He that is Himself life and the Author of life was reckoned among the dead, we do not call those dead who have fallen asleep in the hope of the resurrection and in faith on Him. For how could a dead body work miracles? How, therefore, are demons driven off by them, diseases dispelled, sick persons made well, the blind restored to sight, lepers purified, temptations and troubles overcome, and how does every good gift from the Father of lights[7] come down through them to those who pray with sure faith? How much labour would you not undergo to find a patron to introduce you to a mortal king and speak to him on your behalf? Are not those, then, worthy of honour who are the patrons of the whole race, and make intercession to God for us? Yea, verily, we ought to give honour to them

by raising temples to God in their name, bringing them fruit-offerings, honouring their memories and taking spiritual delight in them, in order that the joy of those who call on us may be ours, that in our attempts at worship we may not on the contrary cause them offence. For those who worship God will take pleasure in those things whereby God is worshipped, while His shield-bearers will be wroth at those things wherewith God is wroth. In psalms and hymns and spiritual songs[8], in contrition and in pity for the needy, let us believers[9] worship the saints, as God also is most worshipped in such wise. Let us raise monuments to them and visible images, and let us ourselves become, through imitation of their virtues, living monuments and images of them. Let us give honour to her who bore God as being strictly and truly the Mother of God. Let us honour also the prophet John as forerunner and baptist[1], as apostle and martyr, *For among them that are born of women there hath not risen a greater than John the Baptist*[2], as saith the Lord, and he became the first to proclaim the Kingdom. Let us honour the apostles as the Lord's brothers, who saw Him face to face and ministered to His passion, *for whom God the Father did foreknow He also did prædestinate to be conformed to the image of His Son*[3], *first apostles, second prophets*[4], *third pastors and teachers*[5]. Let us also honour the martyrs of the Lord chosen out of every class, as soldiers of Christ who have drunk His cup and were then baptized with the baptism of His life-bringing death, to be partakers of His passion and glory: of whom the leader is Stephen, the first deacon of Christ and apostle and first martyr. Also let us honour our holy fathers, the God-possessed ascetics, whose struggle was the longer and more toilsome one of the conscience : *who wandered about in sheepskins and goatskins, being destitute, afflicted, tormented; they wandered in deserts and in mountains and in dens and caves of the earth, of whom the world was not worthy*[6]. Let us honour those who were prophets before grace, the patriarchs and just men who foretold the Lord's coming. Let us carefully review the life of these men, and let us emulate their faith[7] and love and hope and zeal and way of life, and endurance of sufferings and patience even to blood, in order that we may be sharers with them in their crowns of glory.

---

5 Levit. xxvi. 12 : 2 Cor. vi. 16.   6 Wisd. iii. 1.
7 Ps. xl. 9, 10.   8 Ibid. cxvi. 15.   8a διὰ τοῦ νοῦ.
9 1 Cor. iii. 16.   1 2 Cor. iii. 17.   2 1 Cor. iii. 17.
3 *Aster., Hom. in SS. Mart.*   4 Ex. xvii. 6.
5 Judg. xv. 17.   6 Num. xix. 11.   7 Jas. i. 17.

8 Ephes. v. 19.
9 Text, πιστοί. Variant, πίστει in Reg. 1.
1 Almost all read τὸν πρόδρομον Ἰωάννην, ὡς προφήτην, &c.
2 St. Matt. xi. 11.   3 Rom. viii. 29.
4 1 Cor. xii. 24.   5 Ephes. iv. 11.
6 Hebr. xi. 37, 38.   7 Ibid. xiii. 7.

CHAPTER XVI.

Concerning Images [8].

But since some [9] find fault with us for worshipping and honouring the image of our Saviour and that of our Lady, and those, too, of the rest of the saints and servants of Christ, let them remember that in the beginning God created man after His own image [1]. On what grounds, then, do we shew reverence to each other unless because we are made after God's image? For as Basil, that much-versed expounder of divine things, says, the honour given to the image passes over to the prototype [2]. Now a prototype is that which is imaged, from which the derivative is obtained. Why was it that the Mosaic people honoured on all hands the tabernacle [3] which bore an image and type of heavenly things, or rather of the whole creation? God indeed said to Moses, *Look that thou make them after their pattern which was shewed thee in the mount* [4]. The Cherubim, too, which o'ershadow the mercy seat, are they not the work of men's hands [5]? What, further, is the celebrated temple at Jerusalem? Is it not hand-made and fashioned by the skill of men [6]?

Moreover the divine Scripture blames those who worship graven images, but also those who sacrifice to demons. The Greeks sacrificed and the Jews also sacrificed: but the Greeks to demons and the Jews to God. And the sacrifice of the Greeks was rejected and condemned, but the sacrifice of the just was very acceptable to God. For Noah sacrificed, and *God smelled a sweet savour* [7], receiving the fragrance of the right choice and good-will towards Him. And so the graven images of the Greeks, since they were images of deities, were rejected and forbidden.

But besides this who can make an imitation of the invisible, incorporeal, uncircumscribed, formless God? Therefore to give form to the Deity is the height of folly and impiety. And hence it is that in the Old Testament the use of images was not common. But after God [8] in His bowels of pity became in truth man for our salvation, not as He was seen by Abraham in the semblance of a man, nor as He was seen by the prophets, but in being truly man, and after He lived upon the earth and dwelt among men [9], worked miracles, suffered, was crucified,

rose again and was taken back to Heaven, since all these things actually took place and were seen by men, they were written for the remembrance and instruction of us who were not alive at that time in order that though we saw not, we may still, hearing and believing, obtain the blessing of the Lord. But seeing that not every one has a knowledge of letters nor time for reading, the Fathers gave their sanction to depicting these events on images as being acts of great heroism, in order that they should form a concise memorial of them. Often, doubtless, when we have not the Lord's passion in mind and see the image of Christ's crucifixion, His saving passion is brought back to remembrance, and we fall down and worship not the material but that which is imaged: just as we do not worship the material of which the Gospels are made, nor the material of the Cross, but that which these typify. For wherein does the cross, that typifies the Lord, differ from a cross that does not do so? It is just the same also in the case of the Mother of the Lord. For the honour which we give to her is referred to Him Who was made of her incarnate. And similarly also the brave acts of holy men stir us up to be brave and to emulate and imitate their valour and to glorify God. For as we said, the honour that is given to the best of fellow-servants is a proof of good-will towards our common Lady, and the honour rendered to the image passes over to the prototype [1]. But this is an unwritten tradition [2], just as is also the worshipping towards the East and the worship of the Cross, and very many other similar things.

A certain tale [3], too, is told [4], how that when Augarus [5] was king over the city of the Edessenes, he sent a portrait painter to paint a likeness of the Lord, and when the painter could not paint because of the brightness that shone from His countenance, the Lord Himself put a garment over His own divine and life-giving face and impressed on it an image of Himself and sent this to Augarus, to satisfy thus his desire.

Moreover that the Apostles handed down much that was unwritten, Paul, the Apostle of the Gentiles, tells us in these words: *Therefore, brethren, stand fast and hold the traditions which ye have been taught of us, whether by word or by epistle* [6]. And to the Corinthians he writes, *Now I praise you, brethren, that ye remember me in all things, and keep the traditions as I have delivered them to you* [7]."

---

8 Some MSS. have the title "Concerning the adoration of the august and holy images," or "Concerning the holy and sacred images," or "Concerning holy images."
9 Cf. *Petavius, Theol. Dogm.* xv., ch. 12.
1 Gen. i. 26.
2 *Basil, De Spir. Sancto*, ch. 18.   3 Ex. xxxiii. 10.
4 Ibid. xxv. 40: Heb. viii. 5.   5 Ex. xxv. 18.
6 1 Kings viii.
7 Gen. viii. 21.   8 St. John i. 14; Tit. iii. 4.
9 Bar. iii. 38.

1 Basil, in 40 *Mart.*: also *De Spir. Sancto*, ch. 27.
2 Cf. *August., Contr. Donatist.*, bk. iv.
3 *Evagr., Hist.* iv., ch. 27.
4 *Procop., De Bellis*, ii. ch. 12.
5 i.e. *Abgarus*.   6 2 Thess. ii. 15.   7 1 Cor. xi. 2.

CHAPTER XVII.

Concerning Scripture [8].

It is one and the same God Whom both the Old and the New Testament proclaim, Who is praised and glorified in the Trinity: *I am come*, saith the Lord, *not to destroy the law but to fulfil it* [9]. For He Himself worked out our salvation for which all Scripture and all mystery exists. And again, *Search the Scriptures for they are they that testify of Me* [1]. And the Apostle says, *God, Who at sundry times and in diverse manners spake in time past unto the fathers by the prophets, hath in these last days spoken unto us by His Son* [2]. Through the Holy Spirit, therefore, both the law and the prophets, the evangelists and apostles and pastors and teachers, spake.

All Scripture, then, is *given by inspiration of God and is also assuredly profitable* [3]. Wherefore to search the Scriptures is a work most fair and most profitable for souls. For just as the tree planted by the channels of waters, so also the soul watered by the divine Scripture is enriched and gives fruit in its season [4], viz. orthodox belief, and is adorned with evergreen leafage, I mean, actions pleasing to God. For through the Holy Scriptures we are trained to action that is pleasing to God, and untroubled contemplation. For in these we find both exhortation to every virtue and dissuasion from every vice. If, therefore, we are lovers of learning, we shall also be learned in many things. For by care and toil and the grace of God the Giver, all things are accomplished. *For every one that asketh receiveth, and he that seeketh findeth, and to him that knocketh it shall be opened* [5]. Wherefore let us knock at that very fair garden of the Scriptures, so fragrant and sweet and blooming, with its varied sounds of spiritual and divinely-inspired birds ringing all round our ears, laying hold of our hearts, comforting the mourner, pacifying the angry and filling him with joy everlasting: which sets our mind on the gold-gleaming, brilliant back of the divine dove [6], whose bright pinions bear up to the only-begotten Son and Heir of the Husband-man [7] of that spiritual Vineyard and bring us through Him to the Father of Lights [8]. But let us not knock carelessly but rather zealously and constantly: lest knocking we grow weary. For thus it will be opened to us. If we read once or twice and do not understand what we read, let us not grow weary, but let us persist, let us talk much, let us enquire. For *ask thy Father*, he saith, *and He will shew thee: thy elders and they will tell thee* [9]. For *there is not in every man that knowledge* [1]. Let us draw of the fountain of the garden perennial and purest waters springing into life eternal [2]. Here let us luxuriate, let us revel insatiate: for the Scriptures possess inexhaustible grace. But if we are able to pluck anything profitable from outside sources, there is nothing to forbid that. Let us become tried money-dealers, heaping up the true and pure gold and discarding the spurious. Let us keep the fairest sayings but let us throw to the dogs absurd gods and strange myths: for we might prevail most mightily against them through themselves.

Observe, further [3], that there are two and twenty books of the Old Testament, one for each letter of the Hebrew tongue. For there are twenty-two letters of which five are double, and so they come to be twenty-seven. For the letters Caph, Mem, Nun, Pe [4], Sade are double. And thus the number of the books in this way is twenty-two, but is found to be twenty-seven because of the double character of five. For Ruth is joined on to Judges, and the Hebrews count them one book: the first and second books of Kings are counted one: and so are the third and fourth books of Kings: and also the first and second of Paraleipomena: and the first and second of Esdra. In this way, then, the books are collected together in four Pentateuchs and two others remain over, to form thus the canonical books. Five of them are of the Law, viz. Genesis, Exodus, Leviticus, Numbers, Deuteronomy. This which is the code of the Law, constitutes the first Pentateuch. Then comes another Pentateuch, the so-called Grapheia [5], or as they are called by some, the Hagiographa, which are the following: Jesus the Son of Nave [6], Judges along with Ruth, first and second Kings, which are one book, third and fourth Kings, which are one book, and the two books of the Paraleipomena [7] which are one book. This is the second Pentateuch. The third Pentateuch is the books in verse, viz. Job, Psalms, Proverbs of Solomon, Ecclesiastes of Solomon and the Song of Songs of Solomon. The fourth Pentateuch is the Prophetical books, viz. the twelve prophets constituting one book, Isaiah, Jeremiah, Ezekiel, Daniel. Then come the two books of Esdra made into one, and Esther [8]. There

---

8 This chapter is wanting in *Cod. R.* 3547.   9 St. Matt. v. 17.
1 St. John v. 39.   2 Heb. i. 1, 2.   3 2 Tim. iii. 16.
4 Ps. i. 3.   5 St. Luke xi. 10.   6 Ps. lxviii. 13.
7 St. Matt. xxi. 37.   8 Jas. i. 17.

9 Deut. xxxii. 7.   1 1 Cor. viii. 7.   2 St. John iv. 14.
3 *Cyril Hieros., Cat.* 4; *Epiphan., De pond. et mens.*
4 Many copies read Phi.
5 *Writings.*   6 *Joshua the Son of Nun.*
7 *Chronicles.*
8 R. 2428 reads καὶ ἡ Ἰουδιθ, καὶ ἡ Ἐσθήρ: so also in *Cod. S. Hil*, but Epiphanius does not mention the book of Judith, nor does the text require it.

are also the Panaretus, that is the Wisdom of Solomon, and the Wisdom of Jesus, which was published in Hebrew by the father of Sirach, and afterwards translated into Greek by his grandson, Jesus, the Son of Sirach. These are virtuous and noble, but are not counted nor were they placed in the ark.

The New Testament contains four gospels, that according to Matthew, that according to Mark, that according to Luke, that according to John : the Acts of the Holy Apostles by Luke the Evangelist : seven catholic epistles, viz. one of James, two of Peter, three of John, one of Jude : fourteen letters of the Apostle Paul : the Revelation of John the Evangelist : the Canons [9] of the holy apostles [1], by Clement.

CHAPTER XVIII.

Regarding the things said concerning Christ.

The things said concerning Christ fall into four generic modes. For some fit Him even before the incarnation, others in the union, others after the union, and others after the resurrection. Also of those that refer to the period before the incarnation there are six modes : for some of them declare the union of nature and the identity in essence with the Father, as this, *I and My Father are one* [2] : also this, *He that hath seen Me hath seen the Father* [3] : and this, *Who being in the form of God* [4], and so forth. Others declare the perfection of subsistence, as these, *Son of God*, and *the Express Image of His person* [5], and *Messenger of great counsel, Wonderful Counsellor* [6], and the like.

Again, others declare the indwelling [7] of the subsistences in one another, as, *I am in the Father and the Father in Me* [8] ; and the inseparable foundation [9], as, for instance, the Word, Wisdom, Power, Effulgence. For the word is inseparably established in the mind (and it is the essential mind that I mean), and so also is wisdom, and power in him that is powerful, and effulgence in the light, all springing forth from these [1].

And others make known the fact of His origin from the Father as cause, for instance, *My Father is greater than I* [2]. For from Him He derives both His being and all that He has [3] : His being was by generative and not by creative means, as, *I came forth from the*

Father and am come [4], and *I live by the Father* [5]. But all that He hath is not His by free gift or by teaching, but in a causal sense, as, *The Son can do nothing of Himself but what He seeth the Father do* [6]. For if the Father is not, neither is the Son. For the Son is of the Father and in the Father and with the Father, and not after [7] the Father. In like manner also what He doeth is of Him and with Him. For there is one and the same, not similar but the same, will and energy and power in the Father, Son and Holy Spirit.

Moreover, other things are said as though the Father's good-will was fulfilled [8] through His energy, and not as through an instrument or a servant, but as through His essential and hypostatic Word and Wisdom and Power, because but one action [9] is observed in Father and Son, as for example, *All things were made by Him* [9a], and *He sent His Word and healed them* [1], and *That they may believe that Thou hast sent Me* [2].

Some, again, have a prophetic sense, and of these some are in the future tense : for instance, *He shall come openly* [3], and this from Zechariah, *Behold, thy King cometh unto thee* [4], and this from Micah, *Behold, the Lord cometh out of His place and will come down and tread upon the high places of the earth* [5]. But others, though future, are put in the past tense, as, for instance, *This is our God : Therefore He was seen upon the earth and dwelt among men* [6], and *The Lord created me in the beginning of His ways for His works* [7], and *Wherefore God, thy God, anointed thee with the oil of gladness above thy fellows* [8], and such like.

The things said, then, that refer to the period before the union will be applicable to Him even after the union : but those that refer to the period after the union will not be applicable at all before the union, unless indeed in a prophetic sense, as we said. Those that refer to the time of the union have three modes. For when our discourse deals with the higher aspect, we speak of the deification of the flesh, and His assumption of the Word and exceeding exaltation, and so forth, making manifest the riches that are added to the flesh from the union and natural conjunction with the most high God the Word. And when our discourse deals with the lower aspect, we speak of the incarnation of God the Word, His becoming man, His emptying of Himself, His poverty, His humility. For these and such like are imposed upon the Word and

---

9 R. 2428 reads καὶ ἐπιστολαὶ δύο διὰ Κλήμεντος, probably an interpolation.
1 *Trull., Can.* 2 ; *Euseb., Hist. Eccles.* vi., ch. 23, &c.
2 St. John x. 30.   3 Ibid. xiv 9.   4 Phil. ii. 6.
5 Heb. i. 3.   6 Is. ix. 6.
7 περιχώρησις.   8 St. John xiv. 10.
9 τὴν ἀνεκφοίτητον ἵδρυσιν.
1 *Cyril, Thes.*, bk. xxxiv., p. 341.   2 St. John xiv. 28.
3 *Greg Naz., Orat.* 36, and other Greeks.

4 St. John xvi. 28.   5 Ibid. vi. 57.   6 Ibid. v. 19.
7 Text, μετά. Various reading, κατά.
8 Text, πληρούμενα. Variant, πληρουμένης.
9 κίνησιν, motion.   9a St. John xi. 42.   1 Ps. cvii. 20.
2 St. John xvii. 2.   3 Ps. l. 3.   4 Zech. ix. 9.
5 Mic. i. 3.   6 Bar. iii. 38.   7 Prov. viii. 22.   8 Ps. xlv. 7.

God through His admixture with humanity. When again we keep both sides in view at the same time, we speak of union, community, anointing, natural conjunction, conformation and the like. The former two modes, then, have their reason in this third mode. For through the union it is made clear what either has obtained from the intimate junction with and permeation through the other. For through the union [9] in subsistence the flesh is said to be deified and to become God and to be equally God with the Word ; and God the Word is said to be made flesh, and to become man, and is called creature and last [1] : not in the sense that the two natures are converted into one compound nature (for it is not possible for the opposite natural qualities to exist at the same time in one nature) [2], but in the sense that the two natures are united in subsistence and permeate one another without confusion or transmutation   The permeation [3] moreover did not come of the flesh but of the divinity : for it is impossible that the flesh should permeate through the divinity : but the divine nature once permeating through the flesh gave also to the flesh the same ineffable power of permeation [4] ; and this indeed is what we call union.

Note, too, that in the case of the first and second modes of those that belong to the period of the union, reciprocation is observed. For when we speak about the flesh, we use the terms deification and assumption of the Word and exceeding exaltation and anointing. For these are derived from divinity, but are observed in connection with the flesh. And when we speak about the Word, we use the terms emptying, incarnation, becoming man, humility and the like : and these, as we said, are imposed on the Word and God through the flesh. For He endured these things in person of His own free-will.

Of the things that refer to the period after the union there are three modes. The first declares His divine nature, as, *I am in the Father and the Father in Me* [5], and *I and the Father are one* [6] : and all those things which are affirmed of Him before His assumption of humanity, these will be affirmed of Him even after His assumption of humanity, with this exception, that He did not assume the flesh and its natural properties.

The second declares His human nature, as, *Now ye seek to kill Me, a man that hath told you the truth* [7], and *Even so must the Son of Man be lifted up* [8], and the like.

Further, of the statements made and written about Christ the Saviour after the manner of men, whether they deal with sayings or actions, there are six modes. For some of them were done or said naturally in accordance with the incarnation ; for instance, His birth from a virgin, His growth and progress with age, His hunger, thirst, weariness, fear, sleep, piercing with nails, death and all such like natural and innocent passions [9]. For in all these there is a mixture of the divine and human, although they are held to belong in reality to the body, the divine suffering none of these, but procuring through them our salvation.

Others are of the nature of ascription [9a], as Christ's question, *Where have ye laid Lazarus* [1] ? His running to the fig-tree, His shrinking, that is, His drawing back, His praying, and His making *as though He would have gone further* [2].   For neither as God nor as man was He in need of these or similar things, but only because His form was that of a man as necessity and expediency demanded [3]. For example, the praying was to shew that He is not opposed to God, for He gives honour to the Father as the cause of Himself [4] : and the question was not put in ignorance but to shew that He is in truth man as well as God [5] ; and the drawing back is to teach us not to be impetuous nor to give ourselves up.

Others again are said in the manner of association and relation [5a], as, *My God, My God, why hast Thou forsaken Me* [6] ? and *He hath made Him to be sin for us, Who knew no sin* [7], and *being made a curse for us* [8] ; also, *Then shall the Son also Himself be subject unto Him that put all things under Him* [9]. For neither as God nor as man [1] was He ever forsaken by the Father, nor did He become sin or a curse, nor did He require to be made subject to the Father. For as God He is equal to the Father and not opposed to Him nor subjected to Him ; and as God, He was never at any time disobedient to His Begetter to make it necessary for Him to make Him subject [2]. Appropriating, then, our person and ranking Himself with us, He used these words. For we are bound in the fetters of sin and the curse as faithless and disobedient, and therefore forsaken.

Others are said by reason of distinction in thought. For if you divide in thought things that are inseparable in actual truth, to cut the flesh from the Word, the terms

9 *Greg. Naz., Or at.* 39.   1 Is. xlviii. 12.
2 *Supr.* bk. iii., ch. 2.
3 Or, *inhabitation, mutual indwelling.*
4 περιχωροῦσα.   5 St. John xiv. 1.   6 Ibid. **x. 30.**
7 Ibid. vii. 19 ; viii. 40.   8 Ibid. iii. **14.**

9 Vide *supr.*, bk. iii., ch. **21,** 22, 23.
9a προσποίησις, *feigning.*   1 St. John xi. 34.
2 St. Luke xxiv. 28.   3 *Greg. Naz., Orat.* **36.**
4 *Supr.* bk. iii. 24.
5 Text, μετὰ τοῦ εἶναι Θεός.   Variant, μεῖναι.
5a οἰκείωσις καὶ ἀναφορά.   6 St. Matt. xxvii. 46.
7 2 Cor. v. 21.   8 Gal. iii. 13.   9 1 Cor. xv. **28.**
1 *Greg. Naz., Orat.* 36.   2 Ibid.

'servant' and 'ignorant' are used of Him, for indeed He was of a subject and ignorant nature, and except that it was united with God the Word, His flesh was servile and ignorant [3]. But because of the union in subsistence with God the Word it was neither servile nor ignorant. In this way, too, He called the Father His God.

Others again are for the purpose of revealing Him to us and strengthening our faith, as, *And now, O Father, glorify Thou Me with the glory which I had with Thee, before the world was* [4]. For He Himself was glorified and is glorified, but His glory was not manifested nor confirmed to us. Also that which the apostle said, *Declared to be the Son of God with power, according to the spirit of holiness, by the resurrection from the dead* [5]. For by the miracles and the resurrection and the coming of the Holy Spirit it was manifested and confirmed to the world that He is the Son of God [6]. And this too [7], *The Child grew in wisdom and grace* [8].

Others again have reference to His appropriation of the personal life of the Jews, in numbering Himself among the Jews, as He saith to the Samaritan woman, *Ye worship ye know not what : we know what we worship, for salvation is of the Jews* [9].

The third mode is one which declares the one subsistence and brings out the dual nature : for instance, *And I live by the Father : so he that eateth Me, even he shall live by Me* [1]. And this : *I go to My Father and ye see Me no more* [2]. And this : *They would not have crucified the Lord of Glory* [3]. And this : *And no man hath ascended up to heaven but He that came down from heaven, even the Son of Man which is in heaven* [4], and such like.

Again of the affirmations that refer to the period after the resurrection some are suitable to God, as, *Baptizing them in the name of the Father, and of the Son, and of the Holy Ghost* [5], for here 'Son' is clearly used as God; also this, *And lo, I am with you alway, even unto the end of the world* [6], and other similar ones. For He is with us as God. Others are suitable to man, as, *They held Him by the feet* [7], and *There they will see Me* [8], and so forth.

Further, of those referring to the period after the Resurrection that are suitable to man there are different modes. For some did actually take place, yet not according to nature [9], but according to dispensation, in order to confirm the fact that the very body, which suffered, rose again ; such are the weals, the eating and the drinking after the resurrection. Others took place actually and naturally, as changing from place to place without trouble and passing in through closed gates. Others have the character of simulation [1], as, *He made as though He would have gone further* [2]. Others are appropriate to the double nature, as, *I ascend unto My Father and your Father, and My God and your God* [3], and *The King of Glory shall come in* [4], and *He sat down on the right hand of the majesty on High* [5]. Finally others are to be understood as though He were ranking Himself with us, in the manner of separation in pure thought, as, *My God and your God* [3].

Those then that are sublime must be assigned to the divine nature, which is superior to passion and body : and those that are humble must be ascribed to the human nature ; and those that are common must be attributed to the compound, that is, the one Christ, Who is God and man. And it should be understood that both belong to one and the same Jesus Christ, our Lord. For if we know what is proper to each, and perceive that both are performed by one and the same, we shall have the true faith and shall not go astray. And from all these the difference between the united natures is recognised, and the fact [6] that, as the most godly Cyril says, they are not identical in the natural quality of their divinity and humanity. But yet there is but one Son and Christ and Lord : and as He is one, He has also but one person, the unity in subsistence being in nowise broken up into parts by the recognition of the difference of the natures.

CHAPTER XIX.

That God [7] is not the cause of evils.

It is to be observed [8] that it is the custom in the Holy Scripture to speak of God's permission as His energy, as when the apostle says in the Epistle to the Romans, *Hath not the potter power over the clay, of the same lump to make one vessel unto honour and another unto dishonour* [9]? And for this reason, that He Himself makes this or that. For He is Himself alone the Maker of all things ; yet it is not He Himself that fashions noble or ignoble things, but the personal choice of

---

3 *Supr.,* bk. iii. ch. 21.   4 St. John xvii. 5.
5 Rom. i. 4.
6 *Chrysost., Hom.* 1 *in Epist. ad Rom.,* and others.
7 St. Luke ii. 40.   8 Text, χάριτι. Reg. 1, συνέθει.
9 St. John iv. 22.   1 Ibid. xvi. 10.   2 Ibid.
3 1 Cor ii. 8.   4 St. John iii. 13.
5 St. Matt. xxviii. 19.   6 Ibid. 20.   7 Ibid. 9.
8 Ibid. 10.

9 κατὰ φύσιν.   1 κατὰ προσποίησιν.
2 St. Luke xxiv. 28.   3 St. John xx. 17.
4 Ps. xxiv. 7.   5 Heb. i. 3.
6 *Epist. apologetica ad Acacium Melitinæ Episcopum.*
7 Against Platonists. Gnostics, and Manicheans.
8 *Damasc. Dial. cont. Manich.*   9 Rom. ix. 21.

each one[1]. And this is manifest from what the same Apostle says in the Second Epistle to Timothy, *In a great house there are not only vessels of gold and of silver, but also of wood and of earth : and some to honour and some to dishonour. If a man therefore purge himself from these, he shall be a vessel unto honour sanctified, and meet for the master's use, and prepared unto every good work*[2]. And it is evident that the purification must be voluntary : for *if a man*, he saith, *purge himself.* And the consequent antistrophe responds, " If a man purge not himself he will be a vessel to dishonour, unmeet for the master's use and fit only to be broken in pieces." Wherefore this passage that we have quoted and this, *God hath concluded them all in unbelief*[3], and this, *God hath given them the spirit of slumber, eyes that they should not see, and ears that they should not hear*[4], all these must be understood not as though God Himself were energising, but as though God were permitting, both because of free-will and because goodness knows no compulsion.

His permission, therefore, is usually spoken of in the Holy Scripture as His energy and work. Nay, even when He says that *God creates evil things*, and that *there is no evil in a city that the Lord hath not done*, he does not mean by these words[5] that the Lord is the cause of evil, but the word ' evil[6] ' is used in two ways, with two meanings. For sometimes it means what is evil by nature, and this is the opposite of virtue and the will of God : and sometimes it means that which is evil and oppressive to our sensation, that is to say, afflictions and calamities. Now these are seemingly evil because they are painful, but in reality are good. For to those who understand they become ambassadors of conversion and salvation. The Scripture says that of these God is the Author.

It is, moreover, to be observed that of these, too, we are the cause : for involuntary evils are the offspring of voluntary ones[7].

This also should be recognised, that it is usual in the Scriptures for some things that ought to be considered as effects to be stated in a causal sense[8], as, *Against Thee, Thee only, have I sinned and done this evil in Thy sight, that Thou mightest be justified when Thou speakest, and prevail when Thou judgest*[9]. For the sinner did not sin in order that God might prevail, nor again did God require our sin in order that He might by it be revealed as

victor[1]. For above comparison He wins the victor's prize against all, even against those who are sinless, being Maker, incomprehensible, uncreated, and possessing natural and not adventitious glory. But it is because when we sin God is not unjust in His anger against us ; and when He pardons the penitent He is shewn victor over our wickedness. But it is not for this that we sin, but because the thing so turns out. It is just as if one were sitting at work and a friend stood near by, and one said, My friend came in order that I might do no work that day. The friend, however, was not present in order that the man should do no work, but such was the result. For being occupied with receiving his friend he did not work. These things, too, are spoken of as effects because affairs so turned out. Moreover, God does not wish that He alone should be just, but that all should, so far as possible, be made like unto Him.

CHAPTER XX.

That there are not two Kingdoms.

That there are not two kingdoms[2], one good and one bad, we shall see from this. For good and evil are opposed to one another and mutually destructive, and cannot exist in one another or with one another. Each of them, therefore, in its own division will belong to the whole, and first[3] they will be circumscribed, not by the whole alone but also each of them by part of the whole.

Next I ask[4], who it is that assigns[5] to each its place. For they will not affirm that they have come to a friendly agreement with, or been reconciled to, one another. For evil is not evil when it is at peace with, and reconciled to, goodness, nor is goodness good when it is on amicable terms with evil. But if He Who has marked off to each of these its own sphere of action is something different from them, He must the rather be God.

One of two things indeed is necessary, either that they come in contact with and destroy one another, or that there exists some intermediate place where neither goodness nor evil exists, separating both from one another, like a partition. And so there will be no longer two but three kingdoms.

Again, one of these alternatives is necessary, either that they are at peace, which is quite incompatible with evil (for that which is at peace is not evil), or they are at strife, which

---

[1] Basil, Homil. Quod Deus non sit auct. malorum.
[2] 2 Tim. ii. 20, 21.   [3] Rom. xi. 32.
[4] Is. xxix. 10 ; Rom xi. 8   [5] Amos iii. 6.
[6] Text, δισέμφατον. Variant, δυσέμφατον.
[7] Text, τῶν γὰρ ἑκουσίων κακῶν τὰ ἀκούσια, &c.   R. 2930 has τῶν ἀκουσίων τὰ ἑκούσια.
[8] Basil, loc. cit.   [9] Ps. li. 4.

[1] νικητής is sometimes absent.   [2] Athan., Cont. Gentes.
[3] Athan., Cont. omnes hæret.
[4] Damasc., Dial. Cont. Manich.
[5] Text, ἀποτεμνόμενος. Variants, ἀποτεμόμενος and ἀπονεμόμενος.

is incompatible with goodness (for that which is at strife is not perfectly good), or the evil is at strife and the good does not retaliate, but is destroyed by the evil, or they are ever in trouble and distress[6], which is not a mark of goodness. There is, therefore, but one kingdom, delivered from all evil.

But if this is so, they say, whence comes evil[7]? For it is quite impossible that evil should originate from goodness. We answer, then, that evil is nothing else than absence of goodness and a lapsing[8] from what is natural into what is unnatural: for nothing evil is natural. For all things, whatsoever God made, are very good[9], so far as they were made: if, therefore, they remain just as they were created, they are very good, but when they voluntarily depart from what is natural and turn to what is unnatural, they slip into evil.

By nature, therefore, all things are servants of the Creator and obey Him. Whenever, then, any of His creatures voluntarily rebels and becomes disobedient to his Maker, he introduces evil into himself. For evil is not any essence nor a property of essence, but an accident, that is, a voluntary deviation from what is natural into what is unnatural, which is sin.

Whence, then, comes sin[1]? It is an invention of the free-will of the devil. Is the devil, then, evil? In so far as he was brought into existence he is not evil but good. For he was created by his Maker a bright and very brilliant angel, endowed with free-will as being rational. But he voluntarily departed from the virtue that is natural and came into the darkness of evil, being far removed from God, Who alone is good and can give life and light. For from Him every good thing derives its goodness, and so far as it is separated from Him in will (for it is not in place), it falls into evil.

CHAPTER XXI.

The purpose[2] for which God in His foreknow-ledge created persons who would sin and not repent.

God in His goodness[3] brought what exists into being out of nothing, and has foreknow-ledge of what will exist in the future. If, therefore, they were not to exist in the future, they would neither be evil in the future nor

would they be foreknown. For knowledge is of what exists and foreknowledge is of what will surely exist in the future. For simple being comes first and then good or evil being. But if the very exis'ence of those, who through the goodness of God are in the future to exist, were to be prevented by the fact that they were to become evil of their own choice, evil would have prevailed over the goodness of God. Wherefore God makes all His works good, but each becomes of its own choice good or evil. Although, then, the Lord said, *Good were it for that man that he had never been born*[4], He said it in condemnation not of His own creation but of the evil which His own creation had acquired by his own choice and through his own heedlessness. For the heedlessness that marks man's judgment made His Creator's beneficence of no profit to him. It is just as if any one, when he had obtained riches and dominion from a king, were to lord it over his benefactor, who, when he has worsted him, will punish him as he deserves, if he should see him keeping hold of the sovereignty to the end.

CHAPTER XXII.
Concerning the law of God and the law of sin.

The Deity is good and more than good, and so is His will. For that which God wishes is good. Moreover the precept, which teaches this, is law, that we, holding by it, may walk in light[5]: and the transgression of this precept is sin, and this continues to exist on account of the assault of the devil and our unconstrained and voluntary reception of it[6]. And this, too, is called law[7].

And so the law of God, settling in our mind, draws it towards itself and pricks our conscience. And our conscience, too, is called a law of our mind. Further, the assault of the wicked one, that is the law of sin, settling in the members of our flesh, makes its assault upon us through it. For by once voluntarily transgressing the law of God and receiving the assault of the wicked one, we gave entrance to it, being sold by ourselves to sin. Wherefore our body is readily impelled to it. And so the savour and perception of sin that is stored up in our body, that is to say, lust and pleasure of the body, is law in the members of our flesh.

Therefore the law of my mind, that is, the conscience, sympathises with the law of God, that is, the precept, and makes that its will. But the law of sin[8], that is to say, the assault

6 Text, κακοῦσθαι. Variant, κακουχεῖσθαι.
7 Basil, Hom. Deum non esse caus. mal.
8 Text, παραδρομή. Variant, παρα.ροπῇ, cf. *infra*.
9 Gen. i. 31.
1 Basil Hom. Deum non esse caus. mal.
2 Jer., Contr. Pelag.. bk. iii.
3 Damasc., Dialog contra Manich.

4 St. Mark xiv. 21.   5 1 St. John i 7.
6 Rom. vii. 23.   7 Rom. vii. 25.   8 Ibid. 23.

made through the law that is in our members, or through the lust and inclination and movement of the body and of the irrational part of the soul, is in opposition to the law of my mind, that is to conscience, and takes me captive (even though I make the law of God my will and set my love on it, and make not sin my will), by reason of commixture[9] : and through the softness of pleasure and the lust of the body and of the irrational part of the soul, as I said, it leads me astray and induces me to become the servant of sin. But *what the law could not do, in that it was weak through the flesh, God, sending His own Son in the likeness of sinful flesh* (for He assumed flesh but not sin) *condemned sin in the flesh, that the righteousness of the law might be fulfilled in us who walk not after the flesh but in the Spirit*[1]. *For the Spirit helpeth our infirmities*[2] and affordeth power to the law of our mind, against the law that is in our members. For the verse, *we know not what we should pray for as we ought, but the Spirit itself maketh intercession with groanings that cannot be uttered*[3], itself teacheth us what to pray for. Hence it is impossible to carry out the precepts of the Lord except by patience and prayer.

CHAPTER XXIII.

Against the Jews on the question of the Sabbath.

The seventh day is called the Sabbath and signifies rest. For in it God *rested from all His works*[4], as the divine Scripture says : and so the number of the days goes up to seven and then circles back again and begins at the first. This is the precious number with the Jews, God having ordained that it should be held in honour, and that in no chance fashion but with the imposition of most heavy penalties for the transgression[5]. And it was not in a simple fashion that He ordained this, but for certain reasons understood mystically by the spiritual and clear-sighted[6].

So far, indeed, as I in my ignorance know, to begin with inferior and more dense things, God, knowing the denseness of the Israelites and their carnal love and propensity towards matter in everything, made this law : first, in order that *the servant and the cattle should rest*[7] as it is written, for *the righteous man re-*

gardeth the life of his beast[8] : next, in order that when they take their ease from the distraction of material things, they may gather together unto God, spending the whole of the seventh day in psalms and hymns and spiritual songs and the study of the divine Scriptures and resting in God. For when[9] the law did not exist and there was no divinely-inspired Scripture, the Sabbath was not consecrated to God. But when the divinely-inspired Scripture was given by Moses, the Sabbath was consecrated to God in order that on it they, who do not dedicate their whole life to God, and who do not make their desire subservient to the Master as though to a Father, but are like foolish servants, may on that day talk much concerning the exercise of it, and may abstract a small, truly a most insignificant, portion of their life for the service of God, and this from fear of the chastisements and punishments which threaten transgressors. *For the law is not made for a righteous man but for the unrighteous*[1]. Moses, of a truth, was the first to abide fasting with God for forty days and again for another forty[2], and thus doubtless to afflict himself with hunger on the Sabbaths although the law forbade self-affliction on the Sabbath. But if they should object that this took place before the law, what will they say about Elias the Thesbite who accomplished a journey of forty days on one meal[3]? For he, by thus afflicting himself on the Sabbaths not only with hunger but with the forty days' journeying, broke the Sabbath : and yet God, Who gave the law, was not wroth with him but shewed Himself to him on Choreb as a reward for his virtue. And what will they say about Daniel? Did he not spend three weeks without food[4]? And again, did not all Israel circumcise the child on the Sabbath, if it happened to be the eighth day after birth[5]? And do they not hold the great fast which the law enjoins if it falls on the Sabbath[6]? And further, do not the priests and the Levites profane the Sabbath in the works of the tabernacle[7] and yet are held blameless? Yea, if an ox should fall into a pit on the Sabbath, he who draws it forth is blameless, while he who neglects to do so is condemned[8]. And did not all the Israelites compass the walls of Jericho bearing the Ark of God for seven days, in which assuredly the Sabbath was included[9].

As I said[1], therefore, for the purpose of

9 Text, κατὰ ἀνάκρασιν. Variants, ἀνάκρισιν, ἀνάκλισιν. The old translation is 'secundum anacrasin,' i.e. 'contractionem, refusionem per laevitatem voluptatis :' Faber has 'secundum contradictionem per suadelam voluptatis.' The author's meaning is that owing to the conjunction of mind with body, the law of sin is mixed with all the members.
1 Rom. viii. 3, 4. 2 Ibid. 26. 3 Ibid.
4 Gen. ii. 2. 5 Ex. xiii. 6; Num. xv. 35.
6 Greg. Naz., Orat. 44. 7 Deut. v. 14.

8 Prov. xii. 10. 9 Epiph., Exp. Fid., n. 22. 1 Tim. i. 9.
2 Ex. xxiv. 18 : xxxiv. 28. 3 1 Kings xix. 8.
4 Dan. x. 2. 5 Gen. xvii. 12. 6 Lev. xvi. 31.
7 St. Matt. xii. 5.
8 Epiph., Hæres. 30, n. 32, et Hær. n. 82 seqq.: Athan., Hom. circum. et Sabb.
9 Josh. iii. 1 Ath. ib.

securing leisure to worship God in order that they might, both servant and beast of burden, devote a very small share to Him and be at rest, the observance of the Sabbath was devised for the carnal that were still childish and *in the bonds of the elements of the world*[2], and unable to conceive of anything beyond the body and the letter. *But when the fulness of the time was come, God sent forth His Only-begotten Son, made of a woman, made under the law, to redeem them that were under the law that we might receive the adoption of sons*[3]. *For to as many of us as received Him, He gave power to become sons of God, even to them that believe on Him*[4]. *So that we are no longer servants but sons*[5]: no longer under the law but under grace : no longer do we serve God in part from fear, but we are bound to dedicate to Him the whole span of our life, and cause that servant, I mean wrath and desire. to cease from sin and bid it devote itself to the service of God, always directing our whole desire towards God and arming our wrath against the enemies of God : and likewise we hinder that beast of burden, that is the body, from the servitude of sin, and urge it forwards to assist to the uttermost the divine precepts.

These are the things which the spiritual law of Christ enjoins on us and those who observe that become superior to the law of Moses. *For when that which is perfect is come, then that which is in part shall be done away*[6]: and when the covering of the law, that is, the veil, is rent asunder through the crucifixion of the Saviour, and the Spirit shines forth with tongues of fire, the letter shall be done away with, bodily things shall come to an end, the law of servitude shall be fulfilled, and the law of liberty be bestowed on us. Yea[7] we shall celebrate the perfect rest of human nature, I mean the day after the resurrection, on which the Lord Jesus, the Author of Life and our Saviour, shall lead us into the heritage promised to those who serve God in the spirit, a heritage into which He entered Himself as our forerunner after He rose from the dead, and whereon, the gates of Heaven being opened to Him, He took His seat in bodily form at the right hand of the Father, where those who keep the spiritual law shall also come.

What belongs to us[8], therefore, who walk by the spirit and not by the letter, is the complete abandonment of carnal things, the spiritual service and communion with God. For circumcision is the abandonment of carnal pleasure and of whatever is super-

fluous and unnecessary. For the foreskin is nothing else than the skin which is superfluous to the organ of lust. And, indeed, every pleasure which does not arise from God nor is in God is superfluous to pleasure: and of that the foreskin is the type. The Sabbath, moreover, is the cessation from sin ; so that both things happen to be one, and so both together, when observed by those who are spiritual, do not bring about any breach of the law at all.

Further, observe[9] that the number seven denotes all the present time, as the most wise Solomon says, *to give a portion to seven and also to eight*[1]. And David[2], the divine singer when he composed the eighth psalm, sang of the future restoration after the resurrection from the dead. Since the Law, therefore, enjoined that the seventh day should be spent in rest from carnal things and devoted to spiritual things, it was a mystic indication to the true Israelite who had a mind to see God, that he should through all time offer himself to God and rise higher than carnal things.

CHAPTER XXIV.
Concerning Virginity.

Carnal men abuse virginity[3], and the pleasure-loving bring forward the following verse in proof, *Cursed be every one that raiseth not up seed in Israel*[4]. But we, made confident by God the Word that was made flesh of the Virgin, answer that virginity was implanted in man's nature from above and in the beginning. For man was formed of virgin soil. From Adam alone was Eve created. In Paradise virginity held sway. Indeed, Divine Scripture tells that *both Adam and Eve were naked and were not ashamed*[5]. But after their transgression they knew that they were naked, and in their shame they sewed aprons for themselves[6]. And when, after the transgression, Adam heard, *dust thou art and unto dust shalt thou return*[7], when death entered into the world by reason of the transgression, then *Adam knew Eve his wife, and she conceived and bare seed*[8]. So that to prevent the wearing out and destruction of the race by death, marriage was devised that the race of men may be preserved through the procreation of children[9].

But they will perhaps ask, what then is the meaning of " male and female[1]," and " Be fruitful and multiply ?" In answer we shall say that " Be fruitful and multiply[2] " does not

---

2 Gal. iv. 3.   3 Ibid. 4, 5.   4 St. John i. 12.
5 Gal. iv. 7.   6 1 Cor. xiii. 10.   7 *Athan., loc. cit.*
                    8 Ibid.

9 *Greg. Naz , Orat.* 42.   1 Eccl. xi. 2.   2 Ps. xvi
3 V de bk ii. ch. 30.   4 Deut.   5 Gen. ii. 23
6 Ibid. iv. 7.   7 Ibid. 19.
8 Gen. iv. 1.   9 *Greg. Nvs:., De opif., hom.* 16.
1 Gen. i. 27.   2 Ibid i. 28.

altogether refer to the multiplying by the marriage connection. For God had power to multiply the race also in different ways, if they kept the precept unbroken [3] to the end [4]. But God, Who knoweth all things before they have existence, knowing in His foreknowledge that they would fall into transgression in the future and be condemned to death, anticipated this and made " male and female," and bade them " be fruitful and multiply." Let us, then, proceed on our way and see the glories [5] of virginity : and this also includes chastity.

Noah when he was commanded to enter the ark and was entrusted with the preservation of the seed of the world received this command, *Go in*, saith the Lord, *thou and thy sons, and thy wife, and thy sons' wives* [6]. He separated them from their wives [7] in order that with purity they might escape the flood and that shipwreck of the whole world. After the cessation of the flood, however, He said, *Go forth of the ark, thou and thy sons, and thy wife, and thy sons' wives* [8]. Lo, again, marriage is granted for the sake of the multiplication of the race. Next, Elias, the fire-breathing charioteer and sojourner in heaven did not embrace celibacy, and yet was not his virtue attested by his super-human ascension [1]? Who closed the heavens? Who raised the dead [2]? Who divided Jordan [3]? Was it not the virginal Elias? And did not Elisha, his disciple, after he had given proof of equal virtue, ask and obtain as an inheritance a double portion of the grace of the Spirit [4]? What of the three youths? Did they not by practising virginity become mightier than fire, their bodies through virginity being made proof against the fire [5]? And was it not Daniel's body that was so hardened by virginity that the wild beasts' teeth could not fasten in it [6]. Did not God, when He wished the Israelites to see Him, bid them purify the body [7]? Did not the priests purify themselves and so approach the temple's shrine and offer victims? And did not the law call chastity the great vow?

The precept of the law, therefore, is to be taken in a more spiritual sense. For there is spiritual seed which is conceived through the love and fear of God in the spiritual womb, travailing and bringing forth the spirit of salvation. And in this sense must be understood this verse : *Blessed is he who hath seed in Zion and posterity in Jerusalem.* For does it mean that, although he be a whoremonger and a drunkard and an idolater, he is still blessed if only he hath seed in Sion and posterity in Jerusalem? No one in his senses will say this.

Virginity is the rule of life among the angels, the property of all incorporeal nature. This we say without speaking ill of marriage : God forbid! (for we know that the Lord blessed marriage by His presence [8], and we know him who said, *Marriage is honourable and the bed undefiled* [1]), but knowing that virginity is better than marriage, however good. For among the virtues, equally as among the vices, there are higher and lower grades. We know that all mortals after the first parents of the race are the offspring of marriage. For the first parents were the work of virginity and not of marriage. But celibacy is, as we said, an imitation of the angels. Wherefore virginity is as much more honourable than marriage, as the angel is higher than man. But why do I say angel? Christ Himself is the glory of virginity, who was not only-begotten of the Father without beginning or emission or connection, but also became man in our image, being made flesh for our sakes of the Virgin without connection, and manifesting in Himself the true and perfect virginity. Wherefore, although He did not enjoin that on us by law (for as He said, *all men cannot receive this saying* [2]), yet in actual fact He taught us that and gave us strength for it. For it is surely clear to every one that virginity now is flourishing among men.

Good indeed is the procreation of children enjoined by the law, and good is marriage [3] on account of fornications, for it does away with these [4], and by lawful intercourse does not permit the madness of desire to be enflamed into unlawful acts. Good is marriage for those who have no continence : but that virginity is better which increases the fruitfulness of the soul and offers to God the seasonable fruit of prayer. *Marriage is honourable and the bed undefiled, but whoremongers and adulterers God will judge* [5].

CHAPTER XXV.

Concerning the Circumcision.

The Circumcision [6] was given to Abraham before the law, after the blessings, after the promise, as a sign separating him and his offspring and his household from the Gentiles with whom he lived [7]. And this is evident [8],

---

3 Text, ἀπαραχάρακτον. Variant, ἀπαρεγχάρακτον, old trans. "in intransmutationem."
4 Vid *supr.*, bk. ii. ch. 30.
5 Text, αὐχήματα = incieases. We have read αὐχήματα.
6 Gen. vi. 18 ; vii. 1.   7 Cf. *Chrys., Hom.* 28 *on Genesis.*
8 Gen viii. 16.
1 2 ..ings ii. 11.   2 Ibid. iv. 34.   3 Ibid. ii. 14.
4 Ibid. ii. 9.   5 Dan. iii. 20.   6 Ibid vi. 16.
7 Ex. xix. 15 : Num. vi. 2.

8 St. John ii. 1.   1 Heb. xiii. 4.   2 St. Matt. xix. 11.
3 *Simeon Thess., De initiat.*, ch. 33.   4 1 Cor. vii. 2.
5 Heb. xiii. 4.
6 *Just. Martyr., Dial cum Tryph.*, p. 241.
7 Gen. xvii. 10.   8 *Chrys , Hom.* 39 *in Gen.*

for when the Israelites passed forty years alone by themselves in the desert, having no intercourse with any other race, all that were born in the desert were uncircumcised: but when Joshua[9] led them across Jordan, they were circumcised, and a second law of circumcision was instituted. For in Abraham's time the law of circumcision was given, and for the forty years in the desert it fell into abeyance. And again for the second time God gave the law of circumcision to Joshua, after the crossing of Jordan, according as it is written in the book of Joshua, the son of Nun: *At that time the Lord said unto Joshua, Make thee knives of stone from the sharp rock, and assemble and circumcise the sons of Israel a second time*[1]; and a little later: *For the children of Israel walked forty and two*[2] *years in the wilderness of Battaris*[3], *till all the people that were men of war, which came out of Egypt, were uncircumcised, because they obeyed not the voice of the Lord: unto whom the Lord sware that He would not shew them the good land, which the Lord sware unto their fathers that He would give them, a land that floweth with milk and honey. And their children, whom He raised up in their stead, them Joshua circumcised: for they were uncircumcised, because they had not circumcised them by the way*[4]. So that the circumcision was a sign, dividing Israel from the Gentiles with whom they dwelt.

It was, moreover, a figure of baptism[5]. For just as the circumcision does not cut off a useful member of the body but only a useless superfluity, so by the holy baptism we are circumcised from sin, and sin clearly is, so to speak, the superfluous part of desire and not useful desire. For it is quite impossible that any one should have no desire at all nor ever experience the taste of pleasure. But the useless part of pleasure, that is to say, useless desire and pleasure, it is this that is sin from which holy baptism circumcises us, giving us as a token the precious cross on the brow, not to divide us from the Gentiles (for all the nations received baptism and were sealed with the sign of the Cross), but to distinguish in each nation the faithful from the faithless. Wherefore, when the truth is revealed, circumcision is a senseless figure and shade. So circumcision is now superfluous and contrary to holy baptism. For *he who is circumcised is a debtor to do the whole law*[6]. Further, the Lord was circumcised that He

might fulfil the law: and He fulfilled the whole law and observed the Sabbath that He might fulfil and establish the law[7]. Moreover after He was baptized and the Holy Spirit had appeared to men, descending on Him in the form of a dove, from that time the spiritual service and conduct of life and the Kingdom of Heaven was preached.

CHAPTER XXVI.
Concerning the Antichrist[8].

It should be known that the Antichrist is bound to come. Every one, therefore, who confesses not that the Son of God came in the flesh and is perfect God and became perfect man, after being God, is Antichrist[9]. But in a peculiar and special sense he who comes at the consummation of the age is called Antichrist[1]. First, then, it is requisite that the Gospel should be preached among all nations, as the Lord said[2], and then he will come to refute the impious Jews. For the Lord said to them: *I am come in My Father's name and ye receive Me not: if another shall come in his own name, him ye will receive*[3]. And the apostle says, *Because they received not the love of the truth that they might be saved, for this cause God shall send them a strong delusion that they should believe a lie: that they all might be damned who believed not the truth, but had pleasure in unrighteousness*[4]. The Jews accordingly did not receive the Lord Jesus Christ who was the Son of God and God, but receive the impostor who calls himself God[5]. For that he will assume the name of God, the angel teaches Daniel, saying these words, *Neither shall he regard the God of his fathers*[6]. And the apostle says: *Let no man deceive you by any means: for that day shall not come except there come a falling away first, and that man of sin be revealed, the son of perdition: who opposeth and exalteth himself above all that is called God or that is worshipped, so that he sitteth in the temple of God*[7], *shewing himself that he is God;* in the temple of God he said; not our temple, but the old Jewish temple[8]. For he will come not to us but to the Jews: not for Christ or the things of Christ: wherefore he is called Antichrist[9].

First, therefore, it is necessary that the Gospel should be preached among all nations[1]: *And then shall that wicked one be*

---

9 Text, Ἰησοῦς. 1 Josh. v. 2. 2 Ibid. 6.
3 Text, Βατταριτίδι as in MSS.; but in Bib. Sixt. μαδβαρείτιδι is to be read. The desert in which the Israelites dwelt is called "per antonomasiam" Madbara, from the Hebrew מִדְבָּר, desert.
4 Josh. v. 6, 7.
5 Greg. Naz., Orat. 40. Athan., De Sab. et circ.
6 Gal. v. 3.

7 St. Matt. v. 17. 8 See the note in Migne.
9 1 St. John ii. 22.
1 Iren., bk. v. ch. 25: Greg. Naz., Orat. 47.
2 St. Matt. xxiv. 14. 3 St. John v. 43.
4 2 Thess. ii 10, 11, 12.
5 Chrys., Hom. 4 in Epist. 2 Thess. 6 Dan. xi. 37.
7 2 Thess. ii. 3, 4. 8 Cyril of Jerusalem, Cat. 15.
9 Iren., Cyril Hieros., Catech. 15: Greg. Naz loc. cit.
1 St. Matt. xxv. 14.

revealed, even him whose coming is after the working of Satan with all power and signs and lying wonders [2], *with all deceivableness of unrighteousness in them that perish, whom the Lord shall consume with the word of His mouth and shall destroy with the brightness of His coming* [3]. The devil himself [4], therefore, does not become man in the way that the Lord was made man. God forbid! but he becomes man as the offspring of fornication and receiveth all the energy of Satan. For God, foreknowing the strangeness of the choice that he would make, allows the devil to take up his abode in him [5].

He is, therefore, as we said, the offspring of fornication and is nurtured in secret, and on a sudden he rises up and rebels and assumes rule. And in the beginning of his rule, or rather tyranny, he assumes the rôle of sanctity [6]. But when he becomes master he persecutes the Church of God and displays all his wickedness. But he will come *with signs and lying wonders* [7], fictitious and not real, and he will deceive and lead away from the living God those whose mind rests on an unsound and unstable foundation, so that even the elect shall, if it be possible, be made to stumble [8].

But Enoch and Elias the Thesbite shall be sent and shall turn the hearts of the fathers to the children [9], that is, the synagogue to our Lord Jesus Christ and the preaching of the apostles: and they will be destroyed by him. And the Lord shall come out of heaven, just as the holy apostles beheld Him going into heaven, perfect God and perfect man, with glory and power, and will destroy the man of lawlessness, the son of destruction, with the breath of His mouth [1]. Let no one, therefore, look for the Lord to come from earth, but out of Heaven, as He himself has made sure [2].

CHAPTER XXVII.

Concerning the Resurrection.

We believe also in the resurrection of the dead. For there will be in truth, there will be, a resurrection of the dead, and by resurrection we mean resurrection of bodies [3]. For resurrection is the second state of that which has fallen. For the souls are immortal, and hence how can they rise again? For if they define death as the separation of soul and body, resurrection surely is the re-union of soul and body, and the second state of the living creature that has suffered dissolution and downfall [4]. It is, then, this very body, which is corruptible and liable to dissolution, that will rise again incorruptible. For He, who made it in the beginning of the sand of the earth, does not lack the power to raise it up again after it has been dissolved again and returned to the earth from which it was taken, in accordance with the reversal of the Creator's judgment.

For if there is no resurrection, let us eat and drink [5]: let us pursue a life of pleasure and enjoyment. If there is no resurrection, wherein do we differ from the irrational brutes? If there is no resurrection, let us hold the wild beasts of the field happy who have a life free from sorrow. If there is no resurrection, neither is there any God nor Providence, but all things are driven and borne along of themselves. For observe how we see most righteous men suffering hunger and injustice and receiving no help in the present life, while sinners and unrighteous men abound in riches and every delight. And who in his senses would take this for the work of a righteous judgment or a wise providence? There must be, therefore, there must be, a resurrection. For God is just and is the rewarder of those who submit patiently to Him. Wherefore if it is the soul alone that engages in the contests of virtue, it is also the soul alone that will receive the crown. And if it were the soul alone that revels in pleasures, it would also be the soul alone that would be justly punished. But since the soul does not pursue either virtue or vice separate from the body, both together will obtain that which is their just due.

Nay, the divine Scripture bears witness that there will be a resurrection of the body. God in truth says to Moses after the flood, *Even as the green herb have I given you all things. But flesh with the life thereof, which is the blood thereof, shall ye not eat. And surely your blood of your lives will I require; at the hand of every beast will I require it, and at the hand of every man's brother will I require the life of man. Whoso sheddeth man's blood, for his blood his own shall be shed, for in the image of God made I man* [6]. How will He require the blood of man at the hand of every beast, unless because the bodies of dead men will rise again? For not for man will the beasts die.

And again to Moses, *I am the God of Abra-*

---

[2] Text has πέρασι ψεύδους, instead of the received text, τέρασι ψεύδους, cf. *infr.*
[3] 2 Thess. ii. 8, 9, 10.   [4] Jerome on *Daniel*, ch. vii.
[5] *Chrys., Hom.* 3 *in* 2 *Thess.*
[6] Text, ἁγιοσύνην. Variants, ἀγαθωσύνην, δικαιοσύνην. Old trans. "justitiam," but Faber has "bonitatem."
[7] 2 Thess. ii. 9.   [8] St. Matt. xxiv. 24.
[9] Mal. iv. 6: Apoc. xi. 3.   [1] Acts i. 11.
[2] 2 Thess. ii. 8.
[3] 1 Cor. xv. 35—44.

---

[4] *Epist. in Ancor. n.* 89: *Method., Contr. Orig.*
[5] Is. xxii. 13: 1 Cor. xv. 32.   [6] Gen. ix. 3, 4, 5, 6.

ham, the God of Isaac and the God of Jacob : God is not the God of the dead (that is, those who are dead and will be no more), *but of the living*[7], whose souls indeed live in His hand[8], but whose bodies will again come to life through the resurrection. And David, sire of the Divine, says to God, *Thou takest away their breath, they die and return to their dust*[9]. See how he speaks about bodies. Then he subjoins this, *Thou sendest forth Thy Spirit, they are created : and Thou renewest the face of the earth*[1].

Further Isaiah says : *The dead shall rise again, and they that are in the graves shall awake*[2]. And it is clear that the souls do not lie in the graves, but the bodies.

And again, the blessed Ezekiel says : *And it was as I prophesied, and behold a shaking and the bones came together, bone to his bone, each to its own joint : and when I beheld, lo, the sinews came up upon them and the flesh grew and rose up on them and the skin covered them above*[3]. And later he teaches how the spirits came back when they were bidden.

And divine Daniel also says : *And at that time shall Michael stand up, the great prince which standeth for the children of thy people : and there shall be a time of trouble, such trouble as never was since there was a nation on the earth even to that same time. And at that time thy people shall be delivered, every one that shall be found written in the book. And many of them that sleep in the dust of the earth shall awake : some to everlasting life and some to shame and everlasting contempt. And they that be wise shall shine as the brightness of the firmament, and out of the multitude of the just shall shine like stars into the ages and beyond*[4]. The words, *many of them that sleep in the dust of the earth shall awake*, clearly shew that there will be a resurrection of bodies. For no one surely would say that the souls sleep in the dust of the earth.

Moreover, even the Lord in the holy Gospels clearly allows that there is a resurrection of the bodies. *For they that are in the graves*, He says, *shall hear His voice and shall come forth : they that have done good unto the resurrection of life, and they that have done evil unto the resurrection of damnation*[5]. Now no one in his senses would ever say that the souls are in the graves.

But it was not only by word, but also by deed, that the Lord revealed the resurrection of the bodies. First He raised up Lazarus, even after he had been dead four days, and

was stinking[6]. For He did not raise the soul without the body, but the body along with the soul : and not another body but the very one that was corrupt. For how could the resurrection of the dead man have been known or believed if it had not been established by his characteristic properties ? But it was in fact to make the divinity of His own nature manifest and to confirm the belief in His own and our resurrection, that He raised up Lazarus who was destined once more to die. And the Lord became Himself the first-fruits of the perfect resurrection that is no longer subject to death. Wherefore also the divine Apostle Paul said : *If the dead rise not, then is not Christ raised. And if Christ be not raised, our faith is vain : we are yet in our sins*[7]. And, *Now is Christ risen from the dead and become the first-fruits of them that slept*[8], and *the first-born from the dead*[9]; and again, *For if we believe that Jesus died and rose again, even so them also which sleep in Jesus will God bring with Him*[1]. *Even so*, he said, *as Christ rose again.* Moreover, that the resurrection of the Lord was the union of uncorrupted body and soul (for it was these that had been divided) is manifest : for He said, *Destroy this temple, and in three days I will raise it up*[2]. And the holy Gospel is a trustworthy witness that He spoke of His own body. *Handle Me and see*, the Lord said to His own disciples when they were thinking that they saw a spirit, *that it is I Myself, and that I am not changed*[3]: *for a spirit hath not flesh or bones, as ye see Me have*[4]. And when He had said this He shewed them His hands and His side, and stretched them forward for Thomas to touch[5]. Is not this sufficient to establish belief in the resurrection of bodies ?

Again the divine apostle says, *For this corruptible must put on incorruption, and this mortal must put on immortality*[6]. And again : *It is sown in corruption, it is raised in incorruption : it is sown in weakness, it is raised in power : it is sown in dishonour, it is raised in glory : it is sown a natural body* (that is to say, crass and mortal), *it is raised a spiritual body*[7], such as was our Lord's body after the resurrection which passed through closed doors, was unwearying, had no need of food, or sleep, or drink. *For they will be*, saith the Lord, *as the angels of God*[8]: there will no longer be marriage nor procreation of children. The divine apostle, in truth, says, *For our conversation is in heaven, from whence*

7 Ex. iii. 6: St. Matt. xxii. 32.   8 Wisd. iii. 1.
9 Ps. civ. 29.   1 Ibid. 30.   2 Is. xxvi. 18.
3 Ez. xxxvii. 7.   4 Dan. xii. 1, 2, 3.   5 St. John v. 28, 29.

6 St. John xi. 39—44.   7 1 Cor. xv. 16, 17.   8 Ibid. 20.
9 Col. i. 18.   1 1 Thess. iv. 14.   2 St. John ii. 19.
3 St. Luke xxiv. 37.   4 Ibid. xxiv. 39.
5 St. John xx. 27.   6 1 Cor. xv. 35.
7 1 Cor. xv. 42. 44.   8 St. Mark xii. 25.

also we look for the Saviour, the Lord Jesus, Who shall change our vile body that it may be fashioned like unto His glorious body [9] : not meaning change into another form (God forbid !), but rather the change from corruption into incorruption [1].

But some one will say, *How are the dead raised up ?* Oh, what disbelief ! Oh, what folly ! Will He, Who at His solitary will changed earth into body, Who commanded the little drop of seed to grow in the mother's womb and become in the end this varied and manifold organ of the body, not the rather raise up again at His solitary will that which was and is dissolved? *And with what body do they come* [2] *? Thou fool,* if thy hardness will not permit you to believe the words of God, at least believe His works [3]. *For that which thou sowest is not quickened except it die* [4]. *And that which thou sowest, thou sowest not that body that shall be, but bare grain, it may chance of wheat or of some other grain. But God giveth it a body as it hath pleased Him, and to every seed his own body* [5]. Behold, therefore, how the seed is buried in the furrows as in tombs. Who is it that giveth them roots and stalk and leaves and ears and the most delicate beards ? Is it not the Maker of the universe ? Is it not at the bidding of Him Who hath contrived all things? Believe, therefore, in this wise, even that the resurrection of the dead will come to pass at the divine will and sign. For He has power that is able to keep pace with His will.

We shall therefore rise again, our souls being once more united with our bodies, now made incorruptible and having put off corruption, and we shall stand beside the awful judgment-seat of Christ: and the devil and his demons and the man that is his, that is the Antichrist and the impious and the sinful, will be given over to everlasting fire : not material fire [6] like our fire, but such fire as God would know. But those who have done good will shine forth as the sun with the angels into life eternal, with our Lord Jesus Christ, ever seeing Him and being in His sight and deriving unceasing joy from Him, praising Him with the Father and the Holy Spirit throughout the limitless ages of ages [7]. Amen.

---

[9] Philip. iii. 20, 21.

[1] *Nyss., loc. citat.; Epiph., Hæres.* vi. 4.   [2] 1 Cor. xv. 35.

[3] *Epiph., Ancor., n.* 93.   [4] 1 Cor. xv. 35.

[5] Ibid. 36, 37, 38.

[6] See Migne's Preface to John's *Dial., Contr. Manichæos.*

[7] In R. 2924 is read : ἐν τῷ Κυρίῳ ἡμῶν, ᾧ πρέπει πᾶσα δόξα, τιμὴ, καὶ προσκύνησις, νῦν καὶ ἀεὶ, καὶ εἰς τοὺς αἰῶνας τῶν αἰώνων. Ἀμήν. In 2928 : ὅτι αὐτῷ πρέπει δόξα, τιμὴ καὶ προσκύνησις, νῦν καὶ ἀεὶ, &c.

INDEX OF SCRIPTURE PASSAGES.

INDEX OF SUBJECTS.